THE FOOTBALLERS' WHO'S WHO 2010-11

Edited by Barry J. Hugman

Assistant Editors
Gerald Mortimer (text)
Michael Joyce (statistics)

Photographs © Press Association Images

MAINSTREAM PUBLISHING

EDINBURGH AND LONDON

First published in Great Britain in 2010 by
MAINSTREAM PUBLISHING COMPANY (EDINBURGH) LTD
7 Albany Sreet
Edinburgh
EH1 3UG

ISBN 9781845966010

A catalogue record for this book is
available from The British Library

Typeset and designed by
Cheverton Printers, Cromer, Norfolk, NR27 9JW

Printed in Great Britain by
Clays Ltd, St Ives plc

Foreword

Welcome once again to the Footballers' Who's Who – a definitive guide to every one of the PFA members playing first team football throughout the Premier League and the Football League in England and Wales in 2009-10.

As ever, I am extremely pleased to give the PFA's full endorsement and recommendation to this unique publication which is now in its 16th year. Since the inception of the Who's Who, interest in the modern game – at all levels – has continued to grow at a remarkable rate, and this book once again reflects that growth.

Packed full of statistics and profiles on all PFA members, the Footballers' Who's Who provides the background to what the game is all about – the players. Having to deal with 4,000 PFA members, the book gives me a valuable source of information in an easily accessible, attractive and enjoyable format – as it does anybody involved in the game, whether it be an administrator, player, manager, spectator, or commentator. It is especially invaluable for any football 'Brain of Britain' or football quiz aspirant!

The publication is compiled by Barry Hugman, whose record in this field is unsurpassed, and he is aided by a team of close on 100 people who provide him with the invaluable aspects of local information, which gives this book such credibility. It's a fascinating read and an unequalled source of reference. We hope you enjoy it.

Gordon Taylor, OBE
PFA Chief Executive

Acknowledgements

Formerly known as the *Factfile* and now in its 16th edition, we believe that the *PFA Footballers' Who's Who* has become an invaluable resource to all of those involved in football, whether they be fans, the media or all those involved at club level. To this end, I would once again like to express my thanks to **Gordon Taylor**, the chief executive, and all those at the PFA who have genuinely supported and helped to establish the *Who's Who*. Their continuing support is very much welcomed and appreciated.

The task of dealing with the text this year, as in the previous season, was carried out by **Gerald Mortimer**, whilst the stats were handled by **Michael Joyce**, both working in conjunction with myself. As the Derby County contributor, Gerald's profile can be seen below. Michael is the author of *Football League Players' Records, 1888 to 1939*, a title, which is still available from SoccerData, 4 Adrian Close, Beeston, Nottingham NG9 6FL and slots in perfectly with my post-war *Premier and Football League Players' Records*. Having lived in Norfolk for several years, he has supported Arsenal for as long he can remember and has accumulated data for a complete Football League database over many years, using it to produce the player indexes for the Definitive series of club histories and several other publications. He also provides statistical information for the website: www.since1888.co.uk, which includes career details of every English League player since 1888. The editorial team were also lucky to be able to call upon **Jack Luangkhoth** (FA Premier League), **Ceri Stennett** (FA of Wales), and **Marshall Gillespie** (editor of the *Northern Ireland Football Yearbook*). I am also indebted to **Alan Platt**, the Liverpool contributor, who supplied the international honours and produced the Where Did They Go? section. My thanks also go to **Jenny Hugman**, who did the proof reading, and to many Premier and Football League members up and down the country. Finally, I come to the typesetters, **Stephen Ratcliffe** and **Sarah Lines** of Cheverton Printers, info@cheverton.co.uk, who diligently stuck to the task in hand, working long hours in order to make sure that the remarkably tight deadlines were met. For details provided on players, I have listed below, in alphabetical order, the names of the team without whose help this book would not have been possible to produce. Once again, I thank every one of them for all the hard work they put in.

Audrey Adams (Watford): Has supported Watford since primary school days and currently provides the results and statistics for the BBC's Sports Report on Radio 5 Live. Audrey was also the club statistician for The *Ultimate Football Guide*. Regardless of how the club performed last season her devotion to the Hornets remains undimmed.

Stuart Basson (Chesterfield): A PFA Who's Who contributor since its inception, Stuart is the author of three well-received books on the Spireites, contributes regularly to the club programme and edits the history sections of the club's official website. As Chesterfield FC moves to the b2net Stadium in August, Stuart's celebration of the club's ground of 139 years, *Sunset Over Saltergate*, is due for publication. Stuart will share information on past players and the like with other students of football history and can be reached by email at s.basson@sky.com.

Harry Berry (Blackburn Rovers): As a season ticket holder ever since starting work, Harry has followed Rovers for over 50 years, having been born only three miles from Ewood Park and living within 15 miles of the ground all his life. Coinciding with Rovers' good form, 2006 saw Harry's book, *The Men Who Made Blackburn Rovers Since 1945*, published. Has been a road-runner for many years and has completed a few marathons. By profession a financial director, prior to retirement he worked for the largest manufacturer in Blackburn.

Tony Bluff (Doncaster Rovers): Tony first watched the Rovers in 1953 after he moved to the area with his family. The club historian and statistician for the last 26 years, he contributed to the programme for most of those years but now contributes to the club website with historical data and live match reports for every first team game. Over the years there has been very little published on the club's history but Tony has rectified this by doing all the writing whilst ably assisted by colleagues with the photography and records to produce a total of five books over the last few years covering the history of the club. *The Story of Belle Vue* in words and pictures chronicles the fall of Rovers from the Football League 12 years ago and then the renaissance of the club in their meteoric rise from Conference to the Championship in six seasons.

Rob Briggs (Grimsby Town): A former office employee of the Mariners, Rob, who lives a hefty goal-kick away from Blundell Park, has been a contributor to Grimsby's match-day magazine for over 20 years and has also written for the club fanzine and various soccer magazines. He is the co-author (with Dave Wherry) of *Mariner Men: Grimsby Town Who's Who 1892-2007*.

Jim Brown (Coventry City): The club's official statistician and historian and contributor to the programme, he also pens a weekly column in the *Coventry Telegraph* on the club's history and answering reader's queries. He is the author of several books on the history of Coventry City including *Coventry City-the Elite Era (1998 and 2001)*, *The Illustrated History (2000)*, *Ghosts of a Vanished Stadium (2006) and The Seven-Year Itch (2008)*, in addition to being the co-author of the *Breedon Complete Record (1991)*. Jim has been a Coventry fan since 1962 and has almost a complete collection of Coventry programmes since the war, as well as having a large library of football writings. He also carries out research for a number of commercial bodies and has written critically acclaimed books on *Huddersfield Town's Glory Years (1923-26)* and *The Busby Era at Old Trafford (1946-71)*. In 2007 he founded the club's Former Players Association.

Mark Brown (Plymouth Argyle): Mark has been supporting the Pilgrims for 34 years, having been introduced to them at the tender age of five by his Argyle-mad family. Being a season ticket holder with his son Ben, he attends all of Plymouth's home games and as many away games as he can. His wife and young daughter Libby will no doubt in time become converts to the Green Army. Mark has been contributing to the *PFA Footballers Who's Who* for the past 11 years, in which it has been one of the most successful periods in Plymouth's history.

Gavin Buckland (Everton): A life-long Everton supporter of over 30 years and co-author of *Everton: The Ultimate Book of Stats and Facts* and two other football quiz books, Gavin has also worked as a researcher and question-setter on several TV quiz programmes. As the club statistician, he has a trivia and facts column in every Everton home programme and provides factual data for Radio Merseyside. Gavin is also the author of *Everton*

Strange But Blue published in 2007, a collection of the 50 Strangest Everton matches, and is the joint-author of *2008 Reasons Why Merseyside is the Capital of Football*, also published in 2007.

Trevor Bugg (Hull City): As a supporter of the Tigers, Trevor saw his first game in April 1969 and has been contributing to the programme for over 20 years now (I'd have got less for murder!). He is also proud to have been a *Factfile/Who's Who* ever-present since 1995 (is it really that long?!) and is still pursuing a career in football statistics.

Paul Burton (Walsall): Paul has supported Walsall for 35 years, seeing his first match, a 4-0 home defeat at the hands of Plymouth, at the age of four. Despite this inauspicious start he has watched Walsall ever since, having his first season ticket at the age of five. He watches all the home matches and goes to the majority of away ones. Paul, who has seen Walsall play on more than 80 grounds, is an actuary by qualification, his job being that of a fund manager.

Bob Cain (Fulham): Bob has supported Fulham for 39 years during which time he has not missed a single home match in any first team competition and notched up his 1,000th consecutive home game during March 2010. In all he has clocked up almost 1,850 first team games, watching his club play in all four divisions. A strong advocate of all-seater stadiums he has been a contributor to the club programme for 20 years and has also contributed on occasions to the club website.

Tim Carder (Brighton & Hove Albion): Tim is chairman of the Brighton & Hove Albion Collectors' and Historians' Society, an organisation with around 90 members which he founded in 1998 to preserve and promote the history of the club. He is now heavily involved in the provision of a club museum at the Albion's new Community Stadium, scheduled to open in 2011.

Wallace Chadwick (Burnley): A supporter who has followed the Clarets at both ends of the Football League and also in the Premier League, Wallace has been a contributor to the club programme for over 20 years and also to a number of club histories including the definitive *Clarets Chronicles 1882-2007* by his long-time friend and fellow Burnley devotee Ray Simpson.

Paul Clayton (Charlton Athletic): Author of the book *The Essential History of Charlton Athletic*, Paul wrote a regular feature in the club programme between 1993 and 1998, having previously written other articles for the now defunct Charlton Athletic magazine and *Valiant's Viewpoint* (Supporters Club newsletter/fanzine). He has also provided the Charlton statistics for a number of publications, including the *Ultimate Football Guide* from 1987 to its final publication in 1999, along with the Charlton player information for the *Factfile/Who's Who* since its inception in 1995. Paul is a long-standing season ticket holder at The Valley, and rarely misses a game, home or away, despite living in Wiltshire.

Grant Coleby (Exeter City): A member of both the Supporters' Club and Supporters' Trust, Grant has been the Grecians' contributor since the conception of the *Who's Who*, apart from the time the club was in the Conference.

David Copping (Barnsley): Life-long Barnsley fan who was a regular columnist in the club match-day programme for many seasons, Dave also served on the committee that is currently involved in setting up a museum at Oakwell. For many seasons he commentated on both hospital radio and the club videos.

Frank Coumbe (Brentford): Frank has been the Brentford stastician for the *Who's Who* since the start and enjoys providing the biographies each year. Frank holds the Brentford Club record for attending consecutive first team home matches, the total having reached 882 by the end of the 2009-10 season. On the field, Andy Scott's impressive management led the Bees to a comfortable position in League One. As always Frank was helped by his 14-year-old daughter, Sally, for his contribution to this book.

Mick Cunningham (Bournemouth): A supporter of the club since 1966, Mick took over editing the programme in 1995 and in 2007-08 took charge of the club's official website. He also takes all the photos for Bournemouth.

John Curtis (Scunthorpe United): A life-long Scunthorpe fan, John went ten years without missing a Scunthorpe league game home and away. A professional journalist, he is a former editor of the club's award-winning match-day programme and covered United's fortunes for many years as a sports writer for the *Scunthorpe Telegraph*.

Carol Dalziel (Tranmere Rovers): Carol, who has been watching Tranmere Rovers since 1968, is a shareholder with aspirations to buy the club should she win the Lottery. She has been the operator of the electronic scoreboard for the last 20 seasons and is a former contributor to, and assistant editor of, the match-day programme. Carol's 'proper' job was in the logistics department of a local chemical manufacturing and distribution company, where she worked for 27 years before taking recent retirement.

Iain Dalziel (Barnet): Iain has been a Barnet fan since moving to London at a young age in the late 1990s. He has spent the last three years studying history and politics at Nottingham Trent University and is set to graduate this year. Next year he will be back in North London and will be able to attend Barnet games on a more regular basis once again. This is the fourth year he has written for the *PFA Footballers' Who's Who* and Iain is also one of the main contributor's for the popular unofficial Barnet website www.downhillsecondhalf.co.uk.

David Downs (Reading): David has contributed to the Reading FC player profiles for the *PFA Factfile'Who's Who* for the past 15 seasons. He still works at Reading as the Children's Safety Officer, covering all the under 18s activities within the club. David writes a flashback article for the match-day programme and has a weekly column in the *Reading Evening Post*. On match-day afternoons he commentates on Reading's home games for Hospital Radio. Away from football, David is involved in amateur dramatics with Punky Players and has appeared on stage at The Mill in Sonning, playing The Wizard in 'The Wizard of Oz' pantomime in January.

Ray Driscoll (Chelsea): A life-long Blues' fan born and bred two miles away from Stamford Bridge whose 50 years' spectating encompasses the era from Roy Bentley to John Terry, including the 'wilderness years' of the early 1980s – far removed from the present Abramovich days! Like all Chelsea fans he is in 'Dreamland' following a third Premier League title in six years and the club's first 'Double'. An all-round sports 'nut', he has contributed to many football books as well as other sports such as cricket, golf, rugby and tennis. He has also contributed to more 'cerebral' literature such as reference books. He appeared in the 2008 series of BBC's prestigious *Mastermind* quiz, crossing swords with the Grand Inquisitor John Humphrys, an experience almost as painful as suffering a 'Chopper' Harris tackle!

Thomas Dubber (Portsmouth): A fourth generation Pompey die-hard, Thomas has been attending matches at Fratton Park since he was little more than a babe in arms.

His instant recall of goals, matches, players and events, is legend, and provides the basis for some lively discussion amongst his fellow travellers during some of the long Pompey away trips. Thomas was a published author whilst still at school, and his forthcoming undergraduate studies will allow him ample time to continue to pursue his two main passions: Pompey and writing!

Charlotte Egan (Bury): A 17-year-old college student who has supported the club from six months of age, Charlotte's upbringing has revolved around football and Bury FC, with playing women's football for Manchester Centre of Excellence, captaining her school and college side, and with her father previously writing the match reports for Bury's official website. Charlotte is hoping to study History at Lancaster University with straight A's at A Level.

Dean Enderby and **Eddie Collins** (Nottingham Forest): Dean watched his first Nottingham Forest game in April 1988 and has been an avid supporter ever since. He enjoys writing the profiles for this publication and would like to help research for other publications in the future. Eddie has been watching Forest since 1956 and derives much pleasure from being involved in this publication.

Harold Finch (Crewe Alexandra): Now aged 83, Harold still maintains his position as the club historian. A regular supporter since 1934, he has regularly contributed to the club official programme for over 50 years. Has a vast knowledge of the club and its players and misses very few games at league, cup and youth level. The A to Z record of all the players is progressing steadily, a complex task considering the number of players used over the years.

Jack Gaughan (Blackpool): Jack is 19 years old and the editor of www.blackpool.vitalfootball.co.uk, which is the second largest Blackpool website on the internet. Has also been nominated in the top-ten unofficial football writers in the country by the *New Football Pools'* Fanzine. Having written for the *Guardian* recently, Jack studies Journalism at the University of Central Lancashire.

Jon Gibbes (Torquay United): Jon is a life-long Torquay United supporter and a Popside season ticket holder. He co-wrote *Torquay United FC: The Official Centenary History, 1899-1999* with John Lovis and Leigh Edwards and is a regular contributor to the History Room at www.torquayfansforum.com

Paul Godfrey (Cheltenham Town): Paul watched his first Cheltenham Town game at the age of ten, the Robins losing 2-1 to Yeovil Town in an FA Cup fourth round qualifying match. He followed similar near misses and disappointments religiously before events took a dramatic turn in the late 1990s. Having become the club's programme editor in 1990, he was able to witness at first hand the transformation at Whaddon Road brought about by Steve Cotterill and the Board, headed by the chairman, Paul Baker. Paul, who joined the club on a full-time basis in 2001, is now the club secretary and a director, and retains a keen interest in the history of Town.

Frank Grande (Northampton Town): A supporter for over 50 years and club historian and statistician for the past 28 years, Frank has contributed to the programme for 26 years and written five books on the club and players. Over the years he has been instrumental in re-unions and events involving ex-players, plus fund-raising events for the club.

Michael Green (Bolton Wanderers): Michael is a follower of two clubs – Newcastle United (home-town team) and Bolton Wanderers (local club) – and has watched the latter for the past 30 years. He enjoys writing and is looking to

carve out further opportunities, preferably in the fields of football or popular entertainment (music, film, television etc).

Alan Harding (Swindon Town): Alan, who has been supporting Town since 1968, is a season ticket holder, travels home and away, and has been researching match stats and line-up details, plus details of players, since 1981. Is also a former member of the AFS.

Robert Heys (Accrington Stanley): Robert has worked at the club for eight years and is now the chief executive. A life-long supporter of Accrington through the days of non-league football thanks to his father and grandfather, his times with the club has given him many special memories over the years. This is Robert's second year of involvement in the *Who's Who*.

Adrian Hopper (Yeovil Town): Adrian joined Yeovil Town as media manager in 2002 after a long association through a local newspaper he owned. Also known as 'Fat Harry', he is now a devoted Town supporter attending every game, but has been known to have a slight leaning towards a certain team that plays in red at a Theatre!

Martin Jarred (Leeds United): Martin saw his first Leeds United game in 1966, a 2-1 mid-week home win against West Bromwich Albion, and was hooked. A member of the AFS for many years, he collaborated with Malcom MacDonald on several Leeds' books published by Breedon Books, which include four editions of the *Complete Record*, two *Leeds Story Books*, a *Leeds United Cup Book*, *Leeds United, The Complete European Record* and *The Who's Who of Leeds United*, which came out in 2008-09. He is also the co-author, with Dave Windross, of *Citizens and Minstermen, a Who's Who of York City*. A previous sports editor of the *Scarborough Evening News* and *The Press, York*, Martin is now a freelance journalist.

Mike Jay (Bristol Rovers): Mike has seen Rovers play at over 125 different grounds in his 43 years of supporting the Pirates, with the new Wembley and Anfield being his two favourites. He has been a regular contributor for over 32 years to the award-winning Rovers' match-day programme, *The Pirate*. Is also the official club historian, having had four books published on Rovers, the latest being *A Season To Remember: 1973-74* due to be published in November by the History Press. A keen collector of Rovers' memorabilia, he is always adding to his extensive collection of programmes, photos, autographs, etc.

Colin Jones (Swansea City): A fan since the early 1960s and a long-standing contributor to the club's match-day programme, Colin was programme editor at the Vetch Field for four years up to January 2003. Played non-league football before being involved with the training, coaching and administrative side after retiring as a player. In November 2005 he published the *First Comprehensive Player A-Z of Swansea Town/City players from 1912 to 2005*, and in November 2007 published a supplement to Professor David Farmer's book, *The Swans, Town and City*.

Dave Juson and **Gary Chalk** (Southampton): Gary and Dave, in partnership with Duncan Holley and David Bull, make up Hagiology, a collective formed to collate and disseminate accurate historical information about Southampton FC, and which has for some years operated as the Club's official historians. More information and details pertaining to Hagiology's critically acclaimed publications can be found at www.hagiologists.com.

Mat Kendrick (Aston Villa): Mat has been a sports writer in the Midlands for eight of his ten years in journalism and is now the Aston Villa reporter for the *Birmingham Mail*, *Birmingham Post* and *Sunday Mercury* and the associated websites.

Andrew Kirkham (Sheffield United): A Blades' supporter since 1953, and a regular contributor to the club programme and handbook since 1984, Andrew was a member of the AFS and the 92 club. He was also a contributor to *Sheffield United: The First 100 Years* and co-author of *A Complete Record of Sheffield United Football Club 1889-1999, Sheffield United Football Club Who's Who* and the recently published *Sheffield: The Home of Football*.

Geoff Knights (*Macclesfield Town*): Geoff has supported Macclesfield Town since the late 1980s. Until last season, when Geoff was elevated to the rank of life vice president in recognition of his work for the club, he described himself as an ordinary supporter from the terraces, and one who enjoys the friendly atmosphere of a small club. He keeps detailed statistics and records on the club, which have been used over the years in response to media, club, and other enquiries. Geoff also contributes to the match-day programme and is the author of the book *Macclesfield Town Football Club – The League Story so far*. Although there are no official appointments as such, he is acknowledged as the club's statistician and modern-day historian.

Gordon Lawton (Oldham Athletic): Gordon was the first Oldham contributor for the *Factfile/Who's Who*, covering the publication up until 1999 before making his comeback 11 years later. As the publications manager and programme editor at Boundary Park, he has been at the club for over 25 years and his long service and dedication was recognised when the chairman of the Football League, Lord Mawhinney, presented him with an award to honour the occasion. Gordon is Athletic through and through.

Geoff Lea (Wigan Athletic): A life-long supporter for over 30 years who first started watching the club during the non-league days, Geoff is a former editor of the match-day programme and now plays a key role in the production of the official match-day magazine. A press officer for Athletic on match days, he is also the club's statistician and has missed only a handful of games since election into the Football League. Has also worked for a number of radio stations and newspapers following Wigan's progress.

Richard Lindsay (Millwall): Richard has supported the Lions for over 56 years, first living in Peckham off the Old Kent Road and now residing in Bexhill-on-Sea since the loss of his dear wife. Author of *Millwall: A Complete Record* and one of a group of club historians pursuing the MFC Museum project, he collects all kinds of club memorabilia.

John Maguire (Manchester United): John spends most of his time these days producing booklets on his eBay site: *Sportspages-7*. A long-standing hobby, his titles are mainly football based, but other sports are also catered for, with occasional non-sporting titles. Some items are authentically signed. Naturally, Manchester United figure heavily in the football section with its quota of booklets about the players and the club. John dedicates his profiles this season to Sir Bobby Robson – a true legend in every sense of the word.

Rob Mason (Sunderland): Rob is Sunderland's publications officer and club historian. He edits Sunderland's match-day programme *Red and White*, which won both national Programme of the Year awards in 2009-10 to add to the many it has won over the years. Season 2010-11 will be the 25th year that Rob has edited the programme and the 45th season he has been watching 'the Lads'. Rob also edits SAFC's official magazine *Legion of Light*, junior supporters' magazine *24-7*, and has written 14 books on the club. His sons, Ian and Philip, are both

dedicated Sunderland supporters.

Tony Matthews (West Bromwich Albion): Soccer historian, founder of the Hawthorns museum and WBA statistician, he has written/co-compiled over 100 books on football since 1975, including complete records/histories of *Aston Villa, Birmingham City, Leicester City, Stoke City, Walsall, WBA and Wolves; Who's Whos of Arsenal, Aston Villa, Blues, Chelsea, Everton, Liverpool, Manchester United, Nottingham Forest, Sheffield Wednesday, Stoke City, WBA, Wolves and England (World Cup players); Encyclopaedias of Villa, Blues, Huddersfield Town, Manchester United, Sheffield United, Stoke City, Tottenham Hotspur, WBA and Wolves; Albion - 100 Years at The Hawthorns; West Midlands Football (from 1874); WBA v. Wolves: Black Country Derbies; The Unique Double (WBA's achievement in 1930-31); The Ronnie Allen Story; Cyrille Regis: 25 years in Football; Football Oddities; Football Firsts* and two photographic books. Out later this year are his two latest books: *The History of Birmingham City (1875-2010)* and *The Legends of West Bromwich Albion* (both published by DB Publishing, Derby). Tony can be contacted via e-mail at tonymatthews@live.co.uk

Peter Miles and **Dave Goody** (Southend United): Peter and Dave's first venture into publishing, *A Century United – The Centenary History of Southend United*, was launched in 2007 to much critical acclaim, and has already gone to a reprint. Having got the 'bug', they intend to publish further books on both Southend and football in general, and are now working on a book celebrating Southend United's first ever trophy, the 1980-81 Fourth Division Championship, for which further details can be found at www.shrimperpublishing.co.uk. Peter and Dave are both staunch fans of the Shrimpers, and Dave is now taking his two young sons, Matthew and Sam, with him to Roots Hall.

Ian Mills (Arsenal): Ian has been an Arsenal fan since the age of five and was a Highbury North Bank regular for 16 years. He is now a season ticket holder at the new Home of Football. A keen collector of books on Arsenal, including several players' autobiographies, Ian has also been a regular contributor to the Gunners' foremost fanzine, *The Gooner* for the last 12 years and wrote and published his own team's fanzine, *Sunday Bloody Sunday*, for 11 years. A keen historian on all things Arsenal, his favourite all-time player is Dennis Bergkamp. Ian also ran his own football team for 13 and a half years.

Paul Morant (Leyton Orient): Working for an insurance company in London, Paul is an out-and-out Orient fan who rarely misses a game, home or away, and takes great pride in being this publication's Orient contributor. Paul married Miranda in 2005 and their baby son, Nathan, was born in June 2006. Has now been joined by stepson Tyler as an O's fan.

Gerald Mortimer (Derby County): Gerald saw his first game at the Baseball Ground in 1946 and from 1970 spent 32 years covering them for the *Derby Evening Telegraph*. His spell included two league championships as well as four relegations and three promotions. The author of several statistical books on the club, he is delighted that once again there is Clough in charge of County. Gerald did a great job editing the *Who's Who*.

Ron Norris (Queens Park Rangers): A QPR fan for over 20 years, Ron runs and edits the successful unofficial website: www.qpr.net.com/ and has interviewed countless Rangers' stars, past and present, for the site. He also co-wrote and published the successful book *Loftus Road Legends* in 2002.

John Northcutt (West Ham United): Has supported the Hammers since 1959 and is the co-author of *West Ham: A*

Complete Record and *West Ham United: An Illustrated History*. A regular contributor to the club programme, John was the club adviser to *The Ultimate Football Guide*. He also answers all the questions put to the *Vintage Claret* section on the club's web site. In 2003 he compiled the *West Ham United Definitive*, which can be purchased at SoccerData Publications. John has been a season ticket holder at Upton Park for many years and likes to spend his time adding to his array of West Ham memorabilia. His latest book, *On This Day*, was published in August 2008.

Rex Page (Burton Albion): Rex has been Sports Editor of the *Burton Daily Mail* for more years than he cares to remember and never dreamt he would see Burton Albion playing in the Football League after many seasons of covering them at such exotic non-league locations as Desborough and Wootton Blue Cross. He reported his first Albion game in 1968, and after stints at Raymonds News Agency and the *Birmingham Post & Mail*, he has followed their fortunes continuously since 1986.

Simon Parker (Bradford City): Simon has covered Bradford City's fortunes for the *Bradford Telegraph & Argus* since 2000 - a period that has unfortunately coincided with a spectacular fall from grace. Simon, who previously worked for 11 years for *The News, Portsmouth*, has reported on the Bantams in all four divisions. But having covered three relegations and two administrations, he would not object to a bit of over-due success this season. Simon also ghost-wrote *Deano*, the autobiography of Dean Windass.

Les Payne (Rotherham United): First reported on Rotherham United's affairs back in 1968 (Tommy Docherty the first manager he interviewed as a quivering teenager) when working for the local weekly paper. Les has covered their matches from 137 different grounds across those 40-plus years, having done so the past couple of decades for the *Sheffield Star and Green 'Un*, where he is a sports writer.

Steve Peart and **Dave Finch** (Wycombe Wanderers): A former programme editor of the club and a supporter since 1973, Steve put together the player profiles, while the club statistics were supplied by Dave, who for several years was the official Wycombe statistician. Both were authors of *Wycombe Wanderers, 1887-1996: The Official History*, published in 1996. Dave has supported Wycombe regularly since 1964, although he saw his first game at the old Loakes Park ground in 1958. He was part of Wycombe's programme team from 1990 to 2008 and is now on the committee of the Ex-Players' Association.

Steve Phillipps (Rochdale): A Rochdale supporter for over 40 years, and the club's official historian, Steve is the author of *The Survivors: The Story of Rochdale AFC* (1990), *The Definitive Rochdale* (1995) and, more recently, *The Official History of Rochdale AFC*. A founder member of the AFS, away from football he is a university professor.

Terry Phillips (Cardiff City): Now aged 57, Terry is still covering Cardiff City FC as the MediaWales chief sportswriter for the *South Wales Echo*, *Western Mail* and *Wales on Sunday*. Having been a sports journalist for nearly 40 years – *Kent Evening Post* (1970-1977), *Derby Evening Telegraph* (1977-1986), *Gloucester Citizen* (1986-1994) – he has previously covered clubs at all levels, including Brian Clough's Nottingham Forest, Derby County, Gillingham, and Gloucester City. His specialist subjects are Cardiff City FC and Cardiff Devils (Ice Hockey).

Alan Platt (Liverpool/Manchester City): A dedicated football statistician and follower of Liverpool FC since 1960, whilst resident in London he was a member and official of the London branch of the LFC Supporters Club. Has assisted Barry Hugman in an editorial capacity on all his football publications since 1980, namely five updates of the post-war *Football (now titled Premier & Football) League Players' Records*, the two editions of *Premier League: The Players* and, for the last 16 years, the *PFA Footballers' Who's Who* (formerly *The Factfile*). Now resident in Manchester, his main interest today is in non-league football and he keeps detailed records on all the senior semi-professional leagues, having compiled a database of over 6,000 players participating at that level of football. With regards to the Manchester City profiles, when the Who's Who ran into last-minute problems, **Chris Holmes** of the Blues' Heritage Department kindly provided much back-up material for Alan to complete the task.

Kevan Platt (Norwich City): Kevan recently completed 30 years service at Carrow Road, the last 12 of which have seen him act as club secretary. Having watched his first match in September 1968, last season afforded him the opportunity to visit lots of new grounds as the Canaries slipped into the third tier of English football for the first time in 50 years. That enjoyment was, thankfully, short-lived and the League One Championship was compensation for the pain of relegation 12 months previous. Kevan's interest in statistics, particularly those relating to Norwich City, assisted him greatly when acting as the club's programme editor for many years and also in co-authoring the club's centenary edition of *Canary Citizens* with Mike Davage. As a Trustee for the Norwich City Football Club Historical Trust, he is heavily involved in player reunions and Hall of Fame events, something which helps him keep in touch with former players all across the globe. Supporting the Canaries is something of a family passion for Kevan, with his wife Ann and children Lawrie and Alice often accompanying him to away games, and obviously all matches at Carrow Road.

Richard Prime (Hereford United): Richard, the sports editor of *The Hereford Times*, has followed in the footsteps of distinguished journalists such as Ted Woodriffe and Laurie Teague as the paper's Hereford United correspondent. After a modern languages degree at the University of Bristol and careers in the insurance and travel industries, he now has the opportunity to travel the country to feed his addiction to the Bulls.

Derek Quinn (Morecambe): Derek, the club's press officer and local journalist, has been supporting Morecambe for almost 30 years. After watching Trevor Brooking star for FA Cup winners West Ham in a friendly at Christie Park in the 1970s he went on to sell programmes before promotion to a turnstile operator. Missed a few seasons while at University but the lure of the award-winning Christie Park pies proved too much and he got his dream job as sports editor of the local paper, even getting paid to watch his heroes. Now a BBC match commentator and freelance contributor, he spends his spare time following the Shrimps up and down the country, still living the dream after the club's promotion to the Football League for the first time.

Mick Renshaw (Sheffield Wednesday): Has followed Wednesday for over 40 years, despite all the ups and downs of a club that won the First Division title four times in past years, and will continue to do so regardless. Mick, who is a great supporter of European soccer, also produced the club section for *The Ultimate Football Guide*.

Mick Robinson (Peterborough United): Another life-long fan, for a number of years Mick has contributed to

the club programme and was the joint editor of *The Posh*, the official Peterborough history. Was also club statistician for *The Ultimate Football Guide*.

Alan Russell and **Mike Purkiss** (Crystal Palace): A season ticket holder at Crystal Palace for almost 20 years, Alan has reported extensively on the club's reserves for the official Palace website, and local newspapers the *Croydon Guardian* and *Croydon Advertiser*, writing match reports. Alan has also written articles for numerous Palace fanzines and the club's official programme, and away from following Palace has a keen interest in general football history, going to Ryman's league football and watching both Surrey and England play cricket. Mike has supported Palace since 1950 and produced stats on them since 1960, being the author of *Crystal Palace: A Complete History, 1905-1989*. Was the club statistician for *The Ultimate Football Guide* and also contributed to *Premier League: The Players*.

Phil Sherwin (Port Vale): Phil has supported Port Vale for over 40 years and is the club statistician. He has contributed to the club programme for 20 years and writes weekly articles for the local newspaper. Has helped out on numerous books about the club and in 2010 brought out one of his own, *The Port Vale Miscellany*.

David Simpson (Dagenham & Redbridge): The club's official statistician and programme editor, David has supported them since the days of Walthamstow Avenue through the mergers with Leytonstone/Ilford and Dagenham to its current guise. Since the club's formation in 1992 he has missed only five games, home or away, in all first team competitions. When he gets the time he is continuing to research the complete record of Walthamstow Avenue FC from 1900 to their last game in 1988. David has edited all the Football Conference promotion final programmes since the first one in 2003, including the North and South play-off finals.

Mike Slater (Wolverhampton Wanderers): The Wolves' contributor to this publication since its inception, Mike produced a book on the club's history called *Molineux Memories*, which he published in 1988. He has also written two booklets about Wolves, and compiled several quizzes on them. Continues to help out with other Wolves' publications from time to time.

Gordon Small (Hartlepool United): Gordon has supported Pools since October 1965 and for 45 years now has collected and compiled statistics on his adopted club. In 1998 he produced *The Definitive Hartlepool United FC*, and having a wide range of football interests, in 2007 was the author of *The Lancashire Cup - A Complete Record 1879-80 to 2006-07*. For the last two years has been working as a volunteer at the National Football Museum in Preston. Has contributed to all 16 editions of the *PFA Footballers' Who's Who*.

Dave Smith (Leicester City): Dave has been the official Leicester City statistician and historian for many years, as well as being a regular contributor to both the club programme and the club's extensive media guide. He is also the co-author of both *Of Fossils and Foxes* and *The Foxes Alphabet* and is currently working on a new edition of the official club history due to be published in August 2010. Was editor of both *Farewell to Filbert Street* and *Keeping the Faith*, which together charted the final season at Filbert Street and the first campaign at the Walkers Stadium.

Martin Smith (Stoke City): Now in his 41st season as a Stoke supporter, 47-year-old Martin still attends every game he can with his eldest son Perry, and is only usually kept away by watching his youngest son Jack, a 13-year-old national swimming champion, compete around the country. In between watching Stoke City games and attending swimming galas, with wife Angela, he likes to spend time with his daughter Tamsyn, who starts university this year, and reading almost anything on history. *The Oatcake* fanzine is now in its 23rd season and is still involved in its production and content output. On top of that he writes a regular newspaper column, though he has had to reign back on his online involvement on the Oatcake website.

Paul Smith (Tottenham Hotspur): Paul is the webmaster of one of the oldest and most popular unofficial Spurs' web sites – *Spurs Odyssey* (http://www.spursodyssey.com), and a former board member of the Tottenham Hotspur Supporters' Trust. Aged 58 this year, he has followed Spurs home and away and across Europe since the 1960s. Despite his move from Hertfordshire to Derbyshire in 2008, Paul maintains his maximum commitment to the team he loves. He is also a regular contributor to television and radio news networks, including BBC Five Live.

Phil Smith (Milton Keynes Dons): One of a number of former Wimbledon supporters who now follow the Dons in their new surroundings, Phil is a regular contributor to the club's programme and website.

Pete Stanford (Aldershot Town): Pete is a quality engineer by trade and has supported Aldershot Town since its inception in 1992; he was also a supporter of Aldershot FC (from 1979) prior to that. Has been keeping detailed statistical information on both clubs since 1980 and has contributed various articles for the match-day programme over the past few seasons. Is responsible for the fixtures, results and player statistical information in said publication since the 2007-08 season. In the past, Pete has contributed information to the club's unofficial website as well as to other clubs, media bodies (including the Press Association) and publications. In the summer of 2008, Pete became one of the club's two official statisticians, as well as being a member of club's official website team, responsible for squad profiles, news and ex-player articles. Pete is the author of the recently published *The Phoenix has Risen: An A-to-Z of Aldershot Town FC*, the first such project ever undertaken with regards to the 'new' club.

Paul A. Stead (Huddersfield Town): A passionate life-long supporter of his hometown and beloved football club who has followed the fortunes of the Terriers for the last 30 years, Paul is hoping for a new dawn at the club, with an ambitious young manager in charge, Lee Clark, working in tandem with a new chairman. After narrowly missing out on promotion through the play-offs to Millwall in the semi-finals during the 2009-10 season, the potential for success is hopefully just round the corner. Paul is in his 13th year with the *Who's Who*.

David Steele (Carlisle United): David has been involved with the *Who's Who* ever since its inception and has been a regular contributor to the Carlisle United match-day programme for many years, continuing to write articles on an occasional basis. He also pens a weekly column on the club's history for the local newspaper and is the author of *Carlisle United 1974/75 – A Season in the Sun*, which chronicled the club's year in the First Division. David continues to delve into the history of football in general and Carlisle United in particular.

Richard Stocken (Shrewsbury Town): Richard has followed the Shrews for over 50 years now through thick but mainly thin. An avid collector of all things Shrewsbury Town, he has contributed to a number of books and programmes over the years. In his spare time he is a senior manager with one of the big four banks. He has an ambition to see a Wembley victory for the Shrews after three unsuccessful attempts in recent years.

Bill Swann (Newcastle United): Born and raised in Northumberland, a supporter since the early 1950s days of Jackie Milburn, to whom he is distantly related, and a season ticket holder along with his wife and sons, despite the frequent long drives from home in Cheshire, he is a keen collector of memorabilia connected with the club. He has consolidated his information on club matches, teams, scorers, and players into a database for easy access and analysis. Bill assisted in the production of the club's volume in the *Complete Record* series and is a co-author of the *Essential History of Newcastle United*. This is his 15th year as a contributor to this publication.

Colin Tattum (Birmingham City): Colin is the chief sports writer on the *Birmingham Evening Mail* newspaper, with more than 17 years experience in his field, and has special responsibility to cover the day-to-day fortunes of Birmingham City.

Richard and **Sarah Taylor** and **Ian Mills** (Notts County): Richard is a life-long Notts County fan from a Notts County family, travelling the length and breadth of the land in following the Magpies, and has seen them on all but a few current Football League grounds and many non-league grounds too. In the summer, he umpires cricket matches to wile away the close season. Richard realises, to his great surprise, that he has experienced his addiction to these guys in black and white for over 50 years now. Sarah, who graduated with a degree in law a while ago now, is a keen sports fan and a regular visitor to Trent Bridge in the summer. Having seen his first game at Gay Meadow in 1959-60, Ian, who once ran the match-day programme sales, has been hooked ever since and has completed over 1000 consecutive games for County, being presented with a memento by Chris Hull of Nationwide on the pitch in 2002-03. He now sits in the press box at County, doing the press officer's job, after 23 seasons of programme involvement and wanting a change.

Frank Tweddle (Darlington): The club's official historian and statistician, Frank has regularly contributed articles to the Darlington programme for the last 35 seasons. He has avidly supported the Quakers home and away for over 50 years and has seen them play on well over a 120 grounds. As well as being a member of the 92 Club and the AFS he is the author of *Darlington's Centenary History*, published in 1983, and *The Definitive Darlington 1883-2000*, and also produces work for various other football publications. Now retired, Frank can devote even more time to delving into Darlington's fascinating, if mainly undistinguished, past 127 years!

John Vickers (Lincoln City): A life-long Lincoln City supporter, John was appointed as the Imps' media manager in August 2001. He has been in charge of the club's official website since 1998, whilst he has edited their award-winning match-day programme since the 2002-03 season. Coached as a youngster in his back garden by future England international Mick Harford, who lodged with his family during his playing days at Sincil Bank, John edited his first book in 2007, which

charted City's first 100 seasons in the Football League.

Paul Voller (Ipswich Town): A long-time Ipswich fan who started attending matches at Portman Road in 1963, Paul is a member of the executive committee of the Supporters' Club. He was the Ipswich statistician for the *Rothmans Football Yearbook* and the *Football Club Directory* during the 1990s and is the joint author of *The Essential History of Ipswich Town*, which was published in 2001.

Stuart Watson (Ipswich Town): An ambitious young sports journalist, Stuart was handed the position of covering the U's for the *East Anglian Daily Times* in September 2009 after the previous long-term incumbent of the role – Carl Marston – was appointed Ipswich Town reporter for the paper. In what was his debut season of reporting on professional football, home and away, Stuart could not have asked for a better club to cut his teeth at. Players willing to hand out mobile numbers, a media friendly manager in Aidy Boothroyd and an out-spoken chairman in Robbie Cowling more than made up for nightmare journeys to Yeovil and Carlisle, as well as the fact that the Weston Homes Community Stadium is always bitterly cold.

Martin Weller (Gillingham): A third generation Gillingham supporter, son Sam is now the fourth, Martin made his first visit to Priestfield in 1987 and has been hooked ever since. After 15 years in the television industry he became Gillingham FC's media manager in May 2008 and divides his time between following the club home and away, updating the official website, and editing the Gills' multi award-winning match-day programme.

Shaun Wilson (Middlesbrough): A life-long Boro supporter and season ticket holder, who has always had a passion for all types of memorabilia regarding Middlesbrough FC, especially programmes. Previous *Who's Who* contributor Harry Glaspers' *Middlesbrough: A Complete Record* books in the late 80s and early 90s sparked off a huge interest in the club's history and statistics. Has been Middlesbrough FC's official club statistician since the start of the 2007-08 season, where he contributes to the match-day programme and the club's website.

Tony Woodburn and **Martin Atherton** (Preston North End): Both North End fans for well over 40 years, this is Tony and Martin's final year of contributing to the *Who's Who*. They wish to place on record their pride in having been associated with this wonderful work since its inception 16 years ago and they wish Barry, the editorial team, and all the club contributors continuing success in the future.

David Woods (Bristol City): The official Bristol City historian has been an Ashton Gate regular since March 1958, though the first game he can actually recall seeing was the 2-2 draw at Swindon during the 1954-55 Third Division (South) championship campaign. David has been involved with many works on Bristol City, as well as a history of the Bristol Technical School and a couple of books on Bristol Bulldogs Speedway, the most recent of which, *Bristol Speedway The Bulldogs Roar 1928-1978*, was published just a few months ago by Desert Island Books. A graduate of the Open University, David's other interests include geology, history, cricket (Gloucestershire), rugby (Bristol), speedway (Somerset Rebels) as well as tennis, which has seen him visiting the Wimbledon Championships every year since 1973.

Editorial Introduction

Following on from last year's edition, the Who's Who portrays the statistical career record of every FA Barclays Premiership & Coca-Cola Football League player who made an appearance in 2009-10, whether it be in league football, the Football League Cup (Carling Cup), FA Cup (sponsored by E.ON) Community Shield (formerly the Charity Shield), UEFA Champions League, UEFA Cup, Inter-Toto Cup, Johnstone's Paint Trophy, or in the Play-Offs. Not included are Welsh Cup matches. It goes beyond mere statistics, however, with a write up on all of the 2,300 plus players involved, and also records faithfully last season's playing records separately by club.

The work falls into three main sections, all inter-relating. Firstly, the main core, PFA Footballers' Who's Who: A-Z (pages 13 to 452); secondly, the FA Barclays Premiership and Coca-Cola League Clubs: Summary of Appearances and Goals for 2009-10 (pages 453 to 472); and thirdly, Where Did They Go? (pages 475 to 479); lists all players shown in the previous edition who either moved on or did not play in 2009-10. Below is an explanation on how to follow the PFA Footballers' Who's Who. Transfers from 1 July 2010 until going to press in mid-July that involve players in the book are also recorded separately on pages 474/475.

As the title suggests, all players are listed in alphabetical order and are shown by Surnames first, followed by full Christian names, with the name the player is commonly known by shown in bold. Any abbreviation or pseudonyms bracketed.

Birthplace/date: You will note that several players who would be predominately classified as British, were born in places like Germany and India, for example. My book, Premier and Football League Players' Records, which covers every man who has played league football since the war, has, in the past, used the family domicile as a more realistic 'birthplace'. But, for our purposes here, I have reverted to that which has been officially recorded.

Height and Weight: Listed in feet and inches, and stones and pounds, respectively. It must be remembered that a player's weight can frequently change and, on that basis, the recorded data should be used as a guide only, especially as players are weighed several times during the season.

Club Honours: Those shown, cover careers from the Conference and FA Trophy upwards. For abbreviations, read:- European Honours: UEFACL (UEFA Champions League, formerly known as the European Cup), ESC (European Super Cup), ECWC (European Cup Winners' Cup, not contested since 1999) and UEFAC (UEFA Cup, formerly Fairs Cup). English Honours: FAC (FA Cup), FLC (Football League Cup), CS (Community Shield), FMC (Full Members Cup, which took in the Simod and Zenith Data sponsorships), AMC (Associated Members Cup, now known as the FL Trophy, which is currently sponsored by Johnstone's Paint and has previously involved Freight Rover, Sherpa Van, Leyland DAF, Autoglass, Auto Windscreens and LDV Vans), AIC (Anglo-Italian Cup), GMVC (GM Vauxhall Conference), NC (Nationwide Conference), FC (Football Conference), FAT (FA Trophy), FAYC (FA Youth Cup). Scottish Honours: SPD (Scottish Premier Division), S Div 1/2 (Scottish Leagues), SC (Scottish Cup), SLC (Scottish League Cup), SLCC (Scottish League Challenge Cup). Please note that medals awarded to P/FL, FLC, and AMC winners relate to players who have appeared in 25%, or over, of matches, while FAC, UEFACL,

ESC, ECWC and UEFAC winners' medals are for all-named finalists, including unused subs. For our purposes, however, Community Shield winners' medals refer to me who either played or came on as a sub. Honours applicable to players coming in from abroad are now shown at present, but the position continues to be reviewed.

International Honours: For abbreviations, read:- E (England), NI (Northern Ireland), S (Scotland), W (Wales) and RoI (Republic of Ireland). Under 21 through to full internationals give total appearances (inclusive of subs), while schoolboy (U16s and U18s) and youth representatives are just listed. The cut-off date used for appearances was immediately prior to the World Cup Finals taking place.

Player Descriptions: Gives position and playing strengths and, in keeping the work topical and positive, a few words on how their season went in 2009-10. This takes into account key performances, along with value to the team, injuries, honours, and other points of interest etc. Since 1999-2000, trainees were gradually superseded by scholars under the new scholarship scheme, but for our purposes the young players who come through the club are still denoted as trainees.

Career Records: Full appearances, plus substitutes and goals, are given for all FA Barclay Premiership and Coca-Cola League games. If a player who is in the book has played in any of the senior Scottish Leagues, his appearances with the club in question will also be recorded at the point of signing. Other information given, includes the player's source (clubs in the non-leagues, junior football, or from abroad), registered signing dates (if a player signs permanently following a loan spell, for our purposes we have shown the initial date as being point of transfer). Also, loan transfers are only recorded if an appearance is made, while transfer fees are the figures that have been reported in newspapers and magazines and should only be used as a guide to a player's valuation. Appearances, substitutions and goals are recorded by P/FL (Premiership and Football League), FLC (Football League Cup), FAC (FA Cup) and Others. Other matches take in the Play-Offs, FL Trophy, Community Shield and European competitions, such as the European Champions League, UEFA Cup, European Super Cup and Inter-Toto Cup. All of these matches are lumped together for reasons of saving space. Scottish appearances for players on loan to P/FL clubs in 2009-10 are shown at the point of transfer and do not include games following their return to Scotland. That also applies to players transferred from England to Scotland. FA Cup appearances, subs and goals are only recorded when they are made playing for a P/FL club and do not cover appearances made by Conference sides prior to joining or after relegation from the Football League.

Career Statistics are depicted as
Appearances + Substitutes/Goals

Whether you wish to analyse someone for your fantasy football team selection or would like to know more about a little-known player appearing in the lower reaches of the game, the PFA Footballers' Who's Who should provide you with the answer.

Barry J. Hugman, Editor,
PFA Footballers' Who's Who

A

ABBOTT Pawel Tadeusz Howard
Born: York, 2 December 1981
Height: 6'1" **Weight:** 11.12
International Honours: Poland: U21
Pawel finished the season as Oldham's top scorer, netting 13 times in 41 outings. His main strength is the ball holding that, at times, can be sublime. Pawel's ability to score goals from what looks like nothing are another great quality to have in your locker. He missed seven League games in mid-season to undergo a hernia operation in Germany, which was successful. Without him in the Oldham line-up, the Latics may well have struggled throughout the season.
Preston NE (£125,000 + from LKS Lodz, Poland on 16/2/2001) FL 8+17/6 FLC 0+1 FAC 1+3
Bury (Loaned on 9/8/2002) FL 13/5 FLC 2 Others 1
Bury (Loaned on 18/3/2003) FL 4/1
Huddersfield T (Signed on 16/2/2004) FL 83+28/48 FLC 4/2 FAC 2+2/1 Others 3+4
Swansea C (£150,000 on 22/1/2007) FL 9+9/1 FAC 0+1
Darlington (£100,000 on 12/7/2007) FL 31+11/17 FLC 1 FAC 0+2
Oldham Ath (Free on 2/7/2009) FL 38+1/13 FLC 0+1 Others 1

ABDOU Nadjim (Jimmy)
Born: Martigues, France, 13 July 1984
Height: 5'11" **Weight:** 11.3
Now in his second season at the Den, he has signed an extension to his Millwall contract taking him to 2013. Jimmy started off with a goal in the opening game at Southampton, televised by Sky. Injury in the Carling Cup tie ruled him out for four games, but after his return he played through the rest of the season. He is a midfield player who has boundless energy, constantly putting in match-winning displays from central midfield. Jimmy is tenacious and always wins the ball cleanly.
Plymouth Arg (Free from Martigues, France, ex Sedan, on 24/8/2007) FL 22+9/1 FLC 1 FAC 1/1
Millwall (Free on 4/7/2008) FL 74+5/4 FLC 2 FAC 6+1 Others 8/1

ADA OMGBA Patrick
Born: Yaounde, Cameroon, 14 January 1985
Height: 6'0" **Weight:** 13.5
Signed by Crewe in the summer from Histon, Patrick had been a regular

member of the defence in the Blue Square Premier. He made his Crewe debut in the opening game against Dagenham. Patrick lost his place in the side at the end of October after some early struggles and it was not until mid-April that he was back in again, holding his position for all the remaining fixtures.
Crewe Alex (Free from Histon, ex Redbridge, St Albans C, Exeter C, on 24/6/2009) FL 16+2 FLC 1 FAC 1 Others 1

Charlie Adam

ADAM Charles (Charlie) Graham
Born: Dundee, 10 December 1985
Height: 6'1" **Weight:** 13.1
Club Honours: S Div 1 '06; SLC '08; SLCC '06
International Honours: S: 4; B-3; U21-5
There is one man at Blackpool who everybody is talking about – Charlie Adam. The central midfielder won the PFA 'Player of the Month' for January after scoring in four consecutive games and unsurprisingly made it into the PFA Championship 'Team of the Year'. Adam also made a comeback on the international scene, playing twice for Scotland against Japan and the Czech Republic. A £500,000 acquisition from Glasgow Rangers in the summer, Charlie already knew Bloomfield Road well after spending the back end of the previous season on loan and was immediately made vice-captain. As captain Jason Euell only played a bit-part, it was down to Charlie to captain the side – quite a responsibility for a 24-

year-old. His carrying of the ball from midfield frightened defences throughout the season, and he recorded the most shots on (and off) target in the League. Remarkably for a midfielder, he notched 17 goals. This was thanks to David Vaughan and Keith Southern, who back up Charlie and allow him to express himself. His cool penalty gave Blackpool an important lead in the first leg of the play-off semi-final against Nottingham Forest and his brilliant free kick at Wembley put them back in the final against Cardiff.
Glasgow Rgrs (From juniors on 8/5/2004) SL 52+8/13 SLC 3+1 SC 4 Others 13+5/5
Ross Co (Loaned on 31/8/2004) SL 9+2/2 Others 4
St Mirren (Loaned on 31/8/2005) SL 24+5/5 SLC 0+1 SC 4/3 Others 2+1/1
Blackpool (£500,000 on 2/2/2009) FL 54+2/18 FLC 2/1 FAC 1 Others 3/2

ADAM Jamil Buba
Born: Bolton, 5 June 1991
Height: 5'10" **Weight:** 10.0
International Honours: Nigeria: Yth. RoI: Yth
Jamil played most of the season in the Barnsley Academy but the speedy striker was brought into the first team squad more often as the season moved into the final quarter. He then made a couple of appearances as a substitute. Jamil was selected in the Nigerian under-20 squad but, not having played for them, he chose instead to represent the Republic of Ireland, which he did on a number of occasions at under-19 level. He is a natural finisher and was held back to a degree by there being no reserve team at Oakwell. He shows great promise and much is expected.
Barnsley (From trainee on 7/7/2009) FL 0+3 FAC 0+1

ADAMS Daniel (Danny) Benjamin
Born: Manchester, 3 January 1976
Height: 5'8" **Weight:** 13.9
An experienced defender, Danny started the season at Morecambe on the left side of three central defenders. He played most of the early games but lost his place in the side in November and never got it back. Never happy to sit on the bench he was allowed to leave midway through the season and had a spell at Stalybridge Celtic.
Macclesfield T (£25,000 from Altrincham on 31/8/2000) FL 146+2/1 FLC 5+1 FAC 12 Others 3/1
Stockport Co (Signed on 5/3/2004) FL 39/1 FLC 1 FAC 2 Others 1
Huddersfield T (Free on 24/3/2005) FL 68 FLC 3 FAC 3 Others 3

Morecambe (Free on 21/2/2007) FL 96+2 FLC 5 FAC 4 Others 5

ADAMS Nathan Mark
Born: Lincoln, 6 October 1991
Height: 5'9" **Weight:** 10.10
A second-year scholar, Nathan's first team outings for Lincoln in 2009-10 were restricted to just two substitute appearances totalling 16 minutes early on in the campaign. The striker's prolific form for the youth team, however, saw him rewarded with the offer of a professional contract at the end of the season.
Lincoln C (Trainee) FL 0+4

ADAMS Nicholas (Nicky) William
Born: Bolton, 16 October 1986
Height: 5'10" **Weight:** 11.0
Club Honours: Div 1 '09
International Honours: W: U21-4
Talented young midfielder who remained predominantly on the fringe of matters at Leicester in 2009-10, making almost all of his appearances from the bench. He netted his only goal during a rare start in the League Cup at Preston, but had to rely on a January loan to Leyton Orient for much needed match practice. During the six games he played the O's remained unbeaten and although they wanted to extend the deal Nicky returned to Leicester after a month.
Bury (From trainee on 1/7/2006) FL 61+16/14 FLC 3 FAC 8+1/1 Others 4+1
Leicester C (£100,000 + on 17/7/2008) FL 5+25 FLC 3/1 FAC 1+1 Others 3/1
Rochdale (Loaned on 19/11/2009) FL 12+2/1
Leyton Orient (Loaned on 15/1/2010) FL 6

ADAMSON Christopher (Chris)
Born: Ashington, 4 November 1978
Height: 6'1" **Weight:** 11.12
Chris, whose principal role at Hereford was that of goalkeeping coach, waited patiently as a substitute for his first appearance for the Bulls. Unfortunately that start, at Notts County, turned into a nightmare as United conceded five goals, Chris picked up a facial injury that required stitches and then received a red card. Later in the season, a car accident in which he suffered a back injury, also restricted his availability.
West Bromwich A (From trainee on 2/7/1997) FL 12 FAC 2 (Freed on 7/4/2003)
Mansfield T (Loaned on 30/4/1999) FL 2
Halifax T (Loaned on 1/7/1999) FL 7
Plymouth Arg (Loaned on 10/11/2002) FL 1
Sheffield Wed (Free from St Patrick's

Ath on 28/1/2005) FL 9+2 FLC 1
Stockport Co (Free on 9/8/2007) FAC 2 (Freed during 2008 close season)
Hereford U (Free from Ilkeston T on 2/7/2009) FL 1

ADDISON Miles Vivien Esifi
Born: Newham, 7 January 1989
Height: 6'2" **Weight:** 13.3
International Honours: E: U21-1
Derby's Miles won his first England Under-21 cap as a substitute against Greece but the powerful young defender's season was cut short in January. He suffered from foot trouble in previous campaigns and this proved more serious. In order to find a permanent solution, Miles travelled to San Francisco for surgery by a leading podiatrist. The operation was successful but the prognosis was that he could be out of action for up to a year. It was frustrating for him as he started well in the centre of defence, scoring in the opening day defeat of Peterborough and the home win over Plymouth. But he is determined to work hard on his rehabilitation and should come back strongly.
Derby Co (From trainee on 6/7/2007) P/FL 41+3/3 FLC 6 FAC 5/1

ADEBAYOR Sheyi Emmanuel
Born: Lome, Togo, 26 February 1984
Height: 6'2" **Weight:** 11.11
International Honours: Togo: 40
The Togo international striker experienced a mixed season following his transfer from Arsenal to Manchester City in the summer. He started in blistering form with goals in each of his first four Premiership games for City, the last in a 4-2 win over his former club. Sadly he wasted the goodwill with a kick in the face of former colleague Robin Van Persie – for which he was suspended for three games – and an absurd celebration in front of the Arsenal fans, provoking some crowd trouble, that resulted in a £25,000 fine. In December he joined Togo for the African Cup of Nations in Angola, where their team bus was attacked by terrorists, resulting in the death of three staff members. Understandably he was deeply affected by this and subsequently announced his retirement from international football after the Togo team withdrew from the competition. New City manager Roberto Mancini granted him extended leave of absence and he returned in late January to score in three consecutive games. However he was then handed a four game suspension in February after an elbow on Ryan Shawcross in the FA Cup replay defeat at Stoke. He returned

in April to score two doubles in consecutive games, against Burnley and Birmingham, and ended as City's second top scorer with 14 goals.
Arsenal (£5,000,000 from AS Monaco, France on 31/1/2006) PL 86+18/46 FLC 3+2/3 FAC 4+3/4 Others 21+5/9
Manchester C (Signed on 18/7/2009) PL 25+1/14 FLC 2+1 FAC 2

ADEBOLA Bamberdele (Dele)
Born: Lagos, Nigeria, 23 June 1975
Height: 6'3" **Weight:** 12.8
After turning down a new contract with Bristol City, Dele was the first of three new forwards to arrive at Nottingham Forest in the summer. Although Dele never fully established himself in the side, he used his experience to help the younger strike partners. All of his four goals during the season were scored at the City Ground, including the last of the campaign, against Blackpool in the play-off semi-final. He was out of contract at the end of the season.
Crewe Alex (From trainee on 21/6/1993) FL 98+27/39 FLC 4+3/2 FAC 8+2/3 Others 10+1/2
Birmingham C (£1,000,000 on 6/2/1998) FL 86+43/31 FLC 13+4/8 FAC 2+1/2 Others 1+2/1
Oldham Ath (Loaned on 20/3/2002) FL 5
Crystal Palace (Free on 15/8/2002) FL 32+7/5 FLC 5/2 FAC 4
Coventry C (Free on 2/7/2003) FL 115+48/31 FLC 5+3/3 FAC 8+3/2
Burnley (Loaned on 25/3/2004) FL 0+3/1
Bradford C (Loaned on 13/8/2004) FL 14+1/3 Others 1/1
Bristol C (£250,000 on 31/1/2008) FL 48+8/16 FLC 1 FAC 0+2 Others 3
Nottingham F (Free on 7/7/2009) FL 13+20/3 FLC 0+2 FAC 1+1 Others 0+1/1

ADEYEMI Thomas (Tom) Oluseun
Born: Milton Keynes, 24 October 1991
Height: 6'1" **Weight:** 12.4
Tom made his debut as a substitute in Norwich's opening day mauling by Colchester after a string of impressive pre-season displays, culminating in a superb scoring performance against a Manchester United XI at Carrow Road. An athletic midfielder, he likes to break forward in possession of the ball and is also an excellent passer. His progress won national recognition when he was named as 'League One Apprentice of the Year' at the Football League Awards in March.
Norwich C (From trainee on 13/11/2008) FL 2+9 FLC 2 Others 4

ADKINS Sam
Born: Birmingham, 3 December 1990
Height: 5'10" **Weight:** 11.7
Sam's season was restricted to a handful of minutes towards the end of a 1-0 home defeat by Yeovil on a freezing cold February night when Walsall struggled to put two passes together on a snow-covered pitch. He played on the left side of midfield and had little chance to impress. He was released at the end of the season.
Walsall (From trainee on 4/7/2009) FL 0+2

ADOMAH Albert Danquah
Born: Lambeth, 13 December 1987
Height: 6'1" **Weight:** 11.8
Highly-rated winger Albert nearly left Barnet on transfer deadline day in August but the club rejected a £200,000 bid from Blackpool. He remained with the Bees and was once again a fixture on the right wing. He chipped in with five goals, along with numerous assists, giving many League Two left-backs a torrid time. During the season he was offered a record-breaking contract with the club, but chose to decline it.
Barnet (Signed from Harrow Borough on 14/1/2008) FL 104+8/19 FLC 2 FAC 3+1/1 Others 2

AGARD Keiran Ricardo
Born: Newham, 10 October 1989
Height: 5'10" **Weight:** 10.10
The former Everton Academy player made his debut in the Carling Cup win at Hull in September. The speedy forward then made a first Premier League appearance from the bench against Chelsea at Stamford Bridge in December, before a first start for the Toffees against BATE Borisov in the Europa League. The mobile striker will be hoping to develop his Toffees career next season.
Everton (From trainee on 12/10/2006) PL 0+1 FLC 0+1 FAC 0+1 Others 1+2

AGBONLAHOR Gabriel (Gabby)
Born: Birmingham, 13 October 1986
Height: 5'11" **Weight:** 12.5
International Honours: E: 3; U21-15; Yth
In another season of progress, Gabby ended with his highest goals tally for Aston Villa. The Brummie striker scored 16, with ten League goals making him Villa's joint-leading top flight scorer. His most important goal was arguably his winner against Manchester United in December, Villa's first victory at Old Trafford since 1983. Gabby continued his remarkable record in derbies, scoring

in his sixth successive match against local rivals with the winner at Birmingham in September. Although one of the League's quickest players, he is no longer known for his pace alone. Gabby showed his finishing prowess at various times, most notably with a clinically taken brace in the victory at Fulham, and scored in five successive games early in the season. He has worked hard to improve his touch and awareness and spent extra hours in the gym. He suffered frustration in Villa's two trips to Wembley through refereeing injustices. Manchester United's Nemanja Vidic avoided a red card in the Carling Cup final for a professional foul on Gabby, who was brought down in the box by John Obi Mikel in the FA Cup semi-final, only for the Chelsea midfielder's foul to go unpunished. Gabby made his competitive England debut when he started the qualifying win over Belarus, having previously played in friendlies, but was not chosen for Fabio Capello's World Cup squad.
Aston Villa (From trainee on 4/3/2005) PL 147+9/45 FLC 11+1/3 FAC 6/1 Others 8+3/1
Watford (Loaned on 22/9/2005) FL 1+1
Sheffield Wed (Loaned on 28/10/2005) FL 4+4

AGGER Daniel
Born: Hvidovre, Denmark, 12 December 1984
Height: 6'2" **Weight:** 11.11
Club Honours: CS '06
International Honours: Denmark: 31; U21-10; Yth
In his fourth season at Liverpool, the Danish international central defender was again sidelined by injury at the start after surgery for a recurring back injury. He returned in October and starred in the vital 2-0 victory over Manchester United later that month – their best Premiership display in a troubled campaign. He was almost ever-present for the remainder of the season apart from a three-week absence with a calf problem in January. Despite playing more games (36) than ever before, it was not a great campaign for the Dane as, due to defensive deficiencies, Liverpool lost 19 of their 56 matches and lost, or drew, 11 games after taking the lead – a significant number of goals being conceded from set pieces. Daniel is noted for his forward runs and powerful shooting from long range but this was not much in evidence, his only goal coming from a clever back-heel flick from a corner to give Liverpool an early lead in the Europa Cup at Benfica. In the last six games, Daniel was

switched to left-back to cover for the injured Emiliano Insua.
Liverpool (£5,800,000 from Brondby, Denmark, ex Rosenhoj BK, on 13/1/2006) PL 69+8/3 FLC 4/2 FAC 3 Others 31/2

AGYEMANG Patrick
Born: Walthamstow, 29 September 1980
Height: 6'1" **Weight:** 12.0
International Honours: Ghana: 3
Mainly deployed as an impact sub for the first half of the season, Patrick struggled to find a regular place up front in the Queens Park Rangers' side. He did manage to score three goals; including two in two during December however these both came in heavy defeats against Middlesbrough and Watford. Perhaps finding himself frustrated with the opportunities offered at Loftus Road he joined Bristol City on loan in January, spending the remainder of the campaign with them. Patrick fared little better there, though to be fair he had to overcome injury problems which meant that, following his initial five game flurry, he was out of the team until coming on as substitute for Paul Hartley at Scunthorpe on 17 April.
Wimbledon (From trainee on 11/5/1999) FL 68+53/20 FLC 3+2/1 FAC 8+3/1
Brentford (Loaned on 18/10/1999) FL 3+9 FAC 1
Gillingham (£200,000 on 13/1/2004) FL 29+4/8 FLC 1
Preston NE (£350,000 on 17/11/2004) FL 55+67/21 FLC 1+1 FAC 5+1 Others 0+5
Queens Park Rgrs (£350,000 on 3/1/2008) FL 33+21/13 FLC 3+1 FAC 2+2
Bristol C (Loaned on 25/1/2010) FL 5+2

AINSLEY Jack William
Born: Ipswich, 17 September 1990
Height: 5'11" **Weight:** 11.0
Jack made his debut and only appearance for Ipswich in the Carling Cup at Shrewsbury at right-back and although he did not let the team down, was substituted at half-time. He had a successful season as the reserve team skipper.
Ipswich T (From trainee on 23/7/2009) FLC 1

AINSWORTH Gareth
Born: Blackburn, 10 May 1973
Height: 5'9" **Weight:** 12.5
After becoming part of the Queens Park Rangers' coaching staff in 2008-09, Gareth stepped down to a playing role under new boss Jim Magilton but made

only two substitute appearances before joining up with Gary Waddock at Wycombe on loan in November. The talismanic right-winger immediately inspired his team-mates to two consecutive wins over Millwall and Brentford before injury cut short his stay. He returned to Adams Park in February on an 18-month contract but, six minutes into his return, he was red carded against Millwall after a mass pitch brawl. His contribution for the rest of the season was huge, not just for his infectious enthusiasm and leadership, but for his intelligent wing play. He became the bane of League Two left-backs, invariably delivering quality crosses into the danger area and managing to play the full 90 minutes in most games in spite of his advancing years. He was probably the team's most dangerous striker, when pushed up front chasing the game late on, and was voted the Supporters' 'Player of the Season', in spite of playing only 14 games.

Preston NE *(Signed from Northwich Vic, ex Blackburn Rov YTS, on 21/1/1992) FL 2+3 Others 1/1*
Cambridge U *(Free on 17/8/1992) FL 1+3/1 FLC 0+1*
Preston NE *(Free on 23/12/1992) FL 76+6/14 FLC 3+2 FAC 3+1 Others 8+1/1*
Lincoln C *(£25,000 on 31/10/1995) FL 83/37 FLC 8/3 FAC 2 Others 4/1*
Port Vale *(£500,000 on 12/9/1997) FL 53+2/10 FLC 2/1 FAC 2*
Wimbledon *(£2,000,000 on 3/11/1998) P/FL 21+15/6 FLC 1+1 FAC 5+2/1*
Preston NE *(Loaned on 28/3/2002) FL 3+2/1*
Walsall *(Loaned on 5/12/2002) FL 2+3/1*
Cardiff C *(£50,000 on 17/3/2003) FL 9*
Queens Park Rgrs *(Free on 17/7/2003) FL 102+39/21 FLC 2+2/1 FAC 3+2 Others 2*
Wycombe W *(Free on 20/11/2009) FL 12+2/2*

AINSWORTH Lionel Glenn Robert
Born: Nottingham, 1 October 1987
Height: 5'5" **Weight:** 10.5
International Honours: E: Yth
The pacy Huddersfield wingman was looking to establish himself within the first team during the course of the campaign, often being brought on from the substitutes' bench to supply telling crosses into the danger areas. A couple of back-to-back appearances in the League and further call-ups in the Cup competitions gave him some consistency within the side before he was loaned

out to Brentford for three months during the later part of January. Unfortunately, the tricky outside-right was only used as a substitute until being selected to start against Yeovil at the end of April. Having been substituted the loan deal was promptly ended and he went back to the Galpharm Stadium.
Derby Co *(From trainee on 10/9/2005) FL 0+2*
Bournemouth *(Loaned on 4/8/2006) FL 2+5 FAC 0+1 Others 1*
Wycombe W *(Loaned on 23/2/2007) FL 3+4*
Hereford U *(Free on 7/8/2007) FL 13+2/4 FLC 2/3 FAC 2/1*
Watford *(Signed on 22/11/2007) FL 4+11 FLC 3 Others 1+1*
Hereford U *(Loaned on 21/11/2008) FL 7/3*
Huddersfield T *(Free on 26/1/2009) FL 9+16 FLC 0+2 FAC 1+1 Others 1+1*
Brentford *(Loaned on 29/1/2010) FL 1+8*

AJDAREVIC Astrit
Born: Pristina, Kosovo 17 April 1990
Height: 6'1" **Weight:** 12.2
Club Honours: FAYC '07
International Honours: Sweden: Yth
Talented junior Swedish international midfielder who signed a one-year contract at Leicester in the summer following a brief loan spell towards the end of 2008-09. Having failed to break into the first team squad, he linked up with Brighton, on trial, at the close of the January transfer window, before finally trying his luck on loan at Hereford. Unfortunately his time there amounted to just a few minutes on the pitch against Barnet. The tall, long-striding midfielder injured a hamstring early on and his time at Edgar Street was over. Was out of contract at the end of June.
Liverpool *(From trainee, via Falkenbergs, Sweden, on 3/5/2007)*
Leicester C *(Free on 26/3/2009) FL 0+5*
Hereford U *(Loaned on 25/3/2010) FL 0+1*

AKINBIYI Adeola (Ade) Oluwatoyin
Born: Hackney, 10 October 1974
Height: 6'1" **Weight:** 12.9
International Honours: Nigeria: 1
Ade, who arrived at Notts County from Houston Dynamo after his time was up in America, became the last of the name signings under the big money regime that never was. A striker of outstanding reputation at previous clubs, he remained an enigmatic mystery to County fans because they rarely had a chance to see him play. Reunited with his former mentor Steve

Cotterill in February but unable to claim a place in the starting line-up, he was released at the end of the season.
Norwich C *(From trainee on 5/2/1993) P/FL 22+27/3 FLC 2+4/2 FAC 0+2 Others 0+1*
Hereford U *(Loaned on 21/1/1994) FL 3+1/2*
Brighton & Hove A *(Loaned on 24/11/1994) FL 7/4*
Gillingham *(£250,000 on 13/1/1997) FL 63/28 FLC 2 FAC 2/1 Others 0+1*
Bristol C *(£1,200,000 on 28/5/1998) FL 47/21 FLC 5/4 FAC 1*
Wolverhampton W *(£3,500,000 on 7/9/1999) FL 36+1/16 FAC 3*
Leicester C *(£5,000,000 on 28/7/2000) PL 49+9/11 FLC 1/1 FAC 5+1/1 Others 2*
Crystal Palace *(£2,200,000 + on 6/2/2002) FL 11+13/3 FAC 0+4*
Stoke C *(Loaned on 27/3/2003) FL 4/2*
Stoke C *(Free on 15/9/2003) FL 52+7/17 FLC 0+1 FAC 2*
Burnley *(£600,000 on 24/2/2005) FL 38+1/16 FLC 3/2 FAC 1*
Sheffield U *(£1,750,000 on 27/1/2006) P/FL 12+6/3 FLC 2/1*
Burnley *(£750,000 on 3/1/2007) FL 30+40/10 FLC 2+5/2 FAC 1+1/1 (Freed on 2/4/2009)*
Notts Co *(Free from Houston Dynamo on 27/9/2009) FL 1+9 FAC 1*

AKINDE John Job Ayo
Born: Camberwell, 8 July 1989
Height: 6'2" **Weight:** 10.1
Club Honours: FAT '08
Quite why this Bristol City centre-forward, who was signed from Ebbsfleet United in August 2008, continued to be loaned out to other clubs was a mystery to many Ashton Gate fans. Despite City needing to boost a lack-lustre attack, John only made one full appearance, in the disappointing 2-0 Carling Cup defeat by Carlisle. Loaned out to Wycombe in November, where he had a successful spell in 2008-09, the powerful striker's debut, at Huddersfield, was cut short with a twisted ankle after 38 minutes. However, fit again and following a 'Man of the Match' performance against Stockport, his stay was extended for a further month. Sent off in his next game, against Oldham, shortly after scoring his only goal he returned to City. Although John has the precious ability to make goals out of nothing, a further loan spell, at Brentford in February, saw him unable to integrate into the team in his two appearances before returning to Ashton Gate.
Bristol C *(£140,000 from Ebbsfleet U on 1/9/2008) FL 1+13/1 FLC 1+1 FAC 0+2*

Wycombe W (Loaned on 11/3/2009) FL 11/7
Wycombe W (Loaned on 13/11/2009) FL 4+2/1
Brentford (Loaned on 1/2/2010) FL 2

AKINFENWA Saheed Adebayo (Bayo)
Born: Islington, 10 May 1982
Height: 5'11" **Weight:** 13.0
Club Honours: AMC '06
Out-and-out striker Bayo was the darling of the Northampton crowd again this season with his 100 per cent effort and another hatful of goals. As well as knocking the goals in, he also acted as provider for many of his team-mates by holding up the ball coupled with some powerful runs. He was certainly one of the major factors in Town's climb up the division this season and he deservedly won the 'Player of the Season' trophy. Was out of contract in the summer.
Boston U (Free from Barry T, ex FK Atlantas, on 15/10/2003) FL 2+1 Others 1/1
Leyton Orient (Free on 31/10/2003) FL 0+1 FAC 0+1
Rushden & Diamonds (Free on 11/12/2003)
Doncaster Rov (Free on 18/2/2004) FL 4+5/4
Torquay U (Free on 1/7/2004) FL 28+9/14 FLC 0+1 FAC 1 Others 1+1/2
Swansea C (£35,000 + on 13/7/2005) FL 41+18/14 FLC 1+1/1 FAC 2+3/1 Others 6+3/5
Millwall (Free on 15/11/2007) FL 1+6 FAC 1+1
Northampton T (Free on 18/1/2008) FL 78+10/37 FLC 2+2/2 FAC 2 Others 0+1

AKPA AKPRO Jean-Louis
Born: Toulouse, France, 4 January 1985
Height: 6'0" **Weight:** 10.12
A season of two halves for Jean-Louis saw him produce his best form for Grimsby after Christmas. Occasionally seen on the wing as well as in attack, the crowd favourite was at his best when running at defenders, a notable run and shot versus Shrewsbury (3-0) in March ending a run of 25 League Two games without victory. Although not a regular marksman, Jean-Louis was Town's most creative player, claiming eight goal assists. Was out of contract at the end of June.
Grimsby T (Free from FCM Brussels, Belgium, ex Toulouse, Brest - loan, on 8/12/2008) FL 45+11/8 FLC 1 FAC 1 Others 0+2

AKPAN Hope Ini
Born: Liverpool, 14 August 1991
Height: 6'0" **Weight:** 12.6

Having signed professional terms in 2008, the midfielder was a regular for Everton's reserve side in the last campaign and made his first team debut as an early substitute for Jack Rodwell against BATE Borisov at Goodison in the Europa League. An Academy player from the age of 15, Hope will be looking for further opportunities next season.
Everton (From trainee on 13/11/2008) Others 0+1

ALBRIGHTON Marc Kevin
Born: Tamworth, 18 November 1989
Height: 6'2" **Weight:** 12.6
International Honours: E: Yth
Marc was handed his Premier League debut and was a regular member of Aston Villa's squad. Having progressed through the ranks, Mark had a brief substitute appearance against Wigan on the opening day. The exciting young winger also came off the bench in League games against Liverpool and Wolves and the Europa League home tie against Rapid Vienna. Frustratingly, Marc's only senior start, in the FA Cup fourth round victory over Brighton, ended in disappointment when he limped off after injuring himself in setting up the opening goal.
Aston Villa (From trainee on 28/9/2009) PL 0+3 FLC 0+1 FAC 1 Others 1+1

ALCOCK Craig
Born: Truro, 8 December 1987
Height: 5'8" **Weight:** 11.0
The right-back had a great season operating in what was a very young defence at times. Given the Yeovil captain's armband early in the season after injury to the previous skipper, the accomplished Cornwall-born player grew into the role and even notched a goal against Brentford in September. He is now approaching 100 career games for the Glovers since his debut three years ago and will be one of the first names on the team sheet.
Yeovil T (From juniors on 7/7/2006) FL 69+12/2 FLC 0+3 FAC 4 Others 3+1

ALDRED Thomas (Tom) Michael
Born: Bolton, 11 September 1990
Height: 6'2" **Weight:** 13.3
This Scottish youth international came into contention at Carlisle after some promising displays at youth level and a loan spell at Workington. He gave an assured performance on his full debut against Bristol Rovers that earned him a 'Man of the Match' award. Tom made several more appearances in central

defence and will be pushing for a regular berth in the new campaign
Carlisle U (From trainee on 16/12/2008) FL 4+1 Others 0+1

ALESSANDRA Lewis Peter
Born: Bury, 8 February 1989
Height: 5'9" **Weight:** 11.7
It was a disappointing season for Lewis, ravaged by injury and illness. He made only two appearances for Oldham and was even more unfortunate to be sent on loan to Chester, where he picked up a nasty injury. Big things were expected of Lewis following his stunning hat-trick the previous season against promoted Scunthorpe. But it all seemed to go wrong for the young striker, who packs plenty of pace and ability in his locker.
Oldham Ath (From trainee on 3/7/2007) FL 24+24/8 FLC 0+3 FAC 2+1 Others 0+1

[ALEX] DIAS DA COSTA Alex Rodrigo
Born: Niteroi, Brazil, 17 June 1982
Height: 6'2" **Weight:** 14.0
Club Honours: FAC '09, '10; CS '09; PL '10
International Honours: Brazil: 17; U23-8
Chelsea's big centre-back is known as 'The Tank' or 'The Grenade Launcher' for his ferocious tackling and shooting and signed a four-year contract in October, although he missed the first ten weeks following a double hernia operation. Alex was raised in the favelas of Rio, where most boys want to be a Pele or Zico, but his former boss Guus Hiddink described him as 'the best centre-half in Europe'. He replaced the injured Ricardo Carvalho for 13 of the last 14 matches and played superbly as the Blues hit top form to edge the Premier League title by one point. Surprisingly, he scored only one goal, out of the Blues' total of 142, with a towering header against West Ham. He came close to extending the club scoring record as he shuddered the bar at Birmingham with a free kick but Chelsea drew a blank after 34 consecutive matches in which they had scored. Indeed, this was the only Premier League match in which the Champions failed to score. Alex suffered a disappointment at the season's end with his omission from Brazil's World Cup squad by manager Dunga.
Chelsea (Signed from Santos, Brazil, via PSV Eindhoven, on 14/8/2007) PL 57+11/5 FLC 6 FAC 14/1 Others 16+1/2

Alex

ALEXANDER Gary George

Born: Lambeth, 15 August 1979
Height: 5'11" **Weight:** 13.0
Gary is a powerful striker who always gives 100 per cent to Millwall. He is very good in the air and loves to go on surging runs that create chances for himself and his team-mates. He scored a late winner against Leeds that ended their unbeaten run before a heel injury ruled him out until mid-April. On his return, Gary completed 100 appearances for the Lions.
West Ham U (From trainee on 6/7/1998)
Exeter C (Loaned on 19/8/1999) FL 37/16 FLC 1 FAC 3/1 Others 4/2
Swindon T (£300,000 on 11/8/2000) FL 30+7/7 FLC 3 FAC 2+1 Others 2+1/2
Hull C (£160,000 on 21/6/2001) FL 64+4/23 FLC 3/2 FAC 3/2 Others 4/3
Leyton Orient (Signed on 27/1/2003) FL 165+14/52 FLC 2+2 FAC 10/1 Others 2+4/2
Millwall (Free on 5/7/2007) FL 69+17/19 FLC 4/1 FAC 5+2/3 Others 4+3/2

ALEXANDER Graham

Born: Coventry, 10 October 1971
Height: 5'10" **Weight:** 12.7
Club Honours: Div 2 '00
International Honours: S: 40; B-1
Many thought that Graham would struggle, having finally reached the

Premier League and in so doing becoming its oldest debutant at the age of nearly 38, but how wrong they were. He remained one of the first names on the Burnley team-sheet, captaining the side in the extended absence of Steven Caldwell, and possibly proving his value most while absent through injury in February, when his calm influence in the midfield was badly missed. While hardly a speed merchant, Graham remains superbly fit for a player his age, and his amazing penalty record was maintained as he was again the Clarets' second top scorer, four of his seven League goals coming against Hull. Graham again won several of the club's 'Player of the Year' awards. Following Owen Coyle's departure in January, he was given extra responsibility as part of the Turf Moor coaching staff. He also added two more to his collection of Scotland caps during the season.
Scunthorpe U (From trainee on 20/3/1990) FL 149+10/18 FLC 11+1/2 FAC 12/1 Others 13+4/3
Luton T (£100,000 on 8/7/1995) FL 146+4/15 FLC 17/2 FAC 7+1 Others 6+2
Preston NE (£50,000 on 25/3/1999) FL 350+2/52 FLC 19+1/6 FAC 19/5 Others 8+1
Burnley (£200,000 on 31/8/2007) P/FL 122/17 FLC 7+1 FAC 8/2 Others 3/1

AL-HABSI Ali Abdullah Harib

Born: Muscat, Oman, 30 December 1981
Height: 6'5" **Weight:** 13.12
International Honours: Oman: 66
Last season followed a now familiar pattern for Ali in that he played more games in goal for the Oman national team than he did for Bolton. He made just two appearances for the club, both in Cup competitions and ending in distinctly different manners. His first appearance came in a 4-0 Carling Cup defeat at Chelsea, though that particular result certainly was not a slur on Ali's performance. He followed that with a starting role in the 4-0 FA Cup win over Lincoln in January. Despite a lack of first team action, certainly where the Premier League is concerned, Ali once again insisted that he is content as a Bolton player and this certainly bodes well for the future. He is a highly reliable deputy to Jussi Jaaskelainen and is certainly competent enough to take his place when the Finnish legend decides to retire.
Bolton W (Signed from Lyn Oslo, Norway, ex Al-Midhaibi, Al-Nasr Sports Club, on 10/1/2006) PL 10 FLC 2 FAC 2 Others 4

ALIADIERE Jeremie

Born: Rambouillet, France, 30 March 1983
Height: 6'0" **Weight:** 11.8
Club Honours: FAYC '01; PL '04; CS '04
International Honours: France: U21; Yth
Jeremie started the season up front for Middlesbrough after playing most of the previous campaign on the right wing. In September, he hit a vein of form, scoring twice at home to Ipswich and another one at Sheffield Wednesday three days later. He suffered an ankle injury in Gareth Southgate's last game in charge of Boro that kept him out for two months. He returned on Boxing Day against Scunthorpe with his fourth goal of the campaign but this proved to be his last. A broken toe suffered in March at Cardiff brought another spell on the sidelines but he returned to play in the last two games, although Middlesbrough seemed reluctant to take up the option of an extra year on his contract.
Arsenal (From trainee on 4/4/2000) PL 7+22/1 FLC 9+2/8 FAC 3+4 Others 0+4
Glasgow Celtic (Loaned on 1/7/2005) Others 0+2
West Ham U (Loaned on 25/8/2005) PL 1+6 FLC 0+1
Wolverhampton W (Loaned on 14/2/2006) FL 12+2/2

Middlesbrough (£2,000,000 on 10/7/2007) P/FL 69+9/11 FLC 3/1 FAC 5

ALJOFREE Hasney
Born: Manchester, 11 July 1978
Height: 6'0" **Weight:** 12.1
Club Honours: Div 2 '04
International Honours: E: Yth
Hasney joined Oldham on a free transfer from Swindon in March following surgery on his knee. He was a non-playing substitute on 12 occasions before finally making an appearance in the away game at Yeovil, the team against which he sustained the original injury in the previous season. Following this, the central defender was released by the Latics for financial reasons with only one game left in the season.
Bolton W (From trainee on 2/7/1996) P/FL 6+8 FLC 4+2 FAC 0+2
Dundee U (Signed on 9/6/2000) SL 52+2/4 SLC 5+1 SC 5+1/3
Plymouth Arg (Signed on 30/8/2002) FL 109+8/3 FLC 3 FAC 5/2 Others 2
Sheffield Wed (Loaned on 23/9/2004) FL 2 Others 1
Oldham Ath (Loaned on 21/3/2007) FL 5
Swindon T (Signed on 10/8/2007) FL 55+2/2 FLC 2 FAC 5/1
Oldham Ath (Free on 3/2/2010) FL 1

ALLEN Joseph (Joe) Michael
Born: Carmarthen, 14 March 1990
Height: 5'6" **Weight:** 9.10
International Honours: W: 2; U21-11; Yth
An injury affected season for Swansea's promising central midfield player began with a groin strain in the opening match at Leicester. This sidelined him until late October. When fit, Joe was regularly included in John Toshack's Welsh international squad, but after his return from injury, he suffered further knee trouble at Derby and was once more ruled out of the action. As Joe matured as a force in midfield, the more he was tightly marked by the opposition as the playmaker in Swansea's side.
Swansea C (From trainee on 23/8/2007) FL 32+20/1 FLC 3 FAC 5+1 Others 2+1

ALLOTT Mark Stephen
Born: Middleton, 3 October 1977
Height: 5'11" **Weight:** 12.6
Mark made a welcome return to Chesterfield colours in July. His excellent levels of personal fitness help him to show great consistency and only a one-game virus prevented the midfield playmaker from becoming the club's first outfield ever-present for 14 years. Made his 250th League start for the Spireites in the last game of the season.
Oldham Ath (From trainee on

14/10/1995) FL 105+49/31 FLC 7+3/2 FAC 8+7 Others 2+3
Chesterfield (Free on 19/12/2001) FL 205+16/11 FLC 8+1/2 FAC 5 Others 5+3/1
Oldham Ath (Signed on 12/7/2007) FL 78+9/7 FLC 3 FAC 7 Others 3
Tranmere Rov (Free on 2/7/2009)
Chesterfield (Free on 27/7/2009) FL 45/2 FLC 1 FAC 1 Others 3

ALMOND Louis James
Born: Blackburn, 5 January 1992
Height: 5'11" **Weight:** 12.0
One of the bright sparks from the Blackpool Academy, Louis made his first team bow away at Crewe in the League Cup. Following that, impressive performances for the reserves saw him loaned to Cheltenham later in the season, where he proved to be a lively front runner with pace, good touch and an eye for goal. Louis made his Football League debut for Town in the 1-1 home draw with Port Vale at the Abbey Business Stadium. He also started the next game at Macclesfield, but with Cheltenham fighting a battle against relegation from the League manager Mark Yates went with a more experienced forward line for the final weeks of the season, Louis made his last appearance for the club as a substitute in the last match at home to Accrington.
Blackpool (From trainee on 19/3/2010) FLC 0+1
Cheltenham T (Loaned on 19/3/2010) FL 2+2

ALMUNIA Manuel
Born: Pamplona, Spain, 19 May 1977
Height: 6'4" **Weight:** 11.8
Club Honours: FAC '05
Manuel divided opinion among the Arsenal faithful as he endured a mixed season. There were highs for the goalkeeper, most notably in his outstanding first-half performance against Barcelona in the home Champions League quarter-final and the penalty save at home to West Ham. However in the negative column were own goals against both Manchester clubs and an injury time mistake at Birmingham to concede two points among others. He twice had spells out of the side due to injuries at the beginning and the end of the season. Manuel remains a solid shot-stopper but his biggest weakness is his positional sense and his long-term future as Arsenal's number one is uncertain. He played 29 times in the Premier League, keeping ten clean sheets, and seven times in the Champions League, registering a

further three clean sheets.
Arsenal (£500,000 from Celta Vigo, Spain on 19/7/2004) PL 101 FLC 14 FAC 10 Others 36+1

ALNWICK Benjamin (Ben) Robert
Born: Prudhoe, 1 January 1987
Height: 6'2" **Weight:** 13.12
International Honours: E: U21-1; Yth
The former England under-21 International goalie has been at Tottenham for over three years now and has had limited first team opportunities, spending only short periods out on loan. In 2009-10 Ben was on loan early in August and September at Norwich, where he made six appearances and his calm assurance did much to steady the City ship. He also produced several top-class saves before his brief stint was rudely interrupted by a serious head injury sustained in a clash with team-mate Michael Spillane in the League Cup defeat at the hands of Sunderland, followed by a groin injury immediately afterwards. Recalled by Tottenham, Ben spent most of the season on the bench and was unfortunate that his only appearance came in the last game at Burnley, where the defence switched off and conceded four goals. Ben has good reactive skills, is capable of making good saves, and at 23 years of age he has plenty of time to make further progress.
Sunderland (From trainee on 13/3/2004) P/FL 19 FLC 3
Tottenham H (£900,000 on 1/1/2007) PL 1 FLC 1 FAC 1
Luton T (Loaned on 28/9/2007) FL 4
Leicester C (Loaned on 7/1/2008) FL 8
Carlisle U (Loaned on 17/10/2008) FL 6
Norwich C (Loaned on 4/8/2009) FL 3 FLC 2 Others 1

ALSOP Julian Mark
Born: Nuneaton, 28 May 1973
Height: 6'4" **Weight:** 14.0
Club Honours: Div 3 '00
The most remarkable story of Cheltenham's season was the re-emergence of veteran striker Julian. He spent the previous season with Bishop's Cleeve in the Zamaretto League but caught Cheltenham's eye in a pre-season friendly. His height and strength were effective in the early games and Julian completed a fairytale comeback by scoring a last-minute winner at Rochdale in August. He worked hard on his fitness and his tireless work earned him the supporters' 'Player of the Season' award. Against Lincoln in April, Julian broke Martin Devaney's aggregate League scoring record with his 39th goal.

Bristol Rov (£15,000 from Halesowen on 14/2/1997) FL 20+13/4 FLC 2/1 FAC 1/1 Others 2
Swansea C (Loaned on 20/1/1998) FL 5/2
Swansea C (£30,000 on 12/3/1998) FL 73+12/14 FLC 4+2 FAC 6+1/1 Others 5
Cheltenham T (Free on 3/7/2000) FL 99+18/35 FLC 4+1 FAC 8+2/6 Others 6+1/3
Oxford U (Free on 8/7/2003) FL 29+5/5 FLC 1 FAC 1
Northampton T (Free on 22/10/2004) FL 1+6/1 FAC 0+1 Others 2/1 (Freed on 21/10/2004)
Cheltenham T (Free from Bishops Cleeve, ex Forest Green Rov, Tamworth, Newport Co, Cirencester T, on 20/7/2009) FL 21+20/4 FLC 0+1 FAC 1 Others 0+1

ALTIDORE Josmer (Jozy)
Volmy
Born: Livingston, New Jersey, USA, 6 November 1989
Height: 6'0" **Weight:** 12.4
International Honours: USA: 25
The precocious Hull striker arrived in the Premier League on a season's loan with a remarkable record of being the youngest for almost everything - to score in the Major League Soccer play-offs, to score for the United States in his first international start, to score for the USA in the World Cup qualifiers, to score a hat trick for the USA in the World Cup and the first American to score in Spain's La Liga. Jozy made an immediate impact at Hull by setting up the winner against Bolton only 30 seconds after appearing as a substitute. Powerfully built, the forward's first goal came from a free kick on his full debut against Southend in the Carling Cup. Born of Haitian parents, Jozy was granted compassionate leave to lend his support following the country's catastrophic earthquake. Back in England, he netted his only Premier League goal in the superb win against Manchester City in February. Jozy's stay with the Tigers came to an unfortunate end when he was sent off against Sunderland.
Hull C (Loaned from Villareal, Spain, ex New York Red Bulls, Xerez - loan, on 8/8/2009) PL 16+12/1 FLC 1/1 FAC 0+1

AMANKWAAH Kevin Osei-
Kuffour
Born: Harrow, 19 May 1982
Height: 6'1" **Weight:** 12.0
Club Honours: Div 2 '05
International Honours: E: Yth
A strong, right-sided attacking Swindon full-back, he has plenty of pace and likes to get forward when the opportunity arises. Kevin was an almost

permanent fixture in the Town defence until injury with a gluteal strain restricted his appearances to just three outings from the bench during the last quarter of the season. Eventually returned to the side during the League One play-off games, starting the first leg semi-final against Charlton and the Wembley final against Millwall, during which he was loudly booed with each touch by Lions fans following a well-publicised incident earlier in the season.
Bristol C (From trainee on 16/6/2000) FL 35+19/1 FLC 2+1/1 FAC 1+1/2 Others 7+2/1
Torquay U (Loaned on 25/11/2003) FL 6
Cheltenham T (Loaned on 16/8/2003) FL 11+1
Yeovil T (Signed on 3/2/2005) FL 48+5/1 FLC 2 FAC 3 Others 1
Swansea C (£200,000 on 4/8/2006) FL 23+6 FLC 1 FAC 3+1 Others 4+1
Swindon T (Free on 17/7/2008) FL 59+8/5 FLC 2 FAC 3 Others 6+1

AMAYA Antonio
Born: Madrid, Spain, 31 May 1983
Height: 6'4" **Weight:** 13.8
An experienced defender, Antonio was recruited by Wigan in August in a deal that involved Mohamed Diame also joining from Spanish Segunda Liga side Rayo Vallecano. A tall centre-half with good aerial ability both defensively and offensively, he netted on his debut with a header in the Carling Cup tie against Blackpool. The Spaniard endured a frustrating first season at the DW Stadium as opportunities became less frequent and he spent most of the time on the substitutes' bench. His only other starts came in the FA Cup against Hull and Notts County. A tidy defender with good positional sense and ball control, he will hope to push for more opportunities after adjusting to English football.
Wigan Ath (Signed from Rayo Vallecano, Spain, via SS Reyes - loan, on 14/8/2009) FLC 1/1 FAC 2

AMBROSE Darren Paul
Born: Harlow, 29 February 1984
Height: 5'11" **Weight:** 10.5
International Honours: E: U21-10; Yth
After a disappointing season with Charlton when they were relegated to League One, Darren signed for Crystal Palace on a free transfer during the summer and it proved to be an inspired move for both parties. Rejuvenated by the move and playing some of his best football of the past few years, he gave some consistently good displays throughout the campaign and was the club's top scorer with 20 goals. A large

number came from finely struck free kicks, including a sweetly taken one from 35 yards against Aston Villa in the FA Cup. Having been such a good performer in his first season at Palace, it was fitting therefore that it was his well taken goal at Sheffield Wednesday that kept them in the Championship in the final game of the season.
Ipswich T (From trainee on 3/7/2001) P/FL 20+10/8 FLC 2/1 FAC 1+1/1 Others 3+1/1
Newcastle U (£1,000,000 on 25/3/2003) PL 18+19/5 FLC 1+1 FAC 0+2 Others 8+7/1
Charlton Ath (£700,000 + on 11/7/2005) P/FL 78+34/13 FLC 5+3/2 FAC 6+2/2
Ipswich T (Loaned on 11/11/2008) FL 6+3
Crystal Palace (Free on 2/7/2009) FL 44+2/15 FLC 2/2 FAC 5/3

AMEOBI Foluwashola (Shola)
Born: Zaria, Nigeria, 12 October 1981
Height: 6'2" **Weight:** 12.0
Club Honours: Ch '10
International Honours: E: U21-21
Striker Shola started the season in fine form, netting his first ever hat-trick for Newcastle in the second game at home to Reading, followed by the winner in the next game against Sheffield Wednesday. He was Championship 'Player of the Month' for August, but was then sidelined by a stress fracture of the foot until December, scoring three in four games on his return before a hamstring injury further disrupted his season. He returned as a scoring substitute for the vital game against Nottingham Forest in late March and although his casual style continued to frustrate supporters, his goals per game return was impressive and it was rumoured that he was in line for a call up for Nigeria, for whom he became qualified in 2010.
Newcastle U (From trainee on 19/10/1998) P/FL 120+88/42 FLC 6+3/4 FAC 9+6/3 Others 26+15/12
Stoke C (Loaned on 27/3/2008) FL 3+3

AMOS Benjamin (Ben) Paul
Born: Macclesfield, 10 April 1990
Height: 6'3" **Weight:** 11.11
International Honours: E: Yth
An enthusiastic young goalkeeper who arrived at Peterborough on loan from Manchester United as cover for Joe Lewis who was suspended. A former United scholar he made his debut for Posh two days later in a 2–1 defeat against Barnsley before returning to Old Trafford.
Manchester U (From trainee on 5/1/2008) FLC 1

Peterborough U (Loaned on 29/10/2009) FL 1

ANDERSEN Mikkel
Born: Copenhagen, Denmark, 17 December 1988
Height: 6'5" **Weight:** 12.8
International Honours: Denmark: U21-2; Yth
The Danish under-21 goalkeeper, Mikkel was an imposingly tall figure in Bristol Rovers' goal. To enable him to get League experience, Reading initially allowed him out on a short-term loan. His performances were impressive. His bravery and consistent shot-stopping helped Rovers to start the season well. Mikkel was popular with the fans and Rovers were delighted that his loan was extended for the whole of the season. He made a superb penalty save during Rovers' first ever victory over MK Dons and was the 'Young Player of the Season'. Mikkel added Danish under-21 caps and was pressing for a place in the national side for the World Cup.
Reading (Signed from AB Copenhagen, Denmark on 30/1/2007)
Brentford (Loaned on 9/12/2008) FL 1
Brighton & Hove A (Loaned on 6/3/2009) FL 5
Bristol Rov (Loaned on 1/9/2009) FL 39

[ANDERSON] DE ABREU OLIVEIRA Anderson Luis
Born: Porto Alegre, Brazil, 13 April 1988
Height: 5'10" **Weight:** 10.12
Club Honours: PL '08, '09; UEFACL '08; FLC '09, '10
International Honours: Brazil: 8; U23-6; Yth
Anderson was again a regular for Manchester United and scored his first goal for the Reds in the Audi Cup tournament against Boca Juniors, typically from a curling free kick, His first competitive game came in his 78th appearance, against Spurs in September when he latched on a loose ball at the edge of the area and hammered it into the right corner with his left foot. Concern arose about his Old Trafford future in January, when it was reported that the winger was set for a loan to French side Lyon for the rest of the season after allegedly falling out with Sir Alex Ferguson. Anderson was believed to have returned home to Brazil without Ferguson's permission and was fined £80,000. The move to Lyon never materialised and Anderson returned against West Ham in February. As fate would have it, he ruptured the cruciate ligament in his left knee after just 20 minutes and was later ruled out for the rest of the season, which

regrettably included the World Cup finals in South Africa.
Manchester U (Signed from Porto, Portugal, ex Gremio, on 3/7/2007) PL 37+18/1 FLC 9+1 FAC 6+2 Others 21+5

ANDERSON Joe William
Born: Stepney, 13 October 1989
Height: 5'11" **Weight:** 11.5
A left-sided defender who can also play in a more advanced midfield role, some impressive pre-season form saw Joe included in the Fulham squads for the early Europa League ties and being a non-playing substitute for a number of games. His Fulham debut, a brief substitute appearance at the end of extra time in the Carling Cup tie at Manchester City ultimately proved his only senior appearance for the club. Although he continued to appear regularly for the reserves, normally operating in the left-back role, he was sold to Lincoln early in the January transfer window. At Sincil Bank Joe quickly established himself as the first choice left-back, putting in a succession of composed performances in helping the Imps secure their Football League status.
Fulham (From trainee on 9/12/2008) FLC 0+1
Lincoln C (Signed on 4/1/2010) FL 23 FAC 1

ANDERSON Paul
Born: Leicester, 23 July 1988
Height: 5'9" **Weight:** 10.6
Club Honours: FAYC '06; Div 1 '08
International Honours: E: Yth
This lightning quick winger was another player to join Nottingham Forest before the start of the season. Despite being right-footed, he made the majority of his appearances on the left of midfield. A talented player, who seems to be able to run as fast with the ball as without it. Paul can look back on his first permanent season at the City Ground, following his long loan from Liverpool in 2008-09, as a success.
Liverpool (From trainee at Hull C on 6/1/2006)
Swansea C (Loaned on 7/8/2007) FL 22+9/7 FLC 2/1 FAC 3 Others 5/2
Nottingham F (£250,000 on 3/7/2008) FL 57+6/6 FLC 2+1/1 FAC 3+1 Others 1+1

ANDERSON Russell
Born: Aberdeen, 25 October 1978
Height: 5'11" **Weight:** 11.10
International Honours: S: 11; U21-15
Russell's time at Sunderland was wrecked by a knee ligament injury, picked up while on loan at Burnley. When the former Aberdeen captain was

released by Sunderland in January, Derby manager Nigel Clough nipped in to offer him a contract for the remainder of the season. Russell's first six appearances were as a substitute as he rebuilt match fitness, but in March he took over from Jake Buxton in the centre of defence and stayed there until missing the final game through injury. His partnership with Shaun Barker was the most convincing of the many combinations fielded during an injury-ravaged season and he scored his first senior goal for three years in the draw with Crystal Palace that ensured Derby's safety. Russell is an economical defender with sound positioning and swift use of the ball. He was rewarded by a two-year contract.
Aberdeen (From Dyce Juniors on 1/8/1996) SL 263+17/18 SLC 20 SC 23+1/1 Others 4
Sunderland (£1,000,000 on 19/7/2007) PL 0+1 FLC 1
Plymouth Arg (Loaned on 19/2/2008) FL 14
Burnley (Loaned on 26/8/2008) FL 4 FLC 1
Derby Co (Free on 15/1/2010) FL 9+6/1

[ANDERSON] SILVA Anderson de Franca
Born: Sao Paulo, Brazil, 28 August 1982
Height: 6'2" **Weight:** 12.11
The start and end of the season were a disappointment for Anderson but during the middle part he played some of his best football for Barnsley. He was encouraged by the new manager to push forward more. He responded and his 25- yard shot into the top corner in the Carling Cup against Burnley was stunning. At first manager Mark Robins used him more on the right side, where his ability to hold the ball under pressure and then release the runners was seen at its best. He was then used in a floating position off a single striker and his display at Preston, where he again netted from 25 yards, was superb. His form lapsed after that and he found himself more often than not on the bench. He was out of contract at the end of the season and his future is yet to be decided.
Everton (Signed from Nacional, Uruguay, ex Montevideo Wanderers, Racing Santander, Malaga - all loans from Nacional, on 22/1/2007) PL 0+1
Barnsley (Signed on 23/8/2007) FL 78+6/5 FLC 3+1/1 FAC 2

ANDREW Calvin Hyden
Born: Luton, 19 December 1986
Height: 6'2" **Weight:** 12.11
More often used as a substitute early in the season after coming back from

injury, Calvin featured more prominently for Crystal Palace in the New Year after manager Paul Hart took the reins. Calvin improved as the season progressed and scored at Sheffield Wednesday in January's FA Cup win, plus a vital goal at home to Preston in the League. Not always an automatic first choice, the ex-Luton forward will be looking to break into the first team more regularly after signing a new contract in the summer.

Luton T (From trainee on 25/9/2004) FL 26+29/4 FLC 0+2 FAC 4+3/2 Others 3
Grimsby T (Loaned on 4/8/2005) FL 3+5/1 FLC 1
Bristol C (Loaned on 30/1/2006) FL 1+2
Crystal Palace (£80,000 on 18/7/2008) FL 14+20/1 FLC 2 FAC 0+6/1
Brighton & Hove A (Loaned on 30/1/2009) FL 3+6/2 Others 1

ANDREW Daniel (Danny) Kenny
Born: Holbeach, 23 December 1990
Height: 5'11" **Weight:** 11.3
The young Peterborough defender gained a full start in an injury-ravaged team at the end of the season, having earlier been loaned out to Tamworth, Kidderminster and Cheltenham. Mark Yates had been manager of Kidderminster during his loan spell at the club and when Yates took over at Cheltenham in December he made Danny one of his first signings. Danny made his debut in a 0-0 draw at Grimsby and went on to make a series of appearances as cover for the injured Lee Ridley at left-back, as well as one start on the left-hand side of midfield in a home game against Northampton Town before being recalled to his parent club. Was out of contract in the summer.

Peterborough U (From trainee on 1/7/2009) FL 2
Cheltenham T (Loaned on 12/1/2010) FL 9+1

ANDREWS Keith Joseph
Born: Dublin, 13 September 1980
Height: 5'11" **Weight:** 11.5
Club Honours: AMC '08; Div 2 '08
International Honours: RoI: 15; Yth
Keith had a difficult season at Blackburn in 2009-10. His game is based on keeping mobile and marking men out of the game, but out of sorts at times he became a frequent target for unhappy fans. Although often left out of the side, his manager displayed faith by keeping him involved and there were few games in which he did not appear in some capacity. Keith took on the unsung but necessary roles, being brought on to mark Steven Gerrard

when Sam Allardyce deemed it necessary to hang on to a draw, and playing centre-back when the club ran out of players in the home game against Bolton. He also stepped up to convert a penalty against Manchester City, at a time when Blackburn had run out of competent penalty takers.

Wolverhampton W (From trainee on 26/9/1997) P/FL 41+24 FLC 3/1 FAC 4
Oxford U (Loaned on 10/11/2000) FL 4/1 Others 1
Stoke C (Loaned on 9/8/2003) FL 16
Walsall (Loaned on 13/3/2004) FL 10/2
Hull C (Free on 25/5/2005) FL 24+5 FAC 1
MK Dons (Free on 31/8/2006) FL 75+1/18 FLC 2 FAC 3 Others 6/3
Blackburn Rov (£1,300,000 on 28/8/2008) PL 49+16/5 FLC 1+2 FAC 0+2

ANELKA Nicolas
Born: Versailles, France, 14 March 1979
Height: 6'0" **Weight:** 12.3
Club Honours: PL '98, '10; FAC '98, '09, '10; CS '98, '09
International Honours: France: 66; U21; Yth
Although Nicolas relinquished his Golden Boot title to Chelsea team-mate Didier Drogba, he remains one of the most effective players in the Premier League and revelled in his free role under Carlo Ancelotti; using all his experience to find that vital yard of space. Playing slightly behind Didier Drogba, he intelligently uses the full width of the pitch to open space through the middle. He is now the perfect foil for the Ivorian, having worked hard to develop a strong partnership. His three Champions League goals won three closely-fought ties and helped Chelsea to head their qualifying group. During the African Cup of Nations, Nicolas single handedly led the Chelsea attack and responded by scoring four goals during the absence of Drogba and Salomon Kalou. Nicolas underwent a goal drought from January to April but ended it with the

Keith Andrews

crucial winner against Bolton to put the Blues four points clear. In the final League match he scored twice against Wigan to reach double figures. He gained a third FA Cup winners' medal and, along with Ashley Cole, won the 'Double' with a second club. He was selected for France's World Cup squad – his first involvement in the finals.

Arsenal *(£500,000 + from Paris St Germain, France on 6/3/1997) PL 50+15/23 FLC 3 FAC 13+1/3 Others 7+1/2 (£22,900,000 to Real Madrid, Spain on 20/8/1999)*

Liverpool *(Loaned from Paris St Germain, France on 24/12/2001) PL 13+7/4 FAC 2/1*

Manchester C *(£13,000,000 from Paris St Germain, France on 16/7/2002) PL 87+2/37 FLC 4 FAC 5/4 Others 5/4 (£7,000,000 to Fenerbahce, Turkey on 31/1/2005)*

Bolton W *(£8,000,000 from Fenerbahce, Turkey on 31/8/2006) PL 53/21 FLC 1/1 FAC 2+1 Others 2+2/1*

Chelsea *(£15,000,000 on 12/11/2008) PL 74+10/31 FLC 2 FAC 10+2/6 Others 15+10/5*

ANICHEBE Victor Chinedu
Born: Lagos, Nigeria, 23 April 1988
Height: 6'1" **Weight:** 12.8
International Honours: Nigeria: 5; U23-5
A serious knee injury incurred at Newcastle in February 2009 kept the Nigerian international out of action until the New Year. But when the former Academy player returned, he impressed with a series of fine displays on Everton's right wing, rather than as a centre-forward, including a superb goal at Birmingham, until another month-long lay-off with a hip injury sustained against Bolton. Victor returned to positive effect with excellent performances in the final few matches, especially from the bench at Blackburn and at Stoke.

Everton *(From trainee on 5/4/2006) PL 26+50/7 FLC 2+5/1 FAC 4+2 Others 2+9/4*

ANKERGREN Casper
Born: Koge, Denmark, 9 November 1979
Height: 6'3" **Weight:** 14.11
International Honours: Denmark: U21-3; Yth
Casper lost his place as Leeds' first choice goalkeeper following the summer signing of Shane Higgs from Cheltenham. He was on the bench for the first dozen games and replaced the injured Higgs in the last-gasp win at MK Dons in late September. The Dane figured in the next three games but

gave way to Higgs for the high-profile game against Norwich. Higgs aggravated his injury in the 2-1 win against the Canaries and Casper took over for the next five months. He was outstanding in United's FA Cup win at Manchester United and his early penalty save at Tottenham paved the way for Leeds to force a replay. However, a 2-0 home defeat against promotion rivals Millwall in March was the cue for Higgs to play in the remainder of the programme. Was out of contract at the end of June.

Leeds U *(Signed from Brondby, Denmark, ex Koge BK, on 31/1/2007) FL 117+2 FLC 5 FAC 9 Others 9*

ANTHONY Byron Joseph
Born: Newport, 20 September 1984
Height: 6'1" **Weight:** 11.0
International Honours: W: U21-8; Yth
Welsh central defender Byron showed his versatility by combining with a number of different partners in the Bristol Rovers' back four. Byron reads the game well, is a confident man-marker and a strong tackler. Byron passed a personal milestone of 100 League appearances and following injuries and loss of form by team-mates, was switched to right-back late in the season. He clearly enjoyed the role and his accurate passing helped the balance of the side. Byron almost scored a remarkable goal from fully 35 yards, hitting a right-foot shot that rattled the Exeter crossbar. He later signed a new two-year deal.

Cardiff C *(From trainee on 7/7/2003) FLC 1+1/1*

Bristol Rov *(Free on 3/8/2006) FL 105+5/3 FLC 6 FAC 5/1 Others 8/1*

ANTONIO Michail Gregory
Born: Wandsworth, 28 March 1990
Height: 5'11" **Weight:** 12.10
Club Honours: AMC '10
Michail was an unused substitute in Reading's Carling Cup tie against Burton, then used as a second-half substitute in the Carling Cup against Barnsley, and in the Championship fixture against the same opponent. He gave glimpses of his undoubted potential as a speedy and direct right-winger, and at the beginning of September joined Southampton on loan for the remainder of the season. Michail proved a great success at St Mary's and stayed all season. Raw but fast he was soon causing defensive problems and visibly grew in confidence game by game. He was just shaded by Rickie Lambert for the 'Man of the Match' award in the Johnstone's Paint Trophy final, having had a hand in every goal in the 4-1 win. Michail's contract

with Reading was due to expire at the end of the season, but the club exercised their option to retain his services for another year.

Reading *(Free from Tooting & Mitcham on 28/10/2008) FL 0+1 FLC 0+1*

Cheltenham T *(Loaned on 19/2/2009) FL 7+2*

Southampton *(Loaned on 5/10/2009) FL 14+14/3 FAC 3+2/2 Others 5+1/2*

ANTWI Agyei William (Will) Kwabena
Born: Epsom, 19 October 1982
Height: 6'2" **Weight:** 12.8
International Honours: Ghana: 1
Will made his Dagenham debut at Crewe on the opening day of the season. The centre-half paired up with Mark Arber in the heart of the Daggers' four-man defence until he picked up a calf injury in December. He was on the verge of returning to first team action a month later but he suffered a groin strain and did not play again for the remainder of the season. Will is a commanding, no-nonsense defender whose injury coincided with the club's dip in form.

Crystal Palace *(From trainee on 12/7/2002) FL 0+4 FLC 1+2 (Free to Ljungskile SK, Sweden during 2003 close season)*

Wycombe W *(Free from Aldershot T on 6/7/2005) FL 40+2/1 FLC 6 FAC 2/1 Others 5*

Dagenham & Redbridge *(Free from 17/7/2009) FL 19/1 FAC 1 Others 1*

ANYINSAH Joseph (Joe) Greene
Born: Bristol, 8 October 1984
Height: 5'8" **Weight:** 11.0
This powerful forward ended the term as Carlisle's second top scorer despite missing most of the last three months through injury. Perhaps the most memorable of his goals came at MK Dons where, after United had squandered a three-goal lead, Joe was on hand to scramble home the seventh and final goal of the game. A pacy player who operates either up front or on the wing, he came off the bench at Norwich in the final match of the season but this now looks to be his last appearance for United.

Bristol C *(From trainee on 24/10/2001) FL 2+5 Others 0+2*

Preston NE *(Signed on 13/7/2005) FL 0+6 FAC 0+2*

Bury *(Loaned on 9/2/2006) FL 3*

Carlisle U *(Loaned on 20/9/2007) FL 10+2/3 Others 2*

Crewe Alex *(Loaned on 7/3/2008) FL 6+2*

Brighton & Hove A *(Loaned on*

11/9/2008) FL 10+1 FLC 1+1/1 Others 2/1
Carlisle U *(£20,000 + on 9/1/2009) FL 36+11/13 FLC 3 FAC 2+2/1 Others 1+4/1*

ANYON Joseph (Joe)
Born: Poulton-le-Fylde, 29 December 1986
Height: 6'2" **Weight:** 12.3
International Honours: E: Yth
Recovery from a broken leg meant that Joe became the second choice goalkeeper at Port Vale. The form of Chris Martin kept him waiting for his chance, but it duly arrived in February. Unfortunately Joe committed a couple of errors that cost goals in a seven-game stint and returned to the reserves, where he saved a penalty at Sheffield United. Given a free transfer at the end of the season, he eventually signed for Lincoln.
Port Vale *(From trainee on 13/8/2005) FL 108+1 FLC 2 FAC 5 Others 2*

AQUILANI Alberto
Born: Rome, Italy, 7 July 1984
Height: 6'0" **Weight:** 11.7
International Honours: Italy: 11; U21-19; Yth
The Italian international central midfielder was signed by Liverpool in the summer, ostensibly as a replacement for Xabi Alonso. It was a strange signing as Alberto had an injury prone career at AS Roma and was unavailable at the start with an ankle injury. Even when he was fit, manager Rafa Benitez was strangely reluctant to use him. He finally made his debut in late October as a substitute in the Carling Cup defeat at Arsenal but had to wait until December for his first start, against Fiorentina in the Champions League. Used sparingly, only in the last two months did Alberto start to show top form, scoring twice and providing six assists. Thirteen starts made a poor return on the investment but judgement must be reserved until he plays an uninterrupted season. One thing is clear, that he cannot be considered a like-for-like replacement for Alonso, as he is a more attacking midfielder.
Liverpool *(Signed from AS Roma, via Triestina - loan, on 7/8/2009) PL 9+9/1 FLC 0+1 FAC 1+1 Others 3+2/1*

ARBER Mark Andrew
Born: Johannesburg, South Africa, 9 October 1977
Height: 6'1" **Weight:** 12.11
The season was another good one for Mark and he was rewarded for his consistent displays with the Dagenham

'Player of the Year' trophy. The centre-back assumed the responsibility of taking the penalties midway through the season but gave up after missing one at Northampton on Boxing Day. The Daggers' captain led by example, with no suspensions, and missed only one League game as the result of a calf injury against Accrington.
Tottenham H *(From trainee on 27/3/1996)*
Barnet *(£75,000 on 18/9/1998) FL 123+2/15 FLC 4 FAC 3 Others 8/1*
Peterborough U *(Free on 9/12/2002) FL 67+2/5 FLC 1 FAC 3 Others 2*
Oldham Ath *(Free on 27/7/2004) FL 13+1/1 FLC 2 Others 1*
Peterborough U *(Free on 21/12/2004) FL 98+3/3 FLC 3 FAC 8/1 Others 5 (Freed during 2007 close season)*
Dagenham & Redbridge *(Free from Stevenage Borough on 12/2/2008) FL 99/8 FLC 2 FAC 4 Others 4*

Julio Arca

ARCA Julio Andres
Born: Quilmes Bernal, Argentina, 31 January 1981
Height: 5'10" **Weight:** 11.6
Club Honours: Ch '05
International Honours: Argentina: U21; Yth (World Yth '01)
Julio battled through most of the season for Middlesbrough, despite having regular injections in a painful toe injury. Played predominantly in the centre of midfield during previous boss Gareth Southgate's reign, he was used in a variety of positions when Gordon Strachan took the helm. Never a true favourite with the Boro faithful, perhaps due to his links with Sunderland and a penchant for dwelling on the ball in

dangerous areas, Julio fought back with impressive displays towards the end of the season.
Sunderland *(£3,500,000 from Argentinos Juniors, Argentina on 31/8/2000) P/FL 145+12/17 FLC 5/2 FAC 15/4*
Middlesbrough *(£1,750,000 on 9/8/2006) P/FL 81+16/4 FLC 1 FAC 16/1*

ARCHIBALD-HENVILLE Troy Patrick
Born: Newham, 4 November 1988
Height: 6'2" **Weight:** 12.8
Troy was initially signed on loan at the start of the season from Tottenham before making the move to Exeter permanent. He established himself as a regular in the defence before injuring his cartilage in the warm-up before the home game against Southampton in February, which put paid to the rest of his season. He will be looking to continue his good form next season.
Tottenham H *(From trainee on 10/7/2007)*
Exeter C *(Loaned on 20/1/2009) FL 19*
Exeter C *(Loaned on 6/8/2009) FL 13+2 FAC 0+1 Others 1*

ARESTIDOU Andreas
Born: Lambeth, 6 December 1989
Height: 6'1" **Weight:** 13.1
Released by Blackburn, the young goalkeeper signed for Shrewsbury with a view to future development but took his chance well, deputising for the injured Chris Neal in a 1-1 home draw with Bury in November. He kept his place for a second performance at Hereford and in both games showed that he was a good shot-stopper and distributed well. Subsequent progress was hampered by the need for a hernia operation and then the signing on loan of Tottenham keeper David Button. Was out of contract in the summer.
Shrewsbury T *(From trainee at Blackburn Rov on 9/7/2009) FL 2*

ARISMENDI Hugo Diego
Born: Montevideo, Uruguay, 25 January 1988
Height: 6'2" **Weight:** 12.13
International Honours: Uruguay: 2
When Stoke paid a considerable fee to bring the 22 year-old Uruguayan international over from Club Nacional big things were expected by the fans. He made Carling Cup appearances against Blackpool and Portsmouth, during which time fans though he was being acclimatised to the pace of English football. As the season dragged on though there was no indication that he was going to get any more games in the first team and towards the end of the

campaign he was loaned out to League One side, Brighton. Diego was sidelined for four weeks by a thigh injury before making three appearances in Gus Poyet's starting line-up and three more off the bench. However, the midfielder was still looking to come to terms with the hurly-burly of League One football when he found his season abruptly terminated by a red card at MK Dons.
Stoke C (£2,600,000 from Club Nacional, Uruguay on 31/8/2009) FLC 2
Brighton & Hove A (Loaned on 8/3/2010) FL 3+3

ARMSTRONG Christopher (Chris)
Born: Newcastle, 5 August 1982
Height: 5'10" **Weight:** 11.0
International Honours: S: B-1; E: Yth
After being Reading's 'Player of the Year' in 2008-09, Chris had a frustrating campaign in which he made only one appearance, in the 5-1 home win over Burton in the Carling Cup. The left-back spent most of the remainder of the season in the physio's room, being treated for a serious knee injury.
Bury (From trainee on 2/3/2001) FL 33/1 FLC 1 Others 3
Oldham Ath (£200,000 on 22/10/2001) FL 64+1/1 FLC 2 FAC 6 Others 6
Sheffield U (£100,000 on 1/8/2003) P/FL 76+19/6 FLC 5+1 FAC 3+1
Blackpool (Loaned on 13/10/2005) FL 5 Others 1
Reading (£500,000 on 27/8/2008) FL 40/1 FLC 1

ARNASON Kari
Born: Reykjavik, Iceland, 13 October 1982
Height: 6'3" **Weight:** 13.10
International Honours: Iceland: 17
Kari, a full Icelandic international, joined Plymouth in July on a one-year contract after being released by Danish Superliga side Aarhus. Manager Paul Sturrock had plans to play Kari in central midfield but he made his name this season as a strong defender who is comfortable on the ball. He made his debut in August against Derby and established himself as a regular at the heart of the Argyle defence. He unfortunately tore his hamstring at the end of September which meant he was out of action for a month. He scored his first goal against Reading in December at Home Park to become the 500th player to score a League goal since Plymouth became professional in 1903. He signed a two-year contract extension in January after a string of consistent performances, to keep him at the club until the summer of 2012.

Plymouth Arg (Free from Aarhus GF, Denmark, ex Vikingur, Djurgaarden, Esbjerg - loan, on 20/7/2009) FL 32/2 FAC 2

ARNISON Paul Simon
Born: Hartlepool, 18 September 1977
Height: 5'10" **Weight:** 11.2
Club Honours: Div 2 '06
The experienced right-back was recruited in the summer by Colin Todd during the uncertain period while Darlington were still in administration. Paul started the season solidly but a series of niggling injuries restricted him to just 12 starts during the first half of the season. He regained his place towards the end of the campaign and scored his first goal, against Aldershot in March, but after only half-a-dozen more games injury ruled him out for the remainder of the season.
Newcastle U (From trainee on 1/3/1996)
Hartlepool U (Free on 10/3/2000) FL 53+24/3 FLC 2 FAC 2+1 Others 8/2
Carlisle U (Free on 31/10/2003) FL 72+23/1 FLC 4 FAC 1 Others 10
Bradford C (Free on 5/7/2008) FL 25+2 FLC 1
Darlington (Free on 7/8/2009) FL 17+1/1 FLC 1 Others 2

Andrei Arshavin

ARSHAVIN Andrei Sergeyevich
Born: St Petersburg, Russia, 29 May 1981
Height: 5'8" **Weight:** 11.2
International Honours: Russia: 51
The Russian captain is a true world-class talent yet remains a player who can appear almost non-existent in a game for long periods and then in an instant change the course of it. His winner for

Arsenal at Anfield in December was a good example of this. He was often played out of position as Arsenal's forward line was shredded by injuries and also suffered himself with injury as his missed several matches. He tends not to always score the simpler chances and his strikes are often glorious, as witnessed by the opener in the away match against Manchester United and his crucial winner at home to Bolton as the Gunners battled back from 2-0 down to lead the table. A fully fit Andrei is a wonder to behold and it would seem his best placed as a support striker or played just in the hole behind the front men. He played 30 times in the Premier League, contributing ten goals, eight times in the Champions League, scoring twice, and once in the FA Cup.
Arsenal (£15,000,000 from Zenit St Petersburg, Russia on 3/2/2009) PL 37+5/16 FAC 2+2 Others 7+1/2

ARTELL David (Dave) John
Born: Rotherham, 22 November 1980
Height: 6'2" **Weight:** 13.9
The Morecambe defender was, on more than one occasion, the club's goal hero. Twice he scored two goals in a game, against Accrington and Shrewsbury, and was always a threat in the box from Craig Stanley's set pieces. Dave had the distinction of scoring the Shrimps' last ever goal at Christie Park in the play-off victory over Dagenham. He was his normal dependable self and made some vital tackles as his experience proved essential to the club's late play-off charge.
Rotherham U (From trainee on 1/7/1999) FL 35+2/4 FAC 3 Others 1
Shrewsbury T (Loaned on 26/9/2002) FL 27+1/1 FAC 3 Others 5
Mansfield T (Free on 7/8/2003) FL 43+2/5 FLC 2 FAC 5+1 Others 1+1
Chester C (Signed on 29/7/2005) FL 76+4/3 FLC 1 FAC 9 Others 1
Morecambe (Free on 24/7/2007) FL 102+8/13 FLC 5/1 FAC 2+1 Others 10+1/1

ARTETA Mikel
Born: San Sebastian, Spain, 26 March 1982
Height: 5'9" **Weight:** 10.12
Club Honours: SPD '03; SLC '03
International Honours: Spain: U21; Yth
A ruptured cruciate knee ligament sustained at Newcastle in February 2009 kept Everton's Spanish midfield playmaker on the sidelines until the following January. Although injuries to other players forced David Moyes to play the fans' favourite more than he

would initially have liked, Mikel quickly settled back into the style that makes him one of the best midfielders in the Premier League, scoring two beautifully crafted goals against Hull and another at Manchester City. After a further lay-off with a groin strain the former Glasgow Rangers player returned with a goal in a fine display at Blackburn. The 28-year-old plays the game in the finest traditions of the Goodison School of Science, possessing wonderful close control and is a beautiful striker of the ball, especially from free kicks. All Everton supporters will be wishing for a full season from the Spaniard.
Glasgow Rgrs (£5,800,000 from Paris St Germain, France, ex Barcelona, on 1/7/2002) SL 49+1/12 SLC 5 SC 6/1 Others 7/1 (Transferred to Real Sociedad, Spain on 9/7/2004)
Everton (£2,000,000 from Real Sociedad, Spain on 31/1/2005) PL 136+7/24 FLC 5+1 FAC 9+1/2 Others 13+1/4

ARTHUR Kenneth (Kenny) James
Born: Bellshill, 7 December 1978
Height: 6'3" **Weight:** 13.8
Club Honours: S Div 1 '01
The experienced goalkeeper was recruited by Rochdale in the summer and played in every game, helping Dale move into the top three, before suffering a back injury in October. With no other senior 'keeper available, Kenny was patched up to play in the FA Cup tie at Luton but struggled and was out of action for the next two months. With England under-21 'keepers Tom Heaton and Frank Fielding brought in on loan, Kenny spent the rest of Rochdale's promotion campaign on the bench after he regained fitness until reappearing in the penultimate game.
Partick Thistle (From Possil YMCA 0n 01/06/1997) SL 242+1 SLC 14 SC 24 Others 9
Accrington Stanley (Free on 1/6/2007) FL 66 FLC 2 FAC 2 Others 0+1
Rochdale (Free on 3/8/2009) FL 15 FLC 1 FAC 1 Others 1

ARTUS Frankie
Born: Bristol, 27 September 1988
Height: 6'0" **Weight:** 12.10
The Bristol City midfielder returned from Cheltenham for a three-month loan spell at the end of August 2009, having enjoyed a successful spell at the Abbey Business Stadium towards the end of the previous campaign. A good passer of the ball and strong runner in central or wide positions, Frankie played in the centre and on the left-hand side of a four-man midfield for the Robins. He

also made two appearances on the left-hand side of a three-man forward line as Town chopped and changed their team around trying to find the right blend. Having had his time at Whaddon Road cut short by a toe injury sustained against Crewe at the end of October, Frankie joined Chesterfield on loan in January to bring competitiveness to the centre of midfield but was harshly sent off at Morecambe in his second full appearance. Following that, Frankie came back from suspension to find himself on the bench, where he remained unused in the summer. Was out of contract in the summer.
Bristol C (From trainee on 20/4/2006)
Brentford (Loaned on 7/8/2008) FL 0+1 Others 1
Cheltenham T (Loaned on 23/3/2009) FL 9/3
Cheltenham T (Loaned on 27/8/2009) FL 7 Others 1
Chesterfield (Loaned on 21/1/2010) FL 2+1

ASANTE Kyle Emmanuel Kwabena
Born: Chelmsford, 13 November 1991
Height: 5'9" **Weight:** 10.8
Kyle joined Southend as an under-15, having been released by Millwall, and was a second-year scholar. He scored seven times in the opening nine Youth Alliance League matches and was called into the first team squad for the trip to Carlisle in October. Although he remained on the bench for that game, Kyle soon made his debut as a substitute for James Walker in the FA Cup tie at Gillingham. Sadly for the youngster, his progress was halted by severe knee ligament and tendon injuries. To give him time for rehabilitation, Southend extended his developmental deal for a further year.
Southend U (Trainee) FAC 0+1

ASHDOWN Jamie Lawrence
Born: Wokingham, 30 November 1980
Height: 6'3" **Weight:** 14.10
Club Honours: FAC '08
Portsmouth's perennial reserve goalkeeper could have been forgiven for becoming a frustrated figure in the early part of the season. Regular goalkeeper David James succumbed to a troublesome calf injury after just three League games. However, Jamie was as surprised as anyone to find that previously untried goalkeeper Asmir Begovic was preferred in both League and Carling Cup games. Although he started in two fixtures against Stoke, a 4-0 win and a 1-0 defeat, Jamie was increasingly overlooked in favour of Begovic as the season wore on. Despite

the sale of the Bosnian in the January transfer window, Jamie accumulated only five starts in all competitions for Pompey. Was out of contract at the end of June.
Reading (From trainee on 26/11/1999) FL 12+1 FAC 1 Others 2
Bournemouth (Loaned on 22/8/2002) FL 2
Rushden & Diamonds (Loaned on 14/11/2003) FL 19
Portsmouth (Signed on 2/7/2004) PL 41+1 FLC 8 FAC 1 Others 1
Norwich C (Loaned on 20/10/2006) FL 2

ASHWORTH Luke Alexander
Born: Bolton, 4 December 1989
Height: 6'2" **Weight:** 12.8
Luke was used mainly as Leyton Orient's reserve centre-half. He is a solid performer who will be looking to take the next step and be a regular member of the side in the season ahead. Luke scored his first goal for the club in the FA Cup tie at Tranmere.
Wigan Ath (From trainee on 8/7/2008)
Leyton Orient (Signed on 22/8/2008) FL 8+5 FAC 1/1 Others 4

ASKOU Jens Berthel
Born: Videbaek, Denmark, 19 August 1982
Height: 6'3" **Weight:** 13.5
Club Honours: Div 1 '10
Jens trialled with Norwich in the summer, doing enough to earn a two-year contract following his exit from Turkish football where he played for Kasimpasaspor. A rugged central defender, he knows his first job is to prevent the opposition scoring and his pace and bravery allied to his excellence in the air soon made him a favourite with City fans. A broken metatarsal sustained at Yeovil in December and then the consistency of the Gary Doherty/Michael Nelson partnership in a winning Norwich side made it tough for him to win back his place. A real threat at set pieces, he scored two goals in three games early in the season.
Norwich C (Free from Kasimpasaspor, Turkey, ex Holstebro, Silkeborg, on 30/7/2009) FL 21+1/2 FLC 1 FAC 1 Others 3

ASSOU-EKOTTO Benoit Pierre David
Born: Arras, France, 24 March 1984
Height: 5'10" **Weight:** 10.12
International Honours: Cameroon: 4
The Cameroon international, in his fourth season at Tottenham, was another mainstay of a defence that was matched only by Manchester United in the Premier League for the number of home goals (12) conceded. Benoit made

30 starts for Spurs in all competitions and one from the bench, interrupted only by injury that kept him out in January and February. Spurs were scheduled to miss him anyway because Benoit should have been with Cameroon in the African Cup of Nations but his injury prevented him from travelling. He is in the squad for the 2010 World Cup. Benoit is a reliable left-back who combined in excellent style with Gareth Bale in the second half of the season. He is capable of highly skilful play and there are times when he defends in an almost cheeky fashion. Benoit provided a number of assists and scored his first goal for Spurs, and indeed his first senior career goal, in the opening game against Liverpool from a terrific long-range shot.
Tottenham H (Signed from Lens, France on 14/7/2006) PL 75+1/1 FLC 8 FAC 5 Others 7+1

ATKINSON Robert (Rob) Guy
Born: North Ferriby, 29 April 1987
Height: 6'1" **Weight:** 12.0
Apart from hamstring and groin injuries in the autumn, Rob was a regular fixture for Grimsby, deservedly ending the term as captain. Despite the team's struggles on the pitch the central defender maintained form, even allowing for his having several different partners in the back line. A good covering player who reads the game well, Rob was twice selected for the League Two 'Team of the Week' on the FL website, including a scoring performance in May against Barnet (2-0).
Barnsley (From trainee on 5/7/2006) FL 6+2 FAC 2
Rochdale (Loaned on 19/10/2007) FL 0+2
Grimsby T (Loaned on 22/11/2007) FL 24/1 FAC 1 Others 4

Grimsby T (Free on 31/10/2008) FL 67+1/4 FLC 1 FAC 2 Others 2

ATKINSON William (Will) Henry
Born: Driffield, 14 October 1988
Height: 5'10" **Weight:** 10.7
Having featured for Hull in the pre-season Barclays Asia Trophy in Beijing, Will made his full debut for the club in the Carling Cup first visit from Southend in the unusual position at the top of a midfield diamond. Back in his more familiar left-wing role, Will enjoyed two productive loan spells at Rochdale where he ably assisted League Two Dale to their first promotion in 41 years. Playing on either wing he combined superbly with strikers Chris Dagnall and Chris O'Grady, his first spell seeing Dale collect seven wins and a draw from his eight games, Will netting a brace in the 4-1 victory over Morecambe. Reappearing in February he helped Dale stay at the top of the table but had to return to Hull when his loan reached the maximum allowable three months. Having signed a new contract with the Tigers in March and with relegation all but confirmed he was handed his Premier League debut in the final away game at Wigan. Playing on the right wing, he responded with a fine header goal to open City's account in a 2-2 draw and retained his place for the last game against Liverpool.
Hull C (From trainee on 14/12/2006) P/FL 2/1 FLC 1 FAC 0+1
Port Vale (Loaned on 12/10/2007) FL 3+1
Mansfield T (Loaned on 29/1/2008) FL 10+2
Rochdale (Loaned on 20/11/2009) FL 15/3

AURELIO Fabio
Born: Sao Carlos, Brazil, 24 September 1979
Height: 5'10" **Weight:** 11.11
Club Honours: CS '06
International Honours: Brazil: U21
The Brazilian left-back's season with Liverpool was again disrupted by injury and he was not available until late September, by which time Emiliano Insua had laid a claim for the position. Only two of Fabio's 12 starts were at left-back. The remainder were in central or the left of midfield and he was substituted six times. Following the match at Blackburn in March, he was sidelined with a thigh injury for the rest of the season. Out of contract in the summer, he is expected to move on. More of a squad player than a regular in four years at Anfield, he gave good service but like many of the squad

Benoit Assou-Ekotto

players, promised more than he delivered.
Liverpool *(Signed from Valencia, Spain, ex Sao Paulo, on 20/7/2006) PL 50+21/3 FLC 5 FAC 1+3 Others 21+9/1*

AUSTIN Charles (Charlie)
Born: Hungerford, 5 July 1989
Height: 6'2" **Weight:** 13.0
Possibly the discovery of the season, the former bricklayer made the step up to League One in fantastic style at Swindon. Made his League debut as a substitute at Norwich in October before scoring the winning goal on his first start at Carlisle in November and was then involved in every game, hitting 19 League goals in the process. An instinctive finisher with deft control, Charlie appears to know when and where to arrive in the box for maximum impact and is also willing to run all day. Charlie continued to develop, showing an increasing maturity as the season progressed. A Wembley play-off final in his first season looked to be a fitting showplace for his talents but an unfortunate bobble off the notorious pitch ensured that there was no fairytale finish. Was out of contract in the summer.
Swindon T *(Signed from Poole T, ex Thatcham T, Kintbury Rgrs, Hungerford T, on 5/10/2009) FL 29+4/19 Others 3+2/1*

AUSTIN Kevin Levi
Born: Hackney, 12 February 1973
Height: 6'0" **Weight:** 14.0
Club Honours: AMC '06; Div 1 '08
International Honours: Trinidad & Tobago: 1
Kevin found himself on the team sheet for all but four of Chesterfield's 46 League games but started only 13. He was a good option to have for a situation when the defence needed to be shored up by a change and performed consistently at centre-half or left-back when called upon, making up for a lack of pace with good reading of the game and positional awareness. Was out of contract in the summer.
Leyton Orient *(Free from Saffron Walden on 19/8/1993) FL 101+8/3 FLC 4/1 FAC 6 Others 7*
Lincoln C *(£30,000 on 31/7/1996) FL 128+1/2 FLC 9 FAC 6 Others 4*
Barnsley *(Free on 5/7/1999) FL 3 FLC 2+1*
Brentford *(Loaned on 27/10/2000) FL 3*
Cambridge U *(Free on 21/11/2001) FL 4+2 Others 1*
Bristol Rov *(Free on 12/7/2002) FL 52+4 FAC 4+1*
Swansea C *(Free on 2/7/2004) FL 107+10 FLC 5 FAC 13 Others 14+1*

Chesterfield *(Free on 2/8/2008) FL 41+13 FLC 2 FAC 3 Others 2*

Neil Austin

AUSTIN Neil Jeffrey
Born: Barnsley, 26 April 1983
Height: 5'10" **Weight:** 11.11
International Honours: E: Yth
The hard-tackling right-back snapped up by Hartlepool in the close season started by having to prove his fitness but after a spell on the substitutes' bench was quick to establish himself at right-back. Although signed from local rivals Darlington, Neil was soon accepted by the Victoria Park supporters for his wholehearted approach. A player with a powerful shot, in the second half of the season he scored three long-range goals, each good enough to be short-listed for the 'Goal of the Season' award. Neil was honoured to make a

clean sweep of the club's three 'Player of the Year' awards.
Barnsley *(From trainee on 27/4/2000) FL 132+16 FLC 2+1 FAC 11+1 Others 1+1*
Darlington *(Free on 1/7/2007) FL 52+10/5 FLC 2 FAC 3 Others 3*
Hartlepool U *(Free on 2/7/2009) FL 36+3/3 FAC 1 Others 1*

AUSTIN Ryan
Born: Stoke-on-Trent, 15 November 1984
Height: 6'3" **Weight:** 13.8
The powerful and pacy former Crewe trainee fulfilled his dream of a League career when he was offered a one-year contract by incoming manager Paul Peschisolido following Burton's promotion from the Blue Square Premier. Mostly used as a central defender in his non-League days, Ryan revelled in the opportunity to make the right-back position his own with a series of impressive performances. However, tragedy struck in an FA Cup tie at Gillingham in November when he ruptured cruciate knee ligaments for the second time in his career. Ryan underwent surgery in January and hopes to make a full recovery.
Burton A *(From trainee at Crewe Alex on 1/8/2004) FL 18/2 FLC 1 FAC 2/1 Others 1*

AYALA Daniel
Born: Seville, Spain, 7 November 1990
Height: 6'3" **Weight:** 13.3
A Spanish-born graduate of the Liverpool Academy, the teenager made a surprise debut on the opening day at Tottenham as a substitute and started the following game, at home to Stoke. He then returned to the reserves but made further Premiership appearances from the bench. A tall central defender, Daniel has better prospects of making the grade than most other Liverpool youngsters.
Liverpool *(From trainee at Sevilla, Spain on 1/2/2008) PL 2+3*

AYLING Luke David
Born: Lambeth, 25 August 1991
Height: 5'11" **Weight:** 10.6
Brought in by Yeovil as a loan signing in March from Arsenal, the teenager showed some bright spots during the season's run-in. Predominantly a defender but with the ability to sit in as a defensive midfielder, his energy, tackling and vision promises a great career in the game. Out of contract in the summer, he made four appearances in his loan spell from the Emirates.
Arsenal *(From trainee on 2/7/2009)*
Yeovil T *(Loaned on 17/3/2010) FL 1+3*

B

BABEL Ryan Guno
Born: Amsterdam, Holland, 19
December 1986
Height: 6'1" **Weight:** 12.6
International Honours: Holland: 39;
U23-5; U21-5; Yth
The Dutch international forward is
probably the most disappointing of
Liverpool manager Rafa Benitez's many
overseas signings and, after three years
at Anfield, supporters are still waiting to
see some justification for his large fee.
After starting the season on the left
wing at Tottenham, he became a regular
substitute for the first half of the season,
scoring two late goals in the 6-0
thrashing of Hull in September. In
November he scored a goal at Lyon in
the Champions League that might have
transformed Liverpool's season and his
Anfield career. As a late substitute, he
scored with a stunning 25-yard blast in
the 81st minute to give Liverpool the
lead and the chance to salvage their
Champions League campaign. As so
often, Liverpool could not defend a lead
even for nine minutes and slipped out of
the competition. In mid-season, he fell
out of contention even for a place on
the bench and complained to the media
that he was not getting enough
opportunities. Following the breakdown
of a move to Birmingham, he had an
extended run, playing in all but one
game from February to the end of the
season without showing much uplift in
form. A sending off for petulance in the
Europa Cup match at Benfica probably
cost his team dearly as they slipped to
another defeat after taking the lead.
Given Ryan's pace and powerful shot, it
was surprising that Benitez did not use
him as a central striker during the long
absences of the injured Fernando Torres.
*Liverpool (£11,500,000 from Ajax,
Holland on 25/7/2007) PL 30+52/11 FLC
6 FAC 6+2/1 Others 16+17/8*

BAILEY James Joseph
Born: Bollington, 18 September 1988
Height: 6'0" **Weight:** 12.5
James graduated through the youth
ranks at Crewe and was first seen in a
single substitute appearance in 2007-08.
The following year, he broke into the
squad and this season was firmly
established in midfield, although injury
cost him several appearances. James
makes an impact on the team but a first
goal for the club remains elusive. He
joined Derby, at the same time as John
Brayford, shortly after the season ended.

*Crewe Alex (From trainee on 4/5/2007)
FL 44+2 FLC 4 FAC 5*

BAILEY Nicholas (Nicky)
Francis
Born: Putney, 10 June 1984
Height: 5'10" **Weight:** 12.8
Club Honours: FC '05
It was another excellent season for
Charlton's captain who finished as
second top scorer with 13 goals.
However it was his penalty shoot-out
miss in the play-offs that ended the
chance of promotion. Although looking
most comfortable in central midfield, he
was frequently used wide on the left
during a season in which he missed only
two League games due to an ankle
injury. Nicky is a strong tackler with a
good engine and an intelligent passer
of the ball with an eye for goal. He
scored some great goals, including a
spectacular volley against Millwall at the
Valley and a 35-yard looping shot at
Tranmere.
*Barnet (Signed from Sutton U on
2/7/2004) FL 88+1/12 FLC 5/1 FAC 5
Others 4/1*
*Southend U (£175,000 on 1/8/2007)
FL 43+2/9 FLC 3 FAC 5/2 Others 3/1*
*Charlton Ath (£750,000 on 15/8/2008)
FL 86+1/25 FLC 0+1 FAC 4 Others 3/1*

BAIN Kithson Anthony
Born: Grenada, 26 May 1982
Height: 5'10" **Weight:** 12.8
International Honours: Grenada: 25
Kithson was signed for Tranmere by ex-
Jamaica manager John Barnes in
September on a season-long contract,
and made his debut in the home defeat
by Walsall, becoming the first
Grenadian international to play League
football. It was clear he was not fully
match fit and because the squad was
top heavy with attacking players, he
went on loan to Blue Square Premier
Kettering Town in November. On his
return, despite scoring seven goals in
ten outings for the reserves, Kithson,
who is a solid and quick striker, was
given only a handful of substitute
appearances and released at the end of
the season.
*Tranmere Rov (Free from Ball Dogs,
Grenada, ex Queens Park Rgrs,
Grenada, on 9/9/2009) FL 0+10 Others 1*

BAINES Leighton John
Born: Liverpool, 11 December 1984
Height: 5'8" **Weight:** 11.10
International Honours: E: 2; U21-16
After a series of first class displays on
the left flank, a first England cap
against Egypt was the reward for the

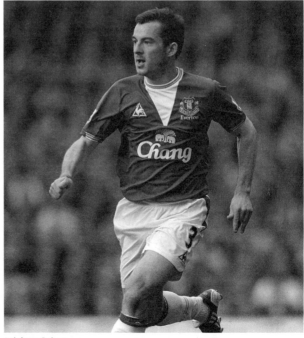

Leighton Baines

full-back who was one of the most consistent performers in an Everton jersey. The former Wigan defender missed just one League match all season, and scored one goal in the top flight – ironically a last-minute winner against his former club at Goodison. Adept at getting forward when partnered by either Diniyar Bilyaletdinov or Steven Pienaar, he provides a speedy and positive presence on the left-hand side of the Everton backline. As an added bonus the locally-born player had one of the highest number of assists for any Premier League defender, often from viciously curled free kicks.

Wigan Ath (From trainee on 4/1/2003) P/FL 140+5/4 FLC 7+2 FAC 6 Others 1+1
Everton (£6,000,000 on 7/8/2007) PL 76+14/2 FLC 1+1 FAC 10/1 Others 12+2

BAINS Rikki Lee
Born: Coventry, 3 February 1988
Height: 6'1" **Weight:** 13.0
The young defender made three starts and two substitute appearances for Darlington during the first couple of months of the season before being allowed out on loan to Blue Square Premier side Gateshead in the New Year. Was out of contract in the summer.

Accrington Stanley (From trainee at Coventry C on 12/9/2006) FL 2+1 (Free to Tamworth on 17/1/2007)
Macclesfield T (Free from Corby T on 29/1/2009) FL 1+1
Darlington (Free on 18/8/2009) FL 3+1 Others 0+1

BAIRD Christopher (Chris) Patrick
Born: Ballymoney, 25 February 1982
Height: 5'10" **Weight:** 11.11
International Honours: NI: 44; U21-6; Yth
Chris enjoyed his best season yet at Fulham where his versatility proved an asset, allowing him to feature more regularly. Although his preferred position is as a central defender, a role in which he was only occasionally deployed, injuries and suspensions amongst the squad saw him establish himself in a previously unfamiliar defensive midfield role operating in front of the back four. He retained this position throughout much of the campaign, although during the absence of John Pantsil, he was selected at right-back for a series of games and also featured there in the Europa League final . Calm under pressure, he is an effective distributor both in the air and on the deck. Chris added to his collection of Northern

Ireland caps with appearances in World Cup qualifiers against the Czech Republic, Poland and Serbia.
Southampton (From trainee on 15/1/2001) P/FL 62+6/3 FLC 4 FAC 5 Others 2
Walsall (Loaned on 26/9/2003) FL 10
Watford (Loaned on 16/3/2004) FL 8
Fulham (£3,000,000 on 17/7/2007) PL 49+11 FLC 3 FAC 4+1 Others 13+3

BAKAYOGO Zoumana
Born: Paris, France, 11 August 1986
Height: 5'9" **Weight:** 10.8
International Honours: Ivory Coast: U23
Zoumana joined Tranmere in what was originally a short-term loan but, despite competition from clubs higher up the League, the arrangement was subsequently extended to the end of the season. After a delay for international clearance, he made his debut against Stockport in October with an immediate impact as he picked up 'Man of The Match' awards in his first two starts. A good utility man, Zoumana's preferred position is left-back, from where he makes pacy runs down the flank. His speed, application and work rate were always impressive, so he soon became a firm favourite with Rovers' fans. He has been offered a new longer-term contract.
Millwall (Free from Paris St Germain, France on 4/8/2006) FL 8+7 FLC 2 FAC 2+2 Others 2 (Freed during 2008 close season)
Tranmere Rov (Free from Alfortville, France on 9/10/2009) FL 29 FAC 5

BAKER Carl Paul
Born: Prescot, 26 December 1982
Height: 6'2" **Weight:** 12.8
International Honours: E: SP-2
Carl started 2009-10 in incredible form for Stockport, with hat-tricks against Brighton and Crewe, and an injury time equaliser from the spot against Southampton. However, tragedy soon followed, his brother Mike dying from leukaemia days before the game at Yeovil. Carl decided to play, though, and scored twice in a 2-2 draw, making it nine goals in just five games. His goal in the home game against Leeds in December was to be his last for the club, as he made the move to Coventry in the January transfer window. Having made a big impact with his good close control and dribbling, after two substitute appearances he was given his first start in a five-man midfield. He had an excellent February playing as a wide man, with his jinking runs and good crosses impressing the fans and winning him several 'Man of the Match' awards.

His high-stepping style had some fans likening him to Coventry legend, Tommy Hutchison and he set up the equaliser at home to Blackpool and Clinton Morrison's goal at Newcastle. However, his early impressive form tailed off along with most of his team-mates and he found himself back on the bench for the last few games.
Morecambe (£30,000 from Southport, ex Prescot Cables, on 30/7/2007) FL 40+2/10 FLC 3/1 FAC 1 Others 2
Stockport Co (£175,000 on 31/7/2008) FL 34+8/12 FLC 2 FAC 2+1/1 Others 3+1/3
Coventry C (Signed on 8/1/2010) FL 14+8

BAKER Harry Kenneth
Born: Bexleyheath, 20 September 1990
Height: 5'11" **Weight:** 12.1
Harry was used as reserve right-winger by Leyton Orient and likes to get the ball down to run at defenders. He was sent out to gain more experience in January with a month's loan at Blue Square Premier Grays but was out of contract during the summer and released.
Leyton Orient (From trainee on 8/1/2009) FL 2+6 Others 3

BAKER Nathan Luke
Born: Worcester, 23 April 1991
Height: 6'3" **Weight:** 12.8
International Honours: E: Yth
Aston Villa loanee Nathan endured an injury-hit spell whilst at Lincoln which restricted the centre-back's appearances to just 18 during his six-month stint at Sincil End. When fit, the England under-19 international showed tremendous potential when putting in a number of commanding performances in the centre of defence.
Aston Villa (From trainee on 18/9/2008)
Lincoln C (Loaned on 23/10/2009) FL 17+1

BAKER Richard (Richie) Peter
Born: Burnley, 29 December 1987
Height: 5'7" **Weight:** 11.6
The young central midfield player made only seven starting appearances for Bury in the season. Quick and competent on the ball and very adept at playing a full part in counter-attacking football, Richie provided vital fresh legs in a further seven substitute appearances. He scored an excellent 85th-minute winner against Rotherham early in the season- his only goal of this campaign. Richie's last appearance for the Shakers was in a 2-0 defeat at Macclesfield in March, meaning he

played no part in the final effort to win promotion or reach the play-offs. Was out of contract at the end of June.
Bury (From trainee at Preston NE on 1/7/2006) FL 68+39/7 FLC 2+3 FAC 8+2/1 Others 4+3

BALANTA Angelo Jasiel
Born: Bogota, Colombia, 1 July 1990
Height: 5'10" **Weight:** 11.11
It was perhaps a frustrating season at Queens Park Rangers for Angelo who, after making the breakthrough in the previous campaign, found himself overshadowed by fellow youth team striker Antonio German in this one. Angelo started the first game but made only three substitute appearances in the remainder of the campaign despite featuring on the bench on numerous occasions.
Queens Park Rgrs (From trainee on 22/1/2008) FL 9+16/2 FLC 1+2/1 FAC 0+1
Wycombe W (Loaned on 14/11/2008) FL 9+2/3

BALDOCK George Henry Ivor
Born: Buckingham, 26 January 1993
Height: 5'9" **Weight:** 10.7
Given a late call to the MK Dons' bench thanks to a raft of senior players being either injured or suspended, George was given the last ten minutes of the Dons' penultimate game against Brighton and in that time showed some neat midfield touches and a willingness to get in and mix it with much more experienced opponents. The first-year Academy scholar did not look out of place and his progress alongside elder brother Sam will be something for the MK fans to look out for.
MK Dons (Trainee) FL 0+1

BALDOCK Samuel (Sam) Edward
Born: Buckingham, 15 March 1989
Height: 5'7" **Weight:** 10.7
Club Honours: AMC '08
International Honours: E: Yth
After netting 12 goals in his breakthrough season with MK Dons, much was expected of Sam under returning boss Paul Ince, but the arrival of Jermaine Easter immediately put his starting place under threat, and spending the first month of the campaign on England under-20 World Cup duty did not help his club's cause. Getting off the scoring mark in early November, eight goals before Christmas showed he was back on song, but a miserable run with injuries then followed and his second half of the season was one that can be filed in the forgettable folder. A very popular player

with the club's fans, he signed an extended deal during the season and will be hoping his stop-start campaign was just one of the seasons to be endured.
MK Dons (From trainee on 20/4/2006) FL 43+23/17 FLC 2/1 FAC 2+2/2 Others 4+7/3

BALDWIN Patrick (Pat) Michael
Born: City of London, 12 November 1982
Height: 6'2" **Weight:** 10.12
Having signed a fresh three-year deal in the summer, the Colchester centre-half and club captain endured a rollercoaster season. In Aidy Boothroyd's first game in charge, at Southampton in September, he was stretchered off with knee and leg injuries. Upon his return to fitness two months later, Pat suddenly found himself out of favour. A loan spell at Bristol Rovers saw him settle in quickly, his assured positional play and strength in the air making him a reliable team member. He also played at full-back, linking up well with the attack. After returning to play in Colchester's 5-0 defeat against Norwich in January he was next loaned to Southend for the rest of the campaign, where he made an immediate impact when netting a last-gasp equaliser against Swindon on his debut. Rugged and determined in the tackle Pat added some much needed steel to an experienced Shrimpers' line-up and as a testament to his impact to the side, unusually for a loan player, he was given the captaincy of the side when Adam Barrett missed the tail-end of the campaign.
Colchester U (From trainee at Chelsea on 16/8/2002) FL 168+24/1 FLC 8 FAC 12 Others 7+3
Bristol Rov (Loaned on 20/11/2009) FL 6
Southend U (Loaned on 29/1/2010) FL 18/1

BALE Gareth Frank
Born: Cardiff, 16 July 1989
Height: 6'0" **Weight:** 11.10
International Honours: W: 24; U21-4; Yth
Gareth started the season with an injury, and even when fit, remained out of the limelight for Tottenham until he made a significant impact for the second half of the season once he became established after Christmas. Gareth plays at left-back or on the left of midfield and it is in the attacking role that he has been most prominent and effective, winning a place in some pundits' teams of the season. He regained his very best form with lightning speed and the ability to leave top defenders trailing before

sending over telling crosses, from which many goals were scored. Gareth is used heavily at free kicks and corners but his three goals were scored from open play. His highlights for Spurs included Premier League goals against Arsenal and Chelsea in successive games. The goal against Chelsea came at the end of a fine run and was scored with his weaker right foot. Gareth makes significant defensive contributions and continues his international career with Wales.
Southampton (From trainee on 19/7/2006) FL 40/5 FLC 3 FAC 1 Others 1
Tottenham H (£5,000,000 on 29/5/2007) PL 38+9/5 FLC 7+2/1 FAC 10 Others 8+2

BALKESTEIN Pim
Born: Gouda, Holland, 29 April 1987
Height: 6'3" **Weight:** 13.3
Pim started the season at the heart of the Ipswich defence and played in the first six league games before falling out of favour and having two loan spells at Brentford. The composed centre-back with good positional sense immediately stiffened up the back line, so much so that the Bees only conceded four goals in his eight appearances before he was recalled by Ipswich. Pim returned to Brentford for a second loan spell in April but was hampered by a groin injury. He then suffered a broken nose in the Bees' penultimate game of the season, at Swindon, which saw him need ten minutes of treatment on the pitch before being carried off. Was not offered a contract for 2010-11.
Ipswich T (£100,000 from SC Heerenveen, Holland on 30/6/2008) FL 23+6 FLC 2+1 FAC 1
Brentford (Loaned on 20/11/2009) FL 8
Brentford (Loaned on 25/3/2010) FL 6/1

BALL Callum Reece
Born: Leicester, 8 October 1992
Height: 6'1" **Weight:** 13.7
Regarded as one of the brightest prospects at Derby's Academy, the young striker was given some experience in the reserve team that won the totesport.com League Central Division. Nigel Clough gave him a brief taste of Championship football as a late substitute in the final game against Cardiff.
Derby Co (Trainee) FL 0+1

BALLACK Michael
Born: Gorlitz, Germany, 26 September 1976
Height: 6'2" **Weight:** 12.8
Club Honours: FLC '07; FAC '09, '10; CS '09; PL '10
International Honours: Germany: 98; U21

Michael showed outstanding early season form as part of Carlo Ancelotti's midfield diamond at Chelsea and soon had three Premier League goals, including a sublime diving header against Burnley. He was an automatic choice until he lost his place after the Champions League elimination at the hands of Inter Milan, when Chelsea's midfield was accused of being 'one paced', but made valuable contributions from the bench – none more so than against Aston Villa in the FA Cup semi-final when his delightful cross was swept home by Florent Malouda for the second goal. Michael replaced injury victim John Obi Mikel in the holding midfield role for the last three League matches and his calm assurance helped to guide Chelsea home, with the Blues scoring 17 goals in the process. He replaced Mikel in the FA Cup final after losing out to the same player 12 months earlier. But his joy at a second consecutive winners' medal and the capture of the 'Double', was tempered by the serious ankle ligament injury he sustained following a heavy challenge that forced him to miss the World Cup finals. This was viewed in Germany as a national calamity as his inspirational captaincy had been a crucial factor in their qualification and led to his being shortlisted for FIFA 'World Player of 2009', one of five Chelsea players so honoured. Michael's contract expired at the end of the season and, after talks stalled, he became a free agent.
Chelsea (Free from Bayern Munich, Germany, ex Chemnitz, Kaiserslautern, Bayer Leverkusen, on 17/1/2006) PL 87+18/17 FLC 9+3 FAC 12+3/5 Others 32+3/4

BANGURA Alhassan (Al)
Born: Freetown, Sierra Leone, 24 January 1988
Height: 5'8" **Weight:** 10.7
International Honours: Sierra Leone: 1
Another surprising acquisition by Ian Holloway in the summer after his release by Watford, Al played 11 times for Blackpool, mainly from the bench. However, when he did play, he was key to the Blackpool midfield. Normally deputising for Keith Southern, Al was the man responsible for playing the destroyer in the midfield three – something he was adept at with Watford. The club had an option of another year on his contract but did not take it up.
Watford (From trainee on 2/6/2005) P/FL 27+35/1 FLC 7+3 FAC 3 Others 1+2
Brighton & Hove A (Loaned on 3/3/2009) FL 6

Blackpool (Free on 14/8/2009) FL 2+7 FLC 2

BANNAN Barry
Born: Glasgow, 1 December 1989
Height: 5'7" **Weight:** 9.7
International Honours: S: B-1; U21-5
The young midfielder quietly went about his business after joining Blackpool on loan from Aston Villa. A box of tricks on the touchline and with a dribbling style that sees him weave in and out of challenges, Barry is always exciting to watch. He also has substance to his play, scoring a fabulous 30-yard goal on the volley at Coventry and contributing two assists. His 20 appearances helped Barry to develop as a player and his raw talent is turning into consistent performances.
Aston Villa (From trainee on 2/7/2008) Others 1+1
Derby Co (Loaned on 13/3/2009) FL 6+4/1
Blackpool (Loaned on 26/11/2009) FL 8+12/1 Others 0+2

BARAZITE Nacer
Born: Arnhem, Holland, 27 May 1990
Height: 6'5" **Weight:** 15.3
International Honours: Holland: Yth
Nacer is a skilful young Dutch playmaker but was sidelined by a shoulder injury for much of the campaign. He did appear for Arsenal as a substitute in the Carling Cup third round tie at home to West Bromwich. Comfortable in possession, he is always looking to receive a pass as well as making one.
Arsenal (From trainee on 2/7/2007) FLC 0+3
Derby Co (Loaned on 20/8/2008) FL 21+9/1 FLC 0+2 FAC 3+1

BARCHAM Andrew (Andy)
Born: Basildon, 16 December 1986
Height: 5'9" **Weight:** 11.11
A tricky left-winger with an eye for goal, Andy made a superb start to life in League One by netting Gillingham's winner in the Carling Cup first round defeat of Plymouth, followed by stunning strikes against Millwall at home and Leeds away. He suffered a loss of form in mid-season but returned a creditable tally of eight goals in all competitions, most notably crashing in a 25-yard drive to level the scores in a 2-2 derby with Charlton at the Valley. Andy swept the board on the club's awards night, winning the 'Player of the Year', 'Players' Player' and supporters' 'Player of the Year' accolades.
Tottenham H (From trainee on 7/7/2005) FLC 1
Leyton Orient (Loaned on 22/11/2007) FL 15+10/1

Gillingham (Signed on 25/9/2008) FL 69+6/13 FLC 2/1 FAC 6+1/3 Others 6

Andy Barcham

BARDSLEY Philip (Phil) Anthony
Born: Salford, 28 June 1985
Height: 5'11" **Weight:** 11.8
Club Honours: FAYC '03
Not a happy season at Sunderland for right-back Phil, who lost his place with the January introduction of Alan Hutton on loan from Tottenham, a player he had previously competed with during a loan spell of his own at Glasgow Rangers. By the latter stages of the season Phil was making it clear that he may need to move on to ensure regular first team football. Things looked so much brighter for Phil until January. As the regular right-back, he was part of Sunderland's bright start to the season but following the introduction of Hutton the ex-Manchester United defender spent most of the time on the bench. Phil returned to the side against Liverpool at Anfield when Hutton was unavailable and was expected to retain his place in the following game when Hutton was ineligible against his parent club Spurs. Instead, Phil found himself back on the bench with Anton Ferdinand preferred.
Manchester U (From trainee on 2/7/2003) PL 3+5 FLC 3+1 FAC 2+1 Others 2+1
Burnley (Loaned on 16/3/2006) FL 6
Glasgow Rgrs (Loaned on 16/8/2006) SL 5/1 Others 2
Aston Villa (Loaned on 8/1/2007) PL 13
Sheffield U (Loaned on 19/10/2007) FL 16
Sunderland (£2,000,000 on 24/1/2008) PL 56+9 FLC 3/1 FAC 3+1

BARKER Christopher (Chris) Andrew

Born: Sheffield, 2 March 1980
Height: 6'0" **Weight:** 11.8
Chris had a very frustrating season at Home Park with Plymouth. He suffered a serious calf tear in a warm-up match against Heart of Midlothian in July and this kept him out of action until the FA Cup third round tie against Newcastle in January. His confidence and strength in defence had been missed and Chris showed his adaptability by playing both as a central defender and at left-back. Towards the end of the season he once again struggled to get into the starting line-up, so his first priority will be to regain full fitness.

Barnsley (Signed from Alfreton T on 24/8/1998) FL 110+3/3 FLC 11+1 FAC 4 Others 0+1
Cardiff C (£600,000 on 12/7/2002) FL 144+15 FLC 9 FAC 8 Others 4
Stoke C (Loaned on 6/8/2004) FL 4
Colchester U (Loaned on 18/8/2006) FL 38 FAC 1
Queens Park Rgrs (Signed on 7/8/2007) FL 25 FAC 1
Plymouth Arg (Free on 9/8/2008) FL 48+6 FLC 1 FAC 3

BARKER Shaun

Born: Nottingham, 19 September 1982
Height: 6'2" **Weight:** 12.8
Derby pursued Shaun relentlessly through the summer until they finally reached an agreement with Blackpool. One of the attractions of the central defender was his excellent fitness record, at Rotherham as well as Blackpool, so it was ironic that he should suffer a thigh strain in pre-season training. The injury troubled him for the first half of the season as he struggled to make an impact. Only past the turn of the year did Derby followers see the real Shaun, a defender capable of dominating games. He is strong in the air and hard to beat on the ground, attributes seen to best advantage when he had a regular partner in the experienced Russell Anderson. Shaun scored five League goals, second only to Rob Hulse, and the way he blossomed earned the supporters' vote for the Jack Stamps' award as 'Player of the Season'. Immediately after the final match, he underwent a knee operation but expected to be fit by the time the players reported back and the feeling is that the best is yet to come from him.

Rotherham U (From trainee on 10/7/2002) FL 119+4/7 FLC 6 FAC 3 Others 1
Blackpool (Signed on 4/8/2006) FL 133+1/5 FLC 5 FAC 6/1 Others 4/2

Derby Co (£1,000,000 on 15/7/2009) FL 33+2/5 FAC 2+1

BARMBY Nicholas (Nick) Jonathan

Born: Hull, 11 February 1974
Height: 5'7" **Weight:** 11.3
Club Honours: FLC '01; UEFAC '01; CS '01
International Honours: E: 23; B-2; U21-4; Yth; Sch
Although in the veteran stage of a glittering career – he is now the 14th oldest player in Hull's history – Nick's continuing value to his home-town team was underlined by the fact that he missed the squad in only one of the Tigers' Premier League matches. He was captain of a youthful line-up in the Carling Cup tie against Southend and appointed team captain by manager Phil Brown in October following the injury to Ian Ashbee and George Boateng's loss of form. Nick's wider contribution to the community was recognised by the University of Hull, who awarded him an honorary degree. Inevitably, he earned the new nickname of 'The Doctor' amongst his team-mates. Following the disappointment of relegation, City supporters hope Nick will continue to contribute his skill and genuine enthusiasm to their midfield, especially as he is only one short of 100 club goals in his career.

Tottenham H (From trainee on 9/4/1991) PL 81+6/20 FLC 7+1/2 FAC 12+1/5
Middlesbrough (£5,250,000 on 8/8/1995) PL 42/8 FLC 4/1 FAC 3/1
Everton (£5,750,000 on 2/11/1996) PL 105+11/18 FLC 2+3/3 FAC 12/3
Liverpool (£6,000,000 on 19/7/2000) PL 23+9/2 FLC 3+4/1 FAC 2+3/1 Others 10+4/4
Leeds U (£2,750,000 on 8/8/2002) PL 17+8/4 FLC 1 FAC 0+2 Others 3/1
Nottingham F (Loaned on 27/2/2004) FL 6/1
Hull C (Free on 6/7/2004) P/FL 90+51/20 FLC 4+1/1 FAC 5+1/1 Others 3/2

BARNARD Lee James

Born: Romford, 18 July 1984
Height: 5'10" **Weight:** 10.10
International Honours: E: Yth
Lee had top scored in both his previous campaigns but an injury-free run in the Southend side in 2009-10 saw him at his prolific best, scoring 17 goals for the club in 27 starts to the end of 2009. This included a first senior hat-trick against Leyton Orient in October. Lee is a natural goalscorer with the uncanny knack of arriving in the danger area at the right moment and his endless

chasing of lost causes had made him a popular figure with the Roots Hall faithful. However, with the club's perilous financial position it was no surprise that he came under close scrutiny from other clubs and during the January transfer window it was Southampton that won the race for his signature. Paired up front with Rickie Lambert, already on 22 goals, for Saints, Lee worked hard to fit in, but it was not until late February he really established himself, netting both goals in a 2-0 win at League One leaders, Norwich. Thereafter he boosted his League scoring tally to 26, and finished the season as the division's third highest scorer.

Tottenham H (From trainee on 3/7/2002) PL 0+3
Exeter C (Loaned on 1/11/2002) FL 3 Others 1
Leyton Orient (Loaned on 5/11/2004) FL 3+5 FAC 1 Others 1
Northampton T (Loaned on 4/3/2005) FL 3+2
Crewe Alex (Loaned on 31/8/2007) FL 9+1/3
Southend U (Signed on 25/1/2008) FL 60+15/35 FLC 3/2 FAC 2+1 Others 4
Southampton (Signed on 22/1/2010) FL 14+6/9 FAC 1+1

BARNES Ashley Luke

Born: Bath, 31 October 1989
Height: 6'0" **Weight:** 11.3
After signing a new two-year contract at the end of 2008-09, the young striker was looking to press home a claim for a first team starting place with Championship Plymouth. He finally made his first start, against Bristol City in October, but due to his lack of action he joined Torquay on loan in February. Returning a month later having made six appearances, he subsequently joined Brighton on loan until the end of the season, scoring on his debut against Tranmere, having been introduced as a substitute ten minutes earlier. He then netted three more times as Albion secured their League One status; the goals included spectacular strikes against Southampton and Bristol Rovers. Although not especially nippy and perhaps lacking the physical presence to lead the line, Ashley demonstrated the striker's art of being in the right place at the right time during his spell in Sussex.

Plymouth Arg (Signed from Paulton Rov on 22/3/2007) FL 15+7/2 FLC 0+2 FAC 1
Torquay U (Loaned on 9/2/2010) FL 6
Brighton & Hove A (Loaned on 25/3/2010) FL 4+4/4

BARNES Corey
Born: Sunderland, 1 January 1992
Height: 5'8" **Weight:** 10.7
This promising young midfielder, now in his second season with Darlington, was thrust into action in November as an emergency right-back following an injury to Paul Arnison. He performed admirably for four consecutive games until loan cover was signed.
Darlington (Trainee) FL 6+3 FAC 1 Others 1

BARNES Giles Gordon
Born: Barking, 5 August 1988
Height: 6'1" **Weight:** 12.13
International Honours: E: Yth
After being released by Derby, wide midfielder Giles trained with West Bromwich for a month before penning an 18-month deal plus a further one year in the club's favour. A ruptured right Achilles tendon had kept him out of action since August and he was not 100 per cent fit when he moved to the Hawthorns, but he quickly got into his swing and made an immediate impact after his 83rd-minute substitute debut in the 1-0 home win over Sheffield Wednesday. He then earned a penalty in his second game as Albion won 2-0 at Swansea.
Derby Co (From trainee on 10/9/2005) P/FL 61+21/10 FLC 2+2/2 FAC 4+3/1 Others 0+2
West Bromwich A (Free on 3/2/2010) FL 1+8

BARNES Sam
Born: Liverpool, 16 October 1991
Height: 6'0" **Weight:** 11.4
With a small squad often suffering injuries and suspensions, Stockport manager Gary Ablett regularly called on second-year scholar Sam as cover on the bench. In April, Sam was surprisingly handed his debut at Leyton Orient and the young defender put in a composed 'Man of the Match' performance at Brisbane Road. He also started the unfortunate 6-0 defeat at home to Huddersfield.
Stockport Co (Trainee) FL 2

BARNETT Charlie John
Born: Liverpool, 19 September 1988
Height: 5'7" **Weight:** 11.7
Club Honours: FAYC '07
An attacking central midfielder who can also play on the left, Charlie failed to find much favour at Tranmere despite signing a one-year contract extension in July. He played most of his football in the reserves, despite – as befits a former Liverpool youth player - having a good first touch, perceptive reading of the game and excellent technique. He was

released by Rovers in May.
Liverpool (From trainee on 7/7/2006)
Tranmere Rov (Free on 5/8/2008) FL 26+10/4 FLC 1+1 FAC 3 Others 2+1

BARNETT Leon Peter
Born: Stevenage, 30 November 1985
Height: 6'1" **Weight:** 11.3
Club Honours: Ch '08
Out of favour at the Hawthorns, tall, central defender Leon made only three starts for West Bromwich in 2009-10, all in the League Cup, before going out on loan to Coventry in early November after it became clear that Ben Turner's injury was serious. He went straight into the team and his experience was evident from the start. A mobile central defender with good ability in the air, his distribution sometimes let him down and after losing his place in January owing to the form of Richard Wood and James McPake he returned in February. Despite being sent off twice in three games, his loan was extended until the end of the season and with McPake injured again Leon played the final six games of the season.
Luton T (From trainee on 28/9/2004) FL 51+8/3 FLC 4 FAC 2+1 Others 3+1
West Bromwich A (£2,500,000 + on 1/8/2007) P/FL 40+5/3 FLC 4 FAC 6
Coventry C (Loaned on 4/11/2009) FL 19+1

BARNETT Moses
Born: Sierra Leone, 3 December 1990
Height: 6'3" **Weight:** 13.2
International Honours: E: Yth
A lively ball-playing left-back who enjoyed getting forward and skilfully linking play, particularly with fellow loanee Jamie Devitt of Hull. He made five loan appearances for Darlington, including two against his namesake team Barnet, before returning to Everton at the beginning of November. Was out of contract in the summer.
Everton (From trainee at Arsenal on 1/5/2008)
Darlington (Loaned on 9/10/2009) FL 4 FAC 1

BARRETT Adam Nicholas
Born: Dagenham, 29 November 1979
Height: 5'10" **Weight:** 12.0
Club Honours: Div 1 '06
Adam has completed his sixth season at Roots Hall and Southend's club captain is now approaching 300 appearances for them. Adam can play at left-back, which exploits his attacking qualities, but in a troubled season was in the heart of the Shrimpers' defence having to contend with seven different centre-back partners. A true fans' favourite, his wholehearted play is universally

admired and the side is poorer in his rare games on the sidelines, his campaign ending slightly early with a troublesome hamstring injury.
Plymouth Arg (From USA football scholarship, ex trainee at Leyton Orient, on 13/1/1999) FL 47+5/3 FLC 4 FAC 6+1 Others 1
Mansfield T (£10,000 on 1/12/2000) FL 34+3/1 FAC 3 Others 2
Bristol Rov (Free on 2/7/2002) FL 90/5 FLC 2 FAC 5/1 Others 2
Southend U (Free on 5/7/2004) FL 244+3/26 FLC 10/1 FAC 16/1 Others 16

BARRON Scott
Born: Preston, 2 September 1985
Height: 5'10" **Weight:** 11.0
Scott's appearances were limited by the outstanding form of Tony Craig and Danny Schofield on the left-hand side of Millwall's team. When he played it was mainly at left-back but he also proved most reliable on the left of midfield. Scott is quick in the tackle and speedy on his overlapping runs. He played his best games in a Millwall shirt in the televised play-off semi-finals against Huddersfield that earned him 'Man of the Match' awards.
Ipswich T (From trainee on 18/3/2004) FL 14+1 FLC 1 FAC 1
Wrexham (Loaned on 8/2/2007) FL 3
Millwall (Free on 9/8/2007) FL 26+23 FLC 2+1 FAC 4+2/1 Others 4

BARRY Gareth
Born: Hastings, 23 February 1981
Height: 6'0" **Weight:** 12.6
International Honours: E: 36; B-1; U21-27; Yth
Mark Hughes stole a march on Liverpool when he signed the influential Aston Villa and England midfielder for Manchester City in the summer. Gareth was a key signing for City and was expected to lift the central midfield department but, despite playing the full season, he did not display quite the high level of performance he showed with his previous club. His first City goal came in the titanic 4-3 battle with Manchester United at Old Trafford and his second was three days later against Fulham. He scored only one more goal all season – in the 1-1 Premiership draw at Stoke – and three goals was a disappointing return from a player who regularly notched up eight or nine for Villa. In club football Gareth normally plays as an attacking midfielder, while for England he is the defensive holding player. After avoiding injury all season, he suffered ankle ligament damage in the penultimate game with Tottenham. It put his participation in the World Cup in doubt but he proved himself fit in

Gareth Barry

make a positive impact. Quickly appointed skipper, the goalkeeper led by example, particularly in United's run to the area semi-final of the Johnstone's Paint Trophy when his penalty saving – seven in three shoot-outs – was crucial. His consistency was reflected in the fact that he was the only Hereford player to feature in each first team match and he was a popular winner of the club's 'Player of the Year' award.
Hereford U (Free from Kidderminster Hrs, ex trainee at Newcastle U, Blyth Spartans, Cambridge U - loan, on 23/6/2009) FL 45+1 FLC 2 FAC 2 Others 4

Adam Bartlett

time to join Fabio Capello's squad.
Aston Villa (From trainee on 27/2/1998) PL 353+12/41 FLC 28/4 FAC 19+2/3 Others 22+4/4
Manchester C (£12,000,000 on 2/6/2009) PL 34/2 FLC 6/1 FAC 2+1

BARRY-MURPHY Brian
Born: Cork, 27 July 1978
Height: 6'0" Weight: 12.4
International Honours: RoI: U21-6; Yth
Brian made an impressive 51 appearances during the season, inevitably putting him at the top of the list. The current longest-serving Bury player, with six seasons at Gigg Lane, Brian is renowned for his outstanding ability from set pieces and his aptitude for playing defence splitting through balls from his position in the centre of midfield. Consistent as ever, BBM was

voted the 'Players' Player of the Season'.
Preston NE (Free from Cork C on 3/8/1999) FL 6+15 FLC 1+3 FAC 1+1 Others 1
Southend U (Loaned on 11/2/2002) FL 8/1
Hartlepool U (Loaned on 30/10/2002) FL 7 FAC 2
Sheffield Wed (Free on 31/1/2003) FL 55+3 FLC 1 FAC 2 Others 6
Bury (Free on 3/8/2004) FL 200+18/13 FLC 5+1 FAC 7+2 Others 11+1

BARTLETT Adam James
Born: Newcastle, 27 February 1986
Height: 6'0" Weight: 11.11
During Hereford's fraught start to the season Adam, with his exceptional reactions, was one of the few players to

BARTLEY Kyle Louie
Born: Stockport, 22 May 1991
Height: 6'1" Weight: 11.12
Kyle was one of the stars of Arsenal's FA Youth Cup winning side and made his Champions League debut in the group game at Olympiacos. A regular for the Gunners' reserve side, he joined Sheffield United in February on a three-month loan deal as central defensive cover and went straight into the side, making his League debut, at Preston. Good in the air and willing to play the ball out of trouble, he appeared in six successive games. Thereafter he made some substitute appearances and was in the starting line-up when Nyron Nosworthy was required at full-back.
Arsenal (From trainee on 2/7/2007) Others 1
Sheffield U (Loaned on 9/2/2010) FL 10+4

BARTLEY Marvin Clement
Born: Reading, 4 July 1986
Height: 5'11" Weight: 12.6
A midfield player who also filled in at

centre-half to great effect for Bournemouth, Marvin started the season on the bench and was in and out of the side for the first half of it. Suspension after a red card cost him his place but in the second half of the season he excelled. Marvin's form was terrific and that earned a deserved new contract for the hard-tackling player.
Bournemouth *(Free from Hampton & Richmond Borough, ex Burnham, Hayes, Didcot T, on 24/7/2007) FL 65+22/2 FLC 1+1 FAC 4+2 Others 4+1*

BARTON Adam James
Born: Blackburn, 7 January 1991
Height: 5'11" **Weight:** 12.2
A young midfielder who was an unused sub for Preston on several occasions before making an impressive debut against Scunthorpe, Adam is a steady and reliable player who hits simple but effective passes and harasses the opposition well. Tall and rangy, he needs to develop physically but he is very mobile. It was unfortunate that a clash of heads ended his first game at half-time but great things are expected of him in years to come.
Preston NE *(From trainee on 8/1/2009) FL 1*

BARTON Joseph (Joey)
Anthony
Born: Huyton, 2 September 1982
Height: 5'9" **Weight:** 11.2
Club Honours: Ch '10
International Honours: E: 1; U21-2
It was another disrupted season for Joey, a talented if aggressive worker in the Newcastle midfield. He was establishing himself on the right flank when he broke a bone in his foot against Plymouth in September and he did not reappear until March, when he came off the bench in the win at Doncaster. His subsequent appearances were primarily as a substitute although when starting against Peterborough in April he scored his first goal for 18 months and his third for the club, all from dead balls. Understandably, given his lack of match practice, he looked rusty, but he showed occasional glimpses of class such as his through ball for Wayne Routledge to score at Plymouth in the title clincher, and hopefully he can deliver such quality more frequently next season in the Premiership.
Manchester C *(From trainee on 5/7/2001) PL 123+7/15 FLC 4/1 FAC 13+1/1 Others 2+3*
Newcastle U *(£5,800,000 on 3/7/2007) P/FL 34+13/3*

BASEY Grant William
Born: Bromley, 30 November 1988
Height: 6'0" **Weight:** 11.11
International Honours: W: 1; U21-1; Yth
Grant is a solid defender, comfortable on the ball and with a powerful shot that he likes to use at set pieces. It was November before Grant started a game for Charlton due to the impressive form of Kelly Youga. After playing a couple of games on the left side of midfield, Grant got his chance in his preferred position of left-back when Youga picked up an injury and he went on to make the position his own until sustaining an horrific ankle ligament injury at Bristol Rovers in February that was to finish his season. Was out of contract at the end of June.
Charlton Ath *(From trainee on 17/7/2007) FL 32+14/1 FLC 2 FAC 2+1 Others 2*
Brentford *(Loaned on 17/7/2007) FL 8 FLC 1 Others 1*

BASHAM Christopher (Chris) Paul
Born: Hebburn, 20 July 1988
Height: 5'11" **Weight:** 12.8
Chris made only two starts for Bolton, both in the Premier League, in what proved to be a season of limited opportunity. The first of these was a result of a tactical reshuffle in the 4-0 home defeat by Chelsea, when Chris was introduced to the team in a bid to stifle Chelsea's diamond formation. His next start came in December in the 1-1 draw at Burnley, where he again played the holding role. Despite making just a handful of further substitute appearance, Chris was happy to sign a contract extension in November. While not a current first team regular, Chris has proved to be a solid performer when called to action. His versatility is also an asset, as proved when moving from defence into the midfield holding role.
Bolton W *(From trainee on 20/10/2007) PL 6+13/1 FLC 0+1 FAC 0+1*
Rochdale *(Loaned on 8/2/2008) FL 5+8*

BASINAS Angelos
Born: Chalkis, Greece, 3 January 1976
Height: 5'11" **Weight:** 11.13
International Honours: Greece: 100
Previously overlooked in his first 12 months at Portsmouth, Greek midfielder Angelos was limited to only two starts before the Blues' FA Cup third round replay at Coventry. However, Angelos was introduced late in the second half at the Ricoh Arena and helped Pompey to snatch victory from the jaws of defeat with an inspired

performance, reversing a 1-0 deficit to a 2-1 extra-time victory. Given this impetus, Angelos then went on to establish himself in the Portsmouth midfield, showing the experience, passing and tackling attributes that have helped him to become Greece's most capped player. His contract expired in the summer.
Portsmouth *(Free from AEK Athens, Greece, ex Panathinaikos, Real Mallorca, on 2/2/2009) PL 10+5 FLC 2 FAC 1+2*

BASSO Adriano
Born: Jundiai, Brazil, 18 April 1975
Height: 6'1" Weight: 11.7
Apart from having a run of four games early in the season, which ended when he pulled a groin muscle during the warm-up before the away match at Newcastle in October, this outstanding goalkeeper was frozen out of the Bristol City side last season after he had declined to sign an extension to his contract which was due to run out at the close of the campaign. City's loss should have been another club's gain but, surprisingly, no one came in for him during the transfer window. Adriano's contract was cancelled by mutual agreement in early March but what a financial loss to City who, had they played him regularly throughout the season, would surely have pulled in a good fee for the best goalkeeper they have had since the days of Mike Gibson some 40 years ago. It was poor business, not just in regard to the money side but also the loss of many points that his presence would probably have prevented. Ashton Gate will not be the same place without this charismatic 'keeper. Hopefully, Adriano will get his wish and be signed by a top club. Certainly his displays between the sticks during the past five seasons are deserving of a bigger stage.
Bristol C *(Free from Woking, ex Atletico Paraense, on 14/10/2005) FL 165 FLC 1 FAC 8 Others 8*

BASSONG Sebastien Aymar
Born: Paris, France, 9 July 1986
Height: 6'2" **Weight:** 11.7
International Honours: France: U21. Cameroon: 3
Sebastien was signed by Tottenham from relegated Newcastle during the summer. The Cameroon International came highly recommended and made a great impact when scoring on his debut in Spurs' 2-1 win over Liverpool in the opening game. Sebastien was thrown in at the deep end at Spurs and was required to cover at centre-back for either Ledley King or Michael Dawson,

making 34 starts and six appearances off the bench in all competitions. He is capable of playing across the back four but is primarily a left-sided centre-back. He is a tight marker, adding strength, pace and aerial ability to his range of skills. Sebastien often pops up in the opposition area at set pieces, and his debut goal was a header, as were most of his opportunities. Sebastien missed selection for the African Cup of Nations but was in the reckoning for the World Cup.
Newcastle U (£1,800,000 from Metz, France on 7/8/2008) PL 26+4 FLC 2 FAC 2
Tottenham H (Signed on 6/8/2009) PL 25+3/1 FLC 3 FAC 7

BASTURK Yildiray
Born: Herne, Germany, 24 December 1978
Height: 5'7" **Weight:** 10.12
International Honours: Turkey: 49
The midfielder arrived at Blackburn at the end of the January transfer window, having been out of the game for a considerable time. He received good reports from the reserve team but then was injured. With games against the leading clubs then arriving it was not until the end of April that he was given a debut at Wolverhampton, but was taken off at half-time when struggling to get to grips with the game.
Blackburn Rov (Loaned from VfB Stuttgart, Germany, ex Wattenscheid 09, VfL Bochum, Bayer Leverkusen, Hertha Berlin, on 27/1/2010) PL 1

BATESON Jonathan (Jon)
Alan
Born: Preston, 20 September 1989
Height: 6'1" **Weight:** 12.2
The former Blackburn apprentice had a debut to forget for Bradford when he was sent off in the last minute of a Carling Cup loss at Nottingham Forest. But Jon learned quickly from that disappointment and emerged as a solid back-up for Bradford's regular right-back Simon Ramsden. He enjoyed a good run in the side over the final couple of months when Ramsden was out of action with an injured calf. Was out of contract in the summer.
Bradford C (From trainee at Blackburn Rov on 10/7/2009) FL 14+7 FLC 1 FAC 1 Others 3+1

BATT Shaun Anthony
Born: Harlow, 22 February 1987
Height: 6'2" **Weight:** 12.6
Peterborough's fleet-footed wide attacker who will trouble any defender with his pace, found it hard to hold down a place at Posh so was loaned out to Millwall at the end of January to gain

valuable playing time and experience. Scoring on his debut at the Den against Southend, his surging runs on to a through ball often outpaced defenders. Unfortunately, Shaun was injured and missed some games when Millwall had an injury crisis at the wrong time of the season, but came back for the play-off final that saw the club climb back into the Championship.
Peterborough U (Signed from Fisher Ath, ex Stevenage Borough, Dagenham & Redbridge, St Albans C - loan, on 28/7/2008) FL 15+35/4 FLC 2+2 FAC 1+5 Others 1
Millwall (Loaned on 25/1/2010) FL 10+6/3 Others 1

BATTH Daniel (Danny)
Tanveer
Born: Brierley Hill, 21 September 1990
Height: 6'3" **Weight:** 13.5
Having progressed through Wolverhampton's Academy to sign professional terms in May, teenage centre-back Danny enjoyed his big breakthrough in a successful season-long loan move to League One side Colchester. One of Aidy Boothroyd's first additions after he took over at the U's, Danny made his League debut in a 2-0 home win over Hartlepool in September. Strong, dominant in the air and appearing instantly at home in senior football, Danny scored his first professional goal in the 1-0 home win over Oldham in February, clinching three points when heading home from a corner.
Wolverhampton W (From trainee on 7/7/2009)
Colchester U (Loaned on 17/9/2009) FL 16+1/1 FAC 1

BAUZA Guillem
Born: Palma de Mallorca, Spain, 25 October 1984
Height: 5'11" **Weight:** 12.6
Club Honours: Div 1 '08
International Honours: Spain: Yth
Following an ankle operation in the summer, Guillem made only one first team appearance, as a substitute for Swansea in the Carling Cup tie against Brighton before a knee cartilage injury kept him out of action until mid-December. A qualified teacher back home in Spain, Guillem is currently taking a Medical Genetics course at Swansea University. Surprisingly introduced into the midfield starting line-up at Queens Park Rangers in March, he also started a few weeks later at home against Scunthorpe.
Swansea C (Signed from Espanyol, Spain, ex Mallorca B, on 26/6/2007) FL 19+30/9 FLC 4+2 FAC 5+3/5 Others 5/2

BAXTER Jose
Born: Bootle, 7 February 1992
Height: 5'11" **Weight:** 11.8
International Honours: E: Yth
The exciting Academy graduate continued his apprenticeship at Goodison after becoming Everton's youngest ever player, aged 16 years 191 days, in the previous campaign. Jose made several appearances from the substitutes' bench and enjoyed a first Goodison start against BATE Borisov in the Europa League. A regular for England teams at youth level, the youngster has been deployed more in an attacking midfield role than as an orthodox centre-forward.
Everton (From trainee on 26/3/2009) PL 1+4 FLC 0+1 Others 1+4

BEAN Marcus Tristam
Born: Hammersmith, 2 November 1984
Height: 5'11" **Weight:** 11.6
Club Honours: Div 2 '09
Brentford's hard-working midfielder suffered a number of short-term injuries during the campaign that restricted his appearances. Nevertheless, he still shows the passion to win the ball and set up chances for his colleagues. Disappointingly, he failed to score a goal, having collected nine in the previous campaign.
Queens Park Rgrs (From trainee on 29/7/2004) FL 44+23/2 FLC 2+1 FAC 2 Others 3+1
Swansea C (Loaned on 17/2/2005) FL 6+2
Swansea C (Loaned on 8/9/2005) FL 9/1
Blackpool (Free on 20/1/2006) FL 19+4/1 FLC 0+1 FAC 0+2 Others 1
Rotherham U (Loaned on 10/8/2007) FL 11+1/1 Others 2
Brentford (Free on 1/7/2008) FL 68+7/9 FLC 1 FAC 6 Others 2

BEATTIE Craig
Born: Glasgow, 16 January 1984
Height: 6'0" **Weight:** 11.7
Club Honours: SPD '04, '06, '07; SC '04, '06; Ch '08
International Honours: S: 7; U21-7
With several competent strikers available for the start of the season, Craig was not part of Roberto di Matteo's plans at West Bromwich and he played in just five games for Albion, scoring three League Cup goals, before signing for Swansea in late August. After arriving at the Liberty Stadium Craig initially struggled with a chest infection, but following his return to fitness he scored in three consecutive games, including the winner at his old club, before being sidelined firstly with a back injury, then a toe injury. The

second half of the season saw him continue to struggle to gain match fitness.
Glasgow Celtic *(From juniors at Glasgow Rgrs on 1/7/2003) SL 18+32/13 SLC 3+2/2 SC 0+4 Others 1+5/1*
West Bromwich A *(£1,250,000 + on 26/7/2007) P/FL 7+24/4 FLC 5+1/3 FAC 1+3*
Preston NE *(Loaned on 4/3/2008) FL 1+1*
Crystal Palace *(Loaned on 27/9/2008) FL 15/5*
Sheffield U *(Loaned on 20/2/2009) FL 1+12/1 Others 2+1*
Swansea C *(£500,000 on 28/8/2009) FL 12+11/3*

BEATTIE James Scott
Born: Lancaster, 27 February 1978
Height: 6'1" **Weight:** 12.0
International Honours: E: 5; U21-5
James' form after signing for Stoke in January 2009 and the goals he scored in the second half of that campaign led to him being widely described as the 'Buy of the Season' by much of the mainstream media. Big things were thus expected of him in the new season. Alas, that has not been the case in what was a hugely frustrating time for both the striker and the Stoke supporters. He started the season looking as if he was carrying some type of injury and never really found the form that so wowed everyone the year before. There were glimpses of what was possible, as he netted twice in the home win over West Ham and helped to harry the Wolverhampton defence into conceding two goals, but unfortunately his season will be most remembered for a well documented occurrence after a 2-0 defeat at Arsenal. This led to James being sidelined for most of the remaining games and in a side struggling for goals this was a major loss for Stoke.
Blackburn Rov *(From trainee on 7/3/1995) PL 1+3 FLC 2 FAC 0+1*
Southampton *(£1,000,000 on 17/7/1998) PL 161+43/68 FLC 11+3/6 FAC 14+1/2 Others 2*
Everton *(£6,000,000 on 5/1/2005) PL 51+25/13 FLC 2+1 FAC 4+1/1 Others 1+1/1*
Sheffield U *(£4,000,000 + on 9/8/2007) FL 57+5/34 FLC 1 FAC 2*
Stoke C *(£3,500,000 on 13/1/2009) PL 27+11/10 FLC 1 FAC 1*

BEAVON Stuart Leigh
Born: Reading, 5 May 1984
Height: 5'7" **Weight:** 10.10
Wycombe's hard-working striker was influential early in the season. A sublime

piece of skill set up Jon-Paul Pittman's goal against Bristol Rovers and Stuart scored his first goal for the club, a 25-yarder at Hartlepool in September, but a groin operation the following month put him out for six weeks. Since joining Wycombe, Stuart has started or been on the bench in equal measure. His urgent, forceful style of play always causes problems for opponents but he will want to improve on his goal tally of three in the coming season. He may miss the start, having suffered a fractured fibula playing in the Berks & Bucks Senior Cup final in May.
Wycombe W *(Free from Weymouth, ex Didcot T, on 19/2/2009) FL 16+17/3 FLC 1 FAC 0+1 Others 1*

BECCHIO Luciano Hector
Born: Cordoba, Argentina, 28 December 1983
Height: 6'2" **Weight:** 13.5
The hard-working Argentine striker built on a fine debut season with Leeds with another positive campaign. Despite missing several games through injury, he was an admirable foil for Jermaine Beckford, notching 15 goals. His early goal output was modest and he damaged ankle ligaments in a 0-0 home draw with Charlton in October, ruling him out for nine games. Once in his scoring stride, he enjoyed doubles at Hartlepool and Carlisle and at home to Oldham. Quick action by the Leeds medical staff saved him from greater danger when he was concussed and swallowed his tongue in the 1-0 defeat at Norwich in March.
Leeds U *(Free from UD Merida, Spain, ex Boca Juniors, RCD Mallorca B, Ciudad de Murcia - loan, Terrassa, Barcelona Atletic, on 1/8/2008) FL 72+10/30 FLC 4+3/2 FAC 5+3/2 Others 3+3/2*

BECKFORD Jermaine Paul
Born: Ealing, 9 December 1983
Height: 6'2" **Weight:** 13.2
Club Honours: Div 1 '07
Another 30 goals for the Leeds' striker saw him named the League One 'Player of the Season' for the second time in succession. High-profile televised goals against Manchester United and Tottenham proved vote winners and he was rarely out of the headlines. He rejected a new contract before the start of the campaign and was transfer-listed. Two unnamed bids were rejected and in mid-July Leeds announced that Jermaine was off the list. He immediately showed his worth by scoring both goals that saw off promoted Exeter on the opening day. Goals continued to flow and four days

after handing in a transfer request, Jermaine became the toast of Elland Road with the goal that knocked Manchester United out of the FA Cup at Old Trafford. A fortnight later, Jermaine withdrew his request and Leeds said he would stay until the end of the season, ruling out any move in the transfer window. Jermaine said he wanted to help Leeds win promotion, and two more FA Cup goals against Tottenham – the second a penalty deep into injury time – further raised his profile. A hamstring injury saw his goal output dip and he was confined to the bench before being restored for the promotion-clinching home game against Bristol Rovers in which, fittingly, he scored the winner.
Leeds U *(Signed from Wealdstone on 15/3/2006) FL 111+15/71 FLC 5+4/4 FAC 9/8 Others 7+1/1*
Carlisle U *(Loaned on 6/10/2006) FL 4/1 Others 1*
Scunthorpe U *(Loaned on 19/1/2007) FL 17+1/8*

Jermaine Beckford

BECKWITH Dean Stuart
Born: Southwark, 18 September 1983
Height: 6'3" **Weight:** 13.4
Central defender Dean found it hard to settle down in his first season at Northampton but became far more assured when Ian Sampson took over as manager, forming a formidable partnership with Craig Hinton at the heart of the Cobblers' defence. Dean is good in the air and likes to prompt attacks from the back.
Gillingham *(From trainee on 7/8/2003)*

FL 0+1 FAC 0+1
Hereford U *(Free on 14/7/2005) FL 92+3/3 FLC 5 FAC 10 Others 3*
Northampton T *(Free on 16/7/2009) FL 37+1 FLC 1 FAC 1 Others 2*

BEDNAR Roman
Born: Prague, Czech Republic, 26 March 1983
Height: 6'4" **Weight:** 13.2
Club Honours: Ch '08
International Honours: Czech Republic: 3; U21-8
The Czech striker was suspended by West Bromwich in May 2009 over well documented off-field allegations. Cautioned by West Midlands Police, the Football Association granted permission for Roman to resume playing following his suspension and he reported back for training in mid-August, returning to the side for the Carling Cup tie against Rotherham shortly afterwards. Three days later, he scored both goals in a 2-2 draw at Sheffield United. In October, playing against Reading, he suffered a back injury (a trapped nerve) which, continued to annoy him for the rest of the season. He also received knee and ankle injuries, had an ongoing hernia problem which requires an operation, but battled on. Although not always a starter for Roberto di Matteo, he still gave a good account of himself and came up with some important goals.
Heart of Midlothian *(Signed from FB Kaunas, Lithuania, ex Bohemians Prague, Mlada Boleslav, on 27/7/2005) SL 33+7/11 SLC 1 SC 1+3/1 Others 4+1/1*
West Bromwich A *(£2,300,000 on 31/8/2007) P/FL 51+31/30 FLC 2 FAC 13/4*

BEEVERS Lee Jonathan
Born: Doncaster, 4 December 1983
Height: 6'1" **Weight:** 12.10
International Honours: W: U21-7; Yth
Having stepped up a division last summer, versatile defender or midfield player Lee made a dream beginning to life at Colchester when starting the first four games of the season at left-back – all of them wins. However, his season was cruelly cut short in his fifth successive start when he badly dislocated his shoulder in the 2-1 defeat at MK Dons. Following surgery, Lee returned to training in February but immediately picked up a knee injury that would keep him out for the rest of the campaign. He returned to reserve team action in the final week of the season.
Ipswich T *(From trainee on 19/3/2001)*
Boston U *(Free on 27/3/2003) FL 71+1/3 FLC 2/1 FAC 5 Others 3/1*

Lincoln C *(Signed on 21/2/2005) FL 154+12/9 FLC 4/2 FAC 5 Others 8+2*
Colchester U *(Free on 3/7/2009) FL 4 FLC 1*

BEEVERS Mark Geoffrey
Born: Barnsley, 21 November 1989
Height: 6'4" **Weight:** 12.9
International Honours: E: Yth
Although still only young, Sheffield Wednesday's Mark has clocked up an impressive number of appearances for his only League club. Tall and commanding, he made the left-sided central defensive position his own after Richard Wood departed. He is solid and reliable, but needs to maintain his concentration levels and also add a more vocal approach to his game. Overall though, he is a very popular member of the squad and has quite a few admirers at clubs higher up the pecking order. Mark is certainly one for the future if he stays at Hillsborough and uses the experience he has gained so far.
Sheffield Wed *(From trainee on 1/12/2006) FL 90+9 FLC 3 FAC 4/1*

BEGOVIC Asmir
Born: Trebinje, Herzegovina, 20 June 1987
Height: 6'5" **Weight:** 15.0
International Honours: Canada: Yth
In what was a breakthrough season for the Bosnian goalkeeper, who broke into the Portsmouth side early on when capitalising on David James' troublesome calf injury. When James returned, Asmir joined Ipswich on loan in October to further his experience and to steady a defence that had conceded 16 goals in the previous six games. In six appearances he was not on the losing side and contributed to Ipswich's first win by making four outstanding saves against Derby. Back at Portsmouth he immediately began to turn heads, establishing himself as the Blues' number one with a string of outstanding performances, making world-class saves and dominating his penalty area with confidence and experience beyond his years. As January arrived, Asmir was a man in demand and eventually moved to Stoke for an undisclosed fee. Tony Pulis had spent almost the entire January transfer window chasing Portsmouth's James and seemed sure to sign him, only to then acquire Asmir at the very last moment after, it appears, he had already agreed a move, in principle, to Tottenham! In a bizarre twist of fate, one of Stoke's first games soon after Asmir's signing was away at Portsmouth, where James lined up for

the home side and Asmir, while wearing a Stoke kit, was presented with the Portsmouth 'Player of the Month' award for January! Asmir waited patiently for his shot at first team football with Stoke, which came when Thomas Sorensen was injured at Chelsea and had to leave the field. Unfortunately for Asmir he went on to concede five goals as the home side completed a 7-0 hammering of Stoke. Thankfully, he then followed up that nightmare debut with two clean sheets, against Everton and Fulham and there is a lot of belief at Stoke that he is being lined up to become the number-one 'keeper in the foreseeable future.
Portsmouth *(From juniors on 19/10/2006) PL 10+1 FLC 3 FAC 3*
Macclesfield T *(Loaned on 23/11/2006) FL 2+1 FAC 1*
Bournemouth *(Loaned on 10/8/2007) FL 8 Others 1*
Yeovil T *(Loaned on 27/3/2008) FL 2*
Yeovil T *(Loaned on 8/8/2008) FL 14*
Ipswich T *(Loaned on 15/10/2009) FL 6*
Stoke C *(£3,250,000 on 1/2/2010) PL 3+1*

BEHAN Denis
Born: Tralee, 2 January 1984
Height: 6'0" **Weight:** 13.5
International Honours: RoI: U23-3; U21
A hard-working and lively striker, Denis joined Hartlepool in the summer as a direct replacement for the departing Joel Porter. Having failed to make the grade at Brentford as a junior, Denis was determined to succeed at his second attempt to break into English football. He started in Pool's first team and soon showed himself to be a fine opportunist scorer. Particularly good from set pieces, his thunderous 35-yard effort against Oldham won the club's 'Goal of the Season' award. Twice sidelined by ankle injuries, against all expectations he was able to return just before the season's end and, as a substitute against Exeter, scored a goal that proved vital in saving Hartlepool from relegation.
Hartlepool U *(Signed from Cork C on 20/7/2009) FL 21+8/6 FLC 2 FAC 1 Others 0+1*

BEHRAMI Valon
Born: Mitrovica, Kosovo, 19 April 1985
Height: 6'1" **Weight:** 12.4
International Honours: Switzerland: 26
If you are in a battle against relegation, as West Ham were, then you need players like Valon in the side. The Swiss international midfield player never stops running and always gives a battling display. In January, against Arsenal in the FA Cup, he was at his best with a dashing, tireless performance in which

he also set up a goal for Alessandro Diamanti. There was another excellent performance against Hull in February, when he scored one goal and was unlucky not to have two more. As the Hammers found themselves in the thick a relegation fight, Valon rose to the occasion. In the vital game against Sunderland in April he won countless tackles and was the engine room of the team. During the season he gained further international caps for his home country Switzerland.
West Ham U (£5,000,000 from SS Lazio, Italy, ex Lugano, Genoa, Verona - loan, on 31/7/2008) PL 48+3/2 FLC 1 FAC 3/1

BELFORD Cameron Dale
Born: Nuneaton, 16 October 1988
Height: 5'11" **Weight:** 12.10
As the understudy to first choice goalkeeper Wayne Brown, Cameron made only three appearances for Bury this season, covering for the injury and suspension of the first choice 'keeper. He did prove reliable, however, producing a fantastic last-minute save against Rotherham and making vital saves in the important Port Vale game.
Bury (From trainee at Coventry C on 18/8/2007) FL 5+4 Others 1

BELHADJ Nadir
Born: Saint-Claude, France, 18 June 1982
Height: 5'9" **Weight:** 10.8
International Honours: France: Yth. Algeria: 44
It was a somewhat sporadic season at Portsmouth for the flying Algerian full-back. The left-sided player helped his country to World Cup qualification, which then pitched them against England in the group stages in South Africa. The highlight of his League season came in December, when he scored the opener for Pompey in a 2-0 victory over Liverpool. Injury limited Nadir's starts to five between September and late January but he forced his way back into contention after that, again scoring against Liverpool, this time at Anfield, and showing the pace and skill that have proved an effective weapon from left-back. However, injury again struck in March to cut Nadir's season short, and, despite his return for the FA Cup final, left his future in the balance as Portsmouth are set to start from scratch in the Championship next season.
Portsmouth (Signed from RC Lens, France, ex RC Lens, Gueugnon, Sedan, Olympique Lyonnais, Sedan - loan, on 1/9/2008) PL 37+11/5 FLC 5 FAC 5+1/1 Others 4+2

Nadir Belhadj

BELL David Anthony
Born: Wellingborough, 21 April 1984
Height: 5'10" **Weight:** 11.6
Club Honours: Div 3 '03
International Honours: RoI: U21-2; Yth
The right-sided midfield player was injured in Coventry's opening League game. David returned to action in late October but took several weeks to gain full match fitness. He was a key player in the impressive run between December and March, with solid but unspectacular performances on the flank showing his close control and crossing ability as well as being the best taker of corners in the club. David scored three excellent goals, all from the edge of or outside the penalty area and all away from home, at Portsmouth, Bristol City and Crystal Palace, the last a winner. His crosses were crucial in producing a number of goals, including the winner at Plymouth.
Rushden & Diamonds (From juniors on 24/7/2001) FL 109+13/10 FLC 4 FAC 5+3 Others 3+2
Luton T (£100,000 on 12/1/2006) FL 62+13/7 FLC 6/1 FAC 7 Others 1
Leicester C (Loaned on 27/3/2008) FL 6
Norwich C (£600,000 on 23/7/2008) FL 12+7 FAC 1
Coventry C (£500,000 on 30/1/2009) FL 28+9/3 FAC 2/1

BELL Lee
Born: Alsager, 26 January 1983
Height: 5'10" **Weight:** 12.0
At the start of last season Lee was used as a second-half substitute at Macclesfield but his performances

ensured that he became a regular starter from September, after which he missed only a few matches when recovering from injury. A speedy and hard-working central midfielder, Lee had some notable performances, including times when he played just in front of the back four. It is rare for Lee to score but he netted two, his second a late winner at Barnet in April. Lee was deservedly voted 'Player of the Year', but was released at the end of the season so that he could seek pastures new.
Crewe Alex (From trainee on 6/2/2001) FL 34+20/3 FLC 0+1 FAC 1+3 Others 1+3 (Signed for Burton A on 31/1/2007)
Mansfield T (Free on 7/8/2007) FL 23/1 FLC 1 FAC 3+1
Macclesfield T (Free on 19/7/2008) FL 74+9/3 FLC 1+2 FAC 3+1 Others 1

BELLAMY Craig Douglas
Born: Cardiff, 13 July 1979
Height: 5'9" **Weight:** 10.12
Club Honours: CS '06
International Honours: W: 58; U21-8; Yth; Sch
The Manchester City and Welsh international striker started the season in the form of his life with a highlight being the September local derby against Manchester United at Old Trafford, where he scored two outstanding goals, the second to make it 3-3 in stoppage time, only for United to score a winner in the sixth additional minute. With so much forward talent at his disposal, manager Mark Hughes used him on the left for many games with Emmanuel Adebayor and Carlos Tevez the central strikers. Here, Craig's pace and willingness to run at defenders set up at least ten assists and his own total of 11 goals made him the club's third top scorer. When his mentor Mark Hughes - at Blackburn and for Wales as well as with City - was dismissed in December, Craig was more upset than most and his form dipped. For a while, he seemed to be out of favour with new manager Roberto Mancini. However, following a short absence with a knee problem he returned with a two-goal flourish in a sensational 4-2 victory at Stamford Bridge over soon-to-be champions Chelsea in February and finished the season back to his best form.
Norwich C (From trainee on 20/1/1997) FL 71+13/32 FLC 6/2 FAC 1
Coventry C (£6,500,000 on 18/8/2000) PL 33+1/6 FLC 3/1 FAC 2/1
Newcastle U (£6,000,000 on 11/7/2001) PL 87+6/27 FLC 3+2/4 FAC 5 Others 24+1/11
Glasgow Celtic (Loaned on 31/1/2005) SL 12/7 SC 3/2

Blackburn Rov (£5,000,000 on 16/6/2005) PL 22+5/13 FLC 3+1/2 FAC 1/2
Liverpool (£6,000,000 on 7/7/2006) PL 23+4/7 FLC 2 Others 8+5/2
West Ham U (£7,500,000 on 10/7/2007) PL 20+4/7 FLC 1/2 FAC 1
Manchester C (£14,000,000 on 20/1/2009) PL 33+7/13 FLC 4+1 FAC 1+2/1 Others 3/2

BELL-BAGGIE Abdulai
Hindolo
Born: Sierra Leone, 28 April 1992
Height: 5'4" **Weight:** 9.10
The teenage winger arrived at Rotherham on loan from Reading after being spotted by Ronnie Moore at a reserve game when he had gone to watch someone else. Small, very quick and with good delivery too, he became an instant fans' favourite with his speed, verve and energy seeing him primarily used as an impact player off the bench. Is a confident young man.
Reading (Trainee)
Rotherham U (Trainee loan on 12/3/2010) FL 2+9 Others 0+1

BELLETTI Juliano Haus
Born: Cascavel, Brazil, 20 June 1976
Height: 5'9" **Weight:** 10.12
Club Honours: FAC '09, '10; CS '09; PL '10
International Honours: Brazil: 23
Yet again, the popular Brazilian full-back with the rocket shot proved a valuable member of the Chelsea squad. Although Branislav Ivanovic became the long-term replacement for injury victim Jose Bosingwa, Juliano switched effortlessly into the midfield holding role whenever Michael Essien, John-Obi Mikel or Michael Ballack were unavailable. His appearances in the second half of the season were limited by a knee injury suffered at Preston in a fourth round FA Cup tie. He reappeared in February against Manchester City but conceded a penalty, was sent off and did not get another chance until the final League match, when he made a late substitute appearance as the Blues were crowned Champions. Seven days later he played a longer part in the FA Cup final and conceded another penalty but Petr Cech spared his blushes with a brilliant save. This may have been his Chelsea swan song as he was strongly linked to a return to Brazil with champions Flamengo.
Chelsea (£3,700,000 from Barcelona, Spain, ex Cruizeiro, Sao Paulo, Atletico Mineiro - loan, Villareal, on 24/8/2007) PL 29+25/5 FLC 11 FAC 6+3 Others 8+12

BEMBO-LETA Djeny
Born: Kinshasa, DR Congo, 9 November 1991
Height: 6'0" **Weight:** 11.6
A youngster making great strides with Oldham following a two-year scholarship at Boundary Park, Djeny was drafted into the first team squad following some dazzling and eye-catching performances with the Latics' reserve side. He made only the one appearance, from the bench for Oldham against Accrington in the Johnstone's Paint Trophy. There will be more to come from this young man.
Oldham Ath (From trainee on 21/4/2010) Others 0+1

BENAYOUN Yossi Shai
Born: Beersheba, Israel, 5 May 1980
Height: 5'10" **Weight:** 11.0
International Honours: Israel: 78
It was an inconsistent season for the occasionally brilliant Israeli international midfielder, who can play on either flank for Liverpool but is probably more comfortable in the centre. Early in the season, he scored his third hat-trick for the Reds in a 4-0 home win over Burnley and his performance in the 2-0 victory over the old enemy Manchester United in October was considered to be his best in a Liverpool shirt. Unfortunately, he constantly alternated between starting and a place on the bench. He was substituted 15 times and his progress was further disrupted by five weeks out with a cracked rib. Although Yossi scored nine goals to match his previous season's efforts there were few match-winning moments. His extra-time goal in the Europa Cup semi-final against Atletico Madrid should have taken Liverpool to the final but, as so often, they failed to defend a lead.
West Ham U (£2,500,000 from Racing Santander, Spain on 27/7/2005) PL 55+8/8 FAC 7 Others 1+1
Liverpool (£5,000,000 on 20/7/2007) PL 55+37/18 FLC 1+3/1 FAC 4+2/3 Others 21+11/7

BENCHERIF Hamza
Born: Paris, France, 2 February 1988
Height: 6'3" **Weight:** 15.8
International Honours: Algeria: Yth
With little opportunity to progress at Nottingham Forest, Hamza moved to Macclesfield in the summer, went straight into the team and quickly established himself as a valuable member. He initially played at centre-back but, after a few matches, moved into central midfield. Always a strong attacking player, Hamza regularly pressed forward and scored five goals, including the winner in the early home

match against Luton and a brace in the 2-1 home victory against Torquay in September. However, Hamza sustained a severely broken ankle at Rochdale in December when he was leading scorer and an ever-present. Hamza returned to training late in the season and his contract was extended to June 2011.
Nottingham F (Signed from Guingamp, France on 16/11/2006)
Lincoln C (Loaned on 2/10/2007) FL 11+1/1 Others 1
Macclesfield T (Free on 6/7/2009) FL 19/5 FLC 1 FAC 1 Others 1

BENDER Thomas Joseph
Born: Harlow, 19 January 1993
Height: 6'3" **Weight:** 10.8
International Honours: W: Yth
A product of the Colchester Academy, left-back or centre-half Tom was handed his senior debut by new manager Aidy Boothroyd as a late substitute in the 2-0 home win over Hartlepool in September. Aged 16 years and 243 days at the time, it made him the second youngest player ever to represent the Essex club. Tom later signed professional terms on his 17th birthday and, while he made no further first team appearances, he featured on the bench on a number of occasions.
Colchester U (From trainee on 27/1/2010) FL 0+1

BENDTNER Nicklas
Born: Copenhagen, Denmark, 16 January 1988
Height: 6'2" **Weight:** 13.0
International Honours: Denmark: 32; U21-4; Yth
The tall Danish striker probably ran the gauntlet of the Arsenal faithful more than any other player during the season. His nadir was reached at home to Burnley where he proceeded to miss a stack of opportunities although, thankfully, the game was won. His moment of redemption came four days later with a hat-trick in the Champions League second round second leg at home to Porto. He also scored late winners at home to Wolverhampton and at Hull, and gave brief hope of a shock when he gave Arsenal the lead in the Champions League quarter-final at the Nou Camp. He remains Arsenal's most potent weapon in the air and has better control with his feet than can often be expected of such a tall player. He needs, though, to add consistency to his game. He played 23 times in the Premier League, scoring six goals, seven times in the Champions League, adding five further goals, and once in the Carling Cup with one goal. Nicklas

was part of the Denmark World Cup squad in South Africa
Arsenal *(From trainee on 1/12/2005) PL 37+44/20 FLC 8+3/4 FAC 5+2/2 Others 15+10/9*
Birmingham C *(Loaned on 4/8/2006) FL 38+4/11 FLC 0+4/2 FAC 1+1*

BEN HAIM Tal
Born: Rishon Le Zion, Israel, 31 March 1982
Height: 5'11" **Weight:** 11.9
International Honours: Israel: 54; U21; Yth
After arriving at Portsmouth late in the summer transfer window, Israeli defender Tal made a strong start to his career on the south coast. Establishing himself as the regular centre-half, Tal grew in stature and confidence and performed equally as well in an unfamiliar role at full-back. However, as a tumultuous season at Pompey drew to a close, Tal became plagued by a number of injuries, leading to a lack of senior football as Portsmouth slid towards a relegation made inevitable by their points deduction.
Bolton W *(Signed from Maccabi Tel Aviv, Israel on 30/7/2004) PL 81+7/1 FLC 6 FAC 9 Others 7*
Chelsea *(Free on 1/7/2007) PL 10+3 FLC 3+2 FAC 2 Others 2+1*
Manchester C *(£4,000,000 on 4/8/2008) PL 8+1 FLC 1 Others 5*
Sunderland *(Loaned on 2/2/2009) PL 5*
Portsmouth *(Signed on 1/9/2009) PL 21+1 FLC 1 FAC 1*

BENITEZ Christian Rogelio
Born: Quito, Ecuador, 1 May 1986
Height: 5'7" **Weight:** 10.12
International Honours: Ecuador: 30
After recovering from summer shoulder surgery and having to jet back to Ecuador on international duty and to be with his father who was in a car crash, Christian made a fine impact coming into the Birmingham team alongside Cameron Jerome. Small but tricky, Christian made the Blues' attack more dynamic. His touch, speed and ability to turn out of tight situations and go past defenders caused opposition teams problems and benefited his team-mates by creating gaps. Did not score as many goals as he should have considering the chances that came his way, and he came out of the team towards the end of the season. Birmingham opted not to make his loan from Mexican club Santos Laguna permanent for $10-million.
Birmingham C *(Signed from Santos Laguna, Mexico, ex El Nacional on 3/6/2009) PL 21+9/3 FLC 1 FAC 3+2/1*

BENJAMIN Joseph (Joe) John
Born: Woodford, 8 October 1990
Height: 5'11" **Weight:** 11.4
Striker Joe found first team opportunities hard to come by due to the number of players used as Northampton tried to find the winning formula. When he did appear he always gave his all and often showed a talent that belied his years. Joe had two separate spells at Blue Square Premier Eastbourne on loan. Was out of contract at the end of June.
Northampton T *(From trainee on 7/1/2009) FL 2+5 Others 0+1*

[BENJANI] MWARUWARI Benjani
Born: Bulawayo, Zimbabwe, 13 August 1978
Height: 6'2" **Weight:** 12.3
International Honours: Zimbabwe: 43
With Manchester City manager Mark Hughes signing three expensive forwards in the summer in the shape of Emmanuel Adebayor, Carlos Tevez and Roque Santa Cruz, it was clear that the Zimbabwean international would be squeezed out of the first team picture at Eastlands but negotiations over a summer transfer to another club fell through. Sure enough, Benjani made only one appearance (as a substitute) under Mark Hughes in the first half of the season. To his credit new manager Roberto Mancini gave him a chance to establish his credentials and Benjani responded by scoring the only goal in a FA Cup win at Middlesbrough in January. However, after a run of five games he went out on loan to Sunderland in January as cover for Kenwyne Jones, Darren Bent and Fraizer Campbell, but played little as the front men stayed fit. He started just one game at home to Birmingham and of his seven substitute appearances the earliest he was introduced was the 73rd minute. Was out of contract at the end of June.
Portsmouth *(£4,100,000 from Auxerre, France on 13/11/2006) PL 62+8/19 FLC 3+1 FAC 2+1*
Manchester C *(£8,000,000 on 31/1/2008) PL 21+2/4 FLC 0+2 FAC 2/1 Others 1+3/2*
Sunderland *(Loaned on 1/2/2010) PL 1+7*

BENNETT Alan John
Born: Cork, 4 October 1981
Height: 6'2" **Weight:** 12.8
Club Honours: Div 2 '09
International Honours: RoI: 2; B-1; U21-1
A centre-back with good positional

sense and ball control Alan joined Brentford on a permanent basis in the summer after he was released by Reading, but following a groin injury in August and an ankle injury in October he was left out of the side. Loaned to Wycombe in February to replace the injured Adam Hinshelwood Alan gave a dominant performance in the centre of the defence on his debut, a 1-0 win at home to Millwall. Continuing to impress until he was recalled one week early by Brentford, he eventually returned Wycombe, on loan again, for the final game of the season, a 3-0 home win against Gillingham where he topped off a superb performance with a headed goal.
Reading *(Signed from Cork C, ex Richmond, on 30/1/2007)*
Southampton *(Loaned on 1/8/2007) FL 10 FLC 1*
Brentford *(Loaned on 7/3/2008) FL 11/1*
Brentford *(Free on 8/8/2008) FL 55+2/1 FLC 2 FAC 5*
Wycombe W *(Loaned on 16/2/2010) FL 5*
Wycombe W *(Loaned on 25/3/2010) FL 1/1*

BENNETT Dale Owen
Born: Enfield, 6 January 1990
Height: 5'11" **Weight:** 12.6
Dale, a product of the Watford Academy, made his full debut for Watford against Barnsley in September at the age of 19. A strong and speedy centre-half who dominates in the air and looks well equipped to deal with the physical aspects of the role, Dale spent most of the season warming the bench. However, as the battle against relegation intensified he was restored to the first team in April and acquitted himself well, giving a series of commanding and assured performances that reflected his development over the season.
Watford *(From trainee on 2/7/2008) FL 8+2 FLC 0+1*

BENNETT Elliott
Born: Telford, 18 December 1988
Height: 5'9" **Weight:** 10.12
Signed from Wolverhampton for a sizeable fee in August, Elliott quickly settled into the Brighton team and started every League match following his arrival. A fleet-footed winger, he showed his adaptability when swapping to the left flank or to right-back as required during the course of a game. Elliott also specialised in long-range goals, his efforts against Gillingham, Charlton and Oldham being particularly memorable, and graduated to the position of dead-ball expert. Voted

runner-up in the 'Player of the Season' poll, he still needs to be more consistent with his delivery.
Wolverhampton W *(From trainee on 2/3/2007)* FLC 2
Crewe Alex *(Loaned on 26/10/2007)* FL 4+5/1 FAC 0+2
Bury *(Loaned on 31/1/2008)* FL 18+1/1
Bury *(Loaned on 30/7/2008)* FL 46/3 FLC 1 FAC 1 Others 4
Brighton & Hove A *(Signed on 20/8/2009)* FL 43/7 FAC 4/2

Elliott Bennett

BENNETT Ian Michael
Born: Worksop, 10 October 1971
Height: 6'0" **Weight:** 12.10
Club Honours: Div 2 '95; AMC '95
Having signed a one-year contract extension with Sheffield United, including duties as a goalkeeping coach, Ian spent much of the season on the bench. He replaced Mark Bunn in October but injured his hand in his third game and made just two further appearances when Bunn was injured. When called upon he was reliable although uncharacteristically he did let a seemingly straightforward shot through his hands for Port Vale's winning goal in the Carling Cup. Was out of contract in the summer.
Newcastle U *(From trainee at Queens Park Rgrs on 20/3/1989)*
Peterborough U *(Free on 22/3/1991)* FL 72 FLC 10 FAC 3 Others 4
Birmingham C *(£325,000 on 17/12/1993)* P/FL 285+2 FLC 38 FAC 16 Others 13
Sheffield U *(Loaned on 9/12/2004)* FL 5
Coventry C *(Loaned on 17/2/2005)* FL 6
Leeds U *(Free on 4/7/2005)* FL 4
Sheffield U *(£100,000 on 27/7/2006)*

P/FL 14+2 FLC 6 FAC 2

BENNETT James Richard
Born: Beverley, 4 September 1988
Height: 5'10" **Weight:** 12.4
Another of Colin Todd's summer signings, James appeared only briefly in midfield at the start of the season. He made his first start in the draw at Grimsby in September but after only five appearances for Darlington was allowed to leave the club in December.
Hull C *(From trainee on 14/12/2006)*
Darlington *(Free on 2/7/2009)* FL 3+1 Others 0+1

BENNETT Joseph (Joe)
Born: Rochdale, 28 March 1990
Height: 5'10" **Weight:** 11.9
After making his debut in the last game of the previous season, Joe was hoping to push on as Middlesbrough got to grips with the Championship. His seasonal bow came when he appeared off the bench in a Carling Cup game at Nottingham Forest in September and he started the next six games in his natural position as an attacking left-back. He was rewarded with a new three-year contract in September but when new boss Gordon Strachan took over, he wanted more steel at the back and Joe reverted to the reserves. He was recalled in March after a spate of injuries but played in an unfamiliar position on the left wing. The experiment was not wholly successful and the England under-19 international was replaced at the break.
Middlesbrough *(From trainee on 6/7/2008)* P/FL 10+3 FLC 0+1

BENNETT Lee
Born: Barnsley, 19 September 1990
Height: 5'10" **Weight:** 12.0
A second-year scholar, Lee's only taste of Football League action came as a stoppage-time substitute in Lincoln's 2-1 victory over Bradford at Valley Parade early on in the season. The midfielder was not offered professional terms by manager Chris Sutton at the end of the campaign.
Lincoln C *(Trainee)* FL 0+1

BENNETT Ryan
Born: Grays, 6 March 1990
Height: 6'2" **Weight:** 11.0
International Honours: E: Yth
Awarded a new four-year contract by Grimsby in the summer of 2009 to end transfer speculation, Ryan began the term in his usual central defensive slot. However, he soon adopted a new advanced role in front of the defence, with license to roam the width of the pitch. When Town's poor form then saw

a change of manager in October, the teenage captain was made available for transfer and signed for Peterborough. Tall but good on the ground, Ryan can play either at full-back or centre-back and impressed the United fans. Was out for a period of time but the club hope to see the best of him this coming season after he comes back to full fitness.
Grimsby T *(From trainee on 18/4/2007)* FL 89+14/6 FLC 3 FAC 4 Others 7
Peterborough U *(Loaned on 29/10/2009)* FL 20+2/1 FAC 1

BENSON Paul Andrew
Born: Southend-on-Sea, 12 October 1979
Height: 6'2" **Weight:** 12.7
Club Honours: FC '07
International Honours: E: SP-1
Paul finished the season as Dagenham's top scorer for the fourth season in succession, adding to his tally in the regular campaign by scoring three times in the play-off semi-final and once in the final at Wembley. He netted four goals in the home game against Shrewsbury in August, a personal best. He is a threat to defences both with his feet and with his head. A regular change in striking partners due to injuries meant he did not forge the same relationship as he had the previous season. In the League game at Morecambe, he broke his nose but a special mask was made to enable him to continue playing.
Dagenham & Redbridge *(Free from White Ensign on 26/5/2005)* FL 95+5/40 FLC 2 FAC 6/5 Others 9/6

BENT Darren Ashley
Born: Wandsworth, 6 February 1984
Height: 5'11" **Weight:** 11.7
International Honours: E: 6; U21-14; Yth
Any other claimants to the accolade of 'signing of the season' will need to have an immensely strong case. Darren's 24 Premier League goals were bettered only by Messrs Rooney and Drogba, whose top two sides provide their strikers with rather more chances than Darren enjoyed as Sunderland achieved 13th place largely thanks to him netting almost half their goals. No other player outside the top seven clubs managed more than ten Premiership goals. With Bent's additional Cup goal also coming against top flight opposition and with goals against Chelsea (home and away), Manchester United and winners Arsenal, Tottenham and Liverpool (the latter with the aid of the infamous beach ball) the striker had a superb season. Nicknamed Dynamite by

Sunderland fans, he scored the quickest goal of the season in only 36 seconds against former club Spurs, scored the all important first goal of the game 15 times and walked off as overwhelming winner of both Sunderland's 'Player of the Year' awards. Given his fifth England cap by Fabio Capello against Brazil in Qatar, Darren was named in England's World Cup squad.

Ipswich T *(From trainee on 2/7/2001) P/FL 103+19/49 FLC 6+1/3 FAC 2+2/3 Others 5+4/2*
Charlton Ath *(£2,500,000 on 3/6/2005) PL 68/31 FLC 4+2/4 FAC 5/2*
Tottenham H *(£16,500,000 on 29/6/2007) PL 32+28/18 FLC 1+3/1 FAC 1 Others 9+5/6*
Sunderland *(£10,000,000 on 5/8/2009) PL 38/24 FAC 2/1*

BENT Marcus Nathan
Born: Hammersmith, 19 May 1978
Height: 6'2" **Weight:** 12.4
International Honours: E: U21-2
After suffering injury just before the season started, Marcus made the bench just once for Birmingham before being loaned out to Middlesbrough, signing a two- month emergency loan deal in October. Unfortunately, of the seven League games he played in, only one of those was a win for the Teesside club. However, due to the shortage of strikers in the Boro squad his loan was extended to the middle of January and he featured in the 2-1 home FA Cup defeat against big spending Manchester City. The young Boro striker Jonathan Franks later cited Marcus as being a great help to him while he was at the club. After Marcus returned to Birmingham, he was soon on the move again, this time on loan to Queens Park Rangers for the rest of the season. At Loftus Road, Marcus only managed to play 135 minutes of football without scoring a goal after injuries disrupted his campaign.

Brentford *(From trainee on 21/7/1995) FL 56+14/8 FLC 7/1 FAC 8/3 Others 5+1/1*
Crystal Palace *(£150,000 + on 8/1/1998) P/FL 13+15/5 FLC 0+2 FAC 0+1*
Port Vale *(£375,000 on 15/1/1999) FL 17+6/1 FLC 1*
Sheffield U *(£300,000 on 28/10/1999) FL 48/20 FLC 5/3 FAC 3/1*
Blackburn Rov *(£1,300,000 + on 24/11/2000) P/FL 22+15/8 FLC 0+1 FAC 5+1/3*
Ipswich T *(£3,000,000 on 23/11/2001) P/FL 51+10/21 FLC 0+2 FAC 4/1 Others 2+1/1*
Leicester C *(Loaned on 1/9/2003) PL 28+5/9 FAC 2/1*

Everton *(£450,000 on 8/7/2004) PL 38+17/7 FLC 1+2/1 FAC 3+1 Others 2+2*
Charlton Ath *(£2,000,000 on 17/1/2006) P/FL 32+14/4 FLC 5/1 FAC 1*
Wigan Ath *(Loaned on 31/8/2007) PL 25+6/7 FAC 1*
Birmingham C *(£1,100,000 on 18/7/2008) FL 16+17/3 FLC 1 FAC 1*
Middlesbrough *(Loaned on 30/10/2009) FL 3+4 FAC 1*
Queens Park Rgrs *(Loaned on 1/2/2010) FL 2+1*

BENTLEY David Michael
Born: Peterborough, 27 August 1984
Height: 5'10" **Weight:** 11.0
International Honours: E: 7; B-1; U21-8; Yth
David was a peripheral figure in the Tottenham squad in the early part of the season because of Aaron Lennon's terrific form on the right flank, where David also plays. At that time, David's appearances were limited to Cup games but he did have a 'Man of the Match' performance in the Carling Cup against Everton, when he dazzled down the right and mesmerised the defence at times, also offering an excellent supply of crosses. Unfortunately for David, he was not always able to take advantage of Lennon's injuries, as he was sidelined on two occasions. David made 19 starts in all competitions and scored four goals, including one in the record 9-1 win against Wigan, when his free kick rebounded off the back of the goalkeeper. This goal was initially counted as an own goal but subsequently awarded to David by the doubtful goals panel. David played regularly in Spurs' successful end of season pursuit of Champions League qualification. He is an England International but his last appearance was in August, 2008.

Arsenal *(From trainee on 8/9/2001) PL 1 FLC 4 FAC 0+3/1 Others 0+1*
Norwich C *(Loaned on 28/6/2004) PL 22+4/2 FLC 0+1 FAC 1*
Blackburn Rov *(Signed on 31/8/2005) PL 96+6/13 FLC 9/2 FAC 8/2 Others 14/4*
Tottenham H *(£15,000,000 on 31/7/2008) PL 31+9/3 FLC 6+1/1 FAC 6+1/1 Others 5/1*

BENTLEY James (Jim) Graham
Born: Liverpool, 11 June 1976
Height: 6'1" **Weight:** 13.0
The Morecambe skipper had a mixed season and made only 27 League starts due to injury and a short spell when he lost his place with boss Sammy McIlroy opting for the pairing of Dave Artell and

Will Haining in the centre of the defence. Jim sat on the bench for 12 successive games. He was still an inspiration when he started, with some typically solid performances. He scored only three goals but all three were match winners. One major development for Jim was off the field when he became the club's reserve team manager after Jeff Udall stepped down from the role. He is expected to combine coaching duties and playing next season.

Morecambe *(Free from Telford U on 31/5/2002) FL 115+1/12 FLC 4/1 FAC 3 Others 7*

BENTLEY Mark James
Born: Hertford, 7 January 1978
Height: 6'2" **Weight:** 13.0
Club Honours: Div 1 '06
An experienced midfield player, Mark's preferred role is on the right but with Gillingham losing a number of defenders to injury and suspension, he found himself deployed more often than not as a makeshift centre-half. Due to the early kick-off time, his 12th-minute strike against Swindon on the opening day of the season was the first goal scored in the Football League. Mark also netted a memorable header to put the Gills two goals up in the 3-2 home victory over Leeds. Was out of contract at the end of June.

Southend U *(Signed from Dagenham & Redbridge on 15/1/2004) FL 70+23/12 FLC 1+1 FAC 0+1 Others 10+1/1*
Gillingham *(Free on 1/8/2006) FL 141+8/9 FLC 4 FAC 10/3 Others 4+2/1*

BENYON Elliot Paul
Born: High Wycombe, 29 August 1987
Height: 5'9" **Weight:** 10.1
This young striker has always had a nose for goal, but worked hard on his stamina and upper-body strength to develop into an all-round forward capable of leading the Torquay line for 90 minutes as opposed to just being a goal poacher. Elliott netted a hat-trick in an FA Cup tie at Stockport, finished the season as the club's top scorer with 15 goals and received the supporters' 'Player of the Season' trophy.

Bristol C *(From trainee on 6/7/2006)*
Torquay U *(Free on 2/7/2007) FL 31+14/11 FLC 0+1 FAC 3/3 Others 2/1*

BERBATOV Dimitar Ivan
Born: Blagoevgrad, Bulgaria, 30 January 1981
Height: 6'2" **Weight:** 12.6
Club Honours: FLC '08, '10; PL '09
International Honours: Bulgaria: 78
With Ronaldo moving on, Sir Alex

Ferguson was hopeful that Dimitar's class and scoring ability could turn him into a new Cantona figure at Old Trafford. All boded well as Dimitar netted his first goal of the season in a 5-0 win at Wigan in August. He then produced one his most memorable performances in a Manchester United shirt in October, against Wolfsburg in the Champions League, and scored in successive Premiership games again Stoke and Sunderland in September. His sublime scissor-kick finish for the first of United's two equalisers against Sunderland was by far the most spectacular, and he rounded off October with another excellent bit of control and clinical finishing against Blackburn in a 2-0 win at Old Trafford. Unfortunately he also sustained an injury that kept him out until December. Returning to action, he scored against Hull in December, then netted the fourth goal in the next game, another 5-0 win in the Premiership against Wigan. Scoring his ninth goal in the Premier League in the 3-1 reverse at Everton, he gave a sterling workmanlike performance in the Carling Cup final win over Aston Villa in February. With a double strike against Bolton in March, Dimitar looked much the player he was at Spurs, but he may still have to win over a certain section of the fans.
Tottenham H (£10,900,000 from Bayer Leverkusen, Germany, ex CSKA Sofia, on 12/7/2006) PL 63+7/27 FLC 7+2/2 FAC 6+1/5 Others 15+1/12
Manchester U (£30,750,000 on 1/9/2008) PL 53+11/21 FLC 2 FAC 3+1/1 Others 7+9/4

BERNER Bruno George
Born: Zurich, Switzerland, 21 November 1977
Height: 6'1" **Weight:** 12.11
Club Honours: Div 1 '09
International Honours: Switzerland: 16; U21; Yth
An experienced former Swiss international who enjoyed a remarkably consistent season at left-back with Leicester. Two of his four strikes during the campaign proved crucial, the opener against Nottingham Forest and the winner against Crystal Palace. Bruno also displayed admirable composure when converting the opening spot kick in the ill-fated knock-out at Cardiff in the play-offs. It was no coincidence that a couple of absent spells due to injury coincided with the Foxes' two worst runs of form in the season.
Blackburn Rov (Signed from FC Basle, Switzerland, ex Grasshoppers Zurich, Real Oviedo, SC Freiburg, on 31/1/2007) PL 3 FLC 1 FAC 2

Leicester C (Free on 12/9/2008) FL 55+12/7 FAC 4 Others 3+1

BERRA Christophe Didier
Born: Edinburgh, Scotland, 31 January 1985
Height: 6'1" **Weight:** 12.10
Club Honours: Ch '09
International Honours: S: 7; B-1; U21-6
Christophe recovered from a hamstring injury to captain Wolverhampton in the Carling Cup but he still missed the first four League games. However, he got in the team and stayed there with some determined performances. Strong in the tackle, good in the air, he was superb in the 1-0 win at Tottenham, having established a fine partnership with Jody Craddock in the centre of Wolves' defence. He continued to represent Scotland from time to time too. When Stoke visited Molineux, the home team had to defend 25 powerful throw-ins, a challenge relished by Christophe, who cleared many of them. He played in the last 19 matches, and was unlucky not to score on the final day, when his header was brilliantly saved by Sunderland's Craig Gordon.
Heart of Midlothian (From Edina Hibs on 1/7/2003) SL 112+11/4 SLC 9+1/1 SC 5+2 Others 6
Wolverhampton W (£2,300,000 on 2/2/2009) P/FL 47 FLC 2 FAC 2

BERRETT James Trevor
Born: Halifax, 13 January 1989
Height: 5'10" **Weight:** 11.13
International Honours: RoI: U21-3; Yth
The season never really took off for the Republic of Ireland under-21 international as the manager rotated the Huddersfield squad around the more experienced players. The midfield player was on the substitutes' bench for most of the season but, when called upon, showed great maturity as a holding midfielder or defender. James had to wait until October to make a start in the defeat at Colchester before being installed in defence for the following game.
Huddersfield T (From trainee on 5/7/2007) FL 20+15/2 FLC 0+1 FAC 2+1 Others 2

BERTRAND Ryan Dominic
Born: Southwark, 5 August 1989
Height: 5'10" **Weight:** 11.0
International Honours: E: U21-5; Yth
Ryan joined Reading on loan from Chelsea at the start of the season and proved one of the best young full-backs in the country. He missed only three of Reading's 54 games and quickly

endeared himself to the crowd as well as the coaching staff with his meticulous defending at left-back. Never beaten for pace and only very rarely in the air, he showed real class in his reading of the game and the reliability of his tackling. Ryan regularly made surging runs down the left before sending in accurate, weighted crosses. He scored his first League goal against Derby's stand-in goalkeeper Robbie Savage during Reading's 4-1 victory. Ryan was third in the supporters 'Player of the Year' poll and continued in the England under-21 team.
Chelsea (From trainee on 10/8/2006)
Bournemouth (Loaned on 3/11/2006) FL 5 FAC 2
Oldham Ath (Loaned on 21/8/2007) FL 21 FLC 1 Others 2
Norwich C (Loaned on 4/1/2008) FL 18 FAC 1+1
Norwich C (Loaned on 6/7/2008) FL 37+1 FAC 1+1
Reading (Loaned on 18/7/2009) FL 44/1 FLC 1 FAC 6

BESSONE Federico (Fede)
Born: Cordoba, Argentina, 23 January 1984
Height: 5'11" **Weight:** 11.13
A squad player for Swansea during the early stages of the season, but after impressing in the derby game against Cardiff, the Argentinian displayed consistent form at left-back, scoring the only goal of the game at the Liberty Stadium against Derby with a rocket left-foot shot. Fede became a regular feature for the Swans in defence but in February he was sidelined with a calf injury. This kept him out of action until mid-April but his overall progress made him the most improved player in the squad.
Swansea C (Free from Espanyol, Spain, ex Barcelona C, Gimnastic de Tarragona - loan, on 30/7/2008) FL 34+2/1 FLC 3 FAC 0+1

BEST Leon Julian Brendan
Born: Nottingham, 19 September 1986
Height: 6'1" **Weight:** 13.3
Club Honours: Ch '10
International Honours: RoI: 7; U21-1; Yth
With Leon in the final year of his contract at Coventry there was always going to be speculation about the big centre-forward's future and his impressive scoring form in early season heightened the speculation. Leon had a golden September with five goals, the pick of which were his cool and controlled finish against Sheffield United and his late equaliser against Middlesbrough. But the best goal of the

season was a stunning free kick at Barnsley. His strong heading ability was later demonstrated with goals against Crystal Palace and at Queens Park Rangers, and his predatory skills were in evidence throughout. Several Premier League clubs were strongly linked to him and in January Newcastle's attractive offer was accepted and Coventry avoided a situation where he could go for a substantially lower fee in the summer. Disappointingly, Leon was mainly restricted to substitute appearances and made little impression, the nearest he got to a goal was when he struck the bar late on in the title clinching win at Plymouth. He did however appear for the Republic of Ireland against Brazil in March, and was also capped at under 21 level.
Southampton (From trainee on 21/9/2004) P/FL 8+7/4 FLC 1+1 Others 1+1
Queens Park Rgrs (Loaned on 17/12/2004) FL 2+3
Sheffield Wed (Loaned on 4/8/2005) FL 2/1
Sheffield Wed (Loaned on 31/1/2006) FL 3+8/1
Bournemouth (Loaned on 4/8/2006) FL 12+3/3 FLC 1 Others 1
Yeovil T (Loaned on 23/11/2006) FL 14+1/10
Coventry C (Signed on 12/7/2007) FL 70+22/19 FLC 3/1 FAC 6+3/3
Newcastle U (Signed on 1/2/2010) FL 6+7

BETSY Kevin Eddie Lewis
Born: Seychelles, 20 March 1978
Height: 6'1" **Weight:** 11.12
International Honours: E: SP-1
Kevin found himself on the Southend bench for the opening games of the season, having been displaced on the right-hand side of the team by the form of Francis Laurent. The need for regular football saw him opt to go out on an extended loan to Wycombe and during his spell there the former Seychelles international surpassed 400 career appearances in English football. His loan spell at Wycombe ended in January and he briefly returned to Roots Hall. However during the transfer window the club allowed him to return to Wycombe on a free transfer. Kevin was a popular returnee to Adams Park and blessed with excellent ball skills and able to keep possession in the tightest of spots, he showed he could play on either wing and deliver searching crosses. His eight assists last season was the highest of any player in the team and he gave several 'Man of the Match' performances, notably in the 3-2 win at MK Dons in April topped with his coolly

taken 94th-minute winner. Also able to play as striker, Kevin vowed to finish his career at Wycombe, having agreed a new two-year deal.
Fulham (£80,000 + from Woking on 16/9/1998) P/FL 3+12/1 FLC 2+1 FAC 0+1 Others 1
Bournemouth (Loaned on 3/9/1999) FL 1+4
Hull C (Loaned on 26/11/1999) FL 1+1 Others 1
Barnsley (£200,000 on 28/2/2002) FL 84+10/15 FLC 2 FAC 6/1 Others 3
Hartlepool U (Loaned on 6/8/2004) FL 3+3/1 FLC 1
Oldham Ath (Free on 10/9/2004) FL 34+2/5 FAC 3 Others 5
Wycombe W (Free on 27/7/2005) FL 70+1/13 FLC 8 FAC 3 Others 7
Bristol C (£150,000 + on 29/1/2007) FL 16+2/1 FLC 1
Yeovil T (Loaned on 5/10/2007) FL 5/1 Others 1
Walsall (Loaned on 31/1/2008) FL 16/2
Southend U (Signed on 8/8/2008) FL 28+15/3 FLC 1+1 FAC 3+1 Others 1
Wycombe W (Free on 1/9/2009) FL 35+4/5 FAC 2

Kevin Betsy

BEVAN Scott Anthony
Born: Southampton, 16 September 1979
Height: 6'6" **Weight:** 15.10
Scott struggled with niggling injuries throughout the season which meant he had to share Torquay's goalkeeping duties with the equally impressive Michael Poke. When he is fully fit, Scott is a commanding and dominant figure between the sticks.
Southampton (From trainee on 16/1/1998)
Huddersfield T (Loaned on 27/7/2002) FL 30 FLC 2 FAC 1 Others 1
Wycombe W (Loaned on 16/1/2004) FL 5
Wimbledon/MK Dons (Free on

12/3/2004) FL 17 FLC 1 Others 1 (Freed on 6/1/2006)
Shrewsbury T (Free from Kidderminster Hrs on 31/1/2008) FL 5
Torquay U (Free on 25/9/2008) FL 17+1 FLC 1 FAC 2 Others 2

BEYE Habib
Born: Paris, France, 19 October 1977
Height: 5'11" **Weight:** 12.6
International Honours: Senegal: 45
Habib failed to live up to expectations during a frustrating first season at Aston Villa. The Senegalese international was signed as cover for Luke Young last summer following injury to Villa's first choice right-back. Habib struggled to settle and after a couple of below par performances, lost his place to Young and converted centre-back Carlos Cuellar. He made only five Premier League starts, one substitute appearance and five Cup starts. Habib has two years of his contract to run and has publicly stated that he may need to move for regular but admits other clubs may be deterred by his wages. Habib was put up for sale at the end of the season.
Newcastle U (£2,000,000 from Olympique Marseille, France, ex Paris St Germain, RS Strasbourg, on 31/8/2007) PL 49+3/1 FLC 2
Aston Villa (Signed on 7/8/2009) PL 5+1 FLC 1 FAC 2 Others 2

BHASERA Onismor
Born: Mutare, Zimbabwe, 7 December 1986
Height: 5'8" **Weight:** 12.0
International Honours: Zimbabwe: 13
A Zimbabwean international, Onismor eventually signed for Plymouth in March after finally securing a work permit. The cultured left-back had been training with Premier League Portsmouth but was unable to secure a permanent deal because of their financial plight. He made his much anticipated debut for the Pilgrims in a 0-0 draw with Barnsley, this being his first competitive match since the previous May. He followed this with a good display and an assist, an excellent in-swinging free kick onto the head of Bradley Wright-Phillips to secure three points at Doncaster.
Plymouth Arg (Free from Kaizer Chiefs, South Africa, ex Tembisa Classic, Maritzburg U, on 12/3/2010) FL 7

BIALKOWSKI Bartosz (Bart) Marek
Born: Braniewo, Poland, 6 July 1987
Height: 6'4" **Weight:** 13.0
Club Honours: AMC '10
International Honours: Poland: U21
Bart had waited patiently to regain his

place in the Southampton goal since recovering from the cruciate ligament injury sustained in January 2006 and when an injury to Kelvin Davis in November gifted him with an eight-match run he acquitted himself with panache, not least by pulling off three penalty saves in the shoot-out in the Johnstone's Paint Trophy tie with Norwich. However, with much to play for, Alan Pardew plumped for experience and Davis supplanted Bart as soon as he was fit. Earlier, in September, he had signed on a week-long emergency loan and made his debut a day later against West Bromwich. He played two games for Barnsley, helping them to maximum points, and showed himself to be a good shot-stopper. His excellent save deep into injury time against Ipswich ensured the Reds a win as they immediately went up field and scored the winner.

Southampton (Signed from Gornik Zabrze, Poland on 4/1/2006) FL 20+1 FLC 4 FAC 3 Others 3
Barnsley (Loaned on 28/9/2009) FL 2

BIDWELL Jake Brian
Born: Southport, 21 March 1993
Height: 6'0" **Weight:** 11.0
International Honours: E: Yth
The left-back became Everton's youngest-ever European player at 16 years 271 days when making an impressive debut against BATE Borisov in the Europa League at Goodison. A regular with the Everton Academy and reserve sides, the defender has also featured for the England under-17 team.
Everton (From trainee on 8/4/2010) Others 1

BIGNALL Nicholas (Nick) Colin
Born: Reading, 11 July 1990
Height: 5'10" **Weight:** 12.10
Nick finally made the breakthrough into Reading's first team and soon showed his qualities as a powerful and pacy striker by scoring twice in three minutes in the 5-1 Carling Cup win over Burton. He made a second start in the Carling Cup tie against Barnsley and then went to Stockport for a loan spell at the end of August, his debut being one to remember as he showed strength and power up front while scoring against Crewe in a 4-1 Johnstone's Paint Trophy win. Against Leyton Orient he raced clear to side-foot the ball home to give County the lead and also scored a header in a 2-2 draw with Hartlepool. However, that would prove to be his last goal in Hatters' colours, returning to Reading just before Christmas after

picking up a knee injury. When fit again he became a regular goal scorer for the reserves, as well as making two further substitute appearances in Championship fixtures against Barnsley and Coventry. Next season should see Nick challenging for a regular place as one of the Royals' strike force.
Reading (From trainee on 2/7/2008) FL 0+1 FLC 2/2
Northampton T (Loaned on 5/11/2008) FL 1+4/1 FAC 0+2
Cheltenham T (Loaned on 15/1/2009) FL 8+5/1
Stockport Co (Loaned on 31/8/2009) FL 11/2 FAC 1 Others 1/1

Andre Bikey

BIKEY Andre Stephane
Born: Douala, Cameroon, 8 January 1985
Height: 6'0" **Weight:** 12.8
International Honours: Cameroon: 24
Cameroon international Andre arrived at Turf Moor in August, just in time to make his Burnley debut in the astonishing home victory over Manchester United. He quickly established himself as a crowd favourite for his muscular and wholehearted efforts, either in central defence or in midfield. Virtually ever-present under Owen Coyle, he struggled to re-establish himself in the side following his absence after the African Cup of Nations in January and the arrival of Brian Laws as manager. Overall he was probably Burnley's most consistent central defender in a season when that area of the team was often problematic, and he would also qualify for the award of 'Best Celebration' after his only goal of the season, in the home

win against Birmingham.
Reading (Loaned from Lokomotiv Moscow, Russia, ex Espanyol, Shannik Yaroslav, on 1/8/2006) P/FL 44+18/6 FLC 4/1 FAC 6 Others 1
Burnley (Signed on 18/8/2009) PL 26+2/1 FLC 2 FAC 1

BILYALETDINOV Diniyar Rinatovich
Born: Moscow, Russia, 27 February 1985
Height: 6'1" **Weight:** 12.2
International Honours: Russia: 33
Signed by Everton from Lokomotiv Moscow, the Russian international had a mixed season, when he was clearly affected by the demands of moving straight from the Russian domestic season to the start of the Premier League in the summer. Employed on the left-hand side of midfield, the 25-year-old provided moments of real quality with his sweet left foot, with a brilliantly struck goal from outside the box against Manchester United being voted the club's 'Goal of the Season' – only for the Russian to produce an even better strike against Portsmouth on the final day. A tall, deceptively quick player who can also produce telling crosses, Everton supporters will be hoping to see the best of this talented Muscovite next season.
Everton (Signed from Lokomotiv Moscow, Russia on 25/8/2009) PL 16+7/6 FLC 1 FAC 2 Others 6+1/1

BINGHAM Billy Christopher
Born: Greenwich, 15 July 1990
Height: 5'11" **Weight:** 11.3
After a season in the reserves, former Crystal Palace youth player Billy made his Dagenham debut as a substitute at home to Lincoln. A skilful midfield player with good vision, he made his second appearance towards the end of October, also as a substitute, then had a month's loan at Blue Square South Grays Athletic in late November and made five appearances for them.
Crystal Palace (From trainee on 7/7/2008)
Dagenham & Redbridge (Free on 13/2/2009) FL 0+2

BIRD David Alan
Born: Gloucester, 26 December 1984
Height: 5'8" **Weight:** 12.2
Long-serving Cheltenham midfielder David again showed his versatility, filling in at right-back, right midfield and central midfield during another season of many changes. David, one of the few locally born players, had another excellent season of unstinting service, although he missed the last few games with a calf injury. He was one of eight

players used at right-back but was equally at home as a defensive midfielder. David's quietly effective contribution was rewarded with the offer of a new contract.
Cheltenham T *(Signed from Cinderford T on 1/2/2001) FL 205+44/8 FLC 7 FAC 15+2 Others 10+3*

BISHOP Andrew (Andy) Jamie
Born: Cannock, 19 October 1982
Height: 6'0" **Weight:** 11.2
International Honours: E: SP-4
Bury's top scorer in the last three seasons, Andy was troubled by injuries sustained in the previous campaign's unavailing attempt at promotion through the play-offs. Making only 12 starting appearances and scoring three goals, Andy struggled to regain his best form and maintain his position in the starting side.
Walsall *(From trainee on 9/8/2002. Freed during 2004 close season)*
Kidderminster Hrs *(Loaned on 18/11/2002) FL 22+7/5 Others 0+1*
Kidderminster Hrs *(Loaned on 5/8/2003) FL 8+3/2*
Rochdale *(Loaned on 20/11/2003) FL 8+2/1 FAC 1*
Yeovil T *(Loaned on 5/2/2004) FL 4+1/2*
Bury *(Free from York C on 1/7/2006) FL 131+23/53 FLC 3+1/1 FAC 10/10 Others 6+1/2*

BISHOP Neal Robert
Born: Stockton, 7 August 1981
Height: 6'0" **Weight:** 12.10
Club Honours: Div 2 '10
Signed from Barnet in the summer, Neal won plaudits from managers, team-mates and supporters for his consistently energetic performances in the centre of Notts County's midfield. A competitive ball winner, he worked tirelessly for the team and always demonstrated a never-say-die attitude. He made a huge contribution towards winning the League Two championship and nobody was more deserving of a winners' medal.
Barnet *(Free from York C, ex Billingham T, Spennymoor U, Gateshead, Whitby T, Scarborough, on 9/7/2007) FL 80+3/3 FLC 2 FAC 8 Others 2*
Notts Co *(Free on 4/7/2009) FL 39+4/1 FLC 1 FAC 6 Others 1*

BJORNSSON Armann Smari
Born: Hofn, Iceland, 7 January 1981
Height: 6'5" **Weight:** 14.2
International Honours: Iceland: 4
A big striker or central defender with ten years experience in Iceland and Norway, Armann joined Hartlepool just

Neal Bishop

ahead of the August transfer deadline and, soon after signing, was promoted to the squad with a handful of substitute appearances. Rewarded with a short run in the starting line-up as a

target man alongside Adam Boyd, he was an immediate success as a striker, scoring three goals in his first five starts. Unfortunately these were his only goals and for the remainder of the season he

was used mainly as a substitute.
Hartlepool U (Free from SK Brann Bergen, Norway, ex UMF Sindri, Lillestrom - loan, Valur, SK Brann Bergen - loan, FH Hafnarfjordur, on 26/8/2009) FL 10+8/3 Others 1

BLACK Adam James
Born: Liverpool, 24 May 1992
Height: 5'11" **Weight:** 11.0
An Accrington youth team player who made just one last-minute substitute appearance when coming off the bench against Cheltenham in October. Used out wide as a striker, Adam went on a work experience loan to non-League Burscough in December and did well.
Accrington Stanley (Trainee) FL 0+1

BLACK Paul Michael
Born: Middleton, 18 January 1990
Height: 6'0" **Weight:** 12.10
Paul came through the youth ranks at Boundary Park to make 13 appearances for Oldham's first team, scoring one stunning goal against Southend. He may well never score a better goal in his career, because he beat three men before smashing in a tremendous shot from 20 yards. A quick-footed full-back with a brain to match, Paul has the talent to construct a very long career.
Oldham Ath (From trainee on 16/1/2008) FL 14+4/1

BLACKBURN Christopher (Chris) Raymond
Born: Crewe, 2 August 1982
Height: 5'7" **Weight:** 10.6
International Honours: E: SP-4
Chris plays centre-half for Aldershot. He is a nephew of legendary Manchester City midfielder Alan Oakes and the cousin of ex-Wolverhampton goalkeeper Michael Oakes. Often used at right-back and playing the occasional game in central midfield, Chris made his 50th start for the club at Crewe in September before losing out to Dave Winfield and Adam Hinshelwood. He regained his place and put in some solid performances but was released after the Shots' play-off semi-final exit, immediately joining Wrexham.
Chester C (Trainee) FL 0+1
Swindon T (Free from Morecambe, ex Northwich Vic, on 10/7/2007) FL 4+3 Others 2/2
Aldershot T (Free on 1/7/2008) FL 72+6 FLC 2 FAC 5 Others 2

BLACKMAN Andre
Alexander-George
Born: Lambeth, 10 November 1990
Height: 5'11" **Weight:** 11.5
Lauded by the Bristol City manager Gary Johnson, when he signed this left-

back from Portsmouth during the close season, Andre's Ashton Gate career came to a mysterious and sudden end after just a couple of appearance's early in the season.
Bristol C (From trainee at Portsmouth on 2/7/2009) FLC 1+1

BLACKMAN Nicholas (Nick) Alexander
Born: Whitefield, 11 November 1989
Height: 6'2" **Weight:** 11.8
A young striker with great potential, his first touch allowing him time in tight positions, Nick joined Oldham on loan from Blackburn in August. He made his Latics' debut in the 2-2 draw with Swindon at Boundary Park before scoring a rasping 30-yard goal in a 1-1 draw at Brentford at the end of August. He went on to make 13 appearances for Latics before fracturing a toe in September. Nick never really recovered from that injury and returned to Ewood Park in January.
Macclesfield T (From trainee on 7/3/2007) FL 1+11/1
Blackburn Rov (Signed on 12/1/2009)
Blackpool (Loaned on 3/3/2009) FL 2+3/1
Oldham Ath (Loaned on 20/8/2009) FL 6+6/1 Others 1

BLACKSTOCK Dexter Anthony Titus
Born: Oxford, 20 May 1986
Height: 6'1" **Weight:** 12.0
International Honours: E: U21-2; Yth
Dexter continued the good form he showed during a brief loan spell in 2008-09 when he signed permanently. He was the regular forward in Nottingham Forest's varied formations and despite not being the biggest, Dexter is very good at holding the ball up to bring his fellow strikers into play. He equalled his best scoring season to date with his last League goal of the season, against Plymouth.
Southampton (From trainee on 24/5/2004) P/FL 15+13/4 FLC 2+2/5 FAC 2+1
Plymouth Arg (Loaned on 13/2/2005) FL 10+4/4
Derby Co (Loaned on 27/10/2005) FL 8+1/3
Queens Park Rgrs (Signed on 11/8/2006) FL 89+21/30 FLC 3/1 FAC 4/1
Nottingham F (Signed on 26/3/2009) FL 36+9/14 FLC 3/1 FAC 1 Others 2

BLAKE Darcy James
Born: New Tredegar, 13 December 1988
Height: 5'10" **Weight:** 12.5
International Honours: W: U21-14; Yth

The comeback kid enjoyed the best season of his career in 2009-10 even though it did not start well. Criticised by manager Dave Jones for not being professional enough in his lifestyle, the versatile Darcy, who can play in midfield, at right-back or centre-back, was sent out on loan to Plymouth in August, making his debut the following day in a 3-1 defeat to Sheffield Wednesday. Early on during his loan spell Darcy suffered a hamstring injury which kept him out for a few games. This attacking right back was sent off for the first time in his professional career during a 1-1 draw with Ipswich. Plymouth appealed the decision but the red card was upheld and he was subsequently banned for three matches. He completed his loan at Plymouth at the end of December and returned to Cardiff after injuries had left the team short of defensive cover. Given a chance, Darcy played 13 successive matches and was a member of the side that fought its way in to the play-offs only to lose in the final. His contract runs until the summer of 2011.
Cardiff C (From trainee on 26/10/2006) FL 26+18 FLC 1+2 FAC 1+6 Others 3
Plymouth Arg (Loaned on 28/8/2009) FL 5+2

BLAKE Robert (Robbie) James
Born: Middlesbrough, 4 March 1976
Height: 5'9" **Weight:** 12.6
Robbie's finest moment of the season, and arguably Burnley's, came in the first home game when his stunning volley proved to be the winning goal against Manchester United. He started the season as a regular in the Clarets' line-up and scored another notable goal to give Burnley the lead (briefly) against fierce local rivals Blackburn at Ewood Park. Still a bag of tricks, his feints and flicks were less effective against Premier League opposition but he remained the man most likely to open up an opposing defence. After December, though, most of his appearances were from the bench and he was rarely a starter under new manager Brian Laws. A firm favourite of the Turf Moor crowd, all the chants at the end-of-season lap of appreciation were for Robbie, whose future at the club looked uncertain, although he was offered a new contract.
Darlington (From trainee on 1/7/1994) FL 54+14/21 FLC 4+2/1 FAC 3+1 Others 3+1/1
Bradford C (£300,000 on 27/3/1997) P/FL 109+44/40 FLC 8+3/4 FAC 7/1 Others 3+1/2
Nottingham F (Loaned on 22/8/2000) FL 9+2/1 FLC 1

49

Burnley (£1,000,000 + on 25/1/2002)
FL 103+17/42 FLC 11/5 FAC 6+1/4
Birmingham C (£1,250,000 on
5/1/2005) PL 2+9/2 FAC 1+1
Leeds U (£800,000 on 26/7/2005) FL
58+19/19 FLC 3+2/1 FAC 2+1 Others 0+2
Burnley (£250,000 on 13/7/2007) P/FL
94+28/19 FLC 7+4/2 FAC 7+1 Others 3

BLAKE Ryan George
Born: Weybridge, 8 December 1991
Height: 5'10" **Weight:** 10.12
International Honours: NI: Yth
A young Brentford left-back who was
on as a substitute in the penultimate
home game of the season, against
Yeovil. Much is expected of this highly-
rated former junior, who was given a
first team squad number at the start of
the campaign, having impressed
manager Andy Scott during pre-season
preparation. Ryan was called up by
Northern Ireland for both the under-18
and under-19 sides.
Brentford (From trainee on 13/8/2009)
FL 0+1

BLANCHETT Daniel
(Danny) William
Born: Wembley, 6 May 1987
Height: 5'11" **Weight:** 11.12
Although principally a left-back, Danny
played most of his extended loan at
Hereford as the left of a defensive trio.
With his ability to read the game and to
pass accurately, he made a strong
impression and it was a disappointment
when he chose not to extend his stay
and return to Peterborough.
Peterborough U (Signed from
Cambridge C, ex Hendon, Northwood,
Harrow Borough, on 20/3/2007) FL
3+4/1 FAC 1 Others 1
Hereford U (Loaned on 17/9/2009) FL
13 FAC 2 Others 1

BLIZZARD Dominic John
Born: High Wycombe, 2 September 1983
Height: 6'2" **Weight:** 13.5
Central midfielder Dominic arrived at
Bristol Rovers from Stockport in the
close season and took time to regain his
match fitness after a series of niggling
injuries. Dominic played on both the
right and left of midfield instead of his
favoured central position and struggled
to impress, being substituted in the
majority of matches. He scored his first
and only goal, a 20-yard strike against
Colchester at the Memorial Stadium. A
niggling hamstring injury ruled him out
of the final four matches.
Watford (From trainee on 19/4/2002)
P/FL 22+7/2 FLC 4+2/1 FAC 1
Stockport Co (Loaned on 8/2/2007) FL 7
MK Dons (Loaned on 22/3/2007) FL 8
Others 2

Stockport Co (Free on 10/8/2007) FL
52+6/4 FLC 1+2/1 FAC 1 Others 1
Bristol Rov (Free on 9/7/2009) FL
22+12/1 FLC 1+1 FAC 1 Others 1

BLOOMFIELD Matthew
(Matt) James
Born: Felixstowe, 8 February 1984
Height: 5'9" **Weight:** 11.3
International Honours: E: Yth
Wycombe's dynamic midfielder suffered
more injury woes last season. A
fractured nose and cheekbone in an
aerial collision against Peterborough in
August, followed by a knee operation,
severely restricted his appearances.
Once he returned at the end of March,
he stayed in the side and his energy and
commitment were key factors in
Wycombe's improved form. Matt scored
a superb goal at home to Swindon in
April. After beating two players with a
weaving run, he curled home a shot
from the edge of the box. He signed a
new one-year contract.
Ipswich T (From trainee on 3/7/2001)
FLC 0+1
Wycombe W (Free on 24/12/2003) FL
153+34/18 FLC 9 FAC 3+5/1 Others
8+2

BOA MORTE Luis
Born: Lisbon, Portugal, 4 August 1977
Height: 5'10" **Weight:** 11.5
Club Honours: PL '98; Div 1 '01; CS
'98, '99
International Honours: Portugal: 28;
U21-28; Yth
On the pre-season tour with West Ham
in China, Luis sustained a bad injury.
Playing against Tottenham in the Asia
Trophy, he suffered anterior cruciate
ligament damage to his knee. After
surgery he had a lengthy eight-month
recovery period. It was a disappointing
setback as he had finished the previous
campaign in top form. Luis was finally
able to return on the last day of the
season in May it was good to see him
back in action and he scored a good
goal against Manchester City.
Arsenal (£1,750,000 + from Sporting
Lisbon, Portugal on 25/6/1997) PL 6+19
FLC 3/2 FAC 2+3/1 Others 2+4/1
Southampton (£500,000 + on
27/8/1999) PL 6+8/1 FLC 0+2 FAC 1
Fulham (£1,700,000 on 31/7/2000)
P/FL 169+36/44 FLC 11+4/6 FAC
16+1/2 Others 10+2/2
West Ham U (£4,500,000 on
5/1/2007) PL 40+29/2 FLC 6 FAC 5+1

BOATENG George
Born: Nkawkaw, Ghana, 5 September
1975
Height: 5'9" **Weight:** 11.7
Club Honours: FLC '04

International Honours: Holland: 4;
U21-18
The longest-serving foreign player in the
Premier League, George was appointed
Hull captain in the light of Ian Ashbee's
long-term injury absence. Strangely, he
was dropped after only two games but
returned in November to lead the
ultimately unsuccessful fight against
relegation. A thunderous 20-yard shot
brought his first goal for Hull, a
sensational winner against Manchester
City that was the supporters' 'Goal of
the Season'. In the following game at
Blackburn, George was sent off for only
the second time since 1997 in the
Premier League. Although the claim for
wrongful dismissal was upheld, George
justifiably saw red against Arsenal in
March due to an uncharacteristic show
of indiscipline. Financial restraints mean
it is unlikely that he will be able to
contribute to City's Championship
campaign but George would leave with
happy memories, as he was runner-up
in the club's and the supporters' club's
'Player of the Season' awards.
Coventry C (£250,000 from
Feyenoord, Holland, ex Excelsior, on
19/12/1997) PL 43+4/5 FLC 3/1 FAC 8/1
Aston Villa (£4,500,000 on 22/7/1999)
PL 96+7/4 FLC 8+1/1 FAC 9 Others 13
Middlesbrough (£5,000,000 on
8/8/2002) PL 177+5/7 FLC 9+1 FAC
13+2/1 Others 16/1
Hull C (£1,000,000 on 17/7/2008) PL
47+5/1 FLC 1 FAC 2+1

George Boateng

BOATENG Kevin-Prince (Kevin)

Born: Berlin, Germany, 6 March 1987
Height: 6'0" **Weight:** 11.9
Club Honours: FLC '08
International Honours: Germany: U21-6; Yth

Having made one substitute appearance for Tottenham before transferring to Portsmouth, the enigmatic Ghanaian midfield playmaker found a new lease of life on the South coast, scoring on his Pompey debut against Bolton and against his former employers, Tottenham. Kevin became an instant hit with fans at Fratton Park, his pace, energy and guile becoming the focal point of the attack. However, following a penalty miss at Stoke, sporadic form and a troublesome ankle injury picked up in January his season looked to end prematurely. Able to return for Pompey's FA Cup semi-final tie at Wembley, he again scored against former club Tottenham with a penalty, but had no such luck in the final against Chelsea, missing a crucial spot-kick just moments before Didier Drogba scored what proved to be a winner for the opposition. Despite that, his performances over the season earned him a place in Ghana's 30-man World Cup squad, where he looks to gain his first international cap.

Tottenham H (£6,000,000 from Hertha Berlin, Germany on 9/8/2007) PL 7+7 FLC 1+4 FAC 1+1 Others 1+2
Portsmouth (£4,000,000 on 28/8/2009) PL 20+2/3 FAC 5/2

BOCO Romauld

Born: Bernay, France, 8 July 1985
Height: 5'10" **Weight:** 11.3
Club Honours: FC '06
International Honours: Benin: 24; U21

The former Accrington utility man was given a short-term contract by Burton in February and made a handful of appearances at right-back and on the right side of midfield. Showed himself to be a busy and tidy player but was not offered a further contract by Burton.

BODDE Ferrie

Born: Delft, Holland, 5 May 1982
Height: 5'10" **Weight:** 12.8
Club Honours: Div 1 '08
International Honours: Holland: U23
The Dutch midfielder returned to action with Swansea after a serious knee injury but after three appearances as a substitute, broke down in his first start against Sheffield United. By January, however, he looked to be back on track for a return and after playing in a reserve game was listed as one on the

bench for the away match at Derby. But in the following match against Peterborough, when he started, he collapsed after 30 minutes with a knee injury. This required further surgery, for which he returned to Holland. Ferrie was undoubtedly a big miss in Swansea's chase for a play-off place.

Swansea C (£50,000 + from ADO Den Haag, Holland on 8/8/2007) FL 52+2/13 FLC 2 FAC 1/1 Others 1+1

BODEN Luke

Born: Sheffield, 26 November 1988
Height: 6'1" **Weight:** 13.1
Luke made five appearances in the Northampton midfield during his one-month loan but sadly his only victory came in a penalty shoot-out against Wycombe in the Johnstone's Paint Trophy. A busy player, he arrived at Sixfields at the time of management change and his loan option was not extended.

Sheffield Wed (From trainee on 5/7/2007) FL 2+13 FLC 1+2 FAC 1
Chesterfield (Loaned on 18/9/2008) FL 4
Northampton T (Loaned on 27/8/2009) FL 4 Others 1

BODEN Scott David

Born: Sheffield, 19 December 1989
Height: 5'11" **Weight:** 11.0
Scott's 30 appearances from the bench this season tell a tale of a player who is a terrific impact substitute for Chesterfield but who made less of a difference when starting. All his six goals were scored when coming off the bench, thanks to speed off the mark and that scorer's knack of being in the right place at the right time. Scott was pleased to sign a two-year contract as the season ended.

Chesterfield (Free from IFK Mariehamn, Finland, ex Sheffield U trainee, on 13/8/2008) FL 8+38/8 FAC 2+1 Others 1

BOERTIEN Paul

Born: Haltwhistle, 21 January 1979
Height: 5'10" **Weight:** 11.2
Burton manager Paul Peschisolido wasted no time in offering his former Derby team-mate a contract at the Pirelli Stadium after he was released by Walsall. Paul did not disappoint with a series of solid displays interrupted only by knee and leg injuries in mid-season. Particularly impressive going forward, Paul scored a memorable first goal for Albion in a 1-1 draw at Bradford, while a strong finish to the campaign was suitably rewarded with a new contract.

Accrington Stanley (Free from Niort, France on 3/8/2006) FL 34+9/3 FLC 2+1 Others 2 (Freed during 2008 close season)

Burton A (Free from Sligo Rov on 24/2/2010) FL 3+5

BOGDAN Adam

Born: Budapest, Hungary, 27 September 1987
Height: 6'4" **Weight:** 14.2
International Honours: Hungary: U21
The young goalkeeper from Bolton joined Crewe on loan in September, making only one appearance, in the home game against Bury, before going back to the Reebok. Way down the pecking order at the Premier League club, the Hungarian under-20 international is seen as a player for the future. He commands the penalty area well, takes crosses cleanly and stands up well in one-on-one situations.

Bolton W (Signed from Vasas, Hungary, via Vecesi - loan, on 1/8/2007)
Crewe Alex (Loaned on 29/9/2009) FL 1

BOGDANOVIC Daniel

Born: Misurata, Libya, 26 March 1980
Height: 6'2" **Weight:** 12.4
International Honours: Malta: 27
An ankle injury during training in the first week under new Barnsley manager Mark Robins put Daniel out of action. He was soon back and in the starting team and was, without doubt, the most natural striker at Oakwell. He benefited most when playing away from home and that is where the majority of his goals came. His two goals at Cardiff were highlights of an impressive season. He comes alive when he sees the opposition net and is dangerous, both in the air or with the ball at his feet. He is out of contract at the end of the season and his future is yet to be decided. He again played international football with Malta.

Barnsley (Signed from Lokomotiv Sofia, Bulgaria, ex Sliema W, Vasas SC, Naxxar Lions, Valletta, Cherno More, Sliema W, Marsaxlokk, Sliema W, Marsaxlokk, Cisco R on 27/1/2009) FL 33+12/16 FLC 2+1/3 FAC 1

BOLASIE Yannick (Yala)

Born: DR Congo, 24 May 1989
Height: 6'2" **Weight:** 13.0
The tricky Plymouth winger linked up with Barnet for the second time last summer, having re-signed on loan, following a successful stint at the club in the second half of the 2008-09 season. Once again, the youngster performed well at Underhill, chipping in with two goals and providing several assists before he returned to Home Park when his loan contract ended in January. He then went onto break into the Argyle first team. An extremely pacy and skilful left winger he made his

51

return to the team away to Barnsley as a 55th-minute substitute and immediately changed the game with his wing wizardry and pace to turn a 1-0 deficit into a 3-1 victory. Two weeks later he scored his first goal for the Pilgrims in a thrilling 4-3 defeat to Sheffield United. He continued to feature in the rest of the campaign on the left-hand side of midfield and will be looking to continue this sort of form into the coming season.

Plymouth Arg (Free from Floriana, Malta on 1/8/2008) FL 8+8/1
Barnet (Loaned on 22/1/2009) FL 17+3/3
Barnet (Loaned on 10/7/2009) FL 14+8/2 FLC 1 FAC 3 Others 2

BOLDER Adam Peter
Born: Hull, 25 October 1980
Height: 5'8" **Weight:** 11.0
Adam managed just five starts in his midfield holding role at Millwall and in March went out on loan to Bradford. Steady and reliable, quick to pick out a forward pass to a colleague, the experienced Adam was among the influx of loan players that Peter Taylor brought to City. Adam added a calm presence to the central area, using the ball intelligently and forming a solid partnership with Lee Bullock and Michael Flynn. He demonstrated his composure by dribbling round a defender and the goalkeeper to score against Morecambe.

Hull C (From trainee on 9/7/1999) FL 18+2 Others 2+1
Derby Co (Signed on 3/4/2000) P/FL 109+57/11 FLC 6 FAC 5+2 Others 1+1
Queens Park Rgrs (Free on 29/1/2007) FL 36+4/2 FLC 1+1
Sheffield Wed (Loaned on 8/2/2008) FL 11+2/2
Millwall (Free on 6/11/2008) FL 33+6 FLC 0+1 FAC 3+1 Others 3+1
Bradford C (Loaned on 5/3/2010) FL 14/1

BOLLAND Paul Graham
Born: Bradford, 23 December 1979
Height: 6'0" **Weight:** 12.6
Paul moved from fellow League Two club Grimsby to Macclesfield in the summer and was mainly used as back-up in midfield, although as the season progressed and the midfield was decimated by injuries, he featured more regularly. A couple of groin injuries and bruised ribs kept him out of contention at times but he made a significant contribution, bringing his experience into play. His one goal came in the 4-1 home victory over Crewe. Paul was released at the end of the season.
Bradford C (From trainee on 20/3/1998) FL 4+8 FLC 2

Notts Co (£75,000 on 14/1/1999) FL 153+19/6 FLC 3+6 FAC 7+1 Others 2+3/1
Grimsby T (Free on 1/8/2005) FL 114+4/13 FLC 5 FAC 5+1/1 Others 9/1
Macclesfield T (Free on 29/6/2009) FL 17+10/1 FLC 1 Others 1

BOND Chad David
Born: Neath, 20 April 1987
Height: 6'0" **Weight:** 11.0
International Honours: W: Yth
Chad, a former trainee with Swansea, was given a contract at the end of the previous season by former manager Roberto Martinez and was regularly included in the squad at the start of the season. However, he made his only starts in the away win at Coventry and in the following Carling Cup tie against Scunthorpe. He is an adaptable player and is capable of playing as a striker or in midfield.
Swansea C (From trainee on 6/7/2005) Others 0+1 (Freed during 2006 close season)
Swansea C (Free from Port Talbot T on 7/8/2008) FL 1 FLC 1

BORE Peter Charles
Born: Grimsby, 4 November 1987
Height: 6'0" **Weight:** 12.2
After an early season hamstring injury, Peter's lack of form as a winger at Grimsby saw him made available for transfer. However, a change of manager and injuries to other players then saw him revert to right-back, a position he was to hold to the season's end. Passing the landmark of a century of games for Grimsby, Peter's regular selection gave him license to aid the attack, his pace and support being recognised with a place in the League Two 'Team of the Week' against Shrewsbury (3-0) on the FL website.
Grimsby T (From trainee on 22/8/2006) FL 72+44/11 FLC 1+2 FAC 1+3 Others 3+4

BORINI Fabio
Born: Bentivoglio, Italy, 29 March 1991
Height: 5'10" **Weight:** 11.9
International Honours: Italy: U21; Yth
Fabio is a quick, mobile Chelsea striker who caused compatriot Carlo Ancelotti to compare him to Filippo Inzaghi, a legendary Italian goalmouth predator. He is equally comfortable alone through the middle or playing off a target man. He made his debut against Tottenham in September as a late substitute and his first start for Chelsea against Queens Park Rangers in the Carling Cup. Sporadic substitute appearances followed and he is likely to feature more prominently in the near future.

Chelsea (From trainee on 4/7/2007) PL 0+4 FLC 1 FAC 0+2 Others 0+1

BORROWDALE Gary Ian
Born: Sutton, 16 July 1985
Height: 6'0" **Weight:** 12.1
International Honours: E: Yth
Gary started the season as first choice left-back under Jim Magilton at Queens Park Rangers and enjoyed his best run in the side since joining the club in January 2009. Something of an unsung hero, he started 20 of the first 23 games and proved an adequately solid presence in the Rangers backline. However Magilton's departure led to his replacements looking at various other options for the position and Gary left to join Charlton on loan in March where he spent the remainder of the season. Signed to fill the problem left-back position with both regulars injured and out for the season and a previous loanee also injured, Gary was immediately put into the team against Gillingham at the Valley and performed very well. Proved to be a strong tackler and good going forward when frequently getting balls into the box.
Crystal Palace (From trainee on 6/12/2002) P/FL 74+24 FLC 7+4 FAC 3+1 Others 1
Coventry C (Signed on 5/7/2007) FL 20+1 FLC 3 FAC 2
Colchester U (Loaned on 25/9/2008) FL 4 Others 1
Queens Park Rgrs (£650,000 + on 27/11/2008) FL 18+3 FLC 2+1 FAC 2
Brighton & Hove A (Loaned on 6/3/2009) FL 11+1
Charlton Ath (Loaned on 18/3/2010) FL 10 Others 2

BOSHELL Daniel (Danny) Kevin
Born: Bradford, 30 May 1981
Height: 5'11" **Weight:** 11.10
Initially selected in Grimsby's midfield at the start of the season, Danny's contribution was soon cut short by two dismissals and suspensions within a month. The frustration then continued under new manager Neil Woods as he rarely figured in Town's match-day squad, and in January was released by mutual consent just six months into a new two-year contract. Signed by Chesterfield on a short-term contract in February to provide options in central midfield, a lack of match sharpness led to a booking within seconds of his debut and saw him largely unused until March. However, when Danny came off the bench on a regular basis to provide fresh legs, he showed neat touches and passing ability to complement Mark Allott in the centre of the Spireites' defence.

Oldham Ath *(From trainee on 10/7/1998) FL 45+25/2 FLC 6/1 FAC 3+3 Others 3/1*
Bury *(Loaned on 24/3/2005) FL 2+4*
Stockport Co *(Free on 1/8/2005) FL 28+5/1 FLC 1/1 FAC 3 Others 1*
Grimsby T *(Free on 24/8/2006) FL 84+15/10 FLC 3 FAC 4+1 Others 11/1*
Chesterfield *(Free on 1/2/2010) FL 3+6*

BOSINGWA Jose
Born: Kinshasa, DR Congo, 24 August 1982
Height: 6'0" **Weight:** 11.11
Club Honours: FAC '09; CS '09
International Honours: Portugal: 23; U21-18
When Chelsea boss Carlo Ancelotti introduced his diamond formation, the onus was on the full-backs to supply the attacking width. They were well served with Ashley Cole marauding on the left and the cavalier Jose bombing down the right. Sadly, the Portuguese star limped off with a serious left knee injury at Aston Villa in October after featuring in the first eight matches. He underwent exploratory arthroscopic surgery but the knee failed to respond and a second operation was required in the spring that ended his Chelsea season and also kept him out of Portugal's World Cup squad in South Africa.
Chelsea *(£16,300,000 from Porto, Portugal, ex Boavista, Freamunde, Boavista, on 9/6/2008) PL 42/2 FAC 4 Others 10+1*

BOSTOCK John Joseph
Born: Camberwell, 15 January 1992
Height: 5'10" **Weight:** 11.11
International Honours: E: Yth
Brentford borrowed John from Tottenham in November, while he was still 17, and he had an outstanding début against Millwall, scoring twice in the first half-hour. The first was a shot from the edge of the box, while the second was direct from a corner. Throughout his stay, John showed outstanding positional sense and exceptional passing ability. Although relying heavily on his left foot, he was deployed mainly on the right side of midfield. His influence on the side diminished towards the end of his stay, as opponents worked out strategies to stop him, but he has huge potential to make it at the top level.
Crystal Palace *(Associated Schoolboy) FL 1+3 FAC 1*
Tottenham H *(£700,000 + on 4/7/2008) Others 0+3*
Brentford *(Loaned on 13/11/2009) FL 9/2 FAC*

BOTHROYD Jay
Born: Islington, 7 May 1982
Height: 6'3" **Weight:** 13.6
Club Honours: FAYC '00
International Honours: E: U21-1; Yth; Sch
The highly talented centre-forward was crucial to everything Cardiff did. The big problem was that when Jay was missing, City had no real alternative. That proved crucial in the Championship play-off final against Blackpool when Cardiff lost 3-2. He was not fully fit, having struggled to shake off a calf strain, and Cardiff gambled but Jay limped off after 15 minutes with Kelvin Etuhu going on out of position. Jay took over as captain when Mark Hudson was out injured and overall had an outstanding season, scoring 13 goals and creating chances for team-mates.
Arsenal *(From trainee on 8/7/1999)*
Coventry C *(£1,000,000 on 13/7/2000) P/FL 51+21/14 FLC 1+5/2 FAC 5/1 (Transferred to Perugia, Italy on 14/7/2003)*
Blackburn Rov *(Loaned on 9/9/2004) PL 6+5/1 FLC 1 FAC 0+1*
Charlton Ath *(Free from Perugia, Italy on 31/8/2005) PL 3+15/2 FLC 0+3/1 FAC 1+3/3*
Wolverhampton W *(Free on 31/7/2006) FL 32+23/12 FAC 3/1 Others 2*
Stoke C *(Loaned on 14/3/2008) FL 1+3*
Cardiff C *(£300,000 on 5/8/2008) FL 75+4/23 FLC 4/1 FAC 6/1 Others 3*

BOUAZZA Hameur
Born: Evry, France, 22 February 1985
Height: 5'10" **Weight:** 12.0
International Honours: Algeria: 15
Perhaps one of the most surprising close season signings in the Championship, Hameur's move to Blackpool raised eyebrows throughout the division. It marked the intentions of the Seasiders and when he played, the Algerian international did not disappoint. A fine goal at home to Peterborough was the highlight, scoring from an impossible position on the by-line. He was, however, restricted to just five first team appearances in the new year because of continuous injury problems. Away at Scunthorpe in April, he came off the bench to change the game, marking his presence when fit. Hameur played in the African Cup of Nations, helping his side reach the semi-finals by scoring an extra-time winner against the Ivory Coast. Was out of contract at the end of June.
Watford *(From trainee on 2/7/2004) P/FL 46+37/9 FLC 8+2/3 FAC 5+1/2*
Swindon T *(Loaned on 7/10/2005) FL*

11+2/2 Others 2/1
Fulham *(£4,000,000 on 8/8/2007) PL 15+5/1 FLC 1 FAC 1*
Charlton Ath *(Loaned on 9/8/2008) FL 22+3/4 FLC 1 FAC 1*
Birmingham C *(Loaned on 9/1/2009) FL 9+7/1*
Blackpool *(Free on 1/9/2009) FL 11+8/1 FLC 0+1*

BOULDING Michael (Micky) Thomas
Born: Sheffield, 8 February 1976
Height: 5'10" **Weight:** 11.4
Micky began last season with high hopes for Bradford but an early injury proved a sign of things to come. He scored in three successive appearances on his return against Northampton, Notts County and Crewe before being sidelined again. Micky scored twice more but found himself out of the picture when Peter Taylor replaced Stuart McCall as Bradford manager. He agreed to terminate his contract early.
Mansfield T *(Signed from Hallam FC on 2/8/1999) FL 28+38/12 FLC 2+2 FAC 2+1 Others 1+1*
Grimsby T *(Free on 24/8/2001) FL 24+11/11 FLC 0+2 FAC 0+2*
Aston Villa *(Free on 9/7/2002) Others 2/1*
Sheffield U *(Loaned on 29/9/2002) FL 3+3 FLC 1/1*
Grimsby T *(Free on 10/1/2003) FL 37+2/16 FLC 1 FAC 1/1 Others 0+1*
Barnsley *(£50,000 on 12/2/2004) FL 27+8/10 FLC 1+1 Others 0+1 (Freed during 2005 close season)*
Cardiff C *(Loaned on 23/3/2005) FL 0+4*
Mansfield T *(Free, having been out of the game for a year and following a short spell at Rotherham U, on 3/8/2006) FL 68+14/27 FLC 2+1/1 FAC 5+1/3 Others 2*
Bradford C *(Free on 4/8/2008) FL 44+21/15 FLC 1+1 FAC 2+1/2 Others 2+1/1*

BOULDING Rory Joseph
Born: Sheffield, 21 July 1988
Height: 6'1" **Weight:** 12.8
Striker Rory made only two appearances as a substitute for Bradford. Younger brother of Michael Boulding, both players agreed to settle up their contracts before the end of the season after being told by manager Peter Taylor that they would not be in his first team plans.
Mansfield T *(From juniors at Rotherham U on 8/8/2006) FL 4+16 FLC 0+1 FAC 2+1/1 Others 0+3*
Bradford C *(Free on 8/8/2008) FL 1+2*

BO-BO PFA FOOTBALLERS' WHO'S WHO

BOUZANIS Dean Anthony
Born: Sydney, Australia, 2 October 1990
Height: 6'1" **Weight:** 13.3
International Honours: Greece: Yth.
Australia: U23-1; Yth
Signed by Liverpool from Sydney FC in 2007, the club saw the young 'keeper as being the best of his age group around. Yet to appear for Liverpool, he joined Accrington on loan in November and made a total of 19 appearances between the posts, enjoying his first taste of League football. A shot-stopper who commands the area with confidence and distributes the ball well, he has played for Australia at all levels up to under-23. Has also appeared for Greece's under-19, but wants to represent Australia.
Liverpool (Signed from NSW Institute of Sport, Australia on 4/10/2007)
Accrington Stanley (Loaned on 26/11/2009) FL 12+2 FAC 3+1 Others 1

BOWDITCH Dean Peter
Born: Bishops Stortford, 15 June 1986
Height: 5'11" **Weight:** 11.7
International Honours: E: Yth
It was a hugely frustrating season for the former Ipswich front man who joined Yeovil in the summer. Scoring in pre-season, he also scored in the opening day win over Tranmere before being carried off with a dislocated shoulder in the second half. Missing three months, he returned and finished as top scorer with ten goals in 30 games, a good return but one he will look to improve given a season free from injury.
Ipswich T (From trainee on 28/7/2003) FL 30+43/8 FLC 5+2/1 FAC 0+1 Others 0+2
Burnley (Loaned on 11/3/2005) FL 8+2/1
Wycombe W (Loaned on 27/1/2006) FL 9+2/1
Brighton & Hove A (Loaned on 1/11/2006) FL 1+2/1 Others 0+1
Northampton T (Loaned on 22/11/2007) FL 7+3/2
Brighton & Hove A (Loaned on 11/2/2008) FL 5
Brentford (Loaned on 31/10/2008) FL 8+1/2
Yeovil T (Free on 30/7/2009) FL 26+4/10

BOWER Mark James
Born: Bradford, 23 January 1980
Height: 5'10" **Weight:** 11.0
An experienced defender brought in by Colin Todd during the uncertain summer period while Darlington were still in administration. He started the season steadily at left-back but after nine games suffered an injury that kept

him out until December, when he returned to captain the side against his old club, Bradford. Alas, a recurrence of the injury ruled him out of the following game and he only appeared briefly towards the end of the campaign. Was out of contract in the summer.
Bradford C (From trainee on 28/3/1998) P/FL 219+12/12 FLC 8 FAC 9+1/1 Others 5
York C (Loaned on 16/2/2000) FL 15/1
York C (Loaned on 30/11/2000) FL 21/1 FAC 3 Others 0+1
Luton T (Loaned on 27/11/2009) FL 16/1
Darlington (Free on 23/7/2009) FL 12+1 FLC 1 Others 1

BOWERY Jordan Nathaniel
Born: Nottingham, 2 July 1991
Height: 6'1" **Weight:** 11.13
The pacy forward stayed on the fringe of contention for Chesterfield until going out on loan to Blue Square Premier Barrow in November, where an injury set back his progress. He made his full League debut late in the season as John Sheridan, impressed with his attitude in training, tried him on the right of midfield. He forced the ball over the line at Macclesfield in March but unobservant officials let play continue and Jordan was denied a maiden goal. This promising lad signed a new two-year contract at the end of the season.
Chesterfield (From trainee on 7/7/2009) FL 2+11 FLC 1 FAC 0+3 Others 0+2/1

BOWMAN Ryan Michael
Born: Carlisle, 30 November 1991
Height: 6'2" **Weight:** 12.0
Ryan progressed through Carlisle's youth ranks and made several substitute appearances towards the end of the term, playing on the wide right in a bid to give him more freedom. Voted the club's YTS 'Player of the Year', this promising striker will be looking to secure a more permanent first team berth next year. Good in the air, with an eye for goal, he has been a regular scorer for the reserves.
Carlisle U (Trainee) FL 0+6

BOWYER Lee David
Born: Canning Town, 3 January 1977
Height: 5'9" **Weight:** 10.6
International Honours: E: 1; U21-13; Yth
Lee had a tremendous campaign, showing he had not lost his fitness, sharpness or know-how. He formed a fine partnership alongside Barry Ferguson in the centre of the park for Birmingham. Lee was effective either making late runs to join the attack or in the general midfield skirmishes. He

passed the ball sensibly and was always in the right positions. During the middle of City's record-breaking 15-game unbeaten run, Lee scored fine winning goals in 1-0 successes over Fulham, Wolverhampton and West Ham in a four-match spell. An underrated member of the team, Lee led by example on and off the pitch.
Charlton Ath (From trainee on 13/4/1994) FL 46/8 FLC 6+1/5 FAC 3/1 Others 2
Leeds U (£2,600,000 on 5/7/1996) PL 196+7/38 FLC 7+1/1 FAC 16/3 Others 38/13
West Ham U (£100,000 on 8/1/2003) PL 10 FAC 1
Newcastle U (Free on 7/7/2003) PL 61+18/6 FLC 1+1 FAC 3+1/1 Others 11+2/4
West Ham U (£250,000 on 12/6/2006) PL 34+7/4 FLC 3+1/1 FAC 1+1 Others 2
Birmingham C (Free on 9/1/2009) P/FL 51+1/6 FLC 1+1/1 FAC 4+1

BOYATA Anga Dedryck
Born: Brussels, Belgium, 8 September 1990
Height: 6'2" **Weight:** 13.2
International Honours: Belgium: U21-1; Yth
A Belgian player of Congolese descent, Dedryck is a product of Manchester City's Academy who was thrust into the limelight early in the New Year following injury to Joleon Lescott and the departure of Kolo Toure to the African Cup of Nations. His debut was in a difficult FA Cup tie at Middlesbrough and he made his Premiership debut as a substitute in the following match against Blackburn. Remarkably, he played in both legs of the Carling Cup semi-final with Manchester United and although City lost out in the last minute of the second leg his performances helped to earn him the accolade of 'Young Player of the Season'. With the return of Lescott and Toure to duty, Dedryck returned to the reserves after a month in the spotlight, his reputation much enhanced.
Manchester C (From trainee on 10/7/2008) PL 1+2 FLC 2 FAC 2

BOYCE Emmerson Orlando
Born: Aylesbury, 24 September 1979
Height: 5'11" **Weight:** 11.10
International Honours: Barbados: 2
A model professional in his fifth season at Wigan, Emmerson is a composed and impressive defender who enjoyed another wonderfully consistent Premiership campaign. Highly competitive and with a great ability to snuff out potential danger, he

54

confirmed his reputation as one of the best signings from the Championship in recent seasons. Reads the game well, tackles under pressure and completes his job with the minimum of fuss. His partnership with Titus Bramble produced a series of impressive displays. He is equally comfortable at right-back, showing his versatility when deputizing for the injured Mario Melchiot. His 100th start for Wigan saw him net in the away victory at Burnley. Having scored one goal in the previous three seasons, Emmerson was something of a lucky omen, scoring two further goals in matches the club did not lose. He reached another landmark with his 100th Premier League start, against Manchester United.

Luton T (From trainee on 2/4/1998) FL 171+15/8 FLC 11 FAC 9+3/1 Others 3
Crystal Palace (Free on 9/7/2004) P/FL 68+1/2 FLC 3 FAC 3 Others 2
Wigan Ath (£1,000,000 on 15/8/2006) PL 107+3/4 FLC 5 FAC 5

BOYD Adam Mark
Born: Hartlepool, 25 May 1982
Height: 5'9" **Weight:** 10.12
The opportunist striker rejoined Hartlepool in May to become the first of manager Chris Turner's many close season signings. A prolific scorer in his first spell at Pools, he scored on his second debut 30 minutes after coming on as substitute against Coventry to clinch a 1-0 extra-time victory in the Carling Cup. Adam held down a place for most of the season and for much of the time was a regular scorer. In the second half of the season he seemed to lose his edge and for several games had to be content with a place on the bench.
Hartlepool U (From trainee on 20/9/1999) FL 89+55/53 FLC 4/1 FAC 6+2/3 Others 9+4/3
Boston U (Loaned on 14/11/2003) FL 14/4
Luton T (£500,000 on 1/8/2006) FL 5+14/1 FLC 2+1/1 FAC 2
Leyton Orient (Free on 8/8/2007) FL 67+10/23 FLC 2+1/2 FAC 5/2 Others 1+2/2
Hartlepool U (Free on 2/7/2009) FL 25+15/7 FLC 1+1/2 FAC 1 Others 0+1

BOYD George Jan
Born: Chatham, 2 October 1985
Height: 5'10" **Weight:** 11.7
International Honours: E: SP-6; S: B-1
George carried on at Peterborough where he had left off the previous season by worrying defenders with his ability on the ball, which made up for his lack of pace. Although finding it

hard at times as the team struggled to come to terms with two promotions in two seasons, he was given the captaincy during the season and made his 144 consecutive League appearance, a club record for the Posh. Was loaned out later in the season to Nottingham Forest and made the jump with ease despite having come from a struggling side. He immediately impressed with a 'Man of the Match' performance on his debut against Swansea before a niggling injury shortly afterwards curtailed his involvement.
Peterborough U (£265,000 from Stevenage Borough on 8/1/2007) FL 138+6/36 FLC 6/5 FAC 10/1 Others 3/1
Nottingham F (Loaned on 2/3/2010) FL 5+1/1

BOZANIC Oliver (Olly) John
Born: Sydney, Australia, 8 January 1989
Height: 6'0" **Weight:** 12.0
International Honours: Australia: Yth
Olly failed to make the breakthrough into Reading's first team despite a string of consistent displays at reserve team level and was allowed to go out on loan, first to Cheltenham and then Aldershot. A slight but clever player, the Australian made his Football League debut on the opening day of the season as Cheltenham defeated Grimsby 2-1 at the Abbey Business Stadium. He made two appearances on the left of midfield and another two on the right-hand side before suffering a knee injury in the 5-4 home defeat to Bradford. The injury cut short his spell at Cheltenham and also prevented him from representing

George Boyd

55

Australia at the FIFA under-20 World Cup in Egypt. An attacking midfielder of Croatian descent, who is the son of ex-Australian international defender Vic Bozanic, Olly is an expert at set pieces and his pace combined with his ability for delivering pin-point crosses make him a handful for opposing defenders. He joined Aldershot at the end of November on a one-month loan and made his debut as a late substitute at Tranmere in an FA Cup second round tie before scoring his first goal in senior football in the Shots' FA Cup second round replay at the EBB Stadium in early December. Having made his first start four days later at Burton, he got a run in the starting line-up from late January to early April, during which time his loan was extended till the end of the season. However, he returned to Reading in late April at his own request and was released by the Berkshire side two weeks later in order to join Australian A-League side Central Coast Mariners in early May.
Reading (Signed from Central Coast Mariners, Australia on 30/1/2007)
Cheltenham T (Loaned on 21/7/2009) FL 4
Aldershot T (Loaned on 26/11/2009) FL 19+6/2 FAC 0+2/1

BRADBURY Lee Michael
Born: Cowes, 3 July 1975
Height: 6'2" **Weight:** 13.10
Club Honours: Div 1 '06
International Honours: E: U21-3
Although Lee made his name as a striker, he is now very much considered to be a right-back and has adapted superbly to the position. A player with a wealth of experience, the promotion season was arguably his finest in a Bournemouth shirt. His consistency and the way he read games were major factors in the success that the side enjoyed.
Portsmouth (Free from Cowes on 14/8/1995) FL 41+13/15 FLC 1+2 FAC 4/2
Exeter C (Loaned on 1/12/1995) FL 14/5
Manchester C (£3,000,000 + on 1/8/1997) FL 34+6/10 FLC 6/1
Crystal Palace (£1,500,000 on 29/10/1998) FL 28+4/6 FLC 3+1/1 FAC 1/1
Birmingham C (Loaned on 25/3/1999) FL 6+1 Others 1+1
Portsmouth (£380,000 on 14/10/1999) FL 90+9/28 FLC 3+2 FAC 2/1
Sheffield Wed (Loaned on 24/12/2002) FL 2+1
Sheffield Wed (Loaned on 1/3/2003) FL 8/3
Derby Co (Loaned on 14/8/2003) FL 1

Derby Co (Loaned on 20/11/2003) FL 6
Walsall (Free on 25/3/2004) FL 7+1/1
Oxford U (Free on 12/7/2004) FL 57+6/9 FLC 2 FAC 4+1/1 Others 2+1
Southend U (Free on 31/1/2006) FL 40+7/5 FLC 2/3 FAC 3/1
Bournemouth (Signed on 24/8/2007) FL 104+9/10 FLC 2 FAC 7 Others 7/2

BRADLEY Mark Simon
Born: Dudley, 14 January 1988
Height: 6'0" **Weight:** 11.5
International Honours: W: 1; U21-14; Yth
A highly frustrating season for Mark, who started 20 consecutive matches for Walsall in central midfield from the middle of September to the end of January but then found time on the pitch restricted to the occasional substitute appearance. His game developed a harder edge as he tried to make more tackles and be more aggressive. His season was summed up by the match at MK Dons – a highly encouraging first 15 minutes but then a major struggle to impose himself on the game. He was an unused substitute for Wales in their World Cup qualifier in Liechtenstein in October. Was released at the end of the season.
Walsall (From trainee on 3/7/2006) FL 65+31/5 FAC 7+1 Others 0+1

BRADSHAW Thomas (Tom) William
Born: Shrewsbury, 27 July 1992
Height: 5'5" **Weight:** 10.12
Making the step up from the youth team, the young striker burst into the Shrewsbury first team as a substitute in the 3-0 away win at Crewe in April. A dream debut saw him score after only a few minutes on the pitch with a superb 25-yard strike, voted 'Goal of the Season' by supporters. He added a second, a tap in, a few minutes later. He certainly looked lively in his five substitute appearances and his full debut in the last match at Port Vale, scoring his third goal and providing the pass for another in the home game against Morecambe in May.
Shrewsbury T (Free from Aberystwyth T on 29/1/2010) FL 1+5/3

BRAIN Jonathan (Jon) Robert
Born: Carlisle, 11 February 1983
Height: 6'3" **Weight:** 14.3
As Macclesfield's first choice goalkeeper, Jon played in all but a handful of matches. Early in the season, Veiga was given the gloves for four matches before Jon was reinstated. Despite the team's struggles, Jon kept 11 clean sheets, and but for his hard

work and reaction saves, the number of goals conceded could have been much higher. Jon always seems to be outstanding against Aldershot and produced a brilliant display in a 0-0 draw at the Recreation Ground in November. Another excellent performance came late in the season at Torquay, who were limited to a single goal. Was out of contract at the end of the campaign.
Port Vale (Free from trainee at Newcastle U, via trials at Carlisle U, on 21/8/2003) FL 58+1 FLC 1 FAC 5 Others 4
Macclesfield T (Free on 7/7/2006) FL 125 FLC 4 FAC 5 Others 5

BRAMBLE Titus Malachi
Born: Ipswich, 31 July 1981
Height: 6'2" **Weight:** 13.10
International Honours: E: U21-10
Having signed a new three-year contract at the start of the season, Titus missed only three League matches for Wigan. After growing in maturity, he has become a rock of the defence, developing into a true professional. Handed the captain's armband in the absence of Mario Melchiot, the centre-half led by example. Big and strong, with an ability to hit long and accurate passes out of defence, he has all the attributes to develop further and become one of the best defenders in the country. His continuing superb form and honest approach saw him achieve cult hero status at the DW Stadium by making a major contribution to Premiership survival and forming effective partnership with first Emmerson Boyce and, after the turn of year, Gary Caldwell. Titus scored two goals, the first against Chelsea as Wigan gained victory over one of the top four in a League game for the first time since promotion. His other goal came in his 250th League appearance, in the win over Arsenal that ensured Premier League status for a sixth season. Titus missed the last two games following surgery on a stress fracture to his right foot.
Ipswich T (From trainee on 24/8/1998) P/FL 41+7/1 FLC 4+1/2 FAC 4+1 Others 4/1
Colchester U (Loaned on 29/12/1999) FL 2
Newcastle U (£5,000,000 on 19/7/2002) PL 96+9/3 FLC 5 FAC 8 Others 38+1/4
Wigan Ath (Free on 17/7/2007) PL 96/5 FLC 3 FAC 5

BRANDON Christopher (Chris) William
Born: Bradford, 7 April 1976
Height: 5'7" **Weight:** 10.3

Titus Bramble

After the injury problems of his first season, Chris was looking forward to making his mark at home-town club Bradford. The skilful midfielder soon scored his first goal against another of his former teams Torquay and weighed in with a last-minute header against Notts County in the Johnstone's Paint Trophy, forcing the game into a penalty shoot-out which City won. Chris can play a variety of roles across the midfield but rarely appeared in the same position for two games running. He found himself out of favour after Peter Taylor became manager and agreed to settle his contract early.
Torquay U (Free from Bradford PA on 5/8/1999) FL 64+7/8 FLC 4/1 FAC 5/1 Others 3
Chesterfield (Free on 9/7/2002) FL 74+5/11 FLC 2+1/1 FAC 2 Others 4/4

Huddersfield T (Free on 5/7/2004) FL 120+15/12 FLC 3+1 FAC 6/2 Others 2+1
Blackpool (Loaned on 21/3/2007) FL 4+1/2
Bradford C (Free on 15/7/2008) FL 18+9/2 Others 2+2/1

BRANDY Febian Earlston
Born: Manchester, 4 February 1989
Height: 5'5" **Weight:** 10.2
Club Honours: Div 1 '08
International Honours: E: Yth
A diminutive striker with an impressive turn of speed, Febian is very comfortable with the ball at his feet and enjoyed considerable success at Gillingham while on a two-month loan from Manchester United. He was most effective when allowed to collect the ball in midfield and run at defenders,

who all too often resorted to physical methods to counter his talents. As a result he won countless free kicks and a number of penalties for the Gills but was often kicked out of matches, his loan spell ending early due to injury. Was out of contract at the end of June.
Manchester U (From trainee on 6/7/2006)
Swansea C (Loaned on 18/1/2008) FL 2+17/3 Others 2
Swansea C (Loaned on 24/7/2008) FL 0+14 FLC 2+2
Hereford U (Loaned on 22/2/2009) FL 14+1/4
Gillingham (Loaned on 5/11/2009) FL 5+2/1 FAC 2/1

BRANSTON Guy Peter Bromley
Born: Leicester, 9 January 1979
Height: 6'0" **Weight:** 13.12
Guy was signed from Kettering Town on a two-year contract by Burton for their first Football League campaign and was quickly awarded the skipper's armband because of his no-nonsense approach and leadership qualities. However, after a promising start to his career at the Pirelli Stadium the brawny defender was suspended three times before the Christmas festivities, which cost him his place in the team. Anxious for regular first team football, Guy joined Torquay United in January on loan until the end of 2009-10. A vastly experienced barn door of a centre-half, he was hugely influential at Torquay and despite lacking pace and quality on the ball his know-how, positional sense and vocal encouragement transformed a leaky defence into a solid unit and a relegation-bound team into a winning team. A red card at Grimsby caused him to miss the last three matches.
Leicester C (From trainee on 3/7/1997)
Colchester U (Loaned on 9/2/1998) FL 12/1 Others 1
Colchester U (Loaned on 7/8/1998) FL 0+1
Plymouth Arg (Loaned on 20/11/1998) FL 7/1 Others 1
Lincoln C (Loaned on 10/8/1999) FL 4 FLC 2
Rotherham U (£50,000 on 15/10/1999) FL 101+3/13 FLC 5+1 FAC 4 Others 2
Wycombe W (Loaned on 19/9/2003) FL 9 Others 1
Peterborough U (Loaned on 25/2/2004) FL 14
Sheffield Wed (Signed on 2/7/2004) FL 10+1 FLC 1 FAC 1
Peterborough U (Loaned on 31/12/2004) FL 4/1
Oldham Ath (Free on 18/2/2005) FL 44+1/2 FLC 1 FAC 2 Others 2

Peterborough U (Free on 24/7/2006) FL 24+2 FLC 1+1/1 FAC 2+1 Others 1
Rochdale (Loaned on 24/8/2007) FL 4 FLC 1 Others 1
Northampton T (Loaned on 15/11/2007) FL 3 FAC 0+1
Notts Co (Free on 1/1/2008) FL 1 (Freed on 30/1/2008)
Burton A (Free from Kettering T on 15/7/2009) FL 18+1 FLC 1 FAC 2 Others 1
Torquay U (Loaned on 31/1/2010) FL 16

BRAYFORD John Robert
Born: Stoke-on-Trent, 29 December 1987
Height: 5'8" **Weight:** 11.2
After being signed from Burton, John missed one League game in almost two full seasons at Crewe. A very capable defender who can adapt to the various positions, John works hard and was made captain in February. He retained the position and was selected in the PFA League Two 'Team of the Season'. John was watched by a number of clubs but moved to Derby, where he was reunited with his former Burton manager Nigel Clough.
Crewe Alex (Signed from Burton A on 1/9/2008) FL 79+2/2 FLC 1 FAC 5 Others 1

BRECKIN Ian
Born: Rotherham, 24 February 1975
Height: 6'0" **Weight:** 12.9
Club Honours: AMC '96
Ian returned to Chesterfield as John Sheridan's first signing and skippered the side from central defence, where his aerial ability was usually to the fore. Sometimes it hardly seemed he had been away. While age has greyed his hair and taken away a little pace, it has brought a great ability to read the game and Ian's experience has enhanced his positional skills.
Rotherham U (From trainee on 1/11/1993) FL 130+2/6 FLC 6 FAC 5 Others 11
Chesterfield (£100,000 on 25/7/1997) FL 208+4/8 FLC 16/1 FAC 9/1 Others 12/1
Wigan Ath (£150,000 on 25/6/2002) FL 92+4 FLC 4 FAC 3+1 Others 1
Nottingham F (£350,000 on 8/7/2005) FL 131+12/12 FLC 4/2 FAC 11 Others 4
Chesterfield (Free on 7/7/2009) FL 41+1 FLC 1 FAC 1 Others 3

BREEN GARY Patrick
Born: Hendon, 12 December 1973
Height: 6'2" **Weight:** 12.0
Club Honours: Ch '05
International Honours: RoI: 63; U21-9
Veteran centre-back Gary combined his playing duties at Barnet with the assistant manager's job after agreeing a

Ian Breckin

one-year deal in July. Injury in Barnet's final pre-season game delayed his first outing in a competitive match until late September. However, Gary was once again a consistent performer for the Bees, marshalling the young defenders in the side and leading by example.
Maidstone U (From juniors at Charlton Ath on 6/3/1991) FL 19
Gillingham (Free on 2/7/1992) FL 45+6 FLC 4 FAC 5 Others 1
Peterborough U (£70,000 on 5/8/1994) FL 68+1/1 FLC 6 FAC 6 Others 6/1
Birmingham C (£400,000 on 9/2/1996) FL 37+3/2 FLC 4 FAC 1
Coventry C (£2,400,000 on 1/2/1997) P/FL 138+8/2 FLC 10+3 FAC 12
West Ham U (Free on 30/7/2002) PL 9+5 FLC 2 FAC 2
Sunderland (Free on 7/8/2003) P/FL 105+2/7 FLC 1 FAC 5 Others 2
Wolverhampton W (Free on 20/7/2006) FL 58+1/1 FAC 4 Others 2
Barnet (Free on 16/12/2008) FL 47 FAC 1

BREZOVAN Peter
Born: Bratislava, Slovakia, 9 December 1979
Height: 6'6" **Weight:** 14.13
International Honours: Slovakia: U21
After trials at Bristol City and Crewe, Peter was expecting to return to his native Slovakia when he received an invitation from Gus Poyet to have a month at Brighton. With Michel Kuipers injured and Graeme Smith suffering a battering to his confidence, Peter was immediately given his chance at Exeter and kept Albion's first clean-sheet for nearly two months, saving a penalty into the bargain. Thereafter, he vied

with Kuipers for the goalkeeper's jersey, the pair making occasional crucial errors, but when his rival broke a finger, Peter established himself. He signed a two-year contract at the end of the season.

Swindon T *(Free from FC Brno, Czech Republic, ex PS Bratislava, Vinorhady Bratislava, SKP Devin, Slovan Breclav, HFK Olomouc, on 1/8/2006) FL 66 FLC 2 FAC 4+1 Others 3*
Brighton & Hove A *(Free, via trial at Crewe Alex, on 4/12/2009) FL 20*

BRIDCUTT Liam Robert
Born: Reading, 8 May 1989
Height: 5'9" **Weight:** 11.7
Combative midfielder Liam joined Stockport on a half-season loan from Chelsea, where he had impressed Hatters' boss Gary Ablett in reserve football. He made his County debut away to Brighton, performing the holding midfield role, and was playing excellently until he was shown a second yellow card for kicking the ball away six minutes from time. On his return, he soon became an integral part of the side, scored his first senior goal in the Johnstone's Paint Trophy tie at Port Vale and was 'Man of the Match' against Southend. Was out of contract at the end of June.
Chelsea *(From trainee on 4/7/2007)*
Yeovil T *(Loaned on 8/2/2008) FL 6+3*
Watford *(Loaned on 27/11/2008) FL 4+2 FLC 1 FAC 0+2*
Stockport Co *(Loaned on 21/8/2009) FL 15 FAC 2 Others 2/1*

BRIDGE Wayne Michael
Born: Southampton, 5 August 1980
Height: 5'10" **Weight:** 11.11
Club Honours: FLC '05, '07; PL '05; FAC '07
International Honours: E: 36; U21-8; Yth
The Manchester City and England left-back endured a torrid season both on and off the pitch. Plagued by injuries – a knee injury in December sidelined him for two months while a groin injury in March kept him out for one month – and poor form, he was a pale shadow of the player he had been at Southampton and Chelsea. No doubt his form was affected by off-field matters as he became the unwilling and blameless participant in that 'John Terry affair' that dominated the media headlines for a month. Naturally shy and diffident, Wayne was so upset by the revelations and the attendant publicity that he announced his premature retirement from international football and refused to shake his former team-mate's hand in the preliminaries

before the match with Chelsea at Stamford Bridge. Although City won 4-2 in sensational fashion it was only a small personal revenge as Chelsea went on to win the Premiership and City missed out on fourth place.
Southampton *(From trainee on 16/1/1998) PL 140+12/2 FLC 10+1 FAC 11*
Chelsea *(£7,000,000 + on 21/7/2003) PL 74+13/1 FLC 15+1/1 FAC 11 Others 24+4/2*
Fulham *(Loaned on 20/1/2006) PL 12*
Manchester C *(£10,000,000 on 7/1/2009) PL 39 FLC 3 FAC 2 Others 6*

BRIDGES Michael
Born: North Shields, 5 August 1978
Height: 6'1" **Weight:** 10.11
Club Honours: Div 1 '96, '99; Ch '05; Div 2 '06
International Honours: E: U21-3; Yth; Sch
Signed on a non-contract basis to cover for a couple of pre-season injuries, Michael came off the bench to play in the MK Dons' opener against Hartlepool, then started in the following 4-1 home Carling Cup defeat by Swindon before remaining on the bench for a few games and leaving the club. He showed some good touches when called into action, but never looked a serious contender for an extended stay.
Sunderland *(From trainee on 9/11/1995) P/FL 31+48/16 FLC 8+3/5 FAC 2*
Leeds U *(£4,500,000 + on 29/7/1999) PL 40+16/19 FLC 3+2 FAC 1+1 Others 17+2/2*
Newcastle U *(Loaned on 2/2/2004) PL 0+6 Others 1+2*
Bolton W *(Loaned on 1/7/2004)*
Sunderland *(Free on 23/9/2004) FL 5+14/1 FAC 0+2*
Bristol C *(Free on 6/8/2005) FL 4+7 FLC 0+1/1 Others 0+1*
Carlisle U *(Signed on 15/11/2005) FL 28+2/15 FLC 0+1*
Hull C *(£350,000 on 31/8/2006) FL 9+13/2 FLC 2/1*
Carlisle U *(Loaned on 25/7/2008) FL 12+18/7 FLC 1+1 FAC 0+1 Others 1/1*
MK Dons *(Free on 8/8/2009) FL 0+1 FLC 1*

BRIDGE-WILKINSON Marc
Born: Nuneaton, 16 March 1979
Height: 5'6" **Weight:** 11.8
Club Honours: AMC '01
Marc was another Carlisle player whose season was disrupted by various injuries. An experienced attacking midfielder, he unfortunately managed just a handful of starts, although he did make rather more appearances coming

on as a substitute. He remains under contract for another year and will be hoping to see more first team action next term.
Derby Co *(From trainee on 26/3/1997) PL 0+1*
Carlisle U *(Loaned on 5/3/1999) FL 4+3*
Port Vale *(Free on 4/7/2000) FL 111+13/31 FLC 3/1 FAC 2+2/1 Others 9/3*
Stockport Co *(Free on 2/8/2004) FL 19+3/2 FLC 1 FAC 2*
Bradford C *(Free on 25/2/2005) FL 87/12 FLC 2/1 FAC 5/1 Others 1*
Carlisle U *(Free on 24/7/2007) FL 70+17/11 FLC 4+1 FAC 5 Others 6+3/3*

BRIGGS Matthew Anthony
Born: Wandsworth, 9 March 1991
Height: 6'1" **Weight:** 11.12
International Honours: E: Yth
Matthew joined Leyton Orient on a month's loan from Fulham in January. Although he played only one game as cover at centre-half, he showed coolness and composure on the ball that belied his lack of age and experience. It was a promising start to his career and now he has to take it on.
Fulham *(From trainee on 24/6/2009) PL 0+1*
Leyton Orient *(Loaned on 15/1/2010) FL 1*

BRIGHT Kris
Born: Auckland, New Zealand, 5 September 1986
Height: 6'2" **Weight:** 12.13
International Honours: New Zealand: 4; Yth
The New Zealand-born striker with four international caps to his credit joined Shrewsbury after a spell playing in Greece. The form of Dave Hibbert initially meant involvement from the bench. This remained the case as he struggled to make an impact in almost 30 games, with just five starts, though often given little time on the pitch. But he never gave up and his first goal was the winner in April against Lincoln, with a further strike in the last match at Port Vale. Given a run in the team, he may provide additional attacking options that the Shrews desperately need.
Shrewsbury T *(Signed from Panserraikos, Greece, ex Waitakere C, New Zealand Knights, Fortuna Sittard, Kristiansund, on 3/8/2009) FL 4+22/2 FLC 0+1 FAC 0+1 Others 1*

BRILL Dean Michael
Born: Luton, 2 December 1985
Height: 6'2" **Weight:** 12.5
Dean had a tough season at Boundary Park. Having joined as Oldham's new first choice goalkeeper, he finished as

reserve to Darryl Flahavan, who was on loan from Crystal Palace. A loss of confidence was to blame for Dean losing his spot and he was not helped by playing behind a defence that was often very shaky. Dean had a good run in which he conceded only one goal in six outings as the Latics put together a series of good results. He made some great saves when on top form, but a lack of consistency was the key as his confidence wavered.

Luton T (From trainee on 15/3/2005) FL 78+3 FLC 5 FAC 6 Others 5
Gillingham (Loaned on 8/12/2006) FL 8
Oldham Ath (Free on 2/7/2009) FL 28 FLC 1 Others 1

BRISLEY Shaun Richard
Born: Macclesfield, 6 May 1990
Height: 6'2" **Weight:** 11.1
Shaun is a tall, young, strong centre-back who firmly established himself at Macclesfield. In the first half of the season, he was in his accustomed centre-back role where he used his strength and height to good effect. As the season progressed and the number of injuries increased, he displayed his versatility by moving to right-back or right wing-back. Although not noted for pace, Shaun made some impressive runs down the flank and was rewarded with a regular berth in the final quarter of the season.
Macclesfield T (From trainee on 8/7/2008) FL 76+5/3 FLC 3/1 FAC 3/1 Others 2/1

BRITTON Leon James
Born: Merton, 16 September 1982
Height: 5'5" **Weight:** 9.10
Club Honours: AMC '06; Div 1 '08
International Honours: E: Yth
Always reliable for Swansea, Leon is not always recognised for his all-round work rate in central midfield and his tireless covering in front of the centre-backs. Midway through the season, he declined to sign an extension to his contract when it was offered but, despite all the rumours over his future when the January window reopened, he remained at the Liberty Stadium. The Swans turned down a request from Wigan – and, therefore, former Swansea manager Roberto Martinez - to take the midfielder on loan just before the March transfer window closed.
West Ham U (From juniors on 21/9/1999)
Swansea C (Free on 13/12/2002) FL 270+25/10 FLC 8+1 FAC 20+2/4 Others 7+3/1

BRIZELL Joshua (Josh) Daniel
Born: Liverpool, 15 October 1991
Height: 5'10" **Weight:** 12.0

A member of Rochdale's successful youth team, Josh played at full-back for the first team in the pre-season friendlies, and with Dale short on numbers early in the season, made his senior debut as a substitute for Marcus Holness in the Carling Cup tie at Sheffield Wednesday. The promising young defender skippered Dale's reserves towards the end of the season.
Rochdale (Trainee) FLC 0+1

BROGAN Stephen Patrick
Born: Rotherham, 12 April 1988
Height: 5'7" **Weight:** 10.4
Stephen could see light at the end of the tunnel as he strove hard to force his way back into Rotherham's first team picture following that 15-month absence after his badly broken leg. Able to play in defence or midfield, he had opportunities, much to the delight of the fans, in mid-season but was to find his way to a regular spot blocked by the form and consistency of those already ahead of him.
Rotherham U (From trainee on 3/8/2006) FL 48+13/4 FLC 1 FAC 4+1/2 Others 1+4

BROMBY Leigh
Born: Dewsbury, 2 June 1980
Height: 6'0" **Weight:** 11.8
International Honours: E: Sch
Because Leigh was not likely to be a first team regular with Sheffield United, after a Carling Cup appearance he was allowed to move to Leeds, thus joining his boyhood heroes at the end of the August transfer window. Having made his debut at centre-back in a 2-0 home win against Stockport, when club skipper Richard Naylor was able to return to action at the end of September after a pre-season injury, Leigh had a spell at right-back. The possessor of a prodigious long throw, he alternated between the two positions, coupled with spells on the bench, for most of the campaign.
Sheffield Wed (Free from Liversedge on 9/7/1998) FL 98+2/2 FLC 8 FAC 6+1 Others 5
Mansfield T (Loaned on 10/12/1999) FL 10/1 Others 1
Norwich C (Loaned on 24/2/2003) FL 5
Sheffield U (Free on 5/7/2004) P/FL 104+5/6 FLC 7+1 FAC 8
Watford (£600,000 on 31/1/2008) FL 35+3/1 FLC 5 FAC 0+1 Others 2
Sheffield U (Free on 13/1/2009) FL 6+6/1 FLC 1 Others 0+1
Leeds U (Signed on 1/9/2009) FL 31+1/1 FAC 5 Others 2

BROOKE Ryan Michael
Born: Holmes Chapel, 4 October 1990
Height: 5'11" **Weight:** 11.1

Having made his breakthrough into Oldham's first team in the previous season, big things where expected of this exciting youngster. As so often happens, events did not go to plan for young Ryan. The striker did make 16 appearances, from which he scored one goal, but it was all a bit hit and miss. Most of Ryan's appearances were from the bench but Oldham have great faith in this youngster and he has been offered a new contract with the club.
Oldham Ath (From trainee on 16/7/2009) FL 2+14/2 FAC 0+1 Others 0+1

BROOKS Kurtney Wayne Cookson
Born: Slough, 14 September 1991
Height: 5'9" **Weight:** 10.2
International Honours: W: Yth
Kurtney made his debut for Watford while still a second-year Academy scholar, coming on as a substitute against Barnet in a Carling Cup tie in August. A midfield player, Kurtney is a Wales under-19 cap. He was released at the end of the season.
Watford (Trainee) FLC 0+1

BROOMES Marlon Charles
Born: Birmingham, 28 November 1977
Height: 6'0" **Weight:** 12.12
International Honours: E: U21-2; Yth; Sch
Marlon joined Tranmere in August initially on a non-contract basis but he signed a permanent deal in September that took him to the end of the season. He is an experienced and versatile defender, able to play at either right or left-back, although he prefers to be centre-back or sweeper. Marlon went straight into the team, making his debut in the first round of the Carling Cup against Grimsby, while the goal he scored in the 2-1 home defeat of Southampton was his first for over four years. It looked as if he was going to be a regular but he picked up a number of yellow cards together with one red and, after serving his suspension, had to wait two months to regain his place because of the form of his replacement. Marlon has been offered a new contract.
Blackburn Rov (From trainee on 28/11/1994) P/FL 24+7/1 FLC 3 FAC 4
Swindon T (Loaned on 22/1/1997) FL 12/1
Queens Park Rgrs (Loaned on 25/10/2000) FL 5
Grimsby T (Loaned on 7/9/2001) FL 13+2 FLC 3/2
Sheffield Wed (Free on 13/12/2001) FL 18+1 FAC 1
Preston NE (Free, via trial at Burnley, on 9/8/2002) FL 59+10 FLC 4 FAC 2

Others 0+2
Stoke C *(Signed on 5/8/2005) FL 36+1/2 FLC 1 FAC 4*
Blackpool *(Free on 3/7/2008) FL 0+1*
Crewe Alex *(Loaned on 26/1/2009) FL 19*
Tranmere Rov *(Free on 8/8/2009) FL 31/1 FLC 1 FAC 3*

BROUGH Michael

Born: Nottingham, 1 August 1981
Height: 6'0" **Weight:** 11.7
International Honours: W: U21-3; Yth
Despite his versatility – he is equally comfortable anywhere across the back four or as a holding midfielder – Michael found opportunities at Torquay limited to a couple of substitute appearances. He played regular Blue Square Premier football during loan spells at Stevenage and then at Mansfield, where he subsequently signed on a permanent basis.
Notts Co *(From trainee on 1/7/1999) FL 67+22/2 FLC 1 FAC 4+5 Others 4 (Freed on 23/1/2004)*
Torquay U *(Free from Forest Green Rov, ex Stafford Rgrs, Stevenage Borough, on 6/6/2008) FL 0+1 FLC 0+1*

BROUGHTON Drewe Oliver

Born: Hitchin, 25 October 1978
Height: 6'3" **Weight:** 12.10
Club Honours: AMC '08; Div 2 '08
Drewe had to start his season late due to a pre-season injury, but on his return to action he was a regular in Rotherham's match-day squad if not always first choice up front. It was clear that his experience was handy to have around and he often made useful second half entrances from the bench. Arriving on loan at Lincoln in February, the striker spent a few weeks at the club and although he failed to find the back of the net during his seven games, his link-up play with Davide Somma went some way to helping preserve the Imps' Football League status. Was out of contract in the summer.
Norwich C *(From trainee on 6/5/1997) FL 3+6/1*
Wigan Ath *(Loaned on 15/8/1997) FL 1+3*
Brentford *(£100,000 on 30/10/1998) FL 1*
Peterborough U *(£100,000 on 17/11/1998) FL 19+16/8 FLC 2 Others 1+1/1*
Kidderminster Hrs *(£50,000 on 22/1/2001) FL 70+24/19 FLC 2 FAC 2/2 Others 5/2*
Southend U *(Free on 13/6/2003) FL 31+1/3 FLC 2/1 FAC 0+2 Others 4+4/5*
Rushden & Diamonds *(Loaned on 14/10/2004) FL 9/4 FAC 1/1*
Wycombe W *(Loaned on 17/12/2004) FL 2+1*

Rushden & Diamonds *(Free on 11/2/2005) FL 43+6/12 FAC 1 Others 1*
Chester C *(Free on 1/7/2006) FL 9+5/2 FLC 1*
Boston U *(Loaned on 26/10/2006) FL 25/8 FAC 1*
MK Dons *(Free on 27/7/2007) FL 2+11 FLC 1/1 FAC 1 Others 2+2*
Wrexham *(Loaned on 25/1/2008) FL 5*
Wrexham *(Loaned on 26/2/2008) FL 11/2*
Rotherham U *(Free on 15/8/2008) FL 39+17/9 FLC 3/1 FAC 2+2/1 Others 4+2/2*
Lincoln C *(Loaned on 16/2/2010) FL 7*

BROWN Aaron Anthony

Born: Birmingham, 23 June 1983
Height: 6'4" **Weight:** 14.7
Freed by Yeovil during the summer, the tall central defender signed a three-month contract with Burton to provide cover before being released in January. Having already played for Redditch United (Conference North), AFC Telford United (Conference North) and Truro City (Southern League Premier Division), as well as Burton, since the start of the season, he reacquainted himself with the Aldershot boss Kevin Dillon when signing as a non-contract player in mid-March. A powerfully-built centre-half, Aaron notched his first goal for the Shots in the win at bottom-placed Darlington less than a fortnight later and his arrival helped to galvanise the spine of the team as they pushed towards the play-offs and eventual defeat at the hands of Rotherham at the semi-final stage.
Reading *(Signed from Tamworth, ex Studley, on 24/11/2005)*
Bournemouth *(Loaned on 17/2/2006) FL 3+4*
Yeovil T *(Free on 11/8/2008) FL 16+7/3 FAC 1 Others 1 (Freed during 2009 close season)*
Burton A *(Free from Redditch U on 28/9/2009) FL 1 FAC 0+2 (Freed on 31/12/2009)*
Aldershot T *(Free from Truro C, via Telford U, on 11/3/2010) FL 12/1 Others 2*

BROWN Aaron Wesley

Born: Bristol, 14 March 1980
Height: 5'10" **Weight:** 11.12
Club Honours: AMC '03
International Honours: E: Sch
The left-back was a regular for Lincoln during the opening stages of 2009-10, but following the arrival of Chris Sutton as manager he found first team opportunities limited and in February had his contract with the Imps terminated by mutual consent. To get match fit he trained with non-League Wrexham and eventually signed a short-

term contract with the Red Dragons that took him through till the end of the season.
Bristol C *(From trainee on 7/11/1997) FL 135+25/12 FLC 3+2 FAC 10+1 Others 12+4*
Exeter C *(Loaned on 6/1/2000) FL 4+1/1*
Queens Park Rgrs *(Free on 5/1/2005) FL 1+2 FLC 1*
Torquay U *(Loaned on 22/3/2005) FL 5*
Cheltenham T *(Loaned on 23/9/2005) FL 3*
Swindon T *(Free on 24/11/2005) FL 36+24/1 FLC 1 FAC 2+1 Others 1*
Gillingham *(Free on 23/7/2007) FL 10+1/1 FLC 1 FAC 1 Others 2/1*
Lincoln C *(Free on 6/8/2008) FL 47+9/2 FLC 2 FAC 1+1/1 Others 1*

BROWN Christopher (Chris) Alan

Born: Doncaster, 11 December 1984
Height: 6'1" **Weight:** 13.4
Club Honours: Div 3 '04; Ch '05, '07
International Honours: E: Yth
Chris appeared in all but three of Preston's 49 matches last year, ending as joint second top scorer with 11 goals, although only six of these came in League matches. He scored all four of the club's goals in the three Carling Cup matches and recorded the first in the 7-0 FA Cup demolition of Colchester. Following the change of manager, he was on the bench as often as starting, but was regularly called on and in this role he produced a stunning lob over the Cardiff 'keeper soon after going on to seal a memorable win. Mobile and aware, Chris is equally adept in finishing with shots or headers and he brings others into play effectively.
Sunderland *(From trainee on 9/8/2002) P/FL 33+33/9 FLC 1/2 FAC 0+2*
Doncaster Rov *(Loaned on 3/10/2003) FL 17+5/10*
Hull C *(Loaned on 9/9/2005) FL 13/1*
Norwich C *(£275,000 on 11/1/2007) FL 11+7/1 FLC 2+1 FAC 3*
Preston NE *(£400,000 on 10/1/2008) FL 56+34/17 FLC 2+1/4 FAC 4/1 Others 1+1*

BROWN Christopher (Chris) Robert

Born: Stockport, 21 February 1992
Height: 6'3" **Weight:** 12.2
Chris, a member of the Rochdale youth team, was an unused substitute in the final game of 2008-09 and appeared in Dale's pre-season friendlies at full-back. He made his senior debut as a late substitute in midfield in the Johnstone's Paint Trophy against Bradford, although his reserve and youth team spot was in central defence. He had loan spells at

61

Bamber Bridge and Droylsden to gain experience. A product of Dale's Centre of Excellence, Chris was shortlisted for the 2010 League Two 'Apprentice of the Year' award and was rewarded with his first professional contract in February.
Rochdale (From trainee on 25/1/2010) Others 0+1

BROWN James Peter
Born: Cramlington, 3 January 1987
Height: 5'11" **Weight:** 11.0
The Hartlepool midfielder or striker will be familiar to Sky Sports Soccer Saturday viewers, with his goals being heralded by Jeff Stelling's "I Feel Good" doll. Having missed most of the previous season with a knee injury, it was good to see him back in contention. James was eased into action but on reaching full match fitness was back on form and had several well-taken goals to his name. Sadly, he was struck by a cruciate knee injury that required surgery and was out of action for several months. Determined to beat his injury problems, he returned to play a part in the run-in.
Hartlepool U (Signed from Chester-le-Street T on 20/9/2004) FL 97+28/27 FLC 5+3/1 FAC 6/3 Others 4+1/2

BROWN Jason Roy
Born: Southwark, 18 May 1982
Height: 5'11" **Weight:** 13.3
International Honours: W: 2; U21-7; Yth
When Paul Robinson was absent with a calf injury at Tottenham near the end of the season, Jason had been limited to odd appearances for Blackburn in Cup games against lower division opposition. It was not an unproductive time as he saved a Dexter Blackstock penalty against Nottingham Forest. His failure to stop a shot from Roman Pavlyuchenko did not augur well but in the next three crucial games he proved himself a solid goalkeeper, particularly decisive in leaving his line to catch the ball flat and calm under pressure. Caught a bit flat footed by a free kick from James McFadden against Birmingham, but it was his only mistake in a solid run of appearances.
Gillingham (From trainee at Charlton Ath on 19/3/2001) FL 126 FLC 8 FAC 3 Blackburn Rov (Free on 6/7/2006) PL 6+3 FLC 3+1 FAC 2

BROWN Lee James
Born: Farnborough, Kent, 10 August 1990
Height: 6'0" **Weight:** 12.6
A young left-back who has come through the youth set up at Queens Park Rangers, Lee enjoyed a loan spell

at Salisbury in the first part of the season and when he returned to Loftus Road he found himself part of the travelling squad on several occasions. Lee made his debut towards the end of the campaign, coming off the bench in an away game against Barnsley to play out the last few minutes.
Queens Park Rgrs (From trainee on 3/7/2008) FL 0+1

BROWN Michael Robert
Born: Hartlepool, 25 January 1977
Height: 5'9" **Weight:** 11.8
International Honours: E: U21-4
After starting the season playing in the opening two League matches for Wigan, Michael was sold to Portsmouth in August following the arrival of Mohamed Diame. Hard working and with a never-say-die attitude, he is an inspirational calming midfielder who adopts a holding role while others advance firmly. He quickly established himself in the heart of Pompey's midfield, his leadership skills earning him the captain's armband for a number of fixtures throughout the season. His tough-tackling, all-action performances earned him iconic status among fans at Fratton Park, as well as the 'Man of the Match' award in the 2-0 home win against Liverpool. Michael scored his first goal for more than four years with a stunning strike against Aston Villa in April, and netted again two weeks later in Portsmouth's last home game of the League season against Wolverhampton. A firm favourite on the south coast, Pompey fans will be hoping the club can retain the services of 'Brown-eye' in what will prove to be a busy summer at Fratton Park.
Manchester C (From trainee on 13/9/1994) P/FL 67+22/2 FLC 2+4 FAC 10+1/2 Others 4
Hartlepool U (Loaned on 27/3/1997) FL 6/1
Portsmouth (Loaned on 19/11/1999) FL 4
Sheffield U (Signed on 17/12/1999) FL 146+5/27 FLC 13+1/3 FAC 6/3 Others 3/2
Tottenham H (£500,000 on 31/12/2003) PL 39+11/2 FLC 4+1/1 FAC 9
Fulham (£1,500,000 on 31/1/2006) PL 40+1 FAC 3
Wigan Ath (Signed on 31/7/2007) PL 47+1/1 FLC 2+1 FAC 2+1
Portsmouth (Signed on 28/8/2009) PL 22+2/2 FLC 2+1 FAC 6

BROWN Nathaniel (Nat) Levi
Born: Sheffield, 15 June 1981
Height: 6'3" **Weight:** 12.1

During the summer, Nat converted his loan from Wrexham into a permanent transfer to Macclesfield, but was unfortunate to suffer a stress fracture of the shin during pre-season, keeping him out of contention until September. After his return he was virtually ever-present and was used as a centre-back, a role he prefers and where he gives his best performances. He scored four goals, all in drawn matches, that helped Macclesfield to keep clear of the relegation zone. Nat always played with his trademark strapping on his left wrist and hand.
Huddersfield T (From trainee on 8/7/1999) FL 56+20 FLC 1+2 FAC 1+1 Others 2+1
Lincoln C (Free on 5/8/2005) FL 86+8/8 FLC 3 FAC 3 Others 5+1/1 (Freed on 26/6/2008)
Macclesfield T (Free from Wrexham on 6/11/2008) FL 66+2/10 FAC 3+1 Others 1

BROWN Scott
Born: Runcorn, 8 May 1985
Height: 5'7" **Weight:** 10.3
International Honours: E: Yth
The midfielder made only one League appearance, in the final match. Scott suffered a career-threatening broken leg while playing for Cheltenham in January 2007, but battled back to make further appearances for Cheltenham and Port Vale before deciding to undergo another operation to remove a metal pin in his leg during the summer. Cheltenham manager Mark Yates offered him the chance to train with the club and Scott impressed the coaching staff enough to earn non-contract terms for the final few weeks, going on as a substitute in the last game against Accrington.
Everton (From trainee on 16/5/2002)
Bristol C (Free on 10/8/2004) FL 48+15/5 FLC 0+1 FAC 0+3 Others 1+3
Cheltenham T (Free on 12/1/2007) FL 13+11 Others 0+1
Port Vale (Free on 21/11/2008) FL 18/1 FAC 1
Cheltenham T (Free, following long-term injury, on 25/3/2010) FL 0+1

BROWN Scott Peter Andrew
Born: Wolverhampton, 26 April 1985
Height: 6'2" **Weight:** 13.1
Goalkeeper Scott was ever-present for Cheltenham and was not short of action as they conceded 79 goals in all competitions. It would have been more without Scott's confident, agile goalkeeping behind a constantly changing defence. Having waited four years for a regular first team chance, he is now established as a League player and was offered an extended contract.

Bristol C *(Free from Welshpool T, ex Wolverhampton W trainee, on 5/12/2003)*
Cheltenham T *(Free on 2/7/2004) FL 92+1 FLC 1 FAC 6 Others 2*

BROWN Simon James
Born: Chelmsford, 3 December 1976
Height: 6'2" **Weight:** 15.0
With only one goalkeeper on Northampton's books, Simon was signed to challenge Chris Dunn for the number-one shirt. He made a couple of first team appearances before agreeing to become goalkeeping coach as well as stand-in 'keeper on the understanding that if he was offered terms by another side he could leave. He did that by moving to Blue Square Premier Cambridge United.
Tottenham H *(From trainee on 1/7/1995)*
Lincoln C *(Loaned on 19/12/1997) FL 1 Others 0+1*
Colchester U *(Free on 20/7/1999) FL 141+1 FLC 7 FAC 9 Others 8+1*
Hibernian *(Signed on 24/6/2004) SL 49 SLC 3 SC 8+1 Others 4*
Brentford *(Signed on 3/7/2007) FL 26 FAC 1 Others 1*
Darlington *(Loaned on 2/8/2008) FL 22 FLC 2 FAC 1 Others 1*
Northampton T *(Free on 11/9/2009) FL 2*

BROWN Troy Anthony
Born: Croydon, 17 September 1990
Height: 5'9" **Weight:** 11.10
Released by Fulham in the summer, he was offered a deal at Ipswich by Jim Magilton before he was relieved of his managerial duties. However, Roy Keane honoured the deal, giving him a year's contract. A central defender who has played for the Welsh under-19s, he made his Ipswich debut as a substitute in the last game of the season.
Ipswich T *(From trainee at Fulham on 30/7/2009) FL 0+1*

BROWN Wayne Jonathan
Born: Kingston, 6 August 1988
Height: 5'9" **Weight:** 12.5
Fulham midfield player Wayne had a loan spell at Bristol Rovers in February, impressing in his home debut against Walsall. He showed ability and composure on the ball before suffering an ankle ligament injury. When fit, he returned for one further brief appearance as substitute. In all the four matches he played, Rovers failed to score. Was out of contract at the end of June.
Fulham *(From trainee on 7/2/2007) PL 0+1 FAC 1*
Brentford *(Loaned on 25/2/2008) FL 7+4/1*

Bristol Rov *(Loaned on 1/2/2010) FL 3+1*

BROWN Wayne Larry
Born: Southampton, 14 January 1977
Height: 6'1" **Weight:** 11.12
Club Honours: FC '04
Bury's very own 'Superman' goalkeeper had a varied season, struggling particularly with his kicking. After an injury received in October, Wayne had difficulty in regaining his previously impeccable form for Bury and wrong decisions against Accrington very nearly proved costly. After a red card at Chesterfield, however, Wayne was able to swing his form around, and reinstated his super-hero status amongst the Shakers' fans towards the end of the season. Was out of contract in the summer.
Bristol C *(From trainee on 3/7/1995) FL 1 (Freed during 1996 close season)*
Chester C *(Free from Weston-super-Mare on 30/9/1996) FL 107 FLC 8 FAC 7 Others 3*
Hereford U *(Free on 5/7/2006) FL 83 FLC 3 FAC 10*
Bury *(Free on 23/7/2008) FL 76 FLC 2 FAC 2 Others 6*

BROWN Wayne Lawrence
Born: Barking, 20 August 1977
Height: 6'0" **Weight:** 12.6
Wayne, an experienced central defender, initially arrived at the Walkers Stadium during the January 2009 transfer window on loan from Hull, which Leicester converted to a permanent deal as the season closed. He regularly turned in a series of uncompromising displays at the heart of the Foxes' defence, using his experience to marshal the troops around him. Sadly, a hamstring problem led to him missing both legs of the play-off semi-final against Cardiff, where his experience might have just tipped the balance.
Ipswich T *(From trainee on 16/5/1996) P/FL 28+12 FLC 3 FAC 2 Others 4+1/1*
Colchester U *(Loaned on 16/10/1997) FL 0+2*
Queens Park Rgrs *(Loaned on 22/3/2001) FL 2*
Wimbledon *(Loaned on 14/9/2001) FL 17/1*
Watford *(Loaned on 30/1/2002) FL 10+1/3*
Watford *(Free on 18/12/2002) FL 24+1/1 FAC 1*
Gillingham *(Loaned on 19/9/2003) FL 4/1*
Colchester U *(Signed on 17/12/2004) FL 138+2/4 FLC 5 FAC 7+1/1 Others 3+1*
Hull C *(£450,000 on 18/7/2007) P/FL 42/1 FLC 4 Others 3*

Preston NE *(Loaned on 27/10/2008) FL 6*
Leicester C *(Signed on 30/1/2009) FL 45+3 FAC 1*

BROWN Wesley (Wes) Michael
Born: Manchester, 13 October 1979
Height: 6'1" **Weight:** 12.4
Club Honours: UEFACL '99, '08; PL '99, '01, '03, '07, '08; FLC '06, '10; FAC '04; CS '07
International Honours: E: 23; U21-8; Yth; Sch
A solid Manchester United central defender, who is commanding in the air, with pace and confidence to match, Wes faced yet another double challenge, vying for one of the central defensive positions while trying to steer clear of niggling injuries. He started the season with only a fleeting number of appearances in the Premiership, but returned to action, missing only six games from November to March. His run was particularly helped by injuries to Rio Ferdinand and Nemanja Vidic, and his partnership with Jonny Evans in central defence was both assured and professional.
Manchester U *(From trainee on 13/11/1996) PL 199+26/3 FLC 21+3 FAC 30+2 Others 53+13/1*

BRUCE Alexander (Alex) Stephen
Born: Norwich, 28 September 1984
Height: 6'0" **Weight:** 11.6
International Honours: RoI: 2; B-1; U21-5
Alex started the season in the Ipswich first team and during the first two months had various central defensive partners before taking over the captaincy. Having had to be substituted early in the home game against Newcastle because of a hernia problem, he later admitted that he was carrying it before the game and should not have played. The injury kept him out of action for a month but then recurred on his return and when he regained full fitness he was unable to get back into the side. Following that, he was loaned to Leicester during the transfer window once it became clear that Aleksandar Tunchev was likely to be out of action for the remainder of the season. An abdominal strain on his full Foxes' debut threatened to turn his loan into a non-event, but he recovered sufficiently to give glimpses of his best form during the play-offs.
Blackburn Rov *(From trainee on 4/7/2002)*
Oldham Ath *(Loaned on 23/12/2004) FL 3+3 FAC 1 Others 1*
Birmingham C *(Signed on 26/1/2005) PL 3+3 FAC 4+2*

*Oldham Ath (Loaned on 28/1/2005) FL
5+1 FAC 1 Others 1*
*Sheffield Wed (Loaned on 10/3/2005)
FL 5+1 Others 3*
*Tranmere Rov (Loaned on 17/8/2005)
FL 10+1 FLC 0+1*
*Ipswich T (Signed on 3/8/2006) FL
112+3/2 FLC 6 FAC 5+1/1*
*Leicester C (Loaned on 1/2/2010) FL
2+1 Others 2*

BRUMA Jeffrey Van Homoet
Born: Rotterdam, Holland, 13
November 1991
Height: 6'1" **Weight:** 13.0
International Honours: Holland: U21-
4; Yth
Strapping centre-back who made his
debut for Chelsea in October when he
came on for the last 23 minutes against
Blackburn in the Premier League. Jeffrey

is a ball-playing central defender of
enormous promise, who has also
featured in midfield and full-back. He
was fast-tracked into the Dutch
international set up having represented
Holland's under-21s as an 18-year-old.
He played at three levels for Chelsea
and was still eligible for the FA Youth
Cup winning team, having been in the
losing side in 2008. He has a reputation
as a dead ball specialist and in the FA
Youth Cup final scored a free kick to
level the first leg at Villa Park. He is the
younger brother of ex-Barnsley
defender Marciano, currently at Willem
II in Holland, and hopes to follow John
Terry in graduating from the Chelsea
Academy to the highest levels of
domestic and international football.
*Chelsea (From trainee on 3/7/2009) PL
0+2 FLC 0+1*

BRUNT Christopher (Chris)
Born: Belfast, 14 December 1984
Height: 6'1" **Weight:** 11.8
Club Honours: Ch '08
International Honours: NI: 26; U23-1;
U21-2
West Bromwich's second top scorer in
2009-10, Chris weighed in with some
crucial late goals, both at home and
away, and was certainly one of the
team's best players over the course of
the season. With his brilliant left foot,
he returned to haunt two of his former
clubs, netting a deadly first-half double,
one of them a precisely delivered 45-
yard lob, to set up a comfortable 5-0
victory at Middlesbrough – Albion's first
on Boro soil for 56 years - and bagging
a fine goal at Hillsborough when Albion
beat Sheffield Wednesday 4-0. He also
equalised at Watford with a rare 95th-
minute header, only to be shown a
yellow card for his over-elaborate
celebrations. Itching to get back in the
Northern Ireland team on a regular
basis, totally committed, Chris was
Albion's most booked player, with nine
yellow cards. He also reached the
personal milestone of 250 career
League appearances during the course
of the season.
*Middlesbrough (From trainee on
6/7/2002)*
*Sheffield Wed (Free on 2/3/2004) FL
113+27/24 FLC 4+1 FAC 4 Others
2+2/1*
*West Bromwich A (£3,000,000 on
15/8/2007) P/FL 89+19/25 FLC 2 FAC
7+5/1*

BRYAN Michael Anthony
Born: Hayes, 21 February 1990
Height: 5'8" **Weight:** 9.2
International Honours: NI: 2; U21-2; Yth
Michael, a right-winger in his first year
as a professional with Watford, made a
big impression in pre-season with his
pace, skill and ability to beat defenders.
He was given little chance to show
what he could do in the early part of
the season and was limited to brief
substitute appearances. However he
came back into contention in the
closing stages and gave a series of
cameo performances, including a first
League start at Coventry that promised
well for the future. Another product of
the Watford Academy, Michael is a
member of the Northern Ireland under-
21 squad.
*Watford (From juniors on 21/11/2008)
FL 1+6*

BUCHANAN David (Dave)
Thomas Hugh
Born: Rochdale, 6 May 1986
Height: 5'8" **Weight:** 10.8

Chris Brunt

International Honours: NI: U21-15; Yth
Despite still waiting for his first goal in
six seasons at Bury Dave, a tenacious
full-back, has won over many Shakers'
fans through his determination,
consistency, and clear desire to win.
Dave has adapted exceptionally well to
his switch of position from central
midfield to left-back under manager
Alan Knill, and developed into one of
the best in that position in League Two,
with his excellent crossing ability and
contribution going forward being extra
attributes. A home-grown talent, Dave's
attitude continues to be thoroughly
professional, as was proved in his
performances at right-back when
covering for the injured captain Paul
Scott. Dave was named the Bury Times
'Player of the Season'.
Bury *(From trainee on 5/7/2005) FL
165+21 FLC 5 FAC 11+2 Others 11*

BUCKLEY William (Will)
Edward
Born: Oldham, 21 November 1989
Height: 6'0" **Weight:** 13.0
Rochdale's most exciting discovery of
the previous term, Will started the
season playing as a striker, but
following the signing of Chris O'Grady
he returned to a position on the wing.
He scored in three consecutive victories
in September but suffered a niggling
thigh strain and played only a few
further games in November before
being sold to Watford in January. A
player who can operate on either flank
and also enjoys playing as a striker, Will
lacked match fitness when he arrived
and a series of niggling injuries delayed
his full debut until the end of March,
when he started against
Middlesbrough. He made a good early
impression with his ability to run at
defenders, and scored his first Watford
goal at Preston before a hamstring
injury at the beginning of April brought
his season to a premature close. Only
21, Will is regarded as a long-term
signing for the Hornets.
Rochdale *(Free from Curzon Ashton on
18/8/2007) FL 41+18/14 FLC 1 FAC 3+1
Others 3+2*
Watford *(Signed on 26/1/2010) FL
4+2/1*

BULL Nikki
Born: Hastings, 26 December 1980
Height: 6'2" **Weight:** 12.8
Club Honours: FC '08
International Honours: E: SP-4
After joining Brentford in the summer,
the former Aldershot stalwart was
selected to keep goal for the Bees in
September. Included in his five-game
run was an incident against Southend,

when he appeared to carry the ball over
the line and the assistant referee
signalled a goal. Nikki then suffered a
shoulder injury that kept him out of
action for six months. He returned,
coincidentally, at Southend and went
on as substitute for the last half-hour,
keeping a clean sheet. He will be
hoping for more luck this coming term.
Aldershot T *(From trainee at Queens
Park Rgrs on 27/5/2002) FL 30 FLC 1
FAC 3 Others 1*
Brentford *(Free on 3/8/2009) FL 5+1
FLC 1*

BULLARD James (Jimmy)
Richard
Born: Newham, 23 October 1978
Height: 5'10" **Weight:** 11.10
Club Honours: Div 2 '03
Under the care of California-based
surgeon Richard Steadman, Jimmy
underwent an operation that included
receiving the ligament of a dead man.
Hull's record signing recovered from his
serious knee injury to make his first start
for the Tigers in November. Demanding
the ball in all areas, Jimmy made a
sensational impact, most notably with
two goals against West Ham and a
famous goal celebration after
converting a penalty at Manchester City
as he mimicked manager Phil Brown's
infamous on-pitch rant from the
previous season. Jimmy's inspiring
return was rewarded with the Barclays
'Player of the Month' award. The smiles
of football's ultimate funny man turned
to tears in December as a new knee
injury suffered at Aston Villa meant
another lengthy spell on the sidelines.
He returned in March but, despite
penalty goals against Arsenal and
Fulham, Jimmy could not produce the
miracle and recapture the sparkling
form of earlier in the term.
West Ham U *(£30,000 from Gravesend
& Northfleet on 10/2/1999)*
Peterborough U *(Free on 6/7/2001) FL
62+4/11 FLC 2 FAC 6/1 Others 3/2*
Wigan Ath *(£275,000 on 31/1/2003)
P/FL 144+1/10 FLC 8/1 FAC 1+3*
Fulham *(Signed on 18/5/2006) PL
37+2/6 FLC 1/1 FAC 1*
Hull C *(£5,000,000 on 23/1/2009) PL
13+2/5*

BULLOCK Lee
Born: Stockton, 22 May 1981
Height: 5'9" **Weight:** 11.7
Lee took on a new role for Bradford as
a defensive midfielder, using his height
to protect the back four. Although it
curtailed his attacking options, he grew
in confidence in the position, producing
a lot of unheralded work and allowing
the likes of Michael Flynn alongside him

more freedom to get forward. His
efforts were certainly appreciated by his
colleagues as Lee was voted the
'Players' Player of the Season'.
York C *(From trainee on 29/6/1999) FL
156+15/24 FLC 5+1/1 FAC 10+2/2*
Cardiff C *(£75,000 + on 11/3/2004) FL
12+20/6 FLC 3+1/2 FAC 0+1*
Hartlepool U *(Free on 20/7/2005) FL
30+27/5 FLC 1+2 FAC 2+1 Others 3/1*
Mansfield T *(Loaned on 30/8/2007) FL 5*
Bury *(Loaned on 5/10/2007) FL 8*
Bradford C *(Signed on 1/1/2008) FL
68+8/5 FLC 2 FAC 1 Others 2+1*

Lee Bullock

BUNN Mark John
Born: Southgate, 16 November 1984
Height: 6'1" **Weight:** 12.2
Mark initially joined Sheffield United on
a one-month loan that was later
extended until January while Paddy
Kenny's situation was clarified. After a
promising and consistent start, the
goalkeeper's form dipped and many
thought he was at fault for some goals
conceded from long range. Rested for a
few games, he returned when Ian
Bennett was injured and again after
Carl Ikeme's injury. On his return, he
was much more assured and confident
and in January his loan was extended to
the end of the season. However, in mid-
March he was recalled by Blackburn as
cover for their injuries.
Northampton T *(From trainee on
8/7/2004) FL 90 FLC 7 FAC 7 Others 2*
Blackburn Rov *(£525,000 on
1/9/2008) FAC 1*

Leicester C (Loaned on 16/2/2009) FL 3
Sheffield U (Loaned on 3/8/2009) FL
31+1 FAC 3

BURCH Robert (Rob) Keith
Born: Yeovil, 8 October 1983
Height: 6'2" **Weight:** 12.13
International Honours: E: Yth
An ever-present at Lincoln for the
second successive season, goalkeeper
Rob's impressive 2009-10 campaign
saw him pick up a number of awards,
including the prestigious 'Player of the
Season' trophy as voted for by the
supporters. His ambition to play at a
higher level, however, saw manager
Chris Sutton begin his search for a new
number one at the end of the
campaign.
Tottenham H (From trainee on
3/7/2002)
Barnet (Loaned on 30/1/2007) FL 6
Sheffield Wed (Free on 11/7/2007) FL
2 FLC 1
Lincoln C (Free on 28/7/2008) FL 92
FLC 2 FAC 5 Others 1

BURGESS Benjamin (Ben)
Keiron
Born: Buxton, 9 November 1981
Height: 6'3" **Weight:** 14.4
International Honours: RoI: U21-2;
Yth
The only way to describe the striker -
who scored eight goals – is by saying he
is like Marmite. Blackpool fans either
love him or loathe him. While always an
aerial presence, Ben's running style does
him no favours with the local boo boys,
who need someone to feed off. It was
another productive season for Ben
however, notching up over 30
appearances for the club. Another 'Pool
player whose career has been hit with
injuries but thankfully this campaign he
has been able to manage his long-
standing knee problems to get on the
pitch as much as possible. Was out of
contract at the end of June.
Blackburn Rov (From trainee on
25/11/1998) FL 1+1 FLC 1
Brentford (Loaned on 16/8/2001) FL
43/17 FLC 2 FAC 2/1 Others 4

Stockport Co (£450,000 on 5/8/2002)
FL 17+2/4 FLC 0+1 FAC 1+1/2 Others 2
Oldham Ath (Loaned on 10/1/2003) FL
6+1
Hull C (£100,000 on 27/3/2003) FL
54+16/24 FLC 3/1 FAC 1
Blackpool (£25,000 on 31/8/2006) FL
83+43/23 FLC 3+1/3 FAC 2+3/1 Others
0+5/2

BURKE Christopher (Chris)
Born: Glasgow, 2 December 1983
Height: 5'9" **Weight:** 10.10
Club Honours: SPD '05; SLC '08
International Honours: S: 2; B-1;
U21-3
Lively, hard-working Cardiff winger who
loves to take on defenders, but is also
prepared to get back and defend. Chris
scored ten goals in his first full
Championship season, having joined
the Bluebirds on a free from Glasgow
Rangers. Cardiff needed him after
Wayne Routledge, on loan from Aston
Villa, left to sign for Queens Park
Rangers and he is under contract until
the summer of 2011. Energetic and
enthusiastic, he demands that the ball is
played to his feet. Appeared in all but
two Championship matches for City
and started in all three play-off
matches. Along with most of his team-
mates, Chris disappointed in the
Wembley play-off final and was
replaced by Ross McCormack just
before the hour mark.
Glasgow Rgrs (From juniors on
19/3/2002) SL 64+32/11 SLC 6+1/1 SC
7+2/2 Others 10+9
Cardiff C (Free on 9/1/2009) FL
46+12/10 FLC 2 FAC 4+1/1 Others 3

BURN Daniel (Dan) Johnson
Born: Blyth, 9th May 1992
Height: 6'6" **Weight:** 13.0
This tall young central defender, who
came through the youth ranks at
Darlington, made his debut at Torquay
in December, coming on after 19
minutes for the injured Mark Bower. He
faced a torrid 70 minutes as the
Quakers struggled and slumped to a 5-
0 defeat. Dan made his full debut,
strangely against Torquay at home, in
early March and showed good
composure on the ball and will be one
to watch in the future.
Darlington (Trainee) FL 2+2

BURNELL Joseph (Joe)
Michael
Born: Bristol, 10 October 1980
Height: 5'10" **Weight:** 11.1
Club Honours: AMC '03
Niggling injuries meant Exeter's utility
man Joe found appearances hard to
come by as the Grecians struggled in

Rob Burch

the bottom half of League One for the majority of the season but he did himself justice when he was called into action. Was out of contract in the summer.
Bristol C *(From trainee on 24/7/1999)* *FL 117+14/1 FLC 3+2 FAC 4+3 Others 17+1/2*
Wycombe W *(Free on 7/7/2004) FL 50+7 FLC 2 FAC 1/1 Others 1+1*
Northampton T *(Free on 4/8/2006) FL 50+7/1 FLC 2 FAC 5+2/1 Others 1 (Freed during 2008 close season)*
Exeter C *(Free from Oxford U on 10/7/2009) FL 4+4*

BURNS Michael John
Born: Huyton, 4 October 1988
Height: 5'10" **Weight:** 11.7
Club Honours: FAYC '07
Midfielder Michael made only one senior appearance for Carlisle when he featured in the Johnstone's Paint Trophy game at Morecambe. He went to Stafford Rangers on loan in January and has since been released by Carlisle. Still young, and possessing good passing skills, he will hope to get back into the League before too long.
Bolton W *(From trainee at Liverpool on 13/7/2007)*
Carlisle U *(Free on 23/1/2009) FL 0+1 Others 1*

BURTON Deon John
Born: Reading, 25 October 1976
Height: 5'9" **Weight:** 11.9
Club Honours: Div 1 '03
International Honours: Jamaica: 56
Deon played all season with the discomfort of a problematic hernia but it did not stop him finishing as Charlton's top scorer with 14 goals. Six of them came from the penalty spot, including two in the 4-4 draw with Millwall at the Valley. Deon is strong and a good target man, even though he is not the tallest of strikers. He was used as a sole striker in the early part of the season but was later partnered up front, usually by Dave Mooney. Deon scored some great goals including an audacious chip at Hartlepool and another one at Leyton Orient the following week. Was out of contract at the end of June.
Portsmouth *(From trainee on 15/2/1994) FL 42+20/10 FLC 3+2/2 FAC 0+2/1*
Cardiff C *(Loaned on 24/12/1996) FL 5/2 Others 1*
Derby Co *(£1,000,000 + on 9/8/1997) P/FL 78+47/25 FLC 6+2/3 FAC 9+1/3*
Barnsley *(Loaned on 14/12/1998) FL 3*
Stoke C *(Loaned on 21/2/2002) FL 11+1/2 Others 2+1/2*
Portsmouth *(Loaned on 9/8/2002) FL 6/3*

Portsmouth *(£75,000 + on 12/12/2002) P/FL 5+5/1 FAC 1+1*
Walsall *(Loaned on 12/9/2003) FL 2+1 FLC 1*
Swindon T *(Loaned on 17/10/2003) FL 4/1*
Brentford *(Free on 4/8/2004) FL 38+2/10 FLC 1 FAC 7 Others 2*
Rotherham U *(Free on 1/8/2005) FL 24/12 FLC 2/1 FAC 1/1*
Sheffield Wed *(£100,000 on 2/1/2006) FL 82+34/23 FLC 3+1/2 FAC 2+2*
Charlton Ath *(Signed on 27/11/2008) FL 47+12/18 FLC 0+1 FAC 3+1 Others 2+1/1*

BUTCHER Calum James
Born: Leigh-on-Sea, 26 February 1991
Height: 6'0" **Weight:** 12.13
Callum had a brief loan spell at Barnet in December, joining on a one-month deal from North London neighbours Tottenham. He featured in three League games and one FA Cup outing for the Bees, but was never on the winning side, joining during a poor spell in the club's season. He returned to Spurs after the Boxing Day defeat at Aldershot.
Tottenham H *(From trainee on 18/3/2009)*
Barnet *(Loaned on 26/11/2009) FL 3 FAC 1*

BUTCHER Richard Tony
Born: Peterborough, 22 January 1981
Height: 6'0" **Weight:** 11.9
Richard returned to Lincoln for a third spell in the summer, but after starting the season as a regular under Peter Jackson the arrival of Chris Sutton as manager saw the midfielder find his first team chances limited. In February he went on loan to Macclesfield when their midfield had been depleted by injury and made an immediate impact when scoring in his first game, the defeat at Bury. He then performed strongly in each of his eight appearances before going back to his parent club. His last last game in a City shirt came as a substitute against the Silkmen on the final day of the season.
Rushden & Diamonds *(From trainee at Northampton T on 26/11/1999. Freed on 1/10/2001)*
Lincoln C *(Free from Kettering T on 19/11/2002) FL 95+9/11 FLC 3 FAC 3 Others 1*
Oldham Ath *(Free on 4/7/2005) FL 32+4/4 FAC 3*
Lincoln C *(Loaned on 6/10/2005) FL 4/1*
Peterborough U *(Signed on 28/6/2006) FL 35+8/4 FLC 2 FAC 4/1 Others 2*
Notts Co *(Signed on 23/7/2007) FL*

75+5/18 FLC 3 FAC 3+1/1 Others 1/1
Lincoln C *(Free on 2/7/2009) FL 10+5 FLC 1*
Macclesfield T *(Loaned on 9/2/2010) FL 8/2*

BUTLER Andrew (Andy) Peter
Born: Doncaster, 4 November 1983
Height: 6'0" **Weight:** 13.6
Andy started the season for Huddersfield where he left off in the previous campaign, producing some solid and dependable displays at centre-back as he formed a new partnership with Peter Clarke at the heart of the defence. A good, strong tackler and header of the ball, Andy showed his ability to be a key member of the squad, but after a spell on the substitutes' bench he joined Blackpool on loan with the prospect of gaining first team football. Brought into the Blackpool side in January after injury problems at the back, he played seven games, including a credible 1-1 draw away at Cardiff, before returning to Huddersfield.
Scunthorpe U *(From trainee on 2/7/2003) FL 123+12/16 FLC 3+1 FAC 10 Others 5*
Grimsby T *(Loaned on 6/10/2006) FL 4 Others 1*
Huddersfield T *(Free on 8/7/2008) FL 52+1/4 FLC 2 FAC 1 Others 1+1*
Blackpool *(Loaned on 7/1/2010) FL 4+3*

BUTLER Thomas (Tommy) Anthony
Born: Dublin, 25 April 1981
Height: 5'8" **Weight:** 10.8
Club Honours: Div 1 '08
International Honours: RoI: 2; U21-15; Yth
The winger missed the start of Swansea's season following a hernia operation but after returning to fitness became a regular inclusion in the first team, either from the bench or in the starting line-up. By April, Tommy had made enough appearances to earn himself a further one-year extension to his playing contract with the Swans.
Sunderland *(From trainee on 25/6/1998) P/FL 16+15 FLC 1+3 FAC 0+1*
Darlington *(Loaned on 13/10/2000) FL 8 FAC 2*
Dunfermline Ath *(Free on 10/9/2004) SL 6+6 SLC 2*
Hartlepool U *(Free on 24/3/2005) FL 31+6/2 FLC 2 FAC 2/1 Others 2+1*
Swansea C *(£50,000 on 4/8/2006) FL 75+51/9 FLC 1+1 FAC 6+3/2 Others 4+3*

BUTT Nicholas (Nicky)

Born: Manchester, 21 January 1975
Height: 5'10" **Weight:** 11.3
Club Honours: FAYC '92; CS '96, '97, '03; PL '96, '97, '99, '00, 01, '03; FAC '96, '04; UEFACL '99; Ch '10
International Honours: E: 39; U21-7; Yth; Sch

Appointed Newcastle club captain for his first ever season outside the top flight, midfield general Nicky had a frustrating time with injuries, beginning when he suffered a partial dislocation of a thumb in a pre-season friendly against Darlington. His first League game came as a substitute in the win at Cardiff in September, but subsequent calf and thigh injuries limited his appearances. Coming on as a substitute during the final home game against Ipswich, he won the penalty that helped to secure the unbeaten record at St James' Park. He was presented with the Championship trophy at the end of the match to bring down the curtain on a successful few years at Newcastle since he has said he will be moving on in the summer.
Manchester U *(From trainee on 29/1/1993) PL 210+60/21 FLC 7+1 FAC 23+6/1 Others 67+13/4*
Newcastle U *(£2,500,000 on 30/7/2004) P/FL 121+13/5 FLC 6+2 FAC 10 Others 15+4*
Birmingham C *(Loaned on 4/8/2005) PL 22+2/3 FLC 3 FAC 2*

BUTTERFIELD Daniel (Danny) Paul

Born: Boston, 21 November 1979
Height: 5'10" **Weight:** 11.10
Club Honours: AMC '98
International Honours: E: Yth

It was a season to remember for Danny who, as well as playing in his usual right-back position, also enjoyed games at centre-back and in midfield for Crystal Palace before turning out as a striker for the FA Cup game against Wolverhampton in January. His memorable performance up front netted him a career first hat-trick and a club record, as his three goals in seven minutes became the quickest hat-trick scored in the history of Palace. Their longest-serving player, signed in 2002, has now played over 250 games in defence for the club. Competing with the promising Nathaniel Clyne for the right-back spot, Danny's experience was the deciding factor late in the season, as he kept his place once the promising Palace youngster had returned from injury. One of several Palace players out of contract.
Grimsby T *(From trainee on 7/8/1997) FL 100+24/3 FLC 13+1 FAC 5+2 Others 1+1/1*

Crystal Palace *(Free on 7/8/2002) P/FL 210+22/6 FLC 15+1 FAC 13+2/3 Others 5+1/1*
Charlton Ath *(Loaned on 2/3/2009) FL 12*

BUTTERFIELD Jacob Luke

Born: Bradford, 10 June 1990
Height: 5'11" **Weight:** 12.3
Jacob began the season in Barnsley's starting team and scored his first League goal in the local derby draw at Sheffield Wednesday on the opening day. Jacob saw more time on the pitch during the season and benefited greatly from it. It was shown when coming on as a half-time substitute against Middlesbrough when his performance changed a deficit at the interval into a 2-1 win. A hard-working midfield player who shows a very good touch, is able to pick a pass and had an eye for a shot. He was rewarded with a new two-year contract at the end of the season.
Barnsley *(From trainee on 2/10/2007) FL 11+15/1 FLC 2+3 FAC 1+2*

BUTTON David Robert Edmund

Born: Stevenage, 27 February 1989
Height: 6'3" **Weight:** 13.1
International Honours: E: Yth
Having been recalled from Crewe where he was on loan, the 21-year-old 'keeper played for the last eight minutes of Tottenham's Carling Cup game at Doncaster before returning to Gresty Road. After returning to Spurs he next went on loan to Shrewsbury, keeping a clean sheet in the early December home win against Rotherham on his debut. His confident handling of crosses and command of the 18-yard box with good kicking saw him make a number of excellent performances, notably when saving a penalty in a 2-2 draw with Macclesfield and a string of top class saves in the 1-1 draw at Burton. His confidence clearly grew in his 26 games and he should have a good career ahead of him.
Tottenham H *(From trainee on 3/3/2006) FLC 0+1*
Bournemouth *(Loaned on 6/3/2009) FL 4*
Dagenham & Redbridge *(Loaned on 16/4/2009) FL 3*
Crewe Alex *(Loaned on 22/7/2009) FL 3*
Crewe Alex *(Loaned on 1/9/2009) FL 7*
Shrewsbury T *(Loaned on 20/11/2009) FL 26*

BUXTON Jake Fred

Born: Sutton-in-Ashfield, 4 March 1985
Height: 5'11" **Weight:** 13.0
Club Honours: FC '09
When Jake dropped out of the League with Mansfield, Nigel Clough was both

surprised and delighted to sign the central defender for Burton. Jake played a big part in Burton's promotion from the Blue Square Premier and was their 'Player of the Year'. Clough was keen enough to sign Jake for Derby in the summer as a squad player but injuries to central defenders meant that he had earlier Championship experience than he expected. He began the season in the first team but his early progress was interrupted by a hernia operation. Having recovered, he had a good run in the side from December onwards, much of it in partnership with Shaun Barker. In the latter stages, he gave way to Russell Anderson but had done enough to be offered a second year. There are no frills on Jake but he can be relied upon to put his body in the way to block shots. As Clough knew, Jake's attitude is right and he is a useful man to have in the squad.
Mansfield T *(From juniors on 21/10/2002) FL 144+7/5 FLC 5 FAC 11+1 Others 5+1 (Freed during 2008 close season)*
Derby Co *(Free from Burton A on 2/7/2009) FL 19/1 FLC 1 FAC 4*

BUXTON Lewis Edward

Born: Newport, Isle of Wight, 10 December 1983
Height: 6'1" **Weight:** 13.10
Lewis had mixed season. The versatile Sheffield Wednesday defender started out as a regular in the side at right-back. He played in a back four and looked to be making the position his own. However, a few errors crept into his game and he came under pressure for his place in the side. He was then injured and, when finally fit, he could not regain his place. For the sake of his Hillsborough career, he could really do with establishing himself in one position and sticking to it. His ability to play in central defence and both full-back positions means he is seen as a utility defender rather than a specialist.
Portsmouth *(From trainee on 9/4/2001) FL 27+3*
Exeter C *(Loaned on 21/10/2002) FL 4 Others 2*
Bournemouth *(Loaned on 10/1/2003) FL 15+2 FAC 1*
Bournemouth *(Loaned on 30/10/2003) FL 24+2 FAC 1+1*
Stoke C *(Free on 24/12/2004) P/FL 40+13/1 FLC 2+1 FAC 4*
Sheffield Wed *(Signed on 17/10/2008) FL 60/1 FAC 1+1*

BUZSAKY Akos

Born: Budapest, Hungary, 7 May 1982
Height: 5'11" **Weight:** 11.9
International Honours: Hungary: 19; U21

Recovered from the previous season's injury problems to play a key role in the Queens Park Rangers' side, Akos featured in over 40 games and despite never quite being able to recapture his blistering best, still managed to score 12 goals in all competitions to finish as Rangers' second top scorer behind Jay Simpson. Arguably the purest footballer at the club, Akos played in wide positions, central midfield and in a supporting front role over the season. He represented Hungary in six World Cup qualifiers, scoring the only goal in their 1-0 win over Denmark.
Plymouth Arg (£25,000 from FC Porto, Portugal, ex MTK Hungaria, on 21/1/2005) FL 65+31/8 FLC 4+1/1 FAC 4
Queens Park Rgrs (£500,000 on 30/10/2007) FL 58+19/21 FLC 5 FAC 3/1

BYFIELD Darren
Born: Sutton Coldfield, 29 September 1976
Height: 5'11" **Weight:** 11.11
International Honours: Jamaica: 7
Freed by Doncaster in the summer, the striker spent a second spell at Boundary Park with Oldham under new manager Dave Penney before moving on to Join Walsall. The move saw Darren returning to the club where he first tasted success nine years before, signing initially until the end of January before Walsall took up the option of signing him for a further 18 months. Popular with supporters, pace and close control are his main threats. Although he was caught offside too many times and failed to convert many of his one-on-one duels with opposing goalkeepers he showed his quality when leaving defenders in his wake.
Aston Villa (From trainee on 14/2/1994) PL 1+6 FLC 1 FAC 0+1 Others 1
Preston NE (Loaned on 6/11/1998) FL 3+2/1 Others 1
Northampton T (Loaned on 13/8/1999) FL 6/1 FLC 1/1
Cambridge U (Loaned on 17/9/1999) FL 3+1
Blackpool (Loaned on 6/3/2000) FL 3
Walsall (Free on 21/6/2000) FL 45+32/13 FLC 2+3/2 FAC 4+2/1 Others 2+2/1
Rotherham U (£50,000 on 27/3/2002) FL 53+15/22 FLC 3+1/1 FAC 2
Sunderland (Signed on 6/2/2004) FL 8+9/5
Gillingham (Free on 23/7/2004) FL 54+13/19 FLC 2/1 FAC 1 Others 1
Millwall (Free on 7/7/2006) FL 28+3/16 FAC 3+1 Others 1
Bristol C (£100,000 on 30/8/2007) FL 17+16/8 FAC 1 Others 0+1
Doncaster Rov (Free on 30/7/2008) FL 3+12 FAC 0+1
Oldham Ath (Loaned on 14/11/2008) FL 8/1
Oldham Ath (Free on 7/8/2009) FL 0+3 FLC 1
Walsall (Free on 28/8/2009) FL 31+6/10 FAC 2 Others 1

BYRNE Clifford (Cliff)
Born: Dublin, 27 April 1982
Height: 6'0" **Weight:** 12.12
Club Honours: Div 1 '07
International Honours: RoI: U21-10; Yth
Dependable right-back Cliff took a while to adjust to Scunthorpe's step back up into the Championship and was out of favour in September, losing his place and the captaincy. Returned at the end of the month and was first choice for the rest of the campaign with his strong-tackling, committed displays. Filled in at centre-half at the turn of the year, a move that coincided with his reclaiming the captain's armband. Unfortunately, his season was blighted by three red cards in the space of 11 League games that saw him serve a total of eight matches in suspensions. Having led his team to Championship survival, he quickly agreed a new two-year contract.
Sunderland (From trainee on 27/5/1999)
Scunthorpe U (Loaned on 21/11/2002) FL 13 FAC 3
Scunthorpe U (Free on 2/7/2003) FL 208+20/7 FLC 8 FAC 20+2 Others 20

Akos Buzsaky

BYRNE Richard (Richie)
Born: Dublin, 24 September 1980
Height: 6'1" **Weight:** 12.4
International Honours: RoI: B-1
A strong and experienced central
defender who is good in the air, Richie
joined Darlington in February but had
the misfortune to score an own goal in
the 3-2 defeat by Chesterfield on his
home debut. Alas the following game
at Bradford saw him leave the field
injured and he appeared in only two
further games as a substitute. Was out
of contract at the end of June.
Dunfermline Ath *(Signed from
Shamrock Rov on 13/9/2003) SL 15+4
SLC 1+1 SC 4+1/1 Others 1*
Aberdeen *(£50,000 on 31/1/2005) SL
44+6/1 SLC 3 SC4/1 Others 2*
Oldham Ath *(Free on 5/9/2008) FL 3+1*
Inverness CT *(Free on 14/1/2009)*
St Johnstone *(Loaned on 19/2/2009)
SL 5*
Darlington *(Free on 1/2/2010) FL 2+2*

BYWATER Stephen Michael
Born: Manchester, 7 June 1981
Height: 6'3" **Weight:** 13.2
Club Honours: FAYC '99
International Honours: E: U21-6; Yth
Nigel Clough identified Stephen as his
senior goalkeeper soon after taking
over as Derby manager during the
previous season and his position was
further strengthened when Roy Carroll
moved to OB Odense. The added
confidence seemed to spur on Stephen,
who had an excellent season. He made
a number of outstanding saves, just as
well as Derby were hardly prolific at the
other end. Equally impressive was his
increased command of the penalty area.
He dealt with crosses and let his
defenders know what was expected,
vital as a high crop of injuries meant
frequent changes to the back four.
Stephen was on target for a full house
of appearances until he hurt his back at
Reading in March. As his replacement,
Saul Deeney, was sent off in the same
game, Derby had to bring in David
Martin from Liverpool on one of the
few loans to justify the term emergency.
With Derby safe in the Championship,
Stephen also missed the last two games
with a rib injury.
Rochdale *(Trainee) Others 1*
West Ham U *(£300,000 + on
7/8/1998) P/FL 57+2 FAC 5 Others 3+1*
Wycombe W *(Loaned on 23/9/1999) FL 2*
Hull C *(Loaned on 23/11/1999) FL 4*
Coventry C *(Loaned on 3/8/2005) FL
14*
Derby Co *(Signed on 12/8/2006) P/FL
127+1 FLC 2 FAC 10 Others 3*
Ipswich T *(Loaned on 31/1/2008) FL 17*

Stephen Bywater

C

CADOGAN Kieron James Nathan
Born: Tooting, 3 August 1990
Height: 6'4" **Weight:** 12.7
Young Kieron was outstanding in the reserves for Crystal Palace in the early part of the season with ten goals in eight matches, and as a result went on loan for a month in November at Burton, playing three times for them in League and FA Cup matches. Back at Selhurst Park, the young winger scored a further eight goals for the reserves and was an unused substitute for a number of first team games. Kieron's form was rewarded with a new contract at the end of the season.
Crystal Palace (From trainee on 14/8/2008) FL 0+4/1
Burton A (Loaned on 21/11/2009) FL 2 FAC 1

CAHILL Gary James
Born: Dronfield, 19 December 1985
Height: 6'2" **Weight:** 12.6

International Honours: E: U21-3; Yth
Taking his fine displays from the previous campaign into the initial stages of last season, Gary began 2009-10 in blistering form for Bolton. He added scoring to his ever-growing list of abilities, notching vital strikes in the wins against Portsmouth and Everton before hitting a great goal in the 3-3 draw with Manchester City in December. His status as one of the most promising centre-halves in the League also grew as the season progressed – a string of fine displays led to strong rumours of an England call and continued links to the Premiership's elite clubs. However, a blood clot in his arm led to a period of inactivity, missing his first game of the season against Fulham in February and not returning until the 4-0 defeat by Manchester United in March. The injury seemed to have taken its toll on Gary as his end-of-season performances fell a little short of his usual standards. Despite this, Gary is still considered to be Bolton's most prized asset and it is hoped that he will continue to ply his trade at the Reebok.
Aston Villa (From trainee on 23/12/2003) PL 25+3/1 FLC 2 FAC 1

Gary Cahill

Burnley (Loaned on 9/11/2004) FL 27/1 FLC 1 FAC 4
Sheffield U (Loaned on 20/9/2007) FL 16/2
Bolton W (£4,500,000 on 30/1/2008) PL 75/8 FLC 4/1 FAC 2/1 Others 4

CAHILL Timothy (Tim) Joel
Born: Sydney, Australia, 6 December 1979
Height: 5'10" **Weight:** 10.11
Club Honours: Div 2 '01
International Honours: Australia: 39; W Samoa: Yth
The Australian is quite simply an Everton idol and in another productive campaign continued to score priceless goals, often away from home. The midfielder's main gift is using his prodigious aerial ability after finding space in the opposition penalty area. During the course of the season, he completed a run of scoring 11 successive headed goals in the Premier League. Deployed as an attacking midfielder for most of the campaign, personal highlights included late winners at Wigan and Blackburn and netting for a second successive season at Manchester City, to complete a hat-trick of headed goals at Eastlands. The consummate Blue also makes no secret of his love for the club off the pitch and captained the side in the absence of Phil Neville, as well as reaching 50 goals and 200 games for the Toffees. The 29-year-old played a major role in ensuring Australia qualified for the World Cup finals for the second successive time with a series of vital goals.
Millwall (Signed from Sydney U, Australia on 31/7/1997) FL 212+5/52 FLC 9+1/1 FAC 10+2/3 Others 10+1/1
Everton (£2,000,000 on 29/7/2004) PL 161+3/45 FLC 8+4/3 FAC 13+1/4 Others 19/4

CAIN Ashley Thomas
Born: Nuneaton, 27 September 1990
Height: 6'2" **Weight:** 12.6
A product of Coventry's Academy, the pacy right-sided flank player made his full debut in the Carling Cup defeat at home to Hartlepool and later made two substitute appearances in away League games. Ashley was on the Coventry bench regularly in the first half of the season before being loaned out, first to Luton in November, where he made one substitute appearance, and later in March to Oxford, where he started one game. Bad weather and niggling injuries limited his opportunities. Coventry released Ashley in April and he had a trial with Port Vale before the end of the season.
Coventry C (From trainee on 29/6/2009) FL 0+7 FLC 1

CAIRNEY Thomas (Tom)
Born: Nottingham, 20 January 1991
Height: 6'0" **Weight:** 11.5
International Honours: S: Yth
In an otherwise miserable season at the KC Stadium, Tom's meteoric progress was the shining light for Hull. He made his senior bow against Tottenham in the pre-season Barclays Asia Trophy in Beijing. A domestic debut followed against Southend and, with an audacious chip, Tom became the first player to progress through the ranks and score for Hull since Gary Bradshaw in March 2002. His Premier League debut came 11 days after his 19th birthday against Wolverhampton. Although competing against some of the game's greatest talents, his composure on the ball in central midfield belied his tender years. Strongly favouring his left foot, Tom added to his goals account with another fine effort at Everton - the club's 'Goal of the Season'. Qualifying for Scotland through his father, his Hull contract was extended to 2013 in March.
Hull C (From trainee on 20/6/2009) PL 10+1/1 FLC 2/1 FAC 1

CALDERON Inigo
Born: Vitoria, Spain, 4 January 1982
Height: 5'10" **Weight:** 12.2
Released by Spanish side Alaves, Inigo had an unsuccessful trial with Gillingham but arrived at Brighton in January and became an instant hit. Slotting into the right-back berth with ease, he played a major role in the defensive improvement in the New Year by mixing enthusiasm, skill and tough-tackling in equal measure. A typical swashbuckling run at Charlton ended with his only goal of the season but a serious hip injury at Southend in April ended his campaign abruptly. Although he was a revelation, bringing a breath of fresh air to the Withdean Stadium, Inigo failed to accept the offer of a contract.
Brighton & Hove A (Free from Deportivo Alaves, Spain, ex Deportivo Alaves, Alicante CF, on 7/1/2010) FL 19/1 FAC 1

CALDWELL Gary
Born: Stirling, 12 April 1982
Height: 5'11" **Weight:** 12.0
Club Honours: SPD '07, '08; SC '07; SLC '09
International Honours: S: 37; B-4; U21-19; Yth; Sch
The former Glasgow Celtic captain was recruited by Wigan on a four-and-a-half year contract in January. A centre-half in the classic mould, Gary was close to

ever-present and would have been closer but for a suspension resulting from a harsh red card. His leadership qualities, reading of the game and precise timing in the tackle make the Scottish international a rock at the heart of defence. A regular for his country he made his club debut at Wolverhampton, becoming a towering presence at the heart of the defence and forming an effective partnership with Titus Bramble. His size and power made him a major scoring threat, particularly from set pieces. His first goal came at Blackburn, closely followed by a goal in the home game against Aston Villa. His younger brother Steve played in the Premier League with Burnley.
Newcastle U (From trainee on 19/4/1999)
Darlington (Loaned on 20/11/2001) FL 4
Hibernian (Loaned on 31/1/2002) SL 10+1 SLC 1
Coventry C (Loaned on 3/7/2002) FL 36 FLC 3 FAC 2
Derby Co (Loaned on 8/8/2003) FL 6+3 FLC 1
Hibernian (Free on 30/1/2004) SL 87+1/5 SLC 6 SC 8/2 Others 2+1
Glasgow Celtic (Signed on 1/7/2006) SL 105+1/5 SLC 8 SC 7+1/2 Others 27+1
Wigan Ath (Signed on 13/1/2010) PL 16/2 FAC 1

CALDWELL Stephen (Steve)
Born: Stirling, 12 September 1980
Height: 6'0" **Weight:** 11.5
Club Honours: Ch '05
International Honours: S: 10; B-3; U21-4; Yth
It was a desperately disappointing season for Burnley skipper Steve, an abdominal injury picked up on pre-season Scotland duty keeping him out for the first two months and then laying him low again after a return to the side that included what was almost the winning goal at home to Aston Villa and a very harsh red card at West Ham a week later. After another three months on the sidelines, he returned at the end of the campaign. Central defence was a major problem area for Burnley in the Premier League and whether Steve, always a solid presence at the back, would have improved matters will never be known. At the end of the season, his contract was not renewed.
Newcastle U (From trainee on 30/10/1997) PL 20+8/1 FLC 3/1 Others 1+5
Blackpool (Loaned on 12/10/2001) FL 6 Others 1/1

Bradford C (Loaned on 7/12/2001) FL 9
Leeds U (Loaned on 2/2/2004) PL 13/1
Sunderland (Free on 19/7/2004) P/FL 75+1/4 FLC 4/1 FAC 1
Burnley (£400,000 on 31/1/2007) P/FL 99+5/5 FLC 7 FAC 5 Others 3

CAMARA Henri
Born: Dakar, Senegal, 10 May 1977
Height: 5'9" **Weight:** 10.8
International Honours: Senegal: 89
After a trial with Sheffield United, free agent Henri was offered a contract, which initially fell through, but eventually he signed to the end of the season. Because of fitness issues he initially played as a substitute and when in the starting line-up he was usually subbed. However his pace, control and vision caused problems for the opposition defences and he produced fine finishing when scoring against Bristol City. Injury at Doncaster effectively ended his season with eight games to go, although he did make two short appearances in subsequent games.
Wolverhampton W (Free from Sedan, France, ex Neuchatel Xamax, Strasbourg, Grasshoper Zurich, on 6/8/2003) PL 29+1/7 FLC 2
Glasgow Celtic (Loaned on 2/8/2004) SL 12+6/8 SLC 0+1 SC 0+1 Others 4+2
Southampton (Loaned on 31/1/2005) PL 10+3/4 FAC 2+1/2
Wigan Ath (£3,000,000 on 10/8/2005) PL 46+23/20 FLC 4+3/3 FAC 1/1
West Ham U (Loaned on 31/8/2007) PL 3+7
Stoke C (Loaned on 2/2/2009) PL 0+4
Sheffield U (Free on 22/10/2009) FL 9+14/4 FAC 2

CAMARA Mohamed (Mo)
Born: Conakry, Guinea, 25 June 1975
Height: 5'11" **Weight:** 11.9
Club Honours: SPD '06; SLC '06
International Honours: Guinea: 79
The veteran left-back signed for Torquay after his release by St Mirren. Mo showed glimpses of quality but a lack of match fitness acted against him. He was replaced at half-time in his second appearance and never again featured in the squad.
Wolverhampton W (Signed from Le Havre, France, ex AS Beauvais, Troyes, OSC Lille, on 11/8/2000) FL 27+18 FLC 2+1 FAC 1+1 Others 2
Burnley (Free on 18/7/2003) FL 90 FLC 7/1 FAC 6+1
Glasgow Celtic (Free on 22/6/2005) SL 19 SLC 3 Others 2
Derby Co (Free on 16/8/2006) P/FL 21 FLC 4/1 FAC 4
Norwich C (Loaned on 20/11/2007) FL 20+1 FAC 1+1

Blackpool *(Loaned on 5/8/2008) FL 14*
St Mirren *(Free on 2/2/2009) SL 10 SLC 1 SC 2*
Torquay U *(Free on 11/2/2010) FL 2*

CAMERON Nathan Benjamin
Born: Birmingham, 21 November 1991
Height: 6'2" **Weight:** 12.0
A product of Coventry's Academy, the youngster made a brief substitute appearance against Hartlepool in the Carling Cup. Two bench-warming appearances came soon afterwards and then he disappeared from view. In April, after being offered a professional contract by Coventry, he went on loan to Nuneaton Town.
Coventry C *(Trainee) FLC 0+1*

CAMP Lee Michael John
Born: Derby, 22 August 1984
Height: 5'11" **Weight:** 11.11
International Honours: E: U21-5; Yth
Following the previous season's loan from Queens Park Rangers, the goalkeeper was instantly installed as number one with Nottingham Forest, immediately showing the assurance that was to last all the way. Lee was behind and helping to organise one of the tightest defences in the Championship. His consistent performances resulted in him being named Forest 'Player of the Year'. He was also voted in as goalkeeper for the PFA 'Championship Team of the Year' and captained Forest towards the end of the season after injury to Paul McKenna.
Derby Co *(From trainee on 16/7/2002) FL 88+1 FLC 2 FAC 4 Others 2*
Queens Park Rgrs *(Loaned on 12/3/2004) FL 12*
Norwich C *(Loaned on 8/9/2006) FL 3*
Queens Park Rgrs *(Loaned on 19/2/2007) FL 11*
Queens Park Rgrs *(£300,000 on 7/8/2007) FL 50 FLC 2 FAC 1*
Nottingham F *(Loaned on 20/10/2008) FL 15*
Nottingham F *(Signed on 3/7/2009) FL 45 FAC 2 Others 2*

CAMPBELL Dudley (DJ)
Junior
Born: Hammersmith, 12 November 1981
Height: 5'10" **Weight:** 11.0
The quick and powerful Leicester striker had a frustrating time at the Walkers Stadium, enjoying only a handful of outings before Nigel Pearson allowed him to join up with both Derby and Blackpool on loan during the season. At Derby, DJ made a dramatic entrance as a substitute when scoring an equaliser deep into stoppage time to earn a point off West Bromwich at Pride Park. He also scored twice in the away win over Peterborough, an important result at the time, before moving on to Blackpool where he had been successful in 2008-09. DJ was clearly at home in Blackpool, scoring over a goal every two games. This time it was to help the Seasiders secure a play-off spot, with braces in crucial games at Scunthorpe and against Nottingham Forest. His pace makes him difficult to stay tight

Lee Camp

73

to, but also a threat when defenders back off him. When presented with chances, DJ invariably snaps them up; this, and his total professionalism were on show away at Peterborough when he still managed to pounce to score the only goal of the game following trouble off the field the day before the game. He will always be remembered by Blackpool supporters as the man who scored a hat-trick in the 4-3 play-off semi-final win over Cardiff that set the club on a path to the Premier League.

Brentford *(Signed from Yeading, ex Stevenage Borough, on 7/6/2005) FL 13+10/9 FLC 1 FAC 4/3*

Birmingham C *(£500,000 on 31/1/2006) P/FL 19+24/9 FLC 2+2/1 FAC 3/2*

Leicester C *(£2,100,000 on 7/8/2007) FL 19+19/4 FLC 3+3/1 FAC 0+1 Others 0+1*

Blackpool *(Loaned on 8/1/2009) FL 20/9*

Derby Co *(Loaned on 26/11/2009) FL 6+2/3*

Blackpool *(Loaned on 1/2/2010) FL 14+1/8 Others 3/3*

CAMPBELL Fraizer Lee

Born: Huddersfield, 13 September 1987
Height: 5'11" **Weight:** 12.4
International Honours: E: U21-14; Yth

Steve Bruce's first signing claimed Sunderland's number nine shirt before the acquisition of Darren Bent but was to make most of his starts on the right of midfield. Fraizer's appetite for hard work won him friends but he had to wait until March for his first League goal which, when it came, was the fastest in the Premier League thus far in the season. Bolton were the opposition, his goal adding to three previous Cup strikes all against teams beginning with the letter B. It sparked a purple patch for Fraizer, whose three further Premier League goals came in his next seven games. He ended the season strongly by starting the final 13 games, comfortably doubling the number of League starts he made prior to that run.

Manchester U *(From trainee on 29/3/2006) PL 1+1 FLC 0+1 Others 0+1*

Hull C *(Loaned on 18/10/2007) FL 32+2/15 Others 3*

Tottenham H *(Loaned on 1/9/2008) PL 1+9/1 FLC 3+1/2 FAC 0+1 Others 5+2*

Sunderland *(£3,500,000 on 11/7/2009) PL 19+12/4 FLC 3/1 FAC 1+1/2*

CAMPBELL Stuart Pearson

Born: Corby, 9 December 1977
Height: 5'10" **Weight:** 10.8

Club Honours: FLC '97, '00
International Honours: S: U21-14

Captain and central midfielder, Stuart was a consistent performer, always featuring on manager Paul Trollope's team-sheets and the only ever-present. Stuart passed 200 League appearances for the Pirates and was always able to create scoring opportunities from his accurate dead-ball crosses. Stuart almost scored his first goal since the 2007 League Two play-off semi-final in a seven goal thriller against Southend at the Memorial Stadium, his shot hitting an opponent on the goal line to secure an injury time 4-3 win. After six seasons at Rovers, the popular and hard-working midfielder signed a new two-year deal. Stuart was the supporters' 'Player of the Season'.

Leicester C *(From trainee on 4/7/1996) PL 12+25 FLC 2+5 FAC 3+3*

Birmingham C *(Loaned on 23/3/2000) FL 0+2*

Grimsby T *(£200,000 on 15/9/2000) FL 154+1/12 FLC 6/1 FAC 7 Others 0+1*

Bristol Rov *(Free on 5/7/2004) FL 221+19/2 FLC 9 FAC 18+1 Others 18+1/1*

CAMPBELL Sulzeer (Sol) Jeremiah

Born: Plaistow, 18 September 1974
Height: 6'2" **Weight:** 14.1
Club Honours: FLC '99; PL '02, '04; FAC '02, '05, '08; CS '02
International Honours: E: 73; B-2; U21-11; Yth (UEFA-U18 '93)

Out of contract with Portsmouth in the summer, Sol joined up with Notts County. So much has been written and spoken about this sorry episode, which turned out to be a mistake and saw him walk away from the club after just one appearance. He then made an incredible return to Arsenal in the January transfer window, signing a one-year deal as back up to the first choice central defensive pairing of William Gallas and Thomas Vermaelen. However, injuries to both allowed him far more appearances than he could have expected, including two in the Champions League against Porto. Despite being 35, Sol's key assets remain his physical strength and his leadership qualities and he was in negotiation to renew his contract for a further year at the end of the season.

Tottenham H *(From trainee on 23/9/1992) PL 246+9/10 FLC 28/4 FAC 28+2/1 Others 2*

Arsenal *(Free on 10/7/2001) PL 133+2/8 FLC 2 FAC 19/2 Others 41/1*

Portsmouth *(Free on 11/8/2006) PL 95/2 FLC 1 FAC 10 Others 5*

Notts Co *(Free on 25/8/2009) FL 1*

Arsenal *(Free on 15/1/2010) PL 10+1 FAC 1 Others 2/1*

CAMPBELL-RYCE Jamal Julian

Born: Lambeth, 6 April 1983
Height: 5'7" **Weight:** 11.10
Club Honours: Div 1 '06
International Honours: Jamaica: 20; Yth

Jamal began the season for Barnsley in his usual wide-midfield position, but with the team struggling he suffered an eye injury in new manager Mark Robins' first game and was out of action for a month. Struggling to find a way back into the starting line-up and finding his chances limited, he joined Bristol City in January for an undisclosed fee. Having a fresh start suited the exciting Jamaican international winger and despite some absences through injury, he proved an unqualified success, especially impressing when, following Jamie McAllister's injury, he played a number of games at wing-back.

Charlton Ath *(From trainee on 9/7/2002) PL 0+3 FLC 0+2*

Leyton Orient *(Loaned on 10/8/2002) FL 16+1/2 FLC 2/1*

Wimbledon *(Loaned on 6/2/2004) FL 3+1*

Chesterfield *(Loaned on 20/8/2004) FL 14 FLC 1 Others 1/1*

Rotherham U *(Signed on 30/11/2004) FL 27+4 FAC 1*

Southend U *(Loaned on 27/9/2005) FL 7+6 FAC 2 Others 1*

Colchester U *(Loaned on 23/3/2006) FL 1+3*

Southend U *(Free on 30/5/2006) FL 40+5/2 FLC 5 FAC 3*

Barnsley *(Signed on 31/8/2007) FL 81+9/12 FLC 2+1 FAC 5+2/1*

Bristol C *(Signed on 19/1/2010) FL 13+1*

CANA Lorik

Born: Pristina, Kosovo, 27 July 1983
Height: 6'1" **Weight:** 13.8
International Honours: Albania: 40

The former Marseille captain proved to be an inspirational figure as Sunderland skipper. Operating in central midfield, his ability to hunt down the ball enabled the Wearsiders to dominate many games, especially in the first half of the season when in tandem with Lee Cattermole before the latter's injuries. A player who collects more than his share of yellow and red cards, Lorik is a tackler and a half but uses the ball effectively too. Off the field Cana (pronounced Sana) is a model professional and leads Albania, for whom he plays at centre-back, a position he started just once for the Black Cats.

Sunderland (£5,000,000 from Marseille, France, ex Paris St Germain, on 24/7/2009) PL 29+2 FLC 2 FAC 2

CANAVAN Niall David Stephen
Born: Leeds, 11 April 1991
Height: 6'3" **Weight:** 13.7
Having turned pro in the summer, Niall quickly found himself in first team contention for Championship newcomers Scunthorpe. A tall left-sided centre-back who is strong in the air, his League debut could not have been a tougher baptism, being introduced as an early substitute at Sheffield Wednesday with his side already 2-0 down. Three days later he started the Carling Cup tie at Swansea and headed the Iron into an early lead. He figured in the next two rounds of that competition as well but did not appear in the first team from November until the end of March. Started three of the final six games of the campaign and netted his first League goal with a close-range strike against Nottingham Forest on the final day.
Scunthorpe U (From trainee on 10/7/2009) FL 4+3/1 FLC 2+1/1

CANHAM Sean Thomas
Born: Exeter, 26 June 1984
Height: 6'1" **Weight:** 13.1
A tall centre-forward signed by Notts County with the hope that he could develop as a League player. He had a successful loan spell at Hayes & Yeading and returned as a better player for having had match experience. Sadly, did not do quite enough to earn a further contract and was released at the end of the season.
Notts Co (Free from Team Bath, ex Exeter C, Tiverton T - loan, on 7/8/2008) FL 7+17/3 FLC 0+2 FAC 3/1 Others 1

CANSDELL-SHERRIFF Shane Lewis
Born: Sydney, Australia, 10 November 1982
Height: 6'0" **Weight:** 11.12
International Honours: Australia: U23; Yth
A versatile player whose preferred position is central defence but who can also play left-back or midfield. He was used in all of those roles at some point in making over 40 appearances for Shrewsbury in what was a good season for him. Shane was a consistently strong performer, especially when playing in central defence after replacing the injured Graham Coughlan. The disappointment is probably that he scored only two goals, his first in the 3-3 Carling Cup tie

against Ipswich, when he played in midfield, and his second in the 3-1 defeat of Hereford from a set piece.
Leeds U (Free from NSW Soccer Academy, Australia on 1/2/2000. Freed during 2003 close season)
Rochdale (Loaned on 8/11/2002) FL 3 FAC 1
Tranmere Rov (Signed from Aarhus GF, Denmark on 24/7/2006) FL 83+4/6 FLC 2/1 FAC 6/1 Others 2
Shrewsbury T (Free on 5/8/2008) FL 68+4/3 FLC 2/1 FAC 1 Others 4/1

Shane Cansdell-Sherriff

CAPALDI Anthony (Tony) Charles
Born: Porsgrunn, Norway, 12 August 1981
Height: 6'0" **Weight:** 11.8
Club Honours: Div 2 '04
International Honours: NI: 22; U21-14; Yth
Having made nine appearances for Cardiff at the start of the season, Tony went out on loan to Leeds in November when it was clear that City had too many full-backs in their squad, including Mark Kennedy and Kevin McNaughton on the left, Paul Quinn, Miguel Comminges, Aaron Morris and Adam Matthews on the right. Due to be a loan with a view to a permanent transfer, Tony played just five times for Leeds before returning to Cardiff in January. Although he made a further nine appearances for Cardiff before the end of the season, he did not figure in the play-offs and was released at the end of the campaign. Has a long throw which can be dangerous.
Birmingham C (From trainee on 9/7/1999)
Plymouth Arg (Free on 3/5/2003) FL

122+19/12 FLC 4 FAC 5+1 Others 0+2
Cardiff C (Free on 1/7/2007) FL 56+6 FLC 8 FAC 6+1
Leeds U (Loaned on 26/11/2009) FL 3 FAC 1+1

CARAYOL Mustapha Soon
Born: Banjul, Gambia, 10 June 1989
Height: 5'11" **Weight:** 12.0
This young Torquay winger, equally at home on either flank, has always possessed speed and trickery in abundance but a lack of discipline and end-product always left him a fringe player. As a result, he was loaned out to Kettering where his stay was interrupted by injury. After a further spell on the bench, he grasped his next chance of first team football at Torquay with both hands, showing improved work rate and finishing his mazy runs with good crosses or shots. The improvement was to an extent that he now appears certain to move on upwards rather than downwards.
MK Dons (From trainee at Swindon T on 10/8/2007) FLC 1 Others 0+1
Torquay U (Free on 24/7/2008) FL 11+9/6 FLC 0+1

CAREW John Alieu
Born: Strommen, Norway, 5 September 1979
Height: 6'5" **Weight:** 14.0
International Honours: Norway: 84; U21; Yth
John strengthened his reputation at Aston Villa by finishing as the club's top scorer for the second successive season. The Norwegian international's tally of 17 goals, including ten in the Premier League, was one better than Gabby Agbonlahor's return. But for injuries, John was convinced he would have topped 20 goals. His highlight was a brilliant hat-trick in the FA Cup quarter-final at Reading to help Villa come from behind to book a semi-final. John has always courted controversy and accidentally struck a young fan after kicking a corner flag to celebrate his winner against Stoke in December. But he is a gentle giant away from the pitch and immediately apologised to the supporter, checking he was not hurt and giving him his shirt as a conciliatory gesture. John is unplayable on his day, according to Martin O'Neill, who would like to see the striker use his 6'5" frame more regularly to hold off defenders and generally bully his opponents. He was preferred to Emile Heskey in the second half of the season. John's contract has one year left and Villa decided to put talks about a new deal on hold.
Aston Villa (Signed from Olympique

Lyonnais, France, ex Lorenskog IF,
Valerenga, Rosenborg, Valencia, AS
Roma - loan, Besiktas, on 24/1/2007) PL
83+20/37 FLC 2+2 FAC 6+2/7 Others
5/4

CAREY Louis Anthony
Born: Bristol, 20 January 1977
Height: 5'10" **Weight:** 11.10
Club Honours: AMC '03
International Honours: S: U21-1
The Bristol City captain joined a small
select band of Ashton Gate players who
have made 500 League appearances for
the club. By the end of the season his
overall total of 583 in League and Cup
took him past Trevor Tainton (581
appearances, 1967-1982) in City's all-
time chart, just leaving the great John
Atyeo (645 appearances, 1951-1966)
some way in front, even if Louis' 32
games in other competitions are added.
Unfortunately, like many at Bristol City
last season, he failed to match his
previous high standards but was
competent in defence for all that.
*Bristol C (From trainee on 3/7/1995) FL
301+11/5 FLC 15+1 FAC 18+1 Others
21+2/1*
*Coventry C (Free on 16/7/2004) FL 23
FLC 3 FAC 1*
*Bristol C (Free on 1/2/2005) FL 185+3/7
FLC 7/1 FAC 8 Others 8+1/1*

CARLE Nicholas (Nick)
Alberto
Born: Sydney, Australia, 23 November
1981
Height: 5'11" Weight: 12.2
International Honours: Australia: 12;
U23-16; Yth
The Australian international found
himself predominantly on the sidelines
in the early part of the season and was
largely used as substitute. In his second
season at Crystal Palace Nick was
hoping to catch Australian eyes and be
part of their World Cup squad but was
largely used as a squad player, scoring
one goal against Blackpool. A move
linking him with a return to the
Australian League with Sydney FC in
January failed to materialise but he
could be set for a return to his
homeland in the future.
*Bristol C (Free on Genclerbirligi,
Turkey, ex Sydney Olympic, Troyes,
Marconi Stallions, Newcastle United
Jets, on 18/1/2008) FL 14+3 Others 3*
*Crystal Palace (£1,000,000 on
16/7/2008) FL 49+10/4 FLC 2+1/1 FAC 5*

CARLISLE Clarke James
Born: Preston, 14 October 1979
Height: 6'1" **Weight:** 12.10
International Honours: E: U21-3
Always an imposing presence in the

centre of Burnley's defence, Clarke
suffered as much as any from the
malaise that affected that part of the
side, which often struggled against the
best the Premier League had to offer.
Still a match for most physically, his
anticipation was sometimes at fault and
he perhaps suffered from the extended
absence of his usual partner at the back
Steve Caldwell. He remained a regular
in the side when fit, but an ankle injury
kept him out for the last two months,
during which he signed a two-year
contract extension. Clarke achieved
brief national fame with success on
Channel 4's 'Countdown', cementing
his reputation as Britain's brainiest
footballer.
*Blackpool (From trainee on 13/8/1997)
FL 85+8/7 FLC 4+1 FAC 3/1 Others 5*
*Queens Park Rgrs (£250,000 on
25/5/2000) FL 93+3/6 FLC 5 FAC 6
Others 5*
*Leeds U (Free on 12/7/2004) FL 29+6/4
FLC 3*
*Watford (£100,000 on 6/8/2005) P/FL
34+2/3 FLC 2/2 FAC 2*
Luton T (Loaned on 1/3/2007) FL 4+1
*Burnley (£200,000 on 17/8/2007) P/FL
95+1/5 FLC 8 FAC 4 Others 3*

Clarke Carlisle

CARLISLE Wayne Thomas
Born: Lisburn, 9 September 1979
Height: 6'0" **Weight:** 11.6
International Honours: NI: U21-9;
Yth; Sch
This experienced and reliable winger
missed the second half of the season
through a recurrent knee injury, but was
Torquay's most consistent performer in
the matches he was able to play. Wayne
is not the fastest winger but works
voraciously, has a good football brain, is

comfortable on the ball and is an
excellent crosser.
*Crystal Palace (From trainee on
18/9/1996) FL 29+17/3 FLC 4+3 FAC 1*
*Swindon T (Loaned on 12/10/2001) FL
10+1/2 FAC 2*
*Bristol Rov (Free on 28/3/2002) FL
62+9/14 FLC 2 FAC 3+2/1 Others 1*
*Leyton Orient (Free on 27/7/2004) FL
27+13/3 FLC 1 FAC 2+3/1 Others 5/1
(Freed on 19/1/2006)*
*Torquay U (Free from Exeter C on
6/6/2008) FL 20+4/2 FLC 1 FAC 3
Others 1+1*

CARLOS Joao
Born: Portugal, 2 April 1989
Height: 5'10" **Weight:** 10.8
Joao signed League registration papers
for Dagenham on a non-contract basis
in November, being dual registered to
play in the Ryman League with
Dartford. The speedy striker made just
one appearance as a substitute at
Rochdale in February, appearing for 15
minutes, before his registration was
cancelled a couple of weeks later. He
also played for Ryman League Concord
Rangers during the season, on loan
from the Darts.
*Dagenham & Redbridge (Free from
Aveley, ex Clapton, Brentwood T, on
3/11/2009) FL 0+1*

CARLTON Daniel (Danny)
Born: Leeds, 22 December 1983
Height: 5'11" **Weight:** 12.4
Impressive in pre-season, Danny was
signed by Bury after his release from
Carlisle as a promising striker but
received an horrific injury in the Carling
Cup first round defeat by West
Bromwich. He was able to return, off
the bench, only in the very late stages
of the season.
*Carlisle U (Signed from Morecambe on
20/7/2007) FL 17+26/3 FLC 2+1 FAC
0+2 Others 2+1*
*Morecambe (Loaned on 12/11/2008)
FL 8/2 FAC 1*
*Darlington (Loaned on 14/1/2009) FL
16+1/4*
Bury (Free on 2/7/2009) FL 1+6 FLC 1

CAROLE Sebastien (Seb)
Born: Pontoise, France, 8 September
1982
Height: 5'6" **Weight:** 11.4
Having been released by Brighton in the
summer, Seb joined Tranmere on a
short-term basis in September, having
been signed by the then-manager, John
Barnes. However, his tricky style of wing
play was perhaps the wrong one for a
side struggling from the off against
relegation and he failed to make any
real impact in an unsettled team. After

his period at Prenton Park was not extended beyond its initial term, the Frenchman arrived in Brighton on trial in January and was subsequently signed on a weekly arrangement for his third spell at the Withdean Stadium. In and out of the team for the remainder of the campaign, Seb was used on either flank by manager Gus Poyet to provide service for the forwards. Blessed with all the tricks in the book with the ball at his feet, Seb still needs to find that final delivery more consistently to make the most of his undoubted gifts.

West Ham U *(Loaned from Monaco, France on 31/1/2004) FL 0+1*
Brighton & Hove A *(Signed from Monaco, France on 12/8/2005) FL 34+6/2 FLC 1 FAC 1*
Leeds U *(Free on 3/8/2006) FL 24+21/3 FLC 3 FAC 2 Others 1+1*
Darlington *(Free on 1/12/2008) FL 3+3 Others 1*
Brighton & Hove A *(Free on 29/1/2009) FL 5+7*
Tranmere Rov *(Free on 19/9/2009) FL 4 Others 1*
Brighton & Hove A *(Free on 11/1/2010) FL 7+2 FAC 0+1*

CARR Stephen

Born: Dublin, 29 August 1976
Height: 5'9" **Weight:** 12.2
Club Honours: FLC '99
International Honours: RoI: 44; U21- 12; Yth; Sch
Made the Birmingham captain, Stephen had a triumphant return to the Premier League. He was highly consistent and hardly let any winger get the better of him due to his pugnacious style and clever positioning. Always liked to dash forward in support and his influence on making the Blues' defence very tight was huge. An on-pitch and dressing room leader, Stephen was banned for the last home match after being found guilty of improper conduct in the derby at Villa.

Tottenham H *(From trainee on 1/9/1993) PL 222+4/7 FLC 23/1 FAC 16+1 Others 6*
Newcastle U *(£2,000,000 on 12/8/2004) PL 76+2/1 FLC 1 FAC 8 Others 20*
Birmingham C *(Free on 23/2/2009) P/FL 48 FLC 1 FAC 4*

CARRAGHER James (Jamie)

Lee Duncan
Born: Bootle, 28 January 1978
Height: 6'1" **Weight:** 13.0
Club Honours: FAYC '96; FLC '01, '03; FAC '01, '06; UEFAC '01; ESC '01, '05; CS '01, '06; UEFACL '05
International Honours: E: 36; B-3; U21-27; Yth

Jamie Carragher

The indefatigable Liverpool central defender clocked up his 600th appearance in December and now has 630 to his credit. At the start of the season, he seemed to be struggling for pace after being run ragged by young West Ham tyro Zavon Hines and it seemed likely that he would need to be rested more often by manager Rafa Benitez. However he was back to his best for the 2-0 home victory over Manchester United in October and went on to clock up a remarkable 53 games, missing only three. One was due to suspension after a sending off at Fulham in October, his first red card in over seven years. Nevertheless this was not a vintage season for Jamie who must share the defensive responsibility for the Reds' dismal record of 19 defeats and 11 failures to protect a lead. Somehow his partnerships with Daniel Agger, Martin Skrtel and Sotiris Kyrgiakos were never as solid as the old one with Sami Hyypia. He was still the best defender in the back four and, as in previous seasons, he was switched to right-back by Benitez for 12 games in mid-season to cover for the prolonged absence of Glen Johnson. In a remarkable development, he was recalled to England's squad for the World Cup finals in South Africa by Fabio Capello, three years after announcing his retirement from international football.

Liverpool *(From trainee on 9/10/1996) PL 421+14/3 FLC 23+5 FAC 33+1 Others 132+1/1*

CARRICK Michael

Born: Wallsend, 28 July 1981
Height: 6'0" **Weight:** 11.10
Club Honours: FAYC '99; PL '07, '08, '09; CS '07, '10; UEFACL '08
International Honours: E: 22; B-1; U21-14; Yth
A highly-rated and composed Manchester United midfield player, Michael had the added incentive of

starting the World Cup year with specific goals for club and country. Making as many appearances as a substitute as starting in August and September, he missed a penalty in the 1- 0 Premier League defeat at Burnley. He notched his first goal of the season in September in the Champions League group game against Wolfsburg in a 2-1 victory at Old Trafford. Due to a defensive crisis, he put his versatility to good use, filling in at centre-back after Gary Neville, himself being played out of position, picked up an injury against West Ham. Despite having never played in defence in his career, Michael's contribution pleased Sir Alex Ferguson and he stepped into defence again in December, one of three alongside Darren Fletcher and Patrice Evra in a 3-1 away win against Wolfsburg in the Champions League. At the end of that month Michael netted his third goal of the season in an emphatic 5-0 home League win over Wigan. Starting the new decade with his first ever Carling Cup goal, coolly side-footing the second in a dramatic 3-1 win (4-3 on aggregate) in the second leg of the semi-final against Manchester City. In February, he was sent off for the first time in his career following two yellow cards in United's 3-2 win against Milan at the San Siro.

West Ham U *(From trainee on 25/8/1998) P/FL 128+8/6 FLC 8 FAC 11 Others 3+1*
Swindon T *(Loaned on 12/11/1999) FL 6/2*
Birmingham C *(Loaned on 23/2/2000) FL 1+1*
Tottenham H *(£3,000,000 on 24/8/2004) PL 61+3/2 FLC 3+1 FAC 6+1*
Manchester U *(£14,000,000 + on 1/8/2006) PL 99+23/12 FLC 4+3/1 FAC 13+1/1 Others 41+4/3*

CARRINGTON Mark Richard
Born: Warrington, 4 May 1987
Height: 6'0" **Weight:** 11.0
One of the later additions to the MK Dons' squad for the season, Mark quickly showed himself to be a hard-working and mobile midfielder who was able to get forward to support the attack whenever a quick break materialised. Given fewer opportunities in the middle part of the season, he began staking a more regular claim late on and was in his most consistent starting run of the campaign when his season was ended three games early after suffering a back injury against Wycombe.
Crewe Alex *(From trainee on 3/7/2006) FL 15+14/2 FLC 1+2 FAC 1+2*

Others 1+1
MK Dons *(Free on 21/7/2009) FL 15+5/4 FLC 1 Others 3/1*

CARROLL Andrew (Andy) Thomas
Born: Gateshead, 6 January 1989
Height: 6'3" **Weight:** 11.0
Club Honours: Ch '10
International Honours: E: U21-5; Yth
This was a season when local boy Andy established himself as the focal point of the Newcastle attack. Tall, strong, and fearless with a neat touch, he led the front line well, being particularly effective when paired with Peter Lovenkrands, and his heading prowess is a major bonus when defending opposition corners. He benefited from regular exposure and scored 15 goals in 21 games towards the end of the season, while he also found the net twice for England under-21s against Macedonia in a European Championship qualifier in October. His performances earned him selection for the PFA Championship 'Team of the Season' and reportedly attracted the attention of Scotland, for whom he qualifies through his Scottish grandmother.
Newcastle U *(From trainee on 4/7/2006) P/FL 39+22/20 FAC 3+5/2 Others 0+2*
Preston NE *(Loaned on 14/8/2007) FL 7+4/1 FLC 0+1*

CARSLEY Lee Kevin
Born: Birmingham, 28 February 1974
Height: 5'10" **Weight:** 11.11
International Honours: RoI: 39; U21-1
Lee began the season as the midfield pivot for Birmingham but then Barry Ferguson and Lee Bowyer played so well in the middle he had to kick his heels on the sidelines. Lee was calm and cool on the ball and did a good job protecting the back four. Unfortunately, he injured his ankle in the January FA Cup tie at Nottingham Forest and only recovered in time for the last few weeks of the season. He announced he was leaving on a free transfer and the Brummie was given a rapturous send-off by the Blues' fans in the last home game.
Derby Co *(From trainee on 6/7/1992) P/FL 122+16/5 FLC 10+3 FAC 12 Others 3*
Blackburn Rov *(£3,375,000 on 23/3/1999) P/FL 40+6/10 FLC 4/1 FAC 4/1*
Coventry C *(£2,500,000 on 1/12/2000) P/FL 46+1/4 FLC 2/1 FAC 3*
Everton *(£1,950,000 on 8/2/2002) PL 153+13/12 FLC 14/1 FAC 8+1 Others 9*
Birmingham C *(Free on 2/7/2008) P/FL 44+4/2 FLC 3/1 FAC 2*

CARSON Scott Paul
Born: Whitehaven, 3 September 1985
Height: 6'3" **Weight:** 13.7
Club Honours: ESC '05
International Honours: E: 3; B-2; U21-29; Yth
Captain of his club, Scott had a very good season, despite conceding plenty of goals. Not helped by several changes at the heart of the West Bromwich defence, he nevertheless produced some brilliant saves – especially in home League games against Bristol City, Ipswich and Peterborough - that kept his side in the game. So impressive was he at one time that people were hinting he could still make Fabio Capello's World Cup squad. Despite being sent off for violent conduct in Albion's 2-0 home defeat by Cardiff in early December, which resulted in a three-match ban, he started more Championship games than any other Baggies' player and was delighted to keep a clean sheet in both League games against his former club Sheffield Wednesday. Now he is looking forward to doing likewise against Aston Villa and Liverpool.
Leeds U *(From trainee on 5/9/2002) PL 2+1*
Liverpool *(£750,000 + on 21/1/2005) PL 4 FLC 1 FAC 1 Others 3*
Sheffield Wed *(Loaned on 10/3/2006) FL 9*
Charlton Ath *(Loaned on 14/8/2006) PL 36 FLC 2*
Aston Villa *(Loaned on 10/8/2007) PL 35 FAC 1*
West Bromwich A *(£3,250,000 on 18/7/2008) P/FL 78 FAC 8*

CARTER Darren Anthony
Born: Solihull, 18 December 1983
Height: 6'2" **Weight:** 12.5
International Honours: E: Yth
It was another frustrating season for Darren as he made only 28 appearances for Preston, almost half of those from the bench, and never established himself as a regular under either manager, his longest run of starts being only three matches. Tall and mobile, the left-sided central midfielder contributed one goal, in the FA Cup trouncing of Colchester, and although he showed commitment to the cause, his overall performances lacked consistency. He publicly stated that his future is probably away from Deepdale and he is still young enough to realise his undoubted potential.
Birmingham C *(From trainee on 13/11/2001) P/FL 28+17/3 FLC 1 FAC 2+3/2 Others 1+1*
Sunderland *(Loaned on 17/9/2004) FL 8+2/1*

West Bromwich A *(£1,500,000 on 5/7/2005) P/FL 30+23/4 FLC 6/1 FAC 3+2/1 Others 0+2*
Preston NE *(£1,250,000 on 10/8/2007) FL 49+31/4 FLC 6 FAC 5/1 Others 1+1*

CARVALHO Alberto Ricardo
Born: Amarante, Portugal, 18 May 1978
Height: 6'0" **Weight:** 12.6
Club Honours: FLC '05, '07; PL '05, '06, '10; CS '09
International Honours: Portugal: 62
Chelsea's classy Portuguese central defender endured another injury-blighted season but it began brightly for Ricardo as he scored with a diving header against Manchester United in the Community Shield at Wembley and was 'Man of the Match'. He was an integral part of the Blues' defence that created a club record of ten consecutive home clean sheets. But he sustained a serious ankle ligament injury at Portsmouth at the end of March that sidelined him for the rest of the season and cost him a second consecutive FA Cup medal. Ricardo received a timely boost when Portugal boss Carlos Queiroz selected him for the World Cup finals squad.
Chelsea *(£16,500,000 + from FC Porto, Portugal, ex Leca, on 30/7/2004) PL 129+6/7 FLC 11 FAC 14/1 Others 49+1/3*

CASKEY Jake Dane
Born: Southend-on-Sea, 25 April 1994
Height: 5'10" **Weight:** 10.0
International Honours: E: Yth
A central midfielder like his father Darren, Jake became the youngest player ever to appear for Brighton in a peacetime match in the last game of the season, just 13 days after his 16th birthday. As a late substitute he demonstrated a great touch and a maturity beyond his years. That debut capped a tremendous end to the season for the youngster, having just agreed a scholarship deal - and future professional contract - and giving a two-goal 'Man of the Match' performance to clinch the Sussex Senior Cup for the reserves. Jake appeared twice for the England under-16 side.
Brighton & Hove A *(Academy) FL 0+1*

CASTILLO Segundo
Alejandro
Born: San Lorenzo, Ecuador, 15 May 1982
Height: 5'10" **Weight:** 12.2
International Honours: Ecuador: 45
The midfielder returned to England with Wolverhampton, albeit on loan from Red Star Belgrade. His debut came in a

2-1 win over Fulham, and his strong tackling and willingness to shoot augured well. He had two short spells in the team, the latter ending in a comprehensive defeat at Chelsea. There was one appearance in December, but with Karl Henry in good form he slipped out of contention and did not make the 18 in 2010. It was no surprise that he left Molineux at the end of the season.
Everton *(Loaned from Red Star Belgrade, Serbia, ex Deportivo El Nacional, on 29/8/2008) PL 5+4 FLC 1 FAC 1+1 Others 1/1*
Wolverhampton W *(Loaned from Red Star Belgrade, Serbia on 31/8/2009) PL 7+1 FLC 1*

CATHCART Craig George
Born: Belfast, 6 February 1989
Height: 6'2" **Weight:** 11.5
International Honours: NI: U21-15; Yth
Craig arrived on loan from Manchester United in September and made his first appearance for Watford against Leicester. A tall centre-half, calm and composed in possession, Craig made a dozen appearances for the Hornets before a knee injury curtailed his loan period in December, and he returned to Old Trafford early in order to undergo surgery. Craig is a Northern Ireland under-21 international.
Manchester U *(From trainee on 7/2/2006)*
Plymouth Arg *(Loaned on 8/8/2008) FL 30+1/1 FLC 1 FAC 1*
Watford *(Loaned on 14/9/2009) FL 12*

CATTERMOLE Lee Barry
Born: Stockton, 21 March 1988
Height: 5'10" **Weight:** 12.0
International Honours: E: U21-16; Yth
Steve Bruce was determined to ensure the England under-21 midfield dynamo followed him from Wigan to Wearside, having previously signed the former Middlesbrough man for the Latics. Right

Lee Cattermole

from Lee's opening day debut, Sunderland supporters could see why Bruce was determined to get his man as Lee bossed the centre of the park in partnership with skipper Lorik Cana. The pairing was a key to Sunderland's bright start only for injuries to seriously restrict Lee's progress as a Black Cat. Indeed, after appearing in the opening five Premier League games, Lee was never able to start more than four games in a row. Having looked the real deal when fully fit, both Bruce and Lee will hope to master the art of staying fit next time round.

Middlesbrough *(From trainee on 2/7/2005) PL 42+27/3 FLC 3 FAC 13+1/1 Others 3+2*
Wigan Ath *(£3,500,000 on 29/7/2008) PL 33/1 FLC 2/1*
Sunderland *(£6,000,000 on 12/8/2009) PL 19+3*

CAULKER Steven Roy

Born: Feltham, 29 December 1991
Height: 6'3" **Weight:** 12.0
International Honours: E: Yth
One of the brightest starlets that the Huish Park faithful have ever seen in a Yeovil shirt, teenage centre-half Steven had a sparkling debut League season with the Glovers. Signed on loan from Tottenham, his cool, composed style allied with a strong tackle, aerial power and reading of the game made him a true fans' favourite and won him just about every 'Player of the Year' trophy going. He was selected several times for the England under-19 squad and may well go all the way to the top.

Tottenham H *(From trainee on 8/7/2009)*
Yeovil T *(Loaned on 16/7/2009) FL 44 FLC 1 FAC 1*

CAVALIERI Diego

Born: Sao Paulo, Brazil, 1 December 1982
Height: 6'2" **Weight:** 13.7
Diego is Liverpool's second choice goalkeeper behind Pepe Reina, although he has yet to make his Premiership debut after two seasons at Anfield. He made four first team appearances, two in the Carling Cup games at Leeds and Arsenal, one in the Champions League against Fiorentina and also in the disastrous FA Cup replay with Reading in January that Liverpool lost in extra time. Although Liverpool lost three of these four games, there is no suggestion that the Brazilian was to blame, the goals being the result of defensive blunders and the failure to build on a lead.

Liverpool *(£3,500,000 from Palmeiras, Brazil on 28/7/2008) FLC 4 FAC 2 Others 2*

CAVE-BROWN Andrew Robert

Born: Gravesend, 5 August 1988
Height: 5'10" **Weight:** 12.2
International Honours: S: Yth
Andrew was used by Leyton Orient mainly as cover for Stephen Purches at right-back and when called upon he never let the team down. Andrew was perhaps unfortunate that when Purches was injured for the end of season run-in, the club signed Eric Lichaj on loan from Aston Villa and he was preferred. Andrew was out of contract during the summer and was released.

Norwich C *(From trainee on 4/7/2006) FLC 1 FAC 0+1*
Leyton Orient *(Free on 8/8/2008) FL 22+7 FAC 1 Others 4*

CECH Marek

Born: Trebisov, Slovakia, 26 January 1983
Height: 6'1" **Weight:** 11.11
International Honours: Slovakia: 35
The Slovakian international played in three different positions for West Bromwich – full-back, central midfield and wide left. Totally committed, he struggled early on with his fitness and, indeed, his form, but came back strongly after Christmas having replaced Joe Mattock at left-back. One of the quickest players in the squad, he scored his first two goals in English football, both of them real beauties, in Albion's 3-1 home League win over Plymouth in September. Said by some to be a 'bit-part player' he was better than that and although approached by the French club Rennes and watched by both Glasgow Celtic and FC Twente, he stayed loyal to the Baggies and, as the season progressed, added to his tally of international caps.

West Bromwich A *(£1,400,000 from Porto, Portugal, ex Inter Bratislava, Sparta Prague, on 21/7/2008) P/FL 32+9/2 FLC 2 FAC 4+1*

CECH Petr

Born: Plzen, Czech Republic, 20 May 1982
Height: 6'5" **Weight:** 14.3
Club Honours: FLC '05, '07; PL '05, '06, '10; CS '05, '09; FAC '07, '09, '10
International Honours: Czech Republic: 72; U21-15
Although regarded as one of the great contemporary goalkeepers, Petr's form was questioned in December as Chelsea conceded some uncharacteristically sloppy goals. Fortunately, this was just a blip as they regained their 'cast iron' reputation – helped by some outstanding goalkeeping from Petr. Earlier, the Blues smashed an 83-year-

old club record by keeping ten consecutive home clean sheets, with Petr between the sticks for seven. Four days after a 'Man of the Match' performance at Wolverhampton, including a string of brilliant saves and two assists, Petr's season was interrupted by a calf injury in an innocuous challenge at the San Siro against Inter Milan and he missed five matches. Apart from Chelsea's first domestic 'Double', individual awards rolled in: Czech 'Player of the Year' for the fourth time and winner of the 'Golden Glove' award after keeping 17 League clean sheets. He played a major role in securing the 'Double' at Wembley by becoming only the third 'keeper to save an FA Cup final penalty and pulling off an amazing reflex save in the first half.

Chelsea *(£9,000,000 from Stade Rennais, France, ex Chmel Blsany, on 19/7/2004) PL 184 FLC 8 FAC 15 Others 56*

CERNY Radek

Born: Prague, Czech Republic, 18 February 1974
Height: 6'3" **Weight:** 13.5
Club Honours: FLC '08
International Honours: Czech Republic: 3
Last year's joint 'Golden Glove' winner found his first team opportunities in goal limited through the season. Radek started the campaign as number one for Queens Park Rangers and was pretty much an ever-present up to Christmas. Then he found himself behind loan signing Carl Ikeme by the turn of the year but came back into the side after Ikeme returned to Wolverhampton and played in the final five games of the season.

Tottenham H *(Loaned from Slavia Prague, Czech Republic, ex Ceske Budejovice, Union Cheb, on 28/1/2005) PL 2+1*
Tottenham H *(Loaned from Slavia Prague, Czech Republic on 1/7/2006) FLC 2 FAC 2 Others 1*
Tottenham H *(Loaned from Slavia Prague, Czech Republic on 1/7/2007) PL 13 FLC 2 FAC 2 Others 3*
Queens Park Rgrs *(Free from Slavia Prague, Czech Republic on 4/7/2008) FL 71 FLC 4 FAC 4*

CHADWICK Luke Harry

Born: Cambridge, 18 November 1980
Height: 5'11" **Weight:** 11.0
Club Honours: PL '01
International Honours: E: U21-13; Yth
A runaway winner of MK Dons' 'Player of the Year' award, picking up both the supporters' and players' trophies, Luke's

displays over the course of the season, and in particular those in the second half of the campaign, lit up what turned out to be a disappointing League One campaign for the Dons. Given plenty of free rein by manager Paul Ince, he was at his best when running at defenders, drawing countless free kicks in dangerous areas, and also showing a very competitive attitude in tracking back and tackling wherever possible. Staying relatively injury free throughout the campaign gave him a consistent starting run, and though his finishing sometimes let him down, that was really the only minus factor on what was an excellent campaign for the likeable crowd favourite.
Manchester U (From trainee on 8/2/1999) PL 11+14/2 FLC 5 FAC 1+2 Others 1+5
Reading (Loaned on 7/2/2003) FL 15/1 Others 1+1
Burnley (Loaned on 15/7/2003) FL 23+13/5 FLC 2/1 FAC 1+1
West Ham U (Free on 5/8/2004) FL 22+10/1 FLC 1 FAC 3
Stoke C (£100,000 on 4/8/2005) FL 46+5/5 FAC 4/1
Norwich C (£200,000 on 14/11/2006) FL 10+7/2 FLC 0+1
MK Dons (Free on 1/10/2008) FL 60+4/8 FLC 0+1 FAC 2+1 Others 5+2

Luke Chadwick

CHALMERS Lewis John
Born: Manchester, 4 February 1986
Height: 6'0" **Weight:** 12.4
Club Honours: FC '08
International Honours: E: SP-10
Lewis is a central midfielder who can play as an emergency centre-half and has a great long throw. He was an emergency right-back for Aldershot in a

couple of early games and had a decent run from October to February, during which he made his 100th appearance for the club. By the beginning of March, Lewis was out of favour and joined Blue Square Premier leaders Oxford on loan until the end of the season. He was released by the Shots.
Aldershot T (Free from Altrincham on 2/7/2007) FL 38+8/1 FLC 1+1 FAC 3 Others 2

CHAMBERS Adam Craig
Born: West Bromwich, 20 November 1980
Height: 5'10" **Weight:** 11.8
International Honours: E: Yth
Adam struggled with injury until November and it was not until Boxing Day onwards that he returned to the central midfield engine room at Leyton Orient. Adam was out of contract in the summer and was offered a new deal.
West Bromwich A (From trainee on 8/1/1999) P/FL 38+18/1 FLC 4+2 FAC 5+1 Others 2+1
Sheffield Wed (Loaned on 19/2/2004) FL 8+3 Others 1
Kidderminster Hrs (Free on 24/3/2005) FL 2
Leyton Orient (Free, via trial at Swansea C, on 29/8/2006) FL 140+5/9 FLC 2+2 FAC 8 Others 5/1

CHAMBERS Ashley Renaldo
Born: Leicester, 1 March 1990
Height: 5'10" **Weight:** 11.6
International Honours: E: Yth
Wycombe signed the 19-year-old Leicester striker on loan in August, in a deal lasting until January. He made his debut as a substitute in the Football League Trophy against Northampton, one of three players to miss their kick in the penalty shoot-out defeat, before making a dramatic League debut at Swindon in September as a substitute and coolly scoring the 89th-minute equaliser. After two more substitute appearances, and with the team struggling, he fell out of favour and returned early to Leicester in November. His next spell on loan was at Grimsby and he regularly missed out due to the limits on the number of loan players permitted in the side. However, when selected the young forward showed potential with his pace and eye for goal, his injury-time turn and shot versus Bournemouth securing a rare Town home victory.
Leicester C (From trainee on 7/9/2007) FL 1+5 FLC 0+1 FAC 0+1 Others 0+1
Wycombe W (Loaned on 21/8/2009) FL 0+3/1 Others 0+1
Grimsby T (Loaned on 21/1/2010) FL 2+2/2

CHAMBERS James Ashley
Born: West Bromwich, 20 November 1980
Height: 5'10" **Weight:** 11.8
International Honours: E: Yth
James spent most of the season at right-back for Doncaster, with just a few games on the other flank when Gareth Roberts was out with injury. Always ready to attack down the flank, his crosses led to a number of goals. Another excellent season from him but he missed the last two games with a knee injury.
West Bromwich A (From trainee on 8/1/1999) P/FL 54+19 FLC 5+1 FAC 1
Watford (£75,000 on 9/8/2004) P/FL 74+16 FLC 8+1/2 FAC 3+1 Others 3
Cardiff C (Loaned on 12/10/2006) FL 7
Leicester C (Free on 3/8/2007) FL 15+9 FLC 2+1
Doncaster Rov (Free on 4/8/2008) FL 77+3 FLC 2+1 FAC 5

CHAMBERS Luke
Born: Kettering, 29 August 1985
Height: 5'11" **Weight:** 11.0
Luke had a disappointing start to Nottingham Forest's campaign after being sent off against Reading on the opening day. He struggled to hold down a regular place but never let the side down when called on, playing either at right-back or in his preferred position in the centre of defence. He bagged three goals during the campaign, including a vital winner against Swansea that briefly put Forest in the automatic promotion places before they had to settle for the play-offs.
Northampton T (From trainee on 3/11/2003) FL 109+15/1 FLC 6+1 FAC 8+3 Others 6+1
Nottingham F (Signed on 30/1/2007) FL 99+19/11 FLC 5/1 FAC 8 Others 3/2

CHANDLER Jamie
Born: South Shields, 24 March 1989
Height: 5'7" **Weight:** 11.3
International Honours: E: Yth
A tenacious midfield player brought in on loan from Sunderland by manager Colin Todd at the start of the season. His non-stop displays and energetic work rate made him a favourite with the Darlington crowd, but after 16 appearances he returned to Sunderland at the end of October. However, he was announced as one of Simon Davey's first signings for 2010-11 just before the end of the season.
Sunderland (From trainee on 12/7/2007)
Darlington (Loaned on 6/8/2009) FL 12+2 FLC 1 Others 1

CHAPLOW Richard David
Born: Accrington, 2 February 1985
Height: 5'9" **Weight:** 9.3
International Honours: E: U21-1; Yth
Richard seemed to be over his injury problems from previous seasons with some promising early performances in Preston's midfield, scoring twice, until he required a hernia operation in February. After missing six games, he failed to re-establish himself and despite some fine performances away from Deepdale he was unable to replicate these achievement levels in home games and began to attract the unwelcome attentions of some fans. At his best a mobile, box-to-box player with excellent passing skills, he will be seeking to revive his career at a new club in the coming campaign.
Burnley (From trainee on 13/9/2003) FL 48+17/7 FLC 3+1 FAC 5
West Bromwich A (£1,500,000 on 31/1/2005) P/FL 25+19/1 FLC 6+2 FAC 5/2 Others 1
Southampton (Loaned on 8/2/2006) FL 11/1
Preston NE (£800,000 on 10/1/2008) FL 57+11/8 FLC 0+3 FAC 3+1

CHARLES Anthony Daniel
Born: Isleworth, 11 March 1981
Height: 6'0" **Weight:** 12.0
Club Honours: FC '08
Primarily a centre-half, Anthony played left-back on several occasions for Aldershot, missing the first seven games due to a back injury before marking his 150th game with a goal against Cheltenham. He was sent off in the club's 1000th competitive fixture, a 6-1 mauling at Burton. Anthony took over as captain after Adam Hinshelwood's departure but the rest of his season was hampered by a groin injury. He played superbly in enough games to be a major influence as the Shots made the play-offs before losing to Rotherham.
Crewe Alex (Signed from Brook House on 22/9/1999. Free to Hayes in October 2001)
Barnet (Free from Farnborough T on 6/1/2005) FL 52+5 FLC 3 Others 2
Aldershot T (Free on 7/7/2007) FL 73+1/6 FLC 1 FAC 6 Others 3

CHARLES Elliott Grant
Born: Enfield, 11 February 1990
Height: 6'2" **Weight:** 12.2
Teenage striker Elliott began his second season at Barnet on the fringes of the first team and was named on the bench several times in the early stages. He showed considerable promise in pre-season, scoring against a strong Arsenal side in a friendly. However, he found his chances limited at Underhill and after

just two substitute appearances and brief loan spells at Ebbsfleet United and Hemel Hempstead Town, he was released in January, later signing for Blue Square Premier outfit Kettering Town.
Barnet (From juniors on 2/7/2008) FL 0+8 FLC 0+1 Others 0+3

CHARNOCK Kieran James
Born: Preston, 3 August 1984
Height: 6'1" **Weight:** 14.7
International Honours: E: SP-11
This steady, reliable left-sided centre-back was unfortunate in that injuries and suspensions seemed to strike at inopportune times and he ended up behind Mark Ellis and Guy Branston in the pecking order at Torquay. Kieran returned for the last three games and looked rock solid as the club continued their run of clean sheets.
Wigan Ath (From trainee on 2/7/2002. Free to Southport on 14/3/2003)
Peterborough U (Signed from Northwich Victoria on 12/7/2007) FL 12 FAC 2 Others 2
Accrington Stanley (Loaned on 17/10/2008) FL 33+1 FAC 2
Torquay U (Signed on 6/8/2009) FL 22+2 FLC 1 FAC 3 Others 2

CHEREL Julien
Born: Caen, France, 8 March 1983
Height: 6'5" **Weight:** 13.5
The sturdy central defender joined Hartlepool on trial early in the season and turned in some good performances for the reserves. In September, he signed a contract to the end of the season. New to English football, he was introduced to the squad among the substitutes. In January, with regular defenders Sam Collins and Gary Liddle both out, he made his League debut against Oldham and gave a creditable performance. Despite this encouraging start, he was soon out of the picture and, at the end of the season, was released on a free transfer.
Hartlepool U (Free from USON Mondeville, France on 25/9/2009) FL 1

CHESTER James Grant
Born: Warrington, 23 January 1989
Height: 5'9" **Weight:** 11.9
After being nominated by Manchester United reserve team manager Ole Gunnar Solskjaer as reserve 'Player of the Year' in the previous season, James was keen to gain some first team experience. With this in mind, the right-sided central defender joined Plymouth on a three-month loan in September. However, in his third appearance for the Pilgrims, James suffered cartilage damage that would

rule him out of action beyond the scheduled end of his loan, so he returned to Manchester United in October.
Manchester U (From trainee on 3/7/2007) FLC 0+1
Peterborough U (Loaned on 2/2/2009) FL 5
Plymouth Arg (Loaned on 19/9/2009) FL 2+1

CHICKSEN Adam Thomas
Born: Milton Keynes, 27 September 1991
Height: 5'8" **Weight:** 11.9
Given his senior debut for MK Dons as a 16-year-old on the opening day of the 2008-09 campaign, Adam had to wait until early April for his taste of senior action under returning boss Paul Ince. A left-footed midfielder more used to filling the full-back berth at Academy level, he continued to feature for the remainder of the season and the more games he got under his belt, the more confident his play became, especially when even younger players were given their chances late on. Signing a two-year deal, he can be expected to feature much more regularly in the first team from now on.
MK Dons (Trainee) FL 4+3 FLC 1 Others 0+1

CHILVERS Liam Christopher
Born: Chelmsford, 6 November 1981
Height: 6'1" **Weight:** 13.5
Club Honours: FAYC '00
Liam appeared in the heart of the Preston defence 23 times last term and although he only started eight games under Darren Ferguson, he was available from the bench for the majority of the other games. Tall and dominant in the air, Liam never shows any emotion on the pitch but nor does he concede much to opponents when challenging for the ball. His partnerships with Youl Mawene and Sean St Ledger are well established, which allowed these three to alternate without seriously upsetting the balance of the side. It was announced at the end of the season that his contract would not be renewed.
Arsenal (From trainee on 18/7/2000)
Northampton T (Loaned on 22/12/2000) FL 7
Notts Co (Loaned on 1/11/2001) FL 9/1 FAC 2
Colchester U (Loaned on 24/1/2003) FL 6
Colchester U (Loaned on 26/8/2003) FL 29+3 FLC 1 FAC 7 Others 5
Colchester U (Free on 6/8/2004) FL 73+2/3 FLC 3 FAC 6+2 Others 2
Preston NE (Free on 13/7/2006) FL 92+5/2 FLC 4 FAC 6

CHIMBONDA Pascal

Born: Les Abymes, Guadeloupe, 21 February 1979
Height: 5'11" **Weight:** 11.11
Club Honours: FLC '08
International Honours: France: 1. Guadeloupe: 3
Having started the season at Tottenham, Pascal was a surprise replacement for Stephen Warnock when the left-back left Blackburn in August. Although predominantly right-footed, he improvised well and it came in extremely useful when he scored a crucial goal, the winner at home to Burnley, when he cut in from the left and from a tight angle used his right foot to curl the ball past Brian Jensen. A footballer who attempts to see the bigger picture, he always prefers to stay upright and move forward, attempting to drag the ball out of the tackle. After switching to his natural right-back position, Pascal lost his place following a game at Stoke in February and, although recalled a month later from then on he was confined to the bench.
Wigan Ath (Signed from Bastia, France on 26/7/2005) PL 37+1/2 FLC 3+1 FAC 2
Tottenham H (Signed on 31/8/2006) PL 64+1/3 FLC 8/1 FAC 6 Others 19
Sunderland (£3,000,000 on 28/7/2008) PL 13 FLC 1 FAC 2
Tottenham H (£3,000,000 on 28/1/2009) PL 1+2 Others 2
Blackburn Rov (£2,000,000 on 27/8/2009) PL 22+2/1 FLC 3+1 FAC 1

CHISHOLM Ross Stephen

Born: Irvine, 14 January 1988
Height: 5'9" **Weight:** 10.3
This industrious midfielder arrived at the club in March from Shamrock Rovers and made his debut as a substitute against Port Vale; thereby being the 50th player to be used by Darlington in the season.
Hibernian (From juniors on 10/2/2007) SL 28+15 SLC 1 SC 0+1 Others 1+1 (Freed during 2009 close season)
Darlington (Free on 2/3/2010) FL 2+1

CHO Won-Hee

Born: Seoul, South Korea, 17 April 1983
Height: 5'10" **Weight:** 11.7
International Honours: South Korea: 30; Yth
The South Korean, in his first full season at Wigan, found his opportunities limited following the appointment of Roberto Martinez as manager. A defensive midfielder who can also play in the back four, he is a tough competitor who is strong in the tackle. Having played only three games from the substitutes' bench, his only start

was in December, away to Manchester United. Keen to pursue his international career in a World Cup final year, he was allowed to return to his former club Suwon Samsung Bluewings during the January transfer window on a one-year loan.
Wigan Ath (Signed from Suwon Samsung Bluewings, ex Ulsan Hyundai Horang-i, Gwangju Sangmu Phoenix, on 11/3/2009) PL 2+3

CHOPRA Rocky **Michael**

Born: Newcastle, 23 December 1983
Height: 5'8" **Weight:** 9.6
International Honours: E: U21-1; Yth
Michael rejoined Cardiff on loan - in two separate spells - from Sunderland in 2009 and completed a transfer back to the Welsh club for 2009-10. He scored 21 goals in League and Cups but was still only Cardiff's second top scorer behind Peter Whittingham. He had scored 12 goals by the end of September, but then went 13 matches without a goal - and netted only one in 17 games. Fired both goals in a 2-1 home win against Cardiff's Welsh rivals Swansea and put the Bluebirds ahead against Blackpool in the play-off final at Wembley, where he was 'Man of the Match', but Cardiff failed to hold on and lost 3-2. Is a natural scorer who relishes the big occasion.
Newcastle U (From trainee on 4/1/2001) PL 7+14/1 FLC 1+2 FAC 1+1/1 Others 1+4/1
Watford (Loaned on 25/3/2003) FL 4+1/5 FAC 1
Nottingham F (Loaned on 6/2/2004) FL 3+2
Barnsley (Loaned on 27/8/2004) FL 38+1/17 FLC 1 FAC 1 Others 1
Cardiff C (£500,000 on 19/7/2006) FL 42/22 FAC 2
Sunderland (£5,000,000 on 13/7/2007) PL 22+17/8 FLC 1+1 FAC 1
Cardiff C (Loaned on 6/11/2008) FL 10+1/5
Cardiff C (Signed on 2/2/2009) FL 49+8/20 FLC 2+1/1 FAC 3+1/2 Others 3/2

CHORLEY Benjamin (Ben) Francis

Born: Sidcup, 30 September 1982
Height: 6'3" Weight: 13.2
Club Honours: FAYC '01
Ben signed for Leyton Orient on a free transfer after rejecting the offer of a new contract at Tranmere. He is an old fashioned centre-half who puts his head or foot in when needed to clear the ball. Ben surprisingly took until three games from the end of season to score his first goal for the club but was captain for the final game at Colchester.

Arsenal (From trainee on 2/7/2001)
Brentford (Loaned on 14/8/2002) FL 2 FLC 1
Wimbledon/MK Dons (Free on 3/3/2003) FL 119+6/5 FLC 6 FAC 5+1 Others 2
Gillingham (Loaned on 26/10/2006) FL 24+3/1
Tranmere Rov (Free on 25/7/2007) FL 75+1/2 FLC 2 FAC 6+1 Others 4
Leyton Orient (Free on 31/7/2009) FL 42/1 FLC 2 FAC 2 Others 1

Ben Chorley

CHRISTOPHE Jean-Francois

Born: Creil, France, 13 June 1987
Height: 6'1" **Weight:** 13.2
Known as 'Jeff' at Roots Hall, in his second campaign at Southend he was rarely out of the midfield alongside Alan McCormack. His only spells out of the team came from minor niggling injuries and suspensions caused by two red cards, at Swindon and, controversially, in the home game with Charlton. Strong and combative, he usually sits in front of the centre-backs and breaks up opposition possession. Managed only one goal in the season.
Portsmouth (Signed from RC Lens, France on 3/8/2007)
Bournemouth (Loaned on 10/8/2007) FL 5+5/1 FLC 1
Yeovil T (Loaned on 10/3/2008) FL 4+1
Southend U (Signed on 1/9/2008) FL 60+9/5 FLC 2 FAC 6/1 Others 1+1

CHURCH Simon Richard

Born: Amersham, 10 December 1988
Height: 6'0" **Weight:** 13.4
International Honours: W: 8; U21-14
Simon added to his growing reputation as a quality striker by scoring goals at

Championship and international level. In 42 appearances for Reading, Simon completed 90 minutes on only nine occasions but his 12 goals included some quality strikes, none better than the last of the season, a superb first-time volley from distance into the top corner of the Preston net in Reading's 4-1 victory. He scored vital FA Cup goals against Liverpool and West Bromwich and his first full international goal for Wales, against Scotland. Simon remains a regular in the Welsh squad and his value to Reading is shown by the signing of a contract extension that will keep him at the Madejski Stadium until 2013.
Reading *(From trainee on 4/7/2007) FL 22+14/10 FAC 5+2/2 Others 1*
Crewe Alex *(Loaned on 19/10/2007) FL 11+1/1 FAC 2*
Yeovil T *(Loaned on 30/1/2008) FL 2+4*
Wycombe W *(Loaned on 28/8/2008) FL 6+3*
Leyton Orient *(Loaned on 17/2/2009) FL 12+1/5*

CISSE Kalifa

Born: Dreux, France, 9 January 1984
Height: 6'1" **Weight:** 12.8
International Honours: Mali: 1; Yth
Kalifa was a regular in Reading's squad during Brendan Rodgers' time as manager but found appearances rarer from February onwards. Niggling injuries, loss of form and the emergence of Jay Tabb as a central midfielder kept Kalifa out for months at a time. But the long-striding Mali international also made a couple of early season appearances at centre-back, a position he filled occasionally as a second half substitute. The highlight of his season was Reading's second goal in the 2-0 win at Sheffield Wednesday in December, starting and finishing the move himself. He has an important role for Reading but midfield competition will be even stiffer next season.
Reading *(£1,000,000 from Boavista, Portugal, ex Toulouse, GD Estoril, on 18/5/2007) P/FL 49+26/3 FLC 3 FAC 4 Others 0+1*

CLAPHAM James (Jamie)
Richard
Born: Lincoln, 7 December 1975
Height: 5'9" **Weight:** 10.11
Club Honours: Div 2 '10
A versatile, skilful and experienced left-sided defender, Jamie made a valuable contribution to Notts County's promotion success. He played at left-back, right-back and on the left of midfield. However, he probably had his best game of the season in the centre of midfield at waterlogged Bury. He

thoroughly deserved his championship medal. Was out of contract in the summer.
Tottenham H *(From trainee on 1/7/1994) PL 0+1 Others 4*
Leyton Orient *(Loaned on 29/1/1997) FL 6*
Bristol Rov *(Loaned on 27/3/1997) FL 4+1*
Ipswich T *(£300,000 on 9/1/1998) P/FL 187+20/10 FLC 19+1/4 FAC 4+3/1 Others 16+2/1*
Birmingham C *(£1,000,000 + on 10/1/2003) PL 69+15/1 FLC 5+2 FAC 3+3*
Wolverhampton W *(Free on 3/8/2006) FL 21+5 FLC 1+1 FAC 1*
Leeds U *(Loaned on 20/8/2007) FL 12+1 FAC 0+1 Others 0+1*
Leicester C *(Free on 31/1/2008) FL 11*
Notts Co *(Free on 19/9/2008) FL 57+13/3 FLC 1 FAC 8 Others 1*

CLARK Benjamin (Ben)

Born: Consett, 24 January 1983
Height: 6'2" **Weight:** 13.0
International Honours: E: Yth; Sch
The utility man who played in a variety of defensive and midfield positions in six seasons at Hartlepool, Ben had a disappointing season. At the start, he was recovering from a hernia operation and on his return was sidelined by a second injury. Eventually match fit, he made a number of substitute appearances and was mainly utilised as cover to Pool's central defenders Sam Collins and Gary Liddle. In the second half of the season Ben made a handful of appearances but struggled to find his best form. A popular player who had always shown a great attitude for the Pool, he was released at the end of the season.
Sunderland *(From trainee on 5/7/2000) P/FL 3+5 FLC 4 FAC 2*
Hartlepool U *(Signed on 22/10/2004) FL 144+18/6 FLC 1 FAC 14+2 Others 5*

CLARK Christopher (Chris)

Born: Aberdeen, 15 September 1980
Height: 5'11" **Weight:** 10.8
International Honours: S: B-3
Chris is an extremely useful member of Plymouth's squad as he can play in a variety of positions. He began the campaign on the substitutes' bench but during the season he became more of a first team regular, playing on the left side of midfield. He showed his versatility by also playing on the right, through the centre and even appeared as a left-back. The fans often showed their appreciation for his work, as he always gives 100 per cent with his seemingly boundless energy. He scored just the one goal, against Bristol City in

the 3-2 victory in March.
Aberdeen *(Signed from Hermes on 16/8/1997) SL 167+32/8 SLC 7+3 SC 16+2/1 Others 5+2*
Plymouth Arg *(£200,000 on 17/1/2008) FL 66+19/1 FLC 0+1 FAC 4/1*

Chris Clark

CLARK Ciaran

Born: Harrow, 26 September 1989
Height: 6'2" **Weight:** 12.0
International Honours: E: Yth
Ciaran deserved his place in Aston Villa's squad and barely put a foot wrong on his winning debut against Fulham in August. His career was held back slightly by the capture of central defenders Richard Dunne and James Collins, so he was in and out of squads. The strong defender captained the reserves to his second and their third successive Premier Reserve League South title. Several clubs asked about a loan but manager Martin O'Neill is keen for him to progress under Villa's coaches. Ciaran is coming through the ranks at international level, being called up for England under-21s after captaining the under-20s and under-19s.
Aston Villa *(From trainee on 2/7/2008) PL 1*

CLARK William (Billy)
Charles
Born: Ipswich, 20 October 1991
Height: 5'10" **Weight:** 11.11
A product of the Ipswich Academy, Billy made his debut as an injury-time substitute in the penultimate home

game against Doncaster. He also came on late in the following game at Newcastle, where he was involved in the build up for Town's late equaliser.
Ipswich T (Trainee) FL 0+3

CLARKE Andre (Jamie)
Nathan Jermaine Everton
Born: Hammersmith, 11 September 1988
Height: 5'10" **Weight:** 11.11
The young striker who joined Lincoln in the summer following his release by Rotherham, scored four goals from his 23 League and Cup appearances, with three coming in the FA Cup ties against AFC Telford United and Northwich Victoria. Placed on the transfer list at his own request after he found first team chances limited under Chris Sutton, Jamie left Sincil Bank by mutual consent in January.
Blackburn Rov (From trainee on 4/7/2007)
Accrington Stanley (Loaned on 8/8/2008) FL 12+3/5 FLC 1 Others 1
Rotherham U (Free on 2/2/2009) FL 7+4/2
Lincoln C (Free on 2/7/2009) FL 14+6/1 FLC 1 FAC 2/3

CLARKE James (Jamie)
William
Born: Sunderland, 18 September 1982
Height: 6'2" **Weight:** 12.9
A regular for Grimsby in the early months of the season, Jamie showed his usual ball-winning skills and shooting from distance as a midfielder. An autumn managerial change then restricted his appearances and he was released by mutual consent in January, subsequently joining Blue Square Premier York.
Mansfield T (From trainee on 5/7/2002) FL 29+5/1 FLC 2 FAC 3+1 Others 2
Rochdale (Free on 5/7/2004) FL 53+10/1 FLC 2 FAC 4 Others 2+2
Boston U (Free on 20/1/2006) FL 42+10/3 FLC 0+1 FAC 1
Grimsby T (Free on 5/7/2007) FL 67+7/3 FLC 1+1 FAC 2 Others 9+2/1

CLARKE Jordan Lee
Born: Coventry, 19 November 1991
Height: 6'0" **Weight:** 11.3
International Honours: E: Yth
A product of the Coventry Academy, the young full-back was given a debut on the opening day as a substitute and three days later made his first start in the Carling Cup tie against Hartlepool. Jordan is an athletic and skilful defender who likes to play on the right and overlap when the team is in possession. Early in the season he was high in Chris

Coleman's plans and even preferred to England under-21 defender Martin Cranie for a few games. He is confident on the ball and came out well in some tough encounters with Middlesbrough's Adam Johnson and Newcastle's Jonas Guttierez, setting up the first goal in the former game. He was unfortunate to be sent off at Derby for two yellow cards, the second for a challenge on Robbie Savage that perhaps a more experienced player would not have made. An ankle injury impeded his progress but he returned near the end of the season and made three substitute appearances. He was selected for England under-19s during the season.
Coventry C (From trainee on 5/8/2009) FL 6+6 FLC 1

CLARKE Leon Marvin
Born: Birmingham, 10 February 1985
Height: 6'2" **Weight:** 14.2
In terms of form, it was a mixed season for this talented if rather unpredictable Sheffield Wednesday striker. Leon has managed to win over the Hillsborough fans by putting in some very committed performances, but his playing style is languid so if things are not going right for him on the pitch it can appear that he is not trying too hard when in fact he is. Leon needs to increase his scoring rate and also to have a little more confidence in his own ability. He really could play at the highest level.
Wolverhampton W (From trainee on 5/3/2004) P/FL 32+42/13 FLC 2+4/1 FAC 1+2/1
Kidderminster Hrs (Loaned on 25/3/2004) FL 3+1
Queens Park Rgrs (Loaned on 31/1/2006) FL 1
Plymouth Arg (Loaned on 23/3/2006) FL 5
Sheffield Wed (£300,000 on 16/1/2007) FL 43+40/18 FLC 1+1 FAC 1+1
Oldham Ath (Loaned on 1/3/2007) FL 5/3
Southend U (Loaned on 31/8/2007) FL 16/8

CLARKE Matthew (Matt)
Paul
Born: Leeds, 18 December 1980
Height: 6'3" **Weight:** 12.7
The Bradford left-sided central defender suffered the ignominy of being substituted after an hour of the 5-0 defeat at Notts County on the opening day and was hardly involved again until December. Having regained his place, he was harshly sent off in a home defeat by Shrewsbury but bounced back to form a good partnership alongside Zesh Rehman. Matt always

gets forward at set pieces and scored against promoted Rochdale. He was released at the end of the season.
Halifax T (From trainee at Wolverhampton W on 5/7/1999) FL 42+27/2 FAC 5+1 Others 2+2
Darlington (Free on 9/7/2002) FL 163+6/13 FLC 5 FAC 6 Others 4
Bradford C (Free on 24/6/2006) FL 82+6/4 FLC 1 FAC 4+1 Others 5
Darlington (Loaned on 27/10/2006) FL 2

CLARKE Nathan
Born: Halifax, 30 July 1983
Height: 6'2" **Weight:** 11.5
Young Nathan had to bide his time for a regular place, as competition was strong in the Huddersfield defence. Once in the side, the centre-half looked assured and composed as he formed a solid partnership with captain Peter Clarke. Nathan is confident in the air, can be a threat at set pieces and also attacks with long throws. As the squad rotated through the season Nathan was often on the substitutes' bench, but remained an important cog in the squad. His two goals came in Cup competitions, the second a wonderful overhead kick for the FA Cup winner against Port Vale.
Huddersfield T (From trainee on 6/9/2001) FL 259+4/8 FLC 8 FAC 15/1 Others 11+2/1

CLARKE Peter Michael
Born: Southport, 3 January 1982
Height: 6'0" **Weight:** 12.0
International Honours: E: U21-8; Yth; Sch
Huddersfield captured Southend's 'Player of the Year' during the summer and the tough-tackling defender was quickly installed as captain. The faith was repaid as the commanding centre-half led his side towards the play-offs. Peter missed only one game as he served a suspension after being sent off in the defeat at Colchester. The captain communicates well and has the ability to stay calm. Peter causes problems at set pieces and scored six goals. He was voted the fans' 'Player of the Year', a great start to his Town career.
Everton (From juniors on 19/1/1999) PL 6+3 FLC 0+1 FAC 4
Blackpool (Loaned on 8/8/2002) FL 16/3
Port Vale (Loaned on 20/2/2003) FL 13/1
Coventry C (Loaned on 13/2/2004) FL 5
Blackpool (Signed on 18/9/2004) FL 84/11 FLC 5/2 Others 1+1
Southend U (£250,000 on 4/8/2006) FL 122+4/10 FLC 6+1 FAC 13/1 Others 4
Huddersfield T (Free on 2/7/2009) FL 46/5 FLC 2 FAC 3 Others 3/1

CLARKE Shane Robin
Born: Lincoln, 7 November 1987
Height: 6'1" **Weight:** 13.3
A locally-born midfielder, Shane enjoyed his most prolific season for Lincoln in terms of games played but ended the campaign on the transfer list as manager Chris Sutton rang the changes ahead of his first full season in charge at Sincil Bank. Comfortable when playing in a holding role, Shane will no doubt be looking to impress in a bid to work his way back into Sutton's plans.
Lincoln C (From trainee on 6/7/2006) FL 45+23 FLC 1+1 FAC 3 Others 2

CLARKE Thomas (Tom)
Born: Halifax, 21 December 1987
Height: 5'11" **Weight:** 12.2
International Honours: E: Yth
After a substitute appearance in Huddersfield's opening day draw at Southend, the home-grown talent adopted a new role in the centre of midfield. The defender flourished there with some 'Man of the Match' performances, thwarting opponents as well as distributing the ball accurately. Injuries seem a regular occurrence for the youngster and knee trouble kept him out for a large chunk of the season. Tom returned for the latter part of the season, this time at right-back.
Huddersfield T (From trainee on 18/1/2005) FL 62+15/2 FLC 1+1 FAC 0+3 Others 3+1
Bradford C (Loaned on 23/10/2008) FL 4+2 FAC 1

CLARKE William (Billy)
Charles
Born: Cork, 13 December 1987
Height: 5'8" **Weight:** 10.1
International Honours: RoI: U21-7
Injury halted Billy's progress at Blackpool after an encouraging start to life by the seaside. Signed on a two-year contract as a winger after being released by Ipswich, Billy's direct running and good delivery made him very difficult for opposition defences to handle. His first League cameo in tangerine came in the very first minute of the Lancashire derby against Preston – a fizzing drive from outside the area. Billy made 18 League appearances, which was disappointing for 'Pool fans who love to watch him play.
Ipswich T (From trainee on 26/1/2005) FL 20+29/3 FLC 0+2/1 FAC 3+2
Colchester U (Loaned on 23/3/2006) FL 2+4
Falkirk (Loaned on 31/1/2008) SL 1+7/1
Darlington (Loaned on 8/8/2008) FL 18+2/8 FLC 2/1 FAC 1 Others 1+1
Northampton T (Loaned on

23/1/2009) FL 5/3
Brentford (Loaned on 23/3/2009) FL 8/6
Blackpool (Free on 3/7/2009) FL 9+9/1 FLC 3/1

CLARKSON David
Born: Bellshill, 10 September 1985
Height: 5'10" **Weight:** 9.13
International Honours: S: 2; B-1; U21-13
After impressing for Bristol City in a 2-2 draw at Preston in the opening game of the season, this Scottish international forward, signed from Motherwell, was laid low by a viral infection and was given few chances to shine thereafter as he was mainly used from the bench. David contributed a number of goals, his close-range header securing all the points at Peterborough in March. Given a decent run in the side, many feel he has all the attributes to be a success south of the border.
Motherwell (From juniors on 1/7/2002) SL 165+54/49 SLC 9+5/4 SC 49+14/4
Bristol C (Signed on 8/7/2009) FL 10+16/4 FAC 1

CLAYTON Adam Stephen
Born: Manchester, 14 January 1989
Height: 5'9" **Weight:** 11.11
International Honours: E: Yth
Adam had two loan spells at Brunton Park, interspersed with a brief return to Manchester City, and in total featured in over half of Carlisle's matches. An attacking midfielder who always looks comfortable on the ball, he showed character at Goodison Park in the FA Cup in creating United's equaliser after his mistake had led to Everton taking the lead. He shone at Wembley in the Johnstone's Paint Trophy final but his best performance was at Brunton Park against MK Dons when his mastery in midfield laid the foundations for United's 5-0 victory. He returned to Manchester at the end of the term but there are hopes he could yet be back at Brunton Park.
Manchester C (From trainee on 3/7/2007)
Carlisle U (Loaned on 2/11/2009) FL 28/1 FAC 2+1 Others 5/2

CLEMENTS Christopher (Chris) Lee
Born: Birmingham, 6 February 1990
Height: 5'9" **Weight:** 10.6
A product of Crewe's youth system, Chris came off the bench in the 90th minute in the FA Cup first round tie at York. The midfielder had been recalled in early September from a loan spell with IBV, the Icelandic club, due to the club having injury problems, but that

was the only first team action the youngster got before being released at the end of the season.
Crewe Alex (From trainee on 30/4/2009) FAC 0+1

CLEVERLEY Thomas (Tom)
William
Born: Basingstoke, 12 August 1989
Height: 5'9" **Weight:** 10.8
Club Honours: Div 1 '09
International Honours: E: U21-6; Yth
Watford's 'Player of the Season' arrived in August for what turned out to be a season's loan from Manchester United and marked his debut at Nottingham Forest with the winning goal. He settled very quickly and soon established his credentials as a player of great skill and quality. Operating from the left wing, but with licence to roam, Tom ended the season with 11 goals, highly creditable for a midfield player. He was sent off at Scunthorpe in February following a rash challenge, but that was a rare blemish. As well as finding success at club level, he established himself as a regular in the England under-21 team. Sadly, Tom's season ended in April when he was carried off against West Bromwich with seriously damaged lateral knee ligaments and he returned to Old Trafford for treatment.
Manchester U (From trainee on 3/7/2007)
Leicester C (Loaned on 16/1/2009) FL 10+5/2
Watford (Loaned on 17/8/2009) FL 33/11 FLC 1 FAC 1

CLICHY Gael
Born: Paris, France, 26 February 1985
Height: 5'9" **Weight:** 10.0
Club Honours: PL '04; CS '04
International Honours: France: 4; B-2; U21-13
Having missed the run in to the previous season, Arsenal's Gael returned to full fitness for the start of the campaign. However, this was by no means a vintage season for the Frenchman. He was injured again in the home win over Tottenham in October and did not return until the Bolton away game in the middle of January. He seemed to suffer defensively more than most as the club changed to a 4-3-3 formation that created more scoring opportunities but also left Arsenal's back four exposed to counter-attacks. Gael at his best remains a fast and skilful attacking full-back but the defensive side of his game is still developing and he will surely face competition for his place, which will hopefully motivate him further, from the promising Kieran Gibbs. He

featured 24 times in the Premier League, nine times in the Champions League and was named in France's World Cup squad.
***Arsenal** (£250,000 from Cannes, France on 6/8/2003) PL 135+19/1 FLC 7+1 FAC 10+5 Others 38+5*

CLINGAN Samuel (Sammy)
Gary
Born: Belfast, 13 January 1984
Height: 5'11" **Weight:** 11.6
International Honours: NI: 24; U21-11; Yth; Sch
The combative midfield player arrived from relegated Norwich in the close season and had a good solid season for Coventry. A player who likes to sit back and control the play he nonetheless is a firm tackler and good passer. The bonus came from his five incredible goals. All were stunning efforts and included a 30-yard free kick at Preston, two wicked bending free kicks against Leicester and Scunthorpe at home, a 25-yard daisy-cutter drive at Watford and a technically superb scissor-kick against Barnsley at home. Unfortunately he missed two and a half months after breaking a metatarsal in his left foot in the home game with Leicester in October and Coventry's form suffered during his absence.
***Wolverhampton W** (From trainee on 18/7/2001)*
***Chesterfield** (Loaned on 8/10/2004) FL 15/2*
***Chesterfield** (Loaned on 31/8/2005) FL 14+7/1 Others 1*
***Nottingham F** (Signed on 24/1/2006) FL 79+6/1 FLC 3 FAC 4+1 Others 3*

Sammy Clingan

***Norwich C** (Free on 28/7/2008) FL 40/6 FLC 1 FAC 2*
***Coventry C** (Signed on 24/7/2009) FL 32+2/5 FAC 2*

CLUCAS Samuel (Sam)
Raymond
Born: Lincoln, 20 August 1990
Height: 5'9" **Weight:** 10.6
The midfielder's only first team outing for Lincoln came in a Johnstone's Paint Trophy match at Darlington early in the season. Sam, who joined City while at Lincoln College, found first team opportunities limited under Chris Sutton and was released at the end of the season.
***Lincoln C** (Free from Nettleham, ex trainee at Leicester C, on 1/8/2009) Others 1*

CLYNE Nathaniel Edwin
Born: Stockwell, 5 April 1991
Height: 5'9" **Weight:** 10.7
International Honours: E: Yth
After admitting a disappointing start, which resulted in Nathaniel losing his place in the Crystal Palace starting side after the season began, his solid performances when he did play saw him the focus of a bid from Wolverhampton in January. The player himself ultimately decided to remain where he was at Palace, stating that he was more likely to play first team football if he stayed there. Voted the Football League 'Young Player of the Season', he scored his first goal for Palace with a fine strike against Reading in December and was capped during the season by England at under-19 level. His ability is sure to attract the attention of Premier League clubs again in the very near future.
***Crystal Palace** (From trainee on 7/5/2009) FL 44+4/1 FLC 1 FAC 8*

COBB Joe Anthony
Born: Leicester, 13 October 1990
Height: 5'11" **Weight:** 12.1
Wycombe signed 18-year-old left-back Joe from Leicester in the summer on a one-year contract. He made his debut as a half-time substitute in the Johnstone's Paint Trophy defeat by Northampton in September, more than holding his own. However, with Craig Woodman virtually ever-present at left-back, Joe made no more appearances and was released at the end of the season.
***Wycombe W** (From trainee at Leicester C on 29/7/2009) Others 0+1*

COHEN Christopher (Chris)
David
Born: Norwich, 5 March 1987
Height: 5'11" **Weight:** 10.11

International Honours: E: Yth
The midfielder continued to improve during his third season with Nottingham Forest. He was used in a variety of positions, including all across midfield as well as at left-back and tackled them all without any fuss. Chris is the kind of player who is a delight for a manager and supporters, one who never seems to have a poor game. He missed only two of the 53 games played by Forest and was their most used player.
***West Ham U** (From trainee on 1/4/2004) P/FL 2+16 FLC 2+1 FAC 0+1*
***Yeovil T** (Signed on 10/11/2005) FL 73+1/7 FLC 1 FAC 2/1 Others 3+1*
***Nottingham F** (Signed on 10/7/2007) FL 125+1/7 FLC 6/1 FAC 8/1 Others 2/1*

COHEN Tamir
Born: Tel Aviv, Israel, 4 March 1984
Height: 6'1" **Weight:** 11.9
International Honours: Israel: 15; U21-12; Yth
Perhaps Bolton's surprise package of the season, Tamir really proved his worth after 18 months of being little more than a squad player. His first start of the season, against Liverpool, saw Tamir claim his first goal in Bolton colours and he maintained a scoring mini-streak with a goal in the following game, a 3-2 victory at Portsmouth. His third goal in four games proved vital when sealing victory at Birmingham and it soon became apparent that Tamir had a real attacking prowess that had not previously surfaced when operating as a fairly staid central midfielder. A thigh strain in the defeat at Aston Villa ruled Tamir out for some time and he appeared sporadically toward the end of the season, although a red card in the victory at West Ham blotted his copybook a little. However, Tamir performed admirably enough over the course of the season to suggest that he can now be considered an important member of the first team squad.
***Bolton W** (£650,000 from Maccabi Netanya, Israel, ex Maccabi Tel Aviv, on 4/1/2008) PL 32+9/5 FLC 0+1 FAC 3+2*

COID Daniel (Danny) John
Born: Liverpool, 3 October 1981
Height: 5'11" **Weight:** 11.7
Club Honours: AMC '02, '04
It was another frustrating season of injury woe for Danny at Blackpool. After battling back from a long-term hamstring injury, the right-back started away at West Bromwich but lasted only 45 minutes before he hobbled off with a recurrence of the snap. He ended up playing the solitary game for the Seasiders and was later released after

12 years at the club.
Blackpool *(From trainee on 24/7/2000)*
FL 227+37/9 FLC 11+3 FAC 18/1 Others
20+1/3

COLACE Hugo Roberto
Born: Buenos Aires, Argentina, 6
January 1984
Height: 5'10" **Weight:** 11.7
International Honours: Argentina: Yth
Hugo had an excellent season for
Barnsley, taking his play to a new level.
He was encouraged to break forward
more and with Nathan Doyle playing
the holding role, did that to great
effect, netting seven times. He scored
the winner with his first goal for the
club, a header in the Carling Cup
against Burnley. This was in addition to
his usual role in midfield that involved
breaking up play and tackling. He
covered every blade of grass and
deservedly won both supporters' and
players' 'Player of the Year' awards.
Barnsley *(Free from Newell's Old Boys,*
Argentina, ex Argentinos Juniors,
Estudiantes de la Plata - loan, Flamengo
- loan, on 5/9/2008) FL 71+4/7 FLC 3/1
FAC 2

COLBACK Jack Raymond
Born: Newcastle, 24 October 1989
Height: 5'9" **Weight:** 11.5
A stunningly successful season-long
loan brought the young midfielder the
Ipswich players' 'Player of the Year'
award. Town boss Roy Keane had seen
Jack's ability during their time at
Sunderland and the flame-haired north
easterner grew in stature the longer the
season went on. Although not really
establishing himself in the first team
until the New Year, from thereon he
was an ever-present, playing mainly on
the left of midfield where he linked up
well with the full-back, both in attack
and defensively. He was always looking
to join the attack and weighed in with
four goals, two of them against
Blackpool. One of these showed his
coolness under pressure when he ran
on to a through pass and calmly lifted
the ball over the 'keeper. He played a
few games at left-back and although he
gave sound defensive displays the team
missed his influence in midfield.
Impressed by how well Jack had done,
Sunderland boss Steve Bruce handed
him a Sunderland and Premier League
debut on the final day of the season at
Wolverhampton but that was to prove
disastrous. Brought on with 13 minutes
left, Jack quickly received a yellow card
and then with 15 seconds of the season
remaining was shown a second yellow
and thus a red ruling him out of the
first game of 2010-11 after a mistimed

challenge as the youngster sought to
impress.
Sunderland *(From trainee on*
18/7/2007) PL 0+1
Ipswich T (Loaned on 6/8/2009) FL
29+8/4 FLC 2 FAC 2/1

COLBECK Philip Joseph (Joe)
Born: Bradford, 29 November 1986
Height: 5'10" **Weight:** 10.12
The former Bradford 'Player of the Year'
began the season at Valley Parade and
played his part in their early wins over
Torquay and Cheltenham before joining
Oldham for an undisclosed fee just
minutes before the August transfer
window shut. Latics' manager Dave
Penney was delighted with the capture
of a winger who is probably the
quickest player in the Football League
over 40 yards. Unfortunately, Joe
suffered a dip in form and only made
28 appearances for Athletic. The step
up in class from League two to League
One may have come as a surprise to Joe
as he suddenly found that defenders
had more pace too!
Bradford C *(From trainee on*
18/7/2006) FL 68+41/8 FLC 2+1 FAC
0+1 Others 3
Darlington *(Loaned on 25/10/2007) FL*
4+2/2
Oldham Ath *(Signed on 1/9/2009) FL*
18+9/1 FAC 1

COLE Ashley
Born: Stepney, 20 December 1980
Height: 5'8" Weight: 10.8
Club Honours: FAC '02, '03, '05, '07,
'09, '10; PL '02, '04, '10; CS '02; '04,
'09; FLC '07
International Honours: E: 78; B-1;
U21-4; Yth
New manager, new system. Carlo
Ancelotti's diamond formation demands
the width be provided by attacking full-
backs and there is nobody better
equipped than Ashley. He scored his
first Chelsea goal at the Bridge against
Burnley with a superb half-volley to
round off a sweet move he instigated
and three days later signed a new
three-year contract. His second goal of
the season was equally eye-catching: a
brilliant diving header against
Tottenham, but then he picked up his
first bad injury, a depressed fracture of
the tibia against Atletico Madrid in
October. He demonstrated to Arsenal
fans just what they are missing with a
barnstorming performance at the
Emirates. Twice in three minutes he
rampaged down the left and curled
over undefendable crosses that were
converted to put Chelsea on the path to
a crucial victory. Even those notoriously
difficult-to-please pundits on Match of

the Day unanimously described Ashley
as the best left-back in the world. His
third goal, against Sunderland, was one
of the outstanding of the season.
Controlling a chipped pass and turning
a defender in one movement, he
stabbed the ball past the advancing
'keeper. Ashley's brilliant season was
brought to a halt in February when he
suffered a fractured ankle at Everton.
Ironically, he was injured in a tackle with
Landon Donovan, a star with England's
Group C rivals the United States.
Fortunately, for club and country, he
recovered to feature in Chelsea's last
three League matches and the FA Cup
final. He had the final say in the Blues'
title campaign, scoring the record 103rd
goal of the League season. Seven days
later he went into the record books as
the first player to gain six FA Cup
winners' medals and, like Nicolas
Anelka, to win the 'Double' with two
clubs.
Arsenal *(From trainee on 23/11/1998)*
PL 151+5/8 FLC 2+1 FAC 19+1 Others
46+3/1
Crystal Palace *(Loaned on 25/2/2000)*
FL 14/1
Chelsea *(Signed on 31/8/2006) PL*
106+5/6 FLC 4+2 FAC 14+1 Others 33

COLE Carlton Michael
Born: Croydon, 12 November 1983
Height: 6'3" **Weight:** 13.4
International Honours: E: 7; U21-19;
Yth
The England international striker was
the top scorer at West Ham. It was a
fine campaign for Carlton, who was a
handful for all defenders with his height
and pace. The opening home game
against Tottenham saw him score a
wonder goal. It was a superb piece of
control, a turn away from the defender
and a fierce shot into the roof of the
net. Further goals followed against
Sunderland and Burnley in November.
He causes panic in defences with his
strength but tellingly brings others into
play. In the game with Burnley, a knee
injury caused him to miss the second
half and it turned out to be a bad injury
as it forced him out of action until
February. He was back to his best
against Hull, being a threat with his
strength and ability to hold up the ball.
In April he turned provider when setting
up goals for Araujo Ilan against both
Sunderland and Wigan. He added to his
collection of England caps during the
campaign.
Chelsea *(From trainee on 23/10/2000)*
PL 4+21/4 FLC 1/2 FAC 1+3/2 Others
0+2
Wolverhampton W *(Loaned on*
28/11/2002) FL 5+2/1

Carlton Cole

Charlton Ath (Loaned on 20/8/2003)
PL 8+13/4 FAC 1/1
Aston Villa (Loaned on 12/7/2004) PL
18+9/3 FLC 1+1 FAC 1
West Ham U (£2,000,000 on
6/7/2006) PL 78+27/26 FLC 4+3/3 FAC
7+1/2 Others 1+1

COLE Jake Stanley
Born: Hammersmith, 11 September
1985
Height: 6'2" **Weight:** 13.0
Goalkeeper Jake signed for Barnet on a
permanent deal in July following his
release by Queens Park Rangers. He had
previously enjoyed a successful loan
spell with Barnet in the latter stages of
2008-09 and was a popular signing. He
took the number-one jersey and
featured in every one of Barnet's
competitive games, putting in a number
of quality performances. At the end of
the season, he was voted the Bees'
'Player of the Year' by the supporters.
Queens Park Rgrs (From trainee on

6/7/2005) FL 4+2 FLC 2
Barnet (Free on 6/3/2009) FL 56 FLC 1
FAC 3 Others 2

COLE Joseph (Joe) John
Born: Romford, 8 November 1981
Height: 5'9" **Weight:** 11.0
Club Honours: FAYC '99; FLC '05; PL
'05, '06, '10; CS '05, '07; FAC '07, '10
International Honours: E: 54; B-1;
U21-8; Yth; Sch
The season was difficult for Chelsea cult
hero Joe as he strove to overcome his
serious cruciate ligament injury. He
made his long-awaited comeback, as
captain, in the Carling Cup against
Queens Park Rangers in September. Joe
scored two Premier League goals, the
first a drive from the edge of the box
against Wolverhampton but the other
was one of the most significant of the
season. In the clash of the top two at
Old Trafford, Joe opened the scoring for
Chelsea with an impudent back-heel
that put them on course for a vital

victory in their pursuit of the title. Joe
did not get a long unbroken run in the
side, mainly due to the excellent form
of other midfield players, and figured in
just over half the League programme.
He came back strongly at the end of the
season, creating Chelsea's final - and
103rd-goal of the League season. The
following weekend he came off the
bench at Wembley to claim his second
FA Cup winners' medal. Joe's inclusion
in Fabio Capello's World Cup squad was
the icing on the cake when his
participation looked far from certain.
Worryingly for Chelsea fans, Joe's
contract talks broke down and he
became a free agent.
West Ham U (From trainee on
11/12/1998) PL 108+18/10 FLC 6+1/1
FAC 10+1/2 Others 2+3
Chelsea (£6,600,000 on 6/8/2003) PL
122+61/27 FLC 12+8/4 FAC 17+7/2
Others 38+17/5

COLEMAN Seamus
Born: Donegal, 11 October 1988
Height: 6'4" **Weight:** 10.8
International Honours: RoI: U23-3;
U21-10
A late mover into the professional game,
Seamus arrived at Everton from Sligo
Rovers in 2009, but following a
promising performance at Bury in pre-
season he developed a serious foot injury
following a blister. After a real baptism
of fire at Benfica in the Europa League,
the Irish defender made three substitute
appearances and was impressive in
matches at Goodison against Tottenham
and Manchester City, showing an
appetite for getting forward with sound
defensive skills. A highly productive loan
spell to Blackpool followed, in which the
right-back was a revelation. His attacking
displays were mesmeric with his goal
away at Scunthorpe a good indication as
to what he can do on the ball, taking
several players on before scoring. But his
defensive capabilities are also as strong,
with the Seasiders conceding just eight
goals in his nine matches – four of which
came away at Newcastle. It is obvious to
all who watch him that Seamus has a
bright future ahead of him.
Everton (Signed from Sligo Rov on
2/2/2009) PL 0+3 FAC 0+1 Others 3
Blackpool (Loaned on 19/3/2010) FL
9/1 Others 3

COLEMAN-CARR Luca Paolo
Born: Epsom, 11 January 1991
Height: 5'8" **Weight:** 11.0
Having made his Football League debut
for Lincoln on the final day of 2008-09,
second-year scholar Luca's only first
team outing during the season came as
a substitute in Lincoln's opening day

victory over Barnet. The left-back was not offered professional terms by manager Chris Sutton at the end of the campaign.
Lincoln C (Trainee) FL 0+2

COLES Daniel (Danny) Richard
Born: Bristol, 31 October 1981
Height: 6'1" **Weight:** 11.5
Club Honours: AMC '03
Danny overcame his knee injury to hold down a regular place for Bristol Rovers. Always a good organiser, the experienced former Bristol City central defender was the pick of the back four. A determined competitor in both penalty areas and strong in the air, Danny scored a firm header at Stockport for his only goal of the season but his best work was his man-marking to restrict the more dangerous strikers in League One. He was sent off for two yellow cards at Brighton.
Bristol C (From trainee on 7/6/2000) FL 141+7/5 FLC 4/1 FAC 8+1 Others 19/1
Hull C (£200,000 on 26/7/2005) FL 26+5 FAC 1
Hartlepool U (Loaned on 1/10/2007) FL 3
Bristol Rov (Signed on 2/11/2007) FL 65/3 FAC 6/2

COLGAN Nicholas (Nick) Vincent
Born: Drogheda, 19 September 1973
Height: 6'1" **Weight:** 13.6
International Honours: RoI: 9; B-1; U21-9; Yth; Sch
Fifteen years after a non-playing loan spell at Grimsby, Nick rejoined the Mariners as their number-one goalkeeper. However, a difficult season was soon hindered by a groin injury and relegation battle, during which the experienced custodian was also Town's skipper from October to February. Nevertheless, at times Nick showed the qualities that had previously brought him international caps, reaching double figures for clean sheets and a place in the League Two 'Team of the Week' against Cheltenham (0-0) on the FL website.
Chelsea (From trainee on 1/10/1992) PL 1
Brentford (Loaned on 16/10/1997) FL 5
Reading (Loaned on 27/2/1998) FL 5
Bournemouth (Free on 9/7/1998)
Hibernian (Free on 29/7/1999) SL 121 SLC 8 SC 16 Others 2
Stockport Co (Loaned on 8/8/2003) FL 14+1 FLC 2
Barnsley (Free on 20/7/2004) FL 99+2 FLC 2+1 FAC 5 Others 4
Dundee U (Loaned on 28/1/2005) SL 1 SLC 1
Ipswich T (Free on 31/1/2008)

Sunderland (Free on 24/7/2008)
Grimsby T (Free on 15/7/2009) FL 35 FLC 1 FAC 1 Others 2

COLLIN Adam James
Born: Penrith, 9 December 1984
Height: 6'3" **Weight:** 12.4
Adam began the campaign as Carlisle's second choice goalkeeper although, on his debut in the Johnstone's Paint Trophy against Morecambe, he ended the game as a hero with three saves in the penalty shoot-out. Making his League debut in November at MK Dons, he retained the number-one spot for the rest of the campaign. Formerly on Newcastle's books, Adam is keen to establish himself at League level having moved to Carlisle from Workington. He works hard at his game, is mature and keen to learn and has the potential to develop into a very good all-round goalkeeper.
Newcastle U (From trainee on 1/8/2003. Freed during 2004 close season)
Carlisle U (Signed from Workington on 9/7/2009) FL 29 FAC 2 Others 5

COLLINS Charlie John
Born: Hammersmith, 22 November 1991
Height: 6'0" **Weight:** 11.11
International Honours: RoI: Yth
Injuries to all the club's front-line strikers meant that Charlie was handed his senior debut for MK Dons in the penultimate game of the season against Brighton, and but for the frame of the woodwork would have marked the occasion with a goal. Also starting in the final game at Walsall, the Republic of Ireland under-19 international showed some neat touches but will clearly need to fill out more physically before being ready for the day to day action of League football.
MK Dons (Trainee) FL 2

COLLINS Daniel (Danny) Lewis
Born: Buckley, 6 August 1980
Height: 6'2" **Weight:** 12.1
Club Honours: FC '04; Ch '05, '07
International Honours: W: 7; E: SP-2
Sunderland's 'Player of the Year' for 2008-09 began the season as captain, playing the first three games in his preferred centre-back role rather than the left-back berth he had most often been seen in during his five years on Wearside. Left out of a Carling Cup tie, Danny was named on the bench at Stoke for the final game before the August transfer window closed and was back at the Britannia Stadium for the Potters next home game having

followed his former Sunderland skipper Dean Whitehead as one of six former Sunderland players to swap the red and white stripes of Sunderland for Stoke. He immediately became the first choice left-back but soon found himself in a sustained battle for that spot with Danny Higginbotham. It was a steady rather than spectacular season for Danny, but for the most part he turned in consistently reliable performances and his versatility, in either a full-back or centre-half role, means that he is valued highly by manager Tony Pulis. His best performance for the Potters probably came in the 1-0 victory over West Ham at Upton Park, where his sterling defensive display kept the home side at bay before he was able to provide the forward ball that put Ricardo in with the chance to score the winning goal. He did not always match that level of performance but looked very impressive whenever he did.
Chester C (Signed from Buckley T on 27/12/2001) FL 12/1 FLC 1
Sunderland (£140,000 on 13/10/2004) P/FL 134+15/3 FLC 5+1 FAC 7+1
Stoke C (£2,750,000 on 1/9/2009) PL 22+3 FAC 4+1

COLLINS James Michael
Born: Newport, 23 August 1983
Height: 6'2" **Weight:** 13.0
International Honours: W: 34; U21-8; Yth
The Welsh international central defender started the season with West Ham before becoming a deadline-day signing for Aston Villa. Although the fans were hoping for a more glamorous arrival following a long summer wait, James easily exceeded their low expectations by being one of Villa's most consistent performers. Making his debut in a derby-day victory over the club's fierce local rivals Birmingham on opposition territory he instantly endeared himself to the claret and blue faithful. James, or 'Ginge' as he is known to his team-mates, has won over the Villa Park public with his no-nonsense displays and formed a formidable partnership with Richard Dunne. Up until the dreadful drubbing at Stamford Bridge in April, Villa boasted the best defence in the Premier League, which was down to James as much as anybody else. Even after that 7-1 shocker at Chelsea, James earned the respect of supporters by using his Twitter social networking internet site to publicly apologise for his personal performance. The heavy defeat was a far cry from the reverse fixture against Carlo Ancelotti's team when he scored his first goal in Villa colours to help

them win 2-1 at Villa Park. James has also grown in stature on the international stage and the proud Welshman even captained his country against Liechtenstein and Sweden in the absence of regular skipper Craig Bellamy.

Cardiff C *(From trainee on 5/4/2001) FL 49+17/3 FLC 5 FAC 4+5/3 Others 4+2*
West Ham U *(£3,200,000 on 5/7/2005) PL 51+3/2 FLC 3+1 FAC 6 Others 1*
Aston Villa *(Signed on 1/9/2009) PL 26+1/1 FLC 5 FAC 5/1*

COLLINS James Steven
Born: Coventry, 1 December 1990
Height: 6'2" **Weight:** 13.6
International Honours: RoI: U21-5
A young striker with an eye for goal

who came on loan from Aston Villa in October and scored two goals in his eight appearances for Darlington before returning to Villa Park.
Aston Villa *(From trainee on 3/7/2009)*
Darlington *(Loaned on 22/10/2009) FL 5+2/2 FAC 1*

COLLINS Lee Harvey
Born: Telford, 28 September 1988
Height: 6'1" **Weight:** 11.10
International Honours: E: Yth
Lee had a superb season in Port Vale's defence and missed only one game, through injury. Calm and composed, he never seemed ruffled even when under pressure. He began the season as one of three centre-halves but as the campaign wore on, he played with equal aplomb at both right and left-

back. Scored just one goal, the last in a 4-0 victory over Grimsby, but it was his defensive duties that earned him the 'Players' Player of the Year' award. He was watched by clubs higher up the League but has another year's contract at Vale.
Wolverhampton W *(From trainee on 2/3/2007)*
Hereford U *(Loaned on 15/11/2007) FL 14+2 FAC 4*
Port Vale *(Free on 1/8/2008) FL 84/2 FLC 4 FAC 5 Others 2*

COLLINS Matthew (Matty) Jeffrey
Born: Merthyr Tydfil, 31 March 1986
Height: 5'9" **Weight:** 11.9
International Honours: W: U21-2; Yth
Apart from making a first team appearance for Swansea at full-back in a Carling Cup tie against Brighton and as deputy for Angel Rangel in an early League game against Watford, the former Fulham trainee had to be content with captaining the club's reserve team, usually from a central midfield position. In mid-April, he played as a trialist in a Bristol Rovers' reserve team game.
Fulham *(From trainee on 4/4/2003)*
Swansea C *(Free on 18/7/2007) FL 3+1 FLC 2*
Wrexham *(Loaned on 2/11/2007) FL 2 FAC 1*

COLLINS Michael Anthony
Born: Halifax, 30 April 1986
Height: 6'0" **Weight:** 10.12
International Honours: RoI: U21-2; Yth
Michael was looking to carry on where the previous season left off, a regular in the Huddersfield side aligned with a good scoring record. Fresh from signing a new contract, the Republic of Ireland under-21 international started in midfield but an untimely sending off in the opening day draw at Southend allowed others to take his place. The attacking midfielder enjoyed a good run in the side, although not scoring as freely as in the previous season. A nasty finger injury kept him out of the side until a substitute appearance in the final League match at Exeter.
Huddersfield T *(From trainee on 11/5/2005) FL 147+26/19 FLC 4+1 FAC 8+4/2 Others 5+2/1*

COLLINS Neill William
Born: Troon, 2 September 1983
Height: 6'3" **Weight:** 13.0
Club Honours: Ch '05, '09
International Honours: S: B-1; U21-7
Neill had the last of many decisive moments before leaving Wolverhampton when taking the sixth

James (Michael) Collins

91

and final penalty in the Carling Cup shoot-out against Swindon, scoring to put the club into the next round. He then joined Preston initially on loan, before signing in January. The rangy centre-half joined Preston as cover for Sean St Ledger's own loan move but sadly he never really got going at Deepdale. He made 17 straight starts but lost his place soon after being signed permanently in January and was not even seen often on the bench. Comfortable in the air, his only goal came from a powerful header versus Ipswich but his future seems almost certain to lie elsewhere and in March he moved to Leeds on loan after their inspirational centre-back Paddy Kisnorbo was ruled out of the League One promotion climax with an Achilles tendon injury. Partnering the skipper Richard Naylor at the heart of the defence, Neill, who had previously won promotion with Sunderland and Wolverhampton, was able to make it a hat-trick when playing in Leeds' final nine league games and being part of the side that went back to the Championship.
Queen's Park (From juniors on 20/3/2001) SL 30+2 SLC 1 SC 2
Dumbarton (Free on 22/7/2002) SL 62+1/4 SLC 3 SC 2 Others 4
Sunderland (£25,000 on 13/8/2004) P/FL 14+4/1 FLC 2 FAC 4/1
Hartlepool U (Loaned on 12/8/2005) FL 22 FLC 2 Others 1
Sheffield U (Loaned on 18/2/2006) FL 2
Wolverhampton W (£150,000 on 2/11/2006) P/FL 74+10/9 FLC 4 FAC 7/1 Others 2
Preston NE (Signed on 1/9/2009) FL 19+2/1 FAC 1
Leeds U (Loaned on 23/3/2010) FL 9

COLLINS Samuel (Sam) Jason
Born: Pontefract, 5 June 1977
Height: 6'3" **Weight:** 14.0
Sam, an experienced Hartlepool central defender, exudes authority as team captain. He was quickly able to build a good understanding with new central defensive partner Gary Liddle. A powerfully-built player, Sam's uncompromising style has long endeared him to supporters and he was voted 'Away Player of the Year'. Rarely absent in his two full seasons at Hartlepool, Sam is rock steady at the back and as captain is able to instil a degree of calm to his fellow defenders.
Huddersfield T (From trainee on 6/7/1994) FL 34+3 FLC 6+1 FAC 3
Bury (£75,000 on 2/7/1999) FL 78+4/2 FLC 5 FAC 0+2 Others 1
Port Vale (Free on 15/7/2002) FL

135/11 FLC 4 FAC 5 Others 5
Hull C (Signed on 3/11/2005) FL 23 FLC 2 FAC 2
Swindon T (Loaned on 28/9/2007) FL 3+1
Hartlepool U (Signed on 31/1/2008) FL 94/3 FLC 5 FAC 3 Others 2

COLLIS Stephen (Steve) Philip
Born: Harrow, 18 March 1981
Height: 6'2" **Weight:** 13.0
Having been at Crewe since the summer of 2008, Steve was unable to claim a regular first team place in 2009-10 and made only one appearance before being released and joining Bristol City on a free transfer. Gary Johnson knew Steve from his Yeovil days and moved in for him after letting the back-up 'keeper Stephen Henderson go out on loan to Aldershot. After not being called upon by City and with both their 'keepers injured, Torquay signed Steve on a seven-day emergency loan to play in the last game of the season. It was only his second match of the season, but he gave a solid performance and kept a clean sheet against champions Notts County. Was out of contract at the end of June.
Barnet (From juniors on 27/8/1999)
Nottingham F (Free on 11/7/2000)
Yeovil T (Free on 6/8/2001) FL 41+2 FAC 0+1 Others 2
Southend U (Free on 3/7/2006) FL 20+1 FLC 2 FAC 3 Others 1
Crewe Alex (Free on 1/7/2008) FL 19 FLC 3 FAC 2 Others 2
Bristol C (Free on 25/1/2010)
Torquay U (Loaned on 7/5/2010) FL 1

COLLISON Jack David
Born: Watford, 2 October 1988
Height: 6'0" **Weight:** 13.10
International Honours: W: 7; U21-7
The Welsh midfield player was keen to establish himself in the West Ham team on a regular basis. In October at Sunderland, he was outstanding as he set up both goals in the 2-2 draw. He was hoping to score more goals himself and in November netted in successive games against Hull and Burnley. In the December home game against eventual champions Chelsea, Jack produced a complete performance as he never stopped running and gave the opposition problems in both defence and attack. Unfortunately, he suffered a knee injury in March that forced him to miss the rest of the season. He had surgery in May and it was a huge disappointment to Jack and the Hammers to learn that, following the operation, he would be out of action for a further nine months. During the

campaign Jack added to his international caps for Wales.
West Ham U (From trainee on 10/8/2007) PL 36+8/5 FLC 1 FAC 3+1

COLLISTER Joseph (Joe) Douglas
Born: Hoylake, 15 December 1991
Height: 6'0" **Weight:** 13.10
Joe, a goalkeeper who developed through the youth system at Tranmere, made his debut against Walsall in October as a second-half substitute to replace the injured Luke Daniels and made his first start a week later at Exeter. He signed his first professional contract in the summer and has shown himself to be an impressive stopper with the ability to organise the defence. Joe's particular strengths are his assurance with high balls and the speed at which he gets down to low shots. He is capable of producing stunning saves and should have a bright future.
Tranmere Rov (From trainee on 28/7/2009) FL 1+2

COLOCCINI Fabricio
Born: Cordoba, Argentina, 22 January 1982
Height: 6'0" **Weight:** 12.4
Club Honours: Ch '10
International Honours: Argentina: 33
There were many who thought that Newcastle centre-back Fabricio would find it difficult to cope with the more rugged nature of the Football League following his club's relegation. However, he adjusted well, coped with the physical challenges, reading the game astutely to compensate for a lack of pace, and was the keystone at the heart of the meanest defence in the Championship, so much so that he was named in the PFA Championship 'Team of the Season'. He even found time to score his first goals for the club with points-winning headers at Cardiff and Watford. He played for Argentina in the friendly against Spain in November, but was not in the final 23 for the World Cup.
Newcastle U (£9,500,000 from Deportivo la Coruna, Spain, ex Boca Juniors, AC Milan, San Lorenzo - loan, Alaves - loan, Atletico Madrid - loan, Villareal - loan, on 15/8/2008) P/FL 71/2 FLC 2 FAC 5

COMLEY James Richard
Born: Holloway, 24 January 1991
Height: 5'10" **Weight:** 12.7
The young Crystal Palace central midfielder was used sparingly this season after making his debut in the previous campaign. Despite being a regular for the reserves, where he

finished with a hat-trick in their last game of the season, James made his only senior appearances as a substitute in the FA Cup matches against Wolverhampton and Aston Villa. He was then released by Palace after their final game of the season.
Crystal Palace (From trainee on 14/8/2008) FL 1+3 FAC 0+2 9/7/2009) FL 29 FAC 2 Others 4

COMMINGES Miguel
Born: Les Abymes, Guadeloupe, 16 March 1982
Height: 5'9" **Weight:** 11.3
International Honours: Guadeloupe: 11
Miguel suffered a series of injuries and made only two appearances for Cardiff, both during August. A versatile player, who can operate in midfield or defence, he is a Guadeloupe international. A serious thigh injury ended the season early for Miguel. He spent time in France in rehabilitation, but was back with City, although not fit to play, for the Championship play-offs. Out of contract in the summer of 2010, he was awarded a new six-month deal to enable him to regain fitness. It looks as if he will move on when that deal ends.
Swindon T (Signed from Reims, France, ex Amiens, on 10/8/2007) FL 32+8 FLC 1 FAC 4 Others 2
Cardiff C (Free on 1/7/2008) FL 10+21 FLC 2+2

COMMONS Kristian (Kris) Arran
Born: Mansfield, 30 August 1983
Height: 5'6" **Weight:** 9.8
International Honours: S: 6
It was a season of intense frustration for Kris and for Derby. Because of recurring hamstring problems, Kris was involved in fewer than half the Championship matches and started only 11 times. Kris is an important player for the Rams who, at least until the arrival of Tomasz Cywka on loan, have nobody who can replicate his best role, playing off the main striker. He was always either injured or striving to achieve match fitness but when he returned to the final game against Cardiff, Kris promptly landed a perfect free kick on Jay McEveley's head. He was due to return early, to work on his fitness before the start of the pre-season programme. It is an important season ahead because supporters want to see more of Kris, as does manager Nigel Clough.
Stoke C (From trainee on 25/11/2001) FL 20+21/5 FLC 1+2 FAC 0+1 Others 1
Nottingham F (Free on 2/7/2004) FL 112+26/32 FLC 5+1 FAC 8+1/5 Others 4+2/1

Derby Co (Free on 6/8/2008) FL 41+13/8 FLC 7/1 FAC 6+2/2

CONLON Barry John
Born: Drogheda, 1 October 1978
Height: 6'3" **Weight:** 13.7
International Honours: RoI: U21-7
Having joined Grimsby on a permanent basis in the summer, Barry was in good form for the Mariners at the start of the season, hitting three goals in the opening five League games. However, two dismissals and subsequent bans then robbed Town of the forward's services when they were short on firepower, and he thereafter saw most outings when coming off the bench under a new manager. It was still a surprise though, when the crowd favourite was made available in the January transfer window and moved to Chesterfield. At Saltergate, Barry gave his new side a different sort of attacking thrust and eight of the next 11 games were won as the team climbed to third place. The burly pivot contributed seven goals - five from the spot- in 14 starts but his impact waned as the team slipped out of the play-off places and he was released at the end of his contract.
Manchester C (From trainee at Queens Park Rgrs on 14/8/1997) FL 1+6 FLC 0+1
Plymouth Arg (Loaned on 26/2/1998) FL 13/2
Southend U (£95,000 on 4/9/1998) FL 28+6/7 FAC 1 Others 1
York C (£100,000 on 20/7/1999) FL 33+15/11 FLC 2+2 FAC 1 Others 0+1
Colchester U (Loaned on 9/11/2000) FL 23+3/8 FAC 1 Others 1
Darlington (£60,000 on 6/7/2001) FL 114+1/39 FLC 4 FAC 4/3 Others 2
Barnsley (Free on 5/7/2004) FL 25+10/7 FLC 3+1/1 FAC 1 Others 1
Rotherham U (Loaned on 14/10/2005) FL 3/1 Others 1
Darlington (Free on 24/7/2006) FL 12+7/6 FAC 1+1 Others 2
Mansfield T (Free on 12/1/2007) FL 16+1/6
Bradford C (Free on 18/7/2007) FL 36+36/17 FLC 2 FAC 2+2 Others 2/1
Grimsby T (Free on 20/3/2009) FL 15+9/10 FLC 1 FAC 1 Others 0+1
Chesterfield (Loaned on 15/1/2010) FL 15+4/7

CONNELL Alan John
Born: Enfield, 15 February 1983
Height: 5'11" **Weight:** 10.8
In many ways it was a frustrating season for Alan, as the majority of his Bournemouth appearances came from the bench. With such a small squad and a transfer embargo, the striker occupied a number of different positions,

particularly on the left of midfield. He finished the season in style by coming off the bench to score the goal that clinched promotion for the club at Burton and netted twice in the final home match against Port Vale. Was out of contract in the summer.
Bournemouth (From juniors at Ipswich T on 9/7/2002) FL 18+36/8 FLC 1+3/1 FAC 3+2/2 Others 0+1
Torquay U (Signed on 14/7/2005) FL 12+10/7 FLC 0+1 FAC 0+2 Others 1
Hereford U (Free on 1/8/2006) FL 33+11/9 FLC 0+1 FAC 4/1 Others 1
Brentford (Free on 3/7/2007) FL 36+8/12 FLC 1 FAC 1 Others 1
Bournemouth (Free on 29/8/2008) FL 25+25/5 FAC 2+1/2 Others 2/1

CONNELLY Ryan Michael
Born: Castlebar, 13 January 1992
Height: 5'10" **Weight:** 11.8
The young Irish midfield player showed up well in Derby's Academy and successful reserve sides. He had his first taste of senior action in the final game against Cardiff. In the process, he became the 40th player to be used during the season, a club record Derby will not be keen to break.
Derby Co (Trainee) FL 0+1

CONNOLLY David James
Born: Willesden, 6 June 1977
Height: 5'8" **Weight:** 11.4
Club Honours: Ch '07
International Honours: RoI: 41; U21
Southampton became the latest port of call for this roving striker in September. Having spent a season out of the game injured, he trained with the Saints for a month before making his debut as a substitute at Oldham in October, scoring minutes after taking the field. Popular from the off, his runs into the box, with or without the ball, unsettle defenders and send a frisson through crowds. Minor injuries have hampered his progress, but he impressed when available and many supporters will be keen to see David stay, despite him being out of contract in the summer.
Watford (From trainee on 15/11/1994) FL 19+7/10 FLC 1 FAC 3+3/4 Others 1/1 (Free to Feyenoord, Holland during 1997 close season)
Wolverhampton W (Loaned on 21/8/1998) FL 18+14/6 FLC 2 FAC 0+1
Wimbledon (Free from Feyenoord, Holland on 27/7/2001) FL 63/42 FLC 1 FAC 4
West Ham U (£285,000 on 8/8/2003) FL 37+2/10 FLC 2/2 FAC 4/2 Others 3
Leicester C (£500,000 on 22/7/2004) FL 48+1/17 FAC 3+2
Wigan Ath (£2,000,000 on 31/8/2005) PL 4+15/1 FLC 2+1/1 FAC 1/1

Sunderland *(Signed on 31/8/2006) P/FL 31+8/13 FLC 0+1 FAC 1+1*
Southampton *(Free on 8/10/2009) FL 9+11/5 FAC 1/2 Others 1+1*

CONNOLLY Matthew Thomas Martin
Born: Barnet, 24 September 1987
Height: 6'1" **Weight:** 11.3
International Honours: E: Yth
Injuries plagued Matthew's campaign and limited the promising young Queens Park Rangers' defender to 19 starts. Despite his problems, he had reasons to be pleased with his performances as he continued to show what a fine prospect he is. January was a particularly good month for Matthew, while it was a tumultuous time at Loftus Road. He put in a string of fine performances and capped it off with a goal of the season contender at Blackpool. He also demonstrated his versatility across the back line once again in a run of three games in March, when he played first right-back, then centre-back and finally left-back.
Arsenal *(From trainee on 1/7/2005) FLC 1+1*
Bournemouth *(Loaned on 23/11/2006) FL 3+2/1 FAC 2*
Colchester U *(Loaned on 16/7/2007) FL 13+3/2*
Queens Park Rgrs *(£1,000,000 on 2/1/2008) FL 66+8/2 FLC 6 FAC 1*

CONNOLLY Paul
Born: Liverpool, 29 September 1983
Height: 6'0" **Weight:** 11.9
Club Honours: Div 2' 04
Paul began the season as Derby's captain but gave way to the more extrovert Robbie Savage in the fourth game. He continued as the regular right-back until the turn of the year with occasional games as a central defender because of injuries. He was equally competent in his emergency position but was one of the victims of Derby's bad spell in December and January, when they lost three successive home games. Paul hardly featured after that as Nicky Hunt arrived on loan from Bolton. Paul joined Sheffield United on loan in March as emergency cover, playing against Blackpool in the evening of the day he signed. He made a series of solid games at right-back, doing well in defence but not being too prominent coming forward. His loan was extended for a week to include the Sheffield derby.
Plymouth Arg *(From trainee on 23/7/2002) FL 156+6/1 FLC 5 FAC 9 Others 1*
Derby Co *(Free on 2/8/2008) FL 56+5/1 FLC 7 FAC 4*
Sheffield U *(Loaned on 16/3/2010) FL 7*

CONNOLLY Reece William
Born: Frimley, 22 January 1992
Height: 6'0" **Weight:** 11.9
Reece is a striker and an ex-Crystal Palace schoolboy who entered his second year as an Aldershot scholar. He made his debut as a substitute at Bournemouth before being loaned to Blue Square Premier side Salisbury. Recalled in April, his mature attitude led to a professional contract, thus becoming the first scholar to sign full pro forms with the club.
Aldershot T *(Trainee) FL 0+3 Others 0+1*

CONNOR Paul
Born: Bishop Auckland, 12 January 1979
Height: 6'1" **Weight:** 11.5
Club Honours: AMC '00, '06
The experienced striker, who joined Lincoln in the summer following his release by Cheltenham, suffered an injury-hit time whilst at Sincil Bank with a serious knee injury picked up in early September keeping him on the sidelines for five months. Paul eventually made 17 League and Cup appearances for the Imps before being released at the end of the season.
Middlesbrough *(From trainee on 4/7/1996)*
Hartlepool U *(Loaned on 6/2/1998) FL 4+1*
Stoke C *(Free on 25/3/1999) FL 18+18/7 FLC 3+3/3 FAC 0+1 Others 2+3*
Cambridge U *(Loaned on 9/11/2000) FL 12+1/5 FAC 1*
Rochdale *(£100,000 on 9/3/2001) FL 76+18/28 FLC 3 FAC 8+1/3 Others 0+2*
Swansea C *(£35,000 on 12/3/2004) FL 51+14/16 FLC 1 FAC 6/3 Others 3/1*
Leyton Orient *(£40,000 on 31/11/2006) FL 20+14/7 FLC 1 FAC 0+3 Others 1*
Cheltenham T *(£25,000 on 15/1/2007) FL 53+26/7 FLC 3 FAC 3+3 Others 3/1*
Lincoln C *(Free on 22/7/2009) FL 8+7 FLC 1 Others 1*

CONSTANTINE Leon Charles
Born: Hackney, 24 February 1978
Height: 6'2" **Weight:** 11.10
A tall, mobile striker, Leon started the season as a first choice for Hereford before a dip in his and the team's form led to a spell on the sidelines. A flurry of goals on his recall in mid-season, including a pair at Burton, showed that, when the ball was placed in the right spot for him he was very likely to hit the target. Leon remained in the side for most of the remainder of the season but a rapid turnover of strike partners made it difficult for him to nail down a specific role in the side.

Millwall *(Signed from Edgware T on 31/8/2000) FL 0+1 Others 1*
Leyton Orient *(Loaned on 27/8/2001) FL 9+1/3 Others 0+1*
Partick T *(Loaned on 11/1/2002) SL 2 SC 1*
Brentford *(Free on 8/8/2002) FL 2+15 FLC 1+1*
Southend U *(Free on 21/8/2003) FL 40+3/21 FAC 2+1 Others 6+1/4*
Peterborough U *(Free on 2/7/2004) FL 5+6/1 Others 1*
Torquay U *(Loaned on 29/10/2004) FL 4/3 FAC 1*
Torquay U *(£75,000 on 10/12/2004) FL 30+8/7 FLC 1 Others 0+1*
Port Vale *(£20,000 on 4/11/2005) FL 71+1/32 FLC 4/2 FAC 7/2 Others 2/2*
Leeds U *(Free on 9/8/2007) FL 1+3/1 FAC 0+2 Others 1/1*
Oldham Ath *(Loaned on 4/3/2008) FL 7+1/2*
Northampton T *(Free on 3/7/2008) FL 21+11/3 FLC 2 FAC 2 Others 1*
Cheltenham T *(Loaned on 20/3/2009) FL 4+2/1*
Hereford U *(Free on 2/7/2009) FL 25+10/6 FLC 1 FAC 1 Others 3/2*

CONVERY Mark Peter
Born: Newcastle, 29 May 1981
Height: 5'6" **Weight:** 10.5
This right-sided midfielder made a surprise return to the club that he left in 2005 after more than 80 appearances in four seasons. He proved he is still an accurate crosser of the ball but failed to really re-establish himself in the Darlington team. New manager Simon Davey did bring him back for the last few games of the season, using his presence down the right to send over dangerous crosses. Was out of contract at the end of June.
Sunderland *(From trainee on 24/3/1999)*
Darlington *(Free on 30/1/2001) FL 38+38/3 FLC 1+1 FAC 0+3 Others 1+3 (Freed during 2005 close season)*
Darlington *(Free from Newcastle Blue Star, ex York C, Cambridge U, Weymouth - loan, on 7/8/2009) FL 9+12 FAC 1 Others 1+1/1*

COOK Jordan Alan
Born: Hetton-le-Hole, 20 March 1990
Height: 5'10" **Weight:** 10.10
One of a trio of young players brought in on loan by Colin Todd from Sunderland at the start of the season. This Hetton-born youngster made four starts and one substitute appearance in Darlington's midfield during the first few weeks of the season before returning to Wearside.
Sunderland *(From juniors on 12/7/2007)*

Darlington (Loaned on 18/8/2009) FL 4+1

COOK Lee
Born: Hammersmith, 3 August 1982
Height: 5'9" **Weight:** 11.7
Injury woes meant that the Queens Park Rangers' crowd favourite found himself battling for fitness for most of early months of the season and he did not return to the first team until late January. The last few months of the campaign saw him mostly used off the bench, although he did manage eight full appearances before the close of the season. Lee scored his only goal in a 1-1 draw against Derby at Loftus Road in March.
Watford (Signed from Aylesbury U on 19/11/1999) FL 31+28/7 FLC 0+2 FAC 2+1
York C (Loaned on 2/10/2002) FL 7/1 Others 1/1
Queens Park Rgrs (Loaned on 20/12/2002) FL 13/1
Queens Park Rgrs (Free on 3/7/2004) FL 109+10/9 FLC 3+1/1 FAC 4
Fulham (£2,500,000 on 20/7/2007)
Charlton Ath (Loaned on 31/1/2008) FL 4+5
Queens Park Rgrs (Signed on 1/8/2008) FL 36+14/2 FLC 3 FAC 1

COOPER Kenny
Born: Baltimore, Maryland, USA, 21 October 1984
Height: 6'3" **Weight:** 14.1
International Honours: USA: 10
The tall American striker joined Plymouth on loan from TSV Munich 1860 in Germany in January until the end of the season. He was familiar to Plymouth's head coach Paul Mariner from their time in America and was looking to gain regular first team experience to force himself into the United States' World Cup squad in South Africa. Unfortunately, it was to be a frustrating time for the USA international, as he appeared only from the substitutes' bench and often for only a few minutes at a time. With good ball control for a tall striker, Kenny did not score during his loan and his season ended with a knee injury. Plymouth decided not to take up the option of signing him permanently.
Manchester U (Signed from Dallas Mustangs, USA on 2/11/2004. Transferred to FC Dallas, USA on 27/1/2006)
Oldham Ath (Loaned on 28/1/2005) FL 5+2/3 FAC 0+1 Others 1
Plymouth Arg (Loaned from TSV Munich 1860, Germany on 28/1/2010) FL 0+7

COOPER Liam David Ian
Born: Hull, 30 August 1991
Height: 6'2" **Weight:** 13.7
International Honours: S: Yth
An immensely promising young left-sided centre-back, Liam gained more experience as he travelled with Hull to China for the Barclays Asia Trophy and appeared as a substitute against Tottenham. Carling Cup appearances against Southend and Everton followed. Liam made his Premier League debut a month after his 18th birthday at Liverpool. Despite a 6-1 defeat, he could hold his head high on a day when a hat-trick from Fernando Torres would have got the better of more experienced defenders. Liam performed admirably as a sub against in-form Arsenal in March and it was no surprise that he was offered – and thankfully agreed to – a new three-year contract. Although born in Hull, he qualifies for Scotland through his grandparents.
Hull C (From trainee on 25/9/2008) PL 1+1 FLC 3

COOPER Shaun David
Born: Newport, Isle of Wight, 5 October 1983
Height: 5'10" **Weight:** 10.10
After having surgery on a hip injury in the summer, it was a long and lonely season for the popular and versatile Bournemouth defender, cum midfielder. Shaun's rehabilitation took longer than anticipated because of the severe winter, but after only 45 minutes of reserve team football, he came back into the team in late March and was able to enjoy the securing of promotion.
Portsmouth (From trainee on 7/4/2001) FL 3+4
Leyton Orient (Loaned on 17/10/2003) FL 9
Kidderminster Hrs (Loaned on 24/9/2004) FL 10 FAC 1 Others 1
Bournemouth (Free on 5/8/2005) FL 136+13/1 FLC 4+1 FAC 9/1 Others 7

COPPINGER James
Born: Middlesbrough, 10 January 1981
Height: 5'7" **Weight:** 10.6
Club Honours: AMC '07
International Honours: E: Yth
Another fine season for Doncaster from James, even though he spent some time playing behind the striker rather than in his usual position on the right of midfield. More of a provider than a marksman he still scored four goals, the most memorable being a fine cross-shot to give the team a victory at local rivals, Barnsley.
Newcastle U (£250,000 + from trainee at Darlington on 27/3/1998) PL 0+1

Hartlepool U (Loaned on 10/3/2000) FL 6+4/3 Others 1
Hartlepool U (Loaned on 25/1/2002) FL 14/2
Exeter C (Free on 2/8/2002) FL 35+8/5 FLC 1 FAC 3 Others 2
Doncaster Rov (£30,000 on 7/7/2004) FL 191+25/21 FLC 8+5/2 FAC 11+4 Others 9+1/3

COQUELIN Francis
Born: Laval, France, 13 May 1991
Height: 5'10" **Weight:** 11.8
Francis is regarded as a defensive midfielder at Arsenal but his limited first team opportunities all occurred at right-back. The young Frenchman made his FA Cup debut at Stoke and appeared twice in the Carling Cup. He also made the bench for the Champions League Group game away to Olympiacos.
Arsenal (Free from Stade Lavallois, France on 18/7/2008) FLC 1+2 FAC 1

CORBETT Andrew (Andy) John
Born: Worcester, 20 February 1982
Height: 6'0" **Weight:** 11.5
Club Honours: FC '09
Andy has been Burton's Mr Versatile for several seasons and was delighted to be given the chance to demonstrate his athleticism and reliability at League level, playing both on the right of midfield and at right-back. His fitness levels and stamina never cease to amaze and justifiably earned him a new contract in May. His lack of genuine quality is sometimes exposed, but Andy could never be accused of not giving it his all. He is the archetypal squad player yet always seems to play a high proportion of games.
Kidderminster Hrs (From juniors on 4/7/2000) FL 3+5 (Transferred to Solihull Borough on 18/11/2002)
Burton A (Signed from Nuneaton Borough on 1/11/2003) FL 32+2/1 FLC 1 Others 0+1

CORK Jack Frank Porteous
Born: Carshalton, 25 June 1989
Height: 6'0" **Weight:** 10.12
International Honours: E: U21-3; Yth
The highly-rated Chelsea and England under-21 midfielder, whose father Alan was a former Coventry assistant manager, arrived at the Ricoh Arena on loan after David Bell's opening day injury. He had scored twice against the Sky Blues for Scunthorpe in 2007-08 and quickly became an ever-present in the Coventry side up until his return to Stamford Bridge at the end of the year. Using the ball intelligently, his confidence grew in his four months at City and although he got some

buffeting from the Championship's more aggressive midfield players he made a good impression with the fans. Jack's next stop was a loan spell at Burnley in January and he impressed in his first full appearance at Aston Villa. A skilful attacking midfielder whose Premier pedigree was often evident in his creative and thoughtful play, Jack was a regular starter by the end of the season and scored the Clarets' equaliser with a powerful header in the final game against Tottenham. He may well be out of Burnley's reach as a permanent signing, but he certainly provided some of the brightest moments of the second half of a troubled season.
Chelsea (From trainee on 5/7/2006)
Bournemouth (Loaned on 3/11/2006) FL 7 FAC 2
Scunthorpe U (Loaned on 17/8/2007) FL 32+2/2 FAC 1
Southampton (Loaned on 21/8/2008) FL 22+1 FLC 2
Watford (Loaned on 2/1/2009) FL 18+1 FAC 2/1
Coventry C (Loaned on 21/8/2009) FL 20+1
Burnley (Loaned on 1/2/2010) PL 8+3/1

CORLUKA Vedran
Born: Derventa, Bosnia, 5 February 1986
Height: 6'3" **Weight:** 13.3
International Honours: Croatia: 37
Croatian international Vedran remains a stalwart of the Tottenham defence, holding the right-back position against all opposition. He has also played as a central defender and while he does not have the pace of some players, he usually comes out on top thanks to guile and the ability to read opponents. Vedran made 35 starts and one substitute appearance in all competitions, heading his only goal in a League match at Bolton. He often gets forward to support his wing player and for set pieces, and there have been occasions when the 'Croatian Triangle' of Vedran, Luka Modric and Niko Kranjcar have used their international understanding to good effect. Vedran played five games for Croatia during the season and now has 37 caps. He suffered an ankle injury in the FA Cup quarter-final against Fulham and played no further part in the season except for the semi-final against Portsmouth.
Manchester C (£7,000,000 from Dinamo Zagreb, Croatia, ex Inter Zapresic - loan, on 10/8/2007) PL 37+1/1 FLC 3 FAC 3 Others 3
Tottenham H (£8,500,000 on 1/9/2008) PL 62+1/1 FLC 6+1 FAC 7

CORNELL David Joseph
Born: Gorseinon, 28 March 1991
Height: 5'11" **Weight:** 11.7
International Honours: W: U21-1; Yth
A former scholar at the club, David made his Swansea debut in the Carling Cup tie against Scunthorpe. Apart from being included in the Wales under-21 squad during the season, David also earned selection for the full Wales international squad to play Scotland in November.
Swansea C (From trainee on 10/7/2009) FLC 1

CORR Barry
Born: Wicklow, 2 April 1985
Height: 6'4" **Weight:** 12.8
International Honours: RoI: Yth
A summer signing, target man Barry was Exeter's first choice striker until suspension and loss of form cost him his starting place. He weighed in with three League goals, including the last-gasp equaliser against Wycombe. Was out of contract in the summer.
Leeds U (From trainee on 11/4/2002)
Sheffield Wed (Free on 18/4/2005) FL 7+10 FLC 1 FAC 1
Bristol C (Loaned on 27/10/2006) FL 1+2 Others 1/1
Swindon T (Signed on 19/3/2007) FL 17+19/10 FAC 2+2 Others 1+1
Exeter C (Free on 4/7/2009) FL 17+17/3 FAC 2/3 Others 1

CORT Carl Edward Richard
Born: Bermondsey, 1 November 1977
Height: 6'4" **Weight:** 12.7
International Honours: E: U21-12
An excellent target man with good passing ability, Carl started the season in the Brentford line-up. He stayed there, apart from missing four games with an ankle injury, until November when it was decided to use him from the bench as a long-standing knee problem was troubling him. This role saw him create and score late goals in many games and his classy performances made him extremely popular with the fans. He returned to the starting line-up in April but a foot injury caused him to miss the last three games.
Wimbledon (From trainee on 7/6/1996) PL 54+19/16 FLC 8+2/7 FAC 6+4/2
Lincoln C (Loaned on 3/2/1997) FL 5+1/1
Newcastle U (£7,000,000 on 6/7/2000) PL 19+3/7 FLC 3/1 FAC 2 Others 0+1
Wolverhampton W (£2,000,000 on 28/1/2004) P/FL 78+16/31 FLC 1 FAC 3+1/1
Leicester C (Signed on 9/8/2007) FL

7+7 FLC 1/1 (Freed on 29/1/2008)
Norwich C (Free from Marbella, Spain on 12/12/2008) FL 7+5/1 FAC 1
Brentford (Free on 4/8/2009) FL 16+12/6 FAC 1+1/1

CORT Leon Terence Anthony
Born: Bermondsey, 11 September 1979
Height: 6'2" **Weight:** 13.4
With the likes of Ryan Shawcross, Robert Huth, Abdoulaye Faye and Danny Higginbotham ahead of him in the Stoke pecking order it was always going to be difficult for Leon to force his way into one of the two centre-half spots and he made only four Cup appearances for the Potters. He played in the three Carling Cup games against Leyton Orient, Blackpool and Portsmouth before making his last ever appearance in a Stoke shirt, a 3-1 FA Cup victory over York. Shortly after that this immensely likeable character, who scored many vital goals when Stoke were promoted to the Premier League, became a January signing for Burnley. He came straight into the side, partnering Clarke Carlisle at the back, and proved effective on occasion at both ends of the pitch, making a number of vital last-ditch clearances and using his aerial power to some effect up front. Leon will now be looking to take Burnley back into the Premiership at the first time of asking.
Millwall (Free from Dulwich Hamlet on 23/1/1998)
Southend U (Free on 11/7/2001) FL 135+2/11 FLC 3 FAC 13/1 Others 8
Hull C (Free on 7/7/2004) FL 85+1/10 FLC 1 FAC 4
Crystal Palace (£1,250,000 on 6/7/2006) FL 49/7 FAC 1
Stoke C (£1,200,000 on 2/11/2007) P/FL 42+2/8 FLC 5+1 FAC 3
Burnley (£1,500,000 on 27/1/2010) PL 15

COTTERILL David Rhys George Best
Born: Cardiff, 4 December 1987
Height: 5'10" **Weight:** 10.11
International Honours: W: 16; U21-11; Yth
Most of David's appearances for Sheffield United were from the bench and although capable of beating the full-back and producing excellent centres he too often ran into trouble. This problem seemed to be accentuated on the few occasions he started a game. Having scored a well-taken penalty and netted his first, and only, United goal from open play at Reading, he joined Swansea on loan in November and the move was made permanent in January for a record fee. The winger,

capable of playing on either flank, impressed as the season went on, scoring spectacular goals at Leicester and in the live SKY TV game at the Liberty Stadium against Newcastle. He suffered a groin strain during a substitute appearance for Wales against Sweden and for a couple of weeks struggled to regain fitness, but he was back into his stride as the campaign ended.
Bristol C (From trainee on 5/1/2005) FL 48+14/8 FLC 1/1 FAC 1 Others 1+1
Wigan Ath (£2,000,000 on 31/8/2006) PL 7+11/1 FLC 1 FAC 1+1/1
Sheffield U (Signed on 8/2/2008) FL 35+19/6 FLC 3 FAC 3 Others 2
Swansea C (Loaned on 24/11/2009) FL 14+7/3 FAC 1/1

COUGHLAN Graham
Born: Dublin, 18 November 1974
Height: 6'2" **Weight:** 13.6
Club Honours: S Div 1 '01; Div 3 '02; Div 2 '04
The vastly experienced Shrewsbury central defender was always determined and an excellent captain. He poses constant danger at set pieces and dominates in the air at the back. A player with influence and when he plays well, so does the team. He gave a number of solid performances, none more so than in Shrewsbury's September victory over Crewe that began a good run, including four consecutive victories with only one goal conceded. He appeared in 39 games, scoring two goals, one of which was a 90th-minute equaliser in the November 1-1 home draw against Bury. Was out of contract in the summer.
Blackburn Rov (£100,000 from Bray W on 14/10/1995)
Swindon T (Loaned on 25/3/1997) FL 3
Livingston (Free on 29/3/1999) SL 53+3/2 SLC 4 SC 2 Others 5
Plymouth Arg (Free on 21/6/2001) FL 177/25 FLC 4 FAC 10 Others 2/1
Sheffield Wed (Signed on 15/7/2005) FL 47+4/5 FLC 2/1 FAC 3
Burnley (Loaned on 22/3/2007) FL 1+1
Rotherham U (Free on 19/7/2007) FL 45/1 FLC 1 FAC 2 Others 1
Shrewsbury T (Signed on 7/8/2008) FL 78/6 FLC 2 FAC 2 Others 7/1

COULSON Michael James
Born: Scarborough, 4 April 1988
Height: 5'10" **Weight:** 10.0
Usually seen on Grimsby's right wing, Michael was operating on the left when his initial strike against Dagenham (1-1) in December ended the Mariners' run of 429 minutes without a League goal. Full of running and combative in attack, the loan player later hit four goals in five

games to maintain Town's fight against relegation, twice earning recognition in the League Two 'Team of the Week' on the FL website. Was out of contract at the end of June.
Barnsley (Free from Scarborough on 24/7/2006) FL 1+15 FLC 2+1 FAC 1+5/2
Grimsby T (Loaned on 19/11/2009) FL 28+1/5

COUNAGO Pablo
Born: Pontevedra, Spain, 9 August 1979
Height: 6'0" **Weight:** 11.6
International Honours: Spain: U21-15; Yth
Pablo suffered along with all the other strikers during Ipswich's prolonged winless run at the start of the season and was not able to produce the consistency of performance to guarantee himself a regular first team place. However, he still maintains his skills in holding the ball up and linking well with his fellow players in and around the box. He scored a memorable goal in the 97th minute to give Ipswich a 3-2 home win against Coventry when he ran on to Connor Wickham's lay-off and lifted the ball over the onrushing 'keeper: this was after Coventry had scored a 95th- minute equaliser. He also produced a consummate piece of skill against Barnsley when he beat the 'keeper to a loose ball out on the touchline and curled in a shot which rebounded off a post for Daryl Murphy to tap into the open net.
Ipswich T (Free from Celta Vigo, Spain on 19/7/2001) P/FL 51+49/31 FLC 7/2 FAC 4+2 Others 7+2/3 (Freed during 2005 close season)
Ipswich T (Signed from Malaga, Spain on 25/7/2007) FL 72+42/23 FLC 3/1 FAC 3+1/2

COUSIN Daniel
Born: Libreville, Gabon, 2 February 1977
Height: 6'1" **Weight:** 13.5
Club Honours: SLC '08; SC '08
International Honours: Gabon: 30
The talented centre-forward soon fell out of favour at Hull at the start of the season and seemed set for a move to Burnley as the summer transfer window came to a close. However, he had to wait until January before securing a loan switch to Greek club Larissa. With minimal opportunities at Hull, the captain of Gabon remained active on the international stage. Daniel scored in a World Cup qualifier against Cameroon in September but suffered a shoulder injury to further dent his City prospects. In January, he became the first Tigers' player to appear in the

African Cup of Nations and became a national hero in another shock win against Cameroon.
Glasgow Rgrs (£750,000 from RC Lens, ex Martigues, Niort, Le Mans, on 1/8/2007) SL 21+7/11 SLC 0+2 SC 1+1 Others 5+7/2
Hull C (£1,500,000 on 1/9/2008) PL 19+11/4 FAC 3/1

COUSINS Mark Richard
Born: Chelmsford, 9 January 1987
Height: 6'2" **Weight:** 12.2
Colchester's popular second choice goalkeeper hardly had a look in last season. Having made 13 appearances the previous campaign, Mark added just two more appearances early in the season. An ever-present on the bench, Mark's opportunities were limited by the fact that new signing Ben Williams enjoyed a superb first season at the club.
Colchester U (From trainee on 1/7/2006) FL 9+2 FLC 1 FAC 1 Others 4

COUTTS Paul Alexander
Born: Aberdeen, 22 July 1988
Height: 5'9" **Weight:** 11.9
International Honours: S: U21-4
A steely hard-tackling midfielder, never one to pull out of a tackle and having a good eye for a defence-splitting pass, Paul left Peterborough when following manager Darren Ferguson to Preston in January. He made an immediate impact, being commanding in central midfield and establishing an excellent partnership with Matthew James from their first game together. Very aware, mobile and able to pass over short and long distance, he celebrated his first ever goal in English football versus Sheffield Wednesday before his season finished early with operations to correct hip and groin problems. Only 21, he was called up by Scotland at that level and North End fans will be looking forward to watching his continuing development in the years ahead.
Peterborough U (Signed from Cove Rgrs on 29/7/2008) FL 47+6 FLC 1 FAC 5 Others 1
Preston NE (Signed on 1/2/2010) FL 13/1

COWAN-HALL Paris Declan Joseph
Born: Hillingdon, 2 October 1990
Height: 5'8" **Weight:** 11.5
Paris was to be restricted to three brief substitute outings on loan to Grimsby from Portsmouth due to tonsillitis and glandular fever. Even then he showed electric pace as a winger, before his season ended early with a hamstring injury.

Portsmouth *(From trainee on 26/7/2008)* **Grimsby T** *(Loaned on 1/1/2010) FL 0+3*

COWIE Donald (Don)
Born: Inverness, 15 February 1983
Height: 5'11" **Weight:** 11.9
International Honours: S: 2
A regular selection for Watford throughout the season, Don turned in a series of hard-working and consistent performances on the right of midfield. He scored excellent goals against Queens Park Rangers and Sheffield United, but was more concerned with creating chances for team-mates as a corner and free-kick specialist. Don was delighted to receive his first international call-up for what was admittedly a depleted Scotland squad against Japan in October and made his debut as a second-half substitute. He did well enough to retain his place for the next match against Wales, which he started.
Ross Co *(From juniors on 23/8/2000) SL 131+26/17 SLC 7+3/3 SC 8+2/3 Others 13+1/1*
Inverness CT *(Free on 1/7/2007) SL 56+3/12 SLC 6 SC 2*
Watford *(£50,000 on 2/2/2009) FL 50+1/5 FLC 2 FAC 1+1*

COX Dean Arthur Edward
Born: Haywards Heath, 12 August 1987
Height: 5'4" **Weight:** 9.8
After four seasons as a regular, Dean will have been frustrated by his final campaign at Brighton as he fell from favour in the New Year and became a peripheral figure with only occasional appearances on the bench. Although nominally a winger, he is at his best when given a free role to roam and use his vision to good effect, with his ability to supply a killer pass. A feisty character on the pitch, Dean rarely found his peak form and was released by Brighton.
Brighton & Hove A *(From trainee on 28/6/2006) FL 121+25/16 FLC 6+1/1 FAC 11+1/3 Others 13+1/2*

COX Samuel (Sam) Peter
Born: Edgware, 10 October 1990
Height: 5'5" **Weight:** 10.3
A diminutive midfielder, Sam was one of the many loan players signed by Cheltenham during Martin Allen's 13-month spell at the club. The teenage Tottenham player arrived at the Abbey Business Stadium at the start of September but had to wait just over a month for his Football League debut, in the League Two away match at Accrington Stanley on his 19th birthday.

As an energetic ball-playing midfielder, he was selected in the centre of midfield but a disastrous afternoon began with early injuries to two defenders, forcing him to play in an unaccustomed role in the back four. He battled bravely against a useful Accrington side, earning the admiration of the travelling supporters, before returning to his parent club in mid-November following Allen's departure. Having spent a few weeks on loan at non-League Histon he moved to Torquay in January and spent a month there on loan, making one start and two substitute appearances before going back to White Hart Lane. Was out of contract at the end of June.
Tottenham H *(From trainee on 8/7/2009)*
Cheltenham T *(Loaned on 1/9/2009) FL 1*
Torquay U *(Loaned on 19/1/2010) FL 1+2*

COX Simon Richard
Born: Reading, 28 April 1987
Height: 5'10" **Weight:** 10.12
Burly striker Simon scored his first West Bromwich goal – a real belter - four minutes from the end of extra time to earn a 4-3 victory in a pulsating Carling Cup tie against Rotherham. Virtually a squad member until late in the season, he had to wait another two months before claiming his first League goal for Albion, a precise, fierce long-range drive in a 5-0 home win over Watford. And before Christmas he struck twice, including the 50th goal of his League career, in a 4-1 victory over Bristol City. He continued to find the net at regular intervals – smashing home a beauty in a 2-0 win over Middlesbrough - and, in fact, whenever Simon scored, Albion did not lose. He is eligible to play for England and the Republic of Ireland through his Irish-born grandmother.
Reading *(From trainee on 22/11/2005) P/FL 0+2 FLC 0+3 FAC 0+4*
Brentford *(Loaned on 11/9/2006) FL 11+2 FLC 1*
Northampton T *(Loaned on 22/3/2007) FL 6+2/3*
Swindon T *(Loaned on 31/8/2007) FL 18+1/8 Others 1+1/1*
Swindon T *(£200,000 on 31/1/2008) FL 62/36 FLC 1/1 FAC 1 Others 3/2*
West Bromwich A *(£1,500,000 on 8/7/2009) FL 17+11/9 FLC 3/1 FAC 3*

COYNE Daniel (Danny)
Born: Prestatyn, 27 August 1973
Height: 5'11" **Weight:** 13.0
International Honours: W: 16; B-1; U21-9; Yth; Sch
Then Middlesbrough manager Gareth Southgate signed the experienced

Welsh international goalkeeper to provide competition for Brad Jones and Jason Steele. An ankle injury to Jones in pre-season saw Danny start the opening games of the season and impress by keeping four clean sheets. However, after a 5-0 home defeat by West Bromwich in September, Jones was recalled. New Boro boss Gordon Strachan picked Danny in December and he played 15 consecutive games before losing his place after a 2-2 draw at Derby. He was called into action in the final game at Leicester, when Jones was sent off with five minutes to go. A good communicator, he still has another year on his contract and will be looking for three games to reach the 500 milestone.
Tranmere Rov *(From trainee on 8/5/1992) FL 110+1 FLC 13 FAC 2 Others 2*
Grimsby T *(Free on 12/7/1999) FL 181 FLC 13 FAC 7*
Leicester C *(Free on 4/7/2003) PL 1+3 FLC 1*
Burnley *(£25,000 on 4/8/2004) FL 39+1 FLC 4*
Tranmere Rov *(Free on 17/7/2007) FL 80 FLC 1 FAC 8 Others 4*
Middlesbrough *(Free on 6/7/2009) FL 22+1 FLC 1 FAC 1*

COZIC Bertrand (Bertie) Edern
Born: Quimper, France, 18 May 1978
Height: 5'10" **Weight:** 12.6
A solid run of form in the first half of the season saw Bertie appear in the majority of Exeter's games. The ball-winning midfielder chipped in with two League goals, including one in a comprehensive win over Brentford in October. Manager Paul Tisdale has described him as the perfect squad player and he will be looking for a new contract in the summer.
Cheltenham T *(Free from Team Bath on 8/8/2003) FL 7/1 FLC 0+1 (Free to Hereford U in March 2004)*
Northampton T *(Free on 3/8/2004) FL 8+6 FLC 1 FAC 1+1 Others 1+1*
Kidderminster Hrs *(Free on 2/2/2005) FL 13+2 (Freed during 2005 close season)*
Exeter C *(Free from Team Bath, ex Team Bath, Aldershot T, on 9/8/2006) FL 35+14/2 FLC 1 FAC 3 Others 1*

CRADDOCK Jody Darryl
Born: Redditch, 25 July 1975
Height: 6'1" **Weight:** 12.4
Club Honours: Ch '09
By his own admission, Wolverhampton's centre-half expected to be a peripheral figure this season. Yet he was captain

for the first four League games, only to miss the next four, partly because of injury. He returned at Everton, where even a head injury only interrupted him for ten minutes. Four successive Wolves' goals in the Premier League were scored by the defender, a remarkable feat - even if two of them prompted appeals for offside. Aged 34, his fitness and ability ensured that nobody showed him up. Goal number five in March made Jody second top scorer for the club. He was an ever-present for the last 18 League games, had another spell as captain and was voted 'Player of the Season' by the supporters. Was out of contract in the summer.
Cambridge U (Free from Christchurch on 13/8/1993) FL 142+3/4 FLC 3/1 FAC 6 Others 5
Sunderland (£300,000 + on 4/8/1997) P/FL 140+6/2 FLC 8+2 FAC 7+2 Others 3
Sheffield U (Loaned on 27/8/1999) FL 10
Wolverhampton W (£1,750,000 on 15/8/2003) P/FL 188+11/13 FLC 9/2 FAC 7+1 Others 2/1
Stoke C (Loaned on 17/8/2007) FL 4

CRAIG Nathan Lee
Born: Bangor, 25 January 1991
Height: 6'0" **Weight:** 11.6
International Honours: W: U21-3; Yth
The promising midfielder has been at Everton since the age of 12 and made his debut as a substitute in the Europa League match at Goodison against BATE Borisov, when several first teamers were rested. The youngster has established a reputation as a dead-ball specialist with the Academy and reserve teams and also received a call-up for the Welsh under-21 squad.
Everton (From trainee on 28/10/2008) Others 0+1

CRAIG Tony Andrew
Born: Greenwich, 20 April 1985
Height: 6'0" **Weight:** 10.13
Tony's season was interrupted by injury. Two of them were facial, caused in the games against Wycombe and Exeter. When he came back to the Millwall side in January, it showed what had been missing. With his tough tackling, he can play at centre-back or left-back and his quick runs down the left are capable of causing chaos in the opposition half. He also scored a couple of goals, the better one a superb dipping volley in the 4-0 victory over Gillingham. Tony passed two milestones in the course of the season as he reached 150 games for Millwall, first in all competitions and then in the League. Like his full-back partner Alan Dunne, he missed the last

three games of the League campaign because of an ankle injury.
Millwall (From trainee on 13/3/2003) FL 75+4/2 FLC 3+2 FAC 2 Others 1
Wycombe W (Loaned on 22/10/2004) FL 14 FAC 2 Others 2
Crystal Palace (£150,000 on 28/6/2007) FL 13 FLC 1
Millwall (Loaned on 27/3/2008) FL 5/1
Millwall (£125,000 on 11/7/2008) FL 72+2/4 FLC 1 FAC 5 Others 7

Stephen Crainey

CRAINEY Stephen Daniel
Born: Glasgow, 22 June 1981
Height: 5'9" **Weight:** 9.11
Club Honours: SPD '02
International Honours: S: 6; B-1; U21-7
The reliable Blackpool left-back held his own against some of the best right-wingers in the Championship despite not being blessed with great pace. His distribution from the back is said to be something that allows the side to play their attractive football. After building a good understanding with the midfield, Stephen is able to bring the likes of Charlie Adam and David Vaughan into the game. He has never enjoyed such regular football in an injury-plagued career until now, and at the age of 29 has plenty still left in the tank. He played 41 League games for Ian Holloway's side and is one of the first names on the team sheet, even though a section of the Bloomfield Road crowd look to get on his back.
Glasgow Celtic (From juniors on 3/7/1997) SL 18+21 SLC 6+1/1 SC 2+3

Others 3+2
Southampton (£500,000 + on 31/1/2004) PL 5
Leeds U (£200,000 on 6/8/2004) FL 51+1 FLC 6 FAC 2 Others 2
Blackpool (Free on 11/7/2007) FL 93+5/1 FLC 3 FAC 2 Others 3

CRANEY Ian Thomas William
Born: Liverpool, 21 July 1982
Height: 5'10" **Weight:** 12.7
Club Honours: FC '06
International Honours: E: SP-7
Ian joined Morecambe on a season-long loan from Huddersfield in the summer and started the campaign in midfield, impressing the Shrimps' fans with his attitude and work rate. He was beginning to hit top form when he suffered an ankle injury and missed the second half of the season after having an operation. Ian returned to Huddersfield, where he was released and signed for Blue Square Premier newcomers Fleetwood in the summer.
Accrington Stanley (£17,500 from Altrincham on 22/6/2004) FL 18/5 FLC 2 FAC 1 Others 2/1
Swansea C (£150,000 on 23/11/2006) FL 24+4 FLC 2 Others 1
Accrington Stanley (£25,000 on 28/9/2007) FL 36/8 FLC 1/1
Huddersfield T (Free on 21/8/2008) FL 23+11/5 FAC 1/1
Morecambe (Loaned on 22/7/2009) FL 16/2 FLC 1 FAC 1+1

CRANIE Martin James
Born: Yeovil, 23 September 1986
Height: 6'0" **Weight:** 12.4
International Honours: E: U21-16; Yth
Coventry signed the England under-21 defender from Portsmouth just after the start of the season. Martin had a good solid first season despite playing out of position at left-back for much of the time. His early performances were in the centre of defence alongside Ben Turner and the pair looked to be building a good partnership until Turner was injured. Then a few less than consistent performances at right-back cost him his place but when Patrick van Aanholt's loan ended, Martin came in at left-back. He scored his first and only goal with a glancing header in the home win over Sheffield United.
Southampton (From trainee on 29/9/2004) P/FL 11+5 FLC 2+1 FAC 3+2 Others 1
Bournemouth (Loaned on 29/10/2004) FL 2+1
Yeovil T (Loaned on 8/11/2006) FL 8
Yeovil T (Loaned on 3/3/2007) FL 3+1
Portsmouth (£150,000 on 5/7/2007) PL 1+1 FLC 1 FAC 2

Queens Park Rgrs *(Loaned on 8/10/2007) FL 6*
Charlton Ath *(Loaned on 1/9/2008) FL 19*
Coventry C *(Signed on 12/8/2009) FL 38+2/1 FAC 2*

CRAWFORD Harrison (Harry)

Born: Watford, 10 December 1991
Height: 6'1" **Weight:** 12.0
Harry was a prolific scorer at youth level for Southend and it was no surprise when he was called into the first team despite still being on scholarship forms. He made his debut as a substitute for Scott Spencer in the home victory over Walsall in March and started the final two matches against Stockport, when he netted his first senior goal, and away to Southampton. He was offered a two-year professional contract and his season was completed by being called up to the Republic of Ireland under-18 squad for their two matches against Macedonia in May.
Southend U *(Trainee) FL 2+5/1*

CRESSWELL Aaron William

Born: Liverpool, 15 December 1989
Height: 5'7" **Weight:** 10.5
A natural left-back who came up through the Tranmere youth system, Aaron is half way through a two-year contract at Prenton Park. He started the season as a regular under John Barnes but suffered a dip in form and was out of the side from October until February. He persevered quietly and without fuss in the reserves, grabbing his chance again with a typically strong, unruffled performance when recalled for the home game against Oldham. Aaron is always a threat at set pieces as well as being a strong yet clean tackler and is impressively calm and assured for his age.
Tranmere Rov *(From trainee on 19/7/2008) FL 21+6/1 FLC 2 FAC 0+1 Others 1*

CRESSWELL Richard Paul Wesley

Born: Bridlington, 20 September 1977
Height: 6'0" **Weight:** 11.8
International Honours: E: U21-4
A player described as a model professional by Stoke manager Tony Pulis, he came on as a substitute in the opening day victory over Burnley and was within a whisker of scoring his first Premier League goal as a Stoke player with a shot that hit the crossbar. He then started in the next match at Liverpool, and also in the League Cup away win at Leyton Orient. Those were his final appearances in a Stoke shirt, but his goals in the club's promotion

campaign two years earlier will be long remembered by the supporters as will his overall contribution to the team, his tireless work rate and willingness to operate in any position asked of him, marking him out very much as a manager's player and a credit to his profession. After joining Sheffield United in September on a three-month loan, the move was made permanent in January. He had a splendid season, making his debut in the evening of the day he signed and starting the next game against Doncaster, cracking a rib as he collided with the post when scoring the equaliser. Once fit he was a regular in the side either as a striker or playing wide on the left. He worked hard, ran into space, created chances and scored goals in a variety ways including a cheeky effort against Plymouth and by scoring four goals in the final five games he finished as the club's top scorer. It came as no surprise when he was voted joint 'Players' Player of the Year'.
York C *(From trainee on 15/11/1995) FL 72+23/21 FLC 3+3 FAC 4+2/3 Others 4*
Mansfield T *(Loaned on 27/3/1997) FL 5/1*
Sheffield Wed *(£950,000 + on 25/3/1999) P/FL 7+24/2 FLC 1+1/1 FAC 0+3*
Leicester C *(£750,000 on 5/9/2000) PL 3+5 FLC 1 FAC 0+2/1 Others 0+2*
Preston NE *(£500,000 on 12/3/2001) FL 164+23/49 FLC 8+2/5 FAC 2+1/3 Others 4+2/1*
Leeds U *(£1,150,000 on 24/8/2005) FL 30+8/9 FLC 1+1/2 FAC 0+2 Others 0+2*
Stoke C *(Signed on 3/8/2007) P/FL 54+20/11 FLC 5+1/2 FAC 2*
Sheffield U *(Signed on 29/9/2009) FL 28+3/12 FAC 2+1/2*

CRESSWELL Ryan Anthony

Born: Rotherham, 22 December 1987
Height: 5'9" **Weight:** 10.5
The tall and determined defender rotated with fellow centre-backs Efe Sodje and Ben Futcher to provide stability in Bury's back four. With his excellent heading ability and good pace, Ryan was also used as another striker during the closing stages of games in which the Shakers were behind. He was said to be devastated when he received a red card at Port Vale for two bookable offences.
Sheffield U *(From trainee on 25/7/2006)*
Rotherham U *(Loaned on 21/9/2007) FL 1+2 Others 1*
Morecambe *(Loaned on 2/11/2007) FL 2*
Macclesfield T *(Loaned on 10/1/2008) FL 19/1*
Bury *(Free on 31/7/2008) FL 43+10/1 FAC 2 Others 4*

CROFT Lee David

Born: Wigan, 21 June 1985
Height: 5'9" **Weight:** 13.1
International Honours: E: Yth
Lee ended his contract at Norwich as 'Player of the Year' and looked like a good summer signing by Derby. The right-winger went straight into the team in the hope that he would run at defenders and put in good crosses. Lee worked hard but, for some reason, could not find the expected effectiveness at Pride Park. He scored his only goal in a convincing home victory over Sheffield Wednesday but disappeared from the team in the New Year and, at times, was not even named among the substitutes.
Manchester C *(From trainee on 2/7/2002) PL 4+24/1 FLC 0+1 FAC 0+3*
Oldham Ath *(Loaned on 12/11/2004) FL 11+1 FAC 3/1 Others 2/1*
Norwich C *(£585,000 on 2/8/2006) FL 86+32/9 FLC 3+2 FAC 7+1*
Derby Co *(Free on 28/7/2009) FL 14+5/1 FLC 1 FAC 1*

CROFTS Andrew Lawrence

Born: Chatham, 29 May 1984
Height: 5'9" **Weight:** 10.8
International Honours: W: 13; U21-10; Yth
Signed in the summer after leaving Gillingham, Andrew proved to be a great acquisition for Brighton by manager Russell Slade. A non-stop midfield dynamo, he started slowly but blossomed in the autumn, especially when new manager Gus Poyet made him captain. Andrew never looked back and revelled in the responsibility, leading by example. As well as feeding his forwards, he also contributed a number of goals himself, notably late winners at Exeter, Torquay and Stockport. In March, Andrew was rewarded with another cap for Wales and was voted Albion's 'Player of the Season' at the end of the campaign.
Gillingham *(From trainee on 6/8/2003) FL 162+12/17 FLC 5+3/2 FAC 3+3 Others 3*
Peterborough U *(Loaned on 19/11/2008) FL 4+5*
Brighton & Hove A *(Free on 2/7/2009) FL 44/5 FLC 1 FAC 5/2*

CROSSLEY Mark Geoffrey

Born: Barnsley, 16 June 1969
Height: 6'0" **Weight:** 16.0
International Honours: W: 8; B-1; E: U21-3
Mark came to Chesterfield as goalkeeping coach and back-up to Tommy Lee but played in the season's opener to become the club's oldest debutant. Mark played three more

times when Lee was rested in December and performed well, using his experience to marshal the defence to good effect. From the sidelines he contributes fully to the team's management during games.

Nottingham F (From trainee on 2/7/1987) P/FL 301+2 FLC 39+1 FAC 32 Others 18
Millwall (Loaned on 20/2/1998) FL 13
Middlesbrough (Free on 25/7/2000) PL 21+2 FLC 5 FAC 3
Stoke C (Loaned on 29/11/2002) FL 1
Stoke C (Loaned on 6/3/2003) FL 11
Fulham (£500,000 on 14/8/2003) PL 19+1 FLC 4
Sheffield Wed (Loaned on 8/11/2006) FL 17/1 FAC 2
Oldham Ath (Free on 10/8/2007) FL 59 FLC 3 FAC 7 Others 1
Chesterfield (Free on 2/7/2009) FL 4

CROUCH Peter James
Born: Macclesfield, 30 January 1981
Height: 6'7" **Weight:** 11.12
Club Honours: Div 1 '04; FAC '06; CS '06
International Honours: E: 38; B-1; U21-6; Yth

Peter was another of Harry Redknapp's signings from former club Portsmouth at the beginning of the season. He was a former Spurs' junior, but without playing senior football. Peter played a part in all Tottenham's Premier League games, with 21 starts and 17 appearances from the bench. He scored eight League goals, but another five in six Cup appearances. These included a hat-trick in the 5-1 Carling Cup win at Preston in September. Peter continues to be a regular for Fabio Capello's England, where his scoring ratio is excellent, and he added goals against Belarus and Egypt. Peter also played in the friendly against Brazil and is in the 23-man squad for the World Cup finals. Peter's height makes him a natural target for high balls and he wins a good proportion before laying off an accurate pass. But he also has good close control together with lightning speed of thought leading to often skilful finishes. Peter was on hand to score Spurs' vital winner at Manchester City, heading home a parried save, that gave Spurs the Champions League qualification place.

Tottenham H (From trainee on 2/7/1998)
Queens Park Rgrs (£60,000 on 28/7/2000) FL 38+4/10 FLC 1+1 FAC 3/2
Portsmouth (£1,250,000 on 11/7/2001) FL 37/18 FLC 1/1 FAC 1
Aston Villa (£4,000,000 + on 28/3/2002) PL 20+17/6 FLC 1+1 Others 4

Peter Crouch

Norwich C *(Loaned on 8/9/2003) FL 14+1/4*
Southampton *(£2,000,000 on 14/7/2004) PL 18+9/12 FLC 1 FAC 5/4*
Liverpool *(£7,000,000 on 20/7/2005) PL 55+30/22 FLC 5/1 FAC 10+1/5 Others 23+10/14*
Portsmouth *(£9,000,000 on 11/7/2008) PL 38/11 FLC 1 FAC 3/1 Others 6+1/4*
Tottenham H *(Signed on 27/7/2009) PL 21+17/8 FLC 2+1/4 FAC 6/1*

CROWE Jason William Robert
Born: Sidcup, 30 September 1978
Height: 5'9" **Weight:** 10.9
Club Honours: Div 1 '03
International Honours: E: Yth; Sch
Signed from relegated Northampton, attacking right-back Jason began as first choice, playing in the first dozen games as Leeds remained unbeaten. He suffered a hamstring injury in a 1-0 win at MK Dons and made only one more start in the next two months. He was in and out of the side and looked set to miss Leeds' FA Cup tie at Manchester United until Leigh Bromby was suspended. Jason played his best game for Leeds in the 1-0 win, making a goal-line clearance to deny Wayne Rooney an equaliser. His season ended prematurely with an ankle operation in April.
Arsenal *(From trainee on 13/5/1996) FLC 0+2 FAC 0+1*
Crystal Palace *(Loaned on 10/11/1998) FL 8*
Portsmouth *(£750,000 + on 7/7/1999) FL 67+19/5 FLC 4 FAC 1+2*
Brentford *(Loaned on 12/9/2000) FL 9 FLC 2*
Grimsby T *(Free on 7/8/2003) FL 64+5/4 FLC 3 FAC 3 Others 1*
Northampton T *(Free on 7/7/2005) FL 170+1/14 FLC 8/1 FAC 10/2 Others 1+3*
Leeds U *(Free on 2/7/2009) FL 16+1 FLC 3 FAC 3+1 Others 3/2*

CRUISE Thomas Daniel
Born: Islington, 9 March 1991
Height: 6'1" **Weight:** 12.8
International Honours: E: Yth
The Englishman with the famous name made his Arsenal debut in the Champions League group game away to Olympiacos. Rated highly by the manager, the left-back impressed but continued to learn his trade in the reserves. Also able to play in the centre of the defence if required, his work rate, strength and ability to join up with the attack down the left side make him a player with a future.
Arsenal *(From trainee on 2/7/2008) Others 1*

CUDICINI Carlo
Born: Milan, Italy, 6 September 1973
Height: 6'1" **Weight:** 12.3
Club Honours: FAC '00; CS '00; FLC '05; FAC '07
International Honours: Italy: U21; Yth
Carlo began the season as Tottenham's first choice goalkeeper, initially because of injury to Heurelho Gomes. He held his place against competition until the Brazilian took over and nailed down the position. Carlo's season ended in October as the result of a serious motor-cycle accident from which he has made a brave recovery, hoping to play in the coming season. Carlo played eight times for Spurs, keeping one clean sheet. He made a number of vital saves without looking spectacular, the result of his excellent positioning and speed of thought.
Chelsea *(£160,000 from Castel di Sangro, Italy, ex AC Milan, Prato, Lazio, on 6/8/1999) PL 138+4 FLC 18 FAC 31 Others 23+2*
Tottenham H *(Free on 26/1/2009) PL 10+1 FLC 1*

CUELLAR Carlos Javier
Born: Madrid, Spain, 23 August 1981
Height: 6'3" **Weight:** 13.3
Club Honours: SC '08; SLC '08
This was a breakthrough period for the Spaniard, who put his injury-affected first season behind him to become an Aston Villa regular. A centre-half by trade, Carlos had limited chances in his specialist position and instead continued his conversion to right-back. His defensive qualities are obvious with timely interceptions, blocks and headers. The attacking skills needed as a modern Premier League full-back are a work in progress for Carlos who is striving to improve his touch and passing. Carlos opened his account for Villa with League goals against Bolton and Manchester United and an FA Cup strike against Blackburn. Although now in his late 20s, the competitive defender still fiercely harbours the ambition to be capped by Spain. Carlos was sent off for the first time in his Villa career after two harsh bookings in the October draw at Everton.
Glasgow Rgrs *(£2,370,000 from CA Osasuna, Spain, ex Calahorra, Numancia, on 5/7/2007) SL 36/4 SLC 4/1 SC 6 Others 19*
Aston Villa *(£7,800,000 on 14/8/2008) PL 60+4/2 FLC 7 FAC 6/1 Others 8*

CULLEN Mark
Born: Ashington, 24 April 1992
Height: 5'9" **Weight:** 11.11
A prolific scorer for Hull's youth team, Mark earned a surprise call-up for the

FA Cup tie at Wigan in January and replaced Kamel Ghilas after 66 minutes. Having been awarded his first professional contract in March, the young Geordie who was rejected by Newcastle as a 14-year-old made his Premier League bow on his 18th birthday as a substitute for George Boateng against, of all teams, Sunderland. He became only the second player, after Portsmouth's Lennard Sowah, to appear in the Premier League having been born after its inception in 1992. Although it came on the day that the Tigers were effectively relegated, Mark started the following game – again at Wigan – and capped a fine performance with his 34th goal of the season at all levels to retain his place for the final game against Liverpool. He was named 'Young Player of the Year' by the club and the supporters' club.
Hull C *(From trainee on 25/11/2009) PL 2+1/1 FAC 0+1*

CUMMINGS Shaun Michael
Born: Hammersmith, 25 February 1989
Height: 6'0" **Weight:** 11.10
Loan signing Shaun made a comfortable debut at right-back for West Bromwich in their televised 2-0 home League win over Ipswich in August. However, after just four games for the Baggies his spell at the Hawthorns was cut short when Chelsea transferred him to Reading. He went straight into the first team to fill the spot at right-back left empty by Liam Rosenior's loan move to Ipswich. He impressed during his initial spell of seven consecutive Championship games, but a dip in form saw him lose his place to Jay Tabb midway through October. Thereafter he only made one more first team start, in the 1-1 home draw with Scunthorpe, though he was an unused substitute on three further occasions. But Shaun continued to apply himself well on the training ground and was rewarded with the captaincy of the reserve team in the second half of the season. A tall, leggy full-back who enjoys the opportunity to go forward, Shaun will need to work hard to regain a regular starting place in Royals' first team.
Chelsea *(From trainee on 4/7/2007)*
MK Dons *(Loaned on 5/8/2008) FL 29+3 FLC 1 FAC 1 Others 0+1*
West Bromwich A *(Loaned on 17/8/2009) FL 3 FLC 1*
Reading *(Signed on 1/9/2009) FL 8*

CUMMINGS Warren Thomas
Born: Aberdeen, 15 October 1980
Height: 5'9" **Weight:** 11.8
International Honours: S: 1; U21-9

The long-serving left-back was ever-present in the Bournemouth side until January and showed admirable consistency. With the transfer embargo the club was under, he would have kept his place but for a rush of blood at Aldershot. He reacted angrily to the ball being thrown at him and ended with a red card. As a result, Rhoys Wiggins was brought in before Warren showed versatility to play centre-half at Shrewsbury.
Chelsea (From trainee on 5/7/1999)
Bournemouth (Loaned on 20/10/2000) FL 10/1 Others 1
West Bromwich A (Loaned on 21/3/2001) FL 1+2
West Bromwich A (Loaned on 25/7/2001) FL 0+2 FLC 0+2
Dundee U (Loaned on 23/8/2002) SL 7+1 SLC 1
Dundee U (Loaned on 16/11/2002) SL 0+3
Bournemouth (Free on 3/2/2003) FL 203+18/6 FLC 6+1/1 FAC 13+1 Others 11

CUMMINS Michael (Micky) Thomas Stephen
Born: Dublin, 1 June 1978
Height: 6'0" **Weight:** 11.11
Club Honours: AMC '01
International Honours: RoI: U21-2; Yth
The experienced midfielder battled hard to get a permanent spot and never let Rotherham down when he did figure and certainly will not forget his fine goal in a brave extra-time defeat at West Bromwich in the Carling Cup. Micky faced strong competition in midfield, which made it hard to hold down a starting place on a regular basis. Was out of contract in the summer.
Middlesbrough (From trainee on 1/7/1995) PL 1+1
Port Vale (Free on 17/3/2000) FL 247+6/31 FLC 7/1 FAC 11/1 Others 16/1
Darlington (Free on 21/7/2006) FL 69+10/10 FLC 1+2 FAC 3+1 Others 3+2
Rotherham U (Free on 4/8/2008) FL 36+14/5 FLC 4/1 FAC 2/1 Others 5+1

CUNNINGHAM Gregory (Greg) Richard
Born: Galway, 31 January 1991
Height: 6'1" **Weight:** 11.7
International Honours: RoI: 1; Yth
A product of the Manchester City Academy, left-back Greg made his bow as a half-time substitute in the FA Cup victory at Scunthorpe in January and later in the season made his Premiership debut, also from the bench, in the 4-1 victory over Birmingham. With the left-back position proving such a problem for City, there may be more

opportunities ahead. Greg made his international debut for the Republic of Ireland in May, against Algeria.
Manchester C (From trainee on 10/7/2008) PL 0+2 FAC 0+1

CURETON Jamie
Born: Bristol, 28 August 1975
Height: 5'8" **Weight:** 10.7
International Honours: E: Yth
Jamie's contribution to Norwich's cause in 2009-10 was not as great as he would have liked, the prolific front pairing of Grant Holt and Chris Martin keeping him on the sidelines. Goals as a substitute in successive games in the autumn against Leyton Orient and Bristol Rovers pointed to a 'super-sub' role for the ever popular striker, but he soon found himself out of Paul Lambert's thinking altogether and spent the last three months of the season on loan at Shrewsbury. A proven and experienced goalscorer, he made his debut in the February away defeat at Bury. Understandably lacking match fitness, having not been involved in first team games at Norwich for some time, it was hoped that he would forge a fruitful partnership with fellow striker Dave Hibbert, but it never quite worked out. Glimpses of his skills and good positional play were evident but despite appearing in 12 league games he was unable to find the net. Was out of contract at the end of June.
Norwich C (From trainee on 5/2/1993) P/FL 13+16/6 FLC 0+1 FAC 0+2
Bournemouth (Loaned on 8/9/1995) FL 0+5 Others 0+1
Bristol Rov (£250,000 on 20/9/1996) FL 165+9/72 FLC 7+1/2 FAC 10/2 Others 6/3
Reading (£250,000 on 21/8/2000) FL 74+34/50 FLC 4+1/1 FAC 5+2/2 Others 6+1/2 (Free to Busan Icons, South Korea during 2003 close season)
Queens Park Rgrs (£95,000 from Busan Icons, South Korea on 2/2/2004) FL 20+23/6 FLC 2/1 FAC 1
Swindon T (Free on 5/8/2005) FL 22+8/7 FLC 0+1 Others 0+1
Colchester U (Loaned on 21/10/2005) FL 7+1/4 FAC 2/3
Colchester U (Free on 2/6/2006) FL 44/23 FLC 0+1 FAC 1/1
Norwich C (£750,000 on 2/7/2007) FL 42+27/16 FLC 2+1/2 FAC 2 Others 2
Barnsley (Loaned on 27/11/2008) FL 7+1/2
Shrewsbury T (Loaned on 17/2/2010) FL 10+2

CURRAN Craig
Born: Liverpool, 23 August 1989
Height: 5'9" **Weight:** 11.9
Still only 20 and in his fifth season with

Tranmere, Craig enjoyed a much better start than a year earlier, fortunately staying injury free this time. A hard-working striker, he is a good finisher and although Rovers' preferred 4-3-3 system did not really suit his style of play, he is always willing to track back, harry the opposition and run until the final whistle. Because of his enthusiasm and determination, Craig is a great favourite of the Prenton Park crowd and has begun to fulfil the potential he has shown since his explosive debut in 2007. He was Rover's second top scorer, with seven goals in all competitions.
Tranmere Rov (From trainee on 29/8/2006) FL 48+49/14 FLC 3+1/1 FAC 6+2 Others 3/1

CURRIE Darren Paul
Born: Hampstead, 29 November 1974
Height: 5'11" **Weight:** 12.7
Any hoped-for improvement in Darren's impact at Chesterfield did not materialise, and his patient approach did not ultimately add the necessary stimulus to the left of midfield. He was a regularly named but unused sub until joining Dagenham on loan in December. The veteran would eventually sign for his former manager, John Still, in January after being freed by Chesterfield. Besides his ability to pinpoint passes he possesses a great talent in being able to put his foot on the ball and look around for options on where to pass, thus slowing the game down. He made his Daggers' debut in AFC Bournemouth in November.
West Ham U (From trainee on 2/7/1993)
Shrewsbury T (Loaned on 5/9/1994) FL 10+2/2
Shrewsbury T (Loaned on 3/2/1995) FL 5
Leyton Orient (Loaned on 16/11/1995) FL 9+1
Shrewsbury T (£70,000 on 7/2/1996) FL 46+20/8 FLC 2+1/1 FAC 3
Plymouth Arg (Free on 26/3/1998) 5+2
Barnet (Free on 13/7/1998) FL 120+7/19 FLC 5/1 FAC 3/2 Others 6
Wycombe W (£200,000 on 11/7/2001) FL 109+17/14 FLC 5 FAC 6+1/5 Others 5
Brighton & Hove A (Free on 5/8/2004) FL 21+1/2 FLC 1
Ipswich T (£250,000 on 10/12/2004) FL 64+19/9 FLC 2 FAC 2 Others 1+1
Coventry C (Loaned on 23/11/2006) FL 6+2
Derby Co (Loaned on 15/3/2007) FL 4+3/1 Others 0+1
Luton T (Free on 4/7/2007) FL 25+6/2 FLC 1+1 FAC 4+1
Chesterfield (Free on 6/8/2008) FL 16+15/3 FLC 0+2/1 FAC 1+2 Others 1+1/1

Dagenham & Redbridge *(Loaned on 23/11/2009) FL 5+11*

CURTIS John Charles Keyworth
Born: Nuneaton, 3 September 1978
Height: 5'10" **Weight:** 11.9
Club Honours: FAYC '95; FLC '02
International Honours: E: B-1; U21-16; Yth; Sch
John can play in midfield or defence and had to appear in both positions during the early part of the season. As Northampton settled under the new management team, John found himself spending most of his days as a substitute although, with his experience and ability to adapt, he can be brought on from the bench without disturbing the balance of the team. Was out of contract in the summer.
Manchester U *(From trainee on 3/10/1995) PL 4+9 FLC 5 Others 0+1*
Barnsley *(Loaned on 19/11/1999) FL 28/2 Others 1+1*
Blackburn Rov *(£2,250,000 on 1/6/2000) P/FL 61 FLC 10 FAC 6 Others 1*
Sheffield U *(Loaned on 3/3/2003) FL 9+3 FAC 1 Others 3*
Leicester C *(Free on 15/8/2003) PL 14+1 FLC 1 FAC 1*
Portsmouth *(Free on 2/2/2004) PL 5+2*
Preston NE *(Loaned on 10/9/2004) FL 12*
Nottingham F *(Free on 3/2/2005) FL 76+3 FLC 1 FAC 8 Others 3*
Queens Park Rgrs *(Free on 3/8/2007) FL 3+1 FLC 0+1 (Freed on 7/3/2008)*
Northampton T *(Free from Wrexham, ex Worcester C, on 29/7/2009) FL 18+1 FLC 0+1 FAC 1*

CURTIS Wayne John
Born: Barrow, 6 March 1980
Height: 6'0" **Weight:** 12.2
Morecambe's longest-serving player made only nine starts in the League season and rarely had the chance to play in his favourite role as an out-and-out striker. Played on the left and the right of midfield his versatility saw him go on as a substitute more than 25 times and chip in with four goals. Wayne was chosen to start the final game of the campaign in the play-off semi-final against Dagenham but, despite his popularity with the fans for his loyalty, was released at the end of the season.
Morecambe *(Free from Holker OB on 3/3/1998) FL 48+55/11 FLC 1+1 FAC 1+1 Others 6+3/1*

CUTHBERT Scott
Born: Alexandria, 15 June 1987
Height: 6'2" **Weight:** 14.0
International Honours: S: B-1; U21-

Scott Cuthbert

13; Yth
Initially used as Swindon's left-back in the season's opener at Gillingham, a shaky performance saw Scott relegated to the bench. A magnificent display at the centre of defence in a Carling Cup tie at Wolverhampton in August soon revitalised his season and he became a fixture at the heart of the Town defence thereafter with a series of strong performances. He formed a solid defensive partnership with Gordon Greer and is a tough tackler who is good in the air.
Glasgow Celtic *(From juniors on 1/8/2004)*
Livingston *(Loaned on 15/12/2006) SL 4/1*
St Mirren *(Loaned on 14/8/2008) SL 28+1 SLC 0+1 SC 4*
Swindon T *(Signed on 13/7/2009) FL 39/3 FLC 1 FAC 3 Others 5*

CYWKA Tomasz
Born: Gliwice, Poland, 27 June 1988
Height: 5'11" **Weight:** 12.0
International Honours: Poland: U21; Yth
The Polish under-21 striker joined Derby from Wigan on loan in March and immediately created a favourable impression. Derby were struggling to find fit forwards at the time and Tomasz likes to play behind the main striker. Although slightly built, he shows considerable strength in holding the ball, especially on the half-turn, when defenders are marking him tightly. There were echoes of Kris Commons in his style and although he did not score, there were frequent cries of "sign him on" from the crowd. That is exactly what Nigel Clough did. Tomasz had an offer from Wigan but felt he would have more chances at Pride Park.
Wigan Ath *(Signed from Gwarek Zabrze, Poland on 4/8/2006) FLC 1 FAC 0+1*
Oldham Ath *(Loaned on 31/10/2006) FL 0+4 Others 1*
Derby Co *(Loaned on 25/3/2010) FL 4+1*

D

DA COSTA Manuel Marouan
Born: Nancy, France, 6 May 1986
Height: 6'3" **Weight:** 12.13
International Honours: Portugal: U21-2
The Portuguese central defender joined West Ham from Fiorentina in September. He struggled at first with the pace and power of the Premier League, then scored his first goal at Hull, coming up with the vital equaliser. It was late in the season when he finally came to the fore. At Everton, he showed superb heading skills and also scored a vital goal. Manuel never looks ruffled and his real strength is his coolness in defence. He grew in confidence in every game and finished the season on a high.
West Ham U (Signed from Fiorentina, Italy, ex Nancy, PSV Eindhoven, Sampdoria - loan, on 31/8/2009) PL 12+3/2 FLC 1

DAGNALL Christopher (Chris)
Born: Liverpool, 15 April 1986
Height: 5'8" **Weight:** 11.9
Free of the injuries that had plagued the previous two seasons and with a permanent place in Rochdale's attack, Chris proved one of the best finishers in League Two, reaching 20 League goals for the first time and becoming one of the few Dale strikers to pass 50 career League goals. His partnership with the taller Chris O'Grady formed the attacking basis of Dale's successful promotion season and together they scored just over half of the 82 goals. It was the first time ever that Rochdale had two players hitting 20 in the same season. A personal highlight for Chris was his hat-trick against Grimsby, his fourth for the club and a tally second only to legendary 1920s centre-forward Albert Whitehurst.
Tranmere Rov (From trainee on 11/7/2003) FL 18+21/7 FLC 0+1 FAC 0+1 Others 1+2
Rochdale (£25,000 on 13/1/2006) FL 124+33/54 FLC 5 FAC 5/1 Others 8+2/5

DAILLY Christian Eduard
Born: Dundee, 23 October 1973
Height: 6'0" **Weight:** 12.10
Club Honours: SC '94, '08, '09
International Honours: S: 67; B-1; U21-34; Yth; Sch
Christian was signed by Charlton in the summer to add experience to the squad. He missed only two games all

season and was assured and reliable in central defence alongside Miguel Llera or Sam Sodje. Good in the air and a great passer of the ball, his consistent performances earned him the accolade of being named as the supporters' 'Player of the Year'. Christian scored Charlton's first goal of the campaign on his debut against Wycombe with a powerful header. He frequently goes forward for set pieces but has not as yet added to his opening day goal. Was out of contract at the end of June.
Dundee U (From juniors on 2/8/1990) SL 110+33/18 SLC 9/1 SC 10+2 Others 8+1/1
Derby Co (£1,000,000 on 12/8/1996) PL 62+5/4 FLC 6 FAC 4+1
Blackburn Rov (£5,300,000 on 22/8/1998) P/FL 60+10/4 FLC 5+1 FAC 4 Others 2
West Ham U (£1,750,000 on 18/11/2001) P/FL 133+25/2 FLC 8/1 FAC 14+6 Others 3+2/1
Southampton (Loaned on 21/9/2007) FL 11
Glasgow Rgrs (Free on 30/1/2008) SL 19+2/2 SLC 1+1 SC 5+1 Others 4+1
Charlton Ath (Free on 31/7/2009) FL 44/1 FAC 1 Others 4

DALEY Luke Aaron
Born: Northampton, 10 November 1989
Height: 5'11" **Weight:** 11.0
This speedy front runner made his first start for the Norwich senior side against Sunderland in the Carling Cup and followed with his full League debut at MK Dons. An unfortunate string of injuries hampered his progress in the second half of the campaign, but this former Academy player has a promising future with his direct running style and extreme pace likely to trouble the best of defenders.
Norwich C (From trainee on 8/4/2008) FL 3+7 FLC 1 Others 1+1

DALEY Omar
Born: Kingston, Jamaica, 25 April 1981
Height: 5'10" **Weight:** 11.0
International Honours: Jamaica: 56
Bradford's speedy Jamaican winger missed the first four months of the season as he recovered from a serious knee injury. He made his first appearance as a substitute at Carlisle in December but it was another month before he was fit enough to start a game. It was a frustrating season for such a lively player, who looks equally effective on the left or right, but there was one bright spot - a 25-yard winning goal against Aldershot at Valley Parade. Unfortunately Omar blotted his copybook when he was sent off at

Chesterfield for an off-the-ball clash and will miss the opening fixture of the new season as he sits out the final game of his suspension.
Reading (Loaned from Portmore U, Jamaica on 19/8/2003) FL 0+6 FLC 0+1
Preston NE (Loaned from Portmore U, Jamaica on 3/8/2004) FL 1+13 FLC 1+2/1
Bradford C (Signed from Charleston Battery, USA on 16/1/2007) FL 82+15/10 FLC 2 FAC 3/1 Others 1+1

DANIEL Colin
Born: Nottingham, 15 February 1988
Height: 6'0" **Weight:** 13.5
Having been on loan at Macclesfield at the end of 2008-09 and then released by Crewe, Colin signed permanently last summer and went straight into the team. He was ever-present until a hamstring injury in March, but recovered to appear in the final matches. One of most consistent performers, Colin filled the wide left midfield berth, pressing forward, assisting with several goals and scoring three. Colin surprised even himself with his first senior goal in the home draw against Bradford, a header for the first time in his career. His goal in the home match against Hereford at the end of December was Macclesfield's 'Goal of the Season', a stunning strike from 35 yards. His contract was extended to June 2012.
Crewe Alex (£20,000 + from Eastwood T on 8/5/2007) FL 9+5/1 FAC 3
Macclesfield T (Free on 24/3/2009) FL 42+4/3 FLC 1 FAC 1 Others 1

DANIELS Charlie
Born: Harlow, 7 September 1986
Height: 5'10" **Weight:** 11.10
Although not a natural left-back, Charlie seemed to excel with an extended run in this position for Leyton Orient. He is an excellent crosser of the ball and a free-kick specialist, so it was surprising that he failed to score a single goal during the season. Charlie was out of contract in the summer and was offered a new deal
Tottenham H (From trainee on 7/7/2005)
Chesterfield (Loaned on 9/3/2007) FL 2
Leyton Orient (Loaned on 4/8/2007) FL 24+7/2 FLC 1+1 FAC 2 Others 1+1
Gillingham (Loaned on 26/8/2008) FL 5/1
Leyton Orient (Free on 9/1/2009) FL 61+1/2 FLC 2 FAC 2 Others 2

DANIELS Luke Matthew
Born: Bolton, 5 January 1988
Height: 6'4" **Weight:** 12.10
International Honours: E: Yth

Scott Dann

A former England Youth international goalkeeper, Luke signed a two-year contract with West Bromwich in July, then made a season-long loan move to Tranmere in order to improve his League experience. As agreed in the deal by then manager John Barnes, he went into the first team immediately, making his debut at Yeovil. Luke handles the ball confidently and is particularly adept at dealing with free kicks, while both his kicking from hands and distribution improved immeasurably. He was virtually ever-present in the Rovers' side until a knock to his back in the home game against Wycombe in mid-April ended his season, leaving Luke facing possible surgery.
West Bromwich A (From trainee on 18/7/2006)
Motherwell (Loaned on 8/2/2008) SL 2
Shrewsbury T (Loaned on 5/8/2008) FL 38 FLC 1 Others 5
Tranmere Rov (Loaned on 21/7/2009) FL 37 FLC 2 FAC 5 Others 1

DANN Scott
Born: Liverpool, 14 February 1987
Height: 6'2" **Weight:** 12.0
Club Honours: Div 2 '07
International Honours: E: U21-2
Scott answered an emergency call to make his Birmingham debut at Hull in September despite not being fully fit and played a blinder. From then on he never looked back and forged a fine partnership with Roger Johnson. Scott's ability to spot danger and act, and his timing in the tackle, were features of a fine rookie season at Premier League level. Showed good composure on the ball and passed it well. A threat at set pieces too, Scott was one of the signings of the Premier League season.
Walsall (From trainee on 6/8/2004) FL 52+7/7 FLC 1+1/1 FAC 7 Others 1
Coventry C (Signed on 31/1/2008) FL 45+2/3 FLC 2/1 FAC 1+1
Birmingham C (Signed on 12/6/2009) PL 30 FLC 1 FAC 4/1

DANNS Neil Alexander
Born: Liverpool, 23 November 1982
Height: 5'9" **Weight:** 12.1
Crystal Palace's creative midfielder was largely seen on the right wing for the majority of the season and used his eye for goal to good effect, getting forward to support the attack whenever possible. After an injury-ridden 2008-09, Neil remained for the large part fit last season but missed Palace's crucial last relegation game of the season at Sheffield Wednesday after being sent off against West Bromwich in the final home match. He formed a key partnership with Darren Ambrose in the centre of the team, finishing as second top scorer for Palace.
Blackburn Rov (From trainee on 3/7/2000) PL 1+2 FLC 2 FAC 1 Others 1
Blackpool (Loaned on 7/8/2003) FL 12/2 FLC 2 Others 1
Hartlepool U (Loaned on 12/3/2004) FL 8+1/1 Others 0+2
Colchester U (Signed on 9/9/2004) FL 70+3/19 FLC 3/1 FAC 5+1/5 Others 4+1/3
Birmingham C (£550,000 + on 26/6/2006) P/FL 11+20/3 FLC 5 FAC 0+3
Crystal Palace (£600,000 on 22/1/2008) FL 57+9/10 FLC 2 FAC 8/2

DAPRELA Fabio
Born: Ticino, Switzerland, 19 February 1991
Height: 5'11" **Weight:** 10.3
International Honours: Switzerland: Yth
West Ham gained the signature of the highly-rated Swiss left-back in July when he joined from the Grasshopper club. Fabio made his first team debut in the FA Cup against Arsenal in January. He gave an excellent performance, looking solid in the tackle and made three storming runs forward. Certainly not out of his depth in the Premier League and one for the future.
West Ham U (Signed from Grasshoppers, Switzerland on 31/7/2009) PL 4+3 FAC 1

DARBY Stephen Mark
Born: Liverpool, 6 October 1988
Height: 6'0" **Weight:** 12.6
Club Honours: FAYC '07
International Honours: E: Yth
Stephen is a right-back and a highly-rated product of the Liverpool Academy who starred in the club's FA Youth Cup successes of 2006 and 2007. Sadly, he has yet to make much impact on the first team, making only three appearances in 2009-10. His first opportunity came in the Champions League home tie with Fiorentina in December, the second in the 1-1 FA

Cup draw at Reading in January and finally his Premiership debut as a 90th-minute substitute for Philipp Degen against Tottenham. In March he was loaned to Swindon following an injury to Kevin Amankwaah and started every game until the end of the season. A young right-back who impressed with his sound and sensible defensive displays, Stephen netted the decisive penalty in the play-off shoot-out at the Valley and made a substitute appearance in the Wembley final.
Liverpool *(From trainee on 26/7/2006) PL 0+1 FLC 0+1 FAC 1 Others 1+1*
Swindon T *(Loaned on 11/3/2010) FL 12 Others 1+2*

DA SILVA Paulo Cesar
Born: Asuncion, Paraguay, 1 February 1980
Height: 5'11" **Weight:** 12.0
International Honours: Paraguay: 70
The Paraguay international defender played in half Sunderland's games but spent most of the second half of the campaign as an unused substitute. A centre-back by trade, Paulo made most of his appearances there but had a few games at right-back. A stocky, experienced player, he reads the game well and is composed in possession. Paulo had tried his luck in Italy when much younger and arrived on Wearside having enjoyed considerable recent success in Mexican football. Although he would have welcomed more game time, Paulo was in the squad for every match following his debut in August. For the coming season, Paulo will be joined in the Sunderland squad by his international team-mate Cristian Riveros.
Sunderland *(Signed from Deportivo Toluca, Mexico, ex Atlantida Sporting Club, Cerro Porteno, Perugia, Lanus, Venezia, Cosenza, Libertad, on 13/7/2009) PL 12+4 FLC 3 FAC 2*

DAVIDSON Callum Iain
Born: Stirling, 25 June 1976
Height: 5'10" **Weight:** 11.8
Club Honours: S Div 1 '97
International Honours: S: 19; U21-2
Preston's captain had yet another injury-plagued season, missing two months from September and another six weeks after a sickening head injury at Peterborough in January which left him minus several teeth. When available, Callum led by example from left-back, with occasional outings in midfield, and took over penalty duties with some success, scoring with all three efforts. On the down side, he was unlucky to be dismissed at Ipswich in conceding a spot kick but his strong tackling,

excellent distribution and willingness to overlap all demonstrated his value to the team and the club. A born leader, Darren Ferguson regularly cited him as a glowing example to the club's-up-and-coming youngsters.
St Johnstone *(From juniors on 8/6/1994) SL 39+5/4 SLC 1 Others 3*
Blackburn Rov *(£1,750,000 on 12/2/1998) P/FL 63+2/1 FLC 3+1 FAC 6 Others 1+1*
Leicester C *(£1,700,000 on 12/7/2000) P/FL 90+11/2 FLC 5+1 FAC 5+1 Others 0+1*
Preston NE *(Free on 6/8/2004) FL 136+12/18 FLC 2+1 FAC 10*

DAVIES Andrew John
Born: Stockton, 17 December 1984
Height: 6'3" **Weight:** 14.8
International Honours: E: U21-1; Yth
It was a season where it just did not happen for Andrew at Stoke and his only appearance in the colours of the Potters came as a substitute in a League Cup tie at Leyton Orient. He did however wear another set of red and white stripes during a three-month loan spell at Sheffield United as emergency central defensive cover. On the evening of the day he signed he equipped himself well in the Sheffield derby at Bramall Lane and playing as a central defender, with one appearance at right-back, he produced eight competent performances before returning early to Stoke.
Middlesbrough *(From trainee on 6/7/2002) PL 39+14 FLC 4+1 FAC 2+1 Others 4*
Queens Park Rgrs *(Loaned on 12/1/2005) FL 9*
Derby Co *(Loaned on 6/7/2005) FL 22+1/3 FAC 1*
Southampton *(£1,000,000 on 9/10/2007) FL 22+1 FAC 2*
Stoke C *(£1,300,000 on 19/8/2008) PL 0+2 FLC 0+1 FAC 1*
Preston NE *(Loaned on 13/2/2009) FL 5*
Sheffield U *(Loaned on 18/9/2009) FL 7+1*

DAVIES Arron Rhys
Born: Cardiff, 22 June 1984
Height: 5'9" **Weight:** 10.0
Club Honours: Div 2 '05
International Honours: W: 1; U21-14
After an injury interrupted spell at Nottingham Forest things looked to be improving for Arron following a good pre-season, but having played in the early rounds of the Carling Cup and struggling with injury he joined Brighton on the last day of the summer transfer window. Despite linking up with his former Yeovil manager, Russell Slade, now in charge at Brighton, on

loan for four months, he was rarely able to reproduce the exciting wing-play that enticed Forest to splash out a large fee on him. It was not the best of times at the Withdean Stadium as the club languished in or around the relegation zone and he returned to the City Ground a month earlier than intended. At the end of January Arron was next loaned to his old club, Yeovil, but found it hard to break into the side and made just ten appearances. On his day, one of the most exciting flank players in League One, he is in desperate need of a decent injury-free run.
Southampton *(From trainee on 11/7/2002)*
Barnsley *(Loaned on 13/2/2004) FL 1+3*
Yeovil T *(Signed on 16/12/2004) FL 76+25/22 FLC 2+1/1 FAC 2+4/2 Others 5/2*
Nottingham F *(Signed on 20/7/2007) FL 12+20/1 FLC 3 FAC 1+4*
Brighton & Hove A *(Loaned on 1/9/2009) FL 7 Others 1*
Brighton & Hove A *(Free on 11/2/2010)*
Yeovil T *(Loaned on 11/2/2010) FL 4+6*

DAVIES Benjamin (Ben) James
Born: Birmingham, 27 May 1981
Height: 5'6" **Weight:** 10.7
Club Honours: FC '04; Div 2 '10
A brilliant signing by Notts County's manager Ian McParland from Shrewsbury in the summer, Ben fulfilled his role as a midfield playmaker in a quite outstanding season. Creator and scorer of goals galore, with breathtaking skill from set pieces, he was the supporters' 'Player of the Year' and selected in the PFA League Two 'Team of the Year'. Ben is rated by many as being among the best players seen at Meadow Lane in recent years.
Walsall *(From trainee at Stoke C on 11/8/1999)*
Kidderminster Hrs *(Free on 1/3/2000) FL 11+1 FLC 1 Others 1*
Chester C *(Free on 7/5/2002) FL 80+9/9 FLC 1+1/1 FAC 6 Others 1+2*
Shrewsbury T *(Free on 6/6/2006) FL 111+1/30 FLC 2 FAC 2 Others 11/1*
Notts Co *(Free on 2/7/2009) FL 45/15 FAC 6/1*

DAVIES Craig Martin
Born: Burton-on-Trent, 9 January 1986
Height: 6'2" **Weight:** 13.5
International Honours: W: 5; U21-8; Yth
Hampered by a knee injury at the start of the season, Craig barely got a look in at Brighton where he played as a reserve forward, making an occasional

appearance from the bench or in the absence of more senior strikers. Despite showing bags of enthusiasm, he was unable to add to the one goal he scored for the club in his first game back in February 2009 and moved to Yeovil on loan towards the end of September. Craig's spell with Yeovil was brief and to the point. Four games in a month's loan in the autumn saw the tall Welsh striker fail to score although the side won two and drew two with him in the side. Back at Brighton he next joined Port Vale on loan in January 2010 until the end of the season. An all-action striker, Craig helped push Vale towards the play-offs by scoring seven goals in just 24 appearances. His willingness to have a shot at any time soon endeared him to his new fans, although with a bit more composure he could play at a much higher level.

Oxford U *(From trainee on 17/2/2005)* FL 23+25/8 FLC 1 FAC 1+2 Others 1+2 *(£85,000 to Verona, Italy on 31/1/2006)*
Wolverhampton W *(Loaned from Verona, Italy on 4/8/2006)* FL 6+17 FLC 1 FAC 3/2
Oldham Ath *(Free on 20/7/2007)* FL 36+8/10 FLC 3/1 FAC 5/1 Others 3/1
Stockport Co *(Loaned on 1/11/2008)* FL 9/5 FAC 4/1
Brighton & Hove A *(Signed on 2/2/2009)* FL 10+11/1 FAC 1+1
Yeovil T *(Loaned on 25/9/2009)* FL 2+2
Port Vale *(Loaned on 15/1/2010)* FL 22+2/7

DAVIES Curtis Eugene
Born: Leytonstone, 15 March 1985
Height: 6'1" **Weight:** 11.13
Club Honours: Div 1 '05
International Honours: England: U21-3
Curtis started the season as Aston Villa's first choice centre-half but ended it on the transfer list after his blossoming career stalled for the first time. His campaign was off to a frustrating start when he dislocated a shoulder during a pre-season game. Villa then had a shortage of centre-backs following Martin Laursen's retirement and the sale of Zat Knight, while James Collins and Richard Dunne were yet to arrive. Curtis played on with pain in Villa's first two Premier League games and two in the Europa League but subsequently needed surgery. It meant that his goal in the memorable 3-1 victory over Liverpool at Anfield in August was the only silver lining in a cloudy season. Curtis made good progress with his rehabilitation, returning for a brief substitute cameo in January's FA Cup win over Brighton, but that was his last appearance. At the end of the season, the £10 million defender

was put up for sale.
Luton T *(From trainee on 2/7/2004)* FL 54+2/2 FLC 2 FAC 3 Others 0+1
West Bromwich A *(£3,000,000 on 1/9/2005)* P/FL 65/2 FLC 2 FAC 6
Aston Villa *(£8,000,000 on 31/8/2007)* PL 45+4/3 FLC 1 FAC 5+1 Others 7+1

DAVIES Kevin Cyril
Born: Sheffield, 26 March 1977
Height: 6'0" **Weight:** 13.6
International Honours: E: U21-3; Yth
While Kevin's goals-per-game ratio will never be as impressive as the Premiership's top strikers, he remains absolutely pivotal to maintaining Bolton's continued stay in the top tier. His goal in the 2-2 draw with Hull in December was his first in ten games, though still committed and powerful performances throughout ensured he would always remain in the starting side. Equally adept playing on the right side of a front three or as the spearhead of the team, Kevin is one of the last of the genuine old-style British centre-forwards. Despite being unfairly labelled as an over-physical player, Kevin's game consists of excellent close control in addition to his undoubted physical prowess and he is, despite his reputation, one of the most fouled Premiership players of recent years. He still retains his ability to notch important goals, not least when capping a fantastic performance in the 2-1 win at West Ham with a bullet header. He also turned his hand to penalty taking, due to the absence of Matt Taylor, in the 4-0 win over Wigan. Kevin rightfully won a number of Bolton's 'Player of the Year' awards.
Chesterfield *(From trainee on 18/4/1994)* FL 113+16/22 FLC 7+2/1 FAC 10/6 Others 9+2/1
Southampton *(£750,000 on 14/5/1997)* PL 20+5/9 FLC 3+1/3 FAC 1
Blackburn Rov *(£7,250,000 on 2/6/1998)* P/FL 11+12/1 FLC 3 FAC 2/1 Others 1
Southampton *(Signed on 18/8/1999)* PL 59+23/10 FLC 3+2/1 FAC 3+5/2
Millwall *(Loaned on 13/9/2002)* FL 6+3/3
Bolton W *(Free on 25/7/2003)* PL 243+4/53 FLC 11+3/2 FAC 13/4 Others 12+1/1

DAVIES Mark Nicholas
Born: Willenhall, 18 February 1988
Height: 5'11" **Weight:** 11.8
International Honours: E: Yth
Season 2009-10 was something of a stop-start one for Mark at Bolton, with injury playing a major part. Having shown considerable promise during the latter stages of the previous campaign,

Mark forced his way into the first team during the initial period. An inventive and probing midfield playmaker, he really caught the eye with some confident displays, scoring his first goal for the club in the Carling Cup victory at Tranmere and also notching in his first FA Cup game against Lincoln. However, an ankle injury sustained in the game at Arsenal saw him spend some time out of action and he figured in just under half of Bolton's League games, starting just five. A player with considerable promise, Mark will be looking to feature more prominently.
Wolverhampton W *(From trainee on 24/2/2005)* FL 12+15/1 FLC 2+1/1 FAC 1+4
Leicester C *(Loaned on 27/11/2008)* FL 5+2/1 FAC 1+1
Bolton W *(£1,000,000 on 26/1/2009)* PL 13+14 FLC 2/1 FAC 0+2/1

DAVIES Scott David
Born: Blackpool, 27 February 1987
Height: 6'2" **Weight:** 11.4
Morecambe's reserve team goalkeeper was again left frustrated by the form of number-one Barry Roche. He made just one appearance, in a 4-1 defeat at Aldershot in October, and he was immediately replaced by Doncaster 'keeper Ben Smith, who was brought on loan for three games. After being left on the bench for three seasons, he was expected to look for another club in the summer in order to attain regular football.
Morecambe *(From juniors on 26/7/2005)* FL 11 Others 3+1

DAVIES Scott Myles Edward
Born: Aylesbury, 10 March 1988
Height: 5'11" **Weight:** 11.13
Club Honours: FC '08
International Honours: RoI: U21-3; Yth
Scott was in the Reading first team squad for the first six games of the season and although his adventurous style of play and long-range shooting was popular with the fans, he failed to get his name on the score-sheet. The young midfielder was then sent out on loan to Wycombe in October to gain match experience and of all the loan signings last season at Adams Park, Scott probably had the most dramatic impact. Wycombe manager Gary Waddock had previously signed him on loan at Aldershot and the central midfielder, with endless energy and drive and a penchant to hit the early ball, normally put defences on the back foot. In his third game, his first half performance against Walsall was simply magnificent. Spotting the 'keeper was off his line at a free kick,

he scored with an incredible 40 yard dipping shot, followed up by a second goal when carefully guiding the ball home from 18 yards. Only a goal-line clearance prevented a first half hat-trick. Scott's loan was increased to the full 93 day period, before he returned to Reading in January. Unable to make it on to the pitch at Reading, Scott, who has been a member of the Republic of Ireland under-21 squad, said in an interview with 4-4-2 magazine: "I do not mind where I play, as long as I am playing and doing well".

Reading *(From trainee on 5/7/2006) FL 3+1 FLC 1*
Aldershot T *(Loaned on 24/7/2008) FL 37+4/13 FAC 3 Others 1/1*
Wycombe W *(Loaned on 16/10/2009) FL 14+1/3 FAC 2/1*
Yeovil T *(Loaned on 16/3/2010) FL 4*

DAVIES Simon

Born: Haverfordwest, 23 October 1979
Height: 5'10" **Weight:** 11.4
International Honours: W: 58; B-1; U21-10; Yth
The first half of the campaign proved frustrating for Fulham's Welsh international midfielder, who twice returned from a long-term foot injury only to quickly suffer another lay off. With more competition for places, it was not until February that he once more established himself as a regular. A player who is comfortable on either flank, he usually started games on the left of midfield where he linked well with the left-sided defenders, Paul Konchesky and Nicky Shorey. Simon was also deployed at right-back on occasions, enjoying a fine game in this position in the home Europa League tie with Wolfsburg. He returned to international action in March, appearing in a friendly against Sweden. Although not a frequent scorer, he produced memorable goals in both the semi-final and final of the Europa League, the latter a well controlled volley at the far post.

Peterborough U *(From trainee on 21/7/1997) FL 63+2/6 FLC 4 FAC 3 Others 3*
Tottenham H *(£700,000 on 10/1/2000) PL 99+22/13 FLC 10+3/3 FAC 10+3/2*
Everton *(£3,500,000 on 26/5/2005) PL 35+10/1 FLC 3 FAC 1+1 Others 3*
Fulham *(£2,500,000 on 24/1/2007) PL 95+6/9 FLC 4 FAC 9+3/2 Others 11/2*

DAVIES Steven (Steve) Gary

Born: Liverpool, 29 December 1987
Height: 6'1" **Weight:** 11.7
Steve continued to offer Derby

supporters tantalising glimpses of his skill, most notably with a lovely goal against Millwall that took the FA Cup replay to a penalty shoot-out. The problem is that if there is an injury to be found, Steve will locate it and his season ended with an ankle operation. He started only seven Championship games, making it 15 starts in the two seasons since he signed from Tranmere. Steve looks as if he could be effective, either on the left or as a central striker, but has to prove it. He was back early at the training ground to work on his basic fitness before the start of pre-season.

Tranmere Rov *(From trainee on 28/7/2005) FL 30+30/5 FLC 2+1 FAC 3 Others 4+1*
Derby Co *(£275,000 + on 3/7/2008) FL 15+22/4 FLC 4+1 FAC 1+3/2*

DAVIS Claude

Born: Kingston, Jamaica, 6 March 1979
Height: 6'3" **Weight:** 14.4
International Honours: Jamaica: 64
After finishing the previous season on loan at Crystal Palace from Derby, the tough-tackling and uncompromising Jamaican international began the campaign as a free transfer capture and back up for Palace's central defensive pairing. He found himself in the side on a fairly regular basis from October, with regular centre-back Paddy McCarthy sidelined with injury. A groin injury for Claude himself kept him out in the latter part of the season and after a red card picked up against Leicester in mid-March, he was used largely as a substitute for the remaining games of the season.

Preston NE *(Signed from Portmore U, Jamaica on 15/8/2003) FL 74+20/4 FLC 4 FAC 5 Others 5*
Sheffield U *(£2,500,000 + on 14/6/2006) PL 18+3 FLC 1*
Derby Co *(£3,000,000 on 25/7/2007) P/FL 25+2 FLC 2 FAC 2*
Crystal Palace *(Free on 2/2/2009) FL 26+2 FAC 5*

DAVIS David Lowell

Born: Smethwick, 20 February 1991
Height: 5'8" **Weight:** 12.4
An athletic and composed midfield player, with the ability to win the ball and also distribute it well, David made six appearances for Darlington on loan from Wolverhampton in October and November.

Wolverhampton W *(From trainee on 7/7/2009)*
Darlington *(Loaned on 22/10/2009) FL 5 FAC 1*

DAVIS Harry Spencer

Born: Burnley, 24 September 1991
Height: 6'2" **Weight:** 12.6
Son of the Crewe assistant manager Steve Davis, Harry progressed through the youth team and was on the substitutes' bench on a number of occasions. A defender who is capable of making progress at League level, he was one of the substitutes used in the final game of the season against Bradford.

Crewe Alex *(Trainee) FL 0+1*

DAVIS Kelvin Geoffrey

Born: Bedford, 29 September 1976
Height: 6'1" **Weight:** 14.0
Club Honours: AMC '10
International Honours: E: U21-3; Yth
It was a close run thing: Kelvin was about to sign for West Ham on 8th July, the day Southampton were taken out of administration. He hesitated, then accepted a new three-year contract at St Mary's. Saints' 'Player of the Season' in 2008-09 and club captain – incoming manager Ian Pardew rated him as the best skipper he has worked with – Kelvin's decision to stick with Southampton was a morale-booster for all involved because he is an exceptional goalkeeper. It was no surprise when he was named in the PFA 'League One Team of the Year' along with team-mates Jason Puncheon and Rickie Lambert .

Luton T *(From trainee on 1/7/1994) FL 92 FLC 7 FAC 2 Others 6*
Torquay U *(Loaned on 16/9/1994) FL 2 FLC 1 Others 1*
Hartlepool U *(Loaned on 8/8/1997) FL 2 FLC 1*
Wimbledon *(£600,000 + on 14/7/1999) FL 131 FLC 7 FAC 8*
Ipswich T *(Free on 6/8/2003) FL 84 FLC 2 FAC 3 Others 4*
Sunderland *(£1,250,000 on 1/7/2005) PL 33 FAC 2*
Southampton *(£1,000,000 on 21/7/2006) FL 159 FLC 5 FAC 10 Others 5*

DAVIS Liam Lloyd

Born: Wandsworth, 23 November 1986
Height: 5'9" **Weight:** 11.7
Liam's speedy wing play was missed by Northampton during the early part of the season, when he was out with an injury that prevented him being restored to the first team until February. He soon got back into his stride, outpacing defenders and scoring goals by cutting inside and sending in low hard shots. He is an exciting player with the ball at his feet for he does not rely only on speed but is also skilful.

Coventry C *(From trainee on 1/7/2006)
FL 3+8 FAC 1*
Peterborough U *(Loaned on
15/9/2006) FL 7 FLC 1*
Northampton T *(Free on 4/7/2008) FL
34+12/6 FLC 2 FAC 1+2 Others 1+1*

DAVIS Sean
Born: Clapham, 20 September 1979
Height: 5'10" **Weight:** 12.0
Club Honours: Div 1 '01
International Honours: E: U21-11
Gary Megson finally got his man on a
free transfer from Portsmouth in the
summer, having been linked with Sean
for many months before that. Sean
made his debut for Bolton in the
opening day defeat by Sunderland and
was harshly sent off for two yellow
cards against Liverpool. This was hardly
the ideal start to Sean's Bolton career
and things got worse when a knee
injury forced him out of action in late
August. Ruled out of the remainder of
the campaign, he went under the
surgeon's knife in April to repair a
damaged knee cartilage. Sean joined
Bolton with high hopes and will be
hoping to shake off his injury woes and
make more of an impression.
Fulham *(From trainee on 2/7/1998) P/FL
128+27/14 FLC 9+5/3 FAC 15+2/2
Others 12/1*
Tottenham H *(£3,000,000 on
10/7/2004) PL 11+4 FLC 1+1*
Portsmouth *(Signed on 12/1/2006) PL
94+8/2 FLC 2 FAC 4+2/1 Others 4+2*
Bolton W *(Free on 2/7/2009) PL 3 FLC 1*

DAVIS Solomon (Sol)
Sebastian
Born: Cheltenham, 4 September 1979
Height: 5'8" **Weight:** 11.0
Club Honours: Div 1 '05; AMC '09
Sol joined his local MK Dons primarily as
back-up left-back to club skipper Dean
Lewington, and after getting several
opportunities to fill in early in the
season was then loaned to Kettering
Town in time to feature in both their FA
Cup first round matches with Leeds.
Recalled at the start of 2010, he was
then a regular on the bench for the
second half of the campaign before
getting a start in the penultimate game
of the season as Lewington was
switched to cover in the centre of the
defence. Was out of contract in the
summer.
Swindon T *(From trainee on
29/5/1998) FL 100+17 FLC 7 FAC 5+1
Others 1*
Luton T *(£50,000 + on 16/8/2002) FL
187+12/3 FLC 10+1 FAC 12+1 Others 6*
MK Dons *(Free on 1/8/2009) FL 5+5
FLC 1 Others 2+1*

DAWKIN Joshua (Josh)
George
Born: St Ives, Cambs, 16 January 1992
Height: 5'9" **Weight:** 10.10
International Honours: W: Yth
Josh is a Welsh under-19 international
attacking wide midfield player who
loves nothing more than to run directly
at defenders, committing them to the
tackle before delivering his cross or
shot. He made his Norwich debut in the
Johnstone's Paint Trophy at Gillingham
and followed that with further
appearances in the competition and in
the FA Cup at Carlisle. His progress was
rewarded with the offer of his first
professional contract at the end of the
season.
Norwich C *(Trainee) FAC 0+1 Others 1+1*

DAWSON Andrew (Andy)
Stuart
Born: Northallerton, 20 October 1978
Height: 5'9" **Weight:** 10.2
A stalwart campaigner dating back to
Hull's days in the Third Division, Andy

matched leading scorer Stephen Hunt
as the Tigers' last remaining ever-
present until a bout of asthma sidelined
him for the trip to Everton in March.
The left-back returned for the visit of
Arsenal to the KC Stadium to make the
400th appearance of his career, with
over 200 League games for the Tigers.
He was named captain for the first time
since November 2006 in new manager
Iain Dowie's first game in charge at
Portsmouth, only to suffer a hamstring
injury during the match. Andy took his
City goals tally into double figures with
a free kick in a thrilling 3-2 win against
Everton in November and faced his
younger brother Michael from the start
of a game for the first time in their
careers in the 0-0 draw at Tottenham in
January. Respect from his colleagues
showed in his 'Players' Player of the
Year' trophy and Andy was third in the
club's and supporters' club's 'Player of
the Year' award.
Nottingham F *(From trainee on
31/10/1995) FLC 1*

Andy Dawson

Scunthorpe U (£70,000 on 18/12/1998) FL 192+3/8 FLC 6 FAC 12/1 Others 12/2
Hull C (Free on 1/7/2003) P/FL 205+7/8 FLC 4+2 FAC 10/2 Others 3

DAWSON Craig
Born: Rochdale, 6 May 1990
Height: 6'0" **Weight:** 12.4
Local lad Craig joined Rochdale from Radcliffe Borough late the previous season and, at 19, was probably looking to further his career in Dale's reserves. However, injury to centre-half Rory McArdle meant that Craig was thrust into the first team on the opening day and never looked back. Partnering the experienced Nathan Stanton at centre-back, Craig immediately looked like a seasoned campaigner, winning several 'Man of the Match' accolades as Dale moved into the top three in October and stayed there, to the delight of Craig as a life-long Dale fan. Apart from his defensive qualities, Craig proved a remarkable scorer, particularly dangerous in the air at free kicks and corners, and in one spell netted eight times in 13 games. After only half a season, he was voted into the best Dale XI of the decade in a poll on the fans' website and followed by becoming the League Two 'Player of the Year' at the League awards night and a member of the PFA League Two 'Team of the Year'. He cleaned up Rochdale's awards as 'Player of the Year', 'Most Improved Player of the Year' and 'Young Player of the Year'.
Rochdale (Signed from Radcliffe Borough on 23/2/2009) FL 40+2/9 FLC 1 FAC 2/1 Others 1/1

DAWSON Michael Richard
Born: Northallerton, 18 November 1983
Height: 6'2" **Weight:** 12.12
Club Honours: FLC '08
International Honours: E: B-2; U21-13; Yth
Michael missed Tottenham's first seven games through injury but once he established himself in the side he became one of the rocks on which the successful bid for Champions League football was based. He made 35 starts and three appearances from the bench and played every minute of 33 of the last 35 games, succumbing only to injury. Michael always seems to have a smile on his face but that takes nothing away from his limpet-like determination and effort. He made so many vital defensive interventions but one of the most notable came against Didier Drogba in the home win over Chelsea.

His trademark long diagonal passes continue to bear fruit and he popped up to score in two games. It was no surprise that he won the Spurs supporters' 'Player of the Season' award and was in Fabio Capello's 30-man World Cup squad.
Nottingham F (From trainee on 23/11/2000) FL 82+1/7 FLC 5 FAC 2 Others 1
Tottenham H (Signed on 31/1/2005) PL 137+9/5 FLC 16+1/1 FAC 20 Others 19+2/1

DAWSON Stephen John
Born: Dublin, 4 December 1985
Height: 5'9" **Weight:** 11.2
International Honours: RoI: U21-1
'Awesome Dawson', the relentless central midfield player, was again in fantastic form for Bury. Chosen as the club's 'Player of the Season' for the second time in succession, he was also named in the PFA 'League Two Team of the Season'. The captain, Stephen provided four goals, including a wonder strike against champions Notts County, and yet another season of outstanding tackles and assists. Manager Alan Knill can only hope that Stephen will wear the Bury shirt in the season ahead.
Leicester C (From trainee on 15/7/2003)
Mansfield T (Free on 5/8/2005) FL 106+11/4 FLC 3+1 FAC 7+1 Others 2
Bury (Free on 5/8/2008) FL 87+1/6 FLC 2 FAC 2 Others 5

DAY Jamie Robert
Born: High Wycombe, 7 May 1986
Height: 5'9" **Weight:** 10.7
The long-serving Peterborough defender had only started two games on his comeback from a back injury before being loaned out to Dagenham in November to aid his comeback and to act as cover for the departed left-back Scott Griffiths. The loan was extended until January and by the end of it he was back to match fitness. What was impressive during his stay with the Daggers was his solid tackling and ability to get down the left to provide good crosses. After return to his parent club, Jamie was released at the end of the season.
Peterborough U (From trainee on 19/8/2003) FL 85+17/5 FLC 4+1 FAC 6 Others 4+1
Dagenham & Redbridge (Loaned on 26/11/2009) FL 8

DEAN Harlee James
Born: Basingstoke, 26 July 1991
Height: 6'3" **Weight:** 12.13
Harlee has the ability to play anywhere down the middle. A product of the

Dagenham youth system, he made his debut against Port Vale as a substitute and slotted into the centre-back position. During the season, he has had loan spells at Braintree Town, from August to October, and Grays Athletic, November until the end of the season, to gain more experience.
Dagenham & Redbridge (From juniors on 1/8/2008) FL 0+1

DEAN Luke Adam
Born: Cleckheaton, 14 May 1991
Height: 5'9" **Weight:** 11.0
Bradford boss Peter Taylor promised to give some of the club's youngsters a first team chance in the closing weeks of the season. First-year professional Luke, who can play central in midfield or up front, was given his debut against Morecambe at Valley Parade. He had a hand in City's second goal, helping clear the ball out of defence in a thrilling counter attack that was finished off by Adam Bolder.
Bradford C (From trainee on 9/7/2009) FL 0+1

DEANE Patrick
Born: Perth, 16 April 1990
Height: 5'11" **Weight:** 12.7
Another of Steve Staunton's New Year recruits, who made his Darlington debut in the away win at Rotherham in January as a substitute. He was only ever used as a substitute, making ten appearances from the bench, with his ability to hold the ball in forward areas of the pitch. Was out of contract at the end of June.
Montrose (From juniors at Hibernian on 1/10/2009) SL 1
Darlington (Free on 15/1/2010) FL 0+10

[DECO] DE SOUZA Anderson Luis
Born: Sao Bernardo do Campo, Brazil, 27 August 1977
Height: 5'9" **Weight:** 11.7
Club Honours: CS '09; PL '10
International Honours: Portugal: 73
Following a disappointing end to his first season in English football, Chelsea's Brazilian-born schemer was reinvigorated just when he was being linked with moves away from the club. Deco was employed at the point of Carlo Ancelotti's diamond, alternating with Joe Cole, where his silky dribbling and clever short passing could create havoc. He scored a sublime goal in the second match at Sunderland, dipping his right shoulder, skipping past a defender and angling a drive in off the post. His other two goals both came against Bolton in the space of four days.

Deco was employed successfully in a deeper role in January while Michael Essien and John Obi Mikel were away at the African Cup of Nations and Juliano Belletti was injured. His intelligent probing and accurate passing gave Chelsea another, rather unexpected dimension. He made a successful return for the final quarter of the season when the Blues needed more zip in midfield and his prompting, shrewd passing and manipulation of the ball coincided with Chelsea's goal rush as they raced to a record total of 103. Deco announced he would retire from international football after the World Cup finals having been a mainstay of his adopted country Portugal. At the end of the season he was linked with a return to Brazil for family reasons, with Fluminense being the most favoured destination
Chelsea (£8,000,000 from Barcelona, Spain, ex Nacional, Corinthians, Corinthians, Corinthians Alagoano, Benfica, Alverca - loan, Salgueiros - loan, Porto, on 30/6/2008) PL 31+12/5 FLC 3/1 FAC 2+1 Others 6+3

DEEGAN Gary
Born: Dublin, 28 September 1987
Height: 5'9" **Weight:** 11.11
A young Irishman signed from Bohemians in the January transfer window, Gary made a positive impression at Coventry in his first three months in English football. Despite being a member of the Bohemians' 2009 title-winning side and voted into the PFAI 'Team of the Season', it was a big step up for the central midfield player nicknamed 'Pit-Bull'. Scored his first goal against Queens Park Rangers with a deflection and was on hand to score the equaliser from close range at Leicester. He looks strong and energetic and appears to have a good future.
Coventry C (Signed from Bohemians, ex Shelbourne, Kilkenny C - loan, Longford T, Galway U, on 4/1/2010) FL 9+8/2

DEEN AHMED Nuru
Born: Freetown, Sierra Leone, 30 June 1985
Height: 5'9" **Weight:** 11.5
International Honours: Sierra Leone: 10
Sierra Leone international Ahmed signed for Barnet at the beginning of the season, having previously been at Macclesfield. He made a great start to his Barnet career and scored a terrific free kick in the early season win at Northampton. However, he fell out of favour under Ian Hendon and did not play from early December until the final two games of the season, when caretaker manager Paul Fairclough

recalled him. He repaid Fairclough with two fine displays at left-back, helping Barnet stay up in the process. Was out of contract at the end of June.
Peterborough U (From trainee at Leicester C on 9/8/2004) FL 4+1 (Free to Aldershot T during 2005 close season)
Macclesfield T (Free from Bishops Stortford, ex Fisher Ath, St Albans C, trial at Bury, on 4/8/2008) FL 19+9 FLC 2 FAC 1+1
Barnet (Free on 11/8/2009) FL 12+4/1 FAC 3 Others 1

DEENEY Saul
Born: Derry, 12 March 1983
Height: 6'1" **Weight:** 12.10
International Honours: RoI: U21-2; Yth
Saul's first League appearance since he was with Notts County in 2006-07 was eventful. Now the second choice goalkeeper at Derby, Saul went on as a substitute at Reading in March when Stephen Bywater suffered back trouble and was sent off 28 minutes later for a professional foul. Happily, Saul was able to play in the last two games of the season when Bywater had a rib injury and showed his competence. He worked under Nigel Clough at Burton and was understudy to the ageless Kevin Poole when they won the Blue Square Premier. Clough saw enough to give him a chance at Derby and he earned a further year on his contract.
Notts Co (From trainee on 8/9/2000) FL 41+1 FLC 2 FAC 4 (Free to Burton A on 7/10/2005)
Notts Co (Free from Burton A on 18/7/2006) FL 7 FLC 4 Others 1 (Freed during 2007 close season)
Derby Co (Signed from Burton A, ex Hucknall T, on 31/7/2009) FL 2+1

DEENEY Troy
Born: Birmingham, 29 June 1988
Height: 5'11" **Weight:** 12.0
Although looking less clinical in front goal, Walsall's Troy exceeded last season's tally of 12 by two. His overall play was improved, notably in supplying precise long-range passes for assists against Millwall and Colchester. His heading improved towards the end of the season and the number of headers he won at home to Hartlepool was particularly pleasing. Proving a handful for defenders, his target for next season will be to top 20 goals. One of two sending-offs was at home to Charlton for two bookings, the first of which was for a pointless dissent. Troy was voted as the Walsall supporters' 'Player of the Season'.
Walsall (Free from Chelmsley T on 27/2/2007) FL 95+28/27 FLC 0+2 FAC 5+2 Others 2+2

Troy Deeney

DEFOE Jermain Colin
Born: Beckton, 7 October 1982
Height: 5'7" **Weight:** 10.4
Club Honours: FLC '08
International Honours: E: 40; B-2; U21-23; Yth; Sch
The Tottenham and England striker had a blistering start to the season, looking stronger, fitter and faster than ever. Jermain was in the running for the Premier League top-scoring position for the early part of the season but his output fell towards the end of the season. Jermain's finest hour came when he scored a magnificent five goals in Spurs' 9-1 demolition of Wigan. In doing so, Jermain became only the fourth man in Spurs history to score five in a competitive match and the third in League games. Jermain scored two other hat-tricks, against Hull in the League and at Leeds in Spurs' fourth round FA Cup replay. Jermain's tally was 18 League goals and six in Cup competitions. He scored five goals for England since June and was in the 23 heading for the finals in South Africa. Jermain's instincts are to run and aim for goal. Many of his goals come from a quick early touch and a powerful shot on target. Jermain is the first Spurs' player since Gary Lineker in 1991-92 to score two or more League hat-tricks in a season.
West Ham U (£400,000 + from trainee at Charlton Ath on 15/10/1999) P/FL 62+31/29 FLC 6+1/6 FAC 4+1/6
Bournemouth (Loaned on 26/10/2000) FL 27+2/18 FAC 1/1 Others 1
Tottenham H (£7,000,000 + on 2/2/2004) PL 88+51/43 FLC 10+5/10 FAC 8+5/5 Others 4+6/6

*Portsmouth (£9,000,000 on
31/1/2008) PL 29+2/15 Others 5/2
Tottenham H (£15,000,000 on
9/1/2009) PL 37+5/21 FLC 3/2 FAC
6+2/5*

DEGEN Philipp
Born: Holstein, Switzerland, 15
February 1983
Height: 6'2" **Weight:** 12.13
International Honours: Switzerland:
29; U21-14
The former Swiss international right-
back is one of the unluckiest players
ever to sign for Liverpool after suffering
three separate injuries which sidelined
him for most of 2008-09. He finally
made his Premiership debut in
September as a 60th-minute substitute
for Glen Johnson in the 4-0 home win
over Burnley. He started in Carling Cup
ties against Leeds and Arsenal and
made his first Premiership start at
Fulham in October where his run of
misfortune continued with a sending-
off for an innocuous challenge. He
enjoyed a run of three games in
January, twice in midfield, but was
substituted on each occasion and made
only sporadic substitute appearances
thereafter. Philipp looks good as an
attacking or overlapping full-back but
clearly former manager Rafa Benitez
had reservations about his defensive
abilities, preferring to switch Jamie
Carragher to cover Glen Johnson's long
absence with injury.
*Liverpool (Free from Borussia
Dortmund, Germany, ex FC Basle, FC
Aarau - loan, on 10/7/2008) PL 3+4 FLC
4 FAC 1 Others 0+1*

DE JONG Nigel
Born: Amsterdam, Holland, 30
November 1984
Height: 5'9" **Weight:** 11.5
International Honours: Holland: 41
Although he did not score a single goal
in his 42 appearances, the Manchester
City and Dutch international holding
midfielder was judged by team-mates
and supporters to be an outstanding
success. A ball winner and prodigiously
hard worker, he played a major role in
propelling and maintaining City's
challenge for the fourth place in the
Premiership that ultimately ended in
disappointment at the final hurdle. He
did not begin as first choice under Mark
Hughes but after making his first start in
the 4-2 win over Arsenal in September,
he never looked back and his
performance in a victory over eventual
champions Chelsea in December was
rated his best in a City shirt. He was in
Holland's squad for the World Cup finals
in South Africa after missing the 2006

Nigel De Jong

competition through injury.
*Manchester C (£18,000,000 from SV
Hamburg, Germany, ex Ajax, on
23/1/2009) PL 46+4 FLC 4+1 FAC 3*

DE LAET Ritchie Ria Alfons
Born: Antwerp, Belgium, 28 November
1988
Height: 6'1" **Weight:** 12.2
Club Honours: FLC '10
International Honours: Belgium: 2
Young Manchester United central
defender Ritchie featured in the Carling
Cup ties against Wolverhampton and
Barnsley and started in the fifth round
against Tottenham. Despite a defensive
injury crisis in November, Sir Alex
Ferguson preferred to bring midfielder
Michael Carrick on for Gary Neville
ahead of Ritchie after the United

captain suffered a groin strain. Ritchie
played his first League game of the
season in December against Wolves and
his second in the 3-0 defeat by Fulham.
*Stoke C (£100,000 from Royal
Antwerp, Belgium on 29/8/2007)
Manchester U (Signed on 9/1/2009) PL
3 FLC 1+2*

DELANEY Damien Finbarr
Born: Cork, 20 July 1981
Height: 6'3" **Weight:** 13.10
International Honours: RoI: 2; U21-1;
Yth
Damien joined Ipswich in the summer
and took a while to settle into the
team. He seemed to be uncomfortable
playing at left-back and was in and out
of the team. He returned to the side
against Derby in October as a central

defender and remained there for the rest of the season, establishing a partnership with Gareth McAuley that was pivotal in the club's improved fortunes. He has good aerial ability, can tackle well and loves to surge forward through the middle of the pitch to join his attack, although he failed to score this season. Injured ankle ligaments at Nottingham Forest in April but hopes to be fit for the new season.
Leicester C *(£50,000 from Cork C on 9/11/2000)* PL 5+3 FLC 1 FAC 1+1
Stockport Co *(Loaned on 15/11/2001)* FL 10+2/1
Huddersfield T *(Loaned on 28/3/2002)* FL 1+1
Mansfield T *(Loaned on 6/9/2002)* FL 7
Hull C *(£50,000 on 18/10/2002)* FL 220+4/5 FLC 7 FAC 8
Queens Park Rgrs *(£600,000 + on 17/1/2008)* FL 52+2/2 FLC 3/1 FAC 2
Ipswich T *(Signed on 2/7/2009)* FL 36 FLC 1 FAC 2

Rory Delap

DELAP Rory John
Born: Sutton Coldfield, 6 July 1976
Height: 6'0" **Weight:** 12.10
Club Honours: AMC '97
International Honours: RoI: 11; B-1; U21-4
Perhaps the most amiable player in the Stoke squad, Rory continues to attract considerable attention because of his awesome ability to propel monster throws into the opposing penalty area. Many teams have become more adept at dealing with the threat, though it remains an integral part of the Stoke armoury and a fearsome weapon to possess. As well as that much vaunted throw-in though, Rory possesses other

qualities, most notably a work rate that sets the standard for all players at the Britannia Stadium. He is a tireless worker for the team and covers the pitch, box-to-box, with an energy that shames many a younger player. If there is one thing that lets Rory down, it is his record of missing chances because of his weak finishing. However, he remains a vital component in a well-oiled Stoke machine that is founded first and foremost on team spirit and a willingness to work for the greater good.
Carlisle U *(From trainee on 18/7/1994)* FL 40+25/7 FLC 4+1 FAC 0+3 Others 12+2
Derby Co *(£500,000 + on 6/2/1998)* PL 97+6/11 FLC 7/2 FAC 2+1
Southampton *(£3,000,000 + on 21/7/2001)* P/FL 118+14/5 FLC 9+1 FAC 7+1 Others 1+1
Sunderland *(Free on 31/1/2006)* P/FL 11+1/1 FLC 1
Stoke C *(Free on 12/10/2006)* P/FL 114+2/4 FLC 2 FAC 6+1

DELFOUNESO Nathan
Born: Birmingham, 2 February 1991
Height: 6'1" **Weight:** 12.4
International Honours: E: U21-1; Yth
Nathan has long been regarded as the brightest young prospect at Aston Villa and underlined his potential with his first Premier League goal. It came in Villa's victory at Portsmouth in April and followed goals in FA Cup ties against Blackburn and Brighton. Nathan, an Academy product, has been used sparingly by manager Martin O'Neill. He scored three goals in three starts and ten substitute appearance and so far has been seen as an understudy to Gabby Agbonlahor. Clubs have enquired about taking him on loan but O'Neill is keen for him develop under the Villa coaches. Nathan's speed, finishing and desire to improve impress the manager and he has progressed through the England age groups, scoring on his under-21 debut in a defeat by Greece.
Aston Villa *(From trainee on 7/2/2008)* PL 0+13/1 FLC 0+1 FAC 4+2/3 Others 3+3/2

DELPH Fabian
Born: Bradford, 21 November 1989
Height: 5'7" **Weight:** 9.7
International Honours: E: U21-4; Yth
Fabian endured a frustrating first season at Aston Villa that ended in agony with a serious cruciate ligament injury sustained in training. Great things were expected of the former Leeds' wonder-boy when he arrived at Villa Park and he started the opening day clash

against Wigan. Unfortunately, Fabian's disappointing debut coincided with a defeat for Villa and knocked his confidence. From then on he was used mainly as a substitute but made three more Premier League starts and four in the Cups. His reputation as a tough midfielder was confirmed by a string of bookings in his early games and Fabian's best performance came in the FA Cup fourth round tie against Brighton, when he scored his first goal in a 'Man of the Match' display.
Leeds U *(From trainee on 11/1/2008)* FL 40+4/6 FLC 3+2 FAC 2 Others 2+1
Aston Villa *(Signed on 4/8/2009)* PL 4+4 FLC 1+1 FAC 4/1 Others 1

DeMERIT Jay Michael
Born: Green Bay, Wisconsin, USA, 4 December 1979
Height: 6'1" **Weight:** 13.5
International Honours: USA: 18
The Watford club captain started the season on a high after starring for the United States in the Confederations Cup in South Africa during the summer. Having defeated European champions Spain in the semi-final – with Jay successfully subduing Fernando Torres – the Americans lost in the final to Brazil. Returning to England, he suffered a setback in September in the form of a bizarre eye injury. A particle of grit was trapped under his contact lens and cut his eye. The wound became infected, and he had to undergo a partial corneal replacement in October. He then had to 'retrain' the eye before being able to return to first team action in December. Jay missed the end of the season through a combination of injury and disappointing form, but was looking forward to a successful World Cup as part of the United States squad. During the season, the American passed the landmark of 200 appearances for Watford and was again voted Watford's 'Community Ambassador' in recognition of his charitable work. Was out of contract in the summer.
Watford *(Free from Northwood, ex University of Illinois, Chicago Fire, on 13/8/2004)* P/FL 164+18/8 FLC 12+1 FAC 13/1 Others 4+1/1

DEMETRIOU Jason
Born: Newham, 18 November 1987
Height: 5'11" **Weight:** 10.8
International Honours: Cyprus: 3
Jason had something of an indifferent season for Leyton Orient. On his day he likes nothing better than attacking either full-back at pace, but struggled at the end of the season to regain his place in the team under the new manager. He was out of contract in the

summer and offered a new deal.
*Leyton Orient (From trainee on
19/7/2006) FL 105+38/10 FLC 5/1 FAC
9+1/2 Others 6+3/1*

DE MONTAGNAC Ishmel
Abendigo
Born: Newham, 15 June 1988
Height: 5'10" **Weight:** 11.5
Club Honours: Div 2 '07
International Honours: E: Yth
Signed on a one-year contract after
being unattached, Ishmel was a bit-part
player for Blackpool in midfield during
the season. He scored a cracking goal in
the Carling Cup against Wigan in the 4-
1 win but off-field matters, coupled
with a sending-off in a reserve game
against Preston, meant that he did not
really get another look in. With that in
mind, the pacy winger joined
Chesterfield on loan for the last ten
games of the season and returned three
goals - all decent strikes - in a spell that
had many plus points. Most effective
with the ball played to his feet, he
worked both wings well and kept his
full-back guessing by crossing and
cutting in with equal effect. If he drifted
out of games from time to time, that
may have been through an
understandable lack of familiarity with
team-mates and established tactical
plans. Ishmel's true level in football is
above the League Two fare that he
usually illuminated with the Spireites.
*Walsall (From trainee on 13/12/2005)
FL 28+55/9 FLC 0+2 FAC 5+4/1 Others
3+2*
*Blackpool (Free on 7/8/2009) FL 1+7
FLC 1+1/1 FAC 0+1*
*Chesterfield (Loaned on 19/3/2010) FL
10/3*

DEMPSEY Clinton (Clint)
Drew
Born: Nacogdoches, Texas, USA, 9
March 1983
Height: 6'1" **Weight:** 12.2
International Honours: USA: 61
After a quiet start to the season, Clint
once more proved an invaluable part of
the Fulham squad, scoring some
notable goals. The absence of Andy
Johnson meant Clint started a number
of games as a forward, although he
also featured regularly in his more
familiar role on the left side of midfield.
His versatility meant that he often
switched roles during a game following
substitutions. Clint is a clever player
who is comfortable on the ball and
displays excellent positional skill that
enabled him to be among the top
scorers again. His tally of nine goals in
all competitions included a vital point-
saving header at Manchester City and a

Clint Dempsey

dipping 25-yard volley at Stoke. A knee
ligament injury sustained at Blackburn
in January initially raised fears that he
would miss the remainder of the season
but he returned to action two months
later, when he produced a brilliant 25-
yard chip to round off a memorable
Europa League comeback against
Juventus. When fit Clint was a regular
for the United States and was in their
23 for the World Cup finals.
*Fulham (£1,500,000 from New
England Revolution, USA, ex Dallas
Texans, Furman University, on
19/1/2007) PL 85+25/21 FLC 3 FAC
7+4/1 Others 6+7/2*

DEMPSEY Gary William
Born: Wexford, 15 January 1981
Height: 5'9" **Weight:** 10.4
This tough-tackling, experienced
midfielder arrived in January and made
his Darlington debut in the first away
win of the season at Rotherham. He
soon impressed with his combative
displays and enjoys getting forward,
being rewarded with his first goal for
the club with a long-range drive in the

home draw against Lincoln in early
February. Was out of contract at the
end of June.
*Dunfermline Ath (Signed from
Waterford U, ex Bray W, on 1/6/2001)
SL 48+32/7 SLC 5+1 SC 7+4/1 Others 1*
*Aberdeen (Signed on 1/4/2005) SL
37+17/2 SLC 3+1 SC 3*
*Yeovil T (Signed on 19/7/2007) FL
10+6/2 FAC 0+1 Others 1 (Transferred
to St Patrick's Ath on 31/1/2008)*
Darlington (Free on 8/1/2010) FL 24/1

[DENILSON] PEREIRA NEVES
Denilson
Born: Sao Paulo, Brazil, 16 February
1988
Height: 5'10" **Weight:** 10.10
International Honours: Brazil: Yth
The Brazilian midfielder still divides
opinion amongst the Arsenal faithful
but he remains a regular in the first
team. He was yet another player to
suffer with injuries, having a constant
back problem. He opened the Gunners'
scoring for the season with a
sensational long-range strike in the 6-1
romp at Everton and enjoyed his best

season in scoring terms so far. He is a link player in the centre of the pitch who does have a good strike in his armoury. He featured 20 times in the Premier League, scoring four goals, seven times in the Champions League, adding one further strike, and once in the FA Cup, scoring one more goal.
Arsenal (£3,400,000 from Sao Paulo, Brazil on 31/8/2006) PL 63+17/6 FLC 11/2 FAC 6/1 Others 20+4/1

DENNEHY Darren John
Born: Tralee, 22 September 1988
Height: 6'2" **Weight:** 13.2
International Honours: RoI: U21-8; Yth
The tall centre-back started the season as Hereford's first choice during his loan spell from Cardiff, but the Bulls' poor start to the campaign did not help his confidence and after losing his place through injury he was unable to regain a spot in the side and returned to his parent club in the New Year. Next stop for Darren was Gillingham in January as cover for the injured Simon King and he made a big impression during his time on loan there. A natural left-footer, who is good in the air and strong in the tackle, he brought strength to a Gillingham defence that looked very porous, particularly away from home. It was no coincidence that the club recorded six clean sheets during his loan spell, while Darren deservedly earned a recall to the Republic of Ireland under-21's for their UEFA Championship qualifier with Armenia.
Everton (From trainee on 1/7/2007)
Cardiff C (Free on 2/7/2008)
Hereford U (Loaned on 13/3/2009) FL 3
Hereford U (Loaned on 1/7/2009) FL 6+1 FLC 1+1 Others 1
Gillingham (Loaned on 21/1/2010) FL 19

DENTON Thomas (Tom)
Ashley
Born: Huddersfield, 24 July 1989
Height: 6'6" **Weight:** 14.0
Lofty striker Tom joined Cheltenham on loan from Huddersfield in July. A target man whose sheer size makes him a handful for defenders, Tom played in a handful of pre-season games and made his debut in a 2-1 Carling Cup by Southend in August. He was a League substitute in the subsequent 1-1 draw at Hereford and made his only League start in the 1-0 victory at Rochdale. He returned to Huddersfield in November and spent the second half of the season back at Wakefield FC on loan.
Huddersfield T (Signed from Wakefield on 18/8/2008)
Cheltenham T (Loaned on 16/7/2009) FL 1+1 FLC 0+1 Others 1

DERRY Shaun Peter
Born: Nottingham, 6 December 1977
Height: 5'10" **Weight:** 10.13
Club Honours: Div 3 '98
Palace captain Shaun led by example from the centre of midfield in the final games of the season as the club battled to avoid relegation after entering administration. A driving performance in the last game at Sheffield Wednesday was his best display of 2009-10 and he was ever-present for the Eagles in all League and Cup matches, missing only the majority of the game at Watford when he went off injured. One of several players out of contract in the summer.
Notts Co (From trainee on 13/4/1996) FL 76+3/4 FLC 4+1 FAC 6+1/1 Others 3
Sheffield U (£700,000 on 26/1/1998) FL 62+10 FLC 4 FAC 6/1
Portsmouth (£300,000 + on 16/3/2000) FL 48+1/1 FLC 4 FAC 1+1
Crystal Palace (£400,000 on 6/8/2002) P/FL 62+21/3 FLC 9 FAC 4 Others 1+2
Nottingham F (Loaned on 24/12/2004) FL 7 FAC 1
Leeds U (Signed on 18/2/2005) FL 71/3 FLC 0+2 FAC 1+1 Others 3
Crystal Palace (Signed on 19/11/2007) FL 111+4 FLC 3 FAC 7 Others 2

DEVANEY Martin Thomas
Born: Cheltenham, 1 June 1980
Height: 5'10" **Weight:** 11.12
Martin started the season in the Barnsley team but soon found himself on the sidelines when manager Simon Davey brought in Adam Hammill. This continued when new manager Mark Robins took over. Following that, Martin joined MK Dons on loan towards the end of October and showed good pace and skill on the flanks when called into action. A headed goal from just outside the area that helped inspire a comeback FA Cup win over Exeter was the undoubted highlight of his short stay, which was ended by injury. Back at Barnsley and fully fit, he forced himself back in the first team squad with the manager admiring his desire and will to get back into the team. At his best he is an exciting winger capable of beating his marker and delivering telling crosses. He also has an eye for goal.
Coventry C (From trainee on 4/6/1997)
Cheltenham T (Free on 5/8/1999) FL 154+49/37 FLC 5+1/1 FAC 6+3/2 Others 8+2/2
Watford (Free on 1/7/2005)
Barnsley (Free on 26/8/2005) FL 117+33/16 FLC 3+1/1 FAC 10+1/2 Others 4
MK Dons (Loaned on 30/10/2009) FL 4+1 FAC 1+1/1

DEVERA JOSEPH (JOE)
Born: Southgate, 6 February 1987
Height: 6'2" **Weight:** 12.0
Joe was once again a regular for Barnet, playing at either right-back or in the centre. Injury delayed his start to the season but once he regained full fitness he was back to being one of the first names on the team-sheet. Well liked by the fans, Joe is regarded highly for his composure, aerial ability and tough tackling.
Barnet (From juniors on 21/11/2005) FL 128+6/1 FLC 4+1 FAC 9+1 Others 5+1

DEVERDICS Nicholas (Nicky) Ferenc
Born: Gateshead, 24 November 1987
Height: 5'11" **Weight:** 11.11
Nicky had something of a frustrating campaign at Barnet, starting only four League games, having been a regular in the previous season. However, when called upon Nicky showed he was more than able at this level and was extremely professional in his attitude. He managed to add a goal to his Barnet tally when appearing as a sub in the 3-0 win over Darlington. His contract was up at the end of the season.
Gretna (Free from Bedlington Terriers, ex Newcastle U trainee, Gateshead, on 30/3/2007) SL 23+8/3 SLC 0+1 SC 1+1
Barnet (From juniors on 25/7/2008) FL 26+19/2 FAC 2+3 Others 1

DEVITT Jamie Martin
Born: Dublin, 6 July 1990
Height: 5'10" **Weight:** 10.6
International Honours: RoI: Yth
On loan from Hull, Jamie showed himself to be a skilful and pacy winger with some exquisite touches out on the right flank during his seven appearances for Darlington. He scored one goal with a driven free kick against Shrewsbury in the Quakers first win of the season in mid-October but then declined a loan extension at Darlington only to sign on loan for Shrewsbury. Having earlier impressed the Shrews, he gave a good performance on his debut against Aldershot in the 3-1 win and then scored his first goal, at Notts County, in a 1-1 draw a week later. Always looking to be involved, he scored again in a 2-0 win against Rotherham. In all he made nine appearances, scoring twice, before returning to Hull and subsequently going on loan to Grimsby. Arguably Town's best loan signing of the campaign, Jamie instantly proved his worth with a debut equaliser at Notts County. The talented winger showed confidence and skill to claim further goals - most being curling shots from the edge of the box - his winner at

Accrington (3-2) after being 0-2 down securing the club's first away victory in League Two for seven months.
Hull C (From trainee on 17/1/2008)
Darlington (Loaned on 15/9/2009) FL 5+1/1 Others 1
Shrewsbury T (Loaned on 22/10/2009) FL 8+1/2
Grimsby T (Loaned on 17/2/2010) FL 15/5

DE VRIES Dorus
Born: Beverwijk, Holland, 29 December 1980
Height: 6'1" **Weight:** 12.8
Club Honours: Div 1 '08
International Honours: Holland: U21
It was another excellent season for the Dutch goalkeeper and included his first penalty save for Swansea since arriving at the Liberty Stadium from Dunfermline in 2007. This came early in the season at Coventry and over the course of Swansea's near miss for a play-off place, Dorus broke Roger Freestone's club record of 22 clean sheets. An agile 'keeper, good on his line, Dorus was considered by manager Paulo Sousa to be good enough for inclusion in the Holland World Cup squad.
Dunfermline Ath (Signed from ADO Den Haag, Holland, ex Stormvogels Telstar, on 1/7/2006) SL 27 SLC 2 SC 5
Swansea C (Signed on 1/8/2007) FL 132 FLC 6 FAC 8 Others 6

Abou Diaby

DIABY Vassiriki **Abou**
Born: Paris, France, 11 May 1986
Height: 6'3" **Weight:** 11.11
International Honours: France: 4; U21-1; Yth

Abou enjoyed his most consistent season to date in the first team as he started to fulfil some of the undoubted promise he has shown so far in his Arsenal career. A tall and commanding presence in the centre of midfield, Abou has started to drive forward in games and is still at his best as an attacking rather than defensive-minded player. He also registered his most prolific scoring campaign and claimed one of the most important goals of the season as his header beat Liverpool at home in February to ensure the Gunners kept their grip on third place in the Premier League. Another player to suffer too frequently from injury, he has shown that if he plays regularly his performances are greatly enhanced and he will be looking to build on this next season. He featured 28 times in the Premier League, with six goals scored, eight times in the Champions League, adding a further strike, and once in the FA Cup. He was in the French squad for the World Cup.
Arsenal (£2,000,000 from Auxerre, France on 20/1/2006) PL 69+23/12 FLC 8+2/1 FAC 8+2 Others 19+7/4

DIAGOURAGA **Toumani**
Born: Paris, France, 10 June 1987
Height: 6'2" **Weight:** 11.5
Out of contract at Hereford in the summer, this hard-working midfielder, nicknamed 'Dave' by the fans, was brought to Peterborough to add a bit of physical bite in the middle of the park. He was a first team regular until Darren Ferguson lost his job, but not part of the new manager's plans he was loaned out to Brentford in January. Having joined the Bees for the rest of the season, the tall midfield ball-winner was a regular in central midfield and displayed good short passing ability, as well as being a glutton for work.
Watford (From trainee on 17/11/2004) P/FL 1 FLC 3 FAC 1+1
Swindon T (Loaned on 23/3/2006) FL 5+3
Rotherham U (Loaned on 12/1/2007) FL 4+3
Hereford U (Free on 9/8/2007) FL 86/4 FLC 3 FAC 8 Others 1
Peterborough U (Signed on 17/6/2009) FL 18+1 FLC 4
Brentford (Loaned on 21/1/2010) FL 20

DIALLO Drissa
Born: Nouadhibou, Mauritania, 4 January 1973
Height: 6'1" **Weight:** 12.0
Club Honours: AMC '08; Div 2 '08
International Honours: Guinea: 1
Former Guinea international Drissa spent the first half of the season with

Cheltenham. The veteran defender played in the centre of defence and at right-back, battling manfully in a struggling side. A change of management in December resulted in Drissa being left out and this coincided with his establishment of business interests in France. He announced his retirement in January and returned to live in Paris.
Burnley (Free from KV Mechelen, Belgium, ex AS Brevannes, Sedan, RFC Tilleur de Liege, on 9/1/2003) FL 14/1 FAC 4/1
Ipswich T (Free on 6/6/2003) FL 39+6 FLC 3 Others 1
Sheffield Wed (Free on 8/7/2005) FL 8+3 FLC 1
MK Dons (Free on 27/7/2006) FL 70/2 FLC 4 FAC 2 Others 6
Cheltenham T (Free on 18/9/2008) FL 44+1/2 FAC 4 Others 1

DIAMANTI **Alessandro**
Born: Prato, Italy, 2 May 1983
Height: 5'11" **Weight:** 11.7
After joining West Ham the exciting Italian midfielder from Livorno quickly became a cult hero when doing the unpredictable and looking to involve the crowd. He has an incredible left foot and soon began to take all free kicks around the box and penalty kicks, scoring from the spot against Liverpool, Arsenal and Chelsea. In February against Hull, Alessandro collected the ball just in his own half, looked up and saw the goalkeeper off his line. He promptly thumped a shot from 50 yards that the goalkeeper just reached to tip over the bar. Moments like that can excite the crowd and he was deservedly named as runner up in the fans' 'Hammer of the Year' awards.
West Ham U (Signed from Livorno, Italy, ex Prato, Empoli - loan, Fucecchio - loan, Fiorentina - loan, Albino Leffe, Prato, on 28/8/2009) PL 18+9/7 FLC 1 FAC 1/1

DIAME Mohamed
Born: Creteil, France, 14 June 1987
Height: 6'0" **Weight:** 12.8
Arriving at Wigan in a deal that brought Antonio Amaya from Spanish side Rayo Vallecano, Mohamed is a strong, aggressive and tireless worker in the centre of the field. Recruited on a three-year deal, he has battled with the condition 'sudden death syndrome' to reach the Premier League. A defensive midfield player, Mohamed blossomed as the club sought a successor to the departed Lee Cattermole and was virtually ever-present. The young Frenchman has perfect tactical positioning, just in front of the

defensive line, and seldom loses his position. He controls with both feet, which makes it easy for him to escape pressure and send accurate passes to the attack. His only goal was at Sunderland, a brilliant individual effort when unleashing a wonderful drive.
Wigan Ath *(Signed from Rayo Vallecano, Spain, ex RC Lens, CD Linares, on 21/8/2009) PL 34/1 FLC 1 FAC 2*

DIAO Salif Alassane
Born: Kedougou, Senegal, 10 February 1977
Height: 6'0" **Weight:** 11.7
Club Honours: FLC '03
International Honours: Senegal: 39
Salif is another one of those players at Stoke who manages to divide opinion among the supporters, as he did at Liverpool, though he is clearly very well regarded by manager Tony Pulis. Injury limited his first team run-outs to 11 during the season but he did achieve the distinction of scoring his first senior goal for over five years, when he managed to get forward deep into injury time at Portsmouth and score a winner that hammered another nail into the coffin of the south coast club. It is hard to know what the future holds for Salif, who was out of contract in the summer.
Liverpool *(£5,000,000 from Sedan, France, ex Monaco, on 9/8/2002) PL 19+18/1 FLC 7+1/1 FAC 1+1 Others 8+6/1*
Birmingham C *(Loaned on 18/1/2005) PL 2*
Portsmouth *(Loaned on 31/8/2005) PL 7+4 FLC 1 FAC 1*
Stoke C *(Signed on 13/10/2006) P/FL 64+10/1 FLC 1 FAC 3+3*

DICKER Gary Richard Perry
Born: Dublin, 31 July 1986
Height: 6'0" **Weight:** 12.2
International Honours: RoI: U21-1; Yth
Signed in the summer after an impressive loan at the end of 2008-09, Gary was a terrific acquisition for Brighton. He was off to a slow start but fought his way into the side and was more or less a regular, although new manager Gus Poyet tried other options, including playing him wide on the left. Albion looked much better with him in the side. Displaying vision in midfield, Gary demonstrated a remarkable ability to work his way out of tight corners before supplying a telling pass. A return of two goals may be disappointing but Gary should be pleased with his contribution.
Birmingham C *(Signed from UCD,*

Ireland on 31/1/2007)
Stockport Co *(Free on 10/8/2007) FL 51+4 FLC 3 FAC 3+1/1 Others 6*
Brighton & Hove A *(Free on 26/3/2009) FL 42+9/3 FAC 4+1*

DICKINSON Carl Matthew
Born: Swadlincote, 31 March 1987
Height: 6'0" **Weight:** 12.0
The ever-popular left-back made only one appearance for Stoke in the 2009-10 season before going on a season-long loan to Barnsley, where he was an instant hit with the Oakwell supporters who marvelled at his never-say-die approach. Giving Barnsley's defence natural balance being a left footer, extremely combative, strong in the tackle, and good in the air, he settled straight into the starting line-up. He was to stay there throughout the campaign. Probably the best indication as to his worth in the side was when he needed an operation that put him out of action for two months towards the end of the season and the Reds' form dipped noticeably. He was also willing to get forward and put in telling crosses, while his personnel highlight had to be the winning goal, a 25-yard free kick, in the final minute against Cardiff. Carl returned to Stoke at the season's end and will be hard to replace at Oakwell.
Stoke C *(From trainee on 3/8/2006) P/FL 31+20 FLC 6 FAC 2+1*
Blackpool *(Loaned on 20/10/2006) FL 7 FAC 2 Others 1*
Leeds U *(Loaned on 16/1/2009) FL 7*
Barnsley *(Loaned on 23/9/2009) FL 27+1/1 FAC 1*

DICKINSON Liam Michael
Born: Salford, 4 October 1985
Height: 6'4" **Weight:** 11.7
Signed from Derby during the summer, it was a hit-and-miss season at Brighton in general and especially for this tall, unconventional forward. Liam shone like a beacon in a struggling side at times with his enthusiastic approach and goal-assists, but his head could also drop. At his best with the ball at his feet, Liam scored spectacular goals against Huddersfield and Stockport, but with his undoubted physical assets and talent he would have been looking to take more of the chances that fell his way. Under new manager Gus Poyet he rather fell out of favour and joined Peterborough on loan in February, scoring on his debut. Unfortunately, games were limited after he picked up a niggling injury. At his best he is a pacy target man who can hold the ball and give others time to get forward.
Stockport Co *(Signed from Woodley*

Sports on 22/12/2005) FL 57+37/33 FLC 1+1 FAC 2 Others 8/2
Derby Co *(£750,000 on 3/7/2008)*
Huddersfield T *(Loaned on 21/8/2008) FL 13/6*
Blackpool *(Loaned on 27/11/2008) FL 5+2/4*
Leeds U *(Loaned on 13/3/2009) FL 4+4*
Brighton & Hove A *(Signed on 15/7/2009) FL 17+10/4 FLC 1 FAC 3+1/2*
Peterborough U *(Loaned on 15/2/2010) FL 9/3*

DICKOV Paul
Born: Livingston, 1 November 1972
Height: 5'6" **Weight:** 11.9
Club Honours: ECWC '94; Div 1 '09
International Honours: S: 10; U21-4; Yth; Sch
The veteran striker only made a couple of substitute appearances for Leicester in 2009-10 before being allowed to try his luck on loan at Derby. At Pride Park, Paul was one of two forwards allowed out on loan from Leicester to Derby, DJ Campbell being the other. Although his finishing lacked the sharpness of his best days, Paul set a splendid example with his professionalism and commitment. He was still willing to chase everything and worry defenders. After he had returned to Leicester his contract was cancelled by mutual consent during the winter and, following a brief trial with Toronto, he signed for Leeds as a free agent. Unfortunately, it did not really work out for Paul at Elland Road and he made just one start for Leeds, a 2-0 home defeat against promotion rivals Millwall.
Arsenal *(From trainee on 28/12/1990) PL 6+15/3 FLC 2+2/3*
Luton T *(Loaned on 8/10/1993) FL 8+7/1*
Brighton & Hove A *(Loaned on 23/3/1994) FL 8/5*
Manchester C *(£1,000,000 on 23/8/1996) P/FL 105+51/33 FLC 9+4/5 FAC 5+4/1 Others 3/2*
Leicester C *(Signed on 22/12/2002) P/FL 81+8/32 FLC 4/2 FAC 4/3*
Blackburn Rov *(£150,000 on 16/6/2004) PL 44+6/14 FLC 3+1/2 FAC 7/1*
Manchester C *(Free on 3/7/2006) PL 9+7 FLC 0+2 FAC 0+1*
Crystal Palace *(Loaned on 31/8/2007) FL 6+3*
Blackpool *(Loaned on 31/1/2008) FL 7+4/6*
Leicester C *(Free on 8/8/2008) FL 4+17/2 FLC 1+2/1 FAC 1+2 Others 1*
Derby Co *(Loaned on 28/8/2009) FL 10+6/2*
Leeds U *(Free on 3/3/2010) FL 1+3*

DICKSON Christopher (Chris) Matthew

Born: Plumstead, 28 December 1984
Height: 5'11" **Weight:** 13.4
International Honours: Ghana: 1
It was a disappointing season for Chris who failed to impress when eventually given a chance in the Charlton side. Unable to break into the squad, he was loaned to Bristol Rovers where he netted twice in 12 games after getting off to a superb start with two well taken goals on his League debut at Brentford. The striker returned to the Valley in December and featured up front in five games, but did not manage to score. He was then loaned to Gillingham for the remainder of the season, where he scored once in nine appearances. Chris is quick for a big man and has an eye for goal, but needs to go to the next level to achieve his aims. Was out of contract at the end of June.
Charlton Ath *(Signed from Dulwich Hamlet, ex Erith & Belvedere, on 12/3/2007) FL 7+21 FLC 0+2 FAC 0+4/2*
Crewe Alex *(Loaned on 17/8/2007) FL 2+1*
Gillingham *(Loaned on 21/9/2007) FL 9+3/7 Others 2/4*
Bristol Rov *(Loaned on 17/9/2009) FL 10+4/4*
Gillingham *(Loaned on 15/2/2010) FL 4+5/1*

DICKSON Ryan Anthony

Born: Saltash, 14 December 1986
Height: 5'10" **Weight:** 11.5
Club Honours: Div 2 '09
The strong-tackling Brentford left-back is a real threat going forward, delivering good crosses into the penalty area. Ryan suffered a knee injury in August that kept him out for seven games and then a hamstring problem in March that meant a further ten games were missed. In between he showed his usual skill and commitment to the side. He scored twice, a header against Norwich and a left-foot shot against Carlisle following a lung-bursting run the length of the pitch in the 90th minute. Ryan was reported to have turned down a new contract at Brentford to pursue his career at a higher club. The Bees, though, would receive a compensation payment as Ryan is under the age of 24.
Plymouth Arg *(From trainee on 1/8/2005) FL 2+3 FLC 0+1 FAC 0+1*
Torquay U *(Loaned on 12/1/2007) FL 7+2/1*
Brentford *(Signed on 16/11/2007) FL 87+10/3 FLC 1 FAC 6 Others 1+1*

DIGARD Didier

Born: Gisors, France, 12 July 1986
Height: 6'0" **Weight:** 11.13
International Honours: France: U21-4
Didier had an injury-plagued start and struggled to maintain any consistency when in the side. He was starting to put a run of games together when Middlesbrough manager Gareth Southgate was relieved of his duties. It would be another month before he was picked by new boss Gordon Strachan but was then sidelined by a back injury. In January, he joined French side Nice on loan until the end of the season and helped them win their fight against relegation.
Middlesbrough *(£4,000,000 from Paris St Germain, France, ex Le Havre, on 16/7/2008) P/FL 19+13 FLC 2/1 FAC 2*

DIKGACOI Kagisho Evidence

Born: Brandfort, South Africa, 24 November 1984
Height: 6'0" **Weight:** 12.11
International Honours: South Africa: 30
Signed from South African club Golden Arrows, Kagisho spent much of the season on the fringes of the Fulham squad and was never selected to start consecutive Premier League games, nor did he feature at all in the Europa League campaign. He suffered some cruel luck at times with a red card on his debut at West Ham and sustaining an ankle ligament injury at Bolton that curtailed a fine display and kept him out for several weeks. A defensive midfielder, he has an imposing presence in the centre of the park, where he is able to break up the opposition play with a timely interception or a crisp tackle before looking to release the ball to a more attack-minded colleague. A regular for South Africa during the past few years, he was in their 23 for the World Cup finals in his native country.
Fulham *(Signed from Golden Arrows, South Africa, ex Bloemfontein Young Tigers, on 27/8/2009) PL 7+5 FLC 0+1 FAC 1+1*

DINDANE Aruna

Born: Abidjan, Ivory Coast, 26 November 1980
Height: 5'9" **Weight:** 12.8
International Honours: Ivory Coast: 54
An eventful first season on English

Aruna Dindane

shores for the Ivorian striker. After joining crisis-stricken Portsmouth on loan in the summer, the striker became an instant hit in the Premier League, with a notable hat-trick in a 4-0 trouncing of Wigan an early sign of his undoubted talent. With pace, skill and strength in abundance, Aruna went on to impress throughout a turbulent season on the south coast before a bizarre set of circumstances left his future in the balance. A contractual dispute between Pompey and his parent club Lens meant Aruna was ineligible to play in a number of games towards the climax of the season unless a fee was met. However, a personal plea from the striker to the Lens hierarchy led to the clause in his contract being waived, allowing Aruna to return to action with a bang as he played a key role in Portsmouth's FA Cup semi-final triumph over Tottenham and inspired the unlikeliest of comebacks against Bolton with two well-taken goals. His return to action and form could not have been better timed as the Ivory Coast's newly appointed coach Sven Goran Eriksson happy to name Aruna in his strongest possible squad for the summer World Cup tournament.
Portsmouth (Loaned from RC Lens, France, ex ASEC Mimosas, Anderlecht, on 28/8/2009) PL 18+1/8 FLC 2/1 FAC 3/1

DIOP Mor **Serigne**
Born: Ghana, 29 September 1988
Height: 6'0" **Weight:** 13.8
This tall French-Ghanaian striker joined Darlington in October after playing in the Ukraine, Belgium and Cyprus. He played mainly as a target man, with his ability to bring the ball down and feed his fellow forwards. He showed neat footwork and a good shot, scoring his first goal in the FA Cup defeat at Barnet in November, but only managed two more in the League. Was out of contract in the summer.
Darlington (Free from SE Ibiza Eivissa, Spain, ex Metalurh Donetsk, Stal Alchevsk - loan, Germinal Beerschot, Apollon Limassol, PAEEK - loan, on 22/10/2009) FL 18+5/2 FAC 0+1/1

DIOP Pape Bouba (**Papa**)
Born: Dakar, Senegal, 28 January 1978
Height: 6'4" **Weight:** 15.7
Club Honours: FAC '08
International Honours: Senegal: 63
It was in many ways a frustrating season for the Portsmouth midfielder. The Senegalese powerhouse known as 'The Wardrobe' spent much of the season on the sidelines battling against a number of niggling injuries. After

starting the season's opening two games, Papa was ruled out until December before a run of games in which he was drafted in and out of the side. Powerful, determined and strong in the tackle, Papa remains a valuable asset to any side.
Fulham (Signed from RC Lens, France on 30/7/2004) PL 70+6/8 FLC 3+1 FAC 4/1
Portsmouth (Signed on 31/8/2007) PL 49+4 FLC 1+1 FAC 9+3 Others 4+1

DIOUF El **Hadji** Ousseynou
Born: Dakar, Senegal, 15 January 1981
Height: 5'11" **Weight:** 11.11
Club Honours: FLC '03
International Honours: Senegal: 57
El Hadji was used primarily as a wide midfield player at Blackburn during 2009-10, on either flank and usually interchanging during the game. He was also played in the hole, behind a lone striker, and given license to roam. Although he was frequently omitted, at times he was crucial to Rovers, mainly because he can retain possession. Two of his three goals were great headers that brought home points against Sunderland and Chelsea but his tally was disappointing. Nobody could ever doubt that El Hadji was devoted to Blackburn's cause and when the pressure was on he worked as hard as anyone. His season closed early to have his tonsils removed.
Liverpool (£10,000,000 from RC Lens, France, ex Sochaux, Stade Rennais, on 17/7/2002) PL 41+14/3 FLC 7/3 FAC 4 Others 9+5
Bolton W (£3,500,000 on 20/8/2004) PL 102+12/21 FLC 3+2 FAC 3+2 Others 6+6/3
Sunderland (£2,600,000 on 29/7/2008) PL 11+3 FLC 1 FAC 1
Blackburn Rov (Loaned on 30/1/2009) PL 37+3/4 FAC 1

DIOUF Mame **Biram**
Born: Dakar, Senegal, 16 December 1987
Height: 6'1" **Weight:** 12.0
International Honours: Senegal: 3; Yth
Signed from Molde in Norway – the club that gave Manchester United Ole Gunnar Solksjaer - and loaned back to them in 2009, Biram said about his shock move: "Playing for United has always been a dream of mine ever since I was a small boy. I hope that when I move in January, I will have a big impact". Signing a work permit in December, the striker made his Reds' debut in the Premier League at Birmingham in January as a substitute for Paul Scholes. Making his home debut in the 3–0 win over Burnley as a

74th-minute substitute for Wayne Rooney, he scored his first goal for United in stoppage time after being played in by Antonio Valencia, looping a header over goalkeeper Brian Jensen.
Manchester U (Signed from Molde FK, Norway, ex Diaraf, on 17/7/2009) PL 0+5/1 FLC 0+1

DI SANTO Franco Matias
Born: Mendoza, Argentina, 7 April 1989
Height: 6'4" **Weight:** 12.4
Club Honours: FAC '09
International Honours: Argentina: Yth
The young man from Argentina was a popular presence at Blackburn in the first half of the season, when his strong running, skill at holding the ball and ability to defend from the front made him a real favourite. On loan from Chelsea, he sometimes lacked composure in the danger areas, but his only goal in the home game against Burnley was a popular one. Franco is still seen as a striker who should make rapid progress with further Premier League experience.
Chelsea (£3,400,000 from Audax Italiano, Chile on 27/1/2008) PL 0+8 FLC 0+2 FAC 0+3 Others 0+3
Blackburn Rov (Loaned on 3/8/2009) PL 15+7/1 FLC 0+1 FAC 1

DISLEY Craig Edward
Born: Worksop, 24 August 1981
Height: 5'10" **Weight:** 11.0
The experienced central midfield player signed for Shrewsbury after being released by Bristol Rovers. An energetic box-to-box player, he likes to get forward into attacking positions. Disappointingly, Shrews' followers did not see the best of him as injuries limited his involvement to 19 games. A knee ligament injury in August kept him sidelined until December. He scored his only goal in February in a 2-0 win against Barnet but sustained an ankle injury at Rotherham later that month that kept him out until the end of a season he will want to forget.
Mansfield T (From trainee on 23/6/1999) FL 106+35/16 FLC 2 FAC 9+1 Others 5
Bristol Rov (Free on 13/7/2004) FL 171+32/25 FLC 5+1/1 FAC 15+1/3 Others 17/2
Shrewsbury T (Free on 2/7/2009) FL 16+2/1 FLC 1

DISTIN Sylvain
Born: Paris, France, 16 December 1977
Height: 6'4" **Weight:** 13.10
Club Honours: FAC '08
After starting the season strongly at Portsmouth, Sylvain earned a move to

Everton at the end of the summer transfer window and quickly took advantage of the absence of others to play most of the season in the centre of defence, missing only a few matches due to a hamstring injury. Cool and calm, the former Manchester City defender provided a powerful screen for goalkeeper Tim Howard and his occasional forays up front were very effective. With keen competition for the central defensive berths at Everton this coming season, he will have to be at his best to retain his place.
Newcastle U (Loaned from Paris St Germain, France, ex Tours, Guegnon, on 14/9/2001) PL 20+8 FLC 2 FAC 5
Manchester C (£4,000,000 from Paris St Germain, France on 4/7/2002) PL 178/5 FLC 7 FAC 16/1 Others 5
Portsmouth (Free on 4/7/2007) PL 77 FLC 4 FAC 9 Others 6
Everton (Signed on 28/8/2009) PL 29 FLC 2 FAC 1 Others 6/2

DJILALI Kieron Stephen Larbi
Born: Lambeth, 22 January 1991
Height: 6'3" **Weight:** 13.2
A right-winger, Kieron can also play on the left side of the pitch and filled both roles for Crystal Palace in the handful of appearances he made during the season. He started the campaign with a loan spell at non-League Crawley in September, before another loan from November to January at League Two Chesterfield where he scored his first ever League goal, an eye-catching strike in the 5-2 defeat of Darlington. After taking a few games to adapt to the requirements of League Two football, the winger showed good vision and pace on the right of midfield and went forward with enthusiasm. Once back in Palace colours he also claimed his first goal for the Eagles with a shot from close range away at Doncaster early in the New Year, and appeared sporadically for the first team during the remainder of the season. Was offered and signed a new deal with Palace in mid-May and will be looking to step up to another level in the coming season.
Crystal Palace (From trainee on 20/8/2008) FL 4+10/1 FLC 1+2 FAC 0+2
Chesterfield (Loaned on 13/11/2009) FL 8/1

DJOUROU-GBADJERE Johan Danon
Born: Abidjan, Ivory Coast, 18 January 1987
Height: 6'3" **Weight:** 13.11
International Honours: Switzerland: 23; U21-2; Yth
Even in an Arsenal team often hampered by injury problems, Johan's

struggles take some surpassing. The defender suffered an injury in pre-season that ruled him out for virtually the entire season. He only returned to the Arsenal squad for the penultimate game of the campaign at Blackburn and made his solitary appearance at home to Fulham the following week.
Arsenal (From trainee on 28/8/2004) PL 38+8 FLC 11+1 FAC 7 Others 11+2
Birmingham C (Loaned on 10/8/2007) PL 13

DOBBIE Stephen
Born: Glasgow, 5 December 1982
Height: 5'10" **Weight:** 10.3
A close season signing from Scottish side Queen of the South, the Swansea front runner scored in consecutive Carling Cup ties at the Liberty Stadium but failed to convince the management for a regular place in the match-day squad. When the transfer window re-opened in January he started a loan spell at Championship rivals Blackpool, scoring on his debut. Stephen was in a difficult situation when loaned to Blackpool in January - he was battling against his parent side for a play-off spot. Four goals from wide of a front three and decent performances from the bench enhanced his reputation and it will be interesting to see where he goes from here.
Glasgow Rgrs (From juniors on 1/8/2000)
Hibernian (Free on 1/7/2003) SL 7+28/2 SLC 2+5/5 SC 1 Others 0+1
St Johnstone (Free on 28/1/2005) SL 12+16/3 SLC 2/2 SC 0+1 Others 1+3/2
Dumbarton (Loaned on 10/8/2006) SL 17/10 SLC 1/1
Queen of the South (Free on 5/11/2007) SL 74+9/47 SLC 2 SC 10+1/7 Others 1
Swansea C (Signed on 1/7/2009) FL 4+2 FLC 1+1/3 FAC 0+1
Blackpool (Loaned on 1/2/2010) FL 6+10/4 Others 0+3/1

DOBIE Robert **Scott**
Born: Workington, 10 October 1978
Height: 6'1" **Weight:** 12.8
International Honours: S: 6;
Having first played for Carlisle 13 years before, the season just gone looks to be Scott's last at Brunton Park. Playing up front, he scored four times in four games early on in the campaign, in a sequence that included matches against both Leeds and Southampton. He finished the campaign in double figures, his best haul for some years and, as ever, showed a willingness to play for the shirt. His contract expired at the end of the season and he now looks likely to move elsewhere.

Carlisle U (From trainee on 10/5/1997) FL 101+35/24 FLC 2+6 FAC 4+1/2 Others 6+1
Clydebank (Loaned on 3/11/1998) SL 6
West Bromwich A (£125,000 + on 11/7/2001) P/FL 57+53/21 FLC 6+4/4 FAC 1+6
Millwall (£500,000 + on 10/11/2004) FL 15+1/3
Nottingham F (£525,000 on 25/2/2005) FL 20+21/3 FLC 1 FAC 0+4 Others 2+1/1
Carlisle U (Signed on 23/1/2008) FL 43+41/12 FLC 3+1/2 FAC 1+5 Others 5+2/3

DODDS Louis Bartholomew
Born: Leicester, 8 October 1986
Height: 5'11" **Weight:** 11.11
Louis had an excellent season in a variety of midfield roles for Port Vale, sometimes in the centre, sometimes on the wing with his best position probably being just behind the front two. He missed only five games and scored eight goals, seven of them before Christmas when the club played with a back five, which meant he had a more central role. Louis has a good shot on him and his most important goal came in the FA Cup replay win at Stevenage.
Leicester C (From trainee on 15/7/2005)
Rochdale (Loaned on 20/2/2007) FL 6+6/2
Lincoln C (Loaned on 31/7/2007) FL 38+3/9 FLC 0+1 FAC 2
Port Vale (Signed on 4/8/2008) FL 70+18/10 FLC 2 FAC 3+1/4 Others 3/1

DOE Scott Mark
Born: Reading, 6 November 1988
Height: 6'1" **Weight:** 12.2
Scott made his Dagenham debut in the opening game at Crewe and played for the first two months of the campaign at right-back before moving to central defence in October where he grew in strength and effectiveness. With Mark Arber he formed a great partnership at the heart of a four-man defence and his aerial ability, along with his well-timed tackles, earned him the runner-up spot in the Daggers' 'Player of the Year' awards.
Dagenham & Redbridge (Free from Weymouth, ex Swindon T trainee, on 13/3/2009) FL 40+2 FLC 1 FAC 1 Others 3

DOHERTY Gary Michael Thomas
Born: Carndonagh, 31 January 1980
Height: 6'2" **Weight:** 13.1
Club Honours: Div 1 '10
International Honours: RoI: 34; U21-7; Yth
Gary clocked up his 200th League

appearance for Norwich during a highly successful season for this resolute and highly experienced central defender. He found himself out of favour in the early days of Paul Lambert's reign as City manager but quickly won back his place and went on to produce a string of fabulous performances at the heart of the Norwich rearguard. A real competitor, he combines strength in the air with an uncanny ability to second-guess his opponent with a tackle, interception or timely block. He also enjoyed his best scoring season for City, notching seven goals including a purple patch of four in three games just before Christmas. Finished third in the fans' 'Player of the Season' vote. Was out of contract in the summer.
Luton T (From trainee on 2/7/1997) FL 46+24/12 FLC 0+3/1 FAC 6+2/2 Others 1+1
Tottenham H (£1,000,000 on 22/4/2000) PL 45+19/4 FLC 3+3 FAC 7+1/4
Norwich C (Signed on 20/8/2004) P/FL 192+10/11 FLC 11+1 FAC 10+1/1 Others 2/1

DOHERTY Thomas (Tommy) Edward
Born: Bristol, 17 March 1979
Height: 5'8" **Weight:** 9.13
Club Honours: AMC '03
International Honours: NI: 9
After three months on the sidelines with a pre-season hamstring injury, Tommy returned to the Wycombe side in October as the holding midfielder under new manager Gary Waddock. Ever-present in the side, Tommy's superb ball skills were undiminished, without hitting the heights of the previous season. All became clear in January when he surprisingly quit the club, unable to reconcile differences with Waddock who had let him go when they were at Queens Park Rangers. He explained to fans that his heart simply was not in it any more and made a surprise move to Hungarian side Ferencvárosi TC, signing a contract until the end of the season.
Bristol C (From trainee on 8/7/1997) FL 155+33/7 FLC 9+1/1 FAC 7+1 Others 18+1/1
Queens Park Rgrs (Signed on 30/6/2005) FL 14+1
Yeovil T (Loaned on 2/3/2006) FL 1
Wycombe W (Loaned on 15/9/2006) FL 23+3/2 FLC 3+1 Others 1
Wycombe W (Free on 22/10/2007) FL 66+4 FLC 1 FAC 2+1 Others 2

DONALDSON Clayton Andrew
Born: Bradford, 7 February 1984

Height: 6'1" **Weight:** 11.7
International Honours: E: SP-2
Clayton has now completed two seasons at Crewe following his transfer from Hibernian. The striker is a difficult opponent but sustained a broken leg at Bournemouth in late August. He was back in the side at Notts County in October and was a regular in attack from then on. Clayton was Crewe's second highest scorer, all his goals being scored in League games.
Hull C (From trainee on 10/2/2003) FL 0+2 Others 0+3/1 (Free to York C on 23/6/2005)
Hibernian (Free on 1/7/2007) SL 11+7/5 SLC 2/1 SC 0+1
Crewe Alex (Free on 18/8/2008) FL 56+18/19 FLC 0+2 FAC 3+1/1 Others 0+2

DONALDSON Ryan Mark
Born: Newcastle, 1 May 1991
Height: 5'9" **Weight:** 11.0
International Honours: E: Yth
Ryan is a striker whose pace and control, allied to his goal sense, mark him out as a promising prospect at his home-town club of Newcastle. He made his first League and home appearance when coming off the bench in the win over Leicester in August, and his full debut came when he led the line in the Carling Cup game at Peterborough in September as part of the club's youngest ever team . Thereafter he was frequently an unused substitute, although he did come off the bench against Ipswich in September, when he played at right-back. He was called up for the England under-19 side in October and scored in the win over Slovenia.
Newcastle U (From trainee on 18/11/2008) FL 0+2 FLC 1 FAC 0+2

DONE Matthew (Matty)
Born: Oswestry, 22 June 1988
Height: 5'8" **Weight:** 10.7
Much had been expected of wide midfielder Matty after Hereford dropped down a tier but he was very much a peripheral figure in the early part of the campaign. When he forced his way back into the squad, his ability to take on defenders and to play on either left or right often made him a dangerous attacker, but he suffered from a lack of a long run in the side and struggled to turn potentially dangerous situations into goals.
Wrexham (From trainee on 3/8/2006) FL 41+25/1 FLC 2+1/1 FAC 3 Others 2
Hereford U (Free on 4/8/2008) FL 31+25 FLC 1+1 FAC 0+2 Others 2+2/1

DONNELLY George John
Born: Liverpool, 28 May 1988
Height: 6'2" **Weight:** 13.0
George joined Stockport on loan from Plymouth in January, replacing the outgoing Peter Thompson. His debut came when he replaced Richie Partridge in the 2-0 defeat at Southampton, and he scored on his home debut against MK Dons – his fine chip over Willy Gueret in goal giving County the lead. He notched a double in the 4-3 victory over Wycombe later in February, but it would be nine more games until he found the back of the net again, a late consolation in the 3-1 loss to Yeovil.
Plymouth Arg (Signed from Skelmersdale U on 20/3/2009) FL 0+2
Stockport Co (Loaned on 29/1/2010) FL 16+3/4

Scott Donnelly

DONNELLY Scott Paul
Born: Hammersmith, 25 December 1987
Height: 5'8" **Weight:** 11.10
Club Honours: FC '08
International Honours: E: Yth
Scott is an industrious central midfielder who can also play on the wing or as a forward. He scored his first goals of the season against Accrington and added another two in Aldershot's next game at Grimsby. Scott scored with an exquisite 'Beckhamesque' 45-yard lob against Cheltenham, contributing to the supporters' September 'Player of the Month' award. Having added to his catalogue of quality goals with a superb 25-yarder at Bury, he ended with 14 in

all competitions. Missed only three games as the Shots exceeded all expectations by reaching the play-offs.
Queens Park Rgrs *(From trainee on 1/3/2006) FL 3+10 FAC 0+1 (Freed on 23/1/2007)*
Aldershot T *(Free from Wealdstone on 1/11/2007) FL 54+9/14 FLC 2 FAC 3/1 Others 4*

DONOVAN Landon Timothy
Born: Los Angeles, California, USA, 4 March 1982
Height: 5'8" **Weight:** 11.5
International Honours: USA: 122; U23-15; Yth
Everton boss David Moyes did good business by signing the American star on a short-term loan deal from Los Angeles Galaxy in the January transfer window. The United States' international made a brilliant impression on Toffees' supporters and was keen to express thanks for the welcome he received. With a hard-working attitude, Landon played mainly on the right flank in his time at Goodison, scoring two goals and providing many opportunities for others. An extension for his loan deal was scuppered but it is not beyond the realms of possibility that the popular American will return at some point in the future.
Everton *(Loaned from Los Angeles Galaxy, USA, ex IMG Soccer Academy, Bayer Leverkusen, San Jose Earthquakes - loan, Bayern Munich - loan, on 1/1/2010) PL 7+3/2 FAC 1 Others 2*

DORAN Aaron Brian
Born: Dublin, 13 May 1991
Height: 5'7" **Weight:** 11.13
International Honours: RoI: Yth
Aaron made an immediate impact after joining MK Dons on loan from Blackburn in October, when scoring and also setting up a goal on his debut in the 2-0 Johnstone's Paint Trophy win over Southend. Given a couple of League starts soon after, he showed some tricky wing skills but generally found it hard going against some very experienced opponents and returned to Blackburn after completing his month. Unable to get a game at Ewood Park, Aaron was next loaned to Leyton Orient towards the end of February, in order to replace another loanee in Nicky Adams. Aaron is a right-winger who likes to run at defenders and playing in a struggling team he was never able to show the fans why Blackburn have faith in him and why he has appeared in the Premiership for them.
Blackburn Rov *(From trainee on 14/5/2008) PL 0+3*
MK Dons *(Loaned on 5/10/2009) FL*

2+2 Others 1/1
Leyton Orient *(Loaned on 22/2/2010) FL 6*

DORRANS Graham
Born: Glasgow, 5 May 1987
Height: 5'9" **Weight:** 11.7
International Honours: S: 3; U21-6; Yth
In March, Graham was named the second best player outside the Premier League – and now he can show how good he is by pitting his wits against the best midfield players around. He was West Bromwich's top scorer with 18 goals, two-thirds of them from dead-ball situations, including eight penalties. Two came in a 4-2 FA Cup win over Newcastle and he was outstanding at times. His passing, work rate, creativeness and all-round play earned praise from opposing players and managers alike as his inspirational performances helped Albion win promotion at the first attempt. Top of his goal list were two wonderful free kicks, both driven home with supreme accuracy, the first from fully 30 yards high into the net in a 3-2 home win over Preston and his second another beauty from outside the box against Doncaster on the day promotion was confirmed. He also grabbed a dramatic late equaliser on the final day of the season against Barnsley while keeping his nerve, and a cool head, as he netted late penalties to seal home and away victories over Blackpool. However, his competitive nature got the better of him in the Carling Cup win over Peterborough when a late lunge on Charlie Lee earned him a second yellow card of the night. He won his first full cap for Scotland in a World Cup qualifier against Holland in September and added two more soon afterwards against Japan and the Czech Republic. Graham, the only Baggies' player to appear in 50 games, was voted Albion's 'Player of the Year' by the club's supporters and was also named in the PFA's 'Championship Team of the Season'.
Livingston *(From juniors on 7/5/2005) SL 63+14/16 SLC 4/1 SC 5+3/3 Others 1+1*
Partick T *(Loaned on 31/8/2005) SL 13+2/5*
West Bromwich A *(£100,000 on 11/7/2008) P/FL 47+6/13 FLC 3/2 FAC 5+2/3*

DOSSENA Andrea
Born: Lodi, Italy, 11 September 1981
Height: 5'11" **Weight:** 12.2
International Honours: Italy: 10; Yth
The Italian international left-back

endured a torrid time in his 18 months with Liverpool following his transfer from Udinese. Lacking the extra pace required to compete in the Premiership, he enjoyed some success as an auxiliary midfielder, scoring wonder goals against Real Madrid and Manchester United towards the end of his first season. In 2009-10, he started only three games, the last in a dismal 2-0 defeat at relegated Portsmouth in December. The following month, he returned to Italy in a £4.25-million deal with Napoli.
Liverpool *(£8,000,000 from Udinese, Italy, ex Verona, Treviso, on 21/7/2008) PL 13+5/1 FLC 2 FAC 2 Others 5+4/1*

DOUGLAS Jonathan
Born: Monaghan, 22 November 1981
Height: 5'10" **Weight:** 12.12
International Honours: RoI: 8; U21-1; Yth
The experienced midfielder arrived at Swindon during the close season after not being offered a further contract at Leeds. Jonathan became the supporters' 'Player of the Season' and was a major contributor to the Swindon side's improved performances. An almost permanent fixture in the centre of midfield, where he orchestrated proceedings with his neat passing game, strong tackling and willingness to either defend or get forward as the need arose. His only failing was his inability to register a goal during the season.
Blackburn Rov *(From trainee on 10/2/2000) P/FL 14+2/1 FLC 1+2 FAC 1+4*
Chesterfield *(Loaned on 26/3/2003) FL 7/1*
Blackpool *(Loaned on 7/8/2003) FL 15+1/3 FLC 3 Others 1*
Gillingham *(Loaned on 10/3/2005) FL 10*
Leeds U *(Signed on 19/8/2005) FL 130+12/10 FLC 8+2/1 FAC 6 Others 7+1*
Swindon T *(Free on 10/7/2009) FL 43 FLC 2 FAC 2 Others 5*

DOUMBE Mathias Kouo
Born: Paris, France, 28 October 1979
Height: 6'1" **Weight:** 12.5
International Honours: France: Yth
Mathias joined MK Dons just ahead of the new season, making his debut at right-back on the opening day against Hartlepool and then alternating between that slot and his more preferred central position. Scoring for first time for the club when netting the only goal in a mid-September derby win at Wycombe, he always looked comfortable when getting forward.

Hibernian (Signed from Paris St Germain, France, ex Nantes, on 26/10/2001) SL 44+1/2 SLC 5 SC 3 **Plymouth Arg** *(Free on 8/6/2004) FL 127+7/4 FLC 3+1 FAC 4* **MK Dons** *(Free on 7/8/2009) FL 29+4/1 FLC 1 FAC 2 Others 3*

DOWNES Aaron Terry
Born: Mudgee, New South Wales, Australia, 15 May 1985
Height: 6'3" **Weight:** 13.0
International Honours: Australia: U23-8; Yth
Having recovered from knee ligament damage, Aaron made a return to Chesterfield's first team in January. He immediately brought reassuring composure to the centre of defence, linking well with Rob Page, but the popular Aussie suffered more damage to the same knee after just seven games, and his season was cruelly cut short. This setback might have crushed lesser men but Aaron is determined to make a return next season.
Chesterfield (Free from Frickley Ath, ex Hampton & Richmond Borough, on 29/7/2004) FL 157+8/10 FLC 5 FAC 6 Others 5/2

DOWNES Aidan
Born: Dublin, 24 July 1988
Height: 5'8" **Weight:** 11.7
International Honours: RoI: U21-3; Yth
The 21-year-old from Dublin was another Yeovil player who will want to forget the season in a hurry. Crocked in a pre-season friendly at Dorchester, he also sustained a shoulder injury and picked up a bug in hospital, meaning that he did not make a start until the April clash with Southend. Equally at home as a second striker or a winger, the Irishman was out of contract in the summer.
Everton (£90,000 from Tolka Rov on 24/1/2006)
Yeovil T (Free on 27/3/2008) FL 20+14/1 FLC 1 FAC 1

DOWNING Paul Michael
Born: Taunton, 26 October 1991
Height: 6'1" **Weight:** 12.6
On loan from West Bromwich, centre-back Paul quickly proved a player of talent at Hereford where his uncle Keith Downing had served with distinction as a player and coach. Paul's ability to read the game and produce a decisively timed tackle added some solidity to the back line before an unlucky sending off at Notts County brought his run in the side to an end.
West Bromwich A (Trainee)
Hereford U (Loaned on 25/1/2010) FL 6

DOWNING Stewart
Born: Middlesbrough, 22 July 1984
Height: 5'11" **Weight:** 10.6
Club Honours: FLC '04
International Honours: E: 23; B-2; U21-8; Yth
Stewart recovered from the bizarre experience of signing for Aston Villa on crutches to become a virtual ever-present during the second half of last season. Martin O'Neill showed faith in the winger last summer by paying a fee that could rise to £12-million although he was nursing a broken foot at the time. Ironically the injury was caused by a challenge from Villa captain Stiliyan Petrov in Stewart's final match at Middlesbrough. Stewart continued his recovery at Villa's Bodymoor Heath training ground and, at the end of November, made his debut as a late substitute in a draw at Burnley. His first start came in early December at Portsmouth in the Carling Cup quarter-final and he capped his full bow with a goal in the 4-2 win. Arguably, Stewart's best performance was in February's 5-2 home victory over Burnley, when he scored twice. Having shown glimpses of his ability to deliver dangerous crosses from dead-ball situations and open up play, his season ended in disappointment when he missed selection for England's World Cup 23.
Middlesbrough (From trainee on 6/9/2001) PL 157+24/17 FLC 6+2/1 FAC 26+1/3 Others 17+1/1
Sunderland (Loaned on 29/10/2003) FL 7/3
Aston Villa (£12,000,000 on 16/7/2009) PL 23+2/2 FLC 4/1 FAC 6

DOWSON David
Born: Bishop Auckland, 12 September 1988
Height: 5'10" **Weight:** 12.1
A bustling forward who came on loan from Sunderland along with Jamie Chandler at the start of the season. He scored in Darlington's opening day defeat at Aldershot but failed to find the net again after a dozen appearances and returned to Wearside after contract at the end of June.
Sunderland (From trainee on 12/7/2007)
Chesterfield (Loaned on 21/2/2008) FL 9+3/3
Darlington (Loaned on 6/8/2009) FL 6+4/1 FLC 1 Others 0+1

DOYLE Kevin Edward
Born: Wexford, 18 September 1983
Height: 5'11" **Weight:** 12.6
Club Honours: Ch '06
International Honours: RoI: 35; U21-11
The most expensive Wolverhampton

signing to date has proved good value. After a hernia operation in July, he had to wait until the fourth League game to start for his new club. His first goal of the season was for the Republic of Ireland in Cyprus, before he scored for Wolves against Fulham. Kevin had a huge disappointment in November. He played in two World Cup play-off matches with France, but Eire went out in controversial circumstances. Kevin's glancing header won the day at Tottenham, and he began playing up front on his own in most matches. His ability to control the ball, beat players and work hard for the team endeared him to the fans. This was typified at home to Liverpool. He played for his country against Brazil in March, and topped the scoring charts for Wolves with nine goals. Kevin was voted 'Player of the Year' by his fellow players, which underlined his unselfish attitude to the team.
Reading (£75,000 from Cork C on 5/8/2005) P/FL 142+12/55 FLC 2+2 FAC 1+3/1 Others 1
Wolverhampton W (Signed on 30/6/2009) PL 33+1/9 FLC 1+1 FAC 0+1

Kevin Doyle

DOYLE Michael Paul
Born: Dublin, 8 July 1981
Height: 5'8" **Weight:** 11.0
International Honours: RoI: 1; U21-8
Midfielder Michael joined Leeds two days before the start of the campaign on a season-long loan from Coventry. In an anchor role best suited to his tackling style, he played in the majority of games and but despite striking the

woodwork from distance several times, failed to score. Perhaps his most telling display was the man-marking job he did on Norwich playmaker Wes Hoolahan at Carrow Road in March.

Glasgow Celtic *(From juniors on 1/8/1998)*
Coventry C *(Free on 4/7/2003) FL 241+6/19 FLC 11+2/1 FAC 18/1*
Leeds U *(Loaned on 6/8/2009) FL 42 FLC 3 FAC 6 Others 1*

DOYLE Nathan Luke Robert
Born: Derby, 12 January 1987
Height: 5'11" **Weight:** 11.11
International Honours: E: Yth
Having played at right-back for Hull against Tottenham in the pre-season Barclays Asia Trophy in China and against Southend in the Carling Cup, Nathan then joined Barnsley on loan until the end of the year. After making his debut as a substitute against Swansea, he had a successful spell at Oakwell where he soon became an integral part of Mark Robins' team. He showed his versatility by playing initially at full-back but then moving to midfield, where his invaluable work often went unseen. Tracking runners, tackling and breaking up play were his strengths. He briefly returned to the Tigers' bench as an unused sub in the FA Cup tie at Wigan before concluding a permanent move to Oakwell during the January transfer window and continuing to work tirelessly in the Reds' midfield throughout the rest of the campaign.
Derby Co *(From trainee on 21/1/2004) FL 4+5 FAC 0+1*
Notts Co *(Loaned on 24/2/2006) FL 12*
Bradford C *(Loaned on 4/8/2006) FL 25+3 FLC 1 FAC 3 Others 1*
Hull C *(Signed on 31/1/2007) P/FL 3+2 FLC 3 FAC 4 Others 0+2/1*
Barnsley *(Free on 18/9/2009) FL 32+2*

DOYLEY Lloyd Collin
Born: Whitechapel, 1 December 1982
Height: 6'0" **Weight:** 11.10
Monday, 7th December 2009 is a date which will be celebrated in Watford folklore. On that day, Lloyd finally ended a nine-year drought and scored his first professional goal on the occasion of his 269th appearance. Fittingly, it was fine effort – a diving far-post header against Queens Park Rangers that inspired an eventual 3-1 victory. Endearingly, Lloyd himself had no idea how to celebrate and had to be encouraged by his team-mates while the stadium erupted around him. It was no surprise when Lloyd's effort was chosen as Watford's 'Goal of the Season' with a landslide vote, while the

Lloyd Doyley

boots he wore fetched £1,900 at a charity auction. 'Lloydinho' is Watford's longest-serving player, having been with the club since he was 12. Deployed at left-back despite being right-footed, he played every minute of every game until he had to go off with a hamstring injury against West Bromwich in April. Typically, he was back before the end of the season, having missed only two matches.
Watford *(From trainee on 8/3/2001) P/FL 235+27/1 FLC 17+1 FAC 6+4 Others 4*

DRAPER Ross James
Born: Wolverhampton, 20 October 1988
Height: 6'3" **Weight:** 15.1
Ross moved from Zamaretto Premier League side Hednesford Town to Macclesfield in the summer, and went straight into the team, making an immediate impact and looking every inch a League player. Usually playing as a central midfielder, Ross had to be versatile when the number of injuries to

midfield players increased. He played all across midfield, coping equally well in a three or four. Ross missed all January following a double hernia repair and an ankle injury in March kept him out for the remainder of the season. His performances were recognized by a two-year contract extension.
Macclesfield T *(Free from Hednesford T, ex trainee at Shrewsbury T, Stafford Rgrs, on 9/7/2009) FL 28+1/1 FLC 1 FAC 1*

DRINKWATER Daniel (Danny) Noel
Born: Manchester, 5 March 1990
Height: 5'10" **Weight:** 11.0
International Honours: E: Yth
The teenager joined Huddersfield soon after the beginning of the season on loan from Manchester United to add an extra dimension to the midfield area and after two substitute appearances was installed in the starting line-up. Danny scored with a rasping drive in the 7-1 mauling of Brighton but, as he adapted to life in the third tier, was often in and out of the side. It was not

until the latter part of the season that Danny came into his own with a rich vein of form and, always a threat at set pieces, scored with a wonderful flighted free kick in the 6-0 mauling of Stockport.

Manchester U (From trainee on 4/7/2008)
Huddersfield T (Loaned on 14/8/2009) FL 27+6/2 FLC 1 FAC 0+1 Others 2

DROGBA Didier Yves Tebily
Born: Abidjan, Ivory Coast, 11 March 1978
Height: 6'2" **Weight:** 13.8
Club Honours: FLC '05, '07; PL '05, '06, '10; CS '05, '09; FAC '07, '09, '10
International Honours: Ivory Coast: 66
A season of personal landmarks – African 'Player of the Year', Chelsea 'Player of the Year', nominee for FIFA 'World Player' and PFA 'Player of the

Year', election into the PFA 'Team of the Year' and, with a final day hat-trick against Wigan, the 'Golden Boot' for 29 Premier League goals. Didier scored from the first day, two goals that beat Hull, until the last, the only goal at Wembley against Portsmouth to clinch the FA Cup and Chelsea's first ever 'Double'. He left for the African Cup of Nations as joint top Premier League scorer with 14 goals and on his return scored Chelsea's next three, including two against Arsenal to make it 12 in 11 matches against them. He scored on other big occasions, as first League goals at Old Trafford and Anfield helped to seal crucial victories in Chelsea's march to the title. His all-round centre-forward play is superb and he does not get the credit for valuable defensive work defending dead-ball situations. He is a superb crosser from either flank

contributing to his ten assists, the fourth best in the Premier League. What made his achievements the more remarkable is that he played with pain for the last third of the season, deferring a much-needed hernia operation until the end of the season and before the World Cup finals. His winner in the FA Cup final made him only the second player to score in three different finals and he has scored in all six matches he has played at Wembley. Didier signed a new deal that keeps him at Chelsea until 2012 and now stands seventh in the club's all-time scoring list.
Chelsea (£24,000,000 from Marseille, France, ex Levallois, Le Mans, Guingamp, on 23/7/2004) PL 133+33/84 FLC 9+6/9 FAC 19+3/10 Others 51+6/28

DRUMMOND Stewart James
Born: Preston, 11 December 1975
Height: 6'2" **Weight:** 13.8
International Honours: E: SP-13
The central midfielder was again one of Morecambe's most consistent performers and was the one solid figure in a midfield that was constantly forced to change because of injuries. Stewart missed only five games, three of them through suspension for a rare red card. After playing more than 400 games for the Shrimps in his two spells, he again proved his value at both ends of the field as he chipped in with nine goals as well as some vital defensive clearances. He was awarded a testimonial at the end of the season.
Chester C (Free from Morecambe on 25/6/2004) FL 85+2/12 FLC 2 FAC 6/1 Others 1+2
Shrewsbury T (Free on 14/7/2006) FL 65+2/7 FLC 1 FAC 3 Others 4/1
Morecambe (£15,000 on 4/1/2008) FL 99+6/21 FLC 1+1 FAC 3 Others 6+1/1

DRURY Adam James
Born: Cambridge, 29 August 1978
Height: 5'10" **Weight:** 11.8
Club Honours: Div 1 '04, '10
Norwich fans were delighted to welcome Adam into the team on a regular basis as he enjoyed his first largely injury-free season since 2006-07. A solid and accomplished left-back, few opponents are able to get the better of him in one-on-one situations and his covering skills contributed to City's excellent defensive record in League One. Norwich's preferred diamond formation also placed an onus on him to get forward whenever possible, a responsibility he thrived upon, creating numerous goals for his team-mates. He now lies 20th in Norwich's all-time appearance lists with over 320.

Didier Drogba

Peterborough U (From trainee on 3/7/1996) FL 138+10/2 FLC 8 FAC 9 Others 10+1
Norwich C (£275,000 on 21/3/2001) P/FL 291+3/3 FLC 11 FAC 14 Others 4

DUBERRY Michael Wayne
Born: Enfield, 14 October 1975
Height: 6'1" **Weight:** 13.6
Club Honours: FLC '98; ECWC '98; ESC '98
International Honours: E: U21-5
Michael was Peter Taylor's major summer signing for Wycombe to replace the departed defender Dave McCracken and was immediately made team captain. It took time for the big man to settle in central defence but he was ever-present until the first week of December, when he was dropped to the substitutes' bench, and then out of the squad completely by new manager Gary Waddock. On 1st February, it was announced that Michael had left Wanderers by mutual consent six months after he arrived on a two-year contract. He immediately signed for Scottish Premier League side St Johnstone, where he was ever-present until the end of the season.
Chelsea (From trainee on 7/6/1993) PL 77+9/1 FLC 8 FAC 12/2 Others 9
Bournemouth (Loaned on 29/9/1995) FL 7 Others 1
Leeds U (£4,000,000 + on 29/7/1999) P/FL 54+4/4 FLC 0+4 FAC 4+2 Others 9+1
Stoke C (Loaned on 15/10/2004) FL 15
Stoke C (Free on 3/3/2005) FL 80/1 FLC 2 FAC 5
Reading (£800,000 on 31/1/2007) P/FL 47+1 FLC 3 FAC 1 Others 2
Wycombe W (Free on 10/7/2009) FL 18 FAC 1

DUFF Damien Anthony
Born: Dublin, 2 March 1979
Height: 5'10" **Weight:** 12.0
Club Honours: FLC '02, '05; PL '05, '06; CS '05
International Honours: RoI: 83; B-1; Yth; Sch
Damien scored the opening goal of the season for Newcastle to earn a point at West Bromwich before being transferred to Fulham and enjoying an outstanding first season at Craven Cottage. He is a tricky winger whose skills can unlock opposition defences with ease and an excellent crosser of the ball, as well as possessing a fierce and accurate shot which resulted in stunning goals against Everton and Birmingham, the latter being voted BBC 'Goal of the Month' for February. In addition to his attacking prowess he is also a competent defender and can

drop back to help the side retain a lead when required. Although normally deployed on the right he also featured on the left flank on a number of occasions. The Irishman made an immediate impact when introduced as a substitute against Russian club, Amkar Perm, where his first touch began a move that resulted in a goal for Bobby Zamora. A regular choice throughout the season for both club and country he featured for the Republic of Ireland in crucial World Cup qualifier and play-off ties as well as a prestige friendly against Brazil at the Emirates.
Blackburn Rov (Signed from Lourdes Celtic on 5/3/1996) P/FL 157+27/27 FLC 16+1/5 FAC 13+5/2 Others 4/1
Chelsea (£17,000,000 on 26/7/2003) PL 63+18/14 FLC 7+1/2 FAC 4+4 Others 21+7/3
Newcastle U (£5,000,000 on 26/7/2006) P/FL 61+8/5 FLC 2+1 FAC 5/1 Others 8+1
Fulham (Signed on 18/8/2009) PL 30+2/6 FAC 4/2 Others 10+4/1

DUFF Michael James
Born: Belfast, 11 January 1978
Height: 6'1" **Weight:** 11.8
Club Honours: FAT '98; FC '99
International Honours: NI: 22
Having moved up from non-League through all the divisions, Michael had to wait for his Premier League debut, a pre-season injury and Burnley's good start to the season keeping him out of the side until December. The arrival of Leon Cort in January again saw him relegated to the bench before a return in March and April. In both spells, he produced several fine performances and as often as not looked the pick of the back four, a never-say-die presence more than making up in 100 per cent effort for any lack of finesse. His display at Hull, where he played most of the match with a bandaged head after an accidental clash with Cort, was typical. Not for the first time, he was perhaps the most under-appreciated player on Burnley's books. Was out of contract at the end of June.
Cheltenham T (From trainee on 17/8/1996) FL 201/12 FLC 6 FAC 15 Others 9
Burnley (£30,000 on 8/7/2004) P/FL 158+15/4 FLC 15+3/1 FAC 8 Others 3

DUFF Shane Joseph
Born: Wroughton, 2 April 1982
Height: 6'1" **Weight:** 12.10
International Honours: NI: U21-1
Long-serving Cheltenham central defender Shane had a frustrating testimonial season, being out for over six months following an Achilles

operation at the end of August. He appeared in the first five games and, after surgery, returned at a crucial time to help Cheltenham stave off the drop. From the end of March, Shane starred as the Robins embarked upon a six-game unbeaten run – their best of the season – that helped them to remain in the League. He was offered a new contract by manager Mark Yates.
Cheltenham T (From juniors on 20/10/2000) FL 184+9/2 FLC 5+1 FAC 9+1 Others 11/1

DUFFY Darryl Alexander
Born: Glasgow, 16 April 1984
Height: 5'11" **Weight:** 12.1
Club Honours: S Div 1'05; SLCC '04; Div 1 '08
International Honours: S: B-2; U21-8
With the departure of leading scorer Rickie Lambert to Southampton it was expected that the Scottish striker would hold down a regular place at Bristol Rovers, but this failed to materialise. He scored twice from the spot against Aldershot in the Carling Cup, but managed just two League goals for Rovers plus an FA Cup goal against Southampton. Many of his appearances continued to be from the bench before he spent a loan spell at Carlisle, scoring once in seven starts before picking up an ankle injury which ended his term there. Returned to Rovers and made a few end of season appearances, scoring at Leeds in the final match, but in general had a disappointing season.
Glasgow Rgrs (From juniors on 1/7/2003) SL 0+1 SLC 0+1 Others 0+1
Brechin C (Loaned on 16/1/2004) SL 8/3
Falkirk (Signed on 25/6/2004) SL 55+2/27 SLC 5/4 SC 1 Others 5/6
Hull C (Signed on 11/1/2006) FL 9+15/3 FLC 0+3/1 FAC 0+1
Hartlepool U (Loaned on 3/11/2006) FL 10/5
Swansea C (Signed on 22/3/2007) FL 17+11/6 FLC 0+2 FAC 1+3 Others 3+2/1
Bristol Rov (Free on 11/7/2008) FL 43+30/17 FLC 3/2 FAC 0+2/1 Others 2
Carlisle U (Loaned on 1/2/2010) FL 7+1/1

DUFFY Mark James
Born: Liverpool, 7 October 1985
Height: 5'9" **Weight:** 11.2
The exciting young winger enjoyed some high points during his first full League season after joining Morecambe from Southport in the middle of the previous campaign. One of the Shrimps' most threatening players, he enjoyed some good games and scored four League goals including a superb chip in

the 5-0 victory over Bournemouth. Although his final ball sometimes lets him down, if he continues to improve as he has done he could be a major player for Morecambe.

Morecambe (Free from Southport on 23/2/2009) FL 28+16/5 FLC 1 FAC 0+2/1 Others 3/1

DUFFY Richard Michael

Born: Swansea, 30 August 1985
Height: 5'10" **Weight:** 10.4
International Honours: W: 13; U21-8; Yth
Richard was signed in the summer from Millwall and was a virtual ever-present in the Exeter back line. His versatility saw him playing in almost every position across the defence, while his positioning and awareness meant that he was rarely caught out of position or on the ball. Richard scored his only goal in the December draw with Gillingham.

Swansea C (From trainee on 3/9/2002) FL 16+2/1 FAC 3+1 Others 1
Portsmouth (£300,000 on 26/1/2004) PL 0+1 FLC 1
Burnley (Loaned on 24/9/2004) FL 3+4/1 FLC 2
Coventry C (Loaned on 27/1/2005) FL 14 FAC 1
Coventry C (Loaned on 1/7/2005) FL 30+2 FAC 2
Coventry C (Loaned on 23/10/2006) FL 13
Swansea C (Loaned on 11/1/2007) FL 8+3 FAC 1
Coventry C (Loaned on 21/3/2008) FL 2
Millwall (Free on 2/2/2009) FL 11+1
Exeter C (Free on 23/7/2009) FL 41+1/1 FLC 1 FAC 1

DUFFY Shane

Born: Derry, 1 January 1992
Height: 6'4" **Weight:** 12.0
International Honours: NI: B-1; U21-3; Yth
The Everton central defender earned a swift promotion through the Academy and reserve teams to make his first team debut as an early substitute against AEK Athens in December, which was quickly followed by a start against BATE Borisov. A hugely promising, tall and strong centre-half in the classic mould, the youngster switched allegiance from Northern Ireland to the Republic in 2010.

Everton (Signed from Foyle Harps YFC on 31/1/2009) Others 1+1

DUGUID Karl Anthony

Born: Letchworth, 21 March 1978
Height: 5'11" **Weight:** 11.7
Karl is a very versatile member of Plymouth's squad. The former captain started the season on the substitutes'

bench but it did not take long for him to force his way back into the starting line-up. During his first couple of games, Karl was often seen in the heart of the Pilgrims' midfield but he also appeared on either the left or right of midfield as well as at right-back, which many Pilgrims' fans think is his best position. He was to reclaim the captain's armband at the end of the season when Carl Fletcher was injured. Karl scored a memorable goal for the Pilgrims at Newcastle in September following a surging run into the box.

Colchester U (From trainee on 16/7/1996) FL 317+68/42 FLC 10+3 FAC 17+6/2 Others 12+5/1
Plymouth Arg (Free on 1/7/2008) FL 79+2/2 FLC 2 FAC 3/1

DUKE Matthew (Matt)

Born: Sheffield, 16 June 1977
Height: 6'5" **Weight:** 13.4
Matt continued his professional rivalry with Wales international Bo Myhill for Hull's goalkeeping position into a sixth season. The former non-League 'keeper regained the gloves in the 11th game at Burnley and could count himself unfortunate to return to the bench at the end of a six-game run that included City's best sequence of results of the campaign. The patient Yorkshireman had to wait until April for a recall at Birmingham, with new manager Iain Dowie praising his calmness under pressure as the Tigers headed towards relegation. Having overcome testicular cancer in recent years, Matt continues to be a staunch and active supporter of the Everyman charity.

Sheffield U (Free from Alfreton T on 26/8/1999)
Hull C (£60,000 from Burton A on 23/7/2004) P/FL 26+3 FLC 4 FAC 2 Others 0+1
Stockport Co (Loaned on 5/8/2005) FL 3
Wycombe W (Loaned on 13/1/2006) FL 5

DUMBUYA Mustapha

Born: Sierra Leone, 7 August 1987
Height: 5'7" **Weight:** 11.0
Mustapha was signed by Doncaster from Blue Square Premier club Grays Athletic during the summer of 2009. A right-back, he showed plenty of pace going forward but he found it hard to get into the team past the incumbent, James Chambers and his deputy James O'Connor. Consequently he only made three substitute appearances, but has been offered another contract.

Doncaster Rov (Free from Ptters Bar T, ex Wingate & Finchley, Maidenhead U, Grays Ath, on 6/8/2009) FL 0+3

DUMIC Dario

Born: Sarajevo, Bosnia, 30 January 1992
Height: 6'2" **Weight:** 14.11
International Honours: Denmark: Yth
This giant central defender from Denmark made a brief appearance at right-back for Norwich in the Johnstone's Paint Trophy tie at Swindon before stating homesickness and a desire to complete a Danish education as reasons for his move back to Denmark, with Brondby, in January. A regular member of the Danish under-19 team, Norwich will receive a sell-on payment in the event that he moves on from Brondby to fulfil his obvious potential.

Norwich C (From trainee on 4/8/2009) Others 0+1

DUNBAVIN Ian Stuart

Born: Huyton, 27 May 1980
Height: 6'2" **Weight:** 13.0
Ian spent the season battling for Accrington's number-one spot with several loanee goalkeepers who joined the squad, but always did a job when called upon in this his third year at the club. Sent off twice in the season for professional fouls in the area, the second at Crewe was rescinded on appeal.

Liverpool (From trainee on 26/11/1998)
Shrewsbury T (Free on 17/1/2000) FL 91+5 FLC 3 FAC 6 Others 7 (Freed during 2004 close season)
Accrington Stanley (Free from Halifax T, following loan period at Scarborough, on 2/8/2006) FL 75+2 FLC 2 FAC 4 Others 4

DUNFIELD Terence (Terry)

Born: Vancouver, Canada, 20 February 1982
Height: 5'10" **Weight:** 11.3
International Honours: Canada: 1; U23-1; Yth; E: Yth
Tough-tackling central midfield player who is a real hard worker with bags of enthusiasm, he won over Shrewsbury fans after a disappointing opening. His first start was delayed until the late November draw with Bury by a dislocated shoulder but a string of 'Man of the Match' performances followed and his first goal, a 40-yard volley, came in the 3-1 win at Bradford in December. He was really on form in January and February and scored his second goal in the 1-0 defeat of Bournemouth, again a cracking long-range shot.

Manchester C (From trainee on 5/5/1999) PL 0+1
Bury (Loaned on 16/8/2002) FL 15/2 FLC 3

Bury (Free on 13/12/2002) FL 48+11/3 FLC 0+1 Others 3+1/1 (Freed during 2005 close season)
Macclesfield T (Free, following injury and a spell with Worcester C, on 31/7/2007) FL 59+2/2 FLC 2 FAC 4/1 Others 1
Shrewsbury T (Free on 26/1/2009) FL 43+4/2 FLC 0+1

DUNK Lewis Carl
Born: Brighton, 21 November 1991
Height: 6'3" **Weight:** 12.2
A young Brighton central defender of some potential, Lewis played youth and reserve football throughout the season before signing a professional contract at the end of April and making his debut at Milton Keynes, where he turned in a faultless display. A ball-playing left-footer, Lewis also enjoyed work experience with Bognor Regis Town.
Brighton & Hove A (Trainee) FL 1

DUNN Christopher Michael
Born: Brentwood, 23 October 1987
Height: 6'4" **Weight:** 12.5
Goalkeeper Chris found it hard to find his form at the start of the season but a change of management and a settled defence in front of him saw him regain his feet again and put in some excellent displays, playing a large part in Northampton's rise up the division. Agile and alert, Chris is commanding in the air but an injury kept him out of the side during the latter part of the season.
Northampton T (From trainee on 8/1/2007) FL 59 FLC 1 FAC 2 Others 4

DUNN David John Ian
Born: Great Harwood, 27 December 1979
Height: 5'10" **Weight:** 12.3
Club Honours: FLC '02
International Honours: E: 1; U21-20; Yth
David was by a considerable margin Blackburn's most productive and constructive forward player. The problem lay in the fact that his chequered history of hamstring injuries made it necessary to nurse him through the season and a flare up of Achilles problems further restricted his playing time. His early form forced the club to change the proposed 4-4-2 system, to use him playing behind a lone striker and by the end of the campaign that had become the preferred method. He was by far the most reliable scorer, with strikes in the home games against Burnley and Birmingham and away at Bolton being demonstrations of his ability to shoot from distance with precision. He also kept his cool when faced with a last-minute penalty against

Aston Villa and a vital penalty at Turf Moor, scoring both comprehensively.
Blackburn Rov (From trainee on 30/9/1997) P/FL 120+16/30 FLC 14+3/5 FAC 11+2/3 Others 3+1
Birmingham C (£5,500,000 on 9/7/2003) P/FL 46+12/7 FLC 2+3 FAC 5+1/
Blackburn Rov (£2,200,000 on 17/1/2007) PL 59+21/11 FLC 6+1/1 FAC 5+1 Others 5+1

DUNNE Alan James
Born: Dublin, 23 August 1982
Height: 5'10" **Weight:** 12.0
Now at right-back, his best position, Alan had a few injuries that meant missing the odd game, but he was soon back to the best form of his career with Millwall. Fast on the break and overlapping down the right side, he also varies his final ball, either a good cross or a cut inside for a shot on goal, as he did at Walsall with a 93rd-minute equaliser. Alan reached 200 appearances in all competitions and the 150 mark in League games for Millwall during 2009-10. He was also voted the fans' 'Player of the Season'. Packs a tremendous shot in either foot and his stoppage-time strike at Walsall won him the club's inaugural 'Goal of the Season' award. He missed the final games of the League campaign through injury.

Millwall (From trainee on 17/3/2000) FL 157+22/14 FLC 9+1/2 FAC 14+2/3 Others 5

DUNNE James William
Born: Bromley, 18 September 1989
Height: 5'11" **Weight:** 10.12
A former Arsenal trainee, James played a bit-part role early on for Exeter before having a decisive impact in the latter part of the campaign. Hard working, good on the ball and with an eye for goal, James' partnership with Liam Sercombe in central midfield coincided with just one defeat in Exeter's last 13 games and he is likely to play a more prominent role next season. He scored superbly in the crucial game at Swindon.
Arsenal (From trainee on 14/9/2007)
Exeter C (Free on 24/7/2009) FL 18+5/3 FAC 1+1 Others 1

DUNNE Richard Patrick
Born: Dublin, 21 September 1979
Height: 6'1" **Weight:** 14.0
Club Honours: FAYC '98; Div 1 '02
International Honours: RoI: 58; B-1; U21-4; Yth (UEFA-U18 '98); Sch
Despite a Manchester City career of over 300 games and four 'Player of the Year' awards, the Republic of Ireland central defender was deemed surplus to requirements following manager Mark

Richard Dunne

Hughes's signings of Kolo Toure and Joleon Lescott in the summer. After starting the first two games he left the club for Aston Villa in late August understandably feeling under-appreciated by the club he had served with such distinction. Richard's dignified refusal to celebrate his emotional first Villa goal against Manchester City out of respect for his former club was a measure of the man. The experienced defender might not have been needed at Eastlands but City's loss was Villa's gain as he became a firm fans' favourite. Rather than sulk about his treatment at his old club, Richard set about trying to prove on the pitch that they were wrong to let him go. His inclusion in the PFA 'Premier League Team of the Year' and status as Villa's players' 'Player of the Season' shows that he achieved his aim in some style. Not only that, but he also managed the considerable feat of filling the boots of retired favourite Martin Laursen. Richard barely put a foot wrong during his first season at Villa Park after signing on August transfer deadline day last season. There was a slight hitch when the paper work did not go through until the following day, but he was worth waiting for. Despite a reputation for carrying too much weight as a youngster, the stocky Irishman now keeps himself in tip-top condition. He is strong in the air, deceptively quick across the floor and his reading of the game is impeccable, giving him a head start on nippier attackers. Remarkably, his appearance in Villa's Carling Cup final team was the first time he had been beyond a semi-final in his career, although it was to end in disappointment when his rare slip led to the goal which turned the match in eventual winners Manchester United's favour. The football fates were also cruel to Richard on the international stage when Thierry Henry's controversial handball squeezed France through to the World Cup finals at the expense of Ireland. Again the former Everton player showed his class by sportingly chatting to Henry after the final whistle. Richard was disappointed that Villa finished a place below Manchester City but had no regrets after two Wembley appearances and a push for the top four. He also played through the pain barrier with head and Achilles injuries towards the end of the season, displaying bravery which added to his emerging reputation among Villa fans as the 'new Paul McGrath'.
Everton *(From trainee on 8/10/1996) PL 53+7 FLC 4 FAC 8*
Manchester C *(£3,000,000 on*

20/10/2000) P/FL 290+6/8 FLC 12 FAC 26 Others 17+1
Aston Villa *(£6,000,000 + on 1/9/2009) PL 35/3 FLC 5 FAC 4*

DYER Alex Craig
Born: Knowsley, 1 June 1990
Height: 5'8" **Weight:** 11.7
With so many midfield players on Northampton's books Alex found first team places at a premium. Despite this when called on for first team duty or as a substitute he always gives a 100 per cent. A skilful player who likes a pop at goal and, despite his limited opportunities, Alex is still responsible for setting up some of the goals scored by Town during the season. Was out of contract in the summer.
Northampton T *(From trainee on 8/11/2007) FL 12+22/3 FLC 1+1 FAC 0+3 Others 3+1*

DYER Kieron Courtney
Born: Ipswich, 29 December 1978
Height: 5'7" **Weight:** 9.7
International Honours: E: 33; B-3; U21-11; Yth
It was another disappointing campaign for the West Ham midfielder. On his day, Kieron has lightning pace and can cause problems for all defenders. If he could only stay fit he would be a great asset. In all his games he showed great promise and looked dangerous but unfortunately he suffered hamstring injuries and rarely completed 90 minutes.
Ipswich T *(From trainee on 3/1/1997) FL 79+12/9 FLC 11/1 FAC 5 Others 5+1/2*
Newcastle U *(£6,000,000 on 16/7/1999) PL 169+21/23 FLC 6+3/3 FAC 17+1/5 Others 30+3/5*
West Ham U *(£6,000,000 on 16/8/2007) PL 7+12 FLC 2 FAC 0+1*

DYER Lloyd Richard
Born: Birmingham, 13 September 1982
Height: 5'10" **Weight:** 11.4
Club Honours: AMC '08; Div 2 '08; Div 1 '09
Speedy left-winger who lost, then regained, his place in Leicester's starting line-up as the season unfolded. He found the net only three times but all proved to be point winners. In particular, Lloyd's speedy burst from midfield at Blackpool to net the winner will be long remembered by the Foxes' travelling faithful.
West Bromwich A *(Signed from juniors at Aston Villa on 9/7/2001) P/FL 2+19/2 FLC 2 FAC 0+2*
Kidderminster Hrs *(Loaned on 5/9/2003) FL 5+2/1*
Coventry C *(Loaned on 22/3/2005) FL 6*

Queens Park Rgrs *(Loaned on 27/9/2005) FL 15*
Millwall *(Free on 31/1/2006) FL 2+4*
MK Dons *(Free on 2/8/2006) FL 82+4/16 FLC 1+3 FAC 2 Others 3+2*
Leicester C *(Free on 11/7/2008) FL 68+9/13 FLC 1+1 FAC 4/1 Others 5*

DYER Nathan Antone Jonah
Born: Trowbridge, 29 November 1987
Height: 5'6" **Weight:** 9.0
Nathan is an exceptionally talented and speedy winger who was Swansea's main attacking outlet in the early part of the season, when half of the first team squad were sidelined through injury. Despite his energy and good work on the flank, his scoring return was poor, with only two goals to show for his enterprise.
Southampton *(From trainee on 13/10/2005) FL 36+20/1 FLC 3+4/2 FAC 2+1*
Burnley *(Loaned on 28/10/2005) FL 4+1/2*
Sheffield U *(Loaned on 27/9/2008) FL 3+4/1*
Swansea C *(£400,000 on 2/1/2009) FL 50+7/4 FLC 2 FAC 3+1/1*

Nathan Dyer

E

EAGLES Christopher (Chris) Mark
Born: Hemel Hempstead, 19 November 1985
Height: 6'0" **Weight:** 10.8
Club Honours: FAYC '03
International Honours: E: Yth
As in his first season with Burnley, Chris had something of a mixed campaign. He had to wait until October for a Premier League start, but once in he pulled out a string of fine performances. Combining his undoubted qualities of speed and footwork on the wing he was more than a match for most even in the top flight, with a more effective final delivery than before. At that stage he looked a clear 'Player of the Year' candidate, but after losing his place at the end of January, he struggled under new boss Brian Laws for more than cameos from the bench. Without Chris or Robbie Blake, the side sometimes looked short of flair as Laws concentrated on tightening things up in the battle against relegation. Still some way short of the finished article, Chris nevertheless proved himself well capable of competing against the best when on top form.
Manchester U (From trainee on 25/7/2003) PL 2+4/1 FLC 2+4 FAC 1 Others 2+2
Watford (Loaned on 21/1/2005) FL 10+3/1
Sheffield Wed (Loaned on 4/8/2005) FL 21+4/3
Watford (Loaned on 6/1/2006) FL 16+1/3 FAC 1 Others 0+1
Burnley (£1,300,000 on 6/8/2008) P/FL 50+27/10 FLC 8+1/1 FAC 6 Others 1+2

EARDLEY Neal James
Born: Llandudno, 6 November 1988
Height: 5'9" **Weight:** 10.7
International Honours: W: 13; U21-9; Yth
Neal was signed by Blackpool for an undisclosed fee from Oldham in the summer and made an instant impact with his attacking philosophy from right-back. Deceptively strong in the tackle, Neal has all the components of a good full-back, albeit being slightly small. His awareness of situations is something that is highly impressive for a player so young and he will be looking to kick on from a decent start. Unfortunately for him, an injury in March coincided with the loan signing of Seamus Coleman and Neal struggled to regain a spot. The season saw him play for Wales three times, contributing to two wins. He came off the bench twice.
Oldham Ath (From trainee on 19/9/2006) FL 108+5/10 FLC 5 FAC 8 Others 3
Blackpool (£350,000 on 7/8/2009) FL 22+2 FLC 1+1 FAC 1

EARNSHAW Robert
Born: Mufulira, Zambia, 6 April 1981
Height: 5'8" **Weight:** 10.10
International Honours: W: 49; U21-10; Yth
The Nottingham Forest striker again finished as top scorer, claiming 15 League goals despite the fact that he struggled to gain a regular spot at the start of the season. His high spot of the season came in December when he scored his first Forest hat-trick in the 5-1 victory over Leicester. Although his career has stuttered at Derby and Forest, Robert's scoring record makes it wise to have him on the field and he continued to add to his Welsh caps.
Cardiff C (From trainee on 4/8/1998) FL 141+37/85 FLC 6+2/10 FAC 11+2/9 Others 5+1/1
Morton (Loaned on 20/1/2000) SL 3/2 SC 1
West Bromwich A (£3,500,000 + on 1/9/2004) PL 22+21/12 FLC 2+1/2 FAC 3+1/3
Norwich C (£3,500,000 on 31/1/2006) FL 41+4/27 FLC 1 FAC 1
Derby Co (£3,500,000 on 29/6/2007) PL 7+15/1 FLC 1 FAC 0+2/1
Nottingham F (£2,650,000 on 30/5/2008) FL 46+18/27 FLC 4/3 FAC 3/2 Others 1+1/2

EASTER Jermaine Maurice
Born: Cardiff, 15 January 1982
Height: 5'8" **Weight:** 12.4
International Honours: W: 8; Yth
Although Jermaine netted 20 goals for MK Dons during his first season at the club, by his own admission he was disappointed that the tally was not more because his output slowed in the second half of the campaign. A mounting catalogue of squad injuries and suspensions undoubtedly had a major part to play in that, but also to be considered was his deployment on several occasions as a wide front player as opposed to his more preferred central slot. A calm and clinical finisher when put in front of goal, his early season form led to a recall to the Welsh international squad during the campaign.

Robert Earnshaw

Wolverhampton W *(From trainee on 6/7/2000)*
Hartlepool U *(Free on 17/3/2001) FL 0+27/2 Others 0+3*
Cambridge U *(Loaned on 6/2/2004) FL 25+14/8 FLC 1 FAC 1 Others 2/1*
Boston U *(Free on 15/3/2005) FL 5+4/3*
Stockport Co *(Free on 14/7/2005) FL 18+1/8 FLC 1 FAC 3/3*
Wycombe W *(£80,000 on 30/1/2006) FL 44+15/21 FLC 7/6 FAC 1/1 Others 2+1*
Plymouth Arg *(£210,000 on 26/10/2007) FL 22+14/6 FLC 1 FAC 2*
Millwall *(Loaned on 26/9/2008) FL 2+3/1 FAC 1*
Colchester U *(Loaned on 20/11/2008) FL 5/2*
MK Dons *(Signed on 14/7/2009) FL 32+4/14 FLC 1/1 FAC 2+1/1 Others 4+1/3*

EASTHAM Ashley Thomas
Born: Preston, 22 March 1991
Height: 6'3" **Weight:** 12.6
The young defender played a role in Blackpool's Carling Cup run - starting away at Stoke in the 4-3 defeat. He also started against Peterborough in the League when the Seasiders were short on defenders before going out on loan to Cheltenham at the end of November. A tall, strong centre-back with excellence balance and positional sense beyond his tender years, Ashley made an immediate impression at the Abbey Business Stadium in a team fighting to stay in the Football League. He produced a string of fine performances in December and January but was unfortunate to be sent off for two yellow cards in a 0-0 draw at Grimsby. Ashley was recalled by Blackpool shortly afterwards and added to the squad for a couple of first team games but once the January transfer window opened he returned to Cheltenham to continue gaining valuable experience.
Blackpool *(From trainee on 20/5/2009) FL 0+1 FLC 1*
Cheltenham T *(Loaned on 26/11/2009) FL 18+2*

EASTMAN Thomas (Tom) Michael
Born: Clacton, 21 October 1991
Height: 6'3" **Weight:** 13.12
A series of impressive reserve team performances led to central defender Tom's promotion to the Ipswich first team ranks in April. He was an unused substitute for four games before finally being given his debut in the last game of the season. Unfortunately he will remember it for all the wrong reasons as he received two yellow cards, for clumsy rather than malicious fouls, and was back in the dressing room after an

hour of play. He now has the dubious distinction of being the first Ipswich player to be sent off on his first appearance for the club.
Ipswich T *(Trainee) FL 1*

EASTMOND Craig Leon
Born: Wandsworth, 9 December 1990
Height: 5'11" **Weight:** 11.8
Craig is one of a number of promising young English players at Arsenal and made his debut in a central-defensive role in midfield at Portsmouth. He went on to start the Premier League games at Bolton and Wigan. Craig appeared four times in the Premier League, once in the FA Cup and twice in the Carling Cup.
Arsenal *(From trainee on 2/7/2009) PL 2+2 FLC 2 FAC 1*

EASTON Brian Neil
Born: Glasgow, 5 March 1988
Height: 6'0" **Weight:** 12.0
Club Honours: S Div 1 '08
International Honours: S: B-1; U21-2
Scotland under-21 international Brian joined Burnley from Hamilton Academical in July on a three-year-deal. Clearly regarded as one for the future, his only appearance was in the Carling Cup win at Hartlepool, where he performed efficiently at left-back. However, he was unable to dislodge Stephen Jordan from the League side and returned to Hamilton on loan in January for the rest of the season.
Hamilton Academical *(From juniors on 8/8/2006) SL 101+1/2 SLC 6+1 SC 6 Others 3*
Burnley *(£350,000 on 14/7/2009) FLC 1*
Hamilton Academical *(Loaned on 29/1/2010) SL 12*

EASTON Craig
Born: Airdrie, 26 February 1979
Height: 5'10" **Weight:** 11.3
International Honours: S: U21-21; Yth
Little was seen of Craig at Swindon, with his first League appearance not coming until late October when he was a substitute at Tranmere. Although he will have been disappointed not to have been more involved, making only two starts and ten substitute appearances, he remained a regular member of the squad throughout and was perhaps unfortunate to be confined to the bench for over 20 games. A strong-running central midfielder, also able to operate wide, who likes to get in the box, Craig has been offered a further contract for the coming season.
Dundee U *(From juniors on 31/8/1995) SL 162+44/12 SLC 15+4/4 SC 19+1/2*
Livingston *(Free on 1/7/2004) SL 24+6/3 SLC 3/1 SC 2/1*

Leyton Orient *(Free on 21/7/2005) FL 65+6/5 FLC 2 FAC 6/1 Others 2*
Swindon T *(Free on 10/8/2007) FL 56+19/8 FLC 2+1 FAC 3+1 Others 5*

EASTWOOD Freddy
Born: Epsom, 29 October 1983
Height: 5'11" **Weight:** 12.0
Club Honours: Div 1 '06
International Honours: W: 10
Freddy's talent shone out again this season but it was clear from day one that he was no longer the first choice striker at Coventry. His first League start was not until early October, owing to the early form of Leon Best and Clinton Morrison, and was in a wide midfield role. When playing wide he always gave his best but looked out of place and managed only one goal, a stunning 25-yard effort against Reading. In December he was switched to a striking role and responded in his first game by scoring three goals, two with his head, against Peterborough, the first League hat-trick by a Coventry player since 2002. It was a golden period for Freddy as he scored the winner at Plymouth a week later, another header, and won several 'Man of the Match' awards. Goals were harder to come by in the last third of the season but he netted with a clever piece of skill against Preston at home.
Southend U *(Signed from Grays Ath, ex trainee at West Ham U, on 4/10/2004) FL 106+9/53 FLC 4+1/4 FAC 6/3 Others 7+2/5*
Wolverhampton W *(£1,500,000 on 13/7/2007) FL 10+21/3 FLC 2/1 FAC 0+2*
Coventry C *(£1,200,000 on 14/7/2008) FL 58+24/12 FLC 2 FAC 6+1*

EASTWOOD Simon Christopher
Born: Luton, 26 June 1989
Height: 6'2" **Weight:** 13.13
Huddersfield goalkeeper Simon spent the first half of the season on loan at West Yorkshire neighbours Bradford where he gained valuable experience. He was ever-present during his time at Valley Parade and came to the fore with his penalty-saving exploits in the Johnstone's Paint Trophy. Simon was the star in shoot-out wins over Notts County and Port Vale when he kept out five spot kicks.
Huddersfield T *(From trainee on 5/7/2007) FL 1*
Bradford C *(Loaned on 25/7/2009) FL 22 FLC 1 FAC 1 Others 4*

EAVES Thomas (Tom) James
Born: Liverpool, 14 January 1992
Height: 6'3" **Weight:** 13.7
This Oldham youngster burst on the

scene this season and made a dramatic impact, which has led to him being tracked by a number of big clubs. A striker, Tom's height and strength are his main attributes but he also has skill in abundance. He made 14 appearances for Oldham, all from the bench, but expectations that Tom has a long career in front of him were reinforced by the fact that Latics offered him a five-year professional contract in May.
Oldham Ath *(From trainee on 6/5/2010) FL 0+15*

EBANKS-BLAKE Sylvan Augustus

Born: Cambridge, 29 March 1986
Height: 5'10" **Weight:** 13.4
Club Honours: FAYC '03; Ch '09
International Honours: E: U21-1
The Wolverhampton striker had scored 37 goals in his first 16 months at the club, but had a miserable opening day this time, missing a chance and suffering a hamstring injury that kept him out for a month. On his third League start, he thundered home a

penalty against Aston Villa but then found goals hard to come by. His header at Chelsea was well saved by Petr Cech and he was unable to score again, despite some good displays. Sylvan lost his place in January, then went from usually coming on as a substitute to not being used at all for six matches. With Wolves struggling at home to Blackburn, he came on and headed a vital equaliser with his first touch, and he was back in the first team on the final day.
Manchester U *(From trainee on 24/2/2005) FLC 1+1/1*
Plymouth Arg *(£200,000 + on 18/7/2006) FL 49+17/21 FLC 4/1 FAC 3+1/1*
Wolverhampton W *(£1,500,000 on 10/1/2008) P/FL 73+11/39 FLC 1+1 FAC 2+3*

EBOUE Emmanuel (Manu)

Born: Abidjan, Ivory Coast, 4 June 1983
Height: 5'10" **Weight:** 11.3
International Honours: Ivory Coast: 50
If a player changed the fans' perception

of him during one season, it was Manu. He had his finest season to date in an Arsenal shirt and contested the right-back berth with Bacary Sagna throughout. He is not the most gifted player, yet has more ability than some give him credit for and his enthusiasm for the game overcomes any perceived lack of talent. Being included in far more games increased his confidence and this was evident as he rounded off a fine team move to score the fourth goal in the Gunners' 5-0 rout of Porto in the Champions League second round home leg. He appeared 25 times in the Premier League scoring once, ten shots in the Champions League, adding two further strikes, and once in the Carling Cup. Having already competed at the African Cup of Nations in January, he was also a part of the Ivory Coast World Cup squad.
Arsenal *(£1,540,000 from Beveren, Belgium, ex ASEC Mimosas, on 1/1/2005) PL 88+31/4 FLC 6+2/1 FAC 11+1/1 Others 35+13/3*

ECCLESTON Nathan Geoffrey

Born: Manchester, 30 December 1990
Height: 5'10" **Weight:** 10.6
Nathan is a teenage striker and a graduate from Liverpool FC's Academy. After good form in the reserves he was called up to the first team squad in October, making his debut as a substitute in the Carling Cup defeat at Arsenal and his Premiership debut in the following game at Fulham, again as a late substitute, before returning to the reserves. In January he joined Huddersfield on a month's loan in order to gain valuable first team experience and to bolster the already young attack force at the Galpharm Stadium. The livewire enjoyed a great start by netting the winner in the away victory over Yeovil and after showing such promise club officials tied up his loan spell until the end of the season. Full of energy and pace his skills were deployed to the right wing as he looked to stretch opponents defences. An uncharacteristic sending off in the away defeat to Gillingham kept him out of the first team action before a return to the fold late in the season as the Terriers pushed for the play-offs.
Liverpool *(From trainee on 27/2/2008) PL 0+1 FLC 0+1*
Huddersfield T *(Loaned on 28/1/2010) FL 4+7/1 Others 0+1*

ECKERSLEY Richard Jon

Born: Worsley, 12 March 1989
Height: 5'9" **Weight:** 11.10
A promising defender, Richard joined Burnley from Manchester United on a

Sylvan Ebanks-Blake

four-year deal shortly before the start of the season. He failed to make the League side, but played in both of the Clarets' Carling Cup games, being sent off at Hartlepool, and also the FA Cup tie at MK Dons. The limited evidence suggested a player of considerable promise but needing to curb his sometimes rash tendencies in the tackle. In March the Burnley defender joined Plymouth on a one-month loan deal as cover for the injured Reda Johnson. The move allowed Richard much-needed match experience. He made his debut at right-back in the 1-1 draw at home to Preston and was nominated as the 'Man of the Match' for his excellent display. Unfortunately he had to go back to Turf Moor after his fourth game for the club (this time as left-back) following an ankle injury suffered in the defeat to Scunthorpe. He returned to Home Park for two more games at the end of the season.
Manchester U (From trainee on 3/7/2007) PL 0+2 FAC 0+2
Burnley (£500,000 on 15/7/2009) FLC 2 FAC 1
Plymouth Arg (Loaned on 5/3/2010) FL 7

Gareth Edds

EDDS Gareth James
Born: Sydney, Australia, 3 February 1981
Height: 5'11" **Weight:** 10.12
International Honours: Australia: U23-2; Yth
A central midfielder who can also play at centre-back or right-back if necessary, Gareth's versatility gave Tranmere a box-to-box midfield option. He was always energetic and hard working as well as being reliable and a calming influence on the younger players. The team's

pragmatic style of play adopted by manager Les Parry suited the former Australian under-23 and youth international and he was always keen to use his strong shooting when he had the opportunity, ending with four goals. Although a firm favourite with Rovers' supporters, Gareth was not offered a new contract at Prenton Park when his previous deal expired.
Nottingham F (From trainee on 19/2/1998) FL 11+5/1 FAC 1
Swindon T (Free on 9/8/2002) FL 8+6 FLC 0+1 FAC 1 Others 2
Bradford C (Free on 14/7/2003) FL 19+4 FLC 1
MK Dons (Free on 23/7/2004) FL 97+25/10 FLC 6+2 FAC 9+1/2 Others 6+1
Tranmere Rov (Free on 2/7/2008) FL 46+23/5 FLC 1+1/1 FAC 8 Others 2+1

EDGAR Anthony James
Born: Newham, 30 September 1990
Height: 5'10" **Weight:** 11.0
The young midfielder is learning his trade with West Ham. He graduated through the youth side to become a regular member of the reserve team before joining Bournemouth on emergency loan in October. He made his debut in a 0-0 draw at Port Vale, but struggled with the physical demands of League Two and returned to Upton Park after staying for a month. In January he made his first team debut for the Hammers against Arsenal in the FA Cup, coming on as a substitute in the 88th minute which was too late for him to make an impact
West Ham U (From trainee on 1/7/2009) FAC 0+1
Bournemouth (Loaned on 1/10/2009) FL 2+1 Others 1

EDGAR David Edward
Born: Kitchener, Ontario, Canada, 19 May 1987
Height: 6'2" **Weight:** 12.0
International Honours: Canada: Yth
Arriving from Newcastle in July on a four-year deal, the Canadian under-20 international had few first team opportunities in his first season with Burnley. Under Owen Coyle, his only start was in the Carling Cup game at Hartlepool, but following Brian Laws' appointment in January he was given a League debut at Manchester United, forming an effective central defensive partnership with Michael Duff and keeping United at bay for much of the game. The arrival of Leon Cort pushed him down the pecking order, though, and he was loaned out to Swansea in late March, making his debut at the Liberty Stadium against Ipswich at centre-back followed by the derby

match against Cardiff at left-back. The following match against Scunthorpe saw him score the Swans' opening goal.
Newcastle U (From trainee on 20/9/2006) PL 11+8/2 FLC 0+2 FAC 2
Burnley (£300,000 on 1/7/2009) PL 2+2 FLC 1 FAC 1
Swansea C (Loaned on 23/3/2010) FL 5/1

EDMAN Erik Kenneth
Born: Huskvarna, Sweden, 11 November 1978
Height: 5'10" **Weight:** 12.6
International Honours: Sweden: 53
Composed and assured at left-back, Erik is a stylish player possessing an effective tackle and with a good turn of pace. Solid, reliable and highly committed, Erik again struggled to make Wigan's starting line-up because of the impressive form of Maynor Figueroa. He made his first start in the Carling Cup tie against Blackpool. A regular on the bench, Erik started against Fulham in November and in the following game against his former club Tottenham, when he had a torrid time against Aaron Lennon. His final appearance in a Wigan shirt was as a substitute at Manchester United in December. Out of contract at the end of the season, he was allowed to re-sign for his former club Helsingborg on a five-year deal in February.
Tottenham H (£1,300,000 from SC Heerenveen, Holland, ex Helsingborg, on 5/8/2004) PL 31/1 FAC 2+1 (Transferred to Stade Rennais, France on 31/8/2005)
Wigan Ath (£500,000 from Stade Rennais, France on 23/1/2008) PL 7+3 FLC 1 FAC 0+1

[EDUARDO] DA SILVA Eduardo Alves
Born: Rio de Janeiro, Brazil, 25 February 1983
Height: 5'9" **Weight:** 11.0
International Honours: Croatia: 29; U21-12
The Croatian striker had a disappointing campaign for Arsenal. The combination of a catalogue of niggling injuries affected any chance of a consistent run in the side and on the occasions he did feature, he appeared severely lacking in confidence in front of goal, no doubt a by-product of his continuing mental recovery from his dreadful injuries sustained in 2008. He was also involved in controversy, being accused of diving to win a penalty in the home leg of the Champions League against Glasgow Celtic. He not only won the penalty but scored from it. He played 24 times in the Premier League, although only 13

of these were starts and contributed just three goals. He made five Champions League appearances, scoring twice, and had two FA Cup outings, scoring the third round winner at West Ham. With the arrival of Maroune Chamakh, the competition for forward places is further increased. *Arsenal (£10,000,000 from Dinamo Zagreb, Croatia, ex Nova Kennedy, Bangu - loan, Inker Zapresic - loan, on 3/8/2007) PL 26+15/6 FLC 4+2/4 FAC 5+2/5 Others 6+7/5*

EDWARDS Akenhaton **Carlos**
Born: Port of Spain, Trinidad, 24 October 1978
Height: 5'11" **Weight:** 11.9
Club Honours: AMC '05; Ch '07
International Honours: Trinidad & Tobago: 78

Carlos played just one competitive game for Sunderland under Steve Bruce before re-joining former boss Roy Keane at Ipswich, along with midfielder Grant Leadbitter, in the August transfer window. He had scored a pre-season winner for Sunderland in Portugal at Portimonense and featured in all but one of the seven warm-up games only to find himself an unused sub in the opening two League games. Left out altogether in the third, Carlos played at right-back on his solitary Sunderland appearance of the season in a Carling Cup win at Norwich before moving on. Despite the new surroundings, although he was in the squad for the majority of games he did not really establish a regular place in the side. With plenty of speed and able to take on defenders one-to-one he lacked consistency and tended to fade in and out of games. His first goal for Town came at Sheffield Wednesday and proved to be the match winner when he picked up a loose ball in midfield and fired in a long-range effort. *Wrexham (£125,000 from Defence Force, Trinidad on 8/8/2000) FL 144+22/23 FLC 4+2/1 FAC 3 Others 6/1*
Luton T (Free on 1/8/2005) FL 64+4/8 FLC 4+1 FAC 1
Sunderland (£1,400,000 on 4/1/2007) P/FL 32+18/5 FLC 2 FAC 3+1
Wolverhampton W (Loaned on 3/10/2008) FL 5+1
Ipswich T (Signed on 1/9/2009) FL 21+7/2 FAC 1+1

EDWARDS David Alexander
Born: Pontesbury, 3 February 1986
Height: 5'11" **Weight:** 11.2
Club Honours: Ch '09
International Honours: W: 19; U21-9; Yth

The versatile, energetic Wolverhampton midfielder took his scoring chance well against Fulham in September. He also netted a fine half-volley for Wales against Scotland in November. David had a ten-match run and was showing his best form yet for the club, producing a typical all-action display when he suffered an ankle ligament injury at Tottenham. That kept him out from December to April, when he came on as a substitute at nearby Arsenal. He did make three more starts, deputizing for the suspended Karl Henry.
Shrewsbury T (From trainee on 5/1/2004) FL 82+21/12 FLC 2 FAC 5/2 Others 3+2/1
Luton T (£250,000 + on 7/8/2007) FL 18+1/4 FLC 2 FAC 4 Others 1
Wolverhampton W (£675,000 on 14/1/2008) P/FL 49+25/5 FLC 2+1 FAC 2

EDWARDS Declan
Born: Dublin, 23 December 1989
Height: 5'10" **Weight:** 12.0
Young Irish striker Declan made his

Stockport debut in the 2-0 home defeat by Bristol Rovers in August, replacing Peter Thompson. In September, he joined Northwich Victoria on loan, and came off the bench during Vics' famous 1-0 FA Cup victory over Charlton. However, various niggling injuries restricted him to just four appearances. *Stockport Co (From trainee on 14/9/2009) FL 0+1*

EDWARDS Michael (Mike)
Born: Hessle, 25 April 1980
Height: 6'1" **Weight:** 12.0
Club Honours: Div 2 '10

Mike is the longest-serving player at Notts County, with over 200 appearances to his credit, mainly in central defence. In the early part of the season, he was in and out of the side, much to the frustration of the supporters and the player himself. However, he maintained a determined and professional attitude and regained his place alongside Graeme Lee as the first choice central defensive

Mike Edwards

partnership. His performances in the second half of the season were brilliantly consistent and his Brazilian bicycle-kick goal to clinch the title was unforgettable.

Hull C *(From trainee on 16/7/1998) FL 165+13/6 FLC 8+1 FAC 11/2 Others 9+1*
Colchester U *(Free on 27/3/2003) FL 3+2*
Grimsby T *(Free on 7/8/2003) FL 32+1/1 FAC 2 Others 1*
Notts Co *(Free on 2/7/2004) FL 195+7/18 FLC 10/1 FAC 10 Others 3*

EDWARDS Philip (Phil) Lee
Born: Bootle, 8 November 1985
Height: 5'10" **Weight:** 11.9
Club Honours: FC '06
At the heart of Accrington's defence for every League and Cup game, Phil was as reliable as ever. Still only 24 but in his sixth season at the club, he can play anywhere along the back four. He was at the heart of the Stanley defence for most of the time and also notched a few goals after becoming the regular penalty taker.

Wigan Ath *(From trainee on 7/7/2005)*
Accrington Stanley *(Free on 31/7/2006) FL 149+7/10 FLC 4+1 FAC 8 Others 8+1/1*

EDWARDS Robert (Rob) Owen
Born: Telford, 25 December 1982
Height: 6'1" **Weight:** 12.0
International Honours: W: 15; Yth
Two red cards at key moments of Rob's season at Blackpool meant he spent the majority of the run-in on the bench but still managed 25 games under his belt. He saw red against Ipswich in the FA Cup and Middlesbrough, meaning Ian Evatt paired Alex John-Baptiste in the centre of defence for long spells. It was unfortunate for the former Wolves' man, who had been playing extremely well. Rob is always a safe bet to win the majority of his headers against the biggest target men and is reliable at corners with his organisation – something that has been made easier since Matt Gilks' inclusion in goal. Was out of contract at the end of June.

Aston Villa *(From trainee on 4/1/2000) PL 7+1 FAC 1*
Crystal Palace *(Loaned on 21/11/2003) FL 6+1/1*
Derby Co *(Loaned on 9/1/2004) FL 10+1/1*
Wolverhampton W *(£150,000 + on 26/7/2004) FL 82+18/1 FLC 6 FAC 2+3*
Blackpool *(£250,000 on 8/8/2008) FL 54+3/2 FLC 4 FAC 0+1 Others 0+1*

EDWARDS Robert (Rob) William
Born: Kendal, 1 January 1973
Height: 6'0" **Weight:** 12.2

Club Honours: Div 2 '00
International Honours: W: 4; B-2; U21-17; Yth
First team coach Rob's experience proved vital as he helped his younger colleagues during the crucial run in which Exeter maintained their League One status. Always calm on the ball, his years of experience were invaluable as the Grecians navigated their way to League One safety. A hamstring injury curtailed his number of appearances. Was out of contract in the summer.

Carlisle U *(From trainee on 10/4/1990) FL 48/5 FLC 4 FAC 1 Others 2+1*
Bristol C *(£135,000 on 27/3/1991) FL 188+28/5 FLC 16+3/1 FAC 13+2 Others 12+1/2*
Preston NE *(Free on 5/8/1999) FL 156+13/4 FLC 13 FAC 10 Others 5/1*
Blackpool *(Free on 2/8/2004) FL 52+6/1 FLC 2 FAC 4+1 Others 4*
Exeter C *(Free on 5/8/2006) FL 61+4 FLC 1 FAC 1 Others 1*

EDWORTHY Marc
Born: Barnstaple, 24 December 1972
Height: 5'8" **Weight:** 11.10
Club Honours: Div 1 '04
The experienced full-back signed for Burton on a one-month contract after being released by Leicester. Marc was in the Albion team that lost to Shrewsbury on their League Two debut, but did not make another appearance.

Plymouth Arg *(From trainee on 30/3/1991) FL 52+17/1 FLC 5+2 FAC 5+2 Others 2+2*
Crystal Palace *(£350,000 on 9/6/1995) P/FL 120+6 FLC 8+1/1 FAC 8 Others 8*
Coventry C *(£850,000 + on 28/8/1998) P/FL 62+14/1 FLC 5 FAC 4*
Wolverhampton W *(Free on 23/8/2002) FL 18+4 FLC 1*
Norwich C *(Free on 8/8/2003) P/FL 69+2 FLC 2+1 FAC 2*
Derby Co *(Free on 6/7/2005) P/FL 75+2 FLC 1+1 FAC 4 Others 0+1*
Leicester C *(Free on 7/11/2008) FL 5 FAC 3*
Burton A *(Free on 7/8/2009) FL 1*

EL-ABD Adam Mohamad
Born: Brighton, 11 September 1984
Height: 5'11" **Weight:** 13.9
It was a good season for the versatile Brighton man, who was the only steady performer in the back five during a turbulent autumn when he filled in admirably at left-back, despite being predominantly right-footed. These performances prompted new manager Gus Poyet to label Adam his most valuable player and the long-serving defender was rewarded with a new contract to 2012. While not especially gifted, Adam gives maximum effort and

commitment to the team, a quality amply demonstrated in December when he played at Wycombe with a broken toe. After a month's recovery he returned to the side as a central defender, capping a sterling campaign with a goal at Gillingham, his first for more than two years.

Brighton & Hove A *(From trainee on 22/12/2003) FL 171+28/3 FLC 4+2/1 FAC 12/1 Others 14*

Adam El-Abd

ELDER Nathan John
Born: Hornchurch, 5 April 1985
Height: 6'1" **Weight:** 11.9
Club Honours: Div 2 '09
The big, strong, physically imposing striker, a good target man, was signed by Shrewsbury from Brentford. Made his debut in the opening game and scored his first goal a week later in the 2-2 draw at Barnet. Up against an in-form Dave Hibbert and struggling to hit his best, he fell out of favour. After playing in 22 games and scoring twice he moved to AFC Wimbledon on January on loan, where he sustained a cruciate ligament tear that will keep him sidelined for at least six months.

Brighton & Hove A *(£10,000 from Billericay T, ex Hornchurch, Aveley, on 1/1/2007) FL 2+20/2 FAC 0+2 Others 1+2*
Brentford *(£35,000 on 31/1/2008) FL 34+10/10 FLC 1 FAC 2/1*
Shrewsbury T *(Signed on 4/8/2009) FL 9+10/2 FLC 1 FAC 0+1 Others 1*

ELDING Anthony Lee
Born: Boston, 16 April 1982
Height: 6'1" **Weight:** 13.10
Club Honours: FC '02
Although Anthony cost Crewe a six-figure fee when he was signed from

Leeds, he was unable to maintain a regular spot up front despite his appearances in the squad. He again lost his place after some early games and went on loan to Blue Square Premier Kettering, where he had a reasonable spell. In January, he moved to Hungary, joining Ferencvaros on a free transfer.
Boston U (From juniors on 6/7/2001) FL 3+5 FAC 0+1 Others 0+1 (Transferred to Stevenage Borough, via loan spell at Gainsborough Trinity, on 12/2/2003)
Boston U (Signed from Kettering T on 16/8/2006) FL 18+1/5 FAC 0+1 Others 0+1
Stockport Co (Signed on 4/1/2007) FL 38+7/24 FLC 2/1 FAC 2 Others 3/1
Leeds U (Signed on 31/1/2008) FL 4+5/1
Crewe Alex (£175,000 on 25/7/2008) FL 14+12/1 FLC 2+2/2 Others 1+2
Lincoln C (Loaned on 5/1/2009) FL 15/3

ELFORD-ALLIYU Lateef
Born: Nigeria, 1 June 1992
Height: 5'8" **Weight:** 10.12
International Honours: E: Yth
Lateef spent a month on loan at Hereford but started only one game during his spell. On that appearance, the young striker showed pace and willingness as well as an ability to run into the right positions. But the physical nature of League Two football at this stage of his development looked a big step for him and he returned to West Bromwich at the end of his stint.
West Bromwich A (From trainee on 10/6/2009)
Hereford U (Loaned on 25/1/2010) FL 1

EL HAIMOUR Mounir
Born: Limoges, France, 29 October 1980
Height: 5'9" **Weight:** 10.3
Mounir was in Barnsley's first team squad at the start of the season but after a change of manager he soon found himself out of the picture. The left-sided full-back or midfielder struggled to make an impression with no reserve team in place and was on the bench only when there were injuries and suspensions. Even then, he failed to get on the pitch. His contact was terminated by mutual consent in the final week of the season.
Barnsley (£200,000 from Neuchatel Xamax, Switzerland, ex SO Chatellerault, Champagne Sports, Yverdon Sport, Alania Vladikavkaz - loan, Schaffhausen, on 10/7/2008) FL 10+8 FLC 1 FAC 1

ELITO Medy Efoko
Born: DR Congo, 20 March 1990
Height: 6'0" **Weight:** 10.6

International Honours: E: Yth
Having started the season completely out of favour with Colchester manager Paul Lambert, the tricky young winger was given a brief chance when Aidy Boothroyd took over. He made four late appearances off the bench, receiving a straight red card for an over-enthusiastic but dangerous lunge in the closing stages of November's 2-2 draw against Exeter. To get more football, Medy joined Cheltenham on loan during March and his arrival gave the team something it had been crying out for all season - genuine pace - and his appearances on the left-hand side of midfield transformed the dynamic of the team at a crucial point of the season. Quick, clever and good on the ball with a fearsome shot, Elito contributed three vital goals including two venomous shots from the edge of the penalty area. In the closing weeks of the season Cheltenham finally hit upon a midfield formation that worked well and Elito burned up and down the left-hand touchline making a key contribution before returning to Colchester at the end of the season.
Colchester U (From trainee on 6/8/2007) FL 7+12/1 FLC 0+1 FAC 0+2 Others 1
Cheltenham T (Loaned on 5/3/2010) FL 12/3

ELLINGTON Nathan Levi Fontaine
Born: Bradford, 2 July 1981
Height: 5'10" **Weight:** 12.10
Club Honours: Div 2 '03
Watford's record signing, Nathan spent the 2008-09 season on loan at Derby and had been expected to make the move permanent. However, the deal fell through and he returned to Watford in time for pre-season training. Looking lean and fit and showing good application, Nathan made 18 appearances in the first half of the season, 16 as a substitute. He scored his first goal for 18 months at Ipswich in October but was sent off at Reading in September. In December he moved to Greece to join Skoda Zanthi on a year's loan in a deal that may become permanent.
Bristol Rov (£150,000 from Walton & Hersham on 18/2/1999) FL 76+40/35 FLC 7/2 FAC 6+1/4 Others 6+1/3
Wigan Ath (£750,000 + on 28/3/2002) FL 130+4/59 FLC 6+1/6 FAC 3+1/2 Others 0+1
West Bromwich A (£3,000,000 on 15/8/2005) P/FL 34+34/15 FLC 6/5 FAC 3+1 Others 0+3
Watford (£3,250,000 on 30/8/2007) FL 20+31/5 FLC 0+1 FAC 1+1 Others 2
Derby Co (Loaned on 28/6/2008) FL 13+14/3 FLC 4/6 FAC 0+1

ELLIOT Robert (Rob)
Born: Chatham, 30 April 1986
Height: 6'3" **Weight:** 14.10
Club Honours: FC '06
Rob started the season as Charlton's first choice goalkeeper and performed consistently well until tearing an adductor muscle at Gillingham in late October which put him out for six weeks. He returned to the side and kept his place with some great performances until sidelined by a groin injury sustained in the home game with Gillingham, when Darren Randolph took over in goal at half-time. Unfortunately Rob was unable to regain his place when he recovered due to the form of his replacement. Rob is powerfully built and agile, very confident at coming for crosses and commands his area well
Charlton Ath (From trainee on 27/1/2005) FL 56+1 FLC 2 FAC 2 Others 1
Notts Co (Loaned on 28/1/2005) FL 3+1
Accrington Stanley (Loaned on 31/7/2006) FL 7 FLC 0+1 Others 3

ELLIOTT Marvin Conrad
Born: Wandsworth, 15 September 1984
Height: 5'11" **Weight:** 12.2
This dynamic Bristol City midfield player looks to have lost some of his sparkle since returning from injury. However, there were signs towards the end of the campaign that he was rediscovering his old form and it is hoped that a summer's rest will restore him to his proper self, as his special brand of athleticism has been much missed during the past two seasons.
Millwall (From trainee on 6/2/2002) FL 119+25/3 FLC 5+1/1 FAC 7+3 Others 3+1
Bristol C (Signed on 31/7/2007) FL 101+11/9 FLC 4/1 FAC 4+1 Others 3

ELLIOTT Stephen William
Born: Dublin, 6 January 1984
Height: 5'8" **Weight:** 11.8
Club Honours: Ch '05, '07
International Honours: RoI: 9; U21-10; Yth
Stephen was very much a peripheral figure at Preston in 2009-10, making only six starts (all of them early in the season) and seven more from the bench. A tireless worker up front, he scored twice before falling down the strikers' pecking order and joining Norwich on loan in early March. Making a handful of appearances as the Canaries pushed for an immediate return to the Championship, he showed himself to be an intelligent striker whose movement off the ball allowed

him to drift away from his marker, as was the case when he scored twice in City's 3-1 win at Huddersfield. Back at Colchester he was released at the end of the season.
Manchester C *(From trainee on 17/1/2001) PL 0+2*
Sunderland *(Signed on 6/8/2004) P/FL 55+26/22 FLC 1+3/1 FAC 3*
Wolverhampton W *(Signed on 20/7/2007) FL 18+11/4 FLC 0+1 FAC 1+1/1*
Preston NE (Signed on 1/9/2008) FL *26+20/7 FLC 3/1 FAC 0+2 Others 0+1*
Norwich C *(Loaned on 4/3/2010) FL 4+6/2*

ELLIOTT Steven (Steve)
William
Born: Derby, 29 October 1978
Height: 6'1" **Weight:** 14.0
Club Honours: AMC '04
International Honours: E: U21-3
Experienced Bristol Rovers' central defender Steve suffered an early season injury that hampered his chances. Steve was patient once he regained his fitness and when the opportunity to resume his place in the back four arose he was at his best with some 'Man of the Match' performances. He hit a superb half-volleyed goal in a televised match against Charlton at the Memorial Stadium. A knee ligament injury curtailed his opportunity to impress in the final matches and he was released after six seasons with Rovers.
Derby Co *(From trainee on 26/3/1997) P/FL 58+15/1 FLC 8+1 FAC 3+2*
Blackpool *(Free on 14/11/2003) FL 28 Others 5*
Bristol Rov *(Free on 5/7/2004) FL 217+1/16 FLC 8/1 FAC 13 Others 17+1*

ELLIOTT Thomas (Tom)
Joshua
Born: Leeds, 9 September 1989
Height: 5'10" **Weight:** 11.0
The tall and athletic Tom was taken on loan from Leeds to cover the numerous injuries Bury suffered in the centre-forward position. Excellent at holding up the ball, Tom's involvement was restricted by injury, although he did contribute one goal in his eight starts.
Leeds U *(From trainee on 29/8/2008) FL 0+3 FLC 1*
Macclesfield T *(Loaned on 27/1/2009) FL 4+2*
Bury *(Loaned on 16/9/2009) FL 7+9/1 Others 1*

ELLIOTT Wade Patrick
Born: Eastleigh, 14 December 1978
Height: 5'9" **Weight:** 11.1
International Honours: E: Sch
Wade played a part in all of Burnley's

Premier League games, appearing less often on the right wing as in the past and more frequently in a central role. Having moved up gradually from non-League, Wade had developed sufficiently to be comfortable in elite company, but inevitably he was often overshadowed by the best at that level. Even so, he could still be a danger going forward as well as providing a degree of steel that had not always been present in his game before. His four goals were all important ones, coming in four of the Clarets' best performances of the season. Possibly the best of them was his curling shot that proved the winner in the early-season home game against Everton.
Bournemouth *(£5,000 from Bashley on 4/2/2000) FL 178+42/31 FLC 6+1 FAC 19/5 Others 9+2/1*
Burnley *(Free on 4/7/2005) P/FL 183+21/17 FLC 8+2 FAC 9+1/1 Others 2/1*

ELLIS Mark Ian
Born: Kingsbridge, 30 September 1988
Height: 6'2" **Weight:** 12.4
Torquay's Mark matured immensely during the course of the season, which included a short early-season loan spell at Blue Square Premier Forest Green. He particularly benefited from the experience and guidance of Guy Branston alongside him as he finally nailed a regular starting place for Torquay. His strength, aerial prowess and battling attitude have always made him a fans' favourite. Improved positional awareness and a curbing of his natural impetuosity have seen him develop into a commanding and extremely promising centre-back.
Bolton W *(From trainee)*
Torquay U *(Free on 1/7/2008) FL 25+2/3 FAC 1 Others 1*

ELLISON Kevin
Born: Liverpool, 23 February 1979
Height: 6'1" **Weight:** 12.8
Signed pre-season from Chester, Kevin made the Rotherham left-wing spot his own save for a late-season stutter. He struck ten goals by Christmas, one direct from a corner, which considerably helped Rotherham to be among the pace-setters in the first half of the season. Then, strangely, he did not find the net again until the end of April but never stopped foraging up and down his flank. Kevin also proved useful, with his height and combativeness, when Rotherham were defending set pieces.
Leicester C *(£50,000 + from Altrincham on 13/2/2001) PL 0+1*
Stockport Co *(£55,000 on 30/11/2001) FL 33+15/2 FLC 1 FAC 1 Others 2*

Lincoln C *(Loaned on 12/3/2004) FL 11 Others 2*
Chester C *(Free on 6/8/2004) FL 24/9 FLC 1 FAC 3/1 Others 2/1*
Hull C *(£100,000 on 12/1/2005) FL 26+13/2 FLC 1 FAC 1*
Tranmere Rov *(Signed on 28/6/2006) FL 26+8/4 FLC 1 FAC 1 Others 2*
Chester C *(Signed on 26/6/2007) FL 75/19 FLC 2 FAC 2 Others 2/1*
Rotherham U *(Free on 15/5/2009) FL 36+3/8 FLC 1+1/1 FAC 2/1 Others 4/1*

ELM David
Born: Broakulla, Sweden, 10 January 1983
Height: 6'3" **Weight:** 14.13
Joined Fulham from Swedish club Kalmar FF, for whom he had impressed in early Champions League qualifiers prior to signing on the September transfer-deadline day. Apart from a substitute appearance in extra time during the Carling Cup at Manchester City, he was rarely named in the squad until the New Year when he appeared in a number of successive games during January and February. He enjoyed an outstanding game at home to Burnley, when he scored his first goal for the club and set up another for Danny Murphy. A tall forward who is impressive both in the air and on the ground, he can hold up the ball for others or play off another striker and is not reluctant to try his luck on goal.
Fulham *(£500,000 from Kalmar FF, Sweden, sex Falkenbergs FF, on 1/9/2009) PL 3+7/1 FLC 0+1 FAC 1+2 Others 0+2*

ELMANDER Johan Erik Calvin
Born: Alingsas, Sweden, 27 May 1981
Height: 6'2" **Weight:** 12.6
International Honours: Sweden: 47; U21-28
Johan was expected to make significant progress for Bolton in 2009-10, having experienced a difficult and disappointing debut campaign in English football. However, the Swedish international struggled once again, certainly in scoring terms. A total of five goals, two of which came in Cup competitions, was a disappointing return for such an expensive signing. Johan's work rate is beyond question, as a series of energetic and mobile displays confirmed. However, Johan simply does not score enough goals. His first goal came in the Carling Cup victory over West Ham and his first League goal of the season was as a substitute in the 5-1 defeat at Aston Villa. Something of a drought followed, until Johan claimed his first League goal in three months in the 4-0 win over Wigan. Despite his

Johan Elmander

lack of goals, Johan shared centre-forward duties with Ivan Klasnic, with Owen Coyle seemingly preferring the Swede's work rate to Klasnic's natural eye for a goal. With rumours of a post-season reshuffle from Coyle, Johan's future at the Reebok was left in the balance.
Bolton W (£8,200,000 from Toulouse, France, ex Holmalunds, Orgryte IS, Feyenoord, Djurgaarden - loan, NAC Breda - loan, Brondby, on 11/7/2008) PL 45+10/8 FLC 1+2/1 FAC 2+3/1

ELOKOBI George Nganyuo
Born: Mogadishu, Somalia, 31 January 1986
Height: 6'0" **Weight:** 13.2
Having missed most of 2008-09 with a knee injury, George came on as substitute in Wolverhampton's third game, at Manchester City, and a

crunching tackle signalling his intent. The strong left-back set up a good chance at home to Hull, but was left out at Blackburn having arrived late. He played in the next seven games, conceding an own goal in the last at Stoke. George was not quite ready yet and only made fleeting appearances in the winter months. He worked hard to improve, and played in the last eight games, during which he looked a lot more accomplished.
Colchester U (Free from Dulwich Hamlet on 12/7/2004) FL 35+4/2 FLC 1+1 FAC 1 Others 4/1
Chester C (Loaned on 27/1/2005) FL 4+1
Wolverhampton W (Signed on 31/1/2008) P/FL 35+6 FLC 3 FAC 1+1

ELPHICK Thomas (Tommy)
Born: Brighton, 7 September 1987
Height: 5'11" **Weight:** 11.7

It was a rocky start for Tommy, his third as a first team regular – but then it was for Brighton as Russell Slade's side fell into the relegation zone. A red card against Stockport was the low point of his campaign. Under new manager Gus Poyet, Tommy showed his character and regained the poise and positional sense that he had shown in previous years, largely eliminating the errors that marred his early season performances. A speedy central defender, equally at home on the ground or in the air, Tommy can be pleased with the way he finished and his personal highlight will surely be scoring at Aston Villa in the FA Cup, one of his four goals.
Brighton & Hove A (From trainee on 8/6/2006) FL 122+4/6 FLC 5/1 FAC 8/1 Others 7+1

EL ZHAR Nabil
Born: Ales, France, 27 August 1986
Height: 5'7" **Weight:** 10.3
International Honours: Morocco: 8; Yth. France: Yth
Nabil is a French-born winger with Liverpool who has eight caps for Morocco. Following a few first team starts in 2008-09, he was expected to make more headway but suffered a hamstring injury at the start of the season and was not called up until December, when he made a brief substitute appearance at Blackburn. He had to wait until March for a few more outings as a substitute before making his only start in the final game at Hull. Nabil is one of a number of young overseas players that manager Rafa Benitez signed to make good what he views as a shortage of local talent, but as yet none of these imports has made the grade.
Liverpool (Signed from St Etienne, France, ex OAC Ales, Nimes Olympique, on 31/8/2005) PL 2+19 FLC 3+1/1 FAC 0+1 Others 0+6

EMERTON Brett Michael
Born: Sydney, Australia, 22 February 1979
Height: 6'1" **Weight:** 13.5
International Honours: Australia: 72; U23; Yth
Blackburn's Brett resumed after a cruciate ligament injury and, perhaps predictably, was not fit to play until September. His season was to be punctuated by niggling leg and thigh problems and he never established himself. Although primarily used on the right of midfield, he was at his best display was in the centre in the Carling Cup tie against Peterborough. He also had a fine game in the same competition against Chelsea when he played on the right,

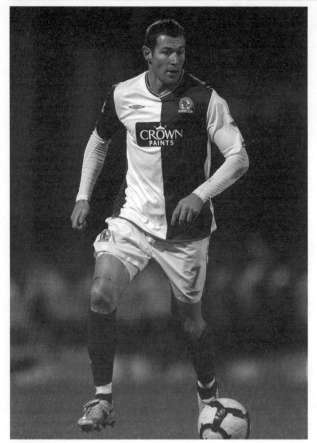

Brett Emerton

but injuries appeared to have taken their toll.
Blackburn Rov *(£2,200,000 from Feyenoord, Holland, ex Sydney Olympic, on 21/7/2003) PL 180+35/9 FLC 13+5/5 FAC 10+4 Others 11+1/1*

EMMANUEL-THOMAS Jay
Aston
Born: Forest Gate, 27 December 1990
Height: 5'9" **Weight:** 11.5
International Honours: E: Yth
A product of the Arsenal Academy, he joined Blackpool on loan at the beginning of the season and scored a great goal against Doncaster when he dribbled his way through the defence and rifled the ball into the net from distance. At Bloomfield Road he was employed as a central midfielder, winger and front man during his time there before going back to his parent club.

Having made his Arsenal debut in the 3-1 FA Cup win at Stoke, he joined Doncaster on loan at the end of February and immediately made his mark in his first start, at Bristol City, by scoring within 90 seconds from a Billy Sharp pass and later getting a second. He received the best accolade of all when the Bristol fans gave him a standing ovation after he was substituted late in the game. Against Derby at the Keepmoat he scored what the media called a 'wonder' goal. He received the ball on the right angle of the penalty area and hit a left-foot thunderbolt into the far corner of the net past a totally bewildered 'keeper. Classed as a midfielder, he played alongside striker Billy Sharp for Rovers and always seemed to have bags of time on the ball. With more experience he will become an even more consistent performer.

Arsenal *(From trainee on 16/7/2008) FAC 1*
Blackpool *(Loaned on 17/8/2009) FL 6+5/1 FLC 1*
Doncaster Rov *(Loaned on 27/2/2010) FL 12+2/5*

EMNES Marvin
Born: Rotterdam, Holland, 27 May 1988
Height: 5'11" **Weight:** 10.5
International Honours: Holland: U21-3; Yth
Marvin began in the Middlesbrough starting line-up, playing up front alongside Jeremie Aliadiere and scored a fine goal in a 3-0 win at Swansea. It proved to be his only one of the campaign. He was a near ever-present in Gareth Southgate's side, despite his lack of goals, but dropped out of the reckoning following the change of manager. A rare appearance as a first-half substitute in an FA Cup tie against Manchester City was short lived as he had to go off with a rib injury 25 minutes later.
Middlesbrough *(£3,200,000 from Sparta Rotterdam, Holland on 21/7/2008) P/FL 15+16/1 FLC 2+1/1 FAC 0+5/1*

ENCKELMAN Peter
Born: Turku, Finland, 10 March 1977
Height: 6'2" **Weight:** 12.5
International Honours: Finland: 12; U21-15
Cardiff's FA Cup final goalkeeper from 2008 was back-up to David Marshall last season and was restricted to six starts, three in the Championship and three in the Carling Cup. Unfairly blamed by fans for an error that led to Nwankwo Kanu's winner in the final, the Finnish international has played in the UK since 1999, for Aston Villa, Blackburn and Cardiff. His contract with Cardiff ended in the summer of 2010 and he was released, but is keen to continue playing in Britain.
Aston Villa *(£200,000 from TPS Turku, Finland on 1/2/1999) PL 51+1 FLC 6 FAC 1 Others 7+1*
Blackburn Rov *(£150,000 on 7/11/2003) PL 2 FLC 1*
Cardiff C *(Free on 10/1/2008) FL 29+3 FLC 4 FAC 6*

[ENRIQUE] SANCHEZ DIAZ Jose Enrique
Born: Valencia, Spain, 23 January 1986
Height: 6'0" **Weight:** 12.0
Club Honours: Ch '10
International Honours: Spain: U21-3
Widely expected to leave Newcastle following relegation, Enrique committed himself to the club and had

Peter Enckelman

an outstanding season, being nominated at left-back in the PFA 'Championship Team of the Season', chosen as his club's 'Player of the Season' and rated by many neutral observers as the best player in the division. Very strong and difficult to knock off the ball, his close control enables him to escape from the tightest of corners and his surprising pace allows him to supplement his attack, forming a dangerous partnership with Jonas Gutierrez. In the crucial home fixture with Nottingham Forest in March, he crowned a fine performance with his first goal at club level, scored with his right foot, although he is strongly left-footed.
Newcastle U (£6,500,000 from Villareal, Spain, ex Levante, Valencia, Celta Vigo - loan, on 17/8/2007) P/FL 75+8/1 FLC 4 FAC 6

EPHRAIM Hogan
Born: Holloway, 31 March 1988
Height: 5'9" **Weight:** 11.0
International Honours: E: Yth
It was an up-and-down season for Hogan who found himself out of the first team picture at Queens Park Rangers for much of it. He spent a month on loan at League One side Leeds, making his debut in a 2-0 win at Oldham. His only other start for the Whites saw him score the opener in the 2-0 Johnstone's Paint Trophy area semi-final victory against Accrington. Back at Loftus Road he finally got a run in the side following the arrival of Neil Warnock. The new manager started Ephraim in all but one of his 14 games in charge and he became a key part of Warnock's strategy. Scored two goals for Rangers during the campaign, both coming in Carling Cup matches against

Exeter and Accrington.
West Ham U (From trainee on 15/4/2005) FLC 0+1
Colchester U (Loaned on 23/11/2006) FL 5+16/1
Queens Park Rgrs (£800,000 on 10/8/2007) FL 52+26/4 FLC 2+1/2 FAC 1+3
Leeds U (Loaned on 26/11/2009) FL 1+2 Others 1/1

ERSKINE Emmanuel **Jacob** Kenneth
Born: Lambeth, 13 January 1989
Height: 6'1" **Weight:** 13.3
A powerful, if somewhat limited forward, Jacob was handed a one-year contract after impressing Mark Stimson with his performance against Gillingham in a pre-season friendly at Bromley. He made his first start against Colchester in the Johnstone's Paint Trophy and a handful of substitute appearances but spent the remainder of the season on loan at Bromley, Bishop's Stortford and Croydon Athletic.
Dagenham & Redbridge (Signed from Croydon Ath on 29/11/2007. Freed during 2009 close season)
Gillingham (Free from Bromley on 4/8/2009) FL 0+4 Others 1+1

ERTL Johannes (Johnny)
Born: Graz, Austria, 13 November 1982
Height: 6'2" **Weight:** 12.8
International Honours: Austria: 7
The Austrian international right-back was often deployed by Crystal Palace in a central midfield role as well as making the occasional appearance at centre-back or in his natural position, and won over the fans with a series of committed performances. Looking comfortable when putting his foot in to break up play, or going forward with the ball at his feet to start an attack, Johnny settled well into the side during his second season at Selhurst Park and indicated he was happy to play the midfield role if it meant a regular place. He scored his first goal for Palace at home to Aston Villa in the FA Cup. Was out of contract at the end of June.
Crystal Palace (Free from Austria Vienna, Austria, ex Sturm Graz, Kalsdorf - loan, on 25/7/2008) FL 32+13 FLC 1+1 FAC 4/1

ESAJAS Etienne
Born: Amsterdam, Holland, 4 November 1984
Height: 5'7" **Weight:** 10.4
Yet another disappointing season for the Dutch left-winger, Etienne was not able to force his way into a struggling Sheffield Wednesday side and only

made a few starts. Most of his appearances were from the substitutes' bench and he failed to influence matches when given the chance. The only time he really lived up to his potential was at Bramall Lane in the local derby, when he went on in the second half and almost snatched a draw from a miserable defeat. Very quick, with a great left foot, he needs to add more determination and grit to be firmly established in the English game. He scored a great goal against Rochdale in the Carling Cup but needs to do more of the same.
Sheffield Wed (Signed from Vitesse Arnhem, Holland on 31/8/2007) FL 28+32/5 FLC 3/3 FAC 1+1

ESPINOZA Giovanny (Gio) Patricio
Born: Charguayaco, Ecuador, 12 April 1977
Height: 6'2" **Weight:** 14.0
International Honours: Ecuador: 90
Signed by Birmingham essentially as defensive cover, Gio was left in the shadow of Scott Dann and Roger Johnson. Made appearances in the early rounds of the Carling Cup and showed he still had to adapt to the speed and physicality of the British game. Had good vision and technically decent, but was released by mutual consent in December.
Birmingham C (Signed from Barcelona SC, Ecuador, ex Aucus, Monterrey, Aucus, LDU Quito, Vitesse Arnhem, Cruzeiro, on 24/6/2009) FLC 2

ESSIEN Michael Kojo
Born: Accra, Ghana, 3 December 1982
Height: 5'10" **Weight:** 12.3
Club Honours: PL '06, '10; FLC '07; FAC '07, '09; CS '09
International Honours: Ghana: 51
For the second successive time, injury robbed Chelsea of Michael's services for half the season. It started so brightly for Michael as he settled at the base of Carlo Ancelotti's midfield diamond, à la Claude Makelele, with licence to drive forward and use his powerhouse shooting. He helped Ghana into the World Cup finals; was one of five Chelsea players shortlisted for FIFA 'World Player 2009' and – alongside club-mate Didier Drogba – was one of three final nominees for 2009 African 'Player of the Year'. He scored with a 35-yard piledriver against Blackburn and followed with two goals against Wolves: he was denied a hat-trick when another drive crashed back off the bar. His fourth of the season came against Apoel Nicosia in the Champions League with a superb swerving drive but he

limped off shortly afterwards with a torn calf muscle and that was his last involvement for the Blues. He recovered in time to make the African Cup of Nations but returned from Angola on crutches after incurring another knee ligament injury – this time in a training session. Following an operation, Michael suffered a setback in his rehabilitation programme and was forced to miss the climax of a remarkable season and declare himself unfit for the World Cup finals. Although Chelsea's glittering midfield created a myriad of chances during the club's record-breaking season, Michael's aggression, raw dynamism and versatility were still missed.
Chelsea (£24,400,000 from Lyon, France on 19/8/2005) PL 106+10/14 FLC 10+2/1 FAC 10+4/1 Others 40+2/5

Mattie Etherington

ETHERINGTON Matthew (Mattie)
Born: Truro, 14 August 1981
Height: 5'10" **Weight:** 11.2
International Honours: E: U21-3; Yth

It was an amazing season for the Stoke left-winger as he not only scooped all three of the major 'Player of the Season' awards at the Britannia Stadium but also found himself, briefly, mentioned as a possible outside bet for a call to the England squad. His consistently good performances on the left side of the pitch, coupled with a good number of goals and assists for team-mates, made him an indispensable member of a team that again coasted towards mid-table security with plenty in the tank to spare. Players willing to take on defenders are an increasingly rare commodity in the Premier League and so Mattie's ability to go past opponents means that he is invaluable in a team not noted for the number of chances created or goals scored.
Peterborough U (From trainee on 15/8/1998) FL 43+8/6 FLC 1+1 FAC 2+1 Others 2
Tottenham H (£500,000 on 10/1/2000) PL 20+25/1 FLC 3+1 FAC 1+1/1
Bradford C (Loaned on 23/10/2001) FL 12+1/1
West Ham U (£1,000,000 on 8/8/2003) P/FL 151+14/16 FLC 7+1 FAC 13+2/1 Others 6+1/1
Stoke C (£2,000,000 on 8/1/2009) PL 45+3/5 FLC 0+1/1 FAC 3/1

ETUHU Dickson Paul
Born: Kano, Nigeria, 8 June 1982
Height: 6'2" **Weight:** 13.4
Club Honours: Div 1 '02
International Honours: Nigeria: 12
A regular choice when fit and available, Dickson again provided a solid foundation to the centre of the Fulham midfield. A tall mobile player who is difficult to shrug off the ball, he reads the game well in order to disrupt the flow of the opposition's attacking moves. Despite his commanding presence in the box at set pieces he is not a regular scorer, although his two goals against FK Vetra and Juventus in the Europa League were both significant. After appearing as a regular starter in the opening weeks of the season he missed much of October through injury. On his return he appeared only intermittently before jetting off to the African Cup of Nations where he was part of the Nigeria squad that finished third. The latter stages of the season saw him back as a regular and in his best form of the season before heading for the World Cup finals.
Manchester C (From trainee on 23/12/1999) FL 11+1 FLC 1
Preston NE (£300,000 on 24/1/2002)

FL 100+34/17 FLC 8 FAC 4/1 Others 0+3
Norwich C *(£450,000 on 11/11/2005)*
FL 57+5/6 FLC 2+1/1 FAC 5
Sunderland *(£1,500,000 on 17/7/2007) PL 18+2/1 FLC 1*
Fulham *(£1,500,000 on 1/9/2008) PL 33+8/1 FAC 7 Others 14/2*

ETUHU Kelvin

Born: Kano, Nigeria, 30 May 1988
Height: 5'11" **Weight:** 11.2
International Honours: E: Yth
Kelvin was signed by Cardiff on a season-long loan from Manchester City. There were high expectations for the winger or striker but he was injured when he crashed into advertising hoardings while playing for Cardiff against Newcastle. He was never able to establish himself because of recurring injury problems. Kelvin returned to Manchester City for treatment but was back with Cardiff for the end of the season, appearing from the substitutes' bench in all three Championship play-off games. He went on for Jay Bothroyd after 15 minutes of the final against Blackpool at Wembley, given a striking role alongside Michael Chopra. That did not work as Cardiff lost 3-2.
Manchester C *(From trainee on 9/11/2005) PL 4+6/1 FLC 0+1 FAC 0+1 Others 0+3*
Rochdale *(Loaned on 5/1/2007) FL 3+1/2*
Leicester C *(Loaned on 5/3/2008) FL 2+2*
Cardiff C *(Loaned on 22/8/2009) FL 7+9 FLC 1 Others 0+3*

EUELL Jason Joseph

Born: Lambeth, 6 February 1977
Height: 6'0" **Weight:** 11.6
International Honours: Jamaica: 3; E: U21-6; Yth
A summer signing for Blackpool after being released by Southampton, the former Wimbledon man was given the captain's armband on arrival. Jason can be employed right across the midfield and up front. It was as a lone striker where he capped his best performance of the season, scoring a 65th-minute winner at home to Newcastle. After that he was the target of some criticism from the home fans as his form dropped but he soon won them over when he taunted the Preston crowd as he was warming up as a substitute in the Lancashire derby. He would have liked to make more of an impact on the pitch but his goal against Newcastle and the winner in a 1-0 win over Ipswich were goals which ultimately helped the Seasiders gain a play-off place.
Wimbledon *(From trainee on 1/6/1995) P/FL 118+23/41 FLC 15+2/4*

FAC 14+5/2 Others 2+2
Charlton Ath *(£4,750,000 on 16/7/2001) PL 102+37/34 FLC 4+3/1 FAC 5+4/2*
Middlesbrough *(Signed on 31/8/2006) PL 9+8 FLC 0+1 FAC 0+2*
Southampton *(Free on 31/8/2007) FL 49+13/5 FAC 3*
Blackpool *(Free on 21/7/2009) FL 23+10/4 FLC 0+1 FAC 1*

EUSTACE John Mark

Born: Solihull, 3 November 1979
Height: 5'11" **Weight:** 12.12
John ended the 2008-09 season on loan at Derby and it was a surprise to see him back in first team contention at Watford. After spending the first month on the bench, he missed only one match for the rest of the season and re-established himself as a mainstay of the team. An experienced defensive midfield player, John was a reliable anchor man protecting what was often a very youthful defence and his maturity, determination and leadership qualities were invaluable. John scored his first goal for Watford in 14 months against Peterborough in December and ended the season with four goals altogether, most of them last-gasp efforts that reflected his never-say-die attitude. John seemed to get stronger and more influential as the season wore on and was outstanding in the closing weeks as the team battled to stave off relegation. Fittingly, his contribution was recognised when he was chosen as the players' 'Player of the Season'.
Coventry C *(From trainee on 5/11/1996) P/FL 62+24/7 FLC 6+2/2 FAC 3+2/1*
Dundee U *(Loaned on 17/2/1999) SL 8+3/1 SC 2*
Middlesbrough *(Loaned on 17/1/2003) PL 0+1*
Stoke C *(Free on 4/8/2003) FL 55+19/5 FLC 3+1 FAC 5+1/1*
Hereford U *(Loaned on 13/10/2006) FL 8*
Watford *(£250,000 + on 31/1/2008) FL 66+6/6 FLC 2 FAC 1 Others 2*
Derby Co *(Loaned on 9/3/2009) FL 6+3/1*

EVANS Chedwyn (Ched) Michael

Born: Rhyl, 28 December 1988
Height: 6'0" **Weight:** 12.0
International Honours: W: 12; U21-13
In the summer, Ched joined Sheffield United and signed a three-year deal with the Blades for a possible £3-million fee. Despite the manager Kevin Blackwell's comments that Ched still had a lot to learn there was plenty of expectation from the fans on his

shoulders. Hard working and sometimes playing behind the front two, Ched found goals hard to come by, although he was unfortunate on several occasions. He injured his collar bone at Peterborough when challenging the goalkeeper and this nearly ended his season, but he did return to score a fine goal at Ipswich in the final game of the campaign.
Manchester C *(From trainee on 3/7/2007) PL 3+13/1 FLC 0+2 Others 2+6*
Norwich C *(Loaned on 22/11/2007) FL 20+8/10*
Sheffield U *(£3,000,000 on 24/7/2009) FL 21+12/4 FAC 2+1*

EVANS Gareth Charles

Born: Stockport, 26 April 1988
Height: 6'0" **Weight:** 12.8
Gareth was a willing worker in the Bradford attack and hardly gave opponents a moment's respite with the way he would chase down seemingly lost causes. He can play out wide on either wing or down the middle. His first goal for City was a beauty, sweeping past three Cheltenham defenders before finishing in the corner. He admits he can lack composure in front of goal at times but there were signs that he was getting that right towards the end of the season, particularly when he scored twice in the final home game against Northampton.
Macclesfield T *(From trainee at Crewe Alex on 28/8/2007) FL 55+27/19 FLC 2+1/1 FAC 2+1 Others 0+2*
Bradford C *(Signed on 2/7/2009) FL 38+5/11 FLC 1 FAC 1 Others 2*

EVANS Jonathan (Jonny) Grant

Born: Belfast, 3 January 1988
Height: 6'2" **Weight:** 12.2
Club Honours: Ch '07; FLC '09, '10; PL '09
International Honours: NI: 20; U21-3; Yth
A solid and reliable Manchester United defender who has come on in leaps and bounds since arriving back from loan spells at from Sunderland, Jonny once again showed the necessary attributes to become one of United's key stars in the forthcoming seasons. Making his first Premiership contribution against Birmingham in the season's opener at Old Trafford in August, he missed only one game in the Reds' successful Carling Cup campaign that ended in glory at Wembley against Aston Villa. Although his appearances were sporadic overall, he can look back on the season with much satisfaction.
Manchester U *(From trainee on*

*12/4/2005) PL 34+1 FLC 11 FAC 3+1
Others 11+4*
*Sunderland (Loaned on 4/1/2007) FL
18/1 FAC 1*
*Sunderland (Loaned on 4/1/2008) PL
15 FAC 1*

EVANS Rhys Karl
Born: Swindon, 27 January 1982
Height: 6'1" **Weight:** 12.2
International Honours: E: U21-2; Yth;
Sch
Highly experienced goalkeeper Rhys
initially joined Bristol Rovers as cover for
first choice Steve Phillips. However, after
Phillips was subsequently loaned out,
Rovers brought in two young 'keepers
on loan, one of whom, Mikkel
Andersen, was to claim the jersey. So
Rhys had to be patient for some action
appearing in various Cup ties where he
pulled off some superb saves at Cardiff
in the Carling Cup. Rhys started just
two League matches when Andersen
was on international duty. A strong
talker and organiser, he will have been
disappointed not to have more action.
Was out of contract at the end of June.
Chelsea (From trainee on 8/2/1999)
Bristol Rov (Loaned on 25/2/2000) FL 4
*Queens Park Rgrs (Loaned on
6/11/2001) FL 11*
*Leyton Orient (Loaned on 10/8/2002)
FL 7*
*Swindon T (Free on 28/7/2003) FL 118
FLC 2+1 FAC 4 Others 3*
*Blackpool (Free on 5/7/2006) FL 32 FLC
3 FAC 5 Others 1*
Bradford C (Loaned on 5/10/2007) FL 4
Millwall (Free on 22/1/2008) FL 21 FAC 1
*Bradford C (Free on 2/8/2008) FL 45
FLC 1 FAC 2 Others 1*
*Bristol Rov (Free on 11/8/2009) FL 3
FLC 2 FAC 1 Others 1*

EVATT Ian Ross
Born: Coventry, 19 November 1981
Height: 6'3" **Weight:** 13.11
The tall central defender was a man
mountain at the heart of Blackpool's
defence. His presence put off even the
biggest of Championship strikers. What
improved in Ian's game in the season
was his ability to anticipate and
intercept balls easily, which is something
that has not been seen since his
midfield days at Chesterfield in the
lower divisions. After battling it out
with Rob Edwards to partner Alex
Baptiste at the back for 'Pool, Ian clearly
won the duel and was an ever-present
in the last three months of the season.
His distribution has come into question
at times, but a brilliant curling effort at
home to Swansea was something a bit
special from a defender.
Derby Co (From trainee on 3/12/1998)

Ian Evatt

P/FL 19+15 FLC 0+2/1 FAC 1
*Northampton T (Loaned on
10/8/2001) FL 10+1 FLC 2*
*Chesterfield (Free on 4/8/2003) FL
84/9 FLC 2 FAC 2/1 Others 1+1*
*Queens Park Rgrs (£150,000 + on
6/6/2005) FL 21+6 FLC 1*
*Blackpool (Free on 3/8/2006) FL
137+5/5 FLC 5 FAC 8/1 Others 7*

EVRA Patrice
Born: Dakar, Senegal, 15 May 1981
Height: 5'8" **Weight:** 11.13
Club Honours: FLC '06, '09; PL '07,
'08, '09; CS '07, '10; UEFACL '08
International Honours: France: 29
A quick, athletic and attack-minded
Manchester United and French
international full-back, Patrice
continued to show just what a key
figure he is in the Reds' defence. Now
renowned as not only one of the best
left-backs in the Premiership, but in the
world, he remained an ever-present as
United went on their perennial search
for trophies. He achieved a notable first
when he captained the Reds to their
Carling Cup final success against Aston
Villa in February. Though he is
renowned for being attack minded, he
finished the campaign without a goal to
his credit, but that did not detract from
his overall performances which were
consistently good. Captaining the team

in the absence of Rio Ferdinand, Gary
Neville and Ryan Giggs, he will
undoubtedly be one of the first names
on the French team-sheet in the World
Cup finals in South Africa.
*Manchester U (£5,500,000 from AS
Monaco, France on 12/1/2006) PL
127+7/1 FLC 5+3 FAC 9+3 Others
37+6/1*

EYJOLFSSON Holmar Orn
Born: Iceland, 6 August 1990
Height: 6'2" **Weight:** 11.8
International Honours: Iceland: U21-
12; Yth
Young West Ham defender Holmar
spent October on loan at Cheltenham
and made his League debut in the 1-1
home draw against Notts County. The
son of former Iceland international
manager Eyjólfur Sverrisson, Holmar is a
versatile defender who made his four
Town appearances at right-back before
injury in a 4-0 defeat by Crewe ended
his loan. For the second half of the
season Holmar was loaned to KSV
Roeselare in Belgium and also played
for Iceland under-21. While at
Cheltenham, he scored his first goal in
an 8-0 win over San Marino in the UEFA
under-21 championships.
*West Ham U (Signed from HK
Kopavogur, Iceland on 1/7/2008)*
Cheltenham T (Loaned on 1/10/2009) FL 4

F

FABIANSKI Lukasz
Born: Kostrzyn nad Odra, Poland, 18 April 1985
Height: 6'3" **Weight:** 13.0
International Honours: Poland: 15; U21
Lukasz remains a good shot-stopper, as he showed in a strong performance in the third round FA Cup victory at West Ham, but he needs to work on crosses into the box to establish himself as first choice goalkeeper at a big club like Arsenal. A lack of experience in the Champions League second round first leg away to Porto, the FA Cup fourth round at Stoke and the Premier League match at Wigan helped condemn the Gunners to defeat in each match. He played four times in the Premier League, keeping two clean sheets, twice in the Champions League, twice in the FA Cup and once in the Carling Cup.
Arsenal (£2,000,000 from Legia Warsaw, Poland, ex Lubuszanin Drezdenko, Sparta Brodnica, Mieszko Gniezno, Lech Poznan, on 6/7/2007) PL 12+1 FLC 10 FAC 7 Others 4+1

[FABIO] PEREIRA DA SILVA Fabio
Born: Rio de Janeiro, Brazil, 9 July 1990
Height: 5'8" **Weight:** 10.3
Club Honours: FLC '10
International Honours: Brazil: Yth
Left-sided Manchester United defender who, like his twin brother Rafael, loves to roam forward, Fabio was given his Premier League debut in August, playing at right-back in United's first home game of the season against Birmingham. In his second start, at home to Wolverhampton in the Carling Cup, he was red carded just short of the half-hour mark for a professional foul on Michael Kightly. Handed his Champions League debut in October against CSKA Moscow in a 1-0 win, he ended the game with an injury but earned plaudits from Sir Alex Ferguson who enthused over his 'fantastic' contribution, particularly as the game was played on an artificial surface. Though being a twin can have its advantages when trying to confuse the opposition, Fabio and his twin Rafael were involved in a case of mistaken identity during the Carling Cup tie against Barnsley, when Fabio received a yellow card for a foul committed by Rafael. United had to appeal against the ban.
Manchester U (Signed from Fluminense, Brazil on 1/8/2008) PL 1+4 FLC 2 FAC 3 Others 2+1

FABREGAS Francesc (Cesc)
Born: Barcelona, Spain, 4 May 1987
Height: 5'9" **Weight:** 10.8
Club Honours: CS '04; FAC '05
International Honours: Spain: 49; U21; Yth
The Arsenal captain again led by example from midfield as he contributed a career best 15 goals in the Premier League and a further 15 assists. He also scored four times in the Champions League, including a priceless equaliser in the home quarter-final against his former team Barcelona. However, he broke a leg in the process of winning the penalty and missed the rest of the campaign. Personal highs for the season were a great goal at home to Tottenham after intercepting an opposition kick-off and a remarkable 30-minute cameo against Aston Villa when he scored with a devastating free kick and then added a second before his tight hamstring again gave way. In all he played 27 times in the Premier League, eight times in the Champions League and once in the FA Cup. Cesc was named in the PFA Premier League 'Team of the Season' and short-listed for the 'Player of the Season'. He was selected for the Spanish World Cup squad.
Arsenal (From trainee on 14/9/2004) PL 168+19/32 FLC 6+4/1 FAC 10+2 Others 53+5/15

FACEY Delroy Michael
Born: Huddersfield, 22 April 1980
Height: 5'11" **Weight:** 13.10
Club Honours: Div 2 '10
International Honours: Grenada: 2
A cult figure with the fans at Notts County and ever popular, he lost his place in the pecking order with so many new arrivals at the club and was allowed to move on loan to Lincoln. At

Cesc Fabregas

145

Sincil Bank the experienced front man scored once in nine games before returning to his parent club and becoming involved in the promotion battle. Playing a very effective strike partner to Lee Hughes up until the season's end, earlier he had scored the 'Goal of the Month' at Bradford in the Johnstone's Paint Trophy. Was out of contract in the summer.
Huddersfield T *(From trainee on 13/5/1997) FL 40+35/15 FLC 1+1 FAC 1+2 Others 2*
Bolton W *(Signed on 4/7/2002) PL 1+9/1 FAC 4*
Bradford C *(Loaned on 8/11/2002) FL 6/1*
Burnley *(Loaned on 1/9/2003) FL 12+2/5 FLC 2*
West Bromwich A *(£100,000 on 30/1/2004) FL 2+7*
Hull C *(Free on 1/7/2004) FL 12+9/4 FLC 1 FAC 2/2 Others 1*
Huddersfield T *(Loaned on 26/2/2005) FL 4*
Oldham Ath *(Free on 24/3/2005) FL 1+8 FLC 1*
Tranmere Rov *(Free on 31/8/2005) FL 30+7/8 FAC 1 Others 3/1*
Rotherham U *(Free on 3/8/2006) FL 37+3/10 FLC 1 FAC 1 Others 1/1*
Gillingham *(Signed on 1/8/2007) FL 27+5/3 FLC 0+1 FAC 1 Others 1*
Wycombe W *(Signed on 27/3/2008) FL 4+2/1 Others 2/1*
Notts Co *(Free on 8/8/2008) FL 51+12/11 FLC 2 FAC 3+1 Others 2/1*
Lincoln C *(Loaned on 26/11/2009) FL 9+1/1*

FAGAN Christopher (Chris)

Born: Dublin, 10 May 1989
Height: 5'8" **Weight:** 10.6
International Honours: RoI: U21-3
A former Manchester United trainee who joined Lincoln on a two-year contract last summer from the Glenn Hoddle Academy in Spain, Chris scored four goals from his 17 League and Cup appearances in 2009-10. However, having failed to hold down a regular first team place under Chris Sutton, the Republic of Ireland under-21 international striker finished the season on loan with Spanish side Jerez Industrial CF.
Manchester U *(From trainee on 10/7/2007. Freed during 2008 close season)*
Lincoln C *(From Glenn Hoddle Football Academy, via trials at Huddersfield T and Hamilton Academical, on 9/6/2009) FL 10+3/3 FLC 0+1 FAC 2/1 Others 0+1*

FAGAN Craig Anthony

Born: Birmingham, 11 December 1982
Height: 5'11" **Weight:** 11.12

Craig missed most of pre-season and the early part of Hull's campaign following a hernia operation. A tenacious performer who prefers the right side, his return in November coincided with the Tigers' best spell of a troubled season. Although regularly used as a forward, it is arguable that Craig was more profitably employed wide in midfield, especially as his work rate helps to protect the right-back. He coolly converted a penalty against Manchester United, while a looping header against Fulham at the end of March briefly revived hopes of survival. Someone who can never be accused of giving anything less than total commitment, Craig's competitive nature got the better of him when he was sent off in the crucial encounter at West Ham in February.
Birmingham C *(From trainee on 20/12/2001) PL 0+1 FLC 0+2 FAC 0+1*
Bristol C *(Loaned on 16/1/2003) FL 5+1/1 Others 1*
Colchester U *(Free on 5/8/2003) FL 55+8/17 FLC 5/3 FAC 10/4 Others 4*
Hull C *(Signed on 28/2/2005) FL 67+13/15 FLC 2+1 FAC 1*
Derby Co *(£750,000 on 12/1/2007) P/FL 29+10/1 FLC 1/1 FAC 3 Others 3*
Hull C *(Signed on 7/3/2008) P/FL 39+16/5 FLC 1 FAC 3 Others 0+3*

FAHEY Keith Declan

Born: Dublin, 15 January 1983
Height: 5'10" **Weight:** 12.8
International Honours: RoI: 2; Yth
On his rookie Premier League season, Keith had to be patient as the Birmingham side remained settled in the early part of the season. He was often used as first substitute and did a good, steady job on either flank. A clever passer with good control and vision, the defensive side of Keith's game improved. Prefers central midfield, but was asked to interpret wide roles for the Blues and it was puzzling why he was often overlooked by the Republic of Ireland.
Aston Villa *(£250,000 from trainee at Arsenal on 30/3/2000. Freed on 11/11/2002)*
Birmingham C *(Signed from St Patrick's Ath, ex Bluebell U, St Patrick's Ath, Drogheda U, on 2/1/2009) P/FL 33+20/4 FLC 0+1 FAC 3+2*

FAIRHURST Waide Simon

Born: Sheffield, 7 May 1989
Height: 5'11" **Weight:** 10.10
Waide had showed up well at the end of the previous season and got another chance in mid-September as partner to Billy Sharp in the Doncaster attack at West Bromwich, scoring after just seven

minutes. In the following match against Ipswich he again scored the first goal but when James Coppinger returned from injury he was relegated to the bench. In October the pacy striker went to Shrewsbury on loan, giving an excellent debut performance in the 3-1 home win against Aldershot while scoring his first goal for the Shrews. Stayed until the Boxing Day game against Macclesfield when his loan spell was ended after he ruptured a ligament in his foot. He had scored four goals in ten games during his time at the ProStar Stadium, including one in the 2-0 defeat of Rotherham in December with a long-range shot when giving his best performance for the Shrews. Back at the Keepmoat Stadium it was March before he was ready to play again.
Doncaster Rov *(From trainee on 4/7/2008) FL 2+7/2 FLC 0+1*
Shrewsbury T *(Loaned on 22/10/2009) FL 10/4*

FALLON Rory Michael

Born: Gisbourne, New Zealand, 20 March 1982
Height: 6'2" **Weight:** 11.10
International Honours: New Zealand: 7. E: Yth
Rory again started the season as the main striker for Plymouth but did not score his first goal until the end of September. The powerful striker is a real handful for an opposition defence and is a genuine presence in the box, often being marked by two defenders. He also uses his height in defensive positions and can often be seen heading the ball away from dangerous situations. Rory had a good consistent run in the starting line-up from December to the end of February, but towards the latter end of the season was often seen on the substitutes' bench. In November, Rory became a national hero when he scored the only goal in the second leg of New Zealand's World Cup qualifier against Bahrain to send them to the World Cup in South Africa for their first appearance at the finals in 28 years.
Barnsley *(From trainee on 23/3/1999) FL 33+19/11 FLC 2+1 FAC 1 Others 2*
Shrewsbury T *(Loaned on 14/12/2001) FL 8+3*
Swindon T *(£60,000 on 14/11/2003) FL 43+32/21 FLC 1+2 FAC 2+2/1 Others 5+2/3*
Yeovil T *(Loaned on 22/2/2005) FL 2+4/1*
Swansea C *(£300,000 on 26/1/2006) FL 34+7/12 FLC 1 FAC 2+1 Others 3/1*
Plymouth Arg *(£300,000 on 19/1/2007) FL 69+52/18 FLC 1+3 FAC 4*

FAUBERT Julien
Born: Le Havre, France, 1 August 1983
Height: 5'10" **Weight:** 11.12
International Honours: France: 1
It was a good campaign for the West Ham right-back. The flying French winger was used at the back to good effect and was voted the 'Most Improved Player' by the fans. His all-round play has been far better this term and his pace has certainly helped him. He was 'Man of the Match' against Hull in February as he made a goal for Carlton Cole with a pinpoint pass and then scored his first goal for the club with a stunning shot into the far corner. It has taken time but Julien has returned to something like the form that won him an international cap for France.
West Ham U (£6,000,000 From Bordeaux, France, ex AS Cannes, on 13/7/2007) PL 51+9/1 FLC 3+1 FAC 3+1

FAURLIN Alejandro Damian
Born: Rosario, Argentina, 9 August 1986
Height: 6'1" **Weight:** 12.6
Scouted and recruited for Queens Park Rangers by Jim Magilton's staff last summer and trumpeted as a big-money signing when he joined in July in a deal reputed to be worth £3.5-million, Alejandro never let the fuss get the better of him and enjoyed a simply sublime debut season in blue and white hoops. While turmoil often raged around the players at Loftus Road, Alejandro remained a consistent presence in midfield, combining Argentine flair and skill with a steely winning attitude that soon won over the Rangers' faithful. For so long it looked as if a first goal might evade him but it finally came, against Sheffield Wednesday in April and a more popular scorer you could not wish to see. His excellent maiden season was rewarded when he was rightly named both the supporters' and players' 'Player of the Season'.
Queens Park Rgrs (£3,500,000 from Instituto de Cordoba, Argentina, ex Rosario Central, Atletico de Rafaela on 8/7/2009) FL 36+5/1 FLC 1 FAC 2

FAYE Abdoulaye Diagne
Born: Dakar, Senegal, 26 February 1978
Height: 6'2" **Weight:** 13.10
International Honours: Senegal: 34
In his first season at Stoke, Abdoulaye was named team captain and led by example with a stunning campaign in the red and white stripes. It was perhaps because he set the bar so high that his second season seemed almost a let-down. He was never fully fit

throughout 2009-10 and this impacted both on his form and his inability to get a decent spell of games in the team. There were certainly flashes of the brilliance and composure that made him such a legend in 2008-09, and he still weighed in with his fair share of goals, but it was not quite the same Abdoulaye. A frustrating campaign for the player himself, when the team were once again exceeding expectations, culminated in an angry set-to with team-mates following the 7-0 rout at Chelsea. Nevertheless, the imposing defender remains a key part of the Stoke defence, a hugely popular character at the club and supporters are all hoping he can get fully fit again and recapture the form that made him such a revelation in his first season.
Bolton W (Signed from RC Lens, France on 3/8/2005) PL 53+7/3 FLC 2 FAC 3 Others 7
Newcastle U (£2,500,000 on 31/8/2007) PL 20+2/1 FLC 1 FAC 1
Stoke C (£2,250,000 on 15/8/2008) PL 66+1/5 FAC 1

FAYE Amdy Mustapha
Born: Dakar, Senegal, 12 March 1977
Height: 6'1" **Weight:** 12.4
International Honours: Senegal: 31
After a productive first season at the Britannia Stadium Amdy found himself very much on the sidelines at Stoke this time and had to make do with a handful of selections on the substitutes' bench and only one first team appearance, in the 1-0 Carling Cup victory at Leyton Orient. Other than that it was the slim pickings of reserve team football for the central midfielder and it was announced at the end of the season that he had been released.
Portsmouth (£1,500,000 from Auxerre, France on 14/8/2003) PL 44+3 FLC 2 FAC 2+1
Newcastle U (£2,000,000 on 25/1/2005) PL 22+9 FLC 1+1 FAC 3 Others 9
Charlton Ath (£2,000,000 on 10/8/2006) P/FL 25+4/1 FLC 3+1 FAC 1
Glasgow Rgrs (Loaned on 31/8/2007) SL 2+2 SLC 1 Others 0+1
Stoke C (£2,250,000 on 15/8/2008) PL 18+3 FLC 1+1

FEATHERSTONE Nicky Lee
Born: Goole, 22 September 1988
Height: 5'9" **Weight:** 11.7
Having featured for Hull against Tottenham in the pre-season Barclays Asia Trophy meeting in Beijing, Nicky - who was a recognised striker - played in the Tigers' 3-1 win against Southend in the Carling Cup in an unfamiliar midfield-anchor role and took the eye

with his precision passing. However, unable to find a place in City's Premier League line-up, he went out on loan to League Two neighbours Grimsby, making his debut in a local derby at Lincoln and performing well in a 0-0 draw. Not afraid to shoot from distance, the right-sided midfielder later returned for a second loan spell, although this ended early due to a lack of senior opportunities.
Hull C (From trainee on 18/12/2006) P/FL 0+8 FLC 4+2 FAC 0+2
Grimsby T (Loaned on 19/11/2009) FL 7+1

FEDERICI Adam Jay
Born: Nowra, Australia, 31 January 1985
Height: 6'2" **Weight:** 14.2
International Honours: Australia: 1; U21-5; Yth
Adam made Reading's goalkeeping spot his own by playing every minute of the Championship fixtures. He missed only two Carling Cup ties and the last 20 minutes of the first FA Cup tie against Liverpool after being injured. Adam proved a reliable, agile and strong last line of defence, making many brave, close-range saves when a goal seemed inevitable. He reserved his best performances for the FA Cup run that took Reading into the quarter-finals but his consistency meant that his name was regularly linked with Premiership clubs. Adam almost repeated his scoring feat of the previous season but his injury-time scissor-kick was saved by the Cardiff goalkeeper. Made his international debut for Australia against New Zealand in May.
Wolverhampton W (Free from Australian Institute of Sport, via trial at Bolton W, on 27/2/2003. Freed during 2003 close season)
Reading (Free from Sassari Torres, Italy, following trial at Leeds U, on 20/1/2005) P/FL 60+3/1 FLC 4 FAC 13
Southend U (Loaned on 25/9/2008) FL 10

FEENEY Liam Julian
Born: Hammersmith, 21 January 1987
Height: 6'0" **Weight:** 12.2
A quick winger who enjoyed an excellent first full season as a League player, Liam showed versatility throughout Bournemouth's promotion campaign, switching between wings on numerous occasions during games. He set up a number of goals as well as scoring some vital ones himself, including a wonderful solo effort to secure three points in an important win at Cheltenham.
Southend U (Loaned from Salisbury C,

ex Hayes, on 26/11/2008) FL 0+1
Bournemouth *(Free from Salisbury C on 2/2/2009) FL 50+8/8 FLC 1 FAC 2 Others 1*

Liam Feeney

FEENEY Warren James
Born: Belfast, 17 January 1981
Height: 5'10" **Weight:** 11.6
International Honours: NI: 34; U21-8; Yth; Sch
Northern Ireland international striker Warren spent more than three years with Cardiff, but was scarcely given a chance, making only six starts without getting on the scoresheet. Loan spells with Swansea and Dundee United were both successful, while during 2009-10 he had a short spell with Sheffield Wednesday. Signed on loan from Cardiff, this experienced striker was not 100 per cent fit and consequently made only one appearance as a substitute while at Hillsborough. Out of contract with Cardiff during the summer and released, a number of clubs including Bristol Rovers, Plymouth and Cheltenham were quick to show interest.
Leeds U *(Signed from St Andrew's BC on 26/1/1998)*
Bournemouth *(Free on 22/3/2001) FL 83+25/36 FLC 1+1 FAC 6+4 Others 3+2/1*
Stockport Co *(Free on 29/7/2004) FL 31/15 FAC 2/2*
Luton T *(£175,000 on 24/3/2005) FL 45+32/8 FLC 4/2 FAC 1+1/1*
Cardiff C *(Signed on 23/2/2007) FL 6+14 FLC 1 FAC 0+1*
Swansea C *(Loaned on 31/8/2007) FL 7+3/5 FAC 1+1/1 Others 0+1*

Dundee U *(Loaned on 7/7/2008) SL 18+5/6 SLC 1+1 SC 1*
Sheffield Wed *(Loaned on 26/11/2009) FL 0+1*

FELLAINI Marouane
Born: Brussels, Belgium, 22 November 1987
Height: 6'4" **Weight:** 13.5
International Honours: Belgium: 21
The charismatic and unusually coiffured Belgian international really found his feet in his second season at Everton and was regarded as being one of the top midfielders in the country until the campaign was prematurely ended with a serious ankle injury against Liverpool at Anfield in February. After patchy early form due to a virus that disrupted pre-season, the big midfielder was deployed in his favourite holding role, where he displayed his ability to break

up play adeptly, no little skill on the ball and fine passing. Around the turn of the year, the former Standard Liege player put in a series of magnificent displays, especially at Arsenal and at home to Manchester City, before the season came to a crashing end at Anfield. A popular presence at Goodison, fans of Everton will be hoping for a swift return for this classy midfielder with huge potential.
Everton *(£15,000,000 from Standard Liege, Belgium on 1/9/2008) PL 48+5/10 FLC 2+1 FAC 6/1 Others 7/1*

FENTON Nicholas (Nicky) Leonard
Born: Preston, 23 November 1979
Height: 5'10" **Weight:** 10.4
International Honours: E: Yth
Another solid season for the experienced Rotherham central

Marouane Fellaini

defender and his partnership with Ian Sharps was as good as anything in League Two. He missed seven games in the second half of the season and Rotherham lost four of them. His outstanding display in the first leg of the play-off semi-final at Aldershot was the most inspirational individual performance of the season. Strangely, for someone so good in the air, he went the entire season without a goal although he was up for every set piece.
Manchester C *(From trainee on 26/11/1996) FL 15 FLC 3+1 Others 1*
Notts Co *(Loaned on 7/10/1999) FL 13/1 Others 1*
Bournemouth *(Loaned on 23/3/2000) FL 8*
Bournemouth *(Loaned on 11/8/2000) FL 4+1*
Notts Co *(£150,000 on 18/9/2000) FL 153+2/9 FLC 7 FAC 12/2 Others 4*
Doncaster Rov *(Free on 27/7/2004) FL 58+5/3 FLC 7 FAC 5/1 Others 4*
Grimsby T *(Signed on 25/8/2006) FL 77+3/6 FLC 1 FAC 5 Others 9/1*
Rotherham U *(Free on 8/8/2008) FL 79+1/1 FLC 6/1 FAC 4 Others 8/1*

FERDINAND Anton Julian
Born: Peckham, 18 February 1985
Height: 6'0" **Weight:** 11.0
International Honours: E: U21-17; Yth
Anton played in both full-back positions and even in midfield as well as his more renowned centre-back role. A regular in central defence in the first half of the season, an injury sustained at Fulham ruled him out for two-and-a-half months, after which he held down a place at left-back. However, his 50th Sunderland start back at his former club West Ham in April proved to be his last of the season. Known to be a huge fan of Michael Jackson, Anton had long promised to perform a Jacko dance if he scored. As he found the back of the net against Tottenham in April, Anton duly performed his tribute to a musical hero… only to realise the goal had been disallowed.
West Ham U *(From trainee on 15/8/2002) P/FL 118+20/5 FLC 6+1 FAC 14 Others 4*
Sunderland *(£8,000,000 on 27/8/2008) PL 50+5 FLC 2+1 FAC 3*

FERDINAND Rio Gavin
Born: Peckham, 7 November 1978
Height: 6'2" **Weight:** 12.1
Club Honours: PL '03, '07, '08, '09; CS '03, '07; FLC '06; UEFACL '08
International Honours: E: 78; B-1; U21-5; Yth
A consummate Manchester United and England central defender, who

Rio Ferdinand

combines great strength in the air with neat skills on the ground, Rio's season was severely hampered by a persistent back injury that cost him dearly for both United and England. He only made five Premier League appearances between August and October and did not return to Premiership action until January in the home game against Hull. Despite United winning 4-0, Rio was then banned for four matches after elbowing an opponent in that game. Fully fit to return for the business part of the season, he was a leading light as United went in search of the domestic title and glory in Europe. A certainty for Fabio Capello's England squad for the World Cup finals in South Africa, Rio looked to be back to his best as the season ended before breaking down prior to the tournament getting underway.
West Ham U *(From trainee on 27/11/1995) PL 122+5/2 FLC 11+1 FAC*
9 Others 9
Bournemouth *(Loaned on 8/11/1996) FL 10 Others 1*
Leeds U *(£18,000,000 on 27/11/2000) PL 54/2 FLC 2 FAC 3 Others 14/1*
Manchester U *(£29,100,000 + on 22/7/2002) PL 219+2/6 FLC 11+1 FAC 23+1 Others 73+1/1*

FERGUSON Barry
Born: Glasgow, 2 February 1978
Height: 5'11" **Weight:** 11.1
Club Honours: SPD '99, '00, '03, '05, '09; SLC '98, '00, '03, '08; SC '00, '02, '03, '09
International Honours: S: 45; U21-12
Outstanding in central midfield, Barry was a hit after his move from Glasgow Rangers to Birmingham. He dictated the tempo and pattern of games for the Blues, taking possession and keeping the ball well, or moving it on at the right moment to the right option.

Tended to sit deeper, but when he did get forward was clever and creative, scoring with a fine curler at Everton in the FA Cup to top off a lovely team move. Named 'Players' Player of the Season', he opted not to rekindle his international career. Was a leader on the pitch and did so much to help the Blues change their style to more of a passing game.
Glasgow Rgrs *(From juniors on 6/7/1994) SL 148+2/24 SLC 15/3 SC 23+2/6 Others 46+1/2*
Blackburn Rov *(£7,500,000 on 30/8/2003) PL 35+1/3 FLC 1/1 FAC 1*
Glasgow Rgrs *(£4,500,000 on 31/1/2005) SL 130+7/20 SLC 7+2/1 SC 9 Others 35/4*
Birmingham C *(£1,200,000 on 17/7/2009) PL 37 FLC 1 FAC 5/2*

FERREIRA Renato **Paulo**
Born: Cascais, Portugal, 18 January 1979
Height: 6'0" **Weight:** 11.13
Club Honours: FLC '05, '07; PL '05, '06, '10; CS '05; FAC '07, '10
International Honours: Portugal: 61
From spending time in the shadows, the ever-reliable Paulo made a welcome return in the last quarter of the season as Chelsea underwent an injury crisis to their full-backs. He initially filled in on the left when Ashley Cole and Yury Zhirkov were sidelined and switched to his more familiar right side when Jose Bosingwa, Branislav Ivanovic, and Juliano Belletti were all laid low by injury. He settled seamlessly back into the side where his familiar, enthusiastic rampaging gave Chelsea the perfect fit for their sometimes narrow style. He even managed to score at Blackburn in the Carling Cup. His drive from a tight angle in the last minute of extra time, only his second goal in English football, sent the match into a penalty shoot-out. Paulo was selected as Bosingwa's replacement in Portugal's World Cup squad.
Chelsea *(£13,200,000 from FC Porto, Portugal on 20/7/2004) PL 92+20 FLC 13+2/1 FAC 13+4/1 Others 23+5*

FERRY Simon
Born: Dundee, 11 January 1988
Height: 5'8" **Weight:** 11.0
Simon joined Swindon on loan from Glasgow Celtic towards the end of August and was immediately installed in the centre of midfield, where he linked up with Jonathan Douglas. Although initially struggling with the pace of the game in League One, having been confined to Scottish reserve team football, he soon adapted and his loan was

Maynor Figueroa

extended to the end of the season. A busy and energetic midfield workhorse, he was always full of running. Netted his first League goal in a victory at Tranmere at the end of October.
Glasgow Celtic *(From juniors on 18/2/2006)*
Swindon T *(Loaned on 27/8/2009) FL 40/2 FAC 3 Others 3*

FIELDING Francis (Frank)
David
Born: Blackburn, 4 April 1988
Height: 6'1" **Weight:** 11.11
International Honours: E: U21-2; Yth
Frank arrived for his second loan spell at Rochdale in February. Taking over from fellow England under-21 international goalkeeper Tom Heaton, he kept up the good work. Dale were beaten only twice in the next ten games and Frank's sixth clean sheet came in the 1-0 victory over Northampton that guaranteed promotion.
Blackburn Rov *(From trainee on 10/7/2006)*
Wycombe W *(Loaned on 28/9/2007) FL 36 FAC 1 Others 2*
Northampton T *(Loaned on 12/9/2008) FL 12 FLC 1 FAC 2*
Rochdale *(Loaned on 6/11/2009) FL 23 Others 2*
Rochdale *(Loaned on 30/1/2010) FL 18*

FIGUEROA Maynor
Born: Jutiapa, Honduras, 2 May 1983
Height: 5'11" **Weight:** 13.4
International Honours: Honduras: 66; U23-8; Yth
Maynor enjoyed another accomplished season at Wigan, playing in 35 Premiership matches. A left-back who can also play in the centre of defence, Maynor is quick, athletic and attack-minded. Continuing to grow in confidence, he played his part as the club safeguarded Premier League status for a sixth season. With his tough tackling, he anticipates well and breaks out of defence with speed and purpose. He made his 50th Premier League start against Sunderland and signed a new improved contract in January as speculation linked him with a move to Sunderland. His only goal won the December 'Goal of the Month' award, etching his name into Barclays Premier League and Wigan history after an incredible demonstration of technique and quick thinking when arrowing a free kick from inside his own half. A Honduran international, Maynor played his part in his country's success in reaching the World Cup finals for the first time since 1982.
Wigan Ath *(Loaned from Deportivo Olimpia, Honduras, ex Deportivo Victoria, on 22/1/2008) PL 1+1*

Wigan Ath *(Signed from Deportivo Olimpia, Honduras on 29/7/2008) PL 73/2 FLC 2 FAC 3+1*

FINNAN Stephen (Steve) John
Born: Limerick, 20 April 1976
Height: 5'10" **Weight:** 11.6
Club Honours: Div 3 '98; Div 2 '99; Div 1 '01; UEFACL '05; ESC '05; FAC '06; CS '06
International Honours: RoI: 53; B-1; U21-8

After a slow start to his Portsmouth career, veteran full-back Steve managed to shake off a number of injuries to play an integral part in a difficult season on the south coast. Ageing limbs may limit Steve's appearances on both the pitch and the training field to a bare minimum but his sharpness of mind and big-match experience helped the defender to grow in stature game by game, excelling in both full-back positions and even as a makeshift centre-half. His future hung in the balance, with his contract expiring at the end of June and his international career seemingly over following his omission from several Republic of Ireland squads by coach Giovanni Trapattoni.

Birmingham C *(£100,000 from Welling U on 12/6/1995) FL 9+6/1 FLC 2+2 Others 2+1*
Notts Co *(Loaned on 5/3/1996) FL 14+3/2 Others 3/1*
Notts Co *(£300,000 on 31/10/1996) FL 71+9/5 FLC 4 FAC 7/1 Others 1*
Fulham *(£600,000 on 13/11/1998) P/FL 171+1/6 FLC 10+1 FAC 18/1 Others 6*
Liverpool *(£3,500,000 on 30/6/2003) PL 134+11/1 FLC 5+1 FAC 12+1 Others 49+4 (Signed by Espanyol, Spain on 1/9/2008)*
Portsmouth *(Signed on 31/7/2009) PL 20+1 FAC 4*

FISHER Thomas (Tom) Michael
Born: Wythenshawe, 28 June 1992
Height: 5'10" **Weight:** 11.7

Young striker Tom, handed his first professional contract by Stockport in the summer, waited until November for his first senior appearance of the season, as a substitute in the 5-0 victory over Tooting & Mitcham in the FA Cup. He also played the last ten minutes in the 1-0 defeat by Brentford.

Stockport Co *(Trainee) FL 0+2 FAC 0+1*

FLAHAVAN Darryl James
Born: Southampton, 9 September 1977
Height: 5'10" **Weight:** 12.1
Club Honours: Div 1 '06

In search of first team football, having

played back-up to Palace's first choice Julian Speroni, Darryl joined Oldham on loan for a large part of the season after making one early League appearance for Palace against Newcastle. He joined Oldham twice on loan with the first spell coming at the tail-end of last year until interrupted by injury. Darryl then re-joined them on loan a second time in March, and was first choice 'keeper for the remaining games through till the end of the season. Small in stature but with great presence and a great personality, Darryl was a huge success at Oldham, making 19 appearances in all. Steadying the Latics through stormy waters as they fought a rearguard action against relegation, Darryl was out of contract at Palace in June and will be looking for pastures new.

Southampton *(From trainee on 14/5/1996. Free to Woking on 13/8/1998)*
Southend U *(Free from Chesham U on 16/10/2000) FL 289+2 FLC 9 FAC 23 Others 28*
Crystal Palace *(Free on 8/7/2008) FL 2 FLC 2*
Oldham Ath *(Loaned on 4/11/2009) FL 18 FAC 1*

FLANAGAN Thomas (Tom) Michael
Born: Hammersmith, 21 October 1991
Height: 6'2" **Weight:** 11.0

Called into the MK Dons' senior squad when injuries decimated the defensive options in mid-February, Tom is a tall and slim right-sided defender who made his League debut when coming on as an 82nd-minute substitute in a game at Carlisle the Dons were losing 5-0 at the time. Helping to maintain that score to the end, he then warmed the bench on several more occasions in between skippering the club's under-18 team.

MK Dons *(Trainee) FL 0+1*

FLEETWOOD Stuart Keith Wakley
Born: Chepstow, 23 April 1986
Height: 5'10" **Weight:** 11.8
International Honours: W: U21-5; Yth

Stuart finally made his Charlton debut in the Carling Cup tie at Hereford last August when he came on as a late substitute. The striker was named on the bench for the next three games but failed to make another appearance, being loaned to Exeter in early September for the rest of the season. Even at his new club he found a starting place hard to come by as manager Paul Tisdale regularly shuffled his forward line. However, his direct and pacy style helped him to bag four League goals,

including the opener against Colchester in April.

Cardiff C *(From trainee on 2/2/2004) FL 1+7 FLC 1+3*
Hereford U *(Free on 30/1/2006) FL 21+6/3 FLC 2/3 FAC 0+2 Others 1*
Accrington Stanley *(Loaned on 31/1/2007) FL 3*
Charlton Ath *(Free from Forest Green Rov on 8/7/2008) FLC 0+1*
Cheltenham T *(Loaned on 26/9/2008) FL 6/2 Others 1*
Brighton & Hove A *(Loaned on 31/10/2008) FL 5+6/1 FLC 1 FAC 1+1*
Exeter C *(Loaned on 18/3/2009) FL 7+2/3*
Exeter C *(Loaned on 1/9/2009) FL 16+11/4 FAC 2 Others 0+1/1*

FLETCHER Carl Neil
Born: Camberley, 7 April 1980
Height: 5'10" **Weight:** 11.7
International Honours: W: 36

After Carl enjoyed a short loan spell at Plymouth in the previous season, manager Paul Sturrock was delighted to sign the Welsh international from Crystal Palace in June on a two-year contract. Carl was pleased and honoured to be named as Plymouth's captain for the season. He was called up for Wales in August but then surprisingly decided to retire from international football to concentrate on his club career for Plymouth. Strong in the tackle with an eye for a pass, Carl was the mainstay in the centre of the Pilgrims' midfield, also popping up with some important goals such as the injury time winner against West Country rivals Bristol City in March. He suffered a nasty knee injury against Blackpool three games later and his influence was seriously missed. His efforts and performances were rewarded at the end of the season as the Plymouth fans nominated him as their 'Player of the Season'.

Bournemouth *(From trainee on 3/7/1998) FL 186+7/19 FLC 6 FAC 15+1/1 Others 9+1/3*
West Ham U *(£250,000 on 31/8/2004) P/FL 32+12/3 FLC 0+1 FAC 4+3 Others 1*
Watford *(Loaned on 16/9/2005) FL 3*
Crystal Palace *(£400,000 on 2/8/2006) FL 50+18/4 FLC 0+2 FAC 3+1*
Nottingham F *(Loaned on 17/10/2008) FL 4+1*
Plymouth Arg *(Free on 20/2/2009) FL 54/5 FAC 2*

FLETCHER Darren Barr
Born: Dalkeith, 1 February 1984
Height: 6'0" **Weight:** 13.5
Club Honours: FAC '04; FLC '06, '10; PL '07, '08, '09; CS '07; UEFACL '08

International Honours: S: 47; B- 1; U21-2

The Manchester United and Scotland midfield player possesses an exquisite touch and passing skills. Darren's absence from the Champions League final against Barcelona at the end of 2008-09 was given as a major reason for United's defeat. Little wonder that he soon consolidated his place in the heart of midfield. Opening his scoring account with a double in the first Manchester derby at Old Trafford – a 4-3 victory for United – he twice put the Reds in front before Michael Owen notched the winner in the sixth minute of added time. Awarded the Barclays 'Man of the Match' award, Darren scored his third goal in November with a stunning half-volley from the edge of the area to give United the lead against Everton. Another plus to his growing repertoire was seeing him – along with fellow midfielders Michael Carrick and Ji-Sung Park – deputising in defence due to an injury crisis that left Patrice Evra the only fit regular. They still managed to keep a clean sheet against West Ham and concede only one goal against Wolfsburg in the Champions League. Despite a red card against Birmingham in the Premiership for a second bookable offence, Darren made his mark on the European stage by scoring in a 4-0 win over AC Milan at Old Trafford in March that sent United through to the last 16.
Manchester U (From trainee on 3/2/2001) PL 133+30/14 FLC 13+1 FAC 13+8/2 Others 43+14/2

FLETCHER Steven Kenneth
Born: Shrewsbury, 26 March 1987
Height: 6'1" **Weight:** 12.0
Club Honours: SLC '07
International Honours: S: 7; B-1; U21-7; Yth

Steven became Burnley's record signing when he joined the Clarets from Hibernian in July. Already an established Scottish international, he very quickly established himself as a fans' favourite with the quality of his forward play, combining a sharp eye for goal with unselfish skill on the ball and the ability to contribute from all areas of the pitch, making him much more than just a target man. He had already notched three Carling Cup goals before his first in the Premier League, in the home win against Birmingham, but from then on he usually looked the Clarets' main threat, registering a very respectable 12 goals in total, a fine tally considering the side's ultimately doomed struggle against relegation. He won several 'Player of the Year' awards and took his

total of full caps to seven, but after breaking his hand during Scotland training he was out of the Burnley side for three games in March. Steven indicated a willingness to drop to the Championship after the Clarets' relegation and if they can keep him he could be a major player in that division next season.
Hibernian (From juniors on 23/3/2004) SL 115+41/43 SLC 5+6/5 SC 11+5/3 Others 5+1/1
Burnley (£3,000,000 on 30/6/2009) PL 35/8 FLC 1+1/3 FAC 1/1

Steven Fletcher (Burnley)

FLETCHER Steven (Steve) Mark
Born: Hartlepool, 26 June 1972
Height: 6'2" **Weight:** 14.9

It was another incredible season of success for the Bournemouth legend. Despite being 37, Steve was involved in every game and was a big influence in the side gaining promotion. The striker passed 600 appearances for the Cherries at the start of the season, and once again, advanced the club's appearances record every time he took the field. A remarkable season became even more memorable when he had a stand named after him at Dean Court.
Hartlepool U (From trainee on 23/8/1990) FL 19+13/4 FLC 0+2/1 FAC 1+2 Others 2+2/1
Bournemouth (£30,000 on 28/7/1992) FL 446+47/87 FLC 30/4 FAC 31+2/9 Others 19+3/5
Chesterfield (Free on 11/7/2007) FL 23+15/5 FAC 1 (Freed during 2008 close season)
Bournemouth (Free from Crawley T on 23/1/2009) FL 50+16/8 FLC 0+1 FAC 0+2

FLETCHER Wesleigh (Wes)
Born: Ormskirk, 28 February 1990
Height: 5'11" **Weight:** 12.6

Mostly seen as a late substitute for Grimsby, Wes claimed an injury-time goal with an angled shot at Rotherham. The teenage forward then made his full bow against Notts County, showing pace and threat before returning to parent club Burnley to earn a new contract.
Burnley (From trainee on 4/7/2009)
Grimsby T (Loaned on 15/1/2010) FL 1+5/1

FLINDERS Scott Liam
Born: Rotherham, 12 June 1986
Height: 6'4" **Weight:** 14.0
International Honours: E: Yth

A commanding goalkeeper who had an impressive first season with Hartlepool after joining them in the summer, Scott is surprisingly agile for a big man. He was off to a great start as it was 233 minutes before he conceded his first goal and an incredible 435 minutes before he conceded an away goal. While at Crystal Palace, Scott spent most of his time in the reserves, although loaned out to five different clubs. Never previously having a lengthy run, he benefited greatly from regular football and, having proved himself an excellent acquisition, was Hartlepool's only ever-present.
Barnsley (From trainee on 2/4/2005) FL 14 FLC 2 FAC 2 Others 1
Crystal Palace (Signed on 17/7/2006) FL 7+1 FLC 2 FAC 3
Gillingham (Loaned on 8/9/2006) FL 9 Others 1
Brighton & Hove A (Loaned on 20/2/2007) FL 12
Yeovil T (Loaned on 11/2/2008) FL 9
Falkirk (Loaned on 14/8/2008) SL 8 SLC 1
Hartlepool U (Free on 2/7/2009) FL 46 FLC 2 FAC 1 Others 1

FLITCROFT David (Dave) John
Born: Bolton, 14 January 1974
Height: 5'11" **Weight:** 13.5

The Rochdale assistant manager made yet another comeback when Dale were short on numbers at the start of the season, being on the bench against Sheffield Wednesday in the Carling Cup and then starting in his old central midfield role against Bradford in the Johnstone's Paint Trophy.
Preston NE (From trainee on 2/5/1992) FL 4+4/2 FLC 0+1 Others 0+1
Lincoln C (Loaned on 17/9/1993) FL 2 FLC 0+1
Chester C (Free on 9/12/1993) FL 146+21/18 FLC 10+1 FAC 7 Others 8/1
Rochdale (Free on 5/7/1999) FL

141+19/4 FLC 5+2 FAC 7+4 Others 9+1 **Macclesfield T** *(Free on 11/7/2003) FL 14+1 Others 1* **Bury** *(Free on 30/1/2004) FL 95+5/4 FLC 2 FAC 4 Others 2 (Freed on 18/11/2006)* **Rochdale** *(Free from Hyde U on 31/1/2007) FL 0+1 Others 1*

FLOOD William (Willo)
Robert
Born: Dublin, 10 April 1985
Height: 5'6" **Weight:** 9.11
International Honours: RoI: U21-18; Yth
After spending most of the first half of the season on the sidelines at Glasgow Celtic, Willo became one of Gordon Strachan's mass influx at Middlesbrough from his former club. After speculation that he was arriving on loan, Willo signed a permanent contract. He quickly impressed the Riverside faithful with his drive and tenacity on the right of midfield. In his second game against Swansea, he hit a wonder goal from the right touchline that sailed over the goalkeeper's head. Afterwards, tongue in cheek, he said he meant it. His season was cut short in March when, against former club Cardiff, he suffered a tear in his posterior cruciate ligament.
Manchester C *(From trainee on 13/4/2002) PL 5+9/1 FLC 2/1 FAC 0+1 Others 1*
Rochdale *(Loaned on 15/3/2004) FL 6*
Coventry C *(Loaned on 19/8/2005) FL 7+1/1*
Cardiff C *(£200,000 on 2/8/2006) FL 5+20/1 FLC 1 FAC 2*
Dundee U *(Loaned on 20/7/2007) SL 33+3/1 SLC 5 SC 3*
Dundee U *(Loaned on 10/7/2008) SL 20 SLC 3 SC 1*
Glasgow Celtic *(Free on 30/1/2009) SL 2+4 SLC 1 Others 1+1*
Middlesbrough *(Free on 13/1/2010) FL 11/1*

FLYNN Jonathan (Johnny)
Joseph
Born: Belfast, 18 November 1989
Height: 6'0" **Weight:** 11.4
International Honours: NI: U21-10; Yth
The Northern Ireland under-21 international joined Accrington on loan from Blackburn in November, but only had limited opportunities in the first team, making just eight appearances. Previously, Johnny had spent time at non-League Chester, where he had impressed as an all-round central defender for the future. Blackburn have high hopes for this youngster.
Blackburn Rov *(Signed from Ballymena U on 12/1/2008)*

Accrington Stanley *(Loaned on 26/11/2009) FL 6+2*

FLYNN Matthew (Matt)
Born: Preston, 10 May 1989
Height: 6'0" **Weight:** 11.8
Matt was on the point of signing for Rhyl when offered the chance to join Rochdale on loan in August, a move that was made permanent shortly afterwards. He made half-a-dozen appearances at right-back in place of the injured Scott Wiseman. For the rest of the season he was an almost permanent substitute, providing cover for the full-backs.
Macclesfield T *(From trainee on 4/7/2007) FL 23+5 FAC 2 Others 1+1*
Rochdale *(Signed on 13/8/2009) FL 7+3 Others 1*

FLYNN Michael (Mike) John
Born: Newport, 17 October 1980
Height: 5'10" **Weight:** 12.10
Club Honours: Div 2 '03
International Honours: W: SP
An outgoing character, Mike was seen as the heartbeat of Bradford's side with his driving runs from midfield and powerful shot. Always keen to have a shot from long range, he scored spectacular goals against Shrewsbury, Rochdale and Dagenham. Mike also proved effective as a striker, playing just off the target man, and scored a winner against Barnet well into stoppage time after coming off the bench to take up that role.
Wigan Ath *(£50,000 from Barry T, ex Newport Co, on 25/6/2002) FL 5+33/2 FLC 0+4 FAC 1+2/1 Others 2*
Blackpool *(Loaned on 20/8/2004) FL 6 FLC 1*
Gillingham *(Signed on 3/2/2005) FL 90+7/19 FLC 4 FAC 3/2 Others 1*
Blackpool *(Free on 6/7/2007) FL 20+8/3 FLC 3 FAC 1*
Huddersfield T *(Free on 29/7/2008) FL 18+7/4 FLC 2/1*
Darlington *(Loaned on 27/11/2008) FL 4 Others 1*
Bradford C *(Free on 5/8/2009) FL 41+1/6 FLC 1 FAC 1 Others 4/2*

FOLAN Caleb Colman
Born: Leeds, 26 October 1982
Height: 6'1" **Weight:** 12.12
International Honours: RoI: 7
After an impressive performance as a lone striker in Hull's narrow opening day defeat at Chelsea, Caleb was surprisingly and unceremoniously dropped after only four games. Amid a very public fall-out with the Tigers' management, the powerful front-runner was allowed to go out on loan to Championship Middlesbrough for

the remainder of the year. He began life at The Riverside on the bench versus West Bromwich, coming on as a first-half substitute, as the Albion ran riot when winning the game 5-0. His fortunes turned from bad to worse as he suffered a torn hamstring in training. He stayed on in an attempt to get fit but new boss Gordon Strachan cut his loan deal short and he returned to his parent club Hull where he remained firmly out of favour. That was until the appointment of Iain Dowie as City's new manager in March and he was rewarded with an immediate recall with a two-goal salvo at Portsmouth. Amazingly, the injury jinx struck again as he was hindered by a hip problem. At the end of a frustrating season, he was selected for the Republic of Ireland's summer training camp.
Leeds U *(From trainee on 2/11/1999)*
Rushden & Diamonds *(Loaned on 5/10/2001) FL 1+5 Others 1*
Hull C *(Loaned on 30/11/2001) FL 0+1*
Chesterfield *(Free on 14/2/2003) FL 57+45/15 FLC 3+1/3 FAC 1+1 Others 2/1*
Wigan Ath *(£500,000 on 26/1/2007) PL 9+6/2 FLC 1*
Hull C *(£1,000,000 on 31/8/2007) P/FL 27+25/11 FLC 1 FAC 3+2 Others 0+3/1*
Middlesbrough *(Loaned on 17/9/2009) FL 0+1*

FOLEY David John
Born: South Shields, 12 May 1987
Height: 5'4" **Weight:** 8.9
Diminutive striker or midfielder for Hartlepool, David was long considered a great prospect. In a disappointing final season at Pool, his outings were restricted to two second-half substitute appearances. He was loaned to Barrow early in the season but an ankle injury cut this short. David was released in February to join USSF club Puerto Rico Islanders and leaves United with two distinctions, the youngest player ever to appear in a League game and the player with the most substitute appearances.
Hartlepool U *(From trainee on 4/7/2006) FL 21+77 FLC 1+6/4 FAC 1+4/1 Others 2+3/2*

FOLEY Kevin Patrick
Born: Luton, 1 November 1984
Height: 5'9" **Weight:** 11.2
Club Honours: Div 1 '05; Ch '09
International Honours: RoI: 2; B-1; U21-9
Wolverhampton's Kevin made a goal-line clearance on the opening day but a knee ligament injury was to keep him out for a month. He never really had much chance in the right-back position, where he had excelled in 2008-09. By

mid-December he had been restricted to two League starts, but he then played 24 times in a row in midfield. Kevin was desperately unlucky not to score on at least two occasions, hitting the inside of a post with a fine shot at Bolton, and cracking the bar at West Ham. Kevin is a good team player and though he was dropped on the last day, he came on as a substitute.
Luton T (From trainee on 8/3/2004) FL 143+8/3 FLC 3+2/2 FAC 8 Others 1+1
Wolverhampton W (£700,000 on 14/8/2007) P/FL 110+4/2 FLC 5 FAC 6

FOLLY Yoann
Born: Paris, France, 6 June 1985
Height: 5'11" **Weight:** 11.0
International Honours: Togo: 1. France: U21-10
Yoann's Plymouth future looked uncertain at the start of the season as he was left out of the Pilgrims' pre-season tour to Scotland. However, he made a surprise return to the starting line-up in October against Middlesbrough, having only appeared once before that in 2009, and produced a composed central midfield performance in a 1–0 victory for the Pilgrims. He retained his place for three of the club's next four games but soon fell out of favour under head coach Paul Mariner before joining Dagenham on an initial one-month loan in February. After making seven appearances for the Daggers, he returned to Plymouth at the end of March because of a midfield crisis at the club. Despite that he was not called upon and it was announced in May that he was being released.
Southampton (£250,000 from St Etienne, France on 31/7/2003) P/FL 12+2 FLC 2+1 FAC 0+1
Nottingham F (Loaned on 7/1/2005) FL 0+1 FAC 1/1
Preston NE (Loaned on 14/3/2005) FL 0+2
Sheffield Wed (Signed on 31/1/2006) FL 41+12 FLC 0+1/1 FAC 0+1
Plymouth Arg (£200,000 on 11/1/2008) FL 11+11 FLC 1 FAC 0+1
Dagenham & Redbridge (Loaned on 26/2/2010) FL 5+2

FON WILLIAMS Owain
Born: Penygroes, 17 March 1987
Height: 6'4" **Weight:** 12.2
International Honours: W: U21-11; Yth
Owain was virtually ever-present in the League for Stockport. He kept a clean sheet on the opening day of the season, although he then missed the next game – a Carling Cup tie at Huddersfield – after being called up to the Wales squad for a friendly against Montenegro. The goalkeeper made a

string of fine saves to help earn a point in the goalless League One game at Huddersfield and all three points in a 1-0 win at Tranmere. Other clean sheets followed against Carlisle, Exeter and Gillingham. However, over the course of the season, Owain was hindered by a poor and ever-changing defence in front of him, conceding four or more goals on six occasions. His ever-present League run ended when young 'keeper Lloyd Rigby was handed his League debut at Southend in the penultimate game.
Crewe Alex (From trainee on 3/7/2006) Stockport Co (Free on 8/8/2008) FL 77 FLC 1 FAC 6 Others 1

FONTAINE Liam Vaughan Henry
Born: Beckenham, 7 January 1986
Height: 6'3" **Weight:** 12.2
Club Honours: Div 2 '05
International Honours: E: Yth
As dependable as ever, this defender is now adding goals to his game. After netting his first ever goal in 2007-08, he notched two more in 2008-09 to which he added another couple last campaign. He certainly deserved his first, when Preston were defeated 4-1 in January, but his second was more contentious - getting the credit for opening the scoring against Nottingham Forest at Ashton Gate in April, when he got a touch to Bradley Orr's 30-yard screamer.
Fulham (From trainee on 5/3/2004) PL 0+1 FAC 1
Yeovil T (Loaned on 13/8/2004) FL 15 FLC 2 Others 1
Kilmarnock (Loaned on 28/1/2005) SL 3 SC 2
Yeovil T (Loaned on 31/8/2005) FL 10 FLC 1 FAC 0+1
Bristol C (Signed on 16/1/2006) FL 141+20/5 FLC 7 FAC 8+1/1 Others 5+

FONTE Jose Miguel da Rocha
Born: Penafiel, Portugal, 22 December 1983
Height: 6'2" **Weight:** 12.8
Club Honours: AMC '10
International Honours: Portugal: U21-3
One of the most consistent performers at Crystal Palace over the last few seasons, the popular centre-back was an automatic first choice in defence after missing the opening game of the season. Unfortunately for Palace fans, the cascading financial problems of the club enabled Southampton to lure him away in January despite the fact that Jose would be stepping down a division. Confident, skilful and subtle, he settled into the Saints' central defence as if he had been running it for a couple of seasons and his contribution

to a side that lifted the Johnstone's Paint Trophy at Wembley and almost achieved play-off form in the last half of the season could not be understated.
Crystal Palace (Signed from Benfica, Portugal, ex Sporting Lisbon, Salgueiros, Felgueiras, Vitoria Setubal, Pacos de Ferreira - loan, Estrela Amadora - loan, on 31/7/2007) FL 75+7/6 FLC 4 FAC 4 Others 1+1
Southampton (Signed on 9/1/2010) FL 21 Others 3

FORBES Adrian Emmanuel
Born: Greenford, 23 January 1979
Height: 5'8" **Weight:** 11.10
Club Honours: AMC '06
International Honours: E: Yth
After an impressive loan spell with Grimsby in the previous season and a subsequent two-year contract, Adrian was then absent at the start of the campaign following a cartilage operation. Indeed, apart from a run in the side during the autumn when he was seen both on the wing and in attack, injury was to further affect his season. The player also suffered a long-term absence with a broken leg.
Norwich C (From trainee on 21/1/1997) FL 66+46/8 FLC 1+4 FAC 2+2
Luton T (£60,000 on 16/7/2001) FL 39+33/14 FLC 1 FAC 5/6 Others 0+1
Swansea C (Free on 2/7/2004) FL 48+21/11 FLC 1 FAC 5+1 Others 6+4/1
Blackpool (Free on 5/7/2006) FL 26+10/1 FLC 1 FAC 5 Others 4
Millwall (Signed on 4/1/2008) FL 6+7 FAC 2+1
Grimsby T (Free on 2/2/2009) FL 16+12/4 Others 2

FORBES Terrell Dishan
Born: Southwark, 17 August 1981
Height: 6'0" **Weight:** 12.8
Club Honours: FAYC '99
Terrell had a steady, reliable season clocking up more than 40 games in this, his fourth season at Yeovil. Despite being only 28, he found himself the senior defender for long periods of 2009-10. His quiet, unassuming style belies his tough tackling and commitment to the cause and the London-born centre-half even managed to break a goal drought that had lasted almost 12 years when he scored in the local derby against Bristol Rovers in October.
West Ham U (From trainee on 2/7/1999)
Bournemouth (Loaned on 18/10/1999) FL 3 FAC 1
Queens Park Rgrs (Free on 24/7/2001) FL 113+1 FLC 6 FAC 3+1 Others 6
Grimsby T (Free on 15/9/2004) FL 33 Others 1
Oldham Ath (Free on 4/7/2005) FL

33+6 FLC 1 FAC 3 Others 1
Yeovil T *(Free on 21/7/2006) FL*
160+3/1 FLC 5 FAC 4+1 Others 9

FORDE David
Born: Galway, 20 December 1979
Height: 6'2" **Weight:** 13.7
David was Millwall's first choice
goalkeeper for a second season and
completed another full campaign
between the posts in League games. His
performances have become even better
this term, with fine saves at crucial
times allied to a commanding presence
when taking crosses. He was always in
charge of his area and achieved 100
appearances for the Lions with a clean
sheet in the 2-0 win over Leeds at
Elland Road in March.
West Ham U *(£75,000 from Barry T on*
1/2/2002. Freed during 2004 close
season)
Cardiff C *(Signed from Derry C on*
2/1/2007) FL 7
Luton T *(Loaned on 24/8/2007) FL 5*
FLC 1
Bournemouth *(Free on 7/3/2008) FL*
11
Millwall *(Free on 7/7/2008) FL 92 FLC 3*
FAC 10 Others 7

FORECAST Tommy Steven
Born: Newham, 15 October 1986
Height: 6'6" **Weight:** 11.11
An early season loan signing by Grimsby
from Southampton following injury to
Nick Colgan, Tommy's debut for the
Mariners was in a forgettable 4-0 home
loss to Crewe. The big goalkeeper
though, was later in good form to earn
a clean sheet at Bury, helping Town to
their initial victory of the term.
Tottenham H *(From trainee on*
22/2/2007)
Southampton *(Signed on 7/7/2008)*
Grimsby T *(Loaned on 14/8/2009) FL 4*

FORSHAW Adam John
Born: Liverpool, 8 October 1991
Height: 6'1" **Weight:** 11.0
The locally-born player has been at
Everton since the age of eight and
earned a place in the starting line-up
for the first time against BATE Borisov in
the Europa League at Goodison, with
the Toffees already having qualified. The
midfielder will be hoping to develop
further in 2010-11.
Everton *(From trainee on 21/1/2010)*
Others 1

FORSTER Fraser Gerard
Born: Hexham, 17 March 1988
Height: 6'0" **Weight:** 11.13
Club Honours: Div 1 '10
The giant Newcastle goalkeeper started
the season on loan with Bristol Rovers

and impressed with his confident
handling and organisation of his
defence. Then, having returned to
Newcastle he was quickly loaned out to
Norwich for the remainder of the
campaign. Largely unknown prior to his
arrival, Fraser quickly set about building
himself an excellent reputation amongst
colleagues, opponents and supporters.
He made some incredible saves during
the campaign, often at critical times in
big matches, and was particularly adept
at denying opposing strikers when
facing them in one-on-one situations.
With his reputation well and truly
enhanced it remains to be seen if
Norwich can persuade Newcastle and
the player himself that another season
with the Canaries would serve his career
best. Collected the players' 'Player of the
Year' award and finished second in the
club's 'Player of the Year' vote.
Newcastle U *(From trainee on*
4/7/2007)
Stockport Co *(Loaned on 3/10/2008)*
FL 6 Others 1
Bristol Rov *(Loaned on 31/7/2009) FL 4*
Norwich C *(Loaned on 28/8/2009) FL*
38 FAC 1 Others 3

Fraser Forster

FORSTER Nicholas (Nicky) Michael
Born: Caterham, 8 September 1973
Height: 5'10" **Weight:** 11.5
International Honours: E: U21-4
Having topped the scoring charts at
Brighton for the third successive season,
Nicky was hopeful of extending his
career with the club in 2009-10,
perhaps with a view to coaching.
However, his desire for a decision on a
new contract transmuted into an
apparent transfer request and he was

omitted until the position was clarified.
By that time Glenn Murray was playing
as a lone forward in a successful new
formation and the veteran striker was
largely restricted to the bench
thereafter. In March he moved to
Charlton on loan and was immediately
thrown into the side, opening his
scoring account for the Addicks with a
match-winning penalty at MK Dons. He
again scored the only goal in the home
win over against Colchester and
featured in all but one of Charlton's
remaining fixtures. Although now aged
36, Nicky's experience enables him to
get into good positions and he can still
be a handful for opposition defenders.
Gillingham *(Signed from Horley T on*
22/5/1992) FL 54+13/24 FLC 3+2 FAC
6/2
Brentford *(£100,000 on 17/6/1994) FL*
108+1/39 FLC 11/3 FAC 8/1 Others
7+1/4
Birmingham C *(£700,000 on*
31/1/1997) FL 24+44/11 FLC 2+2/1 FAC
3+1
Reading *(£650,000 on 23/6/1999) FL*
157+30/60 FLC 10+1/4 FAC 7+1/2
Others 5+4/2
Ipswich T *(Free on 1/8/2005) FL 21+3/8*
FLC 1
Hull C *(£250,000 on 31/8/2006) FL*
26+9/5 FAC 1+1/1
Brighton & Hove A *(£75,000 on*
6/7/2007) FL 88+10/40 FLC 3/1 FAC
9+2/6 Others 7/4
Charlton Ath *(Loaned on 25/3/2010)*
FL 8/2 Others 0+2

FORTE Jonathan Ronald James
Born: Sheffield, 25 July 1986
Height: 6'2" **Weight:** 12.2
Club Honours: AMC '07
International Honours: Barbados: 2;
E: Yth
After struggling to make much
impression at Scunthorpe in 2008-09,
striker Jonathan was more involved
during this campaign, albeit regularly as
a substitute. Of his 28 League
appearances, 22 were from the bench
and his pace troubled tiring defences. A
skilful, direct left-footed player, who can
play centrally or as a winger, he starred
as the lone striker in the 4-0 win at
Crystal Palace in September but
struggled to establish himself due to the
form of strikers Gary Hooper and Paul
Hayes. Jonathan scored three times,
including the equaliser in the Carling
Cup fourth round tie at Manchester
City.
Sheffield U *(From trainee on 7/7/2004)*
FL 2+28/1 FLC 3+2 FAC 0+4
Doncaster Rov *(Loaned on 31/8/2005)*
FL 6+2/4 Others 1

Doncaster Rov (Loaned on 19/11/2005) FL 3+2 Others 1
Rotherham U (Loaned on 9/1/2006) FL 8+3/4
Doncaster Rov (Loaned on 21/7/2006) FL 31+10/5 FLC 3/3 FAC 4 Others 3/1
Scunthorpe U (Signed on 16/7/2007) FL 25+49/6 FLC 4+2/1 FAC 1+3 Others 1+5
Notts Co (Loaned on 13/11/2008) FL 4/4
Notts Co (Loaned on 16/2/2009) FL 11+3/4

FORTUNE Jonathan (Jon)
Jay
Born: Islington, 23 August 1980
Height: 6'2" **Weight:** 11.4
Jon trained with Sheffield United after his release by Charlton to prove his fitness as he recovered from an Achilles injury and was awarded a short-term contract. After two appearances and recovering from further injuries he signed until the end of the season. A regular on the bench, the defender made three starts in January, producing competent performances and scoring against Reading.
Charlton Ath (From trainee on 2/7/1998) P/FL 140+26/7 FLC 13+2/1 FAC 13+1/2
Mansfield T (Loaned on 18/2/2000) FL 4
Mansfield T (Loaned on 31/8/2000) FL 14
Stoke C (Loaned on 31/1/2007) FL 4
Stoke C (Loaned on 7/3/2007) FL 10/1
Sheffield U (Free on 18/9/2009) FL 3+2/1 FAC 1

FORTUNE Quinton
Born: Cape Town, South Africa, 21 May 1977
Height: 5'11" **Weight:** 11.11
Club Honours: CS '03
International Honours: South Africa: 46; U23-18
Quinton was signed by Doncaster on a six-month contract in the summer after returning to this country from a spell of playing in Belgium. He was mostly on the fringe of the squad but, in September, ten minutes after coming on as a substitute at home to Ipswich, he hit a terrific strike from 30 yards to earn a point for his team. He started the next game at Scunthorpe but was sent off with Rovers leading by two goals. They drew 2-2 at the end. He then suffered from a back injury and was released at the end of January.
Manchester U (£1,500,000 from Atletico Madrid, Spain on 27/8/1999) PL 53+23/5 FLC 8 FAC 8+1/1 Others 19+14/4
Bolton W (Free on 28/7/2006) PL 5+1 FAC 1 (Free during 2007 close season)
Doncaster Rov (Signed from Tubize, Belgium, ex Western Province U, Brescia, on 4/8/2009) FL 3+3/1 FLC 0+1

FOSTER Benjamin (Ben)
Anthony
Born: Leamington Spa, 3 April 1983
Height: 6'2" **Weight:** 12.6
Club Honours: AMC '05; FLC '09
International Honours: E: 4
Manchester United's goalkeeper rocketed to prominence after his transfer from Stoke. Ben was given an early chance to shine when Edwin van der Sar was injured for the first two months of the campaign. He started a run of eight consecutive Premier League games in August, and though he bore criticism for conceding goals to Arsenal and Manchester City, Sir Alex Ferguson publicly stated that he believed in his young goalkeeper's ability and potential. Still vying for an England slot with West Ham's Robert Green, Ben won his third cap against Belarus in a 3-0 win and made a brilliant one-handed save from Sergei Omelyanchuk in the second half. Also playing against Brazil in November, at club level he was superseded by Tomasz Kuszczak, before van der Sar returned to full fitness.
Stoke C (Signed from Racing Club Warwick on 25/4/2001)
Kidderminster Hrs (Loaned on 29/10/2004) FL 2
Wrexham (Loaned on 24/1/2005) FL 17 Others 4
Manchester U (£1,000,000 on 22/7/2005) PL 12 FLC 4 FAC 3 Others 4
Watford (Loaned on 2/8/2005) FL 44 FAC 1 Others 3
Watford (Loaned on 10/8/2006) PL 29 FLC 1 FAC 3

FOSTER Daniel (Danny)
Born: Enfield, 23 September 1984
Height: 5'10" **Weight:** 12.10
Club Honours: FC '07
A calm defender who understands his job and does it in a quiet way, Danny joined Brentford from Dagenham in the summer. Despite starting the majority of the Bees' fixtures at right-back, he was never totally certain of his position at the club, with other players being given opportunities to progress. He is also a useful crosser of the ball in attacking situations.
Tottenham H (From trainee on 25/7/2002)
Dagenham & Redbridge (Free on 1/7/2004) FL 69+1/3 FLC 1 FAC 6 Others 1
Brentford (Free on 2/7/2009) FL 32+4 FLC 1 FAC 4 Others 1

FOSTER Stephen
Born: Mansfield, 3 December 1974
Height: 6'1" **Weight:** 12.0
Club Honours: FAT '97; Div 3 '04; Div 1 '07
Stephen started the season where he left off, as a rock in the centre of Darlington's defence with his customary dominating performances. However, after four months of the season he became embroiled in a dispute with the club over the extension of his contract and failed to start a game after the end of November. Eventually, he was allowed to leave at the end of February and joined Blyth Spartans. It was an ignominious end to an outstanding two-and-a-half seasons and over 100 games for Darlington, many as captain.
Mansfield T (From trainee on 15/7/1993) FL 2+3 FLC 2 (Free to Telford U on 22/1/1994)
Bristol Rov (£150,000 from Woking on 23/5/1997) FL 193+4/7 FLC 14 FAC 13 Others 11
Doncaster Rov (Free on 1/8/2002) FL 95/2 FLC 7 FAC 3 Others 3
Scunthorpe U (Free on 19/1/2006) FL 62 FLC 2 FAC 3 Others 1
Darlington (Free on 18/7/2007) FL 91+1/2 FLC 4 FAC 4 Others 7/1

FOSTER Stephen (Steve)
John
Born: Warrington, 10 September 1980
Height: 5'11" **Weight:** 11.8
International Honours: E: Sch
The Barnsley skipper again played more games for the Reds than anyone else during the season and led the team from the front. He is a player who one could say likes to defend. Steve was at his best when playing against a big centre-forward because it was then that his prowess in the air was seen most clearly. He was also a force in the other area and a constant threat from set pieces. He signed a new two-year extension to his contract, taking him to the summer of 2012.
Crewe Alex (From trainee on 19/9/1998) FL 200+18/15 FLC 9+1/2 FAC 10+1/1 Others 4
Burnley (Free on 2/8/2006) FL 7+10 FLC 2 FAC 1
Barnsley (£100,000 on 24/8/2007) FL 121/6 FLC 5 FAC 7/2

FOX Daniel (Danny)
Born: Winsford, 29 May 1986
Height: 6'0" **Weight:** 12.6
Club Honours: Div 2 '07
International Honours: S: 4. E: U21-1
Danny joined Burnley in January from Glasgow Celtic, signing a three-and-a-half year contract. He made an instant impact, scoring spectacularly from a free kick on his debut at home to West Ham, as well as putting in a fine shift at left-back. While never reaching such heights again, he established himself as the Clarets' first choice in that position and looked competent enough

although hampered by the fact that the whole back line often struggled against top-class opposition. A player who can be dangerous on the overlap, Danny may well be able to display more of that side of his game in the Championship next season.
Everton *(From trainee on 10/7/2004)*
Walsall *(Free on 1/7/2005) FL 98+1/6 FLC 4 FAC 11 Others 4*
Coventry C *(£300,000 on 28/1/2008) FL 57/6 FLC 2 FAC 3+1*
Glasgow Celtic *(£1,500,000 on 24/7/2009)*
Burnley *(Signed on 29/1/2010) PL 13+1/1*

FOX David Lee
Born: Leek, 13 December 1983
Height: 5'9" **Weight:** 12.2
International Honours: E: Yth
Having been released by Championship side Blackpool, David was persuaded by manager Paul Lambert to sign a three-year deal with League One outfit Colchester at the start of the season. Things started so well for the central midfield playmaker when he scored a free kick in the opening day 7-1 win at Norwich and again netted a week later against Yeovil. Aidy Boothroyd soon took over as U's boss, though, and David quickly found himself out of favour. Described by Boothroyd as 'probably the best footballer at the club', he seemingly did not fit into the team's more physical style and started just ten games in nine months.
Manchester U *(From trainee on 18/12/2000)*
Shrewsbury T *(Loaned on 8/10/2004) FL 2+2/1 Others 1*
Blackpool *(Free on 20/1/2006) FL 68+26/6 FLC 5 FAC 7/1 Others 0+2*
Colchester U *(Free on 2/7/2009) FL 15+3/3 FAC 2 Others 1*

FOX Nathan James
Born: Leicester, 14 November 1992
Height: 5'10" **Weight:** 12.2
Nathan is the first of the new crop of youngsters from the re-formed Centre of Excellence at Notts County to be given a brief outing with the seniors. A talented left-back or midfield player, he made his debut in a substitute appearance against Darlington and showed some promise for the future.
Notts Co *(Trainee) FL 0+1*

FRAMPTON Andrew (Andy) James Kerr
Born: Wimbledon, 3 September 1979
Height: 5'11" **Weight:** 10.10
Andy found a tough challenge for the left-sided defensive roles at Millwall from Darren Ward and Tony Craig after

picking up an injury in mid-winter. Another player with a superb work-ethic, he always gives 100 per cent, whether on defensive duty or supporting midfield going forward. Andy played his 100th game for Millwall in the FA Cup tie at Staines.
Crystal Palace *(From trainee on 8/5/1998) FL 19+9 FLC 3+1 FAC 2*
Brentford *(Free on 28/10/2002) FL 121+13/4 FLC 2 FAC 15+2/2 Others 11/1*
Millwall *(Signed on 27/6/2007) FL 80+8/4 FLC 4 FAC 12/1 Others 6+1*

FRANCE Ryan
Born: Sheffield, 13 December 1980
Height: 5'11" **Weight:** 11.11
Having had a pre-season trial with Sheffield Wednesday, Ryan moved across the city to sign for Sheffield United as a utility cover player and he made his debut as a wide midfielder on the opening day of the season. He twice made the starting line-up at right-back and made several substitute appearances. Was a regular on the bench until an injury in training brought his season to an early end.
Hull C *(£15,000 from Alfreton T on 24/9/2003) P/FL 76+57/6 FLC 5+1/1 FAC 6+4/1 Others 2/1*
Sheffield U *(Free on 24/7/2009) FL 3+6 FLC 1*

FRANCIS Simon Charles
Born: Nottingham, 16 February 1985
Height: 6'0" **Weight:** 12.6
International Honours: E: Yth
Primarily the right-back at Southend, Simon can also deputise at centre-back or right midfield when needed. His overlapping and delivery of accurate crosses was useful in midfield and from the back. At times during his career at Roots Hall, Simon has struggled to hold down a regular place but this season he was a fixture at right-back and delivered his most consistent performances for the club. In November, Simon passed 150 appearances for Southend and his improved form earned him the fans' 'Player of the Year' award..
Bradford C *(From trainee on 3/5/2003) FL 49+6/1 FLC 1 FAC 1*
Sheffield U *(£200,000 on 16/3/2004) FL 6+6 FLC 2 FAC 0+1*
Grimsby T *(Loaned on 26/9/2005) FL 5 Others 1*
Tranmere Rov *(Loaned on 18/11/2005) FL 16+1/1*
Southend U *(£70,000 on 16/6/2006) FL 138+19/4 FLC 7+3 FAC 8+1/2 Others 4*

FRANCO Guillermo (Guille) Luis
Born: Corrientes, Argentina, 3 November 1976

Height: 6'0" **Weight:** 12.0
International Honours: Mexico: 21
The Mexican striker signed for West Ham in September from the Spanish club Villarreal. Guille is a very intelligent and clever player and he immediately set up a promising partnership with Carlton Cole. He likes to drop deep to cause problems and then pick out Cole with astute passes. He was also on the score sheet with goals against Sunderland in October and Hull in November. Then, against Burnley, he was outstanding as he set up Junior Stanislas for the second goal and scored with a header as the Hammers hit five. After suffering a thigh injury at Tottenham in December he was missing for five games but returned in late February to play a big part in the defeat of Hull. He is the link between the midfield and Cole up front and offers something different to the team. During the campaign he added to his caps for Mexico and helped them reach the World Cup finals. He was in their 23 for South Africa. Was out of contract at the end of June.
West Ham U *(Free from Villareal, Spain, ex San Lorenzo, Monterrey, on 17/9/2009) PL 16+7/5*

FRANCOMB Georgie (George)
Born: Hackney, 8 September 1991
Height: 5'11" **Weight:** 11.5
George is a stylish right-back who, as a second-year scholar, made three first team starts for Norwich. Confident and composed when in possession of the ball, he is a natural competitor and something of a dead-ball specialist with the youth team, scoring more than his fair share of goals. He can also play in the centre of defence or in a holding midfield role with such versatility helping him earn the offer of his first professional contract.
Norwich C *(Trainee) FL 2 Others 1*

FRANKS Jonathan Ian
Born: Stockton, 8 April 1990
Height: 5'9" **Weight:** 11.5
International Honours: E: Yth
After his debut as a substitute in Middlesbrough's last game in the Premier League in 2009, Jonathan was rewarded with a three-year contract. Having been involved with the squad all season, his career took off when Gordon Strachan became manager. Jonathan impressed with his attitude in training and soon made his first start at Barnsley in December. Initially, he featured in an unfamiliar role on the left-wing but stood out through his work and endeavour. He scored his first

senior goal in an impressive 4-1 win at Doncaster. Further goals followed against Preston, and a clincher at Plymouth as Boro strove to reach the play-offs.
Middlesbrough *(From juniors on 6/7/2007) P/FL 9+15/3 FAC 1*

FRASER Thomas (Tommy) Francis Peter
Born: Brighton, 5 December 1987
Height: 5'11" **Weight:** 12.6
The Port Vale midfield player had a good first season and became the youngest captain in the Football League. He was a major player in the centre of the park and at the hub of all of Vale's attacking moves. He always gives 100 per cent and never shirked, also taking the majority of the dead-ball kicks. Tommy scored just one goal, a close-range header against Accrington. He missed three games through suspension and was left out for the last few games.
Brighton & Hove A *(From trainee on 28/6/2006) FL 51+28/2 FLC 3+1 FAC 7+2/1 Others 7+4*
Port Vale *(Free on 2/7/2009) FL 33+5/1 FLC 3 FAC 1 Others 2*

FRAUGHAN Ryan Stephen
Born: Liverpool, 11 February 1991
Height: 5'7" **Weight:** 11.2
Ryan is a central midfielder who can also play in attack and has been on Tranmere's books since the age of 14. Ryan shows great potential and is a fine passer of the ball, with the enviable ability to carve open the opposition defence. He creates plenty of chances for his team-mates and is no slouch himself in front of goal, finding the net three times for the reserves. Ryan has incredible stamina and pace while his work rate is also good. In order to gain some first team experience, Ryan joined Welsh Premier League side Aberystwyth Town on loan in January for the rest of the season and scored three times for them.
Tranmere Rov *(From trainee on 3/1/2009) FL 1+5 FLC 0+1 Others 0+1*

FRECKLINGTON Lee Craig
Born: Lincoln, 8 September 1985
Height: 5'8" **Weight:** 11.0
International Honours: RoI: B-1
Lee had an in-and-out season at Peterborough, not helped by the merry-go-round of managers, each with their own ideas, who never really gave him time to settle. He was signed from Lincoln near the end of the previous season after being on loan at London Road and the fans had high hopes of seeing a repetition of the surging runs

and powerful shots they knew were within his capacity. Lee likes nothing better than to attack from midfield but was more often used in a holding role in that department.
Lincoln C *(From trainee on 3/8/2005) FL 97+27/21 FLC 2+1/1 FAC 5/1 Others 6+3*
Peterborough U *(Signed on 10/2/2009) FL 28+14/2 FLC 4/2 FAC 1*

FREDRIKSEN Jon Andre
Born: Moss, Norway, 5 April 1982
Height: 5'11" **Weight:** 12.0
A skilful left-sided utility player signed by Hartlepool during the close season, Jon was new to English football but looked sharp in the pre-season friendlies and began in the centre of midfield. After two promising performances and a short run, he was relegated to the bench. In the remainder of the season, unable to regain a place, he had to be content with reserve team football.
Hartlepool U *(Free from Sarpsborg 08, Norway, ex Rade, Moss FK, on 13/7/2009) FL 4+8 FLC 1+1*

FREEDMAN Douglas (Dougie) Alan
Born: Glasgow, 21 January 1974

Height: 5'9" **Weight:** 11.2
International Honours: S: 2; B-1; U21-8; Sch
Now a veteran campaigner, his touch, ability and vast experience are valuable assets in Steve Tilson's youthful Southend side and, although not a regular starter due to some niggling fitness issues, Dougie made valuable appearances from the bench. He has been a model professional during his spell at Southend. His willingness to pass on his knowledge and advice to youngsters led to him leaving Roots Hall in February, where he was held in the highest esteem, to be first team coach under Paul Hart at Crystal Palace.
Queens Park Rgrs *(From trainee on 15/5/1992)*
Barnet *(Free on 26/7/1994) FL 47/27 FLC 6/5 FAC 2 Others 2*
Crystal Palace *(£800,000 on 8/9/1995) P/FL 72+18/31 FLC 3+2/1 FAC 2+1 Others 3+2/2*
Wolverhampton W *(£800,000 on 17/10/1997) FL 25+4/10 FAC 5+1/2*
Nottingham F *(£950,000 on 12/8/1998) P/FL 50+20/18 FLC 8+1/4 FAC 3+1/1*
Crystal Palace *(£600,000 on 23/10/2000) P/FL 141+96/64 FLC 14+1/9 FAC 5+5/1 Others 1+2*

Brad Friedel

Leeds U (Loaned on 7/3/2008) FL 9+2/5
Others 3/1
Southend U (Free on 2/9/2008) FL
21+15/6 FLC 0+1 FAC 1+2 Others 0+1

FRIEDEL Bradley (Brad)
Howard
Born: Lakewood, Ohio, USA, 18 May
1971
Height: 6'3" **Weight:** 14.7
Club Honours: FLC '02
International Honours: USA: 82
Aston Villa's veteran goalkeeper
continued to produce performances
that belied his age as part of one of the
meanest defences in the Premier
League. Brad kept 15 clean sheets in
the top flight - a record bettered only by
Petr Cech of Chelsea, and Liverpool's
Pepe Reina, who both kept 17. Having
started a long run of consecutive
Premier League games at Blackburn,
Brad's final game of last season was his
228th in a row. The retired United
States international's unbeatable form
meant frustration for his young
compatriot and understudy Brad Guzan
who has yet to make his full League
debut. Offering a consistently safe pair
of hands, Brad particularly excelled in
the 0-0 draw at Tottenham and 1-0
derby victory over Birmingham with a
string of world-class saves. Brad has 12
months left on his three-year deal but
such has been his form that there is talk
of him agreeing an extension which will
enable him to play top flight football
into his 40s. He puts his longevity in the
game down to practising yoga and a
sensible diet.
Liverpool (£1,000,000 from Columbus
Crew, USA on 23/12/1997) PL 25 FLC 4
Others 1+1
Blackburn Rov (Free on 7/11/2000)
P/FL 288/1 FLC 20 FAC 29 Others 20
Aston Villa (£2,000,000 on 28/7/2008)
PL 76 FLC 1 FAC 6 Others 5

FRIEND George Andrew
Jordan
Born: Barnstaple, 19 October 1987
Height: 6'2" **Weight:** 13.0
Unable to get a regular place at
Wolverhampton, the left-sided defender
was loaned to Millwall, Southend,
Scunthorpe and Exeter in 2009-10. He
did play once for Wanderers, in the
Premier League at Manchester United,
where he was close to opening the
scoring. Having made seven
appearances at Millwall at the start of
the season as cover for Nadjin Abdou,
he moved on to Southend in September
and quickly became a big hit with the
fans for his all-action style and his
accuracy from set pieces, the latter
being highlighted with a superb strike

from a free kick against Southampton
at Roots Hall. Unfortunately, due to
financial constraints at United the
manager, Steve Tilson, was unable to
extend his loan due to the club being
placed under a transfer embargo and
George opted for a spell at Scunthorpe
at the end of October. Arriving at
Glanford Park as cover for left-back he
started two games, but with the team
struggling defensively George was
unable to make much impact and after
six weeks he was recalled to Molineux.
In March, he returned to Exeter, where
he had first made his name, and almost
immediately made a defensive position
his own. Always comfortable on the
ball, his arrival coincided with City
putting together a spell of one defeat in
13 games, George chipping in with a
header in the crucial draw against
Charlton in April. Was out of contract in
the summer.
Exeter C (From juniors on 5/6/2006) FL
4 FLC 1
Wolverhampton W (£350,000 on
1/9/2008) P/FL 5+2 FAC 1
Millwall (Loaned on 11/8/2009) FL 4+2
Others 1
Southend U (Loaned on 18/9/2009) FL
5+1/1
Scunthorpe U (Loaned on 30/10/2009)
FL 2+2
Exeter C (Loaned on 4/3/2010) FL 13/1

FRY Matthew (Matt) Ronald
Born: Longfield, 26 September 1990
Height: 6'1" **Weight:** 12.0
A natural left-footer, Matt joined
Gillingham on loan from West Ham in
October to fill the void left by the
injured Simon King at centre-half. He
made his League debut in the Gills' 2-0
defeat at MK Dons but was
instrumental in helping the back four to
a run of five consecutive clean sheets at
home. Good in the air and fearless in
the tackle, he is also comfortable on the
ball and has good passing skills. Matt
made a big impression at Gillingham
and only injury prevented the club from
extending his loan.
West Ham U (From trainee on
1/7/2009)
Gillingham (Loaned on 15/10/2009) FL
11 FAC 2

FRYATT Matthew (Matty)
Charles
Born: Nuneaton, 5 March 1986
Height: 5'10" **Weight:** 12.4
Club Honours: Div 1 '09
International Honours: E: Yth
Highly-rated striker who continued to
find the net regularly back in the
Championship for Leicester before an
horrendous double fracture of the jaw,

sustained in the home clash with
Doncaster, threatened to bring his
season to a premature end. He
reappeared from the bench in the final
fixture of the regular season and again
in the first leg of the play-offs, before
being restored to the starting line-up in
South Wales, where his strike brought
the Foxes back into contention. Matty
was at his most prolific during the early
weeks of the season, when nominated
for a 'Player of the Month' award, and
still topped the Foxes' overall goal chart
with 13 to his name.
Walsall (From trainee on 28/4/2003) FL
49+21/27 FLC 0+1 FAC 3/2 Others
3+1/1
Carlisle U (Loaned on 18/12/2003) FL
9+1/1
Leicester C (Signed on 10/1/2006) FL
132+24/49 FLC 6+1/2 FAC 6+1/5
Others 2+3/2

FULLER Barry Marc
Born: Ashford, 25 September 1984
Height: 5'10" **Weight:** 11.10
Club Honours: FAT '07
International Honours: E: SP-1
A tough-tackling right-back, Barry is not
the most technically gifted player but
always compensates for his
shortcomings with his energetic and
wholehearted displays. Gillingham's
captain, Barry is never one to shirk a 50-
50 challenge or fail to put his head in
when the boots are flying. As a result
he has collected more than his fair
share of injuries. A broken arm kept
him out for five weeks in March, while
his season was curtailed in April by a
broken nose. A favourite with
Gillingham's supporters, he finished
runner-up in the club's 'Player of the
Year' award. Was out of contract at the
end of June.
Charlton Ath (From trainee on
15/1/2004. Free to Stevenage Borough
on 2/7/2006)
Barnet (Loaned on 14/1/2006) FL 15/1
Gillingham (Free on 28/1/2008) FL
81+2 FLC 3 FAC 6 Others 5

FULLER Joshua (Josh) Piers
Born: Grimsby, 9 February 1992
Height: 5'9" **Weight:** 10.12
Josh continued his development with
selection in Grimsby's first team squad
at the start of the campaign. The right-
sided midfielder showed confidence on
the ball, going on to play his part in a
rare Mariners' victory over Hereford.
Town's ongoing relegation battle and
change of manager thereafter saw Josh
out of favour, apart from in the FA Cup
exit to Bath City.
Grimsby T (From trainee on
18/11/2009) FL 2+4 FAC 0+1 Others 1

FULLER Ricardo Dwayne

Born: Kingston, Jamaica, 31 October 1979
Height: 6'3" **Weight:** 13.3
International Honours: Jamaica: 60
The popular and unpredictable Jamaican striker remains the talisman of this Stoke side and it is hard to imagine how they could perform without him. This was not his most productive season in terms of goals scored – three in the League and eight overall – but his other efforts, in leading the forward line and providing chances for team-mates, more than made amends. Stoke won four League away games and all the winning goals were either scored by Ricardo or set up by him. He is at the heart and soul of everything Stoke try to do and his willingness to harry defenders and plough a lonely furrow up front makes him indispensable. His winning goal at West Ham, where he picked up the ball outside the area and took on the home defence single handed before slotting past Robert Green, was as good an individual flair goal as could have been seen from any Premier League striker last season. Ricardo is a true fans' favourite at Stoke and whenever he gets possession in the final third, everybody is up from their seats in expectation and anticipation.
Crystal Palace (£1,000,000 from Tivoli Gardens, Jamaica on 19/2/2001) FL 2+6
Heart of Midlothian (Loaned on 19/10/2001) SL 27/8 SC 2/2
Preston NE (£500,000 on 1/7/2002) FL 57+1/27 FLC 2+1/2 FAC 2/2
Portsmouth (£200,000 + on 27/8/2004) PL 13+18/1 FLC 3+1 FAC 1+1
Southampton (£340,000 on 5/8/2005) FL 22+9/9 FLC 0+1 FAC 0+1
Ipswich T (Loaned on 24/2/2006) FL 3/2
Stoke C (Signed on 30/8/2006) P/FL 111+30/39 FLC 1+3/1 FAC 8+1/5

FULOP Marton

Born: Budapest, Hungary, 3 May 1983
Height: 6'6" **Weight:** 14.7
International Honours: Hungary: 20; U21-11
The Hungarian international goalkeeper began the season with an opening day clean sheet as Sunderland won at Bolton, but after three games Craig Gordon took over upon his return from injury. This allowed Marton to rest a heel injury of his own before he returned in November when coming on as a sub at Tottenham, his former club, after Gordon suffered a broken arm. A run of ten consecutive starts for Marton followed, which was ended after Chelsea scored seven against him and a

fit again Gordon returned. Soon afterwards he ceased even being on the bench before ending the season in sensational style when answering Manchester City's need for an emergency goalkeeper following injury to Shay Given. Marton played the final three games of the season for City, which included the so called 'Champions League play-off' against Tottenham.
Tottenham H (Signed from MTK Hungaria, Hungary on 8/6/2004)
Chesterfield (Loaned on 11/3/2005) FL 7
Coventry C (Loaned on 28/10/2005) FL 31 FAC 2
Sunderland (£500,000 on 23/11/2006) P/FL 44+1 FLC 2 FAC 3
Leicester C (Loaned on 17/8/2007) FL 24 FLC 3
Manchester C (Loaned on 27/4/2010) PL 3

FURLONG Paul Anthony

Born: Wood Green, 1 October 1968
Height: 6'0" **Weight:** 13.8
Club Honours: FAT '88
International Honours: E: SP-5
One of the oldest players in the Football League, Paul was still a regular in the Barnet team at the age of 41. He could not repeat his scoring record of the previous campaign, but was an important member of the Bees' side and chipped in with several goals. Missed out on the chance to be the oldest ever player to score a hat-trick in the Football League when he scored twice in the home game against Chesterfield but missed a penalty. Popular with Barnet fans and throughout the game, it looks likely Paul will be hanging up his boots after enjoying a great career.
Coventry C (£130,000 from Enfield on 31/7/1991) FL 27+10/4 FLC 4/1 FAC 1+1 Others 1
Watford (£250,000 on 24/7/1992) FL 79/37 FLC 7/4 FAC 2 Others 3
Chelsea (£2,300,000 on 26/5/1994) PL 44+20/13 FLC 3+1 FAC 5+5/1 Others 7/3
Birmingham C (£1,500,000 on 17/7/1996) FL 104+27/50 FLC 11+2/3 FAC 5/3 Others 4
Queens Park Rgrs (Loaned on 18/8/2000) FL 3/1
Sheffield U (Loaned on 8/2/2002) FL 4/2
Queens Park Rgrs (Free on 8/8/2002) FL 137+31/56 FLC 3+1 FAC 2+1 Others 4+1/1
Luton T (Free on 7/8/2007) FL 24+8/8 FLC 3+1/2 FAC 1+1 Others 1/2
Southend U (Free on 3/7/2008) FL 1+2 FLC 1
Barnet (Free on 21/1/2009) FL 52+7/14 FLC 1 FAC 3

FURMAN Dean

Born: Cape Town, South Africa, 22 June 1988
Height: 6'0" **Weight:** 11.6
An exciting young midfielder, Dean was signed by Oldham from Glasgow Rangers in the summer. Dean is a busy box-to-box player with energy to burn. Considered for South Africa's World Cup squad but left out at the last cut, Dean will look to establish himself as a big hitter in League One next season. With 41 appearances for Oldham under his belt in his first season in England, Dean surprisingly failed to score.
Glasgow Rgrs (From trainee at Chelsea on 15/5/2006) SL 0+1
Bradford C (Loaned on 29/8/2008) FL 26+6/4 Others 1
Oldham Ath (Free on 2/7/2009) FL 32+6 FLC 1 FAC 1 Others 1

FUSEINI Ali

Born: Accra, Ghana, 7 December 1988
Height: 5'9" **Weight:** 12.11
With tough competition for central midfield places, Ali found it hard to break into the Millwall side. When he did, he put in his usual battling, hard-working displays. Unfortunately, he suffered a recurring injury problem as well, playing in the first 13 games of the season before being ruled out for two months. Was out of contract in the summer.
Millwall (From trainee on 27/9/2006) FL 57+19/2 FLC 3 FAC 7+2 Others 1+1

FUTCHER Benjamin (Ben) Paul

Born: Manchester, 20 February 1981
Height: 6'6" **Weight:** 12.4
The towering centre-back once again proved himself as a stalwart at the heart of the Bury defence, rotating with Ryan Cresswell and Efe Sodje in accordance with form and injuries. Tough and experienced, he unfortunately could not help the Shakers into the League Two play-offs for what would have been his seventh attempt at the sudden-death stage.
Oldham Ath (From trainee on 5/7/1999) FL 2+8 FAC 0+1 (Free to Stalybridge Celtic on 3/1/2000)
Lincoln C (Free from Doncaster Rov on 7/8/2002) FL 119+2/13 FLC 3 FAC 4/1 Others 1/2
Boston U (Free on 8/7/2005) FL 13+1 FAC 3/1 Others 2
Grimsby T (Signed on 12/1/2006) FL 15+4/2 FLC 1 Others 1+2/1
Peterborough U (Signed on 25/8/2006) FL 22+3/3 FAC 3 Others 2
Bury (Free on 16/7/2007) FL 102+4/2 FLC 3 FAC 4+1/1 Others 9/1

G

GABBIDON Daniel (Danny) Leon
Born: Cwmbran, 8 August 1979
Height: 6'1" **Weight:** 11.2
International Honours: W: 43; U21-17; Yth
For the West Ham central defender, it was another frustrating campaign. With his experience, Danny can always be relied upon to do a good job, either in central defence or covering as a full-back. A succession of niggling injuries meant that he appeared in only ten Premier League games, with his best performance being against Burnley in November. Danny added to his collection of international caps for Wales during the season.
West Bromwich A (From trainee on 3/7/1998) FL 20 FLC 4+1 FAC 2
Cardiff C (£175,000 on 10/8/2000) FL 194+3/10 FLC 8 FAC 11 Others 3
West Ham U (Signed on 5/7/2005) PL 65+5 FLC 5+1 FAC 8 Others 2

Peter Gain

GAIN Peter Thomas
Born: Hammersmith, 11 November 1976
Height: 6'1" **Weight:** 11.0
International Honours: RoI: U21-1; Yth
Peter played as a left-sided midfielder or in the centre of midfield for Dagenham and showed no sign of the knee problems that had cost him eight weeks of the previous season. He is never one to shirk a tackle and while that is one of his strengths, it also led to him being

suspended on two occasions for reaching the requisite number of bookings. Peter's experience shone throughout the season and was of great assistance to the team's younger players.
Tottenham H (From trainee on 1/7/1995)
Lincoln C (Loaned on 31/12/1998) FL 0+3 Others 1
Lincoln C (£15,000 on 26/3/1999) FL 195+29/21 FLC 7+1 FAC 9+1/1 Others 14+2
Peterborough U (Free on 4/7/2005) FL 63+8/9 FLC 2+1 FAC 2+2 Others 2
Dagenham & Redbridge (Free on 17/1/2008) FL 91+1/4 FLC 2 FAC 4 Others 5

GALL Kevin Alexander
Born: Merthyr Tydfil, 4 February 1982
Height: 5'9" **Weight:** 11.1
Club Honours: Div 2 '05
International Honours: W: U21-8; Yth; Sch
Kevin was another player who had previously been on loan at Darlington, in early 2008. His hard running and determination to chase every ball saw him score on his return debut against Accrington and bag another at Cheltenham. However he was released after 11 starts and one outing from the bench, joining Blue Square Premier club York.
Newcastle U (From trainee on 29/4/1999)
Bristol Rov (Free on 22/3/2001) FL 28+22/5 FLC 2 FAC 2+2 Others 2+2
Yeovil T (Free on 4/2/2003) FL 80+43/13 FLC 3+2/1 FAC 9+2/1 Others 3+1/1
Carlisle U (Free on 3/8/2006) FL 54+12/9 FLC 2+1 FAC 3 Others 1+2/2
Darlington (Loaned on 28/1/2008) FL 7+1
Lincoln C (Loaned on 29/7/2008) FL 6+3 FLC 1 Others 0+1
Port Vale (Loaned on 24/2/2009) FL 7
Darlington (Free on 20/8/2009) FL 9+1/2 Others 2

GALLAGHER Paul
Born: Glasgow, 9 August 1984
Height: 6'1" **Weight:** 12.0
International Honours: S: 1; B-1; U21-11
Returning to the Blackburn side after a long spell on loan, the skilful striker who can also operate in a wide role was brought on for the last 15 minutes of the opening game against Manchester City in an unusual central midfield role and looked creative. He was then transferred to Leicester where he mostly found himself playing under Nigel Pearson. Paul demonstrated rare

moments of his class during the campaign, with a smart brace against Crystal Palace, a neat hat-trick against Scunthorpe and a stunning free kick against Nottingham Forest, as well as delivering a host of important set pieces for the Foxes throughout.
Blackburn Rov (From trainee on 5/2/2003) PL 19+42/6 FLC 0+3/1 FAC 5+2/1 Others 2+2
Stoke C (Loaned on 29/8/2005) FL 32+5/11 FAC 3/1
Preston NE (Loaned on 31/8/2007) FL 15+4/1
Stoke C (Loaned on 31/1/2008) FL 2+5
Plymouth Arg (Loaned on 30/8/2008) FL 36+4/13 FAC 1
Leicester C (Signed on 21/8/2009) FL 31+10/7 FLC 1 FAC 1+1 Others 2

GALLAS William Eric
Born: Paris, France, 17 August 1977
Height: 6'1" **Weight:** 12.7
Club Honours: FLC '05; PL '05, '06; CS '05
International Honours: France: 82; U21-11; Yth
William struck up an immediate understanding with his new central defensive partner Thomas Vermaelen and both scored in the crushing opening day win at Everton. He enjoyed his best season to date in an Arsenal shirt as he played every moment of the Premier League campaign until injury thwarted him in February. An ill-fated return against Barcelona in the home Champions League quarter-final only served to worsen the problem and ruled him out for the rest of the season. William is out of contract in June and rumours suggest he may have played his last game for Arsenal. If so, he will be a difficult player to replace as, when fully focused, he remains an excellent centre-half. He featured 26 times in the Premier League, scoring three goals, eight times in the Champions League, scoring one, and once in the FA Cup. He was named in France's World Cup squad.
Chelsea (£6,200,000 from Olympique Marseille, France, ex SM Caen, on 4/7/2001) PL 147+12/12 FLC 13 FAC 17/1 Others 36/1
Arsenal (Signed on 31/8/2006) PL 101/12 FLC 1 FAC 9/1 Others 31/4

GALLINAGH Andrew (Andy) Anthony
Born: Sutton Coldfield, 16 March 1985
Height: 5'8" **Weight:** 11.8
Versatile Andy played an important part as Cheltenham battled successfully against the drop from League Two. A product of the youth team, Andy operated in a number of positions,

starting in the centre of midfield before he was pressed into action as a centre-back then at right-back in a constantly changing team. His consistent performances and diligent attitude earned him the offer of an extended contract.
Cheltenham T (Signed from Stratford T on 30/9/2004) FL 90+16/2 FLC 2+2 FAC 4+2 Others 4+1

Andy Gallinagh

GAMBLE Joseph (Joe) Finbar
Born: Cork, 14 January 1982
Height: 5'6" **Weight:** 11.3
International Honours: RoI: U21-5; Yth
The tenacious central midfielder joined Hartlepool in the January transfer window after training with the club for several weeks. An experienced Cork City player, he first attracted manager Chris Turner's attention when Pool were looking to sign Denis Behan and Colin Healy from the Irish club. Although short of match fitness, Joe went straight into the starting line-up and slotted in well to tighten the midfield. A valuable ball winner who has helped to boost Hartlepool's possession in the centre of the field, from his January debut he was an ever-present to the end of the season.
Reading (Signed from Cork C on 8/8/2000) FL 2+5 FLC 0+2 FAC 1+1 Others 2 (Freed during 2004 close season)
Hartlepool U (Signed from Cork C on 5/1/2010) FL 22/2

GARCIA Richard
Born: Perth, Australia, 4 September 1981
Height: 6'1" **Weight:** 11.2
Club Honours: FAYC '99

International Honours: Australia: 6; U23; Yth
Richard's hopes were cruelly dashed when he damaged knee ligaments in a freak training ground accident at the end of July. It was three months before he returned to Hull's senior ranks and confirmed his recovery by making the most of his aerial ability in scoring both goals in a 2-2 draw against Atalanta in the invitation Achille e Cesare Bortolotti Trophy match played in Bergamo. Having been tried at right-back in the reserves, Richard duly returned to his familiar berth of the right of midfield. That was until history repeated itself in April when he suffered another knee injury in training. As well as ruling Richard out of key matches in City's unsuccessful battle against relegation, it also was a severe blow to his hopes of reclaiming his place in Australia's World Cup squad, although he was boosted by a place in the provisional 31.
West Ham U (From trainee on 16/9/1998) P/FL 4+12 FLC 0+5 FAC 0+1
Leyton Orient (Loaned on 11/8/2000) FL 18/4 FLC 3
Colchester U (Signed on 3/9/2004) FL 62+20/16 FLC 2+1 FAC 7+2/2 Others 5/3
Hull C (Free on 5/7/2007) P/FL 62+17/6 FLC 1+1/1 FAC 4+2 Others 3/1

GARDNER Anthony Derek
Born: Stone, 19 September 1980
Height: 6'5" **Weight:** 13.8
International Honours: E: 1; U21-1
Having enjoyed a productive pre-season and featured in Hull's first two games, the strapping left-sided centre-back's injury jinx struck yet again when he suffered a knee injury in training. Anthony returned in October for the visit of relegation rivals Portsmouth and was appointed captain for the crucial game, a position he held for much of the season. With the influential defender in their ranks, the Tigers maintained their hopes of retaining Premier League status. They suffered a massive blow in February when he sustained ankle ligament damage under no challenge at West Ham. By the time Anthony returned with three games to play, City were all but down.
Port Vale (From trainee on 31/7/1998) FL 40+1/4 FLC 2 FAC 1
Tottenham H (£1,000,000 on 28/1/2000) FL 94+20/2 FLC 13/1 FAC 11+3 Others 3
Hull C (£2,500,000 on 21/8/2008) PL 30 FAC 2

GARDNER Craig
Born: Solihull, 25 November 1986
Height: 5'10" **Weight:** 11.13

International Honours: E: U21-14
Craig sealed a dream move from Aston Villa to Birmingham, his boyhood club, in January and forced his way into the side wide on the right where his thrusting play and aggression made him popular and injected fizz into the side. He scored his first Blues' goal with a smartly taken volley on the run against Everton in March. Energetic and enthusiastic, Craig quickly found his feet and fitted in well.
Aston Villa (From trainee on 2/2/2005) PL 32+27/5 FLC 3 FAC 3+3 Others 11+1/1
Birmingham C (£3,000,000 on 26/1/2010) PL 10+3/1 FAC 0+2

GARDNER Daniel (Danny) Keith
Born: Manchester, 30 November 1989
Height: 6'1" **Weight:** 12.7
A young striker who had been with Glasgow Celtic for a short time, Danny joined Crewe from non-League Flixton in February. He managed two substitute appearances, at Port Vale and in the home game against Accrington, before he was released at the end of the season. Full of running, brave and a hard worker, Dario Gradi reluctantly let him go in order for him to play on a regular basis.
Crewe Alex (Signed from Flixton on 16/2/2010) FL 0+2

GARDNER Ricardo Wayne
Born: St Andrew, Jamaica, 25 September 1978
Height: 5'9" **Weight:** 11.0
International Honours: Jamaica: 109
In another season blighted by injury, Bolton's Ricardo missed the beginning of the campaign with a hamstring injury. He returned to action some five weeks later, making a significant impact on the game when introduced as a half-time substitute in the home draw against Stoke. His first start of the season came in the following game against West Ham and Ricardo went on to make a total of 11 starts in the Premier League. Ricardo could not seem to force himself into the starting line-up on a consistent basis, due to a number of niggling injury problems and fierce competition in midfield. However, he has proved very effective when playing in the central positions, as he did for much of last season, rather than occupying one of the wide berths.
Bolton W (£1,000,000 from Harbour View, Jamaica on 17/8/1998) P/FL 276+57/20 FLC 20+4/2 FAC 20+4 Others 17/3

GARNER Joseph (Joe) Alan
Born: Blackburn, 12 April 1988
Height: 5'10" **Weight:** 11.13
International Honours: E: Yth; Sch
With an array of forwards signed during the summer, Joe started the season playing on the right of midfield and, although it is not his natural position, he did a serviceable job for Nottingham Forest. He started only two games, playing in his preferred position in attack and scored on both occasions, against Blackpool and Scunthorpe. Despite this good end to the campaign, he was surprisingly overlooked for the play-off games against Blackpool.
Blackburn Rov (From trainee on 16/4/2005)
Carlisle U (£140,000 on 19/1/2007) FL 47+2/19 FLC 1 FAC 2 Others 0+1
Nottingham F (£1,140,000 on 28/7/2008) FL 33+13/9 FLC 1+1 FAC 0+3/1

GARRIDO Javier
Born: Irun, Spain, 15 March 1985
Height: 5'10" **Weight:** 11.11
International Honours: Spain: U21-9; Yth
It was another disappointing season for the Spanish-born Manchester City left-back who provides cover for Wayne Bridge. After being frozen out by manager Mark Hughes in the first half of the season, he was given the opportunity of a fresh start when Roberto Mancini took over in December. In his second game of the season, he scored as a substitute with a spectacular free kick in the 3-0 win at Wolverhampton and then enjoyed a run of six games, deputizing for the injured Bridge. Later, he played intermittently without impressing and his future at Eastlands must be in doubt although he has a year remaining on his contract.
Manchester C (£1,500,000 from Real Sociedad, Spain on 3/8/2007) PL 39+10/2 FLC 4 FAC 1 Others 6+2

GARRY Ryan Felix Mayne
Born: Hornchurch, 29 September 1983
Height: 6'2" **Weight:** 13.0
Club Honours: FAYC '01
International Honours: E: Yth
A highly consistent and classy centre-half, Ryan enjoyed an excellent season and, during it, signed an extension to his Bournemouth contract. He still suffered from the minor injury setbacks that have affected his whole career, but forged a great partnership with Jason Pearce at the back. Ryan scored his first senior goal in the opening home match against Rotherham but a couple of minutes before had received a blow to the head and had no recollection of his

maiden strike.
Arsenal (From trainee on 2/7/2001) PL 1 FLC 0+1
Bournemouth (Free on 10/8/2007) FL 60+7/1 FLC 1+1 FAC 3 Others 2

GARVAN Owen
Born: Dublin, 29 January 1988
Height: 6'2" **Weight:** 10.8
International Honours: RoI: U21-15; Yth
The Ipswich season proved to be another one that Owen would prefer to forget. The midfield player was in the starting line-up only twice in the first five games of the season and on both occasions he was substituted at half-time. There then followed a two-month period when he was not included in any squad until mid-November and although he featured in most squads thereafter, he was unable to claim a regular place in the Ipswich side. He is still regarded by the fans as the best passer at the club and despite his limited appearances was still credited with five assists, including setting up both goals in the 2-1 win at Cardiff. Inch perfect passes gave Jon Walters and Jon Stead scoring opportunities that they put away.
Ipswich T (From trainee on 27/5/2005) FL 128+36/13 FLC 2+2/1 FAC 4+3/1

GEARY Derek Peter
Born: Dublin, 19 June 1980
Height: 5'6" **Weight:** 10.8
A serious knee operation kept Derek sidelined for over a year. Having made his return in November, earlier than expected, as a substitute against Barnsley, he subsequently made several starts for Sheffield United at right-back. There, despite his lack of match fitness, he played wholeheartedly both in defence where he was as solid as ever and also going forward where he produced a range of crosses. Sadly a separate, unrelated ankle injury in February sidelined him until he made the bench for the final few games. Was out of contract at the end of June.
Sheffield Wed (Signed from Rivermount Boys Club on 17/11/1997) FL 95+9 FLC 12+2 FAC 4 Others 5
Stockport Co (Free on 2/8/2004) FL 12+1 FLC 1 Others 1
Sheffield U (£25,000 on 22/10/2004) P/FL 82+12/1 FLC 8+1 FAC 11+1

GEOHAGHON Exodus Isaac
Born: Birmingham, 27 February 1985
Height: 6'7" **Weight:** 11.11
International Honours: E: SP-2
Exodus was signed by Peterborough's second manager of the season from his old club Kettering. At 6'7" it is hard for

him to hide but after some of his early performances he probably wishes he could. He took time to settle to the pace of football at Championship level but won over the fans with some fine performances. Brought to London Road as a centre-back, his best games came when he played in midfield, with a surprisingly good touch for such a tall player. Exodus can also hurl the ball a long way and can make any throw within 40 yards of the goal into a something as good as a corner. He was told at the end of the season that he did not figure in the new manager's plans and was placed on the transfer list.
Peterborough U (Signed from Kettering T, ex Redditch U, on 24/11/2009) FL 17+2/1

[GEOVANNI] DEIDERSON GOMEZ Geovanni Mauricio
Born: Aciaca, Brazil, 11 January 1980
Height: 5'9" **Weight:** 10.10
International Honours: Brazil: 1; U23-6
Having sparkled in Hull's first season in the Premier League, the talented attacking midfielder again impressed. Geovanni scored with spectacular 25-yarder in the pre-season Barclays Asia Trophy tournament against Beijing Guoan in China and followed it up with August strikes against Southend in the Carling Cup and Wolverhampton in the Premier League. He further committed himself to the Tigers by agreeing a new two-year deal in September despite a number of offers from abroad. His involvement gradually diminished as the season progressed with, notably, his only goal after the first week of October coming in the FA Cup third round at Wigan. There was reported interest from AEK Athens in March and, away from football, Geovanni continued to work as a pastor at the New Hope Fellowship Church in Hulme, near Manchester.
Manchester C (Free from Cruzeiro, Brazil, ex Cruzeiro, America Brazil, Barcelona, Benfica, on 26/7/2007) PL 2+17/3 FLC 2+1 FAC 0+1
Hull C (Free on 14/8/2008) PL 48+12/11 FLC 0+1/1 FAC 4/1

GERA Zoltan
Born: Pecs, Hungary, 22 April 1979
Height: 5'11" **Weight:** 11.3
Club Honours: Ch '08
International Honours: Hungary: 63; U21-3
One of the players of the season at Fulham, the hard-working left-sided midfielder began as a first choice before finding chances limited in autumn. His fortunes changed after sensational performances in the final Europa League

163

group games against CSKA Sofia and FC Basel, in both of which he netted the winning goals. His six goals made him the second highest Europa League scorer behind Bobby Zamora. Throughout the second half of the campaign, with injuries and inexperience limiting Fulham's attacking options, he was used as a support striker to Zamora. He excelled, particularly in the home leg against Juventus, when his first double for the club included a coolly converted penalty at a vital stage. A competent performer both on the ground and in the air, where his timing often results in him climbing above taller opponents, Zoltan was a regular member of the Hungarian squad throughout the ultimately unsuccessful World Cup qualifying campaign.
West Bromwich A (£1,500,000 from Ferencvaros, Hungary ex Harkany, Pecsi MFC, on 9/8/2004) P/FL 104+32/21 FLC 2+2/1 FAC 8+4/3 Others 2+1
Fulham (Free on 2/7/2008) PL 39+20/4 FLC 3/2 FAC 5+3/1 Others 18/6

[GEREMI] N'JITAP FOTSO Geremi Sorele
Born: Bafoussam, Cameroon, 20 December 1978
Height: 5'11" **Weight:** 12.8
Club Honours: PL '05, '06; CS '05; FLC '07
International Honours: Cameroon: 109
Geremi is an experienced right-sided midfielder and occasional right-back who featured in the Newcastle match squad for most early season games, usually as a substitute, scoring in the Carling Cup home win against Huddersfield. However, his form was not impressive and towards Christmas even bench appearances became rare and it seemed clear that he did not figure in manager Chris Hughton's long-term plans, probably at least in part because he was a high earner. He eventually moved to Ankaragucu in Turkey after a prolonged on-off transfer saga during the January window.
Middlesbrough (Loaned from Real Madrid, Spain, ex Racing Baffousam, Cerro Porteno, Genclerbirligi, on 31/7/2002) PL 33/7 FAC 1
Chelsea (£7,000,000 from Real Madrid, Spain on 1/8/2003) PL 48+24/4 FLC 8 FAC 8+1 Others 10+10
Newcastle U (Free on 14/7/2007) P/FL 38+11/1 FLC 4+1/1

GERKEN Dean Jeffery
Born: Southend-on-Sea , 22 May 1985
Height: 6'3" **Weight:** 13.0
The Bristol City goalkeeper certainly had a challenging job in trying to match the accomplishments of his predecessor,

Adriano Basso. This was always going to be a difficult task no matter who City brought in, but Dean rose to the challenge and proved to be an accomplished shot-stopper. Frequently he kept his side in the game and notched up a number of 'Man of the Match' accolades, none more deserved than that for his display in the drawn game at Ipswich in February. He was not beaten until stoppage time, when he failed to clear with an attempted punch. Fortunately the goal was disallowed as Connor Wickham's long throw had gone in without anyone else touching the ball. Dean certainly proved to be a good signing from Colchester but is not as athletic as Basso and was sometimes troubled by balls to the far post. Stretchered off with a neck injury, sustained in a collision with Nathan Tyson in the 1-1 home draw with Nottingham Forest in April, Dean amazed many by being available for selection just two weeks later and was back between the sticks when Derby were beaten 2-1 in the penultimate game of the season.
Colchester U (From trainee on 12/7/2004) FL 107+2 FLC 6 FAC 5 Others 6
Darlington (Loaned on 15/1/2009) FL 7
Bristol C (Signed on 2/7/2009) FL 39 FLC 2 FAC 2

GERMAN Antonio Timothy
Born: Park Royal, 26 December 1991
Height: 5'10" **Weight:** 12.2
After making his first team debut for Queens Park Rangers in 2008-09, Antonio was unable to get into the side at the start of the new campaign and joined Aldershot on a one-month loan in early October. Antonio, who was the last signing made by Gary Waddock before he departed for Wycombe, made his debut in the Johnstone's Paint Trophy second round tie at Hereford but failed to find the net in four outings before going back to his parent club. Having returned to Loftus Road, the powerfully-built forward capped his first start for the Rs (in mid-February) with a goal against Doncaster. Beginning to make an impact on the first team picture he went on to make five starts and nine substitute appearances under three different managers, scoring the opener in a 2-1 win over Doncaster and a vital equaliser during the home game with Swansea.
Queens Park Rgrs (From trainee on 10/7/2009) FL 5+11/2 FAC 0+1
Aldershot T (Loaned on 5/10/2009) FL 2+1 Others 1

GERRARD Anthony
Born: Liverpool, 6 February 1986
Height: 6'2" **Weight:** 13.1
Club Honours: Div 2 '07
International Honours: Rol: Yth
Anthony signed for Cardiff from Walsall, where he was out of contract, in the summer. A commanding, aggressive and tenacious centre-half, he is strong in the air. Made good progress over the season and firmly established himself at Championship level. One of three central defenders from the start, along with Gabor Gyepes and Mark Hudson, when Darcy Blake stepped in to help out because of injuries he stayed. Anthony missed the play-off semi-finals against Leicester with a calf injury but was fit for the final against Blackpool and selected among the substitutes. He went on in the second half and was thrown into attack at the end but Cardiff lost 3-2.
Everton (From trainee on 10/7/2004)
Walsall (Free on 24/3/2005) FL 157+6/7 FLC 3 FAC 9+1 Others 6
Cardiff C (Signed on 3/7/2009) FL 39/2 FLC 3 FAC 4 Others 0+1

GERRARD Paul William
Born: Heywood, 22 January 1973
Height: 6'2" **Weight:** 14.4
International Honours: E: U21-18
Veteran goalkeeper Paul joined Gary Ablett's coaching team at Stockport in the summer, also registering as a player to help provide competition for Owain Fon Williams. He was first called into action for County against Huddersfield in the Carling Cup in August, when Fon Williams was selected in the Wales national squad, a game lost 3-1. And 3-1 was also the score in his only other game of the season, a defeat in the Johnstone's Paint Trophy at Port Vale.
Oldham Ath (From trainee on 2/11/1991) P/FL 118+1 FLC 7 FAC 7 Others 2
Everton (£1,000,000 + on 1/7/1996) PL 89+1 FLC 6 FAC 3
Oxford U (Loaned on 18/12/1998) FL 16
Ipswich T (Loaned on 16/11/2002) FL 5
Sheffield U (Loaned on 29/8/2003) FL 16
Nottingham F (Free on 25/3/2004) FL 71+1 FLC 4 FAC 5 Others 1
Sheffield U (Free on 20/9/2006) PL 2 FAC 1 (Freed during 2008 close season)
Stockport Co (From retirement on 16/7/2009) FLC 1 Others 1

GERRARD Steven George
Born: Huyton, 30 May 1980
Height: 6'2" **Weight:** 12.4
Club Honours: FLC '01, '03; FAC '01, '06; UEFAC '01; ESC '01; UEFACL '05; CS '06
International Honours: E: 80; U21-4; Yth
The talismanic Liverpool and England

Steven Gerrard

GHILAS Kamel Fathi
Born: Marseille, France, 9 March 1984
Height: 5'10" **Weight:** 11.0
International Honours: Algeria: 16
In the week before the start of the season, Kamel joined Hull on a four-year deal from Celta Vigo, where he had been the previous season's leading scorer with 13 goals despite relegation from La Liga. The speedy right-sided forward soon made a favourable impression, especially with his clinical finish against Bolton in August, earning a first League win at the KC Stadium since the previous December. Despite his bright start and obvious enthusiasm, after his last League start at Burnley in October, most observers were bemused as to why his services were increasingly ignored. In contrast, he was a regular squad member as Algeria reached the World Cup finals for the first time since 1986 but his lack of first team action at Hull meant that he missed selection for the finals in South Africa.
Hull C (Signed from Celta Vigo, Spain, ex Martigues, AS Cannes, Vitoria Guimaraes, on 13/8/2009) PL 6+7/1 FLC 1+1 FAC 1

GIBBS Kieran James Ricardo
Born: Lambeth, 26 September 1989
Height: 5'10" **Weight:** 10.2
International Honours: E: U21-14; Yth
Kieran showed great promise in the previous campaign when he deputised for the injured Gael Clichy at left-back and started this season determined to have more game time in the Arsenal team. The early signs were encouraging and an on-form Kieran was really beginning to press Clichy for his place. However, a broken toe suffered on England under-21 duty ruled him out for the rest of the season. He was fit enough only to make the bench for the last game of the season but did not appear. There were calls from some quarters to include him in England's World Cup squad although he was not eventually picked. Kieran may well have an exciting career ahead of him for both club and country. He played three times in the Premier League, twice in the Champions League and twice in the Carling Cup.
Arsenal (From trainee on 14/9/2007) PL 9+2 FLC 6+1 FAC 5+1 Others 5+1
Norwich C (Loaned on 31/1/2008) FL 6+1

GIBSON Darron Thomas Daniel
Born: Derry, 25 October 1987
Height: 6'0" **Weight:** 12.4
Club Honours: FLC '09, '10
International Honours: RoI: 9; U21-1; Yth

midfielder endured what was probably his least effective season but, as usual, he stood ahead of his midfield colleagues. Although he played in 49 of the 56 games, he was frequently troubled with groin problems. His 12 goals, including three penalties, made him Liverpool's second top scorer but were significantly fewer than the 20-plus he scored in three of the previous four seasons. Two were candidates for 'Goal of the Season' - a curling cross-shot into the roof of the net in a 6-0 victory over Hull and his second goal in the late season 4-0 win at Burnley. More than any other Liverpool player, he suffered from the summer departure of Xabi Alonso whose ball retention and laser passing gave Steven the freedom to play just behind Fernando Torres. In Torres' frequent absences, he lacked the confidence to advance so often. In nearly all the big Premiership and Champions League games of last season his usual dynamism was lacking and, ironically, in the Reds' best Premiership performance, the 2-0 home win over Manchester United in October, he was absent through injury. After Rio Ferdinand's injury, Steven became England's World Cup captain in South Africa.
Liverpool (From trainee on 26/2/1998) PL 340+26/80 FLC 17+3/7 FAC 24+4/10 Others 107+11/35

Athletic Manchester United and Republic of Ireland midfielder who packs a powerful shot, Darron was eager to prove that the reward of a three-year extension to his contract at the end of 2008-09 would be fully justified. Impressing early on with his midfield ability United's young crop of stars came under fire when they lost 1-0 to Besiktas in the Champions League group match, thus ending the Reds' four-year unbeaten home record. Six days after that defeat, Darron rose above the criticism by scoring both goals in a 2–0 win against in-form Tottenham to send United to the semi-finals of the Carling Cup. Still on the goal trail, he went on to score his third goal in a week, netting a fantastic long-range shot in an emphatic 4–0 win at West Ham. The coup de grace should have been another piledriver in the Champions League knockout match against Bayern Munich at Old Trafford but the Germans fought back to seal the tie on the away goals rule.
Manchester U *(From trainee on 12/8/2005) PL 7+11/3 FLC 7+3/2 FAC 3+1/2 Others 4+2/1*
Wolverhampton W *(Loaned on 19/10/2007) FL 15+6/1 FAC 1+2*

with a series of cultured displays, showing good footwork and a willingness to press forward down the flank. Was out of contract in the summer.
Coventry C *(From trainee on 16/6/2004) FL 12+4 FLC 2 FAC 1 (Freed during 2008 close season)*
Oldham Ath *(Loaned on 10/8/2007) FL 2 FLC 1*
Darlington *(Free from Hinckley U on 10/11/2009) FL 22*

GIGGS Ryan Joseph
Born: Cardiff, 29 November 1973
Height: 5'11" **Weight:** 10.9
Club Honours: ESC '91; FAYC '92; FLC '92, '06, '09; PL '93, '94, '96, '97, '99, '00, '01, '03, '07, '08, '09; CS '93, '94, '96, '97, '03, '07, '10; FAC '94, '96, '99, '04; UEFACL '99, '08
International Honours: W: 64; U21-1; Yth; E: Sch
A Manchester United and Welsh international left-winger, who can play

equally as well as a front-line striker, Ryan showed that he still had plenty to aim for. In a pre-season friendly against Hangzhou Greentown, he scored his first hat-trick for the Reds as a second-half substitute. More of a starter than a substitute when the campaign began, he scored United's first goal in an impressive 3-1 Premier League win against Tottenham at White Hart Lane in September, maintaining his record of being the only player to have scored in every Premier League season since its inception in 1992 – and it was his 700th start for the club. Also in September, he scored his 150th goal for United, only the ninth player to do so, against Wolfsburg in his first Champions League game of the season. It was the 14th Champions League season in which he had scored, equalling the record set by Raul for Real Madrid 15 days earlier. On the eve of his 36th birthday in November, he celebrated with his 100th Premier

Ryan Giggs

Stuart Giddings

GIDDINGS Stuart James
Born: Coventry, 27 March 1986
Height: 6'0" **Weight:** 11.8
International Honours: E: Yth
Stuart had been understudy to Steve Staunton throughout his last season at Aston Villa and the new Darlington manager wasted no time in recruiting him from Hinckley Athletic to fill the left-back spot. He made this berth his own for the remainder of the season

League goal in a 4-1 victory over Portsmouth at Fratton Park, only the 17th player to reach the milestone. On the day after his birthday, it was announced that he would be offered an additional one-year contract to run until the end of 2010-11. No doubt this will see him past the 20th anniversary of his first game and goal for United. In December, his appearance against West Ham at Upton Park – where he ended the game playing at left-back – equalled the outfield record of his fellow countryman Gary Speed with 535 Premier League appearances. This was surpassed in December when he played against Aston Villa in a rare 1-0 home defeat. On the same day, Ryan travelled to Sheffield to claim the BBC 'Sports Personality of the Year' award for 2009. In February he broke an arm while playing against Aston Villa, but retuned for the all-important run-in.

Manchester U *(From trainee on 1/12/1990) P/FL 504+84/108 FLC 30+6/9 FAC 57+8/10 Others 129+20/28*

GILBERT Kerrea Kuche
Born: Willesden, 28 February 1987
Height: 5'6" **Weight:** 11.3
Club Honours: Div 1 '09
International Honours: E: Yth
Having made two Premier League appearances for Arsenal in 2009-10, Kerrea was given a Champions League debut in the Group Stage game at Olympiacos before going out on loan to Peterborough in January. An attack-minded right-back who likes nothing more than getting to the opponents by-line and getting a cross in, he was unfortunate that an injury meant he was only able to play in ten matches. Was out of contract at the end of June.

Arsenal *(From trainee on 1/7/2005) PL 2 FLC 5+1 FAC 2 Others 1+1*
Cardiff C *(Loaned on 27/7/2006) FL 21+3 FAC 2*
Southend U *(Loaned on 8/8/2007) FL 5 FLC 1*
Leicester C *(Loaned on 4/8/2008) FL 33+1/1 FLC 2 FAC 1+1 Others 1*
Peterborough U *(Loaned on 15/1/2010) FL 7+3*

GILBERT Eric Peter
Born: Newcastle, 31 July 1983
Height: 5'9" **Weight:** 12.13
Club Honours: Div 2 '04
International Honours: W: U21-12
Having been released by Sheffield Wednesday, Peter joined Oldham and made five appearances at the beginning of the season, showing himself to be a strong-tackling full-back with a good eye for a pass. However, because he wanted more stability than was

afforded by the week-to-week deal with Latics he left before the 1st September transfer deadline to allow himself the chance to find a permanent club. Arriving at Northampton in November, the defender made history by becoming the first Cobbler to be sent off on his debut since Ian McParland in 1992! After putting that behind him he settled down to become an integral part of the back four. Playing at left-back, he often prompted attacks when linking up with Liam Davis as well as cutting out the opposing wing play.

Birmingham C *(From trainee on 1/7/2002)*
Plymouth Arg *(Signed on 8/7/2003) FL 78/1 FLC 2 FAC 2 Others 2/1*
Leicester C *(£200,000 on 3/8/2005) FL 4+1*
Sheffield Wed *(Free on 24/11/2005) FL 39+2 FLC 2*
Doncaster Rov *(Loaned on 9/1/2007) FL 4 Others 1*
Oldham Ath *(Free on 6/8/2009) FL 5 FLC 1*
Northampton T *(Free on 13/11/2009) FL 30 FAC 1*

GILKS Matthew (Matt)
Born: Oldham, 4 June 1982
Height: 6'1" **Weight:** 12.7
It was definitely Matt's breakthrough season in goal for Blackpool after a frustrating time the year before. He was on the brink of leaving the club before Ian Holloway came in and has now firmly dislodged Paul Rachubka as the Seasiders' number one. He played 29 games in the normal season, and each of the last 16. Matt's communication with his back four is second to none and his ability when coming for crosses is unquestioned. His shot-stopping improved tenfold over the course of the season and culminated in him making key stops in each of the last three games to cement Blackpool in the top six.

Rochdale *(From trainee on 4/7/2001) FL 174+2 FLC 4 FAC 9+1 Others 7*
Norwich C *(Free on 5/7/2007)*
Blackpool *(Free on 21/7/2008) FL 30+1 FLC 4 Others 3*
Shrewsbury T *(Loaned on 21/11/2008) FL 4*

GILL Matthew James
Born: Cambridge, 8 November 1980
Height: 5'11" **Weight:** 12.1
When Matthew joined Norwich in July having run out of contract at Exeter, it was something of a homecoming for this midfielder who had been on City's books as a youngster. An efficient player, always looking to keep the ball moving, his impact at Carrow Road was

reduced by a series of injuries that ruled him out for much of the early part of the season. By the time he was fit, the team was almost picking itself and he had to be content with a place on the bench. He will be hoping for better fortunes in his second season with the Canaries.

Peterborough U *(From trainee on 2/3/1998) FL 121+30/4 FLC 3+1 FAC 6+1 Others 3+4*
Notts Co *(Free on 17/6/2004) FL 45+12 FLC 3 FAC 4+1 Others 1*
Exeter C *(Free on 17/1/2006) FL 43/9 FLC 1 FAC 1 Others 1*
Norwich C *(Free on 2/7/2009) FL 5+3 FLC 1 Others 0+1*

GILLESPIE Mark Joseph
Born: Newcastle, 27 March 1992
Height: 6'3" **Weight:** 13.7
This Carlisle youth team goalkeeper went on in stoppage time at Norwich in the last match of the season, thus becoming the club's youngest ever goalkeeper. Much is expected of this youngster, who will be looking to press for a first team place next season.

Carlisle U *(Trainee) FL 0+1*

GILLESPIE Steven
Born: Liverpool, 4 June 1984
Height: 5'9" **Weight:** 11.5
Colchester's record signing failed to get his career at the club off the ground in his second season there. Following an injury-plagued début campaign, the pacy and hard-working striker eventually returned to fitness in September. He then found himself behind the likes of Clive Platt, loanee Kevin Lisbie and new signing Kayode Odejayi in the pecking order in, for him, a frustratingly stop-start campaign. Steven started just ten games all season, with 23 of his appearances coming from the bench. The long-haired Liverpudlian scored twice but often proved a real nuisance to the opposition with his constant running.

Bristol C *(From trainee at Liverpool on 6/8/2004) FL 4+8/1 FLC 0+1 FAC 0+2 Others 1+1*
Cheltenham T *(Loaned on 11/1/2005) FL 10+2/5*
Cheltenham T *(Signed on 11/11/2005) FL 52+22/24 FLC 0+1 FAC 2/2 Others 5+1/2*
Colchester U *(£400,000 on 15/7/2008) FL 16+31/5 FLC 0+1/1 FAC 2+1/1 Others 1+1*

GILLET Kenny Lego
Born: Bordeaux, France, 3 January 1986
Height: 5'10" **Weight:** 12.4
French defender Kenny was heavily

involved in the Barnet team for the third season in succession. He faced competition for his usual left-back role from a number of players, but still appeared in more than 30 games. He ended the season in a centre-back role, where he gave a number of solid displays as the Bees secured their Football League safety. Was out of contract at the end of June.
Barnet *(Free from SM Caen, France on 30/8/2007) FL 89+11 FLC 2 FAC 11 Others 2*

GILLETT Simon James
Born: Oxford, 6 November 1985
Height: 5'6" **Weight:** 11.7
Club Honours: AMC '10
After managing just one start under Alan Pardew's new regime at Southampton, the bright, resolute and industrious midfielder departed on loan for Doncaster, who were troubled by injuries to midfielders. Following his arrival in October, he did so well that there was talk of him signing a permanent deal but it came to nothing and he returned to his parent club in January. Although he made a cameo appearance from the bench in the Johnstone's Paint Trophy final and collected a winner's medal he was not retained at the end of the season.
Southampton *(From trainee on 8/11/2003) FL 23+8 FLC 2+1 FAC 1+2 Others 1+1*
Walsall *(Loaned on 30/9/2005) FL 2*
Blackpool *(Loaned on 9/8/2006) FL 13+1/1 Others 1/1*
Bournemouth *(Loaned on 22/11/2006) FL 7/1*
Blackpool *(Loaned on 31/1/2007) FL 7+10 Others 0+2*
Yeovil T *(Loaned on 21/9/2007) FL 3+1 Others 0+1*
Doncaster Rov *(Loaned on 12/10/2009) FL 10+1*

GILLIGAN Ryan James
Born: Swindon, 18 January 1987
Height: 5'10" **Weight:** 11.7
Ryan has had his best season yet playing in the middle of the Northampton midfield, prompting attacks and helping out in defence. His goal tally is his highest and if some came from the penalty spot, that in turn gave him another feather in his cap. A lot of his goals came from long-range volleys or opportunist chances and he is certainly a player to look out for in the future.
Northampton T *(From trainee at Watford on 12/8/2005) FL 110+48/19 FLC 4+4 FAC 7+1/1 Others 3+2/2*

Ryan Gilligan

GILMARTIN Rene Patrick
Born: Dublin, 31 May 1987
Height: 6'5" **Weight:** 13.6
International Honours: RoI: U21-1; Yth
Although still having a lot to learn, this was perhaps the breakthrough season in Rene's career. He finished the season as Walsall's first choice goalkeeper having many fine games. Still young, he benefited from the club again having a goalkeeping coach. He still needs to work on his kicking and on taking crosses, but it was a highly satisfactory season for him to build on. A complete misunderstanding with Jamie Vincent which gifted Millwall a goal was one incident among a few when communication with his defenders was lacking.
Walsall *(Free from St Kevin's BC on 26/8/2005) FL 34+1 FLC 1 FAC 2 Others 2*

GILMOUR Brian Thomas
Born: Irvine, 8 May 1987
Height: 5'7" **Weight:** 9.4
International Honours: S: Yth
A former Scottish youth international, Brian marked his first season in the Football League by turning in a number of lively showings for Lincoln in the attacking third of the field. Although he only scored twice, one of these proved important, coming in the local derby draw at Grimsby which helped keep the Imps clear of the relegation-bound Mariners.
Glasgow Rgrs *(From juniors on 1/7/2005)*

Clyde *(Loaned on 9/2/2007) SL 13/1*
Queen of the South *(Free on 2/8/2007) SL 14+9/1 SLC 1 SC 2 Others 1 (Freed during 2009 close season)*
Lincoln C *(Free from FC Haka, Finland on 26/11/2009) FL 14+2/2 FAC 1+1*

GILROY Keith
Born: Sligo, 8 July 1983
Height: 5'10" **Weight:** 11.4
Club Honours: FC '09
International Honours: RoI: U21-1; Yth
Injury problems have blighted Keith's time with Burton and severely limited his opportunities during the club's first League season. On his day, Keith is an exciting player when he mixes his dribbling skills and crossing ability from the left wing and will be hoping that new treatment on a persistent hamstring problem will enable him to play a bigger part in the second year of the contract he signed in 2009.
Middlesbrough *(Signed from Sligo Rovers on 5/9/2000. Free to Scarborough on 27/3/2003)*
Darlington *(Free from Scarborough on 24/2/2005) FL 1+1*
Burton A *(Free on 10/8/2005) FL 4+4*

[GIOVANI] DOS SANTOS Giovani Alex
Born: Monterrey, Mexico, 11 May 1989
Height: 5'8" **Weight:** 12.2
International Honours: Mexico: 26; Yth
Giovani is an exciting attacking left-sided midfielder, who has played 23 internationals for Mexico, helping them to qualify for the 2010 World Cup. He made just two starts for Tottenham in Carling Cup ties, and in the second of those, after hitting the bar with a shot, he had to be substituted due to injury. This led to him missing further opportunities apart from a brief appearance at Wolves in December. Giovani spent the second half of the season on loan at Galatasaray where he played 17 games including at home and away in the Europa League against eventual winners Atletico Madrid.
Tottenham H *(£4,700,000 from Barcelona, Spain on 14/8/2008) PL 2+5 FLC 2+1 FAC 0+1 Others 3+1/1*
Ipswich T *(Loaned on 13/3/2009) FL 6+2/4*

GIVEN Seamus (Shay) John James
Born: Lifford, 20 April 1976
Height: 6'1" **Weight:** 13.4
Club Honours: Div 1 '96
International Honours: RoI: 103; U21-5; Yth
Even at the age of 34, the Manchester

City and Republic of Ireland goalkeeper remains one of the top performers in the Premiership and he enjoyed another consistent season, helping his team to their highest placing for 19 years although, in the final analysis, fifth was a disappointment. In December, he made an outstanding penalty save from Frank Lampard to deny Chelsea an equaliser in City's 2-1 victory and in March he made his 400th Premiership appearance. Also in March he became the Republic's most capped player with 103 appearances, an honour he shares with Kevin Kilbane. He was denied the opportunity of playing in the World Cup finals in South Africa through a controversial incident in the play-off match with France in Paris when William Gallas equalised following two handballs by Thierry Henry. In any event he might have missed the finals due to a dislocated shoulder he incurred against Arsenal, ruling him out of City's last three games. Next season he will face a fierce challenge from Joe Hart, returning from a season's loan with Birmingham and World Cup duty with England.
Blackburn Rov (From juniors at Glasgow Celtic on 8/8/1994) PL 2 FLC 0+1
Swindon T (Loaned on 4/8/1995) FL 5
Sunderland (Loaned on 19/1/1996) FL 17
Newcastle U (£1,500,000 on 14/7/1997) PL 354 FLC 12+1 FAC 34 Others 62
Manchester C (£8,000,000 on 2/2/2009) PL 50 FLC 6 FAC 3 Others 6

GIVET-VIAROS Gael
Born: Arles, France, 9 October 1981
Height: 5'11" **Weight:** 11.11
International Honours: France: 13
Gael was never anything other than a warrior, whether playing at left-back or in the centre of Blackburn's defence. Extremely competitive, his strength lies in his ability to spot the ball within his reach and once he has made up his mind, is definite and seldom fails to achieve his objective. Strong in the air, he covers well across the back, cutting out danger. He also profited from the presence of the towering Chris Samba and Steven N'Zonzi to obtain goals at Sunderland and at home against Bolton, as well as being the moral scorer of the goal against Wolverhampton that was credited to Jason Roberts because it brushed off his shirt.
Blackburn Rov (£3,500,000 from Olympique Marseille, France ex AS Monaco, on 16/1/2009) PL 47+1/2 FLC 3 FAC 3+2

Gael Givet-Viaros

GLEESON Stephen Michael
Born: Dublin, 3 August 1988
Height: 6'2" **Weight:** 11.0
International Honours: RoI: 12; U21-10; Yth
Signed on a permanent deal after impressing while on loan at the end of the previous campaign, Stephen's first full season with MK Dons never really kicked into top gear. Stylish on the ball, with a precise and accurate passing range, the hard-tackling defensive midfield slot he was often asked to fill did not really suit his more refined skills, with the result that as the season went on, so his yellow card tally mounted. Picking up further Republic of Ireland under-21 honours during the campaign, he will be hoping for better deployment on the pitch under a different manager.
Wolverhampton W (From trainee on 5/7/2006) FL 0+3 FLC 1 Others 0+1
Stockport Co (Loaned on 3/11/2006) FL 14/2 FAC 3
Hereford U (Loaned on 21/2/2008) FL 3+1
Stockport Co (Loaned on 27/3/2008) FL 4+2 Others 2+1/1
Stockport Co (Loaned on 8/8/2008) FL 17+4/2 FLC 1 FAC 3/1 Others 1
MK Dons (Signed on 25/3/2009) FL 31+3 FAC 3 Others 3+1

GLENNON Matthew (Matt) William
Born: Stockport, 8 October 1978
Height: 6'2" **Weight:** 14.9
The experienced goalkeeper was Stuart McCall's last signing as Bradford manager. Matt cancelled his contract at Huddersfield in January to move across West Yorkshire, making his debut against Bury. It was his first senior appearance for over a year. A very vocal 'keeper with his defenders, Matt played 17 times before making way for Jon McLaughlin. He was released at the end of the season.
Bolton W (From trainee on 3/7/1997)
Bristol Rov (Loaned on 15/9/2000) FL 1
Carlisle U (Loaned on 10/11/2000) FL 29 FAC 3 Others 1
Hull C (£50,000 on 20/6/2001) FL 35 FLC 3 FAC 2 Others 2
Carlisle U (Free on 18/10/2002) FL 76 FLC 1 FAC 4 Others 10
Falkirk (Free on 20/7/2005) SL 21 SC 2
St Johnstone (Signed on 27/1/2006) SL 12/1
Huddersfield T (Free on 29/6/2006) FL 109 FLC 4 FAC 7 Others 2
Bradford C (Free on 13/1/2010) FL 17

GLOVER Daniel (Danny)
Born: Crewe, 24 October 1989
Height: 6'0" **Weight:** 11.3
The striker began the season on the transfer list at Port Vale and made seven appearances on loan for Salisbury City before returning to the Vale in September. He was only restricted to four substitute appearances for the Vale, either side of a month's loan with Rochdale, during which he played for them twice when covering injuries. A decent striker of the ball, he just lacked a bit of consistency and ended the campaign on loan at Stafford Rangers before being released on a free transfer at the end of the campaign.
Port Vale (From trainee on 27/7/2007) FL 20+21/4 FAC 0+3 Others 1+1
Rochdale (Loaned on 26/11/2009) FL 0+2

GOBERN Lewis Thomas
Born: Birmingham, 28 January 1985
Height: 5'10" **Weight:** 11.7
Lewis signed a one-year deal with MK Dons well in time for the new season, making his debut as a substitute in the opening day goalless draw with Hartlepool. A pacy and skilful winger on his day, he flitted in and out of the squad throughout the season, suffering a couple of minor injuries along the way, and netted his only goal with the winner in an FA Cup first round success over Macclesfield.
Wolverhampton W (From trainee on 5/3/2004) FL 6+7/2
Hartlepool U (Loaned on 1/11/2004) FL 1 Others 0+1
Blackpool (Loaned on 24/11/2005) FL 4+4/1
Bury (Loaned on 23/3/2006) FL 7/1
Colchester U (Loaned on 15/11/2009) FL 5+7
MK Dons (Free on 2/7/2009) FL 7+13 FLC 1 FAC 0+1/1 Others 1+3

GOBERN Oscar Lee
Born: Birmingham, 26 January 1991
Height: 5'11" **Weight:** 10.11
A graceful and diligent attacking Southampton midfielder with an eloquent left foot, Oscar was unable to make the transition from the subs' bench to starting line-up early in the season and joined his big-brother Lewis at MK Dons when arriving on loan in September. Linking up well together, the two of them became the first siblings to play for the club after both came on as substitutes in the home game against Gillingham. Oscar had previously filled in well at left-back when replacing injured skipper Dean Lewington against Walsall, and though those two matches were his only involvement, he showed good composure and passing ability in his 70 minutes played. On his return to St Mary's he was confined to making sallies from the bench until January, before being sidelined by injury. As the season ended he was scheduled for a hip operation.
Southampton (From trainee on 20/9/2008) FL 4+6 FLC 0+1 FAC 1+2
MK Dons (Loaned on 17/9/2009) FL 0+1

GODSMARK Jonathan (Jonny)
Born: Ashington, 3 September 1989
Height: 5'6" **Weight:** 10.1
Lively right-winger Jonny made a promising start to his Hereford loan, the winning goal in a Carling Cup success over Charlton being an early highlight, but a spell on the sidelines with a broken arm only five League games into the campaign did not help him or Hereford. He played only rarely after that before returning to Newcastle in the New Year. Was out of contract at the end of June.
Newcastle U (From trainee on 7/7/2008)
Hereford U (Loaned on 6/8/2009) FL 7+1/1 FLC 2/1 FAC 1 Others 0+2

GOHOURI Lohore **Steve** Ulrich
Born: Treichville, Ivory Coast, 8 February 1981
Height: 6'2" **Weight:** 13.12
International Honours: Ivory Coast: 11
Recruited by Wigan after his contract with German club Borussia Moenchengladbach was terminated in January, Steve is a powerful and pacy centre-half, having played over 50 games in the Bundesliga. An Ivorian international, he hoped his move to the Premier League would be a factor in his quest to be a part of the Ivory Coast's squad for the World Cup finals in South

Africa. A fine reader of the game and a clean tackler, he is a threat in the air from set pieces. Steve made his debut in the FA Cup tie at Notts County and his first Premier League starts were against Portsmouth and then Arsenal, as he put in typically solid displays. His first Premier League goal was a dramatic and acrobatic injury-time strike in the final home game against Hull. Just 11 months after recovering from a life-threatening bout of tropical malaria, Steve was rewarded with a two-year contract.
Wigan Ath (Free from Borussia Moenchengladbach, Germany, ex Paris St Germain, Bnei Yehuda, Yverdon Sport, Bologna, Vaduz, Young Boys of Berne, on 12/1/2010) PL 4+1/1 FAC 0+1

GOLBOURNE Scott Julian
Born: Bristol, 29 February 1988
Height: 5'8" **Weight:** 11.8
International Honours: E: Yth
Signed by Exeter in the summer from Reading, Scott played at either left-back or left wing-back. His accurate ball delivery and pace made him an essential part of the City rearguard. Quick to the tackle, he quietly went about his business in a professional manner. There is little doubt that Scott will play an integral part of the City team next season.
Bristol C (From trainee on 5/3/2005) FL 11+3 FLC 1/1
Reading (£150,000 on 3/1/2006) P/FL 1+1 FLC 2+1 FAC 1
Wycombe W (Loaned on 18/8/2006) FL 13+2/1 FLC 3 Others 1
Wycombe W (Loaned on 12/1/2007) FL 18+1 FLC 1
Bournemouth (Loaned on 6/11/2007) FL 5 FAC 2/1 Others 1
Oldham Ath (Loaned on 23/1/2009) FL 7+1
Exeter C (Free on 2/7/2009) FL 30+4 FLC 1 FAC 2 Others 0+1

GOMES Heurelho
Born: Minas Gerais, Brazil, 15 February 1981
Height: 6'3" **Weight:** 12.13
International Honours: Brazil: 10; U23-8
The Tottenham number one has firmly established himself as a favourite with the fans after a difficult start to his Premier League career. Heurelho suffered an early season injury and had a battle to regain the goalkeeper's jersey from Carlo Cudicini, but had clearly won the battle before Carlo's serious injury ended his season. Heurelho played in every Tottenham game between mid-October and May, making a total of 42 full appearances out of 50. He has great speed and

agility and made many spectacular and crucial saves. His most memorable were three genuinely world-class stops against Arsenal in a vital League win and he also saved three penalties against former Spurs striker Darren Bent in the two League games against Sunderland. Heurelho entered the Spurs' history books as the first 'keeper since Pat Jennings to save two penalties in the same game. He is capable of throwing the ball beyond the half-way line and often uses this additional accuracy to the advantage of the team. He was rewarded at the end of the season with a place in the Brazilian World Cup squad.
Tottenham H (£7,000,000 from PSV Eindhoven, Holland, ex Cruzeiro, on 22/7/2008) PL 65 FLC 8 FAC 9 Others 8

GOODALL Alan Jeffrey
Born: Birkenhead, 2 December 1981
Height: 5'9" **Weight:** 11.6
This wholehearted Chesterfield left-back missed the first half of the season because of injury and the good form of others. Coming into the side in January, Alan's positional responsibility was a feature as the team climbed to third but he lost his place after being sent off in the 5-0 defeat by Port Vale in March. Subsequent opportunities were limited and it was no surprise to see him released at the end of his contract.
Rochdale (Signed from Bangor C on 30/7/2004) FL 110+10/8 FLC 2 FAC 4 Others 5
Luton T (Free on 24/7/2007) FL 25+4/1 FLC 3 FAC 2+1 Others 1
Chesterfield (Free on 7/8/2008) FL 38+7/3 FLC 1 FAC 2 Others 1

GOODFELLOW Marc David
Born: Swadlincote, 20 September 1981
Height: 5'8" **Weight:** 10.6
Club Honours: AMC '06; FC '09
Pacy winger with a terrific left foot, Marc was retained by Burton for their first League season but was unable to command a regular place and spent much of the season on loan to Barrow and Kidderminster. His spell at Barrow included an appearance in the third round of the FA Cup at Sunderland. Was out of contract in the summer.
Stoke C (From juniors on 29/1/1999) FL 17+37/6 FLC 3+3/2 FAC 1+6 Others 4/1
Bristol C (£50,000 on 9/1/2004) FL 8+12/4 Others 0+2/1
Port Vale (Loaned on 6/10/2004) FL 4+1
Swansea C (Loaned on 26/11/2004) FL 6/3 FLC 1+1/1
Colchester U (Loaned on 17/3/2005) FL 4+1/1
Swansea C (Signed on 30/6/2005) FL 5+6 Others 2

Grimsby T (Free on 31/1/2006) FL 8+2/1 Others 0+1
Bury (Free on 5/7/2006) FL 2+2 FLC 0+1 Others 0+1
Burton A (Free on 24/1/2007) FL 0+3 Others 1

GOODISON Ian De Souza
Born: St James, Jamaica, 21 November 1972
Height: 6'3" **Weight:** 12.10
International Honours: Jamaica: 113
Possibly Tranmere's most important player – the team struggles to win without Ian – is half way through a two-year contract at Prenton Park and is the longest-serving player, having been a regular in the defence since 2004. His preferred position is at centre-back but he is equally adept at left-back. Possibly not at his best early in the campaign when John Barnes was in charge, he soon came to influence every game in which he played and ran the back four with his usual mixture of calm, assurance and vision. Solid and powerful in the tackle, Ian continues to defy the years and also took great delight in the three goals he scored. Happily, he also got through relatively free of injury.
Hull C (Free from Olympic Gardens, Jamaica on 22/10/1999) FL 67+3/1 FLC 2 FAC 6+1 Others 5 (Free to Seba U, Jamaica during 2002 close season)
Tranmere Rov (Free from Seba U, Jamaica on 20/2/2004) FL 246+7/6 FLC 6 FAC 14 Others 11+2

GOODWIN James (Jim) Michael
Born: Waterford, 20 November 1981
Height: 5'9" **Weight:** 12.2
Club Honours: Div 1 '07
International Honours: RoI: 1; U21-14
The creative midfielder started the season frozen out of the starting line-up after a great debut season during the last campaign as he worked his way back from injury. A substitutes' appearance in the home victory over Yeovil was soon followed by a start in the Johnstone's Paint Trophy tie at Rotherham. The Irish midfielder likes to be at the hub of the action with his strong tackling and probing passes. After five full appearances for the club during the current campaign Jim joined Oldham on loan in early January with a view to playing regular first team football. Having made his debut in the 2-1 defeat to Hartlepool, Jim tore his thigh muscle in his fifth outing with the club and was sidelined for the next 15 games before returning at the tail-end of the season. Jim appeared eight times for the Latics and made many friends at

Boundary Park with his no-nonsense approach before returning to the Galpharm Stadium.
Glasgow Celtic (Signed from Tramore on 25/11/1997) SL 1
Stockport Co (Free on 7/6/2002) FL 81+22/7 FLC 3 FAC 6/1 Others 7/1
Scunthorpe U (Free on 3/8/2005) FL 74+10/6 FLC 0+1 FAC 0+3 Others 3+1/1
Huddersfield T (Free on 8/7/2008) FL 38+4/1 FLC 1+1 FAC 1 Others 2
Oldham Ath (Loaned on 1/1/2010) FL 8

GORDON Benjamin (Ben) Lawrence
Born: Bradford, 2 March 1991
Height: 5'11" **Weight:** 12.6
International Honours: E: Yth
A promising left-back and a regular for Chelsea's reserves, Ben is in his third year at Stamford Bridge and was loaned to Tranmere on transfer deadline day in March. He made his full League debut in Rovers' 3-0 defeat at Brighton but could not be blamed for any of the goals and did enough to start the next game. Ben, who is an under-17 England international, is a calm and confident young defender who reads the game well and has the ability to hold the ball when necessary, but can also deliver telling passes upfield.
Chelsea (From trainee on 9/7/2008)
Tranmere Rov (Loaned on 25/3/2010) FL 4

GORDON Craig Anthony
Born: Edinburgh, 31 December 1982
Height: 6'4" **Weight:** 12.2
Club Honours: SC '06
International Honours: S: 39; U21-5
On his own assessment, this was Britain's most expensive goalkeeper's best season since coming to England three years ago. The Scotland international missed the start of the campaign through injury but was in top form by the time he broke his arm at Spurs in November in a clash with Jermain Defoe. Craig was ruled out for two-and-a-half months but quickly made up for lost time with a string of top class performances. Craig's agility, decision making and composure made him one of the top 'keepers in the Premier League and enabled manager Steve Bruce to proclaim him as his number one ahead of Hungarian international Marton Fulop, who ended the season on loan to Manchester City.
Heart of Midlothian (From juniors on 1/8/2000) SL 138+1 SLC 8 SC 15 Others 14 SL 13 SLC 1
Cowdenbeath (Loaned on 31/8/2001) SL 13 SLC 1
Sunderland (£9,000,000 on 10/8/2007) PL 72 FLC 4 FAC 3

Craig Gordon

GORDON Michael Alexander
Born: Tooting, 11 October 1984
Height: 5'6" **Weight:** 10.4
With a lightning-quick turn of pace, the right-winger's Lincoln career threatened to burst into life in 2009-10. However, having been a regular during Chris Sutton's early days in charge Michael found himself limited to numerous unused substitute appearances which restricted his total tally to just four starts.
Wimbledon (Free from trainee at Arsenal on 11/3/2003) FL 8+11 FLC 1 FAC 0+1 (Freed during 2004 close season)
Lincoln C (Free from Merstham, ex Havant & Waterlooville, Aldershot T, Crawley T, Sutton U, Worthing, Walton & Hersham, AFC Wimbledon, Harrow Borough, Hemel Hemp on 11/11/2009) FL 4+1

GORKSS Kaspars
Born: Riga, Latvia, 6 November 1981
Height: 6'3" **Weight:** 13.5
International Honours: Latvia: 30; U21-12
Queens Park Rangers most used defender, Kaspars struggled to repeat the outstanding form of the previous season in a difficult campaign. He still made 45 starts and was a key part of the R's back four. He began to find more consistency in his game in the final months of the season, when given

171

a settled run with a regular centre-back partner in Damion Stewart and he went on to make 28 consecutive starts from mid-December to the final game of the season. Kaspars scored three times, all headers and all away from home, including the crucial second goal that saw Rangers beat Crystal Palace 2-0 and all but secure their Championship survival.

Blackpool *(Signed from FK Ventspils, Latvia, ex FK Auda, Osters IF, Assyriska FF, on 2/1/2007) FL 47+3/5 FLC 3+1/2 FAC 1+2*
Queens Park Rgrs *(£250,000 on 1/8/2008) FL 70+2/3 FLC 4+1 FAC 4*

GORNELL Terence (Terry) Michael
Born: Liverpool, 16 December 1989
Height: 5'11" **Weight:** 12.4
Having fully recovered from a nasty medial ligament injury during the last close season, Terry started as a regular and was fortunate to remain fit during the entire campaign, enjoying his longest uninterrupted run in the front line at Tranmere. He is a product of the club's youth system and has great potential, being a talented striker who has timing, a good first touch and a killer instinct in front of goal. He is equally comfortable in the air or playing on the ground, while the system employed by Rovers under Les Parry suited his style of play. Terry seemed to improve with each game, no doubt helped by his willingness to take on board any help or advice offered by more experienced colleagues.
Tranmere Rov *(From trainee on 2/7/2008) FL 22+15/3 FLC 1+2 FAC 3+2/1*
Accrington Stanley *(Loaned on 19/9/2008) FL 10+1/4*

GOSLING Daniel (Dan)
Born: Brixham, 2 February 1990
Height: 5'10" **Weight:** 11.3
International Honours: E: U21-2; Yth
A season that was just about to take off for the Everton youngster was ended cruelly at Wolverhampton with a cruciate knee injury that will sideline Dan for the start of the 2010-11 season. Typically it was incurred when ghosting into the area with an opportunity to net a late winner. Used from the bench in the Premier League, the former Plymouth player started in six Europa League matches, either at full-back or in midfield. In the League, Dan netted crucial goals in the win at West Ham and a typical poacher's effort in a memorable Goodison win over Manchester United. A versatile presence, either at the back or in

midfield, all at Everton wish the young star a speedy recovery.
Plymouth Arg *(From trainee on 20/2/2007) FL 13+9/2 FAC 2*
Everton *(£1,000,000 on 14/1/2008) PL 9+13/4 FLC 2/1 FAC 1+5/1 Others 6+1*

GOULDING Jeffrey (Jeff) Colin
Born: Sutton, 13 May 1984
Height: 6'2" **Weight:** 11.11
International Honours: E: SP-1
The striker was in Bournemouth's squad at the beginning of the season and started in the Carling Cup tie at Millwall before sustaining a training ground injury that sidelined him for a number of months. He had a few starts around Christmas before having to settle for a place on the bench. Jeff scored his final goal for the club with an injury-time strike at Notts County to earn a point but was released at the end of the season.
Bournemouth *(Free from Fisher Ath, via Grays Ath - loan, on 1/9/2008) FL 17+27/4 FLC 1 FAC 0+1 Others 2/1*

GOW Alan
Born: Clydebank, 9 October 1982
Height: 6'0" **Weight:** 11.0
Club Honours: S Div 2 '04
International Honours: S: B-1
In August, Glasgow Rangers accepted Plymouth's bid for Alan and when negotiations were complete, he signed a two-year contract with the Championship side. Alan, who is a naturally gifted striker, started his Argyle career well by scoring a late penalty on his debut against Cardiff in August. However, he struggled to cement his place in the starting line-up and most of his appearances were from the substitutes' bench. In February, Alan joined Hibernian on loan until the end of the season. He subsequently suffered from hamstring injuries that restricted his appearances but he has expressed a desire to stay at Hibernian and to leave Plymouth permanently.
Clydebank *(From Gleniffer Thistle on 24/11/2000) SL 3+4 Others 0+1*
Airdrie U *(Free on 1/8/2002) SL 67+17/25 SLC 3+3 SC 3+1/1 Others 3+1*
Falkirk *(Signed on 1/6/2005) SL 64+6/13 SLC 4+1/1 SC 5+1/4*
Glasgow Rgrs *(Free on 1/7/2007) SLC 1 SC 1*
Blackpool *(Loaned on 1/9/2008) FL 10+7/5*
Norwich C *(Loaned on 2/2/2009) FL 8+5*
Plymouth Arg *(Free on 14/8/2009) FL 8+6/2*
Hibernian *(Loaned on 1/2/2010) SL 3+4 SC 0+1/1*

GOWER Mark
Born: Edmonton, 5 October 1978
Height: 5'11" **Weight:** 11.12
Club Honours: FLC '99, Div 1 '06
International Honours: E: SP-4; Yth; Sch
The former Southend wide midfield player scored his first goal for Swansea in the home win over Queens Park Rangers, after missing a penalty in the previous home game against Reading. Mark was sidelined in November and December with back and groin injuries but returned to first team duty in February. From then on, he made regular starts in the centre of midfield, where he was best able to display a good range of passing.
Tottenham H *(From trainee on 1/4/1997) FLC 0+2*
Motherwell *(Loaned on 12/3/1999) SL 8+1/1*
Barnet *(£32,500 on 19/1/2001) FL 10+4/1 Others 1/1*
Southend U *(£25,000 on 25/7/2003) FL 189+14/35 FLC 8/1 FAC 14/3 Others 17+1/2*
Swansea C *(Free on 5/8/2008) FL 57+10/1 FLC 2+2 FAC 2+2*

GOWLING Joshua (Josh) Anthony Izaac
Born: Coventry, 29 November 1983
Height: 6'3" **Weight:** 12.8
A right-sided centre-half, Josh joined Gillingham from Carlisle in pre-season after injury sidelined defensive cornerstone Simon King. Forced to cover, out of position, at left centre-half, Josh struggled for form in his first few starts for the club but settled when returned to his natural position following the arrival of Matt Fry on loan. Far from being a physical player, Josh has good pace and a good range of passing but surprisingly earned two red-cards and 11 yellows which cost him a place in the side during the latter part of the campaign.
Bournemouth *(Free from Herfolge, Denmark, ex West Bromwich A trainee, on 1/8/2005) FL 72+11/1 FLC 3 FAC 4 Others 4*
Carlisle U *(Free on 3/7/2008) FL 3+1 FAC 1 Others 1*
Hereford U *(Loaned on 27/11/2008) FL 13*
Gillingham *(Signed on 20/7/2009) FL 29+1/2 FLC 2 FAC 3 Others 1*

GRABBAN Lewis James
Born: Croydon, 12 January 1988
Height: 6'0" **Weight:** 11.3
After struggling to get first team games at Millwall, Lewis joined Brentford on loan in March and headed home the winner on his debut against Leyton

Orient while deployed as a striker. He was then moved back to a right-sided midfield role, where his attacking attributes proved very useful before he was recalled to the Den for the last game of the League campaign to cover for injuries. When playing wide right of midfield, he is at his best when getting past the full-backs and creating chances for the strikers.
Crystal Palace *(From trainee on 28/7/2006) FL 0+10/1 FLC 0+3*
Oldham Ath *(Loaned on 16/8/2006) FL 1+8 FLC 1*
Motherwell *(Loaned on 31/8/2007) SL 0+5 SLC 0+1*
Millwall *(£150,000 on 21/1/2008) FL 44+11/9 FLC 1+1 FAC 9+1/2 Others 1+1*
Brentford *(Loaned on 25/3/2010) FL 7/2*

GRADEL Max Alain
Born: Abidjan, Ivory Coast, 30 November 1987
Height: 5'8" **Weight:** 12.3
Club Honours: Div 1 '09
A slight but pacy and tricky winger who had few opportunities at Leicester last season, Max joined Leeds on loan in October and became an instant hit. Still only 22, Max has the potential to reach the top if he can add consistency to his undoubted skill. He gave a taste of things to come with an outstanding 15-minute appearance from the bench which earned him the 'Man of the Match' award against Norwich. Capable of either playing on the flanks or as a striker, he continued to thrive as an impact substitute, netting within minutes of coming on in the 4-0 win against Yeovil. His loan deal was extended and he came on to score a late winner to see off Leyton Orient and was also on target in the West Yorkshire derby against Huddersfield after replacing Neil Kilkenny. Towards the end of January Max joined Leeds for an undisclosed fee on a two-and-half-year deal but could not tie down a regular starting position. However, with top scorer Jermaine Beckford out of touch near the end of the season Max was given his chance to lead the attack and responded with some vital goals, although blotting his copybook with his first-half dismissal in the nail-biting final game of the season against Bristol Rovers, which saw ten-man Leeds clinch promotion.
Leicester C *(Signed from Lewisham College, via trials at West Ham U, on 21/9/2005) FL 16+11/1 FLC 1+2 FAC 2/1 Others 0+1*
Bournemouth *(Loaned on 9/8/2007) FL 31+3/9 FLC 1 FAC 2/1 Others 1*
Leeds U *(Signed on 19/10/2009) FL 11+21/6 Others 2+1*

GRAHAM Daniel (Danny) Anthony William
Born: Gateshead, 12 August 1985
Height: 5'11" **Weight:** 12.5
International Honours: E: Yth
Danny joined Watford from Carlisle during the summer in a deal that required Watford to pay a minimum £200,000 in compensation. A striker with a proven scoring record, Danny settled quickly and scored Watford's first goal of the season against Doncaster on the opening day, which was also his debut. He kept up his scoring streak with six goals in his first nine League matches, but the goals rather dried up after that and he scored only two in his next 29 games. In fairness he was often required to play as a lone striker and hold up the ball rather than find the net. Fortunately he regained his confidence and his scoring touch at the end of the season and his goals against West Bromwich and Reading were crucial in staving off relegation. His goal against Albion – a 25-yard right-footed volley – would have been a goal of the season contender had it had been scored earlier. He ended with a total of 14, making him Watford's leading scorer. A player with an excellent work ethic, Danny was involved in all of Watford's matches.
Middlesbrough *(From trainee on 6/3/2004) PL 1+14/1 FLC 0+2/1 FAC 0+2 Others 1+1*
Darlington *(Loaned on 19/3/2004) FL 7+2/2*
Derby Co *(Loaned on 24/11/2005) FL 11+3*
Leeds U *(Loaned on 23/3/2006) FL 1+2*
Blackpool *(Loaned on 2/8/2006) FL 1+3/1*
Carlisle U *(Free on 1/1/2007) FL 89+11/36 FLC 3/1 FAC 5/1 Others 5/2*
Watford *(Signed on 2/7/2009) FL 37+9/14 FLC 2 FAC 1*

GRANDISON Jermaine Mickel
Born: Birmingham, 15 December 1990
Height: 6'4" **Weight:** 13.3
A highly-rated central defender from Coventry's Academy, Jermaine was one of several youngsters given a run-out in the home Carling Cup defeat by Hartlepool in August and played well. A few days later he impressed when coming off the bench at Barnsley and in October had his first League start at home to Reading. Despite failing to stop Grzegorz Rasiak scoring a second-minute goal, he recovered to put in a solid display. The arrival of Leon Barnett restricted his games and he made only two further substitute appearances

despite sitting on the bench over 30 times.
Coventry C *(From trainee on 29/6/2009) FL 1+4 FLC 1 FAC 0+1*

Anthony Grant

GRANT Anthony Paul Shaun Andrew Daure
Born: Lambeth, 4 June 1987
Height: 5'11" **Weight:** 11.3
International Honours: E: Yth
Nominally a central midfielder, Anthony's versatility meant he played at right and left-back, centre-back and right midfield for Southend and did not look out of place in any of those positions. A tigerish midfielder who tends to play the deepest of the quartet, his defensive duties and breaking up of attacking play incurred the attention of referees, bringing 14 yellow cards and spells on the sidelines due to suspension. An extremely skilful player, his passing is second to none at Roots Hall and in a traumatic season, Anthony always fought every inch of the way. For that he was a worthy runner-up in the fans' 'Player of the Year' award. Anthony will not want reminding that his own goal at Bristol Rovers in March was his fourth as a Blues player, an unwanted post-war club record.
Chelsea *(From trainee on 1/7/2005) PL 0+1*
Oldham Ath *(Loaned on 13/1/2006) FL 2*
Wycombe W *(Loaned on 1/8/2006) FL 39+1 FLC 5 FAC 2 Others 1+1*
Luton T *(Loaned on 16/11/2007) FL 1+3 FAC 0+1*
Southend U *(Free on 31/11/2008) FL 61+22/1 FLC 3 FAC 5+1 Others 1*

173

GRANT Gavin Renaldo
Born: Finchley, 27 March 1984
Height: 5'11" **Weight:** 11.0
Gavin is a pacy striker who can play down the middle or wide on the right. He joined Bradford on a non-contract basis in February, linking up with Peter Taylor for a third time after spells together at Stevenage and Wycombe. After nearly a year out of the game for personal reasons, Gavin took time to build up his match fitness but showed his raw speed can be a real threat to full-backs.
Gillingham (Signed from Tooting & Mitcham on 9/12/2005) FL 1+9/1
Millwall (Free on 16/5/2006) FL 1+3 FLC 0+1 Others 2
Wycombe W (Free on 23/7/2008) FL 9+1 FLC 1 Others 0+1
Bradford C (Free on 26/2/2010) FL 7+4

GRANT Joel Valentino
Born: Acton, 27 August 1987
Height: 6'0" **Weight:** 11.1
Club Honours: FC '08
International Honours: Jamaica: Yth
Joel completed his second season with Crewe after joining them from Aldershot. A skilful player who usually occupies the left-wing berth, he missed only handful of games and took his goal tally into double figures as well as creating several assists. With plenty of pace, Joel can also play up front if needed, his hard work and enthusiasm rubbing off on the team.
Watford (From trainee on 9/3/2006) FL 2+5 FLC 1+2 (Freed during 2007 close season)
Crewe Alex (£130,000 from Aldershot T on 1/7/2008) FL 60+11/11 FLC 3+1 FAC 2/1 Others 1

GRANT John Anthony Carlton
Born: Manchester, 9 August 1981
Height: 5'11" **Weight:** 11.9
Club Honours: FC '08
International Honours: E: SP-4
John is a forward with a reasonable scoring ratio for Aldershot and was also the PFA delegate. He played only occasionally, although made his 150th appearance for the Shots against Hereford in February. Later that month, John joined Oxford on loan until the end of the season. John finished with 57 goals in all competitions for the Shots, putting him fourth in their all-time scorers list. He will not be adding to that as he was released by manager Kevin Dillon.
Crewe Alex (From trainee on 7/7/1999) FL 2+5 FLC 1+3 (Free to Hereford U on 19/7/2002)
Shrewsbury T (Free from Telford U on 7/8/2004) FL 10+9/2 FLC 1 Others 0+1

(Freed on 22/3/2005)
Aldershot T (Free from Halifax T on 3/7/2006) FL 33+19/8 FLC 1+1 FAC 3+2/1 Others 0+1

GRANT Lee Anderson
Born: Hemel Hempstead, 27 January 1983
Height: 6'2" **Weight:** 13.4
International Honours: E: U21-4; Yth
Lee had another terrific season in goal for Sheffield Wednesday, playing in every game. Although his defence looked rocky, especially in the early part of the campaign, Lee really impressed. His anticipation and fielding of crosses has improved no end and this, added to his other attributes, makes him a top target for clubs at a higher level. Lee still needs to be more commanding and vocal so that he is the one taking the decisions and helping out his fellow defenders in the penalty area. Hopefully, the Owls will be able to hold

on to him and build a good team. Then he could go on to the highest level.
Derby Co (From trainee on 17/2/2001) FL 69+5 FLC 3 FAC 2
Burnley (Loaned on 15/11/2005) FL 1
Oldham Ath (Loaned on 31/1/2006) FL 16
Sheffield Wed (Free on 24/7/2007) FL 136 FLC 5 FAC 4

GRANT Robert
Born: Liverpool, 1 July 1990
Height: 5'11" **Weight:** 12.0
A product of the Accrington youth set-up, Robert continued to impress as he came of age. Was played up front for the majority of games rather than his usual left-wing position and notched up 18 goals over the campaign. A gifted and naturally left-footed player, he agreed to sign for Scunthorpe at the start of the coming season.
Accrington Stanley (From trainee on 8/2/2008) FL 53+12/15 FLC 1+2/1 FAC 5/2 Others 4/1

Robert Grant

GRAY Andrew (Andy) David

Born: Harrogate, 15 November 1977
Height: 6'1" **Weight:** 13.0
International Honours: S: 2; B-3; Yth
Andy's only start for Charlton was in the Carling Cup defeat at Hereford in August when his penalty kick was saved by the opposing 'keeper. His only other appearances, both as substitute, were either side of that game. He was then sold to Barnsley for an undisclosed fee towards the end of August. Andy is an experienced striker who holds the ball up well and is effective playing on his own up front or with another front man. Making his debut against Leicester a day later, Andy was immediately involved and quickly showed his goal-scoring qualities. Used regularly as a sole striker away from home, his display at Preston was as complete a performance as you would wish to see from a player in that position, but used mainly as a substitute in home games he did not find the target as much as he would have liked.
Leeds U (From trainee on 1/7/1995) PL 13+9 FLC 3+1 FAC 0+2
Bury (Loaned on 11/12/1997) FL 4+2/1
Nottingham F (£175,000 on 2/9/1998) P/FL 34+30/1 FLC 3+4 FAC 4+1
Preston NE (Loaned on 23/2/1999) FL 5
Oldham Ath (Loaned on 25/3/1999) FL 4
Bradford C (Free on 9/8/2002) FL 77/20 FLC 2 FAC 2/1
Sheffield U (Signed on 27/2/2004) FL 56+2/25 FLC 2/2 FAC 5/1
Sunderland (£1,100,000 on 10/8/2005) PL 13+8/1 FAC 0+1
Burnley (£750,000 + on 17/3/2006) FL 68+1/28 FLC 2+1/2 FAC 1
Charlton Ath (£1,500,000 + on 19/1/2008) FL 31+14/9 FLC 1 FAC 0+1
Barnsley (Signed on 21/8/2009) FL 19+11/6 FAC 1

GRAY Danie (Dan) Edward

Born: Mansfield, 23 November 1989
Height: 6'0" **Weight:** 10.12
Dan's ability to play in midfield or at right-back, where his height is an asset, helped him win a regular place on the bench before breaking through into Chesterfield's starting line-up in January. With an eye for a pass and a decent long throw, he was an important member of the team that won seven out of eight to climb to third place but lost his place, briefly, as the team stumbled. Despite this he was offered, and accepted, a new two-year deal in May.
Chesterfield (From trainee on 30/12/2008) FL 36+8 FLC 1 FAC 3 Others 1+2

GRAY David Peter

Born: Edinburgh, 4 May 1988
Height: 6'0" **Weight:** 12.10

International Honours: S: U21-2
Following his successful loan spell at Plymouth in the previous season, David returned to Home Park in September for a further three-month spell. He again made the right-back position his own, starting in 12 out of the next 14 games. His strong defensive work and his attacking runs down the right often resulted in scoring opportunities. He returned to Old Trafford at the end of his loan to try and fight for opportunities of first team action.
Manchester U (From trainee on 17/8/2007) FLC 1
Crewe Alex (Loaned on 22/11/2007) FL 1
Plymouth Arg (Loaned on 2/1/2009) FL 14 FAC 1
Plymouth Arg (Loaned on 19/9/2009) FL 12

GRAY Joshua (Josh) Ian

Born: South Shields, 22 July 1991
Height: 6'1" **Weight:** 11.11
Josh has come through the youth ranks at Darlington and played one full game in 2008-09 before being used more regularly this campaign. He relishes running at defences down the left flank and shows a good burst of speed, clever footwork and a strong shot. He was rewarded with his first goal at Burton on Easter Saturday with a fierce drive from the edge of the penalty area.
Darlington (From trainee on 24/5/2009) FL 11+21/1 FAC 0+2

GRAY Julian Raymond

Born: Lewisham, 21 September 1979
Height: 6'1" **Weight:** 11.10
Having left Fulham during the summer, Julian was a free agent and signed for Barnsley on a monthly contract in September. Made his debut three days later against Swansea and played all his time at Oakwell in the problem left-back position where his passing and ability to get forward was shown to good effect. His opportunities became limited with the arrival of Carl Dickinson on loan and despite doing little wrong he was mainly confined to the bench. After two months his contract was not renewed and he left Barnsley before signing for Walsall in the middle of February and playing in every game thereafter. It took him a while to adapt to the lowest level of League football he has played, but he showed the occasional touch of sheer class be it a high quality left-wing cross or an intelligent pass, although this was perhaps not seen often enough for a player possessing such undoubted ability. His four goals included a calmly placed right-foot volley at Exeter and a superb curling 20-yard right-footed shot

at home to Hartlepool.
Arsenal (From trainee on 13/7/1998) PL 0+1
Crystal Palace (£250,000 + on 21/7/2000) FL 100+25/10 FLC 5+6/1 FAC 6/2 Others 2
Cardiff C (Loaned on 13/10/2003) FL 5+4
Birmingham C (Free on 24/6/2004) P/FL 38+22/3 FLC 7/1 FAC 6/1
Coventry C (Free on 10/7/2007) FL 23+6/4 FLC 2+1 FAC 1
Fulham (Signed on 1/9/2008) PL 0+1 FAC 1+1
Barnsley (Free on 15/9/2009) FL 1+4 FLC 2
Walsall (Free on 12/2/2010) FL 17+1/4 FAC 1

GRAY Michael

Born: Sunderland, 3 August 1974
Height: 5'7" **Weight:** 10.10
Club Honours: Div 1 '96, '99
International Honours: E: 3
For two-thirds of the season, Michael was a vital part of the Sheffield Wednesday side, playing on the right of a four-man midfield. Because of a slight loss of form and the tactical changes to the team he lost his place with a quarter of the season to go. A vastly experienced player with a great left foot, he adds calmness to the side and also takes a good free kick. Unfortunately, his goal tally from midfield has been very sparse, with only one scored during the season. At this stage of his career he really needs to be playing regularly and certainly the team would profit more from using his skills to better advantage.
Sunderland (From trainee on 1/7/1992) P/FL 341+22/16 FLC 23+4 FAC 17+1/1 Others 2
Glasgow Celtic (Loaned on 31/8/2003) SL 2+5 SLC 1 Others 1+1
Blackburn Rov (Free on 28/1/2004) PL 63+1 FLC 6 FAC 1 Others 2
Leeds U (Loaned on 3/2/2005) FL 10
Leeds U (Loaned on 22/3/2007) FL 6
Wolverhampton W (Free on 1/8/2007) FL 33+8/4 FLC 3 FAC 2+1
Sheffield Wed (Free on 9/1/2009) FL 40+3/2 FLC 0+1

GRAY Reece Anthony

Born: Oldham, 1 September 1992
Height: 5'7" **Weight:** 8.8
Another youth team product at Rochdale, Reece was on the first team bench for one game in mid-season. After helping the youth side earn runners-up medals in their Youth Alliance league, he made his first senior appearances as a substitute striker in the last two League matches of the season.
Rochdale (Trainee) FL 0+2

GREEN Daniel (Danny) Richard
Born: Harlow, 9 July 1988
Height: 5'11" **Weight:** 12.0
Danny made his Dagenham debut on the opening day of the season at Crewe. Having signed from Bishop's Stortford, he opened his account with two goals against Torquay in August. He had a dip in form in the middle of the season but came back to terrorise defences with his wing skills in the final two months, during which time he assumed the responsibility for taking the penalties. Danny scored the second goal in the Daggers' play-off final victory at Wembley.
Nottingham F (From trainee at Northampton T on 1/7/2007. Freed during 2008 close season)
Dagenham & Redbridge (Free from Bishops Stortford, on 2/7/2009) FL 45+1/13 FLC 1 FAC 1 Others 3+1/1

GREEN Dominic Ashley
Born: Newham, 5 July 1989
Height: 5'7" **Weight:** 11.5
Peterborough have high hopes for this wide midfielder, who came to the club as one for the future. Although Dominic found it hard to get an extended run in the first team, when picked he showed his potential with tight control and mazy runs. In order to get first team football he was loaned out to Chesterfield and although he took a few games to get his eye in at League Two level, he became more and more influential and grabbed a fine individual goal in the February win over Lincoln. He is an exciting prospect with the ball at his feet, and can cross or cut in with equally good effect.
Dagenham & Redbridge (From West Ham U/Thames Gateway Football Partnership Scheme on 7/8/2007) FL 4+10/1 FLC 1
Peterborough U (£150,000 on 27/8/2008) FL 9+18/2 FAC 1+2 Others 1
Chesterfield (Loaned on 14/1/2010) FL 10/2

GREEN Jamie Paul
Born: Rossington, 18 August 1989
Height: 5'7" **Weight:** 10.7
After his excellent first full season for Rotherham, Jamie was first choice left-back at the start of this one. Tucked into the job with typical enthusiasm and energy but lost his place a couple of months in, shortly after Ronnie Moore's arrival as manager. He made a number of substitute appearances later in the season and always gave everything.
Rotherham U (From trainee on 29/6/2007) FL 49+10/2 FLC 2+1 Others 4

GREEN Paul Jason
Born: Pontefract, 10 April 1983
Height: 5'11" **Weight:** 12.0
Club Honours: Div 3 '04; AMC '07
International Honours: RoI: 2
An uneven season for Paul ended happily when he won his first two caps for the Republic of Ireland, qualifying through grandparents. After an excellent first campaign in Derby's midfield, Paul had a setback in September when a foot injury from the previous season required further surgery. When he returned in November, circumstances dictated that he played wide on the right. He gave it his best shot but was clearly uncomfortable near the touchline and was seen at his best only when he returned to a central position. He also had a competent stint at right-back in the FA Cup replay against Millwall. Given his energy in central midfield, he should better his contribution of two goals. Called into the Irish training camp, Paul did well enough to stay on for two matches. He went on as a substitute against Paraguay before starting and scoring against Algeria.
Doncaster Rov (From trainee on 16/8/2000) FL 161+37/25 FLC 8+3/1 FAC 7+3 Others 11+4/1
Derby Co (Free on 13/6/2008) FL 59+3/5 FLC 7/1 FAC 8/2

GREEN Paul Michael
Born: Birmingham, 15 April 1987
Height: 5'11" **Weight:** 12.0
Having started 2009-10 on the sidelines after undergoing back surgery in the summer, the versatile Lincoln defender marked his return to action on Boxing Day by turning in a sequence of impressive performances during the second half of the season. Although Paul finished the campaign with a broken metatarsal he was rewarded with a new one-year contract.
Aston Villa (From trainee on 19/4/2005)
Lincoln C (Free on 23/1/2007) FL 93+7/3 FLC 2 FAC 5 Others 3

GREEN Robert Paul
Born: Chertsey, 18 January 1980
Height: 6'2" **Weight:** 12.2
Club Honours: Div 1 '04
International Honours: E: 10; B-1; Yth
The West Ham goalkeeper is a model of consistency, having now played in 126 consecutive Premier League games. It was another good campaign for the England 'keeper who made vital saves as the Hammers struggled to avoid relegation. He was outstanding at Manchester City and Aston Villa as he thwarted the attempts of Martin Petrov and Gabby Agbonlahor. Robert is an

Robert Green

excellent shot-stopper who also commands his box well. At times he was playing behind a hesitant defence but his presence steadied their nerves. In the vital game against Wigan he made an amazing save from James McCarthy, who let fly from 30 yards before Robert flung himself full length to push the shot away. During the campaign he maintained his place in the England team and staked his place as England qualified for the World Cup finals. He was one of the three 'keepers Fabio Capello picked to go to South Africa.
Norwich C (From juniors on 3/7/1997) P/FL 222+1 FLC 7 FAC 8 Others 3
West Ham U (£2,000,000 on 18/8/2006) PL 140 FLC 5 FAC 7

GREEN Ryan Michael
Born: Cardiff, 20 October 1980
Height: 5'8" **Weight:** 11.6
International Honours: W: 2; U21-16; Yth
Ryan's return to Hereford, where he was the winning goalscoring hero in the Conference play-off final, was enthusiastically received and he demonstrated that he had lost none of his class. A fine reader of the game, whether at his usual right-back position or at centre-back, where he was regularly deployed in mid-season, he showed that he remained a player of high quality. His ability to time a tackle remained unimpaired and, although his forays forward might be less than in his younger days, a scything run and crucial goal against Cheltenham showed that he could still be a force in opposition penalty areas. Was out of contract at the end of June.
Wolverhampton W (From trainee on 25/10/1997) FL 6+2 FLC 2 FAC 0+2
Torquay U (Loaned on 2/3/2001) FL 10
Millwall (Free on 19/10/2001) FL 12+1
Cardiff C (Free on 14/8/2002) Others 1
Sheffield Wed (Free on 27/11/2002) FL 4 (Free to Hereford U on 8/8/2003)
Bristol Rov (Free from Hereford U on 7/6/2006) FL 64+7 FLC 1 FAC 3+1 Others 8
Hereford U (Free on 2/7/2009) FL 31/1 FLC 2 FAC 1 Others 2

GREEN Stuart
Born: Whitehaven, 15 June 1981
Height: 5'10" **Weight:** 11.4
After previously working with him at Hull and Crystal Palace, Wycombe manager Peter Taylor signed his son-in-law Stuart on a two-year contract after his release from Blackpool in the summer. Used mainly as an attacking central midfielder, with good vision and passing, Stuart started most games until

Taylor's departure in October. He came close to scoring a last-minute equaliser against Leeds in August when his shot was tipped against a post. Under new manager Gary Waddock, he made only two further appearances, one from the bench, before he was dropped from the squad completely, spending the rest of the season in the reserves.
Newcastle U (From trainee on 8/7/1999)
Carlisle U (Loaned on 14/12/2001) FL 16/3
Hull C (£150,000 on 3/7/2002) FL 111+26/24 FLC 2+1 FAC 4+1/1 Others 1/1
Carlisle U (Loaned on 19/2/2003) FL 9+1/2 Others 3
Crystal Palace (£75,000 on 31/8/2006) FL 12+12/4 FLC 1 FAC 2
Blackpool (Free on 31/1/2008) FL 1+5 FLC 0+1 FAC 1
Crewe Alex (Loaned on 14/11/2008) FL 2
Wycombe W (Free on 15/7/2009) FL 10+3 FLC 1 FAC 1

GREENING Jonathan
Born: Scarborough, 2 January 1979
Height: 5'11" **Weight:** 11.7
Club Honours: UEFACL '99; FLC '04; Ch '08
International Honours: E: U21-18; Yth
Having started the season with West Bromwich, playing two games, the midfielder was signed on a season-long loan by Fulham, who had been tracking him throughout the summer. A regular in the match-day squad he enjoyed his best run in the side during an autumn injury to Dickson Etuhu. Although mainly used as a central midfielder he was also deployed on the left side of the midfield four on a number of occasions. An excellent passer of the ball he has the vision to seek out a key cross-field pass to change the axis of attack. Despite often getting into good attacking positions himself he does not possess a good goalscoring record but his only strike of the season was a composed effort in a crowded penalty box and sufficient to gain all three points in the home game against Portsmouth. At the end of the season it was not clear as to whether the loan signing would become a permanent move.
York C (From trainee on 23/12/1996) FL 5+20/2 FLC 0+1 Others 1
Manchester U (£500,000 + on 25/3/1998) PL 4+10 FLC 6 FAC 0+1 Others 3+3
Middlesbrough (£2,000,000 on 9/8/2001) PL 91+8/4 FLC 5 FAC 4+1
West Bromwich A (£1,250,000 on 30/7/2004) P/FL 190+6/7 FLC 6+3/1 FAC 16 Others 3

Fulham (Loaned on 20/8/2009) PL 15+8/1 FLC 1 FAC 2+1 Others 6+1

GREER Gordon
Born: Glasgow, 14 December 1980
Height: 6'2" **Weight:** 12.5
International Honours: S: B-1
Having enjoyed a successful loan at Swindon in the previous season, Gordon became manager Danny Wilson's first signing during the close season. Resuming his role as Town captain, he formed a strong defensive pairing with Scott Cuthbert. His only goal was a thumping last-minute header that secured a home point against Norwich. An uncharacteristically rash challenge in the second leg of the play-offs at Charlton put him out of the Wembley final, where his defensive qualities were sorely missed. A solid central defender, he tackles strongly, is good in the air, but is also comfortable on the ball and distributes it well.
Clyde (Free from Port Glasgow on 28/6/2000) SL 27+3 SLC 0+1 SC 1 Others 1
Blackburn Rov (£200,000 on 23/5/2001) FLC 1
Stockport Co (Loaned on 27/3/2003) FL 4+1/1
Kilmarnock (Signed on 31/8/2003) SL 102+5/4 SLC 8/1 SC 5
Doncaster Rov (Free on 25/7/2007) FL 10+2/1 FLC 1+1 FAC 2 Others 2
Swindon T (Loaned on 26/1/2009) FL 19/1
Swindon T (Free on 2/7/2009) FL 43+1/1 FLC 2 FAC 3/1 Others 4

GREGAN Sean Matthew
Born: Guisborough, 29 March 1974
Height: 6'2" **Weight:** 14.7
Club Honours: Div 2 '00
Oldham's influential captain was the winner of every award going at Boundary Park at the end of the season. Sean played in every minute of every game of the campaign and won the 'Player of the Season' award with a 100 per cent vote. A fantastic captain with a brilliant football brain, Sean is very much the senior player at Boundary Park and the man every other player looks up to. At the age of 36, he was awarded a 12-month extension to his playing contract that will keep him at Boundary Park as a player until next June. In 49 appearances, he scored one goal and is still one of the best in League One.
Darlington (From trainee on 20/1/1991) FL 129+7/4 FLC 8 FAC 7 Others 10+1/1
Preston NE (£350,000 on 29/11/1996) FL 206+6/12 FLC 14 FAC 15/1 Others 10

West Bromwich A *(£1,500,000 on 6/8/2002) Pl/FL 76+3/2 FLC 4 FAC 2*
Leeds U *(£500,000 on 17/9/2004) FL 63+1 FLC 6 FAC 1 Others 3*
Oldham Ath *(Free on 8/11/2006) FL 126+2/1 FLC 4 FAC 5/1 Others 5*

GRELLA Mike
Born: Glen Cove, New York, USA, 23 January 1987
Height: 5'11" **Weight:** 12.2
International Honours: USA: Yth
American striker Mike's learning process at Leeds continued although the bulk of his appearances were from the bench. Regarded by many as the most skilful player at Elland Road, he notched his first Leeds' goal after nine minutes of his first League start against Stockport. Mike's biggest impact was in the FA Cup, scoring in the last minute in the first round as Oldham were eliminated and hitting an extra-time double as Leeds' finally saw off Kettering. His header at Carlisle sent the Johnstone's Paint Trophy Northern Area final to a penalty shoot-out that the Cumbrians won.
Leeds U *(Free from Cary Clarets, USA, ex Duke University, Long Island Rough Riders, on 12/2/2009) FL 3+25/1 FLC 2+1 FAC 1+3/3 Others 3+2/1*

GRELLA Vincenzo (Vince)
Born: Dandenong, Victoria, Australia, 5 October 1979
Height: 6'0" **Weight:** 12.6
International Honours: Australia: 44; U23-17; Yth
It was another season when Vince struggled with a succession of leg injuries that prevented him from ever having a run of games for Blackburn. In the brief glimpses that were possible he displayed the calm ability to control the centre of midfield in a holding role that would make him an automatic choice, but his frequent absences made him a largely forgotten man. He was sent off in an early season game against Aston Villa, which did not help his appearances, but even having played superbly in the late season game against Manchester United he promptly had to be left out because of recurring injury.
Blackburn Rov *(£4,000,000 from Torino, Italy, ex Canberra Cosmos, Carlton, Empoli, Ternana - loan, Parma, on 29/8/2008) PL 25+7 FLC 0+2 FAC 2*

GREULICH Billy
Born: Sunderland, 24 April 1991
Height: 6'3" **Weight:** 12.0
Billy impressed in pre-season friendlies and was signed by Hartlepool just ahead of the August transfer deadline. Still a teenager, the striker had been rejected by a number of League clubs but in 2008-09 was a regular scorer with Northern League team Brandon United. He was leading scorer for Hartlepool's reserves but his first team opportunities were limited to a handful of substitute appearances. Seen as a player for the future, Billy was offered an extension to his initial one-year contract.
Hartlepool U *(Signed from Brandon U on 23/8/2009) FL 0+4 FAC 0+1*

GREY Andre Anthony
Born: Wolverhampton, 26 June 1991
Height: 5'10" **Weight:** 12.3
A young first-year professional midfield player, he made his League debut for Shrewsbury as a substitute in the opening day game against Burton. Played in four League games and one Johnstone's Paint Trophy tie, all from the bench, and had most impact when playing a significant part in the build up to one of the goals in the 2-0 home win against Crewe in September. Subsequently, had spells on loan with Telford and Hinckley United to gain experience. Was out of contract in the summer.
Shrewsbury T *(From trainee on 8/7/2009) FL 0+4 Others 0+1*

GRIFFIN Adam
Born: Salford, 26 August 1984
Height: 5'7" **Weight:** 10.5
Adam was one of a handful of former players who trained with the Stockport squad in the summer before being handed the chance to rejoin County. He scored in his first game back, a 3-1 defeat at Huddersfield in the Carling Cup, but the winger was unable to hold down a regular place because of a string of injuries. In March he required a hernia operation, keeping him out for action until the final three games.
Oldham Ath *(From trainee on 9/8/2003) FL 58+4/3 FLC 2 FAC 4+1 Others 4+1/1*
Oxford U *(Loaned on 10/11/2005) FL 8+1 FAC 2 Others 2*
Stockport Co *(Signed on 20/1/2006) FL 68+23/6 FLC 2+1 FAC 4 Others 1*
Darlington *(Free on 29/7/2008) FL 9+8 FLC 1+1 FAC 1+1 Others 0+1*
Stockport Co *(Free on 1/8/2009) FL 9+9 FLC 0+1 FAC 1 Others 1*

GRIFFIN Andrew (Andy)
Born: Billinge, 7 March 1979
Height: 5'9" **Weight:** 10.10
International Honours: E: U21-3; Yth
Very much out of favour at Stoke, Andy played only three games for the Potters in 2009-10, all of which were in the Carling Cup. However, in one of those games he had the distinction of completing a remarkable fight-back by ten-man City which saw them come from behind to win 4-3 with a goal in the sixth minute of injury time. In January Andy was recruited by Reading on a loan basis to fill the problem right-back spot in their defence. That position had been occupied by five other players at various times prior to Andy's arrival, but he made it his own with a non-stop series of quality displays. A vastly experienced defender, he added stability to Royals' back line. Andy's tackling was strong but precise, and he used his meticulous reading of the game to save his legs on many occasions. He could deliver accurate crosses from the right flank too, though it was his reliability in the full-back position that gave orthodox wide midfielders such as Jimmy Kebe and Jobi McAnuff the confidence to push forward. When Andy left the field after being substituted near the end of Reading's last home game of the season, he received a standing ovation from the packed Madejski Stadium crowd.
Stoke C *(From trainee on 5/9/1996) FL 52+5/2 FLC 4+1 FAC 2*
Newcastle U *(£1,500,000 + on 30/1/1998) PL 63+13/2 FLC 8 FAC 6 Others 14/1*
Portsmouth *(Free on 2/7/2004) PL 38+6 FLC 3+1 FAC 1*
Stoke C *(Loaned on 9/9/2006) FL 32+1/2 FAC 1*
Derby Co *(Signed on 1/8/2007) PL 13+2*
Stoke C *(£300,000 on 11/1/2008) P/FL 32+3 FLC 3+1/1*
Reading *(Loaned on 12/1/2010) FL 21 FAC 4*

GRIFFITH Anthony James
Born: Huddersfield, 28 October 1986
Height: 5'10" **Weight:** 12.0
Club Honours: AMC '07
Anthony had a very good season as Port Vale's central midfield enforcer and his defending went a long way towards breaking up opposition attacks. He took time to get going but soon made the position his own. He filled in as a right-back briefly but soon reverted to midfield. The only downside is that his sort of role brings bookings and his tally of 14 for the season meant that he missed three games through suspension. After being booked at Bournemouth, he was substituted because of the risk of a red card but unfortunately the team missed him and lost 4-0. Anthony was the supporters' 'Player of the Year'.
Doncaster Rov *(Signed from*

Glasshoughton Welfare on 5/9/2005) FL
6 FLC 0+1 Others 2
Darlington (Loaned on 23/11/2006) FL
2+2
Port Vale (Free on 8/5/2008) FL 75+3
FLC 3+1 FAC 5 Others 1+2

GRIFFITHS Scott Robert
Born: Westminster, 27 November 1985
Height: 5'9" **Weight:** 11.2
Club Honours: FC '07
International Honours: E: SP-2
Scott had another great season as
Dagenham's left-back and put in some
top-notch performances in the early
matches which made him a target for
transfer. He even added his first goal for
two seasons before joining
Peterborough in late October on loan.
Signing for the Posh in January for an
undisclosed six figure fee, Scott proved
to be an exciting attacking full back
who loves to push on down the line.
Pacy and good in the tackle, not many
wide men will be looking forward to
face him this coming season.
Dagenham & Redbridge (Free from
Aveley on 12/8/2004) FL 97+1/1 FLC 3
FAC 6 Others 7
Peterborough U (Signed on
23/10/2009) FL 20 FAC 1

GRIMES Ashley James
Born: Swinton, 9 December 1986
Height: 6'0" **Weight:** 11.2
Ashley made only two starts for
Millwall, the second of which was in a
2-1 win over Walsall, and four as a
substitute, as the competition for places
at the club hotted up. He still put in
energetic displays, full of running up
front and likes to feed off the taller
strikers to create chances.
Manchester C (From trainee on
3/7/2006)
Swindon T (Loaned on 22/3/2007) FL
0+4
Millwall (Free on 1/7/2008) FL 6+15/2
FLC 0+2 FAC 0+5/2 Others 1+1

GRITTON Martin Francis
Born: Glasgow, 1 June 1978
Height: 6'1" **Weight:** 12.7
Martin will be hoping that the last year
of his current agreement at Chesterfield
is more productive than the season just
completed. The mobile front man could
not dislodge Jack Lester or Wade Small
in the early season and then found
Barry Conlon signed and preferred to
him when a different attacking option
was explored by Chesterfield. Rather
than take the opportunity to go out on
loan, Martin stayed to keep pressure on
the first teamers by scoring regularly for
the reserves.
Plymouth Arg (Free from Porthleven

on 7/8/1998) FL 15+29/7 FLC 2+2/1
FAC 0+4 Others 3/1
Torquay U (Signed on 8/8/2002) FL
72+21/23 FLC 2 FAC 2+1/3 Others 2
Grimsby T (£5,000 on 24/12/2004) FL
29+20/6 FLC 0+2 FAC 0+1 Others 1
Lincoln C (Signed on 31/1/2006) FL
9+18/3 Others 1+2
Mansfield T (Loaned on 12/1/2007) FL
14+5/6
Macclesfield T (Free on 3/7/2007) FL
40+12/13 FLC 1/1 FAC 3+1/2 Others 3
Chesterfield (Signed on 12/1/2009) FL
21+8/5 FLC 1

GROUNDS Jonathan Martin
Born: Thornaby, 2 February 1988
Height: 6'1" **Weight:** 12.3
After impressing in Middlesbrough's
pre-season matches and with injuries to
Andrew Taylor and Emanuel Pogatetz,
Jonathan took his chance and started
the first few games at left-back. He was
virtually ever-present under Gareth
Southgate but was out of favour when
Gordon Strachan arrived. In January, he
returned to the first team when Sean St
Ledger decided not to turn his loan
from Preston into a permanent move.
He impressed against Doncaster and
Bristol City at centre-half when
partnering David Wheater. With the
loan acquisition of Stephen McManus in
the January transfer window, Jonathan
was back among the substitutes.
Middlesbrough (From trainee on
6/7/2007) P/FL 23+4 FLC 1 FAC 2
Norwich C (Loaned on 1/9/2008) FL
3+2
Norwich C (Loaned on 7/1/2009) FL
11/3

GROVES Daniel (Danny) Charles
Born: Middlesbrough, 10 December
1990
Height: 6'2" **Weight:** 12.0
Another promising young player who
has come through the Darlington youth
ranks and made one brief substitute
appearance in the final game of the
previous season at Chester. This season
he made eight starts and an equal
number from the bench, showing
composure in midfield and gaining
valuable experience for a 19-year-old.
Was out of contract at the end of June.
Darlington (From trainee on 1/7/2009)
FL 8+9 Others 1

GUDJOHNSEN Eidur Smari
Born: Reykjavik, Iceland, 15 September
1978
Height: 6'1" **Weight:** 13.0
Club Honours: CS '00, '05; FLC '05; PL
'05, '06
International Honours: Iceland: 61;

Eidur Gudjohnsen

U21-11; Yth
The Icelandic international striker
arrived on loan from Monaco in
January, after Tottenham allowed
Robbie Keane to go to Glasgow Celtic
on loan. Eidur is an experienced player,
with Premier League appearances at
Bolton and Chelsea. While his
appearances were limited to four starts
and ten off the bench, Eidur is a similar
player to Keane in that he can bolster

midfield due to his excellent reading of the game, skill at intercepting and a creative eye. Eidur scored twice for Spurs and his finest moments came in a vital win at Stoke, where he had the strength to hold the ball against a determined defensive challenge before scoring the first goal, then dummied for Niko Kranjcar's winner. Eidur scored his second in the next Spurs' game, their 3-1 FA Cup quarter-final success against Fulham.

Bolton W (Free from KR Reykjavik, Iceland, ex Valur, PSV Eindhoven, on 6/8/1998) FL 48+7/18 FLC 8+1/3 FAC 4+1/4 Others 4/1
Chelsea (£4,000,000 on 12/7/2000) PL 126+60/54 FLC 8+8/6 FAC 17+8/10 Others 26+10/8 (Transferred to Barcelona, Spain on 3/7/2006)
Tottenham H (Loaned from AS Monaco, France on 28/1/2010) PL 3+8/1 FAC 1+2/1

GUDJONSSON Johannes (Joey) Karl
Born: Akranes, Iceland, 25 May 1980
Height: 5'8" **Weight:** 11.5
International Honours: Iceland: 34; U21-10; Yth
Joey's only League start came in Burnley's game at Tottenham, a 5-0 defeat. Otherwise, his appearances were confined to the Cups and cameos from the bench and while his tenacious midfield play remained intact, little was seen of his renowned shooting from distance. Usually a squad member under Owen Coyle's reign, he fell out of favour under Brian Laws, and in April was suspended by the club after criticising Laws on an Icelandic website. He was released just before the end of the season.
Aston Villa (Loaned from Real Betis, Spain, ex IA Akranes, KRC Genk, MVV Maastricht, RKC Waalwijk, on 27/1/2003) PL 9+2/2
Wolverhampton W (Loaned from Real Betis, Spain on 29/8/2003) PL 5+6 FLC 3/1 FAC 1+1
Leicester C (Free from Real Betis, Spain on 11/8/2004) FL 66+11/10 FLC 5/2 FAC 7/1 (Freed during 2006 close season)
Burnley (£150,000 from AZ Alkmaar, Holland on 22/1/2007) P/FL 43+45/7 FLC 8+2 FAC 4+4 Others 1+2

GUEDIOURA Adlene
Born: La Roche-sur-Yon, France, 12 November 1985
Height: 6'1" **Weight:** 12.8
International Honours: Algeria: 1
Wolverhampton's French-Algerian central midfielder soon confirmed his reputation as being a hard tackler, who

was not afraid to shoot. He had been given the incentive of a three-year contract if he impressed. He hit a volley almost perfectly against Chelsea but was denied by a fine Petr Cech save. One of his shots was deflected in at Burnley, but after six consecutive starts he still needed to fully adapt to the Premier League, as he had the odd lapse in concentration. The last match at home to Sunderland saw Adlene return to the first team, hitting a fine left-footed winner to earn that contract.
Wolverhampton W (Loaned from RSC Charleroi, Belgium, ex Racing Club de Paris, Sedan, US Roye, Noisy-le-Sec, L'Entente SSG, Creteil, KV Kortrijk, on 25/1/2010) PL 7+7/1

GUERET Willy July
Born: St Claude, Guadeloupe, 3 August 1973
Height: 6'1" **Weight:** 13.5
Club Honours: AMC '06, '08; Div 2 '08
Willy completed his third season as MK Dons regular starting goalkeeper, missing just three games throughout including the final two due to a thumb injury. Very agile when making saves, he generally commanded his area well, which was no mean feat considering the ever-changing nature of the back four in front of him. This lack of continuity particularly caused problems at set-piece situations, with the Dons conceding many more goals from high balls being thrown into the box than they would have liked. As such, and being the perfectionist he is, Willy will have been disappointed with the total of goals let in during the campaign.
Millwall (Free from Le Mans, France on 31/7/2000) FL 13+1 FAC 3 Others 2
Swansea C (Free on 5/8/2004) FL 132 FLC 3 FAC 10 Others 10
MK Dons (Signed on 10/8/2007) FL 133 FLC 3 FAC 3 Others 14

GUERRERO Fernando Alexander
Born: Quito, Ecuador, 30 September 1989
Height: 5'7" **Weight:** 11.0
International Honours: Ecuador: 2
There were high expectations of the Ecuador international when he arrived at Burnley on trial in time for the start of the season and he made a good early impression with his electrifying pace and quick thinking, usually in brief substitute appearances, although he did start in both of the Clarets' Carling Cup ties. After September, though, he was rarely seen, and he returned to his parent club Independiente del Valle in March without ever really having the chance to prove his potential in English

football.
Burnley (Loaned from Independiente del Valle, ex Castilla, Emelec - loan, on 6/8/2009) PL 0+7 FLC 2

GUINAN Stephen (Steve) Anthony
Born: Birmingham, 24 December 1975
Height: 6'1" **Weight:** 13.7
International Honours: E: SP-4
Striker Steve was signed to link up with Bayo Akinfenwa in the Northampton front line, but no sooner had they started to gel when Steve was whipped into hospital for a double hernia operation. By the time the experienced front man returned, partner Bayo was out. Steve became the first winner of the 'Tommy Fowler award', made by the family of the Northampton legend in recognition of Steve's fund-raising exploits.
Nottingham F (From trainee on 7/11/1993) P/FL 2+5 FLC 2/1
Darlington (Loaned on 14/12/1995) FL 3/1
Burnley (Loaned on 27/3/1997) FL 0+6
Crewe Alex (Loaned on 19/3/1998) FL 3
Halifax T (Loaned on 16/10/1998) FL 12/2
Plymouth Arg (Loaned on 24/3/1999) FL 11/7
Scunthorpe U (Loaned on 10/9/1999) FL 2+1/1
Cambridge U (Free on 24/12/1999) FL 4+2 FAC 0+2 Others 1
Plymouth Arg (Free on 23/3/2000) FL 15+15/3 FLC 2 FAC 2 Others 0+1
Shrewsbury T (Free on 28/3/2002) FL 4+1 (Free to Hereford U on 15/8/2002)
Cheltenham T (Free from Hereford U on 17/5/2004) FL 79+13/13 FLC 3/1 FAC 8/1 Others 5+3/3
Hereford U (Free on 25/1/2007) FL 76+11/25 FLC 0+3 FAC 2+2
Northampton T (Free on 2/7/2009) FL 19+9/4 FLC 1 FAC 2 Others 2+1/3

GULACSI Peter
Born: Budapest, Hungary, 6 May 1990
Height: 6'3" **Weight:** 13.1
International Honours: Hungary: U21-1; Yth
With special permission from the League and to solve a goalkeeping crisis at Tranmere, Peter was signed from neighbours Liverpool in mid-April and then had his loan extended on a weekly basis until the end of the season. A former Hungarian under-21 international, Peter has yet to make a first team appearance for Liverpool, but showed great promise during his spell at Prenton Park, fitting into the team immediately and conceding only four goals. He has good reflexes as well as displaying exceptional handling and

distribution.
Liverpool *(Free from MTK Hungaria, Hungary on 19/8/2008)*
Hereford U *(Loaned on 2/2/2009) FL 18*
Tranmere Rov *(Loaned on 16/4/2010) FL 5*

GUNNARSSON Aron Einar Malmquist

Born: Akureyri, Iceland, 22 April 1989
Height: 5'10" **Weight:** 11.0
International Honours: Iceland: 17; U21-7
The young Icelandic midfield player, who had made such a big impression at Coventry with his all-action midfield play the previous season, had a tougher second campaign in Championship football. His earlier speciality, the long throw, was not as effective this time but one superb effort did create a goal for Clinton Morrison at home to Cardiff. His form was patchy but he had set high standards and was less combative than the previous years, reflected in his bookings with only three compared to 12. When Sammy Clingan played, Aron generally had more freedom to get into the opposition box but despite some good chances his first and only goal did not arrive until the penultimate game at Middlesbrough.
Coventry C *(Signed from AZ Alkmaar, Holland, ex Thor Akureyri, on 7/7/2008) FL 72+8/2 FLC 2 FAC 7/1*

GUNNARSSON Brynjar Bjorn

Born: Reykjavik, Iceland, 16 October 1975
Height: 6'1" **Weight:** 11.12
Club Honours: Ch '06
International Honours: Iceland: 74; U21-8; Yth
Icelandic international Brynjar was in the Reading squad for all but six of the 54 matches, although he was an unused substitute on 16 occasions and only managed the full 90 minutes in 15 games. He filled in as an emergency right-back for a run of mid-season games, went on from time to time at centre-back and was frequently introduced in the second half to tighten midfield. Brynjar will be most remembered for a magical moment in the FA Cup replay against Liverpool at Anfield. With the score 1-1 in extra time, he scampered down the right, nutmegged Emiliano Insua and sent over an inch-perfect cross for Shane Long to head the winner. Brynjar has signed a one-year contract extension.
Stoke C *(£600,000 from Orgryte IS, Sweden, ex KR Reykjavik, Valerenga, Moss - loan, on 4/1/2000) FL 128+3/16*

FLC 7/1 FAC 7/2 Others 12+1/1
Nottingham F *(Free on 1/8/2003) FL 9+4 FAC 1*
Stoke C *(Free on 19/3/2004) FL 1+2*
Watford *(Free on 2/7/2004) FL 34+2/3 FLC 5 FAC 1+1*
Reading *(Signed on 22/7/2005) P/FL 78+47/9 FLC 4+1 FAC 10+1/1 Others 2*

GUNNING Gavin Jude

Born: Cork, 26 January 1991
Height: 6'0" **Weight:** 12.8
International Honours: RoI: U21; Yth
Gavin signed his first professional contract with Blackburn in the summer of 2009 and made his debut for the Republic of Ireland under-21 team in a UEFA qualifying game in October. A strong defender who is sufficiently versatile to play either in the centre or on the left-hand side of defence, he spent the first month of the season on loan to Tranmere where he showed great potential. His next spell on loan came at Rotherham in late January and the alliance proved beneficial for both player and club. Slotting in at left-back, Gavin proved himself a quick learner. Comfortable on the ball, he generally proved solid defensively, strong in the air and improved positionally as the games ticked by.
Blackburn Rov *(From trainee on 31/11/2008)*
Tranmere Rov *(Loaned on 6/8/2009) FL 6*
Rotherham U *(Loaned on 22/1/2010) FL 21 Others 3*

GUNTER Christopher (Chris) Ross

Born: Newport, 21 July 1989
Height: 5'11" **Weight:** 11.2
International Honours: W: 22; U21-8; Yth
Having spent an impressive spell on loan to Nottingham Forest from Tottenham towards the end of the previous season, Chris returned on a permanent basis and immediately maintained the form he had shown at the City Ground. He was used mainly as a right-back but never looked out of place when he played on the opposite flank. He scored his first League goal to earn a 1-0 victory over Plymouth in September and was named in the PFA 'Championship Team of the Year' while continuing to add to his Welsh caps.
Cardiff C *(From trainee on 25/10/2006) FL 20+8 FLC 3+2*
Tottenham H *(£2,000,000 + on 4/1/2008) PL 3+2 FLC 1 FAC 2+1 Others 6+1*
Nottingham F *(£1,750,000 on 12/3/2009) FL 52/1 FLC 2 FAC 1+1 Others 2*

GUTHRIE Daniel (Danny) Sean

Born: Shrewsbury, 18 April 1987
Height: 5'9" **Weight:** 11.6
Club Honours: Ch '10
International Honours: E: Yth; Sch
A hamstring injury delayed the start of Newcastle midfielder Danny's season, but on recovery he became a regular in the side, initially selected wide right, where his tendency to drift inside unbalanced the team's shape. When he was given a start in the centre of midfield he grasped the opportunity and established himself there. Although his habit to fade from games persists and he lacks real pace, he became a focal point for the side with an impressive tally of goal assists. He scored with a magnificent free kick against West Bromwich in January to earn a vital draw, but his best performance came in the demolition of Barnsley in March when he crowned a 'Man of the Match' display with a brace of goals.
Liverpool *(From trainee on 8/12/2004) PL 0+3 FLC 1+2 Others 1*
Southampton *(Loaned on 5/3/2007) FL 8+2 Others 2*
Bolton W *(Loaned on 5/7/2007) PL 21+4 FLC 2/1 FAC 1 Others 6+1*
Newcastle U *(£2,250,000 on 14/7/2008) P/FL 57+5/6 FLC 3/1 FAC 4+1*

GUTIERREZ Jonas Manuel

Born: Buenos Aires, Argentina, 5 July 1983
Height: 6'0" **Weight:** 11.0
Club Honours: Ch '10
International Honours: Argentina: 16
Assured by Diego Maradona that playing in the Championship would not affect his international future, Jonas was happy to stay at Newcastle and did continue to be selected for Argentina. He is a fleet-footed winger, primarily on the left, with fine close control which makes him a potent attacker, his energy and commitment also sees him tackling back to supplement his defence. He netted his first Newcastle goal in a pre-season friendly against Darlington, and his first competitive goal for the club came against Peterborough in November when he took on five opponents before scoring. In March against Barnsley he scored a stunning goal from 20 yards before delighting the Toon Army by donning the mask that had earned him the nickname 'Spiderman'.
Newcastle U *(Signed from Real Mallorca, Spain, ex Velez Sarsfield, on 15/8/2008) P/FL 57+10/4 FLC 1 FAC 3+2*

GUTTRIDGE Luke Horace
Born: Barnstaple, 27 March 1982
Height: 5'5" Weight: 9.7
Club Honours: Div 1 '06
Midfield general Luke found himself
playing wide for Northampton this time.
With his experience, he soon adapted to
the position, setting up attacks from the
flanks. He is also the club's dead-ball
expert and is involved with most of the
free kicks and corners. Another player
who has suffered with injury this season,
he was out of contract in the summer.
Torquay U (Trainee) FL 0+1
*Cambridge U (Free on 15/8/2000) FL
127+9/17 FLC 1+3 FAC 6+1/1 Others
9+3/2*
*Southend U (Signed on 18/3/2005) FL
59+4/5 FLC 1+1 FAC 1+3 Others 0+3*
*Leyton Orient (Loaned on 23/11/2006)
FL 7/1*
*Leyton Orient (Signed on 30/1/2007)
FL 8+2*
*Colchester U (Free on 11/7/2007) FL
5+9 FLC 1 FAC 1*
*Northampton T (Free on 8/8/2008) FL
47+9/6 FLC 2/1 FAC 3/2 Others 2*

GUY Jamie Lesley
Born: Barking, 1 August 1987
Height: 6'1" Weight: 13.0
Colchester striker Jamie was set to join
Port Vale at the start of the season
following a trial, but the move fell
through after he injured his knee.
During his time out he was involved in
an unsavoury off-field incident and
upon his return he suffered the
embarrassment of being a subbed
substitute in Colchester's 1-1 draw at
Swindon. Loaned to Port Vale, Jamie
made just one start and again found
himself amidst controversy away from
the field. His Colchester contract was
ended by mutual consent in January
and, after finishing the season at Julian
Dicks' struggling non-leaguers Grays
Athletic, he was released by the club.
*Colchester U (From trainee on
31/7/2006) FL 2+50/3 FLC 1 FAC 0+2
Others 1+3*
*Dagenham & Redbridge (Loaned on
3/3/2009) FL 5+4/1*
*Port Vale (Loaned on 6/10/2009) FL
0+3 FAC 0+1 Others 1+1*

GUY Lewis Brett
Born: Penrith, 27 August 1985
Height: 5'10" Weight: 10.8
Club Honours: AMC '07
International Honours: E: Yth
The striker, who was one of Doncaster's
longest-serving players, failed to break
into the first team starting line-up
during the season and was mainly used
as a substitute before being loaned to
Oldham in March. The Latics were

managed by Dave Penney, the man
who had originally signed him for
Rovers. Lewis made a big impact when
he arrived at Boundary Park despite
having been sidelined with injury for
most of 2009-10 up until then. He was
always a threat with his pace and eye
for a goal, his three strikes being the
difference between success and failure
in the relegation scrap at the foot of
League One. Was released by Rovers at
the end of the campaign.
*Newcastle U (From trainee on
3/8/2002) Others 0+1*
*Doncaster Rov (Free on 3/3/2005) FL
74+73/18 FLC 12+1 FAC 8+5/1 Others
8+5/5*
*Hartlepool U (Loaned on 19/2/2009)
FL 4*
*Oldham Ath (Loaned on 15/3/2010) FL
12/3*

GUYETT Scott Barry
Born: Ascot, 20 January 1976
Height: 6'2" Weight: 13.2
Club Honours: FC '04; Div 2 '05
International Honours: E: SP-4
Scott's season as a Bournemouth
central defender was wrecked by injury.
A wholehearted player, he twice started
games with no training behind him
because the transfer embargo left the
Cherries short of numbers. Scott had
two operations during the season,
severely restricting his appearances, and
was released after the campaign.
*Oxford U (Free from Southport, ex
Brisbane C, Gresley Rov, on 9/7/2001)
FL 20+2 FLC 1 FAC 1 Others 1 (Free to
Chester C on 2/8/2002)*
*Yeovil T (Free from Chester C on
30/7/2004) FL 73+16/2 FLC 1 FAC 6
Others 6*
*Bournemouth (Free on 8/8/2008) FL
27+7 FLC 1 FAC 3 Others 2*

GUZAN Bradley (Brad)
Edwin
Born: Chicago, Illinois, USA, 9
September 1984
Height: 6'4" Weight: 14.11
International Honours: USA: 16
Aston Villa's Brad junior ended the
campaign pondering the prospect of a
loan next season after a shortage of
first team opportunities in the Premier
League. Last season his chances were
limited to the knockout competitions,
with the goalkeeper starting Villa's two
Europa League matches against Rapid
Vienna and developing a reputation as
the Cup 'keeper in the Carling Cup and
FA Cup. Brad played in every game en-
route to the Carling Cup final, including
a remarkable performance in the fourth
round win at Sunderland when he
saved four penalties, one in normal time

and three in the shoot-out. Despite his
spot-kick heroics, Brad was left out of
the final against Manchester United,
manager Martin O'Neill going with the
experience of Brad Friedel. Brad Guzan
played in the early stages of the FA
Cup, again losing out to Friedel when
Villa progressed to the quarter and
semi-finals. Despite limited club
opportunites, Brad was in the USA
World Cup squad as understudy to Tim
Howard of Everton.
*Aston Villa (£600,000 from Chivas
USA, USA, ex South Carolina
Gamecocks, Chicago Fire Premier, on
13/8/2008) PL 0+1 FLC 6 FAC 4 Others 7*

GWYNNE Samuel (Sam)
Luke
Born: Hereford, 17 December 1987
Height: 5'8" Weight: 11.3
Now Hereford's longest-serving player,
Sam showed his customary battling
qualities as he enjoyed a couple of
extended spells in the Bulls' side. He, at
last, was given a run in the team in his
preferred central midfield position and
made a good impact with his tenacious
tackling and strong running. He showed
his versatility by turning out on the
flanks and also had a run of games in
the side at right-back. Was out of
contract in the summer.
*Hereford U (From juniors on
24/6/2006) FL 47+15/1 FLC 0+2 FAC
3+2 Others 2+1*

GYEPES Gabor
Born: Budapest, Hungary, 26 June
1981
Height: 6'3" Weight: 13.1
International Honours: Hungary: 26
It was a mixed season at Cardiff for the
Hungarian defender. He made three
appearances for his country, all in World
Cup qualifiers, taking his tally of caps to
26. At club level, Gabor found his first
team appearances limited. He made
only one appearance, starting against
Derby, after the end of March. By the
end of the season Gabor was out of the
reckoning and did not make the 18-
man play-off final squad. Mark Hudson
and Darcy Blake started with Anthony
Gerrard among the substitutes. A solid
defender, he makes up for what he
lacks in pace with power in the air and
strength in the tackle. His City contract
is due to end in 2012.
*Wolverhampton W (Signed from
Ferencvaros, Hungary on 5/8/2005) FL
19+1 FLC 2 FAC 2 (Freed on 24/4/2007)*
*Northampton T (Free, following long-
term injury and trial at Queens Park
Rgrs, on 25/1/2008) FL 15 FLC 1*
*Cardiff C (£200,000 on 19/8/2008) FL
41+2/3 FLC 2 FAC 4*

H

HABER Marcus

Born: Vancouver, Canada, 11 January 1989
Height: 6'3" **Weight:** 13.5
International Honours: Canada: U23-3; Yth
Signed on loan from West Bromwich in February, Canadian-born Marcus appeared five times for Exeter, making his English League debut against Stockport in February. A big target man, he made life uncomfortable for defenders. Was out of contract at the end of June.
West Bromwich A (Signed from Vancouver Whitecaps, Canada on 12/1/2010)
Exeter C (Loaned on 18/2/2010) FL 3+2

HACKETT Christopher (Chris) James

Born: Oxford, 1 March 1983
Height: 6'0" **Weight:** 11.6
Chris had his best season so far with Millwall, playing wide on the right of midfield. Using his speed and trickery, getting himself into positions to put in telling crosses, he also covered back and helped out in defence as part of a tight, compact unit. He reached the 100 game milestone for the Lions. In the League it was against Tranmere and in all competitions at Derby in an FA Cup replay.
Oxford U (From trainee on 20/4/2000) FL 72+53/9 FLC 0+3 FAC 3+3 Others 4+4
Heart of Midlothian (£20,000 on 24/1/2006) SL 1+1
Millwall (Free on 3/8/2006) FL 71+30/5 FLC 4 FAC 8+2 Others 4+2/1

HACKNEY Simon John

Born: Stockport, 5 February 1984
Height: 5'8" **Weight:** 10.3
Club Honours: Div 2 '06
Simon had a rollercoaster season at Colchester. After playing a starring role in the club's superb start to the campaign, the direct and hard-running left-winger slipped down the pecking order once Aidy Boothroyd took over. After being subbed in the 7-0 thrashing by Preston in the FA Cup third round - only his third start under the new manager - Simon was loaned to League Two side Morecambe in March and played eight times. Started off well and claimed the assists for two early goals in a draw with Grimsby and an away win at Hereford. Having chipped in a goal as Morecambe beat Rotherham he was

just beginning to make a real impression when he was recalled by his parent club because of injury problems. Rejuvenated, he started the last two games of the season, scoring at Huddersfield in a 'Man of the Match' display.
Carlisle U (Signed from Woodley Sports on 16/2/2005) FL 78+35/17 FLC 6+1 FAC 3+1 Others 6+7
Colchester U (£105,000 on 26/11/2009) FL 20+14/1 FLC 1/1 FAC 3/1 Others 1
Morecambe (Loaned on 8/3/2010) FL 8/1

Marcus Hahnemann

HAHNEMANN Marcus Stephen

Born: Seattle, Washington, USA, 15 June 1972
Height: 6'3" **Weight:** 16.2
Club Honours: Ch '06
International Honours: USA: 6
When he was signed for a season as one of four Wolverhampton goalkeepers, the impact he was to make seemed unlikely. His respective rivals suffered from injury, went out on loan or briefly lost form, and Marcus made his League debut for Wolves in November. His first touch was to pick the ball out of the back of the net, but he was not to blame, and a week later he was making fine saves against Bolton. His ability and bravery made him popular with the crowd, and his organisational skills and calmness brought stability to the team. At Arsenal he made a string of good saves, but usually it was more his positional sense rather than agility that got him through.
Fulham (£80,000 from Colorado Rapids, USA, ex Seattle Sounders, on 9/7/1999) FL 2 FLC 2

Rochdale (Loaned on 12/10/2001) FL 5 Others 2
Reading (Loaned on 14/12/2001) FL 6
Reading (Free on 14/8/2002) P/FL 276 FLC 9+1 FAC 7 Others 4
Wolverhampton W (Free on 17/6/2009) PL 25 FLC 2

HAINING William (Will) Wallace

Born: Glasgow, 2 October 1982
Height: 5'11" **Weight:** 10.10
Signed from St Mirren days before the start of the season, Will was a buy who excited the Morecambe fans. He was quick to show his class on the ball at centre-half but had a nightmare start as the Shrimps conceded five goals in two successive games. An injury kept him out of action until the end of September and he was injured again in his first game back. He returned to the side from November and helped the Shrimps go on two impressive runs of form. He scored one goal in a 2-2 draw at Macclesfield but ended the season on the bench after picking up another niggling injury.
Oldham Ath (From trainee on 17/10/2001) FL 147+8/11 FLC 4+1 FAC 9+1/1 Others 10
St Mirren (Free on 2/7/2007) SL 46+2/1 SLC 3 SC 7
Morecambe (Free on 7/8/2009) FL 28+4/1 FLC 1 FAC 1 Others 1

HALDANE Lewis Oliver

Born: Trowbridge, 13 March 1985
Height: 6'0" **Weight:** 11.13
International Honours: W: U21-1
A speedy winger who joined Port Vale on loan from Bristol Rovers in August, he soon won over his new fans with his dazzling wing play and scored his first goal against Stockport in the Johnstone's Paint Trophy. He returned to Rovers when his three-month spell was up, but came back to Vale in January on a free transfer. Defences can never leave him alone and he managed another three goals, all in the League.
Bristol Rov (From trainee on 13/10/2003) FL 90+57/15 FLC 2+1 FAC 5+7 Others 9+5/2
Port Vale (Free on 1/9/2009) FL 29+8/3 FLC 1 FAC 3 Others 1+1/1

HALFORD Gregory (Greg)

Born: Chelmsford, 8 December 1984
Height: 6'4" **Weight:** 13.10
International Honours: E: Yth
Having been signed from Sunderland in the summer, Greg impressed at Wolverhampton in pre-season, scoring with a beautiful free kick. Hoping to claim a regular midfield spot, he was used more at right-back though, and

his long throw-in proved a surprise weapon, creating a goal against Fulham. Having started the first nine League games, and been unlucky with a couple of free kick moves, Greg was only used every so often afterwards. He was involved in the victories at Tottenham and West Ham.
Colchester U *(From trainee on 8/8/2003) FL 132+4/18 FLC 4+1/1 FAC 13/5 Others 8+1*
Reading *(£2,000,000 + on 30/1/2007) PL 2+1*
Sunderland *(£2,500,000 on 11/6/2007) PL 8 FLC 1*
Charlton Ath *(Loaned on 31/1/2008) FL 16/2*
Sheffield U *(Loaned on 3/7/2008) FL 31+10/4 FLC 1 FAC 4/3 Others 3/1*
Wolverhampton W *(Signed on 3/7/2009) PL 12+3 FAC 0+1*

HALL Daniel (Danny) Andrew
Born: Ashton-under-Lyne, 14 November 1983
Height: 6'2" **Weight:** 12.7
Despite finishing 2008-09 strongly, Danny found the opportunity to claim a regular place in Chesterfield's defence restricted. His five full appearances were made either side of a loan spell at Darlington in December and, although he performed with commitment and intelligence in these games, lapses in concentration counted against him. At Darlington, the central defender proved to be very strong in the air when playing three games before the freezing weather curtailed his spell there. Was not offered a new contract by Chesterfield upon expiry of his current deal in June.
Oldham Ath *(From trainee on 7/8/2003) FL 57+7/1 FLC 1 FAC 7+1 Others 6*
Shrewsbury T *(Free on 1/7/2006) FL 28+14 FLC 1+1 FAC 2 Others 6*
Gretna *(Free on 10/1/2008) SL 14+1 SC 2*
Chesterfield *(Free on 4/8/2008) FL 30+2/2 FLC 1 FAC 3*
Darlington *(Loaned on 26/11/2009) FL 3*

HALL Fitz
Born: Leytonstone, 20 December 1980
Height: 6'1" **Weight:** 13.4
It was hardly a memorable campaign for Fitz, who only managed 12 starts and two substitute appearances for Queens Park Rangers, and he found himself behind Kaspars Gorkss and Damion Stewart in the pecking order for centre-back places. Looking for a new challenge, Fitz arrived at Newcastle in the January transfer window on loan to the end of the season, with the aim of supplementing the centre-back resources at Newcastle. Tall and angular,

comfortable on the ball with an unhurried yet no-nonsense approach, he fitted into the team comfortably and proved a useful acquisition, although hamstring problems affected his availability. Manager Chris Hughton was reportedly considering making his move permanent in the close season.
Oldham Ath *(£20,000 + from Chesham U, ex Staines T, on 15/3/2002) FL 44/5 FLC 4 FAC 3/1 Others 2+1*
Southampton *(£250,000 + on 14/7/2003) PL 7+4 FLC 1*
Crystal Palace *(£1,500,000 on 12/8/2004) P/FL 75/3 FLC 2 FAC 2 Others 2*
Wigan Ath *(£3,000,000 on 30/6/2006) PL 22+3 FLC 2 FAC 1*
Queens Park Rgrs *(£700,000 on 4/1/2008) FL 44+8/2 FLC 2 FAC 2*
Newcastle U *(Loaned on 29/1/2010) FL 7*

HALL Marcus Thomas Jackson
Born: Coventry, 24 March 1976
Height: 6'1" **Weight:** 12.2
International Honours: E: B-1; U21-8
When Chris Coleman obtained Patrick van Aanholt on loan from Chelsea, it was clear that Marcus' first team appearances for Coventry were going to be limited and although he had a mini-run in September in his favoured left-back position, he failed to reach double figures in appearances in his testimonial season. When he played, he always gave 100 per cent but his marauding runs up the wing were less in evidence than in the past, although a superb cross set up Leon Best's goal against Bristol City. Marcus was given time off when his father died in mid-season and returned for two solid performances at Peterborough and at home to Sheffield Wednesday. A new contract was not forthcoming from Sky Blues and sadly he was not even given a cameo appearance in the final game at home to Watford.
Coventry C *(From trainee on 1/7/1994) P/FL 113+19/2 FLC 14+1/2 FAC 8+2*
Nottingham F *(Free on 7/8/2002) FL 1*
Southampton *(Free on 30/8/2002) Stoke C** *(Free on 6/12/2002) FL 76+3/1 FLC 3 FAC 5*
Coventry C *(Signed on 21/2/2005) FL 125+13 FLC 4+1 FAC 8*

HALLFREDSSON Emil
Born: Hafnarfjordur, Iceland, 29 June 1984
Height: 6'1" **Weight:** 12.6
International Honours: Iceland: 29
Having signed a season long-loan in August from Italian side Reggina, this cultured left-footed midfielder showed very quickly that he was going to be a very useful acquisition to Barnsley. He

was equally at home in the centre of midfield or as a wide man and in either position was able to display his good range of passing. He also showed his ability to find the net and scored some crucial goals. His season was prematurely ended by a broken foot and he returned to Italy for treatment. He continued to be selected for Iceland.
Tottenham H *(Signed from FH Harnarfjordur, Iceland on 1/12/2004. Free to Lyn Oslo, Norway on 20/7/2007)*
Barnsley *(Loaned from Reggina, Italy on 14/8/2009) FL 22+5/3 FLC 2 FAC 1*

HALLS Andrew (Andy) Thomas
Born: Urmston, 20 April 1992
Height: 6'0" **Weight:** 12.2
Although young full-back Andy had been given a run in the Stockport side the previous season, his only senior game in the first six months was the Johnstone's Paint Trophy tie at Crewe, a game eventually won 4-1. His next start was against Charlton in March, but, . following injury to Johnny Mullins he remained in the side for the rest of the season.
Stockport Co *(From trainee on 7/8/2009) FL 12+4 Others 1*

HALLS John
Born: Islington, 14 February 1982
Height: 6'0" **Weight:** 11.4
Club Honours: FAYC '00; Div 2 '09
International Honours: E: Yth
Having helped Brentford win the previous season's League Two title, John signed a two-year deal with Aldershot after a trial. He was used as a right-sided holding midfielder and, as vice-captain, made his debut in the opening day victory over Darlington. Missing nine games with a groin injury that eventually needed an operation, although he returned at Burton in December he was then out for just over four months. John was able to start both legs of the play-off semi-final against Rotherham.
Arsenal *(From trainee on 18/7/2000) FLC 0+3*
Colchester U *(Loaned on 18/1/2002) FL 6*
Stoke C *(Free on 4/10/2003) FL 67+2/2 FLC 2 FAC 3*
Reading *(£250,000 on 19/1/2006) P/FL 1+1/1 FLC 4/1 FAC 2*
Preston NE *(Loaned on 1/11/2007) FL 4*
Crystal Palace *(Loaned on 10/1/2008) FL 5*
Sheffield U *(Loaned on 14/3/2008) FL 5+1*
Brentford *(Free on 25/9/2008) FL 22+1 FAC 1*
Aldershot T *(Free on 29/7/2009) FL 10+6 FLC 1 FAC 0+2 Others 2*

HALMOSI Peter
Born: Szombathely, Hungary, 25 September 1979
Height: 6'0" **Weight:** 11.9
International Honours: Hungary: 30; U21-2
With his only Premier League involvement at Hull being as an unused substitute for the first two months, Peter had to rely on the Cup competitions to stake his claim for a recall. He played in the unfamiliar left-back role in the Carling Cup ties against Southend and Everton before returning to his more recognised left-wing berth at Wigan in the FA Cup. Having retained his place in the national squad, Peter returned to his native Hungary during the January transfer window with a loan move to Szombathelyi Haladas until the end of the season.
Plymouth Arg (£400,000 from Debreceni, Hungary, ex Haldas Szombatheley, Grazer AK, on 12/1/2007) FL 55+4/12 FLC 2 FAC 3+2/1
Hull C (£2,000,000 on 22/7/2008) PL 4+14 FLC 3 FAC 5+1/1

HAMER Benjamin (Ben)
John
Born: Chard, 20 November 1987
Height: 5'11" **Weight:** 12.4
Club Honours: Div 2 '09
After winning a League Two medal as a loan goalkeeper with Brentford the previous season, Ben was the permanent understudy to Adam Federici at Reading. He had only three opportunities to show his prowess. Ben played in the Carling Cup ties against Burton and Barnsley in August and his only other appearance was as a second-half substitute for Federici in the FA Cup tie against Liverpool in front of a capacity Madejski Stadium crowd. Despite signs of nerves, Ben made some safe catches and kept a clean sheet during his 20 minutes of action, thus ensuring a 1-1 draw.
Reading (From trainee on 5/7/2006) FLC 2 FAC 0+1
Brentford (Loaned on 10/8/2007) FL 20 FLC 1
Brentford (Loaned on 1/7/2008) FL 45 FLC 1 FAC 2 Others 1

HAMMILL Adam James
Born: Liverpool, 25 January 1988
Height: 5'11" **Weight:** 11.7
Club Honours: FAYC '06
International Honours: E: Yth
Adam joined Barnsley from Liverpool in August having spent the second half of the previous season on loan at Oakwell. He soon scored a spectacular equaliser at Derby in a match in which Barnsley

went on to record their first League win of the season. It was a strike that was to win Barnsley's 'Goal of the Season'. This livewire winger loved to run at defenders and could take them on either inside or outside, setting problems for the opposition. He also had an eye for goal although his output in the second half of the season was disappointing. His performances won him the Reds' 'Young Player of the Season' award.
Liverpool (From trainee on 31/1/2006)
Dunfermline Ath (Loaned on 18/1/2007) SL 9+4/1 SC 5
Southampton (Loaned on 16/7/2007) FL 12+13 FAC 2+1
Blackpool (Loaned on 23/7/2008) FL 14+8/1 FLC 1
Barnsley (Signed on 2/2/2009) FL 40+13/5 FLC 3 FAC 0+1

Adam Hammill

HAMMOND Dean John
Born: Hastings, 7 March 1983
Height: 6'0" **Weight:** 12.4
Club Honours: AMC '10
The box-to-box midfielder started the opening three games of the season in fine form as Colchester's skipper before he turned down a new deal at the club and signed for League One rivals Southampton. Dean was coaxed to St Mary's at a time when the U's were top of the League with nine points and Saints were bottom with minus nine. However, once established he was made first team skipper and, having led Southampton to a triumphant day at Wembley in the Johnstone's Paint Trophy final and to the verge of the play-offs, he could well be considered a snip. Is a player who moves as cleverly off the ball as when he manoeuvres to gain it and is habitually well placed to

conclude the attacks he initiates.
Brighton & Hove A (From trainee on 10/6/2002) FL 122+14/21 FLC 5/1 FAC 7/2 Others 5+2/2
Leyton Orient (Loaned on 17/10/2003) FL 6+2 FAC 1
Colchester U (£250,000 on 31/1/2008) FL 51+5/5 FLC 2+1 Others 4
Southampton (Signed on 19/8/2009) FL 40/5 FAC 4/1 Others 5

HAMMOND Elvis Zark
Born: Accra, Ghana, 6 October 1980
Height: 5'10" **Weight:** 10.10
International Honours: Ghana: 1
Former Ghana international striker Elvis spent most of the season with Cheltenham. A quick, wiry forward with the ability to pull defenders out of position, Elvis scored three times in the opening five games but was forced out by a niggling ankle problem. After a spell in a two or three-man forward line, he was omitted following the departure of manager Martin Allen. He found the travelling from his London home to be too much and he reached a contract settlement in March.
Fulham (From trainee on 1/7/1999) P/FL 3+8 FLC 0+2
Bristol Rov (Loaned on 31/8/2001) FL 3+4 FLC 0+1
Norwich C (Loaned on 14/8/2003) FL 0+4
Leicester C (£225,000 + on 5/8/2005) FL 32+32/8 FLC 5/1 FAC 1+1/1
Cheltenham T (Free on 12/11/2008) FL 31+15/9 FLC 1/1 FAC 3

HAMSHAW Matthew (Matt) Thomas
Born: Rotherham, 1 January 1982
Height: 5'9" **Weight:** 11.12
Club Honours: Div 2 '10
International Honours: E: Yth; Sch
A right-sided Notts County midfielder or winger, Matt is capable of producing devastating bursts down the flank to provide crosses for the strikers. He was unable to gain a starting place after all the new arrivals but made frequent and valuable contributions as a substitute. Was out of contract at the end of June.
Sheffield Wed (From trainee on 5/1/1999) FL 35+39/2 FLC 6+3/2 FAC 2+1/2 Others 2
Stockport Co (Free on 5/8/2005) FL 35+4/5 FLC 1 FAC 3 Others 1
Mansfield T (Free on 8/8/2006) FL 83+2/6 FLC 2 FAC 7/1 Others 2
Notts Co (Free on 24/7/2008) FL 41+20/3 FLC 1+2 FAC 2+3 Others 1

HANGELAND Brede Paulsen
Born: Houston, Texas, USA, 20 June 1981
Height: 6'5" **Weight:** 14.7

International Honours: Norway: 60; U21-12

Brede remained at Craven Cottage despite widespread speculation that he was wanted elsewhere, subsequently enjoying another outstanding season at the heart of the Fulham defence. The Craven Cottage faithful took further delight from a new long-term contract signed in November. A dominant centre-half who is rarely beaten in the air and is confident moving forward with the ball at his feet, he again formed a formidable defensive partnership with Aaron Hughes. An automatic starting choice throughout the season, when fit he missed only a handful of games due to injury and squad rotation. Having netted only once in his previous 18 months at Fulham, Brede struck three times, including vital Europa League goals against AS Roma and Shakhtar Donetsk. His height and ability to escape his markers make him a significant threat at set pieces. He captained the Norway side that narrowly failed to qualify for the 2010 World Cup finals.
Fulham (£2,500,000 from FC Copenhagen, Denmark, ex FK Vidar, Viking Stavanger, on 22/1/2008) PL 84/2 FLC 1 FAC 9 Others 16/2

HANLEY Grant

Born: Dumfries, 20 November 1991
Height: 6'2" **Weight:** 13.10
International Honours: S: Yth
The young Scottish centre-back looked strong and capable in Blackburn's reserves but was overshadowed by the rise of Phil Jones. It was a surprise that he was called into the team for the final game of the season but he handled John Carew and Emile Heskey, got in his challenges, and looked at ease in the Premiership. He captained the youth team to the semi-finals of the FA Youth Cup.
Blackburn Rov (From trainee on 21/11/2008) PL 1

HANSON James Robert

Born: Bradford, 9 November 1987
Height: 6'4" **Weight:** 12.4
Twelve months earlier, James was stacking shelves in a supermarket and playing part-time football with Guiseley. But he finished his first season as a professional as Bradford's top scorer and 'Player of the Year' - and looking as if he had been in the League for years. The tall centre-forward, who can also operate on the left flank, is very strong in the air and holds the ball up effectively for his team-mates. He was unlucky not to claim a first hat-trick in a home game against Dagenham, scoring

twice with headers and seeing another hit the post.
Bradford C (Signed from Guiseley, ex Eccleshill U, on 21/7/2009) FL 33+1/12 FLC 1 FAC 1 Others 2+1/1

HARDING Benjamin (Ben) Scott

Born: Carshalton, 6 September 1984
Height: 5'10" **Weight:** 11.2
Club Honours: FC '08
International Honours: E: SP-3
Ben is a creative Aldershot midfielder who can play on the left or in the centre. He made his 100th start for the Shots at Bristol Rovers in the first round of the Carling Cup before an ankle ligament injury kept him out for eight weeks. Ben returned in the defeat at Burton, scored direct from a corner against Crewe in April and made one more start, at Morecambe, in the final League game.
Wimbledon/MK Dons (From trainee on 15/10/2001) FL 39+12/6 FLC 1 FAC 1 Others 0+1
Aldershot T (Free on 6/8/2007) FL 57+5/4 FLC 2 FAC 3+2

HARDING Daniel (Dan) Andrew

Born: Gloucester, 23 December 1983
Height: 6'0" **Weight:** 11.11
Club Honours: AMC '10
International Honours: E: U21-4
In his mid-20s and a free agent, Dan became Alan Pardew's first signing for Southampton on arriving at St Mary's late in the summer. A cavalier wing-back, Dan soon struck up a great partnership with Adam Lallana down the Saints' left flank. Although at his best pushing forward, Dan is an effective defender and a good team player. He consented to play at right-back in March, not a comfortable position for him. It was playing there that he earned his Johnstone's Paint Trophy winners' medal, before returning to the left with evident relief.
Brighton & Hove A (From trainee on 28/7/2003) FL 56+11/1 FLC 1+2 FAC 1 Others 4+1
Leeds U (£850,000 on 4/6/2005) FL 20 FLC 1
Ipswich T (Signed on 4/8/2006) FL 70+3/1 FLC 2 FAC 4
Southend U (Loaned on 8/8/2008) FL 19/1 FLC 1
Reading (Loaned on 29/1/2009) FL 3 Others 2
Southampton (Free on 21/7/2009) FL 42/3 FLC 2 FAC 4 Others 5/1

HAREWOOD Marlon Anderson

Born: Hampstead, 25 August 1979

Height: 6'1" **Weight:** 11.0
Club Honours: Ch '10
Marlon moved to Tyneside on a three-month loan to help fire Newcastle back to the Premiership. He is quick and powerful with a striker's instinct, and although not all Toon followers were convinced of his quality, he did score some important goals such as the vital strike against Queens Park Rangers in September that secured a draw. Manager Chris Hughton was considering extending the loan or negotiating a permanent transfer in January when he broke a metatarsal in his foot to rule out any such move. Was out of contract in the summer.
Nottingham F (From trainee on 9/9/1996) P/FL 124+58/51 FLC 12+4/3 FAC 3+2/1 Others 2
Ipswich T (Loaned on 28/1/1999) FL 5+1/1
West Ham U (£500,000 on 25/11/2003) P/FL 123+19/47 FLC 6/3 FAC 13+1/5 Others 7+1/1
Aston Villa (£4,000,000 on 19/7/2007) PL 1+28/5 FLC 3/1 FAC 0+1 Others 5+2/1
Wolverhampton W (Loaned on 24/3/2009) FL 2+3
Newcastle U (Loaned on 24/9/2009) FL 9+6/5

HARGREAVES Christian (Chris)

Born: Cleethorpes, 12 May 1972
Height: 5'11" **Weight:** 12.2
Chris will be remembered as the talismanic midfield general whose skill, work rate, exemplary attitude and larger than life personality had driven Torquay to promotion back into the Football League. At the age of 37, he found it increasingly difficult to drag his body through 90 minutes of play – particularly given his all-action style. Despite this, he contributed fully to the cause, notably when his winner against Northampton ended a long run without a victory. After negotiations to move to a youth coaching role broke down in January, he returned to former club Oxford in an effort to guide them back to the League.
Grimsby T (From trainee on 6/12/1989) FL 15+36/5 FLC 2+2/1 FAC 1+2/2 Others 2+4
Scarborough (Loaned on 4/3/1993) FL 2+1
Hull C (Signed on 26/7/1993) FL 34+15 FLC 1 FAC 2+1/1 Others 3+1
West Bromwich A (Free on 13/7/1995) FL 0+1 Others 0+1
Hereford U (Free on 19/2/1996) FL 57+4/6 FLC 3+1 FAC 1 Others 2
Plymouth Arg (Free on 20/7/1998) FL 74+2/5 FLC 4 FAC 11/2 Others 1

Northampton T *(Free on 7/7/2000) FL 144+7/6 FLC 5+1/1 FAC 11/2 Others 8/2*
Brentford *(Free on 2/7/2004) FL 30/2 FLC 1 FAC 6/1 Others 2*
Oxford U *(Free on 15/7/2005) FL 34+1/1 FAC 3 Others 1*
Torquay U *(Free on 3/8/2007) FL 21+2/3 FAC 2*

HARGREAVES Owen Lee
Born: Calgary, Canada, 20 January 1981
Height: 5'11" Weight: 11.7
Club Honours: PL '08; UEFACL '08
International Honours: E: 42; B-1; U21-3
A seasoned England and Manchester United midfield player, Owen's frustrations continued with his recurring patella tendinitis problems. Having undergone an intensive rehabilitation programme in the United States, he played for one minute plus in the next to last Premier League game against Sunderland.
Manchester U (£17,000,000 from Bayern Munich, Germany, ex Calgary Foothills, on 4/7/2007) PL 17+9/2 FAC 2+1 Others 6+3

HARLEY Jonathan (Jon)
Born: Maidstone, 26 September 1979
Height: 5'9" **Weight:** 10.3
Club Honours: FAC '00
International Honours: E: U21-3; Yth
A left-sided player, at home in midfield or occasionally at left-back, Jon proved a reliable squad man, making most of his appearances for Watford as a substitute. He scored only one goal, but it was a spectacular effort against Sheffield Wednesday in October. A much-travelled player, Jon was linked with Bristol City during the January transfer window, but ended the season at Vicarage Road. A tenacious, terrier-like player in midfield, he was sent off against West Bromwich in April. Was out of contract at the end of June.
Chelsea (From trainee on 20/3/1997) PL 22+8/2 FLC 0+1 FAC 7 Others 1+3
Wimbledon (Loaned on 20/10/2000) FL 6/2
Fulham (£3,500,000 on 8/8/2001) PL 19+6/1 FLC 2 FAC 4+1 Others 4
Sheffield U (Loaned on 30/10/2002) FL 8+1/1 FLC 2
Sheffield U (Loaned on 16/9/2003) FL 5
West Ham U (Loaned on 16/1/2004) FL 15/1 FAC 1
Sheffield U (Free on 4/8/2004) FL 48/2 FLC 3 FAC 5
Burnley (£75,000 on 26/8/2005) FL 116+3/3 FLC 3+1 FAC 3
Watford (Free on 23/7/2008) FL 52+23/2 FLC 3+2 FAC 2+1

HARLEY Ryan Bernard
Born: Bristol, 22 January 1985
Height: 5'9" **Weight:** 11.0
Ryan finished up as Exeter's top scorer with ten goals, including a superb double against Leeds in January. He continued to impress in a playmaking role, where he formed a good partnership with James Dunne and Liam Sercombe. When Exeter won a free kick at Colchester, Ryan stepped up and curled a delicious shot into a postage stamp in the top corner. You would struggle to find a better free kick. He scored the all important goal against Huddersfield that secured League One safety.
Bristol C (From trainee on 6/7/2004) FL 1+1 Others 0+1 (Freed during 2005 close season)
Exeter C (Free from Weston-super-Mare on 29/2/2008) FL 68+7/14 FLC 2 FAC 2+1 Others 1/1

HARPER James Alan John
Born: Chelmsford, 9 November 1980
Height: 5'10" **Weight:** 11.7
Club Honours: Ch '06
James made two full appearances in Carling Cup ties for Reading at the start of the campaign, plus three as a substitute in Championship fixtures. It soon became apparent, however, that he did not fit into plans of new manager Brendon Rodgers and he was allowed to join Sheffield United on loan at the beginning of September. The move was made permanent later in the season. Playing in an attacking midfield role James was a regular in the United side for much of the season, although he missed a few games through injury. Working hard he was always trying to find colleagues with an early ball. He also contributed four goals. Was out of contract in the summer.
Arsenal (From trainee on 8/7/1999)
Cardiff C (Loaned on 29/12/2000) FL 3
Reading (£400,000 on 28/2/2001) P/FL 282+30/25 FLC 15+2/1 FAC 13 Others 4+2
Sheffield U (Free on 1/9/2009) FL 31+3/4 FAC 2

HARPER Stephen (Steve) Alan
Born: Seaham, 14 March 1975
Height: 6'2" **Weight:** 13.0
Club Honours: Ch '10
For the first time in his 16 years at Newcastle, Steve began the season as the club's undisputed first choice goalkeeper. However he was injured in an accidental collision with his own striker Shola Ameobi in the season's opener at West Bromwich, was substituted at half time and taken to hospital for a brain scan. Fortunately he was able to take his place in the side for the rest of the League season, although he was substituted again through injury in the draw at Swansea and was stood down for the final game at Queens Park Rangers to allow his understudy Tim Krul a game. He had a fine season, the highpoint possibly being at Sheffield United in November when he was outstanding in securing the win. Steve conceded just a single goal in his first six matches and achieved a club record 21 clean sheets for the season as custodian in the tightest defence in the Championship.
Newcastle U (Free from Seaham Red Star on 5/7/1993) P/FL 126+7 FLC 12 FAC 9+1 Others 15+2
Bradford C (Loaned on 18/9/1995) FL 1
Hartlepool U (Loaned on 29/8/1997) FL 15
Huddersfield T (Loaned on 18/12/1997) FL 24 FAC 2

Shaun Harrad

HARRAD Shaun Nicholas
Born: Nottingham, 11 December 1984
Height: 5'10" **Weight:** 12.4
Club Honours: FC '09
International Honours: E: SP
The energetic and hard-working former England 'C' international had a memorable first season in the League with Burton, topping their scoring chart with a career-best 22 goals. Shaun scored some spectacular goals to add to the 17 he registered in Burton's promotion campaign. Not always a regular under previous regimes, Shaun quickly won the admiration of manager Paul Peschisolido, was rewarded with a two-year contract and quickly established himself as one of the most feared strikers in League Two.

*Notts Co (From trainee on 22/4/2004)
FL 4+25/1 FAC 1+2*
*Burton A (Free on 10/8/2005) FL
35+7/21 FAC 2/1 Others 1*

HARRIS Kadeem Raymond
Born: Westminster, 8 June 1993
Height: 5'9" **Weight:** 10.6
Youth team winger Kadeem became
the youngest ever player for Wycombe
in the League, making his debut as a
substitute in the Boxing Day match at
Yeovil. At 16 years and 201 days, he
beat the previous record held by Ikechi
Anya by 78 days. Kadeem can play on
either wing and, with very quick feet,
likes to take on players. He made a
second appearance off the bench in the
final game, against Gillingham. He is
being carefully nurtured after coming
through the Wycombe Centre of
Excellence, having joined the club as a
14-year-old.
Wycombe W (Trainee) FL 0+2

Neil Harris

HARRIS Neil
Born: Orsett, 12 July 1977
Height: 5'11" **Weight:** 12.9
Club Honours: Div 2 '01
Neil improved Millwall's goals records,
that he already held, this season to 122
in the League and 135 in all
competitions. In fact, he broke his duck
in the Carling Cup with a hat-trick
against Bournemouth at the Den. He
has been given a new contract to 2012,
a just reward for his work rate. He is still
as good as he was when he first joined
the Lions and now uses his experience
to set up almost as many chances for
others as he creates for himself, often
dropping deep to receive the ball. Neil
won League One's 'Player of the Month'

for February and also played his 400th
game for Millwall in the play-off semi-
final second leg at the Den.
*Millwall (£30,000 from Cambridge C
on 26/3/1998) FL 186+47/93 FLC 6+1
FAC 13+2/2 Others 13+1/3*
*Cardiff C (Loaned on 3/12/2004) FL
1+2/1*
*Nottingham F (Free on 22/12/2004) FL
16+17/1 FLC 2 FAC 1+3 Others 0+2*
*Gillingham (Loaned on 28/8/2005) FL
28+8/6 FAC 1 Others 1+1*
*Millwall (Free on 9/1/2007) FL
81+34/29 FLC 3/4 FAC 6+2/3 Others
5+1/1*

HARRIS Sebastian (Seb)
James
Born: Rochester, Michigan, USA, 5
August 1987
Height: 6'3" **Weight:** 12.11
Striker Seb became the first American
outfield player to wear a Northampton
shirt. Coming from American college
football, he found the gap quite large
but adapted well. First team chances
were few and far between but when
called upon he always threw himself
into the game with hard running and
chasing, plus the odd shot on goal. He
scored the winner against Cheltenham
with a neat back header and performed
a celebration that was as memorable as
the goal.
*Northampton T (Free from Michigan
Bucks, USA, ex Oakland Golden
Grizzlies, on 3/8/2009) FL 0+9/1 FAC
0+1*

HARRISON Daniel (Danny)
Robert
Born: Liverpool, 4 November 1982
Height: 5'11" **Weight:** 12.5
Danny did not start as first choice but
soon got into Rotherham's midfield and
stayed there by dint of his
performances. He is essentially the
water-carrier although his all-round
game matured too. Often did the
unseen work, the nitty-gritty that
typifies a team player. After a mid-
season wobble, he won back his place
and had excellent second half of the
campaign, which included being part of
a nicely-balanced midfield with the
more skilful Josh Walker.
*Tranmere Rov (From trainee on
16/5/2002) FL 89+35/5 FLC 2+1 FAC
8+1 Others 8+3/2*
*Rotherham U (Free on 1/7/2007) FL
103+11/9 FLC 6/2 FAC 5+1 Others
8+1/1*

HARRISON Ryan Andrew
Born: Sherburn-in-Elmet, 13 October
1991
Height: 5'10" **Weight:** 12.0

Manager Peter Taylor sprang a surprise
when he named 18-year-old left-winger
Ryan on the Bradford bench against
Macclesfield. Ryan earned his chance
after some impressive displays for David
Wetherall's youth team and was
rewarded with an appearance as a
substitute for the final 20 minutes.
Bradford C (Trainee) FL 0+1

HARROLD Matthew (Matt)
James
Born: Leyton, 25 July 1984
Height: 6'1" **Weight:** 11.10
Matt's ten goals from 31 starts for
Wycombe comprised five penalties, four
headers and a well-taken shot at
Norwich. He has detractors and
supporters in equal measure among the
fans and, although he will probably
never be a prolific scorer, is extremely
hard working and runs himself into
exhaustion. He plays well as a target
man, whether flicking on to team-
mates or holding the ball until help
arrives. He lost his place to a rampant
Alex Revell in early April and was not
offered a new contract at the end of
the season.
*Brentford (Free from Harlow T on
12/8/2003) FL 11+21/2 FAC 2+3/3
Others 2*
Grimsby T (Loaned on 4/3/2005) FL 6/2
*Yeovil T (Signed on 15/7/2005) FL
30+17/9 FLC 1+2/1 FAC 1+2 Others 1*
*Southend U (£90,000 on 31/8/2006)
FL 25+27/3 FLC 2/2 FAC 2+2/1 Others 1*
*Wycombe W (Signed on 1/9/2008) FL
57+16/17 FAC 4/5*

HARSLEY Paul
Born: Scunthorpe, 29 May 1978
Height: 5'9" **Weight:** 11.10
This versatile midfielder's second season
at Chesterfield was a disappointing
repeat of his first, when early
involvement in the squad gave way to a
prolonged period in the shadows. Paul
was then loaned to Darlington, along
with Danny Hall, at the beginning of
December and made just three
appearances before the freezing
weather cut short his time at Neasham
Road. When it became apparent that he
had no future at Chesterfield, he joined
his old boss Martin Foyle at York City on
loan and was formally released by
Chesterfield as the season ended.
Grimsby T (From trainee on 16/7/1996)
*Scunthorpe U (Free on 7/7/1997) FL
110+18/5 FLC 6 FAC 4+2/1 Others 5+1*
*Halifax T (Free on 1/7/2001) FL 45/11
FLC 1 FAC 3/1 Others 1*
*Northampton T (Free on 8/7/2002) FL
46+13/2 FLC 2 FAC 3+2/1 Others 2+2*
*Macclesfield T (Free on 13/2/2004) FL
105+2/11 FLC 3 FAC 5 Others 11/2*

Port Vale *(Free on 13/7/2006) FL 68+5/6 FLC 4 FAC 3 Others 2*
Chesterfield *(Free on 2/8/2008) FL 7+13/1 FLC 2 FAC 1 Others 0+1*
Darlington *(Loaned on 26/11/2009) FL 3*

HART Danny Gary
Born: Hendon, 26 April 1989
Height: 5'9" **Weight:** 11.5
In his third season at Barnet, the young winger struggled to break into the first team and like the previous two campaigns, was loaned out for much of year. He made a handful of substitute appearances early in the season, before going on loan to Hemel Hempstead Town, where he was a regular and scored a number of goals from midfield
Barnet *(Free from Borehamwood on 14/8/2007) FL 2+4/1 FLC 0+1 Others 0+2 .*

HART Gary John
Born: Harlow, 21 September 1976
Height: 5'9" **Weight:** 12.8
Club Honours: Div 3 '01; Div 2 '02
After extending his Brighton career with a series of remarkable performances at the end of 2008-09, Gary played a relatively minor role, making just two starts in his 19 appearances. Although lacking the pace of ten years ago, he is always combative and continues to give the total effort that has made him such a firm favourite with the Withdean fans. His 12th season with the club was hampered by toe and back injuries, but with his versatility – he is principally a forward but can also play as a winger or full-back – he is still a useful player to have around and has been invited back for pre-season training in July.
Brighton & Hove A *(£1,000 from Stansted on 18/6/1998) FL 298+72/44 FLC 9+3 FAC 10+2 Others 9+5/1*

HART Charles Joseph (Joe) John
Born: Shrewsbury, 19 April 1987
Height: 6'3" **Weight:** 12.9
International Honours: E: 3; U21-21; Yth
A major success on loan from Manchester City, The young goalie was named Birmingham's 'Player of the Season' and earned selection for the England World Cup squad. Behind a solid defence, when he was called upon he was always capable of making a game-defining save. Showed great powers of concentration, agility and sharpness and was error free all season. Joe grew in stature and confidence through the loan and regular football. His handling at corners and crosses improved and his kicking was always firm and sure. Was choked with

Joe Hart

emotion by the way the Blues' fans gave him such an appreciative send off on the last day of the season at Bolton.
Shrewsbury T *(From trainee on 10/8/2004) FL 52 FLC 2 FAC 2*
Manchester C *(£600,000 on 31/5/2006) PL 50 FLC 3 FAC 4 Others 9*
Tranmere Rov *(Loaned on 1/1/2007) FL 6*
Blackpool *(Loaned on 8/4/2007) FL 5*
Birmingham C *(Loaned on 24/6/2009) PL 36 FAC 5*

HART Michael
Born: Airdrie, 10 February 1980
Height: 5'10" **Weight:** 11.6
Michael was a regular in the Preston squad all season, but made only 15 appearances in all, usually as stand-in for Billy Jones, before being released at the end of the season. He played in all three Carling Cup matches but had to

wait until October for his first League start. Following the change of manager at Deepdale, he enjoyed a run of six starts when Billy Jones moved into midfield before returning to the bench for the remainder of the season. Able to play in both full-back slots, Michael is a dependable pro who can always be relied on to cover his flank and to show good commitment in the tackle.
Aberdeen *(From juniors on 1/8/1997) SL 6+10 SLC 0+2 SC 1*
Livingston *(Loaned on 8/3/2000) SL 3*
Livingston *(Loaned on 26/9/2000) SL 16+6 Others 1+1*
Livingston *(Signed on 1/7/2001) SL 24+8 SLC 2 SC 2 Others 1+1*
Aberdeen *(Signed on 24/1/2003) SL 102+5 SLC 5 SC 7+1 Others 5*
Preston NE *(£100,000 on 31/1/2008) FL 17+2 FLC 5 FAC 1*

HARTE Ian Patrick
Born: Drogheda, 31 August 1977
Height: 6'0" **Weight:** 12.4
International Honours: RoI: 64; U21-6
His converted penalty in the opening day game against Brentford was just the first of 18 goals this experienced back-four player scored for Carlisle during the campaign. It was a remarkable total as he became the first defender ever to top the club's scoring charts thanks to a mixture of penalties, goals from open play and, most commonly, strikes from free kicks taken close to the penalty area. Ian was also chosen for the PFA League One 'Team of the Season', the only player nominated from a club in the lower half of the division. It was a testament to his qualities as a defender and his innate professionalism as well as his more obvious scoring abilities.
Leeds U (From trainee on 15/12/1995) PL 199+14/28 FLC 10+2/2 FAC 16+2/3 Others 45/6 (Transferred to Levante, Spain on 12/7/2004)
Sunderland (Free on 29/8/2007) PL 3+5
Blackpool (Free on 11/12/2008) FL 4 FAC 1
Carlisle U (Free on 26/3/2009) FL 48/17 FLC 3/1 FAC 4/1 Others 6+1

HARTLEY Paul James
Born: Baillieston, 19 October 1976
Height: 5'8" **Weight:** 10.1
Club Honours: S Div 1 '99; SPD '07, '08; SC '06, '07; SLC '09
International Honours: S: 25; U21-1
This midfield signing from Celtic proved to be Bristol City's most consistent and inspiring performer last season, despite not always being sure of selection. A skilful player he immediately won over the fans with his fully committed displays. Renowned for his free kicks, he scored with an exquisite effort in the away game at West Bromwich in November. Added to his Scottish international honours by being twice capped in the World Cup qualifiers at the start of the season, when he became the first City player to represent Scotland while at Ashton Gate. Paul was a member of the first squad selected by the new Scottish manager Craig Levein and played the whole of the second half at Hampden Park in March when the Czech Republic were beaten 1-0.
Hamilton Academical (Free from Mill U BC on 9/9/1994) SL 39+8/11 SLC 1+1 SC 1 Others 1+2
Millwall (£400,000 on 4/7/1996) FL 35+9/4 FLC 1+1 FAC 2 Others 1
Raith Rov (£150,000 on 22/8/1997) SL 48+2/13 SLC 2/1 SC 3 Others 1

Hibernian (£225,000 on 23/12/1998) SL 20+16/6 SLC 1+1/1 SC 2+3/1
Morton (Loaned on 20/12/1999) SL 3/1
St Johnstone (£200,000 on 5/7/2000) SL 80+7/12 SLC 5+1/2 SC 4 Others 1
Heart of Midlothian (Free on 1/6/2003) SL 113+5/31 SLC 7+1/3 SC 11/3 Others 10+2/1
Glasgow Celtic (£1,100,000 on 31/1/2007) SL 53+9/3 SLC 3+1 SC 6+1 Others 12+1/1
Bristol C (Free on 6/7/2009) FL 36+4/5 FAC 2

HARTLEY Peter
Born: Hartlepool, 3 April 1988
Height: 6'0" **Weight:** 12.6
A left-sided or central defender, Peter joined Hartlepool after progressing through the junior ranks at Sunderland. Recognising that opportunities were few playing for Sunderland's reserves, he jumped at the chance of a move to his home-town club in the summer. A wholehearted player with a tough, no-nonsense approach, he quickly established himself as automatic choice at left-back in a defence that, for most of the season, picked itself. For his sterling work off the field, he was the recipient of the club's 'Community Player of the Year' award.
Sunderland (From trainee on 25/7/2006) FL 0+1
Chesterfield (Loaned on 21/2/2008) FL 12
Hartlepool U (Free on 2/7/2008) FL 38/2 FLC 2 FAC 1

HASLAM Steven (Steve) Robert
Born: Sheffield, 6 September 1979
Height: 5'11" **Weight:** 11.0
International Honours: E: Yth; Sch
The experienced utility defender joined Hartlepool on trial during the pre-season preparations. Already known to manager Chris Turner from his time in charge at Sheffield Wednesday, Steve impressed sufficiently to be signed on a two-year contract. He began the season as first choice right-back and put in some good performances before being replaced by a now fully-fit Neil Austin, who had originally been earmarked for the position. Subsequently Steve was mainly restricted to a place on the bench, but later made a number of appearances at left-back in place of Peter Hartley.
Sheffield Wed (From trainee on 12/9/1996) P/FL 115+29/2 FLC 10+1 FAC 9+1 Others 5+1 (Free to Halifax T on 13/8/2004)
Northampton T (Free on 27/8/2004) FL 2+1 (Free to Halifax T on 12/10/2004)
Bury (Free on 5/7/2007) FL 50/1 FAC 5

Others 5+1
Hartlepool U (Free on 7/8/2009) FL 15 FLC 2 Others 1

HASSELL Robert (Bobby) John Francis
Born: Derby, 4 June 1980
Height: 5'9" **Weight:** 12.6
Bobby suffered a couple of early season injuries that kept him out of action for a couple of months. However, once he regained his place, his form kept him in the Barnsley team. His late headed equaliser against Newcastle was his first goal in two years, but it is his defensive qualities for which he is most remembered. He is a good reader of the game, making his tackling precise, and is also very good in the air in both penalty areas. It is his comfort on the ball and passing ability that have come on in leaps and bounds in the last 12 months.
Mansfield T (From trainee on 3/7/1998) FL 151+9/3 FLC 6+1 FAC 9 Others 4
Barnsley (Free on 5/7/2004) FL 172+18/5 FLC 5 FAC 14 Others 5

HAVERN Gianluca
Born: Manchester, 24 September 1988
Height: 6'1" **Weight:** 13.0
Due to County's financial problems, Gianluca was another former player who re-signed for Stockport after training with the squad over the summer. Initially a regular in the starting line-up, in October he picked up a shoulder injury. Things got worse when he developed heart problems, needing an operation in the spring to correct a stress-induced tachycardia. Fortunately the defender made a full recovery to play in several reserve games before the season's end.
Stockport Co (From trainee on 25/4/2007) FL 1/1 (Freed on 12/1/2009)
Stockport Co (Free from Mansfield T on 7/8/2009) FL 7 FLC 1 Others 2

HAWKINS Colin Joseph
Born: Galway, 17 August 1977
Height: 6'1" **Weight:** 13.6
International Honours: RoI: U21-9; Yth
The season was a complete disaster for Brighton's robust Irish defender. His only involvement with the first team was against Stockport in August when he came on as a substitute as manager Russell Slade reorganised following Tommy Elphick's dismissal. Two minutes later there was a goalmouth scramble which ended with Colin tugging a visiting forward's shirt, giving away a penalty and earning a red card for himself. After serving a suspension, he

made just one reserve appearance before suffering an Achilles' tendon injury that required an operation and terminated his campaign. He has been invited back for pre-season training in July by manager Gus Poyet, who has yet to see him play.
Coventry C (Signed from Salthill Devon on 25/11/1995. Freed during 1997 close season)
Coventry C (Signed from Shelbourne, ex St Patrick's Ath, Doncaster Rov, Bohemians, on 29/1/2007) FL 13 FLC 1
Chesterfield (Loaned on 27/3/2008) FL 5
Brighton & Hove A (Free on 2/7/2008) FL 17+1 FLC 2 FAC 2 Others 3

HAWLEY Karl Leon
Born: Walsall, 6 December 1981
Height: 5'7" **Weight:** 12.0
Club Honours: Div 2 '06, '10
International Honours: E: SP-2
Arriving from Preston in the summer, Karl showed himself to be an extremely capable Notts County forward with an excellent talent at reading the game and interacting with the players around him. He has a good scoring pedigree but was restricted in the number of appearances due to the outstanding form of the incumbent strikers. He will relish the opportunity to play more regularly with Lee Hughes in the coming season.
Walsall (From trainee on 26/1/2001) FL 0+1 FAC 0+1 Others 0+2
Raith Rov (Loaned on 9/8/2002) SL 15+2/7 SLC 1 SC 1+2/1
Raith Rov (Loaned on 29/8/2003) SL 4+5/2 SLC 1
Carlisle U (Free on 3/8/2004) FL 76+2/34 FLC 2+1 FAC 2 Others 7/4
Preston NE (Free on 1/8/2007) FL 20+10/3 FLC 2+1 FAC 3/2
Northampton T (Loaned on 12/9/2008) FL 11/2
Colchester U (Loaned on 20/3/2009) FL 4
Notts Co (Signed on 3/8/2009) FL 14+17/3 FLC 1 FAC 2+3/1 Others 1

HAWORTH Andrew (Andy)
Alan David
Born: Lancaster, 28 November 1988
Height: 5'8" **Weight:** 10.6
Following a loan at Gateshead, Andy joined Rochdale on loan from Blackburn in January and stayed for the rest of the season. He started on the left wing for two games, making a promising debut in the 4-1 win at Cheltenham. After that, he had to settle for a place on the bench, following Will Atkinson's return and a change to 4-4-3 with less reliance on wide men. Only the woodwork denied Andy a spectacular first League goal in the championship decider against Notts County.

Blackburn Rov (From trainee on 4/7/2007) FLC 1 FAC 0+1
Rochdale (Loaned on 21/1/2010) FL 3+4

HAYES Paul Edward
Born: Dagenham, 20 September 1983
Height: 6'0" **Weight:** 12.2
Five 'Player of the Year' awards summed up Paul's contribution to Scunthorpe's survival in the Championship. A highly skilful, creative striker, his ability to drop deep and thread a pass to split open opposition defences was a key feature of the campaign, forming a superb partnership with 20-goal top scorer Gary Hooper. Despite being more of a creator, he still netted 13 times himself in all competitions. The pick of his goals was a stunning volley in the televised FA Cup tie against Manchester City but he also showed a liking for playing his old club Barnsley, scoring in all three meetings during the season. Started 51 of the club's 52 matches in all competitions but was out of contract and agreed to join Preston.
Scunthorpe U (From trainee at Norwich C on 22/3/2003) FL 68+31/28 FLC 2+1/2 FAC 6+2/4 Others 3+3/1
Barnsley (£150,000 on 11/7/2005) FL 63+12/11 FLC 1+2 FAC 7/5 Others 3+1/2
Huddersfield T (Loaned on 23/2/2007) FL 4/1
Scunthorpe U (Free on 17/7/2007) FL 116+13/34 FLC 5/2 FAC 6/2 Others 9+1/3

HAYLES Barrington (Barry) Edward
Born: Lambeth, 17 May 1972
Height: 5'9" **Weight:** 13.0
Club Honours: GMVC '96; Div 2 '99; Div 1 '01
International Honours: Jamaica: 10; E: SP-2
Veteran striker Barry shouldered much of the burden for Cheltenham's attack. He used his physical presence and ability on the ball to create chances in a struggling side and contributed important goals, including an unlikely last-minute winner at Bury. Barry's seven League goals included three from midfield, either on the right or left. Towards the end of the season, he took turns with equally experienced Julian Alsop to partner Justin Richards up front as Cheltenham cobbled together enough points to stay in the League.
Bristol Rov (£250,000 from Stevenage Borough on 4/6/1997) FL 62/32 FLC 4/1 FAC 5/2 Others 3+2/1
Fulham (£2,100,000 on 17/11/1998) P/FL 116+59/44 FLC 10+2/5 FAC 12+7/6 Others 2+5/2
Sheffield U (Free on 26/6/2004) FL 4 FLC 1

Millwall (Signed on 1/9/2004) FL 49+6/16 FLC 4/1 FAC 1
Plymouth Arg (£100,000 on 1/8/2006) FL 58+4/15 FLC 1 FAC 2+1/1
Leicester C (£150,000 on 1/1/2008) FL 10+18/2 FAC 1 Others 1
Cheltenham T (Loaned on 14/8/2008) FL 6+1/3
Cheltenham T (Loaned on 27/11/2008) FL 5/1 FAC 1
Cheltenham T (Free on 13/7/2009) FL 23+16/7 FLC 1 FAC 0+1 Others 0+1

HAYNES Daniel (Danny) Lewis
Born: Peckham, 19 January 1988
Height: 5'11" **Weight:** 11.11
Club Honours: FAYC '05
International Honours: E: Yt
A close-season signing from Ipswich, while looking more at home on the wing, was frequently employed in a striking role by Bristol City. Danny responded with some highly energetic crowd-pleasing displays but often lacked composure in front of goal, as demonstrated by his return of seven goals. He reserved his best performance for the BBC Match of the Day cameras, being in scintillating form during City's 2-1 home victory over West Bromwich in February.
Ipswich T (From trainee on 2/2/2006) FL 36+78/17 FLC 2+3/2 FAC 5+3
Millwall (Loaned on 26/9/2006) FL 5/2
Bristol C (Signed on 13/7/2009) FL 29+9/7 FLC 2 FAC 1

HAYNES Kyle John
Born: Wolverhampton, 29 December 1991
Height: 5'11" **Weight:** 11.2
The promising young defender made further progress for Cheltenham. Kyle remained a scholarship player but started six games at right-back, including a 5-1 win over Barnet. He also starred in the FA Youth Cup, scoring all the goals from right-back in a 4-0 win at Exeter. Kyle was one of four Cheltenham Academy players to be offered professional contracts and his growing reputation was further underlined when he was named 'Apprentice of the Year' for League Two at the League Awards evening in London.
Cheltenham T (Trainee) FL 8+9 FAC 0+1 Others 0+1

HAYTER James Edward
Born: Sandown, Isle of Wight, 9 April 1979
Height: 5'9" **Weight:** 11.2
James finished as second top scorer for Doncaster after originally starting the

season as the main striker but then playing as partner to Billy Sharp. He is not afraid to go in where it hurts and had a spell out injured but returned to the goal standard when Sharp was injured.
Bournemouth *(From trainee on 7/7/1997) FL 305+53/94 FLC 9+3/4 FAC 18+3/5 Others 12+4/5*
Doncaster Rov *(£200,000 on 25/6/2007) FL 63+36/20 FLC 4+1/1 FAC 2+1/2 Others 2+2/1*

James Hayter

HAZELL Reuben Daniel
Born: Birmingham, 24 April 1979
Height: 5'11" **Weight:** 12.0
'Mr Consistency', Reuben continually impresses with his ability and sound defending. He enjoyed another outstanding season, in which he made 44 appearances at the centre of the Oldham defence. Reuben's secret lies in his athleticism. He is built for speed but can also battle it out with the big forwards. Missing games only through suspension, Reuben never seems to age. He is just a good all-round player.
Aston Villa *(From trainee on 20/3/1997)*
Tranmere Rov *(Free on 5/8/1999) FL 38+4/1 FLC 8 FAC 3 Others 1*
Torquay U *(Free on 10/1/2002) FL 77+7/2 FLC 1 FAC 2 Others 1*
Kidderminster Hrs (Free on 1/8/2004)
Chesterfield *(Free on 2/8/2005) FL 69+3/2 FLC 4 FAC 2 Others 2*
Oldham Ath *(Free on 14/9/2007) FL 116+2/7 FLC 3 FAC 6+1 Others 3*

HEALY Colin
Born: Cork, 14 March 1980
Height: 5'11" **Weight:** 10.7
Club Honours: SPD '01; SLC '01

International Honours: RoI: 13; U21-10
Colin was offered a contract at Portman Road after impressing when playing against Ipswich on their pre-season tour of Ireland. However, once in England he seemed out of his depth and was unable to make an impression or hold down a regular place in the side and joined Falkirk on loan in January.
Glasgow Celtic *(Signed from Wilton U on 7/7/1998) SL 16+14/1 SLC 5+1/2 SC 3+1 Others 3+5*
Coventry C *(Loaned on 29/1/2002) FL 17/2*
Sunderland *(Free on 22/8/2003) FL 16+4*
Livingston *(Signed on 9/3/2006) SL 6+3/2*
Barnsley *(Free on 10/8/2006) FL 0+8 FLC 2 (Freed on 31/1/2007)*
Bradford C *(Loaned on 10/11/2006) FL 2 FAC 2*
Ipswich T *(Signed from Cork C on 24/7/2009) FL 3 FLC 2*
Falkirk *(Loaned on 21/1/2010) SL 17+2/1*

HEALY David Jonathan
Born: Downpatrick, 5 August 1979
Height: 5'8" **Weight:** 11.0
International Honours: NI: 80; B-1; U21-8; Yth; Sch
A player who has never started a League game at Sunderland, David came off the bench seven times for the Black Cats in 2009-10 but never earlier than the 73rd minute. Taken on loan to Ipswich for the second half of the season by Roy Keane, who signed him for Sunderland, David made an immediate impact in a game against Middlesbrough when his right-wing run and low cross gave fellow loanee Daryl Murphy a tap in goal after 23 seconds. He scored his first League goal in 12 months at Scunthorpe when he pounced on a loose ball and scored from a tight angle before a knee injury kept him out of the last three games of the campaign. Was recently made an OBE.
Manchester U *(From trainee on 28/11/1997) PL 0+1 FLC 0+2*
Port Vale *(Loaned on 25/2/2000) FL 15+1/3*
Preston NE *(£1,500,000 on 29/12/2000) FL 104+35/44 FLC 7+1 FAC 7+1 Others 3/1*
Norwich C *(Loaned on 30/1/2003) FL 5/1*
Norwich C *(Loaned on 13/3/2003) FL 5+3/1*
Leeds U *(Signed on 29/10/2004) 82+29/29 FLC 3+1 FAC 3+1/2 Others 1+1*
Fulham *(£1,500,000 on 16/7/2007) PL*

15+15/4 FLC 1+1/1 FAC 2/1
Sunderland *(£8,000,000 on 21/8/2008) PL 0+13/1 FLC 1+3/1 FAC 2+2/1*
Ipswich T *(Loaned on 1/2/2010) FL 5+7/1*

HEATH Joseph (Joe)
Born: Birkenhead, 4 October 1988
Height: 5'11" **Weight:** 11.11
One of former Lincoln manager Peter Jackson' summer signings after arriving on loan from Nottingham Forest, left-back Joe's six months at Sincil Bank were marred by injuries which restricted him to just five League and Cup appearances before he returned to parent club. Is a player who likes pushing forward to join up with the forwards.
Nottingham F *(From trainee on 1/12/2005) FL 9+1 FLC 1 FAC 0+1*
Lincoln C *(Loaned on 26/6/2009) FL 3+1 FAC 1*

HEATH Matthew (Matt) Philip
Born: Leicester, 1 November 1981
Height: 6'4" **Weight:** 13.13
The towering Colchester centre-back started the season on loan at Essex rivals Southend, making six appearances. Commanding in the air, Matt turned in some solid performances in the heart of defence alongside experienced campaigner Adam Barrett, but with his month up he was recalled to the Weston Homes Community Stadium. On his return he was initially limited to coming off the bench under new U's manager Aidy Boothroyd until injuries saw him handed a start against MK Dons in January. Matt retained his place in the team for the next 11 games, but his solid displays were not enough to keep him in the side once other players returned and he failed to feature in the final nine matches.
Leicester C *(From trainee on 17/2/2001) P/FL 42+9/6 FLC 3 FAC 5+2*
Stockport Co *(Loaned on 24/10/2003) FL 8 Others 2*
Coventry C *(£200,000 on 12/7/2005) FL 30+2/1 FLC 2/1*
Leeds U *(Free on 9/11/2006) FL 51+1/4 FLC 2 FAC 3 Others 1+1*
Colchester U *(Loaned on 14/3/2008) FL 29+8 FLC 2/1 FAC 1 Others 5*
Brighton & Hove A *(Loaned on 3/3/2009) FL 6/1*
Southend U *(Loaned on 30/7/2009) FL 4 FLC 2*

HEATON Thomas (Tom) David
Born: Chester, 15 April 1986
Height: 6'1" **Weight:** 13.6

International Honours: E: U21-2; Yth
Having joined Queens Park Rangers on loan from Manchester United in August to provide both back-up and competition in the goalkeeping positions, Tom spent three months at Loftus Road but only featured twice; both appearances were in League Cup games including Rangers' narrow 1-0 defeat at Chelsea. His next spell on loan was at Rochdale and he had a quite remarkable record during his two-and-a-half-month stay there. His debut in goal ended in a defeat, but then Dale launched into a six-match winning streak and the side were not beaten again in any of Tom's other 11 games, conceding just eight goals in total, a run that took them to the top of the table and eventual promotion. In February, it was Wycombe's turn to sign the highly-rated goalkeeper and he remained as first choice until the end of the season. Supporters universally agreed that he is the best 'keeper to appear for the Chairboys since Martin Taylor left in 2003. Above all Tom is decisive, has real presence, commands his area well, and is particularly safe at handling crosses. Some of his instinct saves were verging on the unbelievable, as he showed in the 0-0 home match with Southampton. He saved a penalty on his home debut, against Millwall, and saved another at MK Dons. Had he come on loan sooner, he probably would have saved the six points Wycombe needed to avoid the drop. Was out of contract at the end of June.
Manchester U *(From trainee on 3/7/2003)*
Swindon T *(Loaned on 18/8/2005)* FL 14 FLC 1 FAC 2 Others 2
Cardiff C *(Loaned on 3/7/2008)* FL 21 FLC 2 FAC 1
Queens Park Rgrs *(Loaned on 15/7/2009)* FLC 2
Rochdale *(Loaned on 13/11/2009)* FL 12
Wycombe W *(Loaned on 12/2/2010)* FL 16

HEFFERNAN Dean James
Born: Sydney, Australia, 19 May 1980
Height: 6'1" **Weight:** 12.11
International Honours: Australia: 2
The defender became only the second Australian in Huddersfield's history to don the blue and white shirt after joining from Central Coast Mariners. After a whirlwind trip to England, the left-back made his debut in the victory at Yeovil. Dean tackles strongly and overlaps well, adapting to the rigours of the English game. Minor injuries and tactical changes sometimes kept him out of the side but Dean had a big part

to play. Was out of contract in the summer.
Huddersfield T *(Signed from Central Coast Mariners, Australia, ex St George Saints, Bulli, Sutherland, Wollongong Wolves, Sydney U, Selangor MPPJ, Sutherland, Marconi on 28/1/2010)* FL 15

HEFFERNAN Paul
Born: Dublin, 29 December 1981
Height: 5'10" **Weight:** 10.7
Club Honours: AMC '07
International Honours: RoI: U21-3
The leading scorer for Doncaster in each of his previous four campaigns he failed to get on the score sheet at the beginning of the season. With Billy Sharp brought in and scoring goals he spent a frustrating time on the bench before being loaned out to Oldham. At first he looked rusty, but as time went on he began to look more like his old self before returning to his parent club after four appearances. His next loan spell was at Bristol Rovers, where he scored five goals and led the line well. Using his good positional play and ability to spot a goalscoring chance Paul managed a well-taken effort at Swindon when turning and beating defenders to score from inside the penalty area. One of his best goals, however, came after a powerful run that saw him holding off two Charlton defenders before he hit a powerful shot into the net. Unfortunately for The Pirates he was called back to Doncaster in early April to play at Blackpool following an injury to Sharp. Was released at the end of the season.
Notts Co *(Signed from Newtown, Co Wicklow on 22/10/1999)* FL 74+26/36 FLC 2+3/1 FAC 2+2/1 Others 2+3
Bristol C *(£125,000 + on 16/7/2004)* FL 10+17/5 FLC 0+1 FAC 1/1 Others 2/1
Doncaster Rov *(£125,000 on 8/6/2005)* FL 88+39/36 FLC 6+4/4 FAC 5+7/4 Others 10+1/10
Oldham Ath *(Loaned on 26/11/2009)* FL 4/1
Bristol Rov *(Loaned on 8/2/2010)* FL 11/4

HEGARTY Nicholas (Nick) Ian
Born: Hemsworth, 25 June 1986
Height: 5'10" **Weight:** 11.0
Nick began the term in his usual left-wing role, passing a century of senior outings for the Mariners before a campaign ruined by an ankle injury. Grimsby badly missed his goal assists of the previous season as a relegation battle dawned, and when Nick did eventually return in the spring, a quiet display at Morecambe highlighted a lack of fitness and he remained on the bench thereafter.

Grimsby T *(From trainee on 11/1/2006)* FL 73+19/8 FLC 2 FAC 3+1 Others 9+1/1

HEITINGA John (Johnny) Gijsbert Alan
Born: Alphen aan den Rijn, Holland, 15 November 1983
Height: 5'11" **Weight:** 11.5
International Honours: Holland: 53; U21; Yth
The Dutchman proved yet another inspired David Moyes purchase for Everton after signing just before the close of the August transfer window. After taking time to settle, the international found his feet when selected in his favoured central defensive role, where his no-nonsense approach found favour with Toffees' supporters, for whom he became a cult hero. A strong-tackling defender with good distribution skills, the former Atletico Madrid player also excelled when moved into the pivotal midfield anchor role following Marouane Fellaini's injury, before an unfortunate foot injury picked up at Aston Villa in April ruled him out until the final day. His undoubted leadership skills on the pitch have him singled out as a future captain with some observers.
Everton *(£6,000,000 from Atletico Madrid, Spain, ex Ajax, on 1/9/2009)* PL 29+2 FLC 2 FAC 2

HELGUSON Heidar
Born: Akureyri, Iceland, 22 August 1977
Height: 6'0" **Weight:** 12.2
International Honours: Iceland: 48; U21-6; Yth
Started the first two games of the season for Queens Park Rangers, scoring his only goal for the club in a 1-1 draw at Plymouth. Although he went on to feature in another five games for Rangers, Heidar made a popular return to Vicarage Road in September when rejoining Watford on loan until the end of the season. The Icelandic international striker had scored 64 times during his first spell and marked his second coming with two goals and a 'Man of the Match' performance against Leicester. Unfortunately he sustained a calf injury in that game which caused him to miss the next six matches, but after that he was virtually an ever-present. Heidar finished the season with 11 goals for Watford, including a brace against Scunthorpe and a crucial winner against Plymouth. An excellent professional who has now made more than 200 appearances for Watford, Hornets' fans were hoping his move would be made permanent in the summer.

Watford *(£1,500,000 from SK Lillestrom, Norway, ex Throttur, on 13/1/2000) P/FL 132+42/55 FLC 8+7/5 FAC 8+2/4*
Fulham *(£1,100,000 on 7/7/2005) PL 31+26/12 FLC 3/3 FAC 3*
Bolton W *(Signed on 20/7/2007) PL 3+4/2 FLC 1 Others 2*
Queens Park Rgrs *(£750,000 on 26/11/2008) FL 18+7/6 FAC 0+2*
Watford *(Loaned on 15/9/2009) FL 8+2/5*
Watford *(Loaned on 11/1/2010) FL 18+1/6*

HENDERSON Darius Alexis
Born: Sutton, 7 September 1981
Height: 6'0" **Weight:** 12.8
A regular for Sheffield United from the start of the season the big striker, whether playing alongside another striker or on his own, generally operated as a target man. Good in the air, he worked very hard challenging defenders, holding up the ball well and bringing others into play. Dangerous in the air from crosses he scored 12 goals including two penalties in the 2-2 draw at Barnsley. He missed a spell in December through injury and another few games when sent off at Forest before injury ended his season two games early.
Reading *(From trainee on 15/12/1999) FL 5+66/11 FLC 2+2/2 FAC 1+2 Others 4+1/2*
Brighton & Hove A *(Loaned on 8/8/2003) FL 10/2*
Gillingham *(£25,000 on 2/1/2004) FL 31+5/9 FAC 2+1/1*
Swindon T *(Loaned on 20/8/2004) FL 6/5*
Watford *(£450,000 on 4/8/2005) P/FL 85+20/29 FLC 3 FAC 5+1 Others 3+1/2*
Sheffield U *(£2,000,000 on 24/7/2008) FL 53+11/18 FLC 3/1 FAC 3+1 Others 1*

HENDERSON Ian
Born: Bury St Edmunds, 24 January 1985
Height: 5'8" **Weight:** 10.10
Club Honours: Div 1 '04
International Honours: E: Yth
At the end of the 2008-09, Ian left Luton following their relegation from the Football League and made a surprise switch to Turkish top flight club Ankaragucu. Financial problems at the club saw him leave after only a few months though and in January he signed for Colchester. He made his debut as a substitute against former club Norwich but was sent off for a dangerous tackle in that 5-0 defeat. Played primarily as a right or left-sided midfielder, Ian scored twice in 13 appearances; one a spectacular angled

volley against Wycombe. Incredibly tenacious yet technically gifted, Ian has played in virtually every position on the pitch in the course of his career.
Norwich C *(From trainee on 3/2/2003) P/FL 26+42/6 FLC 4+3 FAC 1+3*
Rotherham U *(Loaned on 12/1/2007) FL 18/1*
Northampton T *(Free on 17/7/2007) FL 9+17 FLC 2+1 FAC 1+2 Others 0+1*
Luton T *(Free on 2/1/2009) FL 14+5/1 (Freed during 2009 close season)*
Colchester U *(Free from Ankaragucu, Turkey on 7/1/2010) FL 6+7/2*

HENDERSON Jordan Brian
Born: Sunderland, 17 June 1990
Height: 6'0" **Weight:** 10.8
International Honours: E: Yth
An outstanding success as he won both the club and Supporters' Association 'Young Player of the Year' awards. Still a teenager as the season closed, Jordan played more games for Sunderland than anybody apart from 'Player of the Year', Darren Bent. Used slightly more in central midfield than on the right flank, the Sunderland-born youngster excelled. Having played only twice for the club before last season, Jordan played every game bar one until injury struck in February. Five games later he was back sooner than predicted and played in all the remaining matches. Notching his first Sunderland goal against Birmingham in the Carling Cup and his first Premier League goal away to Manchester City, Jordan's trademark became his ability to nutmeg defenders as he broke forward to set up yet another attack.
Sunderland *(From trainee on 1/7/2008) PL 23+11/1 FLC 4/1 FAC 2*
Coventry C *(Loaned on 29/1/2009) FL 9+1/1 FAC 3*

HENDERSON Liam Marc
Born: Gateshead, 28 December 1989
Height: 5'11" **Weight:** 12.2
A graduate of the Watford Academy in his second season as a professional, Liam failed to start any matches for Watford this term but made 14 appearances off the bench. A rugged centre-forward, he was an ideal impact substitute, though his continuing failure to score for the first team was a disappointment. However, he was a prolific scorer for the reserves and claimed hat-tricks against Northampton and Colchester and four goals against Stevenage.
Watford *(From trainee on 23/7/2008) FL 0+18 FLC 0+2 FAC 0+1*
Hartlepool U *(Loaned on 16/1/2009) FL 2+6 FAC 0+1*

HENDERSON Stephen
Born: Dublin, 2 May 1988
Height: 6'2" **Weight:** 13.10
International Honours: RoI: U21-5
This Bristol City goalkeeper, who had impressed during the limited opportunities he had in 2008-09, was surprisingly overlooked for much of last season's campaign and after a proposed temporary move to Wycombe fell through at the end of January, he joined Aldershot on a month-long loan as a replacement for the departing Clark Masters. He visibly grew in confidence and excellent performances at Chesterfield in late February and at home against Bradford in early March saw his loan extended to a second month. Stephen returned to Ashton Gate seven days into the second month of his loan, when a 24-hour notice recall clause was invoked as a result of an injury to Dean Gerken. This gave him the opportunity he needed to remind some at the club of his capabilities. A clean sheet at Preston that was followed by another at home to Swansea suggested that Stephen was the better option for City as they attempt to fill the void left by the virtually irreplaceable Adriano Basso. Unfortunately, a 3-0 defeat at Scunthorpe, saw him lose his place as Gerken returned for the final two games of the season.
Aston Villa *(From trainee on 5/5/2006)*
Bristol C *(Free on 25/7/2007) FL 3+2*
Aldershot T *(Loaned on 1/2/2010) FL 8*

HENDERSON Wayne Christopher Patrick
Born: Dublin, 16 September 1983
Height: 5'11" **Weight:** 12.2
Club Honours: FAYC '02
International Honours: RoI: 6; U21-13; Yth
Wayne was goalkeeping substitute for every Preston game last season until finally making his first appearance for the club since August 2007 when he replaced the injured Andy Lonergan in the penultimate match and retained his spot for the final game at Reading. Wayne has fought his way back from a serious back injury and he will be hoping to challenge for a starting place next term, when his all-round abilities as a good organiser of his defence, an excellent shot-stopper and a commanding claimer of crosses can be demonstrated to good effect.
Aston Villa *(From trainee on 27/9/2000)*
Wycombe W *(Loaned on 23/4/2004) FL 3*
Notts Co *(Loaned on 9/8/2004) FL 9 Others 1*
Notts Co *(Loaned on 3/12/2004) FL 2 Others 1*

Brighton & Hove A *(£20,000 on 5/8/2005) FL 52 FAC 2 Others 3*
Preston NE *(£150,000 on 31/1/2007) FL 8+1 FLC 1*
Grimsby T *(Loaned on 27/2/2009) FL 14*

HENDRIE Lee Andrew
Born: Birmingham, 18 May 1977
Height: 5'10" **Weight:** 10.3
International Honours: E: 1; B-1; U21-13; Yth

Lee signed for Derby from Sheffield United on the same day that Jordan Stewart moved in the opposite direction. His experience boosted County's midfield and there were glimpses of his old skill, so valuable to Aston Villa. However, he was unable to command a regular place and became frustrated by a lack of senior action before seeing out his contract on loan to Brighton. Moving in March in an effort to bolster the League One club's midfield and perhaps with a view to extending his career at a lower level, Lee found it difficult at times to get involved. Even so, he showed glimpses of his Premier League pedigree with some accurate long-range passing and memorably creating a goal for Tommy Elphick against Carlisle.

Aston Villa (From trainee on 18/5/1994) PL 202+49/27 FLC 15+3/3 FAC 12+8 Others 14+5/2
Stoke C (Loaned on 29/9/2006) FL 17/3
Stoke C (Loaned on 29/1/2007) FL 9+2
Sheffield U (Free on 27/7/2007) FL 7+10/1 FLC 2+1/2 FAC 3+2/1 Others 0+1
Leicester C (Loaned on 28/2/2008) FL 9/1
Blackpool (Loaned on 15/11/2008) FL 5+1
Derby Co (Signed on 1/9/2009) FL 4+5 FAC 1
Brighton & Hove A (Loaned on 23/3/2010) FL 6+2

HENNESSEY Wayne Robert
Born: Anglesey, 24 January 1987
Height: 6'0" **Weight:** 11.6
Club Honours: Ch '09
International Honours: W: 25; U21-6; Yth

Wolverhampton's Wayne was younger than most Premier League goalkeepers, although he probably had more international experience than many. He made some good saves at Manchester City, keeping the score to a respectable 1-0. He did not really let Wolves down and played for Wales in their 3-0 win over Scotland, only to be at fault for two Chelsea goals a few days later. Wayne was dropped, but was expected to return quickly, only to be kept out by the fine form of Marcus Hahnemann. To

sum up, he played the first 13 League games but only the three FA Cup games after that start. Wayne appeared for Wales in March against Sweden.

Wolverhampton W (From trainee on 7/4/2005) P/FL 93+1 FLC 1 FAC 8 Others 2
Stockport Co (Loaned on 12/1/2007) FL 15

HENRY James
Born: Reading, 10 June 1989
Height: 6'1" **Weight:** 11.11
International Honours: S: Yth; E: Yth

James made just two first team starts for Reading at the beginning of the season, and one as a substitute near the end, but found it difficult to displace more experienced wide players such as Jimmy Kebe and Jobi McAnuff in the starting line-up. Sent out on loan to Millwall to play first team football and score goals, he returned to the Den and did just that in a spell which lasted from September until an injury meant a return to Reading. He scored a brilliant hat-trick in the 5-0 win over Tranmere and then added two last-minute goals after coming on as a sub, which won three points against Colchester and a point at Brentford. He has clever ball control and plenty of pace for a wide midfielder. Back at Reading he was given a two-year extension to his contract, in the anticipation that he will begin to fulfil his undoubted potential with his local club.

Reading (From trainee on 12/6/2006) P/FL 4+6 FLC 5+1/4 FAC 1+1
Nottingham F (Loaned on 22/3/2007) FL 0+1
Bournemouth (Loaned on 2/11/2007) FL 8+3/4
Norwich C (Loaned on 31/1/2008) FL 1+2
Millwall (Loaned on 12/2/2009) FL 15+1/3 Others 1+1
Millwall (Loaned on 10/9/2009) FL 6+3/5

HENRY Karl Levi Daniel
Born: Wolverhampton, 26 November 1982
Height: 6'1" **Weight:** 10.13
Club Honours: Ch '09
International Honours: E: Yth

Karl's good tackle kept Wolverhampton 1-0 up at Wigan, and the combative midfielder soon regained his role as captain. He certainly led by example and played very well at home to Aston Villa, and at Tottenham. He was unable to get forward so much, scoring just one goal, a sweetly-struck shot at Crystal Palace. Karl was influential in a vital win at West Ham and had played every minute of every League game bar one until April. That ended with a harsh

sending off at Arsenal and his abiliy to break up the play was missed during his suspension. He returned for the last two fixtures.

Stoke C (From trainee on 30/11/1999) FL 63+57/1 FLC 4+1 FAC 7+2 Others 1+1
Cheltenham T (Loaned on 13/1/2004) FL 8+1/1
Wolverhampton W (£100,000 on 3/8/2006) P/FL 148+3/6 FLC 5+1 FAC 10/1

Karl Henry

HERBERT Courtney Anthony
Born: Northampton, 25 October 1988
Height: 6'2" **Weight:** 12.8

At the beginning of the season, Courtney was playing non-League football and working in a factory. By September, he was a professional with Northampton, becoming Ian Sampson's first signing when he took over as manager. He repaid his boss' faith by scoring his first goal in a 3-1 victory against Rotherham. One of the fastest players seen at Sixfields in some time, Courtney also has the finishing skills. Injury robbed him of a large part of the season but once back fit and on form he will be a player to watch.

Northampton T (Free from Long Buckby on 23/9/2009) FL 8+15/2 Others 0+1

HERD Benjamin (Ben) Alexander
Born: Welwyn Garden City, 21 June 1985
Height: 5'9" **Weight:** 10.12

Ben is a tenacious, attacking right-back, who was released by Shrewsbury and impressed sufficiently on trial to sign a two-year deal with Aldershot. He made

his debut in the opening day victory over Darlington but a knee ligament injury kept him out for six weeks. Having returned at Torquay in September, he played every minute of every game until being stretchered off at Port Vale in April with an ankle injury. Although missing five games, he was back for the home leg of the play-off semi-final against Rotherham. Ben enjoyed personal glory by winning both the supporters' and players' 'Player of the Year' awards.

Watford *(From trainee on 8/5/2003)*
Shrewsbury T *(Free on 6/6/2005) FL 136+7/3 FLC 5 FAC 5+1 Others 7+2*
Aldershot T *(Free on 25/7/2009) FL 33+1 FAC 3 Others 3*

HERD Christopher (Chris)
Born: Perth, Australia, 4 April 1989
Height: 5'8" **Weight:** 12.0
International Honours: Australia: Yth
A combative, strong, attacking midfielder, Aston Villa's Chris weighed in with some important goals during his loan spell at Lincoln whilst his wholehearted approach made him a firm fans' favourite. Unfortunately, a medial ligament injury sustained in the local derby at Notts County forced the Australian to miss the last month of the campaign.
Aston Villa *(From trainee on 3/7/2007)*
Port Vale *(Loaned on 10/1/2008) FL 11/2*
Wycombe W *(Loaned on 14/3/2008) FL 3+1*
Lincoln C *(Loaned on 26/11/2009) FL 20/4 FAC 2*

HERD Jonathan (Johnny) James
Born: Huntingdon, 3 October 1989
Height: 5'9" **Weight:** 11.13
Highly regarded at Roots Hall, Johnny played well when drafted into the Southend team and looks to have a bright future at left-back, a slot that has been a major headache for manager Steve Tilson in the last couple of seasons. Johnny is attack minded and has a remarkably long throw for a slightly-built player, a weapon that caused major defensive problems for the team's adversaries. Johnny regained his place for the final 11 games and again acquitted himself well. Southend activated a clause in his contract tying him to Roots Hall for a further season.
Southend U *(From trainee on 31/7/2008) FL 22+4 FAC 6 Others 1*

HESKEY Emile William Ivanhoe
Born: Leicester, 11 January 1978
Height: 6'2" **Weight:** 13.12
Club Honours: FLC '97, '00, '01, '03;

FAC '01; UEFAC '01; ESC '01; CS '01
International Honours: E: 58; B-1; U21-16; Yth
Emile's disappointing season with Aston Villa has not stopped the striker from being an important player for England. While the burly front man was in and out of Martin O'Neill's team, he remains a firm favourite of Fabio Capello and was selected in the World Cup squad. Emile has never been a prolific scorer and his tally of three Premier League goals and two in the Cups did little to convince Villa fans who have reservations. O'Neill is a staunch supporter of Emile from their days at Leicester but even the Villa manager generally opted to partner John Carew and Gabby Agbonlahor up front in the second half of the season, knowing they carried a greater goals threat. Emile's three League goals came at home and away against relegated Burnley and at Sunderland, while he scored in the Carling Cup quarter-final and semi-final against Portsmouth and Blackburn. He is famed more for his ability to hold the ball and bring others into play. Many of his striker partners down the years have praised his unselfishness, but Villa have yet to see the best of Emile in this creative role and he was not helped by a succession of niggly injuries.
Leicester C *(From trainee on 3/10/1995) P/FL 143+11/40 FLC 25+2/6 FAC 11 Others 5*
Liverpool *(£11,000,000 on 10/3/2000) PL 118+32/39 FLC 7+5/2 FAC 9+5/6 Others 42+5/13*
Birmingham C *(£3,500,000 + on 2/7/2004) PL 68/14 FLC 5/1 FAC 5/1*
Wigan Ath *(£5,500,000 on 14/7/2006) PL 80+2/15 FLC 2+1 FAC 3*
Aston Villa *(£3,500,000 on 23/1/2009) PL 27+18/5 FLC 5/2 FAC 3+1 Others 2*

HESSEY Sean Peter
Born: Whiston, 19 September 1978
Height: 6'0" **Weight:** 12.8
An innocuous slip on the second day of pre-season training damaged Sean's knee ligaments and he did not play his first match for Macclesfield until mid-December in the 3-1 home victory against Hereford, immediately giving a top performance. Ever-present thereafter, Sean was initially at centre-back but took over from left-back Carl Tremarco, who was recovering from a hernia operation. Equally comfortable with four or five at the back, he was out of contract in the summer.
Leeds U *(From juniors at Liverpool on 15/9/1997)*
Wigan Ath *(Free on 24/12/1997)*
Huddersfield T *(Free on 12/3/1998) FL 7+4 FAC 1*

Kilmarnock *(Free on 31/8/1999) SL 38+6/1 SLC 2 SC 1*
Blackpool *(Free on 12/2/2004) FL 4+2 Others 0+1*
Chester C *(Free on 2/7/2004) FL 70+9/1 FLC 2 FAC 6 Others 5/1*
Macclesfield T *(Free on 9/11/2007) FL 82+4 FLC 2 FAC 3*

HEWSON Sam
Born: Bolton, 28 November 1988
Height: 5'8" **Weight:** 11.11
International Honours: E: Yth
A creative midfield player on loan to Bury from Manchester United, Sam made only one start for the Shakers and six substitute appearances, failing to establish himself in the side. His ten-minute debut performance at Bradford in February set the precedent for further substitute appearances, in which Sam failed to impose himself sufficiently. Was out of contract at the end of June.
Manchester U *(From trainee on 3/7/2007)*
Hereford U *(Loaned on 6/1/2009) FL 9+1/3*
Bury *(Loaned on 1/2/2010) FL 1+6*

HEYWOOD Matthew (Matt) Stephen
Born: Chatham, 26 August 1979
Height: 6'2" **Weight:** 14.0
Club captain Matt's sole outing for Grimsby last term was in a 4-0 defeat at Port Vale. The central defender then suffered a knee injury, his contract later being cancelled in January by mutual consent. At his best he was virtually unbeatable in the air and was an inspiration to those around him as a leader.
Burnley *(From trainee on 6/7/1998) FL 11+2 FAC 1 Others 1*
Swindon T *(Free on 22/1/2001) FL 176+7/8 FLC 5+1 FAC 9/1 Others 10/1*
Bristol C *(Free on 1/7/2005) FL 22+2/2 FAC 0+1*
Brentford *(Signed on 28/7/2006) FL 55+5/2 FLC 2 FAC 2 Others 3*
Grimsby T *(Free on 28/7/2008) FL 17+2 FLC 2 Others 2*

HIBBERT Anthony (Tony) James
Born: Liverpool, 20 February 1981
Height: 5'8" **Weight:** 11.3
Club Honours: FAYC '98
Although no longer an automatic selection for Everton, this loyal one club man has now played in the Premier League for ten successive seasons and this was yet another campaign of effective duty on the right-hand side of the Blues' defence. The full-back passed the landmarks of 200 League and 250 competitive appearances for the Toffees

and celebrated setting a new club record for European appearances by leading the side for the first time against BATE Borisov. A groin strain and hernia operation sidelined the former Academy player in the New Year but he returned to play impressively in the final few League games. A fierce and clean tackler, the locally-born player has improved his forward play substantially over the years.
Everton (From trainee on 1/7/1998) PL 186+15 FLC 12+1 FAC 17 Others 16+4

David Hibbert

HIBBERT David John
Born: Eccleshall, 28 January 1986
Height: 6'2" **Weight:** 12.6
It was an excellent season for the Shrewsbury striker, who put an injury-hit previous campaign behind him to lead the line with 14 League goals and one in the Carling Cup. Making his first start since October 2008, he opened his account against Burton on the first day of the season. A tireless worker, whose height and strength enables him to hold the ball, he has a great shot and is equally lethal in the air. He had a number of good performances and a purple patch in December and January when he bagged five goals in five consecutive games, though a lean spell followed until he scored at Crewe in April in the 3-0 win. Supporters voted him their 'Player of the Year'.
Port Vale (Trainee) FL 2+7/2 Others 1
Preston NE (Free on 6/7/2005) FL 0+10 FAC 1+2
Rotherham U (Loaned on 5/8/2006) FL 12+9/2 FLC 0+1
Bradford C (Loaned on 5/1/2007) FL 4+4
Shrewsbury T (Signed on 18/6/2007) FL 82+23/29 FLC 2+2/1 FAC 1 Others 1+1

HIGGINBOTHAM Daniel (Danny) John
Born: Manchester, 29 December 1978
Height: 6'1" **Weight:** 12.6
When Tony Pulis signed another left-footed centre-half or left-back in Danny Collins just before the end of the August transfer window, it was seen by many as a sign that Danny would not be getting much playing time at Stoke during the season. It was a case, though, of taking your chance when it came along and Danny did just that, as injuries brought him back into contention for the match at Tottenham at the end of October. His superb display in that 1-0 win made him effectively undroppable and between then and the end of the season he was, except when injured, a near permanent fixture in the Stoke defence. His versatility in being able to play at centre-half or left-back make him a valued squad member, with his solid defensive attributes, not to mention his eye for goal whenever he comes up with the other big guns to play an important part in Stoke's array of set-piece routines.
Manchester U (From trainee on 10/7/1997) PL 2+2 FLC 1 Others 1+1
Derby Co (£2,000,000 on 12/7/2000) P/FL 82+4/3 FLC 7+1/1 FAC 3+1
Southampton (Signed on 31/11/2003) P/FL 84+10/4 FLC 4 FAC 7 Others 1
Stoke C (£225,000 on 4/8/2006) FL 45/7 FLC 1 FAC 2
Sunderland (£2,500,000 on 30/8/2007) PL 22/3
Stoke C (£2,500,000 on 1/9/2008) PL 51+1/2 FLC 4/1 FAC 3

HIGGINBOTHAM Kallum Michael
Born: Salford, 15 June 1989
Height: 5'11" **Weight:** 10.10
Out of the picture for much of the previous term and on the transfer list in the summer, Kallum re-established himself in the Rochdale squad from November onwards. While largely used as an impact substitute, he played an important role in Rochdale's promotion, either on the wing or as an extra striker. Having netted a hat-trick for the reserves, Kallum scored the most amazing goal of the season when he controlled a clearance from the Accrington 'keeper and returned it into the net from the half-way line to seal a 4-2 win. Was out of contract at the end of June.
Oldham Ath (Free from Salford C on 1/8/2006)
Rochdale (Free on 19/6/2007) FL 31+38/7 FLC 1+1 FAC 2+2 Others 3+1
Accrington Stanley (Loaned on

17/10/2008) FL 1+4
Accrington Stanley (Loaned on 23/1/2009) FL 4+3

HIGGS Shane Peter
Born: Oxford, 13 May 1977
Height: 6'2" **Weight:** 12.12
Summer signing Shane was one of the key factors behind Leeds' superb start. The former Cheltenham goalkeeper did not finish on the losing side in any of his first 13 appearances, making a penalty save at Southend in September to preserve the unbeaten record. He sustained a thigh injury in the victory at MK Dons, missed two games, and on his return against Norwich aggravated the injury, ruling him out for six months. During his time out of action he signed a contract adding a further year.
Bristol Rov (From trainee on 17/7/1995) FL 10 Others 2 (Free to Worcester C on 11/7/1998)
Cheltenham T (£10,000 from Worcester C on 21/6/1999) FL 235+2 FLC 8 FAC 14 Others 16
Leeds U (Free on 3/7/2009) FL 19 FLC 3

[HILARIO] SAMPAIO Henrique Hilario Alves
Born: Sao Pedro da Cova, Portugal, 21 October 1975
Height: 6'2" **Weight:** 13.5
Club Honours: FLC '07; FAC '09, '10; CS '09
International Honours: Portugal: 1; B; U21
Whenever Petr Cech was indisposed at Chelsea, his impressive deputy Hilario did a sound job in goal. His first action of the season involved walking off the bench to replace the dismissed Cech at Wigan and facing a penalty he could not keep out. He kept three successive clean sheets before Cech's return and, in total, had a respectable six from nine full matches. He was called into the Portugal squad for the first time by Carlos Queiroz at the age of 34 for the World Cup qualification play-off against Bosnia but suffered the disappointment of being excluded from the final squad.
Chelsea (Free from CD Nacional, Portugal, ex Naval, Academica Coimbra, Porto, Estrela Amadoro - loan, Varzim - loan, Academica Coimbra - loan, on 10/7/2006) PL 16+2 FLC 7 FAC 6 Others 3+2

HILL Clinton (Clint) Scott
Born: Huyton, 19 October 1978
Height: 6'0" **Weight:** 11.6
Clint began the season for Crystal Palace as usual at left-back but after an injury to Paddy McCarthy and the transfer of Jose Fonte to Southampton, he found himself in his natural position,

in the centre of a four-man defence partnering either Claude Davis or Matt Lawrence. When Paddy McCarthy returned from injury he once again moved to the left of defence. A player who always gives his all for the cause, with his contract expiring at the end of last season and Palace's future ownership uncertain, he could be set for a future elsewhere within the Championship and has already been linked with other clubs.

Tranmere Rov (From trainee on 9/7/1997) FL 138+2/16 FLC 18/3 FAC 11+1/1
Oldham Ath (Signed on 16/7/2002) FL 17/1 FLC 4 FAC 2 Others 2
Stoke C (£120,000 on 22/7/2003) FL 71+9/3 FLC 2 FAC 2
Crystal Palace (Free on 6/11/2007) FL 114/5 FLC 4 FAC 6+1/1 Others 2

HILL Matthew (Matt)
Clayton
Born: Bristol, 26 March 1981
Height: 5'7" **Weight:** 12.6
Club Honours: AMC '03; Ch '09
Matt was one of four Wolverhampton left-backs with first team experience, and his first appearance was in the Carling Cup. The tidy defender was to start two Premier League games though, acquitting himself well enough at Blackburn and Manchester United. However, he wanted to play more, and was loaned to Queens Park Rangers at the end of January and went on to spend three months in Shepherds Bush playing in 15 out of 16 games during that time. Left-back was a problem position for Rangers throughout the season and Matt's arrival gave them some constancy of selection in that spot for both his managers, Mick Harford and Neil Warnock.

Bristol C (From trainee on 22/2/1999) FL 182+16/6 FLC 8 FAC 15 Others 19+5
Preston NE (£100,000 on 10/1/2005) FL 94+11 FLC 4 FAC 6+1 Others 3
Wolverhampton W (Signed on 1/9/2008) P/FL 15 FLC 1 FAC 1
Queens Park Rgrs (Loaned on 25/1/2010) FL 15+1

HILLS Lee Mark
Born: Croydon, 13 April 1990
Height: 5'10" **Weight:** 11.11
International Honours: E: Yth
The Crystal Palace man arrived at Oldham on loan in November, having had limited appearances at Selhurst Park, with a big reputation as a tough-tackling defender. In his fourth game for the club he proved it when he was sent off following a crunching tackle at Walsall. The subsequent three-game ban ended his loan spell with Oldham

and after returning to his parent club he was back in the first team just before Christmas, being very much part of the squad for the rest of the season, either playing in his favoured left-back role or as a substitute. Having already featured in the FA Cup for Oldham, he was unable to play for Palace in their two games against Premier League opposition. Was unlucky to be sent off for the second time during the season, away to Watford, at the end of March and after catching his studs on the turf in the game at Derby in mid-April he picked up a cruciate ligament injury that has ruled him out until the end of 2010.

Crystal Palace (From trainee on 1/2/2008) FL 24+21/1 FLC 0+1 FAC 1
Colchester U (Loaned on 13/11/2008) FL 1+1
Oldham Ath (Loaned on 4/11/2009) FL 3 FAC 1

HINDS Richard Paul
Born: Sheffield, 22 August 1980
Height: 6'2" **Weight:** 11.0
Club Honours: Div 1 '07
An Owls' supporter all his life, the versatile Sheffield Wednesday defender suffered a series of injuries to frustrate his search for a place in the squad. He only managed a few appearances and even when fit had to make do with a place on the bench for the most part. Richard can play at full-back or in central defence and is a solid, reliable performer wherever he is selected. He really needs a good injury-free season to enable him to get back and stay in the side. Still young enough to re-establish his career at Hillsborough and, hopefully, will stay for a long time to come.

Tranmere Rov (From juniors on 20/7/1998) FL 42+13 FLC 3+5 FAC 5 Others 1
Hull C (Free on 1/7/2003) FL 40+5/1 FLC 1 FAC 1 Others 1+1
Scunthorpe U (Free on 17/3/2005) FL 85+8/8 FLC 3/1 FAC 6 Others 2+1
Sheffield Wed (Free on 5/7/2007) FL 50+13/2 FLC 3+1 FAC 2

HINES Sebastian (Seb) Tony
Born: Wetherby, 29 May 1988
Height: 6'2" **Weight:** 12.4
International Honours: E: Yth
Seb featured prominently in Middlesbrough's defence at the opening of the season and started successive League games against Ipswich and Sheffield Wednesday in September. He was then dropped in favour of loan signing Sean St Ledger. After suffering a knee injury, Seb returned to play a reserve team game against Morecambe in December. After

scoring in the first half, he slid in to clear the ball and suffered ankle and medial knee ligament damage. He was stretchered off and his season was over.

Middlesbrough (From trainee on 2/7/2005) P/FL 2+2 FLC 0+1 FAC 3/1
Oldham Ath (Loaned on 13/2/2009) FL 4

HINES Zavon
Born: Jamaica, 27 December 1988
Height: 5'10" **Weight:** 10.7
International Honours: E: U21-2
The young West Ham striker was a revelation this season as he fought to gain a regular place in the team. He was outstanding against Liverpool in September with his pace and trickery. In November he was on as a substitute against Aston Villa, when his persistence and willingness to chase led to him scoring the winning goal in the last minute. Playing against Manchester United in December he was forced off at half-time with a knee injury that resulted in surgery. It was serious enough to keep Zavon out for the remainder of the campaign.

West Ham U (From trainee on 6/7/2007) PL 5+8/1 FLC 1+2/2
Coventry C (Loaned on 27/3/2008) FL 0+7/1

HINSHELWOOD Adam
Born: Oxford, 8 January 1984
Height: 5'10" **Weight:** 12.10
Following his release from Brighton in the summer, the central defender signed a one-year deal with Aldershot after giving some solid performances as a triallist in the club's pre-season friendlies. Adam's leadership qualities led to him being named captain and he made his debut in the opening day victory over Darlington before suffering ignominy in the club's next two games when giving away two penalties. Having suffered a knee injury in the home League game against Hereford in early September, which kept him out for three weeks, he was persistently hampered by knee and hamstring problems before becoming former Shots' boss Gary Waddock's first January transfer window signing for Wycombe. Straight away, Adam brought stability to a defence badly leaking sloppy goals, but after a solid run in the team injuries saw him miss several games, including the last five of the season. Given the captaincy and offered a new contract, if he can keep free of injuries he will be a key player next season. Has excellent positional play, is composed on the ball, and has good upper body strength.

Brighton & Hove A (From trainee on 28/7/2003) FL 88+11/2 FLC 3 FAC 4

Others 5+2
Aldershot T (Free on 29/7/2009) FL 13+2 FLC 1 FAC 1 Others 1
Wycombe W (Free on 1/1/2010) FL 13/1

HINTON Craig
Born: Wolverhampton, 26 November 1977
Height: 6'0" **Weight:** 12.0
Club Honours: FC '00
Central defender Craig was made club captain on his arrival at Northampton but struggled in the early days, maybe due to the change of defending partner. The new management team settled things by linking him with Dean Beckwith and, as expected, the defence tightened up. Craig plays a captain's game, leading the team by example as one of the busiest players on the field.
Birmingham C (From trainee on 5/7/1996)
Kidderminster Hrs (Free on 12/8/1998) FL 172+1/3 FLC 5 FAC 10 Others 8
Bristol Rov (Free on 20/7/2004) FL 135+18/3 FLC 3 FAC 15+2/3 Others 13+1
Northampton T (Free on 2/7/2009) FL 38+2 FLC 1 FAC 2 Others 3

HIRD Adrian Samuel (Sam)
Born: Askern, 7 September 1987
Height: 6'0" **Weight:** 12.0
Sam, a centre-back, was the one Doncaster player in that position who stayed free of injury throughout 2009-10. He had quite a good season and had a particularly good game at Swansea in the last match of the campaign, when the Swans needed a win but were held to a goalless draw.
Leeds U (From trainee on 13/9/2005)
Doncaster Rov (Free on 8/2/2007) FL 57+25/1 FLC 2 FAC 4+2/1 Others 4+1
Grimsby T (Loaned on 20/11/2007) FL 17 FAC 1

HOBBS Jack
Born: Portsmouth, 18 August 1988
Height: 6'3" **Weight:** 13.4
Club Honours: FAYC '06; Div 1 '09
International Honours: E: Yth
The highly-rated young defender was loaned to Leicester by Liverpool for all of 2008-09 and Jack was quickly made a permanent signing as that campaign drew to a close. He gradually matured during the Championship season, being voted the club's 'Player of the Year', and had inherited the captaincy by the time the play-offs came around. England under-21 manager Stuart Pearce is already keeping an eye on Jack, of whom even greater things are expected next season.

Lincoln C (Trainee) FL 0+1
Liverpool (£750,000 on 19/8/2005) PL 1+1 FLC 2+1
Scunthorpe U (Loaned on 25/1/2008) FL 7+2/1
Leicester C (Signed on 29/7/2008) FL 83+5/1 FLC 2 FAC 4 Others 4

HODGES Lee Leslie
Born: Epping, 4 September 1973
Height: 6'0" **Weight:** 12.1
Club Honours: Div 3 '02; Div 2 '04
International Honours: E: Yth
Lee is a vastly experienced utility defender or midfield player who made two starts, one at left-back and one at centre-back, and a few substitute appearances for Torquay before departing on an extended loan to Truro, where he combined playing duties with two spells as caretaker manager. Was out of contract in the summer.
Tottenham H (From trainee on 29/2/1992) PL 0+4
Plymouth Arg (Loaned on 26/2/1993) FL 6+1/2
Wycombe W (Loaned on 31/12/1993) FL 2+2 FAC 1 Others 1
Barnet (Free on 31/5/1994) FL 94+11/26 FLC 6+1 FAC 6+1/4 Others 4+1
Reading (£100,000 on 29/7/1997) FL 58+21/10 FLC 7+3 FAC 7+1/1 Others 0+2
Plymouth Arg (Free on 17/8/2001) FL 162+33/11 FLC 5/1 FAC 10+2 Others 2+1
Torquay U (Free on 2/7/2008) FL 2+3 Others 0+1

HODSON Lee James Stephen
Born: Borehamwood, 2 October 1991
Height: 5'11" **Weight:** 11.2
International Honours: NI: U21-5; Yth
Lee, a successful graduate of the Watford Academy, made a big impression this term. Strong, quick and two-footed, he was drafted into Watford's depleted defence at right-back at the end of August and kept his place until the end of January. His composure and consistency belied his 17 years and he also demonstrated a mature reading of the game and crossing ability when going forward. Lee laid on three assists against Leicester and was 'Man of the Match' at Ipswich. After a period on the bench, he was pressed into service again, this time at left-back, at the end of the season and again looked comfortable. A local boy, Lee was chosen as Football League 'Apprentice of the Month' in November and was a runner-up as 'Apprentice of the Year'. It was no surprise when Watford offered him a professional contract during the course

of the season. Already a Northern Ireland under-19 international, Lee graduated to the under-21 team during the season.
Watford (From trainee on 6/11/2008) FL 29+3 FLC 2 FAC 1

HOGG Jonathan Lee
Born: Middlesbrough, 6 December 1988
Height: 5'7" **Weight:** 10.8
Jonathan scored on his Darlington debut at Chesterfield in November but failed to find the net again in four further starts before returning to Villa Park. Is a combative midfielder who weighs in with more than his fair share of goals.
Aston Villa (From trainee on 2/7/2008)
Darlington (Loaned on 19/11/2009) FL 5/1

HOILETT David Wayne
Born: Ottawa, Canada, 5 June 1990
Height: 5'8" **Weight:** 11.0
After obtaining a work permit on appeal, the speedy, wide player was eased into the Blackburn squad, although he spent most of the time on the bench. A rare start in the Carling Cup at Gillingham produced a sound performance, topped by a goal from a diving header. It was to be his only score and as the season wore on he ran out of luck in the final third. In the last few moments of the home game against West Ham he had the chance to win the match with a great burst clear of the defenders but his lob landed on the roof of the net. For an inexperienced player he showed real composure when asked to take a penalty in the shoot-out in the Carling Cup quarter-final against Chelsea. Chelsea had just levelled but David showed no nerves and scored emphatically.
Blackburn Rov (From juniors on 4/8/2008) PL 8+15 FLC 3+1/1

HOLDEN Dean Thomas John
Born: Salford, 15 September 1979
Height: 6'0" **Weight:** 11.0
International Honours: E: Yth
The versatile right-back was signed by Shrewsbury from Falkirk and made his debut in the opening game against Burton. He has an all-action style, tackles strongly and is a good distributor of the ball. Dean captained the side when Graham Coughlan was injured. Likes to get forward but, surprisingly, in all his 38 appearances, did not manage to bag a goal. Generally looked comfortable but his robust style did lead to three suspensions, including one for a

sending-off in the 1-0 win against Chesterfield for a professional foul.
Bolton W *(From trainee on 23/12/1997) P/FL 7+6/1 FLC 3+1 FAC 3+1*
Oldham Ath *(Free on 12/10/2001) FL 98+10/10 FLC 2+1 FAC 5 Others 8+1/1*
Peterborough U *(Free on 7/7/2005) FL 54+2/4 FLC 2 FAC 4 Others 5*
Falkirk *(Signed on 2/1/2007) SL 44+4/2 SLC 3 SC 3+3*
Shrewsbury T *(Signed on 26/6/2009) FL 37 FLC 1*

HOLDEN Luke
Born: Liverpool, 24 November 1988
Height: 5'8" **Weight:** 11.0
Luke was signed by Charlton in the summer, on loan from Rhyl with a view to a permanent move at the end of the year. With Charlton running no regular reserve side during the season, it was difficult for the speedy winger to put himself in contention. He made only one appearance, as a second-half substitute in the Johnstone's Paint Trophy at Southampton. Charlton did not take up their option to sign him and he returned to Rhyl at the end of the year.
Charlton Ath *(Free from Rhyl, ex The New Saints, Cammell Laird, Bradford PA, on 1/9/2009) Others 0+1*

HOLDEN Stuart
Born: Aberdeen, 1 August 1985
Height: 5'10" **Weight:** 11.7
International Honours: USA: 14; U23-7; Yth
A United States international attacking midfielder, Stuart signed for Bolton following a successful trial period. Having spent his career in Major League Soccer, Stuart, who was born in Scotland, opted for a move to the Premiership. He made his debut in the 4-0 FA Cup defeat at Spurs but impressed enough to retain his place in the following League game at Wolves, where he was arguably the 'Man of the Match'. Hoping to build upon this impressive form, Stuart's season was cut short when he suffered a fractured fibula playing for the USA in March. Returning to action on the final day of the season, Stuart was set to join the USA World Cup squad for South Africa.
Sunderland *(Free from Clemson Tigers, USA on 5/3/2005. Freed during 2005 close season)*
Bolton W *(Signed from Houston Dynamo, USA on 26/1/2010) PL 1+1 FAC 1*

HOLDSWORTH Andrew (Andy)
Born: Pontefract, 29 January 1984
Height: 5'9" **Weight:** 11.2

Andy suffered a major setback after playing 15 games for Oldham, having joined them in the summer from Huddersfield. He was sidelined with a knee injury that required surgery and had to sit out the remainder of the season. When he did make it on to the pitch the likeable Andy, as ever, put 100 per cent into his game. Good at either full-back position or in midfield, he is an excellent squad member and, when fit, still retains his pace and excellent passing ability.
Huddersfield T *(From trainee on 6/12/2003) FL 214+17/6 FLC 8/1 FAC 12/1 Others 9+1*
Oldham Ath *(Free on 23/7/2009) FL 11+1 FLC 1 FAC 1 Others 1*

HOLLANDS Daniel (Danny)
Timothy
Born: Ashford, Middlesex, 6 November 1985
Height: 5'11" **Weight:** 12.11
It was another good season for Danny, Bournemouth's energetic midfield player. Danny missed the start of the season through injury but was soon back in the side and was handed the captain's armband. Despite some solid performances, it was only when the responsibility of captaincy was taken away from him that he really flourished. His hard work for the team came to the fore and he scored some vital goals, including braces against Rotherham and Notts County. Danny signed a one-year extension to his contract in May.
Chelsea *(From trainee on 12/11/2003)*
Torquay U *(Loaned on 9/3/2006) FL 10/1*
Bournemouth *(Free on 6/7/2006) FL 127+24/17 FLC 0+1 FAC 9+2/2 Others 7+1/2*

HOLMES Lee Daniel
Born: Mansfield, 2 April 1987
Height: 5'7" **Weight:** 10.6
International Honours: E: Yth
It has been another season at Southampton disrupted by injury for Lee. A scheming, fleet-footed winger, with a rich repertoire of passes and crosses, he started the campaign on the bench but was not fit enough to figure in the starting team until mid-season. He then started three matches looking purposeful, notably when playing a key role in the elimination of Ipswich from the FA Cup at St Mary's in January. Then he was sidelined for the rest of the season, this time by a persistent groin problem.
Derby Co *(From trainee on 15/5/2004) FL 26+20/2 FLC 2 FAC 1+3*
Swindon T *(Loaned on 22/12/2004) FL 14+1/1 Others 1*

Bradford C *(Loaned on 4/8/2006) FL 16 FLC 1 FAC 1 Others 1*
Walsall *(Loaned on 11/1/2008) FL 19/4*
Southampton *(Free on 16/7/2008) FL 13+3 FLC 2/2 FAC 1+2 Others 0+1*

HOLNESS Marcus Lewis
Born: Swinton, 8 December 1988
Height: 6'0" **Weight:** 12.2
With injuries afflicting a number of Rochdale defenders early in the season, Marcus, still only 20, played a number of games, mainly as cover for Nathan Stanton at centre-back, partnering the even younger Craig Dawson. Marcus then suffered a long-term injury, being out from November until March. On his return, the strongly-built defender was a regular on the bench but appeared only once.
Oldham Ath *(From trainee on 3/7/2007)*
Rochdale *(Free on 2/10/2007) FL 24+14 FLC 1 FAC 3+1 Others 3+1*

HOLROYD Christopher (Chris)
Born: Macclesfield, 24 October 1986
Height: 5'11" **Weight:** 12.3
Signed by Brighton in January from Cambridge United, for whom he had scored ten Blue Square Premier goals, Chris showed bags of enthusiasm and a good touch but failed to hit the net in his 13 outings, eight of them as a substitute. He was sidelined by a hamstring strain for a time and it was a big step up into League One. Chris needs the boost of seeing the net bulge.
Chester C *(From trainee at Crewe Alex on 5/7/2006) FL 21+26/4 FLC 0+2 FAC 0+1 Others 0+2/1 (Freed during 2008 close season)*
Brighton & Hove A *(Signed from Cambridge U on 30/1/2010) FL 5+8*

HOLT Andrew (Andy)
Born: Stockport, 21 May 1978
Height: 6'1" **Weight:** 12.7
Club Honours: AMC '05
Wide man Andy is one of the best headers of the ball at Northampton and a skilful player, but sadly so much of his season was lost through injury. Since February Sixfield supporters have not seen their long-throw expert causing havoc in the opposition penalty area, but he returned for the final few games of the season as a central defender. Was out of contract in the summer.
Oldham Ath *(From trainee on 23/7/1996) FL 104+20/10 FLC 8 FAC 6+4 Others 3*
Hull C *(£150,000 on 15/3/2001) FL 45+26/3 FLC 1 FAC 1 Others 5+1*
Barnsley *(Loaned on 15/8/2002) FL 4+3 FLC 1*

Shrewsbury T (Loaned on 27/3/2003) FL 9
Wrexham (Free on 3/8/2004) FL 80+1/9 FLC 3 FAC 2/1 Others 7
Northampton T (Free on 11/7/2006) FL 121+22/9 FLC 5+1 FAC 10+1 Others 4

HOLT Grant
Born: Carlisle, 12 April 1981
Height: 6'1" **Weight:** 12.7
Club Honours: Div 1 '10
Signed from Shrewsbury, this energetic and ever-willing striker became the first Norwich player to score 30 goals in a season since Ron Davies in 1964 and only the fact that he missed six games through suspension denied him the chance to break all kinds of Norwich scoring records. Strong in the air, he leads the line superbly with an enormous appetite for hard work – always being willing to close down the opposition and to try to win the ball back in deeper positions. His partnership with Chris Martin and Wes Hoolahan became an almost unstoppable force as all three had their best-ever scoring seasons. Grant's contribution, as player and captain, to Norwich's successful season was immense and all City fans will be hoping he can continue his scoring form into next season. Voted as the club's 'Player of the Season', he missed the last two games of the season to bring forward an ankle operation planned for the summer.
Halifax T (Signed from Workington on 16/9/1999) FL 0+6 FLC 1/1 Others 1 (Free to Barrow during 2001 close season)
Sheffield Wed (Free from Barrow on 27/3/2003) FL 12+12/3 FLC 0+1 FAC 2/1 Others 1+2
Rochdale (Signed on 30/1/2004) FL 75/35 FLC 2/1 FAC 4/5 Others 2/2
Nottingham F (£300,000 on 12/11/2006) FL 74+22/21 FLC 1+2 FAC 5+1/1 Others 3+1/3
Blackpool (Loaned on 20/3/2008) FL 0+4
Shrewsbury T (£170,000 on 14/7/2008) FL 43/20 FLC 1 FAC 1/1 Others 6/7
Norwich C (Signed on 4/8/2009) FL 39/24 FLC 2/3 FAC 2/3 Others 1

HONE Daniel Joseph
Born: Croydon, 15 September 1989
Height: 6'2" **Weight:** 12.0
Despite being a regular during Chris Sutton's early days in charge at Lincoln, centre-back Danny was restricted to just 17 starts in 2009-10 after he found himself edged down the pecking order. Injuries elsewhere in the squad, however, saw the former trainee finish

the season in the starting line-up, putting in some impressive performances.
Lincoln C (From trainee on 6/12/2007) FL 53+6/3 FAC 4 Others 2

HOOLAHAN Wesley (Wes)
Born: Dublin, 10 August 1983
Height: 5'6" **Weight:** 10.3
Club Honours: Div 1 '10
International Honours: RoI: 1; U21-12
This impish Republic of Ireland international continued to defy attempts to buttonhole him as a winger or as an attacking midfielder and operated successfully in a role for Norwich just behind a traditional front two. His skill on the ball and ability to pick a pass created a hatful of goals for his colleagues and for himself as he reached 14 for the season. Once in possession, he can twist and turn away from defenders when it almost looks impossible to do so and he became the player opposition defences singled out to stop playing – if they could. Much admired by his peers, he narrowly lost out in the Football League's 'League One Player of the Year' poll.
Livingston (Signed from Shelbourne on 1/1/2006) SL 14+2 SLC 1 SC 0+2
Blackpool (Signed on 24/7/2006) FL 80+7/13 FLC 2+3/1 FAC 3+1/1 Others 3/1
Norwich C (£250,000 on 18/7/2008) FL 63+6/13 FLC 3/2 FAC 2+2/1 Others 1

HOOMAN Harry James
Born: Worcester, 27 April 1991
Height: 5'11" **Weight:** 12.4
A first-year professional at Shrewsbury, the full-back or central defender had his first taste of League football as substitute in the 3-0 home win against Northampton in September. Harry looked comfortable, making a couple of important tackles to prevent scoring opportunities. He had his full debut in October at Darlington in central defence and made a positive start to his professional career in his four appearances.
Shrewsbury T (From trainee on 9/7/2009) FL 1+1 FAC 1 Others 1

HOOPER Gary
Born: Loughton, 26 January 1988
Height: 5'9" **Weight:** 11.2
Club Honours: FAT '05
After bagging 30 goals in his first season with Scunthorpe, ace marksman Gary showed that he was capable of the step up to the Championship, finishing as the division's third top scorer. His final total of 20 goals included 19 in the League, a particularly impressive record as he started only 31

games because of niggling injuries. A quick forward, he plays off the shoulder of the last defender and with strike partner Paul Hayes providing fantastic service, had plenty of chances in a struggling side. Bagged a hat-trick in the 3-0 home win over Bristol City in mid-April and six goals in his final four games.
Southend U (Free from Grays Ath on 10/8/2006) FL 12+20/2 FLC 3+4/2 FAC 2+2 Others 0+1
Leyton Orient (Loaned on 15/3/2007) FL 2+2/2
Hereford U (Loaned on 28/1/2008) FL 19/11
Scunthorpe U (£125,000 on 16/7/2008) FL 76+4/43 FLC 2+2/1 FAC 4/4 Others 6+1/2

HOPKINSON Bobby Thomas
Born: Plymouth, 3 July 1990
Height: 5'8" **Weight:** 13.8
Bobby is a versatile young midfielder, who can play centrally or on the right, and signed as a non-contract player after a trial with Aldershot. He made his debut as a substitute in the Johnstone's Paint Trophy tie at Hereford and his League baptism came four days later, again as a substitute, against Morecambe, his last appearance for the Shots. Bobby was dual registered with Southern League Premier Division side Farnborough before he was released in March and joined Blue Square South side Havant and Waterlooville.
Aldershot T (Free from Tiverton T, ex trainee at Plymouth Arg, on 24/8/2009) FL 0+1 Others 0+1

HORNE Louis Peter
Born: Bradford, 28 May 1991
Height: 6'2" **Weight:** 12.5
The young left-back made his Bradford debut from the bench against Cheltenham. It was a testing start for the son of the club's youth development officer because City were down to ten men. But operating in a three-man defence Louis used the ball well and played with good composure.
Bradford C (From trainee on 3/9/2009) FL 0+1

HORSFIELD Geoffrey (Geoff) Malcolm
Born: Barnsley, 1 November 1973
Height: 5'10" **Weight:** 11.0
Club Honours: FC '98; Div 2 '99
The experienced striker is also the assistant manager at Port Vale. Unfortunately, injury hampered the playing side and he started only one game, on the opening day against Rochdale. A combination of age catching up with him and a succession

of leg injuries meant he could develop the coaching side. He made a further 11 appearances as a substitute and was always willing to grit his teeth and play through the pain barrier. At the end of the season he retired as a player.
Scarborough *(From juniors on 10/7/1992) FL 12/1 FAC 1 Others 0+2 (Free to Halifax T on 31/3/1994)*
Halifax T *(Free from Guiseley, ex Witton A, on 8/5/1997) FL 10/7 FLC 4/1*
Fulham *(£325,000 on 12/10/1998) FL 54+5/22 FLC 6/6 FAC 8+1/3*
Birmingham C *(£2,000,000 + on 12/7/2000) P/FL 75+33/23 FLC 10+1/3 FAC 1+1 Others 5/2*
Wigan Ath *(Signed on 6/9/2003) FL 16/7 FLC 1*
West Bromwich A *(£1,000,000 on 18/12/2003) P/FL 48+19/14 FLC 2/1 FAC 2+2*
Sheffield U *(Loaned on 13/2/2006) FL 1+2*
Sheffield U *(Signed on 3/7/2006) FLC 0+2/1 (Freed duirng 2008 close season)*
Leeds U *(Loaned on 4/8/2006) FL 11+3/2 FLC 1*
Leicester C *(Loaned on 31/1/2007) FL 9+4/2*
Scunthorpe U *(Loaned on 31/1/2008) FL 11+1*
Lincoln C *(From retirement on 2/1/2009) FL 14+3/1*
Port Vale *(Free on 21/7/2009) FL 1+8 FLC 0+2 FAC 0+1*

HORWOOD Evan David
Born: Billingham, 10 March 1986
Height: 6'0" **Weight:** 11.2
Having been missing from the side for much of the previous term, Evan forced his way back into contention and was Carlisle's regular left-back for most of the campaign. A defender who often looks at his best when going forward, he performed well but perhaps, surprisingly, was not retained at the end of the season.
Sheffield U *(From trainee on 12/11/2004) FLC 0+1*
Stockport Co *(Loaned on 11/3/2005) FL 10*
Chester C *(Loaned on 31/1/2006) FL 1*
Darlington *(Loaned on 13/10/2006) FL 2*
Darlington *(Loaned on 1/1/2007) FL 18 Others 1*
Gretna *(Loaned on 31/8/2007) SL 15/1 SC 1/1*
Carlisle U *(Signed on 17/1/2008) FL 72+3 FLC 2 FAC 6 Others 9+1*

HOSKINS William (Will) Richard
Born: Nottingham, 6 May 1986
Height: 5'11" **Weight:** 11.2
International Honours: E: Yth

An intelligent and mobile Watford striker, at his best playing off a big centre-forward, Will made a slow start after struggling with a back injury in pre-season. He made the majority of his 19 appearances as a substitute and his return of three goals was reasonable in the circumstances. It was disappointing that he remained a bit-part player despite showing greater maturity and an improved work rate. Was out of contract in the summer.
Rotherham U *(From trainee on 16/2/2005) FL 35+38/23 FLC 2+1/1 FAC 1+2 Others 1+1/1*
Watford *(Signed on 5/1/2007) P/FL 25+35/7 FLC 6+2/1 FAC 2/1*
Millwall *(Loaned on 18/9/2007) FL 9+1/2 FAC 2/2*
Nottingham F *(Loaned on 8/2/2008) FL 2*

HOULT Russell
Born: Ashby-de-la-Zouch, 22 November 1972
Height: 6'3" **Weight:** 14.9
A vastly experienced Notts County 'keeper who began the season with two clean sheets in the first two League games and then lost his place to the newly arrived Kasper Schmeichel, Russell was then loaned to Darlington. Brought in to bolster the rearguard of a team that had gleaned only one point from the opening seven League games, he alone could not turn the tide and although he featured in one win and a draw he returned to Meadow Lane after six games. Was out of contract at the end of June.
Leicester C *(From trainee on 28/3/1991) FL 10 FLC 3 Others 1*
Lincoln C *(Loaned on 27/8/1991) FL 2 FLC 1*
Bolton W *(Loaned on 3/11/1993) FL 3+1 Others 1*
Lincoln C *(Loaned on 12/8/1994) FL 15 Others 1*
Derby Co *(£300,000 on 17/2/1995) P/FL 121+2 FLC 8 FAC 7*
Portsmouth *(£300,000 + on 21/1/2000) FL 40 FLC 4*
West Bromwich A *(£500,000 on 5/1/2001) P/FL 189+1 FLC 10 FAC 11 Others 2*
Nottingham F *(Loaned on 16/9/2005) FL 8*
Stoke C *(Free on 31/1/2007) FL 1 FLC 1*
Notts Co *(Loaned on 22/2/2008) FL 14*
Notts Co *(Free on 24/7/2008) FL 19+1 FLC 2 FAC 4 Others 1*
Darlington *(Loaned on 16/9/2009) FL 6*

HOWARD Brian Richard William Brotherton
Born: Winchester, 23 January 1983
Height: 5'8" **Weight:** 11.1
International Honours: E: Yth

Brian's previous season's move to Sheffield United had not worked out and although he played in the Blades' first few games he moved to Reading at the end of the August transfer window. He slotted immediately into a central midfield position, replacing James Harper, who had moved in the opposite direction. Having arrived with the reputation of being a tough, hard-working and competitive player with an eye for goal he quickly set about adding to that well-earned testimonial. He was always one of the first names on the team-sheet, apart from a spell in December when he missed four games after breaking his jaw in the 2-1 defeat at Derby. Such was Brian's resilience that he was back in the side much earlier than expected, continuing to win bruising tackles in midfield, play penetrating through balls for the strikers, and weighing in with the occasional goal.
Southampton *(From trainee on 27/1/2000)*
Swindon T *(Free on 6/8/2003) FL 49+21/9 FLC 3+1 FAC 4/1 Others 4+1*
Barnsley *(Free on 6/7/2005) FL 115+6/27 FLC 2 FAC 10/1 Others 4*
Sheffield U *(£750,000 on 3/10/2008) FL 25+5/2 FLC 1 FAC 1+2 Others 3/1*
Reading *(Signed on 1/9/2009) FL 30+4/2 FAC 3+2/1*

HOWARD Steven (Steve) John
Born: Durham, 10 May 1976
Height: 6'2" **Weight:** 14.6
Club Honours: Div 1 '05, '09
International Honours: S: B-1
The powerful striker enjoyed his best form of the season in the closing weeks, as he rediscovered his goal touch for Leicester. A moment of madness earned Steve a red card against Watford that kept him out of the first leg of the play-off semi-final against Cardiff. Just what a handicap that was to the Foxes was evident from his second leg display, where he proved to be a nightmare for the Welsh defenders.
Hartlepool U *(Free from Tow Law on 8/8/1995) FL 117+25/26 FLC 7+1/1 FAC 5/2 Others 7/3*
Northampton T *(£120,000 on 22/2/1999) FL 67+19/18 FLC 4 FAC 2+1 Others 2*
Luton T *(£50,000 on 22/3/2001) FL 209+3/95 FLC 7/2 FAC 8/5 Others 1*
Derby Co *(£1,000,000 on 27/7/2006) P/FL 57+6/17 FLC 2+1/1 FAC 3 Others 3/2*
Leicester C *(£1,500,000 on 1/1/2008) FL 77+21/24 FLC 3/1 FAC 6 Others 4/1*

HOWARD Timothy (Tim) Matthew

Born: North Brunswick, New Jersey, USA, 6 March 1979
Height: 6'3" **Weight:** 14.12
Club Honours: CS '03; FAC '04; FLC '06
International Honours: USA: 50; U21
The United States international, now firmly established as Everton's first choice goalkeeper, enjoyed another splendid and consistent campaign, despite playing behind a defence unsettled by several injuries. The popular number one became the first Everton player to start every match in two successive Premier League campaigns on the back of a series of impressive displays both home and away. Highlights of the season included equalling a club record by saving three penalties of the four he faced, one of which, in the last minute against Tottenham in early December, acted as a launch-pad for a run of two defeats in the final 24 League games. As an added bonus Tim captained the side for the first time at Chelsea. A vocal and agile

presence at the back, the American has proved himself in particular to be a fine organiser of the defence.
Manchester U (£2,300,000 from New York/New Jersey Metrostars, USA, ex North Jersey Imperials, on 22/7/2003) PL 44+1 FLC 8 FAC 10 Others 14
Everton (Signed on 5/7/2006) PL 148 FLC 7 FAC 10 Others 19

HOWE Jermaine **Renee (Rene)**

Born: Bedford, 22 October 1986
Height: 6'0" **Weight:** 14.3
With goals hard to come by during the course of the season, Rene's five-goal haul from his 21 appearances whilst on loan from Peterborough, saw him finish the campaign second on the Lincoln goalscoring chart. Despite this relatively prolific spell, his loan spell was cut short by a month due to a recurring hamstring injury. In January, the strong, powerful forward was signed on loan by Gillingham to combat their lack of firepower. He may not have scored many goals, only two in 18 appearances, but created many more

with his strong hold-up play and unselfish team work. His opener in the 2-1 home triumph over Southampton was a particularly special moment for Gills' supporters.
Peterborough U (Signed from Kettering T, ex Bedford T, on 19/7/2007) FL 2+13/1 FAC 0+2 Others 1
Rochdale (Loaned on 8/1/2008) FL 19+1/9 Others 2+1
Morecambe (Loaned on 23/7/2008) FL 35+2/10 FLC 1 FAC 1/1 Others 2/1
Lincoln C (Loaned on 3/8/2009) FL 14+3/5 FLC 1 FAC 1+1 Others 1
Gillingham (Loaned on 20/1/2010) FL 18/2

HOWELL Dean George

Born: Burton-on-Trent, 29 November 1980
Height: 6'1" **Weight:** 12.5
A tall left-back, who can also play as a wing-back or on the left of midfield, he missed 28 games from the start of Aldershot's season while recovering from a hip injury. Dean made his first appearance of the season as a substitute in the February defeat at Barnet and scored his first League goal, again as a substitute, in the home victory over Rotherham. Was released at the end of the season.
Notts Co (From trainee on 1/7/1999) FL 0+1
Crewe Alex (Free on 26/7/2000) FL 0+1 (Freed during 2001 close season)
Rochdale (Loaned on 1/3/2001) FL 2+1
Colchester U (Free from Halifax T, ex Southport, Morecambe, on 5/8/2005) FL 1+3 FLC 0+1 (Freed during 2006 close season)
Aldershot T (Free from Rushden & Diamonds, ex Weymouth, Grays Ath, on 11/5/2008) FL 14+3/1 FLC 1
Bury (Loaned on 27/11/2008) FL 0+3

HOWELL Luke Alexander

Born: Heathfield, 5 January 1987
Height: 5'10" **Weight:** 10.5
Club Honours: AMC '08
Luke made more League appearances for MK Dons in his third season than in the previous two put together and without doubt his proven versatility was a key factor in that. Equally at home in the right-back berth or one of the hard-working midfield slots, he never let the team down when called upon, which was often due to the continuing injury problems the Dons suffered throughout the campaign. All told, he continued to be a very valuable member of the first team squad.
Gillingham (From trainee on 25/7/2006) FL 0+1 Others 1
MK Dons (Free on 11/8/2007) FL 34+18/1 FLC 3 FAC 1+1 Others 7

Tim Howard

HOWLAND David
Born: Ballynahinch, 17 September 1986
Height: 5'11" **Weight:** 11.8
International Honours: NI; U21-4
It was a frustrating season for Port
Vale's central midfield player, who was
never able to get into the first team to
show new manager Micky Adams what
he could do because of the form of
Tommy Fraser and Anthony Griffith. He
managed only five appearances, all as a
substitute, and was released on a free
transfer.
Birmingham C (From trainee on
19/11/2004)
Port Vale (Loaned on 23/1/2008) FL
17/1
Port Vale (Free on 4/8/2008) FL 35+9/2
FAC 1+1/1 Others 1+1

HOWSON Jonathan (Jonny)
Mark
Born: Morley, 21 May 1988
Height: 5'11" **Weight:** 12.1
Locally-born midfielder Jonny was
named vice-captain in August and led
the Whites from the start because of
injury to skipper Richard Naylor. The 21-
year-old rose to the occasion, leading
Leeds to eight straight victories. He
operated mainly in central midfield,
although also being deployed on the
right in several games. While physically
stronger than in previous years, his four
League goals were not as many as he
hoped but included the crucial equaliser
as ten-man Leeds clinched promotion
on the final day against Bristol Rovers.
After that game the club extended his
contract to 2012. His long-range strike
in the 2-0 FA Cup win at Oldham was
one of United's goals of the season in
the first game streamed live by the FA's
own website.
Leeds U (From trainee on 10/7/2006) FL
92+28/12 FLC 7+3 FAC 11+1/1 Others
11/3

HOYTE Gavin Andrew
Born: Leytonstone, 6 June 1990
Height: 5'11" **Weight:** 11.0
International Honours: E: Yth
Signed on a month's loan from Arsenal
in October, Gavin ended up staying
with Brighton for the remainder of the
season. Impressing with his speed and
tackling, the teenage full-back was sent
off at Wycombe in his sixth game, a
setback that appeared to knock his
confidence. New manager Gus Poyet
was prompted to bring in Inigo
Calderon at right-back and Gavin was
relegated to the bench. In April he
returned at left-back after a bad injury
to Calderon gave Gavin his chance
again and he finished the season with a
series of very decent performances.

Arsenal (From trainee on 14/9/2007) PL
1 FLC 3
Watford (Loaned on 1/1/2009) FL 6+1
FAC 3
Brighton & Hove A (Loaned on
9/10/2009) FL 16+2 FAC 3

HOYTE Justin Raymond
Born: Leytonstone, 20 November 1984
Height: 5'11" **Weight:** 10.10
Club Honours: CS '04
International Honours: E: U21-18;
Yth
Justin had to be content with a place on
the Middlesbrough bench at the start of
the season as Tony McMahon was
preferred at right-back. Under new
manager Gordon Strachan, Justin
appeared at left-back and in February
was even used as a makeshift central
midfielder at Ipswich, but with limited
success. Following an injury to
McMahon in February, that ruled him
out for the remainder of the term,
Justin saw a way back but the loan
signing from Tottenham of Kyle
Naughton brought even more
competition at right-back. For the final
few games, with Boro pushing for a
play-off spot, Naughton was moved to
the left to allow Justin to play his
natural attacking game down the right.
Justin managed his first goal for Boro in
a 2-1 defeat at Barnsley, with a cross-
cum-shot.
Arsenal (From trainee on 1/7/2002) PL
24+10/1 FLC 14 FAC 4+4 Others 8+4
Sunderland (Loaned on 31/8/2005) PL
27/1 FLC 1 FAC 2
Middlesbrough (£3,000,000 on
21/8/2008) P/FL 40+12/1 FLC 3 FAC 4+1

HREIDARSSON Hermann
Born: Reykjavik, Iceland, 11 July 1974
Height: 6'1" **Weight:** 13.1
Club Honours: Div 3 '99; FAC '08
International Honours: Iceland: 85;
U21-6
Portsmouth's charismatic full-back
continues to prove with each passing
year that he retains the passion, spirit
and commitment that have been
present throughout his long career. The
veteran Icelander excelled for Pompey
at both left-back and centre-half after
missing the first 15 games of the
campaign. He scored a vital goal in a 2-
0 home victory against fellow strugglers
Burnley before having his season
unluckily cut short against Tottenham in
March when he ruptured an Achilles
tendon. A true living legend on the
south coast, his playful and mischievous
antics have made him a popular figure
with all involved at the club and fans
will be hoping he signs a new contract
to keep him at Fratton Park.

Crystal Palace (Signed from IBV,
Iceland on 9/8/1997) P/FL 32+5/2 FLC
5/1 FAC 4 Others 2
Brentford (£850,000 on 24/9/1998) FL
41/6 FLC 2 FAC 2/1 Others 3/1
Wimbledon (£2,500,000 on
14/10/1999) P/FL 25/1 FAC 2
Ipswich T (£4,000,000 + on
19/8/2000) P/FL 101+1/2 FLC 11 FAC 6
Others 9/1
Charlton Ath (£500,000 + on
27/3/2003) PL 130+2/3 FLC 8/1 FAC 9
Portsmouth (Free on 1/6/2007) PL
66+6/6 FLC 2+1 FAC 11+2 Others
3+1/1

HUDDLESTONE Thomas
(Tom) Andrew
Born: Nottingham, 28 December 1986
Height: 6'3" **Weight:** 14.12
Club Honours: FLC '08
International Honours: E: 3; U21-33;
Yth
Tom emerged as a real force for
Tottenham, making more starts than
any other outfield player. He was
rewarded with international
recognition, making his England debut
as a substitute against Brazil in
November and being in the preliminary
30 for the World Cup finals, although
not in the chosen 23. While he can and
occasionally does play at centre-back,
his best position is in the centre of
midfield, where he is renowned for his
pinpoint long passes, often spreading
the play to the flanks but also offering a
telling ball through the middle. He
scored four goals in all competitions,
including two pile-drivers in League
games against Sunderland and Bolton.
The goal against Bolton was enough for
a crucial win as Spurs sought that vital
fourth place.
Derby Co (From trainee on 27/2/2004)
FL 84+4 FLC 2 FAC 3 Others 2
Tottenham H (£1,000,000 on
1/7/2005) P/FL 80+28/6 FLC 10+5/5 FAC
9+3 Others 16+5/2
Wolverhampton W (Loaned on
25/10/2005) FL 12+1/1

HUDSON Kirk
Born: Southend-on-Sea, 12 December
1986
Height: 6'0" **Weight:** 11.2
Club Honours: FC '08
International Honours: E: Sch
Kirk is a quick player, who is most
effective on the right of midfield. He
played his 150th game for Aldershot in
September and scored his first goal of
the season with a sublime turn and
angled shot at Crewe a week later. A
dip in form saw Kirk dropped in March
and he did not start again until the final
game of the regular season at

Tom Huddlestone

Morecambe, prior to coming off the bench in the second leg of the Shots' play-off semi-final defeat by Rotherham. Kirk finished the season with 45 goals for the club, which puts him eighth in the club's all time scorers list, while his 180 games places him tenth in the list of appearances.
Glasgow Celtic (From Ipswich T juniors on 9/7/2003)
Bournemouth (Free on 5/8/2005) FL 0+1 FLC 0+1
Aldershot T (Free on 20/1/2006) FL 59+18/15 FLC 2 FAC 4/2 Others 1+2/1

HUDSON Mark
Born: Bishop Auckland, 24 October 1980
Height: 5'10" **Weight:** 11.3
Released by Rotherham in the summer, Mark signed for Blackpool on a non-contract basis but after playing one game for the club – in the Carling Cup against Crewe – manager Ian Holloway decided not to take a punt on him. Following a brief spell in non-League football with Gainsborough Trinity, he signed for Grimsby to the season's end. His mobility was to earn him a regular start from February onwards, the midfielder linking well with both the defence and attack. Mark's first goal for the Mariners helped secure a vital away win at Accrington (3-2), coinciding with selection for the League Two 'Team of the Week' on the FL website.
Middlesbrough (From trainee on 5/7/1999) PL 0+5 FAC 0+1
Chesterfield (Loaned on 13/8/2002) FL 15+1/1 FLC 1 FAC 0+1 Others 0+1
Carlisle U (Loaned on 10/12/2002) FL 14+1/1
Chesterfield (Free on 21/3/2003) FL 72+5/8 FLC 1 FAC 1 Others 3
Huddersfield T (Free on 7/7/2005) FL 55+6/6 FLC 1+1 FAC 4 Others 2
Rotherham U (Free on 9/7/2007) FL 65+8/14 FLC 2 FAC 3 Others 3+2/1
Blackpool (Free on 10/8/2009) FLC 1 (Freed on 31/8/2009)
Grimsby T (Free from Gainsborough Trinity on 26/11/2009) FL 11+5/2

HUDSON Mark Alexander
Born: Guildford, 30 March 1982
Height: 6'3" **Weight:** 12.6
Relegated with Charlton in the previous season, Mark went desperately close to promotion with Cardiff. Made club captain, he signed for Cardiff after Darren Purse moved to Sheffield Wednesday in the summer and Roger Johnson joined Birmingham. One of three central defenders at City to start the season, along with Gabor Gyepes and Anthony Gerrard, an ankle operation kept him out for three months before he returned for the play-offs. Mark came in for a fair bit of criticism from Cardiff fans but he is strong in the air, did a good job organising those around him and is comfortable in possession. He was outstanding in the play-off semi-final first leg at Leicester, when Cardiff won 1-0, but could not match that level of performance in the second leg or the final against Blackpool.
Fulham (From trainee on 6/4/1999) FLC 2+1
Oldham Ath (Loaned on 25/8/2003) FL 15 Others 1

Crystal Palace (£550,000 on 16/1/2004) P/FL 112+8/7 FLC 8 FAC 6 Others 2
Charlton Ath (Free on 1/7/2008) FL 43/3 FAC 2
Cardiff C (£1,000,000 on 2/7/2009) FL 26+1/2 FLC 1 FAC 2 Others 3

HUGHES Aaron William

Born: Cookstown, 8 November 1979
Height: 6'0" **Weight:** 11.2
International Honours: NI: 76; B-2; Yth

One of the most underrated central defenders in the Premier League, Aaron again set a high standard through the season, forming a formidable central defensive partnership at Fulham with Brede Hangeland. He was also briefly deployed at right-back for two games in January but did not look as comfortable in this role. An excellent reader of play, he is often the last man, timing his tackles and headers to perfection, thus ensuring the ball is put clear of danger. An effective distributor, he is often the starting point for an attacking move. Aaron remained a first choice, missing just a handful of games when the squad was rotated. Captain of Northern Ireland, he led the side throughout their unsuccessful World Cup qualifying campaign. Aaron partners team-mate Chris Baird in central defence when on international duty.

Newcastle U (From trainee on 11/3/1997) PL 193+12/4 FLC 9+1 FAC 15+4/1 Others 39+5/1
Aston Villa (£1,500,000 on 6/8/2005) PL 50+4 FLC 5 FAC 5
Fulham (£1,000,000 on 5/7/2007) PL 101+1 FLC 2 FAC 11 Others 16+1

HUGHES Andrew (Andy) John

Born: Manchester, 2 January 1978
Height: 5'11" **Weight:** 12.1
Club Honours: Div 3 '98

Versatile Andy, who has played most of his career in midfield, found himself mainly at left-back for Leeds after an opening day injury to Ben Parker. He also played several games at right-back to cover for Jason Crowe. His adaptability and commitment ensured his promotion and he made his 100th start in a 3-1 win at Carlisle in April. Was out of contract in the summer.
Oldham Ath (From trainee on 20/1/1996) FL 18+15/1 FLC 1+1 FAC 3+1 Others 1+2
Notts Co (£150,000 on 29/1/1998) FL 85+45/17 FLC 6+1/1 FAC 10/2 Others 2
Reading (Free on 16/7/2001) FL 157+9/18 FLC 7/1 FAC 6+1 Others 3
Norwich C (£500,000 on 21/7/2005) FL 63+9/2 FLC 4 FAC 2+1

Leeds U (Signed on 10/8/2007) FL 88+18/1 FLC 5 FAC 8 Others 5+2

HUGHES Bryan

Born: Liverpool, 19 June 1976
Height: 5'9" **Weight:** 11.2
Club Honours: WC '95

When Derby's midfield was depleted by injuries, they signed Bryan on loan for a month from Hull, where he had dropped out of the picture. He has ample experience and, although clearly short of match action, was one of the better passers in the team. Bryan played three times and was released on his return to Hull. He trained with Sheffield United and played against Derby for their reserves.
Wrexham (From trainee on 7/7/1994) FL 71+23/12 FLC 2 FAC 13+3/7 Others 6+1/1
Birmingham C (£750,000 + on 12/3/1997) P/FL 197+51/34 FLC 17+5/3 FAC 8+5/4 Others 6+2/1
Charlton Ath (Free on 2/7/2004) PL 47+27/5 FLC 5+2 FAC 8/5
Hull C (Free on 30/6/2007) P/FL 27+14/1 FLC 2 FAC 0+1 Others 3
Derby Co (Loaned on 22/10/2009) FL 3

HUGHES Jeffrey (Jeff) Edward

Born: Larne, 29 May 1985
Height: 6'1" **Weight:** 11.0
International Honours: NI: 2; U21-7

The former Lincoln and Crystal Palace winger Jeff made a significant contribution to Bristol Rovers with some superb performances, including important and match-winning goals. Many of his early goals were from the penalty spot and Rovers fans finally seemed to acknowledge his value in the side. Jeff's confidence grew and his ability to play on the left of midfield or full-back was a real bonus. He even filled in at right-back following injury during the home match with Tranmere and did extremely well. His deft finish at home to Swindon, scoring from inside the six-yard box, was a superb piece of skill. He was sent off at Carlisle on Good Friday after conceding a penalty.
Lincoln C (Free from Larne on 24/8/2005) FL 55+8/8 FLC 1 Others 4/3
Crystal Palace (£250,000 on 5/7/2007) FL 4+6
Peterborough U (Loaned on 22/11/2007) FL 2+5/1 FAC 1+1
Bristol Rov (Free on 6/6/2008) FL 87/18 FLC 3 FAC 2/1 Others 2

HUGHES Lee

Born: Smethwick, 22 May 1976
Height: 5'10" **Weight:** 11.6
Club Honours: Div 2 '10

International Honours: E: SP-4

Having been released by Oldham during the summer, Lee became the first striker to score more than 30 goals in a season for Notts County since the legendary Tommy Lawton. He scored from everywhere and created a number for his colleagues. Enjoys hero worship of the Kop where they dance 'The Hughesy' on a regular basis. He has the ability and opportunity to become a legend in his own right at Meadow Lane. Three hat-tricks in the season helped him on his way. He picked up the 'Manager's Player of the Year', 'Players' Player of the Year' and a place in the PFA League Two 'Team of the Year'.
West Bromwich A (£250,000 + from Kidderminster Hrs on 19/5/1997) FL 137+19/78 FLC 10+3/4 FAC 6/2 Others 2/1
Coventry C (£5,000,000 on 9/8/2001) FL 38+4/15 FLC 1+1
West Bromwich A (£2,500,000 on 30/8/2002) P/FL 35+20/11 FLC 2+3/2 (Freed during 2004 close season)
Oldham Ath (Free, following motoring convictions, on 28/8/2007) FL 51+4/25 FLC 1+1 FAC 3/1 Others 1
Blackpool (Loaned on 26/3/2009) FL 2+1/1
Notts Co (Free on 22/7/2009) FL 39/30 FLC 0+1 FAC 5/3

HUGHES Mark Anthony

Born: Dungannon, 16 September 1983
Height: 5'10" **Weight:** 12.4
International Honours: NI: 2; U23-1; U21-12; Yth

Battling midfielder Mark had a solid first full season with Barnet. Very popular with the Underhill faithful for his no-nonsense approach to the game, he was key to Barnet's eventually successful bid to avoid the drop. Near ever-present, Mark scored two goals and also captained the team on a number of occasions. Previously capped by Northern Ireland, if he can continue his form in the new season he may catch his national side's eye again.
Tottenham H (From trainee on 12/7/2001)
Northampton T (Loaned on 27/8/2004) FL 3
Oldham Ath (Free on 19/11/2004) FL 55+5/1 FLC 1 FAC 7 Others 2+3 (Free to Thurrock on 3/11/2006)
Chesterfield (Free from Thurrock on 3/11/2006) FL 2/1 FAC 1 (Free to Stevenage Borough on 11/9/2007)
Chester C (Free on 10/8/2007) FL 64+5/4 FLC 1 FAC 2 Others 3
Barnet (Free on 2/2/2009) FL 48+2/2 FLC 1 FAC 2 Others 2

HUGHES Mark Anthony
Born: Kirkby, 9 December 1986
Height: 6'2" **Weight:** 13.0
Mark became Walsall's first signing of the season and was made club captain. Good organisational ability and reading of the game make up for his slight lack of pace and stamina. Most of his appearances were in the first half of the season before picking up an injury at home to Brighton. When he recovered from this, he was strangely left on the bench at a time when the club had to play left-back Jamie Vincent at centre-half. His one goal was in the 3-2 fight-back at Wycombe, an accurate right- foot shot into the top corner from close range.
Everton (From trainee on 21/12/2004) PL 0+1 FLC 1+1
Stockport Co (Loaned on 13/2/2006) FL 3/1
Northampton T (Signed on 31/1/2007) FL 92+1/4 FLC 5 FAC 6 Others 2
Walsall (Signed on 8/7/2009) FL 24+2/1 FAC 2

HUGHES Richard Daniel
Born: Glasgow, 25 June 1979
Height: 5'9" **Weight:** 9.12
International Honours: S: 5; U21-9; Yth
Portsmouth's perennial utility man and longest-serving player, Richard continues to perform reliably in his defensive midfield position. Although he may find appearances few and far between, he never lets anyone down with his committed and spirited performances, epitomised by his passionate energy, tough tackling and accurate passing.
Arsenal (Free from Atalanta, Italy on 11/8/1997)
Bournemouth (£20,000 on 5/8/1998) FL 123+8/14 FLC 9+1 FAC 8/2 Others 5
Portsmouth (£100,000 on 13/6/2002) P/FL 91+29 FLC 9+3/1 FAC 9+6/1 Others 4
Grimsby T (Loaned on 21/2/2003) FL 12/1

HUGHES Stephen David
Born: Motherwell, 14 November 1982
Height: 5'11" **Weight:** 9.6
Club Honours: Div 1 '10
International Honours: S: 1; U21-12; Yth
Stephen arrived at Norwich in the summer as a Bosman free agent having left Motherwell. A stylish and creative midfielder, he has the variety and vision in his passing game to unlock the meanest of defences and is always looking forward. He earned his first full Scotland cap in an away friendly in

Japan and will hope for similar recognition under the new Scottish management. Was another Norwich player who found his senior opportunities limited in the latter part of the season as Paul Lambert's team attained excellent consistency levels.
Glasgow Rgrs (From juniors on 12/7/1999) SL 41+23/7 SLC 3+4 SC 4+3 Others 7+4
Leicester C (£100,000 + on 31/1/2005) FL 75+16/7 FLC 1+2 FAC 5+1/1
Motherwell (Free on 31/8/2007) SL 64+2/2 SLC 2 SC 5/1
Norwich C (Signed on 23/7/2009) FL 12+17/3 FLC 0+1 FAC 0+1 Others 2+1

HUGHES-MASON Kiernan Peter
Born: Hackney, 22 October 1991
Height: 5'9" **Weight:** 10.8
Kiernan made a solitary substitute appearance for Millwall at the end of August, playing in an attacking wide role. He graduated from the club's youth side that won their league and also reached the FA Youth Cup fifth round. In March he had a loan spell with Cheltenham but was unable to get a game. Was a prolific scorer for the youth team.
Millwall (From trainee on 25/8/2009) FL 0+1

HUGHTON Cian James
Born: Enfield, 25 January 1989
Height: 5'8" **Weight:** 10.5
International Honours: RoI: U21-5
Full-back Cian capped a fine first season of Football League action by not only making more appearances than any other outfield player at Lincoln but also by forcing his way into the Republic of Ireland under-21 side. Named 'Young Player of the Season' by the management team, his form saw him rewarded with a new contract.
Tottenham H (From trainee on 10/7/2007)
Lincoln C (Free on 27/7/2009) FL 41/4 FLC 1 FAC 3 Others 1

HULSE Robert (Rob) William
Born: Crewe, 25 October 1979
Height: 6'1" **Weight:** 11.4
Although he was again Derby's top scorer with 12 Championship goals, it was an unsettled season for Rob. His entry was delayed by a minor groin operation in the summer and he was also the subject of a £4-million bid from Middlesbrough. This dragged on until the final hours of the August transfer window before Rob decided that he was staying at Derby. He was always the likeliest Derby forward to score but had to work hard for his chances as the

service was seldom good enough. Rob was not always first choice and it seemed that the groin problem continued to affect him. He was in for a further operation before the final match. It was hoped that would give him time to recover before pre-season because Derby need a fit Rob.
Crewe Alex (From trainee on 25/6/1998) FL 97+19/46 FLC 6+1/2 FAC 5+1 Others 2/4
West Bromwich A (£750,000 + on 8/8/2003) P/FL 29+9/10 FLC 5+1/3 FAC 1+1
Leeds U (£800,000 + on 8/2/2005) FL 45+7/18 FLC 1+1 FAC 2/1 Others 3/1
Sheffield U (£2,200,000 + on 31/7/2006) P/FL 38+12/8 FAC 0+3
Derby Co (£1,750,000 on 23/7/2008) FL 72+9/27 FLC 5+1 FAC 6+1/3

HUME Iain Edward
Born: Edinburgh, 30 October 1983
Height: 5'7" **Weight:** 11.2
International Honours: Canada: 28; Yth
After being out of action with a fractured skull since November 2008, he made his comeback for Barnsley in late August. He found it a season of rehabilitation with both starts and goals hard to come by. This hard-working fans' favourite found himself playing in a number of positions. He played up front as one of a pair, or behind a target man or wide in midfield. His season's highlights included his two strikes against Peterborough and his winner against Blackpool soon after coming on as a substitute. He again played international football with Canada.
Tranmere Rov (From juniors on 6/11/2000) FL 100+50/32 FLC 4+4 FAC 8+2/3 Others 6+3/2
Leicester C (£500,000 on 31/8/2005) FL 101+21/33 FLC 6/1 FAC 4
Barnsley (£1,200,000 on 1/7/2008) FL 32+18/9 FLC 2+1

HUMPHREYS Richard (Ritchie) John
Born: Sheffield, 30 November 1977
Height: 5'11" **Weight:** 14.6
International Honours: E: U21-3; Yth
Hartlepool club captain and for many years a Victoria Park legend, Ritchie was unfortunate to pick up an Achilles injury in pre-season that meant that he missed the start. Significantly, this was the first time he had been unavailable for selection since joining the club in 2001. On recovering, Ritchie soon settled down in his old position as a central midfielder and, typically, was involved in all remaining first team matches. A player who always gives his best and who always seems to be in the thick of

the action, Ritchie signed an extension to his contract to play in 2010-11, which will be his tenth season at Hartlepool.
Sheffield Wed *(From trainee on 8/2/1996) P/FL 34+33/4 FLC 4+2 FAC 5+4/5*
Scunthorpe U *(Loaned on 13/8/1999) FL 6/2*
Cardiff C *(Loaned on 22/11/1999) FL 8+1/2 FAC 1 Others 1*
Cambridge U *(Free on 2/2/2001) FL 7/3*
Hartlepool U *(Free on 18/7/2001) FL 378+18/30 FLC 12 FAC 25/1 Others 16+2/1*
Port Vale *(Loaned on 8/9/2006) FL 5+2*

HUNT Benjamin (Ben) Robert
Born: Southwark, 23 January 1990
Height: 6'1" **Weight:** 11.0
Former West Ham youngster Ben failed to make any impression for Bristol Rovers, making two very brief substitute appearances in August. The powerfully-built and pacy striker suffered due to a lack of a reserve team at Rovers and Ben had a loan spell at Blue Square North Gloucester City, scoring four times in 12 appearances before joining Newport County on loan. Was out of contract at the end of June.
Bristol Rov *(From trainee at West Ham U on 23/7/2008) FL 0+14 FAC 0+1 Others 0+1*

HUNT David John
Born: Dulwich, 10 September 1982
Height: 5'11" **Weight:** 11.9
Club Honours: Div 2 '09
Brentford's midfield ball-winner, free-kick taker and long-throw expert started the season in the side, playing the first ten games before missing five with a foot injury. Thereafter he was mostly selected as a substitute until late in the season, when a run of injuries led to him featuring again. The highlight of his season was a free kick blasted through the Norwich wall to win the match in August.
Crystal Palace *(From trainee on 9/7/2002) FL 2 FLC 0+1*
Leyton Orient *(Signed on 11/7/2003) FL 57+8/1 FLC 2 FAC 3/1 Others 3+1*
Northampton T *(Free on 24/3/2005) FL 57+16/3 FLC 1 FAC 5+2 Others 2+1*
Shrewsbury T *(Free on 7/8/2007) FL 22+7/2 FLC 1+1 FAC 0+1 Others 1*
Brentford *(Free on 9/1/2009) FL 28+16/5 FLC 1 FAC 0+4 Others 1*

HUNT Lewis James
Born: Birmingham, 25 August 1982
Height: 5'11" **Weight:** 12.8
Club Honours: Div 1 '06
After playing the final games of the

previous season with a broken metatarsal in a foot, only revealed by a post-season scan, Wycombe defender Lewis did not recover fully until mid-September. He immediately resumed at right-back, giving his usual steady performances and pushing up when possible. He lost his place in January to Julian Kelly, on loan from Reading, but deputized extremely well in central defence for injured Adam Hinshelwood for the final five games. Many saw this as his future role at the club but, surprisingly, he was not offered a new contract.
Derby Co *(From trainee on 17/2/2001) FL 8+3 FLC 0+2*
Southend U *(Free on 28/10/2003) FL 126+20/2 FLC 7+2/1 FAC 14 Others 10+1*
Wycombe W *(Free on 5/8/2008) FL 46+1/1 FAC 3*

HUNT Nicholas (Nicky) Brett
Born: Westhoughton, 3 September 1983
Height: 6'1" **Weight:** 13.8
International Honours: E: U21-10
When Nigel Clough was concerned about Derby's right-back position, he signed Nicky on a month's loan from Bolton. This was soon extended until the end of the season. Nicky, delighted to be playing after a lean time at Bolton, settled quickly and looked like a Premiership defender, winning his tackles, using the ball and pressing ahead to deliver crosses. His form dipped at the end of March, perhaps as a result of his previous inactivity, but he recovered to finish the season strongly. He always showed a good professional attitude.
Bolton W *(From trainee on 7/7/2001) P/FL 113+15/1 FLC 11 FAC 9+3 Others 10*
Birmingham C *(Loaned on 3/11/2008) FL 9+2*
Derby Co *(Loaned on 7/1/2010) FL 20+1 FAC 2*

HUNT Noel
Born: Waterford, 26 December 1982
Height: 5'8" **Weight:** 11.5
International Honours: RoI: 3; B-1; U21-3
Noel was a Reading regular at the start of the season and looked as if he had recaptured his excellent form of the previous campaign. As a lively and determined striker, he caused problems for opposing defences, especially in the 3-1 win at Barnsley, their first Championship victory under Brendan Rodgers. Noel scored with a header and from a penalty in that game but was injured after an hour at West Bromwich in October and had to spend the rest of the season with the physiotherapy staff attempting to regain full fitness. He

made good use of his time, joining in many of the community events, and accompanying the youth team on their end of season tour in the United States.
Dunfermline Ath *(Signed from Shamrock Rov, via Waterford U - loan, on 27/1/2003) SL 42+38/8 SLC 2+3/1 SC 2+8/2 Others 1*
Dundee U *(£50,000 on 20/6/2006) SL 59+5/23 SLC 7/5 SC 3+1*
Reading *(£600,000 on 28/7/2008) FL 32+15/13 FLC 2+2/2*

HUNT Stephen James
Born: Southampton, 11 November 1984
Height: 6'1" **Weight:** 13.0
Club Honours: Div 2 '10
At last a season where he managed to maintain fitness and take a regular place in the Notts County side. A tall and talented left-sided defender, he has remarkable composure when he is in possession. Although his preference is to play in the centre of defence, his regular place was at left-back where he played with distinction in a successful defence.
Colchester U *(From trainee at Southampton on 19/7/2004) FL 16+6/1 FLC 2 FAC 1+1 Others 1*
Notts Co *(Free on 31/7/2006) FL 100+12/4 FLC 5 FAC 8/2 Others 2*

HUNT Stephen Patrick
Born: Port Laoise, 1 August 1980
Height: 5'7" **Weight:** 12.6
Club Honours: Ch '06
International Honours: RoI: 25; B-1; U21-1
On his return to the Premier League, Stephen made a superb start with Hull by scoring in his first two games against Chelsea and Tottenham to set the trend that would see him finish as the Tigers' leading scorer. With his energy on the left wing, along with his steady supply of opportunities from set pieces, he was regularly the outstanding performer in a struggling team. His commitment to City was amply demonstrated when he calmly converted a vital penalty against Wolverhampton in January at a time when he was the subject of a £5-million bid from the relegation rivals. Hopes of avoiding the drop were dealt a significant blow in March when Stephen lost his ever-present tag due to a foot injury. An exploratory operation ruled him out for the rest of the season when it was found that ligaments had been detached from the bone. A consolation and an indication of the impact he made in East Yorkshire came with him deservedly winning the club's and the supporters' club's 'Player of the Year' awards.

Crystal Palace *(From trainee on 29/6/1999) FL 0+3*
Brentford *(Free on 6/8/2001) FL 126+10/25 FLC 2+2 FAC 8+3/2 Others 9/3*
Reading *(Free on 30/6/2005) P/FL 109+47/17 FLC 8+1/1 FAC 5+2/3 Others 0+1*
Hull C *(Signed on 13/8/2009) PL 27/6*

HUNTER Garry Paul
Born: Morecambe, 1 January 1985
Height: 6'0" **Weight:** 12.3
The locally-born midfield player was another to find himself in and out of the Morecambe first team. He rarely had a game in his favoured central midfield role and was often used wide on the right. Always popular with the fans for never giving less than 100 per cent, he would have been disappointed to score only twice in the League campaign, although he was another player whose season was hit by niggling injuries. Garry was awarded a new two-year contract and will hope to make more of an impact in the season ahead.
Morecambe *(From juniors on 7/5/2003) FL 68+30/4 FLC 1+3 FAC 2+1 Others 9/2*

HUNTINGTON Paul David
Born: Carlisle, 17 September 1987
Height: 6'3" **Weight:** 12.8
International Honours: E: Yth
Having had an injury-ravaged 2008-09, Paul was hoping to re-establish himself at Leeds last season, but played just once in a Carling Cup tie at Darlington before going to Stockport on loan in September and debuting in the 2-2 draw at Yeovil. He picked up a red card against Southend after a challenge on Lee Barnard, initially deemed fair by the referee but then given by the linesman. Having returned to Elland Road, he re-joined County in the January transfer window after requesting his Leeds' contract be paid up.
Newcastle U *(From trainee on 20/6/2005) PL 10+1/1 FLC 1 FAC 2 Others 1+1*
Leeds U *(Signed on 31/8/2007) FL 16+5/2 FLC 3 FAC 2 Others 6/1*
Stockport Co *(Free on 10/9/2009) FL 26*

HURST Kevan James
Born: Chesterfield, 27 August 1985
Height: 6'0" **Weight:** 11.7
Club Honours: Div 1 '07
Signed by Carlisle from Scunthorpe near the start of the season, Kevan normally featured on the right side of midfield, where he complemented Matty Robson's role on the left flank. Occasionally troubled by injury problems earlier in the term, his season

finally ended in mid-March during the match against Colchester. He therefore missed out on the Johnstone's Paint Trophy final despite having scored a fine goal in the second leg of the Northern final against Leeds. He will now be concentrating on a return to full fitness ready for the new term.
Sheffield U *(From trainee on 24/3/2004) P/FL 0+1 FLC 0+3 FAC 1*
Boston U *(Loaned on 25/3/2004) FL 3+4/1*
Stockport Co *(Loaned on 18/2/2005) FL 14/1*
Chesterfield *(Loaned on 18/8/2005) FL 30+7/4 FLC 1/1 FAC 1+1/1 Others 1*
Chesterfield *(Loaned on 26/7/2006) FL 25/3 FLC 4 Others 1*
Scunthorpe U *(Signed on 31/1/2007) FL 55+11/3 FLC 2 FAC 1+3/1 Others 1+1*
Carlisle U *(Signed on 17/8/2009) FL 30+3/2 FLC 2 FAC 3+1/2 Others 5/1*

HUSBAND Stephen
Born: Dunfermline, 29 October 1990
Height: 6'0" **Weight:** 12.13
The Scottish midfielder was signed from Hearts in the January transfer window but failed to make much of an impact for Blackpool, playing just three games. It was reported that Ian Holloway paid £25,000 for his services, which could rise to close to £100,000. He is, however, highly thought of at Blackpool, who are looking to develop the 19-year-old. Before signing a two-and-a-half-year contract at Bloomfield Road, he spent time on loan at Livingston.
Heart of Midlothian *(From juniors on 1/7/2006)*
Cowdenbeath *(Loaned on 23/12/2006) SL 3+2*
Livingston *(Loaned on 25/8/2009) SL 4+3*
Blackpool *(Signed on 1/2/2010) FL 1+2*

HUSSEY Christopher (Chris) Ian
Born: Hammersmith, 2 January 1989
Height: 5'11" **Weight:** 11.11
Chris was spotted playing for AFC Wimbledon in the Blue Square Premier and in October Coventry fought off stiff competition to sign him, initially on loan but later in the transfer window on a longer contract. Signed as a future prospect for a position that had troubled Chris Coleman since the departure of Danny Fox, Chris made seven substitute appearances before his first start at Reading and was unlucky to have what looked a good goal disallowed in the final minute against Derby. Two days later at Reading, he was given a tough

baptism by Jimmy Kebe and was replaced at half-time. Despite this minor setback great things are expected from a player described as the best left-back in the Conference.
Coventry C *(Signed from AFC Wimbledon, ex Woking, on 19/10/2009) FL 1+7*

HUTCHINS Daniel (Danny) Sean
Born: Northolt, 23 September 1989
Height: 6'0" **Weight:** 12.0
The former Tottenham player joined on a free transfer after an impressive loan spell at Huish Park but found it difficult to break into a fairly settled Yeovil defence. Started five times and came on as a sub in four other matches, but could not force his way past the first choice full-backs Craig Alcock and Nathan Smith. Still only 20, the coming season will be an important one for the youngster.
Tottenham H *(From trainee on 18/7/2007)*
Yeovil T *(Free on 3/3/2009) FL 12+4 FAC 0+1 Others 1*

HUTCHINSON Andrew (Andy) Leslie
Born: Lincoln, 10 March 1992
Height: 5'10" **Weight:** 10.7
A second-year scholar, Andy was restricted to just 11 substitute appearances for Lincoln during 2009-10 with all but one coming prior to Chris Sutton's arrival as manager. An out-and-out striker who has been prolific in front of goal whilst in youth team action, he was rewarded with the offer of a professional contract at the end of the season.
Lincoln C *(Trainee) FL 3+11/1 Others 1*

HUTCHINSON Benjamin (Ben) Lloyd Phillip
Born: Nottingham, 27 November 1987
Height: 5'11" **Weight:** 12.10
A young forward who spent a couple of months on loan at Swindon from Glasgow Celtic, Ben featured in ten League games while at the County Ground but found goals hard to come by. His only successful effort was a cool finish in a 3-2 victory at Brentford at the start of October, which he celebrated with a full-length run of the pitch.
Middlesbrough *(Signed from Arnold T on 31/1/2006) PL 0+8/1 FAC 1*
Glasgow Celtic *(Signed on 31/1/2008) SL 0+5 Others 0+1*
Swindon T *(Loaned on 27/8/2009) FL 6+4/1 FAC 2+1 Others 2*
Dundee *(Loaned on 1/2/2010) SL 5+4/1 SC 1/1*

HUTCHINSON Samuel (Sam) Edward
Born: Windsor, 3 August 1989
Height: 6'0" **Weight:** 11.7
International Honours: E: Yth
Chelsea's very promising young central defender has been blighted by a series of serious knee injuries. Sam, Chelsea's reserve team captain, made his debut as a substitute in the final League match of 2006-07 and could not reappear until August 2009 –two years and four managers apart. He made his first start the following month in a Carling Cup tie against Queens Park Rangers shortly before being called up for the England under-21 squad. He can also play at right-back and it was there that he made his other appearance of the season as a sub, his surging run and cross creating the Blues' fifth goal for Frank Lampard against Stoke.
Chelsea *(From trainee on 10/8/2006) PL 0+3 FLC 1*

HUTH Robert
Born: Berlin, Germany, 18 August 1984
Height: 6'3" **Weight:** 12.12
Club Honours: PL '05, '06
International Honours: Germany: 19; U21-4; Yth
Robert was seen as one of Middlesbrough's jewels in the crown as they bid to regain their Premier League status at the first attempt. The first four League games of the season saw Boro concede no goals, with centre-halves Robert and David Wheater at the fore. Speculation was rife that top flight opposition were poised to bid for his services and Boro's worst fears were confirmed in the last week of the transfer window when he signed for Stoke. The big, uncompromising German defender soon became a favourite with the Stoke supporters and undoubtedly has a keen advocate in manager Tony Pulis. He has maintained a level of performance that has been an essential element in a Stoke defence that has become noted for being tough, disciplined and extremely difficult to break down. For much of the season the manager used him as a right-back and while he did not disappoint in that position it was as a centre-half that he looked at his very best and where he formed a formidable-looking partnership with Ryan Shawcross. Robert fits in extremely well with Stoke's game of pressurising other teams on the ball and is never afraid to put a head or a foot into a dangerous place whenever called upon to do so. He was also a key member of set-piece routines and his three goals during the season all contributed towards the Potters picking up valuable points.

Chelsea *(From trainee on 23/8/2001) PL 23+19 FLC 2 FAC 4+3/1 Others 3+8/1*
Middlesbrough *(£6,000,000 on 31/8/2006) P/FL 44+9/2 FLC 2 FAC 7+1*
Stoke C *(£5,000,000 on 27/8/2009) PL 30+2/3 FAC 5*

HUTTON Alan
Born: Glasgow, 30 November 1984
Height: 6'1" **Weight:** 11.6
Club Honours: SPD '05
International Honours: S: 15; U21-7
Alan's appearances for Tottenham in 2009-10 were once again restricted due to the fact that Vedran Corluka was the clear first choice right-back. After making just one League start and being restricted to mainly playing in Cup games, he was allowed a loan move to Sunderland in January until the end of the season. A direct player with attacking instincts, often combining well with his winger, he went straight into the side and proved a big hit, playing regularly and impressing particularly with his marauding runs which added an extra dimension to Sunderland's attacking options. His form was such that the season ended with the club hoping that a deal may be agreed with Tottenham to bring the Scottish international north. Has occasionally been used by Spurs as cover at left-back, as well as the central defensive positions in an emergency.
Glasgow Rgrs *(From juniors on 1/8/2002) SL 89+5/2 SLC 4 SC 3/1 Others 19+1/1*
Tottenham H *(£9,000,000 on 30/1/2008) PL 20+10 FLC 6 FAC 2 Others 2*
Sunderland *(Loaned on 1/2/2010) PL 11*

HUTTON David Edward
Born: Enfield, 4 December 1989
Height: 5'5" **Weight:** 10.12
International Honours: RoI: Yth
Wide player David joined Cheltenham from Tottenham in the summer, having spent the end of the previous season on loan there. His quick, darting runs from either the right or left of midfield made him a regular in the first third of the season, although he featured more from the bench following the departure of manager Martin Allen. New manager Mark Yates created a different role for the diminutive midfield man, just behind the front two in a midfield diamond that produced a notable 2-0 win at Dagenham. David was used less in the final weeks before being released in the summer.
Tottenham H *(From trainee on 4/7/2008)*
Cheltenham T *(Free on 26/3/2009) FL 19+13/1 FLC 1*

HYDE Jake Matthew
Born: Maidenhead, 1 July 1990
Height: 6'1" **Weight:** 12.4
Young forward Jake signed for Barnet as something of an unknown, having been released by Swindon at the end of the previous season. He quickly made a big impact, scoring a number of early season goals, most notably a stoppage-time winner at home to big spending Notts County. Popular with the supporters, Jake was mainly restricted to the bench in the second half of the season and was released in the summer.
Swindon T *(From trainee on 22/2/2008)*
Barnet *(Free on 2/7/2009) FL 17+17/6 FLC 0+1 FAC 0+2 Others 2/1*

HYDE Micah Anthony
Born: Newham, 10 November 1974
Height: 5'9" **Weight:** 11.5
Club Honours: Div 2 '98
International Honours: Jamaica: 16
Experienced midfielder Micah signed for Barnet in July, shortly after leaving Woking. He was immediately handed the captain's armband and was duly a regular in the first team. He developed a good partnership with fellow central midfielder Mark Hughes and despite maybe not having the pace of his early career, is still as strong as ever in the tackle. Chipped in with two goals, with the Bees winning each time he scored. Was out of contract in the summer.
Cambridge U *(From trainee on 19/5/1993) FL 89+18/13 FLC 3 FAC 7+2 Others 4+1*
Watford *(£225,000 on 21/7/1997) P/FL 235+18/24 FLC 16+1/4 FAC 13 Others 3*
Burnley *(Free on 23/7/2004) FL 95+7/1 FLC 6+1 FAC 5/1*
Peterborough U *(£75,000 on 11/1/2007) FL 56+8 FLC 1 FAC 3 Others 3 (Freed on 28/11/2008)*
Barnet *(Free from Woking on 29/7/2009) FL 41/1 FAC 3/1 Others 1*

HYLTON Daniel (Danny) Thomas
Born: Camden, 25 February 1989
Height: 6'0" **Weight:** 11.2
Club Honours: FC '08
Danny is a young Aldershot forward, who can also play out wide and came through the club's ranks. He started only six League and Cup games, being used more as an impact substitute. He opened his account with a goal against Hereford in September and signed a contract extension in mid-March.
Aldershot T *(From juniors on 16/5/2007) FL 21+29/8 FLC 0+2 FAC 2+1 Others 2*

I

Jabo Ibehre

IBEHRE Jabo Oshevire
Born: Islington, 28 January 1983
Height: 6'2" **Weight:** 12.10
Signed from Walsall by former manager Roberto di Matteo for MK Dons, Jabo scored the winner in his second game of the season at Tranmere, but that was to prove his highlight as he then struggled to make an impact under returning boss Paul Ince and was loaned out to Southend and then Stockport. At Southend, the strong, powerful centre-forward went straight into the starting line-up. However, his spell at Roots Hall was abruptly ended when a red card meant his suspension would exceed the remainder of the loan deal. He did achieve a personal landmark while at Southend when he played his 300th senior career game. Switching to Stockport in January, with the club in need of presence up front, he impressed on his debut against Swindon but was hard done by when receiving two yellow cards in his next game at Carlisle. On his return from suspension he grabbed a brace against Colchester, earning a 2-2 draw. It would be nearly two months until he found the net again, scoring two-in-two against Walsall and champions-elect Norwich.
Leyton Orient (From trainee on 18/7/2001) FL 112+97/36 FLC 3+3/2 FAC 11+5/1 Others 11+1/2
Walsall (Free on 9/7/2008) FL 35+4/10 FLC 1 FAC 1 Others 2/1
MK Dons (Free on 2/7/2009) FL 3+7/1

Others 1+1
Southend U (Loaned on 26/11/2009) FL 4
Stockport Co (Loaned on 18/1/2010) FL 20/5

IBRAHIM Abdisalam (Abdi)
Born: Guriceel, Somalia, 4 May 1991
Height: 6'1" **Weight:** 11.3
International Honours: Norway: Yth
Abdi is a product of the Manchester City Academy who starred in the 2008 FA Youth Cup triumph over Chelsea. Although Somali-born, he joined City from Norway, where his family has lived since 1998. A dynamic midfielder, he made his debut in January in the 4-2 FA Cup victory at Scunthorpe and his Premiership bow as a substitute against Liverpool in February. He is regarded as a great prospect and signed a new four-year contract.
Manchester C (From trainee on 2/7/2008) PL 0+1 FAC 1

IDRIZAJ Besian
Born: Baden bei Wien, Austria, 12 October 1987
Height: 6'2" **Weight:** 12.4
International Honours: Austria: U21-12
The Austrian midfield player or striker was signed after an initial trial period and made an appearance as a substitute in Swansea's Carling Cup tie against Scunthorpe. Besian made just one start, at the Liberty Stadium against Plymouth, but remained a regular among the substitutes and also scored consistently for the club's reserve team. There was much shock and sadness in the world of football when it was announced that Besian had passed away on 14th May after suffering a heart attack in his sleep.
Liverpool (Signed from LASK Linz, Austria, ex Admira Linz, on 30/8/2005. Freed on 31/1/2008)
Luton T (Loaned on 16/3/2007) FL 3+4/1
Crystal Palace (Loaned on 31/8/2007) FL 3+4
Swansea C (Signed from Eilenburg, Germany, ex Wacker Tirol, on 22/8/2009) FL 1+3 FLC 0+1

IFIL Philip (Phil) Nathan
Born: Willesden, 18 November 1986
Height: 5'9" **Weight:** 10.8
International Honours: E: Yth
Phil was one of a number of players to come in from the cold when Aidy Boothroyd replaced Paul Lambert as Colchester manager in September. In and out of the side, Phil still managed 30 appearances – the majority coming

from the bench. Primarily played as an attack-minded right-back, he was also used as a right-winger on occasions. Phil's best spell of form came in December when he scored in successive away games against Brighton and Southend. His excellent crossing also created four goals. Phil was offered a new deal when his contract came to an end in June.
Tottenham H (From trainee on 19/11/2004) PL 3 FLC 1+1
Millwall (Loaned on 12/9/2005) FL 13 FLC 1
Millwall (Loaned on 20/1/2006) FL 3
Southampton (Loaned on 28/9/2007) FL 11+1
Colchester U (Signed on 10/1/2008) FL 40+13/2 FLC 2 FAC 2+1 Others 2

Phil Ifil

IGOE Samuel (Sammy) Gary
Born: Staines, 30 September 1975
Height: 5'6" **Weight:** 10.0
The experienced midfield player showed his class in the early stages of the season for Bournemouth, culminating in two goals against Lincoln. A hamstring problem forced Sammy out of the action and it was an injury that recurred, meaning that he was never able to sustain another run in the side. He was released in the summer after two seasons with Boscombe.
Portsmouth (From trainee on 15/2/1994) FL 100+60/11 FLC 7+5 FAC 2+3
Reading (£100,000 on 23/3/2000) FL 53+34/7 FLC 4+1 FAC 4+2 Others 6+1
Luton T (Loaned on 27/3/2003) FL 2
Swindon T (Free on 14/7/2003) FL 75+4/9 FLC 3+1 FAC 3 Others 3+1
Millwall (Free on 5/8/2005) FL 3+2 FLC 2
Bristol Rov (Loaned on 13/1/2006) FL 10+1/1

Bristol Rov (Free on 1/8/2006) FL
44+17/1 FLC 1+1 FAC 8+3 Others
7+2/4
Hereford U (Loaned on 27/3/2008) FL 4
Bournemouth (Free on 8/8/2008) FL
37+12/3 FLC 2 FAC 4/1 Others 2/1

IKEME Carl
Born: Sutton Coldfield, 8 June 1986
Height: 6'3" **Weight:** 13.9
Club Honours: Ch '09
Unable to get a game at
Wolverhampton, Carl arrived on loan at
Charlton in late October when regular
'keeper Rob Elliot got injured, leaving
only Darren Randolph in reserve. Carl
was preferred to Randolph and played
in five matches before returning to
Molineux. A big and commanding
'keeper, he did well during his short
spell at the club. He next joined
Sheffield United on a one-month loan
to assist in the club's goalkeeping crisis.
After two victories and one clean sheet
he suffered a hamstring injury and
returned early to Wolves. His final loan
spell of the season came at Queens Park
Rangers. Three months there saw Carl
enjoy a run of first team football when
unseating Radek Cerny as first choice
goalkeeper. Improving game by game,
by the time he left Loftus Road in April
he had become a commanding
presence between sticks.
Wolverhampton W (From trainee on
24/9/2004) FL 12+1 FLC 3
Stockport Co (Loaned on 31/8/2005)
FL 9
Charlton Ath (Loaned on 28/10/2009)
FL 4 Others 1
Sheffield U (Loaned on 26/11/2009) FL 2
Queens Park Rgrs (Loaned on
6/1/2010) FL 17

Carl Ikeme

[ILAN] DALL'IGNA Ilan Araujo
Born: Curitiba, Brazil, 18 September
1980
Height: 5'11" **Weight:** 12.0
International Honours: Brazil: 3
The Brazilian striker came to West Ham
in February on a six-month contract
after playing in France with St Etienne.
He made his debut at Burnley as a
substitute and within minutes had
scored his first goal. Quick and elusive,
he went on to score vital goals as West
Ham fought against relegation. He will
best be remembered for his brilliant
equalising goal at Everton in April.
Julian Faubert put over a cross and Ilan
sprang into the box, flew through the
air and thumped a stunning diving
header into the net.
West Ham U (Loaned from St Etienne,
France, ex Paran, Sao Paulo, Atletico
Paranaense, Sochaux, on 1/2/2010) PL
6+5/4

Herita Ilunga

ILUNGA Herita N'Kongolo
Born: Kinshasa, DR Congo, 25 February
1982
Height: 5'11" **Weight:** 11.13
International Honours: DR Congo: 18
The Congolese left-back struggled for
consistency at West Ham. A succession
of injuries made it difficult for him to
rediscover his excellent form of the
previous season. He suffered a broken
jaw at Wolverhampton, followed by
hamstring setbacks. A back injury in the
game against Birmingham in February

forced him to miss the remainder of the
season. His tough tackling and forward
runs were badly missed as the Hammers
fought against relegation.
West Ham U (Signed from Toulouse,
France, ex Stade Rennais, Espanyol, St
Etienne, on 3/9/2008) PL 51 FLC 1/1
FAC 4/2

INCE Clayton
Born: Arima, Trinidad, 13 July 1972
Height: 6'3" **Weight:** 14.2
Club Honours: Div 2 '07
International Honours: Trinidad &
Tobago: 79
Having performed so well over previous
years at Walsall, Clayton's season was
notable for three bad errors. Poor
positioning saw him beaten from long
range at Wycombe and Leeds while a
throw straight to the opposition saw
him gift Southend a goal. Ironically,
Walsall amassed seven points in these
games. Despite occasional lapses in
concentration, he made numerous
excellent saves, his best being a penalty
save at Bristol Rovers followed by an
impressive block of the close-range
follow-up. A highly accomplished
goalkeeper on his day, he occasionally
struggled when crowded at corners. At
the end of the season he retired from
professional football having kept over
100 clean sheets in more than 300
appearances.
Crewe Alex (£50,000 from Defence
Force, Trinidad on 21/9/1999) FL 120+3
FLC 6 FAC 8
Coventry C (Free on 11/7/2005) FL 1
FLC 2 FAC 1
Walsall (Free on 10/7/2006) FL 151+1
FLC 4 FAC 10 Others 3

INGIMARSSON Ivar
Born: Reykjavik, Iceland, 20 August
1977
Height: 6'0" **Weight:** 12.7
Club Honours: Ch '06
International Honours: Iceland: 30;
U21-14; Yth
Ivar missed the first seven games and
the final ten but in between was the
usual reliable and competent centre-
back for Reading, as he has been for the
past seven years. His final appearance
was in a 1-1 draw at Middlesbrough, as
he limped off with a hamstring injury.
Until then, he had been an inspirational
captain. Despite playing alongside
several different partners his
performances were never less than
excellent, the only blemish being a
controversial sending off at Queens Park
Rangers. Having signed a one-year
extension to his contract, Ivar is
Reading's longest-serving player and a
superb ambassador on and off the pitch.

Torquay U (Loaned from IBV Vestmannaeyjar, Iceland on 21/10/1999) FL 4/1
Brentford (£150,000 from IBV Vestmannaeyjar, Iceland on 18/11/1999) FL 109+4/10 FLC 6 FAC 3 Others 13/1
Wolverhampton W (Free on 2/7/2002) FL 10+3/2 FLC 2
Brighton & Hove A (Loaned on 10/2/2003) FL 15
Reading (£100,000 + on 23/10/2003) P/FL 235+3/11 FLC 11+1 FAC 17/1

INGS Daniel (Danny) William
Born: Winchester, 16 March 1992
Height: 5'10" **Weight:** 11.5
Danny is a versatile player and can play as an out-and-out striker or in a deeper role behind the front two. He made his Bournemouth debut in the Johnstone's Paint Trophy at Northampton and further opportunities would have been available but for injury. He was given a three-month professional contract at the end of the season.
Bournemouth (Trainee) Others 0+1

INSUA Emiliano Adrian
Born: Buenos Aires, Argentina, 7 January 1989
Height: 5'10" **Weight:** 12.8
International Honours: Argentina: 1; U23-1; Yth
The young Liverpool and Argentine left-back made enormous strides by starting 44 games. He was fortunate in facing little competition for the left-back position from Fabio Aurelio, who was frequently injured, or Andrea Dossena, who was totally out of favour with then-manager Rafa Benitez. When Emiliano was sidelined with a knee injury late in the season, Benitez was forced to switch Daniel Agger from central defence to cover for him. While he is an excellent attacking full-back, providing six assists, many of the goals Liverpool conceded originated from the flank that he was defending. He scored his only goal so far in the Carling Cup defeat at Arsenal, a wonderful swerving and dipping volley from 25 yards, and made his international debut for Argentina in September.
Liverpool (Signed from Boca Juniors, Argentina on 31/1/2007) PL 43+3 FLC 2+1/1 FAC 3 Others 10

IRELAND Stephen James
Born: Cobh, 22 August 1986
Height: 6'0" **Weight:** 11.5
International Honours: RoI: 6; U21-1; Yth
Manchester City's 'Player of the Year' from the previous season, Stephen suffered a dramatic fall from grace with his future at the club in doubt following

Stephen Ireland

a transfer request in May. Although he started well with a goal in the opening day victory at Blackburn, he was squeezed out of central midfield by the arrival of Gareth Barry and was less effective in the wide positions. Although still a regular performer under manager Mark Hughes, he fell out of favour when Roberto Mancini took over and his appearances became more intermittent. Indeed, in his seven starts in 2010 he was substituted six times. In many ways, Stephen was very unfortunate to lose his attacking midfield place after demonstrating how well he could play there.
Manchester C (From trainee on 14/9/2004) PL 109+29/16 FLC 9+2/2 FAC 11+2/2 Others 13+1/3

IVANOVIC Branislav
Born: Sremska Mitrovica, Serbia, 22 February 1984
Height: 6'0" **Weight:** 12.4
Club Honours: FAC '09, '10; CS '09; PL '10
International Honours: Serbia: 30; U21-33
Although more accustomed to playing in central defence, Serbian international Branislav solved Chelsea's right-back dilemma when swashbuckling Jose Bosingwa was injured in October. Chosen ahead of Juliano Belletti and Paulo Ferreira, he produced a string of accomplished performances as the Blues posted the Premier League's second-best defensive figures. Strong and athletic, Branislav maintained the Blues' attacking options down the right.

His towering presence makes him a threat at set pieces, although he ended with only one goal to his credit, a scrambled effort at Bolton. In March he fell victim to the full-back injury jinx that afflicted Chelsea when torn knee ligaments at Blackburn ruled him out until the final four matches, his calm assurance smoothing ruffled nerves in a difficult run-in. He was one of the most consistent and reliable performers in a record-breaking season for the club. So effective was the big Serb that he was voted in at right-back in the PFA 'Premier League Team of the Season' by his fellow professionals. He was a key player for Serbia as they topped their World Cup qualifying group ahead of favourites France, scoring three goals and, alongside Manchester United's Nemanja Vidic, forming a formidable central defensive barrier.
Chelsea (£10,000,000 from Lokomotiv Moscow, ex Srem Sremska Mitrovica, OFK Belgrade, on 24/1/2008) PL 36+8/1 FLC 5 FAC 6+1 Others 11/2

IWELUMO Christopher (Chris) Robert
Born: Coatbridge, 1 August 1978
Height: 6'3" **Weight:** 13.8
Club Honours: Ch '09
International Honours: S: 2; B-1
The tall, experienced Wolverhampton forward had waited a long time to be in the top flight. A pre-season broken metatarsal prolonged it until 24th October when he was sub and he made a start at Stoke a week later, only to aggravate the injury. Chris made a couple more starts either side of the New Year, and had a volley well saved after coming on as sub against Wigan. He needed regular football and moved to Bristol City on a 28-day emergency loan, proving his worth in the live televised 2-1 game versus West Bromwich when notching his first goal for the club. He then added to his haul with a superb volley on the turn that proved enough to secure all points at Crystal Palace. Chris then returned to Molineux, helping to see out games when he was a sub but unfortunately not being able to register a goal.
St Mirren (From juniors on 5/8/1996) SL 7+19 SLC 0+3/1 SC 1+1/1 Others 0+2 (Free to Aarhus Fremad, Denmark during 1998 close season)
Stoke C (£25,000 from Aarhus Fremad, Denmark on 1/3/2000) FL 40+44/16 FLC 2+4/2 FAC 6+2/4 Others 4+1/1
York C (Loaned on 10/11/2000) FL 11+1/2 FAC 4/1
Cheltenham T (Loaned on 13/2/2001) FL 2+2/1
Brighton & Hove A (Signed on 16/3/2004) FL 10/4 Others 3 (Freed during 2004 close season)

Colchester U (Free from Alemania Aachen, Germany on 6/7/2005) FL 87+5/35 FLC 2 FAC 6/2 Others 2+1
Charlton Ath (Free on 9/8/2007) FL 32+14/10 FLC 0+2 FAC 0+2
Wolverhampton W (£400,000 on 16/7/2008) P/FL 27+19/14 FLC 1+1/2 FAC 2+2
Bristol C (Loaned on 12/2/2010) FL 7/2

IZZET Kemal (Kemi)
Born: Whitechapel, 29 September 1980
Height: 5'8" **Weight:** 10.5
In his tenth season at Colchester, loyal midfielder Kemi produced one of his best ever campaigns. Barely missing a game, he provided the all important but undervalued leg work in front of the back four. Solid, consistent and reliable, the midfielder covers every blade of grass, breaking up attacks and filling in for team-mates when they are out of position. Rewarded with a two-year contract extension in February, he was due a testimonial in the summer. The only disappointments of Kemi's season were his failure to score and a red card at Southampton.
Charlton Ath (From trainee on 11/1/1999)
Colchester U (Signed on 22/3/2001) FL 299+37/18 FLC 9+2/1 FAC 13+2 Others 13+1/2

Kemi Izzet

J

JAASKELAINEN Jussi Albert
Born: Vaasa, Finland, 19 April 1975
Height: 6'3" **Weight:** 12.10
International Honours: Finland: 55;
U21-14; Yth
Jussi maintained his phenomenal run in
the Bolton first team in 2009-10 when
playing every minute of every League
game. Now in his 14th season with the
club, he remains a true Bolton legend.
Having been widely recognised as one
of the Premiership's top 'keepers for
some time, Jussi continues to maintain
his exceptional levels of performance,
with no sign of slipping, at the age of
35. Jussi's consistency has proved to be
a vital element of Bolton's extended stay
in the top flight and, if he can avoid
injury, it is hard to see anyone displacing
him for some time. Notable moments
include his amazing display in the 1-1
FA Cup draw with Spurs, in which he
delivered a goalkeeping master class.

Bolton W (£100,000 + from VPS Vassa,
Finland, ex Mikkelin Palloilijat, on
14/11/1997) P/FL 420+1 FLC 19 FAC 18
Others 13

JACKMAN Daniel (Danny)
James
Born: Worcester, 3 January 1983
Height: 5'5" **Weight:** 10.2
Danny returned for his second stint at
Gillingham, three seasons after leaving
for Northampton, for an undisclosed
fee in August, making his debut as a
substitute in the Carling Cup tie with
Blackburn. Used predominantly as a
left-back in his first spell at the club,
Danny played on the left of central
midfield on his return to Gillingham.
After just a handful of appearances, he
dislocated his shoulder against
Southampton in October but regained
his slot in midfield on his return in late
January.
Aston Villa (From trainee on 4/4/2001)
Cambridge U (Loaned on 14/2/2002)
FL 5+2/1 Others 1+1
Stockport Co (£70,000 on 31/10/2003)
FL 51+9/4 FLC 1 FAC 1 Others 4

Gillingham (Signed on 5/8/2005) FL
65+8/1 FLC 3+1 Others 0+2/1
Northampton T (Free on 30/7/2007) FL
76+6/9 FLC 3+1 FAC 6 Others 1
Gillingham (Signed on 25/8/2009) FL
21+1 FLC 0+1 Others 1

JACKSON John (Johnnie)
Born: Camden, 15 August 1982
Height: 6'1" **Weight:** 13.0
Club Honours: Div 2 '10
International Honours: E: Yth
A highly talented and versatile Notts
County player with an exquisite left
foot, Johnnie played on the left, in the
centre of midfield and also at left-back
after arriving from Colchester in the
summer. Went on loan to Charlton for a
spell in February as he wanted to be
nearer to his home in the south whilst
his wife had their first child. With both
their recognised left-backs being ruled
out for the season with injury, Johnnie
immediately made his debut for
Charlton against Yeovil at the Valley
and impressed with his assured
defending and forward runs down the
left. He retained his place for the next
four games before suffering a torn
hamstring against Stockport which
ended any hopes of a permanent move.
He then returned to Meadow Lane, but
recovered to contribute towards the
final push for the League Two title.
Tottenham H (From trainee on
23/3/2000) PL 12+8/1 FLC 1 FAC 1+2
Swindon T (Loaned on 13/9/2002) FL
12+1/1 FAC 2 Others 2/1
Colchester U (Loaned on 11/3/2003) FL 8
Coventry C (Loaned on 21/11/2003) FL
2+3/2
Watford (Loaned on 23/12/2004) FL
14+1
Derby Co (Loaned on 16/9/2005) FL
3+3
Colchester U (Free on 31/7/2006) FL
92+15/13 FLC 2 FAC 2+1 Others 3
Notts Co (Signed on 17/8/2009) FL
20+4/2 FAC 6/1
Charlton Ath (Loaned on 18/2/2010)
FL 4

JACKSON Marlon Michael
Born: Bristol, 6 December 1990
Height: 6'2" **Weight:** 12.11
The tall Bristol City striker added a little
welcome pace to the Hereford front line
during his loan spell and provided a
lively threat up front. However, his time
at the club was ended by an injury and
he returned to Ashton Gate after just a
couple of starts for the Bulls. Following
that, he joined Aldershot on a similar
deal in late November, thus becoming
the first signing made by the recently-
appointed boss Kevin Dillon. Having
made his debut at Tranmere in an FA

Jussi Jaaskelainen

Cup second round tie, he played mainly as a wide midfielder and scored his first Shots' goal (and his first-ever Football League goal) in his second appearance, at Dagenham in early December. Marlon's loan was eventually extended till end of the season, but a knee injury sustained at the end of January kept him sidelined for four weeks before he came back as a playing substitute at Chesterfield in late February. He was given a spot in the starting line-up in mid-March and, apart from missing the home defeat by Torquay in mid-April, he played in every game, including both legs of the play-off semi-final defeat to Rotherham.
Bristol C (From trainee on 2/7/2009)
Hereford U (Loaned on 21/8/2009) FL 2+3 FLC 0+1 Others 1
Aldershot T (Loaned on 25/11/2009) FL 18+4/1 FAC 2 Others 2

JACKSON Richard
Born: Whitby, 18 April 1980
Height: 5'8" Weight: 10.12
The experienced full-back had to wait a long time to get a contract with League newcomers Burton and then made only a handful of appearances because of injuries. Burton could not accommodate Richard after he trained with them during the summer and he played part-time with his home-town club Whitby Town in the UniBond League. With the squad size diminishing, Richard returned to the Pirelli Stadium and signed an 18-month deal in December. He quickly showed his quality and looked set to hold down the right-back spot but was sidelined from February by a back problem.
Scarborough (From trainee on 27/3/1998) FL 21+1 FLC 2
Derby Co (£30,000 + on 25/3/1999) P/FL 98+20 FLC 5 FAC 2 Others 2
Luton T (Free on 9/8/2007) FL 27+2 FLC 3 FAC 4 Others 1
Hereford U (Free on 4/9/2008) FL 24+1 Others 1 (Freed on 30/4/2009)
Burton A (Free from Whitby T on 1/12/2009) FL 4+1

JACKSON Simeon Alexander
Born: Kingston, Jamaica, 28 March 1987
Height: 5'8" Weight: 11.0
International Honours: Canada: 10; Yth
Gillingham's top scorer in the previous season, Simeon continued his prolific form in League One, netting an opening day hat-trick in the club's sensational 5-0 defeat of Swindon. Notable strikes against Plymouth and Blackburn in the Carling Cup and against promotion contenders Norwich and Charlton saw Simeon reach 12

goals in all competitions by mid-October, his final total being 18 for the campaign. He took his international tally for Canada to ten caps with appearances against Poland and Macedonia in November and was named 2009 Canadian 'Player of the Year' in December.
Rushden & Diamonds (From trainee on 28/4/2006) FL 8+9/5
Gillingham (£150,000 on 31/1/2008) FL 85+16/35 FLC 3/2 FAC 6/1 Others 4+1/4

JACOBS Michael Edward
Born: Rothwell, Northants, 4 November 1991
Height: 5'9" Weight: 11.5
Michael played his first game in Northampton's midfield in a Johnstone's Paint Trophy game against Bournemouth. Despite being named as substitute on several occasions for the first team, he was never called upon to play. He was awarded his first full contract at the end of the season.
Northampton T (Trainee) Others 1+1

JACOBSEN Lars Christian
Born: Odense, Denmark, 20 September 1979
Height: 5'11" Weight: 11.11
International Honours: Denmark: 30; U21-26; Yth
The Dane was one of three right-backs brought in by Blackburn during the close season but was the preferred choice for the first half. Extremely steady, with scarcely a mistake, he was sacrificed primarily because the club preferred the attacking flair of Pascal Chimbonda. Although Lars is not a great force in the opposite half of the field, he can cross with some precision, striking the ball cleanly with little back lift and able to centre without the need to beat his opponent. In the spring he underwent hernia surgery which cost him dear because Michel Salgado had the chance to replace the out of form Chimbonda and never surrendered his position.
Everton (Free from Nuremberg, Germany, ex OB Odense, SV Hamburg, FC Copenhagen, on 26/8/2008) PL 4+1 FAC 0+1
Blackburn Rov (Free on 2/7/2009) PL 11+2 FLC 1+1

JACOBSON Joseph (Joe) Mark
Born: Cardiff, 17 November 1986
Height: 5'11" Weight: 12.6
International Honours: W: U21-15; Yth
Joe joined Oldham in the close season from Bristol Rovers having missed most

of the previous season with injury. His luck did not hold out too well with Oldham either, as he made only 15 appearances before injury struck once again. A combination of hip and groin strains ended his season just as he was looking back to his old self with his strong but fair tackling. Joe's trademark overlaps from full-back make him a danger in any side.
Cardiff C (From trainee on 5/7/2006) FL 0+1 FLC 1
Accrington Stanley (Loaned on 23/11/2006) FL 6/1 Others 1
Bristol Rov (Signed on 15/2/2007) FL 49+24/1 FLC 1+1 FAC 7 Others 2
Oldham Ath (Free on 2/7/2009) FL 14+1

JAGIELKA Philip (Phil) Nikodem
Born: Manchester, 17 August 1982
Height: 5'11" Weight: 12.8
International Honours: E: 3; B-1; U21-6; Yth
The Everton centre-half had incurred a bad cruciate knee injury at the end of the previous campaign and did not make a return to the first team until the end of February. Typically, this courageous and wholehearted performer did not shirk the challenge and despite being understandably rusty, played in the final 13 matches of the season - and Everton did not lose any of the 11 League matches he started. At his best, the former Sheffield United player is one of the most effective English central defenders in the top flight, combining tough tackling with sound reading of the game.
Sheffield U (From trainee on 8/5/2000) P/FL 231+23/18 FLC 16/2 FAC 14/2 Others 3
Everton (£4,000,000 on 5/7/2007) PL 71+9/1 FLC 6 FAC 7 Others 9+3/2

JAIDI Radhi Ben Abdelmajid
Born: Tunis, Tunisia, 30 August 1975
Height: 6'4" Weight: 14.0
Club Honours: AMC '10
International Honours: Tunisia: 101
Surplus to requirements at Birmingham after their promotion, Radhi's League One debut for Southampton was delayed until late September because of work permit complications. That sorted, Saints' defence improved immediately. A striking and dominant defensive presence, more in the English number five mould than the ball-caressing North African model, Radhi can play a bit. He has captained Tunisia to two World Cup finals and, in fact, his defensive partnership with José Fonte towards the end of the season looked world class.
Bolton W (Free from Esperance de

Tunis, Tunisia on 14/7/2004) PL 35+8/8
FLC 3 FAC 2+1 Others 3
Birmingham C (£2,000,000 on
4/8/2006) P/FL 86/6 FLC 4 FAC 3
Southampton (Free on 2/9/2009) FL
26+1/1 FAC 4 Others 3

JAIMEZ-RUIZ Mikhael
Born: Merida, Venezuela, 12 July 1984
Height: 6'1" **Weight:** 11.13
International Honours: Venezuela: 1
Mikhael is a goalkeeper and one of the
few Venezuelans to play in Britain. He
made Aldershot's number-one spot his
own after being Nikki Bull's understudy
in the previous season. Having won the
supporters' 'Player of the Month' award
in October, a dip in consistency saw him
dropped in February and replaced by
Bristol City loanee Stephen Henderson.
He was back in March after Henderson
was recalled by the Robins but was sent
off at Bury in March and replaced by
the recently arrived Jamie Young. It
appeared that Mikhael's season was
over, but he was unexpectedly involved
in the play-off semi-final first leg against
Rotherham as a substitute for the
injured Young. Having started the
second leg, despite becoming a cult
hero for the Shots' fans Mikhael was
released at the end of the season.
Aldershot T (Free from Northwood, ex
CFR Cluj, Ariesul Turda - loan, Barnet,
on 6/8/2007) FL 43+1 FAC 3 Others 2+1

JALAL Shwan Saman
Born: Baghdad, Iraq, 14 August 1983
Height: 6'2" **Weight:** 14.2
International Honours: E: SP-5
Bournemouth's goalkeeper enjoyed a
fine campaign, culminating in two
'Player of the Year' awards. Shwan
missed only two League games in the
Cherries' promotion season, to which
the number of clean sheets he kept,
particularly in the run-in, contributed.
He pledged his future to Bournemouth
by signing an extension to his contract.
Tottenham H (Signed from Hastings T
on 5/7/2001. Freed in April 2004)
Peterborough U (Signed from Woking
on 10/1/2007) FL 8 FLC 2 Others 1
Morecambe (Loaned on 11/1/2008) FL
12
Bournemouth (Free on 8/8/2008) FL
85 FLC 2 FAC 4 Others 3

JAMES Anthony (Tony)
Born: Cwmbran, 9 October 1978
Height: 6'3" **Weight:** 14.2
Club Honours: FC '09
International Honours: W: SP
The stylish defender achieved his dream
of playing in the League with Burton
after previously missing out with
Hereford. Tony's expert reading of the

game and his aerial ability made him a
mainstay and his value was underlined
when he signed a one-year contract
extension in January after Burton
rejected a bid by his former employers.
Soon afterwards, he had particular
delight in heading the winner for
Burton in a 4-3 thriller at Hereford - his
first goal in more than 100 appearances
for the Staffordshire club. Despite
having to play alongside an assortment
of central defensive partners, Tony was
ever reliable and his consistency was
acknowledged when he collected the
'Player of the Year' and 'Players' Player
of the Year' awards.
West Bromwich A (From trainee on
2/7/1997. Freed during 1998 close
season)
Burton A (Free from Weymouth, ex
Hereford U, on 2/7/2007) FL 42/1 FAC 2
Others 1

JAMES Christopher (Chris)
Paul
Born: Wellington, New Zealand, 4 July
1987
Height: 5'9" **Weight:** 11.7

International Honours: E: Yth. New
Zealand: 12; Yth
Chris proved to be something of a
mystery man to Barnet fans. He was
signed in late March, having previously
played in the top flight in Finland and
was expected to be part of New
Zealand's World Cup squad. However,
despite being named in the squad on
several occasions, he was restricted to
just two brief substitute appearances in
Barnet colours. Unfortunately for Chris,
he will not be adding to his 12 New
Zealand caps, having not been selected
in their World Cup squad.
Fulham (From trainee on 22/7/2005.
Freed during 2007 close season)
Barnet (Free from Tampere U, Finland,
ex TPV Tampere - loan, Ilves - loan on
25/3/2010) FL 0+2

JAMES David Benjamin
Born: Welwyn Garden City, 1 August
1970
Height: 6'5" **Weight:** 14.5
Club Honours: FAYC '89; FLC '95; FAC
'08
International Honours: E: 50; B-2;

David James

U21-10; Yth
Portsmouth's and England's veteran number-one goalkeeper continues to defy pundits and age alike as his performances invariably remain at the highest of standards. Approaching 40, he was still one of the Premier League's true stalwarts and most talented performers. David plays like a younger man at the peak of his career. A troublesome calf injury restricted David to only three games between November and January but after being reinstated between the sticks he never looked back and put in some stellar performances, most notably in the FA Cup semi-final against Tottenham and the final against Chelsea. These displays helped him to strengthen his claim for the number-one jersey in England's World Cup campaign in South Africa.
Watford (From trainee on 1/7/1988) FL 89 FLC 6 FAC 2 Others 1
Liverpool (£1,000,000 on 6/7/1992) PL 213+1 FLC 22 FAC 19 Others 22
Aston Villa (£1,800,000 on 23/6/1999) PL 67 FLC 5 FAC 8 Others 4
West Ham U (£3,500,000 on 17/7/2001) P/FL 91 FLC 5 FAC 6
Manchester C (£1,300,000 + on 14/1/2004) PL 93 FLC 1 FAC 6
Portsmouth (£1,200,000 on 15/8/2006) PL 134 FLC 3 FAC 15 Others 6

JAMES Lloyd Roger Stuart
Born: Bristol, 16 February 1988
Height: 5'11" **Weight:** 11.0
Club Honours: AMC '10
International Honours: W: U21-10; Yth
The news that Lloyd had been given a free transfer in May was a shock. In a slightly less ambitious side than Alan Pardew's Southampton, he might have cemented his place in midfield: intelligent, deft and versatile, he has the necessary attributes. However, after the signing of Dean Hammond in August, Lloyd was left to fill in at right-back or right midfield. He weighed in with a couple of sweetly taken goals and remained a squad player, but the longer the season went on the further he fell from first team reckoning.
Southampton (From trainee on 6/12/2005) FL 68+3/2 FLC 5 FAC 4 Others 4+1

JAMES Matthew Lee
Born: Bacup, 22 July 1991
Height: 6'0" **Weight:** 11.12
International Honours: E: Yth
Probably the finest midfield prospect to wear a Preston shirt since a certain David Beckham made a similar trip from Manchester United to Deepdale 15 years earlier, Matthew looked like a

much more experienced player than his 18 years, and an impressive club and career debut was capped by a goal after only ten minutes. He struck up an immediate understanding with Paul Coutts and his awareness and passing ability showed his Old Trafford pedigree. Possessing great stamina, his second goal, hit from distance against Nottingham Forest, also showed his striking potential. Matthew is definitely one to watch for the future.
Manchester U (From trainee on 2/7/2009)
Preston NE (Loaned on 8/2/2010) FL 17+1/2

JANSSON Oscar
Born: Orebro, Sweden, 23 December 1990
Height: 6'1" **Weight:** 11.11
Oscar arrived at Exeter in August on loan from Tottenham to help cure Exeter's goalkeeping injury crisis. He made seven appearances, including the home wins over Tranmere and Hartlepool. Oscar made his English League debut at Gillingham and his Premier League pedigree was evident as he made several superb saves to keep City in matches.
Tottenham H (From trainee on 7/1/2008)
Exeter C (Loaned on 1/9/2009) FL 7

JARA Gonzalo Alejandro
Born: Chile, 29 August 1985
Height: 5'10" **Weight:** 12.2
International Honours: Chile: 34
The hard-tackling, combustible midfield anchorman missed the last three months of the season with a broken foot, suffered in West Bromwich's 2-2 FA Cup draw at Reading in February. Prior to that Gonzalo, who loves to get forward and assist his front men, netted his first goal in English football, from fully 25 yards, to put Albion 2-0 up at Leicester in November. Captain of Chile, he helped his country reach the 2010 World Cup finals by scoring in qualifying victories over Colombia and Venezuela.
West Bromwich A (£1,400,000 from Colo Colo, Chile, ex Huachipato, on 25/8/2009) FL 20+2/1 FLC 1 FAC 3

JARMAN Nathan George
Born: Scunthorpe, 19 September 1986
Height: 5'10" **Weight:** 11.12
A forgettable campaign for Nathan saw him suffer a metatarsal injury on the eve of the season, forcing a two-month absence. The Grimsby forward then unluckily sustained the same injury in his comeback game against Burton and when he eventually returned to action, was seen mostly as a substitute.

Nathan's committed play brought a February dismissal against Macclesfield, while subsequent disciplinary problems meant he was overlooked for Town's relegation run-in.
Barnsley (From trainee on 10/5/2005) FL 1+14 FLC 2 FAC 0+2
Bury (Loaned on 25/11/2006) FL 1+1
Grimsby T (Free on 20/9/2007) FL 32+15/6 FLC 1 FAC 1 Others 3+1/1

Albert Jarrett

JARRETT Albert Ojumiri
Born: Freetown, Sierra Leone, 23 October 1984
Height: 5'11" **Weight:** 11.2
International Honours: Sierra Leone: 2
At the age of 25, Albert is already a well travelled player. He signed for Barnet in August, making them his tenth club, and enjoyed regular first team football with the Bees, operating mainly on the left-wing. Albert scored two goals in his first season at Barnet, one being the winner in the final minute in the last game of the season against Rochdale. Was out of contract at the end of June.
Wimbledon (Signed from Dulwich Hamlet on 17/4/2003) FL 3+6 FLC 0+1
Brighton & Hove A (Free on 5/8/2004) FL 12+11/1 FLC 1+1
Swindon T (Loaned on 20/1/2006) FL 2+4
Watford (Free on 16/8/2006) PL 0+1 FLC 1 (Freed during 2007 close season)
Boston U (Loaned on 16/2/2007) FL 5/2
MK Dons (Loaned on 23/3/2007) FL 2+3
Gillingham (Free, having taken a break from football, on 19/9/2008) FL 11+5 FAC 3 Others 1+1
Barnet (Free on 3/8/2009) FL 33+12/2 FLC 1 FAC 2+1 Others 1+1

JARRETT Jason Lee Mee
Born: Bury, 14 September 1979
Height: 6'0" **Weight:** 12.4
Club Honours: Div 2 '03
The midfield player joined Port Vale on a three-month contract in September. He made an impressive debut in a 0-0 draw at home to Bournemouth as a playmaker, something that had been lacking. Jason then helped Vale to win successive away games at Shrewsbury and Crewe but never managed to live up to his early promise. After being substituted at half-time in a 2-0 home defeat by Morecambe he never appeared again and was released in December.
Blackpool (From trainee on 3/7/1998)
FL 2 FAC 0+1 Others 1
Wrexham (Free on 8/10/1999) FL 1
Bury (Free on 13/7/2000) FL 45+17/4
FLC 0+1 FAC 2+2 Others 3/1
Wigan Ath (£75,000 on 27/3/2002) FL 67+28/1 FLC 7/2 FAC 3 Others 1+1/1
Stoke C (Loaned on 7/1/2005) FL 2 FAC 1
Norwich C (Free on 4/7/2005) FL 6+5 FLC 2+1 FAC 1
Plymouth Arg (Loaned on 24/11/2005) FL 7
Preston NE (Signed on 7/3/2006) FL 12+6/1 FLC 1 Others 1
Hull C (Loaned on 3/11/2006) FL 3
Leicester C (Loaned on 8/2/2007) FL 13
Queens Park Rgrs (Loaned on 2/10/2007) FL 1+1
Oldham Ath (Loaned on 29/1/2008) FL 12+3/3
Brighton & Hove A (Free on 26/11/2009) FL 11+2 Others 1
Port Vale (Free on 29/9/2009) FL 7+2 FAC 2+1 Others 1

JARVIS Matthew (Matt)
Thomas
Born: Middlesbrough, 22 May 1986
Height: 5'8" **Weight:** 11.7
Club Honours: Ch '09
The Wolverhampton winger had a good long-range effort well saved at Manchester City but that was as close as he came despite starting the first eight League games. He was inconsistent with his crossing and was dropped for a short while, but looked dangerous on his return at Chelsea. Matt had another good game at Liverpool and was beginning to look more comfortable. In the New Year he scored four times in 12 matches, all the goals coming away from Molineux. The best was a fine low drive from just outside the area at West Ham.
Gillingham (From trainee on 13/5/2004) FL 78+32/12 FLC 4+1/1 FAC 3+1/1 Others 3/2
Wolverhampton W (Signed on 5/7/2007) P/FL 68+20/7 FLC 0+1 FAC 4/1

Matt Jarvis

JARVIS Ryan Robert
Born: Fakenham, 11 July 1986
Height: 5'11" **Weight:** 11.0
Club Honours: Div 1 '04
International Honours: E: Yth
Ryan works tirelessly as a support forward for Leyton Orient and although he does not always gain a reward in goals for his hard graft he can be guaranteed not to let down the team. Ryan scored the first goal in the last home game against Wycombe that preserved the O's League One status. He was out of contract in the summer and was offered a new deal.
Norwich C (From trainee on 5/8/2003) P/FL 5+24/3 FLC 5/2 FAC 1+3
Colchester U (Loaned on 24/3/2005) FL 2+4
Leyton Orient (Loaned on 16/2/2007) FL 14/6
Kilmarnock (Loaned on 24/8/2007) SL 4+5/1 SLC 1+1
Notts Co (Loaned on 31/1/2008) FL 17/2
Leyton Orient (Free on 8/8/2008) FL 49+24/8 FLC 2+1 FAC 0+4 Others 4/2

JEFFERS Francis
Born: Liverpool, 25 January 1981
Height: 5'9" **Weight:** 11.0
Club Honours: FAYC '98
International Honours: E: 1; U21-16; Yth; Sch
In what was yet another very frustrating and disappointing season for the once exceptional 'fox-in-the-box' striker, he was once again hit by several niggling injuries and at best was only on the fringes of the Sheffield Wednesday side. Even when he played from the start or made an appearance from the bench, he failed to impress. He badly needs a

run in the side, injury-free, and also to once again get back to scoring goals.
Everton (From trainee on 20/2/1998) PL 37+12/18 FLC 2+2/1 FAC 6+1/1
Arsenal (£8,000,000 + on 27/6/2001) PL 4+18/4 FLC 1/1 FAC 7+1/3 Others 1+7
Everton (Loaned on 1/9/2003) PL 5+13 FLC 1 FAC 0+3/2
Charlton Ath (£2,600,000 on 12/8/2004) PL 9+11/3 FLC 2/1 FAC 2/1
Glasgow Rgrs (Loaned on 31/8/2005) SL 4+4 SLC 1+1 Others 2+2
Blackburn Rov (Free on 29/7/2006) PL 3+7 FLC 0+1 FAC 0+1 Others 0+3/1
Ipswich T (Loaned on 2/3/2007) FL 7+2/4
Sheffield Wed (£700,000 on 10/8/2007) FL 28+26/5 FLC 2+1 FAC 3

JEFFERS Shaun Elliot
Born: Bedford, 14 April 1992
Height: 6'1" **Weight:** 11.0
The home grown striker was one of several young Coventry players given a run out in the Carling Cup tie with Hartlepool in August and showed a nice turn of speed despite looking raw. After his debut, he had four more appearances as a substitute but none of them gave him sufficient time to make an impression. Shaun was given a one-year extension to his contract at the end of the season.
Coventry C (Trainee) FL 0+4 FLC 1

JENAS Jermaine Anthony
Born: Nottingham, 18 February 1983
Height: 5'11" **Weight:** 11.2
Club Honours: FLC '08
International Honours: E: 21; B-1; U21-9; Yth
Jermaine's season at Tottenham was severely hampered by two bouts of injury. One came at the start and the other towards the end of the season. On top of that, Jermaine had to deal with the emergence of Tom Huddlestone and Wilson Palacios as the club's central midfielders. Jermaine's qualities are well known, having superb stamina and speed coupled with passing and tackling skills that make him a boon to attack and defence. Jermaine made 13 starts and ten substitute appearances, scoring his one goal in Spurs' 5-0 home win against Burnley. He played the full 90 minutes for England against Brazil, but this was his only International appearance and he missed England's World Cup squad.
Nottingham F (From trainee on 19/2/2000) FL 29/4 FLC 2 FAC 2
Newcastle U (£5,000,000 on 5/2/2002) PL 86+24/9 FLC 3/1 FAC 6+1/1 Others 28+4/1
Tottenham H (£7,000,000 on

31/8/2005) PL 119+16/21 FLC 13/2 FAC 8/2 Others 16+1/1

JENKINS Ross Aden
Born: Watford, 9 November 1990
Height: 5'11" **Weight:** 12.6
International Honours: E: Yth
A young attacking Watford midfield player who made a big impression in his debut season of 2008-09, Ross suffered a setback in October when he sustained a serious back injury that required surgery. He returned to first team action in January and was a regular member of the squad for the rest of the season. Ross has now made more than 50 first team appearances for Watford. He made his England under-20 debut in August.
Watford (From trainee on 19/10/2008) FL 49+4/1 FLC 6 FAC 3+1

JENSEN Brian Paldan
Born: Copenhagen, Denmark, 8 June 1975
Height: 6'1" **Weight:** 12.4
Through all of Burnley's defensive tribulations, 'The Beast' was there at the back, ever-present in the Premier League and seemingly for once without serious competition as the Clarets' first choice 'keeper. At his best, as in the early-season defeat at Stamford Bridge when a series of superb saves kept Chelsea at bay for half the match, Brian could look world class; at other times he looked out of his depth, although in fairness he was not helped by an often shaky back four. He was stretchered off in the Carling Cup defeat at Barnsley and also had to go off with a bizarrely-inflicted injury at home to Wigan, but on both occasions was very quickly back to full fitness.
West Bromwich A (£100,000 from AZ Alkmaar, Holland, ex B93, Hvidovre - loan, on 3/3/2000) FL 46 FLC 4
Burnley (Free on 18/7/2003) P/FL 242+3 FLC 17 FAC 16 Others 3

JEROME Cameron Zishan
Born: Huddersfield, 14 August 1986
Height: 6'1" **Weight:** 13.5
International Honours: E: U21-10
Cameron made himself the first choice striker at Birmingham. Scorer of ten goals, a personal Premier League best, he proved a real handful for defences. His pace, power and movement brought a dynamic edge to the Blues' attack and his partnership with Christian Benitez did so much to forge an incredible 15-match unbeaten run. Cameron won the club's 'Goal of the Season' for a stunning 35-yard strike at Liverpool.
Cardiff C (Signed, following trials at

Huddersfield T, Grimsby, Sheffield Wed, Middlesbrough, on 14/1/2004) FL 65+8/24 FLC 2+2/2 FAC 2/1
Birmingham C (£3,000,000 + on 2/6/2006) P/FL 98+48/34 FLC 4+1/3 FAC 7+1

JERVIS Jake Mario
Born: Wolverhampton, 17 September 1991
Height: 6'4" **Weight:** 12.13
Made a surprise debut in the FA Cup for Birmingham at Everton in January as a substitute. Tall and rangy with a good touch, Jake earned his call-up due to consistent displays in the reserves and he signed a professional contract with the Blues before being loaned out to Hereford in March to gain further experience. With pace to burn, Jake made an impact with a supremely confident finish within minutes of appearing on the pitch as a Hereford substitute against Bradford. His solid temperament was confirmed with a nerveless penalty conversion at Chesterfield as Bulls' fans were left wishing he had arrived earlier in the season.
Birmingham C (From trainee on 11/3/2010) FAC 0+1
Hereford U (Loaned on 19/3/2010) FL 5+2/2

JEVONS Philip (Phil)
Born: Liverpool, 1 August 1979
Height: 5'11" **Weight:** 11.10
Club Honours: FAYC '98; Div 2 '05
Phil is an experienced striker and joined Morecambe on a season-long loan with Ian Craney from Huddersfield in July. His signing was a major boost for boss Sammy McIlroy, who was looking for an experienced front man, and Phil certainly fitted that bill. He scored 20 League and Cup goals and would have had many more had it not been for his uncanny knack of hitting the woodwork, which he did 12 times. He also missed a few games at the end of the year through injury that hampered his hopes of reaching the 20 League goals milestone. Released by Huddersfield at the end of the campaign, McIlroy was keen to sign him for 2010-11.
Everton (From trainee on 10/11/1997) PL 2+6 FLC 1
Grimsby T (£150,000 + on 26/7/2001) FL 46+17/18 FLC 4/2 FAC 3/1
Hull C (Loaned on 5/9/2002) FL 13+11/3 FLC 1 FAC 1
Yeovil T (Free on 21/7/2004) FL 80+4/42 FLC 3 FAC 7/3 Others 1
Bristol C (Free on 19/7/2006) FL 31+12/11 FLC 2+1/2 FAC 5/4 Others 3+1/2

Huddersfield T (Signed on 22/11/2007) FL 29+15/9 FLC 0+1 FAC 4+1/2
Bury (Loaned on 23/3/2009) FL 3+4/2 Others 2
Morecambe (Loaned on 22/7/2009) FL 40/18 FAC 2/1 Others 1+1

JIMENEZ Luis Antonio
Born: Santiago, Chile, 17 June 1984
Height: 6'0" **Weight:** 11.11
International Honours: Chile: 20
Luis joined West Ham from Inter Milan on a season-long loan. A tricky and skilful player, the Chilean midfielder found it difficult to adjust to the pace of the Premier League. He enjoyed his best game for the Hammers against Burnley in December when he gained a penalty that he duly converted. In January he was released back to Inter, from where he subsequently joined Parma.
West Ham U (Loaned from Inter Milan, Italy, ex Palestino, Ternana, Fiorentina - loan, SS Lazio - loan, on 23/6/2009) PL 6+5/1 FAC 1

[JO] ALVES DE ASSIS SILVA Joao
Born: Sao Paulo, Brazil, 20 March 1987
Height: 6'2" **Weight:** 12.4
International Honours: Brazil: 3; U23-7
Loaned to Everton for a second time by Manchester City, the Brazilian failed to do himself justice at Goodison before moving back to City following a breach of club conduct in mid-season – and then went on loan immediately to Galatasaray in Turkey. The striker failed to find the net in League matches at Everton during the season, netting just two goals overall, one in the Europa League and the other at Hull in the Carling Cup.
Manchester C (Signed from CSKA Moscow, Russia, ex Corinthians, on 2/7/2008) PL 6+3/1 FLC 1 FAC 0+1 Others 6+1/2
Everton (Loaned on 2/2/2009) PL 11+1/5
Everton (Loaned on 10/7/2009) PL 6+9 FLC 1+1/1 Others 5+2/1

JOHN Stern
Born: Tunapuna, Trinidad, 30 October 1976
Height: 6'1" **Weight:** 12.12
Club Honours: Ch '07
International Honours: Trinidad & Tobago: 109
Deployed mainly as a substitute for Crystal Palace after signing for them on a free transfer from Southampton prior to the start of 2009-10, the Trinidadian international found himself loaned out to Ipswich for three months from the end of November, as first team

appearances were hard to come by at Selhurst Park following an injury suffered during the first game of the season. At Ipswich, he led the line well, his bustling front-running style certainly ruffling opposing defenders, and he was unlucky to have what looked like a perfectly good goal disallowed against Peterborough. He finally got on the score-sheet when he headed home Liam Rosenior's cross against Coventry. After manager Neil Warnock had moved on and his loan expired at Portman Road at the end of January, Stern found himself back in the first team picture with Palace and a fine second half performance away at Derby in April saw him cap his display with a well taken goal to earn a draw. His one year contract at Palace came to an end at the season's close and he was linked with a move to Kansas City Chiefs in the MLS.
Nottingham F (£1,500,000 + from Columbus Crew, USA on 22/11/1999) FL 49+23/18 FLC 3/2 FAC 4+1
Birmingham C (Free on 8/2/2002) P/FL 42+35/16 FLC 2/3 FAC 1+2/1 Others 3/1
Coventry C (£200,000 on 14/9/2004) FL 65+13/26 FLC 3 FAC 6+1/3
Derby Co (Loaned on 16/9/2005) FL 6+1
Sunderland (£250,000 on 29/1/2007) P/FL 10+6/5
Southampton (Signed on 30/8/2007) FL 39+8/19 FLC 0+3/1 FAC 1+1
Bristol C (Loaned on 24/10/2008) FL 13+11/2 FAC 1+1
Crystal Palace (Free on 30/7/2009) FL 7+9/2
Ipswich T (Loaned on 26/11/2009) FL 5+2/1 FAC 2

JOHN-BAPTISTE Alexander (Alex) Aaron
Born: Sutton-in-Ashfield, 31 January 1986
Height: 5'11" **Weight:** 11.7
Alex had a superb season in tangerine at centre-half, being an integral member Blackpool's successful push to the Premiership. At 24, he reverted from right-back to the middle with the maturity of a defender far older. His pace on the turn is something expected by any top striker and although small, he wins more than his fair share in the air. His greatest attribute however is his tackling. Alex never feels the need to dive in, instead standing up against his man and executing clean tackles. In a season where Ian Holloway had to work out his best defensive pairing, Alex was always first choice and is a firm favourite amongst the supporters.
Mansfield T (From trainee on

5/2/2003) FL 170+4/5 FLC 6 FAC 9/1 Others 8+1
Blackpool (Free on 17/7/2008) FL 63/4 FLC 3 FAC 1 Others 3

JOHN-LEWIS Lenell (Lenny) Nicholas
Born: Hammersmith, 17 May 1989
Height: 5'10" **Weight:** 11.10
Striker Lenell spent the majority of the 2009-10 season on the Lincoln substitutes' bench, restricting his minutes on the pitch somewhat dramatically. Just one goal came his way during the course of the campaign, but it proved to be an important one, a stoppage-time header at Barnet securing the three points.
Lincoln C (From trainee on 21/12/2007) FL 43+29/8 FLC 1 FAC 3+3/1 Others 1+1

JOHNSON Adam
Born: Sunderland, 14 July 1987
Height: 5'9" **Weight:** 9.11
Club Honours: FAYC '04
International Honours: E: 1; U21-19; Yth
After helping England under-21s reach the final of the European Championships in the summer, Adam was hoping to cement himself in the Middlesbrough first team after the departure of Stewart Downing. He soon became one of the stars of the Championship as he regularly won plaudits for his wing play and goals. Playing in his natural position on the left wing, he scored 12 goals before the January transfer window. Speculation was rife that bids from Premier League clubs were forthcoming. Manchester City soon became front runners for his signature but they did not clinch the deal till the last day of the transfer window after tabling a £7m bid. Although the young winger had been recognised as a future star for some time the speed with which he adjusted to playing with a top Premiership team was truly remarkable. Within four months of leaving Middlesbrough he had forced his way into Fabio Capello's initial 30-man squad for the World Cup finals in South Africa with a series of outstanding performances on both wings for the Eastlands club. Although he only scored once - a curling shot into the roof of the net from the edge of the area to secure a stoppage-time equaliser at Sunderland in March – it was considered to be City's 'Goal of the Season'. He also provided nine goal assists - a remarkable statistic considering that he played for less than half the season with City. After the Premiership campaign was over he

made his international debut for the England senior team as a late substitute in the 3-1 victory over Mexico.
Middlesbrough (From trainee on 12/5/2005) P/FL 49+47/13 FLC 5+1/3 FAC 8+6 Others 2+2
Leeds U (Loaned on 17/10/2006) FL 4+1
Watford (Loaned on 14/9/2007) FL 11+1/5
Manchester C (£7,000,000 on 1/2/2010) PL 14+2/1

JOHNSON Andrew
Born: Bedford, 10 February 1981
Height: 5'9" **Weight:** 9.7
International Honours: E: 8; Yth
This was a season Andrew will wish to forget, with injury restricting him to 13 games for Fulham. It started brightly, with three typically predatory goals in the opening two home Europa League ties against FK Vetra and Amkar Perm. His pace and power threatened the Russian defence at every move until he suffered a strong challenge that dislocated a shoulder. Despite making a quicker than expected return to action by mid-September, Andrew lasted only four games before sustaining a further injury that kept him out till the turn of the year. Returning to the side, he played four more games before sustaining a serious knee injury at Blackburn. It required specialist treatment in the United States and immediately ruled him out for the remainder of the season. He is expected to return during the pre-season programme.
Birmingham C (From juniors on 11/3/1998) FL 44+39/8 FLC 6+9/5 FAC 1 Others 1+3
Crystal Palace (£750,000 on 5/8/2002) P/FL 134+6/74 FLC 7/7 FAC 8/2 Others 5/1
Everton (£6,000,000 on 2/6/2006) PL 52+9/17 FLC 4 FAC 2/1 Others 6+1/4
Fulham (£10,500,000 on 7/8/2008) PL 37+2/7 FLC 1 FAC 5/3 Others 4/3

JOHNSON Bradley (Brad) Paul
Born: Hackney, 28 April 1987
Height: 6'0" **Weight:** 12.10
Brad began the season in brilliant form on the left of midfield as Leeds remained unbeaten in League One until mid-October. He used power rather than tricky footwork to get into scoring positions and netted in three successive League wins against Walsall, Tranmere and Colchester in August. Often arriving at the back post with runs from deep he proved a potent aerial weapon. However, an injury in November ruled him out for a month and on his return

he could not recapture the same form. His starting appearances became more sporadic after the New Year, but his ability to occupy a central midfield role and a few games in Leeds' problematic left-back slot ensured his place in the squad.

Cambridge U *(From juniors on 17/11/2004) FL 0+1*
Northampton T *(Free on 23/5/2005) FL 44+9/8 FLC 3/1 FAC 2+1/1 Others 2*
Leeds U *(£250,000 on 9/1/2008) FL 51+21/10 FLC 3+2 FAC 4 Others 5+5*
Brighton & Hove A *(Loaned on 28/10/2008) FL 10/4*

JOHNSON Damien Michael
Born: Lisburn, 18 November 1978
Height: 5'9" **Weight:** 11.2
Club Honours: FLC '02
International Honours: NI: 56; U21-11; Yth
The last survivor of the Birmingham 2002 promotion-winning team, Damien found his chances limited by injury and new additions. A reliable, wholehearted competitor who filled a variety of roles, he made one substitute appearance in the Premier League before he was allowed to leave on a free transfer to Plymouth. It was a real coup for the Championship side to sign the experienced midfielder on a two-and-a-half-year deal in January. An experienced international, Damien is a creative player who has an eye for a pass. He made his debut in the defeat to West Bromwich in February and remained an ever-present for the rest of the season in the centre of the Pilgrims' midfield, scoring two goals during the campaign, one being from the penalty spot.

Blackburn Rov *(From trainee on 2/2/1996) P/FL 43+17/3 FLC 12+3/1 FAC 3+4 Others 0+1*
Nottingham F *(Loaned on 29/1/1998) FL 5+1*
Birmingham C *(Signed on 8/3/2002) P/FL 184+9/4 FLC 5+2 FAC 13+2 Others 1*
Plymouth Arg *(Free on 1/2/2010) FL 20/2*

JOHNSON Edward (Eddie)
Born: Bunnell, Florida, USA, 31 March 1984
Height: 6'0" **Weight:** 12.10
International Honours: USA: 41
Despite some early season promise, the United States' international again struggled to make an impact with regard to regular selection up front for Fulham. Eddie made only four first team appearances, although during his brief appearance against FK Vetra he set up the final goal in a 3-0 win for namesake Andrew. After completing 90 minutes

at Manchester City in the Carling Cup, he came close to scoring his first senior Fulham goal in the final seconds of a 2-2 draw at West Ham. This was his last appearance of the season, despite some confident finishes that brought him three goals in six reserve games. During the January transfer window, he was loaned to Greek club Aris Thessaloniki for the remainder of the season.

Fulham *(£3,000,000 from Kansas City Wizards, USA, ex Dallas Burn, on 30/1/2008) PL 4+4 FLC 1 Others 0+1*
Cardiff C *(Loaned on 26/8/2008) FL 5+25/2 FLC 2 FAC 0+1*

Glen Johnson

JOHNSON Glen McLeod
Born: Greenwich, 23 August 1984
Height: 6'0" **Weight:** 12.0
Club Honours: FLC '05; PL '05; FAC '08
International Honours: E: 22; U21-14; Yth
The England international right-back was signed by Liverpool in the summer from Portsmouth and started in such sparkling form that, within a month, it was clear he could become the Reds' most accomplished right-back since Phil Neal. He scored twice in the first four games, both with blistering shots, and this compared with only four goals from Liverpool's right-backs in the last ten seasons. A brilliant attacking full-back who can outpace his marker and deliver accurate crosses, he also carries a powerful shot from outside the area. Although Glen suffered a calf injury in October and a more serious knee injury against Aston Villa in late December that sidelined him for two months, he finished in good form, scoring a third outstanding goal

in the 3-0 home win over Sunderland. Was a key member of England's World Cup squad, having scored his first goal for the national side, a virtuoso solo effort against Mexico in May.

West Ham U *(From trainee on 25/8/2001) PL 14+1 FAC 0+1*
Millwall *(Loaned on 17/10/2002) FL 7+1*
Chelsea *(£6,000,000 on 22/7/2003) PL 35+7/3 FLC 5+1 FAC 8 Others 13+3/1*
Portsmouth *(Loaned on 11/7/2006) PL 25+1 FAC 2*
Portsmouth *(£4,000,000 on 31/8/2007) PL 58/4 FLC 2 FAC 7 Others 5*
Liverpool *(Signed on 26/6/2009) PL 24+1/3 FLC 0+1 Others 9*

JOHNSON Jemal Pierre
Born: Paterson, New Jersey, USA, 3 May 1984
Height: 5'8" **Weight:** 11.5
Club Honours: AMC '08; Div 2 '08
Although Jemal showed his customary flashes of skill and pace from MK Dons' opening game, with goals and assists proving harder to come by than before he became somewhat of a peripheral figure as the season wore on. He was one of a number of MK Dons' players to switch to Stockport in January, his move being a half-season loan. Initially used as a striker, it was only when he switched to the left wing that he started to find the back of the net. A spectacular curling strike from outside the area won the game 1-0 away to Exeter, and another followed in the 4-3 victory over Wycombe at Edgeley Park. However, he was left out of the squad against Yeovil, with disciplinary reasons cited, and while he returned to the team against Hartlepool he struggled to regain the form he had shown in previous games.

Blackburn Rov *(From trainee on 10/5/2002) PL 0+6 FAC 1+3/1*
Preston NE *(Loaned on 28/10/2005) FL 2+1/1*
Darlington *(Loaned on 10/3/2006) FL 9/3*
Wolverhampton W *(Signed on 17/8/2006) FL 14+6/3 FLC 0+1 FAC 0+3*
Leeds U *(Loaned on 20/2/2007) FL 3+2*
MK Dons *(Signed on 31/8/2007) FL 48+41/11 FLC 3 FAC 2/1 Others 9/2*
Stockport Co *(Loaned on 18/1/2010) FL 14+2/2*

JOHNSON Jermaine
Born: Kingston, Jamaica, 25 June 1980
Height: 5'9" **Weight:** 11.5
International Honours: Jamaica: 53
Last season saw this pacy, attacking player cement his place in the Sheffield Wednesday side. Playing either right or

left of midfield he really looked the part. On occasions he also played as a second striker in a 4-4-2 set up, most notably in Alan Irvine's first match as manager, the win at Barnsley. He also continued to play for Jamaica's full international side and was a far more consistent performer, something which he has lacked in previous seasons.
Bolton W *(£750,000 from Tivoli Gardens, Jamaica on 19/9/2001) PL 4+8 FLC 3 FAC 1+1*
Oldham Ath *(Free on 28/11/2003) FL 31+8/9 FLC 2 FAC 1/1 Others 1 (Freed during 2005 close season)*
Bradford C *(Free from Tivoli Gardens, Jamaica on 24/7/2006) FL 26+1/4 FLC 1 FAC 3*
Sheffield Wed *(£500,000 on 30/1/2007) FL 93+20/11 FLC 4+1/2 FAC 3+1*

JOHNSON John James
Born: Middlesbrough, 16 September 1988
Height: 6'0" **Weight:** 12.0
When Malcolm Crosby joined Northampton as assistant manager, he suggested they bring John from Middlesbrough on loan and he certainly played a part in the club's turn of fortune. The right-back is a strong tackler, loves to get forward and netted a few goals in his stay at Northampton. With first team opportunities being sparse at Middlesbrough, the youngster grabbed his opportunity with both hands.
Middlesbrough *(From trainee on 15/5/2008) PL 0+1*
Tranmere Rov *(Loaned on 24/11/2008) FL 4 Others 1*
Northampton T *(Loaned on 23/9/2009) FL 36/5 FAC 1 Others 1*

JOHNSON Lee David
Born: Newmarket, 7 June 1981
Height: 5'6" **Weight:** 10.7
Club Honours: FAT '02; FC '03; Div 2 '05
International Honours: E: SP-5
This midfielder was having a hard time establishing himself with Bristol City, so he was allowed out on loan to Derby for a month, where his neat touches impressed before he returned to Ashton gate. He silenced the boo boys by scoring the winning goal against West Bromwich on 20 February, but with his father's departure as the City manager in mid-March Lee was only used intermittently as a substitute, which was a great waste of his talent despite the lack of goals in his portfolio.
Watford *(From trainee on 3/10/1998)*
Brighton & Hove A *(Free on 4/9/2000) Others 1/1*

Brentford *(Free on 22/3/2001)*
Yeovil T *(Free on 12/7/2001) FL 115/14 FLC 5/3 FAC 11/2 Others 3+1*
Heart of Midlothian *(£20,000 on 11/1/2006) SL 1+3 SC 1*
Bristol C *(Signed on 9/8/2006) FL 141+13/10 FLC 6 FAC 9 Others 4+4*
Derby Co *(Loaned on 1/1/2010) FL 4 FAC 2+1*

JOHNSON Leon Dean
Born: Shoreditch, 10 May 1981
Height: 6'0" **Weight:** 12.4
In and out of the Wycombe side at the start of the season, Leon had a run of five consecutive games in October in central defence, forming a good partnership with Michael Duberry. He picked up a hip injury in the FA Cup game against Brighton and this turned out to be more serious than thought, requiring an operation that ended his season. He should be fit for the start of 2010-11 when he can expect to be a leading candidate for a central defensive position, especially now that two central defenders have not been offered contracts.
Southend U *(From trainee on 17/11/1999) FL 43+5/3 FLC 1 FAC 1+3 Others 8*
Gillingham *(Free on 15/8/2002) FL 80+18/2 FLC 3 FAC 3+1 Others 3*
Wycombe W *(Free on 3/7/2007) FL 78+1/2 FLC 3 FAC 3 Others 5*

JOHNSON Michael
Born: Urmston, 3 March 1988
Height: 6'0" **Weight:** 12.7
International Honours: E: U21-2; Yth
Two years ago, under the management of Sven Goran Eriksson, the Manchester City midfield player was considered one of the brightest prospects in the country. Since then, his progress has been blighted by injuries and there was no end to his run of bad luck. Sidelined with a groin strain at the start of the season, he returned to action in late September as a substitute in the home game with West Ham and a month later scored his first goal for a year in the Carling Cup victory over Scunthorpe. That was the limit of his involvement as in December it was announced that he had suffered a serious knee injury in training and was out for the rest of the season.
Manchester C *(From trainee on 5/11/2006) PL 36+1/2 FLC 3+1/1 Others 4*

JOHNSON Oliver (Oli) Tobias
Born: Wakefield, 6 November 1987
Height: 5'11" **Weight:** 12.4
Club Honours: Div 1 '10
After a bright beginning to his career at Stockport the previous season, Oli's

2009-10 campaign was very stop-start. His goal in the 4-2 win at Brighton, where he jinked his way past several defenders and the 'keeper, would be his only one of the season for County. Various niggling problems – to his calf, his ankle and picking up a virus amongst them – meant he was unable to get a consistent run in the team. In January he was sold to Norwich, as the club sought the finances to survive. He made an instant impact with the Carrow Road faithful following his transfer with a series of exciting displays, mainly as a substitute, in which he scored four vital goals, including two late strikes against Southend to turn that game in Norwich's favour. Still somewhat raw, as a latecomer to the professional game the striker has that naivety and freshness which allows him to try the unexpected. He likes to run at defenders and with his excellent close control he can be a real handful to even the most experienced of opposition.
Stockport Co *(Free from Nostell Miners Welfare on 17/10/2008) FL 13+27/7 FLC 1 FAC 7+1*
Norwich C *(Signed on 8/1/2010) FL 4+13/4*

JOHNSON Reda
Born: Marseille, France, 21 March 1988
Height: 6'2" **Weight:** 13.10
International Honours: Benin: 3
Having spent some time on trial with Aberdeen, Reda decided to sign a three-year contract with Plymouth from French Third Division side Amiens. The talented young central defender initially struggled to make an impact in the first team and suffered an injury blow in September, when he had to have a cartilage operation. However, when his chance came in December, he put in many impressive performances at the heart of the Pilgrims' defence. After being called up for Benin in August, he was in the national squad for the African Cup of Nations and was severely missed by Plymouth. He returned to make the centre-back position his own, although his progress was unfortunately affected by a groin strain against Sheffield United in February, resulting in him missing three important games.
Plymouth Arg *(Signed from Amiens, France, ex Gueugnon, on 29/7/2009) FL 23+2*

JOHNSON Roger
Born: Ashford, Middlesex, 28 April 1983
Height: 6'3" **Weight:** 11.0
A rock of the Birmingham defence, Roger played in every minute of every

223

Premier League encounter. Strong, determined and physical, he impressed in his rookie top flight campaign and forged a great understanding with Scott Dann in a new-look back line. Often he played on despite taking bad knocks, and his tackling and imposing style made him a favourite with supporters.
Wycombe W *(From trainee on 10/7/2001) FL 146+11/19 FLC 6/1 FAC 6/1 Others 11+3/1*
Cardiff C *(£275,000 on 13/7/2006) FL 112+7/12 FLC 8/1 FAC 9/1*
Birmingham C *(£5,000,000 on 25/6/2009) PL 38 FAC 5*

JOHNSON Simon Ainsley
Born: West Bromwich, 9 March 1983
Height: 5'9" **Weight:** 12.0
International Honours: E: Yth
After looking promising for Bury against Premiership opposition in pre season, the winger was signed on a three-month contract. Having made two appearances in which he made little impact, the club announced that Simon's month-to-month contract had been terminated.
Leeds U *(From trainee on 7/7/2000) P/FL 3+8 FLC 1*
Hull C *(Loaned on 12/8/2002) FL 4+8/2 FLC 0+1*
Blackpool *(Loaned on 13/12/2003) FL 3+1/1 FAC 0+1*
Sunderland *(Loaned on 10/9/2004) FL 1+4*
Doncaster Rov *(Loaned on 6/12/2004) FL 8+3/3*
Barnsley *(Loaned on 24/2/2005) FL 10+1/2*
Darlington *(Free on 29/7/2005) FL 43+23/9 FLC 3/1 FAC 3 Others 3+1*
Hereford U *(Free on 9/8/2007) FL 30+32/5 FLC 1+1 FAC 3+3/1 Others 2*
Bury *(Free on 7/8/2009) FL 1+3 FLC 0+1 Others 1*

JONES Ashlee Ageron
Born: Walthamstow, 4 August 1987
Height: 6'1" **Weight:** 12.5
A young goalkeeper who was signed on loan as cover, Ashlee made one appearance in the four-goal defeat at Notts County in early December. He had similarly been signed by Wycombe the previous season but never left the bench for the Chairboys.
Darlington *(Free from Kingstonian, ex Basingstoke T, Rushden & Diamonds, Potters Bar T, Fisher Ath, Crawley T, Wycombe W - NC, on 29/10/2009) FL 1*

JONES Bradley (Brad)
Born: Armidale, Australia, 19 March 1982
Height: 6'3" **Weight:** 12.3
Club Honours: AMC '04

International Honours: Australia: 2; U23-6; Yth
With the departure of Ross Turnbull to Chelsea in the summer, Brad was looking to establish himself as Middlesbrough's number-one goalkeeper. A pre-season ankle injury let in new signing Danny Coyne who did so well that it was not until after a 5-0 home defeat by West Bromwich in September that Brad regained his place. He was a target for supporters after a below-par performance at Newcastle. New boss Gordon Strachan restored Coyne and Brad's future at the Riverside looked unclear. However, a surprise recall in March vindicated Strachan's faith as Brad impressed with solid displays, including a penalty save at Plymouth.
Middlesbrough *(From trainee on 26/3/1999) P/FL 58 FLC 3 FAC 10+1 Others 4*
Stockport Co *(Loaned on 13/12/2002) FL 1*
Blackpool *(Loaned on 4/11/2003) FL 5 Others 2*
Blackpool *(Loaned on 5/11/2004) FL 12*
Sheffield Wed *(Loaned on 4/8/2006) FL 15*

JONES Christopher (Chris) Trevor
Born: Swansea, 12 September 1989
Height: 5'7" **Weight:** 9.12
International Honours: W: U21-1; Yth
This speedy winger was soon in first team contention for Grimsby following his summer arrival, claiming his initial senior goal against Burton when chasing down a clearance. Seen on both flanks, Chris however appeared just twice following a change of manager, and joined Welsh club Neath on loan in January.
Swansea C *(From trainee on 19/10/2006) FL 0+7 Others 1+1*
Grimsby T *(Free on 25/7/2009) FL 6+1/1 FAC 0+1*

JONES Craig Nicholas
Born: Hereford, 12 December 1989
Height: 6'0" **Weight:** 12.2
Much had been expected of Hereford's Craig after a couple of promising appearances in central midfield towards the end of the previous campaign. And his talents were quickly to the fore when he was selected early in the campaign as a left-sided midfielder willing to get forward. Unfortunately, a long-standing back injury sidelined him for a lengthy spell and it was only towards the end of the season that he forced himself back into the squad. Was out of contract in the summer.
Hereford U *(From juniors at Cardiff C on 7/9/2007) FL 2+2 FLC 1*

JONES Daniel (Dan) Jeffrey
Born: Rowley Regis, 14 July 1986
Height: 6'2" **Weight:** 13.0
Unable to get a game, the Wolverhampton left-back joined Notts County on a temporary loan last September, which was supposed to become permanent. However, when the new financial backers withdrew he was returned to Molineux. Prior to that, he produced some promising performances. His next stop was on loan at Bristol Rovers in February and he made an impressive League debut in the Sky televised home victory over Charlton. Dan is a powerful defender who is able to use his strength and skill to get past defenders to deliver accurate crosses. He was switched to central defence following injuries at Carlisle and looked comfortable using his heading ability to defend set plays, being Rovers' 'Man of the Match'. He can also play on the left side of midfield. Was out of contract at the end of June.
Wolverhampton W *(From trainee on 2/2/2006) FL 9+1 FLC 1*
Northampton T *(Loaned on 7/8/2007) FL 17+6/3 FLC 1+1 FAC 1+2 Others 1*
Northampton T *(Loaned on 7/3/2008) FL 10*
Oldham Ath *(Loaned on 3/10/2008) FL 23/1 FAC 2*
Notts Co *(Loaned on 24/9/2009) FL 7 Others 1*
Bristol Rov *(Loaned on 15/2/2010) FL 17*

JONES Darren Lee
Born: Newport, 28 August 1983
Height: 6'0" **Weight:** 12.6
International Honours: W: Yth; Sch
Centre-back Darren quickly established himself in the Hereford line-up and missed very few games during the season. A wholehearted player who was particularly powerful in the air, he seemed determined to make the most of his opportunity of moving up from the Blue Square Premier and gave everything to the cause. Darren regularly showed off a trademark, raking long pass from the back and also proved a threat from set-piece situations with some useful goals. Was out of contract in the summer.
Bristol C *(From trainee on 22/9/2000) FL 1+1 Others 0+3 (Freed on 17/2/2004)*
Cheltenham T *(Loaned on 25/8/2003) FL 14/1*
Hereford U *(Free from Forest Green Rov, ex Newport Co, on 9/7/2009) FL 40+1/3 FLC 1 FAC 2 Others 3*

JONES David Frank Llwyd
Born: Southport, 4 November 1984
Height: 5'11" **Weight:** 10.10
Club Honours: FAYC '03; Ch '09
International Honours: E: U21-1; Yth
The Wolverhampton midfield playmaker was a substitute at Wigan early in the season and played twice in the Carling Cup. A knee problem then kept him on the sidelines and he returned for the second half of a match in January, coincidentally against Wigan. An FA Cup goal boosted him, and he had a fine spell in which he was not overawed by some of the leading midfield players in the League. David scored the winner against Tottenham, after a splendid team move. His awareness and his ability to try something different kept him in the side for the last 16 matches.
Manchester U (From trainee on 18/7/2003) FLC 2+1 FAC 1
Preston NE (Loaned on 3/8/2005) FL 21+3/3 FLC 1
Derby Co (£1,000,000 on 17/11/2006) P/FL 38+4/7 FLC 1 FAC 2 Others 0+2
Wolverhampton W (£1,200,000 on 11/6/2008) P/FL 47+7/5 FLC 2+1 FAC 3+1/1

JONES Gary Roy
Born: Birkenhead, 3 June 1977
Height: 5'10" **Weight:** 12.0
Rochdale's all-time appearance record holder continued to pile up the milestones, becoming the first Dale player to reach 350 League and 400 appearances in all senior games in the course of the season. More importantly he finally led Dale to promotion from the bottom division at the 36th attempt. His never-say-die attitude in the middle of the park was never better illustrated than at Accrington when, with Dale 2-0 down in the last half-hour, the skipper blasted home his first brace for two years to transform a game that Dale went on to win 4-2. In the process he added another milestone, as the first Rochdale midfielder to score 50 League goals. He was also voted into the PFA League Two 'Team of the Year'.
Swansea C (Signed from Caernarfon T on 11/7/1997) FL 3+5 FLC 0+1
Rochdale (Free on 15/1/1998) FL 123+17/22 FLC 4+1 FAC 6+3 Others 7+2/3
Barnsley (£175,000 on 30/11/2001) FL 56/2 FLC 1
Rochdale (Free on 13/11/2003) FL 236+3/30 FLC 6 FAC 12 Others 12

JONES James (Jamie) Lewis
Born: Kirkby, 18 February 1989
Height: 6'2" **Weight:** 14.4
Jamie is a highly-rated Leyton Orient goalkeeper who commands his area

well and makes difficult saves seem easy. Jamie has already made 50 first team appearances and seems set for a big future in the game.
Everton (From trainee on 4/7/2007)
Leyton Orient (Free on 8/8/2008) FL 56 FLC 1 Others 4

JONES Kenwyne Joel
Born: Point Fortin, Trinidad, 5 October 1984
Height: 6'2" **Weight:** 13.6
International Honours: Trinidad & Tobago: 45; U21
Having been Sunderland's top scorer in his two previous seasons with them, the Trinidad & Tobago international had to be content with being second highest behind the prolific Darren Bent this time round. The two worked together well, at one point Bent inviting Kenwyne to take a second penalty in a big win over Wolves, although that did not go down well with boss Steve Bruce despite the

successful conversion. More commonly, Bent fed off Kenwyne's ability to win balls in the air. Effective in his own box when defending corners, Kenwyne attracted immense media speculation in the January transfer window as Liverpool were rumoured to be seeking his signature but, as always, the player kept a dignified silence and went on to enjoy the second half of the season, making his 100th appearance for Sunderland in the final home game against Manchester United. He had made his debut against them in September 2007.
Southampton (Signed from W Connection, Trinidad on 20/5/2004) P/FL 44+27/19 FLC 4/1 FAC 2+2/2 Others 1
Sheffield Wed (Loaned on 17/12/2004) FL 7/7
Stoke C (Loaned on 14/2/2005) FL 13/3
Sunderland (£6,000,000 + on 30/8/2007) PL 82+12/26 FLC 4/1 FAC 2+1/1

Kenwyn Jones

JONES Michael (Mike) David
Born: Birkenhead, 15 August 1987
Height: 5'8" **Weight:** 10.8
Mike is renowned for his trickery, pace, and ability to beat defenders on either wing. Of his five goals for Bury over the season, the most notable were two superb free kicks at home and away to Hereford. Despite not quite having the same influence as in the previous season, without former fellow winger Elliot Bennett, Mike was consistent when called upon. He received a very harsh red card at home to Burton.
Tranmere Rov (From trainee on 21/4/2006) FL 5+5/1 FAC 0+2 Others 0+1
Shrewsbury T (Loaned on 8/1/2007) FL 3+10/1 Others 0+1
Bury (Free on 5/8/2008) FL 82+5/9 FLC 2 FAC 2 Others 6/2

JONES Nathan Jason
Born: Rhondda, 28 May 1973
Height: 5'7" **Weight:** 10.12
Club Honours: Div 3 '01
This season has seen the veteran defender take a back seat on the pitch because of the form of his understudy Nathan Smith. As Yeovil's assistant manager, Nathan was a regular in the side until January but withdrew from the starting line-up when his deputy impressed. With almost 180 games for Yeovil, and nearly 500 career games in total, the Welsh left-back has oodles of experience. Was out of contract at the end of June.
Luton T (£10,000 from Merthyr Tydfil on 30/6/1995. Freed on 20/12/1995)
Southend U (Free from Numancia, Spain on 5/8/1997) FL 82+17/2 FLC 6+2 FAC 3+1/1 Others 0+3
Scarborough (Loaned on 25/3/1999) FL 8+1
Brighton & Hove A (Free on 7/7/2000) FL 109+50/7 FLC 5+3/1 FAC 6+1 Others 8+1
Yeovil T (Free on 6/7/2005) FL 140+15/2 FLC 6 FAC 8 Others 7+1

JONES Paul
Born: Maidstone, 28 June 1986
Height: 6'3" **Weight:** 13.1
International Honours: E: SP-1
Paul continued with another impressive season and must have saved Exeter at least ten points by his performances. The goalkeeper's command and authority gave his defence confidence. He put him some 'Man of the Match' displays and no Grecians' fan will forget his save from Huddersfield's Gary Roberts on the final day of the season, so important in avoiding relegation.
Exeter C (From trainee at Leyton Orient on 6/7/2005) FL 72 FLC 2 FAC 1 Others 1

JONES Philip (Phil) Anthony
Born: Preston, 21 February 1992
Height: 5'11" **Weight:** 11.2
International Honours: E: Yth
Phil, who was blooded slowly in the Carling Cup, was brought in for the FA Cup tie at Aston Villa and began to look a real prospect for Blackburn. It was the lack of any other centre-back that brought him into the side, against Chelsea and Didier Drogba, at the end of March. He played superbly, was judged 'Man of the Match' and remained in the side for the remainder of the season. A calm player, with no fear of the opposition, he is extremely competitive, jumps well and gets great distance on his headers. Phil is a ferocious tackler with great timing and the speed to cope with fast forwards.
Blackburn Rov (From trainee on 12/10/2009) PL 7+2 FLC 2 FAC 1

JONES Richard (Richie) Glynn
Born: Manchester, 26 September 1986
Height: 6'0" **Weight:** 11.0
Club Honours: FAYC '03; FLC '06
International Honours: E: Yth
The central midfield player struggled at times in his second season at Hartlepool. After a successful first year at the club, this did not go quite so well for the former Manchester United trainee. Briefly transfer listed in the close season, he settled his differences and started in the first team. Although a permanent squad member he could not win an automatic place and was often among the substitutes. Not renowned as a scorer, he excelled himself in February in a 4-1 win over Carlisle with two well-taken goals. Released by Pool at the end of the season, it is understood that several clubs have long been interested in signing him.
Manchester U (From trainee on 4/11/2004) FLC 2+2 FAC 1
Colchester U (Loaned on 27/10/2006) FL 0+6
Barnsley (Loaned on 12/2/2007) FL 1+3
Yeovil T (Loaned on 14/8/2007) FL 6+3 Others 1+1
Hartlepool U (Free on 23/7/2008) FL 58+11/7 FLC 4 FAC 4+1

JONES Robert (Rob) William
Born: Stockton, 30 November 1979
Height: 6'7" **Weight:** 12.2
Club Honours: SLC '07
By his own admission, Scunthorpe's record signing found the switch from the Scottish Premier League to the English Championship to be a big one.

A towering left-sided centre-half, he responded well to being given the captain's armband in September, leading his team to some good wins. Turned in several solid displays, particularly at home, but was exposed away from Glanford Park against pace and movement on the bigger pitches. Remained a regular in the side but lost his place after the arrival of Stockport captain Michael Raynes in February which, combined with niggling injuries, meant he appeared only once in the closing three months.
Stockport Co (Signed from Gateshead on 9/4/2003) FL 14+2/2 FLC 2 Others 1
Macclesfield T (Loaned on 31/10/2003) FL 1
Grimsby T (Free on 30/7/2004) FL 56+4/5 FLC 3 FAC 2 Others 3
Hibernian (Signed on 8/6/2006) SL 96/8 SLC 6/3 SC 10/1 Others 6
Scunthorpe U (Signed on 9/7/2009) FL 28/1 FLC 2 FAC 2

JONES Stephen (Steve) Graham
Born: Derry, 25 October 1976
Height: 5'4" **Weight:** 10.9
International Honours: NI: 29
Steve, who was signed from Burnley on a two-year contract in July, produced numerous hard-working performances for Walsall, giving many left-backs a hard time with his pace and control. His presence coincided with the club's best spells, although a niggling injury meant that he missed many games. He was instrumental in turning a 2-0 deficit at Wycombe into a 3-2 win playing just behind the front two. During a run of eight goals in 11 games, he bagged a brace at home to Exeter; one from 30 yards after advancing from the half-way line, and was denied a hat-trick by a goal-line clearance.
Blackpool (Free from Chadderton on 30/10/1995)
Bury (Free on 23/8/1996. Free to Sligo Rov during 1997 close season)
Crewe Alex (£75,000 + from Leigh RMI, ex Bray W, Chorley, on 4/7/2001) FL 122+37/39 FLC 5+1/4 FAC 4+1/1 Others 2+2/1
Rochdale (Loaned on 5/2/2002) FL 6+3/1
Burnley (Free on 1/8/2006) FL 38+20/6 FLC 3+1 FAC 1+1
Crewe Alex (Loaned on 27/3/2008) FL 2+2/1
Huddersfield T (Loaned on 17/10/2008) FL 2+2
Bradford C (Loaned on 27/11/2008) FL 25+2/3 FAC 1
Walsall (Free on 10/7/2009) FL 25+5/9 FLC 1 FAC 2/1 Others 0+1

Steve Jones

11/3/1999) PL 49+4 FLC 1+3 FAC 7
Cambridge U *(Loaned on 4/10/2002)*
FL 11 Others 3
Burnley *(Free on 23/7/2007) P/FL 69+4*
FLC 9 FAC 1

Stephen Jordan

JONES William (Billy)
Born: Shrewsbury, 24 March 1987
Height: 5'11" **Weight:** 13.0
International Honours: E: Yth
Billy missed only two of Preston's League games last season, one through illness, as he firmly cemented his place as first choice right-back and moved beyond 250 career games despite being only 23. His upbringing at Crewe is still evident, as he is comfortable on the ball and supports the attack well both on the flank and when popping up unnoticed in the box, which brought him four goals. A four-game spell as cover in central midfield in the New Year was less successful and Billy's confidence seemed to suffer for a time before he came back strongly in the final month of the season.
Crewe Alex *(From trainee on 13/7/2004) FL 127+5/8 FLC 5 FAC 2/1 Others 4*
Preston NE *(Signed on 12/7/2007) FL 114+3/7 FLC 5 FAC 3 Others 2*

JONES William (Billy) Kenneth
Born: Chatham, 26 March 1983
Height: 6'0" **Weight:** 11.5
In his third season at Crewe, Billy started as captain and played in the first ten games in the League, Carling Cup and Johnstone's Paint Trophy. He then suffered injury problems and only added one substitute appearance to his total. The competent defender left Crewe in the close season but hopes to further his career elsewhere.
Leyton Orient *(From trainee on 10/7/2001) FL 68+4 FLC 2 FAC 3+1 Others 0+1*
Kidderminster Hrs *(Free on 7/1/2005) FL 10+2 (Free to Exeter C on 6/7/2005)*
Crewe Alex *(£65,000 on 29/5/2007) FL 70+1/8 FLC 4 FAC 5 Others 4/1*

JORDAN Stephen Robert
Born: Warrington, 6 March 1982
Height: 6'0" **Weight:** 11.13
Usually Burnley's left-back, Stephen turned out at centre-half in the season's opening game, but the arrival of Andre Bikey allowed him to resume normal duties afterwards. He was ever-present in the League up to Christmas and on his day, as in the home game against Arsenal when Theo Walcott was hardly allowed a kick, he could be outstanding. Unfortunately, excellent performances in defence were rare for the Clarets this season, and Stephen was frequently caught out by the pace of the Premier League opposition. Injury and then the signing of Danny Fox meant that he rarely featured in the second half of the campaign, and he was released at the end of it on the expiry of his contract.
Manchester C *(From trainee on*

[JORDI GOMEZ] GARCIA-PENCHE Jordi Gomez
Born: Barcelona, Spain, 24 May 1985
Height: 5'10" **Weight:** 11.9
International Honours: Spain: Yth
Roberto Martinez's first signing for Wigan, having played under the manager while on loan at Swansea. Recruited on a three-year deal from Espanyol, the Spaniard is a creative midfielder with good technical ability. Jordi Gomez made his debut in the opening game and started regularly in the first half of the season before losing his place at the turn of the year. He is rarely rushed into doing anything, even in tight situations, and remains cool and

calm on the ball, at times making a difficult game look easy. Fitting in the centre of a five-man midfield, he sometimes struggled to adapt to the pace and the physicality of the Premier League. He netted his only goal in the home match against Birmingham and will hope to improve after a tough baptism in the top flight.
Swansea C (Loaned from Espanyol, Spain, ex Barcelona B, on 4/8/2008) FL 38+6/12 FLC 3+1/2 FAC 3
Wigan Ath (£1,700,000 from Espanyol, Spain on 19/6/2009) PL 11+12/1 FAC 2

[JORDI LOPEZ] LOPEZ FELPETO Jordi
Born: Barcelona, Spain, 28 February 1981
Height: 6'0" **Weight:** 12.2
Jordi Lopez is an experienced Spanish central midfielder who previously played under Swansea boss Paulo Sousa at Queens Park Rangers. He missed most of the pre-season training and when he was introduced to first team action, played in a Swans' team stripped of regular players. Inevitably, he took some time to settle and in February was sidelined with an ankle injury that effectively ended his season.
Queens Park Rgrs (Free from Real Mallorca, Spain, following trials at Portsmouth, Blackburn Rov, Birmingham C, ex Barcelona, Real Madrid, Sevilla, Racing Santander, on 24/2/2009) FL 7+3/1
Swansea C (Signed on 16/7/2009) FL 7+5 FLC 2 FAC 1

JORGENSEN Claus Bech
Born: Holstebro, Denmark, 27 April 1979
Height: 5'11" **Weight:** 11.0
International Honours: Faroe Islands: 10
Claus joined Port Vale in August and played for nothing, as he was hoping to put himself in the shop window. The midfield player made his debut as a substitute in a 0-0 draw at Bradford and made a further four appearances from the bench. The highest profile of these was during the 2-0 Carling cup victory over Sheffield Wednesday. He has the ability to put his foot on the ball but turned down the offer of a short-term contract and left at the end of August. He later joined Blue Square North Fleetwood and had a trial at Cheltenham.
Bournemouth (Free from AC Horsens, Denmark on 12/7/1999) FL 77+10/14 FLC 6/1 FAC 6 Others 1+1
Bradford C (Free on 23/7/2001) FL 41+9/12 FLC 2+1 FAC 1

Coventry C (Free on 5/8/2003) FL 30+22/6 FLC 3+2 FAC 0+5
Bournemouth (Loaned on 23/1/2004) FL 16+1
Blackpool (Signed on 31/8/2006) FL 72+28/6 FAC 1+5 Others 4
Port Vale (Free on 14/8/2009) FL 0+4 FLC 0+1

JOSEPH Marc Ellis
Born: Leicester, 12 November 1976
Height: 6'0" **Weight:** 12.10
International Honours: Antigua & Barbuda: 3
Marc is capable of playing all along the Rotherham back line and actually did so at one time or another, however briefly in some cases. Filled in handily when a defensive vacancy arose and, when not called on to start, was always first choice defensive cover from the substitutes' bench until dropping out of the picture altogether in the final couple of months of the season. He was released at the end of his contract.
Cambridge U (From trainee on 23/5/1995) FL 136+17 FLC 7 FAC 5+2 Others 7+1
Peterborough U (Free on 3/7/2001) FL 60+1/2 FLC 3 FAC 6 Others 3
Hull C (£40,000 on 22/11/2002) FL 81+8/1 FLC 2 FAC 3 Others 1
Bristol C (Loaned on 10/11/2005) FL 3
Blackpool (Signed on 10/1/2006) FL 18+6 Others 1
Rotherham U (Free on 8/7/2007) FL 58+18/4 FLC 2+1 FAC 1+1 Others 3+1

JOYCE Ian Francis
Born: Kinnelon, New Jersey, USA, 12 July 1985
Height: 6'3" **Weight:** 13.7
A popular and capable American goalkeeper, Ian was again understudy to Steve Mildenhall at Southend, in his second campaign at Roots Hall. Ian grabbed some rare opportunities to deputize for the experienced Mildenhall, coming in over the Christmas programme when the number one was sidelined with an injured back. Frustrated by sitting on the bench, Ian was released from his contract in March, allowing him to return to the United States with Colorado Rapids.
Watford (Free from Seton Hall Pirates, USA on 18/10/2007)
Southend U (Free on 11/7/2008) FL 4+1

JOYCE Luke James
Born: Bolton, 9 July 1987
Height: 5'9" **Weight:** 11.4
Luke played at right-back for Accrington at the start of the season before moving into a midfield role

which he made his own for much of the time. Deeply committed and calm on the ball, he is regarded as one of the club's better players.
Wigan Ath (Trainee) FAC 0+1
Carlisle U (Free on 23/3/2006) FL 12+14/2 FLC 0+1 Others 1
Accrington Stanley (Free on 2/7/2009) FL 36+5/1 FLC 2 FAC 2+1 Others 3+1

JUDGE Alan Christopher
Born: Dublin, 11 November 1988
Height: 5'6" **Weight:** 11.3
International Honours: RoI: U21-11
After a successful loan spell with Plymouth during 2008-09 Alan returned to Blackburn and featured regularly for the club during pre-season, including a friendly against Italian giants Roma. He was delighted to rejoin Argyle on loan for the duration of the campaign. Alan continued to feature regularly in midfield, showing his versatility by being able to play on both flanks. He added another three goals to his tally, including his first double in senior football with two in an impressive 4–1 win over Reading in December. However, his work for the Pilgrims could not prevent them from being relegated. He continued to represent the Republic of Ireland under-21s during 2009-10.
Blackburn Rov (From trainee on 24/11/2006) FLC 0+1 FAC 1
Plymouth Arg (Loaned on 30/1/2009) FL 15+2/2
Plymouth Arg (Loaned on 4/8/2009) FL 28+9/5 FLC 1 FAC 2

JULIAN Alan John
Born: Ashford, Middlesex, 11 March 1983
Height: 6'2" **Weight:** 13.5
International Honours: NI: U21-1; Yth
An immensely likeable character with a penchant for the more acrobatic save, Alan was handed Gillingham's goalkeeper's jersey after an excellent pre-season campaign before being replaced between the posts by Simon Royce after a handful of starts. He returned to the team after Royce was injured in a car accident in December and never looked back, seizing the opportunity with both hands and posting a string of impressive match-winning displays. His finest moment came in the home clash with Brighton in April, when he saved Glenn Murray's late penalty to salvage a vital point.
Brentford (From trainee on 4/7/2001) FL 16 FLC 0+1 Others 2 (Free on 1/2/2005)
Gillingham (Free from Stevenage Borough on 17/7/2008) FL 34 FLC 1 FAC 2 Others 2

K

KABBA Steven (Steve)

Born: Lambeth, 7 March 1981
Height: 5'10" **Weight:** 11.12
The experienced striker joined Brentford from Watford just before the start of the season and was a regular in the squad until November. Despite some nice touches he did not pose much of a goal threat and in November he joined Burton on loan for the rest of the season. The deal had been initially for one month, but he stayed until the end of the season after falling out of favour at Griffin Park. Showed all his old skills in a promising start, but was later hampered by a knee problem. Was out of contract in the summer.
Crystal Palace (From trainee on 29/6/1999) FL 2+8/1 FLC 0+1
Luton T (Loaned on 28/3/2002) FL 0+3
Grimsby T (Loaned on 23/8/2002) FL 13/6 FLC 1
Sheffield U (£250,000 on 15/11/2002) P/FL 46+32/18 FLC 1 FAC 6/4 Others 1+2/1
Watford (£500,000 on 26/1/2007) P/FL 13+12/1 FLC 1 FAC 3+1
Blackpool (Loaned on 11/7/2008) FL 12+5/2
Oldham Ath (Loaned on 26/2/2009) FL 7+1
Brentford (Free on 6/8/2009) FL 3+7 FLC 1 Others 1
Burton A (Loaned on 26/11/2009) FL 18+5/6 FAC 1

KABOUL Younes

Born: St-Julien-en-Genevois, France, 4 January 1986
Height: 6'4" **Weight:** 13.9
Club Honours: FLC '08
International Honours: France: U21-18
Younes started the season strongly at Portsmouth as the Blues' first choice centre-half, putting in strong and committed performances, and dominating both penalty areas with consummate ease. He scored impressive goals against Arsenal and Bolton, as well as a vital injury-time equaliser at Sunderland. An early contender for Pompey's 'Player of The Season' award, Younes was snapped up by Tottenham in the January transfer window. He was the last in a line of Portsmouth players signed for Spurs by Harry Redknapp, and the second youth player to re-sign for the club. Many Spurs' fans were sceptical and Younes' chances were limited. However, as Tottenham approached their crucial end of season

he got his chance and played more as a replacement at right-back for Vedran Corluka, than he did in central defence, where he is more comfortable. Younes gave several significant performances in crucial games, such as the League wins over Arsenal, Chelsea and Manchester City, all at right-back. As a central defender he has strength and the desired aerial ability, and at right-back he has shown his pace to good effect, coupled with excellent passing and crossing skills. It was he who provided the cross-shot that led to Peter Crouch's crucial winner at Manchester City and qualification for the Champions League.
Tottenham H (£8,000,000 from Auxerre, France on 12/7/2007) PL 19+2/3 FLC 3+1 Others 3/1
Portsmouth (£5,000,000 on 12/8/2008) PL 36+3/4 FLC 5 FAC 3+1 Others 1+1/1
Tottenham H (Signed on 30/1/2010) PL 8+2

KADAR Tamas

Born: Veszprem, Hungary, 14 March 1990
Height: 6'2" **Weight:** 11.9
Club Honours: Ch '10
International Honours: Hungary: U21-3; Yth
Having recovered from a broken leg which prematurely ended his 2008-09 season, Tamas played in four first team friendlies for Newcastle, but spent most of this season on the bench. Comfortable on the ball, though as yet appearing to lack self-confidence, he made his first team debut in the Carling Cup tie against Huddersfield in August and delivered a fine performance in the FA Cup tie at Plymouth, both in his favoured position of centre-back. He was also used occasionally at full-back. Tamas has never yet been on a losing side for the club and was called up to the Hungarian under-21 side for several European Championship qualifiers.
Newcastle U (Signed from Zalaegerszegi, Hungary on 18/1/2008) FL 6+7 FLC 1 FAC 2

KAKUTA Gael

Born: Lille, France, 21 June 1991
Height: 5'8" **Weight:** 10.3
International Honours: France: Yth
'So this is what all the fuss is about' was the reaction of the football world when super-talented starlet Gael made his Chelsea debut as a substitute against Wolves and immediately illuminated a dark and damp November afternoon. His debut had been delayed by a four-month ban, imposed by UEFA, which had been suspended by the Court of Arbitration for Sport pending an appeal.

His transfer was controversial as Chelsea had been accused of an illegal approach by his previous club, Lens. As a consequence, the Blues were hit by a transfer embargo imposed by UEFA: this was subsequently overturned. In December, Gael made his first start against Apoel Nicosia in the Champions League. He had earlier made headlines when he played a leading role in helping Chelsea to their first FA Youth Cup final for 47 years in 2008 and starred as France reached the European under-17 Championship final. A speedy left-winger with dazzling footwork, he can also play as an attacking central midfielder. Frank Arnesen and his scouts are tasked with scouring the globe to bring the best young talent to Stamford Bridge and Gael, first of the new crop, is poised to make a breakthrough.
Chelsea (From trainee, ex RC Lens, on 4/7/2008) PL 0+1 FLC 0+1 FAC 0+1 Others 1

KALINIC Nikola

Born: Solin, Croatia, 5 January 1988
Height: 6'2" **Weight:** 13.3
International Honours: Croatia: 3; U21-3; Yth
The expensive young Croatian was nursed into first team action because Blackburn manager Sam Allardyce believes overseas players need to acclimatise to the Premiership. Early appearances hinted at the misfortune that was to dog his season and although he displayed a capacity to get into scoring positions, his bad luck was remarkable. He struck the woodwork five times, had efforts at Old Trafford and White Hart Lane ruled out, incorrectly as replays confirmed, had Seb Larsson inadvertently stop on the line his last-minute header at Birmingham, narrowly missed an injury-time winner against Liverpool and saw Martin Fulop produce an incredible save at the same stage of the game against Sunderland. He was also forced to play as a lone striker in a 4-5-1 system that does not suit his style but won the crowd over with his non-stop endeavour, his ability at holding the ball until help arrived and his skill as a pure footballer. His two goals at Villa Park in the semi-final of the Carling Cup, one against Chelsea in the previous round, his beautifully struck opening goal against Bolton and his late header against Wigan hinted at a scoring ability that should make him a valuable member of the team.
Blackburn Rov (£6,000,000 from Hajduk Split, Croatia, via loans at Istra 1961, Sibenek, on 10/8/2009) PL 14+12/2 FLC 6/4 FAC 1/1

KALLIO Toni
Born: Tampere, Finland, 9 August 1978
Height: 6'4" **Weight:** 13.5
International Honours: Finland: 48
Unable to get a game at Fulham, the
Finnish defender spent much of the
season on loan at Sheffield United
following some impressive early season
performances in central defence for
Fulham reserves, where he managed a
couple of goals against Portsmouth and
Chelsea. Joining the Blades on a one-
month loan in late November as
defensive cover, after two competent
appearances at left-back his loan was
extended before being then recalled
to Fulham. His only first team
appearances for Fulham, both at left-
back, came in January when injuries to
both full-backs led to him making a
substitute appearance at Blackburn
followed by a start at left-back the
following week in the FA Cup tie at
Accrington. Then, with the loan signing
of Nicky Shorey completed at the end
of January, the Finn was allowed to
return to Bramall Lane in February, on
loan to the end of the season. However,
after six games, one at centre-back,
injury meant another return to Fulham.
Was out of contract in the summer.
*Fulham (Free from Young Boys of
Berne, Switzerland, ex TPV Tampere, FC
Jazz - loan, HJK Helsinki, Molde FK, on
31/1/2008) PL 2+2 FLC 2 FAC 1*
Sheffield U (Loaned on 26/11/2009) FL 2
Sheffield U (Loaned on 1/2/2010) FL 6

KALOU Salomon
Born: Oume, Ivory Coast, 5 August
1985
Height: 5'9" **Weight:** 10.10
Club Honours: FLC '07; FAC '07, '09,
'10; CS '09; PL '10
International Honours: Ivory Coast: 27
The Ivory Coast striker began on a high
note by scoring the winning kick in the
Community Shield penalty shoot-out
and ended in style by forcing his way
back in for the last three matches of the
League campaign when Chelsea
switched to a three-pronged attack. The
Blues responded with 17 goals as they
surged to a Premier League scoring
record. Salomon's four goals included
his first Chelsea hat-trick, against Stoke.
This gave Salomon his first Premier
League winners' medal followed, seven
days later, by his third FA Cup winners'
medal at the new Wembley. He also
scored consistently before Christmas in
Carling Cup and Champions League
competitions. Having signed a new
three-year contract, he went to the
World Cup with compatriot Didier
Drogba in good heart following such a
tremendous season.

Chelsea *(£8,000,000 from Feyenoord,
Holland, ex Excelsior - loan, on
13/7/2006) PL 71+42/26 FLC 10+5/7
FAC 10+10/5 Others 18+20/5*

KALVENES Christian
Born: Bergen, Norway, 8 March 1977
Height: 6'0" **Weight:** 11.11
With first Stephen Jordan and then
Danny Fox monopolising the left-back
spot for Burnley, Christian was a rare
starter, although he appeared in the
opener at Stoke and then twice in
January when Jordan was injured. A
capable defender, he never really had
the chance to prove himself at the top
level and he left the club in April,
retiring from football to pursue a
business career in his native Norway.
*Dundee U (Signed from SK Brann
Bergen, Norway, ex Asane, Sogndal, on
2/8/2006) SL 47+1/2 SLC 6/1 SC 2*
*Burnley (Free on 7/7/2008) P/FL 24+3/1
FLC 3+1 FAC 5 Others 3*

KAMARA Diomansy Mehdi
Moustapha
Born: Paris, France, 8 November 1980
Height: 6'0" **Weight:** 11.5
International Honours: Senegal: 49
The Senegalese striker struggled to gain
a regular place for Fulham in the early
weeks of the season but a fine
performance in the Europa League tie in
Sofia was capped with a well-taken
opportunist goal. After a couple of
further substitute appearances, he
regained a place playing alongside
Bobby Zamora, a six-match run
producing two further goals. A skilful
player who has excellent ball control
and good positional sense, he was
unfortunate to suffer an injury early in
November after which he made one
further substitute appearance at
Tottenham in January. A few days later
he was loaned to Glasgow Celtic for the
remainder of the campaign.
*Portsmouth (Loaned from Modena,
Italy on 1/9/2004) PL 15+10/4 FLC 2/2
FAC 2*
*West Bromwich A (£1,500,000 from
Modena, Italy, ex Red Star 93,
Catanzaro, on 5/8/2005) P/FL 54+6/21
FLC 3+2/1 FAC 3+1/2 Others 3/1*
*Fulham (£6,000,000 on 16/7/2007) PL
25+24/10 FLC 1+1/1 FAC 0+2 Others
3+1/2*
*Glasgow Celtic (Loaned on 1/2/2010)
SL 8+1/2 SC 1*

KAMDJO Clovis
Born: Cameroon, 15 December 1990
Height: 5'11" **Weight:** 12.2
International Honours: Cameroon:
Yth
The young central defender joined

Barnet on the eve of the season,
following a successful trial after being
released by Reading. He was thrown in
at the deep end, making his debut at
Torquay in August, but showed no
nerves and produced a fine display in a
1-0 away win. Injury in November
limited his first team chances in much
of the second half of the season,
though when called upon he performed
well and could have a bright future at
the club.
*Barnet (From trainee at Reading on
6/8/2009) FL 14+1 FAC 0+1 Others 1*

KAMUDIMBA KALALA
Jean-Paul
Born: Lubumbashi, DR Congo, 16
March 1982
Height: 5'10" **Weight:** 12.1
International Honours: DR Congo: 8
Another player who came back to
Yeovil, the Congolese midfield general
endeared himself once more to the
supporters with his all-action battling
style. Sitting deep in the middle of the
park, his ability to break up attacks and
start ones of his own make him a vital
cog in the team's wheel. More than 70
games in Yeovil colours have produced
just two goals, but his energy and drive
have lifted the team on numerous
occasions.
*Grimsby T (Free from OGC Nice, France
on 25/7/2005) FL 14+7/5 FLC 3/1 FAC 1*
*Yeovil T (Free on 20/7/2006) FL 35+3/1
FLC 1 Others 0+3*
*Oldham Ath (Free on 3/7/2007) FL
14+6 FLC 2/1 FAC 2 Others 2*
*Grimsby T (Loaned on 31/10/2008) FL
21/2 FAC 1*
Yeovil T (Free on 21/8/2009) FL 32+2/1

KANDOL Tresor Osmar
Born: Banga, DR Congo, 30 August
1981
Height: 6'2" **Weight:** 11.7
International Honours: DR Congo: 1
It was a frustrating season for the
Leeds' striker who did not start a single
League One match. Tresor marked his
first appearance for more than a year
with a goal in a Johnstone's Paint
Trophy victory against Darlington and
forced his way back into the squad. He
came off the bench ten times, scoring
the final goals in successive 4-0 wins
against Bristol Rovers and Yeovil. But he
was also sent off for an altercation after
the final whistle against the Glovers and
was handed a three-match ban. He
missed several games because of a
hamstring injury and family problems.
To cap it all he picked up what is
thought to be the quickest red card in
the club's history, dismissed 20 seconds
after going on as an injury-time

substitute at Norwich in March.
Luton T *(From trainee on 26/9/1998) FL 9+12/3 FLC 3+1/2 Others 0+1*
Cambridge U *(Free on 24/8/2001) FL 2+2*
Bournemouth *(Free on 12/10/2001) FL 3+9 FAC 0+2 Others 1/1 (Freed during 2002 close season)*
Darlington *(Loaned from Dagenham & Redbridge on 11/11/2005) FL 6+1/2*
Barnet *(£50,000 from Dagenham & Redbridge, ex Chesham U, Purfleet, Thurrock, on 30/1/2006) FL 27+2/10 FLC 1+1/2 FAC 0+1/2 Others 2/3*
Leeds U *(£200,000 on 23/11/2006) FL 43+26/14 FLC 2 FAC 2+1/1 Others 2+3/1*
Millwall *(Loaned on 7/8/2008) FL 16+2/8 FLC 0+1 FAC 2 Others 1*
Charlton Ath *(Loaned on 30/1/2009) FL 10+3/2*

KANE Anthony (Tony)
Michael
Born: Belfast, 29 August 1987
Height: 5'11" **Weight:** 11.0
International Honours: Rol: U21-5; NI: U21-5; Yth
Released by Blackburn in the summer, Tony signed for Carlisle, having been on loan there towards the end of 2008-09. The versatile full-back had a loan spell with Darlington early on in the season, making four consecutive starts, before returning to Brunton Park. He made his first League start at Charlton on Easter Monday, which was followed by two substitute appearances later in the month, and he will be hoping to enjoy more first team action next year.
Blackburn Rov *(From trainee on 24/11/2004)*
Stockport Co *(Loaned on 2/11/2006) FL 4*
Stockport Co *(Loaned on 9/10/2008) FL 3*
Carlisle U *(Free on 10/2/2009) FL 7+6 Others 1*
Darlington *(Loaned on 18/9/2009) FL 4*

KANU Nwankwo
Born: Owerri, Nigeria, 1 August 1976
Height: 6'4" **Weight:** 13.3
Club Honours: CS '99; FAC '02, '03, '08; PL '02, '04
International Honours: Nigeria: 82; U23 (OLYM '96); Yth (World-U17 '93)
Almost considered royalty in his native Nigeria, it seems even Nwankwo cannot evade the inevitable approach of 'Father Time'. Overflowing with class and skill, he remains one of the most talented members on Portsmouth's roster. The striker is one of the most effective 'off the bench' weapons in world football – an expert in holding up the ball and drawing a foul. His unprecedented

ability to keep the ball glued to his foot is coupled with an uncanny knack for being in the right place at the right time, as seen with his vital last-minute winning goal against Hull. However, ageing limbs seem finally to have caught up with the 33-year-old. The most decorated player in African football history struggled to keep a regular place in Portsmouth's squad and was out of contract at the end of the season.
Arsenal *(£4,500,000 from Inter Milan, Italy, ex Fed Works, Iwuanyanwu National, Ajax, on 4/2/1999) PL 63+56/30 FLC 8/4 FAC 5+11/3 Others 28+26/7*
West Bromwich A *(Free on 30/7/2004) PL 38+15/7 FLC 1+1/1 FAC 3/1*
Portsmouth *(Free on 18/8/2006) PL 54+47/17 FLC 0+6/3 FAC 5+5/4 Others 2+3/1*

KANYUKA Patrick (Pat)
Elamenji
Born: Kinshasa, DR Congo, 19 July 1987
Height: 6'2" **Weight:** 13.10
Central defender Pat joined the Cobblers on a short-term contract following his release from Swindon. It was during Northampton's transitional period and although Pat showed ability and enthusiasm the club needed to turn to experience and his contract was not extended beyond Christmas.
Queens Park Rgrs *(From juniors on 19/7/2004) FL 8+4 FLC 1+1 FAC 1*
Swindon T *(Free on 18/1/2008) FL 19+1/1 FAC 1 Others 2*
Northampton T *(Free on 23/10/2009) FL 3 FAC 1 Others 1*

KAPO Obou Narcisse Olivier
Born: Abidjan, Ivory Coast, 27 September 1980
Height: 6'0" **Weight:** 12.2
International Honours: France: 9
After missing the opening two months of the season through injury, Olivier found first team opportunities limited in his second season at Wigan. Under new management, Olivier was to make just one substitute appearance at Portsmouth. A gifted player who can play on the left side of midfield or in a more advanced role behind the striker, the French international has so much natural ability that the game looks too easy for him at times. He was vocal in his desire to secure a switch during the January transfer window and his wish was granted when he joined French side Boulogne on a six-month loan.
Birmingham C *(£3,000,000 from Juventus, Italy, ex Auxerre, AS Monaco - loan, Levante - loan, on 13/7/2007) PL 22+4/5*

Wigan Ath *(£2,500,000 on 16/7/2008) PL 10+10/1 FLC 1/1 FAC 1*

KARACAN Jem Paul
Born: Lewisham, 21 February 1989
Height: 5'10" **Weight:** 11.6
International Honours: Turkey: U21-3; Yth
After spending much of the previous season out on loan, Jem returned to the Madejski to fight for a regular Reading place. He did so to good effect, making 30 appearances, plus a further 14 as a non-playing substitute. A tough and gritty midfielder, Jem contributed significantly, especially in the second half of the season. His 'Player of the Month' award came as early as August but Jem developed his all-round game under new manager Brian McDermott and enjoyed a long spell alongside Brian Howard and Brynjar Gunnarsson in central midfield. An Academy graduate and Turkish under-21 international, he was unlucky not to score what would have been his only goal of the season in the 3-0 win over Coventry. His shot took the slightest of deflections off Grzegorz Rasiak, who was credited with the score.
Reading *(From trainee on 6/7/2007) FL 34+8/1 FLC 1/1 FAC 5*
Bournemouth *(Loaned on 18/10/2007) FL 11+2/1 FAC 3/1 Others 1*
Millwall *(Loaned on 20/3/2008) FL 7*

KAVANAGH Graham
Anthony
Born: Dublin, 2 December 1973
Height: 5'10" **Weight:** 12.11
Club Honours: AMC '00; Ch '07
International Honours: Rol: 16; B-1; U21-9; Yth; Sch
For Graham, the season began with him primarily in a playing capacity and his last-minute equaliser at Morecambe in the first round kept Carlisle in the Johnstone's Paint Trophy. Gradually, his off-field role began to take precedence with his last playing appearance coming at Wembley in the Johnstone's Paint Trophy final. By the end of the campaign he had become assistant manager. If his playing days now seem to be numbered, he can look back on some fine performances, including the double strike that inspired the victory over Charlton and his midfield master class at MK Dons, where he set up all four United goals in their 4-3 victory.
Middlesbrough *(Signed from Home Farm on 16/8/1991) P/FL 22+13/3 FLC 1 FAC 2+2/1 Others 7*
Darlington *(Loaned on 25/2/1994) FL 5*
Stoke C *(£250,000 + on 13/9/1996) FL 198+8/35 FLC 16+2/7 FAC 6 Others 15/4*

Cardiff C *(£1,000,000 on 6/7/2001) FL 140+2/28 FLC 6+1 FAC 11/3 Others 5*
Wigan Ath *(Signed on 4/3/2005) P/FL 43+5 FLC 4+1 FAC 1+1*
Sunderland *(£500,000 on 31/8/2006) P/FL 10+4/1 FAC 1*
Sheffield Wed *(Loaned on 21/9/2007) FL 7/1 FLC 1*
Sheffield Wed *(Loaned on 31/1/2008) FL 14+2/1*
Carlisle U *(Free on 10/10/2008) FL 62+1/7 FLC 1+1 FAC 7/1 Others 5/3*

KAY Antony Roland
Born: Barnsley, 21 October 1982
Height: 5'11" **Weight:** 11.8
International Honours: E: Yth
The former Tranmere 'Player of the Year' was snapped up by some steel to Huddersfield's midfield. Antony did not disappoint with his no-nonsense approach as he became the main fulcrum of many attacking moves. He is always looking for the ball as he gets through a mountain of work to take a grip on midfield. With his willingness to get forward at every opportunity, he scored seven goals as the Terriers reached the play-offs.
Barnsley *(From trainee on 25/10/1999) FL 156+18/11 FLC 6 FAC 9/1 Others 8*
Tranmere Rov *(Free on 18/7/2007) FL 74+8/17 FLC 1 FAC 8/2 Others 5*
Huddersfield T *(Free on 2/7/2009) FL 38+2/6 FLC 2 FAC 3 Others 3*

KEANE Robert (Robbie) David
Born: Dublin, 8 July 1980
Height: 5'9" **Weight:** 11.10
Club Honours: FLC '08
International Honours: Rol: 99; B-1; Yth (UEFA-U18 '98)
The Irish captain made 25 appearances, scoring nine goals in all competitions for Tottenham, before being allowed to loan move to Glasgow Celtic for the latter part of the season. Four of Robbie's goals came in the 5-0 win over Burnley so his ratio in the remaining games was sparse by his standards. Robbie's contribution has always been about more than goals, as he tracks and tackles back to good effect. He can also play on the left of midfield and often fell back to that position after an attacking substitution. Robbie continues to skipper the Republic of Ireland and scored in the first leg of their tense World Cup play-off against France, which they lost in controversial circumstances. In his time at Celtic, Robbie established himself as a fans' favourite, scoring 16 goals in 19 games.
Wolverhampton W *(From trainee on 26/7/1997) FL 66+7/24 FLC 7+2/3 FAC 3+2/2*

Coventry C *(£6,000,000 on 20/8/1999) PL 30+1/12 FAC 3 (£13,000,000 to Inter Milan, Italy on 31/7/2000)*
Leeds U *(£12,000,000 from Inter Milan, Italy on 22/12/2000) PL 28+18/13 FLC 2/3 FAC 2 Others 6/3*
Tottenham H *(£7,000,000 on 31/8/2002) PL 158+39/80 FLC 14+5/7 FAC 15+4/11 Others 15+4/9*
Liverpool *(£20,300,000 on 29/7/2008) PL 17+3/5 FLC 0+1 FAC 1 Others 6+1/2*
Tottenham H *(£12,000,000 on 2/2/2009) PL 29+5/11 FLC 2+1/2 FAC 1+1/1*
Glasgow Celtic *(Loaned on 1/2/2010) SL 15+1/12 SC 2+1/4*

KEATES Dean Scott
Born: Walsall, 30 June 1978
Height: 5'6" **Weight:** 10.10
Club Honours: Div 2 '07
Battling midfielder Dean was just what Peterborough needed, or so the fans thought, but after Darren Ferguson left new boss Mark Cooper let him go to Wycombe and the team never controlled the midfield again. Dean is the warrior you need, never one to back out of a tackle, always looking to push forward and always talking. Arriving at Adams Park in the January transfer window, the central midfielder went straight into the side and had an impressive debut at Southend. A busy playmaker, with a good eye for a pass, he became the free-kick specialist in the side, laying on four goals. He lost his place for the final six games of the season, as the manager looked to halt a poor run, and was not offered a new contract.
Walsall *(From trainee on 14/8/1996) FL 125+34/9 FLC 15+1/1 FAC 10+4 Others 14+1/3*
Hull C *(Free on 23/8/2002) FL 45+5/4 FLC 1+1 Others 2*
Kidderminster Hrs *(Signed on 10/2/2004) FL 48+1/7 FLC 1 FAC 1 Others 1*
Lincoln C *(Free on 3/8/2005) FL 19+2/4 FLC 2 FAC 1*
Walsall *(Free on 31/1/2006) FL 50+3/15 FLC 2 FAC 2*
Peterborough U *(Free on 12/7/2007) FL 72+12/11 FLC 2+2 FAC 7+1*
Wycombe W *(Free on 21/1/2010) FL 13/1*

KEBE Jimmy Boubou
Born: Vitry-sur-Seine, France, 19 January 1984
Height: 6'2" **Weight:** 11.7
International Honours: Mali: 8
After a stuttering start, Jimmy burst into life under Brian McDermott. His electrifying pace and snappy dribbling took him past defenders on either flank,

though he seems to prefer the right. During McDermott's time as manager, Jimmy scored more goals in open play than anybody else. Two stand out. In the final game, against Preston, he dribbled past four defenders before beating the 'keeper. In execution if not in importance it was the 'Goal of the Season'. In the FA Cup tie at home to West Bromwich, Jimmy gave Reading the lead after only 9.7 seconds – the quickest ever Reading goal. Jimmy was runner-up in the supporters' 'Player of the Year' poll.
Reading *(Signed from RC Lens, France, ex Chateauroux - loan, Boulogne - loan, on 31/1/2008) P/FL 69+19/12 FAC 3+3/2 Others 2*

KEE Billy Rodney
Born: Loughborough, 1 December 1990
Height: 5'9" **Weight:** 11.3
International Honours: NI: U21-5; Yth
Popular young striker who signed on loan from Leicester and made 46 appearances over the course of the campaign for Accrington, notching up nine goals despite more than half of his appearances came from the bench. A stocky, hard-working forward who chases down all goalscoring opportunities in and around the box, he was also called up to the full Northern Ireland side during the season. Released by Leicester at the end of the campaign, it was reported that Billy had signed on for Torquay.
Leicester C *(From trainee on 15/7/2009)*
Accrington Stanley *(Loaned on 21/7/2009) FL 15+22/9 FLC 1+1 FAC 1+2 Others 2*

KELLY Julian James
Born: Enfield, 6 September 1989
Height: 5'9" **Weight:** 10.8
Yet another graduate from the flourishing Reading Academy, Julian played just one first team game for Reading, at right-back in the Carling Cup tie against Barnsley, which was lost 1-2. He was an unused substitute in the next game, by coincidence a 3-1 Championship win at Barnsley. Thereafter a series of niggling injuries, including a dislocated shoulder, kept him out. Clearly in need of first team football Wycombe manager Gary Waddock signed him on an initial one-month emergency loan in February, which was later extended to the season's end. He immediately made the right-back position his own, enjoying a spectacular debut when his cross went into the net for the only goal of the game against Millwall. That earned him

PFA FOOTBALLERS' WHO'S WHO **KE-KE**

a place in League One 'Team of the Week' and his speed and mobility thereafter were eye catching as he formed an excellent partnership with right-winger Kevin Betsy. A hamstring injury sustained against Huddersfield in early April looked to have ended his season but he did start the final game of 2009-10.
Reading (From trainee on 7/7/2008) FL 4+3 FLC 4 FAC 1
Wycombe W (Loaned on 15/2/2010) FL 9/1

KELLY Martin Ronald
Born: Bolton, 27 April 1990
Height: 6'3" **Weight:** 12.2
International Honours: E: Yth
Martin, a defender who can play at right-back or in central defence, is a product of Liverpool's Academy and an England youth international. He made a surprise debut at right-back in the Champions League home tie with Olympique Lyon in October and was praised for his performance despite Liverpool's defeat. Soon afterwards, he was sidelined with a groin injury and made only two more fleeting appearances as a substitute, the second being his Premiership debut against Portsmouth. He is one of several young players at Anfield whose development seemed to have been held up.
Liverpool (From trainee on 18/12/2007) PL 0+1 Others 1+2
Huddersfield T (Loaned on 27/3/2009) FL 7/1

KELLY Shaun David
Born: Liverpool, 11 December 1988
Height: 6'1" **Weight:** 11.4
A promising young defender who was signed by Burton outside the transfer window following the Chester demise, Shaun was used only as cover for Burton's main defenders and was not offered a new contract at the end of the season.
Chester C (From juniors on 23/1/2007) FL 30+9/1 FLC 0+1
Burton A (Free, via trial at Port Vale, on 19/3/2010) FL 2+2

KELLY Stephen Michael David
Born: Dublin, 6 September 1983
Height: 5'11" **Weight:** 12.4
International Honours: RoI: 18; U21-17; Yth
Stephen joined Fulham from Birmingham during the close season but was unable to dislodge regular right-back John Pantsil. Normally used on the right of the back four, he also deputized in an unfamiliar left-back role for the final two Europa League group ties in place of the suspended Paul Konchesky,

enjoying an excellent game in Basel. His best run in the side came early in the New Year but he struggled for consistency as the team went through its worst period of the season. A confident player in possession, he dovetails well with his defensive colleagues. Despite his lack of first team opportunity he continued to be selected regularly by the Republic of Ireland and won further caps in the friendly matches against Brazil and South Africa.
Tottenham H (From juniors on 11/9/2000) PL 29+8/2 FLC 1 FAC 6
Southend U (Loaned on 30/1/2003) FL 10
Queens Park Rgrs (Loaned on 27/3/2003) FL 7 Others 2
Watford (Loaned on 24/9/2003) FL 13
Birmingham C (£750,000 on 18/7/2006) P/FL 75+4 FLC 5+1 FAC 2+1
Stoke C (Loaned on 2/2/2009) PL 2+4
Fulham (Free on 2/7/2009) PL 7+1 FLC 1 FAC 3 Others 9+1

KELTIE Clark Stuart
Born: Newcastle, 31 August 1983
Height: 6'0" **Weight:** 12.7
Having accepted the offer of a new contract at Rochdale in the summer, Clark went on loan to Chester and Gateshead before being freed and joining Lincoln in January. Drafted in to provide some League Two experience by manager Chris Sutton, the midfielder forced his way in to the starting line-up towards the end of the season with some assured performances that saw him rewarded with a new one-year contract at Sincil Bank.
Darlington (Free from Walker Central on 19/9/2001) FL 129+32/9 FLC 3 FAC 8+1/1 Others 5+1/1
Rochdale (Free on 4/8/2008) FL 26+5/1 FLC 1 FAC 2 Others 1+1
Lincoln C (Free, via trial at Darlington and loan spells at Chester C and Gateshead, on 15/1/2010) FL 9+2

KEMPSON Darran Kaya
Born: Blackpool, 6 December 1984
Height: 6'2" **Weight:** 12.13
International Honours: E: SP-2
Arriving from Wrexham in the summer, in what was his third spell at Accrington, Darran successfully partnered Phil Edwards at the heart of the defence for most of the season. A hard-working and no-nonsense defender, he was sent off for a second bookable offence in the FA Cup fourth round against Fulham. Signed for Grimsby at the end of the season following the expiration of his contract.
Crewe Alex (Free from Morecambe, ex trainee at Preston NE, on 14/7/2006) FL 6+1 FLC 0+1 FAC 0+1 Others 1

Bury (Loaned on 23/2/2007) FL 12
Shrewsbury T (Free on 7/8/2007) FL 18+5 FLC 2/1 Others 1 (Freed during 2008 close season)
Accrington Stanley (Loaned on 29/2/2008) FL 8/1
Accrington Stanley (Free from Wrexham on 21/7/2009) FL 40/1 FLC 4 FAC 5 Others 3

KENDALL Ryan Paul
Born: Hull, 14 September 1989
Height: 6'1" **Weight:** 12.8
The young Hull striker joined Bradford on loan and made his senior debut as a substitute against Hereford in March. A pacy forward who holds the ball up well and never gives defenders a moment's peace. Ryan scored his first senior goal with a well-taken lob against Dagenham at Valley Parade, celebrating with an acrobatic cartwheel.
Hull C (From trainee on 24/6/2009)
Bradford C (Loaned on 16/3/2010) FL 2+4/2

KENNEDY Callum Ewan
Born: Chertsey, 9 November 1989
Height: 6'0" **Weight:** 12.6
A regular member of Swindon's squad during the early part of the season, Callum appeared in both Carling Cup games in August. Further League appearances from the bench soon followed, which included some impressive performances and led to Callum starting four games from the end of September before being replaced during the home defeat by Hartlepool. Although restored for first round FA Cup tie, he was later found to be suffering a pelvic stress fracture that brought a premature end to his season. A strong-tackling left-back, he likes to get forward.
Swindon T (From trainee on 22/2/2008) FL 7+5 FLC 1+1 FAC 1 Others 1

KENNEDY Jason Brian
Born: Stockton, 11 September 1986
Height: 6'1" **Weight:** 11.10
Club Honours: FAYC '04
After scoring spectacular goals against Rochdale in each of the previous two seasons, Jason signed for them in the summer and immediately formed a powerful combination with Gary Jones in central midfield. Also teaming up successfully with Jason Taylor when Jones was out injured, he sometimes formed a three-man midfield unit with both of them, when Dale changed their familiar 4-4-2 to 4-3-3 in some games. Close to being ever-present in Dale's drive to promotion he surprisingly failed to score, but his range of passing and

233

intelligent use of the ball was a key element in Dale's success and he won their player's 'Player of the Season' award.
Middlesbrough *(From trainee on 3/2/2005) PL 1+3 Others 1+2*
Boston U *(Loaned on 3/11/2006) FL 13/1*
Bury *(Loaned on 2/3/2007) FL 12*
Livingston *(Loaned on 1/8/2007) SL 18/2 SLC 2 SC 1 Others 1*
Darlington *(Free on 29/2/2008) FL 57+2/7 FLC 2/1 FAC 2 Others 3+2/1*
Rochdale *(Signed on 20/5/2009) FL 40+2 FLC 1 FAC 2 Others 1*

KENNEDY Mark John
Born: Dublin, 15 May 1976
Height: 5'11" **Weight:** 11.9
International Honours: RoI: 34; U21-7; Yth; Sch
Mark settled in at left-back for much of the season at Cardiff. He added experience and ability in possession, helping City turn defence into attack. Not always comfortable against an out-and-out winger, but overall Mark did a solid job for the Bluebirds having the edge on Tony Capaldi in the battle for the left-back slot, while Kevin McNaughton, whose favourite position is left-back, moved over to the right. He played in all three Championship play-off matches. Mark's contract was due to end in the summer of 2010 but he signed a new one-year deal before Cardiff knew whether they would be playing Premier League or Championship football.
Millwall *(From trainee on 6/5/1992) FL 37+6/9 FLC 6+1/2 FAC 3+1/1*
Liverpool *(£1,500,000 on 21/3/1995) PL 5+11 FLC 0+2 FAC 0+1 Others 0+2*
Queens Park Rgrs *(Loaned on 27/1/1998) FL 8/2*
Wimbledon *(£1,750,000 on 27/3/1998) PL 11+10 FLC 4+1/1 FAC 2*
Manchester C *(£1,000,000 on 15/7/1999) P/FL 56+10/8 FLC 5+4/3 FAC 2*
Wolverhampton W *(£1,800,000 on 6/7/2001) P/FL 157+10/12 FLC 3+1 FAC 12/1 Others 3+1/1*
Crystal Palace *(Free on 12/7/2006) FL 42+4/1 FAC 1+1*
Cardiff C *(Free on 11/7/2008) FL 60+6 FLC 1 FAC 5+1 Others 3*

KENNEDY Thomas (Tom) Gordon
Born: Bury, 24 June 1985
Height: 5'10" **Weight:** 11.1
Generally considered one of the best left-backs in the lower divisions, Tom had another excellent season for Rochdale, being virtually ever-present through their promotion campaign. Besides his defensive duties, Tom is

noted for his delivery from set pieces, Craig Dawson in particular often getting on the end of his perfectly placed corners. Tom also netted three times from the spot, most notably against his former club Bury in a 3-0 win. He was voted into the PFA League Two 'Team of the Year' for the third successive season.
Bury *(From trainee on 2/11/2002) FL 131+12/5 FLC 2+1 FAC 7+1/1 Others 3+1*
Rochdale *(Free on 5/7/2007) FL 132/9 FLC 4 FAC 6 Others 9*

KENNY Patrick (Paddy) Joseph
Born: Halifax, 17 May 1978
Height: 6'1" **Weight:** 14.6
International Honours: RoI: 7
Paddy returned to training with Sheffield United on 22 March following his nine-month drugs ban and one month later was available to play. He played in the final two games of the season, showing excellent timing, good command of his area, making some excellent saves on his first appearance in particular and keeping two clean sheets.
Bury *(£10,000 + from Bradford PA on 28/8/1998) FL 133 FLC 5 FAC 7 Others 5*
Sheffield U *(Free on 26/7/2002) P/FL 278 FLC 15 FAC 19 Others 6*

KEOGH Andrew (Andy) Declan
Born: Dublin, 16 May 1986
Height: 6'0" **Weight:** 11.7
Club Honours: Div 1 '07; Ch '09
International Honours: RoI: 13; B-1; U21-9; Yth
The skilful Wolverhampton forward made a big impact at Wigan in the second match. Andy hit the inside of a post and headed in the only goal within six minutes, and could have had a penalty later on. He also struck the bar at Manchester City in the same week. Although playing for the Republic of Ireland again in October, he was being used a bit more sparingly at club level. Andy was still having a good campaign until damaging ankle ligaments in training in December. He was then out for two months and from then on made just four appearances as substitute.
Leeds U *(From trainee on 20/5/2003) FLC 0+1*
Scunthorpe U *(Loaned on 6/8/2004) FL 9+3/2*
Bury *(Loaned on 14/1/2005) FL 4/2*
Scunthorpe U *(Signed on 14/2/2005) FL 69+17/19 FLC 2 FAC 7/3 Others 2/1*
Wolverhampton W *(£600,000 on 23/1/2007) P/FL 79+36/19 FLC 3+3/1 FAC 4+1/3 Others 2*

KEOGH Richard John
Born: Harlow, 11 August 1986
Height: 6'0" **Weight:** 11.11
International Honours: RoI: U21-8
Richard had a fine season at Brunton Park and deservedly collected his share of Carlisle's various 'Player of the Year' awards. For most of the season he filled in at right-back after injury to David Raven but can also play in central defence. Strong in the air and a good tackler, he combines these defensive attributes with the ability to go forward in barnstorming runs that became something of a trademark. Always a threat at set pieces, he scored a number of valuable goals, including a dramatic last-minute header at Walsall to earn a valuable point. Not surprisingly, he is also a fans' favourite and he has been offered a new deal for next term.
Stoke C *(From trainee on 6/11/2005)*
Bristol C *(Free on 26/7/2005) FL 24+16/3 FLC 2 FAC 5+1/1 Others 3+2/1*
Wycombe W *(Loaned on 10/11/2005) FL 2+1*
Huddersfield T *(Loaned on 31/8/2007) FL 9/1 Others 1*
Carlisle U *(Loaned on 22/11/2007) FL 7*
Cheltenham T *(Loaned on 10/3/2008) FL 10*
Carlisle U *(Signed on 21/8/2008) FL 72+1/4 FLC 1+1 FAC 6/1 Others 7/1*

Richard Keogh

KERMORGANT Yann
Born: Vannes, France, 8 November 1981
Height: 6'0" **Weight:** 13.3
The powerful but skilful striker was signed as a free agent by Leicester manager Nigel Pearson during the close season. Yann often impressed in training, but showed an occasional lack

of confidence when thrust into the main fray. He has outstanding aerial ability and showed real class when scoring his first Foxes' goal from 25 yards against Middlesbrough. Sadly, his season will be remembered largely for his would-be audacious chipped penalty in the play-off shoot-out at Cardiff, which he missed to set up the home victory.

Leicester C (Free from Stade Reims, France, ex Vannes OC, SO Chatellerault, Grenoble Foot 38, on 24/8/2009) FL 9+11/1 FLC 0+1 FAC 1+1 Others 0+2

KERR Scott Anthony
Born: Leeds, 11 December 1981
Height: 5'9" **Weight:** 10.12
The midfielder turned in another industrious campaign as Lincoln's club captain when leading by example in the middle of the park. Rewarded with a new one-year contract, Scott made his 200th appearance for the Imps in the 2009-10 season and only the form of goalkeeper Rob Burch stopped him retaining the Club's 'Player of the Season' award. Is a real box-to-box player who relishes winning the ball and driving forward.

Bradford C (From trainee on 4/7/2000) PL 0+1 FLC 0+1 Others 1
Hull C (Signed on 20/6/2001) Others 1 (Free to Scarborough on 7/3/2003)
Lincoln C (Free from Scarborough on 3/8/2005) FL 199+6/8 FLC 5/1 FAC 9 Others 8

KHIZANISHVILI Zurab
Born: Tbilisi, Georgia, 6 October 1981
Height: 6'1" **Weight:** 12.8
Club Honours: SPD '05
International Honours: Georgia: 63
The competent Georgian was never in Sam Allardyce's plans at Blackburn in 2009-10 and played only in the Carling Cup tie at Gillingham, where he took some time to settle and conceded a penalty before going out on a three-month loan to Newcastle in August to provide defensive cover. He made his debut at right-back at Ipswich in September and subsequently settled into a run of games at centre-back. However, this came to an end with the suspension following a sending off at home to Doncaster in October and he returned to Blackburn at the expiry of his loan. After appearing for Rovers in the FA Cup defeat at the hands of Aston Villa he joined Reading on loan in January to add composure and stability to a defence which had looked unsteady at times, mainly due to the number of changes which had been made. It took a while to settle into the team, and when he did so he had to

partner a variety of centre-backs, but the tall, strapping defender soon showed his class, as befits the captain of the Georgia national team. Zurab made a total of 15 appearances in Reading's first team. In every one of those games he played with great confidence, judging his headers and tackles to perfection. His range of passing was interesting to watch too, and he was a perceptible threat at all set pieces. Although he returned to Blackburn at the end of the season, he stated that he would like to stay at Reading if terms could be agreed.

Dundee (Signed from Lokomotiv Tbilisi, Georgia on 8/3/2001) SL 39+3 SLC 3 SC 5
Glasgow Rgrs (Signed on 30/6/2003) SL 39+4 SLC 4+1 SC 2 Others 14
Blackburn Rov (Signed on 31/8/2005) PL 54+8/1 FLC 10+1/1 FAC 10+3 Others 6+1
Newcastle U (Loaned on 17/9/2009) FL 6+1
Reading (Loaned on 25/1/2010) FL 12+3

KIELY Dean Laurence
Born: Salford, 10 October 1970
Height: 6'0" **Weight:** 12.5
Club Honours: Div 2 '97; Div 1 '00; Ch '08
International Honours: RoI: 11; B-1; E: Yth; Sch
Dean officially became West Bromwich's goalkeeper coach in March 2010 after successfully doing the job on a trial basis from the start of the season. He also penned a third one-year extension to his playing contract until 2011. The experienced stopper provided back-up for the majority of the last two seasons and he was called upon to play in three Championship games over the Christmas period because of Scott Carson's suspension, producing excellent displays and helping the Baggies earn seven points towards their promotion bid. Earlier in the season Dean played in three Carling Cup games, keeping a clean sheet against his former club Bury, and also went on as a second-half substitute for Carson when his fellow stopper was shown a red card in the home League game against Cardiff and went off with an injured arm against Middlesbrough.

Coventry C (From trainee on 30/10/1987)
York C (Signed on 9/3/1990) FL 210 FLC 9 FAC 4 Others 17
Bury (£125,000 on 15/8/1996) FL 137 FLC 13 FAC 4 Others 3
Charlton Ath (£1,000,000 on 26/5/1999) P/FL 222 FLC 12 FAC 14
Portsmouth (£500,000 on 25/1/2006) PL 15 FLC 1 FAC 1

Luton T (Loaned on 23/11/2006) FL 11
West Bromwich A (Free on 30/1/2007) P/FL 67+2 FLC 7 FAC 8 Others 3

KIGHTLY Michael John
Born: Basildon, 24 January 1986
Height: 5'9" **Weight:** 9.12
Club Honours: FAT '06; Ch '09
International Honours: E: U21-7
Michael was expected to be one of Wolverhampton's rising stars who could do well in the highest sphere but he continued to be plagued by injuries. His first League start was delayed to 17th October, when he played in draws against Everton, Villa and Stoke but found it difficult against the better defenders and rarely started. He came on as substitute against Birmingham and looked good for 30 minutes despite a 2-1 defeat, only to limp off and be replaced himself. In December his ankle was operated on and it was hoped he would recover well before the season ended but it was not to be.

Southend U (From trainee on 12/12/2003) FL 2+11 FAC 1+2 Others 2+1/1 (Freed during 2005 close season)
Wolverhampton W (Signed from Grays Ath on 17/11/2006) P/FL 84+8/20 FLC 3+1 FAC 1+3/1 Others 2

Kevin Kilbane

KILBANE Kevin Daniel
Born: Preston, 1 February 1977
Height: 6'0" **Weight:** 12.10
International Honours: RoI: 103; U21-11

Kevin's vast experience and incredible versatility was, unfortunately, not enough to prevent Hull's relegation from the Premier League. Named captain for the first time for the visit to Fulham in October, as well as centre-back, left-back, centre midfield and left midfield he added a stint on the right side of midfield for probably the first time in his long career in the late season game against Sunderland. He scored his first City goal in the previous home game against Burnley. Otherwise, Kevin enjoyed a memorable season on the international stage. Having earned his 100th cap against Montenegro in October, he equalled Steve Staunton's Republic of Ireland appearances record in the second leg of the World Cup play-off in France when they were infamously denied qualification by Thierry Henry's 'handball' goal. Along with Shay Given, Kevin broke the record with his 103rd cap against Brazil at Arsenal's Emirates Stadium.

Preston NE *(From trainee on 6/7/1995)* FL 39+8/3 FLC 4 FAC 1 Others 1+1
West Bromwich A *(£1,000,000 on 13/6/1997)* FL 105+1/15 FLC 12/2 FAC 4/1
Sunderland *(£2,500,000 on 16/12/1999)* P/FL 102+11/8 FLC 4 FAC 3+4/1
Everton *(£750,000 on 2/9/2003)* PL 86+18/4 FLC 3 FAC 10/1 Others 3+1
Wigan Ath *(Signed on 31/8/2006)* PL 62+14/2 FLC 4 FAC 4
Hull C *(£500,000 on 16/1/2009)* PL 30+7/1 FLC 0+2 FAC 1 .

KILBEY Thomas (Tom)
Charles
Born: Walthamstow, 19 October 1990
Height: 6'3" **Weight:** 13.8
Tom joined Dagenham for a month on loan from Portsmouth at the start of September. The tall central midfielder made only one appearance for the Daggers before being recalled by the Fratton Park side. His first and last game was in the Johnstone's Paint Trophy first round tie at MK Dons.
Millwall *(Trainee)* Others 0+1
Portsmouth *(£400,000 on 6/2/2008)*
Dagenham & Redbridge *(Loaned on 1/9/2009)* Others 1

KILGALLON Matthew Shaun
Born: York, 8 January 1984
Height: 6'1" **Weight:** 12.5
International Honours: E: U21-5; Yth
Matthew began the season for Sheffield United as he had finished the previous one, showing excellent anticipation, being good in the air, accurate in the tackle and making good use of the ball. As speculation grew about his future as he was out of contract at the end of the

season, his form dipped and there were uncharacteristic errors. He returned to form by December but in January he moved to Sunderland during the January transfer window and debuted immediately away to Everton and added three further appearances before taking up residence on the bench for two and a half months as players returned from injury and suspension. Recalled for the April trip to Hull, Matthew kept his place for the visit of Manchester United but was back on the bench for the one remaining game of the season. A defender ready to attack the ball, Matthew looks to supplement his attack by bursting forward if he sees the opportunity for a quick break.
Leeds U *(From trainee on 10/1/2001)* P/FL 73+7/3 FLC 6+1 FAC 4 Others 3+1
West Ham U *(Loaned on 23/8/2003)* FL 1+2 FLC 1
Sheffield U *(£1,750,000 + on 8/1/2007)* P/FL 105+2/4 FLC 7 FAC 7 Others 3
Sunderland *(Signed on 21/1/2010)* PL 6+1

KILKENNY Neil Martin
Born: Enfield, 19 December 1985
Height: 5'8" **Weight:** 10.8
International Honours: Australia: 2; U23; E: Yth
The injury Neil received in the previous campaign's play-off home game against Millwall left him struggling for full fitness early on. He had to be content with a place on the Leeds' bench and did not start a League game until December, when he marked his return to former club Oldham with a goal. Neil, who went on to pass 100 appearances for Leeds with more regular starts in the second half of season, is thought of as the best passer in the club.
Birmingham C *(From trainee at Arsenal on 27/1/2004)* P/FL 6+20 FLC 3+3 FAC 1+6
Oldham Ath *(Loaned on 19/11/2004)* FL 24+3/4 FAC 3 Others 4/1
Oldham Ath *(Loaned on 10/8/2007)* FL 19+1/1 FLC 1/1 FAC 3/1 Others 1
Leeds U *(Signed on 4/1/2008)* FL 67+14/7 FLC 3+3 FAC 6 Others 11+1/2

KILLEN Christopher (Chris) John
Born: Wellington, New Zealand, 8 October 1981
Height: 5'11" **Weight:** 11.3
Club Honours: SPD '08
International Honours: New Zealand: 31; U23-5; Yth
Chris was one of four Glasgow Celtic players Gordon Strachan brought to Middlesbrough in the January transfer

window. Primarily signed as the target man alongside Scott McDonald, Chris scored in his sixth game, a 2-1 home win over Barnsley. He put away towering headers against Reading and Preston but a virus halted his promising run. After alternating with Lee Miller, Chris started the final game at Leicester at centre-half as injuries shredded the Boro defence – and missed a penalty. Initially signed until the end of the season, Chris stated he would love to earn an extended stay on Teesside.
Manchester C *(Free from Miramar Rangers, New Zealand on 8/3/1999)* FL 0+3
Wrexham *(Loaned on 8/9/2000)* FL 11+1/3
Port Vale *(Loaned on 24/9/2001)* FL 8+1/6 Others 1
Oldham Ath *(£200,000 + on 31/7/2002)* FL 53+25/17 FLC 4+1/1 FAC 3+2/4 Others 2/1
Hibernian *(Free on 26/1/2006)* SL 23+2/16 SLC 2 SC 1+1/2 Others 3/1
Glasgow Celtic *(Free on 31/5/2007)* SL 4+22/2 SLC 2+1/1 SC 0+1 Others 2+8
Norwich C *(Loaned on 2/2/2009)* FL 0+4
Middlesbrough *(Free on 13/1/2010)* FL 15+2/3

KING Andrew (Andy) Philip
Born: Barnstaple, 29 October 1988
Height: 6'0" **Weight:** 11.10
Club Honours: Div 1 '09
International Honours: W: 3 U21-10; Yth
A highly-rated young midfield player who has become a regular senior squad member for Wales, Andy's understated performances for Leicester saw him collect 11 goals during the season, often through timing his arrival in the box to maximum effect. He also demonstrated sound aerial ability in front of goal at times, including what might have been a crucial strike in the play-offs at Cardiff. Surely his development will be monitored closely by a number of top flight clubs over the coming months.
Leicester C *(From trainee on 23/5/2007)* FL 87+12/19 FLC 2+1/1 FAC 5+1/2 Others 5/1

KING Christopher (Chris)
Born: Birkenhead, 14 November 1980
Height: 5'8" **Weight:** 10.1
Made just three appearances for Accrington at the start of the season before picking up an ankle injury that kept him out for the rest of his contract that expired in the New Year. It was a disappointment for both Accrington and Chris after he had been such an important part of the defence in 2008-

09. At his best a confident left-back who enjoys the overlap to deliver crosses to the front men, he is currently looking at League Two or Blue Square Premier sides in respect to the coming season.
Accrington Stanley (Free from The New Saints, ex Stalybridge Celtic, Southport, on 6/8/2008) FL 28 FLC 2 FAC 2 Others 2

KING Craig Stuart
Born: Chesterfield, 6 October 1990
Height: 5'11" **Weight:** 11.12
International Honours: S: Yth
On loan from Leicester, Craig's goal just minutes into his Hereford debut quickly earned him the affections of the fans and his all-action style and willingness to chase everything made the young striker a key member of the side during the first part of his time at Edgar Street. Although not scoring the number of goals his effort deserved, it was significant that twice he was in the right place to follow up and score after a colleague's initial effort had been saved. Injuries impeded his progress in the latter part of the season but he marked himself out as one for the future.
Leicester C (From trainee on 5/9/2008) Others 0+1
Hereford U (Loaned on 17/9/2009) FL 22+4/3 FAC 2 Others 2

KING Gary Ian
Born: Grimsby, 27 January 1990
Height: 5'10" **Weight:** 11.4
Signed following his release from Lincoln in the summer, Gary only had limited opportunities in the Accrington first team during the season. Able to play wide or down the middle with a good turn of pace, he did however manage a couple of goals and with further experience could do well.
Lincoln C (From trainee on 2/7/2008) FL 5+6/1 FLC 0+1
Accrington Stanley (Free on 7/8/2009) FL 3+5/1 Others 1/1

KING Joshua (Josh) Christian Kojo
Born: Oslo, Norway, 15 January 1992
Height: 5'11" **Weight:** 11.7
Young Manchester United footballer of Norwegian and Gambian descent, who usually plays as a forward but can double up as a winger, Josh was signed by United from Valerenga in 2008. After impressing in the reserves, he was rewarded with a place on the bench for the Carling Cup third round tie against Wolverhampton in September. Entering the game as an 81st-minute substitute for the winning scorer Danny Welbeck, Joshua had two opportunities to add to United's lead.

Manchester U (From trainee on 21/2/2009) FLC 0+1

KING Ledley Brenton
Born: Stepney, 12 October 1980
Height: 6'2" **Weight:** 13.6
Club Honours: FLC '08
International Honours: E: 20; B-1; U21-12; Yth
The club captain's battle to play in the centre of Tottenham's defence despite his ongoing knee problems is well documented. Ledley is a one-club player who has now accumulated 241 Premier League appearances, with only eight bookings, in 11 full seasons. When able to play he is inspirational because of the effort he makes to be present and because of his immaculate defending. He still copes with pace, reads the game superbly and is commanding in the air. Fabio Capello picked Ledley for England's World Cup squad and it is a fact that he played more games this season than Rio Ferdinand. He played in Spurs' last four games and five of their last six, leading them to that coveted fourth place. This period included vital wins against Arsenal and Manchester City. Ledley scored twice, one of them at Old Trafford, and played in 19 Premier League games, in nine of which the defence achieved a clean sheet.
Tottenham H (From trainee on 22/7/1998) PL 237+4/10 FLC 20/1 FAC 18+1/3 Others 11

KING Marlon Francis
Born: Dulwich, 26 April 1980
Height: 6'1" **Weight:** 11.12
International Honours: Jamaica: 19
After spending the previous season on loan at Hull and Middlesbrough, Marlon returned to Wigan for the start of the season. A skilful and hard-working striker, he never stopped running and his upper-body strength makes him a formidable opponent. Marlon is also an excellent team player, with his unselfishness in holding the ball and providing openings. Making only one start in the Carling Cup against Blackpool, he was restricted to just a few minutes of play in three League matches as Roberto Martinez used summer signing Jason Scotland as a lone striker. Marlon's contract was cancelled after conviction in a court case resulted in an 18-month prison sentence.
Barnet (From trainee on 9/9/1998) FL 36+17/14 FLC 0+2 FAC 0+1 Others 2+2
Gillingham (£255,000 on 28/6/2000) FL 82+19/40 FLC 6+3/4 FAC 5+1/3
Nottingham F (£950,000 on 27/11/2003) FL 40+10/10 FLC 3/3 FAC 3+1/2

Leeds U (Loaned on 4/3/2005) FL 4+5
Watford (£500,000 on 12/7/2005) P/FL 77+4/36 FAC 2+1 Others 3/1
Wigan Ath (£5,000,000 on 25/1/2008) PL 8+10/1 FLC 1
Hull C (Loaned on 14/8/2008) PL 19+1/5 FLC 0+1 FAC 0+1
Middlesbrough (Loaned on 26/1/2009) PL 9+4/2

KIRK Tyrone Charles
Born: Scunthorpe, 2 January 1986
Height: 5'5" **Weight:** 10.1
The former Scunthorpe trainee signed for Macclesfield in the summer. Tyrone made his senior debut in the first round of the Carling Cup against Leicester at the Moss Rose on the right of midfield. He was replaced at half-time by the more experienced Izak Reid and was loaned to Welsh Premier League side Rhyl nine days later, a move made permanent in January.
Macclesfield T (Free from Stamford AFC on 4/8/2009) FLC 1

KIRKLAND Christopher (Chris) Edmund
Born: Barwell, 2 May 1981
Height: 6'6" **Weight:** 11.7
Club Honours: FLC '03
International Honours: E: 1; U21-8; Yth
Chris is regarded as one of the best all-round goalkeepers in the Premiership and yet again was vital to Wigan. Having suffered with injuries throughout his career, he missed only six League games during the season and made his 100th League start for Wigan in August against Wolverhampton. Tremendously agile for his height, with safe hands and ever growing confidence, he is rated by his manager Roberto Martinez as England's best 'keeper. A terrific shot-stopper, he fills the goal and his presence adds much stability to the defence. He produced many 'Man of the Match' performances as the club maintained their top flight status for a sixth season and his bravery was shown when he played on at West Ham despite having six stitches in a face wound. A superstitious person, Chris insists on wearing a short-sleeved shirt. He missed the final two games following surgery to a finger injury.
Coventry C (From trainee on 6/5/1998) P/FL 24 FLC 3+1 FAC 1
Liverpool (£6,000,000 + on 31/8/2001) PL 25 FLC 6 FAC 3 Others 11
West Bromwich A (Loaned on 18/7/2005) PL 10 FAC 2
Wigan Ath (Signed on 22/7/2006) PL 127 FLC 2 FAC 1

Chris Kirkland

KISNORBO Patrick
(Paddy) Fabio Maxime
Born: Melbourne, Australia, 24 March 1981
Height: 6'2" **Weight:** 11.9
International Honours: Australia: 18; U23-3; Yth

Paddy proved to be Leeds' best summer signing, his move on a two-year deal earning him a recall to the Australian team. He sustained a head wound in the season's opener against Exeter which required 15 stitches and the wound opened when he played against the Republic of Ireland a few days later. After that he wore a headband to protect the scar tissue and it did not stop him from putting in his head where it hurts. Outstanding in the famous 1-0 FA Cup win at Manchester United, the second part of his campaign was punctuated by injury and illness. He was sorely missed as Leeds' previously tight defence began to leak. Paddy's season ended in March when he ruptured an Achilles tendon in the 2-0

televised home defeat by Millwall – an injury that ruled him out of the World Cup. United's 'Player of the Year', he was named in the PFA 'League One Team of the Year'.
Heart of Midlothian *(Signed from South Melbourne, Australia on 2/7/2003) SL 45+3/1 SLC 4 SC 2+1 Others 9/1*
Leicester C *(Free on 15/7/2005) FL 122+4/9 FLC 6+2/1 FAC 4+1/1 Others 1*
Leeds U *(Free on 22/7/2009) FL 29/1 FLC 2 FAC 3 Others 0+1*

KITSON David (Dave) Barry
Born: Hitchin, 21 January 1980
Height: 6'3" **Weight:** 12.11
Club Honours: Ch '06

Having set himself the task of overcoming the disappointment of his first season at Stoke, Dave began 2009-10 in great form. The ground simply exploded when he finally scored his first League goal, against Sunderland, after he had netted away at Leyton Orient a few days earlier. Another goal, against

Bolton, shortly afterwards seemed to have cemented his return and resurgence. Quite what happened then is still a matter of some debate among Stoke supporters. Dave was promptly sent out on loan to Championship Middlesbrough in November, where he started well, finding himself on the score-sheet a week later when notching a brace in a 2-2 draw at Peterborough. The goalscoring continued, when he scored a fine goal in an impressive 5-1 win away at Queens Park Rangers. The striker intimated in press reports that the deal would not become permanent due to his families commitments in the south, and his loan spell duly ended shortly afterwards. After overcoming an injury, he then found his way back into the Stoke side. Having scored a great goal against Manchester City in the FA Cup it looked like he was set to become a permanent fixture in the Stoke side, but several games later he snapped after being substituted in the away defeat at Chelsea and his future was in some doubt at the end of the campaign.
Cambridge U *(Signed from Arlesey T on 16/3/2001) FL 97+5/40 FLC 4/1 FAC 9/2 Others 7+1/4*
Reading *(£300,000 on 30/12/2003) P/FL 111+24/54 FLC 5+1/4 FAC 5+1/2*
Stoke C *(£5,500,000 on 18/7/2008) PL 20+14/3 FLC 3/1 FAC 0+3/1*
Reading *(Loaned on 11/3/2009) FL 9+1/2 Others 0+2*
Middlesbrough *(Loaned on 17/11/2009) FL 6/3*

KLASNIC Ivan
Born: Hamburg, Germany, 29 January 1980
Height: 6'1" **Weight:** 12.6
International Honours: Croatia: 38; U21-3

A Croatian international centre-forward, Ivan made his debut for Bolton in the 3-2 victory at Portsmouth. His first League start came in the hard-fought victory at Birmingham, with his first goal proving to be the decisive strike in the 3-2 victory over Everton. Ivan also scored at Fulham in December, a goal that proved to be the start of a fine run of form. He subsequently scored twice against Manchester City in addition to goals against West Ham and Hull before the end of that month. Ivan started in Owen Coyle's first game in charge but soon found himself back on the bench, with Coyle seemingly preferring the work rate and industry of Johan Elmander, and with Ivan apparently not 100 per cent fit. He returned to the starting line-up during the latter stages of the season, scoring

against Portsmouth and Birmingham, taking his League tally for the season to eight goals from 12 starts, although an additional 15 appearances came from the bench. A huge fan-favourite and a proven instinctive scorer, the Reebok faithful certainly hoped Ivan's deal would be made permanent over the summer.

Bolton W (Loaned from Nantes, France, ex St Pauli, Werder Bremen, on 1/9/2009) PL 12+15/8 FLC 2 FAC 3

KNIGHT David Sean
Born: Houghton-le-Spring, 15 January 1987
Height: 6'0" **Weight:** 11.7
International Honours: E: Yth
David returned to Darlington, where he had played three games on loan from Middlesbrough in 2005-06, this time as first choice 'keeper. After starting the opening nine games, he was replaced by the experienced Russell Hoult on loan from Notts County. He never managed to regain his place and was released in December by new manager Steve Staunton.
Middlesbrough (From trainee on 3/2/2005)
Darlington (Loaned on 30/12/2005) FL 3
Oldham Ath (Loaned on 25/8/2006) FL 2
Swansea C (Free on 31/8/2007) FAC 1 (Freed during 2008 close season)
Middlesbrough (Free from Mansfield T on 1/2/2009)
Darlington (Free on 17/7/2009) FL 7 FLC 1 Others 1

KNIGHT Zatyiah (Zat)
Born: Solihull, 2 May 1980
Height: 6'6" **Weight:** 13.8
International Honours: E: 2; U21-4
Standing at 6'6", the Premier League's tallest defender made his Bolton debut in the opening day defeat by Sunderland. He started the next ten League games before losing his place in the home defeat by Blackburn in November. Returning to action for the 3-3 draw with Manchester City in December, Zat then produced his best performance for the club to date, in the 3-1 victory over West Ham in December. Starting Owen Coyle's first game in charge, at home to Arsenal, Zat remained in the first team for the remainder of the season, making an impressive 35 League starts. After a shaky beginning, his confidence clearly grew and he proved to be a stable and calming influence in the centre of defence, striking up a very promising partnership with Gary Cahill. His first goal for the club came in the vital 1-0 win over Wolverhampton and Zat will be hoping to carry his excellent end of

season form into the new campaign.
Fulham (Signed from Rushall Olympic on 19/2/1999) P/FL 140+10/3 FLC 9 FAC 15+2/1 Others 3+2
Peterborough U (Loaned on 25/2/2000) FL 8
Aston Villa (£4,000,000 on 29/8/2007) PL 38+2/2 FLC 2 FAC 3 Others 9
Bolton W (Signed on 25/7/2009) PL 35/1 FLC 3 FAC 3

Zat Knight

KOMPANY Vincent
Born: Brussels, Belgium, 10 April 1986
Height: 6'3" **Weight:** 14.4
International Honours: Belgium: 30
With the acquisition of so many star signings by Manchester City in the summer, it seemed that the Belgian international defensive midfielder would take a back seat and indeed, due to a foot injury, Vincent did not appear until October. His season was transformed after the arrival of new manager Roberto Mancini in December when an injury to Joleon Lescott and the departure of Kolo Toure for the African Cup of Nations saw him required to fill the gap as an emergency central defender. So well did he perform that he held his place until the end of the season and, in the opinion of many, outshone his more expensive and illustrious colleagues. Not only that but he scored two rare goals – in the 2-0 home win over Portsmouth and the 6-1 thrashing of Burnley.
Manchester C (£6,000,000 from SV Hamburg, Germany, ex Anderlecht, on 22/8/2008) PL 55+4/3 FLC 4+1 FAC 4 Others 8+1

KONCHESKY Paul Martyn
Born: Barking, 15 May 1981
Height: 5'10" **Weight:** 10.12
International Honours: E: 2; U21-15; Yth
Paul continued to be the first choice for Fulham at left-back when available. A consistent performer who is always looking to move forward with the ball, he enjoys an excellent understanding with Fulham's other left-sided players. A crisp tackler who knows exactly how and when to time his challenges, he seldom fails to come away with the ball. Almost ever-present during the first half of the campaign, he suffered an injury blow at Blackburn that kept him out for nearly two months, after which he played some of his best football. Despite his attacking instincts, Paul's goals are rarer than one might expect but usually of the highest quality, such as the stunning strike in the home win against Everton in September. Despite being tipped for further England honours he did not add to his previous caps.
Charlton Ath (From trainee on 25/5/1998) P/FL 91+58/5 FLC 5+4/1 FAC 8+3
Tottenham H (Loaned on 1/9/2003) PL 10+2 FLC 2+1
West Ham U (£1,500,000 on 5/7/2005) PL 58+1/1 FLC 1+1 FAC 7/1 Others 2
Fulham (£2,000,000 on 16/7/2007) PL 96/2 FLC 3 FAC 9 Others 13

Paul Konchesky

KONSTANTOPOULOS Dimitrios (Dimi)

Born: Kalamata, Greece, 29 November 1978
Height: 6'4" **Weight:** 12.2
International Honours: Greece: U21-9
The experienced Greek goalkeeper was number two to Keiren Westwood at Coventry. He made two League starts, at home to Reading and at Derby, and although both games were lost he was not culpable. In fact he saved a Rob Hulse penalty at Pride Park. He played against his old club Hartlepool in the Carling Cup and made two substitute appearances when Westwood had to go off, at home to West Bromwich, when he kept a clean sheet, and at Portsmouth in the FA Cup.
Hartlepool U (Free from SC Farense, Portugal, ex Kalamata, Egaleo, Kalamata, on 22/1/2004) FL 117 FLC 5 FAC 10 Others 7
Coventry C (Free on 10/7/2007) FL 23+1 FLC 1 FAC 2+1
Swansea C (Loaned on 25/10/2008) FL 4 FLC 1 FAC 1
Cardiff C (Loaned on 20/2/2009) FL 6

KORANTENG Nathan Papa Kwabena

Born: Hackney, 26 May 1992
Height: 6'2" **Weight:** 12.5
Youth team wide man Nathan was given limited runs by Peterborough towards the end of the season. He showed good pace, tight ball control and could be one for the future. Nathan went on loan to Blue Square Premier Tamworth during the season to gain senior experience.
Peterborough U (From trainee on 8/3/2010) FL 3+1

KOREN Robert

Born: Ljubljana, Slovenia, 20 September 1980
Height: 5'9" **Weight:** 11.3
Club Honours: Ch '08
International Honours: Slovenia: 45; U21-12
The Slovenian international was not always a preferred choice of manager Roberto di Matteo and Robert had to bide his time before re-establishing himself in West Bromwich's first team. But once he had got back into the side he produced some fine displays, his runs from centre-field giving defenders plenty to think about. He scored some cracking goals, including four at the Hawthorns – a 79th-minute winner which earned the Baggies their first home League victory over Sheffield Wednesday for 35 years; a right-foot stunner in a 3-2 win over Blackpool and two, one a fine individual effort, in the

televised 3-0 defeat of Leicester on Good Friday. Robert captained Slovenia against England at Wembley in September and shortly afterwards scored twice in a World Cup qualifying win over San Marino. Was released in the summer.
West Bromwich A (Free from Lillestrom, Norway, ex NK Drovograd, NK Publikum, on 5/1/2007) P/FL 113+14/16 FLC 2+1/1 FAC 12+4/5 Others 3

KOUMAS Jason

Born: Wrexham, 25 September 1979
Height: 5'10" **Weight:** 11.0
International Honours: W: 34
In his third season with Wigan, Jason surprisingly did not figure in new manager Roberto Martinez's plans, making just ten senior appearances. After producing a 'Man of the Match' performance in the opening game at Aston Villa and netting in the 2-0 win, he was to make only another five Premier League starts. Possessing exceptional skill and technique, he was used either on the left of midfield or where he was most effective – in the middle playing behind the lone striker. After announcing his retirement from international football for Wales in September, he made his 50th League appearance for Wigan in the same week. Jason's last start was in the FA Cup against Notts County in February and he was linked with loan moves to Newcastle and West Bromwich. In the final year of his contract, Jason will be looking for regular football.
Tranmere Rov (From trainee on 27/11/1997) FL 96+31/25 FLC 9+5/2 FAC 9/5
West Bromwich A (£2,500,000 on 29/8/2002) P/FL 103+20/23 FLC 6 FAC 8+1 Others 3
Cardiff C (Loaned on 2/8/2005) FL 42+2/12 FLC 2+1/1
Wigan Ath (£5,600,000 + on 10/7/2007) PL 32+2/2 FLC 1+2 FAC 3+1

KOVAC Radoslav

Born: Prague, Czech Republic, 27 November 1979
Height: 6'2" **Weight:** 13.1
International Honours: Czech Republic: 31; U21-15
The Czech midfielder has the holding role at West Ham. He breaks up the attacks, which gives Scott Parker the freedom to go forward. Playing against Hull in February he had a great game with fine tackling to set up the first goal before he laid on the pass for the third. When the going became tough in the relegation struggle, Radoslav was the

man to have around with some battling performances. His height becomes useful in the opponents' area, shown when he was on hand to head goals against Portsmouth and Wigan.
West Ham U (Signed from Spartak Moscow, Russia, Sigma Olomouc, Sparta Prague, on 2/2/2009) PL 35+5/3 FLC 2 FAC 2

KOVACS Janos

Born: Budapest, Hungary, 11 September 1985
Height: 6'4" **Weight:** 14.10
International Honours: Hungary: U21; Yth
First choice centre-back at Lincoln under the leadership of Peter Jackson, Janos got his 2009-10 season off to a goalscoring start with the winner over Barnet on the opening day. However, following Chris Sutton's arrival at Sincil Bank the Hungarian found his first team chances somewhat limited and he left the club by mutual consent in January.
Chesterfield (Free from MTK Hungaria, Hungary on 11/8/2005) FL 55+2/2 FLC 2 FAC 1 Others 2
Lincoln C (Free on 29/7/2008) FL 59/4 FLC 2 FAC 4 Others 1

KOZLUK Robert (Rob)

Born: Mansfield, 5 August 1977
Height: 5'8" **Weight:** 11.7
International Honours: E: U21-2
Rob signed a new one-year contract during the summer and started the season for Barnsley in his less comfortable left-back position but soon moved over to the right-hand side. The first half of the season saw him as usual giving his all but the acquisition on loan of Ryan Shotton and Carl Dickinson saw his opportunities steadily more limited. A knee injury put him out of action for the second half of the season and he did not reappear until he was an unused substitute in the penultimate game. He was out of contract at the end of the season and released.
Derby Co (From trainee on 10/2/1996) PL 9+7 FLC 3 FAC 2+1
Sheffield U (Signed on 12/3/1999) P/FL 193+20/2 FLC 8+1 FAC 11 Others 3
Huddersfield T (Loaned on 7/9/2000) FL 14
Preston NE (Loaned on 6/1/2005) FL 0+1 FAC 1
Barnsley (Free on 17/7/2007) FL 72+3 FLC 7 FAC 3+1

KRANJCAR Niko

Born: Zagreb, Croatia, 13 August 1984
Height: 6'1" **Weight:** 13.3
Club Honours: FAC '08
International Honours: Croatia: 55; U21-3

Niko Kranjcar

The influential Croatian playmaker started the season at Portsmouth, scoring in a 4-1 Carling Cup win over Hereford before earning a move to Tottenham, where he was reunited with former boss Harry Redknapp. Niko was possibly the club's best value signing of the season and really came to the fore when covering for the injured Luka Modric in a position starting from the left of midfield. Like his compatriot, he would pop up in various positions across the midfield and alongside or even in front of the strikers and was at his best when running with the ball, having the ability to ride tackles. As an attacking midfielder, he can also cover up front, having good passing and shooting skills. Also capable of spectacular goals, such as the final (ninth) goal against Wigan, he was a consistent scorer with eight goals in his 20 starts and eight appearances from the bench, which exceeded his scoring record in three full years at Portsmouth. Niko scored two goals against

Manchester City in December, but his most vital goal was the winner at Stoke, after receiving a pass from the left which had been dummied by Eidur Gudjohnsen. He was unfortunate to finish the season with an ankle injury sustained in the FA Cup semi-final, which he bravely finished, as Spurs had used all their substitutions. Niko is a regular in the Croatia side and scored two goals in seven games this season, with a full record of nine goals in 55 International games.

Portsmouth *(£3,500,000 from Hajduk Split, Croatia, ex Dynamo Zagreb, on 31/8/2006) PL 62+21/9 FLC 5/1 FAC 10/2 Others 2*
Tottenham H *(Signed on 1/9/2009) PL 19+5/6 FAC 5+3/2*

KRUL Timothy (Tim)
Born: Den Haag, Holland, 3 April 1988
Height: 6'2" **Weight:** 11.8
International Honours: Holland: U21-9; Yth
Now installed as understudy to Steve

Harper in the Newcastle goal, Tim had an early opportunity to show his qualities when coming off the bench for the injured Steve at half-time in the season opener at West Bromwich and did not disappoint with a series of outstanding saves to help secure a point. Apart from another substitute appearance against Swansea in November and a start in the final game at Queens Park Rangers, in both of which he was also unbeaten, his games were restricted to the Carling Cup and FA Cup ties, where he continued to impress with his good handling and physical presence in his area. He kept a clean sheet when playing for the Dutch under-21 side against England in August.
Newcastle U *(Signed from ADO Den Haag, Holland on 11/8/2005) P/FL 1+2 FLC 2 FAC 3 Others 1*
Falkirk *(Loaned on 1/1/2087) SL 22 SLC 2 SC 2*
Carlisle U *(Loaned on 21/11/2008) FL 9*

KRYSIAK Artur Lukasz
Born: Lodz, Poland, 11 August 1989
Height: 6'4" **Weight:** 13.1
International Honours: Poland: Yth
The Polish under-19 goalkeeper initially joined Burton on a month's loan from Birmingham and the deal was extended until the end of the season. He had previously gained limited first team experience on loan to Gretna, York, Swansea and Motherwell. Tall and athletic, Artur was Albion's regular goalkeeper for most of the campaign, though he had spells out of the team due to suspension and injury. He was freed by Birmingham and joined Exeter.
Birmingham C *(£60,000 from UKS SMS Lodz, Poland on 26/9/2006)*
Gretna *(Loaned on 31/11/2008) SL 3+1*
Swansea C *(Loaned on 23/9/2008) FL 2*
Burton A *(Loaned on 13/8/2009) FL 38 FAC 1 Others 1*

KUIPERS Michel
Born: Amsterdam, Holland, 26 June 1974
Height: 6'2" **Weight:** 14.10
Club Honours: Div 3 '01; Div 2 '02
It turned out to be a disappointing season for Brighton's veteran Dutchman. Michel started off in terrific form, retaining the goalkeeper's jersey in the face of pressure from the newly-signed Graeme Smith. His campaign started to fall apart when he was sent off at Huddersfield, and although he returned to hold his place, a groin injury in December allowed Peter Brezovan to take over. Blessed with excellent reflexes, Michel vied with Brezovan for a time until a broken finger in training

ruled him out for the rest of the season. After ten years of excellent service, Michel was released but has been promised a testimonial match at Albion's new stadium in 2011.
Bristol Rov *(Free from Blau-Wit Amsterdam, Holland on 20/1/1999) FL 1*
Brighton & Hove A *(Free on 4/7/2000) FL 246+1 FLC 10 FAC 16 Others 14*
Hull C *(Loaned on 29/8/2003) FL 3*
Boston U *(Loaned on 24/11/2005) FL 4*
Boston U *(Loaned on 16/2/2006) FL 11*

Michel Kuipers

KUQI Shefki
Born: Vuqitern, Kosovo, 10 November 1976
Height: 6'2" **Weight:** 13.10
International Honours: Finland: 60
The experienced striker was signed by Swansea on an 18-month contract in the January transfer window from German side Koblenz. Shefki's first three goals all resulted in 1-0 victories away from home but he had to wait until early April before opening his scoring account at the Liberty Stadium, against Scunthorpe.
Stockport Co *(£300,000 from FC Jokerit, Finland, ex HJK Helsinki, on 31/1/2001) FL 32+3/11 FLC 2/1 FAC 1*
Sheffield Wed *(£700,000 + on 11/1/2002) FL 58+6/19 FLC 3 FAC 1*
Ipswich T *(Free on 26/9/2003) FL 69+10/30 FLC 0+2 FAC 2+1/1 Others 3+1/1*
Blackburn Rov *(Free on 1/6/2005) PL 15+19/7 FLC 4+2/1 FAC 1+1*

Crystal Palace *(£2,500,000 on 31/8/2006) FL 46+32/17 FLC 1 FAC 1+3/1 (Freed during 2009 close season)*
Fulham *(Loaned on 31/8/2007) PL 3+7*
Ipswich T *(Loaned on 14/3/2008) FL 2+2*
Swansea C *(Signed from TuS Koblenz, Germany on 26/1/2010) FL 14+6/5*

KURUCZ Peter
Born: Budapest, Hungary, 30 May 1988
Height: 6'1" **Weight:** 12.0
International Honours: Hungary: U21-11
The Hungary under-21 international goalkeeper is developing at West Ham. A regular in the reserve side, Peter was given his first team debut against Manchester United in December. He was on as a second-half substitute and gave an accomplished performance, with a clean sheet against formidable opponents
West Ham U *(Signed from Ujpest, Hungary, via loan at Tatabanya, on 9/2/2009) PL 0+1*

KUSZCZAK Tomasz Miroslaw
Born: Krosno Odrzanskie, Poland, 20 March 1982
Height: 6'3" **Weight:** 13.3
Club Honours: UEFACL '08; FLC '09, '10
International Honours: Poland: 9
Polish international and Manchester United goalkeeper, Tomasz was understandably disappointed after being overlooked in favour of Ben Foster in the 2009 Carling Cup final, and might have seriously looked for other options to further his career. However, he persevered when Edwin van der Sar was injured at the start of 2009-10 and despite initially playing second fiddle to Foster, he kept a clean sheet in his first game – a 1-0 home win over Wolverhampton in the third round of the Carling Cup. Tomasz retained his position for United's Carling Cup fifth round tie against Tottenham, that saw United reach the semi-finals for the second season in succession. He played in the final against Aston Villa, his winners' medal ample reward for missing out 12 months earlier.
West Bromwich A *(Free from Hertha Berlin, Germany on 2/8/2004) PL 30+1 FLC 3 FAC 0+1*
Manchester U *(Signed on 11/8/2006) PL 25+2 FLC 8 FAC 6+1 Others 7+2*

KUYT Dirk
Born: Katwijk, Holland, 22 July 1980
Height: 6'0" **Weight:** 12.1
International Honours: Holland: 62
Despite being signed as a striker, the Dutch international seemed to be regarded by Liverpool's former manager

more as an auxiliary right-sided midfielder. Although a team player par excellence, Dirk seemed to suffer from the collective malaise that gripped Liverpool and his total of 11 goals was a disappointing return from 53 games, considering he played more than usual as a central striker in the absence of Fernando Torres. Unlike his illustrious colleague, most of Dirk's goals are scored from close range, often slotting home loose balls, and he continued his happy knack of scoring against Everton, in both derby games, and producing vital goals in European competitions, where his total of 13 is bettered only by Steven Gerrard and Ian Rush. His best game was in the fourth place contest with Tottenham in January when he scored both goals in a 2-0 victory. He also scored in the 4-1 Europa Cup victory over Benfica with a close-range header from a corner – a curious affair since the linesman disallowed it for offside, only to be overruled by a referee with a better understanding of the laws. Sadly, that was Dirk's only goal in the last 19 matches.
Liverpool *(£9,000,000 from Feyenoord, Holland, ex Quick Boys, FC Utrecht, on 18/8/2006) PL 121+19/36 FLC 1+2 FAC 7+2/2 Others 43+4/13*

KYRGIAKOS Sotirios
Born: Trikala, Greece, 23 July 1979
Height: 6'4" **Weight:** 13.5
International Honours: Greece: 58
An experienced Greek international central defender, Sotirios was a late summer signing by Liverpool as cover for Daniel Agger, Jamie Carragher and Martin Skrtel. He made his debut at Bolton but was selected only intermittently until January, when he had five games deputising for Agger and gave some sterling performances, including his first goal at Stoke. Sotirios is a rugged player, not dissimilar to Skrtel, and unfortunately was sent off in the home derby with Everton. He took a back seat until the closing weeks, when he again performed with distinction and created a second goal against West Ham from a close-range header that hit a post and bounced in off the goalkeeper. In view of his modest fee, the Greek defender was a success and one of few at Anfield who can look back with satisfaction.
Glasgow Rgrs *(£1,750,000 from Panathinaikos, Greece via loan at Agios Nikolaos, on 29/11/2005. Signed by Eintracht Frankfurt, Germany on 1/7/2008)*
Liverpool *(£2,000,000 from AEK Athens, Greece on 21/8/2009) PL 13+1/1 FLC 2 Others 3+2*

L

LABADIE Joss Christopher

Born: Croydon, 31 August 1990
Height: 5'7" **Weight:** 11.2
Equally at home as a defending or attacking midfield player with plenty of stamina, West Bromwich's Joss started his second loan spell at Shrewsbury with a goal on the opening day of the season in a 3-1 win against Burton. His game includes strong tackling and full on action. A great strike from a free kick, his fifth goal for the Shrews came from a dead ball at Morecambe. Later sent off in the same game, he seemed to lose his focus and made his final appearance in the November FA Cup game against Staines. Almost immediately, Joss joined Cheltenham on loan in November, having scored twice against the Robins for Shrewsbury less than two months before. Capable of making box-to-box runs for 90 minutes, he spent three months with Town and was an ever-present during this spell save for a one-match suspension. Cheltenham were reported as wanting to extend the loan but financial restrictions prevented them from doing so and Joss joined Tranmere for his third loan spell of the campaign. Spending the last month or so of the season at Prenton Park, he made his full debut in the home defeat of Exeter, scoring the first of his three valuable goals for the club. Out of contract at the Hawthorns in the summer, having impressed Rovers' physio-turned-manager Les Parry so much in his time in Birkenhead that he was both offered, and then accepted, a permanent deal.
West Bromwich A *(From trainee on 5/7/2008)*
Shrewsbury T *(Loaned on 2/1/2009) FL 1*
Shrewsbury T *(Loaned on 3/8/2009) FL 11+2/5 FAC 1 Others 1*
Cheltenham T *(Loaned on 20/11/2009) FL 11*
Tranmere Rov *(Loaned on 24/3/2010) FL 5+4/3*

LAIRD Marc James Peter

Born: Edinburgh, 23 January 1986
Height: 5'11" **Weight:** 12.12
Marc's central midfield role was hotly contested but his ability when he played could not be faulted. Tall and lithe, he is another of Millwall's box-to-box players and a good ball winner. He played an outstanding part in the FA Cup run in his usual midfield position. Out of contract in the summer, the club have made him an offer of re-engagement.
Manchester C *(From trainee on 23/1/2004)*
Northampton T *(Loaned on 26/1/2007) FL 2+4*
Port Vale *(Loaned on 8/11/2007) FL 7/1 FAC 3*
Millwall *(Free on 9/1/2008) FL 63+12/6 FLC 2+1 FAC 9/1 Others 2+2*

LALLANA Adam David

Born: St Albans, 10 May 1988
Height: 5'8" **Weight:** 11.6
Club Honours: AMC '10
International Honours: E: U21-1; Yth
It has been an outstanding season for the astounding Southampton Academy graduate. Always a scurrying, tight dribbler, he has evolved into a better team member; finding extra poise, involving team-mates to greater purpose, and chasing back and tackling with greater assurance. Scoring is coming more easily too. He helped himself to 20 goals last season, not least the pulsating headed effort that put Saints 2-0 up in the 4-1 win over Carlisle in the Johnstone's Paint Trophy final. Press speculation concerning Adam's future abounds: it is to be hoped he can be retained for another season – at least.
Southampton *(From trainee on 6/12/2005) FL 79+11/17 FLC 6/3 FAC 5/1 Others 5/2*
Bournemouth *(Loaned on 9/10/2007) FL 2+1 Others 1*

LAMBE Reginald (Reggie)

Born: Bermuda, 4 February 1991
Height: 5'7" **Weight:** 10.12
International Honours: Bermuda: 9
A Bermudan international, Reggie's debut and only game for Ipswich came in the Carling Cup at Shrewsbury. He was part of a three-man attack and laid on one of the goals for Connor Wickham.
Ipswich T *(From trainee on 15/7/2009) FLC 1*

LAMBERT Rickie Lee

Born: Liverpool, 16 February 1982
Height: 5'10" **Weight:** 11.2
Club Honours: AMC '10
Rickie had just one match at home to Leyton Orient and scored before his big money transfer from Bristol Rovers to Southampton took place. Joint League One 'Golden Boot' in 2008-09; could he do it for Saints? Yes! He logged 37 goals, 31 of them in League One - a record for the current millennium. Lethal from any angle anywhere within 40 yards of the goal during open play or from free kicks, he combines his ruthlessness with an ability to endure the brutal attentions of 'markers' with almost Zen-like stoicism. He reaped a team-bus full of awards, including 'Man of the Match' for the Johnstone's Paint Trophy final, Saints' 'Player of the Season' and the PFA 'League One Player of the Year', as well as winning a competition run by BBC's Late Kick-Off, for having the hardest kick in the south and south-west, his shot being clocked 80 mph.
Blackpool *(From trainee on 17/7/2000) FL 0+3*
Macclesfield T *(Free on 2/3/2001) FL 36+8/8 FAC 4/2 Others 1*
Stockport Co *(£300,000 on 30/4/2003) FL 88+10/18 FLC 3 FAC 2+1 Others 5+1/1*
Rochdale *(Signed on 17/2/2005) FL 61+3/28 FLC 1 FAC 1 Others 2*
Bristol Rov *(£200,000 on 31/8/2006) FL 114+14/52 FLC 2+1 FAC 13+1/6 Others 10/2*
Southampton *(Signed on 10/8/2009) FL 44+1/30 FLC 2/1 FAC 5/2 Others 6/3*

Rickie Lambert

LAMPARD Frank James

Born: Romford, 20 June 1978
Height: 6'0" **Weight:** 12.6
Club Honours: FLC '05, '07; PL '05, '06, '10; CS '05, '09; FAC '07, '09, '10
International Honours: E: 78; B-1; U21-19; Yth
In sheer numerical terms this was Frank's most productive season, yet he began it at the apex of Carlo Ancelotti's newly introduced diamond formation and then uncharacteristically went ten matches without scoring before smashing home a drive against Atletico Madrid. This goal took his Chelsea tally to 133, overtaking the legendary Jimmy Greaves and putting him fifth in the club's all-time list, behind four England

strikers. Frank moved slightly deeper and was up and running again, the goals and assists flowing. He ended with 27 goals for the season and 157 overall, with only Kerry Dixon and Bobby Tambling having scored more. His haul included another Premier League four-timer, against Aston Villa, and five 'doubles'. He had the most assists in the Premier League with 14, and the third highest number of passes, 1,923. These figures illustrate Frank's massive contribution to Chelsea's record-breaking season of 103 League goals and their first domestic 'Double'. The personal accolades rolled in. He was shortlisted for FIFA 'World Player 2009' and just before Christmas was elected as

Premier League 'Player of the Decade'. He currently stands eighth in the all-time Premier League scoring charts – the only midfield player in the top ten, a phenomenal achievement. As a fitting recognition, he was the recipient of the prestigious 2010 Football Writers' Association Tribute Award, given only to those who have made an outstanding contribution to the game.

West Ham U *(From trainee on 1/7/1995) PL 132+16/24 FLC 14+1/8 FAC 13/2 Others 10/4*
Swansea C *(Loaned on 6/10/1995) FL 8+1/1 Others 1+1*
Chelsea *(£11,000,000 on 3/7/2001) PL 314+6/105 FLC 18+10/11 FAC 41+4/19 Others 80+4/22*

Frank Lampard

LANCASHIRE Oliver (Ollie) James
Born: Basingstoke, 13 December 1988
Height : 6'1" **Weight:** 11.11
A product of the Southampton Academy, Ollie is a big lad who operates as a centre-back and can play a bit. After making two starts early in the campaign, manager Alan Pardew decided that he required more experience and loaned him to Grimsby. The promising defender was to enjoy two loan spells with Grimsby, overcoming a dismissal on his October debut against Accrington to give consistent performances. Ollie's regular selection saw a growing partnership alongside Rob Atkinson despite Town's relegation fight, while his own threat at set pieces was rewarded with a first career goal in April at Darlington. Was released by Saints at the end of the season.
Southampton *(From trainee on 5/7/2006) FL 11+2 FLC 1 FAC 1+2*
Grimsby T *(Loaned on 24/10/2009) FL 9 Others 1*
Grimsby T *(Loaned on 1/2/2010) FL 15+1/1*

Ollie Lancashire

LANGMEAD Kelvin Steven
Born: Coventry, 23 March 1985
Height: 6'1" **Weight:** 13.6
Shrewsbury's longest-serving player, who has been at the club for six years and has played over 250 times, missed only two League games. A strong, dependable central defender, he won the local radio station's 'Player of the Year' award for his consistent and solid performances. Equally comfortable on the ground or in the air, Kelvin captained the side for some of the

season and was voted 'Players' Player of the Year'. A constant danger at set pieces, he scored three goals, including his first for 18 months in the August 3-1 win against Accrington.
Preston NE (From trainee on 26/2/2004) FL 0+1
Carlisle U (Loaned on 27/2/2004) FL 3+8/1
Kidderminster Hrs (Loaned on 4/9/2004) FL 9+1/1 Others 1
Shrewsbury T (Signed on 26/11/2004) FL 210+21/19 FLC 2+3 FAC 4+1 Others 15+1

LANSBURY Henri George
Born: Enfield, 12 October 1990
Height : 6'2" **Weight:** 10.10
International Honours: E: U21-1; Yth
The Arsenal midfield player came to Watford on loan in August and ended up staying the whole season. He made his debut as a substitute against Blackpool in August, but took a little time to settle, partly because it was unclear whether his best position was central midfield or as a supporting striker. An outstanding performance against Sheffield Wednesday in October that included two picture-book goals boosted his confidence, and he continued to show steady improvement and a pleasing attitude and consistency for the rest of the season. Henri scored five excellent goals, with the pick being a 30-yard screamer at Coventry on the last day. Already an England under-19 international, he won his first under-21 cap in November. He returned to Arsenal in time to feature as a second-half substitute in the club's final fixture of the season, the 4-0 home win over Fulham.
Arsenal (From trainee on 2/7/2008) PL 0+1 FLC 0+4
Scunthorpe U (Loaned on 31/1/2009) FL 12+4/4 Others 1+1
Watford (Loaned on 21/8/2009) FL 34+3/5 FLC 0+1 FAC 1

LAPPIN Simon
Born: Glasgow, 25 January 1983
Height: 5'11" **Weight:** 9.6
Club Honours: S Div 1 '06; Div 1 '10
International Honours: S: U21-10
Awarded a new contract in the summer, Simon repaid that in kind by being one of Norwich's most consistent performers. Predominantly playing on the left of a three-man central midfield, his tenacious displays and high work rate, allied to his excellent crossing of the ball, both in open play and from set pieces, made him one of the first names on the team-sheet each week. He also played a few matches at left-back as required and that versatility also

allowed for switches to be made during matches. His unassuming style did not win any individual awards but his overall contribution was second to none.
St Mirren (From juniors on 1/7/1999) SL 136+16/9 SLC 6+1/1 SC 9+2 Others 7+1/2
Norwich C (£100,000 on 31/1/2007) FL 75+3/2 FLC 4+1/1 FAC 3 Others 2
Motherwell (Loaned on 31/1/2008) SL 7+7/2 SC 0+1

LARKIN Colin
Born: Dundalk, 27 April 1982
Height: 5'9" **Weight:** 10.4
International Honours: RoI: Yth
A much-travelled striker or winger, he signed for Hartlepool after showing up well and scoring in a pre-season friendly. Known to Pool's manager Chris Turner from his days as Wolverhampton youth team coach, Colin was signed to give what was a newly assembled squad more attacking options. Early on, he was mainly restricted to substitute appearances but, looking lively as a striker, was soon off the mark with a clever chipped goal against Walsall. A fast-running player, Colin was later utilised more as a right-sided midfielder.
Wolverhampton W (From trainee on 19/5/1999) FL 1+2 FLC 0+1/1
Kidderminster Hrs (Loaned on 14/9/2001) FL 31+2/6 Others 1+1/1
Mansfield T (£135,000 on 9/8/2002) FL 61+31/25 FLC 1 FAC 5+1/1 Others 3+4
Chesterfield (Free on 1/7/2005) FL 58+24/11 FLC 4/2 FAC 3 Others 1+2
Northampton T (Free on 5/7/2007) FL 23+31/3 FLC 1+2/1 FAC 4/1 Others 2
Hartlepool U (Free on 7/8/2009) FL 10+12/1 FLC 0+2 FAC 1 Others 1

LARRIEU Romain
Born: Mont-de-Marsan, France, 31 August 1976
Height: 6'4" **Weight:** 13.11
Club Honours: Div 3 '02
International Honours: France: Yth
Romain, in his tenth season at Home Park, is a true professional and is much appreciated by everyone at Plymouth. To reward him for his long service the popular Frenchman was given the role of club captain at the start of the season. Following on from 2008-09 when he was not the Pilgrims' number-one choice in goal, he trained hard during the close season to ensure that he would be in the starting line-up in August. He made 27 consecutive appearances in goal until David Stockdale arrived on loan in late January to replace him. Romain returned to the team for the final game of the season at home to Peterborough.
Plymouth Arg (Free from ASOA Valence, France, ex Montpellier, on 30/11/2000) FL 263+1 FLC 4 FAC 13 Others 3
Gillingham (Loaned on 22/1/2007) FL 14
Yeovil T (Loaned on 21/9/2007) FL 6 Others 1

LARSSON Sebastian Benet
Born: Eskilstuna, Sweden, 6 June 1985
Height: 5'10" **Weight:** 11.4
International Honours: Sweden: 21; U21-12

Sebastian Larsson

Was a key member of the team nicknamed 'The Unbeatables' for the 15-game sequence without loss that effectively kept Birmingham in the Premier League. Sebastian worked the right flank prodigiously and with a keen eye for a good pass, and excellent dead-ball delivery, fitted in perfectly and unselfishly to the side. Supported the front pair well and also did a disciplined job in helping his full-back.
Arsenal *(From trainee on 1/7/2002) PL 2+1 FLC 4+3 FAC 0+1 Others 1*
Birmingham C *(£500,000 on 4/8/2006) P/FL 120+29/15 FLC 7/2 FAC 8/3*

LAURENT Francis
Born: Paris, France, 6 January 1986
Height: 6'3" **Weight:** 14.0
The tall French winger, in his second season at Southend, was introduced to the club by his agent as a centre-forward but has subsequently found his true position on the right of midfield, where his languid style and burst of pace produced some eye-catching performances and left several League One left-backs turned inside out. His unpredictably and tremendous ball skills have won him cult status amongst the Roots Hall faithful. Francis contributed a useful six goals from the flank, including a brace at home to Brentford in April.
Southend U *(Free from FSV Mainz, Germany, ex Sochaux-Montbeliard B, on 1/9/2008) FL 38+18/9 FAC 3+1/1 Others 1+1*

LAW Nicholas (Nicky)
Born: Plymouth, 29 March 1988
Height: 5'10" **Weight:** 11.6
International Honours: E: Yth
Snapped up from neighbours Sheffield United in the summer having played well against Rotherham late in the previous season while on loan with Bradford. Skilful, elusive and with a touch of quality not overly common in League Two, he had a splendid first half of the season, good enough to catch the eye of opposing players who popped him into the PFA League Two 'Team of the Season' when the time came. Played wide, essentially on the right but could be equally threatening, if not more so, when switched to the left. Was reported to be a mid-season target for Blackpool which Rotherham brushed off but then his form dropped below the early dizzy heights before picking up again late season. For a player of such skill and ability, a return of only two goals was disappointing. Still only 22, he will probably have learned a lot.
Sheffield U *(From trainee on*

17/11/2005) P/FL 2+3 FLC 3+1/1 FAC 0+1
Yeovil T *(Loaned on 16/2/2007) FL 5+1*
Bradford C *(Loaned on 6/10/2007) FL 10/2*
Bradford C *(Loaned on 27/10/2008) FL 30+3/3 FAC 2*
Rotherham U *(Free on 6/7/2009) FL 41+1/2 FLC 2 FAC 3 Others 4*

LAWRENCE Liam
Born: Retford, 14 December 1981
Height: 5'10" **Weight:** 11.3
Club Honours: Ch '05, '07
International Honours: RoI: 8
There is no denying that this was an extremely frustrating campaign for Liam, in which he struggled to make much of an impact on the Stoke team and spent long spells out of the side and on the substitutes' bench. This was surprising, especially given the undoubted impact he had on the side at the end of the previous season after coming back from injury. Many expected him to continue on the right side, where he had such a regular and telling influence in Stoke's resurgence over the past three or four seasons. Liam has said himself that he may need to seek a move if he does not win back a permanent place in the Stoke line-up.
Mansfield T *(From trainee on 3/7/2000) FL 120+16/34 FLC 3 FAC 8/5 Others 4+2*
Sunderland *(Signed on 5/8/2004) P/FL 49+24/10 FLC 3+2 FAC 2*
Stoke C *(£500,000 on 18/11/2006) P/FL 99+14/23 FLC 4 FAC 5+3/1*

LAWRENCE Matthew (Matt) James
Born: Northampton, 19 June 1974
Height: 6'1" **Weight:** 12.12
Club Honours: Div 2 '01
International Honours: E: Sch
After beginning the season as part of the first team squad, Matt found himself out of the picture, transfer listed and criticised by his own manager for his part in a 4-0 defeat for Crystal Palace at home to Scunthorpe in September. A training ground injury then ruled him out of contention for some time but he was back in the team in early January following the sale of Jose Fonte to Southampton. In that return, he moved from right-back to central defence for the remainder of the season, where he was more often than not preferred as partner to Paddy McCarthy. Forming a good understanding with his new partner, he was an integral part of a defence that did not concede too many goals as Palace battled successfully against relegation. His contract at Palace

expired in June.
Wycombe W *(£20,000 from Grays Ath on 19/1/1996) FL 13+3/1 FLC 4 FAC 1 Others 0+1*
Fulham *(Free on 7/2/1997) FL 57+2 FLC 4+1 FAC 2 Others 5*
Wycombe W *(£86,000 + on 2/10/1998) FL 63/4 FLC 4 FAC 6 Others 3*
Millwall *(£200,000 on 21/3/2000) FL 213+11 FLC 9+1 FAC 19 Others 8*
Crystal Palace *(Signed on 3/8/2006) FL 109+12/1 FLC 2+1 FAC 8+1 Others 1+1*

LAWRIE James
Born: Belfast, 18 December 1990
Height: 6'0" **Weight:** 12.5
International Honours: NI: 3; B-1; U21-8; Yth
A skilful forward with Port Vale, he was unable to break through into the first team. However, he spent a lot of time on Northern Ireland international duty at various levels, scoring twice for the under-21 team and helping the under-19s to win the Milk Cup. With Vale, his time was limited to four substitute appearances, 20 minutes being the longest on the opening day. He scored a hat-trick on his final appearance for Vale reserves before ending the season on loan at Kidderminster, where he scored once in 12 games. He was freed at the end of the season.
Port Vale *(From trainee on 12/2/2008) FL 8+9/2 FAC 0+2 Others 0+1*

LEACH Daniel James
Born: Perth, Australia, 5 January 1986
Height: 6'3" **Weight:** 12.13
Tall Australian defender Daniel signed for Barnet after impressing on trial in pre-season. He had previously been playing college football in America and was allegedly discovered via the internet website, YouTube. Daniel found himself in and out of the team, playing at centre-back when selected. During the second half of the season, he had a loan spell at Blue Square South side Dover Athletic. Was out of contract at the end of June.
Barnet *(Free from Portland Timbers, USA ex Brisbane Strikers, Oregon State University, on 21/7/2009) FL 12+1 FLC 1 FAC 1 Others 1*

LEACOCK Dean Graham
Born: Croydon, 10 June 1984
Height: 6'2" **Weight:** 12.4
International Honours: E: Yth
At his best, Dean is Derby's smoothest central defender but he has had regular problems with injuries in the last two seasons. He managed only 13 Championship starts as hamstring and knee injuries restricted him. At one

stage, he produced some accomplished performances at right-back. Dean always looks a player but Nigel Clough's inherited problem is to get him on the pitch regularly. He has passed 100 appearances for Derby and in the hope of stepping up his rate, he reported early for fitness work before pre-season.
Fulham (From trainee on 17/7/2002) PL 8+1 FLC 4
Coventry C (Loaned on 10/9/2004) FL 12+1 FLC 1 FAC 1+1
Derby Co (£375,000 on 11/8/2006) P/FL 81+11 FLC 3 FAC 2 Others 3

Grant Leadbitter

LEADBITTER Grant
Born: Chester-le-Street, 7 January 1986
Height: 5'9" **Weight:** 10.3
Club Honours: Ch '07
International Honours: E: U21-3; Yth; Sch
Grant was sold by Sunderland to former boss Roy Keane at Ipswich along with Carlos Edwards as the August transfer window drew to a close. He had been named on the bench for the opening four Premier League games, coming on for his 50th and final substitute League appearance against Chelsea at the Stadium of Light. There was to be one final game for Grant in his beloved red and white, a Carling Cup tie at Norwich, near neighbours of the club he was about to move to. At Ipswich he quickly settled in to the side, making his presence felt in midfield and taking all the free kicks and corners. He scored on his home debut against Nottingham Forest after 42 seconds when a long throw caused panic in the Forest defence and he volleyed home the loose ball. He tackled back well in his own half, being keen to support his forwards in attack, and was not afraid

to shoot from any distance although his efforts only yielded two more goals during the campaign.
Sunderland (From trainee on 9/1/2003) P/FL 61+50/11 FLC 5+3 FAC 3+1
Rotherham U (Loaned on 23/9/2005) FL 3+2/1 FAC 1 Others 1
Ipswich T (Signed on 1/9/2009) FL 36+2/3 FAC 2

LEARY Michael Antonio
Born: Ealing, 17 April 1983
Height: 5'11" **Weight:** 12.3
International Honours: RoI: Yth
A first team squad member for Grimsby last term, Michael had a run of over a dozen successive starts in Town's midfield during the winter. The tough ball winner likewise offered support to the attack, and while not on the score-sheet himself, his reputation for long-range shooting was maintained when he unluckily saw a 40-yard effort at Notts County cannon off the bar.
Luton T (From juniors on 3/8/2001) FL 9+13/2 FLC 1+1 FAC 1+1 Others 3+2/1
Bristol Rov (Loaned on 31/8/2005) FL 12+1 Others 1
Walsall (Loaned on 6/1/2006) FL 12+3/1 FAC 3/1
Torquay U (Loaned on 3/11/2006) FL 0+2 FAC 1
Brentford (Loaned on 4/1/2007) FL 17
Barnet (Free on 12/7/2007) FL 43+7/3 FLC 1+1 FAC 5+1 Others 1
Grimsby T (Free on 3/7/2009) FL 19+9 FLC 0+1 FAC 1 Others 1+1

LEDLEY Joseph (Joe) Christopher
Born: Cardiff, 23 January 1987
Height: 6'0" **Weight:** 11.7
International Honours: W: 32; U21-5; Yth
Local boy Joe first joined Cardiff as an eight-year-old schoolboy and has been with the club ever since. Out of contract this summer, having spent 18 months in stalemate on new contract talks, Joe waited until he knew where Cardiff would be playing in 2010-11 before deciding what to do and was devastated by their 3-2 defeat by Blackpool in the play-off final. The two Glasgow clubs, Rangers and Celtic, and Premier clubs were all linked with Joe, but he did re-open talks on a new contract with the Bluebirds after the end of the season. The powerful midfielder had operations on both hips in January and February but, remarkably, he was back ahead of schedule and played at the start of April in a 2-1 win against Swansea. He started five times for Wales over the season but did not score.
Cardiff C (From trainee on 29/10/2004)

FL 213+13/25 FLC 10+3/1 FAC 13+1/2 Others 3/1

LEE Alan Desmond
Born: Galway, 21 August 1978
Height: 6'2" **Weight:** 13.9
International Honours: RoI: 10; U21-5
It was a season of rejuvenation for Alan, who finished the previous one on loan to Norwich and looking as if he was set to move on from Crystal Palace. Often forced to play a lone-striking role at Palace under manager Neil Warnock, the big, hard-working Republic of Ireland international became a fans' favourite with a series of committed performances and the ability to win most aerial battles he is involved in. Although he began the season in that lone role, he finished it with more forward support to feed off him, with caretaker manager Paul Hart opting to field two strikers. Alan missed a few vital weeks towards the end of the season with a groin injury but scored the opening goal in Palace's last fixture at Sheffield Wednesday, where they claimed the point they needed to stay in the Championship.
Aston Villa (From trainee on 21/8/1995)
Torquay U (Loaned on 27/11/1998) FL 6+1/2 Others 2/1
Port Vale (Loaned on 2/3/1999) FL 7+4/2
Burnley (£150,000 on 8/7/1999) FL 2+13 FLC 1+1 FAC 0+2 Others 1/1
Rotherham U (£150,000 on 21/9/2000) FL 105+6/37 FLC 5/2 FAC 4+1/1 Others 1/1
Cardiff C (£850,000 + on 15/8/2003) FL 47+39/10 FLC 6/1 FAC 2+2/1
Ipswich T (Signed on 10/1/2006) FL 91+12/31 FLC 2/2 FAC 3+1/1
Crystal Palace (£900,000 on 30/8/2008) FL 43+15/9 FLC 1 FAC 8/1
Norwich C (Loaned on 19/3/2009) FL 6+1/2

LEE Charlie
Born: Whitechapel, 5 January 1987
Height: 5'9" **Weight:** 11.7
Charlie is something of an enigma, having originally joined Peterborough as a midfield player but being used more often as a full-back or centre-half. He seems to relish the challenge of playing centre-half against much taller front men: he may be only 5'9" but is rarely beaten in the air. Charlie, tough in the tackle and with a good eye for a telling pass, may need to be given the chance to concentrate on just one role so that he can settle down
Tottenham H (From trainee on 15/7/2005)
Millwall (Loaned on 16/11/2006) FL 4+1 Others 1

Peterborough U (Free on 27/7/2007)
FL 99+20/13 FLC 4+2 FAC 8+1/1 Others
2+1/1

LEE Chung-Yong

Born: Seoul, South Korea, 2 July 1988
Height: 5'11" **Weight:** 10.12
International Honours: South Korea:
24; U23-7; Yth
Completely disproving the adage that it
often takes foreign players time to
settle in the English game, Chung-Yong
had a fine debut season and much of
Bolton's creative play came through
him. He made his debut as a substitute
on the opening day of the season and
scored a fine first goal for the club in
the 2-1 victory at Birmingham. He was
subsequently rewarded with a place in
the starting line-up against Tottenham
and did not look back from there. A
rapid presence on the wing, Chung-
Yong also possesses a willingness to
take on opposition defenders, as was
proved by the number of goal assists he
provided. His eye for goal was also clear
to see, with particularly impressive
strikes coming in the home wins over
Everton and West Ham. Chung-Yong
retained his place for much of the rest
of the season, so impressive was his
form. He was rested at the very end of
the season but it is no surprise that
fatigue started to show after playing
such a pivotal role in Bolton's
Premiership survival, while also
considering that Chung-Yong would be
involved with South Korea in the World
Cup.
Bolton W (£2,200,000 from FC Seoul,
South Korea on 14/8/2009) PL 27+7/4
FLC 0+2 FAC 3+1/1

LEE Graeme Barry

Born: Middlesbrough, 31 May 1978
Height: 6'2" **Weight:** 13.7
Club Honours: AMC '07; Div 2 '10
Recruited from Bradford by Notts
County in the summer as the central
pivot of the defence, Graeme suffered
an early injury and it took until mid-
season for him to regain his fitness
and form. He then formed an
inseparable defensive barrier with
Mike Edwards and clean sheet after
clean sheet followed. His experience
during the run-in to promotion was
invaluable, as were his goals from set
plays.
Hartlepool U (From trainee on
2/7/1996) FL 208+11/19 FLC 7+2/1 FAC
8+1 Others 13+2/2
Sheffield Wed (Free on 2/7/2003) FL
63+4/5 FLC 1/1 FAC 4 Others 3/1
Doncaster Rov (£50,000 on
13/1/2006) FL 56+4/5 FLC 1 FAC 3
Others 5+1/1

Hartlepool U (Loaned on 14/2/2008)
FL 3
Shrewsbury T (Loaned on 19/3/2008)
FL 4+1
Bradford C (Free on 8/8/2008) FL 44/2
FLC 1 FAC 2/1 Others 1
Notts Co (Free on 2/7/2009) FL 31+1/4
FAC 3 Others 1

LEE Jake Alexander

Born: Cirencester, 18 September 1991
Height: 6'0" **Weight:** 12.7
Second-year scholarship player Jake
made one further League appearance
for Cheltenham, as a substitute in a 0-0
draw at Bournemouth. This locally-born
striker, was top scorer for the youth
team with 11 goals and one of four
scholars to be offered professional
contracts.
Cheltenham T (Trainee) FL 2+2

LEE Kieran Christopher

Born: Stalybridge, 22 June 1988
Height: 6'1" **Weight:** 12.0
It was a fantastic breakthrough season
at Oldham for this ex-Manchester
United starlet. For the early part of the
campaign, Kieran watched from the
sidelines but in the away fixture at
Wycombe, with Athletic short of players
through injury and suspensions, he was
drafted in at full-back. Kieran took to
the job like a duck takes to water.
Quick, solid and with a great range of
passing, nothing fazed him. Oldham
quickly offered the youngster a contract
extension which he duly accepted.
Kieran is very much one for the future.
Manchester U (From trainee on
6/7/2006) PL 1 FLC 0+2/1
Queens Park Rgrs (Loaned on
2/1/2008) FL 2+5 FAC 0+1
Oldham Ath (Free on 14/7/2008) FL
22+9/1 FLC 0+1 FAC 0+2 Others 1+1

LEE Richard Anthony

Born: Oxford, 5 October 1982
Height: 6'0" **Weight:** 12.8
International Honours: E: Yth
Richard was restricted to Carling Cup
appearances at Watford in 2009-10
because of the form and consistency of
Scott Loach in goal but still managed to
excel in the tie at Leeds. A knee injury
ruled him out for five matches in
October, but otherwise he continued to
offer unstinting support and
commitment from the bench. His value
to Watford was underlined when a loan
offer from Wycombe was rejected in
February and he signed a further
contract extension. Enterprising off the
pitch, Richard opened his own
goalkeeping school.
Watford (From trainee on 7/3/2000)
P/FL 89+3 FLC 12 FAC 4 Others 2

LEE Thomas (Tommy) Edward

Born: Keighley, 3 January 1986
Height: 6'2" **Weight:** 12.0
A standout shot-stopper, Tommy was
voted the supporters' 'Player of the
Season' at Chesterfield after the
goalkeeper made match-clinching reflex
saves in too many games to list here. In
front of him, a frequently changed
defence brought communication
problems and led to scary moments but
Tommy had a fine season, and
continues to develop under Mark
Crossley's coaching.
Manchester U (From trainee on
6/7/2005)
Macclesfield T (Loaned on 18/1/2006)
FL 11 Others 1
Macclesfield T (Free on 26/7/2006) FL
51+1 FLC 1 FAC 2
Rochdale (Loaned on 21/3/2008) FL 11
Others 3
Chesterfield (Free on 1/8/2008) FL 70
FLC 2 FAC 3 Others 4

LEE-BARRETT Arran

Born: Ipswich, 28 February 1984
Height: 6'2" **Weight:** 12.10
International Honours: E: SP-1
It was a case of being in the right place
at the right time for Arran. Being a local
lad and a free agent, he was given
permission to train with Ipswich while
he looked for a club. Four games into
the season he found one – Ipswich.
Shane Supple's sudden retirement
meant that Ipswich needed an
experienced 'keeper as cover for
Richard Wright so they signed him on.
Next day he was on the bench at West
Bromwich and then when Wright was
injured in the game at Cardiff, he took
his place between the posts. Arran
made his full debut in the next game at
Bristol City, keeping a clean sheet, and
retained his place in the side until mid-
February when Brian Murphy took over.
Cardiff C (From trainee at Norwich C
on 23/5/2003. Free to Weymouth on
12/7/2005)
Coventry C (Free on 12/1/2007)
Hartlepool U (Free on 3/7/2007) FL 55
FLC 3 FAC 5 Others 2
Ipswich T (Free on 21/8/2009) FL 12+1
FAC 2 s

LEES Thomas (Tom) James

Born: Warwick, 28 November 1990
Height: 6'1" **Weight:** 12.2
A young defender who signed on loan
from Leeds in September, he went on to
make 46 appearances at right-back for
Accrington. Also able to play in the
centre of the defence, Tom is
dependable, has a great attitude and
hunger to learn, and immediately fitted

in well to the back four, keeping his place throughout the season. Tom, who also showed a penchant for solid tackling and getting down the line, stated at the end of the campaign that he had benefited from his time at Accrington, especially with decision making and concentration levels.
Leeds U (From trainee on 20/1/2009)
Accrington Stanley (Loaned on 1/9/2009) FL 39 FAC 4 Others 3

LE FONDRE Adam
Born: Stockport, 2 December 1986
Height: 5'10" **Weight:** 11.4
Rochdale had to sell their previous season's top scorer Adam to rivals Rotherham after just one match, to ease their financial position and what a snip he proved to be. Nicknamed 'The Goal Machine' by the fans, the striker functioned superbly with vital goal after vital goal until slowing down in the final couple of months. Then he scored in each of the play-off semi-finals to help take the Millers to Wembley, where he suffered his second play-off heartbreak in three seasons. He scored in five consecutive matches on two occasions, both times being level with equalling the club record of six and he bagged 30 goals in all, thus becoming the first Rotherham player to reach that mark since Alan Crawford in 1977. His spectacular overhead kick against Lincoln in November was the club's 'Goal of the Season' and he proved ice cool and deadly from the penalty spot, his ten spot-kicks (out of ten) being a record in League games in one season for the club.
Stockport Co (From trainee on 18/2/2005) FL 29+34/17 FLC 1+1/1 FAC 1+4 Others 1+2/1
Rochdale (Loaned on 19/1/2007) FL 7/4
Rochdale (Signed on 3/7/2007) FL 58+33/33 FLC 0+3 FAC 3/4 Others 4+4
Rotherham U (Signed on 11/8/2009) FL 43+1/25 FAC 3/2 Others 4/3

LEGGE Leon Clinton
Born: Bexhill, 1 July 1985
Height: 6'1" **Weight:** 11.3
A tall, commanding old-fashioned centre-half, the 24-year-old joined Brentford from Tonbridge Angels in the summer, a jump of four divisions. After playing in the reserves with an occasional first team game, Leon broke into the League side at the beginning of December and did not miss a game for the remainder of the campaign. His powerful heading was a feature of his play and his positional sense was also sound. He was selected as the FA Cup 'Player of the Second Round' after scoring the winning goal against Walsall.

Brentford (Signed from Tonbridge Angels, ex Eastbourne U, Hailsham T, Eastbourne Borough, Woking, on 3/7/2009) FL 28+1/2 FAC 3/1 Others 1

LEGZDINS Adam Richard
Born: Penkridge, 28 November 1986
Height: 6'0" **Weight:** 12.3
A goalkeeper signed from Birmingham, Adam had to be patient at Crewe. He was unable to break into the senior side in his first season and had to miss time because of a shoulder operation. His wait finally bore fruit with a debut in the Johnstone's Paint Trophy tie against Stockport. A League debut followed at Cheltenham and he played in the final five games of the season, time enough to impress with his consistent performances.
Birmingham C (From trainee on 4/7/2006)
Oldham Ath (Loaned on 27/10/2006) Others 0+1
Crewe Alex (Free on 2/7/2008) FL 6 FLC 1 Others 1

Mikele Leigertwood

LEIGERTWOOD Mikele Benjamin
Born: Enfield, 12 November 1982
Height: 6'1" **Weight:** 13.11
International Honours: Antigua & Barbuda: 3
Stand-in skipper at Queens Park Rangers for much of the season due to the absence of Martin Rowlands and Gavin Mahon, in a season of turmoil at Loftus Road he remained a mainstay of the side regardless of who was picking

the team. Mikele has played at right-back on many occasions as well as his favoured central midfield role. Not always a favourite on the terraces, he did however contribute vital goals through the campaign: four of his five goals helped secure Rangers a total of eight points from two wins and two draws.
Wimbledon (From trainee on 29/6/2001) FL 55+1/2 FLC 4/1 FAC 5
Leyton Orient (Loaned on 19/11/2001) FL 8 FAC 2
Crystal Palace (£150,000 on 2/2/2004) P/FL 41+18/1 FLC 3 FAC 2 Others 4
Sheffield U (£600,000 on 1/7/2006) P/FL 17+4 FLC 2
Queens Park Rgrs (Signed on 31/8/2007) FL 108+14/12 FLC 4+1 FAC 4

LEITCH-SMITH Jay (Ajay)
Born: Crewe, 6 March 1990
Height: 5'11" **Weight:** 12.2
Ajay has progressed through Crewe's youth team to earn a full contract and has so far had one League appearance, as a substitute against Bury in late September. To gain further experience, the promising striker went on loan to Curzon Ashton and performed well there. He has been offered an extended contract and could come to the fore in the months ahead.
Crewe Alex (From trainee on 23/5/2008) FL 0+1

LENNON Aaron Justin
Born: Leeds, 16 April 1987
Height: 5'5" **Weight:** 9.12
International Honours: E: 17; B-2; U21-3; Yth
Aaron was on target to be Tottenham's player of the season, displaying some scintillating wing play until he suffered a groin injury in December that kept him out until late April. Aaron took part in Spurs' last four games and was selected for England's 23-man World Cup squad as he was still regaining match fitness. Aaron is primarily a speedy winger who can play on the left but whose favoured position is on the right. His creative play showed steady improvement, offering many assists but also scoring important goals himself. Aaron hit late winners against West Ham and Birmingham in Spurs' early season unbeaten run that set them on the way to the top four. His third goal was in the 9-1 win against Wigan. On top form, Aaron is capable of leaving the best defenders in his wake.
Leeds U (Trainee) P/FL 19+19/1 FLC 1+2 FAC 1+1
Tottenham H (£1,000,000 on 1/7/2005) PL 114+25/15 FLC 13+4/1 FAC 8+3/1 Others 19+4/1

Aaron Lennon

LENNON Steven
Born: Irvine, 20 January 1988
Height: 5'7" **Weight:** 9.8
International Honours: S: U21-6
Glasgow Rangers' loanee striker Steven found himself operating mainly in a wide role during his time at Lincoln, which saw him score three goals from his 19 appearances. However, he acquitted himself well on each occasion and provided many an opposing defence considerable problems before going back to Ibrox.
Glasgow Rgrs (From juniors on 1/7/2006) SL 0+3
Partick T (Loaned on 16/8/2008) SL 5+3 SLC 0+1
Lincoln C (Loaned on 1/2/2010) FL 15+4/3

LEONARD Ryan Ian
Born: Plympton, 24 May 1992
Height: 6'0" **Weight:** 11.0
Ryan progressed through Plymouth's Centre of Excellence to be rewarded with a two-year scholarship. Regarded as one for the future, he can play at right-back, centre-back or in midfield. His elevation to training regularly with the first team coincided with the return of former player Paul Mariner to Plymouth and, despite still being an apprentice, Ryan made his debut in March as a 73rd-minute substitute against Blackpool.
Plymouth Arg (Trainee) FL 0+1

LESCINEL Jean-Francois
Born: Cayenne, French Guiana, 2 October 1986
Height: 6'2" **Weight:** 12.4
International Honours: Haiti: 1; U23-3
It was a promising first full League season for a player who had to overcome personal tragedy surrounding the earthquake in Haiti. A regular member of the Swindon team for most of the season, he was usually at left-back, where he occasionally looked vulnerable defensively. However,

towards the end of the season had a couple of outings in the centre of defence, where he appeared more accomplished. Physically tall and strong but comfortable when in possession, he has also shown that he is capable of delivering some impressive long passes.
Falkirk (Free from Sedan, France, ex Paris St Germain, on 1/2/2006) SL 8 SC 1 (Freed during 2006 close season)
Swindon T (Free from Guingamp, France on 28/1/2009) FL 29+9 FLC 1 FAC 1 Others 4

LESCOTT Aaron Anthony
Born: Birmingham, 2 December 1978
Height : 5'8" **Weight:** 10.9
International Honours: E: Sch
Bristol Rovers' longest-serving defender could always be relied upon to give one 100 per cent. His performances at left-back were solid and he was a dependable defender. Linking up well with the attack, Aaron contributed two goals, both away from home at Hartlepool and Brentford, which both resulted in wins. He was unfortunate that he suffered a hip injury in February which ruled him out for a while and to aid his return to fitness he was loaned to Cheltenham. At Town, the experienced full-back made an important contribution to the team in the final two months of the season, not only winning and using the ball well but also helping to organise an inexperienced team into a more solid defensive unit. Appearing at both right-back and left-back for the Robins during his loan spell, he would have been ever-present but for a knee injury that sidelined him for five games. Was out of contract at the end of June.
Aston Villa (From trainee on 5/7/1996) FAC 0+1
Lincoln C (Loaned on 14/3/2000) FL 3+2
Sheffield Wed (£100,000 on 3/10/2000) FL 19+18 FLC 3+1 FAC 2
Stockport Co (£75,000 on 14/11/2001) FL 65+7/1 FLC 2+1 FAC 2+1 Others 2+1
Bristol Rov (Free on 25/3/2004) FL 197+10/5 FLC 5+2 FAC 16 Others 12
Cheltenham T (Loaned on 5/3/2010) FL 7+1

LESCOTT Joleon Patrick
Born: Birmingham, 16 August 1982
Height : 6'2" **Weight:** 13.0
International Honours: E: 9; B-1; U21-2; Yth
The England central defender made just one appearance at Everton on the opening day before moving to Manchester City in a big-money deal. He had been clearly unsettled by the much publicised approaches from

Manchester City in the summer, which were initially rebuffed by Everton, but following the Toffees' disastrous opening day 6-1 defeat by Arsenal the transfer was rushed through. Joleon took time to settle in a City shirt and his partnership with Kolo Toure looked decidedly fragile as the team leaked goals and points in the autumn following an electrifying start to the season. These performances ultimately cost manager Mark Hughes his job soon after Joleon was sidelined for two months with a knee injury. He returned to action under new manager Roberto Mancini but after only seven games he succumbed to a hamstring injury which ruled him out for the season and cost him any chance of making Fabio Capello's England squad for the 2010 World Cup. So far the 'dream move' has not paid off for either club or player and it may be that the coming season will see him redeployed at left-back, currently a problem position at the club.
Wolverhampton W (From trainee on 18/8/1999) FL 206+6/13 FLC 7+1 FAC 10 Others 5
Everton (£5,000,000 on 12/6/2006) PL 109+4/14 FLC 9 FAC 8+1/1 Others 12/2
Manchester C (£23,000,000 on 25/8/2009) PL 17+1/1 FLC 4/1 FAC 2

LESLIE Steven William
Born: Glasgow, 5 November 1987
Height: 5'9" Weight: 10.12
Shrewsbury's left-sided midfield player can also play full-back. Steven has pace, puts in a good cross and has a fierce shot. He also played very effectively just behind striker Dave Hibbert for a number of games in January, helping the team to a good spell of results. He scored a creditable six goals including a penalty in the 3-1 defeat of Accrington and two good strikes, securing all three points at Macclesfield in February and in the 2-0 defeat of Barnet three days later. Involved in over 30 games he will be looking to push on and consolidate his career.
Shrewsbury T (From juniors on 1/7/2006) FL 44+40/7 FLC 2+1 FAC 2 Others 3+5/1

LESTER Jack William
Born: Sheffield, 8 October 1975
Height: 5'10" Weight: 11.8

Joleon Lescott

Club Honours: AMC '98
International Honours: E: Sch
Chesterfield missed their talismanic forward as Jack lost about half of the season to a persistent knee injury. He formed decent partnerships with Wade Small and Drew Talbot and the knack of creating goals for others became as important a feature of his play for the Spireites as the ability to score them himself. Jack recovered to return to the side for the season's closing stages and netted in the last game ever played on the Recreation Ground, Saltergate.
Grimsby T (From juniors on 8/7/1994) FL 93+40/17 FLC 13+4/6 FAC 8+1/2 Others 4+4
Doncaster Rov (Loaned on 20/9/1996) FL 5+6/1
Nottingham F (£300,000 on 28/11/2000) FL 73+26/21 FLC 3/3 FAC 1 Others 0+1
Sheffield U (Free on 1/8/2003) FL 26+18/12 FLC 3+1/3 FAC 2/1
Nottingham F (£50,000 on 26/11/2004) FL 42+34/12 FLC 0+1 FAC 1+5 Others 5/1
Chesterfield (Free on 1/8/2007) FL 99+3/54 FLC 2/1 FAC 5/4 Others 4/1

LEVEN Peter McDonald
Born: Glasgow, 27 September 1983
Height: 5'11" Weight: 12.13
International Honours: S: U21-2
After having impressed as a goalscoring midfielder in his first season with MK Dons, it would be fair to say that Peter's second campaign with the club was probably not all that he had hoped for. Missing out early through injury, he then was bumped around in an ever-changing midfield formation, often being given the more defensive as opposed to his preferred left-sided attacking option. As such his previous goal flow was reduced to a trickle, and throw in a couple of other minor injuries sustained during the season and it was very much a stop-start term for the likeable Scot.
Glasgow Rgrs (From juniors on 1/8/2000)
Kilmarnock (Free on 10/7/2004) SL 53+12/5 SLC 7/1 SC 3
Chesterfield (Signed on 7/8/2007) FL 42/6 FLC 1 FAC 1
MK Dons (Free on 1/7/2008) FL 63+8/14 FLC 1 FAC 4 Others 5+3

LEWINGTON Dean Scott
Born: Kingston, 18 May 1984
Height: 5'11" Weight: 11.2
Club Honours: AMC '08; Div 2 '08
Skipper of MK Dons and a very firm favourite with the club's supporters, Dean had a challenging season trying to stand firm in an ever-changing back

251

four and with a seemingly different formation being played in front of him every week. Allied to the fact that he was also in contract discussions that were resolved by him signing a new deal midway through the campaign, it was an unsettling time. But for all that, his all-round ability at left-back, either when defending, surging forward, or indeed his aerial threat at set pieces, continued to make him an essential fixture in the team.
Wimbledon/MK Dons (From trainee on 17/7/2003) FL 287+1/8 FLC 7 FAC 17 Others 20/2

LEWIS Joseph (Joe) Peter
Born: Bury St Edmunds, 6 October 1987
Height: 6'5" **Weight:** 11.12
International Honours: E: U21-5; Yth
Joe capped a good season for him when he swept the Peterborough fans' awards at the end of the campaign. Perhaps it is hard to understand how a goalkeeper from a relegated club can have a good year but Joe played consistently well throughout a disappointing time for Posh. His positional play, handling and kicking all improved, not least because he had plenty of work to do. Still only 22 and hopeful of catching the England manager's eye, to advance his career in that way may mean that he has to move on to a bigger club.
Norwich C (From trainee on 27/10/2004)
Stockport Co (Loaned on 22/3/2007) FL 5
Morecambe (Loaned on 1/8/2007) FL 19 FLC 3
Peterborough U (£400,000 on 7/1/2008) FL 111 FLC 5 FAC 7 Others 1

LEWIS Stuart Allan
Born: Welwyn Garden City, 15 October 1987
Height: 5'10" **Weight:** 11.6
International Honours: E: Yth
A hard-working and energetic young central midfielder, Stuart struggled to hold down a berth at Gillingham amid strong competition from the likes of Curtis Weston, Danny Jackman and Adam Miller, though he did enjoy some success covering for the injured Barry Fuller at right-back. After two seasons at the club he finally opened his account for Gillingham with a sweet right-foot volley to earn a share of the points in a 1-1 draw at Exeter. Was out of contract in the summer.
Tottenham H (From trainee on 19/7/2005. Freed on 31/1/2007)
Barnet (Free on 31/1/2007) FL 2+2
(Free to Stevenage Borough on

20/3/2007)
Gillingham (Free on 28/1/2008) FL 35+16/1 FAC 4+1 Others 3+1

LEWIS Terrell Dayne
Born: Park Royal, 13 August 1988
Height: 5'8" **Weight:** 11.9
Terrell joined Chesterfield after trials in October. The goalscoring midfielder had the right attitude and was a regular reserve but appeared to find the step up to first team football to be just too great. He was released in the summer after a solitary appearance for the Spireites as a 90th-minute substitute in November.
Chesterfield (Signed from Chalfont St Peter on 16/10/2009) FL 0+1

LEWIS Theo Anthony
Born: Oxford, 10 August 1991
Height: 5'10" **Weight:** 10.12
This versatile young player broke into Cheltenham's first team having made two substitute appearances towards the end of the previous campaign. A striker and prolific scorer in the youth team, Theo made a series of substitute appearances, was given a starting chance by acting-manager John Schofield in October and opened his scoring account by giving Cheltenham the lead with a header in an FA Cup tie at Torquay. Theo made a series of appearances in mid-season, in central midfield and wide on the left, and his performances earned him the offer of a first professional contract.
Cheltenham T (Trainee) FL 9+8 FAC 1/1

LICHAJ Eric Joseph
Born: Chicago, Illinois, USA, 17 November 1988
Height: 5'11" **Weight:** 12.6
Sent off in just his second appearance for Lincoln, whilst on loan from Aston Villa, the American full-back returned to Sincil Bank for a second month-long stint which took his final tally to six starting appearances. Still not in contention for a place at Villa, Eric joined Leyton Orient on loan for the last part of the season and made the right-back position his own. Scoring his first ever goal in the win over Stockport at The Matchroom Stadium, he is also the possessor of a long throw that can hurt defences.
Aston Villa (Signed from Universtiy of North Carolina, USA on 18/7/2007)
Lincoln C (Loaned on 22/10/2009) FL 6
Leyton Orient (Loaned on 25/3/2010) FL 9/1

LIDDELL Andrew (Andy) Mark
Born: Leeds, 28 June 1973

Height: 5'7" **Weight:** 11.6
Club Honours: AMC '99; Div 2 '03
International Honours: S: U21-12
The veteran right-winger was persuaded by former Rotherham manager Mark Robins to carry on after leaving Oldham. But after showing typical glimpses of real craft and nous in the handful of appearances he made initially, he eventually succumbed to Achilles surgery by Christmas. From thereon he managed only a brief reserve team comeback, although manager Ronnie Moore involved him behind the scenes, using his experience for the benefit of the squad. Was out of contract at the end of June.
Barnsley (From trainee on 6/7/1991) P/FL 142+56/34 FLC 11+4/3 FAC 5+7/1 Others 2+1
Wigan Ath (£350,000 on 15/10/1998) FL 206+11/70 FLC 11/1 FAC 7/1 Others 14+1
Sheffield U (Free on 7/7/2004) FL 26+7/3 FLC 1 FAC 5/3
Oldham Ath (Free on 29/6/2005) FL 107+18/29 FLC 3+2 FAC 8+1/1 Others 5/3 (Freed on 15/4/2009)
Rotherham U (Free from Bradford PA on 30/7/2009) FL 0+2 FLC 1+1 Others 1

LIDDLE Gary Daniel
Born: Middlesbrough, 15 June 1986
Height: 6'1" **Weight:** 12.6
Club Honours: FAYC '04
International Honours: E: Yth
A versatile player for Hartlepool, having been utilised in a variety of midfield and defensive positions, Gary was moved to central defence with Ben Clark out through injury and formed a successful partnership alongside Sam Collins. Rarely absent in four years at Hartlepool, in April he found himself at the centre of a major controversy, having turned out against Brighton, a game for which he should have been suspended having picked up a tenth booking of the season. There followed a stressful time for Gary and everyone involved, with the Pool being docked three points just two days ahead of the final game of the season and with relegation a distinct possibility. However a goalless draw at Brentford saw Hartlepool safe with Gary being given much encouragement from the club's supporters.
Middlesbrough (From trainee on 14/7/2003)
Hartlepool U (Signed on 18/8/2006) FL 160+6/8 FLC 9 FAC 8+2/2 Others 5/1

LIDDLE Michael William
Born: Hounslow, 25 December 1989
Height: 5'8" **Weight:** 10.10
International Honours: RoI: U21-5

Michael made his Sunderland debut and only appearance of the season in the strangest circumstances. With 19 minutes remaining of the third round FA Cup tie with Blue Square Premier Barrow and Sunderland leading 3-0, manager Steve Bruce called together Michael and another potential young debutant Adam Reed. Michael got the nod having called correctly as Bruce tossed a coin as the fairest way to decide who to provide with a big day. Left-back Michael was an unused sub four times in the Premier League and Reed was on the bench four times, still awaiting his own debut.
Sunderland (From trainee on 18/7/2007) FAC 0+1
Carlisle U (Loaned on 14/11/2008) FL 21+1 FAC 1

LILLIS Joshua (Josh) Mark
Born: Derby, 24 June 1987
Height : 6'0" **Weight:** 12.8
Scunthorpe's reserve goalkeeper Josh again found first team opportunities hard to come by at Glanford Park due to the good form of first choice Joe Murphy, and he spent September on loan at local rivals Grimsby. Becoming Town's third 'keeper in just six games at the start of last term, he experienced a 0-4 loss at Port Vale on his debut, though he had the satisfaction of stopping a penalty. Thereafter Josh produced assured displays, his remaining appearances seeing Grimsby unbeaten in what was otherwise a sorry season for the club. He returned to Scunthorpe, playing twice more before being loaned to Rochdale, where he had a very short but productive loan, appearing in their 4-0 away win over then League leaders Bournemouth. Josh only started eight games during the campaign for Scunthorpe, having his best run at the start of January where good displays against Barnsley and Derby saw him keep fit-again Murphy out of the team for the home match against Cardiff.
Scunthorpe U (From trainee on 2/8/2006) FL 12+5 FLC 3 FAC 1+1 Others 2+2
Notts Co (Loaned on 20/11/2009) FL 5
Grimsby T (Loaned on 1/9/2009) FL 4
Rochdale (Loaned on 30/10/2009) FL 1

LINDEGAARD Andrew (Andy) Rindom
Born: Taunton, 10 September 1980
Height: 5'8" **Weight:** 11.4
Club Honours: FAT '02; FC '03; Div 2 '05
The only local boy in Yeovil's squad, Andy was yet another player to find his way back to the club having previously left. This time around, his stay was brief

and consisted of two starts plus four more as sub. Often unused and on the bench, the versatile defender, cum midfielder, with almost 200 games for the club left in November.
Yeovil T (Signed from Westlands Sports on 5/6/2000) FL 57+32/3 FLC 0+1 FAC 3+2 Others 4
Cheltenham T (Free on 24/7/2007) FL 42+15/2 FLC 3 FAC 2 Others 1
Aldershot T (Loaned on 2/2/2009) FL 6/1
Yeovil T (Free on 7/8/2009) FL 2+3 Others 0+1

LINDFIELD Craig Anthony
Born: Birkenhead, 7 September 1988
Height: 6'0" **Weight:** 11.4
Club Honours: FAYC '06, '07
International Honours: E: Yth
At the time of his release by Liverpool, Craig had picked up an injury that required a double hernia operation. On regaining fitness, he trained with Rochdale before joining Macclesfield in December. Because of postponements in bad weather, Craig had to wait almost a month before making his debut in the 0-0 draw at Port Vale. Initially, he played as a striker but as midfield injuries increased, he often dropped back. Craig scored twice, the first on his third appearance in the 2-2 home draw with Morecambe and the second in the 2-0 home win over Bury. Was out of contract at the end of the season.
Liverpool (From trainee on 9/8/2006)
Notts Co (Loaned on 2/11/2007) FL 3/1 FAC 1
Chester C (Loaned on 18/1/2008) FL 5+2
Bournemouth (Loaned on 22/8/2008) FL 1+2/1 FAC 0+1 Others 0+1
Accrington Stanley (Loaned on 27/1/2009) FL 17+3/2
Macclesfield T (Free on 24/12/2009) FL 12+6/2

LINES Christopher (Chris) John
Born: Bristol, 30 November 1985
Height: 6'2" **Weight:** 12.0
The Bristol Rovers' central midfielder improved considerably over the season. Chris uses his strength and skill to run at opponents and can hit powerful shots with both feet. He was subject of interest from several Championships clubs but accepted an improved long-term deal from Rovers, the club he supported as a schoolboy. His strike from 18 yards against Millwall at the Memorial Stadium was one of his best goals as he reached double figures for the first time in his career. He scored with superb long-range free kicks

against Wycombe and Swindon.
Bristol Rov (From juniors on 26/11/2004) FL 115+10/17 FLC 3 FAC 8+2 Others 3+2

Chris Lines

LINGANZI Amine
Born: Algiers, Algeria, 16 November 1989
Height: 6'1" **Weight:** 12.11
The young Frenchman arrived at Blackburn at the end of January and played for the reserves in central midfield. He was given his debut in the final game of the season and looked comfortable before being substituted at half-time.
Blackburn Rov (Free from St Etienne, France on 28/1/2010) PL 1

LINWOOD Paul Anthony
Born: Birkenhead, 24 October 1983
Height: 6'2" **Weight:** 12.8
After a relegation campaign with Chester in 2008-09, Paul found himself in a similar battle with Grimsby. Positional changes to other players gave him an early season chance in central defence, going on to figure regularly until the New Year. Also seen at right-back in the Christmas home defeat by Port Vale, Paul marked his 26th birthday in October by netting at both ends in a 2-1 defeat at Bournemouth.
Tranmere Rov (From trainee on 3/4/2002) FL 34+10 FAC 4+1 Others 4
Wrexham (Loaned on 26/8/2005) FL 8+1

Chester C (Free on 4/8/2006) FL 118+4/4 FLC 3 FAC 3+1 Others 4/1
Grimsby T (Free on 3/7/2009) FL 23+5/1 FAC 1

LISBIE Kevin Anthony
Born: Hackney, 17 October 1978
Height: 5'9" **Weight:** 10.12
International Honours: Jamaica: 10; E: Yth
Unwanted by Ipswich manager Roy Keane, striker Kevin was loaned back to former club Colchester in a season-long deal. Despite spending the first half of the season playing out of position on the right-wing, Kevin was still able to finish the campaign as United's top scorer with 13, thanks to a combination of coolness from the penalty spot and his dribbling skills in the final third. Unsettled by speculation that he might be recalled or sold by his parent club, Kevin's form dropped off after Christmas. He was dismissed against former club Charlton in April but the decision was quickly overturned.
Charlton Ath (From trainee on

24/5/1996) P/FL 62+93/16 FLC 4+9/3 FAC 2+6
Gillingham (Loaned on 5/3/1999) FL 4+3/4
Reading (Loaned on 26/11/1999) FL 1+1
Queens Park Rgrs (Loaned on 1/12/2000) FL 1+1
Norwich C (Loaned on 9/9/2005) FL 4+2/1
Derby Co (Loaned on 24/2/2006) FL 7/1
Colchester U (Free on 10/8/2007) FL 39+41/17 FAC 1
Ipswich T (£600,000 on 24/7/2008) FL 24+17/6 FLC 2+1/1 FAC 0+1
Colchester U (Loaned on 3/8/2009) FL 35+6/13 FLC 1 FAC 1

LITA Leroy Halirou Bohari
Born: Kinshasa, DR Congo, 28 December 1984
Height: 5'9" **Weight:** 11.2
Club Honours: Ch '06
International Honours: E: U21-9
After Leroy was released by Reading in the summer, Gareth Southgate swooped quickly to bring the pacy

striker to Middlesbrough. He was immediately put in the team for the opening game, despite not having much pre-season training. Although scoring in his fourth game against Doncaster, Leroy struggled for consistency. A return to former club Reading in October reaped dividends as he scored both goals in a 2-0 win. Another brace came in an away game at Queens Park Rangers under new boss Gordon Strachan but he needlessly blotted his copybook by being sent off with Boro 3-0 up at home to Scunthorpe on Boxing Day. For the rest of the season, he was in and out but seemed to make more impact as a substitute. He scored at Doncaster, Derby and Watford, when appearing from the bench.
Bristol C (From trainee on 6/3/2003) FL 44+41/31 FLC 2+1/2 FAC 1+4/3 Others 4+3/2
Reading (£1,000,000 on 15/7/2005) P/FL 60+23/20 FLC 6+2/5 FAC 7+2/7
Charlton Ath (Loaned on 5/3/2008) FL 8/3
Norwich C (Loaned on 2/10/2008) FL 16/7
Middlesbrough (Free on 3/8/2009) FL 23+17/8 FLC 0+1

LITTLE Glen Matthew
Born: Wimbledon, 15 October 1975
Height: 6'3" **Weight:** 13.0
Club Honours: Ch '06
Having been a triallist in Sheffield United's pre-season games Glen was offered a one-season contract. A regular on the bench; initially he had few opportunities but when he did play he showed his experience and awareness, being able to control the ball and use it to set up a colleague. Glen was involved in the last nine games of the season and in particular many felt his second-half appearance at Doncaster played a significant role in United's comeback. Was out of contract at the end of June.
Crystal Palace (From trainee on 1/7/1994. Free to Glentoran on 11/11/1994)
Burnley (£100,000 from Glentoran on 29/11/1996) FL 211+35/32 FLC 11+4 FAC 11+6/3 Others 4+1/1
Reading (Loaned on 27/3/2003) FL 6/1 Others 1
Bolton W (Loaned on 1/9/2003) PL 0+4
Reading (Free on 24/5/2004) P/FL 81+15/5 FLC 3+2 FAC 3+3
Portsmouth (Free on 2/7/2008) PL 4+1 Others 2+1
Reading (Loaned on 9/3/2009) FL 5+3 Others 0+1
Sheffield U (Free on 5/8/2009) FL 7+9 FLC 1 FAC 0+1

Leroy Lita

LITTLE Mark Daniel
Born: Worcester, 20 August 1988
Height : 6'1" **Weight:** 12.11
International Honours: E: Yth
This attack-minded Wolverhampton right-back enjoyed a productive three-month loan spell at Chesterfield, helping the club climb from mid-table to the play-off places, combining steady defensive work with the ability to get forward and provide decent crosses. Still looking for first team football, he was loaned to Peterborough in March and put in some fine displays in his preferred position at full-back. A hard tackler and speedy when pushing forward, Mark has fine positional sense and has a nose for being in the right place at the right time. Injury limited his appearances, but Posh were hoping to make the move a permanent one. Was out of contract in the summer.
Wolverhampton W (From trainee on 26/8/2005) FL 19+8 FLC 1 FAC 3 Others 0+1
Northampton T (Loaned on 10/1/2008) FL 17
Northampton T (Loaned on 22/8/2008) FL 9 FLC 2 Others 1
Chesterfield (Loaned on 5/10/2009) FL 12 FAC 1 Others 1
Peterborough U (Loaned on 3/3/2010) FL 9

LIVERMORE David
Born: Edmonton, 20 May 1980
Height : 5'11" **Weight:** 12.1
Club Honours: Div 2 '01
With just one outing to his name at Brighton, as a substitute in the Johnstone's Paint Trophy, it was clear that David's time at the Withdean Stadium was up. Able to play at left-back or left of midfield, he agreed a deal with the club for his release in February and signed for Barnet. He was involved in the first team from the off and provided good cover in the midfield during the run in. Netted a key goal to the give the Bees a 2-1 win at Darlington in March, but missed the final stages of the run-in due to injury.
Arsenal (From trainee on 13/7/1998)
Millwall (£30,000 on 30/7/1999) FL 269+4/12 FLC 14/2 FAC 18 Others 7
Leeds U (£400,000 on 21/7/2006)
Hull C (£400,000 on 2/8/2006) FL 33+12/5 FLC 4 FAC 3
Oldham Ath (Loaned on 31/1/2008) FL 10/1
Brighton & Hove A (Free on 5/8/2008) FL 12+4 FLC 1+2 FAC 1 Others 3+2/1
Luton T (Loaned on 26/3/2009) FL 8
Barnet (Free on 4/2/2010) FL 11+3/1

LIVERMORE Jake Cyril
Born: Enfield, 14 November 1989
Height : 5'9" **Weight:** 11.10
The 20-year-old Tottenham midfielder had a dream start to the 2009-10 campaign, when he scored against Barcelona in the pre-season Wembley Cup tournament. Jake is a box-to-box midfielder with an eye for goal, as he has proved on loan spells at both Derby and Peterborough. Originally signed for a month, Jake's time at Derby was soon extended to the end of December. He struggled to establish consistency, not easy in a team that was constantly changing because of an unusually high number of injuries, but at times looked the ideal midfield player, strong in possession with a smooth style. When his time with Derby ended, he had a further loan at Peterborough before going back to White Hart Lane and making a very brief substitute appearance at Stoke in March. Has good close control and quick feet.
Tottenham H (From trainee on 23/11/2007) PL 0+1
MK Dons (Loaned on 29/2/2008) FL 0+5
Derby Co (Loaned on 10/8/2009) FL 11+5/1
Peterborough U (Loaned on 8/1/2010) FL 9/1

LIVERSEDGE Nicholas (Nick) James
Born: Hull, 18 July 1988
Height: 6'4" **Weight:** 12.11
Nick put his degree course at Sunderland University on hold to try his hand at professional football after coming through the youth scheme at Darlington. He made a memorable debut at Elland Road against Leeds in the Johnstone's Paint Trophy in October when he was sent off in the dying minutes of the game for a professional foul. He proved a good shot-stopper and went on to make 14 more starts. Was out of contract in the summer.
Darlington (Free from Rotherham U juniors on 2/11/2007) FL 13 FAC 1 Others 1

LIVESEY Daniel (Danny) Richard
Born: Salford, 31 December 1984
Height: 6'2" **Weight:** 13.0
Club Honours: Div 2 '06
One of the few remaining links with Carlisle's year in the Conference, Danny again gave fine service at the heart of the United defence. Good in the air and a strong reliable defender, he was almost ever-present until a hamstring injury against Yeovil in March put him out for a month and caused him to miss

the Johnstone's Paint Trophy final, in which his experience was sadly missed. He has been offered new terms for the season ahead.
Bolton W (From trainee on 17/8/2002) PL 0+2 FLC 1 FAC 3
Notts Co (Loaned on 5/9/2003) FL 9+2 Others 1
Rochdale (Loaned on 6/2/2004) FL 11+2
Blackpool (Loaned on 4/8/2004) FL 1
Carlisle U (Free on 24/12/2004) FL 173+4/13 FLC 10 FAC 10+1 Others 15

LLERA Miguel Angel
Born: Sevilla, Spain, 7 August 1978
Height: 6'4" **Weight:** 13.12
Miguel started as Charlton's first choice centre-half alongside Christian Dailly and looked very assured until 3-0 defeat at Colchester in late September. Sam Sodje was brought in to replace him and kept Miguel out of the side for much of the campaign. Miguel is commanding in the air and loves to get forward for set pieces, scoring four times, including an injury-time equaliser against Swindon on Boxing Day. Miguel was recalled for the second leg of the play-offs against Swindon with Sodje injured but was sent off for a professional foul at the end of normal time.
MK Dons (Free from Hercules Alicante, Spain, ex Recreativo de Huelva, CD San Fernando, Alicante, Gimnastic de Tarragona, on 1/9/2008) FL 34/2 FAC 0+1 Others 2+1
Charlton Ath (Free on 2/7/2009) FL 23+2/4 Others 2

LOACH Scott James
Born: Nottingham, 27 May 1988
Height: 6'1" **Weight:** 13.2
International Honours: E: U21-12
Watford's 'Young Player of the Season', Scott confirmed his standing as one of the best young goalkeepers in the country. He spent the summer at the European under-21 Championships in Sweden as part of the England squad and played in the final which England lost 4-0 to Germany. A lesser character might have suffered a reaction after this disappointment, but Scott simply knuckled down on his return to Watford. Ever-present in the League since November 2008, Scott turned in a series of consistent and sometimes inspired performances. Commendably, he also took responsibility when he conceded soft goals, as he did against Cardiff and Peterborough, and demonstrated a willingness to learn from his mistakes. It was no surprise that Scott was linked with several Premiership clubs during the January transfer window and Tottenham offered

a loan deal with a view to a permanent move in the summer. But Watford turned down all approaches for their most valuable asset, while Scott himself felt he would benefit from playing regularly at Championship level rather than sitting on a Premiership bench. A level-headed and personable young player, Scott became England's first choice under-21 goalkeeper during 2009-2010 and appears to have a fine future.

Watford *(From trainee at Lincoln C on 30/5/2006) FL 76+1 FLC 4 FAC 4*
Morecambe *(Loaned on 1/1/2008) FL 2 Others 1*
Bradford C *(Loaned on 30/1/2008) FL 20*

LOCKHART-ADAMS Kofi Wesley

Born: London, 9 October 1992
Height: 6'1" **Weight:** 12.13
Kofi was the first graduate of Barnet's new Academy to make a first team appearance, when he came off the bench for his debut at Cheltenham. The young central striker was named on the first team bench on a few further occasions during the season, but failed to make another appearance. Highly regarded by the youth set up at the club, Kofi is one for the future.

Barnet *(Trainee) FL 0+1*

LOCKWOOD Adam Brian

Born: Wakefield, 26 October 1981
Height: 6'0" **Weight:** 12.7
Club Honours: FAT '02; FC '03; AMC '07
International Honours: E: SP-2
Adam started the season for Doncaster in his usual position as a centre-back after suffering injury at the end of the previous season. Unfortunately, he was then injured in training at the end of September when he fractured a metatarsal that kept him on the sidelines for some months.

Reading *(From trainee on 19/3/1999)*
Yeovil T *(Free on 17/10/2001) FL 67+6/4 FLC 2+1 FAC 3 Others 2*
Torquay U *(Loaned on 18/11/2005) FL 9/3 FAC 3*
Doncaster Rov *(Free on 3/7/2006) FL 103+18/7 FLC 7 FAC 6+3 Others 6+2*

LOCKWOOD Matthew (Matt) Dominic

Born: Southend-on-Sea, 17 October 1976
Height : 5'9" **Weight:** 10.12
The experienced left-back started just two games for Colchester at the start of the season, one in the FA Trophy under caretaker boss Joe Dunne and another in a 2-1 home win over Walsall soon after Aidy Boothroyd took over. Loan spells at League Two sides Dagenham and Barnet followed. At Dagenham Matt made his debut against Port Vale. The no-nonsense left-back then suffered an ankle injury in training, forcing him to miss the Club's FA Cup tie at Huddersfield, but he returned a week later and made four appearances in total for the Daggers. Arriving at Barnet in January, he scored in his first game away at Morecambe the following day. This was Matt's second spell with the Bees, having had a successful loan spell in the second half of 2008-09. Once again, he acquitted himself well with the Bees, re-establishing himself as the club's first choice left-back when featuring 19 times and chipping in with two goals before returning to Colchester at the end of April. Was released at the end of the season.

Queens Park Rgrs *(From trainee at Southend U on 2/5/1995)*
Bristol Rov *(Free on 24/7/1996) FL 58+5/1 FLC 2+1 FAC 6 Others 4+2*
Leyton Orient *(Free on 7/8/1998) FL 319+9/50 FLC 15/2 FAC 25/2 Others 15/3*
Nottingham F *(Signed on 20/7/2007) FL 11 FAC 1*
Colchester U *(£100,000 on 3/6/2008) FL 6 Others 1*
Barnet *(Loaned on 2/2/2009) FL 12*

Scott Loach

Dagenham & Redbridge *(Loaned on 30/10/2009) FL 4*
Barnet *(Loaned on 22/1/2010) FL 19/2*

LOFT Douglas (Doug) James
Born: Maidstone, 26 December 1986
Height: 6'0" **Weight:** 12.1
A clever central midfield player with a turn of pace, Doug began the season in the Port Vale side but lost his place after suffering a leg injury. He returned for the FA Cup victory at Stevenage and then scored his first Vale goal against Torquay. After that, he was in and out of the side but came back with a bang at Darlington. Vale were losing midway through the second half but Doug came off the bench and scored within a minute with a shot from the edge of the box to inspire a 3-1 victory. He scored in his next game as well, at home to Northampton.
Brighton & Hove A *(Free from Hastings U on 19/1/2006) FL 13+26/2 FLC 1+2 FAC 0+3/1 Others 2+2*
Dagenham & Redbridge *(Loaned on 2/2/2009) FL 10+1*
Port Vale *(Free on 2/7/2009) FL 21+11/3 FLC 3 FAC 2*

LOGAN Conrad Joseph
Born: Letterkenny, 18 April 1986
Height: 6'2" **Weight:** 14.0
Club Honours: AMC '09
International Honours: RoI: Yth
Regular goalkeeping understudy to Chris Weale throughout Leicester's campaign, Conrad finally saw some first team action against Sheffield Wednesday at Hillsborough in March when Weale suffered a badly cut nose. His sole start, though, came in the seasonal closer at home to Middlesbrough, where he showed that his regular pre-match penalty competition against veteran Chris Powell was practice well spent, diving to his right to deny 'Boro and set up a useful home win.
Leicester C *(From trainee on 15/7/2003) FL 19+1 FLC 2*
Boston U *(Loaned on 24/12/2005) FL 10*
Boston U *(Loaned on 20/4/2006) FL 3*
Stockport Co *(Loaned on 10/8/2007) FL 34 FLC 2 Others 5*
Luton T *(Loaned on 20/8/2008) FL 22 FLC 1 FAC 3 Others 4*
Stockport Co *(Loaned on 28/3/2009) FL 7*

LOGAN Richard James
Born: Bury St Edmunds, 4 January 1982
Height: 6'0" **Weight:** 12.5
International Honours: E: Yth; Sch
Exeter fans' favourite Richard was a super sub during the campaign, as he came off the bench no less than 30 times while manger Paul Tisdale chopped and changed his front line. All four of his League goals came as a substitute. Richard will be looking for a new contract for the 2010-11 campaign, as well as more starts in order to show the City faithful what he can do when given a regular place.
Ipswich T *(From trainee on 6/1/1999) P/FL 0+3 FLC 0+1 FAC 0+1*
Cambridge U *(Loaned on 25/1/2001) FL 5/1*
Torquay U *(Loaned on 13/12/2001) FL 16/4*
Boston U *(Free on 30/11/2002) FL 30+5/10 FLC 0+1*
Peterborough U *(Free on 24/9/2003) FL 40+43/15 FLC 0+1 FAC 4+2/2 Others 1+2/2 (Freed during 2006 close season)*
Shrewsbury T *(Loaned on 16/9/2004) FL 5/1 Others 1/1*
Lincoln C *(Loaned on 18/11/2005) FL 8/2*
Exeter C *(Free from Weymouth on 31/1/2007) FL 22+42/8 FLC 0+2 FAC 1 Others 1+1*

LOGAN Shaleum Narval
Born: Wythenshawe, 29 January 1988
Height: 6'1" **Weight:** 12.7
A classy attacking full-back on the books at Manchester City, Shaleum was recruited by then Tranmere manager John Barnes on a season-long loan, and played in the majority of the games. Although a loan player, there was no lack of commitment, enthusiasm or hard work from Shaleum. He was always composed, frequently demonstrated his ability to hold the ball when the team was under pressure and relished any opportunity to make a threatening run down his favoured right wing. Shaleum's only significant injury was a hernia that put him out for a month at the end of the campaign. However, he returned for the last few games in Rovers' fight against relegation and more than played his part in their eventual survival.
Manchester C *(From trainee on 3/7/2006) PL 1 FLC 2*
Grimsby T *(Loaned on 11/10/2007) FL 5/2*
Scunthorpe U *(Loaned on 9/11/2007) FL 4*
Stockport Co *(Loaned on 22/2/2008) FL 6+1*
Tranmere Rov *(Loaned on 24/7/2009) FL 32+1 FLC 1 FAC 5*

LOMAX Kelvin
Born: Bury, 12 November 1986
Height: 5'11" **Weight:** 12.3
Kelvin had another stop-start season at Oldham. A hernia injury did not help the youngster and then, when fit, he found that competition for places in the Latics' defence was fierce, resulting in him making only 15 appearances for the club. He is always competitive, even if lacking a little in height.
Oldham Ath *(From trainee on 12/7/2005) FL 65+17 FLC 1 FAC 4+1 Others 4+2*
Rochdale *(Loaned on 13/9/2007) FL 10*

LONERGAN Andrew (Andy)
Born: Preston, 19 October 1983
Height: 6'4" **Weight:** 13.2
International Honours: RoI: Yth; E: Yth
A groin injury suffered in the 45th minute of Preston's penultimate match brought an end to Andy's proud record of playing every minute of 146 (one and a half) consecutive matches. A local lad, Andy has matured into one of the best goalkeepers outside the Premier League and his development continued last season. A superb shot-stopper, his reflex save against Scunthorpe to preserve the lead brought a sustained standing ovation from the crowd but was simply the best of many during a season in which he was crowned the club's 'Player of the Season'. The final piece of the jigsaw fell into place last term as he showed increased confidence under aerial balls into his box, which he claimed with alacrity to become the complete all-round 'keeper.
Preston NE *(From trainee on 21/10/2000) FL 179/1 FLC 8 FAC 9 Others 2*
Darlington *(Loaned on 20/12/2002) FL 2*
Wycombe W *(Loaned on 6/10/2005) FL 2*
Swindon T *(Loaned on 3/11/2006) FL 1*

LONG Shane Patrick
Born: Kilkenny, 22 January 1987
Height: 5'10" **Weight:** 11.2
International Honours: RoI: 13; B-1; U21-1; Yth
Shane played in 36 of Reading's 54 games but completed the full 90 minutes in only 12 of them. This was hardly surprising as he worked incredibly hard up front, often as the lone striker. Despite not being the tallest, he is a brave target man, able to lay the ball off or hold it, and did his fair share of defending, especially at set pieces. He did not score his first goal until January but what a strike it was, his header from Brynjar Gunnarsson's cross earning Reading a 2-1 FA Cup replay win over Liverpool at Anfield. Soon afterwards he hit a purple patch of seven goals in six matches. Shane is a Republic of Ireland international and has almost reached 150 appearances for Reading.
Reading *(Signed from Cork C on*

19/8/2005) P/FL 50+79/23 FLC 6/1 FAC 10+3/5 Others 2

LOVENKRANDS Peter
Rosenkrands
Born: Copenhagen, Denmark, 29 January 1980
Height: 5'11" **Weight:** 12.8
Club Honours: SPD '03, '05; SLC '02, '03; SC '02; Ch '10
International Honours: Denmark: 21; U21-13; Yth
Released in the summer of 2009, Peter was re-signed by Newcastle on a three-year contract just before the transfer deadline. Used as a wide attacker, his contribution was limited, but when paired up front with a target man he was very effective, adept at anticipating flick-ons, and reading the game astutely to make penetrating runs that his sharp pace and good control enabled him to exploit. He became a regular scorer, netting in five consecutive games in February and March and scoring 11 times in eight games, beginning with a perfect hat-trick against Plymouth in the FA Cup. His father died in January after a long fight against Alzheimer's, and three days later he played against West Bromwich in a vital match, scoring an all-important equalizer.
Glasgow Rgrs (£1,300,000 from AB Copenhagen, Denmark on 1/6/2000) SL 89+40/37 SLC 10+2/4 SC 7+2/5 Others 26+6/8 (Freed on 23/5/2006)
Newcastle U (Free from Schalke 04, Germany on 26/1/2009) P/FL 27+14/16 FLC 1 FAC 1+1/3

LOW Joshua (Josh) David
Born: Bristol, 15 February 1979
Height: 6'1" **Weight:** 12.0
International Honours: W: U21-4; Yth
Talented midfielder Josh spent his second season at Cheltenham, became a regular starter and finished as a player highly popular with the supporters. A fine ball player with the ability to beat opponents and deliver pinpoint passes, Josh began on the bench but quickly broke into the team, appearing in both full-back positions and wide on either the left or right of midfield. Josh scored twice in the confidence-boosting 5-2 win over Bury that went a long way towards ensuring League survival and although faced with a difficult choice at the end of the season as to whether to continue in football or pursue a career in the law, he chose to remain a player and was offered a new contract.
Bristol Rov (From trainee on 19/8/1996) FL 11+11 FLC 0+2 FAC 2+2 Others 2
Leyton Orient (Free on 27/5/1999) FL 2+3/1 FLC 1

Cardiff C (Free on 20/11/1999) FL 54+21/6 FLC 1+1 FAC 2+3 Others 3+1
Oldham Ath (Free on 12/8/2002) FL 19+2/3 FLC 2 FAC 2/1 Others 2
Northampton T (£165,000 on 8/8/2003) FL 90+12/15 FLC 5/1 FAC 8+1/2 Others 8/1
Leicester C (Free on 28/7/2006) FL 12+4 FLC 2+1
Peterborough U (£100,000 on 5/1/2007) FL 26+8/3 FLC 2 FAC 2+2 Others 1
Cheltenham T (Free on 30/8/2008) FL 48+5/4 FLC 0+1 FAC 1 Others 2/2

LOWE Keith Stephen
Born: Wolverhampton, 13 September 1985
Height: 6'2" **Weight:** 13.3
Club Honours: AMC '06
Although he had been expected to fill a central defensive berth on his arrival at Edgar Street, it was as a right-back that Keith made most of his Hereford appearances. His height and long stride made him a useful attacking asset for the Bulls as well as a powerful defender. His ability in the air made him a particular threat from set pieces, bringing an important goal in the home clash with Darlington. Was out of contract at the end of June.
Wolverhampton W (From trainee on 24/11/2004) FL 14 FLC 1+1 (Freed during 2008 close season)
Burnley (Loaned on 26/8/2005) FL 10+6 FLC 2/1
Queens Park Rgrs (Loaned on 31/1/2006) FL 1
Swansea C (Loaned on 10/3/2006) FL 4 Others 2
Cheltenham T (Loaned on 8/9/2006) FL 7+1 FLC 1 Others 1
Cheltenham T (Loaned on 9/1/2007) FL 7+1/1
Port Vale (Loaned on 19/7/2007) FL 24+4/3 FLC 1 FAC 2
Hereford U (Free from Kidderminster Hrs on 22/5/2009) FL 17+2/1 FLC 1 FAC 2 Others 2+1

LOWE Matthew (Matt)
Thomas
Born: Stoke-on-Trent, 20 October 1990
Height: 5'8" **Weight:** 10.1
Matt progressed through the ranks at Macclesfield and was awarded a professional contract in the summer. Regularly featuring as an unused substitute, he eventually made his League debut from the bench at Accrington in March in the fourth of six minutes added time and started for the first time in the 1-1 home draw against Aldershot in April. Matt is a versatile player, who plays right-back and occasionally at centre-back for the

reserves, but his senior games were in midfield, where he makes good use of his long throws.
Macclesfield T (From trainee on 3/7/2009) FL 7+3

Ryan Lowe

LOWE Ryan Thomas
Born: Liverpool, 18 September 1978
Height: 5'11" **Weight:** 11.10
In his debut season at Bury after a move from Chester, Ryan secured the affection and admiration of the Shaker fans. With 20 goals making him the leading scorer this season, Ryan has been extraordinarily consistent and his splendid 78th-minute winner against arch rivals Rochdale ensured his position as the man that Bury could rely on. Ryan played as striker alongside many different partners over the course of the season and created a solid blend with Andy Morrell. His outrageous volley against Crewe was pronounced Bury's 'Goal of the Season' and he was voted 'Player of the Season' by users of the club's official website.
Shrewsbury T (Free from Burscough on 25/7/2000) FL 81+56/23 FLC 2+2 FAC 4+2 Others 7+2/4
Chester C (Free on 22/3/2005) FL 36+4/14 FAC 2/3
Crewe Alex (Free on 2/5/2006) FL 47+17/12 FLC 2/1 FAC 2 Others 6/4
Stockport Co (Loaned on 27/3/2008) FL 4
Chester C (Signed on 2/7/2008) FL 45/16 FLC 1/2 FAC 1 Others 0+1

Bury *(Free on 2/7/2009) FL 34+5/18 FLC 1 FAC 1 Others 1+1*

LOWRY Jamie

Born: Newquay, 18 March 1987
Height: 6'0" **Weight:** 12.0
Jamie started this season on the right side of Chesterfield's midfield, and put in some eye-catching performances. His coolness from the spot helped to put six goals by his name before a cruciate ligament injury struck him down in October, forcing him to miss the rest of the season. The club think very highly of him, though, and offered a new contract.

Chesterfield *(From trainee on 5/7/2006) FL 97+8/11 FLC 2+2 FAC 4 Others 5/1*

LOWRY Shane Thomas

Born: Perth, Australia, 12 June 1989
Height: 6'1" **Weight:** 13.12
International Honours: RoI: U21-2; Yth
Shane got his first taste of first team football at Aston Villa when he came on as a late substitute in both of the Europa League play-off legs against Rapid Vienna at the start of the season. After that the young central defender went out on a three-month loan to Plymouth in September. He went on to make 13 appearances for the Pilgrims, 12 of them in the centre of defence. Unfortunately Shane was sent off in the league game against Swansea which meant he missed one game due to suspension. However, the following game he was back but as an emergency left back against Coventry. He was recalled by Aston Villa who required his services as cover after some injuries to defenders before going out on loan again. This time it was at Leeds, where he featured mainly at left-back for the Yorkshire side. Shane had the misfortune to miss the decisive spot kick in the penalty shoot-out when Leeds were denied a Wembley appearance by Carlisle in the Johnstone's Paint Trophy. Earlier in the season, Shane, who had represented the Republic of Ireland at under-21 and junior level, pledged his allegiance to Australia, the country of his birth, prior to being selected for Australia's provisional 31-man squad for the World Cup.

Aston Villa *(From trainee on 2/7/2008) FAC 0+1 Others 0+2*
Plymouth Arg *(Loaned on 17/9/2009) FL 13*
Leeds U *(Loaned on 28/1/2010) FL 11 Others 1*

LOWTON Matthew John

Born: Chesterfield, 9 June 1989
Height: 5'11" **Weight:** 12.4
Having had a spell on loan at Sheffield United's sister club Ferencvaros Matthew, an academy player, was on the Blades' bench for several games in March as cover for the depleted defence. He made his League debut with a brief substitute appearance at Cardiff and started as a right-sided midfielder in the final game of the season, when he gave an encouraging performance, looking comfortable throughout.

Sheffield U *(From trainee on 20/2/2009) FL 1+1*

LUA LUA Kazenga

Born: Kinshasa, DR Congo, 10 December 1990
Height: 5'11" **Weight:** 12.1
Kazenga moved to Tyneside shortly after his birth and subsequently joined Newcastle, the club for whom his older brother Lomana once played. He is a winger who shares many of the qualities of his brother, displaying trickery and good close control with an eye for goal, and he was called up from the bench in the second Championship game of the season against Reading. He was given starts in the Carling Cup ties against Huddersfield and Peterborough, but a groin injury suffered in the latter sidelined him for a period and on his recovery he failed to make any impact, being loaned out to Brighton for a month in February and playing a part in the team's improvement towards the end of the season. Beating defenders with explosive pace, he quickly became a crowd favourite – nothing excites fans more than a winger flying down the touchline to deliver a pinpoint centre. It was a scenario epitomised against Southampton when Ashley Barnes headed in Kazenga's cross, but the Congolese flier needs to be more consistent in his final product. He returned to Tyneside when a hamstring tear curtailed the move and while he appeared to have made a remarkably quick recovery, the injury then recurred to end his season prematurely.

Newcastle U *(From trainee on 2/5/2008) P/FL 0+6 FLC 2 FAC 0+4*
Doncaster Rov *(Loaned on 26/3/2009) FL 2+2*
Brighton & Hove A *(Loaned on 9/2/2010) FL 9+2*

LUCAS David Anthony

Born: Preston, 23 November 1977
Height: 6'2" **Weight:** 13.10
International Honours: E: Yth

Following his move to Swindon, having been released by Leeds, David established himself as the first choice goalkeeper at the County Ground with a series of commanding displays. A consistent performer throughout the season, he marshals his defence well, commands his area and instils confidence in those in front of him. He was troubled at various times during the season with a hamstring problem and also suffered a damaged shoulder after less than a minute of the play-off semi-final at Charlton but recovered to take his place in the final at Wembley.

Preston NE *(From trainee on 12/12/1994) FL 117+5 FLC 10 FAC 7 Others 11*
Darlington *(Loaned on 14/12/1995) FL 6*
Darlington *(Loaned on 3/10/1996) FL 7*
Scunthorpe U *(Loaned on 23/12/1996) FL 6 Others 2*
Sheffield Wed *(Loaned on 1/10/2003) FL 17 Others 1*
Sheffield Wed *(£100,000 on 14/6/2004) FL 52 FLC 4 FAC 2 Others 4 (Freed during 2006 close season)*
Barnsley *(Free, following long-term injury, on 4/1/2007) FL 2+1*
Leeds U *(Free on 11/9/2007) FL 16 FLC 1 FAC 2+1 Others 4*
Swindon T *(Free on 2/7/2009) FL 41 FLC 2 FAC 2 Others 3*

[LUCAS] PEZZINI-LEIVA Lucas

Born: Dourados, Brazil, 9 January 1987
Height: 5'8" **Weight:** 11.7
International Honours: Brazil: 4; U23-7: Yth
The Liverpool and Brazilian international midfielder is an enigma. After two fairly unimpressive seasons as a squad player, he was the major beneficiary from the summer departure of Xabi Alonso and the non-availability of new signing Emiliano Aquilani. Clearly a favourite of former manager Rafa Benitez, he played in 50 of Liverpool's 56 games, prompting some to claim that he was the most improved player. The majority of supporters remain to be convinced. The problem is that Lucas could not replace Alonso because he is a different type of player. On the few occasions that Benitez played Lucas in a more offensive role, as in the 2-0 home defeat of Manchester United and some Europa Cup games, he looked more effective. His only goal was in the 4-1 Europa Cup defeat of Benfica when he steered Steven Gerrard's pass beyond the goalkeeper.

Liverpool *(Signed from Gremio, Brazil on 26/7/2007) PL 57+21/1 FLC 5/1 FAC 6+2/1 Others 18+12/2*

Lucas

His full range of talents, particularly his composure on the ball, came into their own towards the end of the season and perhaps his only disappointment would have been that he had only one goal himself – a spectacular drive against Burton – to show for his efforts.
Crewe Alex (From trainee on 12/6/1997) FL 343+30/35 FLC 21+4/1 FAC 15+1 Others 4/1
Sheffield Wed (Free on 25/7/2006) FL 33+8 FLC 3+1 FAC 2+1
Crewe Alex (Loaned on 19/2/2008) FL 14
Crewe Alex (Loaned on 20/11/2008) FL 2+1 FAC 1
Hereford U (Free on 5/8/2009) FL 42/1 FLC 2 FAC 2 Others 4

LYNCH Joel John
Born: Eastbourne, 3 October 1987
Height: 6'1" **Weight:** 12.10
International Honours: E: Yth
The left-sided defender started the first seven League games for Nottingham Forest before injury halted his progress. After he recovered, he was unable to regain his place in the side until making two appearances in the last three games. He will be hoping for more chances during the forthcoming campaign.
Brighton & Hove A (From trainee on 3/3/2006) FL 68+11/2 FLC 3 FAC 5+1 Others 5+2
Nottingham F (£200,000 on 25/9/2008) FL 29+4 FLC 2 FAC 1

LUMLEY William (Billy) Daniel
Born: Loughton, 28 December 1989
Height: 6'6" **Weight:** 14.13
With no experienced goalkeeping cover, Billy was signed on loan and made several appearances as a non-playing substitute before being called upon for first team action when Chris Dunn was out injured. Billy's contract was not extended and he was released and allowed to leave Northampton.
Northampton T (Free from Stafford Rgrs, via trial at Swansea C, ex trainee at Wolverhampton W, Glenn Hoddle Football Academy, Grays Ath, on 23/12/2009) FL 2

LUMSDON Christopher (Chris)
Born: Newcastle, 15 December 1979
Height: 5'7" **Weight:** 10.6
Club Honours: Div 2 '06
Chris was another of the experienced players recruited by Colin Todd during the uncertain summer period while Darlington were still in administration. The midfield player or defender started the first three games but unfortunately

suffered an injury in the last of them, against Bury at the Arena, that ruled him out for the remainder of the season.
Sunderland (From trainee on 3/7/1997) P/FL 2 FLC 1+1
Blackpool (Loaned on 3/2/2000) FL 6/1
Crewe Alex (Loaned on 11/9/2000) FL 14+2
Barnsley (£350,000 on 8/10/2001) FL 70+15/13 FLC 2+1 FAC 3+3 Others 2+1
Carlisle U (Free on 12/8/2004) FL 115+8/9 FLC 3 FAC 4+1 Others 12
Darlington (Free on 13/7/2009) FL 2 FLC 1

LUNT Kenneth (Kenny) Vincent
Born: Runcorn, 20 November 1979
Height: 5'10" **Weight:** 10.0
International Honours: E: Yth; Sch
Talented central midfielder Kenny took a little time to settle into his role at Hereford, having played little League football during the previous couple of seasons. But his ability to see and play a pass was evident from the outset and he was the instigator and creative force behind many of Hereford's best moves.

LYNCH Mark John
Born: Manchester, 2 September 1981
Height: 5'11" **Weight:** 11.5
Club Honours: Ch '05
The speedy defender took advantage of an injury to Dale Tonge to reclaim Rotherham's right-back spot in November and he kept the shirt for the remainder of the season except for a handful of occasions. Mark showed his versatility by appearing at left-back as well. Lean and fit, he enjoys making attacking forays and reserved one of his best performances for the play-off final at Wembley. Was out of contract at the end of June.
Manchester U (From trainee on 3/7/2001) Others 1
St Johnstone (Loaned on 25/10/2001) SL 20
Sunderland (Signed on 26/7/2004) FL 5+6 FLC 2
Hull C (Free on 16/6/2005) FL 15+1 FAC 0+1
Yeovil T (Free on 22/8/2006) FL 29+2 FLC 2 FAC 1+1 Others 2+1
Rotherham U (Free on 22/7/2008) FL 28+3/2 FLC 2 FAC 2 Others 3

M

McALLISTER Craig

Born: Glasgow, 28 June 1980
Height: 6'1" **Weight:** 12.7
Exeter's Craig managed a handful of appearances from the subs' bench during the campaign and always did himself justice before joining Barnet on loan in December. The powerful forward arrived at Underhill during a difficult spell in front of goal for the Bees, but was unable to get himself on the score-sheet during his five appearances before returning to his parent club in the New Year. In March he went on loan to Rotherham at a time when the club needed to freshen up their striking options. Although Craig had a useful debut at Dagenham, that proved to be his high spot and he eventually had to settle for the subs' bench before going back to Devon at the end of the season. Was out of contract at the end of June.
Exeter C *(Free from Oxford U, ex Eastleigh, Basingstoke T, Stevenage Borough, Gravesend & Northfleet - loan, Woking, Grays Ath, Rushden & Diamonds - loan, on 5/7/2008) FL 8+26/7 FLC 2 Others 0+1*
Barnet *(Loaned on 26/11/2009) FL 4+1*
Rotherham U *(Loaned on 11/3/2010) FL 7+1*

McALLISTER James (Jamie)** Reynolds

Born: Glasgow, 26 April 1978
Height: 5'11" **Weight:** 11.0
Club Honours: SLC '04
International Honours: S: 1
Jamie signed a two-year extension to his Bristol City contract, despite some less than impressive displays during the past season. He was substituted at half-time when Cardiff came to Ashton Gate and, in winning 6-0, inflicted City's worse home defeat in 86 years. With the manager trying out various formations during the campaign, it could be said that this defender's best displays came when he was deployed on the wing. Unfortunately, injuries disrupted his campaign and a recurrence of his calf problem just before half-time in the televised 2-2 draw with Newcastle in March ended his season.
Queen of the South *(Signed from Bellshill BC on 10/7/1996) SL 17+14 SLC 0+1 SC 2/1 Others 0+2*
Aberdeen *(Signed on 26/5/1999) SL 103+14 SLC 5+3 SC 13+2/1 Others 3+1*
Livingston *(Free on 28/6/2003) SL 34/1*

SLC 5/1 SC 4
Heart of Midlothian *(Free on 2/6/2004) SL 31+16 SLC 5 SC 5+2/2 Others 6*
Bristol C *(Signed on 4/8/2006) FL 135+5/2 FLC 6 FAC 9+1 Others 5+1*

McALLISTER Sean** Brian

Born: Bolton, 15 August 1987
Height: 5'8" **Weight:** 10.7
The energetic, young Sheffield Wednesday central midfielder suffered another season of frustration. Because of injuries he was unable to build on his previous form at Hillsborough. Just when it looked likely that he would regain his place in the side, near to the end of the season, he picked up a stomach strain which kept him out for a few weeks. At his best he adds zest and inspiration to the side, even in his usual central midfield role or occasionally out wide on the right. He wants to stay at Hillsborough, but really needs to be in the side to be able to impress manager Alan Irvine.
Sheffield Wed *(From trainee on 17/7/2006) FL 48+20/4 FLC 3+1 FAC 1*
Mansfield T *(Loaned on 8/9/2007) FL 5+2*

McANUFF Joel (Jobi)** Joshua Frederick

Born: Edmonton, 9 November 1981
Height: 5'11" **Weight:** 11.10
International Honours: Jamaica: 1
Jobi played the first four matches of the season for Watford before moving to Reading at the end of August in a three-year deal and linking up with his former manager Brendan Rodgers. The Jamaican international went straight into the Royals' side and became a permanent fixture for the rest of the season. He made a total of 41 appearances, all in the starting line-up, was rarely substituted, and quickly became a firm favourite with the fans. His exciting wing play on either flank often had the supporters on their feet. Jobi possesses the ability to beat a defender by pace or trickery, then cut into the box to deliver a pinpoint cross or pass. In addition to making so many openings for his team-mates, Jobi also scored a few himself, the best of these being a speedy dribble and accurate finish in the 4-1 domination of Preston on the last day of the campaign.
Wimbledon *(From trainee on 11/7/2000) FL 76+20/13 FLC 2/1 FAC 4+2/1*
West Ham U *(£300,000 on 4/2/2004) FL 4+9/1 Others 0+1*
Cardiff C *(£250,000 on 13/8/2004) FL 42+1/2 FLC 3 FAC 2/1*
Crystal Palace *(£600,000 + on*

7/6/2005) FL 66+9/12 FLC 2 FAC 4/2 Others 2
Watford *(£1,750,000 + on 5/6/2007) FL 68+14/5 FLC 3 FAC 5 Others 2*
Reading *(Signed on 27/8/2009) FL 36/3 FAC 5*

McARDLE Rory** Alexander

Born: Sheffield, 1 May 1987
Height: 6'1" **Weight:** 11.5
International Honours: NI: 2; U21-19; Yth
Rory had the misfortune to dislocate a shoulder in Rochdale's first pre-season friendly and lost his place in central defence to youngster Craig Dawson. When back to fitness, the tall defender played a number of games at right-back while Scott Wiseman was injured but mainly had to make do with a place on the bench except when Dawson, too, was injured in March.
Sheffield Wed *(From trainee on 15/7/2005) FL 0+1*
Rochdale *(Loaned on 26/7/2005) FL 16+3/1 FAC 1*
Rochdale *(Signed on 7/11/2006) FL 125+4/4 FLC 3 FAC 7 Others 7/1*

McAULEY Gareth

Born: Larne, 5 December 1979
Height: 6'3" **Weight:** 13.0
International Honours: NI: 22; B-1; Sch
Once again, Gareth took a while to find his form for Ipswich but once he did, he turned in consistently solid defensive performances and was ever-present during the second half of the season, when he formed a strong defensive partnership with Damien Delaney which was a foundation for the team's improved performance in this period. He also scored five goals during the season, mainly from set pieces, culminating in goals in successive games against Reading and Derby. Against the former he rose unmarked to power home a header from Grant Leadbitter's corner and at Derby he stabbed home a loose ball against another corner. The Ipswich fans chose him as their 'Player of the Year'.
Lincoln C *(£10,000 from Coleraine, ex Linfield, Crusaders, on 5/8/2004) FL 65+7/8 FLC 3 FAC 2 Others 7/2*
Leicester C *(Free on 7/6/2006) FL 70+4/5 FLC 7/1 FAC 3/1*
Ipswich T *(£1,500,000 on 19/6/2008) FL 75+1/5 FLC 2 FAC 4*

McCALLUM Gavin** Kirk

Born: Toronto, Canada, 24 August 1987
Height: 5'9" **Weight:** 12.0
International Honours: Canada: 1; Yth
The previous season's top scorer for

Ryman League Sutton United proved one of the surprise packages of the Hereford season with his goal ratio of better than one in every three starts, despite being deployed as a wide midfielder in many of his appearances. Considerable upper-body strength, pace and a willingness to take on defenders, as well as popping up in the right place in the penalty area, quickly made him one to watch. His ability to score important goals was exemplified with crucial doubles in the home game with Lincoln and at Accrington.
Yeovil T (Signed from Oakville YC, Ontario, Canada on 31/1/2006) FL 0+1 (Freed during 2007 close season)
Hereford U (Free from Sutton U, ex Weymouth, Havant & Waterlooville, on 21/8/2009) FL 20+7/8 FAC 1+1 Others 2

McCAMMON Mark Jason
Born: Barnet, 7 August 1978
Height: 6'5" **Weight:** 14.5
Club Honours: AMC '07
International Honours: Barbados: 5
It was a hugely disappointing campaign, interrupted all too often by injury, that saw the striker make just four starts and 15 substitute appearances in all competitions for Gillingham, during which time he failed to find the net. In February he departed the club for a loan spell with League Two Bradford, starting twice for Peter Taylor's Bantams before returning to Priestfield and sitting out the rest of the season.
Cambridge U (Free from Cambridge C on 31/12/1996) FL 1+3 FAC 0+1 Others 1
Charlton Ath (Free on 17/3/1999) FL 1+3 FLC 0+1
Swindon T (Loaned on 3/1/2000) FL 4
Brentford (£100,000 + on 18/7/2000) FL 46+29/10 FLC 4/1 FAC 3+1/1 Others 3+5/3
Millwall (Free on 27/3/2003) FL 15+7/2 FLC 0+1 FAC 0+1 Others 0+1
Brighton & Hove A (Free on 16/12/2004) FL 19+6/3 FLC 1/1 FAC 0+1
Bristol C (Loaned on 17/2/2006) FL 8+3/4
Doncaster Rov (Free on 2/8/2006) FL 37+17/6 FLC 1+2/3 FAC 5/2 Others 4+4/2
Gillingham (Free on 7/8/2008) FL 24+21/5 FLC 2+1 FAC 0+4 Others 2+2
Bradford C (Loaned on 26/2/2010) FL 2+2

McCANN Christopher (Chris) John
Born: County Meath, 21 July 1987
Height: 6'1" **Weight:** 11.11
International Honours: Rol: Yth
If there was one factor that contributed more than any other towards Burnley's

relegation, it may have been the absence for most of the season of this versatile midfielder, who could have provided the backbone so often lacking in that department. Chris started the season as an automatic choice and signed a new two-year contract in September, but after being carried off with a knee injury in the home game against Sunderland he was out for nearly four months. He played the whole 90 minutes of the FA Cup game at Reading, appearing at left-back, but his Premier League return at Bolton lasted only ten minutes before he was carried off again. He missed the rest of the League season, undergoing cruciate ligament surgery, but was fit to resume duty for the reserves just before the end of the campaign.
Burnley (From trainee on 5/1/2006) P/FL 124+23/18 FLC 11+1/2 FAC 8 Others 3

McCANN Gavin Peter
Born: Blackpool, 10 January 1978
Height: 5'11" **Weight:** 11.0
International Honours: E: 1
Gavin figured sporadically in a Bolton team featuring an increased amount of competition for midfield places during 2009-10. Having made just five League starts, his final appearance came in the 4-2 defeat by Arsenal in January as he was subsequently ruled out for the season to undergo surgery on a troublesome ankle injury. An honest, no-frills midfield battler, it was made clear at the end of the season that Gavin would not be offered a new contract at The Reebok after the year left on his current deal.
Everton (From trainee on 1/7/1995) PL 5+6
Sunderland (£500,000 on 27/11/1998) P/FL 106+10/8 FLC 4+3/2 FAC 11+1/3
Aston Villa (£2,250,000 on 31/7/2003) PL 108+2/3 FLC 12/2 FAC 7
Bolton W (£1,000,000 on 13/6/2007) PL 56+19/1 FLC 4+1 Others 8/2

McCANN Grant Samuel
Born: Belfast, 14 April 1980
Height: 5'10" **Weight:** 12.0
International Honours: NI: 28; U21-11
Creative midfielder Grant had an excellent season, being a regular in Scunthorpe's Championship team and in the Northern Ireland line-up. A cultured, left-footed player, he switched regularly between the centre and a role tucked in on the left, where his passing helped provide a good service to the strikers. After netting regularly with free kicks the previous season, Grant became prolific from open play, scoring nine times during the campaign

including a run of six in seven games in September and October. The pick of them was a stunning 25-yard strike in the home win over Sheffield United.
West Ham U (From trainee on 6/7/1998) PL 0+4
Livingston (Loaned on 27/8/1999) SL 0+4
Notts Co (Loaned on 11/8/2000) FL 2 FLC 1
Cheltenham T (Loaned on 17/10/2000) FL 27+3/3 FAC 2 Others 1
Cheltenham T (£50,000 on 4/10/2002) FL 162+1/32 FLC 6/3 FAC 8/4 Others 12/4
Barnsley (£100,000 on 23/11/2006) FL 28+13/4 FLC 1+1 FAC 1
Scunthorpe U (£100,000 on 15/1/2008) FL 91+8/18 FLC 3/1 FAC 4 Others 7/1

McCARTEN James Phillip
Born: Liverpool, 8 November 1990
Height: 6'3" **Weight:** 12.8
A regular in the Everton reserve side, the young defender was loaned out to Accrington in April, making just one appearance, against Grimsby. Released in the summer, James is a commanding centre-back who is a real threat at set pieces.
Everton (From trainee on 21/10/2008)
Accrington Stanley (Loaned on 11/3/2010) FL 1

McCARTHY Alex Simon
Born: Guildford, 3 December 1989
Height: 6'4" **Weight:** 14.0
The tall goalkeeper joined Yeovil on loan from Championship side Reading at the start of the season and had an impressive debut campaign, keeping a dozen clean sheets. His aerial dominance and shot-stopping of the highest order earned him call-ups to the England under-21 squad, where he was an unused substitute. He returned to the Madejski Stadium after Town's final game, having made 45 appearances and receiving a red card against Stockport.
Reading (From trainee on 2/7/2008)
Aldershot T (Loaned on 2/2/2009) FL 3+1
Yeovil T (Loaned on 24/7/2009) FL 44 FLC 1

McCARTHY Benedict (Benni) Saul
Born: Cape Town, South Africa, 12 November 1977
Height: 6'0" **Weight:** 12.8
International Honours: South Africa: 83
Benni had a frustrating half season at Blackburn before his departure for West Ham in the January transfer window. He never achieved the weight target set for

him and five kilos over he found that Sam Allardyce was never going to play him for the whole 90 minutes. In addition the club decided that the most likely goalscorer at the club was David Dunn, which necessitated a switch to 4-5-1 and left Benni sidelined because he did not have the fitness to play as a lone striker. However, despite his problems he always appeared to be the most potent striker at the club and his goal at Wigan was a fine example of his innate scoring ability. At his best Benni is a top forward who can score from all angles and he made his West Ham debut at Burnley. He looked lively but a knee injury forced him off at half-time. The injury hampered his progress at Upton Park and he only played in one further full game plus a couple of substitute appearances. It was disappointing that he never got to play a key role in as each game he played his partnership with Carlton Cole looked promising.

Blackburn Rov (£2,500,000 from Porto, Portugal, ex Seven Stars, Cape Town Spurs, Ajax Cape Town, Ajax, Celta Vigo, on 2/8/2006) PL 82+27/37 FLC 5+4/6 FAC 6+4/4 Others 10+2/5
West Ham U (Signed on 1/2/2010) PL 2+3

McCARTHY James

Born: Glasgow, 12 November 1990
Height: 5'11" **Weight:** 11.5
Club Honours: S Div 1 '08
International Honours: RoI: 1; U21-5; Yth
Regarded as one of the brightest prospects in British football, James was recruited by Wigan in the summer on a five-year deal. A ball-playing, creative central midfielder with an eye for goal, the Scottish PFA 'Young Player of the Year' for 2009 is one for the future. After making his debut from the substitutes' bench against Manchester United, he netted his first goal in the FA Cup against Notts County. In the following match, he made his first Premier League start, becoming the seventh Wigan player to score on his full Premiership debut and also becoming the youngest scorer for the club in the Premier League An accomplished player with a powerful shot, he made an instant impression on the Premiership, creating opportunities for the lone striker as well as making many intelligent runs behind the defence. Producing a 'Man of the Match' performance against Liverpool at home, he made his senior debut at international level with the Republic of Ireland in February in the friendly against Brazil after rejecting the chance

to play for the country of his birth.
Hamilton Academical (From juniors on 1/8/2006) SL 74+21/13 SLC 6+1/1 SC 6/1 Others 1
Wigan Ath (Signed on 20/7/2009) PL 19+1/1 FLC 1 FAC 2+1/1

McCARTHY Patrick (Paddy) Richard

Born: Dublin, 31 May 1983
Height: 6'1" **Weight:** 12.8
International Honours: RoI: B-1; U21-7; Yth
A usually reliable performer for Crystal Palace, Paddy was forced to miss a large part of the season from November to February because of a persistent shoulder injury. Returning to the side in March, he put in some hard-working and committed performances as he had the previous season, although the goals did not flow as they had during his previous year. Formed a central defensive partnership with Matt Lawrence in the run in to the end of season and his tireless display alongside him in the final game of the season ensured that Palace kept their place in the Championship.
Manchester C (From trainee on 14/6/2000)
Boston U (Loaned on 22/11/2002) FL 11+1
Notts Co (Loaned on 23/3/2003) FL 6
Leicester C (£100,000 on 4/3/2005) FL 69+3/3 FLC 3+2/1 FAC 4+1
Charlton Ath (£650,000 on 10/8/2007) FL 27+2/2 FLC 2/1 FAC 2
Crystal Palace (Signed on 11/7/2008) FL 45+2/3 FLC 4

McCARTNEY George

Born: Belfast, 29 April 1981
Height: 6'0" **Weight:** 12.6
Club Honours: Ch '05
International Honours: NI: 34; U21-5; Yth; Sch
A most disappointing season for the Northern Ireland international, who was persistently troubled by injury and never regained the form he showed in his first spell at Sunderland nor in his time at West Ham. Although he played quite regularly up to the end of February, taking his tally of Sunderland appearances past 200, George failed to match his own standards and did not appear in the final three months of the campaign.
Sunderland (From trainee on 28/5/1998) P/FL 117+17 FLC 6+2 FAC 10+3 Others 2
West Ham U (£600,000 on 8/8/2006) PL 54+7/1 FLC 6 FAC 4
Sunderland (£6,000,000 on 1/9/2008) PL 36+5 FLC 2 FAC 2+1

McCLEARY Garath James

Born: Oxford, 15 May 1987
Height: 5'10" **Weight:** 12.6
The lightning-fast right-winger was a regular in the Nottingham Forest squad for the majority of the season but, unfortunately for him, made only one start, against Doncaster in December in a 3-0 victory. Garath always impressed coming from the bench as his pace unsettled tiring defenders. It was revealed at the end of the season that he had been playing with an ankle injury that required an operation in the close season.
Nottingham F (Signed from Bromley, ex Oxford C, Slough T, on 31/1/2008) FL 18+53/2 FLC 2+1 FAC 2+2

McCOLLIN Andre Stefan

Born: Lambeth, 26 March 1985
Height: 5'7" **Weight:** 12.13
The season never really took off for the 25-year-old striker signed by Yeovil before the previous season. After playing 13 times in his first campaign, he appeared on just three more occasions, all from the bench, although he was used in the opening day victory over Tranmere. He spent a while on loan at Farnborough Town and Dorchester before finishing the season back at Huish Park. Was out of contract at the end of June.
Yeovil T (Free from Fisher Ath on 15/8/2008) FL 0+13/1 FLC 0+1 Others 0+2

McCOMBE Jamie Paul

Born: Pontefract, 1 January 1983
Height: 6'5" **Weight:** 12.6
The Bristol City centre-half made only infrequent appearances in the last campaign. As in the previous season, injuries blighted him, which meant that he did not appear in the first team after the 3-2 defeat by Sheffield United at Ashton Gate in November. His height was much missed in the centre of City's defence.
Scunthorpe U (From trainee on 28/11/2001) FL 42+21/1 FLC 1 FAC 5+1/2 Others 4+1/1
Lincoln C (Free on 11/3/2004) FL 83+4/7 FLC 3/1 FAC 2 Others 7+1
Bristol C (Signed on 26/5/2006) FL 100+19/9 FLC 0+1 FAC 7/2 Others 5

McCOMBE John Paul

Born: Pontefract, 7 May 1985
Height: 6'2" **Weight:** 12.10
A popular central defender who always gave everything for Port Vale, John began the campaign as one of three centre-halves, a policy used until the second half of the season before switching to 4-4-2. John was a casualty

of this at first but fought his way back and missed only six League games. Dangerous from set pieces, he scored four goals, his personal highlight being the winner at Shrewsbury. He was also on the mark against Lincoln, Cheltenham and Bradford in the Johnstone's Paint Trophy, where he produced a cracking finish. Only a lack of pace would prevent him playing at a higher level.

Huddersfield T *(From trainee on 5/7/2004) FL 10+4 FLC 1 FAC 1 Others 4*
Hereford U *(Free on 24/7/2007) FL 23+4 FAC 3+1/1 Others 1*
Port Vale *(Free on 2/7/2008) FL 67+4/5 FLC 4 FAC 4 Others 3/1*

McCONVILLE Sean Joseph
Born: Liverpool, 6 March 1989
Height: 5'11" **Weight:** 11.7
Now in his second year at Accrington, Sean continued where he left off in 2008-09. Although not a regular starter he did feature in the majority of the League and Cup matches during the season. Is a skilful wide man who can play on either flank and will always do his bit for the team.
Accrington Stanley *(Signed from Skelmersdale U on 2/2/2009) FL 16+17/1 FLC 1+1 FAC 3+2 Others 0+1*

McCORMACK Alan
Born: Dublin, 10 January 1984
Height: 5'8" **Weight:** 10.8
International Honours: RoI: Yth; Sch
The Irish midfielder has been a fixture in the side ever since joining Southend on a full-time basis in 2006 after previous loans. One of his strongest assets is a surge into the penalty area to latch on to through balls for strikes on goal. Alan has tremendous energy and his work is unquestionable. He is the heart of the Southend engine room. A vocal presence, his thunderous tackling and will to win often gets him on the wrong side of referees and he again clocked up a double figure tally of yellow cards and was sent off at Hartlepool in March. Despite his disciplinary problems, Alan is an essential part of the team.
Preston NE *(Signed from Stella Maris BC on 14/8/2002) FL 2+9 FLC 0+1*
Leyton Orient *(Loaned on 29/8/2003) FL 8+2 Others 1*
Southend U *(Loaned on 17/3/2005) FL 5+2/2 Others 0+1*
Motherwell *(Loaned on 29/7/2005) SL 24/2 SLC 3 SC 1*
Southend U *(£30,000 on 18/11/2006) FL 128+11/16 FLC 5 FAC 11 Others 3/1*

McCORMACK Ross
Born: Glasgow, 18 August 1986
Height: 5'9" **Weight:** 11.1
International Honours: S: 5; B-1; U21-12; Yth
Cardiff's top scorer in the previous season with 23 League and Cup goals, the arrival of Michael Chopra from Sunderland knocked the Scottish international off track. Manager David Jones never really found how he could fit both players into his starting line-up with success. It was a tough season for Ross, who signed a new long-term contract but was among the substitutes too often for his liking. He was also played wide in midfield and went on from the bench in all three play-off games, including the final against Blackpool at Wembley. Hull were among the clubs who showed interest in the striker before they were relegated.
Glasgow Rgrs *(From juniors on 1/7/2003) SL 3+8/2 SC 0+1/1 Others 0+2/1*
Doncaster Rov *(Loaned on 16/1/2006) FL 12+7/4*
Motherwell *(Signed on 11/7/2006) SL 36+12/10 SLC 4+1/2 SC 4/2*
Cardiff C *(£120,000 on 2/7/2008) FL 53+19/25 FLC 1+2/1 FAC 6+1/2 Others 0+3*

McCRACKEN David
Born: Glasgow, 16 October 1981
Height: 6'2" **Weight:** 11.6
International Honours: S: U21-5
David opted to join MK Dons after his Wycombe contract had expired but soon after he signed, manager Roberto di Matteo departed for West Bromwich and the Scot became one of several new players inherited by returning boss Paul Ince. Coupled with the fact that he had half-a-dozen different central defensive partners throughout the campaign, then it certainly was not easy for the former Scottish Premier League regular. He remained a consistent presence throughout, showing good tackling skills, reassuring composure on the ball and effective passing. A seven out of ten man, he will look to build a solid partnership with the returning Sean O'Hanlon in the season ahead.
Dundee U *(From juniors on 30/6/1998) SL 166+13/8 SLC 13+1 SC 8+1 Others 1*
Wycombe W *(Signed on 9/8/2007) FL 74+2/2 FLC 1 FAC 3 Others 2*
MK Dons *(Free on 2/7/2009) FL 41/1 FLC 1 FAC 2 Others 4*

McCRAE Romone Curtis
Born: Southwark, 28 July 1990
Height: 6'1" **Weight:** 12.7
A young Peterborough midfield player

whose first team action during 2009-10 was at full-back. Tall and rangy, he had limited chances to show his skill when twice coming off the bench for a total of just 55 minutes of playing time.
Peterborough U *(Signed from Crawley T on 27/7/2009) FL 0+2*

McCREADY Christopher (Chris) James
Born: Ellesmere Port, 5 September 1981
Height: 6'0" **Weight:** 11.11
International Honours: E: Sch
Arriving at Northampton from Crewe in the summer, Chris was played at full-back, centre-back and even midfield as manager Stuart Gray tried to find a winning formula. The change of management saw Chris spend most of his time as substitute and realising first team places were at a premium agreed to a loan move to Tranmere in February, in a deal which extended to the end of the season. It was his second spell at Prenton Park and he made his debut in the away game at Gillingham. Steady and effective, Chris turned in some sterling performances to fully play his part in Rovers' fight for First Division survival.
Crewe Alex *(From trainee on 30/5/2000) FL 59+17 FLC 1+1 FAC 1+1*
Tranmere Rov *(Free on 1/8/2006) FL 42/1 FLC 1 FAC 2 Others 2*
Crewe Alex *(Free on 1/7/2007) FL 36+3/2 FLC 2 FAC 2/1*
Northampton T *(Free on 3/8/2009) FL 13+1 FLC 1 Others 2+1*
Tranmere Rov *(Loaned on 21/1/2010) FL 8*

McCRORY Damien Paul
Born: Limerick, 23 February 1990
Height: 6'2" **Weight:** 12.9
International Honours: RoI: Yth
The Plymouth full-back joined Port Vale on loan in August, having been at the club in 2008-09. He made his debut on the left in a 2-2 draw at Hereford and also started the game against Grimsby, which was won 4-0. A steady player with a decent turn of pace, he then reverted to the bench for three games before returning to Plymouth in October. Damien was next loaned to Grimsby and made his debut in a televised Johnstone's Paint Trophy tie at Leeds. Ever-present throughout his loan spell, the attacking full-back also appeared as a left-sided midfielder against Lincoln. The Grimsby management publicly expressed disappointment at being unable to secure his permanent transfer after he had signed for Dagenham for a five-figure fee on the last day of the January

transfer window and he made his debut in the game at home to Northampton. The left-back is as useful attacking down the left as he is in defence and delivered many assists in his four months at the club.
Plymouth Arg *(From trainee on 4/8/2008)*
Port Vale *(Loaned on 8/10/2008) FL 10+2 FAC 2*
Port Vale *(Loaned on 24/8/2009) FL 2+3*
Grimsby T *(Loaned on 9/11/2009) FL 10 Others 1*
Dagenham & Redbridge *(Signed on 1/2/2010) FL 20 Others 3*

McDAID Sean Andrew
Born: Harrogate, 6 March 1986
Height: 5'8" **Weight:** 10.12
Club Honours: AMC '07
Doncaster's Sean missed the entire 2008-09 season with a dislocated kneecap suffered in April 2008. He was still missing when the new season started but after a lot of hard work in rehabilitation, he was back in training in October and took a place on the bench in March, making one substitute appearance. He was released at the end of the season.
Leeds U *(From trainee on 6/3/2003)*
Doncaster Rov *(Free on 28/7/2005) FL 65+15/1 FLC 7+1 FAC 3 Others 6*

McDERMOTT Donal Jeremiah
Born: Dublin, 19 October 1989
Height: 6'6" **Weight:** 12.2
International Honours: RoI: Yth
The Manchester City midfielder struck up a remarkable rapport with Chesterfield's fans when he arrived at Saltergate on loan and gave him a great personal send-off after his skilful and adventurous outlook had lit up the first half of the season. His individualistic genius was evident from the start and Donal added the discipline of team play to that, establishing his credentials as a very quick learner. Despite their best efforts, the club could not extend his loan. After impressing for Chesterfield against Scunthorpe in the Carling Cup, Iron's manager Nigel Adkins brought him to Glanford Park on loan in January to give him a taste of Championship football. A tricky, direct winger who can play on either flank, he found opportunities hard to come by at Scunthorpe and only started four games in his three months at the club. However, he did impress in the win at Sheffield United where a typical mazy run created the winning goal.
Manchester C *(From trainee on 24/10/2007)*
MK Dons *(Loaned on 11/9/2008) FL 0+1*
Chesterfield *(Loaned on 7/8/2009) FL*

13+2/5 FLC 1 Others 1+1
Scunthorpe U *(Loaned on 26/1/2010) FL 4+5*

MacDONALD Charles (Charlie) Lea
Born: Southwark, 13 February 1981
Height: 5'8" **Weight:** 12.10
Club Honours: Div 2 '09
Brentford's hard-working penalty box predator missed the first seven games of the season as he was still suffering from the shoulder injury he sustained the previous March. Thereafter he was a virtual ever-present. Initially he struggled to score consistently but, starting in February, he had a run of ten goals in 14 games and ended the season as Brentford's top scorer with 17 to his name. He scored twice in a game against Gateshead, in the FA Cup, Gillingham, Oldham and Huddersfield. His work rate always impressed, even when he was not hitting the target, and he always gave 100 per cent effort. Charlie signed a new two-year contract that ties him to the club until 2012.
Charlton Ath *(From trainee on 10/11/1998) P/FL 1+7/1 FLC 0+3 FAC 1+1/1 (Freed during 2002 close season)*
Cheltenham T *(Loaned on 16/3/2001) FL 7+1/2*
Torquay U *(Loaned on 15/2/2002) FL 5*
Colchester U *(Loaned on 27/3/2002) FL 2+2/1*
Southend U *(Free from Gravesend & Northfleet, ex Margate, Stevenage Borough, Crawley T, Weymouth, on 15/6/2007) FL 11+14/1 FLC 2+1/1 FAC 2+2/3 Others 0+2*
Brentford *(Free on 10/7/2008) FL 77+1/31 FAC 5/4 Others 1*

McDONALD Clayton Rodney
Born: Liverpool, 6 December 1988
Height: 6'6" **Weight:** 10.12
Clayton signed a two-year contract for Walsall after impressing during a three-month loan spell from Manchester City. Following in the footsteps of his father Rod, who played for Walsall in the early 1990s, he quickly became a crowd favourite with a string of commanding performances, linking up well with a variety of partners in central defence. Thoroughly enjoying his football at the Banks' Stadium, he will have learned from the red card he received at Southend for a poor, two-footed challenge. His one goal was the winner at Leeds, a header that just crept over the line.
Manchester C *(From trainee on 3/7/2007)*
Macclesfield T *(Loaned on 15/8/2008) FL 2*
Chesterfield *(Loaned on 2/2/2009) FL 1+1*

Walsall *(Signed on 1/9/2009) FL 24+2/1 Others 1*

McDONALD Cody Darren John
Born: Witham, 30 May 1986
Height: 5'10" **Weight:** 11.3
Club Honours: Div 1 '10
Having arrived from non-League football midway through the previous season, Cody made steady progress in his first full campaign at Norwich. An instinctive striker with a direct style, once he receives the ball his only thought is to head to the opposition goal and those predatory instincts made him a regular member of City's squad. He continued to display a sharpness and bravery in front of goal, bringing him important strikes in both League and Cup competitions. His contract was extended until 2012 and he will be hoping for more starts than substitute appearances.
Norwich C *(£25,000 from Dartford, ex Witham T, Maldon T, on 2/2/2009) FL 5+19/4 FLC 1+1 FAC 0+2 Others 1+3/1*

McDONALD Kevin David
Born: Carnoustie, 4 November 1988
Height: 6'2" **Weight:** 13.1
International Honours: S: U21-14; Yth
It appeared that this season was going to be a repeat of the previous one for midfielder Kevin, who was given few opportunities to shine until finally establishing a place in the Burnley side in December and maintaining it when Brian Laws replaced Owen Coyle as manager in January. His size and strength always made him a handful, but in truth his Premier League chance may have come a little too soon as he sometimes seemed reluctant to use his assets to the full and often promised more than the final delivery achieved. His shining moment came near the end of the Clarets' match at Manchester City when his only goal of the season earned him a 3-3 draw and a very rare away point.
Dundee *(From juniors on 31/8/2005) SL 86+4/14 SLC 4/1 SC 7+2/1 Others 1+1*
Burnley *(£500,000 on 7/8/2008) P/FL 24+27/2 FLC 4+3/2 FAC 4 Others 0+1*

McDONALD Scott Douglas
Born: Dandenong, Australia, 21 August 1983
Height: 5'8" **Weight:** 12.4
Club Honours: SPD '08; SC '09
International Honours: Australia: 16; U23-3; Yth
It was a hectic last day in the January transfer window for Middlesbrough and their manager Gordon Strachan. Funds

released from Adam Johnson's sale to Manchester City allowed Strachan to raid his former club Glasgow Celtic for Scott McDonald at a reported fee of £3.5-million. As he was recuperating from a hernia operation, Scott had to wait ten days for his Boro debut. Although not 100 per cent fit, he impressed with his movement and work. The chance to break his Boro duck came in his third game at Blackpool with the award of a penalty but his shot was saved. He was rested for three weeks at the end of February, as he had been battling to stay fit after his operation and he came back in a pulsating derby against Newcastle and scored. A slight hamstring strain curtailed his involvement but he started to come back to full fitness as Boro ended the season with some good results, and his partnership with Chris Killen promised well for the future.
Southampton (Signed from Eastern Pride, Australia on 23/8/2000) PL 0+2 FLC 1
Huddersfield T (Loaned on 27/7/2002) FL 7+6/1 FLC 0+1
Bournemouth (Free on 27/3/2003) FL 3+4/1 Others 0+1
Wimbledon (Free on 19/8/2003) FL 0+2
Motherwell (Free on 6/1/2004) SL 96+12/42 SLC 10/1 SC 5+2/2
Glasgow Celtic (£700,000 on 3/7/2007) SL 84+4/51 SLC 7+1/4 SC 7/4 Others 19+6/5
Middlesbrough (£3,500,000 on 1/2/2010) FL 12+1/4

MacDONALD Shaun
Benjamin
Born: Swansea, 17 June 1988
Height: 6'0" **Weight:** 11.4
Club Honours: AMC '06
International Honours: W: U21-22; Yth
Shaun returned to Yeovil for a second season running on loan from Swansea and continued his fine form in the middle of the park, often running the show. The life-long Swans' nut was a favourite with Glovers' fans, who rated him highly, and his partnership with Jean-Paul Kalala in midfield was an integral part of the team's success. Scored three times, including a blinding 30-yard effort against MK Dons and will be sorely missed by the club.
Swansea C (From trainee on 8/4/2006) FL 9+15 FLC 3+1/2 FAC 2+1 Others 6+3
Yeovil T (Loaned on 27/1/2009) FL 4/2
Yeovil T (Loaned on 21/9/2009) FL 31/3 FAC 1

McEVELEY James (Jay)
Michael
Born: Liverpool, 11 February 1985

Height: 6'1" **Weight:** 12.11
International Honours: E: U21-3. S: 3; B-1
When Jay was back in the Derby side as a wide midfield player, he fractured a cheekbone at Middlesbrough in October. In the course of a routine operation to repair this, his heart stopped beating for two minutes and he regained consciousness in intensive care. It was the most alarming moment of an eventful season that began with Jay losing his place at left-back to Dean Moxey. He played some games as a central defender, which may yet prove his best position. It looked like when Derby cleared their lines against Sheffield Wednesday and Jay kept running before banging in Lee Croft's cross for a great team goal. He also scored a snorter to beat Doncaster in the FA Cup. Jay was left-back in the second half of the season but when his contract expired, he was not offered a new deal. He is a good catch for somebody.
Blackburn Rov (From trainee on

8/7/2002) PL 17+1 FLC 4+1 FAC 3 Others 1
Burnley (Loaned on 15/12/2003) FL 0+4 FAC 1
Gillingham (Loaned on 10/3/2005) FL 10/1
Ipswich T (Loaned on 30/8/2005) FL 17+2/1
Derby Co (£600,000 on 29/1/2007) P/FL 77+15/4 FLC 2+1 FAC 2+1/2 Others 3
Preston NE (Loaned on 29/9/2008) FL 7
Charlton Ath (Loaned on 27/11/2008) FL 6

McFADDEN James Henry
Born: Glasgow, 14 April 1983
Height: 5'10" **Weight:** 10.10
International Honours: S: 45; B-1; U21-7
Mercurial on the ball, stayed injury-free and his role coming in off the left was a prime factor in Birmingham's highest finish in 51 years. Dovetailed well with the front two and showed clever invention and creativity when dribbling. His work rate was also high. James'

James McFadden

winning goal against Sunderland in October kick-started the Blues' 15-game unbeaten run. He was also used as a central striker, where he held the ball up well and brought others into play, towards the season's end.
Motherwell *(From juniors on 31/7/1999) SL 52+11/26 SLC 1/1 SC 5+1/5*
Everton *(£1,250,000 on 8/9/2003) PL 53+56/11 FLC 12/3 FAC 7+2/3 Others 7+2/1*
Birmingham C *(£5,750,000 on*

McGINN Stephen
Born: Glasgow, 2 December 1988
Height: 5'7" **Weight:** 10.7
International Honours: S: U21-4
Stephen joined Watford from St Mirren during the January transfer window. Primarily a central midfielder, Stephen is a versatile performer who can also play on either flank. He made his Watford debut as a substitute against Newcastle at the end of February and made a handful of further appearances before the end of the season, including a couple of starts. Very much a long-term signing, Stephen is a Scottish under-21 international.
St Mirren *(From juniors on 15/12/2006) SL 46+28/7 SLC 3/1 SC 4+3*
Watford *(Signed on 15/1/2010) FL 2+7*

McGIVERN Ryan
Born: Newry, 8 January 1990
Height: 6'0" **Weight:** 13.2
Club Honours: FAYC '08
International Honours: NI: 11; B-1; U21-2
Highly-rated young defender loaned to Leicester by Manchester City for the season, he generally found his opportunities limited by the excellent and consistent form of Bruno Berner. Ryan also demonstrated his ability to operate as an emergency central defender as well as adding to his collection of Northern Ireland caps during the campaign.
Manchester C *(From trainee on 14/11/2007)*
Morecambe *(Loaned on 24/10/2008) FL 5/1 Others 1*
Leicester C *(Loaned on 1/9/2009) FL 9+3 FAC 2*

McGLEISH Scott
Born: Barnet, 10 February 1974
Height: 5'9" **Weight:** 11.3
Despite being a veteran forward, Scott still leads the Leyton Orient line very well. Although not tall, he has the spring to beat more physically imposing defenders in the air. Scott scored the winning goal on his return to his first professional club in the televised win at

the Valley against Charlton. He was out of contract in the summer and was offered a new deal.
Charlton Ath *(Free from Edgware T on 24/5/1994) FL 0+6*
Leyton Orient *(Loaned on 10/3/1995) FL 4+2/1 Others 1/1*
Peterborough U *(Free on 4/7/1995) FL 3+10 FLC 0+1 FAC 0+1 Others 3+1/2*
Colchester U *(Loaned on 23/2/1996) FL 1+5/2*
Colchester U *(Loaned on 28/3/1996) FL 9/4 Others 2*
Cambridge U *(Loaned on 2/9/1996) FL 10/7 FLC 1*
Leyton Orient *(£50,000 on 22/11/1996) FL 36/7 FLC 3/1 FAC 1 Others 1*
Barnet *(£70,000 on 1/10/1997) FL 106+28/36 FLC 5/4 FAC 3 Others 7+2/2*
Colchester U *(£15,000 on 11/1/2001) FL 118+26/38 FLC 4 FAC 9+1/2 Others 7+2/7*
Northampton T *(Free on 8/7/2004) FL 106+5/42 FLC 4/2 FAC 10/7 Others 6+1/3*
Wycombe W *(Signed on 26/1/2007) FL 66+9/33 FLC 1+1 FAC 1 Others 3*
Northampton T *(Loaned on 28/10/2008) FL 7+2/1 FAC 2/1*
Leyton Orient *(Signed on 12/2/2009) FL 51+7/18 FLC 0+1 FAC 2*

McGOLDRICK David James
Born: Nottingham, 29 November 1987
Height: 6'1" **Weight:** 11.10
David is a talented, hard-working and energetic striker with plenty of subtle touches. He was a regular member of the Nottingham Forest squad without quite pinning down a starting place. At his best when playing off a main striker, David made the majority of his appearances from the substitutes' bench. He scored his first goal for Forest against Queens Park Rangers in August and ended the campaign with three.
Notts Co *(Associated Schoolboy) FL 2+2*
Southampton *(From trainee on 19/9/2005) FL 49+15/12 FLC 3+3/3 FAC 3+2*
Notts Co *(Loaned on 23/9/2005) FL 4+2 Others 0+1*
Bournemouth *(Loaned on 16/2/2007) FL 12/6*
Port Vale *(Loaned on 31/8/2007) FL 15+2/2 Others 1*
Nottingham F *(£1,000,000 on 29/6/2009) FL 18+15/3 FLC 0+2 FAC 1 Others 0+2*

McGOVERN Jon-Paul
Born: Glasgow, 3 October 1980
Height: 5'7" **Weight:** 9.6
Club Honours: SLC '04
Jon-Paul had an impressive campaign

for Swindon. Having missed the season's opener at Gillingham, he was recalled for the next game and became a fixture in the team for the remainder of the season, starting every game thereafter. Usually operating on the right wing, he worked tirelessly, with his energetic and enthusiastic approach benefiting his strikers as he delivered a regular supply of dangerous crosses. Jon-Paul was credited with being one of the leading providers of assists in League One. His only two goals were both scored in August and away from home, a screamer that started a rout at MK Dons in the Carling Cup and a 30-yard free kick that deceived the goalkeeper at Oldham.
Glasgow Celtic *(From juniors at Heart of Midlothian on 8/6/2000)*
Sheffield U *(Loaned on 13/8/2002) FL 11+4/1 FLC 2/1 FAC 1/1*
Livingston *(Free on 1/7/2003) SL 12+15 SLC 0+3 SC 0+2*
Sheffield Wed *(Free on 3/6/2004) FL 49+4/6 FLC 3 FAC 1 Others 4/2*
MK Dons *(Free on 4/8/2006) FL 42+5/3 FLC 4+1/1 FAC 3 Others 2*
Swindon T *(Signed on 31/8/2007) FL 101+11/5 FLC 3/1 FAC 7/1 Others 9+1*

Jon-Paul McGovern

McGRATH John Matthew
Born: Limerick, 27 March 1980
Height: 5'10" **Weight:** 10.8
Club Honours: FC '09
International Honours: RoI: U21-5
The ebullient midfielder played at the top level with Aston Villa early in his career but eventually dropped into non-League football with Tamworth. But it was after he joined Burton in 2007 that his career again took off. He made more than 100 consecutive

appearances as his sweet left-foot and tough tackling drove the Brewers to their Blue Square Premier success and was virtually ever-present in the Staffordshire club's first season in League Two. John took over the captain's armband after the mid-season departure of Guy Branston, a fitting reward for his unstinting efforts in Burton's engine room.
Aston Villa (Signed from Belvedere YC on 3/9/1999) PL 0+3
Doncaster Rov (Free on 10/7/2003) FL 4+7 FLC 1 FAC 1 Others 1
Shrewsbury T (Loaned on 31/8/2004) FL 7+1
Kidderminster Hrs (Free on 14/1/2005) FL 18+1 (Freed during 2005 close season)
Burton A (Free from Tamworth, ex Limerick, Weymouth, on 1/7/2007) FL 44+1/1 FLC 1 FAC 1 Others 1/1

McGUGAN Lewis Shay
Born: Long Eaton, 25 October 1988
Height: 5'9" **Weight:** 11.6
International Honours: E: Yth
The young Nottingham Forest central midfield player failed to make the expected progress, with only six League starts. He was halted by a fractured cheekbone early in the season and, on his return from injury, had to be content with making the majority of his appearances from the substitutes' bench, although one intervention produced a last-minute equaliser against Cardiff. At his best, Lewis links well between defence and attack. He will be hoping a good pre-season will herald a return to the form he showed earlier in his career.
Nottingham F (From trainee on 15/11/2006) FL 66+31/16 FLC 1+1/1 FAC 7+1/1 Others 2+3

MACHEDA Federico
Born: Rome, Italy, 22 August 1991
Height: 6'0" **Weight:** 11.13
Club Honours: FLC '10
International Honours: Italy: U21-3; Yth
A highly-rated Manchester United forward with a keen eye for the goal, Federico's wonder-boy appearances at the end of 2008-09 might have won him plaudits and the prestigious Jimmy Murphy 'Academy Player of the Year' award but last season was more about consolidation and making advances. Despite limited senior games notably in the Carling Cup and Champions League, he was rewarded with a new four-year contract in December that would tie him to the club until June 2014. On the international front he made his debut for Italy under-21s in a friendly against Russia in August. He

also made his long-awaited introduction against Chelsea in the Premiership in April when he notched United's goal in a 2-1 reverse.
Manchester U (From trainee, ex SS Lazio, on 28/8/2008) PL 3+6/3 FLC 2+1 FAC 1 Others 2

Michael McIndoe

McINDOE Michael
Born: Edinburgh, 2 December 1979
Height: 5'8" **Weight:** 11.0
Club Honours: FAT '02; FC '03; Div 3 '04
International Honours: S: B-2
The Scottish winger had a mixed season and did not fully succeed in winning over Coventry's more critical fans. Michael is a skilful player and when fit was always a first choice on the left wing. He provided numerous assists with crosses, including Leon Best's header at home to Crystal Palace and for Richard Wood at Queens Park Rangers, and he takes a good dead ball. At times he can look a little lightweight and can be muscled out by physical defenders. Despite a good scoring record for previous clubs, he failed to find the net as often as he would have liked, finally scoring his first Coventry goal at home to Plymouth.
Luton T (From trainee on 2/4/1998) FL 19+20 FLC 4+1 FAC 0+3 Others 1 (Free to Hereford U on 20/7/2000)
Doncaster Rov (£50,000 from Yeovil T on 5/8/2003) FL 117+5/28 FLC 10/4 FAC 6/3 Others 4
Derby Co (Loaned on 8/3/2006) FL 6+2
Barnsley (£125,000 on 13/7/2006) FL 18/4 FLC 0+2/1
Wolverhampton W (£250,000 on 23/11/2006) FL 25+2/3 FAC 3 Others 2
Bristol C (Signed on 25/7/2007) FL 88+2/12 FLC 3 FAC 0+1 Others 3/1
Coventry C (Signed on 4/8/2009) FL 38+2/1 FLC 1 FAC 2

McINTYRE Kevin
Born: Liverpool, 23 December 1977
Height: 5'11" **Weight:** 12.2
Club Honours: FC '04
It was another solid season from Shrewsbury's central or left-sided midfield player who is also comfortable at left-back. A player who is always involved, he had particularly good performances in the home game against Burton in August, providing the cross for one of the goals and did the same twice in the 3-0 win against Northampton. His disappointment will be that out of 48 appearances, he found the net only once, a penalty in the 3-1 win at Bradford in December. With his contract ending, it remained to be seen if he features in plans for the new season.
Tranmere Rov (From trainee on 6/11/1996) FL 0+2 (Free to Doncaster Rov on 19/1/1999)
Chester C (Free from Doncaster Rov on 15/5/2002) FL 9+1 FLC 1 FAC 1+1 Others 3
Macclesfield T (Free on 24/12/2004) FL 130+4/16 FLC 2 FAC 7/1 Others 10
Shrewsbury T (£50,000 on 4/1/2008) FL 90+3/3 FLC 2 FAC 2 Others 8/3

Craig Mackail-Smith

MACKAIL-SMITH Craig
Born: Watford, 25 February 1984
Height: 6'3" **Weight:** 12.4
Club Honours: FC '07
International Honours: E: SP-7
Peterborough's Craig found scoring goals harder this season in the Championship than it had been in the surge to League One promotion but that did not inhibit his capacity for work. His non-stop running never gives defenders a chance to settle on the ball

and he has the pace to get in behind most defensive units.
Peterborough U (Signed from Dagenham & Redbridge, ex Arlesey T, on 29/1/2007) FL 129+11/53 FLC 4/1 FAC 9+1/10 Others 1+1

MACKAY Michael
Born: Durham, 11 October 1982
Height: 6'0" **Weight:** 11.6
A hard-working striker, who has maintained a good scoring record in over three years at Hartlepool, Michael was loaned out to Gateshead for the first half of the season with the club having a surplus of strikers. He had only mixed success with the Tynesiders, but on his return initially looked sharp playing for Pool's reserves. To the end of the season Michael was unable to win a regular place in the first team squad, with his sole appearance being at Southampton when he was on as substitute to play just four minutes of football.
Hartlepool U (Signed from Consett, ex Birtley, Durham C, on 8/12/2007) FL 19+30/7 FLC 0+2 FAC 5+2/2 Others 1+2/1

McKAY William (Billy) Robert
Born: Corby, 22 October 1988
Height: 5'9" **Weight:** 10.1
International Honours: NI: U21-6
Billy stepped straight into the Northampton forward line when he signed from Leicester during the close season. Injury to Steve Guinan promoted Billy to the first team where he played off fellow striker Adebayo Akinfenwa. Accrington played a large part in the youngster's debut season at Sixfields. He scored his first League goal against them at the Fraser Eagle Stadium and then hit a brace in the 4-0 home win later in the season.
Leicester C (From trainee on 9/8/2007)
Northampton T (Free on 22/7/2009) FL 29+11/8 FLC 1 FAC 0+1 Others 0+1

MACKEN Jonathan (Jon) Paul
Born: Manchester, 7 September 1977
Height: 5'10" **Weight:** 12.8
Club Honours: Div 2 '00
International Honours: RoI: 1; E: Yth
After signing a new one-year contract during the summer, Jon again played his part for Barnsley throughout the season, although his goal output in the end was slightly down. He was always up for a battle and used all his experience when in possession and scrapping for the ball. His hold-up play and distribution were, as usual, second to none. Defenders always knew they

had been in a game. He was out of contract at the end of the season and was released.
Manchester U (From trainee on 10/7/1996)
Preston NE (£250,000 on 31/7/1997) FL 155+29/63 FLC 12+2/8 FAC 10+5/2 Others 9+3/1
Manchester C (£4,000,000 + on 5/3/2002) P/FL 27+24/7 FLC 1+1/3 FAC 2+2/2 Others 1+1
Crystal Palace (£1,100,000 on 22/6/2005) FL 14+11/2 FLC 2 FAC 0+2 Others 0+1
Ipswich T (Loaned on 31/8/2006) FL 13+1/4
Derby Co (Free on 31/1/2007) P/FL 4+7 FAC 0+2 Others 2
Barnsley (Loaned on 1/11/2007) FL 11/3
Barnsley (£100,000 on 28/1/2008) FL 81+13/18 FLC 4+1/1 FAC 0+1

McKENNA Paul Stephen
Born: Chorley, 20 October 1977
Height: 5'7" **Weight:** 11.12
Club Honours: Div 2 '00
Paul was made Nottingham Forest captain immediately after his arrival from Preston in the summer and promptly impressed the City Ground faithful with his work rate. Playing just in front of the back four, his experience was of great value in helping his young team-mates. He scored his only goal of the season against his former employers. Paul suffered a serious knee injury against Swansea in March that looked like keeping him out for the remainder of the season but surprised everybody by regaining fitness to figure in the play-offs
Preston NE (From trainee on 2/2/1996) FL 400+22/30 FLC 18 FAC 19+2/2 Others 13+2
Nottingham F (£750,000 on 20/7/2009) FL 35/1 FLC 2+1 FAC 1 Others 2

McKENZIE Leon Mark
Born: Croydon, 17 May 1978
Height: 5'11" **Weight:** 11.2
Club Honours: Div 1 '04
The experienced striker recovered from his serious Achilles injury during the summer of 2009 and Coventry extended his contract until he was fit. His final and only appearance of the season was off the bench in the home game against Swansea and a week later he announced that as his contract was not being renewed he was joining Charlton. However, he had a recurrence of the injury and struggled to find full fitness with various setbacks occurring. Leon eventually got fully fit but found it difficult to break into the Charlton side,

making 14 appearances from the bench without actually starting a game. He scored Charlton's only goal in the defeat at Southampton in the Johnstone's Paint Trophy, but after picking up a thigh injury late in the season he played no further part. Was out of contract in the summer.
Crystal Palace (From trainee on 7/10/1995) P/FL 44+41/17 FLC 5+2/1 FAC 2+4
Fulham (Loaned on 3/10/1997) FL 1+2
Peterborough U (Loaned on 13/8/1998) FL 4/3
Peterborough U (Loaned on 30/11/1998) FL 10/5 Others 1/1
Peterborough U (Free on 13/10/2000) FL 83+7/45 FLC 2 FAC 7+1/1 Others 3/4
Norwich C (£325,000 on 15/12/2003) P/FL 47+32/20 FLC 2/2
Coventry C (£600,000 on 31/8/2006) FL 42+20/12 FLC 1+1 FAC 4/2
Charlton Ath (Free on 1/9/2009) FL 0+12 FAC 0+1 Others 0+1/1

McKEOWN James Karl
Born: Sutton Coldfield, 24 July 1989
Height: 6'2" **Weight:** 14.0
International Honours: RoI: Yth
The Republic of Ireland under-19 international goalkeeper was again kept on Peterborough's bench by the form of Joe Lewis. But the two starts and three substitute appearances James made showed just what he is capable of. Good handling, fine positional awareness and good shot-stopping led to James being named as the 'Man of the Match' in a late season game against Blackpool.
Peterborough U (From trainee at Walsall on 25/7/2007) FL 2+4 FLC 0+1

MACKIE James (Jamie) Charles
Born: Dorking, 22 September 1985
Height: 5'8" **Weight:** 11.2
Jamie was again Plymouth's main striker throughout the season, missing only a handful of games. A tricky forward with a fantastic engine and great pace, his final tally of eight goals was a disappointment to him. Playing on the shoulder of the opposition defence, he is always looking for a chance to shoot at goal when sometimes he needs to pick out a pass to a team-mate in a better position. Towards the end of the season and especially following Plymouth's relegation, it was clear that Jamie would not be staying at Home Park and this was confirmed in May when he signed a four-year contract with Queens Park Rangers.
Wimbledon/MK Dons (Signed from Leatherhead on 9/1/2004) FL 8+8 FAC 2+1 Others 1 (Freed during 2005 close season)

Plymouth Arg (£145,000 from Exeter C on 28/1/2008) FL 81+17/16 FLC 1+1 FAC 2

MACKLIN Lloyd Joshua
Born: Camberley, 2 August 1991
Height: 5'9" **Weight:** 12.3
A quick and lively right-winger who can score goals as well as make them, Lloyd was very much a part of the Swindon first team squad in the early part of the season and although only starting two games featured regularly from the bench. Having been forced to leave the field early in a game at Brentford during October, he was later diagnosed with a leg fracture and on his return found others had moved in front of him. Loaned to Torquay, Lloyd spent a month there, showing discipline and working hard, but a lack of match fitness meant that the Gulls did not see him at his best. Was out of contract at the end of June.
Swindon T (From trainee on 12/8/2008) FL 1+10 FLC 1+1 FAC 0+1 Others 0+1
Torquay U (Loaned on 19/2/2010) FL 3+1

McLACHLAN Fraser Malcolm
Born: Knutsford, 9 November 1982
Height: 5'11" **Weight:** 12.7
It was a nightmare season for the desperately unlucky Morecambe midfield player who suffered another broken leg at the beginning of the campaign. He started the first game against Hereford but was injured in the first half and was unable to start another game. After two broken legs in three years he was released at the end of the season.
Stockport Co (From trainee on 11/7/2001) FL 43+10/4 FLC 1 FAC 2 Others 0+1
Mansfield T (Signed on 11/11/2004) FL 23+6 FLC 1 FAC 1 Others 1
Morecambe (Free on 23/3/2006) FL 23+6 FLC 2 FAC 2 Others 1

McLAREN Paul Andrew
Born: High Wycombe, 17 November 1976
Height: 6'0" **Weight:** 13.4
Paul rejoined Tranmere in the summer, signing a two-year contract. An experienced, industrious and quick-thinking central midfielder in his second spell at Prenton Park after spending only one season away, he can deliver telling passes and is a dead-ball specialist with a good record for assists. Paul is skilled at holding the ball and never turned in a performance that was less than reliable. Off the field, Paul is renowned for his willingness to contribute to Rovers'

community initiatives.
Luton T (From trainee on 5/1/1994) FL 137+30/4 FLC 10+4/1 FAC 11/1 Others 9
Sheffield Wed (Free on 11/6/2001) FL 83+13/8 FLC 6+1/1 FAC 2 Others 1
Rotherham U (Free on 2/8/2004) FL 67+5/4 FLC 2 FAC 2/2 Others 1
Tranmere Rov (Free on 3/7/2006) FL 85/5 FLC 1 FAC 6
Bradford C (Free on 31/7/2008) FL 32+2/3 FLC 1 FAC 1 Others 1
Tranmere Rov (Free on 14/7/2009) FL 36+2 FLC 2/1 FAC 2+1

Paul McLaren

McLAUGHLIN Jonathan (Jon) Peter
Born: Edinburgh, 9 September 1987
Height: 6'3" **Weight:** 12.12
The Great Britain Students goalkeeper had to bide his time at Bradford, first behind Simon Eastwood and then Matt Glennon. But once given his chance by Peter Taylor, Jon grabbed it with both hands. He saved a Greg Pearson penalty at Burton and pulled off a stunning late save to deny Barnet's Albert Adomah, arching back to tip his curling shot on to the crossbar. Jon uses his height well and looks particularly strong coming for crosses.
Bradford C (Free from Harrogate T on 5/7/2008) FL 8 18/1/2008) P/FL 64+14/13 FLC 0+1 FAC

McLEAN Aaron
Born: Hammersmith, 25 May 1983
Height: 5'7" **Weight:** 10.8
Club Honours: FAT '06
International Honours: E: SP-5
Aaron was asked to play a little deeper for Peterborough in 2009-10 and it did

not really suit his style of play. He is an out-and-out front man who likes to lead the pack. Good with both feet and surprisingly effective in the air for someone only 5'7", the withdrawn role curtailed his chances in front of goal. An injury kept him out of the last two months of the season. Hopefully he will come back fully fit in the season ahead and again be used in his preferred role.
Leyton Orient (From trainee on 9/7/2001) FL 5+35/2 FAC 0+3 Others 1+1/1 (Free to Aldershot T on 28/3/2003)
Peterborough U (£150,000 from Grays Ath on 31/10/2006) FL 130+8/61 FLC 7/1 FAC 13/7 Others 3/1

MacLEAN Steven (Steve)
Born: Edinburgh, 23 August 1982
Height: 5'10" **Weight:** 11.1
International Honours: S: U21-4
Steve again had a very disappointing time at Plymouth. After giving impressive performances in pre-season he was rewarded with a starting place for the first three games. Following that, he made only one further appearance, against West Bromwich at the Hawthorns in September. Steve was informed by manager Paul Sturrock that he was free to look for a new club and at the end of December, appeared to be joining Scottish Premier League side Heart of Midlothian but was back at Home Park after failing to agree terms. After a month of speculation, Steve finally signed for Aberdeen on loan until the end of the season, scoring his first goal against Hibernian and adding a couple in his next match, a 4–4 draw with Celtic.
Glasgow Rgrs (From juniors on 17/9/1998) SL 0+3 SC 0+1
Scunthorpe U (Loaned on 6/8/2003) FL 37+5/23 FLC 1+1/1 FAC 5 Others 3/1
Sheffield Wed (£125,000 on 27/7/2004) FL 60+23/32 FLC 2 FAC 3/1 Others 1+1/2
Cardiff C (Free on 1/7/2007) FL 6+9/1 FLC 1+1 FAC 1
Plymouth Arg (£500,000 on 18/1/2008) FL 28+13/5 FLC 2 FAC 0+1
Aberdeen (Loaned on 1/2/2010) SL 15+1/5 SC 2

McLEOD Izale (Izzy) Michael
Born: Birmingham, 15 October 1984
Height: 6'0" **Weight:** 11.2
International Honours: E: U21-1
Charlton's Izzy was initially used mainly as a substitute, but started four games in October, scoring three goals in all. The best of those was a great strike against Exeter after the opposing 'keeper had parried Jonjo Shelvey's

cross. Izzy has a good build for a striker, being tall, lean and extremely quick. He is good in the air and his exceptional pace helps him to get past defenders. Unable to keep a regular place, he was loaned to Peterborough in January but sustained a knee injury in training the following month which required surgery and ended his season.
Derby Co *(From trainee on 7/2/2003)* *FL 24+15/4 FLC 1+1*
Sheffield U *(Loaned on 12/3/2004) FL 1+6*
MK Dons *(£100,000 on 4/8/2004) FL 105+11/54 FLC 4+1/3 FAC 8+1/3 Others 5*
Charlton Ath *(£1,100,000 + on 10/8/2007) FL 7+24/3 FLC 4 FAC 3 Others 1/1*
Colchester U *(Loaned on 29/2/2008) FL 0+2*
Millwall *(Loaned on 15/1/2009) FL 5+2/2 FAC 1*
Peterborough U *(Loaned on 10/1/2010) FL 2+2*

McLEOD Kevin Andrew
Born: Liverpool, 12 September 1980
Height: 5'11" **Weight:** 11.3
Club Honours: AMC '06
After struggling with injuries during 2008-09, Kevin was hoping for better at Brighton in 2009-10, but he remained on the fringe of the first team and was never able to demonstrate his best form. While still capable of whipping in a very decent cross from the left flank, he seemed to have lost a yard of pace and was transferred to fellow League One strugglers Wycombe on the last day of the mid-season transfer window. The talented left-winger, who joined on a three month contract until the end of the season, made his debut at Brentford and ran the right-back ragged, crossing for team-mate Kevin Betsy to score. Kevin has very good ball control and a cultured left foot but, after a run of five games, he found himself on the bench. Although he started the final game of the season he was not offered a new contract.
Everton *(From trainee on 24/9/1998) PL 0+5 FLC 1 FAC 0+1*
Queens Park Rgrs *(Loaned on 21/3/2003) FL 8/2 Others 3*
Queens Park Rgrs *(Signed on 18/8/2003) FL 30+29/4 FLC 3+1/1 FAC 2 Others 1/1*
Swansea C *(Signed on 16/2/2005) FL 32+12/7 FLC 2 FAC 1 Others 3+1*
Colchester U *(Free on 30/8/2006) FL 34+18/7 FLC 1 FAC 2*
Brighton & Hove A *(Free on 2/7/2008) FL 13+13 FLC 1+1 FAC 2+1/1 Others 4+1/1*
Wycombe W *(Free on 1/2/2010) FL 8+3*

McMAHON Anthony (Tony)
Born: Bishop Auckland, 24 March 1986
Height: 5'10" **Weight:** 11.6
Club Honours: FAYC '04
Tony started the season as Middlesbrough's right-back after manager Gareth Southgate chose the more steely approach as Boro started life in the Championship. After a brief spell on the bench, he was reinstated under new manager Gordon Strachan. Tony struggled with a foot injury at the turn of the year but battled his way through as Boro's squad was pushed to the limit through injuries. It was not till he was omitted in February against Peterborough that it came to light he had been playing with a stress fracture of the foot, an injury that ruled him out for the rest of the season.
Middlesbrough *(From trainee on 7/2/2005) P/FL 48+3 FLC 1+2 FAC 3+2 Others 4*
Blackpool *(Loaned on 9/11/2007) FL 2*
Sheffield Wed *(Loaned on 21/8/2008) FL 14+1/1*

McMANUS Stephen
Born: Lanark, 10 September 1982
Height: 6'2" **Weight:** 13.1
Club Honours: SPD '07, '07, '08; SLC '06, '09; SC '07
International Honours: S: 22
With the departure of Sean St Ledger back to Preston, the need for an experienced centre-half was at the forefront of Gordon Strachan's mind. After Gary Caldwell turned down a deal to move from Glasgow Celtic to Middlesbrough in favour of Premier League football with Wigan, Strachan turned to out of favour Stephen. He quickly became a fans' favourite at Middlesbrough with his committed defending and seemed to bring the best out of centre-half partner David Wheater, who had been struggling for form since Robert Huth left. Stephen scored with a header in a 2-0 win at Plymouth in April, leaving the Riverside faithful hoping a permanent deal with Celtic can be thrashed out.
Glasgow Celtic *(From juniors on 1/7/2003) SL 148+2/17 SLC 12/1 SC 11 Others 29+1/2*
Middlesbrough *(Loaned on 29/1/2010) FL 16/1*

McNAMEE Anthony
Born: Kensington, 13 July 1984
Height: 5'6" **Weight:** 10.0
Club Honours: Div 1 '10
International Honours: E: Yth
A regular on the right or left wing for Swindon during the early part of the season, he was allowed to move on loan to fellow Division One side,

Norwich in November. Proving to be a skilful, tricky winger with the ability to deliver telling crosses, his move to Carrow Road was made permanent in January. Anthony is a winger from the old school who thrives on good service to him and whilst the Canaries' preferred diamond formation kept him on the sidelines for many weeks, when called upon he excelled to provide vital contributions against Oldham, Southend and Stockport.
Watford *(From trainee on 17/4/2002) P/FL 34+57/2 FLC 6+2 FAC 3+1/1*
Crewe Alex *(Loaned on 21/3/2007) FL 5*
Swindon T *(Signed on 18/1/2008) FL 62+17/3 FLC 3 FAC 2 Others 2+2/1*
Norwich C *(Signed on 26/11/2009) FL 7+10/1*

McNAMEE David Kenneth
Born: Glasgow, 10 October 1980
Height: 5'11" **Weight:** 11.2
Club Honours: SLC '04
International Honours: S: 4; B-1
David, who is a cultured right-back, had another injury-ravaged season with Plymouth. He began well by appearing at right-back in the first five games of the season. He picked up an ankle injury in the game against Derby in August and, unfortunately, was not able to start again until February. He then suffered a groin strain and his final appearances were from the substitutes' bench. David was released at the end of the season.
St Mirren *(From juniors on 1/8/1997) SL 23+1 SLC 1 SC 1*
Blackburn Rov *(£300,000 on 19/2/1999)*
Livingston *(Signed on 31/8/2002) SL 82+3/4 SLC 10+1 SC 7 Others 1*
Coventry C *(£100,000 on 16/6/2006) FL 28+1 FLC 1+1*
Plymouth Arg *(Free on 18/7/2008) FL 11+8 FLC 1 FAC 0+2*

McNAUGHTON Kevin Paul
Born: Dundee, 28 August 1982
Height: 5'10" **Weight:** 10.6
International Honours: S: 4; B-1; U21-1
The 'Silver Fox', who earns his nickname from greying hair, had a season disrupted by injuries at Cardiff. Kevin can play at right-back or left-back and filled both positions over the season but he suffered a number of hamstring injuries that could be triggered by a posture problem. Cardiff's backroom staff worked with him to improve his posture. One of the most consistent defenders in Championship football at his best, he is under contract until the summer of 2011. Finished the season at right-back

and played in all three play-off games, but, along with most of his team-mates, failed to reach his best against Blackpool at Wembley.
Aberdeen *(From juniors on 1/8/1999) SL 165+10/3 SLC 9 SC 13 Others 5*
Cardiff C *(Free on 6/7/2006) FL 133+4/1 FLC 4 FAC 13/1 Others 3*

McNEIL Matthew (Matty)
Born: Manchester, 14 July 1976
Height: 6'5" **Weight:** 14.3
Out of contract striker Matty rejoined Stockport in late 2009, providing a presence up front which the side had been lacking. Playing five games through December, he was unable to find the back of the net. He was then unable to agree terms with the club to extend his short-term contract, leaving in January.
Macclesfield T *(Free from Hyde U, ex Stalybridge Celtic, Runcorn, on 2/3/2006) FL 41+6/6 FAC 2+2 Others 1+1/1*
Stockport Co *(Free on 10/8/2007) FL 36+5/5 FLC 3/1 FAC 4/3 Others 1+1/1*

McNISH Callum Leander
Born: Oxford, 25 May 1992
Height: 6'2" **Weight:** 12.6
A Southampton Academy player since he was 12, Callum signed professional forms on his 17th birthday in May 2008. A long-limbed central midfielder, he is influenced by Patrick Vieira. His introduction to the first team came in a pre-season friendly prior to the 2008-09 season, but he had to wait until last May for a competitive debut, during the second half of Saints' 3-2 home win over Carlisle.
Southampton *(From trainee on 25/9/2009) FL 0+1*

McNULTY James (Jimmy)
Born: Runcorn, 13 February 1985
Height: 6'2" **Weight:** 12.0
International Honours: S: Yth
It was a cruel start to the season for Brighton's Jimmy. Having recovered from the trauma of losing a kidney in February 2009, he succumbed to an ankle injury in training and even missed a game because of wisdom teeth problems before he was finally able to turn out competitively in early October. He received a terrific reception when he made his comeback and performed nobly, but a second ankle injury sidelined him for a further six weeks and then Marcos Painter arrived on loan to establish himself at left-back. Restricted to the role of a substitute, the ball-playing defender joined Scunthorpe on a month's loan in March to provide cover at left-back. Thrown in at the deep end when coming

on as a substitute in the 3-0 defeat at Swansea, he then started in the 3-2 loss at Preston. An ankle injury saw him lose his place but he returned for the final match of the season where he gave an assured performance against Nottingham Forest, combining solid defence with being comfortable on the ball.
Wrexham *(Trainee) Others 0+1 (Freed during 2004 close season)*
Macclesfield T *(Free from Caernarfon T on 1/8/2006) FL 28+6/1 FLC 1 FAC 2+1/1 Others 3*
Stockport Co *(Free on 7/1/2008) FL 37/1 FLC 1 FAC 3 Others 4+1*
Brighton & Hove A *(£150,000 on 2/2/2009) FL 10+3/1 FAC 2 Others 1*
Scunthorpe U *(Loaned on 23/3/2010) FL 2+1*

McPAKE James
Born: Airdrie, 24 June 1984
Height: 6'2" **Weight:** 14.2
The injury-hit centre-half did not appear for Coventry until mid-December after recovering from a pre-season shoulder injury. Before this his appearances had been limited following his move from Scotland in January 2009. His return to action coincided with an excellent run by the Sky Blues and James was on the losing side only once in his first 12 League games – an unlucky injury-time defeat at Ipswich. A no-nonsense, old-school style central defender, James immediately gave Coventry's defence a more solid look and was never afraid to put his body on the line for the cause, with his well-timed last-gasp tackles a particular feature. He scored his first Coventry goal in the televised game at Leicester when, after his poor clearance set up the Foxes' opening goal, he responded with a gutsy display culminating in a finish worthy of a seasoned striker. Injury struck at Reading on Easter Monday but despite playing only 17 League games, he left a strong impression on Coventry's supporters as a very reliable defender.
Livingston *(From juniors on 2/4/2002) SL 82+18/6 SLC 7 SC 9 Others 3*
Morton *(Loaned on 10/1/2006) SL 3+7/2*
Coventry C *(Signed on 31/1/2009) FL 20+1/1 FAC 3*

McPHAIL Stephen John Paul
Born: Westminster, 9 December 1979
Height: 5'10" **Weight:** 12.0
Club Honours: FAYC '97
International Honours: Roi: 10; B-1; U21-7; Yth (UEFA-U18 '98)
Stephen came through terrible times at Cardiff during 2009-10. He was diagnosed with cancer in November and went home to Dublin for

treatment. Later, he suffered a serious thigh injury but fought his way back to play a major role in City's drive for promotion that eventually faltered in the play-off final at Wembley. He joined Cardiff from Barnsley in 2006, having helped the Yorkshire club to promotion via the play-offs and, after one season, signed a new four-year contract that runs out in the summer of 2011. Cardiff's playmaker, he sets the tempo for the team and rarely concedes possession. He finished the season playing alongside Joe Ledley in central midfield.
Leeds U *(From trainee on 23/12/1996) PL 52+26/3 FLC 2+4 FAC 3 Others 15+5*
Millwall *(Loaned on 14/3/2002) FL 3*
Nottingham F *(Loaned on 27/8/2003) FL 13+1 FLC 2*
Barnsley *(Free on 5/7/2004) FL 66+4/4 FLC 2+1 FAC 2 Others 4*
Cardiff C *(Free on 4/7/2006) FL 133+6/3 FLC 9 FAC 7+1 Others 3*

McQUILKIN James Robbie Leonard
Born: Tipton, 9 January 1989
Height: 5'8" **Weight:** 10.8
Although he did not nail down a regular place in the side until February, central midfielder James was not slow in showing the fans what they had been missing with some excellent performances as Hereford ended the season strongly. Despite a slight frame, his powerful, enthusiastic running and astute passing made him an automatic choice, reinforced by his ability to chip in with a couple of important goals. If he develops as expected, he could be the next United player to make an impact on a higher stage.
Hereford U *(Free from Tescoma Zlin, Czech Republic, ex trainee at West Bromwich A, on 1/8/2009) FL 20+2/2 FLC 1*

McQUOID Joshua (Josh) Joseph Brian
Born: Southampton, 15 December 1989
Height: 5'9" **Weight:** 10.10
International Honours: NI: B-1; U21-8; Yth
Josh continued his progress since moving up from Bournemouth's youth team ranks two years earlier. Capable of playing anywhere across the middle or up front, he was an important part of the squad and enjoyed a number of starts. A Northern Ireland under-21 international, he scored his first goal for Bournemouth in the final home game against Port Vale before signing a new one-year deal.
Bournemouth *(From trainee at*

PFA FOOTBALLERS' WHO'S WHO Mc-MA

Brockenhurst College on 8/8/2008) FL
16+36/1 FLC 0+2 FAC 1+5 Others 1+4 4

McREADY John Lewis
Born: South Shields, 24 July 1992
Height: 5'10" **Weight:** 11.7
John is another product of the
Darlington youth scheme and made his
debut as a half-time substitute against
Grimsby at the Arena in late April,
thereby becoming the 53rd player to be
used during the season. He was not
overawed by the step up to first team
level and showed composure on the
ball in midfield and neat footwork. He
made his first start in the penultimate
home game of the season against Notts
County when the Magpies ran out 5-0
winners to take the League Two title.
Darlington (Trainee) FL 3+1

McSHANE Paul David
Born: Wicklow, 6 January 1986
Height: 5'11" **Weight:** 11.5
International Honours: RoI: 22; U21-
6; Yth
Having spent the first half of the
previous season on loan at Hull, Paul
completed a permanent move to the
Tigers on a four-year contract as the
summer transfer window was about to
close. The move would probably have
been concluded earlier had it not been
for a knee injury suffered during
Sunderland's pre-season friendly at
Darlington. By coincidence, his second
debut for Hull came in their visit to
Sunderland, when he was named
captain for the day. At the KC Stadium,
he teamed up with Republic of Ireland
colleagues Kevin Kilbane, Stephen Hunt
and Caleb Folan, and was recalled by
coach Giovanni Trapattoni for the game
against Cyprus in September. As the
international season progressed, Paul
was to feature in one of the most iconic
images in the history of Irish sport as he
was alongside France's Thierry Henry
whose controversial 'handball'
effectively ended the Republic's World
Cup hopes. With Ireland and Hull, Paul
was usually employed at right-back and,
although this did not play to his
strengths, his wholehearted effort and
competitive spirit could not be faulted.
In Iain Dowie's period in charge, he was
selected in his preferred centre-back
role for City's vital relegation clashes at
Portsmouth and Stoke.
*Manchester U (From trainee on
13/1/2003)*
*Walsall (Loaned on 23/12/2004) FL
3+1/1*
*Brighton & Hove A (Loaned on
4/8/2005) FL 38/3 FLC 1 FAC 1*
*West Bromwich A (Free on 10/8/2006)
FL 31+1/2 FLC 3 FAC 4/1 Others 3*

*Sunderland (£1,500,000 + on
27/7/2007) PL 20+4 FAC 1*
*Hull C (Loaned on 1/9/2008) PL 17/1
FAC 2*
*Hull C (Signed on 30/8/2009) PL 26+1
FLC 0+1*

McSHEFFREY Gary
Born: Coventry, 13 August 1982
Height: 5'8" **Weight:** 10.10
International Honours: E: Yth
Gary saw limited opportunity at
Birmingham last season due to new
additions to the squad and the
preference for James McFadden and
Keith Fahey on the left. A willing
worker who causes problems with his
direct running, he showed bright
contributions in the run-outs he got as
a substitute. Was loaned to Leeds in
January until the end of the campaign
and showed glimpses of his undoubted
class. He played both up front and wide
left, but could not make a lasting
impact, scoring just once in nine League
One games. The goal came about when
his mis-hit cross eluded Walsall
goalkeeper Clayton Ince, but was not
enough to stop Leeds sinking to a 2-1
home defeat. Was released by the Blues
at the season's end.
*Coventry C (From trainee on
27/8/1999) P/FL 108+35/44 FLC 7+2/5
FAC 8+2/4*
*Stockport Co (Loaned on 30/11/2001)
FL 3+2/1*
*Luton T (Loaned on 22/8/2003) FL 18/9
FLC 1/1*
*Luton T (Loaned on 18/9/2004) FL
1+4/1*
*Birmingham C (£3,000,000 on
17/8/2006) P/FL 68+15/16 FLC 6+1/3
FAC 4+2/1*
Nottingham F (Loaned on 7/3/2009) FL 4
*Leeds U (Loaned on 29/1/2010) FL
9+1/1 Others 1*

McSTAY Henry Matthew Patrick
Born: Armagh, 6 March 1985
Height: 6'0" **Weight:** 11.12
International Honours: RoI: U21; Yth;
NI; Yth
Making just two substitute
appearances for Morecambe in 2009-
10, it was yet another injury-hit season
for the young Irishman. A versatile
defender, who can play at right-back or
in the centre of the defence, he was
allowed to leave at the end of the
campaign. Wherever he goes, Henry
must be hoping for better luck.
*Leeds U (From trainee on 12/3/2002.
Free to Halifax T on 31/3/2005)*
*Morecambe (Free from Royal Antwerp,
Belgium, ex Portadown, on 30/1/2008)
FL 29+6/1 FLC 0+1 FAC 2/1 Others 2+1*

McSWEENEY Leon
Born: Cork, 19 February 1983
Height: 6'1" **Weight:** 11.3
Out of contract with Stockport, Leon
became Hartlepool manager Chris
Turner's second signing for the new
season. A player able to perform equally
well in a number of different positions,
his versatility was used to advantage.
He started out playing as a striker, then
for most of the time was utilised as a
right-sided midfielder, but also had a try
covering at right-back. In mid-season
Leon was unable to hold a first team
place but after a spell in the reserves he
returned refreshed to turn in some
'Man of the Match' performances.
*Leicester C (Signed from Cork C on
10/8/2001. Freed during 2003 close
season)*
*Stockport Co (Free from Cork C, ex
Scarborough, Hucknall T, Hednesford T,
Hucknall T, Hednesford T, Ilkeston T, on
4/1/2008) FL 33+14/5 FLC 1 FAC 3+1
Others 3+3/1*
*Hartlepool U (Free on 2/7/2009) FL
24+7/1 FLC 2 Others 1*

McVEIGH Paul Francis
Born: Belfast, 6 December 1977
Height: 5'6" **Weight:** 10.5
Club Honours: Div 1 '04; AMC '09
International Honours: NI: 20; U21-
11; Yth; Sch
Paul retuned to Norwich, having left
Luton, for a second spell following a
trial period in the summer and whilst he
did not re-establish himself as a first
team regular, he made some good
contributions in the first part of the
campaign. A good technical player with
that uncanny knack of giving himself
time in possession, this attacking
midfielder then has the skill to deliver
the pass. His best performances came in
the immediate period following Paul
Lambert's arrival at the club, when his
incisive passing created several goals.
He was nearly always in the squad and
played in a variety of positions,
including left-back for the reserves. Was
out of contract in the summer.
*Tottenham H (From trainee on
10/7/1996) PL 2+1/1*
*Norwich C (Free on 23/3/2000) P/FL
148+68/36 FLC 3+5 FAC 7+1/2 Others 3/1*
*Burnley (Loaned on 22/3/2007) FL
6+2/3*
*Luton T (Free on 10/8/2007) FL
24+14/3 FLC 1+3 FAC 3+2 Others 3+3*
*Norwich C (Free on 23/7/2009) FL 4+5
Others 2*

MADDEN Simon Francis
Born: Dublin, 1 May 1988
Height: 5'9" **Weight:** 11.10
International Honours: RoI: U21-3

273

Another New Year recruit for Darlington by Steve Staunton, Simon soon settled into the right-back slot with steady displays of solid tackling and clearing the ball down the line. He likes to overlap and is able to deliver dangerous crosses into the box from deep areas. Was out of contract at the end of June.
Leeds U *(From trainee on 10/5/2006) Others 1 (Freed on 14/4/2008)*
Darlington *(Free from Shamrock Rov on 21/1/2010) FL 13+2*

MADINE Gary Lee
Born: Gateshead, 24 August 1990
Height: 6'2" **Weight:** 11.10
Unable to hold down a regular place at Carlisle, Gary was a surprise loan signing by Coventry in October. The tall striker joined the Sky Blues for a three-month basis and within days was given a first appearance as a substitute near the end of the West Bromwich home game. It was the first of nine appearances from the bench but Gary played less than an hour's football in total and rarely looked like scoring, although he was brought down for a penalty against Doncaster. His time there ended when Carlisle recalled him in January owing to an injury crisis and despite talk of him signing a contract with Coventry the deal never materialised. He then joined Chesterfield on loan at a time when the Spireites were expanding their attacking options. Gary's pace and height were immediately apparent, and matched his keen desire to win, but injury interrupted his progress. Back at Carlisle, he really came into contention at towards the end of the campaign with a number of strikes, including the club's first ever Wembley goal in open play in the Johnstone's Paint Trophy final. At Norwich, he ended the season on a high, scoring in the first minute before raising his overall game to give his best display to date in a Carlisle shirt.
Carlisle U *(From juniors on 13/12/2007) FL 7+38/5 FLC 1+3/1 FAC 2+1/1 Others 1+4/2*
Rochdale *(Loaned on 20/3/2009) FL 1+2*
Coventry C *(Loaned on 19/10/2009) FL 0+9*
Chesterfield *(Loaned on 12/2/2010) FL 2+2*

MAGENNIS Joshua (Josh) Brendan David
Born: Bangor, County Down, 15 August 1990
Height: 6'2" **Weight:** 12.13
International Honours: NI: 2; U21-5; Yth
A big, strong and mobile centre-forward, Josh is a Northern Ireland international who has played in goal and in attack for his country. Having signed for Cardiff at youth level as a goalkeeper, he was switched to striker by Academy manager Neal Ardley. Loaned to Grimsby in October, he was given his debut in Mike Newell's last game as manager and came close to scoring against Rochdale when his shot hit the bar. The teenage striker was then a victim of circumstance under a new management regime, and after a further substitute outing, his month on loan ended early. Raw, but aggressive and quick to learn, he made 11 first team appearances for Cardiff. Left out of the match-day squad for the Championship play-off final against Blackpool, when Jay Bothroyd went off injured after 15 minutes, Cardiff had no natural alternative. Was out of contract at the end of the season and released by the club.
Cardiff C *(From trainee on 1/7/2009) FL 1+8 FLC 0+1/1*
Grimsby T *(Loaned on 14/10/2009) FL 1+1*

MAGHOMA Jacques Honda
Born: Lubumbashi, DR Congo, 23 October 1987
Height: 5'9" **Weight:** 11.7
International Honours: DR Congo: 2
Jacques was the least known of a wave of new signings by Burton manager Paul Peschisolido in readiness for the club's first League season. The Congo-born player had been at Tottenham from a young age until his release in the summer and signed a two-year contract at the Pirelli Stadium. Despite his inexperience, Jacques quickly impressed with performances that embraced skill, pace, energy and an eye for a scoring opportunity. Though never fully established in the first team at Burton, Jacques made a significant contribution until a knee injury forced him to miss the last month of the season.
Tottenham H *(From trainee on 7/7/2005)*
Burton A *(Free on 17/7/2009) FL 24+11/3 FLC 1 FAC 1/1 Others 1*

MAHER Kevin Andrew
Born: Ilford, 17 October 1976
Height: 6'0" **Weight:** 12.5
Club Honours: Div 1 '06
International Honours: RoI: U21-4
Veteran central midfielder Kevin was signed by Mark Stimson last summer with a view to playing the holding role at Gillingham in a midfield diamond, but found himself consigned to the bench as the manager handed the job to promising youngster Jack Payne. As the season wore on, Kevin was brought into the side to add strength and experience to the midfield, although he was little more than a bit-part player once more after Danny Jackman's return to full fitness.
Tottenham H *(From trainee on 1/7/1995)*
Southend U *(Free on 23/1/1998) FL 375+8/22 FLC 18/1 FAC 27/1 Others 25+1/1*
Gillingham *(Loaned on 7/3/2008) FL 7*
Oldham Ath *(Free on 5/8/2008) FL 21+7/1 FLC 1 FAC 1+1 Others 1*
Gillingham *(Free on 2/7/2009) FL 21+5 FLC 2 FAC 0+2 Others 0+1*

MAHON Alan Joseph
Born: Dublin, 4 April 1978
Height: 5'10" **Weight:** 11.5
Club Honours: FLC '02
International Honours: RoI: 2; U21-18; Yth; Sch
A mercurial and talented midfielder, Alan returned to Tranmere in the summer in a move that pleased supporters. It brought a career that began at Tranmere in 1995, full circle. He is experienced, having played in the Premiership and in Portugal, and is a good man to have in any squad as his enthusiasm rubs off on colleagues, especially the younger ones. Alan's passing ability remains second to none but unfortunately he ruptured ankle ligaments in November and struggled to regain full fitness, which meant that his appearances were limited in the second half of the campaign.
Tranmere Rov *(From trainee on 7/4/1995) FL 84+36/13 FLC 12+6/1 FAC 4+2 (Free to Sporting Lisbon, Portugal on 1/7/2000)*
Blackburn Rov *(£1,500,000 from Sporting Lisbon, Portugal on 14/12/2000) P/FL 25+11/1 FLC 4+3 FAC 10*
Cardiff C *(Loaned on 24/1/2003) FL 13+2/2*
Ipswich T *(Loaned on 5/9/2003) FL 7+4/1 FLC 1*
Wigan Ath *(Free on 6/2/2004) P/FL 39+8/9 FLC 6 FAC 3/1*
Burnley *(£200,000 on 23/3/2006) FL 30+37/4 FLC 3+4 FAC 0+3*
Blackpool *(Loaned on 17/3/2009) FL 1*
Tranmere Rov *(Free on 8/7/2009) FL 8+8/1 FLC 2 FAC 1 Others 1*

MAHON Gavin Andrew
Born: Birmingham, 2 January 1977
Height: 6'0" **Weight:** 13.2
Club Honours: Div 3 '99
Gavin started the season in imperious form. His simple ball-winning approach is an unsung job that is only really appreciated when it is not there. His

presence was such a key part of Jim Magilton's early success at Queens Park Rangers and his absence was keenly felt when a cruel knee injury ended his season in early November. He only managed to start six games before this and scored his only goal in a 4-2 win at Derby. Was out of contract in the summer.
Wolverhampton W *(From trainee on 3/7/1995)*
Hereford U *(Free on 12/7/1996) FL 10+1/1 FLC 4*
Brentford *(£50,000 + on 17/11/1998) FL 140+1/8 FLC 8 FAC 5 Others 12*
Watford *(£150,000 + on 4/3/2002) P/FL 180+9/6 FLC 10 FAC 12+1/1 Others 3*
Queens Park Rgrs *(£200,000 on 1/1/2008) FL 45+13/4 FLC 4+1 FAC 3*

MAHOTO Eric Gauthier
Born: Le Havre, France, 21 February 1992
Height: 5'11" **Weight:** 11.5
The highly-rated 18-year-old Frenchman broke into the Portsmouth first team this season with a brief appearance off the bench in a Carling Cup victory over Hereford. Due to the financial situation engulfing Pompey the defensive midfielder moved to French side SC Bastia on the final day of the January transfer window.
Portsmouth *(Signed from Le Havre, France on 15/6/2008) FLC 0+1*

MAIERHOFER Stefan
Born: Vienna, Austria, 16 August 1982
Height: 6'8" **Weight:** 15.6
International Honours: Austria: 10
The Austrian International striker had already played in England this season, for Rapid Vienna at Villa Park. After Wolverhampton signed him he came on for a lively 45 minutes at Blackburn, having three decent scoring attempts and netting the latter. When he came off the bench at Everton it was a different story, as he got sent off. Stefan did not prove as dominant in the air as his size suggested, especially as he was the tallest player in the Premier League. Strangely, his only two starts for Wolverhampton were both at Old Trafford and after being omitted from the 18 he went to Bristol City on a one month loan midway through March. Making his debut in a 2-3 defeat at Plymouth, he was deprived of a goal on being given offside when he put away a rebound off the 'keeper. Then, coming on as a substitute against Nottingham Forest at Ashton Gate on 3 April, he found himself between the sticks a few minutes later after Dean Gerken had been stretchered off following a

collision with Forest's Nathan Tyson.
Wolverhampton W *(Signed from Rapid Vienna, Austria, ex SV Gablitz, Tulin, First Vienna, SV Langenrohr, Bayern Munich, TuS Koblenz, Greuther Furth, on 31/8/2009) PL 1+7/1 FLC 1*
Bristol C *(Loaned on 15/3/2010) FL 1+2*

MAIN Curtis Lee
Born: South Shields, 20 June 1992
Height: 5'9" **Weight:** 12.2
Curtis continued to gain experience at first team level for Darlington, appearing in about half of the games during the season. The majority of his appearances were as a substitute although he did start 12 League games. He possesses an eye for goal and shows neat footwork in tight areas which made him second highest scorer with three goals. A foot operation meant he missed the last few games of the season.
Darlington *(From trainee on 11/9/2009) FL 17+28/5 FLC 0+2 FAC 0+1 Others 0+1*

MAJEWSKI Radoslaw
Born: Pruszkow, Poland, 15 December 1986
Height: 5'7" **Weight:** 10.6
International Honours: Poland: 7
The young central midfielder joined Nottingham Forest on a season-long loan only days before the action started and became a big crowd favourite with his skilful play. He scored with his first touch on his debut against Rushden in a pre-season friendly and his form continued to reach a high level. Radoslaw scored his first League goal against local rivals Derby with a 25-yard volley in September and also hit a memorable goal against West Bromwich in January that was voted Forest's 'Goal of the Season'. His displays helped him to return to the Polish national side and soon after the end of the season his loan was turned in to a permanent move.
Nottingham F *(Loaned from Polonia Warsaw, Poland, ex Znicz Prusszkow, Dyskobolia Grodzisk, on 23/7/2009) FL 31+4/3 FLC 2/1 FAC 1 Others 2*

MAKOFO Serge
Born: Kinshasa, DR Congo, 22 October 1986
Height: 5'11" **Weight:** 12.6
A quick striker, Serge impressed on trial at Burton, where he scored a hat-trick on his first appearance for the reserves. That led to him joining Albion, technically on loan from Grays Athletic because of registration difficulties, but he was unable to force his way into the first team and was released in January.

MK Dons *(From trainee on 14/7/2005) FL 0+1 Others 0+1/1 (Freed during March 2006)*
Burton A *(Loaned from Grays Ath, ex Kettering T, Maidenhead U, Halesowen T, Potters Bar T, Croydon Ath, on 25/9/2009) FL 0+2 FAC 0+2*

Steed Malbranque

MALBRANQUE Steed
Born: Mouscron, Belgium, 6 January 1980
Height: 5'8" **Weight:** 11.7
Club Honours: FLC '08
International Honours: France: U21
Even allowing for the fact that France possess some wonderful footballers, the fact that Steed has never added to his under-21 recognition with a full French cap astonishes those who watch him regularly. Loved by supporters for his glue-like control, Steed did not show new manager Steve Bruce his best form for much of the season when he was employed on the right of midfield. The end of Sunderland's 14-game winless League run coincided with Steed's return to the side after a brief absence, the former Spurs' man re-inventing himself on the left and finishing the season in stunning form.
Fulham *(£5,000,000 from Lyon, France on 14/8/2001) PL 160+12/32 FLC 6+2/2 FAC 17/7 Others 12+2/3*
Tottenham H *(£2,000,000 on 31/8/2006) PL 53+9/6 FLC 9/2 FAC 7+2/1 Others 13+3/3*
Sunderland *(Signed on 1/8/2008) PL 64+3/1 FLC 3+2 FAC 3/1*

MALONE Scott Liam
Born: Rowley Regis, 25 March 1991
Height: 6'2" **Weight:** 11.11
International Honours: E: Yth

Scott was Wolverhampton's Academy 'Player of the Year' in 2008-09 and signed a professional contract with them in February 2009 before gaining some useful experience on a five-month loan to Hungarian First Division side Ujpest Dosza. He was also selected to play for England under-19s this season, his first cap coming against Russia in September in a match played at Shrewsbury. In a mutually beneficial arrangement, Scott became the third Wolves' left-back in recent seasons, following Charlie Mulgrew and George Friend, to spend a loan period at Roots Hall with Southend. Impressing sufficiently in his attack-minded play to secure an extended loan until the end of the season, he eventually lost his place to Johnny Herd and had to be content with a place on the bench, but overall it was a very useful spell in his burgeoning career.

Wolverhampton W *(From trainee on 10/2/2009)*
Southend U *(Loaned on 23/11/2009)*
FL 15+2

MALOUDA Florent Johan
Born: Cayenne, French Guiana, 13 June 1980
Height: 5'11" **Weight:** 11.10
Club Honours: FAC '09, '10; CS '09; PL '10
International Honours: France: 53

From a forlorn figure at the tail-end of 2008 under 'Big Phil' Scolari to one of the most effective players in the Premier League, Florent's renaissance under first Guus Hiddink and then Carlo Ancelotti is remarkable. So consistent was the Frenchman that he replaced the talismanic Joe Cole in the Chelsea side. He scored consistently, including a brilliant 25-yard strike against Wolves, a mazy dribble and firm drive against West Ham and four goals in three days against Portsmouth and Aston Villa to take his Premier League tally into double figures. The beautifully taken brace against Villa earned 'Man of the Match' plaudits in a scintillating team performance. His second successive accolade the following match went a long way to deciding the outcome of the Premier League title, when a surging run at Old Trafford sliced through the Manchester United defence for Joe Cole to back-heel a clever opening goal. A second successive FA Cup semi-final goal at Wembley cemented his award of Barclays 'Player of the Month' for March and, as a measure of his team-mates' regard, he was elected 'Players' Player of the Year' for his 15 goals and eight assists. In February he was forced to stand in as

emergency left-back following injuries to Ashley Cole and Yury Zhirkov, repeating the cover from his Lyon days. A few seasons ago, Chelsea were extremely powerful down the left with Arjen Robben and Damian Duff terrorising defences and now Florent is carving his own niche. His confidence is obvious for all too see as he now plays with a beaming smile on his face and he was happy to sign a four-year contract extension. He went with France to the World Cup in fine fettle.
Chelsea *(£13,500,000 from Lyon, France, ex Chateauroux, Guingamp, on 16/7/2007) PL 66+19/20 FLC 7+1/2 FAC 10+2/3 Others 26+5/3*

MAMBO Yado Massaya
Born: Kilburn, 22 October 1991
Height: 6'3" **Weight:** 13.0

A good prospect from Charlton's Academy, Yado made his first team debut as a substitute in the Johnstone's Paint Trophy against Barnet in October. He was named on the bench on a couple of other occasions but it was to be his only appearance. Tall and well built for his age, Yado is a commanding figure in defence, particularly in the air. To help him gain further experience he had loan spells at Welling United, Dover Athletic and Staines Town and could break into Charlton's side in the next campaign.
Charlton Ath *(Trainee) Others 0+1*

MANCIENNE Michael Ian
Born: Feltham, 8 January 1988
Height: 5'10" **Weight:** 11.7
Club Honours: FAC '09
International Honours: E: U21-21; Yth

Florent Malouda

The central defender, on an extended loan from Chelsea, played in the first eight League matches but with Wolverhampton struggling, changes were made. He came back at Manchester United and did well but the other players in his position were also in form. Michael was used as part of a five-man midfield and when it became a 4-1-4-1 system, he was generally the man in front of the back four. He could tackle well, and was also good on the ball. Sometimes he would come on as a substitute only, but he always seemed to do what was asked of him for the team. It remained to be seen if he was part of Chelsea's plans.
Chelsea (From trainee on 11/1/2006) PL 2+2 FAC 1 Others 0+1
Queens Park Rgrs (Loaned on 17/10/2006) FL 26+2 FAC 2
Queens Park Rgrs (Loaned on 9/8/2007) FL 26+4 FLC 1
Wolverhampton W (Loaned on 27/10/2008) FL 8+2
Wolverhampton W (Loaned on 13/8/2009) PL 22+8 FAC 3

MANGA Marc
Born: Cameroon, 16 January 1988
Height: 5'9" **Weight:** 11.5
Formerly with Bordeaux and Stade Lavallois, French striker Marc had a trial at Hereford before being offered non-contract terms at Rochdale. Said by his manager to offer "something a bit different" up front, Marc made three appearances off the bench in October and November but was not retained.
Rochdale (Free from Stade Lavallois, France, via trial at Hereford U, on 8/10/2009) FL 0+2 FAC 0+1

MANNONE Vito
Born: Milan, Italy, 2 March 1988
Height: 6'0" **Weight:** 11.8
International Honours: Italy: U21-3
Despite being Arsenal's third choice goalkeeper, injuries to Manuel Almunia and Lukasz Fabianski allowed the Italian to stake his claim for the first team. Having kept a comfortable clean sheet against Wigan at home, he produced one of the best goalkeeping displays of recent years as he made several fantastic saves in the 1-0 win at Fulham. His inexperience showed in subsequent games and he found himself back down the pecking order. The Italian under-21 international played five games in the Premier League, keeping two clean sheets, and three times in the Champions League, recording one further clean sheet.
Arsenal (£350,000 from Atalanta, Italy on 15/7/2005) PL 6 Others 3
Barnsley (Loaned on 18/8/2006) FL 1+1 FLC 2

MANSELL Lee Richard Samuel
Born: Gloucester, 28 October 1982
Height: 5'9" **Weight:** 10.10
After early-season injuries and illnesses, Lee re-established himself as Torquay's right-back, where his work and lung-busting stamina made him a constant threat on the overlap. He was moved to a central midfield role on the departure of Chris Hargreaves, a position that suits his all-action tough-tackling box-to-box style. His 'Players' Player of the Season' award reflects the regard he is held in by his team-mates.
Luton T (From trainee on 16/5/2001) FL 35+12/8 FLC 2 FAC 6/2 Others 7
Oxford U (Free on 7/7/2005) FL 44/1 FLC 1 FAC 4 Others 2/1
Torquay U (Signed on 18/7/2006) FL 78+6/6 FLC 1 FAC 7 Others 2

Lee Mansell

MANSET Mathieu
Born: Metz, France, 5 August 1989
Height: 6'1" **Weight:** 13.8
The young Frenchman could hardly have made a more spectacular start to his Hereford career with a goal within minutes of coming on as a substitute against Aldershot in the Johnstone's Paint Trophy and then converting the winning penalty in the shoot-out. His immense physical presence quickly earned him the nickname 'The Beast' among Hereford fans and he proved a handful for opposition defenders with his strong, pacy running and ability in the air. He has all the physical attributes to go a long way in the game.
Hereford U (Free from Le Havre, France on 24/9/2009) FL 16+13/3 FAC 1+1/1 Others 0+2/1

MARIAPPA Adrian Joseph
Born: Harrow, 3 October 1986
Height: 5'11" **Weight:** 12.2
Adrian had the distinction of playing every minute of every match for Watford in 2009-10, a feat that reflected his consistency and value to the side. He switched between right-back and central defence as required and also deputised as team captain for three months while Jay Demerit was ruled out. At the age of only 22, Adrian is regarded as a senior member of the Watford squad, which speaks volumes for his leadership qualities. He clocked up his 100th League appearance for the Hornets against Sheffield Wednesday and marked the occasion with a rare goal – only his second for the club.
Watford (From trainee on 4/7/2005) P/FL 114+18/2 FLC 11+1 FAC 9+2 Others 1

MARIC Goran
Born: Novi Sad, Serbia, 23 March 1984
Height: 6'0" **Weight:** 12.13
A Serbian-born striker with a Spanish passport, Goran had trials at Crystal Palace and Norwich in the summer before signing for City on a one-year contract. He impressed during his trial spell, scoring a couple of goals, but his lazy style did not impress everyone. The Canaries' early season change of manager afforded the burly front man just two appearances in English football before his contract was cancelled and he returned to Spain.
Norwich C (Free from Celta Vigo, Spain, via trial at Crystal Palace and loans at Las Palmas and Barcelona B, on 30/7/2009) FLC 0+1 Others 1

MARNEY Dean Edward
Born: Barking, 31 January 1984
Height: 5'9" **Weight:** 10.7
International Honours: E: U21-1
A series of injuries blighted Dean's attempts to assist Hull in their ultimately unsuccessful attempt to fend off relegation from the Premier League. An impressive display in the League opening day defeat at Chelsea resulted in knee and ankle problems that ruled him out for a month. He returned to play a key role in the Tigers' best sequence of the season. Dean's outstanding work rate in midfield was rewarded with the eventual winner in a thrilling 3-2 success against Everton in November. It was his first Premier League goal since New Year's Day, 2005, when he bagged a brace for Tottenham against Everton. After suffering a calf injury in December, he returned against Arsenal in March for Phil Brown's last game in charge. Dean

retained his place under new boss Iain Dowie before injury again ruled him out of the closing games on the campaign. With relegation confirmed, it appeared his four years in East Yorkshire had come to an end.
Tottenham H *(From trainee on 3/7/2002) PL 4+4/2 FAC 0+3*
Swindon T *(Loaned on 24/12/2002) FL 8+1*
Queens Park Rgrs *(Loaned on 16/1/2004) FL 1+1 Others 1*
Gillingham *(Loaned on 5/11/2004) FL 3*
Norwich C *(Loaned on 2/8/2005) FL 12+1 FLC 2*
Hull C *(£1,000,000 on 18/7/2006) P/FL 102+23/9 FLC 3+3 FAC 6 Others 0+1*

MARQUIS John Edward
Born: Lewisham, 16 May 1992
Height: 6'1" **Weight:** 11.0
John graduated from the youth sides to play just once as a substitute for Millwall in September. Having been in prolific scoring form for the youth team that won its league and reached the fifth round of the FA Youth Cup, he had a successful loan spell at Staines Town towards the end of the season and scored on his debut there. He then added a hat-trick against Thurrock. John won the 'Manager's Young Player of the Year' award from Kenny Jackett.
Millwall *(Trainee) FL 0+1*

MARRIOTT Andrew (Andy)
Born: Sutton-in-Ashfield, 11 October 1970
Height: 6'1" **Weight:** 12.6
Club Honours: Div 4 '92; FMC '92; WC '95
International Honours: W: 5; E: U21-1; Yth
Veteran Andy managed to gain the first team berth for Exeter in the autumn and put in some 'Man of the Match' performances, particularly at Millwall where he made a number of superb saves to keep his team in the game until late on. His experience helped both him and his rival gloves man Paul Jones to have superb seasons.
Arsenal *(From trainee on 22/10/1988)*
Nottingham F *(£50,000 on 20/6/1989) P/FL 11 FLC 1 Others 1*
West Bromwich A *(Loaned on 6/9/1989) FL 3*
Blackburn Rov *(Loaned on 29/12/1989) FL 2*
Colchester U *(Loaned on 21/3/1990) FL 10*
Burnley *(Loaned on 29/8/1991) FL 15 Others 2*
Wrexham *(£200,000 on 8/10/1993) FL 213 FLC 10 FAC 22 Others 13*
Sunderland *(£200,000 + on 17/8/1998) P/FL 2 FLC 3*

Wigan Ath *(Loaned on 1/1/2001) Others 2*
Barnsley *(Free on 13/3/2001) FL 53+1 FLC 2 FAC 1*
Birmingham C *(Free on 13/3/2003) PL 1 (Freed during 2003 close season)*
Coventry C *(Free from Beira Mar, Portugal on 6/8/2004)*
Colchester U *(Free on 20/10/2004) Bury (Free on 5/11/2004) FL 19 FAC 2*
Torquay U *(Free on 2/3/2005) FL 57 FLC 1 FAC 5 Others 1*
Boston U *(Free on 27/7/2006) FL 46 FLC 1 FAC 1 Others 1*
Exeter C *(Free on 2/7/2007) FL 13 FAC 2 Others 1*

MARROW Alexander (Alex) James
Born: Tyldsley, 21 January 1990
Height: 6'1" **Weight:** 13.1
Alex, who joined Oldham on a season-long loan from Blackburn, is a very busy midfield player who can really put himself about. He scored a storming goal against Swindon at Boundary Park that really brought him to the attention of the football fraternity. He is in the Peter Reid mould of player, always wanting to be involved in the action. Alex can sometimes be over zealous, which brings him to the attention of referees.
Blackburn Rov *(Free from Ashton Ath on 21/5/2008)*
Oldham Ath *(Loaned on 6/8/2009) FL 26+6/1 FAC 1 Others 1*

MARSHALL Ben
Born: Salford, 29 March 1991
Height: 6'0" **Weight:** 11.7
A wide Stoke midfield player, Ben was a shining light during the early part of the season on loan at Northampton as the club struggled. His skilful wing play, dribbling ability and eye for the odd goal made him a favourite but he found no place with the new management team and back at the Britannia Stadium he was sent on a month's loan to Cheltenham in the winter of 2009. With the ability to open up defences with his direct running and accurate crossing, Ben produced a 'Man of the Match' display and scored two goals in the team's 5-1 win over Barnet in November. He continued to perform well during his six matches at Town, but returned to parent club just before Christmas. His next stop on loan was at Carlisle in February and he remained at Brunton Park until the end of the season. Having netted at Huddersfield in his second game, throughout his spell with the Blues he showed a willingness to accept responsibility and demonstrated a maturity beyond his

years. Ben returned to the Potteries when the season ended, but he undoubtedly benefited from his time at all three clubs.
Stoke C *(From trainee at Crewe Alex on 9/7/2009)*
Northampton T *(Loaned on 6/8/2009) FL 11+4/2 FLC 1 Others 2*
Cheltenham T *(Loaned on 13/11/2009) FL 6/2*
Carlisle U *(Loaned on 1/2/2010) FL 11+9/3*

MARSHALL David James
Born: Glasgow, 5 March 1985
Height: 6'3" **Weight:** 13.0
Club Honours: SPD '04; SC '04
International Honours: S: 5; B-1; U21-10; Yth
David made more than 100 appearances for Norwich over two seasons before joining Cardiff - and played 50 times for the Bluebirds last season. Still only 25, he is a Scottish international goalkeeper who continues to improve. He has razor-sharp reflexes and an ability to make difficult saves look easy, but needs to be a bigger presence in his own area. The Scot was Cardiff's play-off semi-final hero during a penalty shoot-out against Leicester at home, saving spot kicks from Yann Kermorgant and Martyn Waghorn as the Bluebirds qualified for Wembley. David played three times for Scotland during the season - in World Cup defeats by Norway and Holland, as well as their friendly 3-0 defeat by Wales at Cardiff City Stadium.
Glasgow Celtic *(From juniors on 1/8/2002) SL 34+1 SLC 2 SC 3+1 Others 8+1*
Norwich C *(£750,000 on 17/1/2007) FL 94 FLC 4 FAC 7*
Cardiff C *(£500,000 on 12/5/2009) FL 43 FAC 4 Others 3*

MARSHALL Jordan
Born: Gateshead, 10 May 1993
Height: 5'11" **Weight:** 11.7
Jordan is another product of the youth team and made his debut as a substitute in the penultimate home game against Notts County to become the 54th player to represent Darlington in the season. It was a torrid baptism for the hard-running young forward as County cruised to a 5-0 win to take the League Two title.
Darlington *(Trainee) FLC 0+3*

MARSHALL Marcus Joseph
Born: Hammersmith, 7 October 1989
Height: 6'2" **Weight:** 12.10
Marcus joined Rotherham on loan from Blackburn in January, ostensibly to bring extra pace and mobility to the front

line. Played on the right wing and was initially used as an impact player off the bench, having a degree of success. He marked his full debut in March by setting up the winning goal at Dagenham through pace out wide and showed a willingness to defend in the air at set pieces, not the forte of too many wingers. Had a brief spell down the middle late in the season, showed promising flashes but was less successful there. Was out of contract at the end of June.
Blackburn Rov (From South Nottingham College on 27/1/2007) FLC 0+1
Rotherham U (Loaned on 22/1/2010) FL 13+9 Others 0+1

MARSHALL Mark Anthony
Born: Manchester, Jamaica, 5 May 1987
Height: 5'7" **Weight:** 10.7
Despite appearing as a substitute in the season opener, Mark spent much of the time on the fringes of first team action at Swindon and was sent on loan to Hereford to gain much needed match practice. At Edgar Street, the lively winger made a highly favourable impression as he helped to spark a mini-revival at the club, his dangerous running and crossing creating plenty of chances for his fellow forwards. He also showed himself to be a nerveless performer from the penalty spot as Hereford progressed in the Johnstone's Paint Trophy. Back at Swindon he gave some sterling performances, none more so than at Brighton where he gave an impressive display of strong-running wing play when appearing from the bench to help his side to victory. His only start came in the win at Southampton where he again put in an excellent performance. Was released at the end of the season.
Swindon T (Free from Eastleigh, ex Carshalton Ath, Grays Ath, on 15/8/2008) FL 1+18 FLC 0+2 FAC 0+1 Others 1+1
Hereford U (Loaned on 17/9/2009) FL 8 Others 2

MARTIN Aaron
Born: Newport, Isle of Wight, 29 September 1989
Height: 6'3" **Weight:** 12.0
International Honours: E: Sch
Capped for England schoolboys, Southampton's Aaron learned his game with nearby Eastleigh's youth development system. Aged 20, he signed an 18-month contract in November and, having impressed in the reserves, was sent on loan to Blue Square Premier club Salisbury City. A

tall, strong centre-back with good anticipation, he played in the final two games of the season, looking anything but a non-League player.
Southampton (Signed from Eastleigh on 4/11/2009) FL 2

MARTIN Alan
Born: Glasgow, 1 January 1989
Height: 6'2" **Weight:** 11.11
International Honours: S: U21-7; Yth
A young 'keeper who joined Accrington on loan from Leeds at the start of the season and made ten appearances between the posts before returning to his parent club in October. The Scottish youth and under-21 goalie had been at Barrow on loan during 2008-09 and was ready for a taste of League Two football. Back at Elland Road, he was a regular on the bench in the absence of Shane Higgs and hopes for a first team opportunity before too long.
Motherwell (From juniors on 23/12/2006)
Leeds U (Free on 31/8/2007)
Accrington Stanley (Loaned on 31/7/2009) FL 7 FLC 2 Others 1

MARTIN Carl Clarke
Born: Camden, 24 October 1986
Height: 5'8" **Weight:** 10.4
After several periods on trial at Crewe, Carl was eventually offered a contract in October. A defender with a good turn of pace, he had only limited opportunities to play in the senior side in his first season at the club. It is hoped he will develop and become a regular in the season ahead.
Crewe Alex (Free from Wealdstone on 6/10/2009) FL 1+5/1

MARTIN Christopher (Chris) Hugh
Born: Beccles, 4 November 1988
Height: 5'10" **Weight:** 11.7
Club Honours: AMC '09; Div 1 '10
International Honours: E: Yth
Having spent the whole of the previous season on loan at Luton, this former Norwich scholar returned to Carrow Road with a point to prove and did exactly that. After a slow start to the campaign Chris emerged as a vital cog in City's promotion seeking outfit and contributed over 20 goals in the process. He has great technique and touch, allowing him to create space in tight situations, often affording him the inch of space he needs to get his shots away. Good with his back to goal, he also established himself as Norwich's dead-ball expert, scoring from a number of excellently placed free kicks. His emerging talent was recognised with a new contract during the season.

Norwich C (From trainee on 17/4/2007) FL 52+15/21 FLC 1+2 FAC 3+2/5 Others 3/2
Luton T (Loaned on 7/8/2008) FL 39+1/11 FLC 2 FAC 3 Others 5+1/2

MARTIN Christopher (Chris) Joseph
Born: Mansfield, 21 July 1990
Height: 6'0" **Weight:** 13.5
Chris had an excellent season as Port Vale's 'keeper, conceding just 43 goals in his 39 League appearances. An excellent handler, he commanded his area well and marshalled a defence that had the best record for nine years. His personal highlight came when he saved a penalty in a 1-1 draw at Northampton. He was left out for a seven-game spell in February after his standards dipped slightly in his first full season as the club's number-one goalkeeper but returned all the stronger. His only blemish came when he misjudged a long throw in at Lincoln to knock the ball into his own net. Chris was Vale's 'Young Player of the Year'.
Port Vale (From trainee on 18/4/2008) FL 51+1 FLC 3 FAC 3 Others 3

MARTIN David Edward
Born: Romford, 22 January 1986
Height: 6'1" **Weight:** 13.7
Club Honours: Div 1 '09
International Honours: E: Yth
The son of former West Ham player Alvin, David was brought to Tranmere from Liverpool on a month's loan in October. A highly-rated goalkeeper, he made his debut in the home game against Stockport and showed immediately that he has excellent all-round ability. He is particularly gifted at kicking and also 'talks' well. Then, following an injury to first choice goalkeeper Shane Higgs, Leeds picked up David on loan in December. He sat on the bench a dozen times for the Whites, keeping a clean sheet in his only appearance, a victory against another of his former loan clubs, Accrington, in the Johnstone's Paint Trophy. Then he was off to Derby and was one of the few loans that justified the term emergency. Derby were suddenly short of goalkeepers when Stephen Bywater suffered a back injury at Reading and his deputy, Saul Deeney, had been sent off in the same game. David arrived and gave two competent displays before Bywater regained fitness. At Derby he showed that he had good hands and was willing to take charge of crosses into the box. Was out of contract in the summer.
Wimbledon/MK Dons (From trainee on 19/1/2004) FL 17 FLC 1 FAC 3 Others 4

Liverpool *(Signed on 13/1/2006)*
Accrington Stanley *(Loaned on 23/2/2007) FL 10*
Leicester C *(Loaned on 7/8/2008) FL 25 FLC 2 FAC 3*
Tranmere Rov *(Loaned on 16/10/2009) FL 3*
Leeds U *(Loaned on 26/11/2009) Others 1*
Derby Co *(Loaned on 12/3/2010) FL 2*

MARTIN David (Dave) John

Born: Erith, 3 June 1985
Height: 5'9" **Weight:** 10.10
A wide left Millwall player who has pace and trickery to outfox the most experienced of defenders, he went out on loan to Derby in February with the prospect of a permanent deal, having played against them in two FA Cup ties. On loan for the remainder of the season with a fee agreed for a permanent move, the left-winger was used mainly as a substitute and also helped the reserves to win their league. He started the final game against Cardiff and scored his first goal for Derby with a low cross shot.
Crystal Palace *(£25,000 from Dartford, ex Slade Green, on 23/1/2007) FL 2+12 FLC 1*
Millwall *(£50,000 + on 31/1/2008) FL 60+15/9 FLC 2 FAC 7+1 Others 4+1*
Derby Co *(Loaned on 9/2/2010) FL 2+9/1*

MARTIN Joseph (Joe) John

Born: Dagenham, 29 November 1988
Height: 6'0" **Weight:** 13.0
Joe, son of former England man Alvin Martin, has had a tricky time of it at Blackpool since his move from Tottenham in 2008. He joined the club as a left-sided midfielder but has reverted to left-back, deputising when Stephen Crainey is unavailable. Unfortunately he played in only nine games, three of which were in the Cups. The season before could have been his big one, but he was mismanaged by both Simon Grayson and Tony Parkes. He is only 21 and possesses good positioning, distribution and pace from the full-back position. Joe was on the end of a rough penalty decision away at West Bromwich, when he fouled Giles Barnes outside the area, ultimately costing Blackpool an away point. Was out of contract in the summer.
Tottenham H *(From trainee on 5/12/2005)*
Blackpool *(Signed on 27/3/2008) FL 15+7 FLC 3 FAC 0+1*

MARTIN Lee Robert

Born: Taunton, 9 February 1987
Height: 5'10" **Weight:** 10.3

International Honours: E: Yth
An expensive summer signing of whom much was expected, Lee failed to find any consistency in his performances and did not really fit into the Ipswich team either on the left of midfield or as an out-and-out attacker. After starting against Sheffield Wednesday in November he had only four cameo roles as a substitute in the remainder of the season.
Manchester U *(From trainee on 15/2/2005) PL 1 FLC 2*
Glasgow Rgrs *(Loaned on 11/8/2006) SL 4+3 SLC 0+2 Others 1*
Stoke C *(Loaned on 26/1/2007) FL 4+9/1 FAC 1*
Plymouth Arg *(Loaned on 5/10/2007) FL 10+2/2*
Sheffield U *(Loaned on 11/1/2008) FL 5+1 FAC 2+1*
Nottingham F *(Loaned on 13/8/2008) FL 9+4/1 FLC 1*
Ipswich T *(Signed on 6/7/2009) FL 9+7/1 FLC 1 FAC 0+1*

MARTIN Richard William

Born: Chelmsford, 1 September 1987
Height: 6'2" **Weight:** 12.13
Joined Yeovil as deputy to first choice goalkeeper Alex McCarthy and was used sparingly, appearing just five times in total. Started against Oxford and Bournemouth in the Cups, Southampton and Swindon in the League and also came on when McCarthy was dismissed against Stockport. Was out of contract in the summer.
Brighton & Hove A *(From juniors on 3/9/2004)*
Manchester C *(Free on 10/9/2007)*
Yeovil T *(Free on 21/7/2009) FL 2+1 FAC 1 Others 1*

MARTIN Russell Kenneth Alexander

Born: Brighton, 4 January 1986
Height: 6'0" **Weight:** 11.8
Club Honours: Div 1 '10
As the Peterborough club captain, Russell failed to make the starting line up in the first four games, then after a run of ten starts was again placed on the bench. A dependable right-back who reads the game well, Russell can also play in midfield and is a defender who would much sooner play his way out of trouble than resort to the big boot. It came as something of a surprise when he was allowed to move to Norwich on loan to team up again with his former boss at Wycombe, Paul Lambert. The move became permanent in January and his desire to push forward at every opportunity gave the Canaries an additional weapon. Equally

important was the fact that he also looked rock solid in defence when displaying positional awareness, good concentration levels and excellent passing skills out of defence.
Wycombe W *(Free from Lewes on 4/8/2004) FL 88+28/5 FLC 7+1 FAC 5 Others 12+1*
Peterborough U *(Signed on 4/7/2008) FL 54+2/1 FLC 3+2 FAC 4 Others 1*
Norwich C *(Signed on 26/11/2009) FL 26 Others 1*

MARTIS Shelton

Born: Willemstad, Curacao, Netherlands Antilles, 29 November 1982
Height: 6'1" **Weight:** 12.11
International Honours: Netherlands Antilles: 3
The tall Netherlands Antilles central defender scrambled in his first ever West Bromwich goal in the 1-1 home draw with Newcastle on the opening day of the season and followed up with his second by equalising in the Baggies' 3-1 home win over Plymouth a month later. Despite that, he was unable to hold down a regular position in the team and signed for Doncaster in the January transfer window on a three-and-a-half-year contract. Prior to that, Doncaster had been through a rough time for centre-halves through injury. After relying on loan players in the first half of the season they signed Shelton, who'd had a loan spell at the Rovers in the previous season and he did well. He also scored the winner in the penultimate game of the season at home to local rivals Scunthorpe with a fine looping header in the 89th minute in a seven-goal thriller.
Darlington *(Free from FC Eindhoven, Holland, ex Feyenoord, Excelsior, on 5/8/2005) FL 41+1/2 FLC 1 FAC 1 Others 1*
Hibernian *(Free on 10/8/2006) SL 27 SLC 4+1 SC 2*
West Bromwich A *(£50,000 on 13/7/2007) P/FL 18+4/2 FLC 2 FAC 1*
Scunthorpe U *(Loaned on 4/1/2008) FL 3 FAC 1*
Doncaster Rov *(Loaned on 1/11/2008) FL 5/1*
Doncaster Rov *(Signed on 1/2/2010) FL 13+1/1*

MASCHERANO Javier Alejandro

Born: Santa Fe, Argentina, 8 June 1984
Height: 5'10" **Weight:** 12.1
International Honours: Argentina: 57; U23-18; Yth
In common with many of his team-mates the Liverpool and Argentine holding midfielder failed to achieve the

high performance levels expected of a world class player on a consistent basis. When he started the season below par, it was allleged that he was unsettled by the club's rejection of a summer move to Barcelona. It may have been more from the struggle of his national team, which he captains, to qualify for the World Cup finals. This was resolved only in the last minute of the final qualifying game. Javier is Liverpool's ball winner but he collected nine cautions and two red cards, the worst record in the Premier League, and was suspended for four games in mid-season. An infrequent scorer, due to his deep position, his 30-yard shot at Everton took a deflection off Joseph Yobo and was credited as an own goal. He scored one undisputed goal in the away leg of the Europa Cup tie to Unirea Urziceni with another bullet shot from outside the area. For the last three games, manager Benitez deployed him as a makeshift right-back, having lost so many players to injury and being

unwilling to deploy his reserves. For all his faults, Javier is a key player and, if he leaves, would be very difficult to replace.
West Ham U (Loaned from Corinthians, Brazil, ex River Plate, on 31/8/2006) PL 3+2 Others 2
Liverpool (£18,600,000 from Corinthians, Brazil on 31/1/2007) PL 90+3/1 FLC 1+1 FAC 3+2 Others 37+1/1

MASON Joseph (Joe)
Born: Plymouth, 13 May 1991
Height: 5'9" **Weight:** 11.11
International Honours: RoI: Yth
Joe, a striker with excellent movement, began his career as a youth player with home-town club Plymouth at the age of ten. A regular scorer for the youth team, he made the step up to the reserves with similar ease. He signed his first professional contract in May and immediately set about breaking into the first team. Joe began the season training with the squad and made his

competitive debut against Sheffield United in December. He signed an extension to his contract in January, scored his first professional goal against Sheffield United and went on to add another two. He represented Republic of Ireland under-19's, scoring twice in six appearances.
Plymouth Arg (From trainee on 5/8/2009) FL 5+14/3

MASON Ryan Glen
Born: Enfield, 13 June 1991
Height: 5'9" **Weight:** 10.0
International Honours: E: Yth
Ryan arrived at Yeovil on loan with a reputation of being an exciting prospect at Tottenham and he certainly did not disappoint. Playing either in the hole or in midfield, the lightly-built Ryan was a big creative influence going forward and scored twice in his first three games, including a beauty against Exeter in August. He eventually left in March after scoring six times in 29 games but making four others in his time at Yeovil.
Tottenham H (From trainee on 10/7/2008) Others 0+1
Yeovil T (Loaned on 16/7/2009) FL 26+2/6 FAC 1

MASSEY Gavin Alexander
Born: Watford, 14 October 1992
Height: 5'11" **Weight:** 11.6
Gavin, a skilful striker in his first year as a Watford Academy scholar, made a last-gasp debut as an 85th-minute substitute in the final match of the season at Coventry. Is seen as a youngster who could go a long way in the game.
Watford (Trainee) FL 0+1

MASTERS Clark John
Born: Hastings, 31 May 1987
Height: 6'3" **Weight:** 13.12
Clark is a giant goalkeeper who is very vocal and has a big kick. Having been released by Southend, he joined Aldershot following the departure of long-serving Nikki Bull. He made his debut in the Carling Cup first round at Bristol Rovers but the form of Mikhael Jaimez-Ruiz limited Clark to one more appearance as a substitute. Although sent off from the bench in the home victory over Bournemouth in January for violent conduct, this was rescinded on appeal. Clark joined Blue Square Premier Hayes and Yeading on a free transfer in January.
Brentford (From trainee on 27/6/2006) FL 11+1 FAC 2 Others 2
Southend U (Signed on 11/1/2008)
Aldershot T (Free on 23/7/2009) FL 0+1 FLC 1

Javier Mascherano

MATEJOVSKY Marek
Born: Brandys nad Labem, Czech Republic, 20 December 1981
Height: 5'10" **Weight:** 11.3
International Honours: Czech Republic: 15
It was a disappointing season for Czech international Marek, who could never be sure of a starting place at Reading, except for a run of 11 games leading to the Boxing Day fixture at Plymouth. Reading were heavily beaten 4-1 and for the next game Marek was replaced in midfield by Jay Tabb. Marek made only one more appearance, as a late substitute in the 5-0 home win over Sheffield Wednesday. While his appearances were also curtailed by injury, he failed to score and showed only glimpses of the incisive passing that characterised his earlier years with Reading.
Reading (£1,400,000 from Mlada Boleslav, Czech Republic, ex Mlada Boleslav, Jablonec, on 11/1/2008) P/FL 34+17/2 FLC 2 FAC 1 Others 2

MATIC Nemanja
Born: Sabac, Serbia, 1 August 1988
Height: 6'4" **Weight:** 12.13
Club Honours: FAC '10
International Honours: Serbia: 2; U21-10
An elegant left-sided midfielder, Nemanja impressed for Serbia at the European under-21 Championships. A broken foot delayed any impact at Chelsea following his transfer from Kosice in Slovakia. Nemanja took the brave gamble as a 17-year-old to leave his native Serbia and try his luck in Slovakia. His outstanding form caught the eye of Chelsea, who snapped him up on a three-year contract after an earlier trial with Middlesbrough. It took him three months to overcome his foot injury and he made his debut as a substitute, alongside Gael Kakuta, against Wolves in November. A further substitute appearance against Watford in the FA Cup followed and his third, and final, outing came on that emotional final day of the League season when the Blues clinched the title with the rout of Wigan. Nemanja sees himself filling the holding midfield position where his heading ability and powerful shooting are valuable attributes. He is now a full Serbian international.
Chelsea (£1,500,000 from MFK Kosice, Slovakia, ex Kolubara Lazarevac, on 18/8/2009) PL 0+2 FAC 0+1

MATTHEWS Adam James
Born: Gorseinon, 13 January 1992
Height: 5'10" **Weight:** 11.3

International Honours: W: U21-1; Yth
Adam emerged from Cardiff's trainee ranks last season. His contract includes a clause that entitled him to a new, improved deal after 25 appearances. Talks began soon after he achieved that mark, but nothing had been finalised by the end of the season. He has a current deal that ends in the summer of 2011. Manchester United and Arsenal both showed interest in Adam, who plays at right-back or on the right of midfield. United were said to be ready for a £4-million deal, but he faded out of the first team picture and was not involved at all in the 18 for the Championship play-off final against Blackpool. He remains a player with a big future - and much is expected during 2010-11.
Cardiff C (From trainee on 14/1/2009) FL 24+8/1 FLC 1 FAC 2

MATTIS Dwayne Antony
Born: Huddersfield, 31 July 1981
Height: 6'1" **Weight:** 10.10
International Honours: RoI: U21-2; Yth
Operating in central midfield, the greatest tribute to Dwayne is how much he is missed by Walsall when he is not on the pitch. A strong tackler, he is responsible for carrying out a lot of the harrying of opponents. One of his two goals, a left-foot drive into the corner of the net, was the winner against his home-town club, Huddersfield. His other goal came in the 2-1 victory over Leeds. Troubled by an Achilles injury late in the season he was released at the end of his contract and joined Chesterfield.
Huddersfield T (From trainee on 8/7/1999) FL 50+19/2 FLC 1+2 FAC 3+1 Others 4/1
Bury (Free on 30/7/2004) FL 93+4/11 FLC 4/1 FAC 8/5
Barnsley (£50,000 + on 11/1/2007) FL 3+1 FLC 1
Walsall (Loaned on 28/9/2007) FL 4
Walsall (Free on 4/8/2008) FL 67+4/6 FLC 1 FAC 3 Others 3

MATTOCK Joseph (Joe) William
Born: Leicester, 15 May 1990
Height: 5'11" **Weight:** 12.5
Club Honours: Div 1 '09
International Honours: E: U21-5; Yth
Attacking left-back Joe was ecstatic when told by his agent that West Bromwich were interested in him. He handed in a transfer request to chairman Milan Mandaric, which infuriated him then manager Nigel Pearson. However, he signed a three-year contract at the Hawthorns, citing Richard Stearman as his motivation for leaving the Walkers Stadium, and was

booed when he returned there with Albion in November. Good on the ball and strong going forward, he made his Baggies' debut in a 2–0 Carling Cup win at Bury and despite losing his place a couple of times, mainly to Marek Cech, played his part in helping Roberto di Matteo's team regain their Premiership status at the first attempt. His first Albion goal – a late one - earned the team a 2-2 draw at Reading in the fourth round of the FA Cup.
Leicester C (From trainee on 25/4/2007) FL 54+12/1 FLC 3 FAC 4
West Bromwich A (Signed on 10/8/2009) FL 26+3 FLC 1+1 FAC 2+1/1

Joe Mattock

MAWENE Youl
Born: Caen, France, 16 July 1979
Height: 6'2" **Weight:** 12.6
A cult figure at Preston, Youl continued to be a rock at the heart of the defence when available. He was out for two months either side of Christmas following an accidental collision with team-mate Andy Lonergan and he had only just come back from another short injury break when his season ended early as he returned to France on compassionate leave. A superb reader of a tackle, Youl's lack of pace is more than made up for by his positional sense and his ability to shepherd forwards to where he wants them. On the verge of 200 appearances for North End, all at Deepdale we hope he will add many more in the future.
Derby Co (£500,000 from RC Lens, France, ex Caen, on 4/8/2000) P/FL 54+1/1 FLC 2 FAC 4
Preston NE (Free on 3/8/2004) FL 164+10/8 FLC 6 FAC 10 Others 7

MAY Benjamin (Ben) Steven
Born: Gravesend, 10 March 1984
Height: 6'1" **Weight:** 12.6
It was very much a season to forget for Scunthorpe's giant target man. After impressing with a hatful of goals pre-season, Ben was hoping to push strongly for a starting place but it never came and he spent the early part of the campaign sidelined with ankle injuries and the second half out of favour. His only first team appearance came in the last game of 2009, when he was introduced as an 87th-minute substitute in the home defeat by West Bromwich. He was released at the end of the season.
Millwall (From juniors on 10/5/2001) FL 43+35/4 FLC 4+1/1 FAC 7+2/2 Others 2+1/2
Colchester U (Loaned on 27/3/2003) FL 4+2
Brentford (Loaned on 25/8/2003) FL 38+3/7 FAC 1 Others 1
Colchester U (Loaned on 6/8/2004) FL 5+9/1 FLC 0+2/1
Brentford (Loaned on 3/12/2004) FL 7+3/1 FAC 4+2
Scunthorpe U (Loaned on 28/9/2007) FL 0+5
Scunthorpe U (£100,000 on 18/1/2008) FL 11+29/3 FLC 0+1 FAC 0+1/1 Others 2+2/1

MAYBURY Alan Paul
Born: Dublin, 8 August 1978
Height: 5'11" **Weight:** 11.12
Club Honours: FAYC '97
International Honours: RoI: 10; B-1; U21-8; Yth
Alan had a disappointing second season at Colchester, making only three appearances altogether. A regular at right-back in the latter part of the previous season, the former Republic of Ireland international suddenly found himself behind new signing Lee Beevers at the start of the campaign when Paul Lambert was in charge and then trailing John White once Aidy Boothroyd took over.
Leeds U (Free from St Kevin's BC on 17/8/1995) PL 10+4 FLC 1 FAC 2 Others 1
Reading (Loaned on 25/3/1999) FL 8
Crewe Alex (Loaned on 8/10/2000) FL 6
Heart of Midlothian (£100,000 on 12/10/2001) SL 110+2/4 SLC 7 SC 5 Others 10
Leicester C (£100,000 on 6/1/2005) FL 83+2/3 FLC 6+2 FAC 8+1
Aberdeen (Loaned on 31/1/2008) SL 13 SC 3+1 Others 2
Colchester U (Free on 12/12/2008) FL 26+1 FLC 1 Others 1

MAYNARD Nicholas (Nicky) David
Born: Winsford, 11 December 1986

Height: 5'11" **Weight:** 11.0
Nicky's goal for Bristol City at Queens Park Rangers on Boxing Day deservedly received the plaudit as the best Football League goal of 2009. Unfortunately, a storming start to the season, in which he had ten goals by the end of October, tailed off until two goals in a 3-2 defeat at Plymouth in March sparked off a renaissance that saw him net with another outstanding strike in the televised 2-2 home draw with Newcastle four days later. Despite being described by many as a scorer of outstanding goals, rather than as a regular scorer, he collected 20 goals, as the Championship's joint top marksman, by the end of the campaign. With a goal in the Carling Cup, Nicky can be well satisfied in netting 21 times. Surprisingly, he missed out on the Bristol City supporters' 'Player of the Year' award but had the consolation of picking up their 'Young Player' prize for the second successive time.
Crewe Alex (From trainee on 9/6/2005) FL 52+7/31 FLC 3/2 FAC 0+1 Others 2+2/1
Bristol C (£2,250,000 on 1/8/2008) FL 74+11/31 FLC 3/1 FAC 3

Nicky Maynard

MAYOR Daniel (Danny) John
Born: Leyland, 18 October 1990
Height: 6'0" **Weight:** 11.12
A highly regarded right-winger who can also perform on the opposite flank, Danny was given his first team debut for Preston as a substitute at Bristol City and followed this with a similar appearance in the FA Cup tie against Chelsea, not being overawed by the occasion. Fast, tricky and direct, he started the final four games of the

season and showed real potential. This coming season will be an important one in his long-term development.
Preston NE (From trainee on 16/12/2008) FL 4+3 FAC 0+1
Tranmere Rov (Loaned on 5/3/2009) FL 3

Tyrons Mears

MEARS Tyrone
Born: Stockport, 18 February 1983
Height: 5'11" **Weight:** 11.10
International Honours: Jamaica: 1
Owen Coyle's first signing after Burnley's promotion to the Premier League, Tyrone signed a three-year contract and in his first year at Turf Moor played in every League game and was one of the few truly consistent performers in the side. While the rest of the back four often struggled, he remained composed at right-back, rarely conceding possession and often being the provider further forward, contributing more than his fair share of assists. Hardly ever looking out of place among the elite, he was even suggested as possible cover for England at right-back, despite having - by a misunderstanding as it turned out - previously earned one cap for Jamaica; however, Burnley's lowly League position probably did him no favours in that respect. Tyrone won several of the club's 'Player of the Year' awards at the end of the season.
Manchester C (From juniors on 5/7/2000) FL 0+1
Preston NE (£175,000 on 10/7/2002) FL 50+20/4 FLC 2+2 FAC 5+2 Others 2
West Ham U (£1,000,000 + on 5/7/2006) PL 3+2 Others 1
Derby Co (£1,000,000 on 31/1/2007) P/FL 33+8/2 FLC 1+1 FAC 2 Others 3
Burnley (Signed on 30/6/2009) PL 38 FAC 1

MEDLEY Luke Anthony Cleve
Born: Greenwich, 21 June 1989
Height: 6'1" **Weight:** 13.5
Forward Luke spent the majority of the campaign on loan at Blue Square South side Woking. He returned to Barnet late in the season and made a single appearance from the substitutes' bench in Ian Hendon's final game in charge at Accrington. His contract expired after the end of the season.
Bradford C *(From trainee at Tottenham H on 2/7/2007)* FL 1+8/2
Barnet *(Free on 7/8/2008)* FL 5+14/1 FLC 1 FAC 1 Others 0+1

MEITE Abdoulaye (Abdou)
Born: Paris, France, 6 October 1980
Height: 6'0" **Weight:** 12.12
International Honours: Ivory Coast: 48
Abdou was plagued by irritating hamstring, back and calf injuries all season and played in only a third of West Bromwich's games, although he was absent for a few weeks while on international duty in the African Cup of Nations. When passed fit, the rugged, no-nonsense defender had to fight for his place at the heart of Albion's back four and looked solid enough most of the time but was occasionally caught out by the quicker and more direct strikers who opposed him. Last year, he was part of the Ivory Coast team at a World Cup qualifier·with Malawi when a stampede at the Houphouet-Boignynarena arena saw a wall collapse, tragically killing at least 22 people and injuring more than 130.
Bolton W *(£1,000,000 from Olympique Marseille, France, ex Red Star 93, on 10/8/2006)* PL 56 FLC 4 FAC 3+1/1 Others 5+1/1
West Bromwich A *(£2,000,000 on 10/8/2008)* P/FL 34+4 FLC 2+1 FAC 2

MELCHIOT Mario
Born: Amsterdam, Holland, 4 November 1976
Height: 6'2" **Weight:** 11.11
Club Honours: FAC '00; CS '00
International Honours: Holland: 22; U12-13; Yth
Captain of Wigan, Mario is an experienced right-back capable of getting forward and delivering a fine cross. His attacking forays are a feature and he was given much freedom down the right and relished it. Tall, strong, fast and direct, he is good in the air and on the ground. His link with Charles N'Zogbia created countless chances down the right but he does not neglect his defensive duties. Mario's strong tackling and sense of anticipation make him a fans' favourite and he is a permanent fixture in the side when fit.

His appearance against one of his former clubs, Birmingham in December, was his 250th Premier League start. His final home game against Hull was his 100th for Wigan. Out of contract at the end of the season, he was released.
Chelsea *(Free from Ajax, Holland on 5/7/1999)* PL 117+13/4 FLC 9 FAC 14+2 Others 9+1/1
Birmingham C *(Free on 19/7/2004)* PL 55+2/2 FLC 3 FAC 7 *(Freed during 2006 close season)*
Wigan Ath *(Free from Stade Rennais, France on 5/7/2007)* PL 96+1 FLC 2 FAC 2

MELLIGAN John (JJ) James
Born: Dublin, 11 February 1982
Height: 5'9" **Weight:** 11.4
Club Honours: Div 3 '04
International Honours: RoI: U21-1; Yth
JJ started the season as first choice on the right of Leyton Orient's midfield but lost his place in the team after being sent off at Norwich. Unable to regain a regular shirt, his contract was terminated in February and he returned to Ireland to join Dundalk.
Wolverhampton W *(From trainee on 11/7/2000)* FL 0+2
Bournemouth *(Loaned on 30/11/2001)* FL 7+1 FAC 1
Kidderminster Hrs *(Loaned on 13/9/2002)* FL 10/5 Others 2/2
Kidderminster Hrs *(Loaned on 3/12/2002)* FL 18+1/5 Others 1
Kidderminster Hrs *(Loaned on 3/10/2003)* FL 5/1 Others 1
Doncaster Rov *(Loaned on 17/11/2003)* FL 21/2
Cheltenham T *(£25,000 on 13/7/2004)* FL 101+13/15 FLC 4/1 FAC 9/1 Others 8/1
Leyton Orient *(Free on 27/7/2007)* FL 64+19/6 FLC 5/1 FAC 5+1/1 Others 3/1

MELLIS Jacob Alexander
Born: Nottingham, 8 January 1991
Height: 5'11" **Weight:** 10.12
Club Honours: AMC '10
International Honours: E: Yth
An elegant, assured, versatile young midfielder, Jacob came to Southampton on loan from Chelsea in August. He had a couple of runs in the side but with the Dean Hammond and Morgan Schneiderlin's central midfield partnership improving with every game, he found the opportunities limited and returned to Stamford Bridge in January.
Chelsea *(From trainee on 4/7/2008)*
Southampton *(Loaned on 14/8/2009)* FL 7+5 FLC 1 Others 1+1

MELLOR Neil Andrew
Born: Sheffield, 4 November 1982
Height: 6'0" **Weight:** 13.7
Club Honours: FLC '03

Despite being the most natural finisher at the club and ending as joint second top scorer, Neil was once more something of a disappointment at Preston last term and was released in the summer. Six goals in eight games early in the season suggested he might have found the consistency as a scorer he had previously lacked but sadly he only contributed a further five after the end of September, despite being a regular in the squad, either as a starter or increasingly as an impact substitute. Able to finish effectively with either foot, Neil shows excellent commitment to the cause and is always a willing runner but his goal tally does not reflect the number of opportunities he finds himself presented with.
Liverpool *(From trainee on 8/2/2002)* PL 7+5/2 FLC 6/3 FAC 1+1 Others 1+1/1
West Ham U *(Loaned on 7/8/2003)* FL 8+8/2 FLC 1+1 FAC 0+3
Wigan Ath *(Loaned on 19/1/2006)* PL 3/1 FLC 1 FAC 1
Preston NE *(Signed on 31/8/2006)* FL 63+50/30 FLC 3+3/3 FAC 2+6/1 Others 1+1

MENDEZ-LAING Nathaniel Otis
Born: Birmingham, 15 April 1992
Height: 5'10" **Weight:** 11.11
The pacy Wolverhampton winger made a surprise debut against Swindon in the Carling Cup. He looked as good as anyone in the first half, beating three players in one run. Not bad for someone a few months past his 17th birthday.
Wolverhampton W *(From trainee on 10/9/2009)* FLC 1

MENDY Arnaud
Born: Evreux, France, 10 February 1990
Height: 6'3" **Weight:** 13.8
Arnaud first attracted notice when he scored a spectacular equaliser in Derby's final pre-season friendly, against Stoke. The defender helped the reserves to win their title and made a fleeting substitute appearance at the end of a 3-0 victory over Sheffield Wednesday in October. On loan to Grimsby, he was one of three debutants in Mike Newell's final game as manager and had little chance to show his capabilities as a box-to-box midfielder in a 1-2 home defeat to Rochdale. Due to what was going on at Blundell Park, the Frenchman then had his loan spell cut short and a further loan to Rotherham in March fell through because it was not registered in time.
Derby Co *(Signed from Rouen, France on 5/9/2008)* FL 0+1
Grimsby T *(Loaned on 16/10/2009)* FL 1

MENDY Bernard

Born: Evreux, France, 20 August 1981
Height: 5'11" **Weight:** 12.2
International Honours: France: 3; U21; Yth
Hull's second season in the Premier League proved to be a stop-start affair for the popular former France international. Although a regular in the squad throughout the ill-fated campaign, Bernard failed to start in more than two consecutive League games until the final three games of the season after recovering from a hamstring problem. As in 2008-09, his duties on Hull's right flank were split between midfield and defence. At full-back, his speed off the mark continued to be a match for the very best while, in the more advanced role, his willingness to run at defenders was a valuable asset in the Tigers' attacking armoury. Unfortunately, the end of City's two-year top flight experience appears to have brought his stay in Hull to a premature conclusion.
Bolton W (Loaned from Paris St Germain, France, ex SM Caen, on 27/2/2002) PL 20+1 FLC 1 FAC 1
Hull C (Free from Paris St Germain, France on 18/7/2008) PL 30+19/2 FLC 2 FAC 3+2

MENSAH John

Born: Obuasi, Ghana, 29 November 1982
Height: 5'11" **Weight:** 12.11
International Honours: Ghana: 62
On a season-long loan from Lyon, the vice-captain of Ghana showed he is an awesome defender but was unfortunately plagued by injury. With John in the side, Sunderland invariably looked stronger but the African was unable to play regularly. His best run of the season saw him play six consecutive games but even then he was substituted in four of them. Other than that run, John never started more than two games in a row and completed the full 90 minutes just six times. He scored his only goal in a 4-3 defeat at Manchester City but often looked a threat in the box and came close to adding to his tally several times.
Sunderland (Loaned from Olympique Lyonnais, France, ex MCB Accra, Bologna, Bellinzona, Genoa, Chievo, Modena, Chievo, Cremonese, Stade Rennais, on 28/8/2009) PL 14+2/1 FLC 1

MERIDA Francisco (Fran)

Born: Barcelona, Spain, 4 March 1990
Height: 5'11" **Weight:** 13.0
International Honours: Spain: U21; Yth
Fran is a gifted player who has not been able to force his way into the Arsenal team and played out another season as only a bit-part player in the squad. While his first team appearances were limited he did create two memorable moments. The first was his sublime goal in the Carling Cup win over Liverpool and his other goal was even more important as he scored Arsenal's second in their 2-0 win at Bolton. Fran played four times in the Premier League, picking up a goal in the process, once in the Champions League, once in the FA Cup and twice in the Carling Cup, adding a further goal. He joined Atletico Madrid on a free transfer at the end of the season.
Arsenal (From trainee on 19/3/2007) PL 0+6/1 FLC 5+3/1 FAC 1 Others 1

MEYLER David

Born: Cork, 29 May 1989
Height: 6'3" **Weight:** 11.9
International Honours: RoI: U21-7
Midfielder David was making a big name for himself at Sunderland and had just received a new contract and a first senior call up by the Republic of Ireland to their May training camp when he sustained a cruciate ligament injury in the final home game. Now expected to be ruled out until 2011, the former Cork City player will miss the start through injury for the second season running. He was flown home from Sunderland's training camp in Portugal last summer with an ankle injury and unluckily sustained an injury to the other ankle on his return to training. His long-awaited debut eventually arrived in the final game of 2009, with his energetic and committed style immediately making him look at home at senior level.
Sunderland (Signed from Cork C on 25/7/2008) PL 9+1 FAC 2

MICHALIK Lubomir (Lubo)

Born: Cadca, Slovakia, 13 August 1983
Height: 6'4" **Weight:** 13.0
International Honours: Slovakia: 4
Despite getting only limited game time for Leeds, Lubo was still hoping to earn a place in Slovakia's World Cup squad. Confined to the bench for Leeds' opening games, he marked his first League start with a goal in the 2-0 win against Stockport. He had a run in the side in November while skipper Richard Naylor was injured but paid the price for a bad mistake at Carlisle in the Northern Area final of the Johnstone's Paint Trophy and did not start another game.
Bolton W (Signed from FC Senec, Slovakia, ex Cadca, on 31/1/2007) PL 8+3/1 FLC 1+1 FAC 1 Others 3
Leeds U (Loaned on 9/3/2007) FL 7/1

Leeds U (£500,000 on 31/1/2008) FL 39+10/1 FLC 5 FAC 6+1 Others 8

[MICHEL] MADERA Miguel Marcos

Born: Lena, Spain, 8 November 1985
Height: 6'0" **Weight:** 11.5
Signed by Birmingham from Sporting Gijon in January, Michel was for a long time pursued by Alex McLeish. A tall, technically accomplished midfielder, Michel showed a good range of short and long passing and rarely wasted possession. He had to make do with cameo spells coming off the substitutes' bench as the Blues were performing so well on his arrival. But on his two starts, he helped create goals at Sunderland and Portsmouth with his slide-rule through balls.
Birmingham C (£3,000,000 from Sporting Gijon, Spain on 11/1/2010) PL 3+6

[MIDO] AHMED HOSSAM Abdel Hamid

Born: Cairo, Egypt, 23 February 1983
Height: 6'0" **Weight:** 12.10
International Honours: Egypt: 51; Yth
The Egyptian striker joined West Ham on loan from Middlesbrough in February. An experienced player who has served many European clubs, the Hammers were hoping he would score the goals to ease their relegation fears. Mido came on as a substitute at Burnley, looked keen and proved a nuisance to the defenders but was unlucky with one shot that hit a post. He gave a battling display at Chelsea and in all of his games he never stopped trying but he ended the season without scoring.
Tottenham H (Loaned from AS Roma, Italy, ex Zamalek, KAA Gent, Ajax, Celta Vigo - loan, Olympique Marseille, on 26/1/2005) PL 4+5/2 FAC 0+2/1
Tottenham H (Loaned from AS Roma, Italy on 1/7/2005) PL 24+3/11
Tottenham H (£4,500,000 from AS Roma, Italy on 15/9/2006) PL 7+5/1 FLC 2+2/3 FAC 2+1/1 Others 2+2
Middlesbrough (£7,000,000 on 16/8/2007) PL 13+12/6 FLC 1+1/1 FAC 2+3
Wigan Ath (Loaned on 23/1/2009) PL 10+2/2
West Ham U (Loaned on 1/2/2010) 5+4

MIKEL John Obi

Born: Jos, Nigeria, 22 April 1987
Height: 5'11" **Weight:** 12.8
Club Honours: FLC '07; FAC '07, '09; CS '09; PL '10
International Honours: Nigeria: 34
Although Chelsea took the headlines

with a record-breaking 103 goals during the Premier League season, they still needed the assurance of a reliable holding midfield player to screen the back four and John Obi filled the role to perfection. He is an imposing figure with his solid physique and calm, unflustered style, being the fulcrum for attacks launched from deep that allow the more attacking midfielders to play closer to the front players. For the second successive season Michael Essien was earmarked for the anchor role but injury again wrecked his season and John Obi stepped in to assume the role once so brilliantly undertaken by Claude Makelele. Just like 'Maka', he is not a threat to the opposition goal having yet to score in his 110 Premier League matches. He went to Angola for the African Cup of Nations, helped Nigeria to third place and returned in February to assist Chelsea's pursuit of their first 'Double' but suffered a blow four matches from the end when knee and ankle injuries curtailed his season. The injuries also spoiled his hopes in the

World Cup finals. John Obi signed a new five-year deal with Chelsea in August.
Chelsea *(£12,000,000 + from Lyn Oslo, Norway, via Manchester U, on 18/7/2006) PL 85+25 FLC 8+2 FAC 15+1/2 Others 22+7*

MILDENHALL Stephen (Steve) James
Born: Swindon, 13 May 1978
Height: 6'4" **Weight:** 14.0
Steve was again Southend's first choice goalkeeper, his second campaign at Roots Hall being marked by consistent application and performances. Arguably, his best display was a clean sheet at home to Leeds. Steve deputised as captain in place of Adam Barrett in the Carling Cup tie at Cheltenham and in the FA Cup tie against Gillingham, although a 3-0 reverse, he made his first penalty save for Southend. He missed the Christmas fixtures with a back and pelvic injury but returned with impressive form in a struggling and inexperienced side. Steve was third in the supporters' 'Player of

the Year' award.
Swindon T *(From trainee on 19/7/1996) FL 29+4 FLC 2 FAC 2 Others 1*
Notts Co *(£150,000 on 16/7/2001) FL 75+1 FLC 5/1 FAC 6 Others 3*
Oldham Ath *(Free on 1/12/2004) FL 6*
Grimsby T *(Free on 6/7/2005) FL 46 FLC 3 FAC 1 Others 4*
Yeovil T *(Free on 7/7/2006) FL 75 FLC 2 FAC 2 Others 6*
Southend U *(Free on 4/8/2008) FL 78 FLC 3 FAC 6 Others 2*

MILES John Francis
Born: Bootle, 28 September 1981
Height: 5'10" **Weight:** 12.9
Club Honours: Div 2 '08
This was John's third season with Accrington. A tricky, attacking right-sided midfielder and master of corner kicks, he was a key member of the team for most of the campaign. It has been said previously that when he plays well the whole team goes to another level. Was sent off at home to Barnet in the FA Cup second round.
Liverpool *(From trainee on 27/4/1999)*
Stoke C *(Free on 28/3/2002) FL 0+1*
Crewe Alex *(Free on 16/8/2002) FL 0+5/1 FLC 1 FAC 2 Others 0+2*
Macclesfield T *(Signed on 27/3/2003) FL 75+47/21 FLC 4 FAC 3+3/1 Others 3+4*
Accrington Stanley *(Free on 16/7/2007) FL 86+9/6 FLC 3+1 FAC 6+1/1 Others 4+1*
MK Dons *(Loaned on 24/1/2008) FL 7+5*

John Obi Mikel

John Miles

MILIJAS Nenad
Born: Belgrade, Serbia, 30 April 1983
Height: 6'2" **Weight:** 12.11
International Honours: Serbia: 16
The Croatian international made several scoring attempts in a superb debut for

Wolverhampton against West Ham. He was showing an abundance of skill, but found it hard to adjust to the pace in England and was dropped after five games. Returning, he made both goals at Stoke and his free kicks always posed a threat. He scored a beautiful goal from 30 yards that swerved past the Bolton goalkeeper, the first of two he got in December. Nenad lost his place to David Jones in January, and had no first team action for two months, although he did subsequently manage a few outings as a substitute and showed glimpses of why Wolves bought him.
Wolverhampton W *(Signed from Red Star Belgrade, Serbia, ex Zemun, on 15/6/2009) PL 12+7/2 FLC 0+1 FAC 2*

MILLAR Kirk
Born: Belfast, 7 July 1992
Height: 5'9" **Weight:** 10.8
Being promoted to first team status following a great run in Oldham's youth and reserve teams, Kirk made six appearances at the back end of the season. He could be described as an out-and-out flying winger but this probably does him an injustice. He is a skilful player who loves to take defenders on with his pace and fleetness of foot. Small in stature but with a big heart, Kirk is one to watch.
Oldham Ath *(From trainee on 21/4/2010) FL 2+4*

MILLER Adam Edward
Born: Hemel Hempstead, 19 February 1982
Height: 5'11" **Weight:** 11.6
Club Honours: FAT '07
International Honours: NI: Yth; E: SP-1
The attacking midfielder endured a topsy-turvy season with Gillingham, starting on a high with a goal in the opening day defeat of Swindon before falling out of favour and spending two months on loan with Dagenham. With the loan extended to the middle of January, the combative Adam, who wears a distinctive headband, proved a rock in the Daggers' midfield but with the club unable to afford his wages to sign him on a permanent basis he returned to Kent after eight appearances. Frequently prone to controversy, Adam surprised fans by winning back his place in the Gills' side in February and scored crucial goals against MK Dons, Brighton and Leeds. Was out of contract in the summer.
Queens Park Rgrs *(£50,000 from Aldershot T, ex trainee at Ipswich T, Canvey Island, Gravesend & Northfleet on 15/11/2004) FL 10+5 FLC 1*
Peterborough U *(Loaned on 23/9/2005) FL 2 (Free to Stevenage*

Borough on 23/1/2006)
Gillingham *(Signed from Stevenage Borough on 22/11/2007) FL 80+9/13 FLC 2 FAC 4 Others 2*
Dagenham & Redbridge *(Loaned on 10/11/2009) FL 8*

MILLER Ian Jonathan
Born: Colchester, 23 November 1983
Height: 6'2" **Weight:** 12.2
Ian was one of only two players who remained at the club at the start of the season after Darlington went into administration the previous February. He took over the captaincy at the end of November when Steve Foster was in

dispute with the club and continued to lead by example. Strong in the air and very quick at covering ground to tackle onrushing forwards, he missed a handful of games towards the end of the season after undergoing a hernia operation. This took his Darlington total past 100 appearances, but he failed to add to the four goals he had previously scored for the Quakers.
Ipswich T *(Signed from Bury T on 23/9/2006) FL 0+1*
Boston U *(Loaned on 3/11/2006) FL 12*
Darlington *(Loaned on 9/2/2007) FL 7/1*
Darlington *(Signed on 31/7/2007) FL 74+15/4 FLC 3 FAC 2 Others 2+1/1*

Ian Miller

MILLER Ishmael Anthony
Born: Manchester, 5 March 1987
Height: 6'3" **Weight:** 14.0
Club Honours: Ch '08
Sidelined for well over half the season, burly striker Ishmael returned, on cue, to help West Bromwich clinch promotion, netting two important goals in the process. He played his first competitive game after a 13-month lay-off when he entered the fray as a 77th-minute substitute in the 3-1 home League defeat by Nottingham Forest in early January. Ishmael then claimed his first senior goal for 16 months when he helped Albion beat Blackpool 3-2 at Bloomfield Road and repeated his feat by netting in another 3-2 victory over the Seasiders in the return fixture in March. The 'big fella' was certainly missed during the first half of the season and hopefully he will be fully fit and raring to go when the Premiership starts.
Manchester C (From trainee on 9/3/2005) PL 3+14 FLC 0+1 FAC 0+2
West Bromwich A (Signed on 15/8/2007) P/FL 39+25/14 FLC 1/2 FAC 3+3/5

MILLER Lee Adamson
Born: Lanark, 18 May 1983
Height: 6'2" **Weight:** 11.7
Club Honours: S Div 1 '03
International Honours: S: 3
Lee was part of a busy transfer deadline day for Middlesbrough and manager Gordon Strachan. Lee was due to be out of contract in the summer, but once Boro bid £500,000 he was on his way. Lee travelled south to Teesside and signed a permanent deal till 2012 with the option of a further year. The tall centre-forward struggled to get into any rhythm as fellow signing Chris Killen was invariably preferred but Lee will be aiming for a place once the new season starts.
Falkirk (From juniors on 9/6/2000) SL 61/27 SLC 3/1 SC 6 Others 3/2
Bristol C (£300,000 on 30/7/2003) FL 34+15/8 FLC 3+2/1 FAC 3 Others 1
Heart of Midlothian (Loaned on 11/1/2005) SL 17+1/8 SLC 1 SC 4/3
Dundee U (£225,000 on 3/6/2005) SL 23+14/8 SLC SC 0+1 Others 1
Aberdeen (Free on 31/8/2006) SL 109+10/29 SLC 5/2 SC 10+1/2 Others 9
Middlesbrough (£500,000 on 1/2/2010) FL 6+4

MILLER Shaun Robert
Born: Alsager, 25 September 1987
Height: 5'10" **Weight:** 11.8
A product of the Crewe youth system, Shaun is a regular in the first team squad. He normally occupies one of the

striking positions and contributed his fair share of goals, all of them in the League. A hard worker for the side, Alex are hoping his goal tally will increase in the season ahead.
Crewe Alex (From trainee on 3/7/2006) FL 47+41/15 FLC 1+1 FAC 4+1/3 Others 1+3

MILLER Thomas (Tommy) William
Born: Easington, 8 January 1979
Height: 6'1" **Weight:** 11.12
A player who was expected to add much needed drive and goals into Sheffield Wednesday's midfield, unfortunately Tommy's season was wrecked by injury. Having missed most of pre-season after picking up a thigh injury, he got into the side when fit, but not in his favoured central midfield role. He was played out wide right, sometimes left, in a basic 4-2-4 team pattern. This position did not really suit his skills and after a disappointing run of games in the side, he picked up a leg injury and was out for a long stretch. Eventually he got back fit and in the side, scoring his only goal of the campaign at Preston. Unfortunately, this was followed by his sufffering a hamstring injury that kept him out to the end of the season.
Hartlepool U (From trainee on 8/7/1997) FL 130+7/35 FLC 6/3 FAC 5/1 Others 12/5
Ipswich T (£800,000 + on 16/7/2001) P/FL 101+16/30 FLC 5+2/2 FAC 3+2/3 Others 7+3/2
Sunderland (Free on 2/7/2005) P/FL 30+3/3 FAC 2
Preston NE (Loaned on 14/11/2006) FL 4+3
Ipswich T (Free on 7/8/2007) FL 58+11/10 FLC 3+1/1 FAC 2
Sheffield Wed (Free on 2/7/2009) FL 10+10/1 FLC 2

MILLS Daniel (Danny) Peter
Born: Croydon, 2 June 1991
Height: 6'4" **Weight:** 13.0
Signed from non-League Crawley, the young Peterborough forward was loaned to Torquay in September, playing twice, and then to Rushden to gain first team experience. The tall striker, who has pace to burn and a fine shot, was finally give a chance at Posh when starting once and twice coming off the bench in three of the last five games. Despite not getting on the score-sheet he is seen as one for the future.
Peterborough U (Signed from Crawley T on 23/7/2009) FL 1+2
Torquay U (Loaned on 25/9/2009) FL 0+2

MILLS Gregory (Greg) Adam
Born: Leicester, 18 September 1990
Height: 5'9" **Weight:** 11.7
Derby's Greg was in the middle of a loan to Solihull Moors when injuries to forwards forced the club to recall the young striker. He was on the bench four times and made two brief appearances, both in away games, before resuming with Solihull. Back at Derby, Greg helped the reserves to finish at the top of the table and also had a brief spell on loan with Macclesfield in February, making just one substitute appearance when he replaced Craig Lindfield for the final quarter of an hour in the defeat at Bury. Greg spent the rest of his time at the Moss Rose as an unused substitute. At the end of the season, the speedy attacking wide midfielder was offered another year on his contract.
Derby Co (From trainee on 7/7/2009) FL 0+2
Macclesfield T (Loaned on 29/1/2010) FL 0+1

MILLS Joseph Nathan
Born: Swindon, 30 October 1989
Height: 5'9" **Weight:** 11.0
Club Honours: AMC '10
Joseph, or 'Fish' as he is known to his Southampton team-mates, is a cultured, slick-tackling, smooth-running left wing-back – presently the position occupied by Dan Harding. Joseph has done well when called upon and was able to make up for last year's disappointment – of missing the Johnstone's Paint Trophy final through injury while on loan to Scunthorpe – when he returned to Wembley with the Saints in March and earned a winners' medal in the same competition.
Southampton (From trainee on 1/11/2006) FL 14+10 FLC 1+1 FAC 1+2 Others 2+1
Scunthorpe U (Loaned on 23/2/2009) FL 13+1

MILLS Matthew Claude
Born: Swindon, 14 July 1986
Height: 6'3" **Weight:** 12.12
International Honours: E: Yth
Matthew represented a major investment for Reading when he was signed from Doncaster. Even so, the competition from other central defenders meant he was never certain of a regular place until Brian McDermott took over as manager in December. Once established, Matt showed just how good a centre-back he is. A tall, solid and imposing figure, he can win the ball in the air and on the ground with great authority. His confidence and maturity meant he was given the captain's armband in the

absence of Ivor Ingimarsson in the closing weeks of the season. No mere hoofer out of defence, Matt can pass accurately to his wide players and weighed in with a couple of neatly taken goals.

Southampton *(From trainee on 16/7/2004) FL 3+1 FLC 2*
Coventry C *(Loaned on 18/9/2004) FL 4 FLC 1*
Bournemouth *(Loaned on 21/2/2005) FL 12/3*
Manchester C *(£750,000 on 31/1/2006) PL 1+1*
Colchester U *(Loaned on 26/1/2007) FL 8+1*
Doncaster Rov *(£300,000 on 14/8/2007) FL 70+5/3 FLC 1 FAC 4 Others 6*
Reading *(£2,000,000 on 5/8/2009) FL 22+1/2 FLC 1 FAC 6*

MILLS Pablo Simeon Ishmael
Born: Birmingham, 27 May 1984
Height: 6'0" **Weight:** 11.6
International Honours: E: Yth
Pablo took his Rotherham appearances beyond 100 during the season. He showed his versatility by playing in midfield and also having good, if brief, spells in central defence. This time, he was one of two central midfielders, having been the holding player in a three-man midfield the season before, and took a little time to adjust to the extra demands. Another to lose his place early in the second half of the season but won it back for the run-in and gave some steady displays, adding extra defensive capability when the team was under pressure. Was out of contract in the summer.
Derby Co *(From trainee on 16/7/2002) FL 40+18 FLC 1 FAC 5 Others 0+1*
MK Dons *(Loaned on 31/8/2005) FL 16/1 Others 3/1*
Walsall *(Loaned on 10/2/2006) FL 14*
Rotherham U *(Free on 3/8/2006) FL 127+9/3 FLC 7+1 FAC 5 Others 7*

MILNE Andrew Alexander
Born: York, 30 September 1990
Height: 5'11" **Weight:** 11.6
International Honours: S: Yth
This promising, young defender made his Darlington debut at right-back in the home game against Bradford in December but was injured in the following game at Torquay, so his loan was curtailed and he returned to Leeds for treatment. However, he returned to the Quakers in March after recovering and made ten more appearances before the end of the season. Was out of contract at the end of June.
Leeds U *(From trainee on 6/7/2009)*
Darlington *(Loaned on 26/11/2009) FL 12+1*

MILNE Kenneth (Kenny)
Born: Alloa, 26 August 1979
Height: 6'2" **Weight:** 12.8
International Honours: S: U21-1
After rupturing knee ligaments in the second game of the 2008-09 season, Scunthorpe defender Kenny battled back to make an emotional return to action as a substitute in the FA Cup third round after 16 months out of action. He came through that game well but it was not until two months later that he made the starting line-up. A left-footed, committed centre-half who is strong in the air, Kenny shone in the home wins over Peterborough and Bristol City but his rehabilitation meant he was not capable of playing two games in a week and he figured in just four League games all season. Was out of contract at the end of June.
Heart of Midlothian *(From Edinburgh U on 2/8/1997) SL 6+6 SLC 0+1*
Cowdenbeath *(Loaned on 9/10/2098) SL 24/6 SC 1*
Cowdenbeath *(Loaned on 11/1/2002) SL 9*
Partick T *(Signed on 13/6/2002) SL 58+8/1 SLC 4+1/1 SC 5 Others 1*
Falkirk *(Free on 1/7/2005) SL 90+5/4 SLC 7 SC 7*
Scunthorpe U *(Free on 6/8/2008) FL 5 FLC 1 FAC 0+2*

James Milner

MILNER James Philip
Born: Leeds, 4 January 1986
Height: 5'9" **Weight:** 11.0
International Honours: E: 8; U21-46; Yth
James metaphorically and literally went from waiting in the wings to being the centre of attention during a scintillating breakthrough season for Aston Villa and England. He ended as one of the most talked about and sought after players in the Premier League. Villa manager Martin O'Neill unlocked James' potential by moving him from the right wing to the centre of midfield as soon as Stewart Downing was fit. James responded by taking his goals tally to double figures for the first time, with 12 in League and Cups as well as 12 assists. James was regarded as a potential star at Leeds and Newcastle and is now living up to his billing. Comfortable with both feet, James' switch allowed him to have a greater impact, displaying his passing range, vision and ability to thread team-mates in on goal. Another asset is his work rate, with the former county schoolboy cross-country runner able to make box-to-box runs from first whistle to last. He was the PFA 'Young Player of the Year', was named in the Premier League 'Team of the Season' and was Villa supporters' 'Player of the Season'. This

was not lost on England coach Fabio Capello who gave James his senior debut as a substitute against Holland after his record number of appearances for the under-21s and took him to South Africa for the World Cup finals. Villa entered the summer trying to fend off interest in James after Manchester City sparked a transfer scramble with a £20 million bid.

Leeds U *(From trainee on 12/2/2003) PL 28+20/5 FLC 1 FAC 1+4*
Swindon T *(Loaned on 4/9/2003) FL 6/2*
Newcastle U *(£3,600,000 on 7/7/2004) PL 72+22/6 FLC 6/1 FAC 5+3/2 Others 17+11/2*
Aston Villa *(Loaned on 31/8/2005) PL 27/1 FLC 3/2 FAC 3*
Aston Villa *(£12,000,000 on 29/8/2008) PL 67+5/10 FLC 6/4 FAC 7+1/3 Others 5+1/1*

MILNER Marcus Raglan Webb
Born: Kingston, Jamaica, 28 November 1991
Height: 5'10" **Weight:** 12.3
A young attacking midfielder, and a second-year scholar at Roots Hall, Marcus is well on his way to being another graduate from Ricky Duncan's excellent Youth Academy at Southend. Although the youth team failed to retain the Academy League title, Marcus contributed well apart from an error of judgment against Queens Park Rangers that brought a three-game suspension and a red card. He impressed enough to gain a further one-year developmental deal and was on the first team bench for the last game at Southampton, going on for the final few minutes as a substitute for Stuart O'Keefe.
Southend U *(Trainee) FL 0+1*

MIRFIN David Matthew
Born: Sheffield, 18 April 1985
Height: 6'2" **Weight:** 14.5
For the second successive season, David was the most consistent performer in a struggling Scunthorpe defence, adjusting well to the demands of Championship football after a baptism of fire in the 4-0 opening day defeat at Cardiff. A big centre-half who is strong in the air and committed on the ground, he missed just nine League games all season after shaking off a pre-season ankle injury that saw him sidelined for the early matches. Netted his first League goal for the club with a late header against Crystal Palace in February and was rewarded for his efforts by winning one of the club's main 'Player of the Year' awards.
Huddersfield T *(From trainee on*

6/12/2003) FL 141+20/9 FLC 4 FAC 6+2 Others 5+1/3
Scunthorpe U *(£150,000 on 13/8/2008) FL 69+1/1 FLC 3 FAC 4 Others 9/1*

MITCHEL-KING Mathew (Mat) John
Born: Reading, 12 September 1983
Height: 6'4" **Weight:** 13.1
Recruited from Histon after previous service with Cambridge City and Cambridge United, he joined Crewe in June and made his debut in the opening game of the season. A central defender, Mat had a good spell in the side before dropping out of favour for a period. He came back late in the season but has still to open his goals account for the club.
Crewe Alex *(Free from Histon, ex Mildenhall T, Cambridge C, on 30/6/2009) FL 31+1 FLC 1 FAC 1 Others 1*

MKANDAWIRE Tamika Paul
Born: Mzuzu, Malawi, 28 May 1983
Height: 6'0" **Weight:** 12.3
International Honours: E: SP-2
Tamika is a ball-playing centre-half who also scores his fair share of goals for Leyton Orient. He is dangerous at set pieces with his brave headers but is equally accomplished at beating defenders before scoring from outside the penalty area. Tamika was out of contract in the summer and was offered a new deal.
West Bromwich A *(From trainee on 18/5/2002)*
Hereford U *(Free on 14/7/2004) FL 39/2 FLC 2 FAC 4 Others 1*
Leyton Orient *(Free on 27/7/2007) FL 114/15 FLC 5 FAC 5 Others 2*

Tamika Mkandawire

MODRIC Luka
Born: Zadar, Croatia, 9 September 1985
Height: 5'9" **Weight:** 10.8
International Honours: Croatia: 41; U21-15; Yth
The magical Tottenham midfielder was in great form in the first four games, in which they had a 100 per cent record to top the early table. Unfortunately, Luka was injured in the fourth game and was out of action until December. After his return, he played a full part in helping Spurs to fourth place and Champions League qualification. The Croatian is most often nominally on the left of midfield but tends to use almost every blade of grass, primarily providing the creative spark for the attack, but also popping up in crucial defensive positions. Luka's great skill is his ability to hold and carry the ball through the tightest of marking. His excellent peripheral vision offers great passing skill, particularly over the short to mid-range, and he scored three goals in the Premier League, one of which was a spectacular strike at Turf Moor where even opposition fans applauded his skill. Luka also played in the centre of midfield for some of Spurs' vital end of season games. His international career continues for Croatia, who missed him for their vital games as they failed to qualify for the 2010 World Cup.
Tottenham H *(£15,500,000 from Dinamo Zagreb, Croatia, ex NK Zadar, Zrinjski Mostar - loan, Inter Zapresic - loan, on 3/7/2008) PL 55+4/6 FLC 3+1 FAC 9/1 Others 3+1/1*

MOKOENA Aaron Tebomo
Born: Johannesburg, South Africa, 25 November 1980
Height: 6'2" **Weight:** 12.6
International Honours: South Africa: 100
After a slow start to his career on the south coast with Portsmouth, midfield player Aaron went from strength to strength after scoring a late winner against Coventry in the FA Cup. Injuries and the sale of Younes Kaboul led to him being frequently used as a centre-back, the position he occupies for his country, South Africa. Aaron excelled, putting in heroic performances in both the FA Cup semi-final against Tottenham and the final against Chelsea. Strong, committed and a great leader, he epitomised the spirit of Pompey in what was a season of unprecedented turbulence for the club as a points deduction for entering administration pointed them towards relegation.

Aaron's next job after this was to lead out South Africa on their own soil in the World Cup finals.
Blackburn Rov (£300,000 from KRC Genk, Belgium on 4/1/2005) PL 55+46 FLC 6+4 FAC 17+1/2 Others 5+5
Portsmouth (Free on 2/7/2009) PL 21+2 FLC 2+1 FAC 4/1

MOLESLEY Mark Clifford
Born: Hillingdon, 11 March 1981
Height: 6'1" **Weight:** 11.7
International Honours: E: SP-4
Injuries meant it was a torrid season for the popular midfield player. Mark started in fine style with a wonder goal on the opening day of the season and was a regular as Bournemouth enjoyed a fine start. He had a niggling foot problem and, after battling to play through the pain, was eventually forced to have surgery. That proved to be unsuccessful and a second operation was required. As a result, he missed the last seven months.
Bournemouth (Free from Grays Ath, ex Hayes, Cambridge C, Aldershot T, Stevenage Borough, on 17/10/2008) FL 32+7/5 FLC 1 FAC 2 Others 1+1

MOLONEY Brendon Anthony
Born: Killarney, 18 January 1989
Height: 6'1" **Weight:** 11.12
Club Honours: Div 2 '10
International Honours: RoI: U21-5
Having crossed the River Trent on a six-month loan, he began the season for Notts County, scoring a spectacular individual goal in the opening day thrashing of Bradford. Settled in well as first choice right-back where his thrusting attacking runs helped to develop goals for his team-mates before being recalled by Nottingham Forest at the end of December. He then joined Championship side Scunthorpe on loan in January and was thrown in at the deep end when coming on as a substitute in the home win over Sheffield Wednesday within hours of arriving at the club. A strong, quick full-back who can play on either side, he was brought into the starting line-up at left-back at West Bromwich in February but 20 minutes in was the victim of a strong challenge which saw him damage his knee ligaments, an injury that kept him out for the rest of the season.
Nottingham F (From trainee on 3/3/2006) FL 11+4
Chesterfield (Loaned on 11/1/2008) FL 8+1/1
Notts Co (Loaned on 1/7/2009) FL 18/1 FLC 1
Scunthorpe U (Loaned on 27/1/2010) FL 1+2

Andy Monkhouse

MONCUR Thomas (TJ) James
Born: Hackney, 23 September 1987
Height: 5'10" **Weight:** 12.8
A Wycombe right-back who had four starts in August and September, his only appearances, before falling out of favour and leaving the club on the same day that Peter Taylor was sacked. He signed non-contract terms for Chesterfield in February, after a successful trial, but left after a month and joined Cray Wanderers.
Fulham (From trainee on 30/9/2005)
Bradford C (Loaned on 29/1/2008) FL 6+1
Bradford C (Loaned on 8/8/2008) FL 11+3 FLC 0+1 FAC 2 Others 1
Wycombe W (Free on 2/1/2009) FL 4+2

MONK Garry Alan
Born: Bedford, 6 March 1979
Height: 6'0" **Weight:** 13.0
Club Honours: AMC '06; Div 1 '08
Swansea's club captain was one of three players given a red card in the fiery Carling Cup tie against Scunthorpe at the Liberty Stadium early in the season. A cool, composed central defender, Garry unfortunately suffered during the season with calf injuries, plus a recurring back injury, that forced him to miss a number of games when he would far rather have been playing.
Torquay U (Trainee) FL 4+1
Southampton (Signed on 23/5/1997) PL 9+2 FLC 1 FAC 0+1
Torquay U (Loaned on 25/9/1998) FL 6

Stockport Co (Loaned on 9/9/1999) FL 2 FLC 2
Oxford U (Loaned on 12/1/2001) FL 5
Sheffield Wed (Loaned on 13/12/2002) FL 15
Barnsley (Free on 21/11/2003) FL 14+3 FAC 4/1
Swansea C (Free on 2/7/2004) FL 163+1/3 FLC 8/1 FAC 11 Others 17/1

MONKHOUSE Andrew (Andy) William
Born: Leeds, 23 October 1980
Height: 6'1" **Weight:** 11.6
Andy is an attacking left-sided midfielder who, in four seasons, has made over 150 appearances for Hartlepool. Although this was not the best of seasons for his club, for Andy personally it was memorable as he finished the campaign as the Hartlepool top scorer with 11 goals. A player who at times wears his heart on his sleeve, Andy is a master dribbler who is often utilised playing as an old-style winger and in this role is always a threat when running at opposition defences.
Rotherham U (From trainee on 14/11/1998) FL 68+60/9 FLC 7/3 FAC 2+6 Others 3+1/1
Swindon T (Free on 24/7/2006) FL 9+1/2 Others 0+1
Hartlepool U (Signed on 23/11/2006) FL 131+7/26 FLC 4+1/1 FAC 4+4/1 Others 1

MONTGOMERY Graeme
Born: Enfield, 3 March 1988
Height: 6'1" **Weight:** 11.0
Graeme spent most of the season

sitting on the bench for Dagenham but still managed to appear in almost a third of their League Two games. The left-winger has the ability to deliver pinpoint crosses with his left foot. He scored his first goal for the Daggers in the fifth minute of injury time in April, then repeated the feat with an injury-time winner against Hereford in the next home game, both after leaving the bench.

Dagenham & Redbridge *(£5,000 + from Wealdstone on 1/1/2009) FL 4+18/2 FLC 0+1 FAC 0+1 Others 1+2*

Nick Montgomery

MONTGOMERY Nicholas (Nick) Anthony

Born: Leeds, 28 October 1981
Height: 5'9" **Weight:** 11.8
International Honours: S: B-1; U21-2
Nick, currently the longest-serving Blades player, had what many considered his best season for Sheffield United. First choice in midfield and missing only through a knee injury in October, which typically kept him out of the side for less time than expected, he worked incredibly hard for the full 90-plus minutes. Never shirking a challenge

and breaking up the oppositions' attacks in defence he was always available going forward if needed. His distribution improved and in March he scored with a long-range shot against Blackpool, his first League goal since December 2005. He was voted jointly the 'Players' Player of the Season'. Out of contract at the end of the season, he signed a new three-year deal during the summer.

Sheffield U *(From trainee on 7/7/2000) P/FL 230+64/8 FLC 12+4/2 FAC 19+4 Others 3*

MONTROSE Lewis Robert Egerton

Born: Manchester, 17 November 1988
Height: 6'0" **Weight:** 12.0
Peter Taylor's first signing of the summer for Wycombe was Lewis, a young midfield player captured from Wigan on a two-year deal. He started the first four League games as the central midfield anchor man, and made three more appearances before dropping out of favour, not helped by a cartilage operation that put him out for several weeks in November. After a substitute appearance at Stockport in February, Lewis started the last seven games, showing a remarkable improvement on his previous performances and coinciding with the team's good run of results. He has an athletic build, will run for ever and has a keen eye for a pass.

Wigan Ath *(From trainee on 5/7/2007) FLC 1+1*
Cheltenham T *(Loaned on 24/9/2008) FL 5 FAC 2/1 Others 1*
Chesterfield *(Loaned on 26/2/2009) FL 11+1*
Wycombe W *(Free on 2/7/2009) FL 11+3 Others 1*

MOONEY David (Dave)

Born: Dublin, 30 October 1984
Height: 5'10" **Weight:** 11.11
International Honours: RoI: U23-2
Dave was a member of Reading's first team squad for just three games in August, being an unused substitute in the 0-0 championship draw at Swansea, then playing as a central striker in Carling Cup ties against Burton and Barnsley. He revealed glimpses of his goalscoring potential by netting twice against League Two newcomers Burton, but was unable to press his claim for a regular place at senior level and in October he joined Charlton on loan. Technically, Dave had two spells on loan at Charlton during the campaign, interrupted in between by a knee injury which sidelined him for a couple of weeks. Overall his period at the Valley

was very successful with six goals scored, including one in the play-offs, his strike on the turn against Gillingham, being a contender for goal of the season. His movement on and off the ball was very good but he needs to develop the physical side of his game. Played with a variety of partners but probably had the most success alongside Deon Burton.

Reading *(£350,000 from Cork C, ex Shamrock Rov, Longford T, on 22/8/2008) FLC 2+2/2*
Stockport Co *(Loaned on 16/1/2009) FL 2*
Norwich C *(Loaned on 6/3/2009) FL 8+1/3*
Charlton Ath *(Loaned on 16/10/2009) FL 20+8/5 Others 3/1*

MOORE Byron Curtis

Born: Stoke-on-Trent, 24 August 1988
Height: 6'0" **Weight:** 10.10
Another product of the Crewe youth system, Byron has been around the squad since his first senior game in 2007-08. A front player who can operate effectively on either wing and although not yet a high scorer, he has made many chances for his colleagues. Byron had to miss the last few games of the season after an injury sustained at Torquay.

Crewe Alex *(From trainee on 2/5/2007) FL 60+41/9 FLC 5/1 FAC 4 Others 2*

MOORE James Christopher (Chris)

Born: Newcastle, 17 January 1984
Height: 5'9" **Weight:** 12.0
Chris passed up the chance of a visit to Wembley with Whitley Bay in the FA Trophy to realise his ambition of signing professionally with Darlington in March. He became the 51st player to be used during the season and the 20th and last to be signed by manager Steve Staunton. He soon impressed with his darting runs down the right and accurate crosses which produced several goals, although he has yet to find the net himself.

Darlington *(Free from Whitley Bay, ex Newcastle U trainee, Bishop Auckland, on 12/3/2010) FL 8+3*

MOORE Darren Mark

Born: Birmingham, 22 April 1974
Height: 6'2" **Weight:** 15.6
International Honours: Jamaica: 3
Darren, now in the veteran stage of his career, again played in the majority of Barnsley's games. The giant of a defender always liked a battle against other big forwards. Strong and powerful in the air he was a handful in the opponents' penalty area, although

his only goal, at Swansea, was a disappointing return. His season was disrupted throughout, with a foot injury being the main problem. Darren was out of contract at the end of the season and released but quickly agreed to join a former Derby team-mate, Burton manager Paul Peschisolido.
Torquay U *(From trainee on 18/11/1992) FL 102+1/8 FLC 6 FAC 7/1 Others 8/2*
Doncaster Rov *(£62,500 on 19/7/1995) FL 76/7 FLC 4 FAC 1 Others 3/1*
Bradford C *(£310,000 + on 18/6/1997) P/FL 62/3 FLC 6/1 FAC 2*
Portsmouth *(£500,000 + on 15/11/1999) FL 58+1/2 FLC 5 FAC 2*
West Bromwich A *(£750,000 on 15/9/2001) P/FL 93+11/6 FLC 4 FAC 8*
Derby Co *(£500,000 on 26/1/2006) P/FL 71+9/3 FLC 2/1 FAC 4+1 Others 3/1*
Barnsley *(Free on 19/7/2008) FL 70+3/2 FLC 3*

MOORE Luke Isaac
Born: Birmingham, 13 February 1986
Height: 5'11" **Weight:** 11.13
Club Honours: FAYC '02
International Honours: E: U21-5; Yth
Three of Luke's goals for West Bromwich were scored in the League games against Peterborough, two in a 3-2 win at London Road and one in the 2-0 home victory at the Hawthorns. Niggling injuries, especially early in the season, and then towards the end of the campaign, seriously affected Luke's game and with so many other strikers vying for selection, he had his work cut out to hold down a regular place. He unfortunately missed a penalty in the 2-0 home win over Ipswich, 'keeper Richard Wright blocking his spot-kick with his outstretched left leg.
Aston Villa *(From trainee on 13/2/2003) PL 36+51/14 FLC 2+4/1 FAC 3+2*
Wycombe W *(Loaned on 11/12/2003) FL 6/4*
West Bromwich A *(£3,500,000 on 22/2/2008) P/FL 31+26/5 FLC 2 FAC 2+1*

MOORE Simon William
Born: Isle of Wight, 19 May 1990
Height: 6'3" **Weight:** 12.2
Brentford's third choice goalkeeper had to wait until the final minute of the last game of the season, against Hartlepool, to leave the bench and make his League début. He replaced Wojciech Szczesny for the five minutes of stoppage time, but did not have a save to make.
Brentford *(From Farnborough on 11/8/2009) FL 0+1*

MORENO Marcelo
Born: Santa Cruz, Bolivia, 18 June 1987
Height: 6'2" **Weight:** 12.13
International Honours: Brazil: Yth. Bolivia: 17
The Bolivian international arrived at Wigan from Ukrainian side Shakhtar Donetsk on the last day of the January transfer window on a six-month loan. A centre-forward with good positional sense and plenty of strength to compete with the physical aspect of the English game, he spent the first half of the season on loan at Werder Bremen, having his contract cancelled. Marcelo made his debut in the away match against Sunderland, his first start coming at home against Bolton in February. He struggled to adapt to the pace of English football and a calf injury against West Ham in April marked the end of his loan. The first foreign player to play for the Brazilian under-20 side, He is known as Marcelo Martins when representing Bolivia but as Marcelo Moreno at club level.
Wigan Ath *(Loaned from Shakhtar Donetsk, Ukraine, ex Vitoria, Cruzeiro, Werder Bremen - loan, on 1/2/2010) PL 9+3*

MORGAN Christopher (Chris) Paul
Born: Barnsley, 9 November 1977
Height: 5'10" **Weight:** 12.9
The Blades' captain had another excellent season. First choice in the centre of Sheffield United's defence, because of injuries he played alongside seven different partners and performed in his usual wholehearted and fearless manner. Always very good in the air, Chris showed first-class anticipation and, although happy to clear his lines with a hefty swing of the boot if necessary, he tried to play the ball out of defence. He missed a few games due to a rib injury and others through suspension having accumulated sufficient yellow cards. Despite his aerial threat in the opposition's area he scored only twice, one being a last-minute equaliser against Ipswich. Chris, who was voted the supporters' 'Player of the Season', signed a one-year extension to his contract.
Barnsley *(From trainee on 3/7/1996) P/FL 182+3/7 FLC 14/1 FAC 9 Others 4*
Sheffield U *(Free on 1/8/2003) P/FL 232+7/13 FLC 11/1 FAC 17/1 Others 3*

MORGAN Craig
Born: St Asaph, 18 June 1985
Height: 6'1" **Weight:** 12.7
Club Honours: AMC '05
International Honours: W: 20; U21-12; Yth
Peterborough's Welsh international grew in stature as the season wore on and once he got to the pace of a higher division he more than held his own in the centre of defence. Good in the air, strong in the tackle and with an eye for a pass that can quickly turn defence into attack, he has all the equipment. Craig extended his lead as Peterborough's most capped player and if he carries on in this vein of form, there are many more honours to come.
Wrexham *(From trainee on 10/7/2003) FL 33+19/1 FLC 1/1 FAC 1+1 Others 9*
MK Dons *(Signed on 5/7/2005) FL 41+2 FLC 2 FAC 4 Others 2*
Wrexham *(Loaned on 16/10/2006) FL 1 Others 1*
Peterborough U *(Free on 23/11/2006) FL 122+3/4 FLC 5 FAC 12+1 Others 1*

MORGAN Dean Lance
Born: Enfield, 3 October 1983
Height: 5'11" **Weight:** 11.2
Released by Luton, after a loan spell with Grays Athletic, Dean joined MK Dons on a monthly deal two months into the season and after making his debut as a substitute at Oldham in late September flitted around the first team scene, scoring his first goal in a win at former club Leyton Orient in mid-December. A skilful player at his best on the ball, after failing to make a significant impression he was loaned out to Aldershot in late March. A pacy left-footer, who can play as a winger or a forward, Dean was re-united with his ex-Reading coach (and now Shots' boss) Kevin Dillon. His arrival helped to strengthen the spine of the team as they pushed towards the play-offs, and scoring his first Aldershot goal to crown a 'Man of the Match' performance in the victory over Rotherham on Easter Monday cemented his place as the fans' favourite. He went on to score a last-minute winner at Cheltenham in the Shots' penultimate away game that was reminiscent of Gazza's goal for England against Scotland in Euro '96. The following week, Dean scored another wonder goal, this time drilling the ball home at the end of a mazy run in the home win over Lincoln that secured the Shots' place in the play-offs. His loan was extended at the start of May to enable him to take part in the final, but he could not prevent an aggregate semi-final defeat by Rotherham.
Colchester U *(From trainee on 8/8/2001) FL 23+48/6 FLC 1 FAC 0+3 Others 1+1*
Reading *(Free on 28/11/2003) FL 13+18/3 FLC 0+1 FAC 1+2*
Luton T *(Free on 21/7/2005) FL 54+34/11 FLC 8+1/1 FAC 1+2 Others*

0+1 *(Freed during 2009 close season)*
Southend U *(Loaned on 16/11/2007)*
FL 6+2 FAC 3/3
Crewe Alex *(Loaned on 7/3/2008) FL
7+2/1*
Leyton Orient *(Loaned on 28/8/2008)
FL 18+14/5 FAC 1+1*
MK Dons *(Free from Grays Ath on
28/9/2009) FL 1+8/1 FAC 0+1/1 Others
1+1*
Aldershot T *(Loaned on 25/3/2010) FL
8+1/4 Others 2*

MORGAN Kerry David
Born: Merthyr Tydfil, 31 October 1988
Height: 5'10" **Weight:** 11.3
A former trainee with Swansea who
impressed in pre-season matches and
was given two first team starts, against
Reading in the League and Scunthorpe
in the Carling Cup. Kerry is an
exceptionally quick winger and, despite
his lack of height, is also extremely
brave. He signed on loan for Blue
Square South side Newport County in
September and this was extended to
the end of the season. Kerry remained a
regular fixture in the side that won the
championship and promotion under
Dean Holdsworth.
Swansea C *(From trainee on
24/7/2008) FL 1+2 FLC 1+1*

MORGAN Marvin Newlon
Born: Manchester, 18 April 1983
Height: 6'4" **Weight:** 12.0
Marvin is a strong, tall forward, who is
a handful for defenders and is
Aldershot's record signing, from
Woking. He took just three minutes to
open his account in a 'Man of the
Match' performance against
Darlington on the opening day and
scored again in the Carling Cup tie at
Bristol Rovers. His good start earned
him the supporters' 'Player of the
Month' award in August. Having been
the subject of interest from
Peterborough and ex-Shots' boss Gary
Waddock at Wycombe, he made his
50th start for the Shots at Accrington.
Marvin's importance to the team is
reflected by the fact that he top-scored
with 16 goals in all competitions and
wore the captain's armband on several
occasions in the absence of Anthony
Charles.
Aldershot T *(Signed from Woking, ex
Wealdstone, Yeading, on 9/7/2008) FL
58+14/21 FLC 2/2 FAC 5+1/1 Others
2+1*

MORGAN Mark Paul Thomas
Born: Belfast, 23 October 1978
Height: 6'1" **Weight:** 12.1
International Honours: NI: U21-1
Having spent the whole of 2008-09 on

Paul Morgan

loan at Macclesfield, Paul made the
move permanent last summer. Other
than missing two short spells through
injury, the Town captain has been the
first choice at centre-back throughout
the season. Paul is one of those clever
players who make the game look easy
in an undemonstrative yet extremely
effective way. But there is plenty of
effort in his professional approach to
the game.
Preston NE *(From trainee on 9/5/1997)
FLC 1*
Lincoln C *(Free on 17/7/2001) FL
203+9/2 FLC 6 FAC 5+1 Others 14*
Bury *(Free on 16/7/2007) FL 20 FLC 1
FAC 1*
Macclesfield T *(Free on 15/7/2008) FL
73+2/1 FLC 2 FAC 3 Others 1*

MORGAN Westley (Wes)
Nathan
Born: Nottingham, 21 January 1984
Height: 6'2" **Weight:** 14.0
A big and strong central defender, Wes
was a regular member of the
Nottingham Forest defence for the
seventh consecutive season. A huge
favourite with the club's supporters who
love his never-say-die attitude and his
surging forays into midfield. Despite
being only 26, Wes made his 300th
appearance for his local club.
Nottingham F *(Signed from Central
Midlands League side, Dunkirk, on
5/7/2002) FL 267+17/10 FLC 16 FAC 18
Others 6+2/1*
Kidderminster Hrs *(Loaned on
27/2/2003) FL 5/1*

Wes Morgan

MORISON Steven (Steve)
William
Born: Enfield, 29 August 1983
Height: 6'2" **Weight:** 12.0
Steve joined Millwall from Stevenage
Borough, where he was their leading
scorer. After a period spent settling in,
he quickly became a crowd favourite
who gave of his best in each game,
with deceptive pace and good body
strength. Goals were hard to come by
at first but he did not let his head drop

and, as the side became more settled, so
he prospered, ending the season as top
scorer in League games with 20 goals. He
also won League One's 'Player of the
Month' award for March after scoring in
all five games. Steve scored the first goal
in the League One play-off semi-final
victory that took the Lions to Wembley
for the second year running.
*Northampton T (From trainee on
7/7/2003) FL 7+16/3 FLC 0+2 Others 0+2
(Free to Bishops Stortford on 22/10/2004)*

*Millwall (Signed from Stevenage
Borough on 5/6/2009) FL 42+1/20 FLC 1
FAC 5/2 Others 3/1*

MORRELL Andrew (Andy)
Jonathan
Born: Doncaster, 28 September 1974
Height: 5'11" **Weight:** 12.0
With nine League goals making him the
second top scorer at Bury, the
ceaselessly hard-working Andy formed
a great strike partnership with Ryan
Lowe. Persistent and experienced, Andy
was named the 'Mentor of the Season'.
Scoring two goals in a game on three
occasions, the most notable perhaps in
a 4-2 win at Accrington, Andy, at the
age of 36, was generally replaced
around the 70-minute mark.
*Wrexham (Free from Newcastle Blue
Star on 18/12/1998) FL 76+34/40 FLC
3/1 FAC 1+2 Others 2+3/2*
*Coventry C (Free on 2/7/2003) FL
53+45/17 FLC 5+1/2 FAC 4+3*
*Blackpool (Signed on 16/8/2006) FL
57+21/21 FLC 2+3 FAC 4+1/3 Others
3/1*
*Bury (Free on 11/8/2008) FL 56+17/18
FLC 0+1 FAC 1 Others 3+1*

MORRIS Aaron John
Born: Cardiff, 30 December 1989
Height: 6'1" **Weight:** 12.4
International Honours: W: U21-5; Yth
The young Cardiff defender, who can
play centre-half or full-back, made only
one first team appearance and that was
in the final Championship game of the
season when City had already qualified
for the play-offs and made major
changes to their team. A Wales under-21
international, his contract ran out at the
end of 2009-10 and he was released.
*Cardiff C (From trainee on 25/11/2008)
FL 0+1 FLC 0+1*

MORRIS Glenn James
Born: Woolwich, 20 December 1983
Height: 6'0" **Weight:** 11.3
Glenn was mainly used as reserve
goalkeeper by Leyton Orient but when
called upon to replace the injured Jamie
Jones, he never let the team or himself
down. Glenn was out of contract in the
summer and released.
*Leyton Orient (From trainee on
4/3/2003) FL 121+3 FLC 5+2 FAC 8
Others 11*

MORRIS Ian
Born: Dublin, 27 February 1987
Height: 6'0" **Weight:** 11.2
Club Honours: Div 1 '07
International Honours: RoI: U21-1; Yth
After his excellent displays as an
emergency left-back in the 2008-09
play-offs, Scunthorpe midfielder Ian

was hoping to be back in favour at the Championship club during 2009-10. A skilful, left-footed player with a good range of passing, he started at left-back in the opening day defeat at Cardiff but only made the starting line-up once more and was allowed to join League Two Chesterfield on loan in November. At Saltergate he immediately impressed the supporters with his versatility, work rate and stamina, as well as his ability to contribute equally to creating and defending on the left of midfield. He brought valued consistency to the team in an understated but effective manner before returning to Glanford Park after a couple of months when the clubs could not agree to extend the deal. Ian made just one substitute appearance for the Iron in the closing three months of the campaign.
Leeds U (From trainee on 4/3/2005)
Blackpool (Loaned on 23/9/2005) FL 21+9/3 Others 1
Scunthorpe U (Signed on 31/8/2006) FL 44+32/7 FLC 2 FAC 3+2 Others 6+3/1
Carlisle U (Loaned on 26/3/2009) FL 4+2
Chesterfield (Loaned on 26/11/2009) FL 7

MORRIS Lee
Born: Blackpool, 30 April 1980
Height: 5'10" **Weight:** 11.2
Club Honours: FC '09
International Honours: E: U21-1; Yth
Much was expected of Lee at Edgar Street after a promising pre-season, but Hereford had a poor start to the campaign and the pacy striker lost his place in the side after failing to find the net in the early games. He had a spell on loan at Mansfield but then returned to Hereford for one more start and a handful of substitute appearances before ending the season on loan at Forest Green.
Sheffield U (From trainee on 24/12/1997) FL 14+12/6 FAC 1+5/2 Others 0+1
Derby Co (£1,800,000 + on 15/10/1999) P/FL 62+29/17 FLC 1+4/1 FAC 2+2
Huddersfield T (Loaned on 8/3/2001) FL 5/1
Leicester C (£120,000 on 2/2/2004) FL 2+8
Yeovil T (Free on 3/8/2006) FL 23+11/5 FLC 1+1 FAC 1 Others 3/1 (Freed on 29/2/2008)
Hereford U (Free from Burton A on 27/7/2009) FL 5+7 FLC 1 Others 1

MORRISON Clinton Hubert
Born: Tooting, 14 May 1979
Height: 6'1" **Weight:** 11.2
International Honours: RoI: 36; U21-2

The experienced striker had a good second season at Coventry and featured in all their competitive games, starting 38 times in the League. For the second season running, he reached double figures in League goals and must have been disappointed to score only once in the final 14 games. His goals came in spasms, with six in the first nine games then three in four around Christmas. In between there were long droughts but his all-round level of performances was good. His best goals were all against Ipswich, his great chip and a diving header at home and then a curling shot at Portman Road. Throughout the season, Clinton performed well, always giving 100 per cent and using his strength against some of the most physical defenders in the division. Clinton was acting captain when Stephen Wright was unavailable and always led by example. His contract expired this summer.
Crystal Palace (From trainee on 29/3/1997) P/FL 141+16/62 FLC 16+3/9 FAC 4/1 Others 0+1
Birmingham C (£4,250,000 + on 3/8/2002) PL 56+31/14 FLC 2+1/1 FAC 6+1/1
Crystal Palace (£2,000,000 on 26/8/2005) FL 96+28/41 FLC 2+2 FAC 3+1 Others 3
Coventry C (Free on 7/8/2008) FL 78+13/21 FLC 2+1/2 FAC 6+1

MORRISON James Clark
Born: Darlington, 25 May 1986
Height: 5'10" **Weight:** 10.5
Club Honours: FAYC '04; Ch '08
International Honours: S: 5; E: Yth
Out of action until March with heel and knee injuries, Scottish international wide midfielder James bounced back in style as West Bromwich headed back to the Premiership. He became the 21st player to score for Albion during the season when he rifled in a brilliant opener in the 3-0 home League win over Leicester in the live televised game on Good Friday and immediately his enthusiastic presence seemed to inspire players around him. Unfortunately he was sidelined again towards the end of the campaign but said: "I will be raring to go next season.. I want to win back my place in the Scotland team".
Middlesbrough (From trainee on 14/7/2003) PL 40+27/3 FLC 3+1/1 FAC 6+7/1 Others 11+3/3
West Bromwich A (£1,500,000 on 9/8/2007) P/FL 59+17/8 FLC 2 FAC 5+2/2

MORRISON Michael Brian
Born: Bury St Edmunds, 3 March 1988
Height: 6'0" **Weight:** 12.0

Club Honours: Div 1 '09
International Honours: E: SP-8
Michael is a young defender who is now equally at home in the centre of defence or at right-back. In fact, he spent most of the Leicester campaign in the right-back slot, where he again proved solid and dependable. Although he only contributed the occasional strike, two of them opened the course to victory against Sheffield United and Scunthorpe. Michael looks set to become a mainstay of the Foxes' back four over the coming seasons.
Leicester C (Signed from Cambridge U on 4/7/2008) FL 62+4/5 FLC 4 FAC 3+2/1 Others 3

MORRISON Sean Joseph
Born: Plymouth, 8 January 1991
Height: 6'4" **Weight:** 14.0
The young central defender began the season as a regular member of the Swindon first team, scoring his first senior goal in the victory over Southampton during August. But after a loss of form and other more experienced players later limiting his appearances he spent a successful loan period at Southend. Sean arrived at Roots Hall in November under the emergency loan player rule when Southend were temporarily placed under a transfer embargo. His Southend career did not get off to a particularly auspicious start, being red carded for a professional foul within 31 minutes of his debut at Yeovil. However, suspension served he formed a very solid partnership with the experienced Adam Barrett and his commanding presence ensured that manager Steve Tilson requested a second month extension. Having performed very well it was no surprise that with some solid experience under his belt he was recalled to the County Ground at the end of his loan spell. Unfortunate to suffer a late season injury when receiving a kick to the leg in a reserve game during April, he is a player of whom much more is expected.
Swindon T (From trainee on 22/2/2008) FL 27+4/2 FLC 2 Others 2
Southend U (Loaned on 14/11/2009) FL 8

MORSY Samy (Sam) Sayed
Born: Wolverhampton, 10 September 1991
Height: 5'9" **Weight:** 12.0
Sam is a central midfield player with Port Vale. He was still an apprentice when he made his debut, for the last six minutes of a 4-0 victory over Lincoln in February. Tigerish in the tackle, he can also play at right-back and has a

promising future. At the end of the season his progress was rewarded with the 'Youth Player of the Year' award and he was offered his first professional contract.
Port Vale (Trainee) FL 0+1

MOSES Victor
Born: Lagos, Nigeria, 12 December 1990
Height: 5'10" **Weight:** 11.12
International Honours: E: Yth
Widely tipped to have a big future ahead of him, and watched by a number of clubs in the Premier league, it was only a matter of time before Victor moved on from Crystal Palace. The right-sided midfielder has been capped by England at youth level and was a regular in the Palace team, with a notable performance coming at the end of last year away at Reading, where he starred in a 4-2 win, claiming two of the goals himself. With several clubs rumoured to be interested in his signature, following a spell of six goals in eight games he was snapped up by Wigan in the January transfer window. A naturally gifted player who can play in a number of positions, but at his best playing on the wide left, he made his Premier League debut when coming off the bench in the away match at Sunderland and made his first start in the away match against Fulham. Appearing as a sub for most of the games, his biggest impact came when setting up a late winner in the Burnley match which went a long way in ensuring the club's top flight status. He netted his first goal for the club in the final home game of the season against Hull.
Crystal Palace (From trainee on 27/12/2007) FL 42+16/11 FLC 4 FAC 3+2 Others 1+1
Wigan Ath (Signed on 1/2/2010) PL 2+12/1

MOSS Darren Michael
Born: Wrexham, 24 May 1981
Height: 5'10" **Weight:** 11.6
International Honours: W: U21-4; Yth
After joining Morecambe in the summer, the former Crewe and Shrewsbury defender had a mixed season. Darren started it as first choice right-back but as the Shrimps conceded goals far too easily he lost his place in September and struggled to regain it. Found himself on the bench until the end of February, when he was back in for the suspended Laurence Wilson. Darren ended the season in the side, usually at left-back as Wilson was pushed forward into midfield, and looked extremely solid. The highlight of

his season was a stunning goal in a 1-0 victory over Dagenham that won him the 'Goal of the Season' trophy.
Chester C (From trainee on 14/7/1999) FL 33+9 FLC 1+1 FAC 4 Others 1
Shrewsbury T (Free on 24/7/2001) FL 84+13/10 FLC 1+1 FAC 4 Others 8/1
Crewe Alex (Free on 2/3/2005) FL 54+5/2 FLC 1 FAC 1 Others 2/1
Shrewsbury T (Free on 7/8/2007) FL 56+4/2 FLC 2 FAC 1 Others 6
Morecambe (Free on 2/7/2009) FL 13+3/1 FLC 1 Others 3

MOULT Louis Elliot
Born: Stoke-on-Trent, 14 May 1992
Height: 6'0" **Weight:** 13.5
After working his way up through the Stoke Academy and reserve team ranks, Louis was on the first team substitutes' bench on several occasions towards the end of the season. He had two late runs in the Carling Cup games at Leyton Orient and Portsmouth before making

his League debut as a substitute in a 1-1 draw at Burnley. The local lad will be looking to make even more of an impact in the near future.
Stoke C (From trainee on 22/3/2010) PL 0+1 FLC 0+2

MOUSINHO John Michael Lewis
Born: Isleworth, 30 April 1986
Height: 6'1" **Weight:** 12.7
After being something of a fringe player at times in the previous season, John was one of the key members of Wycombe's midfield, his 39 starts only bettered by captain Craig Woodman. With an all-action style, chasing down and tackling one minute, going on attacking runs the next, he came to embody the spirit needed in a relegation fight. Disappointingly, he scored only once, a close-in effort against Brighton in December. He also played many games at right-back, filling

John Mousinho

in admirably, and was rewarded with the offer of a further contract.
Brentford (Free from Notre Dame University, USA on 7/10/2005) FL 45+19/2 FLC 3 FAC 2 Others 2+1
Wycombe W (Free on 23/6/2008) FL 58+15/3 FLC 2 FAC 3 Others 1

MOUSSA-NYINZAPA Franck

Born: Brussels, Belgium, 24 July 1989
Height: 5'8" **Weight:** 10.8
International Honours: Belgium: Yth
Franck was in his fourth season at Southend, having made his debut as a 16-year-old in 2006. A skilful midfielder, capped at under-18 level by Belgium, Franck was the only Southend player to start all 53 matches. Although his expressed preference is central midfield, Franck became an automatic choice on the left and this season added scoring to his repertoire, netting a very useful six goals for the Shrimpers. Highly regarded at Roots Hall for his skill and industry, Franck was out of contract at the end of the season.
Southend U (From trainee on 8/3/2007) FL 74+16/7 FLC 5+1/1 FAC 3+2 Others 2
Wycombe W (Loaned on 17/10/2008) FL 7+2

MOUSSI Guy

Born: Bondy, France, 23 January 1985
Height: 6'2" **Weight:** 12.13
Guy is a French-born midfielder who operates just in front of Nottingham Forest's back four. He approaches the job with a minimum of fuss, linking play from defence and apparently never ruffled as he finds time to make a pass to a team-mate. In the excitement of scoring his first goal in England against Barnsley in the last minute to earn a 1-0 victory, he jumped into the crowd and was sent off as this was deemed a second bookable offence.
Nottingham F (Free from SCO Angers, France on 8/7/2008) FL 35+7/3 FLC 2 FAC 1

MOUYOKOLO Steven

Born: Melun, France, 24 January 1987
Height: 6'3" **Weight:** 13.5
Having fought off reported competition from Arsenal, Wigan and Bolton to conclude his move from Boulogne the previous January, the lanky defender made his eagerly awaited Premier League debut in the auspicious circumstances of Hull's opening day visit to Chelsea. A last-gasp defeat in a game when he played out of position at right-back promised much although, as well as settling in to his new surroundings, he appeared to struggle

to come to terms with the physical demands of the English game in the first half of the season. After being restored to centre-back against Wolverhampton in January, Steven became arguably Hull's most consistent performer throughout the second half of the term. His confidence boosted by a powerfully headed goal in the following game at the KC Stadium to earn a draw against Chelsea, the speedy Frenchman justifiably retained his place at the heart of the Tigers' defence for the rest of their campaign. He remained calm under increasing pressure and although City dropped down to the Championship, his many impressive displays were noted around the Premiership.
Hull C (Signed from Boulogne, France, ex Chateauroux, Gueugnon, on 1/7/2009) PL 19+2/1 FLC 1 FAC 1

MOXEY Dean William

Born: Exeter, 14 January 1986
Height: 5'11" **Weight:** 11.0
International Honours: E: SP-3
Dean's career has advanced at the gallop. Successive promotions from the Blue Square Premier and League Two with Exeter were followed by a jump into the Championship with Derby. He started at left-back ahead of Jay McEveley and held the position for the first half of the season. Then a few errors crept in and it was time for a rest. Dean is still learning at Championship level but time is on his side. He has a good left foot and enough pace to get forward. Experience will add poise.
Exeter C (From trainee on 5/7/2007) FL 41+2/4 FLC 0+1/1 FAC 1/1 Others 1
Derby Co (£300,000 on 26/6/2009) FL 27+3 FLC 1 FAC 3

MUAMBA Fabrice Ndala

Born: Kinshasa, DR Congo, 6 April 1988
Height: 6'1" **Weight:** 11.10
International Honours: E: U21-25; Yth
Fabrice really established himself as one of Bolton's pivotal performers in 2009-10 with a number of excellent displays at the heart of the midfield, particularly from the turn of the year onward. A no-frills type of player, one of those who rarely attract the plaudits, Fabrice is strong in the tackle and acts as a formidable protective barrier to the defence. That he appeared in all but two of Bolton's League games, starting 35, tells its own story and he is developing into a consistently effective player. He hit his first goal for the club, an enthusiastically celebrated strike in the 4-0 victory over Wigan having

previously gone 59 League games without scoring. In what was a considerable battle for midfield places, Fabrice proved himself to be first choice throughout the season.
Arsenal (From trainee on 8/4/2006) FLC 2
Birmingham C (£2,000,000 on 2/8/2006) P/FL 67+4/2 FLC 3+1 FAC 4
Bolton W (£5,000,000 + on 23/6/2008) PL 68+6/1 FLC 4 FAC 5

MUJANGI BIA Geoffrey

Born: Kinshasa, DR Congo, 12 August 1989
Height: 5'9" **Weight:** 11.3
International Honours: Belgium: 2; U21-6
Loaned from RSC Charleroi, he twice came on for Wolverhampton as a substitute, and his speed and willingness to shoot was encouraging. Geoffrey started the FA Cup replay at Crystal Palace but it was to be a disappointing night for him and the team. He gained invaluable experience by coming on against Chelsea, and he started the last away match, at Portsmouth. It was agreed that he would be loaned to Wolves again for the 2010-11 season.
Wolverhampton W (Loaned from RSC Charleroi, Belgium on 21/1/2010) PL 1+2 FAC 1+1

MUKENDI Vinny

Born: Manchester, 12 March 1992
Height: 6'6" **Weight:** 13.0
A Macclesfield second-year trainee, Vinny scored regularly for the youth and reserve teams last season, using his pace to good advantage. He became a regular member of the senior side from the end of March, scoring his first goal in the home win against Chesterfield in April. Vinny is highly regarded and was awarded his first professional contract for two years.
Macclesfield T (From trainee on 13/4/2010) FL 8+2/1

MULLIGAN Gary Thomas

Born: Dublin, 23 April 1985
Height: 6'1" **Weight:** 12.3
International Honours: RoI: Yth
First team places at Northampton have been scarce for striker Gary, despite netting several goals for the reserves, including a hat-trick. Gary was signed by Stuart Gray at the start of the season and made a handful of appearances but was handed only a few substitute appearances by the new management team. Was out of contract in the summer.
Wolverhampton W (From trainee on 9/7/2002) FL 0+1

Rushden & Diamonds (Loaned on 13/10/2004) FL 12+1/3
Sheffield U (Free on 6/7/2005) FLC 1+1
Port Vale (Loaned on 23/9/2005) FL 8+2/1 FAC 1 Others 1
Gillingham (Free on 31/1/2006) FL 74+33/15 FLC 1+2 FAC 4+3/1 Others 2+1/1
Northampton T (Free on 9/7/2009) FL 2+7 Others 3

MULLIGAN Nathan Michael
Born: Middlesbrough, 15 September 1986
Height: 5'10" **Weight:** 11.5
Nathan is a product of the Middlesbrough Academy and had drifted out of the professional game after a serious illness threatened to end his career. However, Steve Staunton showed faith in this talented young player by signing him from Northern League side Norton and Stockton Ancients. His skill soon shone through and he gave some classy displays on the right, delivering telling crosses. He scored his first Darlington goal with a neat header in the shock win at Rochdale in April, in the game that finally confirmed Darlington's relegation to the Blue Square Premier. Was out of contract at the end of June.
Darlington (Free from Norton Ancients & Stockton, ex trainee at Middlesbrough, on 29/10/2009) FL 10+6/1

MULLIN John Michael
Born: Bury, 11 August 1975
Height: 6'0" **Weight:** 11.10
A widely travelled and experienced Accrington central midfielder, John was out with an ankle injury for much of the season but was still a popular figure around the club. At his best a composed and intelligent player who holds the ball while looking for the right pass, he only made four appearances as the campaign drew to a close. Was out of contract in the summer.
Burnley (From trainee on 18/8/1992) FL 7+11/2 FAC 2
Sunderland (£40,000 + on 12/8/1995) P/FL 23+12/4 FLC 5+1 FAC 2+1
Preston NE (Loaned on 13/2/1998) FL 4+3 Others 1
Burnley (Loaned on 26/3/1998) FL 6
Burnley (Free on 20/7/1999) FL 38+39/8 FLC 2+1 FAC 5+1/1 Others 1
Rotherham U (£150,000 on 5/10/2001) FL 159+21/12 FLC 7+1 FAC 5/2 Others 2
Tranmere Rov (Free on 27/6/2006) FL 43+7/5 FLC 1 FAC 1+2 Others 1+1
Accrington Stanley (Free on 6/8/2008) FL 26+8 FLC 1 FAC 2 Others 1

MULLIN Paul
Born: Burnley, 16 March 1974
Height: 6'3" **Weight:** 14.6
Club Honours: FC '06
Accrington legend Paul left for Morecambe in August as the club's all-time record appearance holder, with over 400 outings in a Stanley shirt, and will always be remembered fondly at the Crown Ground. The experienced striker made an immediate impression at Morecambe with his ability to hold the ball up for others as well as score vital goals himself, including a header in the excellent 2-1 win over Notts County where he was marked during the game by Sol Campbell. Finishing the season with 12 goals, having linked up well with Phil Jevons, he was regularly praised by Sammy McIlroy throughout the season for his amazing fitness levels and seen as a great example to the youngsters.
Accrington Stanley (Signed from Radcliffe Borough, ex Accrington Stanley, Darwen, Trafford, Clitheroe, on 24/8/2000) FL 129/33 FLC 5/3 FAC 4/1 Others 3+1/1
Bradford C (Loaned on 20/3/2009) FL 5+1
Morecambe (Signed on 31/8/2009) FL 36+2/12 FAC 2 Others 2

MULLINS Hayden Ian
Born: Reading, 27 March 1979
Height: 6'0" **Weight:** 11.12
International Honours: E: U21-3
Ever reliable Hayden proved his worth to the Portsmouth crowd this season with a number of spirited performances in a variety of positions. As well as occupying his usual central midfield role, Hayden excelled in a more unfamiliar position at full-back. His energy, commitment and tough tackling made him a firm favourite at Fratton Park and many Blues' fans are hopeful his services will be retained for the forthcoming Championship campaign, during what is guaranteed to be an eventful summer on the south coast.
Crystal Palace (From trainee on 28/2/1997) FL 219+3/18 FLC 24/2 FAC 9 Others 2
West Ham U (£600,000 on 22/10/2003) P/FL 152+28/4 FLC 10 FAC 15+2/3 Others 6
Portsmouth (£1,000,000 on 26/1/2009) PL 30+5 FLC 2 FAC 4+2

MULLINS John (Johnny) Christopher
Born: Hampstead, 6 November 1985
Height: 5'11" **Weight:** 12.7
Despite a few niggly injuries, Johnny was a mainstay of the Stockport

Johnny Mullins

defence in a difficult season, switching between his preferred right-back spot and centre-half when circumstances required it. His only goal of the season was a finely placed header to give County the lead against Leeds at Edgeley Park, a game they eventually lost 4-2. With the departure of Michael Raynes to Scunthorpe in the January window, Johnny took over the captain's armband and, at the season's end, scooped all of the 'Player of the Year' awards.

Reading (From trainee on 17/12/2004)
Kidderminster Hrs (Loaned on 17/12/2004) FL 21/2
Mansfield T (Free on 5/6/2006) FL 81+5/4 FLC 3/1 FAC 5+1 Others 2
Stockport Co (Free on 9/7/2008) FL 67+2/4 FLC 1+1 FAC 6 Others 3

MULUMBU Youssuf

Born: Kinshasa, DR Congo, 25 January 1987
Height: 5'10" **Weight:** 10.3
International Honours: DR Congo: 8. France: U21-2; Yth
A strong, forceful, ball-winning central midfielder with a terrific engine, Youssuf scored an excellent first goal for West Bromwich in the televised 2-0 home League win over Ipswich in August. A month later he headed a goal in a comprehensive 5-0 win at Middlesbrough and four weeks after that bagged a real corker to seal a 3-1 home victory over Reading. Linking up superbly with Graham Dorrans, Chris Brunt, Robert Koren and others, he

certainly looked the part and although he missed several games during the second half of the season with a leg injury, he was around, and at his best, when promotion was confirmed. During the campaign Youssuf added to his collection of caps with the DR Congo.
West Bromwich A (Signed from Paris St Germain, France, via Amiens - loan, on 4/2/2009) P/FL 37+9/3 FLC 0+2 FAC 3+1

MURPHY Brian

Born: Waterford, 7 May 1983
Height: 6'0" **Weight:** 13.1
Club Honours: AMC '06
International Honours: RoI: U21-3; Yth
Brian signed for Ipswich in late 2009 once Bohemians' season had ended but had to wait until the January transfer window to finalise matters. He was due to take his place as a substitute at Leicester in January but damaged his knee ligaments in the warm-up and finally made his debut at Sheffield Wednesday, keeping a clean sheet that owed much to a point-blank save to deny Wednesday a goal. He commands his area and handles crosses well but would be disappointed with his kicking when under pressure.
Manchester C (From trainee on 13/5/2000. Freed during 2003 close season)
Peterborough U (Loaned on 2/5/2003) FL 1
Swansea C (Free from Waterford on 8/8/2003) FL 13 FLC 1 Others 4 (Freed

during 2006 close season)
Ipswich T (Signed from Bohemians, ex Shelbourne, on 10/1/2010) FL 16

MURPHY Daniel (Danny) Benjamin

Born: Chester, 18 March 1977
Height: 5'10" **Weight:** 11.0
Club Honours: FLC '01, '03; FAC '01; UEFAC '01; ESC '01; CS '01
International Honours: E: 9; U21-5; Yth; Sch
Once again a key motivator for the Fulham side, a captain inspiring by example, Danny's presence was sorely missed when he was not available. A competitive central midfielder, he enjoys good partnerships with both Dickson Etuhu and Chris Baird, often feeding off short passes to begin forward moves where his use of the ball is a crucial asset to the team. A tireless worker on and off the ball, he also chips in with his fair share of goals, including vital strikes against Basel and, with a superb individual goal, Manchester United. His captain's responsibility extends to taking penalties, where his calm manner is usually successful. His significant previous European experience was a vital factor in the club's run to the Europa League final.
Crewe Alex (From trainee on 21/3/1994) FL 110+24/27 FLC 7 FAC 7/4 Others 15+2/4
Liverpool (£1,500,000 + on 17/7/1997) PL 114+56/25 FLC 15+1/11 FAC 11+4/3 Others 38+10/5
Crewe Alex (Loaned on 12/2/1999) FL 16/1
Charlton Ath (£2,500,000 on 12/8/2004) PL 54+2/7 FLC 4+1/2 FAC 2+1/1
Tottenham H (£2,000,000 on 31/1/2006) PL 7+15/1 FLC 3 FAC 1 Others 2+1
Fulham (Signed on 31/8/2007) PL 91+5/15 FLC 2/1 FAC 7+2/2 Others 13/2

MURPHY Daryl

Born: Waterford, 15 March 1983
Height: 6'0" **Weight:** 12.13
Club Honours: Ch '07
International Honours: RoI: 9; U21-1
Restricted to three cup appearances in the first half of the campaign for Sunderland, the Republic of Ireland international enjoyed just five minutes of Premier League action before Christmas. Given three consecutive starts at the turn of the year, including two in the league, like goalkeeper Marton Fulop his final Sunderland appearance of the season came in the 7-2 hammering at Chelsea. Re-joining

Youssuf Mulumbu

his former boss Roy Keane on loan at Ipswich on 1st February, Daryl scored on his debut against Middlesbrough when he swept in David Healy's cross after just 23 seconds. He went on to score in the next two games, notched a double against Cardiff and the match-winner against Barnsley. In the Cardiff game he turned in Jack Colback's square ball and knocked in the rebound after David Marshall had blocked Owen Garvan's long-range effort. Indeed, but for Marshall's heroics he would have recorded a hat-trick. Is good in the air, leads the line well and can shoot with both feet.

Luton T *(Signed from Southend U, Waterford on 14/11/2000. Freed on 18/4/2002)*
Sunderland *(£100,000 from Waterford U on 2/6/2005) P/FL 60+50/14 FLC 5+4 FAC 4+1*
Sheffield Wed *(Loaned on 24/11/2005) FL 4*
Ipswich T *(Loaned on 1/2/2010) FL 18/6*

MURPHY Joseph (Joe)
Born: Dublin, 21 August 1981
Height: 6'2" **Weight:** 13.6
Club Honours: Div 1 '07
International Honours: RoI: 2; U21-14; Yth (UEFA-U16 '98)
Joe's fourth season as Scunthorpe's number one showed no sign of him losing his status as the club's first choice goalkeeper. He figured in 40 of the 46 games back in the Championship and was a consistent performer. Playing behind the division's worst defence, he was certainly kept busy and saved two penalties in the opening six League matches of the season. With excellent distribution backing up his reputation for being capable of pulling off stunning saves, Scunthorpe fans were delighted when their side's Championship survival triggered another year on his contract. Joe was also involved in the Republic of Ireland squad as back-up during the campaign.
Tranmere Rov *(From trainee on 5/7/1999) FL 61+2 FLC 8 FAC 3 Others 1*
West Bromwich A *(Signed on 17/7/2002) P/FL 3+2 FLC 1*
Walsall *(Loaned on 8/10/2004) FL 25 Others 2*
Sunderland *(Free on 11/8/2005)*
Walsall *(Loaned on 21/10/2005) FL 14 Others 2*
Scunthorpe U *(Free on 2/8/2006) FL 172 FLC 5 FAC 8 Others 10*

MURPHY Luke John
Born: Macclesfield, 21 October 1989
Height: 6'2" **Weight:** 11.7

Luke made his bow in the previous season after making the move from Crewe's youth team ranks and has now become a regular in the senior squad. Tall and intelligent, he provides a link between midfield and the front line. Still young, he has already made considerable progress at League level.
Crewe Alex *(From trainee on 23/5/2008) FL 27+14/4 FLC 1 FAC 2+1/1*

MURPHY Peter James
Born: Liverpool, 13 February 1990
Height: 6'0" **Weight:** 11.10
A young defender in his second year as a pro at Accrington after coming through the youth system, he was something of a squad player for much of this season but coped well when called upon. Peter can perform anywhere along the back four and also in midfield, being a ball-winner who always looks for the right pass.
Accrington Stanley *(From trainee on 8/8/2008) FL 8+7 FLC 1+1 FAC 1+1 Others 3+1*

MURPHY Peter Michael
Born: Dublin, 27 October 1980
Height: 5'11" **Weight:** 12.10
Club Honours: Div 2 '06
Ever since his arrival back in 2001, Peter has been a regular in the Carlisle line-up, whether in central defence, left-back or in midfield. This season, he more often than not found himself on the bench, particularly in the second half of the year. He remains under contract, however, and as the club's longest-serving player will be looking to regain a regular place in the side.
Blackburn Rov *(From trainee on 15/7/1998)*
Halifax T *(Loaned on 26/10/2000) FL 18+3/1 FAC 1 Others 2*
Carlisle U *(Free on 10/8/2001) FL 260+19/10 FLC 9+1/1 FAC 11 Others 22+1/2*

MURPHY Rhys Philip Elliot
Born: Shoreham, 6 November 1990
Height: 6'1" **Weight:** 12.0
International Honours: E: Yth
The young Arsenal striker joined Brentford on loan in November but found it difficult to adapt to life in League One and returned to his parent club after sustaining an injury. A fast and energetic player, who has thrived on half-chances in and around the box at youth and reserve team level, it was a disappointing time for him.
Arsenal *(From trainee on 2/7/2008)*
Brentford *(Loaned on 24/11/2009) FL 1+4 FAC 0+1*

MURRAY Glenn
Born: Maryport, 25 September 1983
Height: 6'2" **Weight:** 12.7
Club Honours: Div 2 '06
Blessed with a great touch and balance, Glenn divides opinion among Brighton supporters with his sometimes relaxed style. The situation was hardly helped early on by a hernia operation and an apparent desire to leave the club but he settled and turned in some outstanding performances, especially at Southampton in new manager Gus Poyet's first game, and at Wycombe, where he scored four times. Of his 14 goals, 12 were away from Withdean, a statistic that led to him netting an away supporters' award. Latterly used quite successfully as a lone striker, Glenn is undoubted talent but needs to improve a disciplinary record that brought two red cards and seven games spent on the sidelines through suspension.
Carlisle U *(Free from Barrow on 17/12/2004) FL 3+24/3 FLC 1 FAC 0+1 Others 1+6/1*
Stockport Co *(Loaned on 2/8/2006) FL 11/3*
Rochdale *(Signed on 20/10/2006) FL 50+4/25 FLC 2/1 FAC 3 Others 1*
Brighton & Hove A *(£300,000 on 25/1/2008) FL 63+13/32 FLC 3+1/1 FAC 4/2 Others 2*

MURRAY Paul
Born: Carlisle, 31 August 1976
Height: 5'9" **Weight:** 10.8
International Honours: E: B-1; U21-4; Yth
Experienced central midfield player, hard working and a good organiser, his best spell for Shrewsbury was in early season with some strong performances. Always looking to get an attack moving, when he played well, so did the team with good results including defeats of Crewe, Lincoln and Northampton in September. As the partnership of Terry Dunfield and Kevin McIntyre was preferred after the New Year, most of Paul's 29 appearances in League and Cup were in the first half of the season. Was out of contract at the end of June.
Carlisle U *(From trainee on 14/6/1994) FL 27+14/11 FLC 2 FAC 1 Others 6+1*
Queens Park Rgrs *(£300,000 on 8/3/1996) P/FL 115+25/7 FLC 8/1 FAC 9*
Southampton *(Free on 2/8/2001) PL 0+1*
Oldham Ath *(Free on 12/12/2001) FL 93+2/15 FLC 2 FAC 3 Others 4+1 (Freed during 2004 close season)*
Carlisle U *(Free from Beira Mar Aveira, Portugal on 8/5/2006) FL 14/1*
Gretna *(Free on 7/6/2007) SL 31+1/1 SC 2*
Shrewsbury T *(Free on 7/8/2008) FL 56+3/2 FLC 1 FAC 2 Others 3*

MURRAY Scott George
Born: Aberdeen, 26 May 1974
Height: 5'10" **Weight:** 11.0
Club Honours: AMC '03
International Honours: S: B-2
The vastly experienced right-winger signed for Yeovil upon his release from Bristol City and endured a frustrating season, making 28 appearances and scoring twice. Having spent more than a decade at Ashton Gate, he suffered a niggling injury in pre-season and lost his place to others. He reached two career milestones during the campaign, hitting 500 matches and 100 goals with a double against Brighton. That was a highlight of a mixed season for the Scottish winger. Was out of contract in the summer.
Aston Villa (£35,000 from Fraserburgh on 16/3/1994) PL 4
Bristol C (£150,000 on 12/12/1997) FL 193+31/46 FLC 10+3 FAC 13+1/7 Others 18+2/8
Reading (£650,000 on 9/7/2003) FL 25+9/5 FLC 3+1 FAC 2
Bristol C (£500,000 on 25/3/2004) FL 91+39/28 FLC 6 FAC 7+2/2 Others 7+3/1
Cheltenham T (Loaned on 15/9/2008) FL 12+1/2 FAC 3/1
Yeovil T (Free on 2/7/2009) FL 10+10/2 FLC 1 Others 1

MURTAGH Kieran Zac
Born: Wapping, 29 October 1988
Height: 6'2" **Weight:** 12.8
The elegant midfield player had a reasonable second season with Yeovil, almost doubling his total of career League games. The 21-year-old scored his first ever goal with a stunning long-range strike at Huddersfield and added further goals against Carlisle and Wycombe. His ability to hit long, accurate passes combined with a fearsome shot is excellent and he would have played far more for Yeovil were it not for the form of other loan signings in the team.
Yeovil T (Free from Fisher Ath, ex Charlton Ath trainee, on 3/7/2008) FL 29+24/3 FLC 2 FAC 2 Others 2

MURTY Graeme Stuart
Born: Saltburn, 13 November 1974
Height: 5'10" **Weight:** 11.10
Club Honours: Ch '06
International Honours: S: 4; B-1
After another season blighted by injury, Graeme was not retained by Southampton in the summer. This was a pity because although a veteran he still had the ability that made him a legend with Reading. The right-back continues to read the game well and makes the right pass, having made the

tackle. And, moreover, he could still knock over a dangerous cross. Alas, before August was out Graeme had damaged a medial ligament. He returned in November, looked good but then sustained an ankle injury that required a major operation. Meanwhile, he has been moonlighting on the BBC's Late Night Extra programme, to good effect.
York C (From trainee on 23/3/1993) FL 106+11/7 FLC 10/2 FAC 5+1 Others 6+2
Reading (£700,000 on 10/7/1998) P/FL 295+11/2 FLC 9 FAC 15+1 Others 6+2
Charlton Ath (Loaned on 6/1/2009) FL 8
Southampton (Free on 5/8/2009) FL 5+1 FLC 2 FAC 1

MUSTAFI Shkodran
Born: Bad Hersfeld, Germany, 17 April 1992
Height: 6'0" **Weight:** 11.7
International Honours: Germany: Yth
It was something of a coup for Everton's David Moyes to sign the German under-17 international from Hamburg in the summer and having been named as a substitute on a number of occasions, the centre-half made his Everton debut against BATE Borisov in the Europa Cup, when a reserve team was fielded with the Toffees having qualified.
Everton (Signed from SV Hamburg, Germany on 10/7/2009) Others 0+1

MUTCH Jordon James
Born: Derby, 2 December 1991
Height: 5'9" **Weight:** 10.3
International Honours: E: Yth
On loan from Birmingham, it was apparent from his first few minutes in a Hereford shirt that the midfielder was a quality performer with a range of passing as well as talent and composure on the ball. A cannonball 35-yard free kick at Northampton, which brought a follow-up goal after the ball was parried, gave an indication of his striking power during his stay at Edgar Street. Jordan's next loan came at the end of January when Doncaster were suffering injuries in midfield. A big well-made lad and still only 18 years of age, he made a scoring debut from the bench against Middlesbrough following a terrific strike from 30 yards. Used mainly as a substitute in the early part of his time at the club he started the last four games of the season and was well worth his place in the team. He played particularly well against Scunthorpe and scored when he stole in at the far post to slam a cross into the net. While at the club he was called up for England under-19s.
Birmingham C (From trainee on

5/5/2009) FLC 0+1
Hereford U (Loaned on 2/10/2009) FL 3 FAC 1 Others 1
Doncaster Rov (Loaned on 25/1/2010) FL 5+12/2

M'VOTO Jean-Yves
Born: Paris, France, 6 September 1988
Height: 6'4" **Weight:** 14.9
A tall centre-back, Jean-Yves was loaned to Southend for six months in August and featured in half a dozen games before a hip injury curtailed his run and necessitated his return to Sunderland. Shrimpers' manager Steve Tilson was sufficiently impressed to ask them to loan the player again when the transfer window reopened in January. Initially he looked out of form and ponderous, but improved considerably as the season came to a close.
Sunderland (Signed from Paris St Germain, France on 17/1/2008)
Southend U (Loaned on 7/8/2009) FL 15+2/1 FLC 2

MYHILL Glyn (Bo) Oliver
Born: Modesto, California, USA, 9 November 1982
Height: 6'3" **Weight:** 14.6
International Honours: W: 8; E: Yth
Still relatively young in goalkeeping terms, Bo began the season by becoming the 40th player to make 250 appearances for Hull and ended it just two games short of his 300th career outing. Having signed a new three-year contract with the Tigers in September, he added a World Cup appearance in Wales' win in Liechtenstein before suffering a medial knee ligaments in the closing stages of City's goalless draw with Portsmouth in October. After missing six Premier League games, Bo returned to join Hull's ultimately unsuccessful battle against relegation but not without enhancing his own admirable reputation. It was lifted to new heights in January at Tottenham with arguably the finest performance by a 'keeper in Premier League history and probably by a City goalie since the legendary Tony Norman, also at White Hart Lane, in 1981. Although the Tigers return to the Championship in 2010-11, it wouldn't be a surprise if Bo continued his career in the top flight.
Aston Villa (From trainee on 28/11/2000)
Bradford C (Loaned on 22/11/2002) FL 2
Macclesfield T (Loaned on 8/8/2003) FL 15 FLC 1
Stockport Co (Loaned on 22/11/2003) FL 2 Others 1
Hull C (£50,000 on 12/12/2003) P/FL 257 FLC 5 FAC 11 Others 4

N

[NANI] ALMEIDA DA CUNHA Luis Carlos
Born: Praia, Cape Verde, 17 November 1986
Height: 5'9" **Weight:** 10.7
Club Honours: CS '07; PL '08, '09; UEFACL '08; FLC '09, '10
International Honours: Portugal: 36; U21-10
Manchester United winger with an abundance of skill, Nani was on hand to open the scoring in the 2009 FA Community Shield against Chelsea at Wembley. United eventually lost on penalties after a 2–2 draw and Nani suffered a dislocated shoulder. Although the injury was expected to keep him out of the start of the season, he recovered in time play 17 minutes for Portugal against Liechtenstein and

started in United's opening Premier League match against Birmingham four days later. In that match, he provided an assist for Wayne Rooney's winning goal in the 34th minute, but was replaced by Ryan Giggs at half-time. With Ronaldo moving to Real Madrid in the close season, the pecking order for set-play duties intensified. Nani was quick to lay claim to the role when he scored his first Premiership goal of the season from a free kick at Wigan, the final goal of an emphatic 5-0 win. Sent off in the Premier League match against Aston Villa in February, he remained a regular throughout the campaign. Nani saved his best performance for the Champions League game against Bayern at Old Trafford in April. Despite his two goals, United went out on the away goals rule.
Manchester U (£15,000,000 from Sporting Lisbon, Portugal on 3/7/2007) PL 42+20/8 FLC 9/3 FAC 4/3 Others 25+6/3

NARDIELLO Daniel (Danny) Antony
Born: Coventry, 22 October 1982
Height: 5'11" **Weight:** 11.4
International Honours: W: 3; E: Yth; Sch
The striker has struggled with injuries for two seasons at Blackpool. He only participated in five League games throughout the season but did help the team secure a very late win against Watford when he played a part in both injury time goals, a game won 3-2. He went on loan to Bury and also to Oldham. Arriving at Bury in November, following a debut goal against Notts County, Danny went on to score a further three goals and his presence up front was sorely missed upon his return to the Seasiders in December to cover for injuries. In March he joined Oldham on loan and looked the business but after just two games an ankle injury meant he was off back down the M55 to Blackpool. A busy forward who looks to have goals a plenty in him, it must be hoped that he can stay on the pitch and clear of injury which seems to have dogged him for most of his career. Was out of contract in the summer.
Manchester U (From trainee on 1/11/1999) FLC 1+2 Others 0+1
Swansea C (Loaned on 24/10/2003) FL 3+1 Others 1/1
Barnsley (Loaned on 27/1/2004) FL 14+2/7
Barnsley (Free on 16/7/2004) FL 41+51/21 FLC 1+2 FAC 2+3 Others 4+1/3
Queens Park Rgrs (Free on 3/8/2007) FL 4+4
Barnsley (Loaned on 24/1/2008) FL 8+3/1 FAC 2
Blackpool (Free on 8/8/2008) FL 1+6 FLC 1/1 FAC 1
Hartlepool U (Loaned on 30/1/2009) FL 8+4/3
Bury (Loaned on 13/11/2009) FL 6/4
Oldham Ath (Loaned on 5/3/2010) FL 2

NASH Carlo James
Born: Bolton, 13 September 1973
Height: 6'5" **Weight:** 14.1
Club Honours: Div 1 '02
The great form and fitness of Tim Howard meant the sight of the former Manchester City goalkeeper warming the substitutes' bench was a regular feature at Everton last season. The veteran stopper was rewarded with one game, a match against BATE Borisov in the Europa League when, having qualified already, David Moyes rested most of the first team. With his contract up in the summer, his future was unclear.
Crystal Palace (£35,000 from Clitheroe

Nani

on 16/7/1996) FL 21 FLC 1 Others 3
Stockport Co (Free on 7/6/1998) FL 89
FLC 5 FAC 4
Manchester C (£100,000 on
12/1/2001) P/FL 37+1 FLC 2 FAC 1
Middlesbrough (£150,000 on
14/8/2003) PL 3 FLC 2
Preston NE (£175,000 on 24/3/2005)
FL 82 FLC 2 FAC 5 Others 5
Wigan Ath (£300,000 on 28/6/2007)
FLC 1
Stoke C (Loaned on 4/3/2008) FL 10
Everton (Signed on 1/9/2008) Others 1

NASRI Samir
Born: Marseille, France, 26 June 1987
Height: 5'10" **Weight:** 11.11
International Honours: France: 15;
U21-4; Yth
Samir had the misfortune to break a leg
in pre-season, so did not feature for
Arsenal until October. He is a skilful,
quick passer of the ball and can turn a
game with a flash of brilliance but, as
with most players of his ilk, he can be
inconsistent. When Cesc Fabregas was
sidelined with injury, Samir assumed the
central midfield playmaker role. He was
close to perfection when he played this
position against Porto in the Champions
League second round home leg as he
prompted and probed all night. He
capped his evening by slaloming

Samir Nasri

through the Porto defence to score a
memorable goal of genuine quality.
Given his ability, he should score more.
Samir appeared 26 times in the Premier
League, scoring twice, six times in the
Champions League where he added
three further goals and once each in the
FA and Carling Cups. He was
surprisingly left out of the French World
Cup squad.
Arsenal (£13,500,000 from Olympique
Marseille, France on 24/7/2008) PL
50+5/8 FLC 1 FAC 3+3 Others 16/4

NAUGHTON Kyle
Born: Sheffield, 11 November 1988
Height: 5'11" **Weight:** 11.7
International Honours: E: U21-6
Kyle was one of two Sheffield United
players who signed for Tottenham in
the summer of 2009. Whilst Kyle
Walker started the season on loan back
at United, the other Kyle stayed with
Spurs. However, his opportunities were
extremely limited and he made only one
full appearance in the Carling Cup
game at Doncaster, where he played at
right-back. He also made two brief
appearances from the bench and was
utilised at right-back, where his instincts
are to go forward. The England under-
21 international, who played in four
games at that level during the

campaign, then became a transfer
deadline signing for Middlesbrough as
Gordon Strachan looked to inject some
pace into the club's backline. Having
signed a loan deal till the end of the
season, he immediately went into the
team at right-back, with Justin Hoyte
moving over to the left. In March his
lack of match fitness caught up with
him a little and Strachan took him out
of the firing line for a few games, but in
April he was recalled and with both full-
backs given a licence to get forward
more, a 1-0 home win over Sheffield
Wednesday, was his best game yet.
Unlucky not to get on the score-sheet,
the pacy defender certainly impressed
the Boro fans.
Sheffield U (From trainee on
14/3/2007) FL 39+1/1 FLC 0+3/1 FAC
3+1/1 Others 3
Gretna (Loaned on 15/1/2008) SL 18
SC 1
Tottenham H (Signed on 22/7/2009) PL
0+1 FLC 1 FAC 0+1
Middlesbrough (Loaned on 1/2/2010)
FL 12+3

NAVARRO Alan Edward
Born: Liverpool, 31 May 1981
Height: 5'9" **Weight:** 12.6
Club Honours: AMC '08; Div 2 '08
Although Alan got off to a slow start
at Brighton after being released by MK
Dons and was left out for a
considerable spell, he went on to
prove his worth in a holding role in
front of the back four, winning over
the Withdean fans at the same time.
The hard-working midfielder
established himself following the
arrival of Gus Poyet as manager,
playing in an understated manner but
usually improving the team with his
presence. A 'player's player', Alan
always looks to make a tackle or to
take the ball from his defenders to
feed it forward.
Liverpool (From trainee on 27/4/1999)
Crewe Alex (Loaned on 22/3/2001) FL
5+3/1
Crewe Alex (Loaned on 9/8/2001) FL 7
FLC 2
Tranmere Rov (£225,000 on
9/11/2001) FL 35+10/1 FAC 4+2/1
Others 0+1 (Freed on 13/5/2005)
Chester C (Loaned on 20/8/2004) FL 3
FLC 1
Macclesfield T (Loaned on
16/12/2004) FL 11/1
Macclesfield T (Free from Accrington
Stanley on 11/10/2005) FL 55+4/2 FLC 1
FAC 6 Others 5
MK Dons (Free on 10/8/2007) FL
70+7/4 FLC 3 FAC 2 Others 6+1
Brighton & Hove A (Free on 1/8/2009)
FL 31+5 FLC 1 FAC 2+1 Others 1

NAYLOR Richard Alan
Born: Leeds, 28 February 1977
Height: 6'1" **Weight:** 13.7
Richard, who had a successful loan spell with Leeds from Ipswich the previous season, joined permanently in July but missed the start of the season with a back injury that required an operation. Even when he returned, he had to bide his time on the bench before making his first appearance at the end of September against Carlisle. After four successive defeats, Richard rallied his troops by scoring both goals in a crucial 2-1 win at Yeovil in April. Five games later the boot was on the other foot as he headed into his own net at Charlton.
Ipswich T (From trainee on 10/7/1995) P/FL 232+42/37 FLC 13+10/1 FAC 8+6/1 Others 7+6/1
Millwall (Loaned on 29/1/2002) FL 2+1
Barnsley (Loaned on 4/3/2002) FL 7+1
Leeds U (Free on 15/1/2009) FL 51/3 FAC 3 Others 7

NAYSMITH Gary Andrew
Born: Edinburgh, 16 November 1978
Height: 5'7" **Weight:** 11.8
Club Honours: SC '98
International Honours: S: 46; B-1; U21-22; Sch
Gary had a very frustrating season. A cruciate ligament injury the previous season sidelined him until autumn and his return for Sheffield United was delayed further by injuries picked up while playing in the reserves. He made his first appearance of the season one year and four days after his last one. Playing on the left in the final two games he looked as if he had never been away, performing with assurance and confidence.
Heart of Midlothian (Signed from Whitehill Welfare on 17/6/1996) SL 92+5/3 SLC 5/1 SC 10 Others 7/1
Everton (£1,750,000 on 20/10/2000) PL 113+21/6 FLC 6+1/1 FAC 11+3
Sheffield U (£1,000,000 on 10/7/2007) FL 77+2 FLC 3 FAC 6

N'DIAYE Alassane
Born: Montbeliard, France, 25 February 1990
Height: 6'4" **Weight:** 14.2
Signing professional terms with Crystal Palace in June, the tall young French central midfield player was promoted by Neil Warnock after arriving at Palace during the previous season and playing for the reserves in a defensive or offensive central role. He proved to have a good knack of getting forward at the right time to support the attack, and weighed in with his first goal in September, a header that was good enough to give Palace an away win over

West Bromwich. Alassane could be a bit more assertive when in possession but shows great promise for the future.
Crystal Palace (Free from Toulouse, France on 7/8/2009) FL 12+14/3 FLC 2 FAC 1

NEAL Christopher (Chris)
Michael
Born: St Albans, 23 October 1985
Height: 6'2" **Weight:** 12.4
A young goalkeeper signed from Preston, he had an assured debut in the opening day 3-1 win against Burton and went on to save a penalty and a point in the 2-2 draw at Barnet a week later. Opportunities to gain much needed League experience were hampered by a groin injury and then a broken finger. As a result, Shrewsbury signed David Button on loan from Tottenham and his good form meant that Chris was confined to the bench, making just ten starts during the season.
Preston NE (From trainee on 23/12/2004) FL 0+1
Shrewsbury T (Loaned on 21/9/2006) Others 1
Shrewsbury T (Free on 2/7/2009) FL 7 FLC 1 FAC 1 Others 1

NEAL Lewis Ryan
Born: Leicester, 14 July 1981
Height: 6'0" **Weight:** 11.2
A left-sided midfield player with a fine left foot and the ability to go past people that turns him into an out-and-out left-winger, Lewis signed for Shrewsbury in the close season after a short-term deal at Carlisle ended. A pre-season ankle sprain delayed his debut until early September against Bradford. His best spell was in October when he scored his two goals, against Darlington in the 2-1 reverse and in the 3-1 win against Aldershot. He had a season that split opinions with Shrews' followers and did not consistently make the hoped for impact.
Stoke C (From juniors on 17/7/1998) FL 29+41/2 FLC 2+1 FAC 3+3 Others 1+2/1
Preston NE (Signed on 3/8/2005) FL 24+41/5 FLC 1 FAC 5+2
Notts Co (Loaned on 31/10/2008) FL 4 FAC 2
Carlisle U (Free on 31/1/2009) FL 15+1/2
Shrewsbury T (Free on 2/7/2009) FL 21+8/2 FAC 1 Others 1

NEILL Lucas Edward
Born: Sydney, Australia, 9 March 1978
Height: 6'1" **Weight:** 12.0
Club Honours: Div 2 '01
International Honours: Australia: 53; U23-13; Yth

The captain of Australia joined Everton on a one-year deal from West Ham in September, but his spell at Goodison lasted just four months before he moved on to Galatasaray. A versatile defender, who was used either at right-back or in the middle of the Toffees' backline, Lucas' time at Everton was hampered by being ineligible for the Europa League, but he did make a sound impression when fully fit with his combative and committed style.
Millwall (Free from Australian Academy of Sport on 13/11/1995) FL 124+28/13 FLC 6+1 FAC 4 Others 11+1
Blackburn Rov (£1,000,000 on 7/9/2001) PL 184+4/5 FLC 12/1 FAC 17/1 Others 10/1
West Ham U (£1,500,000 on 23/1/2007) PL 79/1 FLC 5 FAC 5
Everton (Free on 17/9/2009) PL 10+2 FLC 1+1 FAC 1

NEILSON Robert (Robbie)
Born: Paisley, 19 June 1980
Height: 5'8" **Weight:** 11.0
Club Honours: SC '06
International Honours: S: 1; U21-1
Following his move south of the border, the experienced right-back took time to settle into English football with Leicester. Robbie did, however, enjoy the distinction of becoming the 1,000th different first-class player – a number amassed over more than a century of League football.
Heart of Midlothian (From Glasgow Rangers BC on 25/10/1996) SL 189+11/1 SLC 13+1 SC 15+4 Others 14+2/1
Cowdenbeath (Loaned on 22/12/1999) SL 8
Queen of the South (Loaned on 27/8/2002) SL 13 SLC 2 Others 2
Leicester C (Free on 1/7/2009) FL 19 FLC 1 FAC 1

NEILSON Scott Steven
Born: Enfield, 15 May 1987
Height: 6'0" **Weight:** 12.11
Former plumber Scott was one of several non-League players to join Bradford at the start of the season. The right-winger signed from Cambridge City as a direct replacement for Oldham-bound Joe Colbeck. He scored on his first start with a deflected goal to complete a comeback win at Rochdale in the Johnstone's Paint Trophy. On Peter Taylor's arrival as manager, Scott returned to Cambridge, this time to United for a loan spell, and helped them pull away from the Blue Square Premier relegation zone.
Bradford C (Signed from Cambridge C, ex Hertford T, Ware, on 28/8/2009) FL 18+5/1 FAC 1 Others 4/1

NELSEN Ryan William
Born: Christchurch, New Zealand, 18 October 1977
Height: 6'1" **Weight:** 14.0
International Honours: New Zealand: 41; U23-2
Blackburn's captain had a season in which injury punctuated his appearances. A knee injury suffered in the final pre-season game with Dundee United kept him out of the season opener and when he returned at Sunderland a recurrence of the problem forced him to limp off at half-time. It was the end of October before he returned at Peterborough in the Carling Cup but from then on he was quickly back to his best. Always the man to take the responsibility of getting under the ball, Ryan is a formidable opponent in the air and has a rare ability to judge the flight and bounce of high balls. His playing time was further disrupted by a severe calf injury suffered against Bolton in February which kept him out for six weeks. However, he returned with a month of the season left, proving his fitness to lead New Zealand at the

World Cup finals. For a man who had only one Premier League goal to his credit, four goals were a crucial contribution to a side that could not score. They came from set pieces, starting with a vital one in the home game against Portsmouth.
Blackburn Rov (Free from DC United, USA on 10/1/2005) PL 140+3/5 FLC 13+1 FAC 11+2 Others 7

NELSON Michael John
Born: Gateshead, 28 March 1980
Height: 6'2" **Weight:** 13.12
Club Honours: Div 1 '10
The former Hartlepool captain arrived at Carrow Road in July to bring strength and resolve to the Norwich defence which some observers said had been missing since Malky Mackay's departure. It was not until the autumn that Michael established himself in the City side and even then an injury halted his run of games, but from mid-December onwards he was a virtual ever-present. Powerful in the air and strong in the challenge he never allows a striker an easy ride, being prepared to

throw his body into a block or tackle. His distribution improved as he settled into the team and he scored a contender for Norwich 'Goal of the Season' with an acrobatic scissor-kick on his return to Hartlepool. He also netted City's promotion clinching effort at Charlton and Championship clincher against Gillingham seven days later.
Bury (Free from Bishop Auckland on 22/3/2001) FL 68+4/8 FLC 4 FAC 3 Others 5
Hartlepool U (£70,000 on 10/7/2003) FL 255+4/14 FLC 13 FAC 20/2 Others 14
Norwich C (Free on 2/7/2009) FL 28+3/3 FAC 2 Others 3

NEVILLE Gary Alexander
Born: Bury, 18 February 1975
Height: 5'11" **Weight:** 12.8
Club Honours: FAYC '92; PL '96, '97, '99, '00, '01, '03, '07, '09; FAC '96, '99, '04; CS '96; UEFACL '99; FLC '06, '09, '10
International Honours: E: 85; Yth (UEFA-U18 '93)
Veteran Manchester United full-back, who is equally effective as a central defender, Gary's season was more about sporadic appearances rather than a regular role in the team. Having started the Premier League campaign as a substitute in the 1-0 reverse at Burnley in August, in October he was sent off for a tackle on Adam Hammill in United's 2-0 win at Barnsley in the Carling Cup. He played in an unfamiliar role at centre-back due to a long-term injury to Rio Ferdinand and various minor injuries to Nemanja Vidic and Jonny Evans but was back to his best in his familiar right-back position as the season reached its exciting climax. Was out of contract at the end of June.
Manchester U (From trainee on 29/1/1993) PL 377+20/5 FLC 22+2 FAC 44+3 Others 120+10/2

NEVILLE Philip (Phil) John
Born: Bury, 21 January 1977
Height: 5'11" **Weight:** 12.0
Club Honours: FAYC '95; PL '96, '97, '99, '00, '01, '03; FAC '96, '99, '04: CS '96, '97, '03; UEFACL '99
International Honours: E: 59; B-1; U21-7; Yth; Sch
Despite being injured for three months up to Christmas, the former Manchester United player continued to set the highest standards as Everton's club captain, both on and off the pitch. The England international started the season either in a central defensive or midfield role until a knee injury sustained at Fulham in September sidelined him for more than three months. On coming back the skipper

Ryan Nelsen

returned to his usual right-back berth and it was no coincidence that this coincided with a change in fortunes for the Toffees. A neat and tidy tackler who uses the ball simply but effectively, he is a perfect role model both on and off the pitch. A charity run in partnership with his wife has raised more than £20-million for a children's hospital.
Manchester U *(From trainee on 1/6/1994) PL 210+53/5 FLC 16+1 FAC 25+6/1 Others 50+25/2*
Everton *(£3,500,000 on 4/8/2005) PL 164+2/3 FLC 8+1 FAC 14 Others 18*

Erik Nevland

NEVLAND Erik
Born: Stavanger, Norway, 10 November 1977
Height: 5'10" **Weight:** 11.9
International Honours: Norway: 8; B-2; U21-2; Youth
Fulham's Norwegian striker was again on the fringes of first team action but always gave a committed performance when called upon, linking particularly well with Bobby Zamora. His opportunist finishing in finding the right penalty-box positions was typified in his four goals, most notably at Accrington, where his early strike helped calm nerves in a tricky Cup tie and at Everton, where he latched on to a poor back pass to finish neatly. Although he rarely started successive games, Erik was often used as substitute, his hustling style harassing tired opponents in the latter stages of games. Out of contract in the summer, the popular player was expected to return to his home country.
Manchester U *(Signed from Viking*

Stavanger, Norway on 15/7/1997) PL 0+1 FLC 0+2/1 FAC 2+1 (Transferred to Viking Stavanger, No on 6/1/2000)
Fulham *(£1,800,000 from Groningen, Holland on 31/1/2008) PL 18+34/9 FLC 0+2 FAC 3+1/1 Others 2+7*

NEWEY Thomas (Tom) William
Born: Huddersfield, 31 October 1982
Height: 5'10" **Weight:** 10.6
Tom provided a solid performance in his Bury debut against arch rivals Rochdale and covered well for the injuries to fellow full-backs Paul Scott and Dave Buchanan. After their full recovery towards the end of the season, however, Tom found himself as third choice full-back, but was consistently reliable whenever Bury called upon his services.
Leeds U *(From trainee on 4/8/2000)*
Cambridge U *(Loaned on 14/2/2003) FL 6 Others 1*
Darlington *(Loaned on 27/3/2003) FL 7/1*
Leyton Orient *(Free on 8/8/2003) FL 34+20/3 FLC 1+1 FAC 2+2 Others 3*
Cambridge U *(Free on 21/1/2005) FL 15+1*
Grimsby T *(Free on 28/7/2005) FL 142+5/3 FLC 5/1 FAC 6 Others 12*
Rochdale *(Loaned on 2/8/2006) FL 1+1 1 Others 3*
Bury *(Free on 28/8/2009) FL 29+3 FAC 1 Others 3*

NGALA Bondz Bondzanga
Born: Newham, 3 October 1989
Height: 6'0" **Weight:** 12.3
The teenage central defender began the season with West Ham as reserve team captain. He was on the fringe of the first team and made his senior debut in October when coming on as a substitute in a Carling Cup tie at Bolton, before being loaned to Championship side Scunthorpe in November. Opportunities were hard to come by at Glanford Park and he made just two substitute appearances at centre-half as the Iron lost heavily at Blackpool and Watford. In March, Plymouth finally completed the loan signing of Bondz and the powerful central centre-back made his debut against Ipswich and impressed head coach Paul Mariner with a mature performance. He was an ever-present for the remainder of the campaign and built up a useful defensive partnership with fellow youngster Reda Johnson. Was out of contract in the summer.
West Ham U *(From trainee on 26/2/2008) FLC 0+1*
MK Dons *(Loaned on 14/11/2008) FL 1+2*
Scunthorpe U *(Loaned on 6/11/2009) FL 0+2*
Plymouth Arg *(Loaned on 18/3/2010) FL 9*

N'GOG David
Born: Paris, France, 1 April 1989
Height: 6'3" **Weight:** 12.6
International Honours: France: U21-12; Yth
David is a young French striker of Cameroon descent. In his second season with Liverpool, he played in more games – 37 with 19 as a substitute – than expected. He scored eight goals and was Liverpool's 'Young Player of the Year', although his only rival for that accolade was left-back Emiliano Insua. His first goal of the season came in the final minute of a 4-0 victory over Stoke and his second was the winner in a scrappy 1-0 Carling Cup victory over Leeds. His most memorable goal came in stoppage time to clinch a vital 2-0 victory over champions Manchester United and although he scored the only goal in the Champions League away match against Debrecen of Hungary, the result was not enough to ensure continued participation. He courted controversy in the home match against Birmingham when, after scoring the first goal, he earned a dubious penalty, enabling Steven Gerrard to salvage a 2-2 draw from the spot. By the end of the season David tired and it was surprising

Bondz Ngala

that he was often preferred to Dirk Kuyt in the striker's role. During the season, he turned down an invitation to play for Cameroon in the 2010 African Cup of Nations.

Liverpool *(£1,500,000 from Paris St Germain, Francis on 30/7/2008) PL 12+26/7 FLC 4/1 FAC 1+1 Others 6+6/3*

N'GUESSAN Diombo (Dany)

Born: Paris, France, 11 August 1987
Height: 6'1" **Weight:** 12.3

Dany is a powerful young winger who can also operate as a striker. He made a scoring debut for Leicester from the bench in the seasonal opener against Swansea and chipped in with further occasional strikes as the campaign unfolded. As a youngster making a step up of two divisions from Lincoln, he understandably spent most of his time on the bench but he can be expected to make more of an impact during the seasons ahead.

Glasgow Rgrs *(Signed from Auxerre, France on 7/7/2005)*
Boston U *(Loaned on 19/8/2006) FL 13+10/5 FLC 1 FAC 1 Others 0+1*
Lincoln C *(Free on 24/1/2007) FL 70+21/15 FLC 2 FAC 3+1/1 Others 1+1*
Leicester C *(Signed on 2/7/2009) FL 16+11/3 FLC 2/1 FAC 1+1/2 Others 0+1*

NICHOLAS Andrew (Andy) Peter

Born: Liverpool, 10 October 1983
Height: 6'2" **Weight:** 12.8

Shortly after Ronnie Moore arrived as Rotherham's manager, Andy was given his chance at left-back and had a nine-game run. However, he then lost his place after a 2-0 defeat at Shrewsbury, when he was substituted, and never got back in the team, going out eventually on loan to Blue Square Premier Mansfield. Was out of contract in the summer.

Swindon T *(From trainee at Liverpool on 21/7/2003) FL 105+21/4 FLC 2/1 FAC 5 Others 7+1/1*
Chester C *(Loaned on 18/3/2005) FL 5*
Rotherham U *(Free on 24/8/2008) FL 26 FLC 3+1 FAC 4 Others 3*

NICHOLLS Alexander (Alex)

Born: Stourbridge, 9 December 1987
Height: 5'10" **Weight:** 11.0

A frustrating season for Alex at Walsall as the signing of Steve Jones meant he lost his place on the right wing, although he was a virtual ever-present in the squad. Highlights of his season included scoring the winner in the fight-back at Wycombe from a narrow angle. His best performance was at home to

Brentford, scoring the first with a guided side-foot shot before making the second with a perfect cross. Towards the end of the season Alex played in his preferred role of centre-forward, although a lack of physical presence gave him little chance in the air.

Walsall *(From trainee on 3/7/2006) FL 69+40/12 FLC 2+1/1 FAC 2+7/1 Others 2+4/1*

NICHOLSON Barry

Born: Dumfries, 24 August 1978
Height: 5'7" **Weight:** 9.2
International Honours: S: 3; U21-7

Barry demonstrated his passing abilities in Preston's first five games of the season, scoring against Morecambe in the Carling Cup, before suffering a serious leg fracture against Peterborough that effectively ended his season at first team level in August. Able to ghost into the box and a good finisher, he combines this with excellent mobility and he breaks down many opposition attacks with his disruptive presence. He made a surprise return in the final game of the season but only lasted 14 minutes before reopening the fracture. It is hoped he can return to his former influential position in the season ahead.

Glasgow Rgrs *(From juniors on 3/7/1995) SL 3+5 SLC 1 Others 0+2*
Dunfermline Ath *(Signed on 2/8/2000) SL 172+2/23 SLC 12/2 SC 21/6 Others 1*
Aberdeen *(£250,000 on 7/6/2005) SL 101+1/13 SLC 7/4 SC 9/4 Others 6*
Preston NE *(Free on 3/7/2008) FL 30+11/3 FLC 2/1 FAC 0+1 Others 1+1*

NICHOLSON Kevin John

Born: Derby, 2 October 1980
Height: 5'8" **Weight:** 11.5
International Honours: E: Yth; Sch

Kevin, a cultured left-back, has tremendous ball-playing qualities, superb crossing ability and an extremely long throw that makes him a constant threat from set pieces, clearly seen in Torquay's televised comeback to obtain a 2-2 draw at future champions Notts County. Not the fastest defender, he can look vulnerable, particularly if lacking defensive cover from his winger. This led to his being dropped in the middle of the season, but he battled his way back into favour and showed that he can defend as he was part of the back line that smashed a club record with seven consecutive clean sheets.

Sheffield Wed *(From trainee on 22/10/1997) FL 0+1*
Northampton T *(Free on 26/1/2001) FL 6+1*
Notts Co *(Free on 8/3/2001) FL*

74+21/3 FLC 4+1 FAC 2+2/1 Others 4
(Freed during 2004 close season)
Torquay U *(Free from Forest Green Rov, ex Scarborough, on 3/8/2007) FL 23+4 FLC 1 FAC 1+2 Others 2*

NIELSEN Gunnar

Born: Torshavn, Faroe Islands, 7 October 1986
Height: 6'4" **Weight:** 13.7
International Honours: Faroe Islands: 2; U21-10

Gunnar is a goalkeeper from the Faroe Islands who followed manager Mark Hughes from Blackburn to Manchester City. He was not expected to challenge for a first team place but made a surprise Premiership debut in April as a substitute for the injured Shay Given in the 0-0 draw at Arsenal. However, manager Robert Mancini chose not to risk playing him in the three remaining Premiership games with fourth place and Champions League qualification at stake and signed Marton Fulop on an emergency loan. Gunnar made his international debut for the Faroes in March.

Blackburn Rov *(Signed from BK Frem, Denmark, ex HB Torshavn, on 2/7/2007)*
Manchester C *(Signed on 2/1/2009) PL 0+1*

NIMANI Frederic

Born: Marseille, France, 8 October 1988
Height: 6'3" **Weight:** 13.10
International Honours: France: U21-6

Frederic was Brian Laws' first signing, joining Burnley in January on a five-month loan from AS Monaco. Much was made of his potential but two brief substitute appearances at Bolton and Aston Villa showed little more than nuisance value up front by virtue of his size. After the Villa game he never even made the bench, and he left at the end of the season having made little impression beyond reserve level.

Burnley *(Loaned from AS Monaco, France, ex Lorient - loan, Sedan - loan, on 22/1/2010) PL 0+2*

NIMELY-TCHUIMENI Alex

Born: Monrovia, Liberia, 11 May 1991
Height: 5'11" **Weight:** 11.4
International Honours: Liberia: Yth. E: Yth

The Liberian-born striker is a product of the Manchester City Academy who made his Premiership debut as a substitute at Burnley in April. Although he had previously played for Liberia's youth teams, he chose to represent his adopted country and was called up for the 2009 FIFA under-20 World Cup in Egypt, where England failed to qualify

from their group.
Manchester C (From trainee on 2/7/2008) PL 0+1

Derek Niven

NIVEN Derek Dunbar
Born: Falkirk, 12 December 1983
Height: 6'1" **Weight:** 11.2
Chesterfield's Derek had the honour of scoring the last ever goal at Saltergate, seconds from the end of the 2-1 win over Bournemouth in May. His personal game improved but his season was mixed, as the club struggled to find the right blend in central midfield. Despite never really being assured of a starting place, his commitment, tenacity and vibrant passion for the game remained constant.
Raith Rov (From juniors at Stenhousemuir on 10/7/2000) SL 0+1
Bolton W (Signed on 29/11/2001)
Chesterfield (Free on 12/12/2003) FL 234+21/17 FLC 7+2/2 FAC 5+2 Others 7+1/1

NOBLE Mark James
Born: West Ham, 8 May 1987
Height: 5'11" **Weight:** 12.0
International Honours: E: U21-20; Yth
Mark is the longest-serving player at West Ham, although he is only 22. The midfielder is a local lad and wears his heart on his sleeve. He started the season with a flourish by scoring one goal at Wolverhampton and setting up another. Mark is always prepared to

run, hustle and put in important tackles. During the year, a stomach bug and some niggling injuries saw him miss vital games but he was back to his best towards the end of the campaign with terrier-like tackling and clever passing. At Everton he hit the bar and was unlucky not to score at Fulham, where he also laid on a goal for Carlton Cole.
West Ham U (From trainee on 1/7/2004) P/FL 102+13/10 FLC 4+4 FAC 10/3 Others 0+3
Hull C (Loaned on 10/2/2006) FL 4+1
Ipswich T (Loaned on 18/8/2006) FL 12+1/1

NOBLE Ryan Andrew
Born: Sunderland, 6 November 1991
Height: 5'11" **Weight:** 11.0
International Honours: E: Yth
A prolific striker at youth and reserve level, the Sunderland youngster made his debut and only senior appearance as a 71st-minute substitute in the FA Cup third round against Blue Square Premier Barrow, going close three times in his brief cameo. An unused sub in four Premier League games, Ryan had a spell on loan at Watford but was not used despite making the Championship side's bench half a dozen times. Top scorer for Sunderland under-18s and reserves, he was the Barclays Premier Reserve League North's top scorer with ten goals from seven starts, plus six as sub. In total, including friendlies, Ryan scored 46 times. At one point, he hit three hat-tricks in a month, culminating with one in the FA Youth Cup at Hillsborough.
Sunderland (From trainee on 20/7/2009) FAC 0+1

NOBLE-LAZARUS Reuben Courtney
Born: Huddersfield, 16 August 1993
Height: 5'11" **Weight:** 13.5
Reuben spent most of the season starring in Barnsley's under-18 team but, as the season came towards an end he again found himself on the first team bench on a number of occasions. Still a 16-year-old, he made a couple of appearances and, in limited time on the field, again showed glimpses of his undoubted talent as a striker.
Barnsley (Trainee) FL 0+4

NOLAN Edward (Eddie) William
Born: Waterford, 5 August 1988
Height: 6'0" **Weight:** 13.5
International Honours: RoI: 3; U21-13
Signed as a centre-half for the future in 2009, Eddie has appeared most often as cover for Callum Davidson in

Preston's problematic left-back position. Fourteen of his 18 games last season were there, but he also made one appearance in his favoured position and three at right-back. Still developing as a mobile defender who likes to support the attack, he is a regular member of the Republic of Ireland squad so it was something of a surprise when he rejoined former mentor Alan Irvine on loan at Sheffield Wednesday for the rest of the season in February. From thereon, Eddie played in every game at right-back and looked comfortable despite coming into a struggling side. The highlight of his stay was his first ever, and so far only, goal in his career, at home against Watford. He advanced with the ball and beat two defenders before slotting the ball past the 'keeper in a vital win. His future looks promising as he can play in either full-back positions and also in central defence.
Blackburn Rov (From trainee on 12/9/2005) Others 0+1
Stockport Co (Loaned on 16/3/2007) FL 2+2
Hartlepool U (Loaned on 22/11/2007) FL 11 FAC 1
Preston NE (£100,000 on 7/10/2008) FL 33+7 FLC 2 FAC 1+1 Others 2
Sheffield Wed (Loaned on 19/2/2010) FL 14/1

Kevin Nolan

309

NOLAN Kevin Anthony Jance
Born: Liverpool, 24 June 1982
Height: 6'0" **Weight:** 14.0
Club Honours: Ch '10
International Honours: E; U21-1; Yth
After an unimpressive first few months during Newcastle's relegation season, Kevin stayed on Tyneside and his outstanding form in midfield made a major contribution to the club bouncing straight back into the Premiership. Highly influential through his strong and forceful play, coupled with his experienced reading of the game, in March he was chosen as the Four Four Two Championship 'Player of the Year' and was named best player in the Football League by Match Magazine, as well as being selected for the PFA Championship 'Team of the Season'. He scored in pre-season friendlies against Darlington and Huddersfield to set down a marker that his drought of the previous season was over and continued his scoring form into the Championship, ending the season as joint top scorer. This included a first career hat-trick at Ipswich in September. He also captained the side when Nicky Butt and Alan Smith were absent.
Bolton W (From trainee on 22/1/2000) P/FL 257+39/40 FLC 10+5/4 FAC 13+7/4 Others 11+3/2
Newcastle U (£4,000,000 on 30/1/2009) P/FL 54+1/17 FLC 1+1/1 FAC 2

NOONE Craig Stephen
Born: Liverpool, 17 November 1987
Height: 6'3" **Weight:** 12.7
After struggling to make an impact at the start of Plymouth's Championship campaign he was loaned to League One Exeter on a three-month loan deal. Winger Craig arrived in September and immediately made an impact with some impressive wing play. He chipped in with two vital goals, including a wonderful lob at Leyton Orient, and did so well at St James' Park that Argyle recalled him early in November. However, once again he only appeared from the substitutes' bench before making three starts in February. An extremely tricky and pacy left-winger, he put in a 'Man of the Match' performance against Leicester and scored the equalizing goal, which he started and finished. After suffering ankle and shin injuries in the game against Preston he had a frustrating end to the season, including a further knee injury, and only appeared once more from the bench.
Plymouth Arg (Signed from Southport, ex Skelmersdale U, Burscough, on 14/8/2008) FL 6+32/2 FLC 0+1 FAC 0+2
Exeter C (Loaned on 10/9/2009) FL 7/2

NORRIS David Martin
Born: Stamford, 22 February 1981
Height: 5'7" **Weight:** 11.6
Club Honours: Div 2 '04
The season could not have started any worse for David because in Ipswich's first game, at Coventry he damaged knee ligaments and this kept him on the sidelines for four months. He returned to the side in the last game of 2009 and once he had gained full match fitness he played in most of the remaining games. He can play anywhere in midfield although is more effective in the middle and is an enthusiastic tackler. Sometimes his enthusiasm gets the better of him and he concedes free kicks in dangerous positions. He has still to replicate the form he showed at Plymouth in Ipswich colours but has not yet played a full season even though he has now completed two-and-a-half campaigns with them.
Bolton W (£50,000 from Boston U on 2/2/2000) FLC 3+1 FAC 1/1
Hull C (Loaned on 4/3/2002) FL 3+3/1
Plymouth Arg (Free on 8/10/2002) FL 216+10/27 FLC 5 FAC 11/1 Others 0+1
Ipswich T (£2,000,000 on 31/1/2008) FL 68+2/5 FLC 1+1 FAC 3

NORTH Daniel (Danny)
Jamie
Born: Grimsby, 7 September 1987
Height: 5'9" **Weight:** 12.2
Due to injuries and suspensions Danny was Grimsby's only available forward in late summer, hitting the winner against Hereford to give the Mariners a rare home victory. The stocky striker later found opportunities limited under new management, and his contract was ended by mutual consent in January. Danny had a trial with Scunthorpe before joining Blue Square North Alfreton Town.
Grimsby T (From trainee on 2/7/2006) FL 44+37/17 FLC 0+3/1 FAC 4+2 Others 7+3/1

NORWOOD James Thomas
Born: Eastbourne, 5 September 1990
Height: 5'9" **Weight:** 11.4
International Honours: E: Sch
A former England schoolboy international, James secured a one-year deal at Exeter after impressing for Eastbourne Town as a striker. He made his debut in August at Leeds, coming on for the last 20 minutes and impressed with his touch and positional sense. He will be hoping for more opportunities next season.
Exeter C (Free from Eastbourne T on 25/7/2009) FL 2+1 FLC 0+1

NOSWORTHY Nyron Paul
Henry
Born: Brixton, 11 October 1980
Height: 6'0" **Weight:** 12.0
Club Honours: Ch '07
A new contract and a 100th League start for Sunderland were highlights for the ex- Gillingham defender who spent most of the first half of the season on the bench at the Stadium of Light before featuring in all six December fixtures. However Nyron was to play just once more before moving on loan to Sheffield United for the second half of the season following Sunderland's purchase of Blades' centre-back Matt Kilgallon. Joining the Blades in February, he played mainly at centre-back but with some games at right-back and although, showing great determination, was a regular in the side. Deceptively fast when needed he always seemed to have time on the ball and although his methods were occasionally unorthodox the result was nearly always successful. Good in the air, strong and accurate in the tackle, and showing good anticipation, his unusual throw-in technique also caused problems for defenders.
Gillingham (From trainee on 30/12/1998) FL 151+23/5 FLC 6+2/1 FAC 7+7 Others 1+2
Sunderland (Free on 2/7/2005) P/FL 103+11 FLC 8+1 FAC 2
Sheffield U (Loaned on 1/2/2010) FL 19

NOUBLE Frank Herman
Born: Lewisham, 24 September 1991
Height: 6'3" **Weight:** 12.13
International Honours: E: Yth
Having been released by Chelsea, the young West Ham striker continued to impress and after a series of substitute appearances he finally made a start, against Arsenal in the FA Cup. It was a tough baptism but he showed enough endeavour and strength to suggest he will be a good player in the future. The following week against Aston Villa, due to injuries he was the lone striker and was a real threat playing against more experienced defenders. In an effort to gain further experience, Frank was loaned to West Bromwich as back-up when injuries ruled out key players. The tall, powerful and pacy London-born striker made his debut for Albion in the 2-0 home League win over Scunthorpe, coming twice close to scoring and giving the visitors' defence plenty to think about. In mid-March he joined Swindon on the one-month emergency loan deal as a boost to Town's striking options due to injuries to Billy Paynter and Vincent Pericard. He made his debut for Swindon against

Championship-chasing Norwich and after starting twice was used mainly from the bench. Having previously been capped for England at under-17 level, Frank played for the under-19 side in a 3–1 victory over Finland in a UEFA championship qualifying round game in Slovenia. Much is expected from him in the future.
West Ham U (From trainee at Chelsea on 21/7/2009) PL 3+5 FLC 0+1 FAC 1
West Bromwich A (Loaned on 9/2/2010) FL 3
Swindon T (Loaned on 19/3/2010) FL 3+5

NOVAK Lee Paul
Born: Newcastle, 28 September 1988
Height: 6'0" **Weight:** 12.4
What a season for the 20-year-old, signed originally from Gateshead. Lee spent the early part of the season being introduced from the Huddersfield substitutes' bench as he made the step into full-time football. He caught the eye with his non-stop running and his wholehearted approach was appreciated by fans and management alike as he eventually earned a starting place. His determination to find the net was rewarded with memorable goals in the derby draw at Leeds and the 'Goal of the Season' in the defeat at Swindon. Injury kept him out during the latter part of the season but he returned from the bench to score vital late winners against Walsall and Colchester.
Huddersfield T (Free from Gateshead, ex Newcastle Blue Star, on 4/2/2009) FL 24+13/12 FLC 1 FAC 3/2 Others 3+1

NOWLAND Adam Christopher
Born: Preston, 6 July 1981
Height: 5'11" **Weight:** 11.6
The former Preston man signed for Blackpool on a non-contract basis in August having been released by Notts County. A midfield playmaker, with a good range of passing skills, he managed only one game for the Seasiders, a 2-1 Carling Cup win at Crewe which he marked with a goal, before joining AFC Fylde and then moving to the USA with FC Tampa Bay.
Blackpool (From trainee on 15/1/1999) FL 18+51/5 FLC 1+5/1 FAC 2+2/1 Others 0+2
MK Dons (Signed on 29/6/2001) FL 35+21/5 FLC 2+1 FAC 2/2
West Ham U (£75,000 on 28/1/2004) FL 5+10/1 FLC 2
Gillingham (Loaned on 29/9/2004) FL 3/1
Nottingham F (£250,000 on 5/11/2004) FL 5 FAC 0+1

Preston NE (Free on 27/8/2005) FL 9+5/3 (Freed on 10/1/2008)
Gillingham (Loaned on 21/9/2007) FL 4+1 Others 0+1
Stockport Co (Loaned on 9/11/2007) FL 4
Notts Co (Free from Lancaster C on 24/7/2008) FL 16+4 FAC 0+1
Blackpool (Free on 10/8/2009) FLC 1/1

NUGENT David James
Born: Liverpool, 2 May 1985
Height: 5'11" **Weight:** 12.13
Club Honours: FAC '08
International Honours: E: 1; U21-14; Yth
After a few fleeting early season performances, David found himself out of favour at Portsmouth and was loaned out to Burnley for the remainder of the campaign on the August deadline day. After a debut at Liverpool, he scored two spectacular goals on his first home appearance against Sunderland, but appeared mainly as a substitute up to Christmas as Owen Coyle often opted for a 4-5-1 formation. Starting opportunities were more frequent after Brian Laws took over, and David's wholehearted and fearless displays up front signalled his most consistent run since local boy Pompey brought him into the Premier League.
Bury (From trainee on 8/3/2003) FL 58+30/18 FLC 2+1 FAC 3+1/1 Others 3+4/1
Preston NE (Signed on 11/1/2005) FL 83+11/33 FLC 2 FAC 5+1/2 Others 5/2
Portsmouth (£6,000,000 on 11/7/2007) PL 18+16/3 FLC 2+2/2 FAC 4+3/1
Burnley (Loaned on 1/9/2009) PL 20+10/6

NURSE Jonathan (Jon) David
Born: Bridgetown, Barbados, 1 March 1981
Height: 5'10" **Weight:** 12.6
International Honours: Barbados: 4
Jon scored Dagenham's first and last goals of the season. He was on the mark from 20 yards in the opening fixture at Crewe and scored the winning goal in the play-off final at Wembley. Normally a forward, Jon has played most of the time on the left, cutting in and scoring his highest season's total since joining the Daggers three years ago. He played in numerous positions and even turned out at right-back in the FA Cup first round tie at Huddersfield.
Dagenham & Redbridge (Free from Stevenage Borough, ex Sutton U, Woking - loan, on 9/7/2007) FL 69+33/12 FLC 1 FAC 2+3/1 Others 6+3/1

NUTTER John Robert William
Born: Burnham, 13 June 1982
Height: 6'2" **Weight:** 12.10
Club Honours: FAT '05, '06, '07
International Honours: E: SP-3
A steady if unspectacular full-back, John enjoyed a solid season for Gillingham that saw him clock up his 100th appearance for the club in the 3-1 home defeat of Stockport. That match also saw the left-back net a stunning left-foot volley to notch up only his second goal in Gillingham colours. John is very comfortable coming forward, supplied a number of assists for team-mates and also made a couple of appearances on the left side of midfield.
Wycombe W (Trainee) FL 1
Gillingham (Signed from Stevenage Borough, ex Aldershot T, St Albans C - loan, Grays Ath, on 22/11/2007) FL 98+6/2 FLC 3 FAC 5+2 Others 6

NYATANGA Lewin John
Born: Burton-on-Trent, 18 August 1988
Height: 6'2" **Weight:** 12.8
International Honours: W: 33; U21-10
A close-season signing for Bristol City from Derby, Lewin added to his haul of Welsh caps by playing against England and Scotland at the start of the campaign. He is a good, solid performer, either at left-back or as a central defender. Was a member of the Welsh squad for the March internationals and came on as a substitute at the Liberty Stadium, Swansea where Sweden won 1-0 in March.
Derby Co (From trainee on 10/9/2005) P/FL 57+6/4 FLC 6 FAC 6 Others 0+1
Sunderland (Loaned on 19/10/2006) FL 9+2
Barnsley (Loaned on 13/2/2007) FL 10/1
Barnsley (Loaned on 27/7/2007) FL 24+1 FLC 2
Barnsley (Loaned on 31/1/2008) FL 16/1
Bristol C (Signed on 14/7/2009) FL 33+4/1 FAC 1

N'ZOGBIA Charles
Born: Le Havre, France, 28 May 1986
Height: 5'7" **Weight:** 11.0
International Honours: France: U21-13; Yth
Charles is a skilful, pacy left-footed player whose abilities were best used at Wigan on the wing. He is most effective as an attacking midfielder and was used down the right as a great option where he could use his pace and fine control to offer a direct threat when cutting in. The opening game against Aston Villa was his 100th Premier League start and

Steven Reid, David Dunn and Brett
Emerton to put injuries behind them, so
he became a regular starter in
Blackburn's midfield and, by the end of
the season, the vital heartbeat of the
team. For a youngster, he has enormous
composure, is calm on the ball and
always able to move it on profitably
when under pressure. An assiduous
coverer and ball winner, he uses his
great height to advantage, pushing
forward to nod on high crosses.
Perhaps less conspicuous as a scorer
than he ought to be, given his heading
ability. He scored the club's finest goal
of the season, a thunderous 30-yard
strike against Everton that perhaps
heralds another facet to the game of a
young man who appears to have a
great future. Unexpectedly, he was
voted Blackburn's 'Player of the
Season'.
Blackburn Rov *(Signed from Amiens,
France on 30/6/2009) PL 33/2 FLC 5*

Steven N'Zonzi

Charles N'Zogbia

he went on to miss only two League
games. A talented player who is able to
carry the ball at pace and has an eye for
goal, his return of five League goals
equalled his record in the Premiership
and his best goal was the injury-time
winner at home to Arsenal. His
performances over the season played a
major part in the club maintaining top
flight status. Charles was named both
the Junior Stripes' 'Player of the Year'
and supporters' 'Player of the Year'.
Newcastle U *(Signed from Le Havre,
France on 3/9/2004) PL 86+32/9 FLC*

7+1 FAC 8+2 Others 13+5/1
Wigan Ath *(£6,000,000 on 2/2/2009)
PL 48+1/6 FAC 0+3/2*

N'ZONZI Steven
N'Kemboanza
Born: Paris, France, 15 December 1988
Height: 6'3" **Weight:** 11.11
International Honours: France: U21-5
Steven came to Blackburn from playing
at the bottom of the French Second
Division and was intended to be used in
emergencies. Opportunity emerged for
him with the failure of Vince Grella,

O

OAKES Stefan Trevor
Born: Leicester, 6 September 1978
Height: 5'11" **Weight:** 12.4
Club Honours: FLC '00
It was an injury-hit second season at
Lincoln for the experienced midfielder
who failed to hold down a regular first
team place. At his best, comfortable
anywhere in the midfield, and a player
who was always looking to make a
pass, he left the club by mutual consent
in March.
*Leicester C (From trainee on 3/7/1997)
P/FL 39+25/2 FLC 7+1/2 FAC 5+2*
*Crewe Alex (Loaned on 17/3/2003) FL
3+4*
Walsall (Free on 18/7/2003) FL 1+4
*Notts Co (Free on 17/2/2004) FL
42+3/5 FLC 0+1 FAC 2+1/1*
*Wycombe W (Free on 6/7/2005) FL
83+23/5 FLC 9/3 FAC 4/1 Others 2+3*
*Lincoln C (Free on 2/7/2008) FL
32+12/1 FLC 2 FAC 1*

OAKLEY Matthew (Matt)
Born: Peterborough, 17 August 1977
Height: 5'10" **Weight:** 12.1
Club Honours: Div 1 '09
International Honours: E: U21-4
Classy midfielder and Leicester club
captain who kept operating throughout
the season despite being hampered by
niggling injuries. Unusually he did not
trouble the scorers at all during 2009-
10 and had to concede defeat late in
the campaign, as injury kept him on the
fringe of the squad during the play-offs.
A good pre-season could see him return
to maximum effectiveness in the
forthcoming season.
*Southampton (From trainee on
1/7/1995) P/FL 238+23/14 FLC 21+2/2
FAC 22+3/4 Others 1*
*Derby Co (Free on 4/8/2006) P/FL
55+1/9 FLC 1 FAC 2 Others 3*
*Leicester C (£500,000 on 11/1/2008)
FL 102+1/8 FLC 2 FAC 4 Others 1*

OASTLER Joseph (Joe) James
Born: Portsmouth, 3 July 1990
Height: 5'10" **Weight:** 11.4
Joe is a versatile young Queens Park
Rangers' player who can perform as a
centre-back or in midfield. He came
through the youth set up at Loftus Road
and spent time on loan at Salisbury this
season. Towards the end of the
campaign, he often featured on the
bench before finally making his debut
as a substitute, coming on in a home
game against Watford to play the last
20 minutes.

*Queens Park Rgrs (From trainee at
Portsmouth on 23/7/2008) FL 0+1*

OBADEYI Temitope Ayoluwa
Born: Birmingham, 29 October 1989
Height: 5'10" **Weight:** 11.10
International Honours: E: Yth
The young Bolton striker spent three
months on loan at Swindon, showing
himself to be a strong, pacy forward
who usually played down the middle
but could operate down either flank.
Used mainly in a wide role, he scored
twice in his time at Town, with his
League debut goal coming from close
range against Southend at the end of
August. That was followed by an
emphatic finish to earn a point in the
home draw with Colchester during
September before going back to the
Reebok at the end of November. In the
winter transfer window, Temitope was
signed on loan by Rochdale in order to
bolster attacking options for their
promotion run-in and he made his
debut as substitute in the televised
game at Bury. Playing out on the wing,
he scored his first Dale goal in his
second start in place of the injured Joe
Thompson, but spent the rest of the
campaign as an almost permanent
substitute.
*Bolton W (From trainee on 3/11/2006)
PL 0+3*
*Swindon T (Loaned on 14/8/2009) FL
9+3/2 FLC 1 FAC 1*
*Rochdale (Loaned on 30/1/2010) FL
5+6/1*

OBERTAN Gabriel
Born: Pantin, France, 26 February 1989
Height: 6'1" **Weight:** 12.6
Club Honours: FLC '10
International Honours: France: U21-
9; Yth
The talented Manchester United winger
who can also play in the centre of
midfield or as a striker, Gabriel went to

Gabriel Obertan

the Clairefontaine Academy in France and was named as France's best player at the 2009 Toulon Tournament before joining United from Bordeaux. After just three reserve games, he made his senior debut in the United's 2–0 away win over Barnsley in the Carling Cup in October. His Premier League debut followed at the end of the month in the 2–0 home win over Blackburn and he had his first taste of the Champions League that same week, replacing Federico Macheda in the 82nd minute in the 3–3 draw against CSKA Moscow. His first Premier League start was in a 3-0 win over Wolves in December.
Manchester U (Signed from Bordeaux, France, via Lorient - loan, on 8/7/2009) PL 1+6 FLC 2 FAC 1 Others 1+2

OBIKA Jonathan Chiedozie
Born: Enfield, 12 September 1990
Height: 6'0" **Weight:** 12.0
International Honours: E: Yth
Jonathan's goals last season went a way to ensuring that Yeovil stayed up and it was great news to the fans that he returned to the club with his good pal and team-mate Ryan Mason. By the time he went back to Tottenham in February, he had increased his stock by scoring seven times in 14 starts, plus 11 more as sub. Three times he came on for Yeovil and scored as a replacement and he repeated the feat in April when playing for his new loan side Millwall. Arriving in February, Jon started all his dozen League games from the bench, salvaging a point for the Lions with a 93rd-minute headed equaliser at his previous club. Tall and extremely fast with good footwork and the strength to hold off defenders, he is seen as one for the future.
Tottenham H (From trainee on 12/1/2009) Others 1+1
Yeovil T (Loaned on 19/3/2009) FL 10/4
Yeovil T (Loaned on 11/8/2009) FL 13+9/6 FLC 0+1 FAC 1 Others 0+1/1
Millwall (Loaned on 12/2/2010) FL 0+12/2

O'BRIEN Alan
Born: Dublin, 20 February 1985
Height: 5'10" **Weight:** 11.3
International Honours: Rol: 5; B-1; Yth
Alan started Swindon's first game of the season at Gillingham before appearing off the bench in most of their games in August. A troublesome hamstring injury put paid to most of his season and it was in the FA Cup at the end of November before the speedy Irishman was seen again. Started twice during December, with a couple of further substitute appearances, before the

injury again curtailed his involvement, although he recovered sufficiently to come off the bench in the final League game at Millwall and also took part in the end of season play-offs. A lightning-quick winger, he usually operates on the left flank.
Newcastle U (From trainee on 24/4/2002) PL 1+4 FAC 0+3 Others 0+1
Carlisle U (Loaned on 30/9/2005) FL 2+3/1
Hibernian (Signed on 1/7/2007) SL 20+27 SLC 0+1 SC 1+3 Others 1
Swindon T (Free on 3/7/2009) FL 3+6 FLC 0+1 FAC 0+1 Others 1+2

O'BRIEN Andrew (Andy)
James
Born: Harrogate, 29 June 1979
Height: 6'3" **Weight:** 12.4
International Honours: Rol: 26; U21-8; E: U21-1; Yth
The pre-season signings of Sam Ricketts and Paul Robinson suggested that there would be fierce competition for defensive places at Bolton and Andy did not figure as much as he would have liked last season. His first League appearance came when starting in the 2-0 home defeat by Blackburn in November and sporadic appearances followed before Andy returned to action in the 0-0 draw at home to Fulham, as a result of Gary Cahill's blood clot. However, Andy again lost his place and, despite returning to the team in impressive style during the 4-0 win over Wigan, he made just six League appearances in total.
Bradford C (From trainee on 28/10/1996) P/FL 113+20/3 FLC 5 FAC 8 Others 4
Newcastle U (£2,000,000 on 28/3/2001) PL 114+6/6 FLC 4+1 FAC 7+3/1 Others 32+5
Portsmouth (£2,000,000 on 7/7/2005) PL 30+2 FLC 3 FAC 2
Bolton W (Signed on 14/8/2007) PL 67+5/1 FLC 1+1 FAC 4+1 Others 7+1

O'BRIEN James (Jamie)
Born: Dublin, 8 June 1990
Height: 6'0" **Weight:** 11.8
International Honours: Rol: Yth
The former Ireland under-16 captain was given a pre-season trial at Bradford after being released by Birmingham. The energetic midfielder, who works best on either the left or right of a central three, did enough to earn an initial month's contract which was then extended until November. Jamie continued the good work, including scoring the winning penalty in a shoot-out win over Notts County in the Johnstone's Paint Trophy, and was rewarded with a full 18-month deal. He

missed two months of action after a nose operation to repair a damaged sceptum.
Birmingham C (From trainee on 13/6/2007)
Bradford C (Free on 4/8/2009) FL 15+8/2 FLC 0+1 FAC 1 Others 2+1

O'BRIEN Luke
Born: Halifax, 11 September 1988
Height: 5'9" **Weight:** 11.7
Local boy Luke enjoyed another long run in the Bradford side and played every game until March. Mainly a left-back, he was also converted to a left-sided midfielder when Peter Taylor became the Valley Parade boss. The more advanced role allowed him to exploit his attacking tendencies and he has shown great energy down the flank. His goal at home to Barnet in front of the Kop was particularly special for a player who had grown up supporting the team from that same end of the ground.
Bradford C (From trainee on 4/7/2007) FL 75+5/2 FLC 1 FAC 4 Others 4+1

Luke O'Brien

O'CALLAGHAN George
Born: Cork, 5 September 1979
Height: 6'1" **Weight:** 11.5
International Honours: Rol: Yth
The Irish midfielder arrived at Yeovil in the summer and started six of the first seven games but a loss of form and injury meant he would only make two more starts before leaving the club. His 15 appearances did not produce any goals from his central midfield berth and he left Huish Park, later to play for Waterford United.
Port Vale (From trainee on 10/7/1998) FL 22+12/4 FLC 2 FAC 1+2 Others 0+1 (Freed on 30/3/2002)

Ipswich T *(Signed from Cork C on 17/1/2007) FL 4+8/1 FAC 1*
Brighton & Hove A *(Loaned on 31/8/2007) FL 13+1 FAC 1 Others 2*
Tranmere Rov *(Free on 15/7/2008) FL 4+2 FLC 1 Others 1 (Freed on 17/2/2009)*
Yeovil T *(Signed from Dundalk on 24/7/2009) FL 7+5 FLC 1 FAC 0+1 Others 1*

O'CONNOR Garry Lawrence
Born: Edinburgh, 7 May 1983
Height: 6'1" **Weight:** 12.2
International Honours: S: 16; U21-8
Was an important player for Birmingham in the early part of the season when they opted for a lone striker role. Big, strong and good at keeping the ball, Garry headed the winner at Hull in September in what was a key victory for the Blues. In November, he required surgery on his groins and hips which kept him out for the remainder of the season.
Hibernian *(From Salvesen BC on 1/7/1999) SL 115+23/46 SLC 9+2/5 SC 9+5/6 Others 3/1 (Transferred to Lokomotiv Moscow, Russia on 7/3/2006)*
Peterhead *(Loaned on 25/8/2000) SL 4/2 Others 1*
Birmingham C *(£2,700,000 from Lokomotiv Moscow, Russia on 17/7/2007) P/FL 20+29/9 FLC 5+1/2 FAC 1/1*

O'CONNOR James Francis Edward
Born: Birmingham, 20 November 1984
Height: 5'10" **Weight:** 12.5
Club Honours: FAYC '02; AMC '07
Normally a right-back, James found himself moved into the middle of the Doncaster back line as a short-term measure because of injuries in the centre-back ranks. He impressed so much that he continued there as centre-back partners came and went either through injury or returning to their parent clubs after a loan period. He returned to right-back for the last two games when James Chambers was injured and kept up the high standard he had shown all season. James won a number of 'Man of the Match' awards for his displays and was voted by the fans as their 'Player of the Season'.
Aston Villa *(From trainee on 24/4/2004)*
Port Vale *(Loaned on 3/9/2004) FL 13 Others 2*
Bournemouth *(Free on 18/2/2005) FL 43+2/1 FLC 1 FAC 1 Others 1+1*
Doncaster Rov *(£130,000 on 19/5/2006) FL 143+7/2 FLC 6 FAC 11/1 Others 8*

O'CONNOR James Kevin
Born: Dublin, 1 September 1979
Height: 5'8" **Weight:** 11.6
Club Honours: AMC '00
International Honours: Rol: U21-9; Yth
A good solid season for this combative central midfielder, James imposed himself on the Sheffield Wednesday midfield, and also captained the side when Darren Purse was unavailable. He scored an opportunist goal against Newcastle on Boxing Day, appearing unnoticed in the penalty area to head in. This goalscoring part of his game is something he needs to improve. Although known as a hard-tackling midfielder, he needs to get up more into attacking positions to support the strikers. Overall he has been a good consistent player for the Owls in his second season with them. Needs to kick on still more for next season and, of course, improve his scoring rate.
Stoke C *(From trainee on 5/9/1996) FL 176/16 FLC 9/3 FAC 8+1 Others 16+1/3*

O'CONNOR Kevin Patrick
Born: Blackburn, 24 February 1982
Height: 5'11" **Weight:** 12.0
Club Honours: Div 2 '09
International Honours: Rol: U21-6
Brentford's long-serving captain had an extremely consistent season. Playing as the central midfield ball-winner, he kept things simple when laying off short passes and driving the side forward. It looked as if Kevin would be ever-present for the season but, after playing every minute of all the first 43 League and Cup matches of the campaign, he sustained an ankle injury in the game at Millwall in April that forced him off the

West Bromwich A *(Signed on 8/8/2003) P/FL 27+3 FLC 5+1 FAC 1+1*
Burnley *(Loaned on 29/10/2004) FL 12+1*
Burnley *(£175,000 on 24/3/2005) FL 117+9/11 FLC 6+1 FAC 3*
Sheffield Wed *(Free on 22/7/2008) FL 79+6/3 FLC 1+1 FAC 2*

James O'Connor (Doncaster Rovers)

field and kept him out of the next three games. He returned for the final five matches and scored against Tranmere, his first League goal in open play for over two years. Kevin scored two penalties in a match against Southend in September and also played a few games at right-back.
Brentford *(From trainee on 4/3/2000)*
FL 308+36/29 FLC 10+1/4 FAC 25+2/4 Others 13+5/2

O'CONNOR Michael Joseph
Born: Belfast, 6 October 1987
Height: 6'1" **Weight:** 11.8
International Honours: NI: 9; B-1; U21-3; Yth
Midfielder Michael quickly adjusted to life in the Championship with a number of excellent early season displays for Scunthorpe that helped to restore him to the full Northern Ireland squad. A combative player who also has an excellent range of passing, he impressed in the centre of midfield or when tucked in on the right side. His competitive edge saw him collect ten yellow cards by mid-January and he then was handed a three-match ban for violent conduct which was spotted on video after the match against Watford in February. Fell out of favour after that, starting just one game in the closing two months, but will expect to have a big part to play in 2010-11.
Crewe Alex *(From trainee on 27/7/2005) FL 65+12/3 FLC 5/3 FAC 3 Others 4*
Lincoln C *(Loaned on 6/3/2009) FL 9+1/1*
Scunthorpe U *(£250,000 on 6/7/2009) FL 23+9/2 FLC 3+1*

Michael O'Connor

O'CONNOR Shane
Born: Cork, 14 April 1990
Height: 5'9" **Weight:** 11.8
A summer telephone call to Roy Keane paid dividends when, after a trial, Shane was offered a one-year contract by Ipswich. He made his debut at Shrewsbury in the Carling Cup when he came on as a half-time substitute for Jack Ainsley. Shane did not appear in another first team squad until he made his full debut at Sheffield Wednesday in February and impressed so much that he retained his midfield place for most of the remaining games of the season. He has plenty of pace which enables him to track back with opposing wingers and make surging runs down the opposition flanks when his ball control makes it difficult to dispossess him.
Ipswich T *(From trainee at Liverpool on 28/7/2009) FL 11+1 FLC 0+1*

O'DEA Darren
Born: Dublin, 4 February 1987
Height: 6'1" **Weight:** 13.1
Club Honours: SPD '07; SLC '09
International Honours: RoI 2; U21-9
Incoming manager Brendan Rodgers used his contacts to secure Glasgow Celtic centre-back Darren on loan to Reading at the beginning of September. He replaced Matt Mills at the heart of the Royals' defence for a run of six games when the manager was struggling to pick a settled side, then made two more appearances, at left-back and as a substitute, before returning to Scotland. He was at the Madejski during a period of great transition, so was able to show only rare indications of his ability as a strong defender. During his time with Reading, he made his Republic of Ireland debut, entering as a late substitute in the 1-0 victory over South Africa.
Glasgow Celtic *(Signed from Home Farm on 1/8/2005) SL 32+13/3 SLC 3/1 SC 8+2/1 Others 3+5*
Reading *(Loaned on 1/9/2009) FL 7+1*

ODEJAYI Olukayode (Kayode) Ishmael
Born: Ibadon, Nigeria, 21 February 1982
Height: 6'2" **Weight:** 12.2
International Honours: Nigeria: 1
After an impressive pre-season at Barnsley, Kayode began 2009-10 in the starting line-up. However, very quickly Kayode found himself on the substitutes' bench and then on the sidelines altogether. Strong and powerful he always gave his all, but found himself constantly under pressure in front of goal. It was no surprise when Kayode moved to Colchester on loan in

September and the powerful Nigerian striker scored six goals in a sensational 12 League starts, including a brilliant brace against Charlton. It was more goals than he had scored in nearly three years at his previous club and saw United sign him permanently as soon as the January transfer window opened. Although Kayode's form dropped off slightly in the New Year, he did add three more goals to his tally and was badly missed when an ankle injury kept him out for seven games in March and April.
Bristol C *(From trainee on 17/7/2000) FL 0+6 Others 1 (Free to Forest Green Rov on 28/9/2002)*
Cheltenham T *(£25,000 from Forest Green Rov on 5/6/2003) FL 100+48/30 FLC 5+1/1 FAC 7+3/2 Others 7+3/1*
Barnsley *(£200,000 on 5/6/2007) FL 32+40/4 FLC 3+1 FAC 4+2/1*
Scunthorpe U *(Loaned on 26/2/2009) FL 1+5/1*
Colchester U *(Signed on 16/9/2009) FL 19+9/9 FAC 3/1*

O'DONNELL Daniel (Danny)
Born: Rainford, 10 March 1986
Height: 6'2" **Weight:** 11.11
Having arrived at Crewe on loan from Liverpool and after signing a full contract, Daniel spent four seasons at Gresty Road. The defender was called upon to fill several positions and had an extended run in the side before dropping out in the last few games. Was not offered a new contract by Crewe.
Liverpool *(From trainee on 25/11/2004)*
Crewe Alex *(Signed on 8/8/2006) FL 89+14/3 FLC 3+2 FAC 4 Others 5/1*

O'DONOVAN Roy Simon
Born: Cork, 10 August 1985
Height: 5'7" **Weight:** 10.4
International Honours: RoI: B-2; U21-9; Yth
The strong and hard-working front man had two contrasting loan spells with League One sides. An Autumn spell at Southend brought a single goal from three starts plus a further appearance off the bench, but he later made the Shrimpers suffer with a hat trick against them in the colours of Hartlepool. They were three of nine goals Roy scored in 15 games to help keep Hartlepool up as Southend went down. His success for Chris Turner's side meant the Irishman was in demand as his Sunderland contract came to a close. Unable to add to his Sunderland appearances in his final season, being an unused sub at Norwich in the Carling Cup and at

home to Barrow in the FA Cup, he was out of contract at Sunderland in the summer.
Coventry C *(From trainee on 13/8/2002. Freed on 1/12/2004)*
Sunderland *(£500,000 + from Cork C on 10/8/2007) PL 4+13 FLC 0+1 FAC 1*
Dundee U *(Loaned on 1/8/2008) SL 7+4/1 SLC 1+1*
Blackpool *(Loaned on 9/1/2009) FL 11+1*
Southend U *(Loaned on 16/9/2009) FL 3+1/1 Others 1*
Hartlepool U *(Loaned on 23/2/2009) FL 15/9*

OFFIONG Richard
Born: South Shields, 17 December 1983
Height: 5'11" **Weight:** 12.0
Club Honours: S Div 1 '08
International Honours: E: Yth
Great things were expected of this player when he was recruited by Carlisle early in the campaign after a successful spell at Hamilton. Unfortunately, he seldom played to his full potential with a disappointing haul of just one goal in nearly 20 appearances, the majority admittedly coming on as a substitute. In March he went on loan to Swedish side Ostersunds FK where it is hoped he will be able to recapture the form and confidence he showed north of the border.
Newcastle U *(From trainee on 26/9/2001. Freed on 26/7/2004)*
Darlington *(Loaned on 29/11/2002) FL 7/2 FAC 2/2*
Motherwell *(Loaned on 31/11/2003) SL 0+9 SC 0+1*
York C *(Loaned on 12/3/2004) FL 2+2*
Doncaster Rov *(Free from Istanbulspor, Turkey on 12/8/2005) FL 2+3 FLC 0+1 FAC 1 Others 2/1*
Hamilton Academical *(Free on 29/7/2006) SL 85+8/38 SLC 5+1/3 SC 4+1 Others 1/1*
Carlisle U *(£75,000 on 25/8/2009) FL 2+13/1 FLC 1 Others 2+1*

O'FLYNN John
Born: Cobh, 11 July 1982
Height: 5'11" **Weight:** 11.11
International Honours: RoI: U21-6
Despite scoring 16 goals in all competitions, John had a slightly disappointing campaign at Barnet. Following an explosive debut season, much was expected of the Irish forward. However, injury hampered his start to the season and his form in front of goal suffered as a result. Still a popular figure at the club, John turned down a move to Shrewsbury in the January transfer window, but with his contract at an end he is likely to be

playing elsewhere in 2010-11.
Peterborough U *(From trainee on 3/7/2001. Freed on 21/12/2001)*
Barnet *(Free from Cork C on 2/9/2008) FL 63+7/29 FAC 5/4 Others 2/1*

O'FLYNN Stephen (Steve) Joseph
Born: Mallow, 27 April 1982
Height: 6'1" **Weight:** 13.8
Striker Steve joined Northampton on a short-term contract from Limerick after over ten seasons in League of Ireland football. The tall front man is not afraid to get stuck in and is full of running but the change to League football may need a little more time than the four months spent so far.
Northampton T *(Free from Limerick, ex trainee at Wimbledon, Cork C, Limerick, Cork C, Derry C, Galway U, on 5/1/2010) FL 0+5*

OFORI-TWUMASI Seth Nana
Born: Accra, Ghana, 15 May 1990
Height: 5'8" **Weight:** 11.3
International Honours: E: Yth
Nana joined Dagenham from Chelsea on a month's loan in November. The young right-back likes to get forward and scored two goals in his spell with the Daggers. The loan was extended by a month but he returned to Stamford Bridge at the start of January. Was out

of contract at the end of June.
Chelsea *(From trainee on 6/7/2007)*
Dagenham & Redbridge *(Loaned on 13/11/2009) FL 8/2*

OGOGO Abumere (Abu) Tafadzwa
Born: Epsom, 3 November 1989
Height: 5'8" **Weight:** 10.0
Abu made his Dagenham debut as a substitute at Crewe on the opening day. The former Arsenal youngster was sent off for a bad tackle at Macclesfield in October and after that found it hard to get back in the side. But he forced his way in during January and made the right-back position his own for the remainder of the season, scoring a couple of goals in the process.
Arsenal *(From trainee on 14/9/2007)*
Barnet *(Loaned on 15/11/2008) FL 7+2/1*
Dagenham & Redbridge *(Free on 2/7/2009) FL 27+3/2 FLC 0+1 Others 4*

O'GRADY Christopher (Chris) James
Born: Nottingham, 25 January 1986
Height: 6'1" **Weight:** 12.8
International Honours: E: Yth
Having appeared for Oldham in the second match of the season, against Carlisle, a week or so later the powerful front man joined Rochdale on loan and immediately struck up a terrific

Chris O'Grady

understanding with fellow striker Chris Dagnall, who scored six times in their first six games together. Chris himself took a little longer to get on the scoresheet, but hit a purple patch as Dale powered to the top of the table, netting 12 in 12 games around the turn of the year, including a hat-trick at Cheltenham. Fortunately Dale were able to afford his permanent transfer in January and Chris continued to hammer in the goals, often demonstrating surprising control for a big man. Having netted the winner against Northampton which guaranteed promotion, Chris ended the campaign on 22 goals.

Leicester C (From trainee on 3/8/2004) FL 6+18/1 FLC 1/1
Notts Co (Loaned on 24/9/2004) FL 3+6 FAC 0+1 Others 1
Rushden & Diamonds (Loaned on 12/8/2005) FL 20+2/4 FLC 1 Others 2
Rotherham U (£65,000 on 19/1/2007) FL 46+5/13 FLC 1 FAC 2/1 Others 1/1
Oldham Ath (Signed on 4/6/2008) FL 3+10 FLC 3 Others 0+1
Bury (Loaned on 17/10/2008) FL 3+3
Bradford C (Loaned on 2/1/2009) FL 0+2
Stockport Co (Loaned on 2/2/2009) FL 17+1/2
Rochdale (Signed on 21/8/2009) FL 43/22 FAC 2

O'HANLON Sean Philip
Born: Southport, 2 January 1983
Height: 6'1" **Weight:** 12.5
Club Honours: AMC '08; Div 2 '08
International Honours: E: Yth
Having been a tower of strength at the back for MK Dons in each of his first three seasons with the club, it is no coincidence that the defensive frailties came during a campaign when Sean was unavailable for selection until late February due to a knee injury. Given a careful reintroduction to first team duty, he showed what had been missing when putting in an outstanding display in the 1-1 draw at champions-elect Norwich in early April, and with the team having fallen out of the play-off picture by then, was given one more start before being signed off early to prepare himself fully for a new season.
Everton (From trainee on 26/2/2000)
Swindon T (£150,000 on 23/1/2004) FL 97+2/9 FLC 1+1 FAC 5/1 Others 5+1
MK Dons (Free on 27/7/2006) FL 117+8/11 FLC 3+2/1 FAC 4 Others 10/1

O'HARA Jamie Darryl
Born: Dartford, 25 September 1986
Height: 5'11" **Weight:** 12.4
Club Honours: FLC '08
International Honours: E: U21-7; Yth
Jamie made one start for Tottenham in

the Carling Cup at Doncaster, scoring his only goal of the season for the club. He did make a couple of appearances off the bench, but spent most of his season on loan at Portsmouth where he won many accolades for his performances before his season ended with an FA Cup final appearance against Chelsea. At Pompey, Jamie swept the 'Player of the Season' accolades in 2009-10, winning a record number of trophies after his commitment, energy and guile endeared him to the fans. As the focal point of the Portsmouth side, his game is epitomised by pinpoint set-piece deliveries, a cultured left-foot and a tireless work rate, Jamie laid on a vital late equaliser against Sunderland, as well as scoring a goal of the season contender against Hull. Popular and charismatic, he returned to Tottenham in the summer and is sure to enjoy a bright future in the game.
Tottenham H (From trainee on 29/9/2004) PL 15+19/2 FLC 6+3/3 FAC 2+1 Others 5+5/2
Chesterfield (Loaned on 13/1/2006) FL 19/5
Millwall (Loaned on 24/8/2007) FL 10+4/2 Others 1
Portsmouth (Loaned on 28/8/2009) PL 25+1/2 FAC 3/1

OKAI Julian Ebenezer
Born: Rochford, 26 February 1993
Height: 5'6" **Weight:** 10.0
A second-year scholar at Southend, Julian's consistent form on the left of midfield for the youth team accelerated him to the first team squad due to the club's ongoing financial struggles. He shone in the pre-season Toomey Trophy youth team competition at Roots Hall, scoring a brilliant goal in the final against Everton. Julian made his debut as a last-minute substitute for Francis Laurent in the FA Cup tie at Gillingham before returning to his highly successful season in the Academy side.
Southend U (Trainee) FAC 0+1

OKAKA CHUKA Stefano
Born: Castiglione del Lago, Italy, 9 August 1989
Height: 6'1" **Weight:** 13.1
International Honours: Italy: U21-2; Yth
A January loan signing from AS Roma, Stefano first came to the attention of Fulham when he scored the winning goal against them in a Europa League tie in Rome in November. The Italian under-21 international was considered a useful addition to the Fulham squad and wasted little time in opening his scoring account with a well-taken effort

in the FA Cup tie against Notts County. A quick player who possesses a firm strike, he has the confidence to try the unorthodox, a feature of his first Premier League goal, a clever back-heel from a low cross to deceive Wigan goalkeeper Chris Kirkland. Soon after arriving at Craven Cottage, he was selected for the Italian under-21 team against Hungary and scored the winning goal.
Fulham (Loaned on 1/2/2010) PL 3+8/2 FAC 0+2/1

O'KANE Eunan
Born: Derry, 10 July 1990
Height: 5'8" **Weight:** 13.4
International Honours: NI: U21-3
Initially signed by Torquay on a short-term deal from Everton, Eunan showed more than enough promise to secure a two-year contract despite not being able to nail a regular starting place. Most of his appearances were wide on the right of midfield, but showed signs that his more natural position may be in central midfield or in the hole. He has an excellent first touch, a good football brain and a great eye for a pass.
Everton (Free from Maiden C on 31/8/2007. Freed during 2009 close season)
Torquay U (Signed from Coleraine on 13/1/2010) FL 5+11/1

O'KEEFE Joshua (Josh) Adam
Born: Whalley, 22 December 1988
Height: 6'3" **Weight:** 13.1
International Honours: RoI: U21-1
It was the end of November before Josh started a game in the centre of the Walsall midfield. So keen was he to make a good impression that over-enthusiasm saw him booked in the first minute. He lost his place when Dwayne Mattis was fit, which was unfortunate as his full debut had been quite impressive. A run of seven consecutive starts in February and March coincided with Walsall's worst spell of the season and he was unlucky as his efforts were not supported by the rest of the team. Josh was released at the end of the season.
Blackburn Rov (From trainee on 16/1/2006)
Walsall (Free on 13/7/2009) FL 8+5

O'KEEFE Stuart Antony Alan
Born: Eye, 4 March 1991
Height: 5'8" **Weight:** 10.2
Stuart is an agile and skilful central midfielder and was handed a three-year deal by manager Steve Tilson following good progress in the previous season, his first for Southend. Stuart continued

to be a regular on the bench for the Shrimpers and contributed well when given the opportunity. Featuring either in central midfield or on the right, he started the final two games and did not look out of place.
Southend U (From trainee on 31/10/2008) FL 4+6 FAC 1+1 Others 0+1

OKUONGHAE Magnus Erharuyi
Born: Nigeria, 16 February 1986
Height: 6'3" **Weight:** 13.4
Towering centre-back Magnus made an effortless step up from League Two club Dagenham to League One Colchester last season. Such was his seamless transition, Magnus was handed the captain's armband early on in the campaign and missed only two games all season. Quick, strong in the air and a good leader of an ever-changing back line, Magnus was rewarded with a contract extension until 2012 in December after being tipped to play at a higher level by manager Aidy Boothroyd.
Rushden & Diamonds (From trainee on 6/7/2005) FL 15+7/1 FLC 0+1 Others 0+1 (Free to Aldershot T on 15/8/2006)
Dagenham & Redbridge (Free from Crawley T, ex St Albans C, on 9/7/2007) FL 54+1/2 FLC 1 FAC 3 Others 4
Colchester U (Free on 2/7/2009) FL 44 FLC 1 FAC 3 Others 1

O'LEARY Kristian (Kris) Denis
Born: Port Talbot, 30 August 1977
Height: 6'0" **Weight:** 13.4
Club Honours: Div 3 '00; AMC '06
International Honours: W: Yth
Kris joined Leyton Orient on loan from Swansea in September. The midfielder struggled to regain his match fitness after a long-term injury and started only one game before returning to the Liberty Stadium at the end of his loan.
Swansea C (From trainee on 1/7/1996) FL 238+46/10 FLC 13 FAC 15+4/1 Others 21+2
Cheltenham T (Loaned on 23/11/2006) FL 5/1
Leyton Orient (Loaned on 31/8/2009) FL 1+2

O'LEARY Stephen Michael
Born: Barnet, 12 February 1985
Height: 5'10" **Weight:** 11.8
Club Honours: Div 1 '05
International Honours: RoI: Yth
Stephen suffered another frustrating season through injury. He broke a small bone in a toe on his Bradford debut and the problem got worse when he came back too early after it was wrongly

diagnosed. A central midfielder who likes to have time on the ball, he finally got his chance again in February when Peter Taylor took over as manager and played in a memorable 3-1 win at leaders Rochdale.
Luton T (From trainee on 3/8/2004) FL 30+15/3 FLC 2+1 FAC 2+2 Others 2+1
Tranmere Rov (Loaned on 21/10/2005) FL 19+2/3 Others 1
Hereford U (Free on 26/8/2008) FL 11+4/1 FAC 1 Others 1
Bradford C (Free on 6/8/2009) FL 4+3

OLI Dennis Chiedozie
Born: Newham, 28 January 1984
Height: 6'0" **Weight:** 12.2
Club Honours: FAT '05, '06
International Honours: E: SP-5
A lightning-fast Gillingham forward with good presence in the air, Mark Stimson utilised Dennis' pace to good effect, either as a right-winger or in a more conventional striking role. Unfortunately while Dennis' speed may have unsettled defences, his shooting was a little less effective leading to a return of just three goals for the season. That said, his scrambled goal to give Gillingham a 2-1 lead against Charlton at the Valley was a special moment for the 3,000 strong travelling support. Was out of contract in the summer.
Queens Park Rgrs (From juniors on 24/10/2001) FL 8+15 FLC 0+1 FAC 1+2 Others 2+1
Swansea C (Free on 6/8/2004) FL 0+1 Others 1 (Freed on 24/11/2004)
Cambridge U (Free on 9/9/2004) FL 4/1
Gillingham (Signed from Grays Ath on 12/11/2007) FL 60+29/11 FLC 1+1 FAC 2+1 Others 3+1/1

OLIVER Luke John
Born: Acton, 1 May 1984
Height: 6'6" **Weight:** 14.6
International Honours: E: SP-1
Dubbed the best central defender at Wycombe by manager Peter Taylor, this giant of a centre-half was an automatic choice until the manager's departure in October. After a spell on the bench he was recalled to the side by new manager Gary Waddock in November, when Leon Johnson became injured, and kept his place until the end of the year. However, with the defence leaking goals he was in and out of the side again until Peter Taylor took him on loan to Bradford in March. He made his debut in a home win over Aldershot where his aerial power came to the fore, particularly defending corners, and playing as a makeshift centre-forward he scored twice in that role before Wycombe called him back four weeks later as cover for injuries. Was not

offered a new contract at the end of the season and signed a two-year deal at Bradford.
Wycombe W (Free from Brook House on 2/7/2002) FL 0+4 (Free to Woking on 25/2/2004)
Yeovil T (Signed on 6/7/2005) FL 0+3 (Free to Stevenage Borough on 27/1/2006)
Wycombe W (Free from Stevenage Borough on 30/1/2009) FL 20+11 FLC 1 FAC 1
Bradford C (Loaned on 3/3/2010) FL 7/2

OLOFINJANA Seyi George
Born: Lagos, Nigeria, 30 June 1980
Height: 6'4" **Weight:** 11.10
International Honours: Nigeria: 41
Having attracted interest from AS Monaco earlier in the summer, Seyi's desire for regular first team football took him to Hull on a four-year contract. He wore the number 44 shirt in recognition of Nigeria and former City legend Jay-Jay Okocha. With impressive composure on the ball for such a powerfully-built central midfielder, he enjoyed a superb debut in the late defeat at Chelsea on the opening day. Unfortunately and somewhat surprisingly, his first team involvement gradually declined. After scoring in the win against his former club Stoke in November, he was to start in only two more Premier League games despite the demands of the Tigers' unsuccessful struggle against relegation. Seyi also experienced mixed fortunes on the international stage. He was a member of the Nigeria squad that reached the semi-finals of the African Cup of Nations in Angola although, due to illness, he appeared only in the third and fourth place play-off.
Wolverhampton W (£1,700,000 from SK Brann Bergen, Norway on 6/8/2004) FL 123+12/16 FLC 3+1 FAC 6/1 Others 2/1
Stoke C (£3,000,000 on 29/7/2008) PL 14+4/2 FLC 2 FAC 1
Hull C (£3,000,000 on 6/8/2009) PL 11+8/1

OLSSON Jonas
Born: Landskrona, Sweden, 10 March 1983
Height: 6'5" **Weight:** 13.5
International Honours: Sweden: 1; U21-23
West Bromwich's vice-captain had an excellent season, admitting: "it was one of his best for several years". He was certainly the mainstay of the Baggies' defence as they finished runners-up in the Championship. Strong in the air, capable and competitive on the ground, Jonas scored some vital goals from set

pieces, including two in the 3-1 home victory over Doncaster in September. He also backed up his goalkeeper Scott Carson on numerous occasions, clearing several goal-bound shots off the line, including a later effort in the promotion-clinching victory at Doncaster in April. Still awaiting his first full cap, Jonas was included in the Swedish squad for the friendly against Wales at Swansea's Liberty Stadium in March, but never came off the bench. He will be hoping for better luck as a Premiership player.
West Bromwich A (£800,000 from NEC Nijmegen, Holland, ex Landskrona, on 2/9/2008) P/FL 71/6 FLC 2 FAC 4/2

OLSSON Martin Tony Waikwa
Born: Gavle, Sweden, 17 May 1988
Height: 5'7" **Weight:** 12.11
International Honours: Sweden: 1; U21-10
It was always likely to be a make or break season at Blackburn for left-back Martin and his chance appeared remote early in the season when Pascal Chimbonda arrived to take over from Stephen Warnock. Martin had to go on in the home leg of the Carling Cup semi-final against Aston Villa, when Lars Jacobsen was injured, and gave an encouraging display, with a refreshing desire to get forward to use his speed wide on the left. In the following game against Fulham, he was used on the left of midfield because Morten Gamst Pedersen was injured and produced a performance of such verve that he remained in the side for the rest of the season, occasionally in his old role of full-back but most often in midfield. He struck a vital goal in the home game against Hull, from an impossible angle on the by-line, and an overhead-kick in the second leg of the Carling Cup tie at Villa Park was a classic example of technique and was voted Blackburn's 'Goal of the Season'.
Blackburn Rov (Signed from Hogaborgs BK, Sweden on 31/1/2006) PL 25+7/1 FLC 8+1/2 FAC 4 Others 0+1

OMOZUSI Elliott Junior
Born: Hackney, 15 December 1988
Height: 5'11" **Weight:** 12.9
International Honours: E: Yth
Elliott arrived at Charlton on loan from Fulham at the end of October to deputise for the injured Frazer Richardson. He looked a little rusty at first but improved the more he played and but for Richardson's return would probably have seen his loan period extended. Elliott is a solid defender and was effective going forward down the right.

Fulham (From juniors on 20/12/2005) PL 8 FLC 0+2 FAC 1
Norwich C (Loaned on 24/7/2008) FL 20+1 FLC 1 FAC 2
Charlton Ath (Loaned on 30/10/2009) FL 7+2 FAC 1

O'NEIL Gary Paul
Born: Bromley, 18 May 1983
Height: 5'10" **Weight:** 11.0
Club Honours: Div 1 '03
International Honours: E: U21-9; Yth
Gary was felt by many Middlesbrough fans to be one of the players on his way out after the club suffered relegation. Despite speculation that former club Portsmouth were poised to sign him, the transfer window came and went with Gary still at the club. He showed his commitment after suffering with a groin injury for most of the campaign. He even returned from a hernia operation, and was playing within two weeks of having 38 staples in his wound. In December, the club exercised the option of extending his contract by a further two years. New manager Gordon Strachan wasted no time in handing Gary the captain's armband, as he was looking for experience to lead the team. The all-action midfielder tried in vain to take his team into the play-offs but too many draws cost them. In April he found himself stranded on 99 games, as it was agreed at the time of his signing that £1-million would be paid to former club Portsmouth if he played 100. A fee was renegotiated in order for Gary to play the last three games but he suffered a groin injury in training after his 100th appearance. He was the Middlesbrough official supporters club 'Player of the Year'.
Portsmouth (From trainee on 5/6/2000) P/FL 142+33/16 FLC 7+4/1 FAC 7+1
Walsall (Loaned on 26/9/2003) FL 7
Cardiff C (Loaned on 24/9/2004) FL 8+1/1
Middlesbrough (£5,000,000 on 31/8/2007) P/FL 88+3/8 FLC 1+1 FAC 7+1

O'NEILL Luke Marcus
Born: Slough, 20 August 1991
Height: 6'0" **Weight:** 11.4
International Honours: E: Yth
The promising young right-back had limited opportunities to impress at Leicester during 2009-10, making his only start at Macclesfield in the Carling Cup and adding just a solitary bench outing to that tally as the season unfolded. To further his experience in the game he joined Tranmere in February on a one-month loan, making his debut in the home game against

Leyton Orient. Although he played only four games for the club, it was apparent from his skill, commitment and endeavour that Luke should have a great future in the game. His steady approach and assurance belied his 18 years.
Leicester C (From trainee on 5/9/2008) FL 0+1 FLC 1 Others 1
Tranmere Rov (Loaned on 18/2/2010) FL 4

O'NEILL Ryan
Born: Dungannon, 19 January 1990
Height: 6'0" **Weight:** 12.13
International Honours: NI: U21-9; Yth
The Northern Irish right-back signed for Barnet after being released by Premier League side West Ham at the end of the previous campaign. Ryan began the season in the first team, with first choice right-back Joe Devera injured. Although he clung on to his first team place for a while, the return of Devera limited his chances and he was confined to the substitutes' bench for much of the campaign. Was out of contract at the end of June.
West Ham U (From trainee on 20/7/2007)
Barnet (Free on 8/7/2009) FL 11+4 FLC 1

ONUOHA Chinedum (Nedum)
Born: Warri, Nigeria, 12 November 1986
Height: 6'2" **Weight:** 12.4
International Honours: E: U21-21; Yth
Nedum is a Manchester City defender and one of a number of younger players whose progress has been hindered both by injuries and the influx of expensive signings. Partly due to a thigh injury he did not make his first appearance of the season until November, as a substitute. He had two starts in central defence in December in what proved to be Mark Hughes' last games in charge. Under Roberto Mancini, he was given occasional outings at right-back and scored twice, at Scunthorpe in the FA Cup in January and at Burnley in April where City won 6-1. At the age of 23, he needs to be playing regular first team football and following public criticism of his manager, may have to look elsewhere.
Manchester C (From trainee on 16/11/2004) PL 72+22/3 FLC 4+2 FAC 6/1 Others 7/1

ORLANDI Andrea
Born: Barcelona, Spain, 3 August 1984
Height: 6'0" **Weight:** 12.2
The former Barcelona 'B' team player was used in a central midfield role by

Swansea manager Paulo Sousa and became a regular inclusion during the first half of 2009-10, showing a wide variety of skill on the ball, with excellent close skills. A hamstring injury at Derby kept him sidelined during the last third of the campaign, and when Andrea returned to fitness he scored his first goal of the season direct from a corner in the derby game at Cardiff.
Swansea C (Free from Deportivo Alaves, Spain, ex Barcelona - loan, Aris Salonika, on 31/8/2007) FL 29+20/2 FLC 3 FAC 3+3 Others 3

ORMEROD Brett Ryan
Born: Blackburn, 18 October 1976
Height: 5'11" **Weight:** 11.4
Club Honours: AMC '02
Much like Keith Southern, Brett is a player you immediately think of when Blackpool are mentioned. His spirit and hard work for the cause is something at 33 and has to be admired. Quoted as saying a Blackpool promotion to the Premiership would top playing in the FA Cup final for Southampton, Brett will want to add to his impressive 11 goals from the right wing this season. Many fans questioned his move from Preston in January 2009, but constant running and a knack of being in the right place at the right time has made him a crowd favourite once again at Bloomfield Road. He sealed 'Pool's play-off place with a brave headed goal against Bristol City on the final day and put them ahead for the first time in the Wembley final against Cardiff with what turned out to be the winner.
Blackpool (£50,000 from Accrington Stanley on 21/3/1997) FL 105+23/45 FLC 8/4 FAC 5+1/5 Others 7+2/8
Southampton (£1,750,000 on 7/12/2001) P/FL 62+37/12 FLC 6+1/6 FAC 6+4/1
Leeds U (Loaned on 23/9/2004) FL 6
Wigan Ath (Loaned on 18/3/2005) FL 3+3/2
Preston NE (Free on 30/1/2006) FL 37+25/13 FLC 1 FAC 1+2/1 Others 2
Nottingham F (Loaned on 7/3/2008) FL 13/2
Oldham Ath (Loaned on 14/10/2008) FL 2+3
Blackpool (Free on 30/1/2009) FL 34+17/13 FLC 2 FAC 1/1 Others 3/1

ORR Bradley James
Born: Liverpool, 1 November 1982
Height: 6'0" **Weight:** 11.12
Another good season from this Bristol City defender, despite being the target of a hot-head fan following the 6-0 home defeat by Cardiff in January, when the free programmes handed out

at this game rained down on the pitch. Bradley was quite the wrong person to pick out as he certainly could never be faulted for lack of effort or commitment. Indeed, so committed is Bradley that, in taking exception to some comments critical of the team being aired on Radio Bristol shortly after one of the home games earlier in the season, he took the trouble to phone in and give an impassioned defence.
Newcastle U (From trainee on 12/7/2001)
Burnley (Loaned on 29/1/2004) FL 1+3
Bristol C (Loaned on 20/7/2004) FL 204+25/12 FLC 5+1/1 FAC 12 Others 8

OSBORNE Karleigh Anthony Jonathan
Born: Southall, 19 March 1988
Height: 6'2" **Weight:** 12.8
Club Honours: Div 2 '09
This solid Brentford centre-back was a regular in the squad for the first few months of the season but did not make any appearances. He then dropped out of contention as other central defenders went ahead of him in the pecking order. Karleigh, producing some impressive defensive displays, returned to first team action in March and started 11 of the last 13 games, a run in which Brentford lost only once.

Bradley Orr

Brentford *(From trainee on 27/6/2006)*
FL 76+18/5 FLC 2+2 FAC 2+2 Others 5

OSBORNE Leon Aiden
Born: Doncaster, 28 October 1989
Height: 5'10" **Weight:** 10.10
Leon, who can play on the left wing or as a central striker, started Bradford's Johnstone's Paint Trophy win over Notts County in October. However, he was given a real opportunity once Peter Taylor took over as manager. Having played in the same position, Taylor recognised the 20-year-old's talent and rewarded him with several games towards the end of the season.
Bradford C *(From trainee on 5/7/2008)*
FL 6+9 FAC 1+2 Others 1+1

OSBOURNE Isaac Samuel
Born: Birmingham, 22 June 1986
Height: 5'10" **Weight:** 11.12
After having played out of position at right-back for large parts of the previous two seasons, the home-grown Coventry midfield player was there again on the opening day of the season owing to injuries. Another injury, to David Bell, saw Isaac switched in game two to the right of midfield. It seemed he was destined for another season of frustration being played out of his favourite central midfield role but first Aron Gunnarsson's mixed form gave him a chance in the middle and then Sammy Clingan's injury in October enabled him to play the anchor role to good effect. Isaac is a strong ball-winner, good at short distribution and always adds a competitive edge to Coventry's midfield. Sadly in early November he picked up a knee injury and missed the rest of the season.
Coventry C *(From trainee on 10/7/2003)* FL 101+21 FLC 7 FAC 6
Crewe Alex *(Loaned on 20/10/2006)* FL 2 FLC 1 Others 1

OSBOURNE Isaiah
Born: Birmingham, 5 November 1987
Height: 6'2" **Weight:** 12.7
Aston Villa's Isaiah was Gordon Strachan's second loan signing a week after he took charge at Middlesbrough. Isaiah was also on the sheet of paper, along with eight other players, that Strachan was photographed holding when entering the Riverside on his first day. Billed by the manager as a 'continuity player', the midfielder made his debut in a 1-0 defeat at Crystal Palace. He played a further eight games before returning to Villa Park at the end of his two-month loan.
Aston Villa *(From trainee on 11/11/2005)* PL 7+3 FLC 4 FAC 1+1 Others 2+2

Nottingham F *(Loaned on 3/3/2009)* FL 7+1
Middlesbrough *(Loaned on 5/11/2009)* FL 9

OSEI-KUFFOUR Jonathan (Jo)
Born: Edmonton, 17 November 1981
Height: 5'7" **Weight:** 10.6
Club Honours: FAYC '00
Jo had to adapt quickly to a variety of different forward partners for Bristol Rovers following the departure of the previous season's leading scorer Rickie Lambert. He is a tricky front runner who uses his pace to get behind defences. Jo scored twice in a first ever victory at Yeovil, his first charging down a clearance from the 'keeper and his second turning cleverly inside the penalty area to score. One of his best goals was a clever finish at Southampton and he was Rovers' leading scorer with 14 goals.
Arsenal *(From trainee on 18/7/2000)*
Swindon T *(Loaned on 24/8/2001)* FL 4+7/2 FLC 1 Others 1
Torquay U *(Free on 18/10/2002)* FL 111+37/29 FLC 2+1/1 FAC 5+1/1 Others 3+1/2
Brentford *(Free on 6/7/2006)* FL 38+1/12 FLC 2/1 FAC 1 Others 2/1
Bournemouth *(Free on 3/7/2007)* FL 39+5/12 FLC 2/1 FAC 2 Others 3/1
Bristol Rov *(Signed on 30/8/2008)* FL 68+15/25 FLC 2 FAC 2

O'SHEA James (Jay)
Born: Dublin, 10 August 1988
Height: 6'0" **Weight:** 11.0
International Honours: RoI: U21-7
Having been signed from Galway United, Jay made a dream debut as a substitute for Birmingham on the opening day of the season at Manchester United. Involved in the squad early on and showing useful, probing wing play as more players became available he dropped out of the picture. Loaned to Middlesbrough in March in order to bolster the club's attacking options, Jay was brought in as an emergency loan signing in March after being on Boro's radar in the summer. Making his debut for Middlesbrough when coming off the bench in a 1-1 home draw with Crystal Palace, he only played one more game, starting in a 2-0 away win at Plymouth, before returning to St Andrews after his loan spell had expired. A tricky right-sided winger, Jay will be hoping to push on for a regular first team place at Birmingham this coming campaign.
Birmingham C *(Signed from Galway U, ex Home Farm, Bray W, on 10/8/2009)* PL 0+1 FLC 2

Middlesbrough *(Loaned on 25/3/2010)* FL 1+1

O'SHEA John Francis
Born: Waterford, 30 April 1981
Height: 6'3" **Weight:** 11.12
Club Honours: PL '03, '07, '08, '09; CS '03, '07; FAC '04; FLC '06, '09; UEFACL '08
International Honours: RoI: 62; U21-13; Yth (UEFA-U16 '98)
As a central defender, John has presence, composure and silky defensive skills. His versatility and overall performances were rewarded when he captained Manchester United for the first time in their opening Premier League game against Birmingham. He celebrated his 350th appearance by scoring his first League goal in over two years, against Stoke, firing a header in a 2-0 win. At international level he was ever-present for the Republic of Ireland, but they unfortunately failed to qualify for the World Cup. An infamous moment in football history came during a crunch clash with Italy, when John was elbowed in the forehead by Giampaolo Pazzini, who earned the fastest sending-off by an Italian. After receiving treatment, John played for the full 90 minutes. Unfortunately, his season was interrupted by injuries. He played in the away defeat by Chelsea in the Premiership in November and made a comeback in the Champions League quarter-final against Bayern Munich, who went through on away goals.
Manchester U *(Signed from Waterford U on 2/9/1998)* PL 170+66/10 FLC 24+1/2 FAC 18+6/1 Others 60+16/2
Bournemouth *(Loaned on 18/1/2000)* FL 10/1 Others 1

OSHODI Edward (Eddie)
Abdullai Mobalaji Olatunji Afo
Born: Brent, 14 January 1992
Height: 6'0" **Weight:** 11.9
International Honours: E: Yth
Eddie, a strapping centre-half, made his Watford debut as a substitute against Coventry in September while still a second-year Academy scholar. An England under-17 international, Eddie was awarded a professional contract before the end of the season.
Watford *(From trainee on 29/1/2009)* FL 0+1

OSMAN Abdul Haq Bin Seidu
Born: Accra, Ghana, 27 February 1987
Height: 6'0" **Weight:** 11.0
This was midfield player Abdul's best season at Sixfields so far, taking on the role of a defensive central midfield player. Several times he has been

named 'Man of the Match' with his constant running, timely tackling and the odd pot shot at goal. Is certainly one of the most improved players at Northampton.
Gretna (Free from Maidenhead U, ex Hampton & Richmond Borough, on 1/7/2007) SL 16+2/1 SLC 1 SC 1
Northampton T (Free on 24/7/2008) FL 60+6/4 FLC 3+1 Others 1+2

Abdul Osman

OSMAN Leon
Born: Billinge, 17 May 1981
Height: 5'8" **Weight:** 11.0
Club Honours: FAYC '98
International Honours: E: Yth; Sch
The midfielder continued to consolidate his role as a regular member of the Everton team and he also captained the club for the first time. Another product of the prolific Everton Academy, he was deployed mostly in a central midfield role during the season, and was reaching top form before being sidelined with a foot injury in the autumn. His personal highlights in the League were two brilliantly taken goals against Stoke at Goodison and Arsenal at the Emirates. A player with immaculate technique and two quick feet, Leon extended his stay at Goodison into a third decade during the season, having been in the FA Youth Cup winning side in 1998.
Everton (From trainee on 18/8/1998) PL 169+23/25 FLC 10+3/2 FAC 13+2/4 Others 16+2/2
Carlisle U (Loaned on 4/10/2002) FL 10+2/1 Others 3/2
Derby Co (Loaned on 26/1/2004) FL 17/3

OSTER John Morgan
Born: Boston, 8 December 1978
Height: 5'9" **Weight:** 10.8
Club Honours: Ch '06
International Honours: W: 13; B-1; U21-9; Yth
Signed by Doncaster as a free agent in the summer on a short-term contract, John played so well that he was offered and signed a contract in January for the rest of the season. He proved to be a hard-working asset in midfield and took over Brian Stock's role when he was injured as playmaker of the team. He eventually opened his goals account in March at Peterborough when, after initiating the move, he arrived in the six-yard box to tap in and seal the win. His season ended when he went down with a hamstring injury in the warm-up before the penultimate match against Scunthorpe.
Grimsby T (From trainee on 11/7/1996) FL 21+3/3 FAC 0+1/1
Everton (£1,500,000 on 21/7/1997) PL 22+18/1 FLC 4+1/1 FAC 2+3/1
Sunderland (£1,000,000 on 6/8/1999) P/FL 48+20/5 FLC 9+2/1 FAC 7+3 Others 2
Barnsley (Loaned on 19/10/2001) FL 2
Grimsby T (Loaned on 1/11/2002) FL 10/5
Grimsby T (Loaned on 21/2/2003) FL 7/1
Leeds U (Loaned on 5/11/2004) FL 8/1
Burnley (Free on 28/1/2005) FL 12+3/1 FAC 2+1
Reading (Free on 2/8/2005) P/FL 29+47/2 FLC 6/1 FAC 8
Crystal Palace (Free on 11/8/2008) FL 27+4/3 FLC 1/1 FAC 1
Doncaster Rov (Free on 7/8/2009) FL 36+4/1 FLC 2 FAC 2

O'TOOLE John (John-Joe) Joseph
Born: Harrow, 30 September 1988
Height: 6'2" **Weight:** 13.7
International Honours: RoI: U21-5
When Aidy Boothroyd took over as Colchester manager in September he made it his first task to bring John-Joe across from his former club Watford on loan. The box-to-box midfielder was soon affectionately nicknamed a 'brawler' by his boss, his battling style helping the U's to numerous narrow victories but also earning him ten yellow cards before the New Year. Colchester made the move permanent in the January transfer window but John-Joe's season was to end in disappointment when he was stretchered off at Charlton with knee ligament damage. He is not due back until next Christmas.
Watford (From trainee on 27/9/2007) FL 37+20/10 FLC 0+4/1 FAC 2+2/1 Others 0+1

Sheffield U (Loaned on 25/2/2009) FL 5+4/1
Colchester U (Signed on 1/9/2009) FL 30+1/2 FAC 2/1

OTSEMOBOR Jon
Born: Liverpool, 23 March 1983
Height: 5'10" **Weight:** 12.7
Club Honours: Div 1 '10
International Honours: E: Yth
Jon made 13 League appearances for Norwich before his move to Southampton in January, scoring with a header against Wycombe. With his pace and power giving him all the attributes needed to be a top-class Football League right-back, he arrived in Southampton with the reputation of being an excellent defender. However, it was soon evident why this former Liverpool trainee had become surplus to requirements at Carrow Road after some inconsistent displays with the Saints let him down. Jon was not offered a new contract in May.
Liverpool (From trainee on 23/3/2000) PL 4 FLC 2
Hull C (Loaned on 13/3/2003) FL 8+1/3
Bolton W (Loaned on 2/2/2004) PL 1
Crewe Alex (Loaned on 30/9/2004) FL 14/1 FLC 1
Rotherham U (Free on 1/8/2005) FL 4+6 FLC 1+1/1 Others 2
Crewe Alex (Free on 18/1/2006) FL 43 FLC 3 FAC 1 Others 3
Norwich C (Free on 3/7/2007) FL 88+5/2 FLC 5 FAC 2+2 Others 1+1
Southampton (Signed on 14/1/2010) FL 19

OWEN Gareth David
Born: Cheadle, Staffordshire, 21 September 1982
Height: 6'1" **Weight:** 11.6
International Honours: W: Yth
Experienced and with a calm head under pressure, Gareth helped Port Vale to achieve their best defensive record for nine years. At first he was one of three centre-halves but did equally as well when they reverted to a flat back four. He suffered for his efforts and missed eight games through injury. A blow in the eye socket at Bradford in the Johnstone's Paint Trophy led to him playing a couple of games in a mask, which brought its own problems in the pouring rain at Barnet. A back injury kept him out for a couple of games but he remained a very important member of the defence.
Stoke C (From trainee on 5/7/2001) FL 1+4
Oldham Ath (Loaned on 16/1/2004) FL 15/1
Torquay U (Loaned on 1/7/2004) FL 2+3 FLC 1

Gareth Owen

Oldham Ath *(£50,000 on 19/3/2005) FL 26 FLC 1 FAC 2+1*
Stockport Co *(Signed on 4/7/2006) FL 82+1 FLC 4 FAC 3 Others 5+1*
Yeovil T *(Loaned on 17/10/2008) FL 7*
Port Vale *(Free on 25/11/2008) FL 52 FLC 3 FAC 2 Others 2*

OWEN Michael James
Born: Chester, 14 December 1979
Height: 5'9" **Weight:** 11.2
Club Honours: FAYC '96; FLC '01, '03, 10; FAC '01; UEFAC '01; ESC '01; CS '01
International Honours: E: 89; B-2; U21-1; Yth; Sch
Veteran striker who won many top honours with Liverpool, Michael's arrival at Manchester United was one of the most fascinating transfer stories of the summer. His management company 'Wasserman Media Group' sent out a 34-page brochure advertising Michael's talents to potential clubs and Sir Alex Ferguson signed him on a two-year deal. With Michael stating the move had come 'out of the blue', he was handed the number seven shirt recently vacated by Ronaldo. And what a start he made, scoring on his debut against a Malaysian XI, and adding three more goals in pre-season games. He made his League debut for the Reds as a substitute against Birmingham in August, and scored his first

competitive goal against Wigan in a 5–0 away win. His second - and first at Old Trafford - came against Manchester City as a substitute for Dimitar Berbatov. Michael's goal came in the sixth minute of stoppage time, which caused a furore in City's ranks, and meant he scored in his fourth derby, having netted in the Merseyside derby, El Classico in Spain and the Tyne–Wear derby. After notching a goal against Barnsley in the Carling Cup in October, he scored his first Champions League goal for United in the 3–3 draw against CSKA Moscow. Still hoping to impress Fabio Capello for the 2010 World Cup finals, he was boosted by a hat-trick in December in the 3-1 away win against Wolfsburg in the Champions League – his first hat-trick since 2005. Playing in the Carling Cup final, Michael netted the equaliser against Aston Villa but pulled up with a hamstring injury that ended his season and dashed any World Cup hopes.
Liverpool *(From juniors on 18/12/1996) PL 193+23/118 FLC 12+2/9 FAC 14+1/8 Others 48+4/23 (£11,000,000 to Real Madrid, Spain on 20/8/2004)*
Newcastle U *(£16,000,000 from Real Madrid, Spain on 31/8/2005) PL 58+13/26 FLC 2+1/3 FAC 5/1*
Manchester U *(Free on 3/7/2009) PL 5+14/3 FLC 3+1/2 FAC 0+1 Others 3+4/4*

OWUSU-ABEYIE Quincy Jamie
Born: Amsterdam, Holland, 15 April 1986
Height: 5'11" **Weight:** 11.1
International Honours: Ghana: 12. Holland: U21-8; Yth
In a brief spell at Portsmouth that consisted of 11 appearances, there was enough time for Quincy to write himself into folklore at Fratton Park. The speedy winger came off the bench to fire Pompey to a 4-1 FA Cup victory at bitter rivals Southampton in February, scoring a classy opener and laying on two more goals. His skill and trickery grabbed the attention of Qatar side Al-Sadd and he was transferred to them in March.
Arsenal *(From trainee on 2/7/2004) PL 1+4 FLC 6+4/2 FAC 0+3 Others 1+4 (Signed by Spartak Moscow, Russia on 31/1/2006)*
Birmingham C *(Loaned from Spartak Moscow, Russia on 7/8/2008) FL 12+7/2 FLC 1+1/1*
Cardiff C *(Loaned from Spartak Moscow, Russia on 2/2/2009) FL 0+5*
Portsmouth *(Loaned from Spartak Moscow, Russia on 28/1/2010) PL 3+7 FAC 0+1/1*

OXLADE-CHAMBERLAIN Alexander (Alex) Mark David
Born: Portsmouth, 15 August 1993
Height: 5'11" **Weight:** 11.0
The son of former England star Mark Chamberlain, Alex has been with Southampton since he was seven. He slipped into first team contention in March, making his debut at St Mary's as a substitute in the 5-0 win over Huddersfield. Then aged 16 years and 199 days, the agile midfielder became the Saints' second youngest debutant after Theo Walcott. In his 15 minutes of action to date Alex has demonstrated tight dribbling, impish ball-skills, nerve and breathtaking acceleration. He looks a likely prospect.
Southampton *(Trainee) FL 0+2*

OXLEY Mark Thomas
Born: Rotherham, 2 June 1990
Height: 5'11" **Weight:** 11.7
International Honours: E: Yth
Signed by Grimsby from Hull on loan to put pressure on regular goalkeeper Nick Colgan, Mark's senior debut was in a 2-0 loss at Dagenham. The teenager then returned at Easter on an emergency loan deal when all of Town's custodians were injured, playing his part in a 3-2 win at Accrington – Grimsby's first away victory in League Two since the previous September.
Hull C *(From trainee at Rotherham U on 1/8/2008)*
Grimsby T *(Loaned on 25/2/2010) FL 3*

P

PACHECO Daniel
Born: Malaga, Spain, 5 January 1991
Height: 5'6" **Weight:** 10.8
International Honours: Spain: Yth
Daniel is a young Spanish-born
attacking midfielder who signed for
Liverpool in 2007 from the Barcelona
youth team. He made his debut in
December as a second-half substitute
for Alberto Aquilani in the last
Champions League game at home to
Fiorentina, when Liverpool's elimination
was confirmed. He made six further
substitute appearances, including his
Premiership debut in late December at
Wolverhampton. He is perhaps the
most promising of Liverpool's
youngsters waiting for a breakthrough.
Liverpool (From trainee, ex Barcelona,
Spain, on 22/2/2008) PL 0+4 Others 0+3

PACK Marlon
Born: Portsmouth, 25 March 1991
Height: 6'0" **Weight:** 11.9
With influential midfielder Tommy
Doherty injured, Wycombe signed the
young midfielder on loan from
Portsmouth in August as cover. He
made his debut in the Johnstone's
Paints Trophy first round game against
Northampton and then had a run of
seven League starts, extending his loan
to a second month, before new
manager Gary Waddock surprisingly
decided not to extend the deal further.
As the midfield lynch pin, Marlon
displayed extraordinary maturity for his
age, controlling play and being able to
spot and deliver a killing pass. In
January he joined Dagenham on loan
and after a slow start showed enough
ability for manager John Still to keep
him on for the maximum 93 days. The
midfielder has good ability in the air
and is strong in the tackle. Marlon
scored in his last game for the Daggers
at Port Vale with a header.
Portsmouth (From trainee on
4/7/2009)
Wycombe W (Loaned on 31/8/2009) FL
7+1 Others 1
Dagenham & Redbridge (Loaned on
7/1/2010) FL 17/1

PAGE Robert (Rob) John
Born: Rhondda, 3 September 1974
Height: 6'0" **Weight:** 12.5
Club Honours: Div 2 '98
International Honours: W: 41; B-1;
U21-6; Yth; Sch
Rob got the clean slate he craved for at
Chesterfield after his trials in 2008-09

and responded with more displays that
showed character and determination.
The vastly experienced Welsh
international linked well with Aaron
Downes at the heart of the Spireites'
defence and, while the most physical
and pacy opponent caused problems,
Rob enjoyed a far more productive
season than before and was offered -
and accepted - a new contract for the
season ahead.
Watford (From trainee on 19/4/1993)
P/FL 209+7/2 FLC 17 FAC 12+1 Others
6/1
Sheffield U (£350,000 on 8/8/2001) FL
106+1/1 FLC 7 FAC 11 Others 3
Cardiff C (Free on 3/7/2004) FL 8+1
Coventry C (Free on 22/2/2005) FL
69+1/1 FLC 3 FAC 3
Huddersfield T (Free on 22/1/2008) FL
18/1 FAC 2
Chesterfield (Free on 2/8/2008) FL
54+1/1 FLC 1 FAC 1 Others 3+1

PAINTER Marcos
Born: Sutton Coldfield, 17 August
1986
Height: 5'11" **Weight:** 12.4

Club Honours: Div 1 '08
International Honours: RoI: U21-7; Yth
The former Birmingham defender made
his return to first team action at
Swansea in a Carling Cup tie against
Scunthorpe, after almost ten months on
the sidelines with a knee injury.
Following a handful of first team
appearances for the Swans he moved to
League One side Brighton in January on
loan for the rest of the season. Quickly
establishing himself in the left-back
berth, he made a significant
contribution to the team's improvement
in the latter half of the season, being
solid in defence and always looking to
get forward. Although he missed three
games with a knee injury, such was his
impact that he ended the campaign
with an agreement to move to Sussex
on a permanent basis despite suffering
a cartilage injury.
Birmingham C (From trainee on
14/7/2005) P/FL 3+2 FLC 2+1 FAC 2+1
Swansea C (£50,000 on 16/11/2006)
FL 66+2 FLC 3 FAC 3+1 Others 4
Brighton & Hove A (Loaned on
13/1/2010) FL 18+1

Wilson Palacios

PALACIOS Wilson Roberto
Born: La Ceiba, Honduras, 29 July 1984
Height: 5'10" **Weight:** 11.3
International Honours: Honduras: 69
While still recovering from the personal tragedy of the loss of his brother, Tottenham's Wilson will probably look back on this season as a high point in his career. The Honduran International played a full part in their qualification for the World Cup and is in their squad for the finals. He played seven games for Honduras during the season. On the domestic front, Wilson remains a mainstay in Tottenham's central midfield and played in 42 of their 50 games, starting 37 times. A great tackler and chaser of the ball, scoring his first senior goal in the 5-1 win at Hull, Wilson's creative skills are also developing and he makes many astute passes. He has occasionally been used to cover other positions, such as right-back. Unfortunately, his tenacity attracts the attention of referees and he was booked ten times, leading to his absence from two of Spurs' crucial run-in games.
Birmingham C (Loaned from Olimpia, Honduras, ex Deportivo Victoria, on 31/8/2007) PL 4+3 FLC 0+1
Wigan Ath (£1,000,000 from Olimpia, Honduras on 11/1/2008) PL 37 FLC 2 FAC 2
Tottenham H (£12,000,000 on 30/1/2009) PL 40+4/1 FLC 3 FAC 6+1 Others 1

PALMER Christopher (Chris) Louis
Born: Derby, 16 October 1983
Height: 5'7" **Weight:** 10.12
A summer signing from Walsall, Chris is a hugely versatile player, blessed with two good feet and capable of playing on either wing or in both left and right-back roles for Gillingham. Unfortunately that versatility was probably his undoing as he failed to hold down a regular berth in any of those positions. His crossing and set-piece play were useful weapons in the Gills' arsenal and he netted his first goal for the club with a rasping late volley in the defeat at Swindon.
Derby Co (From trainee on 3/7/2003)
Notts Co (Free on 2/7/2004) FL 48+6/5 FLC 1/1 FAC 4+1 Others 0+1
Wycombe W (Free on 1/8/2006) FL 23+10 FLC 2+3 FAC 1+1 Others 2
Darlington (Loaned on 9/8/2007) FL 4 FLC 1
Walsall (Free on 7/8/2008) FL 41+3/1 FLC 1 FAC 1 Others 2
Gillingham (Free on 6/7/2009) FL 16+4/1 FLC 1+1 FAC 3 Others 2

PANCRATE Fabrice
Born: Paris, France, 2 May 1980
Height: 6'1" **Weight:** 11.9
Club Honours: Ch '10
Signed by Newcastle as a free agent after being released by Paris St Germain, Fabrice made a stunning early impact against Watford in December when he crashed a shot in off the crossbar after outwitting a couple of defenders with a delightful piece of skill. Primarily a right-winger, he is versatile enough to operate in a number of positions, and in January he came on as a substitute for Enrique at left-back. He failed to live up to his early promise however, and the arrival of Wayne Routledge in the January transfer window cast doubt on his Tyneside future. His contract was not renewed when it expired at the end of the season.
Newcastle U (Free from Paris St Germain, France, ex Louhans-Cuiseaux, Guingamp, Le Mans, Real Betis - loan, Sochaux - loan, on 21/11/2009) FL 5+11/1 FAC 3

PANTHER Emmanuel (Manny) Ugochukwu Ezenwa
Born: Glasgow, 11 May 1984
Height: 6'0" **Weight:** 13.7
International Honours: S: Yth
Signed by Morecambe on a season-long loan from Exeter in the early weeks of the season, Manny made an immediate impression as a holding midfielder to stop the Shrimps leaking goals. He was one of the team's top performers until he unfortunately suffered a broken toe after being involved in a collision with Sol Campbell, in his only League Two game for Notts County, that put him out of action for three months. He struggled to regain his place and match fitness after the injury and ended the season on the bench. Was out of contract at the end of June.
St Johnstone (From juniors on 1/7/2001) SL 8+3 SC 0+1
Partick T (Free on 1/7/2003) SL 6+15/2 SLC 2 Others 2+1/2 (Freed during 2005 close season)
Brechin C (Loaned on 18/2/2005) SL 3+5/1
Exeter C (Free from York C on 8/8/2008) FL 15+7/2 Others 0+1
Morecambe (Loaned on 18/8/2009) FL 14+5 Others 0+1

PANTSIL John
Born: Berekum, Ghana, 15 June 1981
Height: 5'10" **Weight:** 10.10
International Honours: Ghana: 58
The Ghanaian international continued to be first choice at right-back for Fulham when fit, missing only one

Premier League game before sustaining a knee injury against Chelsea in December. This caused him to miss the African Cup of Nations and appeared at one stage to threaten his involvement in the World Cup. However, a quicker than expected recovery saw him back in contention by April and he soon re-established himself as first choice. A wholehearted defender who is quick to turn defence into attack, he is assured in the air and on the ground, where he is rarely beaten for pace. A firm favourite with the Craven Cottage crowd, John was voted 'Footballer of the Year' by the Ghanaian Sports Writers Association before heading for the World Cup finals.
West Ham U (£1,000,000 from Hapoel Tel Aviv, Israel, ex Berekum Arsenal, Liberty Professionals, Berekum Arsenal, Widzew Lodz, Maccabi Tel Aviv, on 7/8/2006) PL 7+12 FLC 1+2 FAC 1+1
Fulham (Signed on 18/7/2008) PL 59 FLC 0+1 FAC 2 Others 9+1

John Pantsil

[PAPA WAIGO] N'DIAYE Papa Waigo
Born: Saint-Louis, Senegal, 20 January 1984
Height: 6'1" **Weight:** 11.9
Club Honours: AMC '10
International Honours: Senegal: 15
The news last September that this Senegalese striker was Southampton-bound on loan, following promptings on internet fan-forums, soon had the faithful Googling YouTube to witness his outlandish goal celebration. It was soon seen live, or rather an edited, English referee-friendly version of it. Although Papa Waigo had spent his

entire career in Italy, shuttling between various Serie A and B sides, he adapted well to League One football. Busy, quick and nimble, with seemingly prehensile boots, the striker was a great crowd pleaser, if something of a square peg. He had his moments though: managing ten tribal dances, one of them after netting at Wembley in the Johnstone's Paint Trophy final. He then returned to Italy, leaving Southampton a slightly greyer place.
Southampton *(Loaned from Fiorentina, Italy, ex Verona, Cesena, Genoa, Lecce - loan, on 2/9/2009) FL 11+24/5 FAC 3/1 Others 4+2/4*

PARK Ji-Sung
Born: Seoul, South Korea, 25 February 1981
Height: 5'9" **Weight:** 11.0
Club Honours: FLC '06, '10; PL '07, '08, '09
International Honours: South Korea: 88; U23-20
A highly competitive Manchester United midfielder, who can play equally as well on either flank, Ji-Sung began the season by signing a three-year contract extension in September, keeping him at the club until 2012. At the end of January, he scored his first goal of the season in a 3-1 win against Arsenal. Though he had to wait until March to net his next goal – the third in a 4-0 win over AC Milan in the Champions League at Old Trafford, he was a massively inspirational player for United. The phrase unsung hero sums him up perfectly. In March, he scored a crucial winner in the north-west derby against Liverpool, heading in a Darren Fletcher cross from close range.
Manchester U *(£4,000,000 from PSV Eindhoven, Holland, ex Kyoto Purple Sanga, on 11/7/2005) PL 70+31/12 FLC 6/1 FAC 10+2/1 Others 16+13/2*

PARKER Benjamin (Ben)
Brian Colin
Born: Pontefract, 8 November 1987
Height: 5'11" **Weight:** 11.6
International Honours: E: Yth
What promised to be a big season at Leeds for Ben was wrecked by injury. He signed an extension to his contract in July and, in the opening game against Exeter, his surging run from right-back paved the way for Leeds' first goal. But with less than half-an-hour gone, he went off with a hamstring injury and was out for eight months, during which time he suffered a hip problem that required surgery. He made his comeback as a substitute in the 3-0 defeat at Swindon in April but a calf injury against MK Dons ended a season to forget.

Leeds U *(From trainee on 16/11/2004) FL 31+6 FLC 4 FAC 4/1 Others 5*
Bradford C *(Loaned on 28/7/2006) FL 35+4 FAC 1 Others 1*
Darlington *(Loaned on 27/2/2008) FL 13 Others 1*

PARKER Joshua (Josh)
Kevin Stanley
Born: Slough, 1 December 1990
Height: 5'11" **Weight:** 12.0
A youth prospect who generally plays as a wide man or forward but, after two cameo appearances off the bench, was given his full debut for Queens Park Rangers by Neil Warnock at right-back in a 1-0 victory at Barnsley, where he put in a solid performance.
Queens Park Rgrs *(From trainee on 2/7/2009) FL 1+3*

PARKER Keigan
Born: Livingston, 8 June 1982
Height: 5'7" **Weight:** 10.5
International Honours: S: U21-1; Yth
In the summer Keigan left Huddersfield

for the short trip over the Pennines to Oldham, scoring a terrific curling 30-yard free kick against Middlesbrough in pre-season. At that stage it all looked well for the Scottish striker, but a loss of form, however, meant that many of his 29 appearances were made from the bench at Boundary Park and late in the season Keigan was sent out on loan to Bury where the injury jinx struck after only two games. The bright Scotsman was then released at the end of the season, thus ending a dismal 12 months for him.
St Johnstone *(From juniors on 1/8/1998) SL 80+44/23 SLC 7+3 SC 3+3 Others 3+1/2*
Blackpool *(Free on 21/7/2004) FL 96+45/34 FLC 6+2/1 FAC 6+2/2 Others 7+1/4*
Huddersfield T *(Free on 4/8/2008) FL 14+6/2 FLC 1+1 Others 1*
Hartlepool U *(Loaned on 2/3/2008) FL 9*
Oldham Ath *(Free on 22/7/2009) FL 17+10/2 FLC 0+1 FAC 1*
Bury *(Loaned on 17/3/2010) FL 2*

Scott Parker

PARKER Scott Matthew
Born: Lambeth, 13 October 1980
Height: 5'7" **Weight:** 10.7
Club Honours: Div 1 '00; FLC '05
International Honours: E: 3; U21-12; Yth; Sch
This was a fine season for the West Ham midfielder as he sparkled throughout. Playing against Burnley in December he stormed forward at every opportunity, set up Luis Jiminez for a penalty and Jack Collison for the first goal and was a superb 'Man of the Match'. The clash with Chelsea in December saw him rally the troops and lead the tackling, giving another towering display. As the season progressed, Scott was at the heart of everything good and in the vital clash with Wigan, scored a stunning winning goal. His performances in this campaign put him head and shoulders above any other West Ham player and he deservedly won the 'Hammers of the Year' award as chosen by the fans. Scott's fine form saw him named in the 30-man England squad to prepare for the World Cup finals but, sadly, was one of those omitted from the 23 taken to South Africa.
Charlton Ath (From trainee on 22/10/1997) P/FL 104+24/9 FLC 8+2/1 FAC 4+3
Norwich C (Loaned on 31/10/2000) FL 6/1
Chelsea (£10,000,000 on 30/1/2004) PL 8+7/1 FLC 3 FAC 1 Others 7+2
Newcastle U (£6,500,000 on 15/6/2005) PL 54+1/4 FLC 4/1 FAC 3/1 Others 9+2
West Ham U (£7,000,000 on 7/6/2007) PL 75+2/4 FLC 4+1 FAC 3

PARKES Thomas (Tom) Peter Wilson
Born: Sutton-in-Ashfield, 15 January 1992
Height: 6'3" **Weight:** 12.3)
The Leicester youngster broke into the League ranks in a hugely successful spell on loan to Burton. Despite his inexperience, the big and brave central defender quickly caught the eye with a series of commanding displays. He scored the first goal of his senior career in the 2-0 victory at Aldershot in March. Like most young players, his form wavered at times but Tom looks to have a very bright future in the game.
Leicester C (From trainee on 6/10/2009)
Burton A (Loaned on 22/1/2010) FL 21+1/1

PARKIN Jonathan (Jon)
Born: Barnsley, 30 December 1981
Height: 6'4" **Weight:** 13.12
Known as 'The Beast', Jon continued to be idolised by the Preston fans last

season and repaid their support by ending as leading scorer with 13 goals. These included a hat-trick in the 7-0 rout of Colchester in the FA Cup and he also stood in for Callum Davidson on penalty duties, scoring with three out of four attempts: the one he failed was coolly side-footed home after Frankie Bunn's save rebounded to him. A formidable physical presence, Jon is much more than just a battering ram, showing a delicacy of touch and awareness of team-mates that comes as something of a surprise to those who only seek the wrapping rather than the complete package. Jon flourished under Darren Ferguson and inspires both fans and colleagues alike with his work ethic and good humour.
Barnsley (From trainee on 5/1/1999) FL 8+2 FLC 1+1 FAC 0+1
Hartlepool U (Loaned on 7/12/2001) FL 0+1
York C (Free on 7/2/2002) FL 64+10/14 FAC 2 Others 2/1
Macclesfield T (Free on 20/2/2004) FL 63+2/30 FLC 1/1 FAC 4+1/1 Others 7/4
Hull C (Signed on 12/1/2006) FL 40+7/11 FLC 1+2 FAC 2/1
Stoke C (Loaned on 10/3/2007) FL 5+1/3
Stoke C (£250,000 on 3/7/2007) P/FL 4+25/2 FLC 2/1 FAC 1+1
Preston NE (£250,000 on 30/8/2008) FL 56+26/21 FLC 1 FAC 2+1/3 Others 2

PARKIN Samuel (Sam)
Born: Roehampton, 14 March 1981
Height: 6'2" **Weight:** 13.0
Club Honours: AMC '09
International Honours: S: B-1. E: Sch
Hopes were high when Sam signed a one-year deal in July. With a good scoring record at Walsall's level, it was hoped he would prove an ideal partner for Troy Deeney. Sam started the first six games of the season, scoring twice, before losing his place when Darren Byfield joined. Injury and a loss of form limited him to only eight starts and his lack of success in the air was particularly disappointing. He was released at the end of the season.
Chelsea (From juniors on 21/8/1998)
Millwall (Loaned on 12/9/2000) FL 5+2/4
Wycombe W (Loaned on 24/11/2000) FL 5+3/1 FAC 0+3/1 Others 2/1
Oldham Ath (Loaned on 22/3/2001) FL 3+4/3
Northampton T (Loaned on 4/7/2001) FL 31+9/4 FLC 2/1 FAC 0+2 Others 2
Swindon T (Signed on 8/8/2002) FL 120+4/67 FLC 4+1/3 FAC 6 Others 5+2/3
Ipswich T (£450,000 on 29/7/2005) FL 17+5/5
Luton T (£325,000 on 25/8/2006) FL

34+16/10 FLC 3 Others 1+2
Leyton Orient (Loaned on 23/10/2008) FL 12+1 FAC 2
Walsall (Free on 16/7/2009) FL 7+17/3 FLC 1 FAC 0+1 Others 0+1

PARNABY Stuart
Born: Bishop Auckland, 19 July 1982
Height: 5'11" **Weight:** 11.4
Club Honours: FLC '04
International Honours: E: U21-4; Yth; Sch
Stuart made his first appearance of the season for Birmingham at left-back in the St Andrew's derby against Aston Villa, filling an emergency call very well. Stephen Carr's form thereafter at right-back meant he had to be a patient watcher. Stuart recovered from a nagging back problem caused by one leg being slightly shorter than the other and when he did see further action was sound, determined and bright, and liked to bound forward.
Middlesbrough (From trainee on 21/7/1999) PL 73+18/2 FLC 5+3 FAC 11+1/1 Others 13+3/1
Halifax T (Loaned on 23/10/2000) FL 6
Birmingham C (Free on 3/7/2007) P/FL 29+13 FLC 6 FAC 2

PARRETT Dean Gary
Born: Hampstead, 16 November 1991
Height: 5'10" **Weight:** 11.8
International Honours: E: Yth
Dean is an aggressive and creative midfielder who joined Aldershot on a one-month loan from Tottenham to cover for the injured Ben Harding. He made his debut at Crewe and performed admirably during his loan, although he had a bout of tonsillitis and was away for a time as captain of England under-19 side.
Tottenham H (From trainee on 3/12/2008) Others 1+1
Aldershot T (Loaned on 17/9/2009) FL 4

PARRISH Andrew (Andy) Michael
Born: Bolton, 22 June 1988
Height: 6'0" **Weight:** 11.0
The young Morecambe defender was largely seen as a squad player at the start of the campaign but after coming into the side in September at right-back, was a virtual ever-present with some excellent performances. He grew in stature as the season progressed and picked up one of the supporters' Player of the Year' awards after being recognised as Morecambe's most improved player. Played most of the season at right-back but started the last game at centre-half, a position boss Sammy McIlroy thinks will suit him for the future. Andy signed a new contract

towards the end of the season.
Bury *(From juniors at Bolton W on 23/9/2005) FL 29+14/1 FLC 1+1 FAC 3 Others 5*
Morecambe *(Free on 2/7/2008) FL 44+4 FLC 1 FAC 2 Others 4+1*

PARRY Paul Ian
Born: Chepstow, 19 August 1980
Height: 5'11" **Weight:** 11.12
International Honours: W: 12
Paul had a frustrating first season at Preston after a protracted summer transfer, a fine start interrupted then only six games by a hamstring injury and then another injury at Christmas saw him out for the rest of the season with tendinitis. Prior to this, the left-footed former Cardiff man had demonstrated his pace and shooting ability on the right wing, scoring twice with powerful strikes against Barnsley and Middlesbrough. His skill on the ball can light up the dullest day and all at Deepdale are looking forward to seeing Paul add to his meagre tally of 17 League appearances for North End.
Cardiff C *(£75,000 from Hereford U on 9/1/2004) FL 148+43/24 FLC 10+5/2 FAC 8/1*
Preston NE *(Signed on 3/8/2009) FL 12+5/2 FLC 1+1*

PARTINGTON Joseph (Joe) Michael
Born: Portsmouth, 1 April 1990
Height: 5'11" **Weight:** 12.0
International Honours: W: U21-3; Yth
The Welsh under-21 international found much of his season with Bournemouth to be frustrating. International calls meant he had no sustained runs in the side and was mainly employed from the bench. A player who is extremely comfortable on the ball with a great range of passing, he captained the reserves on a number of occasions.
Bournemouth *(From trainee at Brockenhurst College on 8/8/2008) FL 10+18/2 FAC 0+1 Others 0+1*

PARTRIDGE Richard (Richie) Joseph
Born: Dublin, 12 September 1980
Height: 5'8" **Weight:** 10.10
International Honours: RoI: U21-8; Yth (UEFA U18'98)
Out of contract at Chester, Richie signed for MK Dons after impressing during pre-season. Making a couple of starts and four substitute appearances, he showed good ability on the ball but never really threatened and after being loaned to Kettering, playing in their FA Cup matches with Leeds, he joined Stockport on a free transfer in mid-January. Joining a club who he

previously had a fine record of scoring against, Richie made his debut against Swindon shortly after and his only goal of the season came when he opened the scoring in the 4-3 win over Wycombe.
Liverpool *(From trainee on 16/9/1997) FLC 1+2*
Bristol Rov *(Loaned on 22/3/2001) FL 4+2/1*
Coventry C *(Loaned on 27/9/2002) FL 23+4/4 FLC 2 FAC 2*
Sheffield Wed *(Free on 5/8/2005) FL 6+12 FLC 1/1 FAC 1*
Rotherham U *(Free on 3/8/2006) FL 30+3/3 FLC 1/1 FAC 1 Others 1*
Chester C *(Signed on 2/7/2007) FL 49+15/5 FLC 1 Others 3/2*
MK Dons *(Free on 21/7/2009) FL 1+3 Others 1*
Stockport Co *(Free on 18/1/2010) FL 20+2/1*

PATERSON James (Jim) Lee
Born: Airdrie, 25 September 1979
Height: 5'11" **Weight:** 13.6
International Honours: S: U21-9
Still under contract until June 2011, Jim started the season well for Plymouth. He showed his versatility in the first five games by playing at left-back, left midfield and central midfield. The popular left-footed player was in and out of the starting line-up and his final appearance was against Preston in December. Due to his lack of first team action, he was loaned to Scottish Premier League Aberdeen but had to return at the end of March because of an Achilles tendon injury.
Dundee U *(From juniors on 3/7/1996) SL 64+37/4 SLC 6+4/1 SC 4+6/2*
Motherwell *(Free on 14/7/2004) SL 91+17/5 SLC 9+1/1 SC 5+4*
Plymouth Arg *(Signed on 31/1/2008) FL 25+12/1 FLC 2*
Aberdeen *(Loaned on 1/2/2010) SL 7 SC 2*

PATERSON Martin Andrew
Born: Tunstall, 13 May 1987
Height: 5'9" **Weight:** 11.5
International Honours: NI: 11; U21-2; Yth
Martin's season was shattered when he tore a medial knee ligament in Burnley's Carling Cup tie at Barnsley in September. He had started the season well, linking with new signing Steven Fletcher up front, and was established in the Northern Ireland side, taking his full cap total to 11 before the injury. It was four months before he was fit to play, at first as a substitute. After a late consolation goal at Aston Villa he returned to the starting line-up, featuring mainly out wide and

showing all his old qualities. Never one to recognise a lost cause, he was one of the Clarets' most consistent performers in the closing stages of the season.
Stoke C *(From trainee on 27/6/2006) FL 2+13/1 FLC 0+1*
Grimsby T *(Loaned on 23/11/2006) FL 15/6*
Scunthorpe U *(Signed on 9/8/2007) FL 34+6/13 FLC 1/1 FAC 1*
Burnley *(£1,000,000 on 3/7/2008) P/FL 56+10/16 FLC 8+1/5 FAC 4+1/1 Others 3/1*

PATERSON Matthew (Matt)
Born: Dunfermline, 18 October 1989
Height: 5'10" **Weight:** 10.9
International Honours: S: Yth
A Southampton Academy graduate, Matt has been a prolific goalscorer at youth and reserve level and it was hardly a surprise when opened Saints' scoring account in the League One curtain raiser at St Mary's, a 1-1 draw with Millwall. However, having brought in Rickie Lambert, Alan Pardew experimented with a number of forward combinations, and Matt found himself holding down a place as a substitute until January, when he left for Southend in part exchange for Lee Barnard. He immediately went into the side, making his debut against Wycombe, but despite there being a lack of goals at Roots Hall he was unable to gain a regular place and was mainly consigned to contributions from the bench. Although a willing worker, when called upon he managed only one goal and that was a consolation strike in a 3-1 reversal at MK Dons.
Southampton *(From trainee on 8/7/2008) FL 5+13/2 FLC 1+1 FAC 1+1*
Southend U *(Free on 22/1/2010) FL 9+7/2*

PATULEA Adrian Marian
Born: Targoviste, Romania, 10 November 1984
Height: 5'11" **Weight:** 12.1
Adrian joined Leyton Orient on a free transfer from Lincoln during the summer. He scored on his first start in the Carling Cup win at Colchester but despite a bright beginning, the Romanian striker struggled to earn even a place in the squad as the season developed, although he scored five goals for the reserves in their victory over Eastbourne Borough.
Lincoln C *(Free from Petrolul Ploiesta, ex Rapid Bucharest, Astra Ploiesta, on 5/9/2008) FL 17+14/11 FAC 1 Others 1*
Leyton Orient *(Free on 2/7/2009) FL 4+17/1 FLC 2/1 FAC 1+1 Others 1+1/1*

PAVLYUCHENKO Roman
Anatolevich
Born: Mostovskoy, Russia, 15
December 1981
Height: 6'2" **Weight:** 12.4
International Honours: Russia: 34;
U21-12; Yth
In his second season at Tottenham, the
Russian International striker again
struggled to win a regular place, with
competitors such as Jermain Defoe,
Peter Crouch and Robbie Keane for the
two striking positions. In the first half of
the season, Roman's only two starts
were in the Carling Cup and he scored
in the 5-1 win at Doncaster. His next
Spurs' goal came in January at the start
of a spectacular run of form in which he
scored six in four games and a total of
nine goals in eight games, having
started five. Forcing his way into the
side in this spell with his first three goals
coming from substitute appearances
within minutes of his arrival on the
pitch, Roman has built up more of an
understanding with colleagues and has
speed, movement and deft finishes in
his repertoire. Sadly, the goals dried up
again as the season ended. Roman
played in seven full Internationals since
August, scoring three times.
*Tottenham H (£14,000,000 from
Spartak Moscow, Russia, ex Dynamo
Stavrapol, Rotor Volgograd, on
1/9/2008) PL 27+17/10 FLC 7+1/7 FAC
4+4/7*

PAYNE Jack Stephen
Born: Gravesend, 5 December 1991
Height: 5'9" **Weight:** 9.2
A very promising youngster, this was a
breakthrough season for Jack in which
he stepped up from the Gillingham
youth team to be a valuable first team
player. Jack started the season in his
preferred central midfield role,
operating at the back of a diamond
formation in front of the back four.
Having a calm head on young
shoulders, his passing, vision and ability
to read the play are major assets of his
game. The 18-year-old was called upon
to deputize for captain Barry Fuller at
right-back for the final games of the
campaign and was named 'Young
Player of the Year' for the second
season running.
*Gillingham (From trainee on
23/2/2009) FL 14+7 FLC 0+1 Others 1*

PAYNE Joshua (Josh) James
Born: Basingstoke, 25 November 1990
Height: 6'0" **Weight:** 11.9
The young energetic West Ham central
midfielder only managed to play in one
Carling Cup tie for the Hammers and to
gain further experience he was loaned

out during the campaign to both
Colchester and Wycombe. Arriving at
Colchester on a one-month loan in
October to provide cover for the illness-
hit Kemi Izzet, he made just two starts
and a substitute appearance before
returning to his parent club. At
Wycombe things got off to a better
start altogether. Coming in on a one-
month loan in January, Josh enjoyed a
very impressive debut in the 1-1 draw at
Southend, which earned him a place in
the League Two 'Team of the Week'. As
the match went on, Josh became
increasingly influential with his elegant
passing and attacking threat, crowned
by a stunning 25-yard goal. However,
after two more starts he was dropped
to the bench and then from the squad,
before returning to Upton Park without
a further extension. Was out of contract
at the end of June.
*West Ham U (From trainee on
2/7/2008) PL 0+2 FLC 1*
*Cheltenham T (Loaned on 24/9/2008)
FL 9+2/1 FAC 2*
*Colchester U (Loaned on 22/10/2009)
FL 2+1*
Wycombe W (Loaned on 22/1/2010) FL 3/1

PAYNTER William (Billy)
Paul
Born: Liverpool, 13 July 1984
Height: 6'1" **Weight:** 12.0
Billy had a magnificent season at
Swindon. Operating as a lone striker
during the early part of the campaign,
he initially found goals hard to come by
and was even relegated to the bench
and rested. Two goals at Tranmere at the
end of October and the emergence of
strike partner Charlie Austin really
brought the best out of Billy as he was
pressed into a more forward role and
responded by hitting a career best 29
goals in all competitions. Injury restricted
his effectiveness during the play-off
games. A hard-working player who
holds the ball up well, is good in the air
and is dangerous when running at
defenders, he hit some spectacular
goals. Long-standing rumours were
proved to be correct when it was
announced that he was moving to
Leeds.
*Port Vale (From trainee on 1/7/2002)
FL 119+25/30 FLC 2+1 FAC 4+2/3
Others 5/1*
*Hull C (£150,000 on 9/11/2005) FL
11+11/3 FAC 1*
*Southend U (£200,000 on 5/8/2006)
FL 5+4 FLC 2/1*
*Bradford C (Loaned on 31/1/2007) FL
15/4*
*Swindon T (Signed on 31/8/2007) FL
102+18/45 FLC 3/3 FAC 7+1/3 Others
4+2*

PEACOCK Lee Anthony
Born: Paisley, 9 October 1976
Height: 6'0" **Weight:** 12.8
Club Honours: AMC '97, '03
International Honours: S: U21-1; Yth
After recovering from a troublesome
back injury, Lee's only Swindon
appearances during 2009-10 were
from the bench. Having found it hard
to break into the Town side, it was no
real surprise when he was allowed to
join Grimsby during January. At
Blundell Park, Lee was initially seen in
Town's midfield, but after a move to
the attack saw him hit both goals in a
local derby versus Lincoln to become a
crowd hero, he alternated between
both positions thereafter. Appointed
club captain from February to April, Lee
was occasionally absent with fitness
problems, robbing the Mariners of his
battling qualities and leadership at a
crucial time.
*Carlisle U (From trainee on 10/3/1995)
FL 52+24/11 FLC 2+3 FAC 4+1/1 Others
6+4*
*Mansfield T (£90,000 on 17/10/1997)
FL 79+10/29 FLC 4/1 FAC 4 Others 4/2*
*Manchester C (£500,000 on
5/11/1999) FL 4+4 FAC 1+1*
*Bristol C (£600,000 on 10/8/2000) FL
131+13/54 FLC 4/3 FAC 11/1 Others
16/5*
*Sheffield Wed (Free on 2/7/2004) FL
37+14/6 FLC 2+1/2 Others 3/1*
*Swindon T (Free on 20/1/2006) FL
104+21/20 FLC 1+1 FAC 6+2 Others
2+1/1*
*Grimsby T (Free on 29/1/2010) FL
14+3/2*

PEARCE Alexander (Alex)
James
Born: Wallingford, 9 November 1988
Height: 6'0" **Weight:** 11.10
International Honours: S: U21-2; Yth
After a series of loan moves to lower
division clubs, Alex spent the whole
season with Reading in a bid to
establish himself at centre-back. He was
a permanent fixture for the first half of
the campaign and was entrusted with
the captaincy, despite there being
several older players in the side. He was
sufficiently mature to do that job
confidently but was not such a regular
choice when Brian McDermott took
over as manager. His 28 appearances
and four goals represent another
important stage in the development of
this talented young player, one of the
golden generation of Academy
graduates. Alex's muscular physique, his
determination and commitment mark
him as an outstanding talent for the
future.
Reading (From trainee on 19/10/2006)

P/FL 37+4/5 FLC 4+2/1 FAC 2+3 Others 1
Northampton T *(Loaned on 9/2/2007)*
FL 15/1
Bournemouth *(Loaned on 2/11/2007)*
FL 11 Others 1
Norwich C *(Loaned on 31/1/2008) FL*
8+3
Southampton *(Loaned on 30/10/2008)*
FL 6+3/2

PEARCE Ian Anthony
Born: Bury St Edmunds, 7 May 1974
Height: 6'3" **Weight:** 14.4
Club Honours: PL '95
International Honours: E: U21-3; Yth
Released by Fulham in the 2008 close
season, Ian moved into non-League
football first with Oxted and then
Kingstonian before joining Lincoln as
assistant to manager Chris Sutton.
Following that, the experienced former
Chelsea centre-back registered as a
non-contract player in October and
went on to play 11 times before a back
injury brought his playing time to a
close in March.
Chelsea *(From juniors on 1/8/1991)*
P/FL 0+4 Others 0+1
Blackburn Rov *(£300,000 on*
4/10/1993) PL 43+19/2 FLC 4+4/1 FAC
1+2 Others 6+1
West Ham U *(£1,600,000 + on*
19/9/1997) P/FL 135+7/9 FLC 8 FAC
10+1/1 Others 1+1
Fulham *(£400,000 + on 23/1/2004) PL*
55+2/1 FLC 3 FAC 2 (Freed during 2008
close season)
Southampton *(Loaned on 22/2/2008)*
FL 1
Lincoln C *(Free from Kingstonian, ex*
Oxted & District, on 27/9/2009) FL 5+5
FAC 0+1

PEARCE Jason Daniel
Born: Hillingdon, 6 December 1987
Height: 5'7" **Weight:** 11.3
It was another superb season for the
wholehearted central defender, who
was an absolute rock at the back for
Bournemouth. He was highly consistent
throughout and halfway through the
campaign, was named as team captain.
He broke a bone in his foot in late
February in a training ground accident
but returned to captain the side to a
memorable promotion.
Portsmouth *(From trainee on*
4/7/2006)
Bournemouth *(Signed on 10/8/2007)*
FL 113+3/4 FLC 3 FAC 7+1/1 Others 4

PEARCE Krystian Mitchell
Victor
Born: Birmingham, 5 January 1990
Height: 6'1" **Weight:** 12.0
International Honours: E: Yth
Taken on loan from Birmingham, the

centre-half was only twice selected by
Peterborough to start and was allowed
to return to City. The games he did
figure in showed him to be a more than
capable defender who read the game
well, was good in the air and quick to
react. His next loan spell was at
Huddersfield, joining in mid-January,
and he spent a frustrating time there,
making only a brief substitute
appearance in the 5-0 mauling at
Southampton. The adaptable defender
played as an assured second-half left-
back, being solid in the air and a good
passer of the ball. Despite any
disappointment, a bright future lies
ahead of him
Birmingham C *(From trainee on*
2/3/2007)
Notts Co *(Loaned on 8/11/2007) FL 8/1*
FAC 1
Port Vale *(Loaned on 31/1/2008) FL*
11+1
Scunthorpe U *(Loaned on 19/8/2008)*
FL 36+3 FAC 2 Others 4+2/1
Peterborough U *(Loaned on*
20/7/2009) FL 0+2 FLC 2+1
Huddersfield T *(Signed on 20/1/2010)*
FL 0+1

PEARSON Gregory (Greg)
Edward
Born: Birmingham, 3 April 1985
Height: 5'11" **Weight:** 12.0
Club Honours: FC '09
Greg proved a success in his first season
in the League despite being on a part-
time contract to enable him to continue
a physiotherapy degree course at
university. Top scorer in Burton's Blue
Square Premier promotion campaign
with 20 goals, the pacy front runner,
signed from Bishop's Stortford, made
the transition with relative ease and was
second in Burton's scoring chart with
14, including the history-making first
scored at League level. Greg had spells
out as Paul Peschisolido rotated his
strikers but the Burton manager had no
hesitation in offering Greg a new deal
to run until 2012.
West Ham U *(From trainee on*
24/5/2004)
Lincoln C *(Loaned on 20/8/2004) FL*
1+2
Rushden & Diamonds *(Free on*
6/7/2005) FL 16+6/1 FLC 1 FAC 1+2
Others 1/1 (Freed on 31/1/2007)
Burton A *(Signed from Bishops*
Stortford on 29/7/2008) FL 24+18/14
FLC 1 FAC 0+2 Others 0+1

PEARSON Stephen Paul
Born: Lanark, 2 October 1982
Height: 6'0" **Weight:** 11.1
Club Honours: SPD '04, '06, '07; SC '04
International Honours: S: 10; B-1; U21-1

In terms of appearances, it was
Stephen's best season for Derby,
although he ended it with a knee
operation that could delay his availability
at the start of the new campaign.
Playing on the left of midfield, Stephen
eats up the ground effortlessly. He
seems to be everywhere, such is his
stride. If he could finish off the moves,
he would be some player. A single goal,
in the last away game at Bristol City, is a
poor return for a player who creates so
many good positions for himself.
Defenders do not like playing against
him because Stephen has a surge that
can leave them standing. If he can
become better with the final ball or the
shot, more Scotland caps beckon.
Motherwell *(From juniors on 1/8/2000)*
SL 68+12/12 SLC 3/1 SC 4+1 Others 1
Glasgow Celtic *(£350,000 on*
9/1/2004) SL 22+34/6 SLC 3+1 SC 5+1
Others 6+4/1
Derby Co *(£750,000 on 11/1/2007)*
P/FL 71+11/2 FLC 1+1 FAC 7+1 Others
3/1
Stoke C *(Loaned on 27/3/2008) FL 3+1*

PEDERSEN Morten Gamst
Born: Vadso, Norway, 8 September
1981
Height: 5'11" **Weight:** 11.0
International Honours: Norway: 58;
U21-18; Yth
Morten Gamst started in fine form and
was a vital component of the Blackburn
side because he was involved in so
much set-piece play, with his long
throws and dead-ball delivery. After a
month his form dipped and by the start
of winter he was regularly omitted.
Over the Christmas period, he scored a
vital goal in the home game against
Sunderland and shortly afterwards his
season was transformed when he was
moved inside. More involved and with
greater options, he was a vital
component in a string of home
victories. Has the talent to score more
goals than he achieved, particularly as
he has fine technique in dead-ball
situations. His free kick against
Peterborough was one of the goals of
the season and he proved that he could
be lethal from open play with a
magnificent volley against Wigan. He
had the misfortune to strike the
woodwork three times. Whenever he
plays he is tremendously hard working,
with a high-tackle count and great
heading ability. Out of contract at the
end of the season, he did not sign the
deal offered.
Blackburn Rov *(£1,500,000 from*
Tromso, Norway on 27/8/2004) PL
180+12/27 FLC 14+4/5 FAC 14+3/5
Others 11+2/1

PELLICORI Alessandro
Born: Cosenza, Italy, 22 July 1981
Height: 5'11" **Weight:** 11.11
Alessandro joined Queens Park Rangers in the summer from Italian side Avellino but failed to make a real impact on the first team despite scoring on his debut in a 5-0 Carling Cup rout at Exeter. That proved to be the striker's only goal of the season as, after ten further appearances, nine of which were off the bench, he returned to Italy, joining Mantova on loan.
Queens Park Rgrs (From Avellino, Italy, ex Cosenza, Lecce, Avellino - loan, Varese - loan, Foggia - loan, Benevento - loan, Grosseto, Catanzaro, Piacenza, Cesena, Gross on 30/7/2009) FL 1+7 FLC 0+2/1

Lee Peltier

PELTIER Lee Anthony
Born: Liverpool, 11 December 1986
Height: 5'10" **Weight:** 12.0
Brought in during the close season from Yeovil, the young defender made an impact in his first year with Huddersfield. Firmly installed at right-back, he was very assured as the side pushed towards the play-offs. Lee tackles and heads solidly, defending without any real fuss. Only an ankle injury kept him out late in the season before a return for the final few matches. Lee proved his versatility by deputising at left-back and was voted 'Players' Player of the Season'.
Liverpool (From trainee on 25/11/2004) FLC 3 Others 1
Hull C (Loaned on 16/3/2007) FL 5+2
Yeovil T (Signed on 7/8/2007) FL 68+1/1 FLC 3 FAC 3 Others 2
Huddersfield T (Signed on 1/7/2009) FL 42 FLC 2 FAC 3 Others 3

PENN Russell Anthony
Born: Dudley, 8 November 1985
Height: 5'11" **Weight:** 11.5
International Honours: E: SP-9
The attack-minded midfield player became Burton's record signing when he moved from Kidderminster Harriers. The England semi-pro international had missed out on League football earlier in his career with Scunthorpe but his ambition was fulfilled when Burton made their League Two debut at Shrewsbury. Initially deployed on the right of midfield, Russell produced his best form once he was offered the more central position in which he thrived in his Kidderminster days, when he often proved a thorn in Burton's side. As well as being a combative and creative player, Russell weighed in with useful goals.
Burton A (£200,000 from Kidderminster Hrs, ex trainee at Scunthorpe U, on 9/7/2009) FL 34+6/4 FLC 1 FAC 2 Others 1

Russell Penn

PENNY Diego Alonso Roberto
Born: Lima, Peru, 22 April 1984
Height: 6'6" **Weight:** 11.13
International Honours: Peru: 6
Diego retained the number-one shirt at Burnley, but was clearly second choice goalkeeper behind Brian Jensen, and later third after Nicky Weaver arrived on loan. His only start was in the Carling Cup game at Hartlepool but he stood in on two other occasions when Jensen had to go off injured. Clarets fans were never really had the chance to gauge his potential in English football, and at present his prospects at Turf Moor do not seem bright.
Burnley (Signed from Coronel

Bolognesi, Peru on 7/8/2008) P/FL 1+1
FLC 1+1

PERCH James Robert
Born: Mansfield, 29 September 1985
Height: 5'11" **Weight:** 11.5
James missed Nottingham Forest's opening to the season because of an injury sustained during pre-season. He made his first start against Birmingham in the FA Cup in January. The tall, versatile defender, who is happy playing on either side of the back four, scored his only goal of the season against Queens Park Rangers and by the end of the season was one of the first names on the team-sheet.
Nottingham F (From trainee on 9/11/2002) FL 163+27/12 FLC 4+2/1 FAC 15+2 Others 8/1

PERICARD Vincent de Paul
Born: Efok, Cameroon, 3 October 1982
Height: 6'1" **Weight:** 13.8
Club Honours: Div 1 '03
Freed by Stoke in the summer, Vincent turned up at Carlisle in October on a three-month contract and his time at Brunton Park coincided with some of the club's best results of the campaign. Adding focus to the attack, he looked comfortable in the lone-striker role with his ability to hold the ball up front until support arrived, netting on his home debut and producing a decent scoring ratio during his time at the club. He will best be remembered, however, for his extraordinary back-heeled volley against Norwich in the FA Cup, a piece of skill that even most Brazilians would have envied. At the end of his contract he was a surprise arrival at Swindon, but a persistent hamstring strain and the form of fellow Swindon strikers Billy Paynter and Charlie Austin meant that he was largely confined to making late appearances from the bench and starting just two games. Very skilful for such a big man, he likes to drop deep and bring others into the game.
Portsmouth (£400,000 from Juventus, Italy, ex St Etienne, on 22/7/2002) P/FL 21+23/9 FLC 2+1/1 FAC 1+1
Sheffield U (Loaned on 16/9/2005) FL 3+8/2
Plymouth Arg (Loaned on 10/2/2006) FL 1+4/4
Stoke C (Free on 21/7/2006) P/FL 20+18/2 FLC 4/2 FAC 2+1
Southampton (Loaned on 14/3/2008) FL 1+4
Millwall (Loaned on 21/2/2009) FL 2
Carlisle U (Free on 13/10/2009) FL 10/4 FAC 4/2 Others 2
Swindon T (Free on 14/1/2010) FL 2+12 Others 0+2

PERKINS David Philip
Born: Heysham, 21 June 1982
Height: 6'2" **Weight:** 12.0
International Honours: E: SP-9
David's second season at Colchester started in glorious fashion when he came off the bench to curl in a free kick at Norwich in an opening day 7-1 victory. However, following a handful of further substitute appearances, the central midfielder handed in a transfer request at the end of August, stating that he wanted to move back nearer the north. Sent out on loan, he enjoyed a decent three-month spell at Chesterfield, operating mostly in central midfield and netting once against his former club, Rochdale. He showed a willingness to be busy with the ball at his feet and an ability to pass it, and win it too. Back at the Weston Homes Community Stadium and not part of Aidy Boothroyd's plans, he returned to his native North West in January when joining Stockport on loan. He went straight into the team against Swindon and the only game he missed for the rest of the season was the 2-2 draw with his parent club. David's all-action and consistent performances in midfield saw him awarded numerous 'Man of the Match' awards.
Rochdale (Signed from Morecambe on 22/1/2007) FL 54+4/4 FLC 1/1 FAC 1 Others 3/1
Colchester U (£150,000 on 15/7/2008) FL 35+8/6 FLC 1+1 FAC 1 Others 2+2/1
Chesterfield (Loaned on 2/10/2009) FL 11+2/1 FAC 1
Stockport Co (Loaned on 18/1/2010) FL 22

PERRY Christopher (Chris) John
Born: Carshalton, 26 April 1973
Height: 5'9" **Weight:** 11.1
Club Honours: AMC '10
Chris was restricted to 19 starts for Southampton. Radhi Jaidi proved his most formidable hurdle to a regular place in central defence. Now a veteran, Chris was, when called upon, his inimitable self, steady, influential, invariably in the right place and seldom short of ideas. He was released at the end of the season, hardly a surprise given the signing of four centre-backs over the season, but he remains capable of holding down a place in a better than average team.
Wimbledon (From trainee on 2/7/1991) PL 158+9/2 FLC 21 FAC 24/1
Tottenham H (£4,000,000 on 7/7/1999) PL 111+9/3 FLC 13 FAC 9 Others 4/1
Charlton Ath (£100,000 on 1/9/2003) PL 69+7/3 FLC 3 FAC 4+1

West Bromwich A (Free on 1/8/2006) FL 23 FLC 1 Others 3
Luton T (Free on 6/7/2007) FL 35/1 FLC 3 FAC 4 Others 2
Southampton (Free on 27/3/2008) FL 55+3/2 FLC 3 FAC 5 Others 3+1

PETERS Jaime Bryant
Born: Pickering, Ontario, Canada, 4 May 1987
Height: 5'8" **Weight:** 11.6
International Honours: Canada: 22: U23-1: Yth
Jaime enjoyed his best season at Ipswich in terms of appearances and showed his versatility by playing in both full-back positions as well as in various midfield roles. He was particularly effective at left-back where he more than held his own against speedy wingers, forcing them to change wings or to be substituted. A surprising element of his defensive play was his ability in the air, where he was often able to out-jump taller opponents. He scored his only goal of the season at Crystal Palace.
Ipswich T (Signed from Kaiserslautern, Germany on 6/8/2005) FL 48+28/3 FLC 1 FAC 5+1
Yeovil T (Loaned on 30/1/2008) FL 12+2/1
Gillingham (Loaned on 24/1/2009) FL 1+2

PETROV Martin Petiov
Born: Vratsa, Bulgaria, 15 January 1979
Height: 5'11" **Weight:** 12.1
International Honours: Bulgaria: 78
The Manchester City and Bulgarian left-winger was a Sven Goran Eriksson signing and was unlikely to be a favourite of manager Mark Hughes. So it proved, with Martin starting on the bench, but when he finally won a starting place in September he responded by scoring in three consecutive matches against West Ham, Wigan and Fulham before losing his place again. Under Roberto Mancini, he was given a run of five games at the turn of the year, scoring again in the 2-0 home win over Stoke. The signing of Adam Johnson probably signalled the end of his career at Eastlands and, on his last appearance in February, he suffered a knee injury that required surgery. Martin was released at the end of the season.
Manchester C (£4,700,000 from Atletico Madrid, Spain, ex CSKA Sofia, Servette, VfL Wolfsburg, on 3/8/2007) PL 46+13/9 FLC 1+1 FAC 6/1 Others 4+1/2

PETROV Stiliyan Alypshev
Born: Sofia, Bulgaria, 5 July 1979
Height: 5'9" **Weight:** 12.1

Club Honours: SPD '01, '02, '04, '06; SLC '01, '06; SC '02, '04, '05
International Honours: Bulgaria: 94
Stiliyan was almost ever-present for Aston Villa, leading by example and playing in 37 of the 38 Premier League games. His appearance record was all the more impressive as he was plagued by a series of knocks and, in the later stages of the season, fatigue. In the early part of the campaign, the Bulgarian international showed the form that won him Villa's awards in the previous season. As tiredness took its toll, and Villa continued to challenge on three fronts, Stiliyan started to fade. He had the honour of leading Villa out at Wembley twice in their first appearances there for a decade, although the Carling Cup final and FA Cup semi-final ended in defeats by Manchester United and Chelsea. Stiliyan has found his best position at Villa as a holding midfielder, offering protection to the back four, and excels in breaking up opposition attacks and prompting Villa forward. Having enjoyed success under Martin O'Neill at Glasgow Celtic, the skipper is now the Villa manager's trusted dressing-room lieutenant. Stiliyan is a year into a four-year deal.
Glasgow Celtic (£2,000,000 from CSKA Sofia, Bulgaria on 29/7/1999) SL 215+13/55 SLC 9+5 SC 15+3/5 Others 49+2/4
Aston Villa (£6,500,000 on 30/8/2006) PL 125+6/4 FLC 11+1 FAC 8/1 Others 8/1

PHILLIPS James (Jimmy) Peter
Born: Stoke-on-Trent, 20 September 1989
Height: 5'6" **Weight:** 9.11
Burton quickly snapped up the skilful and pacy young winger on a two-year contract after he had been given a free transfer by Stoke. Jimmy scored his first career goal in the second game of the campaign in the Carling Cup at Reading and also marked his first season at Burton with a superb strike in the 2-1 defeat of Grimsby that earned the club's 'Goal of the Season' accolade. Jimmy's form wavered at times and he was hampered by niggling back and muscular problems, but much is expected of him in his second season at the Pirelli Stadium.
Stoke C (From trainee on 4/7/2008)
Burton A (Free on 1/8/2009) FL 19+5/1 FLC 0+1/1 FAC 1 Others 0+1

PHILLIPS Kevin Mark
Born: Hitchin, 25 July 1973
Height: 5'7" **Weight:** 11.0
Club Honours: Div 1 '99; Ch '08
International Honours: E: 8; B-1

Primarily used in an impact role coming off the Birmingham substitutes' bench, he adapted superbly. Kevin would pick up the pace of a game quickly and had lost none of his sharpness and predatory positioning, plus his deadly finishing. Memorably scored twice in five minutes late on to win the St Andrew's derby against Wolverhampton in February, and scrambled a stoppage-time equaliser against Arsenal in March to ensure Birmingham's 15-game unbeaten run - a top flight club record - remained intact.

Watford (£10,000 from Baldock on 19/12/1994) FL 54+5/24 FLC 2/1 FAC 2 Others 0+2
Sunderland (£325,000 + on 17/7/1997) P/FL 207+1/113 FLC 9+1/5 FAC 14/10 Others 3/2
Southampton (£3,250,000 on 14/8/2003) PL 49+15/22 FLC 2/1 FAC 4+1/2 Others 2/1
Aston Villa (£750,000 + on 6/7/2005) PL 20+3/4 FLC 1+1/1 FAC 1+1
West Bromwich A (£700,000 on 22/8/2006) FL 60+11/38 FLC 1 FAC 4+2/5 Others 3/3
Birmingham C (Free on 5/8/2008) P/FL 26+29/18 FLC 2+1 FAC 1+3

PHILLIPS Mark Ian
Born: Lambeth, 27 January 1982
Height: 6'2" **Weight:** 13.0
Club Honours: Div 2 '09
A commanding Brentford centre-half who is good in the air, Mark was a regular in the side until the end of October when he sustained an ankle injury at Exeter. After missing 12 games, he was not immediately restored to the side but, when he was, managed only a further four appearances before being sidelined by a knee injury. Mark missed another ten games before being used as a substitute in the final three matches of the campaign. Was out of contract in the summer.
Millwall (From trainee on 3/5/2000) FL 60+7/1 FLC 3+1 FAC 1+1 Others 1
Darlington (Loaned on 22/3/2007) FL 7+1
Brentford (Free on 14/8/2008) FL 47+8/1 FLC 1 FAC 2 Others 2

PHILLIPS Matthew (Matt)
Born: Aylesbury, 13 March 1991
Height: 6'0" **Weight:** 12.10
International Honours: E: Yth
Once again Matt had to be content with an equal share of starts and substitute appearances for Wycombe, 18 each in the League, as the club carefully controlled his exposure in what was a very difficult season on the pitch. His skill is undoubted with perfect ball

control, pace and excellent crossing from his favoured right-wing spot. He is always looking to shoot and his five goals included a snap 25-yarder against Bristol Rovers in August and a beautiful left-foot curler from 20 yards in the final game against Gillingham. He was named as one of the top six apprentices in the country by the PFA and in May was called into the England under-19 squad for a three-match tournament in Ukraine.
Wycombe W (From trainee on 31/7/2008) FL 37+38/8 FLC 0+1 FAC 4/1 Others 2+1

PHILLIPS Steven (Steve) John
Born: Bath, 6 May 1978
Height: 6'1" **Weight:** 11.10
Club Honours: AMC '03
Shrewsbury signed the vastly experienced goalkeeper on loan from Bristol Rovers as cover for the injured Chris Neal and he eventually played in 11 games. Made his debut in the 3-1 win at Accrington at the end of August and quickly bred confidence into the back line with a string of assured performances, impressing particularly in the 2-0 victory against Crewe. That was the beginning of a run of three consecutive clean sheets and he made a number of excellent saves in the 1-1 draw at Notts County, his last Shrewsbury appearance before signing for Crewe on loan. Making his Crewe debut in the York City FA Cup first round match, Steve played in all games until 17th April after which he underwent surgery on a shoulder injury. Was out of contract at the end of June.
Bristol C (Signed from Paulton Rov on 21/11/1996) FL 254+3 FLC 12 FAC 17 Others 23
Bristol Rov (Free on 25/7/2006) FL 136 FLC 4 FAC 14 Others 11
Shrewsbury T (Loaned on 26/8/2009) FL 11
Crewe Alex (Loaned on 2/11/2009) FL 28 FAC 1

PICKEN Philip (Phil) James
Born: Droylsden, 12 November 1985
Height: 5'9" **Weight:** 10.7
Phil began and ended the campaign as Chesterfield's first team full-back but slipped out of the picture between December and March following an ankle injury, while several loanees were played in his position. He did not let the side down at all when called on, playing at left and right-back with equal determination and aplomb, but his height perhaps counted against him at this level. Was one of ten players released as the club rang the changes in

the 2010 close season.
Manchester U (From trainee on 2/7/2004)
Chesterfield (Free on 19/8/2005) FL 133+7/2 FLC 5+1 FAC 3 Others 4+2
Notts Co (Loaned on 8/1/2009) FL 22

PIDGELEY Leonard (Lenny) James
Born: Twickenham, 7 February 1984
Height: 6'4" **Weight:** 13.10
International Honours: E: Yth
Lenny arrived from Millwall to begin the campaign as Carlisle's first choice custodian. He kept a clean sheet on an early return to the Den and gave some confident performances but lost his place after the home defeat by Swindon. He returned for two Johnstone's Paint Trophy matches, including the win at Leeds where he pulled off a string of fine saves, but has not been offered terms for the new season.
Chelsea (From trainee on 11/7/2003) PL 1+1
Watford (Loaned on 16/9/2003) FL 26+1 FAC 2
Millwall (Loaned on 28/11/2005) FLC 1
Millwall (Signed on 12/6/2006) FL 55 FLC 1 FAC 8 Others 1
Carlisle U (Free on 8/7/2009) FL 17 FLC 3 FAC 2 Others 2

PIENAAR Steven
Born: Johannesburg, South Africa, 17 February 1982
Height: 5'10" **Weight:** 10.6
International Honours: South Africa: 46
The South African continued to be one of Everton's star men in another impressive campaign. After starting the season brightly, especially in Europe, the skilful midfielder picked up a nasty knee injury at Portsmouth at the end of September which sidelined him for almost two months. In Mikel Arteta's absence he is Everton's main creative presence and he hit peak form in mid-season, netting three times in four League matches, one a stunning chip against Arsenal at the Emirates and the other a brilliant free kick against Manchester City. Operating on either wing or in the centre of midfield, the former Ajax star kept up those high standards until the end of the season. Steven's main strengths are great skill on the ball and the ability to do the unexpected and it was no surprise that David Moyes was keen for him to sign a new contract at the end of the season.
Everton (£2,000,000 from Borussia Dortmund, Germany, ex Ajax Cape Town, Ajax, on 25/7/2007) PL 82+4/8 FLC 3 FAC 9 Others 14+1/3

334

PILKINGTON Anthony Neil James
Born: Blackburn, 3 November 1987
Height: 5'11" **Weight:** 12.0
International Honours: Rol: U21-1
Huddersfield's tricky and skilful winger started in fine style with the opening goal of the season in the draw at Southend. Anthony is capable of being a match winner with his natural ability to run defences ragged and deliver quality crosses. He can play on either flank and is a danger at set pieces. Anthony managed eight goals in the play-off season and continued to find great scoring positions. Is one of Town's crop of young players who could play at a higher level.
Stockport Co (Free from Atherton Collieries on 19/12/2006) FL 63+14/16 FLC 1+2 FAC 3+2/1 Others 5+1/2
Huddersfield T (Signed on 26/1/2009) FL 58+1/9 FLC 2 FAC 2 Others 4/2

PILKINGTON Daniel (Danny) Luke
Born: Blackburn, 25 May 1990
Height: 5'9" **Weight:** 11.10
Danny was a regular for Stockport in the early season, playing each game on either wing, albeit often as a substitute. He scored his first goal in County colours in the 1-1 draw against Brighton, a missile from 25 yards into the top left corner that was voted 'Goal of the Season' by the Edgeley faithful. In February, he suffered a fractured fibula in training that kept him out for two months but, despite the setback, he still collected one of the club's 'Young Player of the Year' awards.
Stockport Co (Free from Chorley, ex Myerscough College, Atherton Collieries, Kendal T, on 3/7/2008) FL 10+22/1 FLC 0+1 FAC 1 Others 1+1

PINTADO Gorka
Born: San Sebastian, Spain, 24 March 1978
Height: 6'0" **Weight:** 13.1
Gorka was in his second season at the Liberty Stadium but the former Granada striker struggled in front of goal for Swansea. He was sent off in the Carling Cup tie against Scunthorpe and received a second red card later in the season at Derby for a poor tackle when the Swans were leading 1-0 against ten men. It provoked a communal scuffle and both clubs were charged with failing to control their players. Despite his work rate, Gorka's failure to find the net led to him losing his place when Shefki Kuqi arrived.
Swansea C (£100,000 from Granada CF, Spain, ex Real Union Club de Irun, CA Osasuna, CD Leganes, UE Figueres,

UDA Gramenet, on 16/6/2008) FL 25+47/7 FLC 2+2/1 FAC 2+1/1

PIPE David Ronald
Born: Caerphilly, 5 November 1983
Height: 5'9" **Weight:** 12.4
International Honours: W: 1; U21-12; Yth
Starting the season on right-hand side of Bristol Rovers' midfield, David showed up well with his wholehearted forays to support his team-mates. Always a popular player with the fans, regretfully a well publicised off-field matter saw him suspended by Rovers and going to Cheltenham on loan in December. The former Welsh international defender proved to be a powerful and muscular defender with a burst of pace, and his presence immediately improved the team. He was a key contributor as the Robins ground out some important points in the fight against relegation around the turn of the year and it was no secret that the club wanted to extend his loan until the end of the season.

Unfortunately, financial restrictions prevented them from doing so. Was out of contract at the end of June.
Coventry C (From trainee on 8/11/2000) FL 11+10/1 FLC 1+2 FAC 0+1
Notts Co (Free on 15/1/2004) FL 138+3/4 FLC 5 FAC 7 Others 1
Bristol Rov (£50,000 on 30/7/2007) FL 78+8/3 FLC 5 FAC 7 Others 2
Cheltenham T (Loaned on 26/11/2009) FL 7+1

PIQUIONNE Frederic
Born: Noumea, New Caledonia, 8 December 1978
Height: 6'2" **Weight:** 12.1
International Honours: Martinique; France: 1; B-1
The 31-year-old French striker had a highly impressive debut season in the Premier League. On loan at Portsmouth from Lyon, Frederic scored 11 goals in a turbulent season on the south coast and became a vital component of the Blues' side with his pace, strength and aerial prowess. He

Frederic Piquionne

scored a vital brace against Birmingham in the FA Cup quarter-final and also hit the opener at Wembley against Tottenham in the semi-final. A firm favourite at Pompey, he will certainly be a player in demand this summer after his loan expired.
Portsmouth (Loaned from Olympique Lyonnais, France, ex Golden Star, Nimes, Stade Rennais, St Etienne, AS Monaco, on 5/8/2009) PL 26+8/5 FLC 2+2/3 FAC 6+1/3

PIRES Loick Barros Paiva
Born: Lisbon, Portugal, 20 November 1989
Height: 6'2" **Weight:** 13.4
Although Loick can play as either a left-winger or as a centre-forward, Leyton Orient used him mainly as a cover player in 2009-10 and he always gave his best when called upon. Loick was top scorer for the reserves but was released when his contract expired.
Leyton Orient (From trainee on 5/7/2008) FL 0+15 FLC 0+1 FAC 1 Others 2+1

PITMAN Brett Douglas
Born: St Helier, Jersey, 31 January 1988
Height: 6'0" **Weight:** 11.4
It was a sensational season for Brett, a home-grown talent since he came across from Jersey. His 28 goals were absolutely crucial to Bournemouth's promotion from League Two. His all-round game improved once again and not only was he top scorer but also took all the set pieces and created a number of goals. Brett won a monthly PFA award and was named as the club's 'Player of the Season'. His strike in the home game against Burton was selected as the 'Goal of the Season'.
Bournemouth (Signed from St Paul's on 1/7/2005) FL 101+71/55 FLC 1+3 FAC 5+5/1 Others 5+4/2

PITTMAN Jon-Paul
Born: Oklahoma City, Oklahoma, USA, 24 October 1986
Height: 5'9" **Weight:** 11.0
International Honours: E: SP-1
Jon-Paul finished as joint top scorer at Wycombe, with ten goals, after another season of uncertainty over his place, with 21 starts and 21 substitute appearances. He is the only natural scorer at the club, capable of moments of the sublime skill and always liable to terrorise defences with his blistering acceleration. He possesses a fearsome shot and his best goal was undoubtedly at home to Bristol Rovers when, with his back to goal, he turned his man and smashed the ball into the net from 20

yards with his left foot. His best known goal was in the 1-1 draw at Leeds in January when he sprinted past his man on the left wing before shooting into the far corner.
Nottingham F (Signed from Brackley Ath, via trial at Aston Villa, on 1/7/2005) FAC 0+1 Others 0+1
Hartlepool U (Loaned on 13/1/2006) FL 2+1
Bury (Loaned on 4/8/2006) FL 5+4/1 FLC 1
Doncaster Rov (Free on 5/1/2007) Others 0+1 (Freed during 2007 close season)
Wycombe W (Signed from Crawley T on 2/2/2009) FL 32+27/10 FLC 1 FAC 1+1/1 Others 1/2

PLATT Clive Linton
Born: Wolverhampton, 27 October 1977
Height: 6'4" **Weight:** 13.0
Target-man Clive once again led Colchester's line to good effect. A focal point of Aidy Boothroyd's direct approach, the quietly spoken Midlander caused a lot of problems for opposition defences with his aerial threat and ability to hold the ball. Starting 39 games, Clive had seven assists and scored nine goals, including a fine brace against Exeter, the second of which came from an uncharacteristic long run and finish.
Walsall (From trainee on 25/7/1996) FL 18+14/4 FLC 1+2/1 FAC 0+1 Others 1+6
Rochdale (£70,000 + on 5/8/1999) FL 151+18/30 FLC 5/1 FAC 13/5 Others 7/1
Notts Co (Free on 7/8/2003) FL 19/3 FLC 3 FAC 3/3
Peterborough U (Free on 7/1/2004) FL 35+2/6 FLC 1 FAC 1
MK Dons (Free on 13/1/2005) FL 91+11/27 FLC 2+1 FAC 6+1/2 Others 1
Colchester U (£300,000 on 12/7/2007) FL 109+16/25 FLC 4 FAC 2+1/1 Others 2+1/1

PLESSIS Damien
Born: Neuville-aux-Bois, France, 5 March 1988
Height: 6'3" **Weight:** 12.1
International Honours: France: U21-1; Yth
A young French defensive midfielder with Liverpool, Damien made only one appearance, in the Carling Cup away to Arsenal in October, coincidentally the venue where he made a promising Premiership debut two seasons earlier. Sadly, at the age of 22, he has simply not progressed as far as was once anticipated by the supporters.
Liverpool (Signed from Lyon, France on 31/8/2007) PL 3 FLC 3/1 Others 1+1

PLUMMER Matthew (Matt) Robert
Born: Hull, 18 January 1989
Height: 5'11" **Weight:** 11.3
A young defender who arrived at Darlington from Hull along with assistant manager Dean Windass and performed competently in central defence during the first three months of the season. He settled well alongside Ian Miller or Steve Foster when deputizing for one or the other, showing strength in the air and a solid tackle. However, after 12 appearances for Darlington, eight of them starts, he was released by Steve Staunton in December.
Hull C (From trainee on 14/12/2006)
Darlington (Free on 2/7/2009) FL 5+3 FLC 0+1 FAC 1 Others 2

PLUMMER Tristan Daine
Born: Bristol, 30 January 1990
Height: 5'6" **Weight:** 10.8
A hard-working and enthusiastic young Bristol City forward, Tristan pepped up the Hereford attack during his month's loan and showed himself a nerveless performer from the penalty spot. He converted three times from 12 yards, one of these at Aldershot when he also scored the only goal from open play of his month at Edgar Street. Tristan next signed on loan for Gillingham in January as Mark Stimson sought to inject life into his struggling side. After making his debut in the 0-0 draw with Colchester, the pacy left-winger sadly was injured in his second appearance, at Hartlepool, and returned to Ashton Gate, thus terminating the remainder of his loan. Was out of contract at the end of June.
Bristol C (From trainee on 26/5/2007)
Luton T (Loaned on 7/8/2008) FL 0+5 FLC 1+1/1 Others 0+1
Hereford U (Loaned on 21/8/2009) FL 4+1/3 FLC 1/1 Others 1
Gillingham (Loaned on 21/1/2010) FL 2

POGATETZ Emanuel (Manny)
Born: Steinbock, Austria, 16 January 1983
Height: 6'2" **Weight:** 12.13
International Honours: Austria: 37; U21-11; Yth
The season could not end quickly enough at Middlesbrough for the Austria captain as he suffered badly with injuries. After undergoing knee surgery in April, it was not until the last day of October that Manny made his comeback. In that game, against Plymouth, he challenged for a high ball with Pilgrims' defender Shane Lowry and suffered a fractured cheekbone.

This was a recurrence of the injury he suffered in a UEFA Cup tie at Basel in 2006. Despite having an operation, and initially being ruled out for six weeks, he returned within three, playing with a protective mask. Mainly used by Gordon Strachan at left-back, Manny impressed the new boss with his attitude. Unfortunately in March he suffered a nasty blow to his patella, on the same knee that required surgery the previous summer, and was forced to miss the rest of the season.
Middlesbrough *(£1,800,000 from Bayer Leverkusen, Germany, ex Grazer AK, on 28/6/2005) P/FL 119+4/4 FLC 4+1 FAC 21 Others 9*

POKE Michael Harold
Born: Staines, 21 November 1985
Height: 6'1" **Weight:** 12.3
Torquay signed Michael in September on a long-term loan from Southampton, his third loan spell at Plainmoor, because of Scott Bevan's injury problems. He was again a consistent and reassuring presence between the sticks before his own season was interrupted by niggling injury problems. Was out of contract at the end of June.
Southampton *(From trainee on 9/1/2004) FL 3+1*
Northampton T *(Loaned on 18/10/2005) Others 2*
Torquay U *(Loaned on 1/9/2009) FL 28+1 FAC 1*

POLLITT Michael (Mike) Francis
Born: Farnworth, 29 February 1972
Height: 6'4" **Weight:** 14.0
A reliable and experienced Wigan goalkeeper, Mike was restricted to four League appearances by the consistency of Chris Kirkland. The longest-serving player, having been involved in Athletic's five seasons in the Premier League, his other starts were in the domestic Cups against Blackpool and Notts County. A solid performer who commands his area well, when called upon he was his usual confident self, making difficult saves easy with his tremendous positioning and quick reflexes. His last appearance against Chelsea in the final game extended his record as the oldest player to represent Wigan in the Premier League. Out of contract at the end of the season, he was not offered a new deal.
Manchester U *(From trainee on 1/7/1990)*
Bury *(Free on 10/7/1991)*
Lincoln C *(Loaned on 24/9/1992) FL 5 FLC 1*
Lincoln C *(Free on 1/12/1992) FL 52*
FLC 4 FAC 2 Others 4
Darlington *(Free on 11/8/1994) FL 55 FLC 4 FAC 3 Others 5*
Notts Co *(£75,000 on 14/11/1995) FL 10 Others 2*
Oldham Ath *(Loaned on 29/8/1997) FL 16*
Gillingham *(Loaned on 12/12/1997) FL 6*
Brentford *(Loaned on 22/1/1998) FL 5*
Sunderland *(£75,000 on 23/2/1998)*
Rotherham U *(Free on 14/7/1998) FL 92 FLC 4 FAC 7 Others 5*
Chesterfield *(Free on 15/6/2000) FL 46 FLC 3 FAC 1 Others 4*
Rotherham U *(£75,000 on 29/5/2001) FL 175 FLC 11 FAC 6*
Wigan Ath *(£200,000 on 30/6/2005) PL 31+4 FLC 9 FAC 3*
Ipswich T *(Loaned on 15/11/2006) FL 1*
Burnley *(Loaned on 11/1/2007) FL 4*

POOK Michael David
Born: Swindon, 22 October 1985
Height: 5'11" **Weight:** 11.10
Former Swindon player Michael made the short journey to Cheltenham for the start of what was to prove an eventful campaign for the midfield man. He started off in the centre of midfield but suffered an ankle injury in only the third game. Despite returning after only a month, the problem clearly affected his mobility. Michael's game is based on strong running, tackling and simple use of the ball and it was not until the second half of the season that Town fans began to see the best of him. He wrote his name into club folklore by claiming a stunning hat-trick in the remarkable 6-5 win at Burton in March. Michael's performances earned him the 'Players' Player of the Season' award and he was offered a new contract.
Swindon T *(From trainee on 5/8/2005) FL 85+24/3 FLC 1+2/1 FAC 6+2 Others 5+1*
Cheltenham T *(Free on 22/7/2009) FL 31+4/5 FLC 1 FAC 1*

POOLE David Andrew
Born: Manchester, 25 November 1984
Height: 5'8" **Weight:** 12.0
Club Honours: FAYC '03
Like Adam Griffin, David had trained

Michael Pook

with the Stockport squad in the summer after being released by Darlington and was eventually offered a deal to rejoin the Hatters for a second spell. He was a regular fixture in the County team, scoring his only goal of the season in the 5-0 FA Cup win over Tooting & Mitcham, although he had to miss a number of games through suspension. The right-winger first received a straight red card in the 4-2 defeat by Leeds, then picked up two bookings in a 1-0 loss at Bristol Rovers.
Manchester U (From trainee on 2/7/2002)
Yeovil T (Free on 6/7/2005) FL 21+8/2
Stockport Co (£10,000 on 15/9/2006) FL 43+10/6 FLC 1 FAC 2+1/1 Others 2+1
Darlington (Free on 29/7/2008) FL 18+8/1 FLC 1+1 Others 2
Stockport Co (Free on 7/8/2009) FL 29+7 FLC 1/1 FAC 2/1 Others 1+1

POOLE James Alexander
Born: Stockport, 20 March 1990
Height: 5'11" **Weight:** 12.3
The quick and skilful attacking midfield player joined Bury on loan from Manchester City and was a threat when making appearances from the bench. James received a straight red card for a late tackle in the final game at Rotherham.
Manchester C (From trainee on 2/7/2008)
Bury (Loaned on 25/3/2010) FL 4+5

POOLE Kevin
Born: Bromsgrove, 21 July 1963
Height: 5'10" **Weight:** 12.11
Club Honours: FLC '97; FC '09
The modern Peter Pan of football is still going strong 25 years after making his debut for Aston Villa. The goalkeeping coach at Burton added to his long list of League appearances after an injury to regular 'keeper Artur Krysiak. Despite being 46, making him the oldest player in the League, Kevin showed he had lost none of his fitness or agility with fine displays at the end of the campaign, including a 'Man of the Match' performance in the 3-0 defeat of Grimsby that prompted manager Paul Peschisolido to declare him 'a freak of nature'. Kevin, who originally joined Burton as an emergency signing in the summer of 2006, has now made more than 120 appearances for the club and has no intention of hanging up his gloves after signing a new one-year contract in his dual role.
Aston Villa (From apprentice on 26/6/1981) FL 28 FLC 2 FAC 1 Others 1
Northampton T (Loaned on 8/11/1984) FL 3

Middlesbrough (Signed on 27/8/1987) FL 34 FLC 4 FAC 2 Others 2
Hartlepool U (Loaned on 27/3/1991) FL 12
Leicester C (£40,000 on 30/7/1991) P/FL 163 FLC 10 FAC 8 Others 12
Birmingham C (Free on 4/8/1997) FL 56 FLC 7 FAC 2 Others 2
Bolton W (Free on 25/10/2001) PL 4+1 FLC 7 FAC 4
Derby Co (Free on 1/8/2005) FL 6 FAC 1
Burton A (Free on 2/7/2006) FL 5+1 FLC 1

POOLE Matthew (Matty) Ian
Born: Lancaster, 22 October 1990
Height: 5'11" **Weight:** 12.4
A young attack-minded midfielder, who can also play up front, Matty signed a one-year deal after coming through the club's junior sides but failed to make a League start in 2009-10. However, he came off the bench in the Carling Cup defeat at Preston and came close to scoring with a late shot that was well saved by Andy Lonergan. Until suffering an injury late in the season, he was a regular in the reserve side and top scorer with the youth team before being released at the end of the campaign.
Morecambe (Signed from Lancaster C Youth Academy on 24/7/2009) FLC 0+1

POPE Thomas (Tom) John
Born: Stoke-on-Trent, 27 August 1985
Height: 6'3" **Weight:** 11.3
Was the summer's major signing when brought in from Crewe in a deal reported to be worth, with various add-ons, £150,000, thus equalling Rotherham's record. The striker had a good pre-season, with a few goals that looked promising, and when he got off the mark with a cracker at West Bromwich in the Carling Cup followed a few days later by his first League goal at Macclesfield, things looked good. However, Tom then simply could not find the net and went four months before his next goal. It affected his confidence but he continued to try and to give his all, setting up several goals for Adam le Fondre. Lost his place in March and a few weeks later suffered the dreaded broken metatarsal, thus ending his season.
Crewe Alex (Free from Biddulph Victoria on 4/10/2005) FL 32+24/17 FLC 4 FAC 0+2 Others 2
Rotherham U (Signed on 4/6/2009) FL 26+9/3 FLC 2/2 FAC 2

PORRITT Nathan John
Born: Middlesbrough, 9 January 1990?
Height: 5'9" **Weight:** 11.9

A skilful ball player, Nathan arrived at Darlington on loan from Middlesbrough four games into the season. He operated mainly down the left flank but failed to establish himself in the side and after five consecutive appearances, returned to the Riverside.
Middlesbrough (From trainee on 7/7/2008)
Darlington (Loaned on 18/8/2009) FL 4+1 Others 1

PORTER Christopher (Chris) John
Born: Wigan, 12 December 1983
Height: 6'1" **Weight:** 13.2
Rest was prescribed for the hip injury that troubled Chris when he first joined Derby. He knew in pre-season that it had not worked, so he had an operation that kept him out until December. The striker returned as a substitute and scored a precious goal at Watford to give Derby their first away win. Chris gradually eased himself back into contention with his strength and ability to hold the ball. There was always a feeling that more is to come and that needs him fighting fit after a good pre-season.
Bury (From Queen Elizabeth Grammar School OB, Blackburn on 3/3/2003) FL 48+23/18 FLC 2 FAC 2+1/2 Others 2
Oldham Ath (£100,000 on 13/7/2005) FL 52+14/28 FAC 6/3 Others 2+1
Motherwell (Free on 3/7/2007) SL 55+43/27 FLC 2 SC 2/2
Derby Co (£400,000 on 2/2/2009) FL 14+12/7 FAC 3+1

POTTER Darren Michael
Born: Liverpool, 21 December 1984
Height: 6'1" **Weight:** 12.0
International Honours: RoI: 5; B-1; U21-11; Yth
A skilful Sheffield Wednesday central midfielder who can also put a good tackle in was not at his best in 2009-10. Occasional glimpses of his great passing ability were seen but he does need to get more involved in games. Can use either foot well and has a terrific shot, but again he is sometimes reluctant to use it. He scored a really classy goal against Blackpool as Hillsborough, stopping and then shifting his balance to beat the goalkeeper into the corner of the net. Darren really needs to involve himself more in games and take control of the midfield. Then his true worth will be realised.
Liverpool (From trainee on 18/4/2002) PL 0+2 FLC 4+1 FAC 1 Others 5+4
Southampton (Loaned on 27/1/2006) FL 8+2 FAC 1+1
Wolverhampton W (£250,000 on

*17/8/2006) FL 46+10 FLC 2+1 FAC 6/1
Others 2*
***Sheffield Wed** (Signed on 15/1/2009)
FL 63/5 FLC 2 FAC 1*

POTTER Luke Alexander

Born: Barnsley, 13 July 1989
Height: 6'2" **Weight:** 12.7
Luke started the season with a number of appearances in the Barnsley team but then suffered a knee injury that put him out. While he was unavailable, Ryan Shotton and Carl Dickinson were signed on loan, so his opportunities became more limited. However it was an injury to Dickinson that was to give him an extended run at left-back and saw him develop into a useful player. He was always willing to put his body on the line and, given time, can produce telling passes. He can also play in the centre of defence, his preferred position. He signed a two-year extension to his contract, taking it to the summer of 2012.
***Barnsley** (From trainee on 27/5/2009)
FL 13+2 FLC 2*

POWELL Christopher (Chris) George Robin

Born: Lambeth, 8 September 1969
Height: 5'10" **Weight:** 11.7
Club Honours: Div 1 '00, '09
International Honours: E: 5
The veteran left-back became Leicester's first ever 40-year-old outfield player during the campaign. Occasionally called on to exchange his coaching duties for a playing role, he never looked out of place as he used his head to save his legs when necessary. Chris keeps threatening to hang up his playing boots for good but if manager Nigel Pearson can persuade him to register for just one more season, he could yet become the club's oldest ever player.
***Crystal Palace** (From trainee on 24/12/1987) FL 2+1 FLC 0+1 Others 0+1*
***Aldershot T** (Loaned on 11/1/1990) FL 11*
***Southend U** (Free on 30/8/1990) FL 246+2/3 FLC 13 FAC 8 Others 21*
***Derby Co** (£750,000 on 31/1/1996) P/FL 89+2/1 FLC 5 FAC 5/1*
***Charlton Ath** (£825,000 on 1/7/1998) P/FL 190+10/1 FLC 8+1 FAC 8/1*
***West Ham U** (Free on 10/9/2004) FL 35+1 FAC 3 Others 3*
***Charlton Ath** (Free on 16/7/2005) PL 25+2 FLC 2 FAC 5*
***Watford** (Free on 4/7/2006) PL 9+6 FAC 2+1*
***Charlton Ath** (Free on 9/8/2007) FL 16+1/1 FLC 2*
***Leicester C** (Free on 23/8/2008) FL 14+5 FLC 3 FAC 0+1 Others 2+1 .*

POWELL Daniel Vendrys

Born: Luton, 12 March 1991
Height: 6'2" **Weight:** 13.3
Loaned out to Forest Green Rovers for the majority of the campaign, Daniel returned to MK Dons after the early completion of the Blue Square Premier programme and was immediately thrown into action as all the club's main strikers were injured for the penultimate game against Brighton. Showing plenty of pace and strength on the right flank, he also started in the final game at Walsall, scoring with an acrobatic overhead-kick, and during both games showed that his season playing regular first team football had a beneficial effect on his all-round level.
***MK Dons** (From trainee on 11/2/2009)
FL 2+7/2*

POWELL Darren David

Born: Hammersmith, 10 March 1976
Height: 6'3" **Weight:** 13.2
Club Honours: Div 3 '99
Experienced central defender Darren was signed by MK Dons just ahead of the season to help plug the gap left by the long-term injury of Sean O'Hanlon, and throughout the campaign was called upon regularly to provide strength and stability at the heart of the defence. At his best when facing up to tall and imposing attackers, he was unable to escape the injury jinx that affected the squad throughout the campaign, but was fortunately fit and healthy at the tail-end when the Dons had to call on a number of Academy products to make up the numbers. His determined play helped carry the club through a testing last few games without any long-term damage being inflicted on those new faces brought into the fray. Was out of contract at the end of June.
***Brentford** (£15,000 from Hampton on 27/7/1998) FL 128/6 FLC 7 FAC 4 Others 10+1/2*
***Crystal Palace** (£400,000 on 8/8/2002) P/FL 53+2/2 FLC 9+1/1 FAC 3 Others 0+3/1*
***West Ham U** (Loaned on 19/11/2004) FL 5/1*
***Southampton** (Free on 4/7/2005) FL 42+1/2 FAC 6*
***Derby Co** (Free, via trial at Charlton Ath, on 21/11/2008) FL 5+1 FLC 1 FAC 0+1 (Freed on 21/1/9)*
***Brentford** (Free, via trial at Leeds U, on 21/3/2009) FL 3+1*
***MK Dons** (Free on 7/8/2009) FL 19+5 FLC 0+1 FAC 2 Others 1*

POWER Alan Thomas Daniel

Born: Dublin, 23 January 1988
Height: 5'7" **Weight:** 11.6

International Honours: RoI: U21-1
The tough-tackling midfielder has spent two years at Hartlepool without being able to establish himself as a first team squad member. A regular in the successful reserve side, where he was played at right-back as an experiment, he made two very brief first team substitute appearances, on both occasions taking to the field in added time as the match was nearing completion. At the end of the season he was one of seven players released by Hartlepool.
***Nottingham F** (From trainee on 10/4/2006) Others 1*
***Hartlepool U** (Free on 2/7/2008) FL 0+6 FLC 1 Others 1*

PRATLEY Darren Antony

Born: Barking, 22 April 1985
Height: 6'0" **Weight:** 10.13
Club Honours: Div 1 '08
The all-action Swansea central midfield player missed the start of the season following a shoulder operation in the summer but, after returning to the first team, gradually recovered the exciting form of the previous campaign, scoring two goals in the home defeat of neighbours Cardiff, followed by two further goals at Sheffield Wednesday. Swans' turned down an offer from Nottingham Forest when the January transfer window opened and by the end of the season, Darren had topped the club's scoring charts.
***Fulham** (From trainee on 29/4/2002) PL 0+1 FLC 0+1*
***Brentford** (Loaned on 22/2/2005) FL 11+3/1 Others 2*
***Brentford** (Loaned on 30/8/2005) FL 25+7/4 FAC 4 Others 2*
***Swansea C** (£100,000 on 23/6/2006) FL 130+13/17 FLC 1+1/1 FAC 7/1 Others 4+2*

PREECE David Douglas

Born: Sunderland, 26 August 1976
Height: 6'2" **Weight:** 12.11
The goalkeeper signed for Barnsley on a one-year contract with an option of a second year in July, having been a free agent after he was released by Danish club OB Odense. That second year was taken up before the first finished. David was included in the starting line-up as new manager Mark Robins took charge for the first time, at Watford, replacing the injured Luke Steele. Later in the season he again took over when Steele was suspended. On his limited opportunities he showed a good temperament. He was also a good shot-stopper and was unlucky when he replaced Steele, sent off against Newcastle, who then went

on the rampage.
Sunderland *(From trainee on 30/6/1994)* .
Darlington *(Free on 28/7/1997) FL 91 FLC 4 FAC 7 Others 2*
Aberdeen *(£300,000 on 29/7/1999) SL 86+3 SLC 7 SC 10 (Freed during 2005 close season)*
Barnsley *(Free from OB Odense, Denmark, ex Silkeborg, on 20/7/2009) FL 5+1 FLC 1*

PRESTON Daniel (Dan)
Sean
Born: Birmingham, 26 September 1991
Height: 5'11" **Weight:** 12.4
After making his Birmingham debut when coming on for the last ten minutes of the Carling Cup tie at Sunderland in September, the tall, uncomplicated centre-half who is not afraid to stand his ground was loaned to Hereford to further his football education. There was no doubting that Dan had a baptism of fire when he was drafted in to play in a 5-0 defeat at Notts County. He proved that he was not scarred by the experience when turning in a composed display in Hereford's win at Cheltenham in his next outing, showing that he could handle the physical aspects of the game. He played twice more before returning to St Andrews.
Birmingham C *(Trainee) FLC 0+1*
Hereford U *(Loaned on 26/2/2010) FL 4*

PRICE Jason Jeffrey
Born: Pontypridd, 12 April 1977
Height: 6'2" **Weight:** 11.5
Club Honours: Div 3 '00; AMC '07
International Honours: W: U21-7
Having been freed by Doncaster in the summer, Jason joined Millwall on a permanent basis after being on loan for the final eight games in 2008-09. He was a regular member of the first team squad, appearing 20 times prior to going out on loan to Oldham at the beginning of February. An experienced striker who is sharp in the box, Jason was brought in to add pace and height to the Latics' forward line which was depleted by the absence of Pawel Abbott. Immediately Jason's height caused problems for opposing defenders and he led the line well even though he preferred to play out wide. Scored with a good header at Swindon and looked to be enjoying his stay with Oldham but was then allowed to move on to Carlisle on loan in March. He made his debut with a typically bustling performance against Colchester, which he capped off with a debut goal, then netted three more times before returning to the Den in time for the

League One play-offs. Was out of contract at the end of June.
Swansea C *(Free from Aberaman on 17/7/1995) FL 133+11/17 FLC 10/1 FAC 4/1 Others 4+1/1*
Brentford *(Free on 6/8/2001) FL 15/1 FLC 2 Others 1*
Tranmere Rov *(Free on 8/11/2001) FL 34+15/11 FAC 5/4*
Hull C *(Free on 1/7/2003) FL 45+30/13 FLC 3/1 FAC 3+1/1 Others 2/1*
Doncaster Rov *(Signed on 24/1/2006) FL 59+34/17 FLC 2+1 FAC 4+4/1 Others 9+1/5*
Millwall *(Free on 26/3/2009) FL 11+12/4 FLC 0+1 FAC 1+2/2 Others 2*
Oldham Ath *(Loaned on 1/2/2010) FL 7/1*
Carlisle U *(Loaned on 10/3/2010) FL 8+1/4*

PRICE Lewis Peter
Born: Bournemouth, 19 July 1984
Height: 6'3" **Weight:** 13.6
International Honours: W: 7; U21-10; Yth
Derby's Lewis joined Brentford on a season-long loan but, unfortunately, it did not work out well for him. Having started the campaign in goal for the Bees and, initially, impressing with his shot-stopping ability, he was left out for five games following a poor performance against Bristol Rovers in September. Lewis regained his place but when Brentford signed Wojciech Szczesny on loan from Arsenal in November, he was again omitted and appeared only in Cup games and two League matches in December when Szczesny was injured. He added a further Welsh cap as a substitute against Montenegro in August but was released by Derby at the end of his contract.
Ipswich T *(From juniors at Southampton on 9/8/2002) FL 67+1 FLC 4 FAC 3*
Cambridge U *(Loaned on 19/11/2004) FL 6*
Derby Co *(£200,000 on 27/7/2007) PL 6 FAC 3*
MK Dons *(Loaned on 28/10/2008) FL 2 FAC 1*
Luton T *(Loaned on 2/2/2009) FL 1 Others 1*
Brentford *(Loaned on 8/7/2009) FL 13 FAC 4 Others 1*

PRINGLE Benjamin (Ben)
Philip
Born: Newcastle, 27 May 1989
Height: 6'1" **Weight:** 11.13
After helping Ilkeston Town to win promotion from the UniBond Premier Division, Ben joined Derby in the summer. It was planned that the

midfield player should be part of a development squad but he had an early taste of senior action. He was used as a substitute in the opening game against Peterborough and started the disappointing Carling Cup defeat by Rotherham. He spent most of the season helping the reserves to win their league but ended all smiles. He won the Sammy Crooks award as 'Young Player of the Year' and was voted 'Man of the Match' when he made his first League start against Cardiff on the final day.
Derby Co *(Signed from Ilkeston T, ex trainee at West Bromwich A, Newcastle Blue Star, Morpeth T, on 21/7/2009) FL 1+4 FLC 1*

PRISKIN Tamas
Born: Komarno, Slovakia, 27 September 1986
Height: 6'2" **Weight:** 13.3
International Honours: Hungary: 25
A big money signing from Watford, Tamas had trouble finding the consistency of performance and scoring which would have guaranteed him a regular place in the Ipswich team. His first goal came in the Carling Cup at Peterborough, when he also missed a penalty, and his only other goal came at Doncaster after he had come on as substitute. He had opportunities to add to his tally, particularly in one-on-one situations with the opposing 'keepers, but was unable to take them and joined Queens Park Rangers on loan in January. The Hungarian international striker joined up with Rangers at the start of February and became a key part of Neil Warnock's system in the closing months of the season. His first and only goal was in a battling performance at Deepdale when Rangers came back from two down to secure a 2-2 draw, Tamas grabbing the equaliser.
Watford *(Signed from Gyori ETO, Hungary on 11/8/2006) P/FL 46+20/15 FLC 8/3 FAC 4+3/1 Others 0+2*
Preston NE *(Loaned on 7/3/2008) FL 4+1/2*
Ipswich T *(Signed on 7/8/2009) FL 9+8/1 FLC 1/1 FAC 0+1*
Queens Park Rgrs *(Loaned on 1/2/2010) FL 13/1*

PROCTER Andrew (Andy)
John
Born: Blackburn, 13 March 1983
Height: 6'2" **Weight:** 12.4
Accrington's longest-serving player has now been at the Crown Ground for ten years, making over 300 appearances. The central midfielder was made captain at the start of the season and played in all but a couple of first team matches. Is a box-to-box player who

likes to get up with the attack whenever he can.
Accrington Stanley *(Free from Great Harwood T on 21/2/2002) FL 154+13/21 FLC 4 FAC 8 Others 7/1*

PROCTOR Jamie Thomas
Born: Preston, 25 March 1992
Height: 6'2" **Weight:** 12.3
A young striker of undoubted potential who is comfortable on the ball and takes up good positions, Jamie was included on the bench on three occasions before being given his Preston debut as a 72nd-minute substitute in the final game. Able to play through the middle or on the right, the 18-year-old was a regular scorer in the reserves and will be looking for more first team opportunities in the near future.
Preston NE *(From trainee on 23/2/2010) FL 0+1*

PROSSER Luke Barrie
Born: Enfield, 28 May 1988
Height: 6'2" **Weight:** 12.4
Central defender Luke began the season on the transfer list at Port Vale and joined Salisbury City on loan. He made 12 appearances for them but was recalled after six weeks to cover for injuries. A tall defender, who is useful in the air, he made his first appearance for Vale in a 1-1 draw against Cheltenham. His next appearance against Rotherham was memorable because he scored, was booked and then sent off all within eight minutes. He played only one further game, against Huddersfield in the FA Cup, and spent the last month of the campaign on loan at Kidderminster before being freed.
Port Vale *(From trainee on 1/7/2006) FL 29+4/2 FAC 1+1 Others 1*

PROUDLOCK Adam David
Born: Telford, 9 May 1981
Height: 6'0" **Weight:** 13.0
International Honours: E: Yth
Apart from an ankle ligament injury in October, Adam was a regular squad member for Grimsby last term, latterly being used mainly as a substitute. The lack of matches overall was a frustration for the player given Town's position and goal drought, especially as the direct forward had scored twice in three games immediately prior to his injury.
Wolverhampton W *(From trainee on 15/7/1999) FL 42+29/13 FLC 4+2/2 FAC 2+3/2 Others 0+2*
Clyde *(Loaned on 1/8/2000) SL 4/4 SLC 2/1*
Nottingham F *(Loaned on 19/3/2002) FL 3*
Tranmere Rov *(Loaned on 25/10/2002)*

FL 5 Others 1
Sheffield Wed *(Loaned on 13/12/2002) FL 3+2/2*
Sheffield Wed *(Signed on 6/9/2003) FL 37+13/9 FLC 1+2/2 FAC 3/3 Others 5+1/3*
Ipswich T *(Free on 10/10/2005) FL 3+6*
Stockport Co *(Free on 17/8/2006) FL 32+24/11 FLC 2/1 FAC 2+2/3 Others 1+1/1*
Darlington *(Free on 29/7/2008) FL 3+5 FLC 1 Others 2*
Grimsby T *(Signed on 6/11/2008) FL 36+19/9 FLC 1 FAC 1 Others 1/1*

PRUTTON David Thomas
Born: Hull, 12 September 1981
Height: 6'1" **Weight:** 11.10
International Honours: E: U21-25; Yth
The popular midfielder could not nail down a regular place in Leeds' starting line-up, making just one League One start for the Whites in a 2-0 away win against Oldham in December. Towards the end of the following month he moved to Colchester on loan, marking his debut with a goal in a 2-0 triumph against MK Dons. Unavailable for the following game against former club Leeds, David was released after that match and immediately signed for the U's on a short-term deal. A regular in the second half of the season, he started off on the right of midfield before becoming a regular in his natural central position. Scoring twice more, while his visionary passing created four goals, he was offered a new deal in the summer.
Nottingham F *(From trainee on 1/10/1998) FL 141+2/7 FLC 7 FAC 5*
Southampton *(£2,500,000 on 31/1/2003) P/FL 65+17/3 FLC 4+1/1 FAC 6+1/1*
Nottingham F *(Loaned on 30/1/2007) FL 11+1/2 Others 0+1*
Leeds U *(Free on 10/8/2007) FL 47+18/4 FLC 3 FAC 1 Others 8+1*
Colchester U *(Free on 26/1/2010) FL 18+1/3*

PUGH Daniel (Danny) Adam
Born: Manchester, 19 October 1982
Height: 6'0" **Weight:** 12.10
Danny spent another season on the fringe of the Stoke team and he made only one League start. He did, however, find the back of the net in that one start, scoring a close-range diving header past Arsenal. His versatility in being able to play all the left-sided positions, as well as in the centre of midfield, make him one of those players the manager loves to have in the squad, although Danny has been unfortunate to see other players occupying all the spots himself he can slot into. He has

always been there when needed and manager Tony Pulis cited him as an example of the type of great squad player he loves to have at the club.
Manchester U *(From trainee on 18/7/2000) PL 0+1 FLC 2 FAC 0+1 Others 1+2*
Leeds U *(Signed on 20/7/2004) FL 34+16/5 FLC 6/1 FAC 0+1*
Preston NE *(£250,000 on 6/7/2006) FL 50+2/4 FLC 2/1 FAC 3*
Stoke C *(£500,000 on 2/11/2007) P/FL 37+17/1 FLC 5+1/1 FAC 2+3*

PUGH Marc Anthony
Born: Bacup, 2 April 1987
Height: 5'11" **Weight:** 11.5
Marc, although predominantly used as a left-winger at Hereford, was equally at home on either flank with his ability to cross with either foot. Deceptively pacy and with lots of skill, he was one of United's success stories of the season with his impressive 13 goals making him top scorer. Two goals on the opening day at Morecambe set the tone and he continued to find the target regularly, scoring in five of Hereford's last six away matches as his talents proved perfect for the Bulls' counter-attacking style. He was runner-up in Hereford's 'Player of the Year' poll.
Bury *(From trainee on 1/7/2006) FL 30+11/4 FLC 0+1 FAC 4/1 Others 1*
Shrewsbury T *(Signed on 20/7/2007) FL 27+17/4 FAC 1 Others 0+1*
Luton T *(Loaned on 12/9/2008) FL 3+1*
Hereford U *(Free on 25/3/2009) FL 47+2/14 FLC 1 FAC 1+1 Others 3*

PULIS Anthony (Tony) James
Born: Bristol, 21 July 1984
Height: 5'10" **Weight:** 11.10
International Honours: W: U21-5
Having failed to make a single Football League appearance at Southampton in 2008-09 after joining them from his father's club, Stoke, the midfielder spent six weeks at Lincoln on loan in 2009-10. He was going quite well until an ankle injury sustained early on in a 2-0 defeat at Rotherham in November brought about an abrupt end to his City career.
Portsmouth *(From trainee on 26/3/2003) FLC 0+1*
Stoke C *(Free on 23/12/2004) FL 0+2 FLC 2 FAC 0+2*
Torquay U *(Loaned on 24/12/2004) FL 1+2*
Plymouth Arg *(Loaned on 10/3/2006) FL 0+5*
Grimsby T *(Loaned on 23/11/2006) FL 9*
Bristol Rov *(Loaned on 8/2/2008) FL 0+1*
Southampton *(Signed on 29/8/2008)*
Lincoln C *(Loaned on 7/10/2009) FL 7 FAC 1*

Jason Puncheon

PUNCHEON Jason David Ian
Born: Croydon, 26 June 1986
Height: 5'8" **Weight:** 12.2
Having impressed whilst on loan from Plymouth the previous season, Jason returned to MK Dons on a season-long loan, and for the first half of the campaign generally dictated the team's displays. It was clear that when he played well, the Dons played well. Given plenty of freedom to roam by manager Paul Ince, he scored some spectacular left-footed goals and it was no coincidence that the team fell away from the play-off picture once he was recalled by Plymouth to be sold to Southampton. Along with Saints' team-mates Rickie Lambert and Kelvin Davies, Jason made the PFA's League One Team of theYear'. With his blistering pace, tight ball control and an eye for the main chance, he made quite an impression on the St Mary's faithful when the Dons visited in October, and scored with a wicked 20-yard free kick. Versatile, he can play on either wing, behind the front two or as a striker.
Wimbledon/MK Dons (From trainee on 16/10/2004) FL 15+19/1 FLC 2+1 FAC 1+1 Others 2+1 (Freed on 20/1/2006)

Barnet (Free from Lewes, ex Fisher Ath, on 3/8/2006) FL 71+7/15 FLC 3/1 FAC 9/1 Others 3
Plymouth Arg (£250,000 on 10/7/2008) FL 5+1 FLC 1
MK Dons (Loaned on 24/10/2008) FL 8+1/1
MK Dons (Loaned on 12/1/2009) FL 18/3 Others 2
MK Dons (Loaned on 4/8/2009) FL 23+1/7 FLC 0+1 FAC 2+1 Others 4/1
Southampton (Signed on 30/1/2010) FL 19/3

PURCELL Tadhg
Born: Dundrum, 9 February 1985
Height: 5'10" **Weight:** 11.11
Tadhg was one of the few successes of a dismal season for Darlington and ended as top scorer with nine goals after joining in January from Shamrock Rovers. The striker possesses a strong shot in either foot and scored on his debut in the win at Rotherham in January. After netting five in his first seven games for the Quakers, he was more closely marked by opposition defences and his goals per game ratio slowed.
Darlington (Free from Shamrock Rov, ex Leicester Celtic, UCD, Kilkenny C, on 8/1/2010) FL 22/9

PURCHES Stephen Robert
Born: Ilford, 14 January 1980
Height: 5'11" **Weight:** 12.0
Stephen was Leyton Orient's team captain and a regular choice at right-back. He always leads by example and has made more than 100 appearances for the team he supported as a boy. Stephen was out of contract in the summer and was released.
West Ham U (From trainee on 6/7/1998)
Bournemouth (Free on 4/7/2000) FL 221+23/10 FLC 6 FAC 16+1 Others 11/2
Leyton Orient (Free on 25/7/2007) FL 107+3/5 FLC 3 FAC 7 Others 0+2

PURSE Darren John
Born: Stepney, 14 February 1977
Height: 6'2" **Weight:** 12.8
International Honours: E: U21-2
Signed from Cardiff in the close season to add stability and leadership to the Sheffield Wednesday line-up, this experienced centre-half got off to an unsteady start. His decision-making and hesitation were a real surprise both to him and the management at the time. However, he soon got to grips with his own form and went on to have a very good season as captain and, a few little injuries apart, he aided the younger players around him in the Owls'

defence. Scored his only goal of the season against Coventry at home in October. Overall, Darren proved to be a good, solid, dependable player and a much needed strong leader of the team.
Leyton Orient (From trainee on 22/2/1994) FL 48+7/3 FLC 2 FAC 1 Others 7+1/2
Oxford U (£100,000 on 23/7/1996) FL 52+7/5 FLC 10+1/2 FAC 2
Birmingham C (£800,000 on 17/2/1998) P/FL 143+25/9 FLC 17+2/2 FAC 6 Others 6+1
West Bromwich A (£500,000 + on 18/6/2004) PL 22 FAC 2
Cardiff C (£750,000 on 2/8/2005) FL 103+8/10 FLC 8/2 FAC 4
Sheffield Wed (Free on 2/7/2009) FL 39/2 FLC 1 FAC 1

Darren Purse

Q

QUASHIE Nigel Francis
Born: Peckham, 20 July 1978
Height: 5'10" **Weight:** 12.4
Club Honours: Div 1 '03
International Honours: S: 14; E: B-1;
U21-4; Yth
Nigel looked a little ring-rusty after
joining MK Dons on loan from West
Ham, which was hardly surprising as he
was making his first appearance of the
season when making his debut in late
November against Carlisle. He soon got

into the swing of things, netting a very
late winner at Leyton Orient in mid-
December, and by the time he left to
eventually join Queens Park Rangers he
was covering plenty of midfield ground
in generally orchestrating the Dons' play
from deep. Returning to the club he left
in 1998 on a short-term deal in January,
Nigel made his re-debut against former
club Nottingham Forest in a game that
ended in a 5-0 defeat. With his
appearances being restricted to a
further three games, he dropped out of
the side.
*Queens Park Rgrs (From trainee on
1/8/1995) P/FL 50+7/3 FLC 0+1 FAC 4/2*
Nottingham F (£2,500,000 on

*24/8/1998) P/FL 37+7/2 FLC 7/1 FAC
1+1*
*Portsmouth (£200,000 + on 7/8/2000)
P/FL 140+8/13 FLC 8/1 FAC 6+1*
*Southampton (£2,100,000 on
20/1/2005) P/FL 37/5 FAC 1/1*
*West Bromwich A (£1,200,000 on
31/1/2006) P/FL 26+3/1 FLC 1*
*West Ham U (£1,500,000 on
8/1/2007) PL 7 FAC 1*
*Birmingham C (Loaned on
21/10/2008) FL 8+2 FAC 1*
*Wolverhampton W (Loaned on
23/1/2009) FL 3*
*MK Dons (Loaned on 24/11/2009) FL
6+1/2 Others 1*
*Queens Park Rgrs (Free on 22/1/2010)
FL 4*

QUEUDRUE Franck
Born: Paris, France, 27 August 1978
Height: 6'0" **Weight:** 12.4
Club Honours: FLC '04
International Honours: France: B-1
Began the season in the Birmingham
team at centre-half, playing with great
sense and calm in the opening six
matches before a hamstring injury
suffered, when captaining the team in
the St Andrew's derby against Villa in
September, put him out of action. With
Scott Dann getting fit and with Liam
Ridgewell doing so well at left-back,
Franck's chances were therefore limited
as the Blues started to pick up good
results. With Colchester mounting a
League One promotion assault, Aidy
Boothroyd made something of a coup
when bringing Franck in on loan in
March. Playing at centre-back, the
Frenchman was head and shoulders
above everyone in his debut against
Wycombe, but he struggled in the
following game at Exeter when picking
up a hamstring injury. Supposedly fit for
Millwall, after being subbed with the
same problem he failed to make
another appearance. Was released at
the season's end.
*Middlesbrough (£2,500,000 from RC
Lens, France, ex Meaux, on 12/10/2001)
PL 145+5/11 FLC 11+1/1 FAC 14 Others
18+5*
*Fulham (£2,000,000 on 28/7/2006) PL
28+1/1 FAC 3*
*Birmingham C (£2,000,000 on
3/8/2007) P/FL 43+4/3 FLC 1+1 FAC 2*
Colchester U (Loaned on 25/3/2010) FL 3

QUINN Alan
Born: Dublin, 13 June 1979
Height: 5'9" **Weight:** 11.7
International Honours: RoI: 8; U21-8;
Yth (UEFA-U18 '98)
Alan was unable to force his way into
new manager Roy Keane's plans at
Ipswich and despite scoring at

Nigel Quashie

Alan Quinn

Paul Quinn

Shrewsbury in the Carling Cup, made only a handful of appearances in the first team in the first half of the season. **Sheffield Wed** *(Signed from Cherry Orchard on 6/12/1997) P/FL 147+10/16 FLC 14/1 FAC 6+1 Others 2* **Sunderland** *(Loaned on 3/10/2003) FL 5+1* **Sheffield U** *(Free on 7/7/2004) P/FL 76+21/11 FLC 6+2 FAC 3+1* **Ipswich T** *(£400,000 on 19/1/2008) FL 50+19/3 FLC 5/1 FAC 1+1*

QUINN Paul Charles
Born: Wishaw, 21 July 1985
Height: 6'0" **Weight:** 11.3
International Honours: S: U21-3
A tenacious Cardiff right-back who was never able to establish himself in the starting line-up. Paul signed from Scottish Premier League club Motherwell during the summer. Kevin McNaughton's switch from left to right in defence was always going to prove a problem for Paul - and the emergence of talented trainee Adam Matthews increased competition on that side. Having signed a three-year contract for the Bluebirds, he was in the Championship play-off squad and went on during the semi-finals but was an unused substitute in the final against Blackpool at Wembley Stadium.
Motherwell *(From juniors on 12/5/2002) SL 150+11/3 SLC 10+2/1 SC 8* **Cardiff C** *(£300,000 on 4/7/2009) FL 16+6 FLC 2 FAC 2*

QUINN Stephen
Born: Dublin, 4 April 1986
Height: 5'6" **Weight:** 9.8
International Honours: RoI: U21-9
Playing in midfield or wider on the left, Stephen was involved in all but one of Sheffield United's games, some from the bench, playing with great energy, never shirking a tackle, and able to show good vision in passing to the more forward players, although too often the pass went awry. A good striker of the ball, he managed only four goals, half his previous season's tally, and having signed a one-year extension to his contract, Stephen will look to improve in this area in the coming season. He played some of the season with a toe injury that required a close season operation.
Sheffield U *(From trainee on 6/7/2005) P/FL 111+10/15 FLC 7+1/1 FAC 9+1 Others 3* **MK Dons** *(Loaned on 23/9/2005) FL 6 Others 0+1* **MK Dons** *(Loaned on 11/11/2005) FL 7+2 FAC 1 Others 0+2* **Rotherham U** *(Loaned on 21/1/2006) FL 16*

R

RACCHI Daniel (Danny) Craig
Born: Elland, 22 November 1987
Height: 5'8" **Weight:** 10.4
The young and adaptable Danny, able both in midfield and at full-back, has good crossing ability and a fine attitude. Danny made just ten starts for Bury, being used most commonly to run at defenders in the latter stages of games. He failed to make as big an impact as hoped for at the beginning of the season. Was out of contract in the summer.
Huddersfield T (From trainee on 1/7/2006) FL 0+6
Bury (Free on 29/7/2008) FL 10+33 FLC 1 FAC 1+1 Others 2+2/1

RACHUBKA Paul Stephen
Born: San Luis Obispo, California, USA, 21 May 1981
Height: 6'1" **Weight:** 13.5
International Honours: E: Yth
After being an ever-present in the last two seasons, the American goalkeeper played just 21 games for Blackpool this campaign. New manager Ian Holloway could not decide who was the better 'keeper between Paul or Matt Gilks, and it was the latter who triumphed after a spell rotating the pair. Noted for his shot-stopping ability, Paul played magnificently in the 1-0 away win at Nottingham Forest in September, when the Seasiders had him to thank for pulling off a string of good stops to keep the home side at bay.
Manchester U (From trainee on 7/7/1999) PL 1 FLC 0+1 Others 0+1
Oldham Ath (Loaned on 23/11/2001) FL 16 Others 1
Charlton Ath (Signed on 20/5/2002)
Huddersfield T (Loaned on 2/3/2004) FL 13 Others 3
MK Dons (Loaned on 6/8/2004) FL 4
Northampton T (Loaned on 3/9/2004) FL 10 FLC 1
Huddersfield T (Free on 5/11/2004) FL 63 FLC 2 FAC 3 Others 3+1
Peterborough U (Loaned on 22/12/2006) FL 4
Blackpool (Free on 31/1/2007) FL 116 FLC 2 FAC 3 Others 3

RACON Thierry Norbert
Born: Villeneuve-St-Georges, France, 1 May 1984
Height: 5'10" **Weight:** 10.7
Probably the most naturally gifted player at Charlton, Thierry had a fine season in central midfield, building up a great partnership with his more defensive partner Jose Semedo. The Frenchman links the play between midfield and attack and is very comfortable on the ball with good passing ability. Equally comfortable in a 4-5-1 or 4-4-2 system, Therry is very difficult to dispossess when on the ball and also has a powerful shot, scoring with a brilliant volley from the edge of the penalty area at Bristol Rovers in February.
Charlton Ath (Signed from Guingamp, France, ex Olympique Marseille, Lorient - loan, on 24/8/2007) FL 56+3/4 FLC 2 FAC 1+1 Others 2+1
Brighton & Hove A (Loaned on 20/3/2008) FL 8

RAE Alexander (Alex) Scott
Born: Glasgow, 30 September 1969
Height: 5'9" **Weight:** 11.12
Club Honours: Div 1 '99; SPD '05; SC '05
International Honours: S: B-4; U21-8
Linking up with his former Wolverhampton team-mate Paul Ince when joining MK Dons pre-season as first team coach, Alex made his first senior appearance since October 2007 when coming on as a second-half substitute in the Johnstone's Paint Trophy area final defeat at Southampton. The club's mounting injury problems then necessitated him starting two League games in April, showing up well in a holding midfield role in the first before being the victim of a harsh red card in the final home game of the season against Brighton. Despite advancing years, he was able to show plenty of glimpses of the ability that has allowed him to make close on 600 League appearances in his career.
Falkirk (Free from Bishopbriggs on 15/6/1987) SL 71+12/20 SLC 5/1 SC 2+1
Millwall (£100,000 on 20/8/1990) FL 205+13/63 FLC 13+2/1 FAC 13/6 Others 10/1
Sunderland (£750,000 on 14/6/1996) P/FL 90+24/12 FLC 12+1/3 FAC 7 Others 0+2
Wolverhampton W (£1,200,000 on 21/9/2001) P/FL 88+19/15 FLC 4+1/4 FAC 2+2/1 Others 2+1/1
Glasgow Rgrs (Free on 19/5/2004) SL 22+12/1 SLC 2+1 SC 1+1 Others 3+2
Dundee (Free on 1/7/2006) SL 24+2/3 SLC 1 SC 2 Others 1
MK Dons (Free on 2/7/2009) FL 2+1 Others 0+1

RAE Gavin Paul
Born: Aberdeen, 28 November 1977
Height: 5'11" **Weight:** 10.7
International Honours: S: 14; U21-6
An energetic and committed box-to-box midfield player, Gavin has played a leading role in establishing Cardiff as major promotion challengers over the last three seasons. Under contract with Cardiff until the summer of 2011, he finished the season on a low note after having ankle and knee operations but is set to be fit for the start of the new campaign. His final appearance was during the 2-1 win against Swansea at home, although he went off just after the hour. He was injured and missed the Championship play-off final against Blackpool. Gavin started the season well with two goals in his first six games, but failed to find the net again in 42 appearances.
Dundee (Signed from Hermes on 1/8/1996) SL 174+17/23 SLC 9+1 SC 16/2 Others 6/1
Glasgow Rgrs (£250,000 on 1/1/2004) SL 16+12/3 SLC 2 SC 2 Others 4+3
Cardiff C (Free on 6/7/2007) FL 107+16/6 FLC 9/1 FAC 11

[RAFAEL] PEREIRA DA SILVA Rafael
Born: Rio de Janeiro, Brazil, 9 July 1990
Height: 5'8" **Weight:** 10.3
Club Honours: FLC '09, '10; PL '09
International Honours: Brazil: Yth
Manchester United full-back, who excels in getting forward down the right, Rafael ended on a high when both he and team-mate Jonny Evans were shortlisted for the PFA 'Young Player of the Year' award. That honour went to Aston Villa's Ashley Young but Rafael had done enough to be handed a two-year extension to his contract, tying him to the club until 2013. Netting his first goal of the season, and his second overall in a 5-0 Premiership win over Wigan, he beat several players before placing the ball in the right corner. Used sparingly in the Premiership, Rafael won his first honour of the season when he played in the 2-1 Carling Cup win against Aston Villa at Wembley. His dreams of a second final of the season were ended when he was sent off early in the second half of the Champions League tie against Bayern Munich.
Manchester U (Signed from Fluminense, Brazil on 1/8/2008) PL 20+4/2 FLC 9 FAC 2 Others 6+3

RAMAGE Peter Iain
Born: Whitley Bay, 22 November 1983
Height: 6'1" **Weight:** 12.2
Peter never gives anything less than 100 per cent and is becoming something of a cult favourite at Loftus Road as a result. Queens Park Rangers' first choice right-back for the best part of two

seasons now, but perhaps is more suited to playing centre-back. Injuries and suspensions finally gave him a chance for a short run in that position for the last four games of 2009-10, where he excelled despite being sent off against Newcastle in the campaign closer. The first of his two goals was an opening day strike that secured a point against Blackpool and he was also on the mark when Rangers came from two down to draw at Preston.
Newcastle U (From trainee on 15/7/2003) PL 45+6 FLC 4+1 FAC 4+1 Others 6+2
Queens Park Rgrs (Free on 28/5/2008) FL 59+5/2 FLC 3 FAC 3

RAMSDEN Simon Paul
Born: Bishop Auckland, 17 December 1981
Height: 6'0" **Weight:** 12.4
Simon joined Bradford from Rochdale and set a high standard throughout his first season, being a consistent performer at right-back and also filling in as a centre-half when injuries dictated. He can also deliver a good cross and pushed forward to score against Cheltenham and Northampton, although both goals came courtesy of deflections. Simon took over the captaincy before suffering a calf injury that ruled him out of the closing weeks of the season.
Sunderland (From trainee on 7/8/2000) FAC 0+1
Notts Co (Loaned on 16/8/2002) FL 21+11 FLC 1 FAC 1
Grimsby T (Free on 2/8/2004) FL 31+6 FLC 2 FAC 0+1 Others 1
Rochdale (Free on 30/1/2006) FL 107+5/6 FLC 4 FAC 1 Others 7
Bradford C (Free on 2/7/2009) FL 30+1/1 FLC 1 Others 3

RAMSEY Aaron
Born: Caerphilly, 26 December 1990
Height: 5'9" **Weight:** 10.7
International Honours: W: 11; U21-12
Aaron had a fantastic campaign for Arsenal until a terrible injury at Stoke in February brought it to a premature end. Aaron has long been regarded as one of the most talented prospects in Wales and he started to flourish in the Arsenal midfield. He is extremely composed on the ball with a good range of passing and also has a keen eye for goal. He scored a wonderful goal at Portsmouth in December and quickly followed this up by turning the FA Cup tie at West Ham in Arsenal's favour with the equaliser. He is set to be a key player for both the Gunners and Wales for years to come and it is hoped he makes a full recovery as quickly as possible, having

undergone surgery to fix fractures to his tibia and fibula in his right leg. Aaron made 18 appearances in the Premier League, scoring three times, six in the Champions League and two in the FA Cup, scoring one goal. He was also ever-present in the Carling Cup run.
Cardiff C (From trainee on 3/1/2008) FL 11+5/1 FLC 0+1 FAC 3+2/1
Arsenal (£4,800,000 on 17/6/2008) PL 8+19/3 FLC 6 FAC 3+3/1 Others 5+7/1

RANDALL Mark Leonard
Born: Milton Keynes, 28 September 1989
Height: 6'0" **Weight:** 12.12
International Honours: E: Yth
Arsenal's Mark has been on the fringes of the first team squad for a while now and the midfielder is finding it difficult to make the breakthrough. He appeared as a substitute in Carling Cup wins over West Bromwich and Liverpool and also went out on loan to MK Dons in mid-January. After a slowish start he came to the fore late on in the campaign as his fellow midfielders began dropping like flies due to injuries and suspensions. Very comfortable on the ball, as befitting his illustrious roots, he became much more competitive in the tackle as the season wore on, and finished the campaign showing the best form of his stadiummk stay.
Arsenal (From trainee on 7/2/2007) PL 0+2 FLC 4+5 Others 0+2
Burnley (Loaned on 31/1/2008) FL 2+8
MK Dons (Loaned on 15/1/2010) FL 12+4 Others 1+1/1

RANDOLPH Darren Edward
Born: Dublin, 12 May 1987
Height: 6'1" **Weight:** 12.3
Club Honours: FC '06
International Honours: RoI: B-1; U21-10
Starting the campaign as understudy to Rob Elliot in Charlton's goal, Darren was overlooked in late October when Elliot was injured and Carl Ikeme, brought in on loan, was preferred. Darren did play in the FA Cup defeat at Northwich as Ikeme was Cup-tied but did not feature again until replacing an injured Elliot at half time against Tranmere in January. The same thing happened against Gillingham in mid-March but this time Darren kept his place with some fine displays, despite Elliot recovering fitness. Big and strong, he can sometimes appear hesitant in coming off his line, but is a commanding presence in his own goal area.
Charlton Ath (From trainee on 24/12/2004) P/FL 12+2 FLC 2 FAC 2 Others 2
Gillingham (Loaned on 18/8/2006) FL 3 FLC 1

Bury (Loaned on 8/2/2008) FL 14
Hereford U (Loaned on 5/8/2008) FL 13 FLC 1

RANGEL Angel
Born: Tortosa, Spain, 28 October 1982
Height: 5'11" **Weight:** 11.9
Club Honours: Div 1 '08
Swansea's classy, attacking right-back was troubled with groin and Achilles injuries during the close season and, as a result, missed most of the pre-season training. He was clearly below his best form when the new season began. With rumours also circulating over his departure from the Swans, it was no wonder that it took the defender some months to regain his form. Early in the season he received a red card against Scunthorpe in a hectic Carling Cup tie.
Swansea C (Signed from Terrassa, Spain, ex Tortosa, Reus, Girona, Sant Andreu, on 10/8/2007) FL 119+2/3 FLC 3+3 FAC 7 Others 4

RANGER Nile
Born: Wood Green, 11 April 1991
Height: 6'2" **Weight:** 13.3
Club Honours: Ch '10
International Honours: E: Yth
Nile is a striker with fine close control, adept at holding the ball up, whose scoring record for Newcastle's junior sides in the previous season earned him a call-up for the pre-season friendly at Shamrock Rovers in which he scored. After three substitute appearances and a start in the Carling Cup against Huddersfield, he won the 'Man of the Match' award and received a huge ovation from the Toon Army on his first senior League start against Leicester in August, and his first club goal came against Coventry in December. Despite his evident promise he was used primarily as a substitute and his season came to a premature end in April when he sustained an ankle injury in a reserve match. He was selected for the England under-19 side in the European Championship finals and he scored against Slovenia.
Newcastle U (From trainee at Southampton on 15/4/2009) FL 4+21/2 FLC 2 FAC 1+2

RASIAK Grzegorz
Born: Szczecin, Poland, 12 January 1979
Height: 6'3" **Weight:** 13.3
International Honours: Poland: 37
An awkward customer in the penalty-box, Polish international Grzegorz is a master in the art of goal-grabbing, but having spent the 2008-09 season on loan at Watford he did not relish the prospect of grabbing them in League One for Southampton and after three

appearances he was transferred to Reading. Arriving shortly after the start of the season, his acquisition was intended to beef up Royals' strike force following the departure of Kevin Doyle and the last-minute failure to sign Watford striker Tommy Smith. The move was successful to a certain extent as Grzegorz played 34 times for Royals' first-team, completing the full 90 minutes on just ten occasions, but scoring nine goals in the process. He faced keen competition for the striker's role as Reading used a 4-5-1 formation, but even a switch to a more adventurous 4-4-2 meant that he was often overlooked in favour of Simon Church and Shane Long, and occasionally Noel Hunt. His height means that his heading is his greatest attribute, and that is how the majority of his goals are scored. But his most memorable moment of the campaign must surely be that exquisite defence-splitting pass which enabled strike partner Church to score Reading's second goal in the 2-2 FA Cup draw with West Bromwich.
Derby Co (Free from Dyskobolia Grodzisk, Poland, ex Warta Poznan, GKS Belchatow, Odra Wodzislaw, on 24/9/2004) FL 41/18 FLC 0+1 FAC 2/1 Others 1
Tottenham H (Signed on 31/8/2005) PL 4+4 FAC 1
Southampton (£2,000,000 on 8/2/2006) FL 58+20/28 FLC 2+1/1 FAC 4/3 Others 0+2/1
Bolton W (Loaned on 31/1/2008) PL 2+5
Watford (Loaned on 15/8/2008) FL 12+9/8 FLC 0+1 FAC 2+1/2
Reading (Signed on 27/8/2009) FL 14+15/9 FAC 3+2

RAVEN David Haydn
Born: West Kirby, 10 March 1985
Height: 6'0" **Weight:** 11.6
International Honours: E: Yth
It was a frustrating campaign for David who, after holding a regular place at Carlisle until early October, missed much of the season through injury. On his return to the right-back berth, he settled back into the side with some typically sound displays but having reached the end of his contract has now been given a free transfer.
Liverpool (From trainee on 20/5/2002) PL 0+1 FLC 2 FAC 1
Tranmere Rov (Loaned on 31/1/2006) FL 11
Carlisle U (Free on 3/8/2006) FL 134+2/1 FLC 7 FAC 6 Others 5

RAVENHILL Richard (Ricky) John
Born: Doncaster, 16 January 1981

Height: 5'11" **Weight:** 11.3
Club Honours: Div 3 '04; Div 2 '10
Nearly ever-present after arriving from Darlington in the summer, Ricky filled the essential role of midfield anchor-man for Notts County with aplomb. A tenacious tackler, he just ran and ran, causing everyone to wonder from where he could find so much energy. Although not often found in the opposition penalty area, he scored one of the goals of the season with a superb volley against Morecambe.
Barnsley (From trainee on 29/6/1999)
Doncaster Rov (Free on 18/1/2002) FL 58+40/9 FLC 6+3/1 FAC 5+1 Others 4
Chester C (Loaned on 9/7/2006) FL 1+2
Grimsby T (Free on 31/8/2006) FL 15+2/2 FAC 0+1 Others 2
Darlington (Signed on 16/1/2007) FL 75+13/6 FLC 3 FAC 2+1 Others 5
Notts Co (Free on 22/5/2009) FL 40/3 FLC 1 FAC 6 Others 1

Michael Raynes

RAYNES Michael Bernard
Born: Wythenshawe, 15 October 1987
Height: 6'4" **Weight:** 12.0
An influential figure in the Stockport dressing room, despite his tender age of 21, Michael was given the captain's armband and shouldered a lot of responsibility as the club endured administration. His only goal of the season came against Hartlepool, placing a header over the 'keeper from distance after a cross from Liam Bridcutt, and in January his fine form earned him a move to Scunthorpe. Given a rude awakening to the Championship when handed a debut out of position at right-back in the 5-1 defeat at Leicester, Michael soon got switched to his more

accustomed centre-half role and began to impress with his aerial dominance and obvious leadership and organisational qualities. He was beginning to settle down well when an ankle injury in mid-April brought his season to a premature end.
Stockport Co (From trainee on 8/3/2005) FL 123+17/5 FLC 1+1 FAC 9+1 Others 6+1
Scunthorpe U (Signed on 1/2/2010) FL 12

REDMOND Shane Patrick
Born: Dublin, 23 March 1989
Height: 6'2" **Weight:** 12.11
International Honours: RoI: U21-13
The promising goalkeeper was signed on a six-month loan from Nottingham Forest and was in Burton's team on the day they made their Football League debut away to Shrewsbury. However, after a disappointing display, Shane lost his place in the team and had to wait until November for his next chance. Showed much better form, but his Burton career was cut short when he suffered a broken hand in an FA Cup tie at Gillingham in November. He returned to the City Ground before a second spell on loan, this time to Darlington, saw him become the fifth goalkeeper to be used by the club during a desperate season when he made his debut in January. He proved to be an agile shot-stopper making a number of stunning reaction saves at point-blank range and had his initial loan extended to the end of April. Was out of contract in the summer.
Nottingham F (From trainee on 26/5/2006)
Burton A (Loaned on 7/7/2009) FL 3 FAC 1
Darlington (Loaned on 26/1/2010) FL 19

REECE Charles (Charlie) Thomas
Born: Birmingham, 8 September 1988
Height: 5'11" **Weight:** 12.0
Midlander Charlie managed to make an impression on Bristol Rovers' manager and fans with some eye-catching performances in the last few matches of the season. Despite being a regular member of the squad, many of Charlie's appearances were as a substitute. Strong in the tackle, Charlie can play in a central role or on the right of midfield and he uses his passing skill to good effect. Made his full start of the season at Gillingham and worked very hard in closing down opponents. He has signed a new two-year contract and is expected to challenge strongly for a starting place.
Bristol Rov (From Filton College on 5/6/2007) FL 6+10 FLC 0+1 Others 0+1

REED Stephen Leslie

Born: Barnstaple, 18 June 1985
Height: 5'9" **Weight:** 12.6
Stephen moved to Macclesfield from Blue Square South side Weymouth in the summer. He made one appearance in the second round Johnstone's Paint Trophy defeat by Carlisle at left-back. However, with Carl Tremarco and Sean Hessey settled in the full-back positions there were no opportunities for Stephen and he went on loan to Blue Square Premier side Grays Athletic and from December to the end of the season, to his former club Weymouth. Was out of contract in the summer
Yeovil T (From juniors on 26/9/2002) FL 4+4 FLC 0+1 Others 1+1
Torquay U (Free on 3/3/2006) FL 21+5 FAC 3 Others 1 (Freed on 6/2/2007)
Macclesfield T (Free from Weymouth, ex Tiverton T, Weston-super-Mare, Cambridge U, on 3/7/2009) Others 1

REGAN Carl Anthony

Born: Liverpool, 14 January 1980
Height: 6'0" **Weight:** 11.5
International Honours: E: Yth
The tall and athletic former MK Dons' full-back, Carl initially held down a regular place after joining Bristol Rovers in the summer. A pacy wing-back and a strong tackler Carl reads the game well and was part of a back four for the first seven months of the season before injury sidelined him. He missed ten games but returned following a team-mate's suspension.
Everton (From trainee on 19/1/1998)
Barnsley (£20,000 on 15/6/2000) FL 31+6 FLC 5
Hull C (Free on 15/8/2002) FL 33+5 FLC 1 FAC 1 Others 1 (Freed on 25/3/2004)
Chester C (Free from Droylsden on 18/3/2005) FL 43+4 FLC 1 FAC 4
Macclesfield T (Free on 4/7/2006) FL 54+4/2 FLC 2 FAC 4 Others 1+1
MK Dons (Signed on 31/1/2008) FL 32+4/1 FLC 0+1 Others 3
Bristol Rov (Free on 2/7/2009) FL 32+3 FLC 2 FAC 1 Others 1

REHMAN Zeshan (Zesh)

Born: Birmingham, 14 October 1983
Height: 6'2" **Weight:** 12.12
International Honours: Pakistan: 6; E: Yth
An eloquent and passionate player, Zesh was named Bradford's club captain for the work he does within the local community. The Pakistan international defender was used mainly as a centre-half although he has played at right-back on occasions, a position he admits is not his favourite. Zesh had some testing times during a disappointing season for the club but

never shirked his responsibilities. His community efforts were also acknowledged with an award from the Football League.
Fulham (From trainee on 7/6/2001) PL 18+3 FLC 6+1/1 FAC 2
Brighton & Hove A (Loaned on 29/9/2003) FL 6/2 Others 1
Brighton & Hove A (Loaned on 14/11/2003) FL 3+2 Others 1
Norwich C (Loaned on 31/1/2006) FL 5
Queens Park Rgrs (Free on 8/8/2006) FL 40+6 FLC 2 FAC 1
Brighton & Hove A (Loaned on 22/3/2007) FL 8
Blackpool (Loaned on 31/7/2008) FL 0+3 FLC 0+1
Bradford C (Free on 23/11/2009) FL 52+3/2 FLC 1 FAC 1 Others 2

REID Andrew (Andy) Matthew

Born: Dublin, 29 July 1982
Height: 5'7" **Weight:** 11.12
International Honours: RoI: 27; U21-15; Yth (UEFA-U16 '98)
Having shed weight during the summer, Andy showed his best form in the first half of the season, excelling as Sunderland started brightly as much of his interplay with Steed Malbranque brought roars of approval from the Stadium of Light crowd. His four early season goals included a sublime chip at Norwich in the Carling Cup and a classic free kick against West Ham. Operating mainly on the left flank with the occasional outing in central midfield, Andy was badly missed by Sunderland following his final appearance of the season at Portsmouth in early February. Andy picked up a hamstring injury at Fratton Park, followed by a calf problem sustained during his rehabilitation.
Nottingham F (From trainee on 16/8/1999) FL 121+23/21 FLC 6+2/1 FAC 6/2 Others 2/1
Tottenham H (Signed on 31/1/2005) PL 20+6/1 FLC 1
Charlton Ath (£3,000,000 on 17/8/2006) P/FL 36+2/7 FLC 2/1
Sunderland (£4,000,000 on 31/1/2008) PL 49+17/4 FLC 4+2/2 FAC 2+2

REID Izak George

Born: Stafford, 8 July 1987
Height: 5'6" **Weight:** 8.9
Izak was virtually ever-present for Macclesfield until he picked up an ankle injury at Port Vale at the beginning of March that put him out for a month. His pace serves him well at right-back and right wing-back, allowing him to take the ball down the flank, often passing several opponents on the way.

Izak always works hard and his pace is missed when he is out.
Macclesfield T (From trainee on 4/7/2006) FL 83+25/4 FLC 1+2 FAC 3 Others 3+1

REID Kyel Romaine

Born: Deptford, 26 November 1987
Height: 5'10" **Weight:** 12.5
International Honours: E: Yth
Signed by Sheffield United after a pre-season trial, having been released by West Ham, Kyel found it difficult to break into the first team, making a few sub appearances and a start in the Carling Cup. He used his speed to attack opponents but his final ball was often wasted and he moved on loan to Charlton in January until the end of the season as a recognised left-winger was needed at the club. Kyel immediately made his debut and featured in all but three of the remaining games. With a penchant for running at defenders and crossing from the by-line or cutting inside, he also has a powerful shot and found the net four times, his best goal being his late winner at Southend after coming on as a sub and setting up Akpo Sodje for the equaliser.
West Ham U (From trainee on 2/12/2004) PL 1+2 FLC 1+4/1 FAC 0+1
Barnsley (Loaned on 23/11/2006) FL 12+14/2
Crystal Palace (Loaned on 27/3/2008) FL 0+2
Blackpool (Loaned on 27/11/2008) FL 7
Wolverhampton W (Loaned on 16/1/2009) FL 3+5/1 FAC 1
Sheffield U (Free on 2/7/2009) FL 0+7 FLC 1
Charlton Ath (Loaned on 29/1/2010) FL 11+6/4 Others 1

REID Paul Mark

Born: Carlisle, 18 February 1982
Height: 6'2" **Weight:** 12.4
International Honours: E: Yth
A host of injury problems blighted Paul throughout a frustrating season at Colchester. Having broken his kneecap in March 2008, the commanding centre-back suffered numerous setbacks in his recovery process before eventually returning to the side at the end of October. Paul then played 11 games around the turn of the year but just as he was looking to make a starting place his own, a back problem caused chaos with the rest of his campaign. Various related muscle strains kept him out for another three months before he made a promising return for the final three games of the season.
Carlisle U (From trainee on 19/2/1999) FL 17+2 Others 3
Glasgow Rgrs (£200,000 on 1/7/2000)

Preston NE *(Loaned on 29/1/2002) FL 0+1/1*
Northampton T *(Loaned on 31/12/2002) FL 19*
Northampton T *(£100,000 on 19/6/2003) FL 33/2 FLC 2 FAC 3 Others 2+2*
Barnsley *(Signed on 19/7/2004) FL 107+7/3 FLC 4/2 FAC 6/1 Others 4/1*
Carlisle U *(Loaned on 27/3/2008) FL 1*
Colchester U *(Free on 7/8/2008) FL 35+3/1 FLC 2 FAC 2 Others 1*

REID Reuben James
Born: Bristol, 26 July 1988
Height: 6'0" **Weight:** 12.2
Signed in the summer, the midfielder did very well when making his West Bromwich debut in a 2-0 Carling Cup win at Bury in August. In the next round he produced another excellent display in the 4-3 extra-time win over his former club, Rotherham, before being substituted in the 79th minute. However, after that he struggled to get into the first team, making just five more substitute appearances - four in the Championship plus his 100th at club level - before being loaned out to relegation threatened Peterborough. Reuben, who gave up the chance of a professional cricket career with Gloucestershire, found it hard to settle in a struggling side, spending most of the time at London Road keeping the bench warm.
Plymouth Arg *(From Millfield School on 18/1/2006) FL 1+6 FLC 1+2 FAC 2*
Rochdale *(Loaned on 26/1/2006) FL 0+2*
Torquay U *(Loaned on 22/3/2007) FL 4+3/2*
Wycombe W *(Loaned on 31/8/2007) FL 1+10/1 Others 1*
Brentford *(Loaned on 31/1/2008) FL 1+9/1*
Rotherham U *(Free on 5/8/2008) FL 38+3/18 FLC 4/1 FAC 1+1 Others 4*
West Bromwich A *(Signed on 31/7/2009) FL 0+4 FLC 2 FAC 0+1*
Peterborough U *(Loaned on 6/1/2010) FL 5+8*

REID Steven John
Born: Kingston, 10 March 1981
Height: 6'1" **Weight:** 12.4
Club Honours: Div 2 '01
International Honours: RoI: 23; U21-2; E: Yth
It was anticipated that Steven would be back in the Blackburn side after two seasons where he had played little, but as might have been anticipated it was difficult for the midfield player to recover match fitness. He was limited to Carling Cup action and scored a penalty against Peterborough but at

Nottingham Forest demonstrated just how much his lay-off had cost him when unchallenged he mistimed a header and conceded a penalty as he handled the ball. After going on loan to Queens Park Rangers, he was given a start against Fulham in January and came on in the second half against Wigan but it became increasingly obvious that he required a long run of games to get his timing back. It was no surprise that he was allowed to move on loan, joining West Bromwich. Steven's first Albion goal was enough to seal a vital victory over Coventry in March, the right wing-back sliding home the only goal of the game in the 22nd minute to make it seven home League successes on the spin for the Baggies. Manager Roberto di Matteo had handed him his debut against his previous loan club, Queens Park Rangers, a week earlier and as the season progressed he proved to be a very capable replacement for Gianni Zuiverloom. A player who loves to get forward, Steven had the misfortune to score an own-goal in the penultimate League game of the season at Crystal Palace. Was out of contract in the summer.
Millwall *(From trainee on 18/5/1998) FL 115+24/18 FLC 5+2 FAC 10/1 Others 10+1*
Blackburn Rov *(£1,800,000 + on 30/7/2003) PL 91+22/6 FLC 7+4/2 FAC 4+4 Others 1+1*
Queens Park Rgrs *(Loaned on 19/11/2009) FL 1+1*
West Bromwich A *(Loaned on 5/3/2010) FL 10/1*

REINA Jose (Pepe) Manuel
Born: Madrid, Spain, 31 August 1982
Height: 6'2" **Weight:** 13.8
Club Honours: ESC '05; FAC '06; CS '06
International Honours: Spain: 20; U21-20; Yth
The Liverpool and Spain goalkeeper is one of the best in the world and would be an automatic selection for almost any international team other than Spain, for whom he understudies Iker Casillas. In a season when Liverpool's defence displayed alarming deficiencies, Pepe alone maintained his usual high standards and was blameless for any of the 19 defeats. Remarkably he recorded 21 clean sheets, 17 of them in the Premiership, and again won the 'Golden Gloves' award – this time shared with Petr Cech of Chelsea – for the fourth time in five seasons. Unsurprisingly he was voted Liverpool's 'Player of the Season'. Highlights included an outstanding performance against Everton at Goodison Park which

helped his team to an unlikely 2-0 victory despite being outplayed by their Merseyside rivals. He also performed heroics in the Europa Cup matches against Unirea, Lille and Benfica when an away goal could have precipitated elimination for Liverpool. He signed a new six-year contract in April and was in Spain's squad for the World Cup finals.
Liverpool *(£6,000,000 from Villareal, Spain on 6/7/2005) PL 182 FLC 1 FAC 8 Others 68*

RENDELL Scott David
Born: Ashford, Middlesex, 21 October 1986
Height: 6'1" **Weight:** 12.5
On a season-long loan to Torquay from Peterborough, Scott scored on the opening day of the season but struggled to hold down a regular starting place early on. Established himself in the centre-forward role before Christmas and hit a rich vein of form that was interrupted by a broken arm. He returned after injury in a slightly withdrawn role, showing that in addition to his scoring prowess, he is adept at linking play as he is at playing as a more traditional target man.
Peterborough U *(£115,000 from Cambridge U, ex Aldershot T, Forest Green Rov, Hayes, Crawley T, on 18/2/2008) FL 5+8/4 FLC 0+1 Others 0+1*
Yeovil T *(Loaned on 17/10/2008) FL 5 FAC 0+1*
Torquay U *(Loaned on 28/7/2009) FL 28+7/12 FLC 1 FAC 2+1/1 Others 1+1*

REO-COKER Nigel Shola Andre
Born: Thornton Heath, 14 May 1984
Height: 5'8" **Weight:** 10.5
International Honours: E: U21-23; Yth
Nigel's most notable contribution at Aston Villa was a training ground incident that was described as a 'contretemps' by the manager and saw Villa's combative midfielder being sent home from training and dropped from the squad for a game. It was an episode that summed up a season of frustration for Nigel, who had performed impressively as Villa won the pre-season Peace Cup in Spain. He was disappointed to lose his place to youngster Fabian Delph on the opening day of the Premier League and that set the tone for his stop-start campaign. His highlight was an inspirational performance in Villa's win over Liverpool at Anfield. Nigel struggled to break up the central midfield partnership of James Milner and captain

Stiliyan Petrov and was limited to six League starts with three in the Cups and one substitute appearance. His cause was not helped by an ankle injury that ruled him out for most of the second half of the season. Nigel, a tough-tackling energetic midfielder, was made available for transfer at the end of the season, although Villa stood little chance of recouping the money they paid for him in 2007.
Wimbledon *(From trainee on 15/7/2002) FL 57+1/6 FLC 2+1 FAC 2+1*
West Ham U *(£575,000 on 23/1/2004) P/FL 113+7/11 FLC 4 FAC 9+1 Others 5+3*
Aston Villa *(£8,500,000 on 16/7/2007) PL 61+11/1 FLC 3/1 FAC 4 Others 9/1*

REVELL Alexander (Alex) David
Born: Cambridge, 7 July 1983
Height: 6'3" **Weight:** 12.0
A popular figure at Southend, Alex recovered from a broken leg last season but found himself on the bench at Roots Hall in the opening weeks of the season. It was still a surprise to many that he was loaned on a four month spell to Swindon, a rival Division One club in September. Despite some solid performances and two well-taken strikes at Brentford at the start of October the hard-working forward was not signed on a permanent basis due to a tight control of club finances and returned to Southend. Wycombe manager Gary Waddock had been chasing the big striker for some time, finally managing to secure him on a 93 day emergency loan at the end of January. Alex scored a penalty on his debut, in the 3-2 win at Bristol Rovers, but scored no more until a purple patch in April netted him five goals in three games. That run was started the week before with a 'Man of the Match' performance against Hartlepool at home when he chased everything down, caused constant mayhem in the penalty area and ran himself into the ground. He was offered a new contract at the end of the season but decided to sign for Leyton Orient instead.
Cambridge U *(From trainee on 21/4/2001) FL 19+38/5 FLC 0+1 FAC 0+2 Others 1+5 (Freed during 2004 close season)*
Brighton & Hove A (Free from Braintree T on 17/7/2006) FL 48+11/13 FLC 3 FAC 4/3 Others 4+1/2
Southend U *(£150,000 on 30/1/2008) FL 25+9/4 FLC 1+2 FAC 4 Others 0+2*
Swindon T *(Loaned on 1/9/2009) FL 7+3/2 Others 2*
Wycombe W *(Loaned on 22/1/2010) FL 11+4/6*

RHODES Jordan Luke
Born: Oldham, 5 February 1990
Height: 6'1" **Weight:** 11.3
Club Honours: Div 2 '09
Jordan proved to be a bargain buy for Huddersfield. The striker, who was signed on a long-term contract, found the net regularly and enjoyed the perfect start as he stepped off the bench on the opening day to score the equaliser at Southend. A naturally gifted player, he stretched opposing defences with his direct running and energetic displays. As well as being the top scorer with 23 goals, the best return since 2004-05, he also put himself in the record books for scoring the fastest headed hat-trick against Exeter at the Galpharm Stadium in just over eight minutes, breaking the previous record set by Dixie Dean for Everton in the 1930s.
Ipswich T *(From trainee on 22/8/2007) FL 0+10/1*
Rochdale *(Loaned on 19/9/2008) FL 5/2*
Brentford *(Loaned on 23/1/2009) FL 14/7*
Huddersfield T *(Signed on 31/7/2009) FL 43+2/19 FLC 2/3 FAC 3/1 Others 3*

RIBEIRO Christian Michael
Born: Neath, 14 December 1989
Height: 5'11" **Weight:** 12.2
International Honours: W: 1; U21-8; Yth
Having made just one appearance for Bristol City early on, the young defender went off on loan to Stockport in late November, making his debut in the 3-1 home defeat to Exeter. His loan was extended the following month, but, at the end of December, Bristol City manager Gary Johnson recalled him as cover for injured players. His next stop on loan was at Colchester in January and the speedy young right-back made an impressive debut at Gillingham before suffering a groin injury three days later against MK Dons and returning to his parent club. Reintroduced into the City team by caretaker boss Keith Millen, he gave a number of outstanding displays and was twice voted as 'Man of the Match' before being subbed in a 3-0 defeat at Scunthorpe on 17th April. Made his debut for Wales in the match against Croatia in May.
Bristol C *(From trainee on 30/1/2007) FL 5 FLC 2*
Stockport Co *(Loaned on 21/11/2009) FL 7*
Colchester U *(Loaned on 22/1/2010) FL 2*

RICHARDS Ashley Darel Jazz
Born: Swansea, 12 April 1991
Height: 6'1" **Weight:** 12.4

International Honours: W: 1; U21-4
The young first-year professional impressed for Swansea in either full-back position or when he was included in central midfield at Doncaster in late September. Ashley is a terrific athlete and gained honours at under-21 level for Wales during the season. The Swansea-born youngster attracted the attention of several clubs and his consistency saw him voted 'Young Player of the Year' with the Swans.
Swansea C *(From trainee on 3/7/2009) FL 10+5*

RICHARDS Eliot Allen
Born: New Tredegar, 10 September 1991
Height: 5'9" **Weight:** 11.9
International Honours: W: Yth
Young striker Eliot graduated from the Bristol Rovers' Academy, where he was a regular scorer. The teenager spent a large part of the season on the Rovers' bench, finally making a brief substitute appearance at Gillingham. He followed this up with several other appearances from the bench in the last month of the season and made a favourable impression. He is expected to challenge strongly for a place in the starting line-up.
Bristol Rov *(From juniors on 11/7/2009) FL 0+5*

RICHARDS Garry
Born: Romford, 11 June 1986
Height: 6'3" **Weight:** 13.0
A powerful no-nonsense right-sided centre-half, Garry is not the most cultured of players but is physically strong, dominant in the air and rarely found wanting. Like many of Gillingham's players he experienced a turbulent season, starting as a first choice due to Simon King's injury, before losing his place through injury and loss of form. He returned to the starting side in February and was a vital member of the team until an ankle injury sustained against Millwall in April put him out for the rest of the campaign. Was out of contract at the end of June.
Colchester U *(From trainee on 4/7/2005) FL 15+5/1 FAC 1 Others 3*
Brentford *(Loaned on 9/2/2007) FL 10/1*
Southend U *(£50,000 on 10/8/2007) FL 8+2 FLC 2 FAC 1 Others 1*
Gillingham *(£70,000 on 25/11/2008) FL 54+12/3 FLC 2 FAC 3 Others 5+1*

RICHARDS Justin Donovan
Born: West Bromwich, 16 October 1980
Height: 5'10" **Weight:** 11.0
Striker Justin embarked on his third spell as a League player when joining Cheltenham from Kidderminster

Harriers in the summer. He was involved in all but three games and was top scorer with 15 goals – the second highest total in one season, behind Julian Alsop, since promotion to the League in 1999. The sort of striker who comes alive in the penalty area with the ability to turn defenders and get shots away from unlikely angles, Justin held the Cheltenham attack together despite having a number of partners, including alternating veterans Barry Hayles and Alsop. He made a handful of wide midfield appearances and proved the club's most adept penalty taker for years. He scored twice on two occasions – in the 5-4 home defeat by Bradford and the remarkable 6-5 victory at Burton – and his form in front of goal earned him the offer of a new contract.
West Bromwich A (From trainee on 8/1/1999) FL 0+1 FAC 0+1
Bristol Rov (£75,000 on 19/1/2001) FL 3+13 Others 0+1 (Free to Stevenage Borough on 13/12/2002)
Colchester U (Loaned on 21/10/2002) FL 0+2 Others 0+1
Peterborough U (Free from Woking on 31/7/2006) FL 4+9/1 FLC 2 Others 0+1 (Freed during 2007 close season)
Boston U (Loaned on 11/1/2007) FL 3
Cheltenham T (Free from Kidderminster Hrs, via loan at Oxford U, on 3/7/2009) FL 39+5/15 FLC 1 FAC 1 Others 1

RICHARDS Marc John
Born: Wolverhampton, 8 July 1982
Height: 6'0" **Weight:** 12.7
International Honours: E: Yth
Leading scorer for Port Vale with 23 goals, Marc had an excellent season leading the front line and achieved the 20-goal landmark for the first time in his career. It could have been even more, because he missed two penalties out of the seven that he took. A powerful player, who can hold the ball up and create space for others, he failed to start only two games but came on as a substitute in both. His personal highlight was at Chesterfield when Vale produced their best performance of the season to win 5-0, largely thanks to a superb hat-trick by Marc. A lobbed shot, a thumping header and a blistering 25-yard shot really pushed Vale into play-off contention that afternoon.
Blackburn Rov (From trainee on 12/7/1999) FLC 1+1
Crewe Alex (Loaned on 10/8/2001) FL 1+3 FLC 0+1/1
Oldham Ath (Loaned on 12/10/2001) FL 3+2 Others 1/1
Halifax T (Loaned on 12/2/2002) FL 5
Swansea C (Loaned on 22/11/2002) FL 14+3/7

Northampton T (Free on 7/7/2003) FL 35+18/10 FLC 3 FAC 0+4/2 Others 4+2/1
Rochdale (Loaned on 24/3/2005) FL 4+1/2
Barnsley (Free on 31/8/2005) FL 51+18/18 FLC 1 FAC 5+2 Others 4
Port Vale (Free on 8/8/2007) FL 94+11/35 FLC 4+1/2 FAC 5+1/1 Others 3+1/1

RICHARDS Matthew (Matt) Lee
Born: Harlow, 26 December 1984
Height: 5'8" **Weight:** 11.0
International Honours: E: U21-1
Having been freed by Wycombe, Matt earned a two-year contract with Walsall after a fine pre-season. He played for most of the start of the season on the left of midfield and then at left-back. As the team's dead-ball specialist he became the regular taker of corners and free kicks. Possessing a powerful shot, he scored superb and precise free kicks at Southampton and at home to Stockport. Netting two other goals, he also rattled the bar on a number of occasions. He finished the season in central midfield. It was here that he was at his best.
Ipswich T (From trainee on 31/1/2002) FL 118+30/8 FLC 5+1 FAC 6+2/1 Others 4+2
Brighton & Hove A (Loaned on 21/9/2007) FL 28 FAC 3 Others 2
Brighton & Hove A (Loaned on 21/7/2008) FL 23/1 FLC 3/1 FAC 2 Others 4
Walsall (Free on 4/8/2009) FL 39+1/4 FLC 1 FAC 2 Others 1

RICHARDS Micah Lincoln
Born: Birmingham, 24 June 1988
Height: 5'11" **Weight:** 13.0
International Honours: E: 11; U21-14
Micah is another Manchester City youngster who has lost his way in recent seasons. He can play at right-back or in central defence and was a regular member of the England squad two years ago but last season struggled to hold his place at City. Although he started as first choice right-back, he lost his place to Pablo Zabaleta in the dramatic 4-3 defeat by Manchester United at Old Trafford. He returned in November and scored his first goal of the season in the 3-3 draw at Bolton. Under Roberto Mancini, he was switched to central defence for three games to cover for the absent Kolo Toure and scored a wonder goal in the 4-1 home win over Blackburn in January. Carrying the ball out of defence, he swept past five players before laying off the ball to Benjani,

whose shot hit the post only for Micah to follow up. That should have given him confidence but, troubled by knee problems, he lost his right-back slot to Zabaleta again and played only intermittently for the remainder of the season. Although overlooked by Fabio Capello for the England squad, he remains a regular member of Stuart Pearce's under-21 side.
Manchester C (From trainee on 4/7/2005) PL 116+7/5 FLC 7 FAC 13/1 Others 15

RICHARDS William (Will) Stanley
Born: Knighton, 18 December 1991
Height: 6'2" **Weight:** 12.4
The youth team player had his initial taste of senior football with Shrewsbury as a substitute in the 2-0 reverse in the Johnstone's Paint Trophy at Accrington in October. His usual position in the youth team is in central midfield and he may be one for the future at Town.
Shrewsbury T (Trainee) Others 0+1

RICHARDSON Frazer
Born: Rotherham, 29 October 1982
Height: 5'11" **Weight:** 12.1
International Honours: E: Yth
Signed in the summer, Frazer was first choice right-back at Charlton for most of the campaign, putting in some solid performances, but picked up a thigh strain at Gillingham in October that kept him out for a few weeks, followed by a hamstring problem. He finally shook off his injuries and returned to the side in mid-January where he stayed for the remainder of the campaign. Frazer is a strong tackler and likes to go forward down the right flank to put crosses into the box. He scored his only goal against Gillingham at the Valley with a 20-yard daisy-cutter.
Leeds U (From trainee on 2/11/1999) P/FL 122+27/3 FLC 11/1 FAC 5 Others 7+1/1
Stoke C (Loaned on 10/1/2003) FL 6+1
Stoke C (Loaned on 8/11/2003) FL 6/1
Charlton Ath (Free on 9/7/2009) FL 37+1/1 Others 2

RICHARDSON Kieran Edward
Born: Greenwich, 21 October 1984
Height: 5'9" **Weight:** 10.11
Club Honours: FAYC '03; FLC '06; PL '07
International Honours: E: 8; U21-12
A regular for most of the season, Kieran made most of his appearances to solve what became Sunderland's problematic left-back position rather than in his preferred midfield berth. Often asked to change position during the course of a match, Kieran always put the team

Kieran Richardson

ahead of himself and showed his versatility, but will no doubt look to tie down a regular place in one position in the season ahead as he seeks to push himself back into international reckoning. Only twice was he asked to play in the position he excelled in during pre-season – as an attacking midfielder backing up a lone striker. Kieran operated in this role away to Everton and Aston Villa, rating the performance at Villa as his best of the season. His only goal of the season came against West Ham.
Manchester U *(From trainee on 21/8/2003) PL 20+21/2 FLC 11+2/3 FAC 8+2/4 Others 5+12/2*
West Bromwich A *(Loaned on 29/1/2005) PL 11+1/3*
Sunderland *(£5,500,000 on 16/7/2007) PL 74+4/8 FLC 3+1 FAC 3*

RICHARDSON Leam Nathan
Born: Leeds, 19 November 1979
Height: 5'7" **Weight:** 11.4
Club Honours: AMC '04; FC '06
Kept out for much of 2009-10 with injury, Leam only made three appearances for Accrington, coming on as a last-minute sub against Oldham in the Johnstone's Paint Trophy in September and making two starts in the final two League games of the season in May. The defender, who can play at right or left-back, has been at Stanley for five years but is out of contract this summer.
Blackburn Rov *(From trainee on 31/12/1997) FLC 1*
Bolton W *(£50,000 on 13/7/2000) P/FL 5+8 FLC 3+1 FAC 1*
Notts Co *(Loaned on 9/11/2001) FL 20+1 FAC 1*
Blackpool *(Loaned on 20/12/2002) FL 20 FAC 1*
Blackpool *(Free on 15/7/2003) FL 44+7 FLC 2 FAC 1/1 Others 7+2*
Accrington Stanley *(Free on 12/8/2005) FL 78+10/1 FLC 4 FAC 2+2 Others 3+1*

RICHMAN Simon Andrew
Born: Ormskirk, 2 June 1990
Height: 5'11" **Weight:** 11.12
Port Vale's right-sided midfield player missed the first part of the season through injury. This meant that he struggled to make the first team with loan signing Lewis Haldane occupying his role and was used as a substitute only six times. He was a regular in the reserves but was given a free transfer at the end of the season.
Port Vale *(From trainee on 17/4/2008) FL 26+22/5 FLC 0+2 FAC 2 Others 0+1*

RICKETTS Michael Barrington
Born: Birmingham, 4 December 1978
Height: 6'2" **Weight:** 11.12
Club Honours: FLC '04
International Honours: E: 1
Michael joined Tranmere on a one-year deal in August and claimed that the presence of the then manager John Barnes was his main reason for the move to his 11th professional club. A striker who converted to the role from midfield, he made his debut against one of his previous clubs, Bolton, as a substitute in the Carling Cup tie and scored the first of his two goals for Rovers at Exeter. Despite his obvious natural talent and ability to read the game, Michael faced competition from the sheer number of forwards at Prenton Park and having failed to fully adapt to Rovers' style of play or to make an appearance after November, had his contract cancelled by mutual consent in January.
Walsall *(From trainee on 13/9/1996) FL 31+45/14 FLC 2+4 FAC 2+2 Others 3+1/1*
Bolton W *(£500,000 on 17/7/2000) P/FL 63+35/37 FLC 0+4/3 FAC 4+3/4 Others 1+2/2*
Middlesbrough *(£2,200,000 on 31/1/2003) PL 12+20/3 FLC 3+2/1 FAC 2*
Leeds U *(Free on 8/7/2004) FL 10+15 FLC 3+1/2*
Stoke C *(Loaned on 22/2/2005) FL 1+10*
Cardiff C *(Loaned on 31/8/2005) FL 17/5*
Burnley *(Loaned on 30/1/2006) FL 12+1/2*
Southend U *(Signed on 27/7/2006) FL 0+2*
Preston NE *(Free on 12/1/2007) FL*

7+7/1 FAC 2
Oldham Ath *(Free on 10/7/2007) FL 8+1/2 FLC 2 Others 1 (Freed on 31/1/2008)*
Walsall *(Loaned on 2/11/2007) FL 12/3 FAC 4/2*
Walsall *(Free from trials in USA with Columbus Crew and San Jose Earthquakes on 30/7/2008) FL 25+3/9 FLC 1/1 FAC 1/1 Others 2/1*
Tranmere Rov *(Free on 14/8/2009) FL 7+5/2 FLC 0+1 FAC 1+3*

RICKETTS Samuel (Sam)
Derek
Born: Aylesbury, 11 October 1981
Height: 6'0" **Weight:** 11.12
Club Honours: AMC '06
International Honours: W: 38; E: SP-4
A highly versatile Welsh international, Sam made his debut for Bolton on the opening day of the season following his move from Hull. He retained his place for much of the first half of the season but found himself on the bench for Owen Coyle's first game in charge. Sam made occasional appearances during the latter stages of the season, with 31 starts in total over the course of a campaign in which his versatility was a real bonus. Primarily a full-back, he covered every defensive position during the course of the season and, in the 2-1 victory at Stoke, occupied the midfield holding role. A needless red card following two rash fouls in the 4-0 loss at Sunderland was most uncharacteristic and Sam's season, much like the team as a whole, fizzled out toward the end. Despite this, Sam is seen as a valuable member of the squad and will be hoping to figure more consistently.
Oxford U *(From trainee on 20/4/2000) FL 32+13/1 FLC 1 Others 2 (Free to Telford U on 7/7/2003)*
Swansea C *(Free from Telford U on 22/6/2004) FL 85+1/1 FLC 2 FAC 6 Others 11/2*
Hull C *(£300,000 on 18/7/2006) P/FL 111+2/1 FLC 4+1 FAC 8 Others 3*
Bolton W *(Signed on 25/7/2009) PL 25+2 FLC 3 FAC 3*

RIDGEWELL Liam Matthew
Born: Bexleyheath, 21 July 1984
Height: 5'10" **Weight:** 11.0
Club Honours: FAYC '02
International Honours: E: U21-8; Yth
Came back from a broken leg in September and filled in at left-back as an emergency so well, he made himself Birmingham's first choice there for the rest of the season. Liam's defensive skills, reading of the game and competitive nature were allied to an impressive adventurous streak. Had the

Liam Ridgewell

knack of scoring important goals by drifting into the right positions, notably a stoppage-time winner at Derby in the FA Cup fifth round and at home to Tottenham to force a draw. His goal that never was at Portsmouth - the linesman did not see that the ball crossed the line - might have changed the course of that FA Cup quarter-final Birmingham's way had it been allowed to stand.
Aston Villa *(From trainee on 26/7/2001) PL 66+13/6 FLC 6+3 FAC 3+2*
Bournemouth *(Loaned on 11/10/2002) FL 2+3*
Birmingham C *(£2,000,000 on 3/8/2007) P/FL 101+1/5 FLC 4 FAC 7/1*

RIDLEY Lee
Born: Scunthorpe, 5 December 1981
Height: 5'9" **Weight:** 11.
Club Honours: Div 1 '07
Defender Lee was a regular member of Cheltenham's squad in his third

season since joining from Scunthorpe. Lee spent most of the season at left-back and scored his only goal on the opening day – a long-range, right-footed shot against Grimsby that proved highly significant as Cheltenham finished only one place above the Mariners in the battle to avoid relegation. A solid, hard-working player with a dangerous long throw, Lee was one of the few genuinely left-footed players in the squad. After a calf injury, he faced competition from loan signing Danny Andrew, although Lee fought back. Was out of contract at the end of June.
Scunthorpe U *(From trainee on 3/7/2001) FL 87+13/2 FLC 1+1 FAC 6+2/1 Others 5+2*
Cheltenham T *(Signed on 24/7/2007) FL 58+4/1 FLC 2 FAC 5+1 Others 2*
Darlington *(Loaned on 22/11/2007) FL 6*
Lincoln C *(Loaned on 4/1/2008) FL 15*

RIERA Alberto (Albert)
Born: Mallorca, Spain, 15 April 1982
Height: 6'1" **Weight:** 12.1
International Honours: Spain: 16; U21-15; Yth
The Liverpool and Spanish international left-winger seemed an excellent signing for manager Rafa Benitez in 2008 but sadly, in common with so many players, he failed to reproduce that early form and ended the season on the transfer list. After playing in most of the early fixtures his appearances became more intermittent and although he was given a run of three games in January, following an injury to Yossi Benayoun, he was substituted in all three. In March he was suspended after making comments about Benitez's management style to the Spanish media. He might have attracted more sympathy if he had shown form to make the manager select him. A transfer to Spartak Moscow fell through in April but it seemed inconceivable that he would remain at Anfield.
Manchester C (Loaned from Espanyol, Spain, ex Real Mallorca, Bordeaux, on 11/1/2006) PL 12+3/1 FAC 4
Liverpool (£8,000,000 from Espanyol, Spain on 1/9/2008) PL 33+7/3 FLC 1 FAC 2+1/1 Others 9+3/1

[RIGA] MUSTAPHA Rahamat Riga
Born: Accra, Ghana, 10 October 1981
Height: 5'10" **Weight:** 11.0
International Honours: Holland: U21
Having struggled to break into the Bolton first team the previous season, Riga found fewer still chances. Making only three substitute appearances, one in the League and two in the FA Cup, he simply did not make enough of an impression to be utilised to a greater degree. Despite showing glimpses of real pace and skill during his time at the club, it appeared that he was deemed to be surplus to requirements.
Bolton W (Free from Levante, Spain, ex Vitesse Arnhem, RBC Roosendaal - loan, Sparta Rotterdam, on 1/8/2008) PL 2+16 FLC 1 FAC 0+3

RIGBY Lloyd Joseph
Born: Preston, 27 February 1989
Height: 6'2" **Weight:** 12.0
Having signed for Stockport in the summer of 2008, it was more than 12 months before Lloyd made his first team debut, starting in goal in a Johnstone's Paint Trophy game against Crewe. He was on course for a clean sheet until the third minute of injury time, when Calvin Zola knocked in a rebound. His League debut came at Southend and again he performed admirably despite County losing 2-1. He also kept goal for the final game of the season, a 3-0 home defeat by Tranmere.
Rochdale (From trainee on 5/7/2007. Freed on 26/3/2008)
Stockport Co (Free from Vauxhall Motors on 28/8/2009) FL 2 Others 1

RIGG Sean Michael
Born: Bristol, 1 October 1988
Height: 5'10" **Weight:** 10.2
The left-sided midfielder made just one start for Bristol Rovers, in the Carling Cup victory over Aldershot, and frustrated at the lack of opportunities he secured a long-term loan deal at League Two Port Vale which started in November and was extended until the end of the season. A pacy player, who can play either on the wing or up front, he was mainly used as an impact player from the bench despite scoring after just seven minutes in his first start for the club at Grimsby. He followed that up with another in the next game against Burton but managed just one more before the season's end. Always liable to cause problems for the opposition, he was freed by Rovers in the summer and offered a two-year deal by Vale.
Bristol Rov (Free from Forest Green Rov on 2/6/2006) FL 15+42/2 FLC 1+3 FAC 2+5 Others 1+6/1
Port Vale (Loaned on 24/11/2009) FL 9+17/3

RIGGOTT Christopher (Chris) Mark
Born: Derby, 1 September 1980
Height: 6'3" **Weight:** 12.2
Club Honours: FLC '04
International Honours: E: U21-8; Yth
Another injury-riddled season for the Middlesbrough centre-back. Chris had to undergo ankle surgery in May to solve a long-standing problem but suffered a relapse in September and again had to go under the surgeon's knife. He came back in November and after a couple of reserve games, made his return to the first team as a substitute for Manny Pogatetz at home to Scunthorpe on Boxing Day. He retained his place for the following games but his injury jinx struck again, when he pulled a hamstring in the last minute against Swansea in February. He battled back to fitness and featured in a couple of games at the end of the season to cover for the injured David Wheater. Another Boro player to be out of contract in the summer, manager Gordon Strachan stated in the local media, that he hoped a deal could be reached to keep the experienced defender at the club.
Derby Co (From trainee on 5/10/1998)
P/FL 87+4/5 FLC 7/1 FAC 2/1
Middlesbrough (£1,500,000 + on 31/1/2003) P/FL 95+9/5 FLC 10+2 FAC 10+1/1 Others 21/2
Stoke C (Loaned on 29/2/2008) FL 9

RIGTERS Maceo
Born: Amsterdam, Holland, 22 January 1984
Height: 5'10" **Weight:** 13.0
International Honours: Holland: U21-9
Blackburn's forgotten man had to be brought back into the squad when injuries disrupted a thin playing staff. The striker was due to join Kilmarnock on loan during the January transfer window, but the failure to sign a replacement for Benni McCarthy caused the move to be dropped. Ironically, Maceo's first team season was limited to 15 minutes in the FA Cup at Villa Park.
Blackburn Rov (Signed from NAC Breda, Holland, ex SC Heerenveen, FC Dordrecht, on 12/7/2007) PL 0+2 FLC 0+1 FAC 1+1 Others 1+2
Norwich C (Loaned on 19/3/2008) FL 0+2
Barnsley (Loaned on 8/8/2008) FL 4+15 FLC 1 FAC 1

RIISE Bjorn Helge Semundseth
Born: Aalesund, Norway, 21 June 1983
Height: 5'9" **Weight:** 11.0
International Honours: Norway: 22; U21-16
The brother of former Liverpool defender Jon Arne Riise, Bjorn Helge arrived at Fulham on a free transfer from Norwegian side Lillestrom in July, making his first senior appearance as a substitute in the opening Europa League game against FK Vetra. Although a rare starter in Premier League fixtures, he appeared more regularly in Cup and European games. While normally deployed on the right of midfield, he was also used on the left and as a central midfielder. A competitive player who harries opponents into conceding possession, he can also get in behind defences to provide key passes and crosses. A regular choice for Norway, he featured in the key World Cup qualifier against Slovakia and a friendly against South Africa during the autumn.
Fulham (Signed from Lillestrom, Norway, ex Aalesund, Viking Stavanger, Standard Liege, FC Brussels - loan, on 22/7/2009) PL 5+7 FLC 1 FAC 2+1 Others 7+5

RITCHIE Matthew (Matt) Thomas
Born: Gosport, 10 September 1989
Height: 5'8" **Weight:** 11.0

Club Honours: Div 2 '10
Notts County tried very hard to sign Portsmouth's Matt on a permanent deal at the start of the season, but he went there on an extended loan instead. He was the regular first choice wide-left midfielder in the first third of the season but lost his place when his form slipped and returned to Portsmouth at the end of December. County were unable to make a further loan deal due to the transfer embargo, it being a classic case of the 'embargo' disadvantaging the player rather than the club! Swindon manager Danny Wilson was a confirmed admirer of Matt and brought him to the County Ground on loan in February. Four appearances from the bench gave brief glimpses of his ability on the left wing but following a hat-trick for the reserves side was recalled by parent club, who were suffering a chronic shortage of players due to their well publicised difficulties. Having forced his way into the Portsmouth midfield to make his Premier League debut at Wigan, he put in an assured performance and was given another opportunity against Aston Villa ten days later. Cultured and confident, Matt looks sure to have a bright future in the game.
Portsmouth *(From trainee on 4/7/2008) PL 1+1*
Dagenham & Redbridge *(Loaned on 26/9/2008) FL 36+1/11 FAC 3/1 Others 0+1*
Notts Co *(Loaned on 1/9/2009) FL 12+4/3 FAC 1+1 Others 0+1*
Swindon T *(Loaned on 11/2/2010) FL 0+4*

RIZA Omer Kerime
Born: Edmonton, 8 November 1979
Height: 5'9" **Weight:** 11.2
International Honours: Turkey: U21
After a lengthy ban imposed by the Turkish FA was lifted late in 2008-09 his enthusiasm to re-ignite his career earned him a contract at Shrewsbury. Omer has good pace and plays either in midfield or as a striker. Unfortunately, he suffered ankle ligament damage in his third game of the season, at Dagenham, and although he returned to play in the November draw with Torquay, he struggled to make a real impact and left the club in January. He next turned up at Aldershot on a non-contract basis in late February and made his sole appearance as a second-half substitute in the home defeat to Burton. Any hopes Omer may have had of playing any further part in the campaign were ended by a knee operation in April and his time at the EBB Stadium was ended for good.

Arsenal *(From trainee on 1/7/2098) FLC 0+1*
West Ham U *(£20,000 on 7/12/2099)*
Barnet *(Loaned on 20/10/2000) FL 7+3/4 FAC 1 Others 2/1*
Cambridge U *(Loaned on 2/3/2001) FL 10+2/3*
Cambridge U *(Free on 9/8/2002) FL 43+3/11 FLC 2 FAC 3+2/1 Others 4+1/4 (Freed during 2003 close season)*
Shrewsbury T *(Free from Trabzonspor, Turkey, ex Denilizpor, on 17/4/2009) FL 1+9 FLC 0+1 Others 1+2*
Aldershot T *(Free on 25/2/2010) FL 0+1*

ROBERTS Anthony (Tony) Mark
Born: Holyhead, 4 August 1969
Height: 6'0" **Weight:** 12.0
Club Honours: FC '07
International Honours: W: 2; B-2; SP; U21-2; Yth
The Dagenham goalkeeper had another ever-present season. Tony rolled back the years and made countless great saves throughout the year. Despite his age, coming up to 40, he keeps super fit by being the goalkeeping coach at Arsenal for their reserve and youth 'keepers during the week. He has now clocked up over 450 appearances for the Daggers and signed a one-year extension to his contract. Tony was voted third in the 'Player of the Year' awards.
Queens Park Rgrs *(From trainee on 24/7/1987) P/FL 122 FLC 11 FAC 10+1 Others 2*
Millwall *(Free on 6/8/1998) FL 8 (Free to St Albans on 7/4/1999)*
Dagenham & Redbridge *(Free from Atlanta Silverbacks, USA on 12/7/2000) FL 132 FLC 3 FAC 7 Others 9*

Tony Roberts

ROBERTS Gareth (Gary) Michael
Born: Chester, 18 March 1984
Height: 5'10" **Weight:** 11.9
Club Honours: FC '06
International Honours: E: SP-4
Huddersfield's skilful winger signed an extension to his contract during the summer and rewarded the Galpharm faithful with some outstanding displays. When Gary is on his game, he provides a real threat to defences, always willing to make probing runs and deliver quality crosses. Gary scored some terrific goals during the play-off season, none better than the volley in the local derby with Leeds and a sublime chip in the mauling of Stockport. He even netted a rare header in the FA Cup win over Dagenham. A cleverly taken goal in the final League game at Exeter was Huddersfield's 100th of the campaign.
Accrington Stanley *(Free from Welshpool, ex Denbigh T, Bala T, Rhyl, Bangor C, on 1/2/2005) FL 14/8 FLC 2*
Ipswich T *(Signed on 17/10/2006) FL 40+14/3 FLC 1 FAC 4*
Crewe Alex *(Loaned on 12/2/2008) FL 4*
Huddersfield T *(£250,000 on 31/7/2008) FL 83+3/16 FLC 3/2 FAC 4/2 Others 4*

ROBERTS Gareth Wyn
Born: Wrexham, 6 February 1978
Height: 5'7" **Weight:** 12.6
Club Honours: FAYC '96; AMC '07
International Honours: W: 9; B-1; U21-10
Gareth had a good and steady season at left-back for Doncaster, taking over the captaincy when Brian Stock and then Martin Woods went down with long-term injuries. He won the club's award for 'Goal of the Season' for his tremendous strike at Peterborough that set them on the winning trail.
Liverpool *(From trainee on 22/5/1996. £50,000 to Panionios, Greece on 15/1/1999)*
Tranmere Rov *(Free from Panionios, Greece on 5/8/1999) FL 276+5/13 FLC 22 FAC 21+1 Others 12/2*
Doncaster Rov *(Free on 3/7/2006) FL 130+11/6 FLC 6 FAC 7+1 Others 9+1*

ROBERTS Gary Steven
Born: Chester, 4 February 1987
Height: 5'8" **Weight:** 10.5
International Honours: E: Yth
The talented one-time Crewe midfielder was given a chance by Rotherham after being let go by Yeovil. Initially on trial for a month, during which he scored one of League Two's most amazing goals, a quickly taken free kick from near the half-way line at Bradford when he spotted that the goalkeeper had

strayed off his line. He earned an extended stay and was encouraged to knuckle down and keep his place in midfield. But after being injured during the incident in which he was sent off against Torquay in February for a second booking, he never got back in the side and was released before the end of the season.

Crewe Alex *(From trainee on 7/7/2004) FL 110+12/11 FLC 2 FAC 4 Others 5*
Yeovil T *(Signed on 22/8/2008) FL 27+3/2 FLC 1 FAC 2 Others 1*
Rotherham U *(Free, via trial at Brighton & Hove A, on 12/11/2009) FL 11+2/3 FAC 2*

ROBERTS Jason Andre Davis
Born: Acton, 25 January 1978
Height: 5'11" **Weight:** 12.7
International Honours: Grenada: 22

The striker continued in the same vein at Blackburn as previous seasons, often being brought into the team because his strength and ability to hold the ball under pressure causes problems and just as often omitted because of his lack of goals. He had golden moments, such as his two-goal appearance from the bench in the home game against Portsmouth and his sweetly struck 20-yarder against Everton. His best performance was reserved for the penultimate game of the season when his strength and focus unsettled the Arsenal central defenders, paving the way for an unexpected victory. In the January honours list, he received the MBE in recognition of his charity work in Grenada and the East End, which allows under-privileged children relief from their position through playing football.

Wolverhampton W *(£250,000 from Hayes on 12/9/1997)*
Torquay U *(Loaned on 19/12/1997) FL 13+1/6 Others 1*
Bristol C *(Loaned on 26/3/1998) FL 1+2/1*
Bristol Rov *(£250,000 on 7/8/1998) FL 73+5/38 FLC 6/3 FAC 6/7 Others 3*
West Bromwich A *(£2,000,000 on 27/7/2000) P/FL 75+14/24 FLC 3+1/2 FAC 6 Others 2/1*
Portsmouth *(Loaned on 1/9/2003) PL 4+6/1 FLC 2/3*
Wigan Ath *(£2,000,000 on 13/1/2004) P/FL 93/37 FLC 4+2/4 FAC 2+2/2*
Blackburn Rov *(£3,000,000 on 3/7/2006) PL 55+44/19 FLC 2+2 FAC 4+3/1 Others 5+2/2*

ROBERTS Stephen (Steve) Wyn
Born: Wrexham, 24 February 1980
Height: 6'0" **Weight:** 12.7
Club Honours: AMC '05, '07

International Honours: W: 1; U21-4; Yth

Steve made only two appearances in central defence for Walsall before announcing his retirement from the professional game due a long-standing back injury. His season was over before the end of August, his last appearance seeing him substituted 20 minutes before the end of the 0-0 home draw with Gillingham. He now works as a carpenter. A talented artist, his limited edition print of Fernando Torres was sold in the Liverpool club shop.

Wrexham *(From trainee on 16/1/1998) FL 143+7/6 FLC 3 FAC 7+1/1 Others 11+1/1*
Doncaster Rov *(Free on 4/7/2005) FL 58+15/1 FLC 6 FAC 2+2 Others 7+2*
Walsall *(Free on 27/7/2008) FL 16/1 FLC 2 FAC 1 Others 2*

Chris Robertson

ROBERTSON Christopher (Chris)
Born: Dundee, 11 October 1985
Height: 6'3" **Weight:** 11.8

The powerful young defender had an excellent season for Torquay in which he started as right-back, moved to his more regular position of centre-back on Lee Mansell's return to fitness but became right-back as Mansell went into central midfield. The central role would appear to be better suited to his physique but Chris settled into the full-back role so well in his second spell that you could now say he is equally at home in either position.

Sheffield U *(From trainee on 27/10/2001)*
Chester C *(Loaned on 31/1/2006) FL 0+1*
Torquay U *(Free on 8/3/2007) FL 54/3 FLC 1 FAC 2 Others 2*

ROBERTSON Gregor Aedan
Born: Edinburgh, 19 January 1984
Height: 6'0" **Weight:** 12.4
International Honours: S: U21-15

Gregor established himself on the left side of John Sheridan's Chesterfield team and was an important if underrated player. After breaking a leg against Carlisle in the Johnstone's Paint Trophy in November, Gregor's season ended and the Spireites were unable to properly replace his versatility and ability to get forward and defend in equal measure.

Nottingham F *(From juniors at Heart of Midlothian on 8/2/2001) FL 25+11 FLC 2+2 FAC 4*
Rotherham U *(Free on 5/8/2005) FL 46+7/1 FLC 4*
Chesterfield *(Free on 11/7/2007) FL 74+9/3 FLC 2 FAC 5+1 Others 4+1*

ROBERTSON Jordan
Born: Sheffield, 12 February 1988
Height: 6'0" **Weight:** 12.6

After playing in Sheffield United's pre-season games, Jordan made a substitute appearance in the Carling Cup before moving on loan to Bury. Having made just four appearances, scoring on his debut in a 1-0 away win at Darlington, his loan was cut short when he was sentenced to 32 months imprisonment for driving offences and released by the club.

Sheffield U *(From trainee on 6/7/2006) FLC 0+2*
Torquay U *(Loaned on 4/11/2006) FL 5+4/2 FAC 1+1/2*
Northampton T *(Loaned on 26/1/2007) FL 9+8/3*
Dundee U *(Loaned on 28/8/2007) SL 12+2/3 SLC 3/1 SC 1*
Oldham Ath *(Loaned on 26/2/2008) FL 2+1/1*
Southampton *(Loaned on 27/9/2008) FL 8+2/1*
Bury *(Loaned on 13/8/2009) FL 4/1 Others 1*

[ROBINHO] DE SOUZA Robson
Born: Sao Vicente, Brazil, 25 January 1984
Height: 5'8" **Weight:** 9.6
International Honours: Brazil: 74; U23-8

The most expensive player in English football, the Brazilian-born Manchester City striker endured a nightmare, dogged by injuries and poor form. Although he started the first three games, he was withdrawn in each of them before he was diagnosed with an ankle problem that sidelined him until November. Even when fit, he was little used by manager Mark Hughes, who preferred the in-form Emmanuel

Adebayor, Craig Bellamy and Carlos Tevez. Most of Robinho's outings were on the left wing rather than in his preferred position in the centre. After Mark Hughes' departure in December, Roberto Mancini gave him the chance to start in the centre in the Boxing Day match with Stoke. Sadly, his performance was so lame he was replaced early in the second half and although he scored his only goal in the 4-2 FA Cup victory against City, that was probably his last game for City. To enable him to have some match practice to win a place in Brazil's World Cup squad – which he did - he was loaned to his former Brazilian club Santos for the remainder of the season and even if that move does not materialise into a full transfer, it seems unlikely that he will return to Eastlands.
Manchester C (£32,500,000 from Real Madrid, Spain, ex Santos, on 1/9/2008) PL 36+5/14 FLC 1 FAC 1/1 Others 10/1

ROBINSON Andrew (Andy)
Mark
Born: Birkenhead, 3 November 1979
Height: 5'8" **Weight:** 11.4
Club Honours: AMC '06; Div 1 '08
Andy found himself on the fringes of the Leeds' squad in 2009-10, failing to make a League One start for the Whites, but scoring in his only full appearance, a 2-1 Johnstone's Paint Trophy win against Darlington. Given an opportunity for more football, he arrived for his second spell at Tranmere in mid-March on loan; his wages being covered by a special collection held by the supporters' 'Les Aid' Fund. However, his first game for the club in the 3-0 away defeat at Brighton ended prematurely when he was sent off and he also suffered a groin injury in the same match, which delayed his home debut by almost one month. However, the spectacular goal Andy scored against Millwall at Prenton Park proved to be vital in Rovers' fight to avoid relegation and left the fans feeling it was money very well spent
Tranmere Rov (Free from Cammell Laird on 11/11/2002) Others 0+1
Swansea C (Free on 14/8/2003) FL 159+33/43 FLC 2+1 FAC 14+3/5 Others 14/6
Leeds U (Free on 7/8/2008) FL 20+18/2 FLC 3+1/2 FAC 2/1 Others 3+3/2
Tranmere Rov (Loaned on 25/3/2010) FL 3+2/1

ROBINSON Anton Dale
Born: Harrow, 17 February 1986
Height: 5'9" **Weight:** 10.3
International Honours: E: SP-2
Anton is a versatile player and filled

every midfield role for Bournemouth during the season, sometimes changing in the course of a game. He also filled in at right-back to great effect. Since coming out of non-League football, Anton has improved with every week and his reward for a great season was the 'Players' Player of the Year' award.
Millwall (From trainee on 23/4/2004) FAC 1 (Freed during 2005 close season)
Bournemouth (Free from Weymouth, ex Exeter C, Eastbourne Borough, Fisher Ath, on 2/2/2009) FL 59+2/5 FLC 1 FAC 2 Others 2

ROBINSON Jack
Born: Warrington, 1 September 1993
Height: 5'11" **Weight:** 10.8
International Honours: E: Yth
A member of the Liverpool Academy, left-back Jack became the youngest ever debutant for the club at the age of 16 years and 250 days when he was an 87th-minute substitute in the Reds' final match at Hull, remarkably without having played in the reserve team. It is to be hoped that he enjoys more first team action in the future than most players from Liverpool's Academy.
Liverpool (Academy) PL 0+1

ROBINSON Jake David
Born: Brighton, 23 October 1986
Height: 5'9" **Weight:** 10.4
The experienced striker signed for Shrewsbury after being released by Brighton. He likes the ball on the ground and his pace can cause problems to a defence, playing off a target man. Jake enjoyed an excellent debut in the 3-1 opening day win against Burton, scoring his first goal, and scored again against Ipswich in the Carling Cup three days later. He had his best spell in the first two months of the season when all his four goals came. By his own admission he lost his way a little around the turn of the year but was involved in a creditable 34 games.
Brighton & Hove A (From trainee on 22/12/2003) FL 61+62/13 FLC 1+5/1 FAC 7+3/4 Others 6+3/4
Aldershot T (Loaned on 10/2/2009) FL 19/4
Shrewsbury T (Free on 2/7/2009) FL 15+19/3 FLC 1/1 FAC 1

ROBINSON Paul Mark James
Born: Barnet, 7 January 1982
Height: 6'1" **Weight:** 12.1
Paul's first game of the season for Millwall was at Barnet after he recovered from injury. Unfortunately, he received a further ankle injury and this put him out until the away game with Stockport, where he scored the opening goal. From that point, he played in all

the League games until the end of the season. He was given a new contract until 2013 and also got the captain's arm band back. Paul revels in being a central defender with guile and he seldom puts a foot wrong, being brave in the air and dangerous at set pieces in the opponents' penalty area. Having scored the second goal of the play-off win over Huddersfield with a typical set-piece header that took the Lions to Wembley for the second year running, he then scored the winning goal against Swindon in the final.
Millwall (From trainee on 25/10/2000) FL 197+8/13 FLC 7/1 FAC 23+1/2 Others 7+3/3
Torquay U (Loaned on 23/12/2004) FL 12

ROBINSON Paul Peter
Born: Watford, 14 December 1978
Height: 5'9" **Weight:** 11.12
Club Honours: Div 2 '98; Ch '08
International Honours: E: U21-3
In what was a competitive battle for defensive places at Bolton, Paul made 24 League starts last season following his move from West Bromwich. This despite the challenge for the left-back berth from established performer Jlloyd Samuel, with Owen Coyle seemingly preferring Paul to the former Aston Villa man. Recognised as an old school full-back, Paul certainly brought some much needed tenacity and bite to the back line and while this resulted in needless tackles at times, his style complemented the purer approach of Gary Cahill. He is perhaps not the fastest of full-backs and is not as attack-minded as Samuel, so it is testimony to Paul that his other qualities led to him completing the season as the first choice left-back.
Watford (From trainee on 13/2/1997) P/FL 201+18/8 FLC 15+1/1 FAC 10+2 Others 5
West Bromwich A (£250,000 on 14/10/2003) P/FL 211+3/4 FLC 6 FAC 15/1 Others 3
Bolton W (Loaned on 12/12/2009) PL 24+1 FAC 2

ROBINSON Paul William
Born: Beverley, 15 October 1979
Height: 6'2" **Weight:** 13.4
Club Honours: FAYC '97; FLC '08
International Honours: E: 41; U21-11
Paul had a season of highs and lows for Blackburn, perhaps typified by the Carling Cup quarter-final against Chelsea when his saves in the penalty shoot-out from Michael Ballack and Gael Kakuta made him the hero, overshadowing a missed punch that gifted an equaliser to Fabio Ferreira. At times he was the epitome of solid excellence, as in the game towards the

end of the season when he made a couple of outstanding saves to defy a Manchester United side desperate for a win to keep their title hopes alive. In games against Fulham and Hull his contribution was crucial but there were moments when he was far less assured. He was beaten by long-range shots like those by Robbie Blake in the home game against Burnley and Michael Essien at Chelsea. Yet his ability to pull off the outstanding save and his enthusiasm for the game made him a vital player. He was also an unlikely key instrument in attacking play, the accuracy of his delivery resulting in him taking all free kicks in his own half.
Leeds U (From trainee on 13/5/1997) PL 93+2 FLC 5/1 FAC 7 Others 12
Tottenham H (£1,500,000 on 16/5/2004) PL 137/1 FLC 10 FAC 12 Others 16
Blackburn Rov (£3,500,000 on 28/7/2008) PL 70 FLC 7 FAC 3

Paul Robinson (Blackburn Rovers)

ROBINSON Theo Larayan Ronaldo
Born: Birmingham, 22 January 1989
Height: 5'11" **Weight:** 11.8
The young striker was drafted in from Watford to add scoring potential to Huddersfield. Theo started the opening game and kept the goals flowing through the early part of the season, a two-goal haul in the Carling Cup defeat at Newcastle being a highlight. Often brought on from the bench to stretch defences, his lively displays gave him the 'super sub' tag. He was restored to the starting line-up and ended the regular season with a healthy 15 goals.
Watford (From trainee on 5/2/2007) P/FL 0+5 FLC 1

Hereford U (Loaned on 9/8/2007) FL 32+11/13 FLC 2/1 FAC 6/2 Others 0+1
Southend U (Loaned on 24/1/2009) FL 20+1/7
Huddersfield T (Signed on 3/7/2009) FL 17+20/13 FLC 1+1/3 FAC 0+3 Others 0+1

ROBSON Barry Gordon George
Born: Inverurie, 7 November 1978
Height: 5'11" **Weight:** 11.0
International Honours: S: 8; B-2
As soon as the January transfer window opened, Gordon Strachan took little time in raiding former club Glasgow Celtic for players to bolster his Middlesbrough side. Barry was due to sign the same day as Gary Caldwell, who decided at the last minute to join Wigan. An undisclosed fee was renegotiated for Barry and despite the combative midfielder being sent off on his home debut against Swansea, Boro fans took to him immediately. When regular captain Gary O'Neil was injured, Barry took the armband. He was soon scoring goals, five in his 19 games. These included a brace of penalties at home to Queens Park Rangers and a left-foot thunderbolt in a derby against Newcastle. This goal was voted the Garmin 'Goal of the Season' by fans on the official website.
Glasgow Rgrs (From juniors on 10/7/1995)
Inverness CT (Signed on 15/10/1997) SL 102+33/17 SLC 7+4/2 SC 11+3/7 Others 6+1/1
Forfar Ath (Loaned on 1/10/1999) SL 25/9 SC 3/1
Dundee U (£50,000 on 1/7/2003) SL 139+6/32 SLC 9+1/1 SC 9/3 Others 8+2/3
Glasgow Celtic (£1,250,000 on 31/1/2008) SL 31+11/4 SLC 1+1 SC 0+1 Others 8+2/3
Middlesbrough (Signed on 13/1/2010) FL 18/5

ROBSON Matthew (Matty) James
Born: Spennymoor, 23 January 1985
Height: 5'10" **Weight:** 11.2
A close season signing by Carlisle from Hartlepool, Matty impressed from the start with his enthusiasm and positive attitude. A left-sided midfielder who loves to take on his man, particularly on the outside, he also demonstrated an eye for goal. His superb individual effort against Bradford in the Johnstone's Paint Trophy was voted Carlisle's 'Goal of the Season' while his long-range strike at Walsall was chosen as the runner-up. Injuries occasionally kept him out of the side but he will be looking to

progress his career in the new campaign.
Hartlepool U (From trainee on 16/3/2004) FL 90+45/9 FLC 9+2 FAC 9+3/1 Others 11+1
Carlisle U (Free on 2/7/2009) FL 39/4 FLC 3 FAC 4 Others 7/3

ROBSON-KANU Hal
Born: Acton, 21 May 1989
Height: 5'7" **Weight:** 11.8
International Honours: E: Yth. W: 1; U21-1
After gaining experience with a number of lower division clubs, Hal set out to win a regular place in Reading's squad. His decision was largely successful, as he was one of several young players to benefit from the League ruling that the number of substitutes be increased from five to seven. Hal made four starts, went on as a substitute 13 times and was an unused substitute for another 19 matches. So he was very much involved in the action, as befits a young striker who can play down the middle but was often used wide on the right. There, he can use his strength and speed to deliver crosses as well as driving into the box. Hal, already an England under-19 international, had an unexpected bonus at the end of the season when he was called into the Wales under-21 squad for a friendly against Austria, before making his full international debut just five days later, against Croatia.
Reading (From trainee on 4/7/2007) FL 4+13 FAC 0+1
Southend U (Loaned on 31/1/2008) FL 6+2/3
Southend U (Loaned on 21/8/2008) FL 12+2/2 Others 1
Swindon T (Loaned on 26/1/2009) FL 20/4

ROCHA Ricardo Sergio
Born: Braga, Portugal, 3 October 1978
Height: 6'0" **Weight:** 12.8
International Honours: Portugal: 6
In a bizarre start to his career at Portsmouth, Portuguese defender Ricardo was sent off in two of his first three starts for the club. However, as the season reached its climax, he grew in stature, putting in a spectacular performance in the FA Cup semi-final against Tottenham that earned him the 'Man of the Match' award. Strong, committed and calm, Ricardo is a firm favourite with the Fratton Park faithful, who will be hoping the club can retain his services for the Championship campaign that now faces them.
Tottenham H (£3,300,000 from Benfica, Portugal, ex Famalicao, Sporting Braga, on 25/1/2007) PL 13+1

FLC 0+1 FAC 3 (Freed during 2009 close
season)
Portsmouth (Free from Standard Liege,
Belgium on 3/2/2010) PL 10 FAC 2

ROCHE Barry Christopher
Born: Dublin, 6 April 1982
Height: 6'4" **Weight:** 12.6
International Honours: Rol: Yth
The giant goalkeeper swept the board
at Morecambe's 'Player of the Year'
awards night for the second season
running. His second year with the
Shrimps was every bit as successful as
his first with some superb
performances, often keeping his side in
games when they were far from at their
best. He enhanced his growing
reputation with a number of penalty
saves, including one against Crewe
when his side were 3-1 down with ten
men and turned it around to win 4-3
with three goals in the last four
minutes. Morecambe boss Sammy
McIlroy was often quoted as calling
Barry the best goalkeeper in League
Two and was happy when he signed a
new two-year deal at the end of May.
Nottingham F (From trainee on
29/6/1999) FL 10+3
Chesterfield (Free on 5/8/2005) FL 126
FLC 5 FAC 4 Others 5
Morecambe (Free on 30/7/2008) FL 88
FLC 2 FAC 4 Others 6

Barry Roche

RODALLEGA Hugo
Born: Valle del Cauca, Colombia, 25
July 1985
Height: 5'11" **Weight:** 11.5
International Honours: Colombia: 31
A Colombian international, Hugo
finished as Wigan's top scorer with ten
League goals, becoming only the third

player to reach double figures in their
five seasons in top flight football. Hugo
is a skilful striker with pace to burn and
has the killer instinct needed in that
position. He is strong in the air, very
mobile and has clever movement. His
first touch is outstanding and he can
play in various positions. Hugo's goal in
the opening match against Aston Villa
was an astonishing piece of power and
technique, smashing in a remarkable
right-foot volley. He was also on target
as Wigan achieved a first victory over
one of the top four teams in 34
attempts by beating Chelsea. His most
important goal was a stoppage-time
winner over Burnley that went a long
way towards the club retaining their
status. Hugo became only the second
player in the club's Premier League
history, after Maynor Figueora, to start
every League game.
Wigan Ath (£4,500,000 from Necaxa,
Mexico, ex Boca Juniors de Cali,
Deportivo Cali, Monterrey, Atlas - loan,
on 28/1/2009) PL 47+6/13 FLC 0+1 FAC
2+1

RODGERS Luke John
Born: Birmingham, 1 January 1982
Height: 5'7" **Weight:** 11.2
Club Honours: Div 2 '10
International Honours: E: SP-2
Arriving at Notts County from Yeovil
during the summer, Luke enjoyed a
remarkable season after signing,
following a number of goals in pre-
season friendlies. He took until the end
of September to open his League
account and did it in style with a hat-
trick at Lincoln. After a short period out
of the side, he became the regular
partner for Lee Hughes and his electric
pace caused all sorts of problems for
opposing defenders. Late in the season,
he was scheduled to leave for a
lucrative contract with New York Red
Bulls but the deal faltered and was
delayed, allowing him to participate in
clinching the League Two
championship.
Shrewsbury T (From trainee on
10/7/2000) FL 122+20/52 FLC 3/1 FAC
6+1 Others 9+2/5
Crewe Alex (Free on 26/7/2005) FL
18+20/9 FAC 1
Port Vale (£30,000 on 17/1/2007) FL
45+14/15 FLC 1+1/2 FAC 3/1 Others
1+1/1
Yeovil T (Free on 24/11/2008) FL
10+12/3
Notts Co (Free on 21/7/2009) FL
27+15/13 FLC 1 FAC 0+5

RODGERS Paul Leo Henry
Born: Edmonton, 6 October 1989
Height: 5'10" **Weight:** 10.7

By switching Paul from a wing-back to a
wide midfield player, Northampton
benefited from some outstanding
performances by the youngster. His
improved form is coupled with the
club's rise up the table. His speedy wing
play caught out several opposing
defenders over the season.
Arsenal (From trainee on 2/7/2007) FLC 1
Northampton T (Free on 23/1/2009) FL
33+9 FAC 2 Others 2

RODRIGUEZ Jay Enrique
Born: Burnley, 29 July 1989
Height: 6'1" **Weight:** 11.0
Burnley's super-sub from the promotion
season signed a new two-year contract
at the start of 2009-10, but it proved a
disappointing campaign for him. He
appeared in both of the side's Carling
Cup ties before an injury on reserve
duty ruled him out for several months,
after which he was loaned out to
Barnsley for a month in February. Jay
made a dramatic debut for Barnsley a
day later at Preston and, as a substitute
in added time, scored with his only
touch of the game in the Reds'
impressive 4-1 victory. From thereon he
was used mainly as a substitute and
showed plenty of energy and skill when
called upon. Returning to Turf Moor, he
ended the season as an occasional sub
but never saw Premier League action,
having clearly slipped down the pecking
order of Clarets' strikers. Regardless, Jay
remains a promising talent and has
plenty of time to recover from the
season's disappointments.
Burnley (From trainee on 4/7/2007)
P/FL 2+24/2 FLC 1+4/2 FAC 0+4/1
Others 0+3
Stirling A (Loaned on 11/1/2008) SL
10+1/3 SC 0+1
Barnsley (Loaned on 1/2/2010) FL
1+5/1

RODRIGUEZ Maximiliano
(Maxi) Ruben
Born: Rosario, Argentina, 2 January
1981
Height: 5'11" **Weight:** 12.6
International Honours: Argentina: 36
Liverpool signed the experienced
Argentine international winger on a
free transfer from Atletico Madrid
during the January transfer window
and, although ineligible for the Europa
Cup matches, he showed good form on
both flanks in the remaining
Premiership games, starting with a
substitute appearance at Stoke followed
by his full debut at Wolverhampton a
week later. His crosses provided former
Atletico team-mate Fernando Torres
with two goals in his early games and
he scored his first goal in the 4-0 away

win at Burnley. Ironically, his new team was eliminated in the semi-final of the Europa Cup by his former team, with Maxi watching helplessly.
Liverpool (Free from Atletico Madrid, Spain, ex Newell's Old Boys, Real Oviedo - loan, Espanyol, on 13/1/2010)
PL 14+3/1

RODWELL Jack Christian
Born: Southport, 11 March 1991
Height: 6'1" **Weight:** 12.8
International Honours: E: U21-11; Yth
This exciting product of the Everton Academy enhanced his reputation as one of the brightest home-grown talents in England in an excellent campaign. Although nominally a central defender, the England under-21 international played in midfield in the first half of the season when, although hampered by a groin injury on

occasions, he showed his great potential, displaying pace and composure on the ball, as well as strong tackling skills. With senior players returning, Jack was primarily used as a substitute in the second half of the season, making some important cameos from the bench, including a brilliant run and sweetly struck goal against Manchester United. One of the brightest young stars in the domestic game is on a long-term contract at Goodison.
Everton (From trainee on 15/3/2008)
PL 26+21/2 FLC 3 FAC 2+3/1 Others 6+3/2

ROONEY John Richard
Born: Liverpool, 17 December 1990
Height: 5'10" **Weight:** 11.1
John did not have the comfort of an extended run for Macclesfield and many

of his appearances came as a substitute. In the early part of the season he played up front and scored twice, in the Johnstone's Paint Trophy loss at Carlisle and with a thunderbolt from outside the area in the 2-0 victory at Cheltenham. Later, when the Macclesfield midfield was depleted by injury, John was used there. He often played wide but his best performances come in a more central role. John is the brother of Manchester United and England star, Wayne.
Macclesfield T (From trainee on 5/8/2008)
PL 25+16/3 FLC 1+1 FAC 1+1 Others 0+1/1

ROONEY Luke William
Born: Bermondsey, 28 December 1990
Height: 5'8" **Weight:** 11.7
A highly-rated youngster, Luke is an attacking midfielder who signed his first professional deal with Gillingham in the summer. He was used predominately on the right of midfield by Mark Stimson and netted moments into his League debut, scoring the Gills' second after coming off the bench in a 3-0 home win over Exeter. Then, one month later, Luke scored on his first League start in the club's 4-1 defeat by Southampton; his audacious chip at St Marys was later voted 'Goal of the Season' by the club's supporters.
Gillingham (From trainee on 17/7/2009) FL 2+11/2 FLC 0+1 Others 2

ROONEY Wayne Mark
Born: Liverpool, 24 October 1985
Height: 5'10" **Weight:** 12.4
Club Honours: FLC '06, '10; PL '07, '08, '09; CS '07; UEFACL '08
International Honours: E: 60; Yth
Manchester United and England striker Wayne started the World Cup season with a golden scoring spree and never stopped. Opening his account in the FA Community Shield, he then notched the only goal of the opening Premier League game against Birmingham, his 99th for United. He then became the 20th player to pass 100 for United, with two against Wigan. Wayne scored his first hat-trick in three years in a 4-1 victory at Portsmouth and went one better with all four goals against Hull, three of them coming in the last ten minutes to set a personal best. Continuing his rich vein, particularly with his head, he nodded the winner in the second minute of stoppage time against Manchester City to take United into the Carling Cup final. Another landmark was his 100th Premier League goal, against Arsenal at the Emirates. After two headers against Milan, the fifth in succession with his head sealed the Carling Cup final

Jack Rodwell

Wayne Rooney

against Aston Villa. Wayne was absolutely central to United's continuing challenge but, with a World Cup coming, there were always injury scares. He damaged ankle ligaments against Bayern in Munich and was expected to be out for three weeks. Typically, he recovered to play in the second leg of the tie. He limped away from the final Premiership game against Stoke but celebrated a notable double, the Football Writers 'Footballer of the Year' and the PFA 'Player of the Year'.
Everton (From trainee on 20/2/2003) PL 40+27/15 FLC 4+2/2 FAC 4
Manchester U (£20,000,000 + on 31/8/2004) PL 173+16/91 FLC 7+4/4 FAC 18+5/11 Others 54+5/25

ROSE Daniel (Danny) Lee
Born: Doncaster, 2 July 1990
Height: 5'8" **Weight:** 11.11
International Honours: E: U21-8; Yth

volley following a half-clearance by the goalkeeper. Danny was on the Spurs' bench 22 times during the season, being used on three occasions.
Tottenham H (From trainee at Leeds U on 25/7/2007) PL 1/1 FLC 0+1 FAC 1+2
Watford (Loaned on 24/3/2009) FL 3+4
Peterborough U (Loaned on 29/9/2009) FL 4+2

ROSE Michael Charles
Born: Salford, 28 July 1982
Height: 5'10" **Weight:** 11.2
Club Honours: Div 2 '05; Div 1 '10
Michael was an almost ever-present member of the Stockport side at left-back during the first half of the season, once switching to centre-half against Walsall where he performed admirably. Having scored a trademark free kick against Exeter in November, a hernia problem flared up in December and he was forced to play through the pain, scoring his only goal from open play for County away to Gillingham. At the end of January the combative left-back agreed a loan move to Norwich, and scored on his debut in a 2-1 win over Hartlepool. He played nine successive games in the absence of Adam Drury of which City won six and his wholehearted style was much appreciated by colleagues and supporters. His long throw was a most useful weapon too.
Manchester U (From trainee on 9/9/1999. Freed during 2001 close season)
Yeovil T (Free from Hereford U, ex Chester C, on 14/5/2004) FL 37+4/1 FLC 2 FAC 3+1 Others 0+1
Cheltenham T (Loaned on 25/8/2005) FL 3
Scunthorpe U (Loaned on 1/1/2006) FL 15 FAC 1
Stockport Co (Free on 8/7/2006) FL 94+10/8 FLC 2 FAC 5+1/1 Others 9+2
Norwich C (Loaned on 29/1/2010) FL 11+1/1

ROSE Richard Alan
Born: Tonbridge, 8 September 1982
Height: 6'0" **Weight:** 11.9
One of the few players to be retained at Hereford following the previous season's relegation, Richard suffered from his versatility in the early part of the campaign when he was drafted in as a right-back, left-back and centre-back for short stays in the side. It was only towards the end of the season that this popular performer was given an extended run in the side. His displays at centre-back led many to believe that Hereford would have achieved rather more during their disappointing season had he been a regular there.

Danny, who is a former Leeds' trainee signed by Tottenham three years ago, is an attacking left-sided midfielder. In the last year he has progressed from the England under-19s to the under-21 side, scoring his first goal at that level in November against Portugal in a European Championship qualifier. Doncaster-born, he achieved a dream in making his Spurs' debut as a substitute at Doncaster in the 5-1 Carling Cup win. He subsequently had a short loan at Peterborough, but got lost in the hustle and bustle of Championship football despite showing glimpses of what he was capable of. Back at White Hart Lane opportunities were limited, but he made his first start, against Leeds in the FA Cup, and then most spectacularly started against Arsenal. Not only did Spurs beat their rivals, but Danny scored what was potentially the 'Goal of the Season' with a magnificent

Gillingham *(From trainee on 10/4/2001) FL 44+14 FLC 3+1 FAC 1 Others 1*
Bristol Rov (Loaned on 13/12/2002) FL 9
Hereford U (Free on 27/7/2006) FL 122+9/2 FLC 7 FAC 7+3 Others 4+1

ROSE Romone Alexander Aldolphus

Born: Reading, 19 January 1990
Height: 5'9" **Weight:** 11.5
The young Queens Park Rangers' forward signed for Northampton on loan at the start of the season, making one full appearance and one as a substitute before returning to Loftus Road when the new management team took control. He thus joins a small band of Northampton players who have failed to play for 90 minutes for the club. Next stop for Romone was a move to Cheltenham on a month's loan in October. A quick, right-sided player who can operate at both right-back and in midfield, he made only one first team appearance for the Robins, playing on the right-hand side of midfield in a League Two match at Accrington. However, his time at the club coincided with a turbulent period in which manager Martin Allen was replaced by acting boss John Schofield, and with numerous changes to the team taking place at the same time, Romone was allowed to return to Rangers after completing just under a month at the club. Having made his debut two years ago, he managed just one short appearance in 2009-10, when coming off the bench during the final game of the campaign against Newcastle.
Queens Park Rgrs (From trainee on 8/7/2008) FL 0+4 FAC 0+1
Northampton T (Loaned on 6/8/2009) FL 0+1 FLC 1
Cheltenham T (Loaned on 8/10/2009) FL 1

ROSENIOR Liam James

Born: Wandsworth, 9 July 1984
Height: 5'9" **Weight:** 11.8
Club Honours: AMC '03
International Honours: E: U21-7; Yth
Having played just six games for Reading in the right-back position at the beginning of the season, it soon became apparent that the signing of Shaun Cummings from Chelsea made Liam surplus to requirements and he was allowed to join Ipswich on loan, where he stayed for the remainder of the season. There, he quickly established himself as the team's regular right-back, producing sound defensive displays allied with an attacking intent that produced several excellent crosses for the strikers to feed

off. Indeed, it was from one of his teasing right-wing crosses that fellow full-back David Wright headed high into the net for the goal that confirmed the club's first win of the season. His only goal came at Barnsley in October when the 'keeper could only parry Grant Leadbitter's free kick and Liam headed the loose ball into the net. Unfortunately, there was a sting in the tail to his season as he was unable to sustain his level of performance over the whole campaign and rarely featured in the last two months of the season. Was out of contract in the summer.
Bristol C (From trainee on 15/8/2001) FL 2+20/2 FAC 0+1 Others 2+3/1
Fulham (Free on 7/11/2003) PL 76+3 FLC 3+2/1 FAC 8
Torquay U (Loaned on 19/3/2004) FL 9+1
Reading (Signed on 31/8/2007) P/FL 62+2 FLC 1 FAC 2 Others 2
Ipswich T (Loaned on 2/9/2009) FL 26+3/1 FAC 2

ROSICKY Tomas

Born: Prague, Czech Republic, 4 October 1980
Height: 5'10" **Weight:** 10.3
International Honours: Czech Republic: 71; U21-2
After a very long absence with a catalogue of injuries, Tomas made a very welcome return to the Arsenal team as a substitute at Manchester City and scored in the 4-2 defeat. The Czech Republic captain retains a great passing ability and shoots well. He was in talks about his extending his contract, although questions remain over his long-term fitness as his Arsenal career to date has been blighted by injury. He made 24 appearances in the Premier League, scoring three goals, played seven times in the Champions League and once in the Carling Cup.
Arsenal (£6,800,000 from Borussia Dortmund, Germany, ex Sparta Prague, on 25/5/2006) PL 51+18/12 FLC 1+1 FAC 4+1/2 Others 14+4/2

ROTHERY Gavin Marc

Born: Morley, 22 September 1987
Height: 5'9" **Weight:** 10.12
This hard-working central midfielder made two appearances for Carlisle, both in the Johnstone's Paint Trophy. Dogged by injuries, a spell on loan to Barrow followed and he has since been released from Brunton Park.
Leeds U (From trainee on 28/9/2005. Freed on 14/4/2008)
Carlisle U (Free from Harrogate T, ex York C, on 12/2/2009) FL 0+2 FLC 0+2 Others 1+1

ROUSE Domaine

Born: Stretford, 4 July 1989
Height: 5'6" **Weight:** 10.10
With his skill, pace, and outstanding shooting ability Domaine, a powerful striker, was seen as a very talented prospect for Bury. After a fantastic performance at Hereford in August, there was speculation about off-the-field matters and Domaine was released the following month by mutual consent.
Bury (From trainee on 6/11/2007) FL 1+11 FLC 0+1 Others 0+2/1

ROUTLEDGE Wayne Neville Anthony

Born: Sidcup, 7 January 1985
Height: 5'6" **Weight:** 10.7
Club Honours: Ch '10
International Honours: E: U21-12; Yth
Queens Park Rangers' star man in the early months of the season, Wayne really looked to have found his form as part of Jim Magilton's buccaneering side, scoring five times in the opening eight fixtures including a hat-trick against Exeter in the Carling Cup. A lucrative move to Newcastle for both club and player proved too hard for either to resist and Wayne made the switch to St James Park in January. It was soon clear that he would add strength to Newcastle's wide midfield options and his pace and direct running were immediately evident when he made his debut the following day against Crystal Palace and gained an assist towards Nile Ranger's goal. His good close control and acceleration make him a constant threat, and he demonstrated his powerful shooting when opening his goal account with a 30-yard volley in the win over Coventry in February.
Crystal Palace (From trainee on 9/7/2002) P/FL 83+27/10 FLC 5+2 FAC 2+1 Others 3
Tottenham H (£2,000,000 on 7/7/2005) PL 3+2
Portsmouth (Loaned on 30/1/2006) PL 3+10
Fulham (Loaned on 31/8/2006) PL 13+11 FLC 1 FAC 3/1
Aston Villa (£1,250,000 on 30/1/2008) PL 0+2 FLC 0+1 Others 2+3
Cardiff C (Loaned on 20/11/2008) FL 9/2
Queens Park Rgrs (£600,000 on 5/1/2009) FL 43+1/3 FLC 2+1/4 FAC 2
Newcastle U (Signed on 26/1/2010) FL 15+2/3

ROWE Daniel (Danny)

Born: Wythenshawe, 9 March 1992
Height: 6'0" **Weight:** 11.12
This was Danny's first full season as a

professional and, while a regular on the Stockport bench, he had to wait until January to get a game. That was as a substitute for fellow winger Richie Partridge against Brighton and he would replace the same man twice more, against Gillingham and Oldham.
Stockport Co (From juniors on 7/8/2009) FL 0+7

ROWE Thomas (Tommy)
Born: Manchester, 1 May 1989
Height: 5'11" **Weight:** 12.11
Peterborough signed Tommy from Stockport during the close season. A very talented midfield player, he had to contend with a scrap for his preferred position wide on the left with club star George Boyd. Once Boyd went on loan to Nottingham Forest, Tommy made that spot his own and benefited from the extended run. He has good close control and an eye for a defence-splitting pass. His pace takes him round full-backs and he can deliver a telling cross.
Stockport Co (From trainee on 23/3/2007) FL 60+12/13 FLC 1 FAC 2+4 Others 4+2
Peterborough U (Signed on 12/5/2009) FL 26+6/2 FLC 3/1

ROWELL Jonathan (Jonny) Michael
Born: Newcastle, 10 September 1989
Height: 5'7" **Weight:** 11.2
The young midfield player looked to have established himself in Hartlepool's squad at the start of the season. Although he made a number of substitute appearances, he was only to start one first team game, a Johnstone's Paints Trophy match against Grimsby that resulted in an embarrassing home defeat. Almost ever present for the reserves, there was great disappointment that Jonny did not make further progress and he was released at the end of the season.
Hartlepool U (From trainee on 24/8/2008) FL 3+9 Others 1+1

ROWE-TURNER Lathaniel Alanzo
Born: Leicester, 12 November 1989
Height: 6'1" **Weight:** 13.0
A young left-back signed from Leicester just before the January transfer window closed, Lathaniel was quickly thrust into a struggling Torquay team and asked to concentrate on defending solidly rather than overlapping. Stuck to his task admirably despite some initial problems and will be a better player for the experience.
Leicester C (From trainee on 27/10/2007)

Cheltenham T (Loaned on 17/10/2008) FL 1
Torquay U (Signed on 1/2/2010) FL 5+1

ROWLANDS Martin Charles
Born: Hammersmith, 8 February 1979
Height: 5'9" **Weight:** 10.10
Club Honours: Div 3 '99
International Honours: RoI: 5; U21-8
Queens Park Rangers' club captain and now longest-serving player, Martin endured another cruel season that, for the second year running, was ended with a cruciate ligament injury. Having recovered from the one he suffered in 2008, Martin returned to action for the start of this season but managed only seven appearances before he suffered the same fate again. To make matters even worse, the injury occurred while he was on international duty for the Republic of Ireland, having been given a rare chance to prove himself in Giovanni Trapattoni's side.
Brentford (£45,000 from Farnborough T on 6/8/1998) FL 128+21/20 FLC 8+3/1 FAC 7+2 Others 17/2
Queens Park Rgrs (Free on 6/8/2003) FL 179+15/33 FLC 9/4 FAC 6 Others 3

ROWNEY Christopher (Chris)
Born: Ashton-under-Lyne, 14 February 1991
Height: 5'6" **Weight:** 10.1
The young midfield player earned rave reviews while a member of Oldham's youth team. He found it hard to make the step up to first team level and spent all but two games plying his trade in the reserves. Good on the ball, he runs from box to box as well as any player, but was released at the end of the season.
Oldham Ath (From trainee on 2/7/2009) FL 0+1 Others 0+1

ROYCE Simon Ernest
Born: Forest Gate, 9 September 1971
Height: 6'2" **Weight:** 12.8
A vastly experienced goalkeeper, Simon started the season on the Gillingham bench after losing his place in the side to Alan Julian but was restored to the starting line-up after just a handful of games. He clocked up his 100th appearance for the Gills in October and was an ever-present from then until mid-December, when minor injuries incurred in a car accident ended his season prematurely. Was out of contract in the summer.
Southend U (£35,000 from Heybridge Swifts on 15/10/1991) FL 147+2 FLC 9 FAC 5 Others 6
Charlton Ath (Free on 2/7/1998) PL 8
Leicester C (Free on 17/7/2000) PL

16+3 FLC 1 FAC 4
Brighton & Hove A (Loaned on 24/12/2001) FL 6
Queens Park Rgrs (Loaned on 24/8/2002) FL 16 Others 1
Charlton Ath (Free on 4/7/2003) PL 1
Luton T (Loaned on 29/10/2004) FL 2
Queens Park Rgrs (Free on 13/11/2005) FL 63 FLC 1 FAC 3
Gillingham (Free on 19/4/2007) FL 94+1 FLC 3 FAC 6 Others 5

RUDD Declan Thomas
Born: Diss, 16 January 1991
Height: 6'3" **Weight:** 11.11
International Honours: E: Yth
This former Norwich Academy player represented England at under-19 level in the UEFA Championships and extended his Canary contract last summer before being a regular member of the first team squad. His debut came as a first-half substitute at Gillingham when Fraser Forster was shown a red card. He impressed everyone with his calm authority, good communications and obvious goalkeeping ability. In his five starts, City won four and drew one, scoring 19 goals and conceding only three – impressive figures. He has a tremendous future in the game and will surely be in line for under-21 selection in the not too distant future.
Norwich C (From trainee on 24/7/2008) FL 4+3 FAC 1

[RUI MARQUES] MARQUES Rui Manuel
Born: Luanda, Angola, 3 September 1977
Height: 5'11" **Weight:** 12.0
International Honours: Angola: 19
Central defender Rui Marques began as Leeds' longest-serving player, having joined in 2005. He finished on the winning side in all six of his early season appearances in partnership with Paddy Kisnorbo but suffered an Achilles injury on international duty for Angola in September. On his return to fitness, he was down the pecking order at Leeds but despite failing to start a game since the 2-1 win at Colchester at the end of August, he figured in the African Cup of Nations. Returning with an injury he did not feature for Leeds again.
Leeds U (Signed from CS Maritimo, Portugal, ex SSV Ulm 1846, VfB Stuttgart, on 5/8/2005) FL 85+5/4 FLC 4 FAC 3 Others 3
Hull C (Loaned on 23/3/2006) FL 1

RUNDLE Adam
Born: Durham, 8 July 1984
Height: 5'10" **Weight:** 11.2
Rochdale's regular left-winger for the past three seasons started the season in

Alex Russell

his familiar position but lost his starting place when Will Buckley was switched to the left flank. Adam made a goalscoring return against Grimsby when Buckley was injured, but was then loaned to Rotherham when Jason Taylor moved the other way. Arriving at the Don Valley Stadium in November, he was asked to start three of his four appearances on the right flank rather than his more usual left. Substituted in each of his four appearances he then went back after a month and made one further start for Dale before being allowed to join Chesterfield in the January transfer window. Agreeing to a short-term deal, as Chesterfield sought to keep their promotion campaign alive, he operated with commitment on the midfield wings and was often pulled central during in-game tactical changes. Despite proving to be a good crosser and decent with a dead ball at his feet, ultimately, there was not quite enough

in evidence to persuade the club to offer Adam a longer deal.
Darlington *(Trainee) FL 8+9*
Carlisle U *(Free on 31/12/2002) FL 25+19/1 FLC 1 Others 4+1/2 (Freed on 19/8/2004)*
Mansfield T *(Free from Dublin C on 14/1/2005) FL 45+8/9 FLC 1 FAC 3*
Rochdale *(Free on 5/7/2006) FL 95+32/17 FLC 5/1 FAC 5+2 Others 8+1/1*
Rotherham U *(Loaned on 23/11/2009) FL 4*
Chesterfield *(Free on 1/2/2010) FL 12+4*

RUSSELL Alexander (Alex) John
Born: Crosby, 17 March 1973
Height: 5'9" **Weight:** 11.7
Alex was a regular in the Exeter midfield and helped inspire his team-mates with his experience and guile. He also scored with a stupendous free kick on the opening day at Leeds to send the 2,800

travelling City fans wild. Was out of contract at the end of June.
Rochdale *(£4,000 from Burscough on 11/7/1994) FL 83+19/14 FLC 5/1 FAC 1+1 Others 2+3*
Cambridge U *(Free on 4/8/1998) FL 72+9/8 FLC 7+1 FAC 6 Others 3*
Torquay U *(Free on 9/8/2001) FL 152+1/21 FLC 4 FAC 4/1 Others 2*
Bristol C *(Free on 1/7/2005) FL 42+14/6 FLC 1 FAC 4+3 Others 1+2*
Northampton T *(Loaned on 31/8/2007) FL 11+2/1 Others 1*
Cheltenham T *(Free on 11/1/2008) FL 31+5/2 FLC 2/1 FAC 2*
Exeter C *(Free on 27/2/2009) FL 34+2/1 FLC 1 FAC 2*

RUSSELL Darel Francis Roy
Born: Stepney, 22 October 1980
Height: 5'11" **Weight:** 11.9
Club Honours: Div 1 '10
International Honours: E: Yth
Darel enjoyed an excellent season as Norwich earned promotion back to the Championship. Playing mostly as the defensive point of a diamond midfield formation, his tenacious and combative style broke up countless opposition attacks and his greatly improved distribution allowed him to be the starting point for much of his team's forward momentum. An excellent team player, his contribution was much appreciated by his colleagues and the fans. Moved past 250 senior games for the Canaries in this, his second spell at the club and, with his contract expired, many hope he has more to offer at Carrow Road.
Norwich C *(From trainee on 29/11/1997) FL 99+33/7 FLC 8/2 FAC 6+1*
Stoke C *(£125,000 on 8/8/2003) FL 166+5/16 FLC 4+1 FAC 6*
Norwich C *(Signed on 31/7/2007) FL 102+10/11 FLC 4/1 FAC 5+1 Others 2*

RYAN James (Jimmy)
Born: Maghull, 6 September 1988
Height: 5'11" **Weight:** 10.10
Club Honours: FAYC '07
International Honours: RoI: U21-4; Yth
Playing at the heart of the Accrington midfield for most of this his second season, Jimmy has continued to live up to his reputation as a flair player who rarely fails to excite. An attacking player with good shooting ability with either foot, he is a crowd favourite on the terraces. Is also the club's free-kick specialist.
Liverpool *(From trainee on 5/7/2006)*
Shrewsbury T *(Free on 14/8/2007) FL 1+3 FLC 2 Others 1*
Accrington Stanley *(Free on 6/8/2008) FL 77+6/13 FLC 2+1 FAC 7/1 Others 3+1*

S

SABORIO Alvaro Alberto
Born: San Carlos, Costa Rica, 25 March 1982
Height: 6'0" **Weight:** 12.2
International Honours: Costa Rica: 55
Signed on loan from Swiss club FC Sion, the forward netted twice for Costa Rica when they beat Mexico in a World Cup qualifier in September. Unfortunately, he was never able to reproduce his impressive international form for Bristol City and, with personal problems at home, his agreement with both City and FC Sion was cancelled in January.
Bristol C (Loaned from Sion, Switzerland, ex Deportivo Saprissa, on 1/9/2009) FL 11+8/2 FAC 0+2

SADLER Matthew (Mat)
Born: Birmingham, 26 February 1985
Height: 5'11" **Weight:** 11.6
International Honours: E: Yth
Mat joined Stockport on loan from Watford in January as a replacement for Michael Rose, who had moved to Norwich. His appearance in the 2-0 defeat at Southampton was his first senior game in over a year. Largely used at left-back, Mat put in one of his best performances for County in the 1-0 defeat at Bristol Rovers while playing as a centre-half.
Birmingham C (From trainee on 12/4/2002) P/FL 49+2 FLC 6 FAC 3+1
Northampton T (Loaned on 21/11/2003) FL 7 Others 1
Watford (£750,000 + on 25/1/2008) FL 29+1 FLC 2 FAC 1 Others 2
Stockport Co (Loaned on 29/1/2010) FL 20

SAGANOWSKI Marek
Miroslaw
Born: Lodz, Poland, 31 October 1978
Height: 5'10" **Weight:** 12.0
International Honours: Poland: 33
As footballing enigmas go, Marek is a giant. A natural predator, he is a master at running at and through defences and possesses a murderous finish. Then again, since joining Southampton, his lack of consistency has been hard to understand. One might assume that scoring in League One would be relatively easy for an established Polish international, but Marek appeared out of sorts from the off, and was soon restricted to the odd interventions from the bench. In January he departed for Atromitos FC of the Greek Super League on a free transfer.
Southampton (£680,000 from Vitoria

Guimaraes, Portugal, ex LKS Lodz, Feyenoord - loan, SV Hamburg - loan, Wisla Plock, Odra Wodzislaw, Legia Warsaw, on 31/1/2007) FL 42+26/19 FLC 1+1 FAC 1 Others 2+1

SAGNA Bacary
Born: Sens, France, 14 February 1983
Height: 5'11" **Weight:** 11.5
International Honours: France: 17; U21-12
Bacary found his position as Arsenal's first choice right-back under more threat than ever before as Manu Eboue shared the responsibilities. Bacary played when the Gunners needed a more defensive minded full-back and Eboue when they were looking to attack more regularly. In truth, just like his full-back partner Gael Clichy, Bacary suffered a below par season overall and the change in Arsenal's system to a 4-3-3 appeared to have adversely affected him. He did remind Gunners' fans just what he is capable of with a pinpoint cross in the last minute of injury time to set up a vital late winner in the home game against Wolverhampton. He played 34 times in the Premier League and eight times in the Champions League. Bacary was named in the French World Cup squad.
Arsenal (£6,000,000 from Auxerre, France on 18/7/2007) PL 94+5/1 FLC 1+1 FAC 7 Others 23+2

SAHA Louis Laurent
Born: Paris, France, 8 August 1978
Height: 5'11" **Weight:** 11.10
Club Honours: Div 1 '01; FLC '06; PL '07, '08
International Honours: France: 18; U21; Yth (UEFA U-18 '97)
Careful handling by David Moyes enabled the French international to remain largely injury free and he had an excellent season overall, with flashes of real class and quality in the course of

Louis Saha

scoring 15 goals for Everton in all competitions. The forward was especially potent in the first half of the campaign, when highlights included braces at Goodison against Sigma in the Europa League and Blackburn. Although his form dipped slightly thereafter, the former Fulham striker still struck some crucial goals, notably two in a brilliant performance in the win over Chelsea. Possessing all the attributes associated with a great striker, supporters at Goodison hope Louis remains injury free for another productive campaign.
Newcastle U *(Loaned from Metz, France on 8/1/1999)* PL 5+6/1 FAC 1/1
Fulham *(£2,100,000 from Metz, France on 29/6/2000)* P/FL 100+17/53 FLC 3+3/6 FAC 10+1/3 Others 5+4/1
Manchester U *(£12,825,000 on 23/1/2004)* PL 52+34/28 FLC 9/7 FAC 6+4/3 Others 9+10/4
Everton *(Signed on 1/9/2008)* PL 36+21/19 FLC 2 FAC 3+1/2 Others 4+2/2

Sean St Ledger-Hall

ST LEDGER-HALL Sean
Patrick
Born: Birmingham, 28 December 1984
Height: 6'0" **Weight:** 12.0
International Honours: RoI: 12
The 2009-10 season was a strange one for Sean and his final few appearances for Preston seemed to suggest he was feeling the strain. After appearing in seven of the club's first eight games, he was loaned to Middlesbrough in a move that was expected to become permanent at Christmas. Signed on a three-month emergency loan in September by then Boro manager Gareth Southgate, he made his debut on the same day when replacing right-

back Tony McMahon with eight minutes to go in a 3-1 win at Sheffield Wednesday. However his home debut was a nightmare, when the Boro defence shipped five goals in a 5-0 home drubbing by West Bromwich. Despite netting in an early game versus Coventry, Sean never really settled alongside centre-half partner David Wheater and in December, despite an attempt by new boss Gordon Strachan to keep him at the club, he decided not to make the move permanent and returned to Deepdale. Going straight back in the team and looking like he had never been away, he produced some strong performances in the heart of the defence before a number of uncharacteristic errors in late season cost important goals and mystified the Deepdale faithful. An operation planned for the summer might offer some explanation and hopefully Sean will be back on top form this coming term.
Peterborough U *(From trainee on 18/7/2003)* FL 77+2/1 FLC 1 FAC 6 Others 5
Preston NE *(£225,000 on 12/7/2006)* FL 150+4/9 FLC 5 FAC 4 Others 2/1
Middlesbrough *(Loaned on 15/9/2009)* FL 14+1/2

SALGADO Miguel (Michel)
Angel
Born: As Neves, Spain, 22 October 1975
Height: 5'9" **Weight:** 11.11
International Honours: Spain: 53; U21-10; Yth
It was a surprise that Michel elected to finish his career at Blackburn after a glittering period with Real Madrid and a greater one when manager Sam Allardyce insisted he would not be introduced to the Premier League too soon because he needed time to adjust. Early Cup appearances proved little but in a League debut at Everton, he struggled to cope with the pace of the game. Behind the scenes he gained the admiration of players for the manner in which he did not complain about lack of playing time, his determination to train hard and the influence he had on the youngsters. By the start of February, the form of Pascal Chimbonda had dipped so much that Michel was handed the right-back shirt and never looked back. After a slow start, he grew in stature every week and by the time Rovers drew with Manchester United in April he had become a firm favourite. Extremely competitive, he has the ability to keep his position, especially in frantic finales when the defence is stretched. He can

also spot the chance to intercept and has the coolness to play the ball from danger. Despite his age, he is ever willing to join in attacks and has the commendable virtue of chasing back when caught upfield, ensuring that the defence has some time to re-form.
Blackburn Rov *(Free from Real Madrid, Spain, ex Celta Vigo, Salamanca - loan, on 19/8/2009)* PL 16+5 FLC 4/1 FAC 1

SAM Lloyd Ekow
Born: Leeds, 27 September 1984
Height: 5'8" **Weight:** 10.7
International Honours: E: Yth
Lloyd was a fixture on the right wing for Charlton, playing in the majority of games. When on top of his game he is a handful for any defender as he likes to run at them with the ball. He is skilful and quick and can play either on the right or left wing. He is exciting to watch and is a good crosser of the ball. Lloyd possesses a powerful shot and scored four times during the campaign, his best return so far. His goal against Brentford in September was voted the supporters' 'Goal of the Season'. Was out of contract at the end of June.
Charlton Ath *(From trainee on 5/7/2002)* P/FL 95+24/6 FLC 3+2/1 FAC 6+1 Others 3
Leyton Orient *(Loaned on 15/1/2004)* FL 5+5
Sheffield Wed *(Loaned on 24/8/2006)* FL 4
Southend U *(Loaned on 12/3/2007)* FL 0+2

SAMBA Christopher (Chris)
Veijeany
Born: Paris, France, 28 March 1984
Height: 6'5" **Weight:** 13.3
International Honours: Congo: 20
Chris towered over Blackburn, not only literally but metaphorically, being the player who is most crucial to the side Sam Allardyce has constructed. His role would challenge the most gifted of players since he is required to get forward at any opportunity to use his great height in support of the attack. In defence he is capable of becoming a true world-class performer. He is superb in the air and tackles with the precision that comes from great timing. At present there are inconsistencies in his game, although this may be explained because the reliance on him in attack can be detrimental to his defensive duties. His goal tally remains less than it should be because although he is capable of the clinical finish he displayed against Aston Villa, he can also miss the odd chance or two as

the last-minute miss in the home game against Sunderland demonstrated. He did produce one moment of sheer magic at White Hart Lane, when his acrobatic goal-line clearance from Roman Pavlyuchenko illustrated a big man with rare agility and split second precision. It earned the accolade from Harry Redknapp that Chris was the only man in the world who could have made the clearance.
Blackburn Rov *(£396,000 from Hertha Berlin, Germany, ex Rouen, Sedan, on 26/1/2007) PL 111+1/10 FLC 7 FAC 8+1/1 Others 4/1*

SAMMONS Ashley George
Born: Solihull, 10 November 1991
Height: 5'9" **Weight:** 11.3
International Honours: E: Yth
A busy central midfielder, Ashley likes to get on the ball and spray passes around. Made his senior debut for Birmingham at Sunderland in the Carling Cup in September and performed creditably. A local lad who came through the Academy, the more experienced Blues' players meant his chances from then on were few and far between.
Birmingham C *(From trainee on 15/11/2008) FLC 1*

SAMUEL Jlloyd
Born: San Fernando, Trinidad, 29 March 1981
Height: 5'11" **Weight:** 11.4
International Honours: Trinidad & Tobago: 2. E: U21-7; Yth
Last season proved to be frustrating for Jlloyd as he started only 12 League games, the majority coming in the initial stages of the campaign. Having been one of the mainstays of the team during the previous season, the increased competition for places saw Jlloyd spending a considerable amount of time on the bench. He offers a greater attacking threat to the team when playing, especially impressing on the left wing in the FA Cup victory over Sheffield United. However, a red card in the 4-0 home defeat by Chelsea proved to be a low point and Owen Coyle appeared to prefer the defensive qualities of Paul Robinson's game than Jlloyd's natural attacking tendencies.
Aston Villa *(From trainee on 2/2/1999) PL 144+25/2 FLC 15+1/1 FAC 7+1 Others 5+2*
Gillingham *(Loaned on 26/10/2001) FL 7+1*
Bolton W *(Free on 30/6/2007) PL 64+7 FLC 5 FAC 3 Others 4*

SANDELL Andrew (Andy) Charles
Born: Calne, 8 September 1983
Height: 5'11" **Weight:** 11.9
Andy is a left-footed Aldershot midfielder or winger who can also play as a striker and has a very useful long throw. Starting the season at left-back he scored in the opening day win over Darlington. He was a revelation in his new position, twice winning supporters' 'Player of the Month' awards, and scored a 25-yard screamer at Dagenham, following it with a cracking free kick in 4-0 demolition of Barnet. Andy ran Ben Herd close for the 'Player of the Year' title. Hamstring and groin injuries limited him towards the end of the season and he played only in the first leg of the play-off semi-final against Rotherham.
Bristol Rov *(Signed from Bath C on 16/5/2006) FL 20+16/3 FLC 1 FAC 3+1 Others 3+4 (Freed on 31/8/2007)*
Aldershot T *(£10,000 from Salisbury C on 14/11/2008) FL 53+5/7 FLC 1 FAC 3 Others 1*

SANKOFA Osei Omari Kwende
Born: Streatham, 19 March 1985
Height: 6'0" **Weight:** 12.4
International Honours: E: Yth
Osei completed his second campaign at Southend as a utility defender capable

Chris Samba

367

of playing either at right-back or at centre-back. He was unable to dislodge Simon Francis at full-back and Osei also suffered a frustrating time, having been extensively sidelined with a series of niggling Achilles and tendinitis injuries. He was fit again from February but could not force his way in, although it was still a surprise that this handy squad member was released.

Charlton Ath *(From trainee on 8/11/2002) P/FL 12+3 FLC 2+2*
Bristol C *(Loaned on 27/9/2005) FL 8 Others 1*
Brentford *(Loaned on 21/1/2008) FL 10+1*
Southend U *(Free on 3/7/2008) FL 33+6 FLC 0+1 FAC 2 Others 2*

SANSARA Netan Nico

Born: Darlaston, 3 August 1989
Height: 6'0" **Weight:** 11.13
Netan looked all set to start the season as Walsall's left-back until he picked up an injury in late pre-season. It was the end of October before he played and this started a run of 12 consecutive starts. The home defeat by Southampton was an important lesson as he struggled to cope with a far more experienced opponent. Good in the tackle but sometimes passed too easily, his best position might be midfield where his passing would be more valuable. He was released at the end of the season.

Walsall *(Free from Darlaston T on 2/7/2008) FL 24+3 FLC 1 FAC 2*

SANTA CRUZ Roque Luis

Born: Asuncion, Paraguay, 16 August 1981
Height: 6'3" **Weight:** 12.12
International Honours: Paraguay: 69
The Paraguayan international striker endured a frustrating first season following his summer transfer from Blackburn to Manchester City because of a succession of niggling injuries. Sidelined by a knee injury at the start, he did not appear until late September and scored his first City goal in the 5-1 Carling Cup victory over Scunthorpe in October. The highlight of his season was scoring twice in the thrilling 4-3 win over Sunderland in December, but he could not build on this as his knee injury flared again and his mentor Mark Hughes was dismissed after the match. He made intermittent appearances under Roberto Mancini – mostly as substitute – but scored only one more goal, in the 2-1 win at Fulham in March. City have such an embarrassment of forward talent in Emmanuel Adebayor, Craig Bellamy and Carlos Tevez that, even when fit, it is difficult to see how

Roque might win a regular place.
Blackburn Rov *(£3,500,000 from Bayern Munich, Germany, ex Olimpia Asuncion, on 31/7/2007) PL 53+4/23 FLC 3+3/4 FAC 3+1/1 Others 3/1*
Manchester C *(£17,500,000 on 22/6/2009) PL 6+13/3 FLC 1/1 FAC 0+2*

SAPPLETON Reneil (Ricky) St Aubin

Born: Kingston, Jamaica, 8 December 1989
Height: 6'1" **Weight:** 14.5
International Honours: Jamaica: Yth
The big, burly Leicester striker started last season on loan at Macclesfield, with his move made permanent at the end of January. His season was punctuated by a series of injuries and he never made more than five consecutive appearances. Two knee cartilage operations sidelined him from March to the end of the season but Ricky scored seven goals in 26 appearances. Two of his best goals came from 20-yard strikes in the home draws against Barnet and Morecambe and he was joint top scorer with Emile Sinclair.
Leicester C *(From trainee at Queens Park Rgrs on 10/8/2007) FL 0+1*
Bournemouth *(Loaned on 12/8/2008) FL 1+2/1 FLC 0+1*
Macclesfield T *(Free on 28/8/2009) FL 18+6/7 FAC 0+1 Others 1*

SAUNDERS Matthew

Born: Chertsey, 12 September 1989
Height: 5'11" **Weight:** 11.5
The talented midfielder joined Lincoln on loan from Fulham when the January transfer window opened and, with the exception of a brief spell on the sidelines through injury, established himself as a regular first team player at Sincil Bank. Weighing in with some important goals, Matthew was one of the club's most consistent performers during the second half of the season.
Fulham *(From trainee on 4/3/2009)*
Lincoln C *(Loaned on 1/1/2010) FL 17+1/3 FAC 1*

SAUNDERS Neil Christopher

Born: Barking, 7 May 1983
Height: 6'0" **Weight:** 12.6
Attacking midfielder Neil found appearances for Exeter hard to come by this season and made only a handful of contributions, mainly from the bench. However, he did himself justice whenever he had the opportunity. Was out of contract in the summer.
Watford *(From trainee on 1/1/2002. Freed during 2003 close season)*
Exeter C *(Free from Team Bath, ex Barnet, Harlow T, on 12/7/2008) FL 17+6/3 Others 0+1*

SAUNDERS Sam Daniel

Born: Greenwich, 29 August 1983
Height: 5'6" **Weight:** 11.4
Club Honours: FC '07
A skilful right-sided midfield player and free-kick specialist, Sam joined Brentford in the close season. It was a frustrating time for him as, although he kicked off on the right flank, he was often left out as a succession of different players were tried in his position. When he did play, he had no luck in front of the goal, hitting the woodwork on a number of occasions, both from free kicks and in open play. Sam finally scored his first Brentford goal direct from a free kick in the penultimate home game against Yeovil.
Dagenham & Redbridge *(Free from Carshalton Ath, ex Welling U, Hastings T, Ashford, on 10/5/2005) FL 61+1/14 FLC 2 FAC 4 Others 2/1*
Brentford *(Free on 2/7/2009) FL 15+11/1 FLC 1 FAC 1+1 Others 1*

SAVAGE Basir (Bas) Mohammed

Born: Wandsworth, 7 January 1982
Height: 6'3" **Weight:** 13.8
Now established as something of a cult figure at Tranmere, Bas endured a tough time thanks to a re-ruptured Achilles tendon injury sustained in the close season. It kept him sidelined for most of the campaign and meant a long, hard slog back to match fitness, well documented in physio turned manager Les Parry's feared programme notes. A tall, athletic and uncompromising centre-forward, Bas finally had his first start in 11 months at Bristol Rovers, but sadly Tranmere fans did not get to witness his trademark moonwalk goal celebration for one last time before he was released as soon as the campaign ended. Still has a penchant for dying his hair blue.
Reading *(£20,000 from Walton & Hersham on 7/2/2002) FL 6+10 FLC 1 FAC 1 (Freed during 2005 close season)*
Wycombe W *(Loaned on 2/9/2004) FL 2+2 Others 1*
Bury *(Loaned on 11/2/2005) FL 5*
Bristol C *(Free from Walton & Hersham, via trial at Coventry C, on 25/11/2005) FL 15+8/1*
Gillingham *(Free on 28/9/2006) FL 8+6/1 Others 0+1*
Brighton & Hove A *(Free on 2/2/2007) FL 31+5/9 FLC 0+1 FAC 3 Others 1+1/1*
Millwall *(Free on 25/2/2008) FL 9+2/2*
Tranmere Rov *(Free on 15/7/2008) FL 48+7/9 FAC 4 Others 3*

SAVAGE Robert (Robbie) William

Born: Wrexham, 18 October 1974

Height: 6'1" **Weight:** 11.11
Club Honours: FAYC '92; FLC '00
International Honours: W: 39; U21-5;
Yth; Sch
Ignored and isolated by Paul Jewell,
who signed him for Derby, Robbie's
rehabilitation under Nigel Clough was
complete. He took over the captaincy
from Paul Connolly in August and
missed only one match, the FA Cup tie
against Millwall at the Den when he
was suspended. He was a vital presence
in the centre of midfield and appeared
in every Championship match, once as
substitute in deference to his age at a
busy time, to become Derby's first ever-
present since Martin Taylor, now the
club's goalkeeping coach, in 1993-94.
Robbie gave his enthusiasm to Derby
and was often the safest passer in
midfield. Not the least of his
achievements, given his style, was to go
through nine matches without a
caution to avoid a second suspension.
Robbie was the club's 'Player of the
Year' and is working hard on a media
career for the future. It helps that he
never stops talking.
*Manchester U (From trainee on
5/7/1993)*
*Crewe Alex (Free on 22/7/1994) FL
74+3/10 FLC 5 FAC 5 Others 8/1*
*Leicester C (£400,000 on 23/7/1997)
PL 160+12/8 FLC 15+2 FAC 12/1 Others
2+1*
*Birmingham C (£2,500,000 on
30/5/2002) PL 82/11 FLC 1/1 FAC 5*
*Blackburn Rov (£3,100,000 on
9/1/2005) PL 74+2/1 FLC 7 FAC 5+1
Others 10+1/2*
*Derby Co (£1,500,000 on 9/1/2008)
P/FL 81+3/3 FLC 2+2 FAC 7*
*Brighton & Hove A (Loaned on
3/10/2008) FL 6 Others 1*

SAWYER Gary Dean
Born: Bideford, 5 July 1985
Height: 6'0" **Weight:** 10.8
A consistent left-back with Plymouth,
Gary, who also played at centre-back
and left of midfield during the season,
has a cultured left foot and is
dangerous from set plays as evidenced
by popping up for a late winner at
Cardiff on Boxing Day. Out of contract
in the summer, at the end of March
Gary joined fellow Championship club
Bristol City on loan for the remainder of
the season and it was not until the
penultimate game that this defender
made his debut. He could be pleased
with his performance in a 2-1 win
against Derby on 24th April and
keeping his place for the Sky television
game at Blackpool, he again gave an
impressive display in a 1-1 draw as he
looked to earn himself a permanent

deal at Ashton Gate.
*Plymouth Arg (From trainee on
8/7/2004) FL 88+7/5 FLC 3 FAC 7+1*
Bristol C (Loaned on 25/3/2010) FL 2

Gary Sawyer

SAWYER Lee Thomas
Born: Leytonstone, 10 September 1989
Height: 5'9" **Weight:** 11.11
International Honours: E: Yth
Having set Roots Hall alight during a
sparkling loan spell at Southend in
2008-09, winning many admirers with
his industrious and creative work in the
middle of the park and an eye for goal,
Lee returned to the club in September
for a second loan spell. However, unable
to dislodge Alan McCormack and Jean-
Francois Christophe from the centre of
midfield he had to be content with a
handful of impact appearances from the
bench before going back to Stamford
Bridge. Released by Chelsea, the young
central midfielder then signed for Barnet
on a short-term contract in January and
scored on his first home start against
Torquay. Despite showing many signs of
promise in a Barnet shirt, Lee quickly
moved on after failing to agree contract
terms with the club.
Chelsea (From trainee on 6/7/2007)
*Southend U (Loaned on 18/8/2008) FL
11+1/1 Others 1/2*
Coventry C (Loaned on 26/1/2009) FL 1+1
*Wycombe W (Loaned on 19/3/2009) FL
8+1/1*
*Southend U (Loaned on 14/7/2009) FL
0+6 FLC 0+2 Others 1*
Barnet (Free on 14/1/2010) FL 4+3/1

SCANNELL Damian
Born: Croydon, 28 April 1985
Height: 5'10" **Weight:** 11.7
Brother of Crystal Palace player Sean,
Damian is in his third campaign at

Southend and has yet to command a
regular place although his powerful
running and attacking flair provide
useful contributions from the bench. A
natural winger, his forte is getting to
the by-line and delivering telling
crosses. His time at Roots Hall has been
blighted by niggling injuries and an
extended run during February and
March that produced his finest form to
date was sadly ended by an ankle injury
that prematurely finished his season. He
was out of contract at the end of the
season.
*Southend U (£5,000 from Eastleigh, ex
Fisher Ath, on 31/12/2007) FL 21+32/2
FLC 1 FAC 1+2 Others 0+1*
*Brentford (Loaned on 27/11/2008) FL
1+1*

SCANNELL Sean
Born: Croydon, 19 September 1990
Height: 5'9" **Weight:** 11.7
International Honours: RoI: U21-6;
Yth
Largely out of the starting side and used
as a substitute under Neil Warnock, the
Republic of Ireland wide midfield player
or striker came into his own for Crystal
Palace later in the season under
replacement Paul Hart. Sean was used
in his preferred role as a striker or as a
support man to Alan Lee up front,
dropping just off him in a wide role and
often filling the role vacated by Victor
Moses when he left in February. Sean's
brother Damien plays for Southend.
*Crystal Palace (From trainee on
6/2/2008) FL 37+37/6 FLC 0+3 FAC
2+1/1 Others 1*

SCHARNER Paul Josef
Herbert
Born: Scheibbs, Austria, 11 March
1980
Height: 6'3" **Weight:** 12.13
International Honours: Austria: 30;
U21-7; Yth
One of the longest-serving players at
Wigan, there is a maverick streak to
Paul and not just in his occasional
choice of hair colour. He started the
season in the heart of the back four
before moving at the point of a
midfield five, playing just behind the
lone striker. A good passer of the ball
and effective in the air in both penalty
boxes, he was again key to Wigan's
most effective displays as they
maintained their Premier League status
for a sixth season. Quick, tough
tackling and strong in the air, he
produced some solid and determined
performances in the first half of the
season. Paul scored four League goals
and was on target as the club
registered their first League victory over

one of the top four sides in five seasons with a last-minute goal against Chelsea. The holder of the club record for Premier League appearances, he played his 150th game against Manchester City in March. Out of contract at the end of the season, he rejected the offer of new terms. **Wigan Ath** *(£2,000,000 from SK Brann Bergen, Norway on 6/1/2006) PL 130+15/14 FLC 5+1/2 FAC 5/1*

SCHMEICHEL Kasper Peter
Born: Copenhagen, Denmark, 5 November 1986
Height: 6'0" **Weight:** 12.0
Club Honours: Div 2 '10
International Honours: Denmark: U21-17; Yth
Signed by Notts County from Coventry in the summer as the first part of the doomed Middle Eastern consortium package, Kasper put all external issues

aside and proved himself a top goalkeeper and a model professional in every respect. Twenty-four clean sheets in the League were his greatest testament and he was soon adored by the fans and respected by all at the club. Selected for the PFA League Two 'Team of the Year' and a recipient of two 'Player of the Month' awards, he was reported to be joining Leeds in the summer.
Manchester C *(From trainee on 9/11/2004) PL 7+1 FLC 1 Others 1*
Darlington *(Loaned on 13/1/2006) FL 4*
Bury *(Loaned on 23/2/2006) FL 15*
Bury *(Loaned on 24/8/2006) FL 8*
Bury *(Loaned on 21/10/2006) FL 6*
Falkirk *(Loaned on 11/1/2007) SL 15 SLC 1 SC 1*
Cardiff C *(Loaned on 26/10/2007) FL 14*
Coventry C *(Loaned on 14/3/2008) FL 9*
Notts Co *(Signed on 14/8/2009) FL 43 FAC 5 Others 1*

Morgan Schneiderlin

SCHNEIDERLIN Morgan
Born: Obernai, France, 8 November 1989
Height: 5'11" **Weight:** 11.11
Club Honours: AMC '10
International Honours: France: Yth
Morgan has been representing France perennially from under-16 level, and was called up for their under-20 squad for the 2010 Toulon Tournament. Something of an achievement for a League One player, especially as the Fédération Française de Football, Morgan's agent and Morgan himself all expressed reservations about his remaining with Southampton after relegation. Nevertheless, Morgan's attitude has been as admirable as his midfield alliance with Dean Hammond has proved formidable. He has

Paul Scharner

Paul Scholes

SCHOLES Paul

Born: Salford, 16 November 1974
Height: 5'7" **Weight:** 11.10
Club Honours: PL '96, '97, '99, '00, '01, '03, '07, '08, '09; FAC '96, '99, '04; CS '96, '97, '03; UEFACL '08; FLC '09, '10
International Honours: E: 66; Yth (UEFA-U18 '93)

Veteran Manchester United central midfield dynamo whose imaginative distribution makes him the fulcrum of the team, Paul started his 15th Premier League season eager to prove that there was still plenty on offer. Although more a scorer of great goals rather than a great scorer, he notched the winner in the 77th minute away to Beşiktaş, which gave the Reds a winning start to their European campaign. In November, he hit his second goal, again in the Champions League, in the 3-3 draw with CSKA Moscow. His first Premier League goal came in December, in the 4-0 win at West Ham. It was his 99th and another landmark was his first goal in the Carling Cup for seven years in a 3-1 win in the Manchester derby. He hit the opener in United's semi-final, second leg against City, with the Reds winning the tie 4-3 on aggregate. In February, he scored another Champions League goal against AC Milan in a 3–2 win, both United's first goal and first victory in the San Siro. It also made Paul the first ever player to score against Inter and Milan there in the Champions League. Talking of landmarks, Paul became the 19th player in Premier League football to score 100 goals in a 1-0 win against Wolverhampton at Molineux in March. He is a legend already and will be at Old Trafford for another season.
Manchester U (From trainee on 29/1/1993) PL 366+78/101 FLC 14+7/9 FAC 28+13/13 Others 121+16/26

SCHUMACHER Steven (Steve) Thomas

Born: Liverpool, 30 April 1984
Height: 5'10" **Weight:** 11.0
International Honours: E: Yth

Steve has been consistently unlucky with injuries in his three seasons with Crewe. The midfield player again had to miss a number of games through injury but, when fit, was an integral part of the team. He has a steadying influence on the young players around him and is a willing last-ditch tackler. Was out of contract in the summer.
Everton (From trainee on 12/5/2001)
Carlisle U (Loaned on 31/10/2003) FL 4 FAC 1 Others 1/1
Bradford C (Free on 6/8/2004) FL 110+7/13 FLC 3/1 FAC 7/1 Others 2+1

continued to part opponents from the ball with surgical precision and distribute with sagacity, while endeavouring to become more robust, without losing that certain je ne sais quoi.
Southampton (£1,200,000 from RC Strasbourg, France on 27/6/2008) FL 58+9/1 FLC 3+1 FAC 4+1 Others 4

SCHOFIELD Daniel (Danny) James

Born: Doncaster, 10 April 1980
Height: 5'10" **Weight:** 11.3

Danny's season at Yeovil ended in August when he joined Millwall on a two-year deal. He had played five times, scoring once against Leyton Orient, and rather aptly made his last appearance against his boyhood side Huddersfield at the Galpharm Stadium. Having joined the London side to add experience to the left side of their midfield, where his fine ball control and crossing ability was a revelation, he was quickly up to speed when producing impressive and match-winning displays while exhibiting a controlling influence on those around him. He weighed in with seven important League goals, the most noteworthy being the last-minute equaliser at Charlton. Unfortunately, injury meant he missed the important penultimate game against Tranmere.
Huddersfield T (£2,000 from Brodsworth MW on 8/2/1999) FL 205+43/39 FLC 9+1 FAC 13+2/1 Others 16+1/6
Yeovil T (Free on 3/7/2008) FL 38+5/5 FLC 2 FAC 2
Millwall (Loaned on 1/9/2009) FL 28+8/7 FAC 2+2/2 Others 2

Crewe Alex (Signed on 29/5/2007) FL 59+14/7 FLC 1+2 FAC 0+1 Others 4/1

SCHWARZER Mark

Born: Sydney, Australia, 6 October 1972
Height: 6'5" **Weight:** 13.6
Club Honours: FLC '04
International Honours: Australia: 74; Yth
The Australian international goalkeeper made the most appearances for Fulham, missing only three games through injury in September. In good form throughout, he has a calming influence on those in front of him by dominating his penalty box and regularly exercising good judgement about whether to come for the ball or leave a clearance to those in front of him. Mark displays quick reactions, often managing to reach shots that appear to have beaten him. Again among the top Premier League goalkeepers, with 12 clean sheets – fewer than in the previous campaign - his outstanding displays earned vital points at Bolton and Liverpool among others. A vital penalty save in the home Europa League game against AS Roma was to prove significant in the outcome of the group stage. Once again Mark continued to be first choice for Australia, helping them qualify for a second successive World Cup and in their 23 for the finals.
Bradford C (£350,000 from Kaiserslautern, Germany, ex Blacktown, Marconi, Dynamo Dresden, on 22/11/1996) FL 13 FAC 3
Middlesbrough (£1,500,000 on 26/2/1997) P/FL 367 FLC 26 FAC 32 Others 21
Fulham (Free on 2/7/2008) PL 75 FLC 1 FAC 10 Others 18

SCIMECA Riccardo (Riccy)

Born: Leamington Spa, 13 June 1975
Height: 6'1" **Weight:** 12.9
Club Honours: FLC '96
International Honours: E: B-1; U21-9
Cardiff's central midfielder was forced to retire during the season, having suffered from recurring groin injuries. He had a series of operations and made a number of comebacks, but kept breaking down. Making only six appearances over the season, Riccy's final match was in a 2-0 win at his former club West Bromwich in December. He went off at half-time and did not play again. He remained close to the squad and was with Cardiff at the play-off final against Blackpool. Riccy has not decided on what he will do now his playing career is over.
Aston Villa (From trainee on 7/7/1993)

PL 50+23/2 FLC 4+3 FAC 9+1 Others 5+2
Nottingham F (£3,000,000 on 23/7/1999) FL 147+4/7 FLC 8/1 FAC 5 Others 2
Leicester C (Free on 5/7/2003) PL 28+1/1 FLC 1 FAC 1
West Bromwich A (£100,000 on 24/5/2004) PL 29+6 FLC 2+1 FAC 2
Cardiff C (Free on 13/1/2006) FL 60+10/6 FLC 2+1 FAC 2+2

SCOTLAND Jason Kelvin

Born: Morvant, Trinidad, 18 February 1979
Height: 5'9" **Weight:** 11.9
Club Honours: Div 1 '08
International Honours: Tinidad & Tobago: 41
One of two players to join Roberto Martinez at Wigan from his previous club Swansea, striker Jason signed a three-year deal. Strong and pacy, he is a difficult front runner to shake off; Jason possesses a terrific shot with either foot. Made his Premier League debut as a late substitute in the opening match and his first start came in the win over Chelsea, Wigan's first victory over a top four side in 34 attempts. Playing as a lone striker, Jason is undoubtedly very talented and a proven scorer but things just never quite clicked at the DW Stadium as a first goal in Wigan colours continued to elude him. The arrival of Marcelo Moreno was a hammer blow to his chance of keeping a starting place. His only goal arrived at Fulham in April and Jason will be hoping for a better campaign ahead after a season adjusting to top-level football. Away from football, Jason fronts his own four-piece reggae band 'The Jiggs' alongside fellow players Titus Bramble and Emilie Heskey.
Dundee U (Signed from Defence Force, Trinidad & Tobago, ex San Juan Jabloteh, on 16/7/2003) SL 21+29/8 SLC 3+2/1 SC 2+3
St Johnstone (Signed on 27/8/2005) SL 65+1/33 SLC 4/4 SC 6/2 Others 5
Swansea C (Signed on 2/8/2007) FL 82+8/45 FLC 2+3/1 FAC 6+1/5 Others 1+2/2
Wigan Ath (£2,000,000 on 18/7/2009) PL 14+18/1 FLC 1 FAC 3/1

SCOTT Joshua (Josh) Daniel

Born: Camden, 10 May 1985
Height: 6'1" **Weight:** 12.0
Josh made his debut for Dagenham as a substitute at Crewe on the opening day of the season, having joined in the summer from Hayes & Yeading. A number of injuries meant he was in and out of the side and could not really forge the partnership with Paul Benson

that he would have liked. A beefy forward who is hard to shake off the ball, he scored four goals in the play-off semi-final first leg victory over Morecambe and ended his first League season's scoring with double figures.
Dagenham & Redbridge (Free from Hayes & Yeading U on 2/7/2009) FL 36+4/10 FLC 0+1/1 FAC 1 Others 3+1/5

SCOTT Paul

Born: Wakefield, 5 November 1979
Height: 5'11" **Weight:** 12.8
The right-back and sometimes captain once again proved solid and reliable in the Bury defence. Intimidating and ruthless, Paul is an excellent tackler, taking the ball cleanly, and his driven attitude ensures that he is efficient in regaining possession. After struggling to regain his place in the side following an injury early on in the season, Paul re-established himself as the first choice at right-back and battled it out for the captaincy with midfielder Stephen Dawson. Was out of contract at the end of June.
Huddersfield T (From trainee on 3/7/1998) FL 18+14/2 FLC 1+1 FAC 1 Others 1+1
Bury (Free on 20/8/2004) FL 204+9/13 FLC 7 FAC 11+2/2 Others 7+1/1

SCOWCROFT James Benjamin

Born: Bury St Edmunds, 15 November 1975
Height: 6'1" **Weight:** 12.2
International Honours: E: U21-5
James joined Leyton Orient on a free transfer from Crystal Palace part-way through the pre-season training and took a while to gain full match fitness. He showed why he has played at a higher level with some nice touches and headers but the striker was unlucky not to score during the season. James was released at the end of his contract in the summer.
Ipswich T (From trainee on 1/7/1994) P/FL 163+39/47 FLC 21+4/7 FAC 9+1 Others 7+3/1
Leicester C (£3,000,000 on 31/7/2001) P/FL 127+6/24 FLC 6+1/1 FAC 7/3
Ipswich T (Loaned on 15/2/2005) FL 3+6
Coventry C (Free on 11/7/2005) FL 37+4/3 FLC 0+1 FAC 3
Crystal Palace (£500,000 on 27/7/2006) FL 66+17/14 FAC 2 Others 0+1
Leyton Orient (Free on 21/7/2009) FL 13+13 FLC 1 FAC 1 Others 1+1

SEABORNE Daniel (Danny) Anthony

Born: Barnstaple, 5 March 1987

Height: 6'0" **Weight:** 11.10
Centre-half Danny was again a virtual ever-present in the heart of the Exeter defence when producing a number of outstanding performances in 2009-10 before a big money move to League One rivals Southampton in the January transfer window. His ability to read a game and deal with dangerous balls into the box with aplomb had impressed the Saints, who did not hang around and allow others to come in for him. Combining physical presence with admirable anticipation, it will be interesting to see how much better Danny can get.
Exeter C (From trainee on 6/7/2005) FL 48+4/1 FLC 2 FAC 3 Others 2
Southampton (Signed on 13/1/2010) FL 11+5

SEARLE Stuart Andrew
Born: Wimbledon, 27 February 1979
Height: 6'3" **Weight:** 12.4
Stuart joined MK Dons as back-up to regular starting goalkeeper Willy Gueret, and played that role admirably until eventually getting his chance in the Easter Monday game at Bristol Rovers. Making his League debut at the age of 31, a good early tip-over settled any nerves, and though ending up on the losing side it was only a heavily deflected shot that beat him on the day. After returning to the bench, he started the final two games of the season, again through injury, and showed commendable handling and kicking skills in addition to dealing well with any shots that came his way.
Chelsea (Signed from Basingstoke T, ex Aldershot T, Carshalton Ath, on 13/7/2007)
Watford (Free on 23/1/2009)
MK Dons (Free on 17/7/2009) FL 3

SEARS Frederick (Freddie)
David
Born: Hornchurch, 27 November 1989
Height: 5'8" **Weight:** 10.1
International Honours: E: U21-3; Yth
It was another frustrating season for the young West Ham striker. Having joined Crystal Palace on loan for the entire season as the campaign started, he was recalled to his parent club in January when a series of injuries struck the Hammers. Prior to going back to Upton Park, he had scored an infamous goal that was not, at Bristol City, the ball clearly crossing the line but missed by all the officials present. Freddie was then snapped up on another loan by Coventry, who had just sold Leon Best in the January transfer window. Signed until the end of the season, most of his opportunities were from the bench and

playing in a side that was struggling for confidence the lack of goal chances did not help him. Freddie ended the season back at West Ham, having picked up an ankle injury in training.
West Ham U (From trainee on 11/7/2007) PL 5+20/1 FLC 2 FAC 1+3
Crystal Palace (Loaned on 20/6/2009) FL 11+7 FLC 1
Coventry C (Loaned on 12/2/2010) FL 3+7

SEDGWICK Christopher (Chris) Edward
Born: Sheffield, 28 April 1980
Height: 5'11" **Weight:** 10.10
Chris looked to be on his way to Barnsley in January after a successful five-year career at Preston but when this fell through he was soon back in the side, before making way for Danny Mayor in the final few games. Chris continued to demonstrate his willingness to cover every blade of grass from his right-wing berth and despite a lack of pace and a tendency to delay crosses at times, Chris remained a great favourite of the Deepdale crowd and is both a model professional and a fine example to younger players. His future seems to lay elsewhere, but with over 250 appearances for North End and more than 500 in all, he will be an asset to whichever club captures him in the coming season.
Rotherham U (From trainee on 16/8/1997) FL 195+48/17 FLC 10+2/3 FAC 8+5 Others 2+2/1
Preston NE (£300,000 on 23/11/2004) FL 207+22/12 FLC 5+1 FAC 13/2 Others 5+1

SEIP Marcel
Born: Winschoten, Holland, 5 April 1982
Height: 6'0" **Weight:** 13.3
Marcel again started the season as a first choice centre-back for Plymouth and was an ever-present for the first six games of the campaign, but after a 1-3 defeat at home to Sheffield Wednesday in August he was placed on the transfer list. The Dutchman then signed for Blackpool on a month's loan and to the Argyle fans' amazement he was given permission to play against his parent club. Rubbing salt into the wound, he actually scored the opening goal in a 2-0 victory over the Pilgrims. His loan was extended for a further two months and when that expired in January he was loaned out to Sheffield United for the remainder of the season.
Marcel began well, showing good anticipation and distribution, but after two starts he suffered a hamstring injury and when fit again he was

competing with fellow loanees Kyle Bartley and Nyron Nosworthy. From thereon he spent much of the time on the bench, making just four more appearances.
Plymouth Arg (Free from SC Heerenveen, Holland, ex BV Veendam, on 31/8/2006) FL 114+3/6 FLC 4 FAC 7
Blackpool (Loaned on 29/9/2009) FL 7/2
Sheffield U (Loaned on 30/12/2009) FL 5+1 FAC 1+1

SEMEDO Jose Victor Moreira
Born: Setubal, Portugal, 11 January 1985
Height: 6'0" **Weight:** 12.8
International Honours: Portugal: U21-5
Jose had a great season in Charlton's central midfield, building up a good partnership with Therry Racon. A versatile player, Jose can play at right-back, central defence or midfield but was used mainly in a defensive midfield role, in both 4-5-1 and 4-4-2 systems, where his physical presence was seen to best effect. He reads the game well, is comfortable on the ball and a strong tackler. Jose missed a few games early season with a pelvic injury but otherwise was a fixture in the side and scored his first goal for the club at Tranmere after a mazy run from the half-way line.
Charlton Ath (Free from Sporting Lisbon, Portugal, ex Casa Pia, Fereinse, Cagliari - all loan spells from Sporting Lisbon, on 9/8/2007) FL 75+18/1 FLC 3+1 FAC 2 Others 3

SENDEROS Philippe Sylvain
Born: Geneva, Switzerland, 14 February 1985
Height: 6'1" **Weight:** 13.10
Club Honours: FAC '05
International Honours: Switzerland: 39; U21; Yth
The Swiss international central defender endured another frustrating campaign at Arsenal as Thomas Vermaelen's arrival pushed him further down the pecking order. Although Philippe played twice in the Carling Cup, he struggled to make an impact and was loaned to Everton for six months in the January transfer window. The Toffees were in the midst of an injury crisis, but after making his debut at Wigan in January he made just two further appearances until being sidelined following a hip injury sustained at Sporting Lisbon. When fit again, Phil Jagielka's return from long-term injury effectively ended his chance of further first team appearances. Was out of contract at the end of June.
Arsenal (£2,500,000 from Servette,

Switzerland on 18/7/2003) PL 54+10/4
FLC 18 FAC 14+1 Others 19+1
Everton (Loaned on 26/1/2010) PL 1+1
Others 1

SEOL Ki-Hyeon
Born: Seoul, South Korea, 8 January
1979
Height: 6'0" **Weight:** 11.7
International Honours: South Korea:
83; U23-21
An impressive start to the season
brought a well-taken goal in Fulham's
opening Europa League game against
FK Vetra but once again the South
Korean found himself on the fringe of
the first team squad, with his only full
appearance coming in the Carling Cup
tie at Manchester City. It was also at
Eastlands a month later that he made
his final brief substitute appearance for
the club, after which he made
occasional reserve team appearances
before his Fulham contract was
cancelled by mutual consent in January.
He signed for South Korean side Pohang
Steelers. Despite a lack of opportunities,
he initially continued to represent South
Korea and featured in a Craven Cottage
friendly against Serbia in November
although he missed the 2010 World
Cup after sustaining a knee injury.
Wolverhampton W (Signed from
Anderlecht, Belgium on 1/9/2004) FL
50+19/8 FLC 3/1 FAC 4/1
Reading (£1,000,000 + on 12/7/2006)
PL 24+6/4 FAC 4
Fulham (Signed on 31/8/2007) PL
6+12/1 FLC 4 FAC 0+2 Others 0+2/1

SERCOMBE Liam Michael
Born: Exeter, 25 April 1990
Height: 5'10" **Weight:** 10.10
A former trainee, Liam forced his way
into the Exeter team in the second half of
the season. Confident on the ball, his
midfield partnership with James Dunne
and Ryan Harley coincided with City's one
defeat in their last 13 games. Only 20, he
is likely to play a more prominent role
next season. Liam has racked up almost
50 League appearances for City and
scored once last season, at Wycombe.
Exeter C (From trainee on 25/3/2008)
FL 41+16/3 FLC 1 FAC 0+1 Others 1

SERRAN Albert
Born: Barcelona, Spain, 17 July 1984
Height: 6'0" **Weight:** 12.10
Albert was one of the unluckiest players
on the Swansea playing staff. Shortly
after the start of the season, he
suffered an ankle ligament injury at the
training ground and this kept him out
of action until late October. Then, after
replacing the injured Angel Rangel
against Crystal Palace, he was

unfortunate to receive a red card for
what was deemed to be violent
conduct. Swansea appealed and the
decision was overturned at a
disciplinary hearing. In January he
suffered a hamstring injury which once
more kept him out of the squad before
returning to first team action during the
latter stages of the season.
Swansea C (£80,000 from Espanyol,
Spain, ex Cartagena - loan, on
7/8/2008) FL 13+6 FLC 3 FAC 3

SEVERIN Scott Derek
Born: Stirling, 15 February 1979
Height: 5'11" **Weight:** 12.6
International Honours: S: 15; U21-10
Scott, the former Aberdeen captain and
Scottish international, joined Watford on
a free transfer during the summer. A
versatile midfield player who can operate
in a holding role or as the playmaker,
Scott brought valuable experience to the
youthful Watford squad. He suffered a
groin injury in September and struggled
to regain his place once he had
recovered. In January he returned to
Scotland, on loan to Kilmarnock for the
remainder of the season.
Heart of Midlothian (Signed from
Musselburgh Ath on 22/5/1997) SL
135+15/13 SLC 8+1/1 SC 3+4 Others
5+2/1
Aberdeen (Free on 24/6/2004) SL
163+3/12 SLC 8 SC 13 Others 7
Watford (Free on 21/7/2009) FL 4+5
FLC 1/1 FAC 1
Kilmarnock (Loaned on 1/2/2010) SL
13+1 SC 2

SHACKELL Jason Philip
Born: Stevenage, 27 August 1983
Height: 5'11" **Weight:** 11.9
Club Honours: Ch '09
Jason, a centre-back, signed on loan
with Doncaster in the early part of
2009-10 because of injuries in that
department and did so well that the
deal was extended to cover the full
season. However, in late January he
suffered a groin injury in the FA Cup tie
at Derby. Three weeks later he returned
to the starting line-up, but lasted just 15
minutes. An operation was necessary
and he missed the rest of the campaign.
Norwich C (From trainee on 28/1/2003)
P/FL 112+7/3 FLC 8 FAC 4
Wolverhampton W (£500,000 on
1/9/2008) FL 3+9 FAC 1
Norwich C (Loaned on 10/2/2009) FL
14
Doncaster Rov (Loaned on 14/8/2009)
FL 20+1/1 FAC 2

SHAHIN Jammal
Born: Grimsby, 19 December 1988
Height: 5'11" **Weight:** 12.0

On target for Grimsby in their 2006
Midlands Floodlit Youth Cup final
triumph over Walsall, Jammal was
playing for Armthorpe Welfare before a
successful return trial at Blundell Park.
Handed a debut in manager Mike
Newell's last game in charge against
Rochdale, the two-footed left-winger
showed good control and pace against
his marker. Jammal's brief senior run,
however, was ended by the arrival of
loan players, and he was not called
upon thereafter.
Grimsby T (Free from A & G Auto
Repairs, ex trainee at Grimsby T,
Armthorpe Welfare, Lincoln
International FC, on 12/10/2009) FL 4+1
FAC 1 Others 1

SHARP William (Billy) Louis
Born: Sheffield, 5 February 1986
Height: 5'8" **Weight:** 12.2
Club Honours: Div 1 '07
Although scoring in his one Sheffield
United appearance, in the Carling Cup,
Billy's chances seemed limited at Bramall
Lane and he moved on a season-long
loan to Doncaster. For whatever reason,
Billy was apparently down the list of
strikers at United and even when he
made the team he was usually played
wide on the right. His record at
Scunthorpe said he could score goals so
he was brought to the Keepmoat
Stadium, signing the requisite forms just
15 minutes before the deadline. It was
a good decision and Billy proved the
doubters wrong by scoring 15 League
goals before succumbing to an injury in
late March that curtailed his season. His
worth to the team was recognised by
his team-mates when they voted him
the 'Players' Player of the Season'.
Sheffield U (From trainee on 7/7/2004)
FL 0+2
Rushden & Diamonds (Loaned on
21/1/2005) FL 16/9
Scunthorpe U (£100,000 on
18/8/2005) FL 80+2/53 FLC 4/1 FAC 7/1
Others 1+1/1
Sheffield U (£2,000,000 on 7/8/2007)
FL 38+13/8 FLC 4+1/3 FAC 6+2/2
Doncaster Rov (Loaned on 1/9/2009)
FL 32+1/15 FAC 2

SHARPS Ian William
Born: Warrington, 23 October 1980
Height: 6'4" **Weight:** 13.8
The Rotherham captain enjoyed another
good season in central defence. His
partnership with Nick Fenton was once
again a key factor in the club's success
in reaching the League Two play-off
final, not least when they were reunited
late in the season after being split up
for a few games. Ian missed only three
games, was consistent, determined and

his reading of situations was excellent as befits someone with the experience of close on 400 career games behind him. The real surprise was that he did not score from a set piece all season. He went close often enough.
Tranmere Rov (From trainee on 5/7/1999) FL 163+7/6 FLC 7/1 FAC 7 Others 9
Rotherham U (Free on 3/8/2006) FL 160/8 FLC 8/1 FAC 7+1 Others 12/2

Ian Sharps

SHARRY Luke Irvin
Born: Leeds, 9 March 1990
Height: 5'10" **Weight:** 12.12
Bradford gave central midfielder Luke his chance to shine in the Johnstone's Paint Trophy. Luke made a bright appearance from the bench in a thrilling win over Notts County and started his first game in the next round at home to Port Vale, although he was substituted at half-time. Was out of contract at the end of June.
Bradford C (From trainee on 10/7/2008) FL 0+2 Others 1+1

SHAW Jonathan (Jon)
Steven
Born: Sheffield, 10 November 1983
Height: 6'1" **Weight:** 12.9
International Honours: E: SP-6
Jon came off the bench in Rochdale's first two games of the season but following the signing of Chris O'Grady the tall striker was soon loaned to Barrow and then Gateshead. His contract was cancelled by mutual consent in January so that he could join Blue Square Premier Mansfield after only a handful of appearances in 18 months at Spotland.
Sheffield Wed (From trainee on

2/7/2003) FL 8+10/2 FLC 0+1 FAC 0+2 Others 1+2 (Freed on 8/11/2004)
York C (Loaned on 14/11/2003) FL 5+3
Rochdale (£60,000 from Halifax T, ex Burton A, on 8/7/2008) FL 5+2/1 FLC 1+1 FAC 1+2 Others 0+1

SHAWCROSS Ryan James
Born: Buckley, 4 October 1987
Height: 6'0" **Weight:** 12.0
International Honours: E: U21-2
It was a season of contrasting fortunes for one of the most outstanding young talents in the English game at the moment. On the plus front, Ryan's unstintingly good form at the heart of the Stoke defence brought him to the attention not only of England manager Fabio Capello but also several top clubs, with fees of £15-million and more

being mentioned. However, the most documented incident of his season was the tackle that left Arsenal's Aaron Ramsey with a broken leg. Just about every neutral observer agreed that it was an accident and Ryan's own reaction showed how genuinely distraught he was by it. Some have tried to blame him for what happened, but far from being an aggressive player Ryan is instead wholehearted and has no malice in his game. Stoke fans hope that he stays at the heart of the defence for many seasons to come and, with any luck, he will get the England cap he deserves in the not too distant future.
Manchester U (From trainee on 6/7/2006) FLC 0+2
Stoke C (£1,000,000 + on 9/8/2007) P/FL 94+5/12 FLC 4/1 FAC 6/1

Ryan Shawcross

SHEARER Scott
Born: Glasgow, 15 February 1981
Height: 6'3" **Weight:** 14.8
International Honours: S: B-1
It was a difficult year for Wycombe's first choice goalkeeper, with a constantly changing defence in front of him and a higher standard of strikers to deal with. Scott still managed to put in some top-class performances, a penalty save against Oldham in December and, most notably, the 1-0 home defeat to Norwich in January when he made save after brilliant save until the winner 12 minutes from time. However, there were probably a few too many goals conceded as a result of indecision on Scott's part. As a result Wycombe manager Gary Waddock obtained the services of Tom Heaton on loan and Scott had made his last appearance in February, being released in May.
Albion Rov (Signed from Tower Hearts on 6/7/2000) SL 47+2/1 SLC 1 SC 2 Others 1
Coventry C (Signed on 7/7/2003) FL 37+1 FLC 3
Rushden & Diamonds (Loaned on 18/2/2005) FL 3
Rushden & Diamonds (Loaned on 10/3/2005) FL 10
Bristol Rov (Free on 29/7/2005) FL 47 FLC 1 FAC 3 Others 2
Shrewsbury T (Loaned on 25/10/2006) FL 20 FAC 2 Others 2
Wycombe W (Free on 3/7/2007) FL 62+1 FLC 1 FAC 4

SHEEHAN Alan Michael Anthony
Born: Athlone, 14 September 1986
Height: 5'10" **Weight:** 11.2
International Honours: RoI: U21-5; Yth
Allowed to join Oldham on loan from Leeds, Alan immediately became a fans' favourite with his all-round game plan. Fast and strong, with a great football brain, he lit the team up in his nine appearances and was sorely missed when he returned to Elland Road. Unable to settle, Alan next moved to promotion chasing Swindon on loan in December. A left-sided full-back, who is also able to play on the right, he put in some solid defensive performances and was also good going forward with a range of passes and accurate dead-ball deliveries. Sidelined for a month with a hamstring tear sustained in the home victory over Gillingham during January, Alan recovered sufficiently to resume a regular spot before the end of the season. Unfortunately, he was not fully fit when appearing in the Wembley play-off final.
Leicester C (From trainee on 24/9/2004) FL 20+3/1 FLC 4+1/1 FAC 1

Mansfield T (Loaned on 8/9/2006) FL 9+1 Others 1
Leeds U (Free on 31/1/2008) FL 21/2 FLC 1 FAC 1 Others 0+1
Crewe Alex (Loaned on 23/3/2009) FL 3
Oldham Ath (Loaned on 1/9/2009) FL 8/1 Others 1
Swindon T (Loaned on 26/11/2009) FL 22/1 FAC 2 Others 2

SHELLEY Daniel (Danny) Steven
Born: Stoke-on-Trent, 29 December 1990
Height: 5'10" **Weight:** 11.0
Another product of the Crewe youth system, Danny made his debut in the previous season. He gained further valuable experience and is proving to be versatile, having appeared in several positions including full-back and midfield. His development should continue.
Crewe Alex (From trainee on 27/1/2009) FL 10+12/1 FAC 2/1

SHELVEY Jonjo
Born: Romford, 27 February 1992
Height: 6'1" **Weight:** 11.2
International Honours: E: Yth
Jonjo started the first 12 League games for Charlton operating just behind sole striker Deon Burton. It was a successful spell with Jonjo scoring twice and putting in some influential performances. He was then left out as Charlton switched to 4-4-2 and never got a real run in the side after that, only starting seven more games plus a handful of substitute appearances. Jonjo scored twice more during the season, including a great volley from the edge of the penalty area against Swindon. Jonjo loves to get forward and is always looking for the ball, taking throws, corners and free kicks. He has a powerful shot and is not afraid to use it from long range when appropriate. Was sold to Liverpool in May and should have a big future in the game.
Charlton Ath (From trainee on 13/3/2009) FL 35+7/7 FLC 1 FAC 3+1/1 Others 1+1

SHERIDAN Cillian
Born: Baillieborough, Co. Cavan, 23 February 1989
Height: 6'5" **Weight:** 13.10
International Honours: RoI: 2; U21-9
In August, Cillian joined Plymouth on a six-month loan from Glasgow Celtic. In total, he played 14 times for the Pilgrims but unfortunately failed to find the net. When the tall striker returned to Celtic in January, he was immediately out on loan again, this time to St Johnstone for the rest of the season.

The Republic of Ireland international scored twice in St Johnstone's 5-1 defeat of Hibernian and scored the opener in their 4-1 victory against Glasgow Rangers.
Glasgow Celtic (Free from Belvedere, ex Bailieboro Celtic, on 10/2/2006) SL 6+8/4 SLC 0+1 SC 0+1 Others 1+2
Motherwell (Loaned on 2/2/2009) SL 9+4/2 SC 1+1
Plymouth Arg (Loaned on 14/8/2009) FL 5+8 FAC 0+1

SHEVCHENKO Andrei Mykolayovich
Born: Dvirkivshchyna, Ukraine, 29 August 1976
Height: 6'0" **Weight:** 11.5
Club Honours: FLC '07
International Honours: Ukraine: 94; U21-7; Yth
The expensive Chelsea career of Andrei Shevchenko finally came to an end shortly before the close of the summer transfer window. His former AC Milan boss Carlo Ancelotti, with whom he had shared so much success, could not guarantee him regular first team football and he returned to Ukraine with his first club, Dynamo Kiev. He made his swansong in Chelsea's second match, at Sunderland, leaving the bench for the last five minutes. Andrei achieved a long-held ambition by scoring at Wembley in a World Cup qualifier for Ukraine that temporarily frustrated England and he lifted his total of European competition goals to 62, the fourth highest. Although Ukraine lost their play-off to Greece, he took his international appearance tally to 94 and goals to 43 – both national records. Despite the fact that he will be approaching his 36th birthday, Andrei has a burning ambition to lead his country on home soil in Euro 2012 which would be a fitting tribute to a national hero.
Chelsea (£30,800,000 from AC Milan, Italy, ex Dynamo Kiev, on 4/7/2006) PL 30+18/9 FLC 6/5 FAC 5+2/3 Others 12+4/5

SHIELS Dean Andrew
Born: Magherafelt, 1 February 1985
Height: 5'11" **Weight:** 9.11
Club Honours: SLC '07
International Honours: NI: 9; U21-6
Dean started the season for Doncaster in fine form and netted five goals in the early months but, following a short spell out with injury, he found himself in and out of the starting line-up in the latter stages of the season. An all-action player, he is a firm favourite with the fans.
Arsenal (From trainee on 1/7/2002)
Hibernian (Free on 1/7/2004) SL

Ryan Shotton

79+38/24 SLC 10+1/4 SC 9+1/3 Others
3+4
Doncaster Rov *(£50,000 on 2/2/2009)*
FL 31+19/7 FLC 1 FAC 2

SHOREY Nicholas (Nicky)
Born: Romford, 19 February 1981
Height: 5'9" **Weight:** 10.10
Club Honours: Ch '06
International Honours: E: 2; B-1
The left-back struggled to establish
himself at Aston Villa in 2009-10
despite starting the campaign in Martin
O'Neill's first team with five consecutive
League games at left-back, having
regained his place with a consistent run
at the end of the previous year.
Although a cultured ball player, known
for his crossing ability and tendency to
push forward, there were still doubts
over his defensive qualities and Nicky
sought first team football elsewhere last
November after losing his Villa place to
new signing Stephen Warnock. Allowed
to move on loan to Nottingham Forest
in November as Forest were without a
recognised left-back, he helped the club
remain undefeated during his spell
there. Sent off against Reading on his
last appearance Nicky returned to Villa

and was subsquently loaned to Fulham.
Injuries to both regular full-backs had
prompted Fulham boss Roy Hodgson to
bring in Nicky at the end of the January
transfer window and he was pushed
straight into action, deputizing at left-
back for the injured Paul Konchesky. An
outstanding debut against Portsmouth
was followed by a series of assured
performances and even bought
speculation of a possible return to the
England side. Nicky reads the game well
and moves forward confidently with the
ball, being an excellent attacking asset
when providing pinpoint crosses into
the box. Unlucky to lose his place
following Konchesky's earlier than
expected return to fitness in March,
Nicky deputised as right-back at Hull,
after which he remained a squad player
before going back to Villa Park.
Leyton Orient *(From trainee on
5/7/1999) FL 12+3 FAC 1*
Reading *(£25,000 on 9/2/2001) P/FL
267/12 FLC 12 FAC 13 Others 4*
Aston Villa *(£3,500,000 on 8/8/2008)
PL 22+2 FLC 2 FAC 3 Others 10*
Nottingham F *(Loaned on 24/11/2009)
FL 9*
Fulham *(Loaned on 1/2/2010) PL 9 FAC 2*

SHOTTON Ryan Colin
Born: Fenton, 30 September 1988
Height: 6'3" **Weight:** 13.5
One of quite a few Stoke squad players
whose only first team appearance came
in the club's three-match Carling Cup
campaign. After appearing in the 1-0
win at Leyton Orient, Ryan joined fellow
defender Carl Dickinson in a loan deal
that took them to Barnsley. The move
was eventually extended to cover the
rest of the season and the pair brought
stability to the Tykes' defence. Tall and
pacy, he was very good with the ball at
his feet, having started at right-back,
and when injuries struck he moved to
centre-back where he was equally
comfortable. Very good in the air, he
was always a threat from set plays but
unfortunately his only goal was wiped
out when the match at Plymouth was
abandoned. He also possesses a long
throw that caused problems for
opposition defences.
Stoke C *(From trainee on 28/3/2007)
FLC 1+1*
Tranmere Rov *(Loaned on 29/8/2008)
FL 33/5 FAC 3 Others 3/1*
Barnsley *(Loaned on 23/9/2009) FL 30
FAC 1*

SHOWUNMI Enoch Olusesan
Born: Kilburn, 21 April 1982
Height: 6'3" **Weight:** 14.10
Club Honours: Div 1 '05
International Honours: Nigeria: 2
Big Enoch, fully recovered from the
blood clot on his lung that blighted his
previous season, returned to play his
part in Leeds' fine start. Mainly a
substitute, he scored the only goal in his
one start in the Carling Cup victory at
Darlington in August. He moved to
Falkirk on New Year's Day.
Luton T *(Signed from Willesden
Constantine on 5/9/2003) FL 40+62/14
FLC 1+1/1 FAC 2+4 Others 3+1/1*
Bristol C *(Free on 4/7/2006) FL
38+12/13 FLC 2 FAC 5+1/3 Others 3/2*
Sheffield Wed *(Loaned on 31/1/2008)
FL 6+4*
Leeds U *(Free on 9/7/2008) FL 3+12/2
FLC 2+4/3 FAC 0+3 Others 2+2/1*

SHROOT Robin Alexander
Born: Hammersmith, 26 March 1988
Height: 5'9" **Weight:** 11.5
International Honours: NI: U21-4
Signed initially on a season-long loan
from Birmingham, Robin's skill and
trickery earned him a place in Burton's
team for their historic first League
appearance at Shrewsbury. He showed
his adaptability by playing in both wide
midfield positions but international calls
cost him a regular place in the team
and, with a surfeit of attacking players,

Albion decided to end the loan agreement with the Premier League club prematurely in October, with manager Paul Peschisolido decreeing: "Things have not worked out".
Birmingham C *(£20,000 from Harrow Borough, ex Staines T, AFC Wimbledon, on 2/1/2009) FAC 1*
Walsall *(Loaned on 6/3/2009) FL 0+5*
Burton A *(Loaned on 1/7/2009) FL 4+3*

SHUKER Christopher (Chris) Alan
Born: Liverpool, 9 May 1982
Height: 5'5" **Weight:** 10.1
Chris, a fast and talented right-winger, started only 21 games, largely because his attacking, wide style was not a natural fit for the 4-3-3 system introduced by Tranmere manager Les Parry. He has the ability to turn a game with moments of skill and relishes the chance to run past defenders to deliver telling crosses into the box, but he sometimes seems to lack belief in himself. Away from football, Chris is a keen rider and owns several horses. After four years at Prenton Park, he was not offered a new contract.
Manchester C *(From trainee on 21/9/1999) P/FL 1+4 FLC 0+1/1*
Macclesfield T *(Loaned on 27/3/2001) FL 6+3/1*
Walsall *(Loaned on 26/2/2003) FL 3+2*
Rochdale *(Loaned on 7/8/2003) FL 14/1 FLC 1*
Hartlepool U *(Loaned on 13/12/2003) FL 14/1 FAC 1*
Barnsley *(Signed on 17/3/2004) FL 93+7/17 FLC 4/1 FAC 6 Others 2+2*
Tranmere Rov *(Free on 17/7/2006) FL 106+17/14 FLC 4 FAC 8+2/2 Others 5+2/2*

SIDIBE Mamady (Mama)
Born: Bamoko, Mali, 18 December 1979
Height: 6'4" **Weight:** 12.4
International Honours: Mali: 12
Big Mama remains one of those players at Stoke who can split the opinions of supporters straight down the middle. Absolutely nobody doubts his unstinting efforts, tremendous work and genuine commitment to Stoke but the debate remains over whether he is the best partner for Ricardo Fuller. Mama's great strength's are his tireless work, selfless efforts and ability to defend from the front, while acting as a nuisance factor to opposing defenders. Where he falls short is in the number of goals he scores, with just two coming last season. Both were vital strikes but there are other strikers chomping at the bit. His efforts are nonetheless well appreciated and, most importantly of

all, his biggest supporter and admirer is manager Tony Pulis.
Swansea C *(Free from CA Paris, France, ex Racing Club Paris, on 27/7/2001) FL 26+5/7 FLC 0+1 FAC 2/1 Others 1*
Gillingham *(Free on 9/8/2002) FL 80+26/10 FLC 4+1/1 FAC 3+1/2*
Stoke C *(Free on 5/7/2005) P/FL 148+18/24 FLC 5+1/1 FAC 11+1/1*

SIDWELL Steven (Steve) James
Born: Wandsworth, 14 December 1982
Height: 5'10" **Weight:** 11.2
Club Honours: FAYC '00, '01; Ch '06
International Honours: E: U21-5; Yth
It was a frustrating season for Steve, who lost his Aston Villa place following winger James Milner's conversion to central midfield. Steve was a regular starter during the first third of the season but from December onwards he was restricted to Cup games and substitute appearances. The flame-haired dynamo failed to do himself justice and did not perform sufficiently well to force himself back into the team. Strangely, his most notable contribution was as an unused substitute in the 5-1 victory over Bolton at Villa Park last November. While he was warming up, he retrieved a ball that had gone out of play and his clever thinking allowed Gabby Agbonlahor to take a quick throw from which Milner scored. Steve's only League start in the second half of the season ended in humiliation when Villa were hammered 7-1 by his old club Chelsea at Stamford Bridge. He was put up for sale by Villa at the end of the season.
Arsenal *(From trainee on 2/7/2001)*
Brentford *(Loaned on 23/10/2001) FL 29+1/4 FAC 2 Others 3*
Reading *(£250,000 on 21/1/2003) P/FL 164+4/29 FLC 7/1 FAC 9+1 Others 2*
Chelsea *(Free on 3/7/2007) PL 7+8 FLC 3+2/1 FAC 3 Others 0+2*
Aston Villa *(£5,000,000 on 10/7/2008) PL 23+18/3 FLC 0+3 FAC 5+3/1 Others 6*

SIGURDSSON Gylfi Thor
Born: Reykjavik, Iceland, 9 September 1989
Height: 6'1" **Weight:** 12.2
International Honours: Iceland: 1; U21-8; Yth
The cold statistics of 20 goals scored from midfield in 43 games pay scant tribute to the electrifying effect Gylfi has on Reading. Deservedly voted the fans' 'Player of the Year', the young Icelander proved the most exciting graduate to emerge so far from the Royals' Academy. Having furthered his

education of lower division clubs such as Crewe and Shrewsbury, Gylfi became one of the most creative and perceptive players in the Championship and a target for Premiership clubs. Coolness personified, he has the knack of converting crucial penalties as well as delivering deadly free kicks. In the 2-0 home win over Bristol City, he took all of the dead-ball kicks, corners from both sides, was brought down for the penalty, scored the penalty, netted Reading's second goal, and totally dominated the game. It was a surprise that he was not also on the gate taking the money. Gylfi has two years remaining on his contract with Reading but they will do well to hold on to this supremely talented yet essentially reserved young man.
Reading *(From trainee on 6/7/2007) FL 32+6/16 FLC 1+2/1 FAC 5+1/3*
Shrewsbury T *(Loaned on 16/10/2008) FL 4+1/1 Others 1*
Crewe Alex *(Loaned on 27/2/2009) FL 14+1/3*

Gylfi Sigurdsson

SILLS Timothy (Tim)
Born: Romsey, 10 September 1979
Height: 6'1" **Weight:** 14.0
The powerful and intelligent centre-forward had been the focal point of the team as Torquay won promotion from the Blue Square Premier, where his aerial prowess and ability to lead the line far outweighed his lack of pace. Tim looked to have established himself at League level when he scored in three consecutive appearances in September and October but a further goal drought saw him lose his place to Scott Rendell and, after a spell on the bench, he took the opportunity to join Blue Square title chasers Stevenage in January on an 18-month deal.
Oxford U *(£50,000 from Aldershot T,*

ex Kingstonian, on 31/1/2006) FL 9+4/1
Hereford U (Free on 10/7/2006) FL
22+14/2 FLC 2 FAC 4 Others 1
Torquay U (Free on 2/7/2007) FL
12+6/2 FLC 1/1 FAC 1+2 Others 2/1

SILVESTRE Mikael Samy
Born: Chambray-les-Tours, France, 9
August 1977
Height: 6'0" **Weight:** 13.1
Club Honours: PL '00, '01, '03, '07; CS
'03, '07; FAC '04; FLC '06; UEFACL '08
International Honours: France: 40;
U21; Yth (UEFA-U18 '96)
Mikael stayed at Arsenal the previous
summer despite not being an
unqualified success in his first season.
While his experience is not in question,
his pace and general reading of the
game clearly are and he again
struggled in the first team. However,
with injuries reducing Arsenal's centre-
back options in April, he was called
upon far more often than would
normally have been expected. He
scored in the 3-2 reverse at Wigan but
with Arsenal set to make defensive
additions this summer Mikael, out of
contract, is likely to leave. He made 12
appearances in the Premier League,
scoring once, three in the Champions
League, two in the FA Cup and was
ever-present in the Carling Cup run.
Manchester U (£4,000,000 from Inter
Milan, Italy on 10/9/1999) PL 225+24/6
FLC 13+1 FAC 19+2/1 Others 69+8/3
Arsenal (£750,000 on 21/8/2008) PL
21+5/3 FLC 4 FAC 4 Others 8+1

SIMEK Franklin (Frank)
Michael
Born: St Louis, Missouri, USA, 13
October 1984
Height: 6'0" **Weight:** 11.6
International Honours: USA: 5; Yth
Making his way back from long-term
injury, this very popular Sheffield
Wednesday right-back found it difficult
to regain his once established place in
2009-10. A solid defender, Frank is also
very adept at getting forward and is a
great crowd favourite. He was also
trying to win back his place in the
United States international side in time
for the World Cup, and was back in
their squad for a friendly in March.
Sorely missed by the Owls when
unavailable for selection, Frank is a
reliable, skilful, enthusiastic player. Was
out of contract in the summer.
Arsenal (From trainee on 1/7/2002) FLC 1
Queens Park Rgrs (Loaned on
19/10/2004) FL 5
Bournemouth (Loaned on 24/3/2005)
FL 8
Sheffield Wed (Free on 3/8/2005) FL
113+6/2 FLC 7 FAC 4

SIMONSEN Steven (Steve)
Preben Arthur
Born: South Shields, 3 April 1979
Height: 6'3" **Weight:** 13.2
International Honours: E: U21-4; Yth
Yet another frustrating season for Steve
as he spent most of it on the
substitutes' bench kicking his heels,
before finishing off the campaign on
loan at play-off chasing Sheffield United
in the Championship. He made only
seven appearances between the sticks
for Stoke but was on the winning side
five times, including a 1-0 win at
Tottenham and a 3-2 home victory over
Fulham. In the Tottenham game in
particular 'Simmo' was in superb form
and pulled off a string of superb saves
to keep Stoke in contention until Glenn
Whelan's 87th-minute winner. There is
no doubt that Stoke fans would be
happy to see him stay as cover, given
his superb form whenever he was called
upon. In March, Steve signed for
Sheffield United on a one-month loan
and although he conceded a goal five
minutes into his debut at Doncaster and
had to wait for six games for his first
Blades' win, his performances were
excellent. Showing good positioning
and command of his area he made
goalkeeping look easy. His loan was
extended for a week to include the
Sheffield derby.
Tranmere Rov (From trainee on
9/10/1996) FL 35 FLC 4 FAC 3
Everton (£3,300,000 on 23/9/1998) PL
28+2 FLC 2 FAC 5
Stoke C (Free on 6/8/2004) P/FL 160+6
FLC 10 FAC 10+1
Sheffield U (Loaned on 19/3/2010) FL 7

SIMPSON Daniel (Danny)
Peter
Born: Eccles, 4 January 1987
Height: 5'8" **Weight:** 11.10
Club Honours: Ch '07, '10
Danny was recruited by Newcastle on a
six-month loan from Manchester United
as defensive cover and quickly settled
into the side, delivering a 'Man of the
Match' performance against Queens
Park Rangers in September. The fact
that he became a regular in the
Championship's meanest defence is
testament to his consistency, and he
was always ready and willing to
supplement his attack with pacy runs
down the wing, followed by dangerous
crosses. He contributed a first goal for
the club with a delightful curled effort
against Peterborough in November.
Although principally a right-back, he
demonstrated a welcome flexibility by
also appearing occasionally at left-back
and centre-back. His performances
earned him a permanent move in the

January transfer window.
Manchester U (From trainee on
10/1/2006) PL 1+2 FLC 1 FAC 0+1
Others 2+1
Sunderland (Loaned on 29/1/2007) FL
13+1
Ipswich T (Loaned on 21/3/2008) FL
7+1
Blackburn Rov (Loaned on 5/8/2008)
PL 10+2 FLC 3 FAC 5
Newcastle U (Signed on 14/8/2009) FL
39/1 FLC 1 FAC 1

Danny Simpson

SIMPSON Jacob (Jake)
David
Born: Oxford, 27 October 1990
Height: 5'11" **Weight:** 12.0
Given a 12-month contract by
Shrewsbury after being released by
Blackburn, the wide-right midfield
player grew in confidence and began to
show his ability, especially in the second
half of the season after recovering from
calf and knee injuries that kept him
sidelined for some weeks. Voted 'Young
Player of the Season', he has pace, can
put in a great cross and has a really
strong throw in. He was involved in 18
League games and did particularly well
in April against Crewe, providing a cross
for a goal, and Lincoln. Was out of
contract in the summer.
Shrewsbury T (From trainee at
Blackburn Rov on 2/7/2009) FL 14+4
FAC 0+1 Others 0+1

SIMPSON Jay Alistaire
Frederick
Born: Enfield, 27 December 1988
Height: 5'11" **Weight:** 13.4
International Honours: E: Yth
An Arsenal Academy graduate, Jay
spent the season on loan at Queens
Park Rangers, for the most part with
great success. He finished the season as

top scorer at Rangers having bagged himself 13 goals in all competitions, 12 of which came in the Championship. Eight of those were scored in his first 15 appearances, when he spearheaded Jim Magilton's attacking style of play to great effect. A hamstring injury later in the season seemed to slow him down a little and he failed to score in the closing 11 games of the season.
Arsenal (From trainee on 2/7/2007) FLC 1+2/2
Millwall (Loaned on 31/8/2007) FL 34+7/6 FAC 4/1 Others 1/1
West Bromwich A (Loaned on 1/1/2009) PL 9+4/1 FAC 3+1/1
Queens Park Rgrs (Loaned on 27/8/2009) FL 34+5/12 FLC 1 FAC 2/1

SIMPSON Joshua (Josh)
Richard
Born: Harlow, 6 March 1987
Height: 5'10" **Weight:** 12.2
International Honours: E: SP-2
Midfield player Josh joined Peterborough from Blue Square Premier Histon and was used only sparingly, mainly as a substitute. He is an attacking midfielder but was sometimes used in the holding role. His personal highlight of the season was scoring two goals, including the equaliser, in the remarkable recovery from 4-0 down to gain a 4-4 draw against Cardiff.
Peterborough U (Signed from Histon, ex Cambridge C, Cambridge U, Cambridge C, on 5/11/2009) FL 8+13/2

SIMPSON Michael
Born: Nottingham, 28 February 1974
Height: 5'9" **Weight:** 10.8
Club Honours: AIC '95; FC '09
Vastly experienced and hard-working midfield player who fought back from a serious knee injury to resume his career with Burton in 2007. Michael was one of the key players in Burton's rise to the League in a central midfield partnership with John McGrath and won a new contract in 2009, scoring twice in the early-season defeat of Northampton. Renowned for his tackling, closing down and efficient use of the ball, he was unfortunate to have his season interrupted by a broken foot in January, but came back to make six more appearances at the end of the campaign. However, 36-year-old Michael was released by the Pirelli Stadium club in May.
Notts Co (From trainee on 1/7/1992) FL 39+10/3 FLC 4+1 FAC 2+1 Others 7+3
Plymouth Arg (Loaned on 4/10/1996) FL 10+2
Wycombe W (£50,000 on 5/12/1996) FL 267+18/16 FLC 14+1 FAC 23+2/4 Others 14

Leyton Orient (Free on 6/7/2004) FL 105/4 FLC 2 FAC 7 Others 4
Burton A (Free on 2/7/2007) FL 20+4/2 FLC 1 FAC 2

SIMPSON Robbie
Born: Poole, 15 March 1985
Height: 5'10" **Weight:** 11.6
The young striker joined Huddersfield on a three-year deal after leaving Coventry to spearhead the attack. Unfortunately, a long-term thigh muscle problem restricted Robbie to five starts and the accomplished striker was seen mostly in bit parts from the bench. He holds the ball up well and is good with his head, as seen by his goal in the Johnstone's Paint Trophy win over Rotherham in his second start.
Coventry C (£40,000 + from Cambridge U, ex Cambridge C, on 1/7/2007) FL 24+37/4 FLC 2+4/3 FAC 2+2
Huddersfield T (£300,000 on 1/7/2009) FL 4+9 FLC 0+2 Others 1/1

SINCLAIR Dean Michael
Born: Luton, 17 December 1984
Height: 5'9" **Weight:** 11.3
Club Honours: FC '05
International Honours: E: SP-5
Unable to hold down a place at Charlton, Dean re-joined his former club Barnet on a month's loan at the beginning of December 2009. A popular figure during his first spell at the club, much was expected upon his return. However, his time at Underhill was hindered with injuries and suspensions and he left the club at the turn of the year, having played in four games. Dean's second loan spell from Charlton, this time at Grimsby at the end of January, saw him involved in yet another relegation battle, the tough midfielder's presence helping to keep Town in the fight for survival. After initially overcoming fitness problems, he hit two goals versus Shrewsbury (3-0) to end a club record 25 League games without victory, only to frustratingly suffer a hamstring injury in the run-in. Was out of contract in the summer.
Norwich C (From trainee on 7/5/2003) FL 1+1
Barnet (Free on 11/8/2004) FL 81+5/8 FLC 4/1 FAC 4/2 Others 3/1
Charlton Ath (£125,000 on 31/7/2007) FLC 1+1/1
Cheltenham T (Loaned on 6/10/2007) FL 12/1 Others 2
Cheltenham T (Loaned on 21/8/2008) FL 2+1
Grimsby T (Loaned on 8/1/2009) FL 9/1
Barnet (Loaned on 26/11/2009) FL 2+1/1 FAC 0+1
Grimsby T (Loaned on 28/1/2010) FL 16/3

SINCLAIR Emile Anthony
Born: Leeds, 29 December 1987
Height: 6'0" **Weight:** 11.1
Having been on loan at Macclesfield for the second half of 2008-09, Emile made the move permanent in the summer. Predominately a striker, he sometimes played wide right in midfield where he made many speedy runs. He did not score until the end of September but completed the season as joint top scorer with Ricky Sappleton on seven. Three of Emile's goals were against Hereford, including a brace in home fixture, the first from a 30-yard run and a shot from 20 yards. At Hereford, he weaved through the defence to score the second in a 2-0 victory in the first match after the untimely death of manager Keith Alexander. Emile's contract was extended by two years.
Nottingham F (From juniors at Bradford C, ex Harrogate College, on 10/7/2007) FL 0+15/1 FLC 0+2 Others 0+1
Brentford (Loaned on 22/11/2007) FL 1+3
Macclesfield T (Loaned on 15/1/2009) FL 6/1
Macclesfield T (Free on 27/2/2009) FL 41+12/7 FAC 1 Others 1

SINCLAIR Scott Andrew
Born: Bath, 26 March 1989
Height: 5'10" **Weight:** 10.10
International Honours: E: Yth; Sch
A highly promising young winger, Scott was on a nine-month loan at Wigan from Chelsea. At home wide on the right or through the middle, his searing pace remains a constant threat for defenders and he is harnessing it to a more clinical style in front of goal. He made his Wigan debut from the substitutes' bench in the opening match at Aston Villa and his only Premier League start was at Portsmouth. His only goals were netted against Hull, in the away League game and again in the FA Cup tie. Scott's decisions in the final third need to be improved but, at just 21, he gives every sign of having an exciting future.
Bristol Rov (Schoolboy) FL 0+2
Chelsea (From trainee on 28/3/2006) PL 1+4 FLC 3+2/1 FAC 2+1 Others 0+1
Plymouth Arg (Loaned on 17/1/2007) FL 8+7/2 FAC 2+1/2
Queens Park Rgrs (Loaned on 6/11/2007) FL 8+1/1
Charlton Ath (Loaned on 28/2/2008) FL 0+3
Crystal Palace (Loaned on 27/3/2008) FL 6/2 Others 2
Birmingham C (Loaned on 6/1/2009) FL 8+6
Wigan Ath (Loaned on 6/8/2009) PL 1+17/1 FLC 1 FAC 3/1

SKARZ Joseph (Joe) Peter
Born: Huddersfield, 13 July 1989
Height: 5'11" **Weight:** 13.0
The young Huddersfield defender started the season as the regular left-back in the side, but was duly challenged to match his previous first team exploits from the season before as others looked to take over. Joe, who defends with much determination and links well when going forward, is a no-nonsense defender, who can also distribute the ball with accuracy. As the season progressed he continued to be involved within the side, but as more experienced players were utilised within the rearguard of the team he was loaned out to Shrewsbury in January and settled in very quickly. Quite calm for such a young player, he had an excellent game in his debut, a 2-1 win against Dagenham. Solid in defence and dependable, he has a high work rate and is always looking to get an attack moving. He gave a number of confident displays and was a regular until the end of the season.
Huddersfield T *(From trainee on 28/2/2007) FL 60+8/1 FLC 3 FAC 5+1 Others 3+1*
Hartlepool U *(Loaned on 26/3/2009) FL 5+2*
Shrewsbury T *(Loaned on 21/1/2010) FL 20*

SKRTEL Martin
Born: Handlova, Slovakia, 15 December 1984
Height: 6'4" **Weight:** 12.12
International Honours: Slovakia: 38
The Liverpool and Slovakian international central defender did not enjoy the best of seasons, in common with most of his team-mates. Although he started as first choice, his previous dominance in the air came under scrutiny as Liverpool's defence was increasingly vulnerable to headers from set pieces. He lost his previously automatic place to Daniel Agger in late October although, in a brief return, he scored his first goal for the Reds in a 2-2 draw against Manchester City with an opportunistic flick from a corner. He returned to regular duty in January when Jamie Carragher switched to cover at right-back. Sadly his season ended prematurely in February when he broke a metatarsal in his right foot in the 3-1 Europa Cup away victory against Unirea Urziceni.
Liverpool *(£6,500,000 from Zenit St Petersburg, Russia, ex Trencin, on 14/1/2008) PL 49+5/1 FLC 1+1 FAC 4+1 Others 17+1*

SKUSE Cole
Born: Bristol, 29 March 1986
Height: 6'1" **Weight:** 11.5
Bristol City's midfield dynamo is one of the few to have graduated from the Ashton Gate Academy. A wholehearted box-to-box player who has endeared himself to most fans, though some might suggest a lack of vision in his passing and a tendency to play safe. A regular throughout the 2009-10 campaign, Cole should be able to look forward to a long and successful football career. Selected as the Bristol City supporters' 'Player of the Year', it is difficult not to think of this being a case of choosing one of their own, given the scoring exploits of Nicky Maynard and the many excellent displays by Paul Hartley.
Bristol C *(From trainee on 29/4/2005) FL 137+51/6 FLC 5+2 FAC 9+1 Others 3+2*

SLOCOMBE Sam Oliver
Born: Scunthorpe, 5 June 1988
Height: 6'0" **Weight:** 11.11
Scunthorpe's third choice goalkeeper had his first tastes of senior football with two contrasting substitute appearances. Coming on early in the Carling Cup third round tie with Port Vale in September, Sam impressed with a number of fine stops and excellent kicking as his side kept a clean sheet. His League debut came at Blackpool in November after number-one Joe Murphy had been sent off and he was beaten by a free kick within seconds of coming on, going on to concede two more in a 4-1 defeat.
Scunthorpe U *(Free from Bottesford T on 15/8/2008) FL 0+1 FLC 0+1*

SLORY Andwele (Andy) Cedric
Born: Paramaribo, Surinam, 27 September 1982
Height: 5'7" **Weight:** 9.4
International Honours: Holland: 2
On as an 80th-minute substitute for Robert Koren, the Dutch international midfielder's neat header back across goal enabled Chris Brunt to grab a late equaliser at Watford in April as West Bromwich charged on towards promotion. Before that, Andy had played in five League games, giving a good account of himself in each one, especially as a late substitute at Blackpool, while being somewhat unlucky not to score in the 1-1 draw at Cardiff before going off injured. Prior to joining Albion, Andy had scored over 50 goals in Dutch football.
West Bromwich A *(Free from Feyenoord, Holland, ex SC Telstar, Stormvogels, Excelsior, on 1/2/2010) FL 1+5 FAC 1+5*

SMALL Wade Kristopher
Born: Croydon, 23 February 1984
Height: 5'7" **Weight:** 11.6
Freed by Sheffield Wednesday in May 2009, Wade signed for Charlton in the summer on a non-contract basis and made his debut in the Carling Cup at Hereford on the wide left. It was the only game the tricky winger played for the Addicks and on being released he joined Chesterfield to provide pace to their attack. He did that to good effect, linking well with Jack Lester, before missing most of October after injuring an ankle. Unfortunately, Wade seemed to lose a little of the spark that made him such a danger after that and he struggled to find a role in the wake of tactical changes following the January signing of Barry Conlon. Despite that, he was offered a new contract in May.
Wimbledon/MK Dons *(From trainee on 17/7/2003) FL 88+11/12 FLC 3 FAC 10/1 Others 3/2*
Sheffield Wed *(Signed on 2/6/2006) FL 37+31/7 FLC 2/1 FAC 2+2*
Blackpool *(Loaned on 13/3/2009) FL 4+1/1*
Charlton Ath *(Free on 10/8/2009) FLC 1*
Chesterfield *(Free on 28/8/2009) FL 24+3/4 FAC 1 Others 1/2*

Deane Smalley

SMALLEY Deane Alfie
Born: Oldham, 5 September 1988
Height: 6'0" **Weight:** 11.10
If pace is an asset, Oldham's Deane has it in abundance and is very highly thought of at Boundary Park for obvious reasons. Having recovered from a troublesome back problem, Deane was immediately installed out on the right flank, where his pace and height caused every defence problems. He has

terrific spring when jumping for high balls, stemming from his skill as a gymnast in his younger days. He scored three goals from 31 appearances and could easily have had many more.
Oldham Ath *(From trainee on 3/7/2007) FL 64+38/10 FLC 3+1/1 FAC 8 Others 1+1*

SMALLING Christopher Lloyd
Born: Greenwich, 22 November 1989
Height: 6'4" **Weight:** 14.0
International Honours: E: U21-4; Yth
An outstanding young prospect who might have made more of an impact at Fulham but for the form and consistency of the first choice pairing of Brede Hangeland and Aaron Hughes. Initially out of the squad, he was called into action for the European tie in Sofia and was named 'Man of the Match', a feat he repeated in his first Premier League action of the season at Chelsea, where he handled the threat of Didier Drogba admirably. A cool central defender, he competes well for the ball and has excellent distribution. His impressive displays both for the first team and reserves were obviously monitored and in January he signed a pre-contract agreement that will take him to Manchester United in the summer. He also featured at England under-21 level four times.
Fulham *(Signed from Maidstone U on 2/7/2008) PL 9+4 FLC 1 FAC 1 Others 4*

SMITH Adam James
Born: Waltham Forest, 29 April 1991
Height: 5'8" **Weight:** 10.7
With no regular full-backs fit, Wycombe signed this young Tottenham defender on a month's loan at the start of the season. He gave a good account of himself in the opening day's defeat at Charlton, not overawed by the big crowd, showing plenty of energy and willing to push forward. He started the next two League games, home to Leeds and Southend, and also the Johnstone's Paint Trophy first round match against Northampton, before returning to White Hart Lane and then on to Torquay for another spell on loan. Despite being right-footed, this promising young player's best performances were at left-back, although he did also appear at right-back for Torquay. Combined defensive poise and composure with attacking flair and a willingness to overlap as he held a regular first team place from mid-November to mid-February. After a period of illness further opportunities were limited.
Tottenham H *(From trainee on 1/5/2009)*
Wycombe W *(Loaned on 7/8/2009) FL 3 Others 1*

Torquay U *(Loaned on 20/11/2009) FL 16 FAC 2*

SMITH Alan
Born: Rothwell, West Yorkshire, 28 October 1980
Height: 5'9" **Weight:** 11.10
Club Honours: FLC '06; Ch '10
International Honours: E: 19; B-1; U21-10; Yth
This season saw the transition of Alan from an ineffective striker into a fine defensive midfield player, whose performances were an important factor in Newcastle winning the Championship. His strong, no-nonsense tackling and reading of the game enabled him to form a useful shield in front of his defence, and his simple get-and-give style ensured ball retention and provided the springboard for counter attacks. His commitment to the Toon cause was evident from the start and as vice-captain he led the side out for the opening game at West Bromwich in the absence of Nicky Butt. In February he even played games wearing a mask to protect a shattered cheekbone. It was fitting that the Championship trophy was presented jointly to him and Nicky after the home draw with Ipswich.
Leeds U *(From trainee on 26/3/1998) PL 148+24/38 FLC 4+2 FAC 11+4/4 Others 28+7/14*
Manchester U *(£7,000,000 on 26/5/2004) PL 43+18/7 FLC 4+2/1 FAC 2+6 Others 12+6/4*
Newcastle U *(£6,000,000 on 3/8/2007) P/FL 61+10 FLC 2+1 FAC 4*

SMITH Benjamin (Ben) James
Born: Newcastle, 5 September 1986
Height: 6'1" **Weight:** 12.11
Club Honours: AMC '07
Once again the young goalie understudied the ageless Neil Sullivan at Doncaster. Playing in the Carling Cup games in the early part of the season, Ben found himself in the firing line against Tottenham and gave an excellent display. He was certainly not to blame for the five goals that were put past him. To keep his hand in he went out on loan to Morecambe in October, playing three games for the Shrimps and conceding seven goals in the process. Despite that, he looked solid for the most part and made some good saves. Back at Doncaster, he gave a good display in the last match of the season at Swansea before being released.
Doncaster Rov *(Free from N/C at Stockport Co, ex trainee at Newcastle U, on 4/8/2006) FL 14+1 FLC 3 FAC 4 Others 6+1*

Lincoln C *(Loaned on 17/11/2007) FL 9*
Morecambe *(Loaned on 16/10/2009) FL 3*

SMITH Emmanuele (Manny)
Born: Birmingham, 8 November 1987
Height: 6'2" **Weight:** 12.3
Manny produced another excellent season of strong performances at the heart of the Walsall defence. He flourished towards the end of the season, relishing his partnership with Clayton McDonald. Never shirking a challenge he showed that he would not be pushed around by opposing forwards. His first goal for the club, a volley from a well worked corner at Millwall, was followed by headed goals in successive home matches. He signed a two-year contract at the end of the season after reportedly attracting interest from a number of clubs.
Walsall *(From Solihull College on 19/9/2005) FL 57+9/4 FLC 1+1 FAC 2 Others 1*

SMITH Gary Stephen
Born: Middlesbrough, 30 January 1984
Height: 5'8" **Weight:** 10.8
This tenacious, strong-tackling Darlington midfielder was a fixture in the team, along with his namesake Jeff Smith, during the first half of the season with his energetic displays and quick passing. He fell out of favour after the turn of the year but regained his place towards the end of the campaign, playing in the final 14 games. More of a provider than a scorer, he weighed in with one vital goal in the win at Rotherham in January. After Easter he signed a new one-year contract to keep him at the club next season.
Middlesbrough *(From trainee on 6/7/2002)*
Wimbledon *(Loaned on 22/3/2004) FL 10+1/3*
MK Dons *(Free on 6/8/2004) FL 47+24/5 FLC 0+1 FAC 3+2/1 Others 3/3*
Brentford *(Free on 1/8/2007) FL 28+5/1 FLC 0+1 FAC 0+1 Others 1*
Darlington *(Free on 2/7/2009) FL 32+2/1 FLC 1 FAC 1 Others 2*

SMITH Graeme Meldrum
Born: Edinburgh, 8 June 1983
Height: 6'1" **Weight:** 12.4
International Honours: S: B-1
Arriving at Brighton from Motherwell in the summer, Graeme had to play second fiddle to Michel Kuipers and only made his entrance when the Dutch goalkeeper was sent off at Huddersfield. Faced with an immediate penalty kick, he was cautioned for having a feel of the ball before taking up his position, and went on to pick the

ball out of the net five times, although he did save another penalty. Graeme demonstrated excellent reflexes in his Albion career, but playing behind a highly suspect defence did little for his confidence and it was a relief all round when he ended his nightmare and returned north of the border in the New Year to rebuild his career with Hibernian.
Glasgow Rgrs (From juniors on 13/7/1999)
Ross Co (Loaned on 10/12/2003) SL 20 SC 1
Motherwell (Free on 25/6/2005) SL 126+1 SLC 8 SC 10
Brighton & Hove A (Free on 2/7/2009) FL 5+1 FAC 2+1 Others 1

SMITH Jack David
Born: Hemel Hempstead, 14 October 1983
Height: 5'11" **Weight:** 11.5
Jack joined Millwall after his contract expired at Swindon during the summer. Although playing along the back four, his best position is right-back. Is always happy to get forward to support the midfield, Jack's recovery to his defensive position is outstanding.
Watford (From trainee on 5/4/2002) FL 23+2/2 FLC 0+1 FAC 2
Swindon T (Free on 5/8/2005) FL 134+4/9 FLC 4 FAC 7 Others 4
Millwall (Free on 7/8/2009) FL 30+1 FLC 2 FAC 4+1/1 Others 3

SMITH James (Jimmy) Dean
Born: Upton Park, 7 January 1987
Height: 6'1" **Weight:** 10.8
International Honours: E: Yth
Jimmy joined Leyton Orient on a free transfer from Chelsea having impressed in the previous season while on loan. He started the season well in midfield and scored the winning goal in the 2-1 away win at Bristol Rovers. Jimmy remained first choice until December but struggled for most of the rest of the season to claim a regular place. That will be his aim for the forthcoming season.
Chelsea (From trainee on 26/3/2005) PL 0+1
Queens Park Rgrs (Loaned on 27/9/2006) FL 22+7/6 FAC 2
Norwich C (Loaned on 10/8/2007) FL 6+3
Sheffield Wed (Loaned on 3/7/2008) FL 3+9 FLC 1
Leyton Orient (Free on 2/2/2009) FL 49+7/2 FLC 2 FAC 1 Others 1

SMITH Jamie Paul
Born: Leytonstone, 16 September 1989
Height: 5'6" **Weight:** 10.5
A promising young attacking midfielder with an excellent eye for a pass, Jamie was taken on by Brighton following his release from Crystal Palace but made

only two brief appearances. The first was at Huddersfield, a disastrous game in which goalkeeper Michel Kuipers was sent off and Jamie was sacrificed in order to bring on back-up 'keeper Graeme Smith. His second involvement was as a late substitute at Wycombe in December but he was offered a new contract.
Crystal Palace (From trainee on 11/7/2008)
Brighton & Hove A (Free on 4/8/2009) FL 1+1

SMITH Jeffrey (Jeff)
Born: Middlesbrough, 28 June 1980
Height: 5'10" **Weight:** 11.8
Jeff, along with his namesake Gary, was very much a fixture in the Darlington side during the first half of the season but after a dispute with manager Steve Staunton he left the club in March. His strong running at defenders and willingness to chase every ball endeared him to the crowd, but he failed to score for all his effort.
Hartlepool U (From trainee on 3/7/1998) FL 2+1 Others 1 (Free to Barrow in October 1999)
Bolton W (Free from Bishop Auckland on 21/3/2001) P/FL 1+1 FLC 2 FAC 4
Macclesfield T (Loaned on 23/11/2001) FL 7+1/2
Scunthorpe U (Loaned on 16/1/2004) FL 1
Rochdale (Loaned on 20/2/2004) FL 1
Preston NE (Signed on 4/3/2004) FL 0+5
Port Vale (Free on 5/7/2004) FL 65+23/5 FLC 4+1/1 FAC 5+1 Others 1+3/1
Carlisle U (£60,000 on 26/1/2007) FL 41+14/2 FLC 1+2 FAC 3+2 Others 2
Darlington (Free on 13/7/2009) FL 22+2 FLC 1 FAC 1 Others 1+1

SMITH Khano
Born: Paget, Bermuda, 10 January 1981
Height: 6'3" **Weight:** 13.8
International Honours: Bermuda: 24
The Bermudian international left-winger became Chris Sutton's first permanent signing as Lincoln manager in October after a five-week trial spell at Sincil Bank. Having been released by New York Red Bulls in the close season he arrived at Lincoln following a trial at Southend. Although known for his pace and delivery, and ability to play down the middle, he failed to force his way into the first team set-up, apart from six appearances, and left the club in January following the conclusion of his short-term contract. He returned to America and signed on for New England Revolution in March.

Lincoln C (Free from New York Red Bulls, USA, ex Champlain Beavers, Lees-McCrae Bobcats, Carolina Dynamo, Dandy Town Hornets, New England Revolution, on 23/10/2009) FL 4+1 FAC 1

SMITH Korey Alexander
Born: Hatfield, 31 January 1991
Height: 5'9" **Weight:** 10.10
Club Honours: Div 1 '10
Having made his full senior debut on the last day of the previous season, this all-action Norwich midfielder obviously hoped for further outings. A pre-season injury delayed his return to the first team, but in his first game back he scored against Wycombe and became a virtual ever-present thereafter. This former City Academy player combines a tremendous work rate when the opposition has the ball, with quick feet and passing skills when in possession. Korey's contribution became increasingly influential and his desire to break forward brought him four goals, including a late winner at Wycombe. His rapid progress was rewarded with an improved and extended contract.
Norwich C (From trainee on 6/8/2008) FL 37+2/4 FLC 0+1 FAC 2

Korey Smith

SMITH Michael John
Born: Newcastle, 17 October 1991
Height: 5'11" **Weight:** 11.2
A tall, gangly striker who has come through the youth ranks at Darlington, he figured in four games towards the end of the season, all as a substitute, before starting against Notts County in late April for the first time in the

humiliating home 5-0 defeat that saw County crowned as League Two champions. He made his debut as a substitute against Hereford on Easter Monday, showing good footwork when holding up the ball, and thereby became the 52nd player to be used in this frustrating season.
Darlington (Trainee) FL 3+4/1

SMITH Nathan Colin
Born: Enfield, 11 January 1987
Height: 6'0" **Weight:** 12.0
It was a season of two halves for the attacking Yeovil left-back who was signed in March 2008 from non-League football. Initially on the bench in the first half of the season, he deputised for assistant manager Nathan Jones in his preferred position and made it his own with some quality performances. Surging runs are a feature of the six-footer's game and the ex-Potters Bar defender linked up well with Andy Welsh on the flank.
Yeovil T (Free from Potters Bar T on 23/3/2008) FL 65+9/1 FLC 1+1 Others 1

SMITH Paul Daniel
Born: Epsom, 17 December 1979
Height: 6'4" **Weight:** 14.0
Paul had to be content as Nottingham Forest's back-up goalkeeper to Lee Camp but was rewarded with an extension to his contract to the summer of 2012. With Forest's play-off position secure, he made his only League start on the last day of the regular season, against Scunthorpe.
Charlton Ath (Free from Walton & Hersham on 2/7/1998. Free to Walton & Hersham during 1999 close season)
Brentford (Free from Carshalton Ath on 27/7/2000) FL 86+4 FLC 3 FAC 6 Others 8+1
Southampton (£250,000 + on 28/1/2004) P/FL 14+1 FLC 2 FAC 4
Nottingham F (£500,000 on 13/7/2006) FL 120 FLC 8/1 FAC 10 Others 3

SMITH Philip (Phil) Anthony
Born: Harrow, 14 December 1979
Height: 6'1" **Weight:** 13.12
International Honours: E: SP-1
The consistent form of fellow goalkeeper David Lucas kept Phil consigned to the Swindon bench for most of the season but he performed well when called upon, most noticeably against Charlton in the second-leg of the play-offs when he came off the bench after only one minute to help his side to the final with a string of top quality saves. On his day, he is a very reliable goalkeeper, although he has occasionally been prone to unforced errors.

Millwall (From trainee on 17/1/1998) FL 5 (Freed during 2001 close season)
Swindon T (Free from Crawley T, ex Folkestone Invicta, Dover Ath, Margate, on 28/7/2006) FL 76+1 FLC 1 FAC 5 Others 5+1

SMITH Ryan Craig Matthew
Born: Islington, 10 November 1986
Height: 5'10" **Weight:** 10.10
International Honours: E: Yth
After signing for Crystal Palace on a free transfer before the start of the season, Ryan was used as an infrequent midfield substitute on the left or right. With no sign of him breaking into the first team, his short-term contract that expired in January was not renewed and after a short break without a club, he appeared in Major League Soccer in America during March at Kansas City Wizards, where he scored on his debut.
Arsenal (From trainee on 26/11/2004) FLC 2+4
Leicester C (Loaned on 30/9/2005) FL 10+7/1 FAC 2
Derby Co (Signed on 4/8/2006) FL 5+10 FLC 1+1 FAC 1+2
Millwall (£150,000 on 21/3/2007) FL 14+9 FLC 1
Southampton (Free on 3/10/2008) FL 7+6 FAC 1
Crystal Palace (Free on 26/8/2009) FL 0+5 FLC 0+1

SMITH Thomas (Tommy) Jefferson
Born: Macclesfield, 31 March 1990
Height: 6'1" **Weight:** 12.2
International Honours: New Zealand: 4. E: Yth
Due to Ipswich's uncertain start, Tommy struggled to make the starting line-up until September and October when he played in five consecutive games at the heart of the defence and began to grow in confidence. Dominating in the air at the back and threatening the opposition at set pieces, a hand injury sustained in training allowed the Gareth McAuley-Damien Delaney partnership to be established and Tommy was unable to get a look in. The left-footed central defender then joined Brentford on loan in January and impressed alongside Leon Legge at the heart of the Bees' defence. Was recalled by Town in mid-March due to an injury to Delaney and played in the last three games. Tommy made his international debut for New Zealand in a game against Mexico and was challenging to be in their squad for the World Cup in South Africa.
Ipswich T (From trainee on 10/8/2007) FL 13+3 FLC 1
Brentford (Loaned on 7/1/2010) FL 8

SMITH Thomas (Tommy) William
Born: Hemel Hempstead, 22 May 1980
Height: 5'8" **Weight:** 11.4
International Honours: E: U21-1; Yth
As Watford's 'Player of the Season' for the previous two terms, Tommy was an obvious transfer target in the summer of 2009. The only surprise was his eventual destination of Portsmouth after he had seemingly been bound for Reading. Before leaving Vicarage Road, he continued to be fully focused and turned in excellent goalscoring performances in his last two matches to ensure that he departed in style. Unfortunately, injuries left Tommy frustrated throughout the season, as his appearances for Portsmouth were obviously limited. However, his pace, energy and commitment when playing either up front or in midfield made him a firm favourite with the Fratton Park fans. Was out of contract in the summer.
Watford (From trainee on 21/10/1997) P/FL 114+35/33 FLC 7+3/1 FAC 5+3/2
Sunderland (Signed on 25/9/2003) FL 22+13/4 FAC 3+1/4 Others 0+2
Derby Co (From trainee on 29/7/2004) FL 88+2/20 FLC 2 FAC 5/1 Others 2
Watford (£500,000 on 30/8/2006) P/FL 123+1/27 FLC 4 FAC 8+1/1 Others 2
Portsmouth (Signed on 27/8/2009) PL 12+4/1 FAC 2

SMITHIES Alexander (Alex)
Born: Huddersfield, 25 March 1990
Height: 6'1" **Weight:** 13.4
International Honours: E: Yth
The 19-year-old home-grown talent completed every League and Cup game as he firmly established himself as Huddersfield's number-one goalkeeper. His safe handling and great saves earned rave reviews and he commands his area with great maturity. Alex caught the eye of many Premier League scouts but there was no movement in the transfer window and he went on keep 17 clean sheets. He was 'Young Player of the Season' and a fantastic asset to Huddersfield.
Huddersfield T (From trainee on 3/3/2007) FL 74+1 FLC 2 FAC 3 Others 5

SNO Evander
Born: Dordrecht, Holland, 9 April 1987
Height: 6'1" **Weight:** 12.8
Club Honours: SPD '07, '08
International Honours: Holland: U23-2; U21-15
After impressing for Ajax in their 4-0 demolition of Bristol City in a pre-season friendly, this midfielder joined the Ashton Gate club on a season-long

loan. While not playing in his best position, he performed well enough early on in the season, without looking the answer to City's midfield problems. As City's form faded so did his and, ultimately, this signing proved, as had so many of City's previous foreign imports over the years, to be unsuccessful.
Glasgow Celtic (Signed from Feyenoord, Holland, ex Ajax, NAC Breda - loan, on 21/6/2006) SL 10+20/1 SLC 2+2 SC 3+2 Others 5+5 (Signed by Ajax, Holland on 21/8/2008)
Bristol C (Loaned on 1/9/2009) FL 16+8/3 FAC 1 (Loaned from Ajax, Holland on 1/9/2009)

Rob Snodgrass

SNODGRASS Robert (Rob)
Born: Glasgow, 7 September 1987
Height: 6'0" **Weight:** 12.2
International Honours: S: U21-2; Yth
Just before the start of the season Rob signed a four-year contract with Leeds. Once again he proved a most creative attacking influence and his double sent Watford out of the Carling Cup. That set up a televised home tie with Liverpool in which he gave a sparkling display, followed by a last-minute winner at MK Dons. He was called into the Scotland squad by George Burley for the October friendly in Japan, but missed the trip after sustaining ankle and knee injuries against Carlisle. The bulk of his appearances were on the right of midfield, but he also operated on the left, while some of his most effective games were at the tip of a diamond formation when manager Simon

Grayson opted to use that system. Rob was chosen for the PFA 'League One Team of the Year'.
Livingston (From juniors on 1/7/2003) SL 48+31/15 SLC 4+1/1 SC 5+2/1 Others 0+1
Stirling A (Loaned on 31/1/2007) SL 12/5 Others 2+1/2
Leeds U (Free on 28/7/2008) FL 65+21/16 FLC 6/4 FAC 7+1 Others 8/1

SOARES Louie Pierre
Born: Reading, 8 January 1985
Height: 5'9" **Weight:** 10.3
Club Honours: FC '08
International Honours: Barbados: 2
Louie is a Barbadian international midfielder, who can also play as a winger or at right-back. Having scored in the opening day victory over Darlington, he played his 150th game for Aldershot at Crewe in September. Scored a late equaliser in the Johnstone's Paint Trophy at Hereford, the first in a run of five goals in six games, and started every game until dropping to the bench in mid-February. Despite netting nine times he was not involved in the play-off semi-final against Rotherham.
Reading (From trainee on 3/7/2004)
Bristol Rov (Loaned on 6/5/2005) FL 0+1
Barnet (Free on 5/8/2005) FL 14+6/1 FLC 2 FAC 1 Others 1+1 (Freed during 2006 close season)
Aldershot T (Free on 2/7/2006) FL 58+13/10 FLC 2 FAC 5+1/1 Others 2/1

SOARES Thomas (Tom)
James
Born: Reading, 10 July 1986
Height: 6'0" **Weight:** 11.4
International Honours: E: U21-4; Yth
Tom made three Carling Cup appearances on the wing for Stoke early on, but was unable to force his way into Premier League contention. This led to a loan move to Sheffield Wednesday in November, which eventually was extended through to the end of the season. At Hillsborough the skilful young central midfielder was used in a right-sided role in a four-man midfield, but was unable to have a regular run in the side, appearing from the substitutes' bench on numerous occasions.
Crystal Palace (From trainee on 9/9/2004) P/FL 128+21/11 FLC 5+1/1 FAC 1+2 Others 4
Stoke C (£1,250,000 on 1/9/2008) PL 5+2 FLC 2+1 FAC 1
Charlton Ath (Loaned on 16/1/2009) FL 10+1/1
Sheffield Wed (Loaned on 26/11/2009) FL 17+8/2 FAC 1

SODJE Idoro Akpoeyere (Akpo) Ujoma
Born: Greenwich, 31 January 1981
Height: 6'2" **Weight:** 12.8
Akpo's injury jinxed spell at Hillsborough ended with a loan move to Charlton in November. Despite being a very popular player with the Wednesday fans for his endeavours, it was a disappointing last 18 months for him and the club. At his best, a pacy, foraging, athletic centre-forward and a real goal threat, the big striker arrived at the Valley, making his debut against MK Dons as a late substitute. The following week he scored with a terrific volley at Yeovil, netting again three days later against Bristol Rovers. He made his first start against Swindon on Boxing Day, but his loan period ended after only one more game and he returned to Hillsborough in February. Featuring in most of Wednesday's remaining games, scoring three more goals, all of them coming in consecutive matches, he joined Charlton on a permanent basis in May 2010.
Huddersfield T (Free from Erith & Belvedere on 1/9/2004) FL 1+6 Others 1+1
Darlington (Free on 24/3/2005) FL 18+25/9 FLC 0+1 FAC 1 Others 0+1
Port Vale (Free on 1/7/2006) FL 41+5/14 FLC 4/1 FAC 1/1 Others 1+1
Sheffield Wed (£500,000 on 30/8/2007) FL 18+23/9 FLC 0+2 FAC 1
Charlton Ath (Loaned on 14/11/2009) FL 2+7/2
Charlton Ath (Loaned on 1/2/2010) FL 8+8/3 Others 0+1

SODJE Efetobore (Efe)
Born: Greenwich, 5 October 1972
Height: 6'1" **Weight:** 12.0
Club Honours: GMVC '96; Div 1 '06
International Honours: Nigeria: 9
Efe, as he is better known, remains one of the most popular players at Gigg Lane. At the age of 37, he continues to be solid at centre-back for Bury, operating as the rock in the back four. Outstanding at heading, making those much needed tackles, and lifting team spirit, Efe's role at the club both on and off the pitch is invaluable. The sale of his famous 'Against All Odds' bandana is a popular choice in the commercial shop, and he does, as his headgear states, seem to secure points when they seem to have flown away, including his equalising bullet-like header against play-off rivals Port Vale.
Macclesfield T (£30,000 from Stevenage Borough on 11/7/1997) FL 83/6 FLC 6 FAC 6/1 Others 1
Luton T (Free on 12/8/1999) FL 5+4 FLC 1 FAC 2+1 Others 1

Colchester U (Free on 23/3/2000) FL 3
Crewe Alex (Free on 21/7/2000) FL
86+12/3 FLC 6+2 FAC 6+3/1 Others 2
Huddersfield T (Free on 7/8/2003) FL
61+6/5 FLC 3 FAC 1 Others 4+1
Yeovil T (Free on 23/3/2005) FL 23+2/3
FLC 1+1 FAC 1+1 Others 1
Southend U (Signed on 6/1/2006) FL
35+2/2 FLC 4
Gillingham (Free on 7/8/2007) FL 12+1
FLC 1 FAC 1 Others 1
Bury (Free on 15/2/2008) FL 95+1/10
FLC 2 FAC 2 Others 3

SODJE Onome
Born: Warri, Nigeria, 17 July 1988
Height: 5'10" **Weight:** 10.12
Signed a one-year contract from York in
July 2009 and made his Barnsley debut
in mid-August as a substitute against
Coventry. In November, he joined Blue
Square Premier Oxford on a month's
loan and soon after he returned to
Oakwell, moved on again when he
joined the Slovakian team, FC Senica, in
January.
Barnsley (Free from York C, ex trainee
at Charlton Ath, Gravesend &
Northfleet, on 18/6/2009) FL 0+1

SODJE Samuel (Sam)
Okeremute
Born: Greenwich, 29 May 1979
Height: 6'0" **Weight:** 12.0
International Honours: Nigeria: 4
A transfer deadline day signing, Sam
soon replaced Miguel Llera in the
heart of the Charlton defence to play
alongside Christian Dailly. He was
generally preferred to Llera
throughout the season but missed five
games through suspension after
receiving red cards against Yeovil and
Swindon. He also struggled with a
knee injury towards the end of the
campaign. Sam is a strong-tackling
central defender who is good in the
air and also has an eye for goal,
scoring four times, all with headers.
He received a call up from Nigeria for
their World Cup qualifiers but was not
selected to play. Was out of contract
in the summer.
Brentford (Free from Margate, ex
Stevenage Borough, on 2/7/2004) FL
83/12 FAC 14/2 Others 3
Reading (£350,000 + on 14/7/2006) PL
2+1 FLC 1+1 FAC 2+1/1
West Bromwich A (Loaned on
16/3/2007) FL 7/1 Others 3
Charlton Ath (Loaned on 31/8/2007)
FL 20+7/2
Watford (Loaned on 26/9/2008) FL 1
Leeds U (Loaned on 26/3/2009) FL 5
Others 2
Charlton Ath (Free on 1/9/2009) FL
24+3/4 FAC 1 Others 1

SOLANO Nolberto (Nobby)
Albino
Born: Lima, Peru, 12 December 1974
Height: 5'8" **Weight:** 10.8
International Honours: Peru: 95; Yth
Arriving at Leicester from Universitario de
Deportes of Peru, Nobby is a Skilful and
highly experienced wide midfield player
who can occasionally operate as an
emergency full-back. It was in this more
defensive role that he found himself
asked to play when Michael Morrison
was injured late in the season and he
held on to his starting place for Leicester's
play-off semi-finals against Cardiff.
Though he has yet to score a senior goal
for the Foxes, he despatched his spot kick
in the shoot-out in the Welsh capital with
maximum efficiency to suggest there is
still plenty to come from the Peruvian
international. Unusually, he was given a
standing ovation by both sets of fans
when making his Foxes' debut against
former club Newcastle in January.
Newcastle U (£2,763,958 from Boca
Juniors, Argentina, ex Cristal Alianza
Lima, Sporting, Deportivo Municipal, on
17/8/1998) PL 158+14/29 FLC 10+2
FAC 19/2 Others 27+4/7
Aston Villa (£1,500,000 on 29/1/2004)
PL 44+5/8 FLC 2/1 FAC 1
Newcastle U (£1,500,000 on
31/8/2005) PL 52+6/8 FLC 5+1/2 FAC 6
Others 10+1
West Ham U (Signed on 31/8/2007) PL
14+9/4 (Freed during 2008 close
season)
Leicester C (Free from Universitario de
Deportes, Peru, ex AEL Larissa, on
22/1/2010) FL 6+5 Others 2

SOLLY Christopher (Chris)
James
Born: Rochester, 20 January 1991
Height: 5'8" **Weight:** 10.7
Chris made his full debut for Charlton at
right-back against Hereford in the Carling
Cup and then featured in the next two
League games when coming off the
bench. He started, again on the right, in
the Johnstone's Paint Trophy game with
Barnet in October, then later that month
suffered a knee injury in training that
required surgery and sidelined him for
nearly three months. A good tackler,
Chris is predominately right sided but can
play on the left when required or in
midfield. He started both the games at
Walsall and Millwall at left-back, his other
appearances all coming off the bench.
Charlton Ath (From trainee on
21/7/2008) FL 2+8 FLC 1 Others 1

SOMMA Davide Enrico
Born: Johannesburg, South Africa, 26
March 1985
Height: 6'3" **Weight:** 12.13

A South African-born striker of Italian
heritage, Davide signed a one-year deal
with Leeds after arriving from American
Soccer League side San Jose
Earthquakes. His first, and only, taste of
action for Leeds was as a second-half
substitute against Darlington in the
Johnstone's Paint Trophy, when he
pulled up after only a few minutes with
a hamstring injury, leaving United to see
out the game with ten men. He
recovered to score regularly in the
reserves and was loaned out to
Chesterfield and Lincoln to gain more
experience of the English game. At
Chesterfield he showed purpose and
willingness up front immediately, but
having had a penalty kick saved just
eight minutes into his debut he was
never seen to effect during his time
there. Lincoln was a different matter
and it is safe to say that Davide's goals
went a long way to securing Lincoln's
Football League status for the start of
the 2010-11 season. The South African
bagged an impressive nine goals from
his 14 appearances, although his season
ended on a sour note when he was sent
off on the final day of the season
against Macclesfield.
Leeds U (Free from San Jose
Earthquakes, USA, ex CD Logrones,
Perugia, Pro Vasto, Olbia, on 1/9/2009)
Others 0+1
Chesterfield (Loaned on 26/11/2009)
FL 1+2
Lincoln C (Loaned on 25/2/2010) FL
14/9

SONG Alexandre (Alex)
Dimitri
Born: Douala, Cameroon, 9 April 1987
Height: 6'0" **Weight:** 12.0
International Honours: Cameroon:
22; U23-3. Yth. France: Yth
If the previous season was the
breakthrough one for Alex, this
campaign firmly cemented his growing
reputation. He was arguably Arsenal's
'Player of the Year' and gave several
commanding displays in the defensive
midfield role just in front of the back
four. A strong tackler, Alex also has both
skill and confidence on the ball and
possesses a good shot as well as
deceptive pace. He is able to drop back
and play in the centre of defence and
was used there late in the season when
Arsenal were beset by injuries in that
department. Unfortunately injury also
struck him late in the season and his
absence was acutely felt as Arsenal's
Premier League and Champions League
hopes evaporated. From a player many
Gunners' fans were questioning four
years ago, he has become one of the
first names on the team-sheet and there

is a feeling that he is only going to get better. Alex played 26 times in the Premier League, scoring once, ten times in the Champions League and once each in the FA and Carling Cups. Having featured prominently at the African Cup of Nations he was a key member of Cameroon's World Cup squad.
Arsenal (£2,500,000 from Bastia, France on 16/8/2005) PL 57+16/2 FLC 11/1 FAC 5 Others 21+6/1
Charlton Ath (Loaned on 30/1/2007) PL 12

SONKO Edrissa (Eddy)
Born: Essau, Gambia, 23 March 1980
Height: 5'9" **Weight:** 11.0
International Honours: Gambia: 14
Eddy was never really able to live up to his undoubted talent during his spell at Hereford. After missing pre-season, he took some time to achieve full fitness and then had to play in a central midfield role rather than his preferred flank position. Injury set him back again and, although he produced an inspirational performance during United's vital win at Cheltenham, he was unable to establish a regular place.
Walsall (Signed from Xanthi Skoda, Greece, ex Anderlecht, Roda JC Kerkrade, on 1/8/2007) FL 30+7/5 FAC 4+1
Tranmere Rov (Free on 11/7/2008) FL 29+9/5 FLC 1 FAC 2+1 Others 3+1/1
Hereford U (Free on 19/9/2009) FL 5+5 FAC 1 Others 1+1

SONKO Ibrahima
Born: Bignona, Senegal, 22 January 1981
Height: 6'3" **Weight:** 13.7
Club Honours: Ch '06
International Honours: Senegal: 4; U21
With so many centre-backs at Stoke the odds were always stacked against Ibrahima being able to force his way into a regular starting position for the club in 2009-10 and after figuring in the 1-0 Carling Cup win at Leyton Orient he went out on a season-long loan to fellow Premier League side Hull. There, the giant defender became a most unfortunate victim of circumstance as City's struggles in the Premier League continued. He was signed on a season's loan as a direct replacement for the extremely popular Michael Turner following the latter's controversial transfer to Sunderland. Ibrahima then started a run of five consecutive games when he was made captain in the second game, had three different partners and two of the four defeats were of the heavy variety. The Senegal international, who at times

trained with the youth team, then became the forgotten man. It was a major surprise when he was recalled by new manager Iain Dowie against Fulham, but he came through an incredible test of his character with flying colours as the 2-0 win was City's only clean sheet of the year. Further assured displays in three more Premier League outings helped to repair his tarnished reputation. Ibrahima is the cousin of Arsenal defender Bacary Sagna while another cousin, Daniel Bocande, is a former FC Metz midfielder.
Brentford (Free from Grenoble, France, ex St Etienne, on 9/8/2002) FL 79+1/8 FLC 3/1 FAC 6 Others 2
Reading (Free on 5/7/2004) P/FL 122+5/8 FLC 4 FAC 5
Stoke C (£2,000,000 on 29/8/2008) PL 7+7 FLC 2 FAC 1
Hull C (Loaned on 1/9/2009) PL 9

SORDELL Marvin Anthony
Born: Pinner, 17 February 1991
Height: 5'10" **Weight:** 12.6
A product of the Watford Academy, Marvin is a powerful and pacy centre-forward. In his first year as a professional, he made his first start at Swansea in August and claimed his first senior goal at Leeds in the Carling Cup. With further opportunities at a premium, Marvin joined up with Tranmere on transfer deadline day in January, initially on a one-month loan deal which was later extended to two. Acquired both to give himself some first team experience and to cover for the injured Terry Gornell, he impressed immediately with his clever runs and direct approach to goal, prior to going back to Vicarage Road. Marvin clearly benefited from his time at Prenton Park and was included in Watford's first team squad for the last few matches, claiming his first League goal for Watford at Coventry on the last day of the season.
Watford (From trainee on 1/7/2009) FL 1+5/1 FLC 0+1/1
Tranmere Rov (Loaned on 1/2/2010) FL 6+2/1

SORENSEN Thomas Lovendahl
Born: Fredericia, Denmark, 12 June 1976
Height: 6'4" **Weight:** 13.10
Club Honours: Div 1 '99
International Honours: Denmark: 86; B-1; U21-24; Yth
Despite suffering a dislocated elbow in one of the last games of the season, at Chelsea, Thomas was rewarded for another stellar season at Stoke with a

well deserved selection for Denmark's World Cup squad in South Africa. The goalkeeper's status as a firm favourite with Stoke fans remained undiminished, especially when his sequence of saving three penalties, against Portsmouth, Arsenal and Wigan, in quick succession led to the Potters picking up some extra crucial points. His shot-stopping abilities are well appreciated but it is the way in which he commands his area and organises his defence that has made Thomas such an integral part of a Stoke defence that allowed a team short on goals to perform well beyond a level many predicted in their second season in the Premier League. There were constant rumours during the season linking Thomas with a move to Bayern Munich, but Stoke fans hope these are not true. Despite the acquisition of promising young Bosnian 'keeper Asmir Begovic, fans hope to see Thomas at Stoke next season.
Sunderland (£500,000 + from Odense BK, Denmark, via Vejle BK - loan, Svendborg - loan, on 6/8/1998) P/FL 171 FLC 13 FAC 13
Aston Villa (£2,250,000 on 8/8/2003) PL 139 FLC 13 FAC 6
Stoke C (Free on 1/8/2008) PL 68+1 FAC 5

SOUTHAM Glen Andrew James
Born: Enfield, 10 June 1980
Height: 5'7" **Weight:** 11.6
Club Honours: FC '07
International Honours: E: SP-12
After a relatively injury-free five years at Dagenham, central midfielder Glen was struck down with an ankle problem at Hereford on the first day of training. He missed most of the pre-season with the problem and then found it difficult to make an impression in the early games. After losing his place in the side as Hereford struggled, he was released from Edgar Street in the autumn and returned to his first club, Bishop's Stortford.
Dagenham & Redbridge (Free from Bishops Stortford on 8/5/2004) FL 61+14/3 FLC 1 FAC 3+2 Others 6/1
Hereford U (Free on 27/7/2009) FL 5+1 FLC 2 Others 0+1

SOUTHERN Keith William
Born: Gateshead, 24 April 1981
Height: 5'10" **Weight:** 12.6
Club Honours: AMC '04
Keith, known as 'Gnashers', typifies everything that is right about Blackpool. The tenacious central midfielder joined from Everton in 2002 and goes about his job with a quiet professionalism but certainly lets the opposition know that

he is there. Keith enjoyed his best season yet, showing he can adapt to a five-man midfield with ease and supporting the two flair players of the team, David Vaughan and Charlie Adam, extremely capably. The 43 League starts Keith managed show he is integral to the Tangerines. He made two substitute appearances, most notably coming on at half-time against Sheffield United with the scores at 0-0. The game ended 3-0, with Keith said to be one of the main catalysts of the thumping. He missed just one match through suspension and finished the campaign off with a 'Man of the Match' performance in the play-off final win over Cardiff.
Everton (From trainee on 21/5/1999)
Blackpool (Free on 8/8/2002) FL 257+27/24 FLC 5+4/1 FAC 14+1/2 Others 14+1/4

SOWAH Lennard Adjetey
Born: Hamburg, Germany, 23 August 1992
Height: 5'10" **Weight:** 11.2
Lennard made Premier League history by becoming the first player to appear in the competition having been born after its inception. He made his debut for Portsmouth in a home match against Blackburn and continued for several games in his preferred left-back position, where he grew in confidence, putting in steady and assured performances that typify the bright future that appears to be ahead of him.
Portsmouth (Trainee) PL 3+2

SPARROW Matthew (Matt) Ronald
Born: Wembley, 3 October 1981
Height: 5'11" **Weight:** 10.6
Club Honours: Div 1 '07
After scoring twice in the play-off final to win his side promotion to the Championship, Matt started the season as first choice on the right side of midfield for Scunthorpe during August. But he fell out of favour and started only three League games in the following five months. Returned to the side in February and was a regular for the rest of the season, either on the right or switched into the centre of midfield. A hard-working, energetic player who likes to run with the ball he netted only one League goal during the campaign, but his 90th-minute equaliser at home against Reading in April was priceless, guaranteeing his club's Championship status for another season.
Scunthorpe U (From trainee on 30/7/2001) FL 275+61/37 FLC 11+5/1 FAC 21+3/1 Others 18+2/3

SPEARING Jay Francis
Born: Wallasey, 25 November 1988
Height: 5'6" **Weight:** 11.0
Club Honours: FAYC '07
Jay is another graduate of the Liverpool Academy who does not appear to receive the first team opportunities his talent deserves. A midfielder in the mould of Steven Gerrard, he made his first starting line-up in the Carling Cup tie at Leeds in September and also played in the following round of the competition at Arsenal in October. In between these games he made his Premiership debut at Sunderland and received good reviews despite his team's limp performance in a 1-0 defeat. Sadly that was the limit of his first team action, apart from two brief substitute appearances in December. In March he was loaned to Championship team Leicester for the remainder of the season. Joining City to boost the Foxes' late promotion push, Jay soon settled as an effective cog in their midfield, becoming the club's 100th different marksman of the new millennium when opening his account against Watford in April. Jay looked more comfortable as his loan spell progressed and could be a real asset to some club next season if Liverpool again look to widen his experience.
Liverpool (From trainee on 9/8/2006) PL 1+2 FLC 2 Others 0+2
Leicester C (Loaned on 23/3/2010) FL 6+1/1 Others 1+1

SPECTOR Jonathan Michael Paul
Born: Chicago, Illinois, USA, 1 March 1986
Height: 6'0" **Weight:** 12.8
International Honours: USA: 25; Yth
Jonathan showed his versatility by playing for West Ham in a number of defensive positions. Normally a right-back, he covered at left-back on numerous occasions. He always gives a competent performance such as the one at Aston Villa in January. His best game of the season was against Sunderland in April when he coped admirably with Sunderland's threat and played some fine passes. Jonathan likes to go forward and a superb run against Burnley saw him brought down for a penalty that was duly converted. He was a regular in the United States team and was in their squad of 23 for the World Cup finals.
Manchester U (Signed from Chicago Fire, USA on 13/11/2003) PL 2+1 FLC 0+1 FAC 1 Others 1+2
Charlton Ath (Loaned on 11/7/2005) PL 13+7 FLC 1+1 FAC 2
West Ham U (£500,000 on 16/6/2006) PL 56+31 FLC 2+1 FAC 1+2 Others 1

SPENCE Jordan James
Born: Woodford, 24 May 1990
Height: 6'2" **Weight:** 12.7
International Honours: E: Yth
The talented young West Ham full-back, who is still learning his trade, joined Championship side Scunthorpe on loan in August for the first half of the season. Playing at right-back, he impressed in his opening games with good pace, strong tackling and a willingness to get forward, but his confidence seemed to be knocked after conceding an early penalty in the home derby against Doncaster. After four weeks out of the team, he had a difficult afternoon in the 3-0 defeat at Peterborough in October and did not play for the club again, returning to the Hammers at the turn of the year. A regular in the reserve team he finally made his first team debut in May against Manchester City when coming on as a substitute too late to make an impression. With a big future predicted for Jordan, who has been capped by England youth at all levels, he will be looking to become a regular member of the Hammers' squad in 2010-11.
West Ham U (From trainee on 20/7/2007) PL 0+1
Leyton Orient (Loaned on 25/11/2008) FL 20 FAC 1
Scunthorpe U (Loaned on 17/8/2009) FL 9 FLC 2

SPENCE Lewwis Gavin
Born: Kennington, 29 October 1987
Height: 5'11" **Weight:** 11.9
After missing pre-season through a foot injury, Wycombe's left-footed midfielder played 20 minutes as a substitute in the Johnstone's Paint Trophy tie against Northampton before joining Forest Green Rovers on a month's loan in September. He featured in six games for the Blue Square Premier side before returning to Adams Park and spending the rest of the season in the reserves. Lewwis does have a sweet left foot but was released in May.
Crystal Palace (From trainee on 28/7/2006) FL 1+1 FLC 0+1
Wycombe W (Free on 30/7/2008) FL 21+9/2 FLC 1 FAC 2 Others 1+1

SPENCER Damian Michael
Born: Ascot, 19 September 1981
Height: 6'2" **Weight:** 14.5
Damian is a striker who joined Aldershot on loan from Blue Square Premier Kettering in February and made his debut as a substitute at Chesterfield. After nine appearances from the bench, he started at Cheltenham in late April and his loan was extended at the start of May to enable him to take part in the

play-offs. Damian signed a one-year contract extension at Kettering after the first leg of the play-offs and returned without having scored for the Shots.
Bristol C *(From trainee on 14/6/2000) FL 8+5/1 FLC 0+1 Others 1+3/1*
Exeter C *(Loaned on 22/3/2001) FL 2+4*
Cheltenham T *(Free on 7/8/2002) FL 120+104/35 FLC 1+4 FAC 8+11/2 Others 6+9/2 (Freed during 2009 close season)*
Brentford *(Loaned on 20/3/2009) FL 3+2/1*
Aldershot T *(Loaned from Kettering T on 27/2/2010) FL 3+9 Others 0+2*

SPENCER Scott Kernaghan
Born: Manchester, 1 January 1989
Height: 5'11" **Weight:** 12.8
The former Everton youngster signed for Rochdale on non-contract terms in August, making his debut from the bench against Cheltenham. Although looking quite sharp in the reserves, he never progressed beyond being a substitute for the first team. In fact, was on the bench for 20 consecutive games before being released and subsequently signing a short-term six-month deal for Southend. He quickly impressed with some impact appearances from the bench and went on to contribute four goals for the club before injury curtailed his season prematurely. With a . tremendous work rate and willingness to chase lost causes, Scott can only get better.
Everton *(From trainee at Oldham Ath on 8/6/2006)*
Macclesfield T *(Loaned on 7/3/2008) FL 0+3*
Rochdale *(Free on 14/8/2009) FL 0+4 Others 0+1*
Southend U *(Free on 12/1/2010) FL 5+7/4*

SPERONI Julian Maria
Born: Buenos Aires, Argentina, 18 May 1979
Height: 6'0" **Weight:** 11.5
International Honours: Argentina: U23; Yth
Julian proved once again to be one of Crystal Palace's finest performers of the season with a number of good goalkeeping displays that proved to be more important as the season wore on and they were forced into administration. Winning numerous 'Man of the Match' accolades, the two-time Palace 'Player of the Year' was a strong candidate to make it three in a row which he did. He made his 150th career appearance for the Eagles just before the end of the season in the last home game against West Bromwich and missed only one game through

injury. With one year left on his Palace contract, he is sure to attract attention during the next year from Premier League clubs.
Dundee *(Signed from Platense, Argentina on 1/6/2001) SL 92 SLC 5 SC 12 Others 4*
Crystal Palace *(£750,000 on 14/7/2004) P/FL 150+1 FLC 8 FAC 8 Others 2*

Julian Speroni

SPICER John William
Born: Romford, 13 September 1983
Height: 5'11" **Weight:** 11.7
International Honours: E: Yth
John started the season in the Doncaster midfield but was unable to keep his place and was relegated to the bench. After making some fleeting appearances he went out on loan to Leyton Orient in March and showed an ability to play anywhere across the midfield, whether it be in the holding role or further forward. Back at Doncaster, John was released at the end of the season.
Arsenal *(From trainee on 2/7/2001) FLC 0+1*
Bournemouth *(£10,000 on 10/9/2004) FL 43/6 FLC 2/1 FAC 5/1*
Burnley *(£35,000 on 26/8/2005) FL 31+38/4 FLC 5/1*
Doncaster Rov *(Free on 22/7/2008) FL*

35+15/1 FLC 2+1 FAC 4+1
Leyton Orient *(Loaned on 25/3/2010) FL 9/1*

SPILLANE Michael Edward
Born: St Helier, Jersey, 23 March 1989
Height: 5'9" **Weight:** 11.10
Club Honours: AMC '09; Div 1 '10
International Honours: RoI: U21-7; Yth
This current Republic of Ireland under-21 international returned from a season-long loan at Luton determined to grab his opportunity at Norwich. His versatility may have previously hindered his progress, but he now seems to have settled into a defensive role. He enjoyed an excellent run in the senior team until he suffered a nasty hamstring injury against Bristol Rovers in October. It kept him out until mid-February, by which time the settled Canary line-up made it difficult for him to break back into the side. Seen mostly as a right-back, although he can also operate at the heart of the defence, his fierce tackling and strength in the air make him a formidable opponent. Having played much of his junior football in midfield, he is comfortable on the ball, something highlighted with a superb solo effort, voted as the club's 'Goal of the Season', against Leyton Orient at Carrow Road. It was also his first for Norwich.
Norwich C *(From trainee on 2/8/2006) FL 20+6/1 FLC 3+2 FAC 1+1 Others 1*
Luton T *(Loaned on 7/8/2008) FL 35+4/3 FLC 1 FAC 3/1 Others 6*

SPILLER Daniel (Danny)
Born: Maidstone, 10 October 1981
Height: 5'9" **Weight:** 12.3
After impressing in a pre-season trial at Wycombe last summer, having been released by Millwall, Danny signed a short-term contract and even offered, refreshingly, to play for free during that period. He had just one chance to impress, in the 4-0 Carling Cup home defeat to Peterborough, when he played the 90 minutes. Despite putting in a good shift, with so many contracted midfielders at the club he was released and then played one game for Welling United before joining Dagenham. Initially signing for three months, he did well enough to be offered a contract that took him to the end of the season. Disappointingly, the creative midfielder picked up a hamstring injury in February and did not make any more appearances for the Daggers.
Gillingham *(From trainee on 10/7/2000) FL 89+41/6 FLC 3+2 FAC 2+1 Others 2*
Millwall *(Free on 5/7/2007) FL 6+2/1 FLC 1 FAC 0+1*

Wycombe W (Free on 5/8/2009) FLC 1
Dagenham & Redbridge (Free on 11/9/2009) FL 7+3

SPRING Matthew John
Born: Harlow, 17 November 1979
Height: 5'11" **Weight:** 11.5
Matthew did not feature for Charlton as much as expected during the campaign due to the great form of Jose Semedo and Therry Racon. The central midfielder had a run of five consecutive games starting in late September when Semedo was injured, and also started two more in succession in late December. All his other appearances were from the bench apart from three starts in the Carling Cup and Johnstone's Paint Trophy. Matthew is a strong tackler and likes to get forward whenever possible. He possesses a powerful shot but did not manage to feature on the score-sheet this campaign. Was out of contract at the end of June.
Luton T (From trainee on 2/7/1997) FL 243+7/25 FLC 16/1 FAC 18+1/3 Others 4 FLC 2
Leeds U (Free on 2/7/2004) FL 4+9/1 FLC 2
Watford (£150,000 on 19/8/2005) P/FL 38+7/8 FLC 4+1 Others 3/1
Luton T (£200,000 + on 18/1/2007) FL 58/10 FLC 4/2 FAC 5 Others 1/1
Sheffield U (Loaned on 1/8/2008) FL 8+3/1 FLC 2
Charlton Ath (Free on 9/1/2009) FL 19+6/2 FLC 1 Others 2

SPROULE Ivan
Born: Castlederg, 18 February 1981
Height: 5'9" **Weight:** 10.5
International Honours: NI: 11
Ashton Gate's very own version of the 'Road Runner', Ivan was frequently used as a substitute to wreak havoc in the opposition defence with his electric pace. Many Bristol City regulars felt the Northern Ireland international should have been used more frequently from the start, but his finishing often left much to be desired. Towards the end of the season, one of his runs, much to the delight of the Ashton Gate regulars, set up the injury-time winner against Swansea.
Hibernian (Signed from Institute, ex Omagh T, on 1/3/2005) SL 35+36/12 SLC 5+1 SC 10+1/4 Others 4+2/2
Bristol C (£500,000 on 7/7/2007) FL 57+51/6 FLC 1+3 FAC 4 Others 0+2

SPURR Thomas (Tommy)
Born: Leeds, 13 September 1987
Height: 6'1" **Weight:** 11.5
Tommy continued to hold down the left-back role in Sheffield Wednesday's

back four, although not always at his best. He is a popular player, both for his enthusiasm and enterprise. His raids into enemy territory are great to see but his final ball into the box still needs some work. Has improved on his defensive duties and has captained the side on several occasions. Scored his only goal of the season at Barnsley and will hope to increase his tally to help the team more. Can provide cover in central defence as he originally started out in that position.
Sheffield Wed (From trainee on 18/7/2006) FL 160+6/5 FLC 6 FAC 6/1

STAM Stefan
Born: Amersfoort, Holland, 14 September 1979
Height: 6'2" **Weight:** 12.9
International Honours: Holland: U21
The big Dutch defender has had a stop-start first season at Yeovil, with long spells on the treatment table restricting him to just 20 games, but he did manage a goal against Exeter in January. Sidelined with various injuries, the former Oldham centre-half will be hoping for a better forthcoming season. He is a player whose experience could be vital in a young looking Yeovil defence.
Oldham Ath (Free from Huizen, Holland, ex VV Grasshoppers, AFC 34, AZ Alkmaar, PSV Eindhoven, FC Eindhoven, ADO Den Haag, on 16/2/2005) FL 84+13/1 FLC 2+1 FAC 9 Others 2+1
Yeovil T (Free on 2/7/2009) FL 18/1 FLC 1 Others 1

STANISLAS Felix **Junior**
Born: Eltham, 26 November 1989
Height: 6'0" **Weight:** 12.2
International Honours: E: U21-2; Yth
Junior plays on either flank with West Ham but was usually employed on the left. He provides the team with an extra dimension and much needed width. In the fierce London derby with Millwall in August he was the hero, scoring twice to knock the Lions out of the Carling Cup. Against Hull in November, he was at the heart of most things with his pace and made two of the goals. The game with Burnley in November saw him at his best as he scored the second goal and set up the fourth for Guille Franco. As the season progressed, with West Ham struggling against relegation, Junior found it difficult to maintain a consistent performance.
West Ham U (From trainee on 11/7/2007) PL 18+17/5 FLC 1/2 FAC 1
Southend U (Loaned on 27/11/2008) FL 6/1 FAC 3/2

STANLEY Craig
Born: Bedworth, 3 March 1983
Height: 5'8" **Weight:** 10.5
International Honours: E: SP-4
The former Hereford player started the season at Morecambe on the bench due to the signing of Ian Craney but made an immediate impact with a goal against his former club on the opening day after taking the field. He struggled to pin down a place in the early stages but he came to the fore with some excellent performances and became one of the Shrimps' most important players towards the end of the campaign. His free kicks and corners were often deadly and he provided the assists for almost half of Morecambe's goals in the second half of the season. Full of energy in his role of a box-to-box midfielder, he signed a new contract.
Walsall (From trainee on 23/7/2002. Freed on 28/7/2003)
Raith Rov (Loaned on 21/7/2003) SL 18+1/1 SC 1 Others 3/1
Morecambe (Free from Hereford U, ex Telford U, on 15/7/2006) FL 94+11/11 FLC 4 FAC 5 Others 7

STANSFIELD Adam
Born: Plymouth, 10 September 1978
Height: 5'11" **Weight:** 11.6
Club Honours: FAT '02
International Honours: E: SP-5
Fans' favourite Adam finished the season as Exeter's second top scorer, including a double against Tranmere and the winner against Southend. Knee ligament damage ruled him out in February for a month before he was diagnosed with bowel cancer in March. All City fans are wishing Adam a speedy recovery and hope to see him in a Grecian's shirt again next season.
Yeovil T (Signed from Elmore on 8/11/2001) FL 7+25/6 FAC 0+2 Others 0+2 (Freed during 2004 close season)
Exeter C (Free from Hereford U on 22/6/2006) FL 51+13/17 FLC 1 FAC 1+2/1 Others 2

STANTON Nathan
Born: Nottingham, 6 May 1981
Height: 5'9" **Weight:** 11.3
International Honours: E: Yth
Nathan remained a stalwart in the centre of Rochdale's defence for a fourth season, passing 150 appearances for the club despite a couple of red cards, the second of which resulted in a four-match ban. With Nathan providing the experience alongside 'rookie' Craig Dawson, Dale's defence certainly did their bit in ensuring the long-awaited promotion, conceding fewer than 50 goals and with only the two other promoted sides bettering them in the

goals against column.
Scunthorpe U *(From trainee on 19/3/1999) FL 215+22 FLC 9 FAC 16+2 Others 11+1/1*
Rochdale *(Free on 25/7/2006) FL 138+1 FLC 3 FAC 5 Others 7*

STAVRINOU Alexander (Alex) Michael

Born: Harlow, 13 September 1990
Height: 5'9" **Weight:** 10.6
International Honours: Cyprus: Yth
A product of Charlton's Academy, Alex made his full debut in the Carling Cup at Hereford and made another appearance from the bench against Barnet in the Johnstone's Paint Trophy. An intelligent midfielder, Alex reads the game well and is a good passer of the ball. To gain further experience he was loaned out to Ebbsfleet United in November where he remained for the rest of the season.
Charlton Ath *(From trainee on 7/8/2009) FLC 1 Others 0+1*

STEAD Jonathan (Jon) Graeme

Born: Huddersfield, 7 April 1983
Height: 6'3" **Weight:** 11.7
International Honours: E: U21-11
Jon suffered, like all the other strikers at Ipswich, from the poor start and was unable to put together a run of games, instead having to make do with appearances from the substitutes' bench or being substituted himself. He scored at Plymouth and Cardiff after joining the action in the second half, with the latter goal leading to him starting every game in December. Having opened the scoring in the first minute against Blackpool with a low shot from just outside the box, Jon got two more against Queens Park Rangers, a team he cannot stop scoring against. However, he only played in the game because the club had appealed against a harsh red card he had received in the previous game. After the appeal failed and his suspension was increased to four games, he struggled to regain his form when he returned to the side and joined Coventry on loan in the January transfer window. City desperately needed some firepower and Jon's record looked promising. He began well with two goals in his first three starts, but thereafter his scoring form eluded him and although he always gave 100 per cent and did a lot of chasing he was unable to stop the Sky Blues' slump down the table. After being injured against Derby and ruled out for the season with cartilage problems, Jon returned to Portman Road to consider his future.
Huddersfield T *(From trainee on*

30/11/2001) FL 54+14/22 FLC 5/2 FAC 2 Others 2
Blackburn Rov *(£1,200,000 on 2/2/2004) PL 32+10/8 FLC 0+1 FAC 1+3*
Sunderland *(£1,800,000 on 16/6/2005) P/FL 22+13/2 FLC 2+1 FAC 2*
Derby Co *(Loaned on 13/10/2006) FL 15+2/3*
Sheffield U *(£750,000 + on 11/1/2007) P/FL 24+15/8 FLC 4/2 FAC 4/1*
Ipswich T *(£600,000 on 1/9/2008) FL 39+22/18 FAC 0+2/1*
Coventry C *(Loaned on 15/2/2010) FL 9+1/2*

STEARMAN Richard James Michael

Born: Wolverhampton, 19 August 1987
Height: 6'2" **Weight:** 10.8
Club Honours: Ch '09
International Honours: E: U21-4; Yth
Richard was one of many central defenders at Wolverhampton, which was perhaps why he was to play in both full-back positions. He also lashed in a goal at home to Hull with a finish that a striker would have been proud of. Richard did well in the early part of the season but his willingness to play in any position did not help him establish a regular place. It turned sour in January, after he conceded a penalty against Wigan, being dismissed too. Richard was rarely seen after that.
Leicester C *(From trainee on 30/11/2004) FL 94+22/7 FLC 8+2/4 FAC 3+1*
Wolverhampton W *(Signed on 3/7/2008) P/FL 44+9/2 FLC 2 FAC 3*

STECH Marek

Born: Prague, Czech Republic, 28 January 1990
Height: 6'3" **Weight:** 14.0
International Honours: Czech Republic: Yth
Marek, a tall goalkeeper, signed for Bournemouth on a seven-day emergency loan from West Ham when the Cherries had no fit 'keepers. He made one appearance, a 5-0 defeat at Morecambe, but could take no blame for any of the goals.
West Ham U *(From trainee on 16/7/2008)*
Wycombe W *(Loaned on 12/3/2009) FL 2*
Bournemouth *(Loaned on 11/12/2009) FL 1*

STEELE Jason

Born: Newton Aycliffe, 18 August 1990
Height: 6'2" **Weight:** 12.6
International Honours: E: Yth
On loan from Middlesbrough, the young goalkeeper performed heroics between the sticks in his time at

Northampton. The first teenager to play in goal for the Cobblers since 1978 he was signed when regular 'keeper Chris Dunn picked up a long-term injury. Jason only once conceded more than one goal in a game and kept several clean sheets in his stay. Having won England international caps at almost every junior level, it would be no surprise to seeing him keeping goal for his country in years to come.
Middlesbrough *(From trainee on 1/9/2007)*
Northampton T *(Loaned on 27/2/2010) FL 13*

STEELE Luke David

Born: Peterborough, 24 September 1984
Height: 6'2" **Weight:** 11.12
Club Honours: FAYC '03
International Honours: E: Yth
Chosen as Barnsley's number-one goalkeeper, Luke was put out by a broken finger when new manager Mark Robins took over. On his recovery he regained his place immediately, being first choice throughout the season. Although his shot-stopping was excellent, he suffered some lapses against the cross ball during the second half of the season but he will be happy to add plenty of much-needed appearances as his career develops.
Peterborough U *(From trainee on 26/9/2001) FL 2*
Manchester U *(£500,000 on 4/3/2002)*
Coventry C *(Loaned on 11/9/2004) FL 32 FLC 2 FAC 2*
West Bromwich A *(Signed on 10/8/2006) FL 2*
Coventry C *(Loaned on 23/12/2006) FL 5 FAC 2*
Barnsley *(Free on 14/2/2008) FL 63 FLC 4 FAC 4*

STEINSSON Gretar Rafn

Born: Siglufjordur, Iceland, 9 January 1982
Height: 6'2" **Weight:** 12.4
International Honours: Iceland: 38
Gretar was in and out of the Bolton team during the initial stages of the season, with his first start seeing him surprisingly employed on the right wing in the 3-2 win at Portsmouth, where he impressed. Despite having previously displayed a willingness to press forward, Gretar struggled a little when occupying the same position in the following game. Reverting to his more natural right-back position, Gretar flitted in and out of the first team until he figured in Owen Coyle's first game in charge and stayed in the starting line-up for much of the remainder of the season. This run coincided with his best form of the

season and, a red card at Everton aside, Gretar ended the campaign with a number of the strong, full-blooded displays for which he is now known. A cult favourite on the terraces, Gretar plays with passion and pride – qualities that have endeared him greatly to the Bolton fans in his career at the club to date.

Bolton W (£3,500,000 from AZ Alkmaar, Holland, ex IA Akranes, Young Boys Berne, on 17/1/2008) PL 78+2/3 FLC 2 FAC 4/1

STEPHENS Dale Christopher
Born: Bolton, 12 June 1989
Height: 5'7" **Weight:** 11.3
Signed from Bury in the summer of 2008, Oldham sent him out on a three-month loan to Rochdale to get him match fit and he made a goalscoring debut when coming off the bench to complete a remarkable Rochdale comeback from 3-0 down at Morecambe. He then started a couple of games in central midfield before returning to Boundary Park. Once in the Oldham team he never looked back, bursting on to the scene in mid season as a ball-playing midfielder with a terrific eye for a goal. Reminding many of Glenn Hoddle when he was in full flow, there is certainly a long career ahead for this young man.

Bury (From trainee on 5/7/2007) FL 6+3/1 FAC 3
Oldham Ath (Free on 5/7/2008) FL 24+2/2
Rochdale (Loaned on 14/8/2009) FL 3+3/1

STEPHENS David Rhys Remington
Born: Welwyn Garden City, 18 October 1991
Height: 6'4" **Weight:** 14.7
International Honours: W: Yth
A product of the Norwich Academy, this giant central defender made his senior debut for the club in the Johnstone's Paint Trophy tie at Gillingham, acquitting himself well as the Canary rearguard came under some late pressure. Very accomplished with the ball at his feet, David is quick over the ground and decisive in the tackle, attributes which attracted the interest of Lincoln, who took him on a youth loan for the last couple of months of the season. Although having to bide his time at Sincil Bank, when he did get the chance he grasped it, producing three commanding performances at the season's end.

Norwich C (From trainee on 4/8/2009) Others 0+1
Lincoln C (Loaned on 19/3/2010) FL 3

STEVENS Danny Robert
Born: Enfield, 26 November 1986
Height: 5'4" **Weight:** 9.0
This very talented and skilful young winger was a regular starter for Torquay, normally on the left, in the first two months of the season but subsequently found most of his opportunities were from the bench. Danny's potential, despite his slight stature, earned him an extended contract.

Luton T (From trainee at Tottenham H on 18/3/2005) FL 0+1
Torquay U (Free on 3/8/2007) FL 16+11/1 FLC 1 FAC 0+3 Others 1+1/2

STEWART Damion Delano
Born: Jamaica, 8 August 1980
Height: 6'3" **Weight:** 13.8
International Honours: Jamaica: 55
Along with Kaspars Gorkss, Damion is considered Queens Park Rangers' first choice centre-back. The big Jamaican made 35 starts, partnering Gorkss for 31 of them. He added two more goals to bring his Rangers' career total to 13. The first came in the dying moments of an FA Cup exit against Sheffield United and he competed the scoring in a vital 2-0 win over Plymouth that helped Rangers move away from their relegation rivals. His season was ended early during the opening seconds of the game at Crystal Palace when a clash of heads left Damion with a nasty injury that kept him hospitalised for several days. Fortunately he made a full recovery and will be back in the side in time for next season.

Bradford C (Signed from Harbour View, Jamaica on 5/8/2005) FL 20+3/1 FLC 0+1 FAC 0+1 Others 1
Queens Park Rgrs (Free on 31/7/2006) FL 147+4/9 FLC 9+1/3 FAC 7/1

STEWART Jordan Barrington
Born: Birmingham, 3 March 1982
Height: 5'11" **Weight:** 11.12
International Honours: E: U21-1; Yth
On the last day of the summer transfer window Jordan moved to Sheffield United from Derby, Lee Hendrie going in the opposite direction. On the bench for many games, he was initially used as a left-sided midfielder, with the occasional start at left-back or in midfield. In and out of the starting line-up he looked to have established himself at left-back, where he was particularly good coming forward, until, with nobody near him, he injured a cruciate ligament to end his season with five games to go.

Leicester C (From trainee on 22/3/2000) P/FL 86+24/6 FLC 4+2 FAC 8+3
Bristol Rov (Loaned on 23/3/2000) FL 1+3

Watford (£125,000 on 5/8/2005) P/FL 92+13/2 FLC 4 FAC 5 Others 3
Derby Co (Free on 29/7/2008) FL 26/2 FLC 5 FAC 2
Sheffield U (Signed on 1/9/2009) FL 15+8

STEWART William **Marcus** Paul
Born: Bristol, 7 November 1972
Height: 5'10" **Weight:** 11.0
Club Honours: Ch '05
International Honours: E: Sch
Veteran Marcus showed his Premier League experience by putting in some solid performances in the Exeter attack and contributed two League goals. Marcus scored a second-half penalty in the 1-0 win over Carlisle. A virtual ever-present this term, all Grecian fans will be hoping he pens a new deal for 2010-11.

Bristol Rov (From trainee on 18/7/1991) FL 137+34/57 FLC 11/5 FAC 7+1/4 Others 16+1/14
Huddersfield T (£1,200,000 + on 2/7/1996) FL 129+4/58 FLC 18/7 FAC 9/3
Ipswich T (£2,500,000 on 1/2/2000) P/FL 65+10/27 FLC 4+2/1 FAC 4/2 Others 8/7
Sunderland (£3,250,000 on 30/8/2002) P/FL 77+25/31 FLC 5+1/4 FAC 7+2/2 Others 2/2
Bristol C (Free on 29/7/2005) FL 16+11/5 FLC 1 Others 1
Preston NE (Loaned on 21/3/2006) FL 4 Others 1
Yeovil T (Signed on 30/8/2006) FL 66+1/12 FAC 1/1 Others 6/1
Exeter C (Free on 8/8/2008) FL 71+6/9 FLC 2 FAC 2 Others 1

STIRLING Jude Barrington
Born: Enfield, 29 June 1982
Height: 6'2" **Weight:** 11.12
Club Honours: AMC '08; Div 2 '08
A long-standing groin injury caused Jude to miss the first five months of the season, not appearing for MK Dons until coming on as a substitute in the late December loss at Huddersfield. He then regularly came off the bench over the next two months, showing his usual strength and commitment, but with no reserve team available to sharpen up his match fitness was loaned out to Grimsby in late March. Becoming the 42nd different player to wear a Town shirt last term, the big central defender impressed on his loan debut to help earn a rare League Two victory over Bournemouth, before remaining in contention as a squad player.

Luton T (From trainee on 9/7/1999) FL 6+4 FAC 0+2 Others 0+1 (Free to Stevenage Borough on 22/2/2002)

Oxford U *(Free from Grays Ath, ex St Albans C, Hornchurch, Dover Ath, Tamworth, on 5/8/2005) FL 6+4 FLC 1 FAC 0+1 Others 2*
Lincoln C *(Free on 19/1/2006) FL 0+6*
Peterborough U *(Free on 12/7/2006) FL 14+8 FLC 1+1 FAC 2 Others 0+2*
MK Dons *(Signed on 8/1/2007) FL 48+43/5 FLC 4 FAC 1+1 Others 9+3*
Grimsby T *(Loaned on 19/3/2010) FL 2+2*

STOCK Brian Benjamin
Born: Winchester, 24 December 1981
Height: 5'11" **Weight:** 11.2
Club Honours: AMC '07
International Honours: W: 2; U21-4
Brian began the season in central midfield for Doncaster but after only seven games he suffered an ankle injury that kept him out until January. He came back for a further seven games but his back trouble flared up again and he missed the rest of the season until the penultimate game against Scunthorpe when he was listed on the bench but started in place of John Oster, who was injured in the warm-up. He won his first cap for Wales in September in a World Cup qualifier against Russia but had to withdraw from subsequent squads before playing against Croatia.
Bournemouth *(From trainee on 25/1/2000) FL 113+32/16 FLC 5/1 FAC 11/1 Others 7+4/1*
Preston NE *(£125,000 on 14/1/2006) FL 5+3/1*
Doncaster Rov *(£125,000 on 12/9/2006) FL 126+1/14 FLC 3/1 FAC 12/3 Others 8+1/2*

STOCKDALE David Adam
Born: Leeds, 20 September 1985
Height: 6'3" **Weight:** 13.4
International Honours: E: SP-1
David started the season as second choice goalkeeper for Fulham, being given a brief three-match run in the side in September following an injury to Mark Schwarzer and enjoying an outstanding display in the Europa League tie in Sofia. A confident goalkeeper, who is at ease under pressure and both handles and distributes the ball well, he sustained an injury which kept him out of reserve team action for a number of weeks after which he found himself alternating with Pascal Zuberbuhler for the first team substitute goalkeeper role. At the start of January David was loaned to Championship side Plymouth for the remainder of the season and immediately replaced long-standing goalkeeper Romain Larrieu. Starring in his debut, a 1-0 victory at home to Derby, head coach Paul Mariner was

delighted to retain the services of David until the end of April. He even had to overcome the indignity of conceding an unfortunate goal when he rolled the ball in front of him and the Sheffield United striker Richard Cresswell ran up from behind to tap it into the empty net. Apart from this error the Argyle fans were very impressed with David during his time at Home Park.
York C *(From trainee on 9/8/2005) FL 0+1*
Darlington *(Free on 8/8/2006) FL 46+1 FLC 3 FAC 2 Others 2*
Fulham *(£600,000 on 4/6/2008) PL 1 FLC 1 Others 1*
Rotherham U *(Loaned on 21/11/2008) FL 8*
Leicester C *(Loaned on 3/3/2009) FL 8*
Plymouth Arg *(Loaned on 22/1/2010) FL 21*

STOCKDALE Robert (Robbie) Keith
Born: Redcar, 30 November 1979
Height: 5'11" **Weight:** 11.3
International Honours: S: 5; B-2; E: U21-1
One of Grimsby's more consistent performers during a forgettable season, Robbie was a regular choice at right-back early in the campaign. A hernia problem in September then sadly robbed the Mariners of the experienced player's services for six months and, upon his return, Robbie was restricted to the substitutes' bench. Was out of contract in the summer.
Middlesbrough *(From trainee on 2/7/1998) P/FL 62+13/2 FLC 8+1 FAC 7 Others 1*
Sheffield Wed *(Loaned on 13/9/2000) FL 6*
West Ham U *(Loaned on 23/10/2003) FL 5+2 FLC 1 FAC 1*
Rotherham U *(Free on 20/2/2004) FL 43/1 FLC 2*
Hull C *(Free on 31/1/2005) FL 12+2*
Darlington *(Loaned on 25/2/2006) FL 3*
Tranmere Rov *(Free on 3/7/2006) FL 78+2 FLC 2 FAC 4 Others 2*
Grimsby T *(Free on 29/7/2008) FL 27+1 FLC 2 FAC 1/1*

STOCKLEY Jayden Connor
Born: Poole, 15 September 1993
Height: 6'2" **Weight:** 12.6
A highly-rated schoolboy, Jayden was part of the Bournemouth Centre of Excellence but was promoted to the under-18 squad and then received a shock first team call. He made his debut against Chesterfield and also played at Northampton in the Johnstone's Paint Trophy, when the club had to ask his headmaster for permission to take him out of school. When Bournemouth did not have enough players to fill the bench at Shrewsbury, he was rushed

from his home and made it at 3.30. At the end of the season, Jayden was awarded a five-year contract, including a two-year scholarship and a guaranteed three years as a professional.
Bournemouth *(Schoolboy) FL 0+2 Others 0+1*

STOCKLEY Samuel (Sam) Joshua
Born: Tiverton, 5 September 1977
Height: 6'0" **Weight:** 12.0
Sam put in steady performances at right-back for Port Vale and had his best game in the 2-1 Carling Cup victory at Sheffield United. After a couple of games on the sidelines, he was recalled in the unfamiliar role of left-back and helped the club to a run of seven games without defeat. After a match at Dagenham in October, he suddenly announced his retirement owing to a persistent eye injury that kept giving him double vision. He studied broadcast journalism before resuming his career as a player-coach with Ferencvaros in Hungary.
Southampton *(From trainee on 1/7/1996)*
Barnet *(Free on 31/12/1996) FL 177+5/2 FLC 10 FAC 4 Others 11*
Oxford U *(£150,000 on 13/7/2001) FL 39+2 FLC 1 FAC 1 Others 1*
Colchester U *(Free on 30/8/2002) FL 129+12/3 FLC 5 FAC 14+1 Others 10+1*
Blackpool *(Loaned on 17/3/2006) FL 3+4*
Wycombe W *(Free on 26/7/2006) FL 51+5/1 FLC 3+1 FAC 2+1 Others 2*
Port Vale *(Free, via trial with Dallas, USA, on 31/7/2008) FL 29+2 FLC 3 FAC 0+1 Others 2*

STOJKOVIC Vladimir
Born: Loznica, Serbia, 29 July 1983
Height: 6'5" **Weight:** 14.7
International Honours: Serbia: 32
The Serbian international goalkeeper became Wigan's first signing in the January transfer window following his move from Sporting Lisbon on loan until the end of the season. An experienced 'keeper, he was recruited as cover for Richard Kingson while the Ghanaian was on duty at the African Cup of Nations. An eccentric character, the FA Cup afforded him a chance of regular action, appearing in both games against Notts County. Handed his first Premier League start against Everton, the World Cup bound 'keeper was to play in four League games following injuries to Chris Kirkland. A good shot-stopper, he produced some uncertain displays and was never on a winning side. Following the end of his loan, he was not offered a contract.
Wigan Ath *(Loaned from Sporting Lisbon, Portugal, ex Red Star Belgrade,*

Leotar - loan, Zemun, Red Star Belgrade, Nantes, Vitesse Arnhem - loan, Getage - loan, on 7/1/2010) PL 4 FAC 2

STOKES Christopher (Chris) Martin Thomas
Born: Trowbridge, 8 March 1991
Height: 5'7" **Weight:** 10.2
International Honours: E: Yth
The young full-back joined Crewe on loan from Bolton in mid-March and made his debut at Torquay. In the following game, at home to Notts County, he was injured and, as a result, was forced to return to Wanderers.
Bolton W (Trainee)
Crewe Alex (Loaned on 12/3/2010) FL 2

STOOR Fredrik Olof Esaias
Born: Stockholm, Sweden, 28 February 1984
Height: 6'0" **Weight:** 12.6
International Honours: Sweden: 11
The Swedish international defender once again failed to break into first team contention at Fulham, his only start coming in the Carling Cup tie at Manchester City. A week later he was loaned to Derby, where the right-back position was a source of concern to Derby manager Nigel Clough. Remaining at County until the start of the New Year, Fredrik gave a series of steady performances, concentrating on his job at the back and defending in a solid unfussy way, before returning to Craven Cottage. Despite producing some sound displays in the reserves, his only first team action came as a late substitute in the end of season games at Everton and Arsenal.
Fulham (£1,500,000 from Rosenborg, Norway, on 15/8/2008) PL 0+4 FLC 3 FAC 3
Derby Co (Loaned on 25/9/2009) FL 10+1

STRAKER Anthony Othneal
Born: Ealing, 23 September 1988
Height: 5'9" **Weight:** 11.11
Club Honours: FC '08
International Honours: E: Yth
Anthony is an Aldershot player of Barbadian descent who has pace and the ability to deliver crosses. Having lost his left-back spot to Andy Sandell at the beginning of the season, his first appearance was as a substitute in September. He stayed at left-back until Sandell was fit again, then moved into midfield. In his new position, he played in all but one of the remaining games and scored his first League goal with a cheeky back-heel in the ill-tempered victory over Bournemouth before signing a contract extension to 2012.

Aldershot T (From trainee at Crystal Palace on 6/8/2007) FL 64+5/2 FAC 6 Others 3

STREVENS Benjamin (Ben) John
Born: Edgware, 24 May 1980
Height: 6'1" **Weight:** 11.0
Club Honours: FC '05, '07
A neat and tidy target man who joined Brentford in the close season, Ben suffered a broken fibula a week before the campaign started but recovered in time to make his debut in November. He was then a regular in the side until March, playing alongside Charlie MacDonald. Despite showing some neat touches Ben did not present enough of a goal threat and lost his place to Carl Cort in the last couple of months of the season.
Barnet (Free from Wingate & Finchley on 13/1/1999) FL 44+25/9 FLC 4+2 FAC 1+1 Others 2+2 (Freed during 2006 close season)
Dagenham & Redbridge (Free from Crawley T on 1/12/2006) FL 85+7/29 FLC 1+1/1 FAC 5+1/4 Others 2+2/1
Brentford (Free on 2/7/2009) FL 20+5/6 FAC 3+1

STRIDE Darren Neil
Born: Burton-on-Trent, 28 September 1975
Height: 6'0" **Weight:** 13.5
Club Honours: FC '09
The longest-serving player in the club's history, Darren achieved his ambition of playing for Burton in the League 17 years after making his debut for the Brewers in an FA Cup qualifying tie. He is one of the most iconic players in the club's history, making a record 654 appearances and scoring 124 goals. During his career, Darren went from being a marauding wide midfield player to a more central role before becoming a cornerstone of the Burton defence. Renowned for his never-say-die attitude, injuries sadly took a toll on Darren and his influence diminished in recent seasons. He was unable to command a place in the starting side, other than as cover for absent colleagues, and had to wait until 26th September to make his full League debut at Bournemouth. His long association with the club, where he was variously labelled 'Captain Marvel' and 'Mr Burton Albion', came to an end in May when he was not offered a new contract.
Burton A (From juniors on 3/8/1993) FL 5+4

STURRIDGE Daniel Andre
Born: Birmingham, 1 September 1989
Height: 6'2" **Weight:** 12.0

International Honours: E: U21-5; Yth
With the premium being put upon home-grown talent, Chelsea moved quickly to secure out of contract young striker Daniel from Manchester City. A confident, bright goal-poacher with silky left-footed dribbling skills, Daniel fitted well into Chelsea's style of play and he was given his chance in the FA Cup. He responded superbly, scoring four opportunist goals in three matches against Championship sides Watford, Preston and Cardiff and making a short substitute appearance in the final to gain a medal. He scored his first Premier League goal for the Blues with a superb solo effort against Stoke in January, a tribunal set his initial fee at £3.5-million rising to a maximum of £6.5-million dependent on club and international appearances.
Manchester C (From trainee on 2/9/2006) PL 5+16/5 FLC 1 FAC 1+1/1 Others 5+3
Chelsea (£3,500,000 + on 3/7/2009) PL 2+11/1 FLC 1 FAC 3+1/4 Others 0+2

SULLIVAN John Denis
Born: Worthing, 8 March 1988
Height: 6'2" **Weight:** 14.0
International Honours: E: Yth
John was released by Brighton in the summer and joined Millwall as goalkeeping cover for David Forde. Unfortunately, his only game came in the Johnstone's Paint Trophy defeat at Barnet, where he was severely exposed by some lacklustre defending.
Brighton & Hove A (From trainee on 28/6/2006) FL 13 FLC 1 FAC 1 Others 2
Millwall (Free on 2/6/2009) Others 1

SULLIVAN Neil
Born: Sutton, 24 February 1970
Height: 6'0" **Weight:** 12.1
International Honours: S: 28
Even at 40 years of age, this stalwart goalkeeper belied his age, which he maintains is irrelevant, in order to keep out the young bloods waiting to replace him under the Doncaster goal. An excellent season for the maestro and he will continue in 2010-11.
Wimbledon (From trainee on 26/7/1988) P/FL 180+1 FLC 18 FAC 25
Crystal Palace (Loaned on 1/5/1992) FL 1
Tottenham H (Free on 5/6/2000) PL 64 FLC 8 FAC 9
Chelsea (Free on 29/8/2003) PL 4 FLC 2 FAC 1+1
Leeds U (Free on 5/8/2004) FL 95 FLC 8 FAC 4 Others 3
Doncaster Rov (Loaned on 23/11/2006) FL 3
Doncaster Rov (Free on 19/2/2007) FL 150 FLC 3 FAC 8 Others 6

SUMMERFIELD Luke John

Born: Ivybridge, 6 December 1987
Height: 6'0" **Weight:** 11.0
Luke was delighted to be offered a new two-year contract extension in June and through hard work and training during the close season he started the first two games of the season. Initially on the right of midfield he was switched into the centre, displaying passing ability and endeavour before finding himself out of favour. To get regular football, Luke moved on loan to League One side Leyton Orient, where he impressed when providing perfect cover in central midfield for the injured Adam Chambers. A ball player who is equally at home breaking up attacks or starting his own team's offensive, he returned to Home Park in December to force his way back into his favoured central midfield position.
Plymouth Arg (From trainee on 1/8/2005) FL 53+19/3 FLC 2+3/2 FAC 4+3
Bournemouth (Loaned on 20/3/2007) FL 5+3/1
Leyton Orient (Loaned on 25/9/2009) FL 14 Others 1

SUMULIKOSKI Velice

Born: Struga, Macedonia, 24 April 1981
Height: 6'0" **Weight:** 12.2
International Honours: Macedonia: 65
The Macedonian national captain joined Preston in the summer and was a member of all but one of the squads, making 18 appearances, until the change of manager in January. After that, he disappeared off the scene. A holding midfielder, he showed glimpses of his undoubted class but was never given a consistent run in the side and so failed to make any real impression. He captained his country at Hampden but his future at club level was uncertain as the season drew to a close.
Ipswich T (£600,000 from Bursaspor, Turkey, ex NK Publikum, Slovacko, Zenit St Petersburg, on 28/1/2008) FL 32+10/1 FAC 1
Preston NE (Signed on 5/8/2009) FL 9+6 FLC 2 FAC 0+1

SUNU Gilles

Born: Chateauroux, France, 30 March 1991
Height: 6'0" **Weight:** 12.11
International Honours: France: Yth
The young French striker, who has great pace and a keen eye for goal, made his debut for Arsenal when playing the whole game in the Carling Cup third round tie at home to West Bromwich before making his Champions League debut in the Group Stage game at Olympiakos. With opportunities rare and a need to gain experience, Gilles

went to Derby on loan in February. Capable of playing in the centre of attack as well as on the right, where he was more often used, there were glimpses of his ability and sound education he is receiving at Arsenal. Despite all his talent he found it hard to have a sustained impact on games, but will have gained from having played in the Championship.
Arsenal (From trainee on 10/4/2008) FLC 1 Others 0+1
Derby Co (Loaned on 19/2/2010) FL 6+3/1

SUPPLE Shane

Born: Dublin, 4 May 1987
Height: 5'11" **Weight:** 11.12
Club Honours: FAYC '05
International Honours: RoI: U21-1; Yth
Having been on the bench for the first three games of the season and played in the Carling Cup tie at Shrewsbury, it came as a complete shock to everyone at Ipswich when Shane announced that he had fallen out of love with football and was retiring from the game with immediate effect. The goalkeeper returned to Ireland.
Ipswich T (From trainee on 28/6/2004) FL 32+2 FLC 2 FAC 2
Falkirk (Loaned on 31/1/2008) SL 4
Oldham Ath (Loaned on 18/3/2009) FL 5

SURMAN Andrew (Drew) Ronald Edward

Born: Johannesburg, South Africa, 20 August 1986
Height: 5'10" **Weight:** 11.5
International Honours: E: U21-4
Having been signed from Southampton in the summer, Drew, a neat and tidy midfielder, came on as a substitute for Wolverhampton at Wigan in the first away game, and there were glimpses of his passing ability. He seemed to make it to the first team every so often, his three League starts coming against Chelsea, Manchester United and Manchester City. His involvement ceased after February but he is young enough for more opportunities.
Southampton (From trainee on 23/8/2003) P/FL 116+17/15 FLC 6+1 FAC 4/2 Others 1
Walsall (Loaned on 28/1/2005) FL 10+4/2
Bournemouth (Loaned on 3/8/2005) FL 24/6 FLC 2 FAC 1 Others 1
Wolverhampton W (£1,200,000 + on 2/7/2009) PL 3+4 FLC 1 FAC 1

SWAIBU Moses

Born: Islington, 9 May 1989
Height: 6'2" **Weight:** 11.11
Had it not been for the fact that he was forced to miss five games through suspension, having been sent off twice

during the second half of the campaign, the centre-back would have been a virtual ever-present for Lincoln during the course of 2009-10. Moses is making his name as a fast, strong defender who can both tackle and pass well.
Crystal Palace (From trainee on 5/7/2007. Freed during 2008 close season)
Lincoln C (Free from Bromley on 23/1/2009) FL 39+5/1 FLC 1 FAC 2 Others 1

SWAILES Daniel (Danny)

Born: Bolton, 1 April 1979
Height: 6'3" **Weight:** 13.7
Club Honours: AMC '08; Div 2 '08
Having missed practically all of the previous season with ankle ligament injuries, Danny began the campaign at MK Dons with a six-month deal and made his long-awaited comeback in a Johnstone's Paint Trophy win over Dagenham in early September. Given sporadic opportunities after that the central defender had a short spell at Northampton on loan over the Christmas period. At that time, the club were going through a transitional period and with Danny not being 100 per cent fit things did not go to plan. The lanky defender then returned to Stadiummk before being released and signing a six-month contract with Stockport. After making his debut in the 1-0 defeat to Swindon he became an almost permanent fixture in the side.
Bury (From trainee on 9/7/1997) FL 154+10/13 FLC 4+3 FAC 9+1 Others 10+3/1
Macclesfield T (£40,000 on 14/1/2005) FL 94/5 FLC 3 FAC 6 Others 8+1
MK Dons (Signed on 20/8/2007) FL 43/4 FLC 2 FAC 1 Others 6+1/1
Northampton T (Loaned on 26/11/2009) FL 3
Stockport Co (Free on 18/1/2010) FL 20

SWALLOW Benjamin (Ben) Owen

Born: Barry, 20 October 1989
Height: 5'8" **Weight:** 10.10
Welsh teenage left-sided midfield player Ben became a regular squad member for Bristol Rovers. Ben made an impressive debut in a Carling Cup victory over Aldershot when on as a substitute for the final 20 minutes. He impressed with three long-range shots and excited the fans with his ability to run at and go past defenders before delivering crosses into the penalty area. Towards the end of the season, after a long period without any action, Ben made some promising starts and must be considered as a challenger for a regular starting place.
Bristol Rov (From juniors at Cardiff C

*on 5/7/2008) FL 6+17 FLC 0+2 FAC 0+1
Others 1*

SWEENEY Antony Thomas
Born: Stockton, 5 September 1983
Height: 6'0" **Weight:** 11.9
Noted for his versatility, Antony has, over the years, played in just about every outfield position for Hartlepool. A product of the club's youth system, he was signed as a trainee in 2000 and has now made almost 300 first team appearances. A player who always shows great enthusiasm, he spent most of the season turning out in the centre of midfield, but when needed was moved to play equally well in other positions. At the back end of the season, he was limited to a spell on the bench, usually being utilised as a second-half replacement to add fresh legs in midfield.
Hartlepool U (From trainee on 10/1/2002) FL 221+32/34 FLC 12/1 FAC 17 Others 11+1/2

Peter Sweeney

SWEENEY Peter Henry
Born: Glasgow, 25 September 1984
Height: 6'0" **Weight:** 12.0
International Honours: S: B-1; U21-8; Yth
Peter was a near ever-present in Grimsby's midfield until seeing out the term as a substitute. Despite Town's relegation fight the skilful playmaker maintained form, having his best return of goals in a season to date. Indeed, most of these were scored from outside the box, his stunning 20-yard volley at his old club Leeds deservedly being voted the 'Johnstone's Paint Trophy Ultimate Finish' for goal of the round with 49 per cent of the vote.
Millwall (From juniors on 13/12/2000) FL 45+14/5 FAC 3+4 Others 0+1
Stoke C (Signed on 5/7/2005) FL 18+17/2 FLC 1+1 FAC 3+1
Yeovil T (Loaned on 31/1/2007) FL 5+3
Walsall (Loaned on 22/11/2007) FL 7
Leeds U (£250,000 on 10/1/2008) FL 6+3
Grimsby T (Free on 20/3/2009) FL 44+4/4 FLC 1 Others 2/2

[SYLVINHO] SILVIO DE CAMPOS Junior
Born: Sao Paulo, Brazil, 30 June 1974
Height: 5'8" **Weight:** 10.6
International Honours: Brazil: 6
The former Arsenal and Brazilian international left-back is a veteran at the age of 35 and could have ended his career on a high as he was a member of the victorious Barcelona team in the 2009 Champions League final. Despite his pedigree, his signing by Mark Hughes for Manchester City on a one-year contract in the summer was curious as City already had two experienced players in Wayne Bridge and Javier Garrido plus two promising reserves competing for the left-back slot. He made his City debut in the Carling Cup victory over Scunthorpe in October and in mid-season had a run of six Premiership games, deputizing for Wayne Bridge. His appearances were occasional under Roberto Mancini but he scored a stunning long-range goal in the 4-2 FA Cup victory at Scunthorpe. Mancini granted Silvinho a sentimental farewell appearance in the final match at West Ham and he is now expected to retire and return to his native country.
Arsenal (£4,000,000 from Corinthians, Brazil on 20/7/1999) PL 46+9/3 FLC 2 FAC 4+2 Others 14+3/2 (Signed by Celta Vigo on 25/7/2001)
Manchester C (Free from Barcelona on 24/8/2009) PL 6+4 FLC 1+1 FAC 2+1/1

SYMES Michael
Born: Great Yarmouth, 31 October 1983
Height: 6'3" **Weight:** 12.4
Accrington's leading goalscorer hit the back of the net 19 times during the season. Came to Accrington on loan from Shrewsbury at the end of 2008-09 before signing permanently in the summer following his release. He started off as a sub but took his chance and staked a regular spot after Paul Mullin left for Morecambe, forging a great strike partnership with Bobby Grant. A hard-working player, he signed for Bournemouth following the expiration of his contract at the Crown Ground.
Everton (From trainee on 13/2/2002)
Crewe Alex (Loaned on 24/3/2004) FL 1+3/1
Bradford C (Free on 6/8/2004) FL 6+9/3 FLC 1 FAC 1 Others 0+1
Stockport Co (Loaned on 31/1/2006) FL 0+1
Shrewsbury T (Free on 4/8/2006) FL 33+29/14 FLC 3 FAC 3+1 Others 8+2/4
Macclesfield T (Loaned on 11/1/2008) FL 10+4/1
Bournemouth (Loaned on 14/11/2008) FL 3+2
Accrington Stanley (Free on 20/3/2009) FL 46+2/14 FLC 1/1 FAC 5/3 Others 4/2

SZCZESNY Wojciech Tomasz
Born: Warsaw, Poland, 18 April 1990
Height: 6'5" **Weight:** 13.3
International Honours: Poland: 1; U21-6
There is no question that the goalkeeping position at Arsenal is currently a problem area and out of the four current incumbents Wojciech is regarded as the best prospect. He made a string of fine saves in his debut in the Carling Cup third round win over West Bromwich when keeping a clean sheet and appeared three times for the reserves before going on loan to Brentford in November. Eventually staying for the rest of the season, Wojciech proved to be a superb shot-stopper who commanded his penalty area well, seeing danger early and dealing with it. Some of his saves defied belief and many opponents could not believe they had failed to score when he thwarted them. He missed just two games, due to a back injury, and was acknowledged by most Brentford fans as being the best goalkeeper the club have had for many years. Wojciech returned to Arsenal with the potential to succeed at the top level.
Arsenal (From trainee on 4/7/2007) FLC 1
Brentford (Loaned on 20/11/2009) FL 28

T

TAARABT Adel
Born: Marseille, France, 24 May 1989
Height: 5'11" **Weight:** 12.0
International Honours: Morocco: 7. France: 3; Yth
Exciting young Moroccan international Adel spent another year on loan at Loftus Road from Tottenham. Capable of entertaining and frustrating in equal measure, he became something of a talismanic figure in the Queens Park Rangers' side whoever was managing it. Neil Warnock, in particular, took a shine to Adel and openly admitted playing a formation designed to suit his talents as an attack-minded midfielder. He scored seven times in 32 starts and his blockbusting solo effort against Preston was voted 'Goal of the Season' by Rangers' supporters. He was also named as the club's 'Young Player of the Season' and despite the occasional histrionics, will surely be fondly remembered by the Loftus Road crowd.
Tottenham H (Signed from RC Lens, France on 5/1/2007) PL 0+9 FLC 0+1 FAC 0+2 Others 0+3
Queens Park Rgrs (Loaned on 13/3/2009) FL 5+2/1
Queens Park Rgrs (Loaned on 23/7/2009) FL 32+9/7 FLC 0+2 FAC 0+1

TABB Jay Anthony
Born: Tooting, 21 February 1984
Height: 5'5" **Weight:** 9.7
International Honours: RoI: U21-10
It was not until the final third of the season that Jay found a place in the Reading team, where he looked comfortable, produced his best form and won the wholehearted approval of the fans. He was on the bench in the early part of the campaign, then was left out of the squad altogether before being used as an emergency right-back for a spell of ten games around November. He did well but was dropped when Andy Griffin arrived from Stoke on loan. Jay did not start until the FA Cup replay at West Bromwich but then stayed in the side as a dynamic, ball-winning midfielder. His terrier-like tackling saved countless situations for the Royals and he can give and take bruises with the best. But Jay is not merely a destructive force. He is adept at short and long passing with his creative play setting up regular openings.
Brentford (From trainee on 23/7/2001) FL 95+33/20 FLC 1+2 FAC 12+5/1
Others 6+2/3
Coventry C (Free on 17/7/2006) FL 83+12/11 FLC 4+1/1 FAC 4
Reading (£300,000 on 20/1/2009) FL 33+4 FLC 0+1 FAC 2+1 Others 2

TABERNER Daniel (Danny) Andrew
Born: Bolton, 17 June 1993
Height: 6'2" **Weight:** 12.0
Rochdale's youth team goalkeeper, Danny was promoted to the first team squad when reserve Matty Edwards was injured. When first choice Kenny Arthur then suffered a back injury, and with any loan 'keeper ineligible, 16 year old Danny found himself thrust into the side to face Luton in a televised FA Cup replay. Though Dale were beaten, Danny made a number of fine saves and will be hoping for further opportunities. He was named LFE 'Apprentice of the Month' for December.
Rochdale (Trainee) FAC 1

TABIRI Joseph (Joe) Owusu
Born: Kingsbury, 16 October 1989
Height: 5'9" **Weight:** 11.9
A young midfielder, Joe began the season very much in Barnet's first team squad, yet struggled to force his way into midfield on a regular basis. Shortly after starting the Boxing Day game away to Aldershot, Joe was loaned out to Dover Athletic, where he spent the remainder of the season, scoring a few key goals in their play-off push. Was out of contract at the end of June.
Barnet (From Protec Football Academy on 10/8/2007) FL 6+6 FLC 1 Others 0+1

TABOR Jordan Benjamin
Born: Oxford, 9 September 1990
Height: 5'10" **Weight:** 12.6
Former Chelsea trainee Jordan joined Cheltenham on trial in the summer and impressed then manager Martin Allen. He was offered non-contract terms and spent the first three months at the Abbey Business Stadium, making one appearance at left-back in the Johnstone's Paint Trophy against Torquay. He was released in October and spent some time in the United States before joining the Nike Academy.
Cheltenham T (From trainee at Chelsea on 18/7/2009) Others 1

TAINIO Teemu
Born: Tornio, Finland, 27 November 1979
Height: 5'8" **Weight:** 10.12
Club Honours: FLC '08
International Honours: Finland: 51; U21-20; Yth
The Finland international scored his only goal for Sunderland on his solitary appearance of the season, a well-taken opening strike in a big Carling Cup win at Norwich in August. He soon left the Stadium of Light though on a season-long loan to newly promoted Birmingham, where a combination of his own injuries and City's good fortune in going long periods with an unchanged team restricted Teemu to half a dozen appearances. The clever, energetic Teemu started well enough, fitting in nicely to the Blues' style of play and distributing the ball sensibly. He showed great awareness and combative nature at Hull, the game after making his debut out of position at right-back against Villa at St Andrew's before injuring his knee at Liverpool in November and requiring surgery. When fit again, Teemu was unable to break back into the side.
Tottenham H (Free from Auxerre, France on 12/7/2005) PL 48+13/3 FLC 3+3 FAC 5+2 Others 7+2
Sunderland (£4,000,000 on 28/7/2008) PL 18+3 FLC 1/1 FAC 0+1
Birmingham C (Loaned on 1/9/2009) PL 5+1

TAIWO Solomon (Sol) Oladiran
Born: Lagos, Nigeria, 29 April 1985
Height: 6'0" **Weight:** 12.10
Sol began the season for Dagenham in excellent form, playing in the playmaker role in the heart of the Daggers' midfield and taking all the set pieces. Having excelled for the club in the Carling Cup first round tie at Cardiff, after the game the Bluebirds made the Daggers an offer they could not refuse and he joined David Jones' side before the August transfer window closed. The tenacious, hard-working central midfield player was never able to establish himself with City, losing confidence early on and making only two starts, the second of those being in the final Championship match of the season when they were already in the play-offs and had left out a lot of key players. Sol delayed a knee operation to play in that match against Derby, having the surgery the following week. Was on crutches at Wembley Stadium at the play-off final against Blackpool, but he did go out on to the pitch with his club-mates pre-match.
Dagenham & Redbridge (Free from Sutton U, ex Bromley, Lindsey Wilson College, Maidenhead U, Weymouth, Bromley, on 5/10/2007) FL 47+7/4 FLC 2/1 FAC 3/1 Others 4
Cardiff C (£250,000 on 25/8/2009) FL 2+6 FAC 0+2

TAIWO Thomas (Tom) James
William
Born: Leeds, 27 February 1990
Height: 5'7" **Weight:** 10.10
Tom initially arrived at Carlisle on loan
from Chelsea before signing a
permanent deal early in the New Year.
Very much an engine-room type of
player, he works hard for the full 90
minutes and soon became a crowd
favourite with his never-say-die
approach. His is not always an attacking
brief but the first goal of his career,
scored against Hartlepool, occasioned
wild celebrations.
Chelsea (From trainee on 6/7/2007)
Port Vale (Loaned on 29/8/2008) FL

2+2 Others 1
Carlisle U (Signed on 1/7/2009) FL
30+5/1 FLC 3 FAC 3 Others 4+2

TALBOT Andrew (Drew)
Born: Barnsley, 19 July 1986
Height: 5'10" **Weight:** 11.0
Club Honours: AMC '09
A succession of niggling injuries and
illnesses prevented Drew from enjoying
anything like a consistent run in
Chesterfield's side, which was invariably
better for his inclusion. His willingness
to chase a lost cause from the midfield
wings recovered chances for others and
his keenness to get among defenders
saw him lead the scoring charts for a

good part of the season.
Sheffield Wed (Signed from Dodworth
MW on 19/2/2004) FL 5+24/4 FAC 1
Others 0+3/1
Scunthorpe U (Loaned on 12/1/2007)
FL 2+1/1
Luton T (£250,000 on 26/1/2007) FL
33+16/3 FLC 2+1/2 FAC 4+3 Others 3+1
Chesterfield (Free on 27/11/2009) FL
43+4/8 FLC 1 FAC 1 Others 3/4

TAMAS Gabriel Sebastian
Born: Brasov, Romania, 9 November
1983
Height: 6'2" **Weight:** 12.2
International Honours: Romania: 43
A member of Romania's 2008 European
Championship squad, Gabriel had an
uneasy two-match settling in period at
West Bromwich, being booked on his
debut in a 3-1 home League defeat by
Nottingham Forest and having a tough
time in the 2-2 draw at Newcastle. But
after that the capable, hard-tackling,
experienced central defender played
with great determination and
commitment alongside Jonas Olsson
during the last four months of the
season. His two goals for Albion were
both beauties - a wonderfully struck
86th-minute equaliser at Reading in
March and a powerful header from
Chris Brunt's wicked free kick in the 1-1
draw at Crystal Palace, which created a
new points' record of 90 in a season for
the club.
West Bromwich A (Loaned from
Auxerre, France, ex Bastov, Dynamo
Bucharest, Galatasaray, Spartak
Moscow, Dynamo Bucharest - loan,
Celta Vigo, on 1/1/2010) FL 23/2 FAC
2+1

TANSEY Gregory (Greg)
James
Born: Huyton, 21 November 1988
Height: 6'1" **Weight:** 12.3
Greg was another young, but consistent,
virtual ever-present in Stockport's
midfield – if not in his preferred central
position, then doing a makeshift job on
either flank. He picked up two goals
through the season, first with a low drive
from 25 yards in a 2-1 win over Leyton
Orient and then with a trademark free
kick at Swindon, when he curled the ball
around the defensive wall.
Stockport Co (From trainee on
28/7/2006) FL 41+19/3 FLC 1 FAC 2+3
Others 3+2

TATE Alan
Born: Easington, 2 September 1982
Height: 6'1" **Weight:** 13.9
Club Honours: AMC '06; Div 1 '08
Alan proved himself to be 'mister
adaptable' in Swansea's playing squad

Tom Taiwo

and gave creditable performances in either full-back positions or at centre-back when he covered for the injured Garry Monk. He also captained the side in Monk's absence. During March he played through the pain barrier with an ankle injury which, in late April, forced him to undergo an operation that meant he missed the remainder of the season and ruled him out for three months. He remained extremely popular with the fans, who voted him the 'Supporters' Player of the Year' at the end of season awards.
Manchester U (From trainee on 18/7/2000)
Swansea C (Loaned on 22/11/2002) FL 27
Swansea C (Loaned on 24/10/2003) FL 9 Others 1
Swansea C (Free on 6/2/2004) FL 189+17/5 FLC 7 FAC 17+1 Others 14

TAUNDRY Richard Daniel
Born: Walsall, 15 February 1989
Height: 5'9" Weight: 12.10
Richard started only five games in the first half of the season but was an ever-present from February onwards. Walsall supporters relished the full commitment his performances showed. His first goal for his home-town club was the winner at Bristol Rovers, neatly placing the ball into the corner of the net from 12 yards. This was followed by two further goals, one of which, a thunderbolt at home to Millwall, was voted Walsall's 'Goal of the Season'. Towards the end of the season, he formed a good partnership with Matt Richards in central midfield that bodes well for the future.
Walsall (From trainee on 6/7/2007) FL 63+26/3 FLC 2 FAC 2 Others 3

TAVERNIER James Henry
Born: Bradford, 31 October 1991
Height: 5'9" Weight: 11.0
After six seasons with Leeds, whom he joined at the age of nine, James signed for Newcastle two years ago and progressed steadily through the Academy, making his first team debut in the early season friendly win at Huddersfield. His competitive debut came a few weeks later when he was left-back in the club's youngest ever side fielded, against Peterborough in the Carling Cup. He is an adaptable player and although he is most comfortable at full-back or centre-back, he has also featured at centre-forward for the youth team.
Newcastle U (From trainee on 18/7/2009) FLC 1

TAYLOR Aaron Mark
Born: Lancaster, 9 March 1990
Height: 5'8" Weight: 11.9

A teenage striker who was given a new one-year contract after impressing in the previous campaign, he became yet another Morecambe player whose campaign was ruined by injury. Having failed to make a single start and being reduced to three substitute appearances, Aaron was released at the end of the season.
Morecambe (From juniors on 2/7/2008) FL 7+13/2 FAC 1/2 Others 1+1

TAYLOR Alastair William
Born: Sheffield, 13 September 1991
Height: 6'1" Weight: 10.5
This promising Academy player was given his debut as a substitute in Barnsley's final home game against Queens Park Rangers. He can play either wide or in the centre of midfield. A lot is expected of him in the forthcoming seasons.
Barnsley (Trainee) FL 0+1

TAYLOR Andrew (Andy)
Born: Blackburn, 14 March 1986
Height: 5'11" Weight: 11.7
International Honours: E: Yth
Left wing-back Andy joined Sheffield United in the summer and was in the side from the first game of the season. Hard-working in defence, he tried to make good use of the ball but was less prominent going forward. He was out of the side for two spells through injury and on the second occasion regained his place only after Jordan Stewart was injured. His season ended two games early when he suffered ankle ligament damage in the Sheffield derby.
Blackburn Rov (From trainee on 2/7/2004)
Queens Park Rgrs (Loaned on 13/1/2006) FL 1+2
Blackpool (Loaned on 15/2/2006) FL 3
Crewe Alex (Loaned on 20/10/2006) FL 4 FLC 1 Others 1
Huddersfield T (Loaned on 31/1/2007) FL 7+1
Tranmere Rov (Signed on 16/11/2007) FL 67+2/3 FLC 1 FAC 7 Others 4
Sheffield U (Free on 15/7/2009) FL 22+4 FLC 1 FAC 3

TAYLOR Andrew Derek
Born: Hartlepool, 1 August 1986
Height: 5'10" Weight: 10.12
Club Honours: FAYC '04
International Honours: E: U21-13; Yth
Andrew started on Middlesbrough's bench as the more physical presence of Jonathan Grounds was preferred at left-back. He fought his way into the starting line-up, but in only his third start suffered an ankle ligament injury in a home game against Ipswich and was out until November. He recovered

to take his place on the bench but early in the New Year suffered another injury blow when he had to undergo a double hernia operation. Although back in the squad in late January, Andrew never had a run of games in the first team.
Middlesbrough (From trainee on 2/8/2003) P/FL 87+17 FLC 5 FAC 12 Others 1+2
Bradford C (Loaned on 2/8/2005) FL 24 Others 2

TAYLOR Ashton (Ash) John
Born: Bromborough, 2 September 1990
Height: 6'0" Weight: 12.12
International Honours: W: Yth
After a promising end to the previous season, Ash was thrown straight into the team in August due to the lack of defenders in the Tranmere squad and showed himself more than equal to the challenge. A versatile young player, he was used most often in a deep-lying midfield role where both his height and solid defensive qualities lent an extra layer of protection to the back four. Still only 19, Ash is sometimes tempted to do something over spectacular with his passing but is at his most effective when keeping it simple and is beginning to realize this for himself.
Tranmere Rov (From trainee on 24/12/2008) FL 27+7/1 FLC 1+1 FAC 5/1 Others 1

TAYLOR Christopher (Chris) David
Born: Oldham, 20 December 1986
Height: 5'11" Weight: 11.0
Chris had an indifferent season this time round having enjoyed three years of being Oldham's star player. He suffered a long spell with a mystery illness that kept him out of the side. On his day Chris can terrify any defence, but he was obviously not firing on all cylinders. He scored just the one goal from 33 appearances, a dramatic drop from previous seasons, but still has great pace and skill. Will be looking for a return to form in the new season.
Oldham Ath (From trainee on 15/7/2004) FL 160+14/20 FLC 4+1 FAC 11/1 Others 5

TAYLOR Cleveland Ken Wayne
Born: Leicester, 9 September 1983
Height: 5'8" Weight: 11.5
Club Honours: Div 1 '07
International Honours: Jamaica: Yth
The previous season's 'Player of the Year' played for Carlisle in the opening game of the season against Brentford before signing for the Bees a few days later. Joining on a performance-related fee, the experienced outside-right struggled to

establish himself in the team and dropped out of the match-day squad altogether in December before joining Burton on loan for the rest of the season. The flying winger impressed at Burton, his pace and shooting ability adding an extra dimension to the attack, and he made regular appearances on both flanks for the Football League newcomers.
Bolton W (From trainee on 5/8/2002) FAC 0+2
Exeter C (Loaned on 9/8/2002) FL 1+2
Scunthorpe U (Free on 16/1/2004) FL 121+53/15 FLC 4+2 FAC 4+6 Others 4+1
Carlisle U (£50,000 on 31/1/2008) FL 52+9/3 FLC 1 FAC 2+1 Others 0+1
Brentford (Signed on 14/8/2009) FL 8+4/1 FAC 1+1 Others 1
Burton A (Loaned on 14/1/2010) FL 23+1/4

TAYLOR Danny George
Born: Chester, 5 September 1991
Height: 5'10" **Weight:** 9.6
A young right-back, Danny made the step up from the Shrewsbury youth team for his League debut in the 1-1 draw at Burton in January. He took the opportunity presented by Dean Holden's suspension and had an excellent game. He showed good positional play and did everything asked of him. Danny looked equally comfortable in two further games when Holden was injured and should be a good prospect for the future.
Shrewsbury T (From juniors on 5/10/2009) FL 2+1

TAYLOR Jason James Francis
Born: Droylsden, 28 January 1987
Height: 6'1" **Weight:** 11.3
Began the season with high hopes and was first choice in Rotherham's midfield at the start. However, he was to play only four times and never figured at all once Ronnie Moore arrived in September. Having been a Rochdale target the previous January, Jason moved to Spotland on loan at the end of November, as cover for the injured Gary Jones, and subsequently signed up for the remainder of the season. A strong presence in the centre of Dale's midfield, partnering first Jason Kennedy and then the fit again Jones, he could hardly have had a better start as the club won each of his first six games and were unbeaten in 11. His progress was interrupted somewhat by being ineligible to play against his parent club and then a suspension following a red card at Accrington, but he was back in the side as Dale clinched their promotion to League One.
Oldham Ath (From trainee on 18/2/2006)

Stockport Co (Free on 17/3/2006) FL 98+6/6 FLC 3 FAC 8 Others 2+3
Rotherham U (Free on 15/1/2009) FL 11+6/1 FLC 1 Others 2+1
Rochdale (Loaned on 20/11/2009) FL 23/1

TAYLOR Jonathan (Jon) Peter
Born: Liverpool, 23 December 1989
Height: 5'11" **Weight:** 12.0
The youth team player made his League debut for Shrewsbury in the 1-0 win at Chesterfield in January as a late substitution and had another run against Accrington, again as a substitute, later that month. Playing wide midfield, he looked as if he could develop into a fast and exciting player in the future.
Shrewsbury T (From juniors on 5/10/2009) FL 0+2

Kris Taylor

TAYLOR Kris
Born: Stafford, 12 January 1984
Height: 5'9" **Weight:** 13.5
Club Honours: Div 2 '07
International Honours: E: Yth; Sch
Port Vale's left-back made the position his own after arriving on trial. A quick player, he began as left wing-back and shot to prominence with a superb 30-yard goal in the Carling Cup victory over Sheffield Wednesday. His forays down the wing always caused problems for opposition defenders, but that was curbed when the team switched to a flat back four in which he was confined

to defensive duties. He scored three League goals and all were important, being the winners in 2-1 victories. The first was at local rivals Crewe, and the others came on the run-in to the end of the season. One was another 30-yard screamer at Accrington and the other a long cross-shot against Notts County that crept in at the far post.
Manchester U (From trainee on 2/2/2001)
Walsall (Free on 19/2/2003) FL 58+22/6 FLC 3 FAC 3+1 Others 4
Hereford U (Free on 24/7/2007) FL 60+10/2 FLC 1+2 FAC 6+2/1 Others 2
Port Vale (Free on 7/8/2009) FL 38+3/3 FLC 3/1 FAC 3 Others 2

TAYLOR Maik Stefan
Born: Hildesheim, Germany, 4 September 1971
Height: 6'4" **Weight:** 14.2
Club Honours: Div 2 '99; Div 1 '01
International Honours: NI: 78; B-1; U21-1
Had to play second fiddle to Joe Hart but appeared for Birmingham in both Manchester City matches due to the conditions of the former's loan. Maik kept a clean sheet at St Andrew's and reminded everyone of his good, all-round goalkeeping skills. Despite his age, he was clearly as fit as he ever has been and his sharpness and saves for the reserves were top class. Had an unhappy time of it in the 5-1 defeat at Eastlands, but could hardly be blamed for the goals.
Barnet (Free from Farnborough on 7/6/1995) FL 70 FLC 6 FAC 6 Others 2
Southampton (£500,000 on 1/1/1997) PL 18
Fulham (£800,000 + on 17/11/1997) P/FL 183+1 FLC 22 FAC 20 Others 6
Birmingham C (£1,500,000 on 8/8/2003) P/FL 214 FLC 7 FAC 17

TAYLOR Martin
Born: Ashington, 9 November 1979
Height: 6'4" **Weight:** 15.0
Club Honours: FLC '02
International Honours: E: U21-1; Yth
Martin came to Watford on a free transfer from Birmingham during the January transfer window. A 6'4" centre-half with a wealth of Premiership experience, Martin was short of match sharpness on his arrival, but went straight into the first team and played a full part in Watford's successful struggle against relegation. He scored two valuable goals, against Bristol City and Leicester, and was a steadying influence in a young defence.
Blackburn Rov (From trainee on 13/8/1997) P/FL 68+20/5 FLC 17 FAC 13+2/1 Others 3+2
Darlington (Loaned on 18/1/2000) FL 4

Stockport Co (Loaned on 23/3/2000) FL 7
Birmingham C (£1,250,000 on
2/2/2004) P/FL 91+8/2 FLC 11 FAC
6+1/1
Norwich C (Loaned on 4/11/2007) FL 8/1
Watford (Free on 29/1/2010) FL
17+2/2

TAYLOR Matthew (Matt)
James
Born: Chorley, 30 January 1982
Height: 6'1" **Weight**: 12.4
Club captain Matt was an ever-present
in the Exeter defence. With his
intelligent reading of the game, aerial
prowess and never-say-die attitude, it
was not hard to see why the Grecians
faithful voted him the 'Player of the
Year'. He chipped in with five League
goals, including one on the final day of
the season against Huddersfield that
helped secure City's League One status.
Exeter C (Free from Team Bath, ex
Burscough, Rossendale U, Matlock T,
Hucknall T, Guiseley, on 6/6/2007) FL
75+2/7 FLC 2 FAC 3/2 Others 2

TAYLOR Matthew (Matt)
Simon
Born: Oxford, 27 November 1981
Height: 5'10" **Weight:** 11.10
Club Honours: Div 1 '03
International Honours: E: U21-3
Following an impressive first full season
in Bolton's midfield, Matt started with
high hopes of continuing his fine scoring
form. His first goal came from the
penalty spot in the 3-2 victory at his
previous club Portsmouth, swiftly
followed by another penalty in the home
draw with Stoke. Matt started every
game until he dropped to the bench in a
tactical reshuffle designed to stifle
Chelsea's diamond formation – a game
that Bolton lost 4-0. Despite regaining
his place soon after, Matt fell out of
favour toward the end of the season
before figuring in the run in. His set-
piece prowess served him well yet again
when a trademark free kick, plus another
strike, secured three vital points in a 2-1
win at Stoke. Perhaps the pick of his
goals was a fine free kick in the draw at

Burnley in December and Matt finished
the season in a good run of form with
his total of eight goals ensuring he
ended the season as Bolton's joint-top
League scorer along with Ivan Klasnic.
Luton T (From trainee on 9/2/1999) FL
127+2/16 FLC 6 FAC 10/1 Others 1
Portsmouth (£400,000 + on 3/7/2002)
P/FL 139+40/23 FLC 13+1/3 FAC
10+1/3
Bolton W (£4,500,000 on 17/1/2008)
PL 78+9/21 FLC 3 FAC 4 Others 3

TAYLOR Robert (Rob) James
Born: Shrewsbury, 16 January 1985
Height: 6'0" **Weight:** 12.8
The left-sided Port Vale midfielder had
his best season so far. He only started
around half the games but scored ten
goals, mainly when given a free rein on
the left. Has blistering pace and, if he
adds some consistency, could play at a
higher level. Vale never lost when Rob
scored and his first goal came in the
victory over Championship side
Sheffield Wednesday in the Carling
Cup. His best performance was in the
stunning 5-0 victory at Chesterfield, and
he scored the first goal with a low shot.
His confidence was sky high that
afternoon and he was just unstoppable.
His strike at Hereford was the club's
'Goal of the Season' and he can be a
great substitute with his ability to
change a losing situation in an instant.
Port Vale (Free from Nuneaton
Borough, ex Ludlow T, Stourport Swifts,
Solihull Borough, Redditch U, on
3/6/2008) FL 35+24/11 FLC 3+1/1 FAC
2 Others 2/1

TAYLOR Ryan Anthony
Born: Liverpool, 19 August 1984
Height: 5'8" **Weight:** 10.4
Club Honours: Ch '10
International Honours: E: U21-4; Yth
Ryan began the season as first choice
right-back for Newcastle, but from
November Danny Simpson claimed the
shirt and thereafter Ryan's appearances
were usually from the bench. Although
primarily a full-back, he is a fine crosser
of the ball and on occasions was
deployed on the right of midfield, his
adaptability making him a useful squad
player. His first ever Toon goal came
courtesy of a lovely strike against
Crystal Palace in August, and was
followed a month later by a long-range
free kick against Ipswich, an experience
the Toon Army had been awaiting for
some time, given his reputation as
something of a dead-ball specialist.
Tranmere Rov (From trainee on
3/4/2002) FL 82+16/14 FLC 5+1/1 FAC
9+1/2 Others 8/2
Wigan Ath (£750,000 + on 21/7/2005)

Matt Taylor (Bolton Wanderers)

PL 38+18/6 FLC 4/1 FAC 3
Newcastle U *(£6,000,000 on 2/2/2009) P/FL 27+14/4 FLC 1 FAC 3*

TAYLOR Ryan David
Born: Rotherham, 4 May 1988
Height: 6'2" **Weight:** 10.10
Ryan started the season as first choice striker at Rotherham, but it proved a largely frustrating time and he became a regular substitute, earning only the odd start. Looking to revitalize himself, he went to Exeter on loan on the last day of the March transfer window and his tenacity, work rate and ability to bring players into the game saw him involved in City's end of season relegation escape. On returning from Exeter, the young striker immediately figured in Rotherham's three League Two play-off matches, which culminated in him scoring twice - his first goals of the season - at Wembley, albeit in a losing cause. However, he had come back a different and more confident player and hopefully he can finally fulfill his promise.
Rotherham U *(From trainee on 3/8/2006) FL 42+56/10 FLC 2+3 FAC 3+2 Others 6+2/2*
Exeter C *(Loaned on 25/3/2010) FL 3+4*

TAYLOR Steven Vincent
Born: Greenwich, 23 January 1986
Height: 6'1" **Weight:** 13.0
Club Honours: Ch '10
International Honours: E: B-1; U21 29; Yth
Steven is a strong and solid centre-back whose sound partnership with Claudio Coloccini at the heart of Newcastle's defence laid the foundation for winning the Championship. Honoured to captain the side for the first time in the Carling Cup tie with Peterborough in September, his season was disrupted by injury as a hamstring problem incurred in training in October sidelined him for a month, and then he sustained medial ligament damage to his knee in the League clash with West Bromwich in January. He hoped to return to the side before the end of the term, but he suffered a broken jaw in a controversial training ground incident, bringing his season to a close. He was chosen as the city's 'Sports Personality of the Year' in March by Sport Newcastle.
Newcastle U *(From trainee on 30/11/2003) P/FL 125+7/8 FLC 9 FAC 9/1 Others 20+4/1*
Wycombe W *(Loaned on 12/12/2003) FL 6*

TAYLOR Stuart James
Born: Romford, 28 November 1980
Height: 6'4" **Weight:** 13.4

Club Honours: PL '02; FAC '03
International Honours: E: U21-3; Yth
At the age of 29, Stuart has been a permanent cover goalkeeper at each of his three Premiership clubs and the majority of his first team appearances have been on loan to lower division sides. He was signed for Manchester City on a free transfer from Aston Villa by Mark Hughes in the summer to provide cover for Shay Given whilst the promising Joe Hart was on a season-long loan at Birmingham. Due to Given's fitness and consistency, Stuart played only once, in the FA Cup victory at Scunthorpe in January. Sadly for him, when Given was injured at the end of the season, Stuart was also unavailable through injury and the three Premiership games he might have played in went to Marton Fulop, on loan from Sunderland. Was out of contract at the end of June.
Arsenal *(From trainee on 8/7/1998) PL 16+2 FLC 4 FAC 3 Others 3+2*
Bristol Rov *(Loaned on 24/9/1999) FL 4*
Crystal Palace *(Loaned on 9/8/2000) FL 10*
Peterborough U *(Loaned on 15/2/2001) FL 6*
Leicester C *(Loaned on 18/11/2004) FL 10*
Aston Villa *(£1,000,000 on 1/7/2005) PL 9+3 FLC 3 Others 2*
Cardiff C *(Loaned on 13/3/2009) FL 8*
Manchester C *(Free on 2/7/2009) FAC 1*

TAYLOR-FLETCHER Gary
Born: Widnes, 4 June 1981
Height: 5'10" **Weight:** 11.7
International Honours: E: Sch
The midfielder, who has also been employed as a striker, had a consistent season for Blackpool. He struggled with injuries in September and October but overcame them and was a regular starter for Ian Holloway's team. His best display in tangerine came away at recently relegated Middlesbrough, where he tortured on-loan defender Sean St Ledger, scoring two superb goals in a 3-0 win. He will be slightly disappointed to end with only the seven goals despite playing in a more advanced role. Other wingers are sharper and quicker than Gary but his intelligence and seemingly endless time on the ball means he is a key player for Blackpool and was on the spot with a close-range header to equalise for a second time in the thrilling play-off final victory over Cardiff.
Hull C *(Loaned from Northwich Vic on 16/3/2001) FL 1+4*
Leyton Orient *(£150,000 from Northwich Vic on 9/7/2001) FL 10+11/1 FLC 1/1 FAC 2*
Lincoln C *(Free on 14/8/2003) FL*

77+3/27 FLC 1+1/1 FAC 3 Others 8/3
Huddersfield T *(Free on 14/7/2005) FL 69+13/21 FLC 2+1/3 FAC 4/1 Others 3/1*
Blackpool *(Signed on 20/7/2007) FL 100+12/17 FLC 5+1/1 FAC 2 Others 3/1*

TEALE Gary Stewart
Born: Glasgow, 21 July 1978
Height: 6'0" **Weight:** 11.6
Club Honours: Div 2 '03
International Honours: S: 13; B-1; U21-6
Gary had an awkward role for Derby, as a very right-footed player on the left of midfield. He had to check back before delivering his crosses but the one thing he guaranteed was hard work. Even when he was being given stick by the crowd, by no means unusual, he never hid and always wanted the ball. He started the season with goals in the first two games but that was unlikely to continue. When his contract expired, he was not offered a new deal but he leaves the memory of an honest professional.
Clydebank *(From juniors on 19/6/1996) SL 52+16/14 SLC 3+1 SC 1 Others 4*
Ayr U *(£70,000 on 2/10/1998) SL 94+7/13 SLC 5+1/1 SC 10/3 Others 4/1*
Wigan Ath *(£200,000 on 14/12/2001) P/FL 121+41/8 FLC 9+5 FAC 4+3 Others 2/2*
Derby Co *(£600,000 on 11/1/2007) P/FL 65+22/4 FLC 4+3/1 FAC 6+3 Others 0+1*
Plymouth Arg *(Loaned on 19/2/2008) FL 8+4*
Barnsley *(Loaned on 15/8/2008) FL 2+1*

TEHOUE Jonathan Kahne
Born: Paris, France, 3 May 1984
Height: 5'10" **Weight:** 12.8
Jonathan joined Leyton Orient after impressing on trial in the reserves. A skilful striker with a work ethic, he was due to sign for Huddersfield in the summer but was unable to complete the deal because of a contract issue with his previous club. Although lacking match fitness, Jonathan proved to be a real fans' favourite. He was unfortunate to sustain an injury at Southampton on Easter Monday that ended his involvement. Jonathan signed a new contract during the season.
Leyton Orient *(Free Konyaspor, Turkey, ex Bastia, Apoel Nicosia, RE Virton, FC Brussels, Kasimpasa, on 12/1/2010) FL 5+11/2*

TEIXEIRA Filipe de Andrade
Born: Paris, France, 2 October 1980
Height: 5'8" **Weight:** 10.4
Club Honours: Ch '08
International Honours: Portugal: U21
Filipe contributed well when making his only League start of the season as West Bromwich whipped Watford 5-0 at

home in late October. The classy midfielder, who has penned a three-year contract at the Hawthorns, plus a further year's option in the club's favour, joined Barnsley on loan in February after being restricted to just one start and eight substitute appearances in the League. Made his debut a day later and was impressive in the 4-1 victory at Preston, playing mainly wide on the right where he showed his considerable talent. His first touch was superb and his ability to beat a player with either a shrug of the shoulder or just a turn that they were not expecting was exciting to watch. He soon became a firm favourite at Oakwell and the fans were disappointed that he had to go at the end of the campaign.
West Bromwich A *(£600,000 from Academica de Coimbra, Portugal, ex Felgueiras, Istres, Paris St Germain, Uniao Leiria - loan, on 25/7/2007) P/FL 26+23/5 FLC 4+1 FAC 8*
Barnsley *(Loaned on 1/2/2010) FL 14*

TEJAN-SIE Thomas (Tommy) Malcolm
Born: Camden, 23 November 1988
Height: 5'6" **Weight:** 11.9
Tommy joined Blue Square Braintree Town on a month's loan to gain experience at the start of the season. Having returned to Dagenham, the youngster impressed as a substitute against Darlington in October and started his first League game of the season against Bradford a week later. Tommy, who can operate on the left of midfield or in the centre, was a regular on the bench throughout the campaign.
Dagenham & Redbridge *(Free from trainee at Leicester C on 29/11/2007) FL 1+3 FAC 1 Others 0+3*

TERRY John George
Born: Barking, 7 December 1980
Height: 6'0" **Weight:** 12.4
Club Honours: FAC '00, '07, '09, '10; FLC '05, '07; PL '05, '06, '10; CS '05, '09
International Honours: E: 60; U21-9
It seemed to be a season when John was permanently in the headlines, culminating in the loss of the precious England captaincy following off-field controversy; this after some inspirational displays as he led England to the World Cup finals. But he did not allow the negative publicity to affect his club performances. Indeed, at the height of the furore he scored the winning goal at Burnley with a bullet-like header. The pre-season period opened with protracted rumours of a move away from Chelsea but he agreed

John Terry

a new five-year deal that tied him to the club until 2013-14. There were plenty of positives for the iconic Chelsea skipper. He was voted 'Club Defender of the Year' by UEFA, based on 2008-09 Champions League performances, was one of five Chelsea players shortlisted for FIFA 'World Player 2009', was elected into the 'FIFA/FIFPro World XI', the only player to feature every year, skippered the Blues for the 300th time and eventually passed Ron Harris' club record of 324 matches as captain and lifted the Premier League trophy for the third time. The one-match suspension imposed following the red card at

Tottenham ruined his ever-present record but he marshalled the Chelsea defence to the second best defensive record in the League with 32 goals conceded. The first of his two League goals, back in November, was one of the pivotal moments in the title race – his header against Manchester United clinching three very valuable points as the Blues finished just one point ahead of their fierce rivals. John overcame a late injury scare, the curse of the metatarsal, to lead the Blues to their second successive FA Cup and become the first Chelsea captain to steer the club to the domestic 'Double'.

Chelsea (From trainee on 18/3/1998) PL 296+13/19 FLC 23+2/1 FAC 38+5/10 Others 80/8
Nottingham F (Loaned on 23/3/2000) FL 5+1

TEVEZ Carlos Alberto
Born: Buenos Aires, Argentina, 5 February 1984
Height: 5'10" **Weight:** 10.10
Club Honours: PL '08, '09; UEFACL '08; FLC '09
International Honours: Argentina: 52; U21; Yth
Few players live up to the hype surrounding their signing but the Argentine international forward exceeded all expectations following his controversial move from Manchester United to Manchester City in the summer. After a disappointing season at Old Trafford, United manager Alex Ferguson declined to meet the fee for Carlos demanded by the agency holding the player's rights and thus he was free to go across the city in a rare move between the two clubs. Although the exact fee was never disclosed, it was assumed to be a British record. Although not a prolific scorer with his previous clubs and despite a slow start - only two goals in his first 12 Premiership games – he went on to score 29 in 42 games, including hat-tricks against Blackburn and Wigan and six doubles. Unsurprisingly he was voted City's 'Player of the Season' by both supporters and his colleagues. He was outstanding in both legs of the Carling Cup semi-final against fierce rivals United, scoring both goals in City's 2-1 home victory and an equaliser in the second leg at Old Trafford but it was not enough for City to prevail. But for a three-week hiatus in February when he was allowed to return to Argentina on compassionate leave, City might have achieved more than fifth place in the Premiership. During his absence they were dumped out of the FA Cup by Stoke and dropped four vital points in the race for fourth place.
West Ham U (Loaned from Corinthians, Brazil on 31/8/2006) PL 19+7/7 FAC 1 Others 2
Manchester U (Loaned from Corinthians, Brazil on 10/8/2007) PL 31+3/14 FAC 2/1 Others 6+6/4
Manchester U (Loaned from Corinthians, Brazil on 1/7/2008) PL 18+11/5 FLC 5+1/6 FAC 3/2 Others 5+5/2
Manchester C (£25,000,000 from Corinthians, Brazil, ex Boca Juniors, on 14/7/2009) PL 32+3/23 FLC 6/6 FAC 0+1

THEOKLITOS Michael
Born: Melbourne, Australia, 11 February 1981
Height: 6'0" **Weight:** 12.2
Signed on a free transfer from Melbourne Victory in the summer, Michael had the misfortune to make his one and only appearance for Norwich in the 7-1 home defeat by Colchester on the opening day of the season. He arrived with the reputation of being the top goalkeeper plying his trade in Australia and 90 minutes damaged his reputation. Consigned to the reserves, he cancelled his contract in March and returned to Australia.
Blackpool (Free from Auckland Kingz, New Zealand, ex Bulleen Zebras, South Melbourne, on 6/8/2002) FL 2 FAC 1 (Freed during 2003 close season)
Norwich C (Free from Melbourne Victory, Australia, ex South Melbourne, Bulleen Zebras, on 8/7/2009) FL 1

THIRLWELL Paul
Born: Washington, 13 February 1979
Height: 5'11" **Weight:** 11.4
International Honours: E: U21-1
The Carlisle captain again found his season disrupted by injury that kept him out of the side for nearly four months. Otherwise he carried out his allotted duties as a holding player in midfield, breaking up attacks, winning the ball and creating the platform for others to take the game forward. It is not always a role that is properly appreciated but he does whatever is expected of him.
Sunderland (From trainee on 14/4/1997) P/FL 55+22 FLC 6+2/1 FAC 5+2
Swindon T (Loaned on 8/9/1999) FL 12
Sheffield U (Free on 30/7/2004) FL 24+6/1 FLC 2+1 FAC 2+1
Derby Co (Signed on 5/8/2005) FL 15+6 FAC 2
Carlisle U (Free on 8/9/2006) FL 95+10/5 FLC 6+1 FAC 1 Others 4+1

Carlos Tevez

THOMAS Casey Elliot
Born: Port Talbot, 14 November 1990
Height: 5'10" **Weight:** 10.9
International Honours: W: U21-1; Yth
A first-year professional, Casey impressed for Swansea during pre-season matches, scoring in a friendly against Steve McClaren's future Dutch Champions, FC Twente. An exceptionally quick forward who had a short loan spell at Blue Square South side Newport County in September before returning to the Swans, he made his League debut as a substitute in the opening game at the Liberty Stadium against Middlesbrough
Swansea C (From trainee on 10/7/2009) FL 0+1

THOMAS Daniel (Dan) Anthony
Born: Poole, 1 September 1991
Height: 6'2" **Weight:** 12.13
Youth team goalkeeper and a local lad, Dan was promoted to Bournemouth's first team ranks after the departure of Ryan Pryce. He made his debut in the Johnstone's Paint Trophy at Northampton and started the FA Cup game against Notts County. Dan made his full League debut in the final match against Port Vale, kept a clean sheet in a 4-0 win and was handed his first professional contract in the summer.
Bournemouth (Trainee at Brockenhurst College) FL 1+1 FAC 1 Others 1

THOMAS Hendry
Born: La Ceiba, Honduras, 23 February 1985
Height: 5'11" **Weight:** 12.8
International Honours: Honduras: 39; U23-2
A Honduran international, Hendry arrived at Wigan in the summer after a delay concerning a work permit. The cousin of Genoa striker David Suazo, he joined from Deportivo Olimpia, from where Wigan also unearthed the talents of Wilson Palacios and Maynor Figueroa. In a solid start to his Athletic career, Hendry carried out the holding midfield role with considerable aplomb, having good presence of mind and the awareness to pick out pass, quickly turning defence into attack. His strength and pace are also seen as key elements in his style of play. A tendency to dive into tackles cost Hendry a number of bookings and a thigh strain forced him out of the final six games.
Wigan Ath (Signed from Deportivo Olimpia, Honduras on 2/7/2009) PL 27+4 FLC 0+1 FAC 1

THOMAS Jerome William
Born: Wembley, 23 March 1983
Height: 5'10" **Weight:** 11.10

Club Honours: FAYC '00, '01
International Honours: E: U21-2; Yth
Free agent Jerome joined West Bromwich on a two-year deal, plus a further year's option in the club's favour. Fast and direct with good close control on either flank, he made his debut for the Baggies in a 3-2 Carling Cup win at Peterborough and a month later crowned a 'Man of the Match' display with his first goal for the club in a 5-0 victory at Middlesbrough. He was then sent off when he returned to his former club Arsenal in a 2-0 Carling Cup defeat. Following a tussle with Jack Wilshere, he was ordered off by referee Lee Mason. He received a second red card later in the season for serious foul play at Plymouth which resulted in a five-match ban. On his return following his first suspension, Jerome's brilliant brace saw Albion come from behind to end a three-game winless run with a 3-1 victory over Reading.
Arsenal (From trainee on 3/7/2001) FLC 1+2
Queens Park Rgrs (Loaned on 27/3/2002) FL 4/1
Queens Park Rgrs (Loaned on 29/8/2002) FL 5+1/2
Charlton Ath (£100,000 on 2/2/2004) P/FL 74+29/7 FLC 6+1 FAC 4+5
Portsmouth (Loaned on 15/8/2008) PL 0+3
West Bromwich A (Free on 14/8/2009) FL 22+5/7 FLC 1 FAC 1/1

THOMAS Joel
Born: Caen, France, 30 June 1987
Height: 6'1" **Weight:** 12.4
Rapid French striker Joel signed for Paul Lambert at Colchester from Scottish Premier League side Hamilton in the summer. His career at the Essex club never really got off the ground though and, after making seven substitute appearances, he was loaned back to his former club.
Hamilton Academical (Signed from Kaiserslautern, Germany, ex Bordeaux B, on 15/8/2008) SL 10+16 SLC 0+2/1 SC 0+1
Colchester U (£125,000 on 20/7/2009) FL 0+4 FAC 0+2 Others 0+1
Hamilton Academical (Loaned on 29/1/2010) SL 2+9/3

THOMAS Michael David
Born: Manchester, 12 August 1992
Height: 5'10" **Weight:** 11.0
Michael is a Macclesfield trainee centre-back who performs equally well when in the centre of midfield. He made four brief senior appearances, all in away games from the substitutes' bench, totalling 29 minutes of normal time. His first appearance, at Burton at the end

of September, was his League debut.
Macclesfield T (Trainee) FL 0+4

THOMAS Simon Vaughn
Born: Stratford, 21 July 1984
Height: 5'6" **Weight:** 11.13
A non-League signing, Simon spent the majority of the previous season in the Crystal Palace reserve side, never quite impressing enough to look like a member of the first team squad. Having begun 2009-10 on loan at Ebbsfleet United for a month, before returning to Palace's reserves, where he scored during the second game, he then signed for Darlington on loan for three months from October. The tall striker was one of Steve Staunton's first signings and he scored on his debut in Darlington's first League win of the season, against Shrewsbury at the Arena, but failed to find the net again and returned south after eight appearances. His contract at Palace was cancelled in January by mutual consent and after a trial at Colchester, Simon signed for Billericay Town.
Crystal Palace (Signed from Boreham Wood, ex Thurrock, Aveley, Wivenhoe T, Redbridge, on 22/7/2008) FL 0+1
Rotherham U (Loaned on 13/2/2009) FL 2 Others 0+1
Darlington (Loaned on 13/10/2009) FL 7/1 FAC 1

THOMAS Wayne Junior Robert
Born: Gloucester, 17 May 1979
Height: 5'11" **Weight:** 11.12
Club Honours: AMC '10
The news that Wayne was not offered a new contract by Southampton in the summer was disappointing but hardly unexpected. Since his £1-million transfer from Burnley in 2007, he has been cruelly unlucky with injuries, making just 52 starts – he sat out the last 12 games last season with a calf strain. He will be recalled at St Mary's as an immense presence in central defence, coupling intuition with pace to great effect and, when called upon, making some cracking contributions as a right wing-back.
Torquay U (From trainee on 4/7/1997) FL 89+34/5 FLC 2+1/1 FAC 7/1 Others 6+4
Stoke C (£200,000 + on 5/6/2000) FL 188+1/7 FLC 7+1 FAC 10/1 Others 10
Burnley (Free on 4/7/2005) FL 46+4/1 FLC 2 FAC 1+1
Southampton (£1,000,000 on 16/8/2007) FL 39+6 FLC 3 FAC 6/1 Others 4+1/1

THOMAS Wesley (Wes) Alexander Nevada
Born: Barking, 23 January 1987
Height: 6'1" **Weight:** 11.10

Wes scored his first Dagenham goal against Torquay as an 84th-minute substitute. He added to his appearance total this season, either from the bench or by trying to forge a partnership in attack with Paul Benson. The striker joined Blue Square Premier Rushden & Diamonds in April on a month's loan and returned to the Daggers, sitting on the bench for the last game of the season.
Dagenham & Redbridge (Free from Fisher Ath, ex trainee at Queens Park Rgrs, Waltham Forest, Thurrock, on 1/9/2008) FL 4+24/3 FLC 1 FAC 0+1 Others 1

THOMAS-MOORE Ian
Ronald
Born: Birkenhead, 26 August 1976
Height: 5'11" **Weight:** 12.0
International Honours: E: U21-7; Yth
One of Tranmere's most experienced players was their 'Player of the Year' in 2009-10. Ian was named captain by John Barnes and was exemplary in the role, especially in situations that called for a calm head. At the age of 33, Ian is still sharp in the box and has a true poacher's instinct. He scored a number of important goals and maintained a 100 per cent record from the penalty spot. Amazingly, he scored over a quarter of the team's goals. The son of former Rovers' manager Ronnie, Ian added his wife's surname to his own when he married in July 2009.
Tranmere Rov (From trainee on 6/7/1994) FL 41+17/12 FLC 3+2/1 FAC 1+1 Others 0+1
Bradford C (Loaned on 13/9/1996) FL 6
Nottingham F (£1,000,000 on 15/3/1997) P/FL 3+12/1 FLC 0+2 FAC 1
West Ham U (Loaned on 26/9/1997) PL 0+1
Stockport Co (£800,000 on 31/7/1998) FL 83+10/20 FLC 8/2 FAC 3/1
Burnley (£1,000,000 on 20/11/2000) FL 170+22/37 FLC 6+1/1 FAC 17/12
Leeds U (£50,000 + on 24/3/2005) FL 20+39/2 FLC 3+2/3 FAC 1
Hartlepool U (Free on 12/7/2007) FL 22+2/6 FLC 2/1 FAC 2/1 Others 2/1
Tranmere Rov (Free on 31/1/2008) FL 98+4/26 FLC 2/1 FAC 7+1/1 Others 3+2/1

THOMPSON Gary Kevin
Langrish
Born: Kendal, 24 November 1980
Height: 6'1" **Weight:** 12.2
International Honours: E: SP-5
After struggling to establish himself in his first season at Scunthorpe, 2009-10 started in a similar vein for winger Gary. He spent most of the first four months of the season on the substitutes' bench but was rewarded for his consistent

scoring at reserve level with a first start at Barnsley in December. He did not look back and was one of the first names on the team-sheet for the rest of the campaign. Very fast and direct, he switched between the wing and up front, bagging an impressive nine goals in his closing 18 games of the season, including a stunning late strike to earn a draw in the final game against Nottingham Forest.
Morecambe (From Lancaster & Morecambe College on 1/8/1999) FL 36+4/7 FLC 2+1/1 FAC 1 Others 3
Scunthorpe U (Free on 24/7/2008) FL 37+23/12 FLC 2+1 FAC 3+1 Others 4+1

THOMPSON John Paul
Born: Dublin, 12 October 1981
Height: 6'1" **Weight:** 11.11
Club Honours: Div 2 '10
International Honours: RoI: 1; U21-11; Yth
John is Notts County's club captain and had the proud privilege of lifting the Division Two championship trophy. Preferred as a central defender by the previous manager, he moved over to fill the right-back berth with distinction. The genial Irishman contributed to a record-breaking sequence of clean sheets as promotion was secured.
Nottingham F (Signed from Home Farm, ex River Valley Rgrs, on 6/7/1999) FL 100+29/7 FLC 6+2 FAC 5+3 Others 3+1
Tranmere Rov (Loaned on 25/10/2006) FL 5 FAC 2
Tranmere Rov (Loaned on 31/1/2007) FL 7
Oldham Ath (Free on 13/7/2007) FL 6+1 FLC 2 FAC 0+1 Others 1+1
Notts Co (Free on 17/10/2008) FL 73+2/2 FLC 1 FAC 8 Others 1

THOMPSON Joseph (Joe)
Born: Rochdale, 5 March 1989
Height: 6'0" **Weight:** 9.7
Only turning 21 towards the end of the season, local lad Joe became an important part of the Rochdale side, reaching his 100th-career appearance as Dale finally achieved promotion to League One. Generally operating on the right flank in Dale's usual 4-4-2 formation, later in the season he was sometimes given a free role behind the main strikers when Dale went with a three-man midfield. Joe had his best scoring return to date, unusually for a wide man netting several times in powerful headers, as when claiming the winner immediately after coming on as substitute at Shrewsbury.
Rochdale (From trainee on 5/7/2007) FL 57+34/12 FLC 1 FAC 2+1/2 Others 4+2

THOMPSON O'Neil Anthony
Michael Tyrone
Born: Kingston, Jamaica, 11 August 1983
Height: 6'4" **Weight:** 12.2
International Honours: Jamaica: 21
After a very successful trial match against Manchester City, O'Neil was signed by Simon Davey for Barnsley on a two-year deal from Norwegian club Notodden FK for an undisclosed fee. Although he made his debut at Watford in new manager Mark Robins' first match in charge, he found appearances very scarce and joined Burton on a one-month loan in January. Yet again, he was sparingly used, playing just twice, before returning to Oakwell. A huge and powerful man, the Jamaican's performances were in the centre of defence where he showed he was very solid, but his preference is in midfield, where he will hope to have opportunities in 2010-11.
Barnsley (Signed from Notodden FK, Norway, ex Boys' Town, on 7/8/2009) FL 1 FLC 0+1
Burton A (Loaned on 18/1/2010) FL 1+1

THOMPSON Peter
Born: Belfast, 2 May 1984
Height: 5'9" **Weight:** 13.6
International Honours: N: 8; U21-4
Despite 18 months at Edgeley Park, Peter struggled to find scoring form following his big-money move to Stockport from Irish League side Linfield. At his best when playing off a big strike partner, he was instead often forced to play on his own up front. He had to wait until Halloween for his first goal, which was a deflection from a Carl Baker shot; however, after all his bad luck through the season, he deserved a bit of good fortune. Two more goals followed before, in the January transfer window, he made the switch back to Linfield on loan for the rest of the season.
Stockport Co (£100,000 + from Linfield on 29/7/2008) FL 26+15/5 FLC 1+1 FAC 2+2/1 Others 1+1

THOMPSON Steven (Steve)
Howard
Born: Paisley, 14 October 1978
Height: 6'2" **Weight:** 12.10
Club Honours: SC '03; SPD '05; SLC '05
International Honours: S: 16; U21-12
Increased competition in Burnley's forward ranks made life difficult for Scottish international Steve and he made only one Premier League start, winning 'Man of the Match' honours for his performance at home to Stoke. He appeared in half the League games from the bench, though, and more often than

not impressed, hitting a rich scoring vein at the end of the season with four goals in his final six appearances. He was the type of big target man the Clarets generally lacked and probably deserved to be seen a good deal more than he was this season. Was out of contract in the summer.
Dundee U (From juniors on 1/8/1996) SL 81+52/18 SLC 10+4/9 SC 6+8/4
Glasgow Rgrs (Signed on 1/1/2003) SL 21+41/17 SLC 3+2/3 SC 0+5 Others 2+11/3
Cardiff C (Signed on 10/1/2006) FL 71+26/16 FLC 0+2 FAC 3+4/1
Burnley (Free on 1/9/2008) P/FL 24+30/11 FLC 1 FAC 4+3/3 Others 2+1/1

THOMPSON Tyrone l'Yungo
Born: Sheffield, 8 May 1982
Height: 5'9" **Weight:** 11.2
Most of Tyrone's opportunities for Torquay were in the holding midfield role but he also had a few games in the hole behind a single striker away from home. Despite being a reliable squad member, he did not quite do enough to earn a renewed contract.
Sheffield U (From trainee on 10/7/2000) FLC 1+1 FAC 1
Lincoln C (Loaned on 18/10/2002) FL 0+1 Others 2
Huddersfield T (Free on 7/8/2003) FL 1+1 (Freed during 2004 close season)
Torquay U (Free from Crawley T, ex Scarborough, Halifax T, on 24/5/2008) FL 17+7 FLC 1 FAC 2 Others 2

THOMSON Jake Samuel
Born: Portsmouth, 12 May 1989
Height: 5'11" **Weight:** 11.5
International Honours: Trinidad & Tobago: 2; Yth. E: Yth
A Southampton Academy graduate and England under-17 international, Jake is a clever and versatile attacking midfielder who is at his best on the wings. He featured as a substitute early in the season, getting four short excursions into first team action before travelling to Egypt with Trinidad and Tobago for the FIFA under-20 World Cup. Soon after his return from the Caribbean he was loaned to Torquay, where his tremendous pace and skill on the ball were used to best effect when cutting in from a position wide on the left. However, an unwillingness to chase back saw him slip out of first team contention and back at St Mary's he was released in the summer.
Southampton (From trainee on 25/5/2006) FL 6+8 FLC 1+1
Bournemouth (Loaned on 15/1/2009) FL 6/1
Torquay U (Loaned on 27/10/2009) FL 13+2/1 FAC 3

THORNE George Louis Elliot
Born: Chatham, 4 January 1993
Height: 6'2" **Weight:** 13.1
International Honours: E: Yth
George, a tall, upright midfielder, became West Bromwich's youngest League debutant for 49 years when, at the age of 16 years 319 days, he came on as an 88th-minute substitute in the 4-0 win at Sheffield Wednesday in late November. In April 1960, Baggies' legend Bobby Hope was just 16 years 219 days when he played his first League game for the Baggies against Arsenal. A member of Albion's Academy since 2004, George has wonderful ability on the ball and looks set for a bright future.
West Bromwich A (From trainee on 2/3/2010) FL 0+1

THORNE Peter Lee
Born: Manchester, 21 June 1973
Height: 6'0" **Weight:** 13.6
Club Honours: Div 2 '96; AMC '00
Bradford's top scorer in his first two seasons at the club, Peter suffered a very frustrating campaign. He willingly took a pay cut to remain with City and was handed the captain's armband, though his reign started with a 5-0 defeat at Notts County on the opening day. Peter was dogged with injuries to his back, hamstring and knee and was able to start only five games. His final appearance was from the bench at Accrington in Peter Taylor's first game in charge before the recurring knee problems made up his mind about retiring. An immensely popular figure with his team-mates and the fans at Valley Parade, he finished just a couple short of 200 career goals.
Blackburn Rov (From trainee on 20/6/1991) Others 0+1
Wigan Ath (Loaned on 11/3/1994) FL 10+1
Swindon T (£225,000 on 18/1/1995) FL 66+11/27 FLC 5+1/4 FAC 4+2 Others 1+1/1
Stoke C (£350,000 + on 25/7/1997) FL 147+11/65 FLC 12+1/6 FAC 5+1 Others 9+3/9
Cardiff C (£1,700,000 on 13/9/2001) FL 116+10/46 FLC 4/3 FAC 6+1/1 Others 6/1
Norwich C (Free on 4/7/2005) FL 15+21/1 FLC 2+1/1 FAC 1+2
Bradford C (Free on 27/7/2007) FL 67+10/31 FLC 0+1 FAC 2+1/1 Others 1+2

THORNHILL Matthew (Matt) Mark
Born: Nottingham, 11 October 1988
Height: 5'9" **Weight:** 12.0
A Nottingham Forest midfielder with a

promising reputation, Matt agreed a half-season loan deal at Brighton before the start of the campaign, but showed only glimpses of his best form despite the expectations of manager Russell Slade. By November he was no longer in the Albion first team squad, and the following month he returned to the City Ground a month early. Still unable to get a game at Forest, he joined Cheltenham on loan for the final three months of the season. A talented player with vision and passing ability as well as excellent mobility around congested League Two midfields, his arrival helped to galvanise the Robins into a more balanced outfit. Capable of winning the ball and making creative use of it, Matt's contribution to Cheltenham's efforts to stay in the Football League was highly significant and he played in every game of the loan spell save for a couple of minor injury setbacks.
Nottingham F (From trainee on 13/12/2007) FL 18+20/5 FLC 1+2 FAC 2+1
Brighton & Hove A (Loaned on 21/7/2009) FL 3+4 FLC 1 Others 1
Cheltenham T (Loaned on 21/1/2010) FL 16+1/3

THORNTON Kevin Anthony
Born: Drogheda, 9 July 1986
Height: 5'7" **Weight:** 11.0
International Honours: RoI: Yth
Not long after the central midfielder joined Nuneaton, he felt that he was good enough to have another crack at League football. Nuneaton manager Kevin Wilkin and Northampton boss Ian Sampson were team-mates at Sixfields and agreed on a short-term contract for Kevin. Sadly his stay was interrupted by injury and suspension but he showed what he had to offer with a cracking 25-yard goal that came from nothing.
Coventry C (From trainee on 9/7/2003) FL 19+31/2 FLC 0+2 FAC 0+3 (Freed on 2/7/2009)
Brighton & Hove A (Loaned on 26/9/2008) FL 4+8 FLC 1 Others 2
Northampton T (Free from Nuneaton T, ex trial at Port Vale, Boyne Rov, Coventry Sphinx, on 8/1/2010) FL 4+7/1

THORNTON Sean
Born: Drogheda, 18 May 1983
Height: 5'10" **Weight:** 11.0
Club Honours: Ch '05; AMC '07
International Honours: RoI: U21-12; Yth
Sean is a very skilful midfielder who likes nothing better than shaping the play. He is always a willing worker for Leyton Orient and constantly looks for the ball. Sean proved his worth for the big occasion by scoring twice in the 2-1 home win over the champions Norwich

but was out of contract in the summer and was released.

Tranmere Rov *(Trainee) FL 9+2/1 FAC 0+1 Others 0+1*
Sunderland *(Signed on 4/7/2002) P/FL 28+21/9 FLC 4 FAC 5+4 Others 1+1*
Blackpool *(Loaned on 7/11/2002) FL 1+2 Others 1*
Doncaster Rov *(£175,000 on 14/7/2005) FL 38+21/2 FLC 3+2/1 FAC 4+2 Others 4+3/1*
Leyton Orient *(Free on 9/8/2007) FL 76+15/11 FLC 1+2 FAC 5+1 Others 1+1*
Shrewsbury T *(Loaned on 12/9/2008) FL 5/1 Others 1*

THORPE Lee Anthony
Born: Wolverhampton, 14 December 1975
Height: 6'1" **Weight:** 12.4
This experienced journeyman striker made Darlington his 11th club when he was signed by Colin Todd in the summer. He immediately impressed with his prodigious aerial leaps to win the ball and his willingness to chase and harry defenders. Injury problems limited him to nine starts for the Quakers before being released to join Fleetwood Town in early March. He scored just one goal which was enough to beat one of his former clubs, Lincoln, in the Johnstone's Paint Trophy in September.
Blackpool *(From trainee on 18/7/1994) FL 2+10 FLC 0+1 FAC 1 Others 1*
Lincoln C *(Free on 4/8/1997) FL 183+9/58 FLC 5+1/1 FAC 14/1 Others 9+1/7*
Leyton Orient *(Free on 3/5/2002) FL 42+13/12 FLC 2/1 FAC 1 Others 1+1*
Grimsby T *(Loaned on 6/2/2004) FL 5+1*
Bristol Rov *(Free on 12/3/2004) FL 25+10/4 FLC 1/1 FAC 0+1 Others 4/1*
Swansea C *(Signed on 8/2/2005) FL 9+9/3*
Peterborough U *(Loaned on 30/9/2005) FL 6 FAC 1 Others 1*
Torquay U *(Free on 13/2/2006) FL 49+2/11 FLC 1 FAC 3+1 Others 1*
Brentford *(Free on 4/7/2007) FL 17+2/4 FAC 2*
Rochdale *(Free on 31/1/2008) FL 23+13/6 FLC 0+1 FAC 2+1 Others 3+1/1*
Darlington *(Free on 7/8/2009) FL 7+1 FLC 1 Others 1/1*

THORVALDSSON Gunnar Heidar
Born: Vestmannaeyjar, Iceland, 1 April 1982
Height: 6'0" **Weight:** 11.11
International Honours: Iceland: 21
Gunnar joined Reading on loan from Danish Superliga club Esbjerg at the beginning of 2010 to boost the chances of avoiding relegation and perhaps even reaching the play-offs. However, the

move could not be termed a success. First Gunnar, a cousin of club captain Ivor Ingimarsson, had to wait for international clearance and could not be registered in time for the FA Cup tie against Liverpool. Then, despite training assiduously with the squad, he could not force his way into the team on anything but a spasmodic basis. He made only two starts, at Nottingham Forest and Sheffield United, both Championship games being lost, and a further three appearances as a substitute. Despite being used as a striker, he failed to score and returned to his club at the end of the season.
Reading *(Loaned from Esbjerg, Denmark, ex IBV Vestmannaeyjar, Halmstads, Hannover 96, Valerenga - loan, on 1/1/2010) FL 2+2 FAC 0+1*

THRELFALL Robert (Robbie) Richard
Born: Liverpool, 28 November 1988
Height: 5'11" **Weight:** 11.2
Club Honours: FAYC '06, '07
International Honours: E: Yth
Arriving at Northampton on loan from Liverpool in August, Robbie's run as a full-back came at the same time that there were changes to the management. Stuart Gray had signed him, but left at the time his loan spell was up for renewal. Regardless of the situation and despite his short stay, Robbie had showed some neat touches and solid defending. In February, the left-back was Peter Taylor's first loan signing as Bradford manager and he wasted no time making an impact. Scoring a superb free kick on his debut in an impressive win at League Two leaders Rochdale, despite admitting that he rarely got the chance to take set pieces in the reserves at Anfield, he proved that the strike was no fluke with an even better curler from another free kick against Port Vale. Was out of contract in the summer.
Liverpool *(From trainee on 26/7/2006)*
Hereford U *(Loaned on 2/11/2007) FL 6+3 FAC 3*
Hereford U *(Loaned on 30/7/2008) FL 3 FLC 1*
Stockport Co *(Loaned on 5/1/2009) FL 1+1*
Northampton T *(Loaned on 21/8/2009) FL 1+3 Others 1*

THURGOOD Stuart Anthony
Born: Enfield, 4 November 1981
Height: 5'8" **Weight:** 11.10
Club Honours: FAT '05, '06
International Honours: E: SP-5
Stuart made his Dagenham debut at Crewe on the opening day of the season. He soon became a Daggers' favourite with his fearless tackling in the

heart of the midfield. Stuart suffered a cartilage problem in October and rested it for a month. In his comeback game in a County Cup tie, he jarred the knee again and this time an operation was necessary in December. This forced him to miss the rest of the season.
Southend U *(Free from Shimizu-S-Pulse, Japan on 30/1/2001) FL 49+30/1 FLC 1 FAC 5+1 Others 1+2 (Freed during 2003 close season)*
Gillingham *(Signed on 22/11/2007) FL 11+1 (Freed on 13/3/2008)*
Dagenham & Redbridge *(Free from Grays Ath on 2/7/2009) FL 17 FLC 1 FAC 1*

TIERNEY Marc Peter
Born: Prestwich, 23 August 1985
Height: 5'11" **Weight:** 11.2
The tough-tackling left-back was one of Colchester's most impressive and consistent performers of the season. Very few wingers got the better of Marc, who is both rock-solid in defence and a big threat going forward. Sent off for a petulant kick of the ball at Oldham in November, Marc showed far more discipline on his return from suspension. His crunching tackles and committed displays made him a firm fans' favourite and also saw him linked to a host of Championship clubs. He was considering a contract extension offer at the end of the season.
Oldham Ath *(From juniors on 8/8/2003) FL 21+16 FLC 2+1 FAC 2+2 Others 2+1*
Shrewsbury T *(Free on 15/1/2007) FL 78+1/1 FLC 3 FAC 2 Others 6*
Colchester U *(£150,000 on 27/11/2008) FL 67/1 FAC 3*

TILL Peter
Born: Walsall, 7 September 1985
Height: 5'11" **Weight:** 11.4
Peter started the season promisingly in Walsall's 1-0 victory at Brighton, in which he constantly looked to take on the left-back. The form of Steve Jones then kept him out of the side, as did a number of injuries. His best performance saw him produce some excellent wing play, creating both goals with jinking runs and perfect crosses in the 2-2 home draw with Leyton Orient. While always trying to create chances he was not helped by a number of poor pitches over the winter, making close control difficult and was released at the end of the season.
Birmingham C *(From trainee on 4/7/2005) FLC 0+1*
Scunthorpe U *(Loaned on 6/10/2005) FL 6+2 FAC 1 Others 1*
Boston U *(Loaned on 13/1/2006) FL 10+6/1*
Leyton Orient *(Loaned on 6/10/2006) FL 4 Others 1*

Grimsby T *(Free on 23/11/2006) FL 63+9/4 FLC 3 FAC 3+1 Others 8/2*
Chesterfield *(Loaned on 16/1/2009) FL 14+2*
Walsall *(Free on 24/7/2009) FL 18+10 FAC 0+1 Others 1*

TIMAR Krisztian
Born: Budapest, Hungary, 4 October 1979
Height: 6'2" **Weight:** 13.10
International Honours: Hungary: 4; U21
Krisztian began 2009-10 strongly for Plymouth with a goal against Crystal Palace just five minutes into the season. It had been thought that the Hungarian international could re-discover his fine defensive form of a couple of years ago, but he once again found himself out of the team and upon the opening of the January transfer window he was sent out on loan to League One Oldham for a month. However, after just 105 minutes in total of first team action, having launched himself into tackles and proving to be strong in the air, Krisztian suffered a hamstring tear and he returned to Plymouth. With the injury being serious enough to rule him out for the remainder of the campaign, it would be yet another setback.
Plymouth Arg *(£75,000 from Ferencvaros, Hungary, having started his career there, ex MTK Hungaria, BKV Elore, Videoton, Jokerit, Tatabanya, Nyiregyhaza Spartacus, on 18/1/2007) FL 63+12/5 FLC 4 FAC 3*
Oldham Ath *(Loaned on 1/1/2010) FL 2*

TIMLIN Michael Anthony
Born: New Cross, 19 March 1985
Height: 5'9" **Weight:** 11.8
International Honours: RoI: U21-8; Yth
Michael began the season occupying a central midfield spot at Swindon but following the arrival of Simon Ferry, he found it hard to break into the first team. Although he remained a regular member of the squad, he was mainly restricted to appearances from the bench. A consistent performer able to occupy any midfield position, he has also performed capably at left-back. Michael received an offer of a contract extension at the end of the season.
Fulham *(From trainee on 27/7/2002) FLC 2+1 FAC 0+1*
Scunthorpe U *(Loaned on 24/2/2006) FL 0+1*
Doncaster Rov *(Loaned on 23/3/2006) FL 3*
Swindon T *(Loaned on 23/11/2006) FL 18+6/1 FAC 1*
Swindon T *(Free on 13/3/2008) FL 53+19/3 FLC 2 FAC 2+2 Others 4+1*

TINDALL Jason
Born: Mile End, 15 November 1977
Height: 6'1" **Weight:** 11.1
Bournemouth's assistant manager has retired from the game twice but an injury crisis that was present throughout the season meant he was on the bench to ensure that the side had the minimum number of substitutes required. He also made two appearances in the Johnstone's Paint Trophy.
Charlton Ath *(From trainee on 18/7/1996)*
Bournemouth *(Free on 3/7/1998) FL 129+42/6 FLC 4+3 FAC 8+3 Others 4+2*
Bournemouth *(Free from Weymouth as assistant manager in September 2008 before signing as a player on 23/2/2009) FL 0+2 Others 1+1*

TIPTON Matthew John
Born: Bangor, 29 June 1980
Height: 5'11" **Weight:** 13.7
International Honours: W: U21-6; Yth
Matthew returned to Macclesfield for his third spell when he signed from Blue Square North side Droylsden last summer. With younger strikers given preference, many of Matthew's appearances were from the substitutes' bench. He scored five goals, the first three in August, and his tally included three penalties. When used he showed that he still had an eye for goal, would hassle defenders and cause problems in the box. Was out of contract at the end of the season.

Oldham Ath *(From trainee on 1/7/1997) FL 51+61/15 FLC 3+4 FAC 4+7/1 Others 3+3/1*
Macclesfield T *(Free on 13/2/2002) FL 114+17/41 FLC 3+1/1 FAC 8+1/5 Others 6+1/3*
Mansfield T *(Free on 5/8/2005) FL 4*
Bury *(Free on 26/8/2005) FL 15+9/3 FAC 1+1 (Freed during 2007 close season)*
Macclesfield T *(Loaned on 31/8/2006) FL 15+18/4*
Macclesfield T *(Signed from Droylsden, ex Hyde U, on 24/7/2009) FL 11+20/5 FLC 0+1 FAC 0+1 Others 1*

TODD Christopher (Chris) Richard
Born: Swansea, 22 August 1981
Height: 6'0" **Weight:** 11.4
The powerful and committed centre-back fought a battle with leukaemia to play his part in Torquay's promotion from the Blue Square Premier. Chris was a regular starter in the first two months of the new campaign but subsequently lost his place and, after a spell on the bench, went out first on a short-term loan to Salisbury then on a long-term loan to Newport County. Was out of contract at the end of June.
Swansea C *(From trainee on 6/7/2000) FL 39+4/4 FLC 1 FAC 1 Others 1 (Freed during 2002 close season)*
Exeter C *(From Drogheda U on 31/1/2003) FL 12*
Torquay U *(Signed on 14/7/2007) FL 9/1 FLC 1 Others 1*

Sam Togwell

TOGWELL Samuel (Sam) James

Born: Beaconsfield, 14 October 1984
Height: 5'11" **Weight:** 12.4
If one player typified Scunthorpe's never-say-die attitude in the Championship, it was midfielder Sam. Playing in the centre of the park, he complemented the Iron's more creative players with his high-energy, industrious style which made him a regular throughout the campaign up until the closing month when he was hampered by a groin problem. Scored a fantastic strike on his return to his first club, Crystal Palace, in September but his proudest moment came when he captained the team in the absence of Cliff Byrne during March, leading his side to three straight League wins that ultimately took them to survival.
Crystal Palace (From trainee on 31/8/2004) FL 0+1 FLC 1+2
Oxford U (Loaned on 22/10/2004) FL 3+1 FAC 1
Northampton T (Loaned on 24/3/2005) FL 7+1 Others 2
Port Vale (Loaned on 10/11/2005) FL 26+1/2 FAC 2/2 Others 1
Barnsley (Signed on 18/7/2006) FL 54+12/2 FLC 1+1 FAC 3+2
Scunthorpe U (Free on 14/8/2008) FL 67+14/4 FLC 1+3 FAC 5/1 Others 6+2/1

TOLLEY Jamie Christopher

Born: Ludlow, 12 May 1983
Height: 6'0" **Weight:** 11.3
International Honours: W: U21-12
Central midfielder Jamie arrived at Edgar Street looking to rebuild his career after being released by Macclesfield. But his progress was not helped by Hereford's early season form and he endured a long spell out of the side. Just as he was finally getting back into his stride with a run in the team in January, his season was interrupted by injury and he made only one further appearance, against his old club Macclesfield, before being released.
Shrewsbury T (From trainee on 9/1/2001) FL 142+18/14 FLC 3+2 FAC 5+3/2 Others 8+1/1
Macclesfield T (Signed on 11/8/2006) FL 56+7/3 FLC 3 FAC 2+3 Others 1
Hereford U (Free on 15/7/2009) FL 6+4 FLC 0+1 Others 1+1

TOMKINS James Oliver Charles

Born: Basildon, 29 March 1989
Height: 6'3" **Weight:** 11.10
International Honours: E: U21-7; Yth
James continued to learn his trade at West Ham and the youngster gained vital experience in the pressure cooker environment of a relegation campaign.

James is a solid central defender and is good in the air. Against Chelsea in December he gave a controlled display alongside his captain Matthew Upson. This was followed up with an excellent performance at Tottenham which showed that he was maturing fast. As the season progressed he was rested as the Hammers relied upon more experienced defenders in their fight to avoid relegation.
West Ham U (From trainee on 3/4/2006) PL 38+3/1 FLC 2 FAC 4
Derby Co (Loaned on 27/11/2008) FL 5+2 FLC 1

James Tomkins

TOMLIN Gavin Glenrick

Born: Gillingham, 13 January 1983
Height: 6'0" **Weight:** 12.2
Gavin found his feet again in League football and proved himself a valuable member of Yeovil's starting 11, playing either up front, in the hole or even on the right wing at times. His versatility and wholehearted attitude brought him almost 40 games and seven goals including strikes in the first and last games of the season. Despite missing an early season spot kick, he volunteered to continue taking them, showing once again that the ex-Brentford man is more determined than ever to make a name in League One.
Brentford (Free from Windsor & Eton, ex Ashford T, Tooting & Mitcham, Aylesbury U, Staines T, St Albans C - loan, Yeading, on 1/8/2006) FL 6+6 FLC 1 Others 1+1 (Freed on 30/1/2007)
Yeovil T (Free from Fisher Ath on 23/7/2008) FL 58+19/14 FLC 3/1 FAC 0+2 Others 2/1

Gavin Tomlin

TONER Ciaran

Born: Craigavon, 30 June 1981
Height: 6'1" **Weight:** 12.4
International Honours: NI: 2; U21-17; Yth; Sch
Awarded a further contract by Rochdale in the summer, Ciaran spent a large part of the campaign on the sidelines suffering from shin splints. He eventually made his return, from the bench, at the end of November but with the Dale riding high in the table, was unable to force his way into the side and had to wait until replacing the ineligible Jason Taylor for the 4-0 victory over Rotherham in March. Figuring in further games either wide on the left of the midfield four or as part of a three-man midfield, he put in a 'Man of the Match' performance in the 4-1 victory over his former club Grimsby as Dale headed for promotion. Was out of contract at the end of June.
Tottenham H (From trainee on 14/7/1999)
Peterborough U (Loaned on 21/12/2001) FL 6 FAC 1
Bristol Rov (Free on 28/3/2002) FL 6
Leyton Orient (Free on 7/5/2002) FL 41+11/2 FLC 2 FAC 1 Others 2
Lincoln C (Free on 4/8/2004) FL 10+5/2 FLC 0+1 Others 1
Cambridge U (Loaned on 19/3/2005) FL 6+2
Grimsby T (Free on 18/7/2005) FL 80+14/14 FLC 2 FAC 3+1 Others 5+3/1
Rochdale (Free on 4/8/2008) FL 39+11/1 FLC 0+1 FAC 2 Others 4

TONGE Dale

Born: Doncaster, 7 May 1985
Height: 5'10" **Weight:** 10.6
Dale made the Rotherham right-back spot his own, his attacking play and link-ups with Nicky Law ahead of him

down the right, being a feature of the team's play in the early part of the season. His midfield pedigree as a youngster helped in this respect but his defending improved as well. However, a foot injury was to trouble him from mid-season and appearances became sporadic. His campaign was ended prematurely in March by the need for an operation.
Barnsley (From trainee on 2/7/2004) FL 30+15 FLC 4 FAC 3+2 Others 0+1
Gillingham (Loaned on 20/3/2007) FL 3
Rotherham U (Free on 23/7/2007) FL 88+9/1 FLC 5 FAC 5 Others 8/1

TONGE Michael William
Born: Manchester, 7 April 1983
Height: 6'0" **Weight:** 11.10
International Honours: E: U21-2; Yth
For the second successive season

Michael was unable to force his way into regular contention as a first team player at Stoke and was reduced to just three Carling Cup appearances in 2009-10. In order to get regular football he went on one loan spell to a struggling Preston side and then a much more positive one with Derby, where he created a very good impression and had the media talking about a possible permanent move to Pride Park. There was no doubt that Michael did well at Deepdale in his seven games for Preston before Christmas, showing his class in central midfield and helping to add solidity to a previously fragile area of the team, but it was at Derby where he stood out. Looking for more class in midfield, County brought in Michael during February and he played in 19 consecutive League and FA Cup

matches to the end of the season, usually on the right of midfield. He was always comfortable on the ball, seeing possibilities more quickly than some around him, and won the club's 'Goal of the Season' award for his spectacular hit against Watford in March.
Sheffield U (From trainee on 16/3/2001) P/FL 234+28/21 FLC 15+3/3 FAC 17+2 Others 3
Stoke C (£2,000,000 on 1/9/2008) PL 1+9 FLC 2+1 FAC 1
Preston NE (Loaned on 19/11/2009) FL 7
Derby Co (Loaned on 1/2/2010) FL 18/2 FAC 1

TOOTLE Matthew (Matt) James
Born: Widnes, 11 October 1990
Height: 5'9" **Weight:** 11.0
Matt, another product of Crewe's fruitful youth system, made his senior debut in the Carling Cup game against Blackpool. Playing at full-back and also in midfield, he quickly found a regular spot in the League Two side and held his place.
Crewe Alex (From trainee on 2/7/2009) FL 26+2/1

TORRES Fernando Jose
Born: Madrid, Spain, 20 March 1984
Height: 5'11" **Weight:** 12.4
International Honours: Spain: 72; U21-10; Yth
In a disastrous season for Liverpool, only one outfield player enhanced his reputation and that was the Spanish international striker who is considered one of the finest forwards in the world. Troubled by a hernia for most of the season and sidelined for three long periods, Fernando remained the leading scorer by a wide margin, with 22 goals from 32 appearances. He started in electrifying form with three goals in the first four games, followed by two at West Ham and a hat-trick in the 6-0 rout of Hull. His big match temperament was displayed again with the opening goal against Manchester United in October before the first of his long injury lay-offs started in November. Returning in December he scored a stoppage-time winner in a fourth place contest at Aston Villa, his 50th League goal in only 72 appearances, before succumbing to injury again early in the FA Cup replay defeat by Reading. When he returned in late February he scored twice in each of four consecutive home games against Portsmouth, OSC Lille, Sunderland and Benfica. His first goal against Sunderland was probably the Reds' 'Goal of the Season'. Receiving the ball on the left touchline he

Fernando Torres

outwitted his marker, moved inside and curled a shot into the top corner from the edge of the box. His performance in the second leg Europa Cup match with Benfica was even more remarkable. Despite appearing only half-fit, he finished off a brilliant five-man move to give Liverpool a 3-0 lead and clinched victory with a deft chip over the goalkeeper as well as heading away a goal-bound Benfica free kick to prevent a killer second away goal. A knee operation ended his season and without him, Liverpool's challenge for fourth place and Europa Cup success simply collapsed with four blanks in the last seven games. He was able to go to the World Cup in Spain's squad.
Liverpool (£26,500,000 from Atletico Madrid, Spain on 27/7/2007) PL 69+10/56 FLC 2+1/3 FAC 5+1/1 Others 26+2/12

TORRES Sergio Raul
Born: Mar del Plata, Argentina, 8 November 1983
Height: 6'2" **Weight:** 12.4
The Peterborough midfielder did not figure in the earlier season plans of the manager and was loaned out to Lincoln, spending almost two months at Sincil Bank and producing a number of impressive performances which saw him weigh in with two goals. A serious ankle ligament injury forced his premature return to his parent club, but he was able to figure in a few games at the end of the season before being placed on the transfer list.
Wycombe W (Signed from Basingstoke T, ex Atletico Banfield, Molesey, on 26/8/2005) FL 57+29/6 FLC 2+3 FAC 2 Others 4+1
Peterborough U (£150,000 on 14/7/2008) FL 17+7/1 FLC 1 FAC 1+1
Lincoln C (Loaned on 17/9/2009) FL 7+1/1 FAC 1/1

TOSIC Dusko
Born: Zrenjanin, Serbia, 19 January 1985
Height: 5'11" **Weight:** 12.4
International Honours: Serbia: 9
A Serbian left-back who joined Queens Park Rangers on loan from Portsmouth towards the end of the season. He played in the final five fixtures and put in consistently strong performances that helped Rangers move away from relegation danger and secure their Championship safety. Was out of contract in the summer.
Portsmouth (Free from Werder Bremen, Germany, ex OFK Belgrade, Sochaux, on 12/2/2010)
Queens Park Rgrs (Loaned on 25/3/2010) FL 5

TOSIC Zoran
Born: Zrenjanin, Serbia, 28 April 1987
Height: 5'7" **Weight:** 10.12
Club Honours: FLC '10
International Honours: Serbia: 21; U21-17
Manchester United midfielder and winger who is nicknamed 'Bambi' due to his lean build, Zoran had few opportunities to build on the promise of his limited appearances in the previous season. He scored his first senior goal for the Reds in an emphatic 8–2 victory over Hangzhou Greentown during the pre-season campaign in Asia and followed that with his first two international goals for Serbia against South Africa. He made a sole substitute appearance for United against Barnsley in the Carling Cup before moving to Koln until June.
Manchester U (Signed from Partizan Belgrade, Serbia, ex Proleter Zrenjanin, Banat Zrenjanin, on 15/1/2009) PL 0+2 FLC 0+2 FAC 0+1

TOURE Kolo Abib
Born: Sokoura Bouake, Ivory Coast, 19 March 1981
Height: 5'10" **Weight:** 11.13
Club Honours: CS '02, '04; FAC '03, '05; PL '04
International Honours: Ivory Coast: 76
After seven successful seasons with Arsenal, the Ivory Coast international central defender completed a move to Manchester City in the summer, citing differences with other Arsenal defenders as a reason for leaving. He was immediately appointed captain by City manager Mark Hughes but his season did not work out as well as hoped. His partnership with another new signing, Joleon Lescott, was expected to strengthen City's defence and provide a platform for a top-four challenge. In practice, the partnership proved fragile despite an excellent start and by mid-December City had leaked 27 goals in 17 games and were losing unexpected points to weaker teams, a major factor in Hughes' dismissal. In January, Kolo departed for a month to the African Cup of Nations and shortly after his return to Eastlands he was dropped by new manager Roberto Mancini in favour of Vincent Kompany, although he returned to first team duty in March following an injury to Lescott. He scored twice, in the Carling Cup victory over Fulham and in the 3-3 home draw with Burnley.
Arsenal (Signed from ASEC Mimosas, Ivory Coast on 18/2/2002) PL 203+22/9 FLC 7 FAC 21+4/3 Others 64+5/2
Manchester C (£14,000,000 on 29/7/2009) PL 31/1 FLC 3/1 FAC 1

TOWNSEND Andros Darryl
Born: Chingford, 16 July 1991
Height: 6'0" **Weight:** 12.0
International Honours: E: Yth
Four times an unused sub at Tottenham, to further his experience the midfielder spent periods on loan at Leyton Orient and MK Dons during 2009-10. Having joined Orient on a six-month deal at the very start of the season, Andros quickly showed his pace on the left flank, especially when getting the ball and taking on the opposition. Before going back to White Hart Lane he had scored a cracker of a goal against Yeovil, where had previously spent some time on loan. In mid-January, Andros was snapped up by MK Dons and had the good fortune to make his debut in a 5-0 win at Hartlepool before playing the next eight games. During his time at the Stadiummk, he showed some flashing pace and skill down the flanks, which delighted the crowd.
Tottenham H (From trainee on 5/12/2008)
Yeovil T (Loaned on 19/3/2009) FL 10/1
Leyton Orient (Loaned on 5/8/2009) FL 17+5/2 FLC 2 Others 1+1
MK Dons (Loaned on 14/1/2010) FL 8+1/2

TOWNSEND Michael John
Born: Walsall, 17 May 1986
Height: 6'2" **Weight:** 13.12
Tall, strong defender Michael was an important figure in the heart of the Cheltenham defence and was virtually ever-present for the first half of the season apart from a short spell out with a calf injury. He had four partners in the centre of defence at Cheltenham, under three different managers, searched for the right combination to lift them clear of the relegation zone. Michael took on the job of senior central defender alongside less experienced players Andy Gallinagh and Ashley Eastham. He achieved plenty of success against League Two forwards, despite a generally disappointing season for his team. The defender was linked with a number of clubs when his contract ended in the summer.
Cheltenham T (From trainee at Wolverhampton W on 10/1/2005) FL 127+7/6 FLC 4 FAC 4 Others 3+1
Barnet (Loaned on 21/10/2008) FL 13 FAC 2

TOZER Ben Peter Anthony
Born: Plymouth, 15 March 1990
Height: 6'1" **Weight:** 12.11
Ben is a promising young Newcastle centre-back who made his first team debut when manager Chris Hughton fielded the club's youngest ever side in

the Carling Cup tie against Peterborough in September. He did not look out of place, and a month later he made his League debut when appearing as a late substitute in the win against Doncaster.
Swindon T *(Trainee) FL 1+1 FLC 1 FAC 2 Others 2*
Newcastle U *(£250,000 + on 8/1/2008) FL 0+1 FLC 1*

TRAORE Armand
Born: Paris, France, 8 October 1989
Height: 6'1" **Weight:** 12.12
International Honours: France: U21-4; Yth
Having spent the previous campaign on loan at Portsmouth, Armand returned to Arsenal. The French left-back took advantage of injuries to both Gael Clichy and Keiran Gibbs to make several first team appearances. Armand is a strong attacking full-back but still needs to work on the defensive aspects of the position. He appeared nine times in the Premier League, once in the FA Cup and twice in the Carling Cup.
Arsenal *(Signed from AS Monaco, France on 16/10/2006) PL 10+2 FLC 11+1 FAC 4 Others 2*
Portsmouth *(Loaned on 21/8/2008) PL 14+5/1 FLC 0+1 FAC 2 Others 6*

TREACY Keith Patrick
Born: Dublin, 13 September 1988
Height: 6'0" **Weight:** 13.2
International Honours: RoI: U21-5; Yth
Arriving from Blackburn, the young left-footed winger who can play on either side, joined the Blades on a six-month loan and was in the starting line-up for the first nine Championship games. Playing wide on the left he worked hard, producing useful crosses and scoring with a fine 25-yard shot, his first League goal, against Leicester. The arrival of loanee Richard Cresswell and the number of other essential loan players on the Blades' books, saw Keith's opportunities become limited and he returned early to Ewood Park. His next stop on loan was at Preston at the beginning of February and although he took some time to shine it was mainly due to a lack of match fitness. Once he started playing regularly, he showed to good effect his abilities to ghost pass defenders with pace and close control to deliver telling crosses. He scored twice in successive matches, the opener in a defeat at Selhurst Park followed by a stunning injury-time winner against Scunthorpe when he cut in from the right wing to fire a left-foot curler inside the far post. One of a number of exciting wingmen at

Deepdale, he was called up by the Republic of Ireland for summer internationals and great things are expected of him in the years to come.
Blackburn Rov *(From trainee on 20/10/2005) PL 2+10 FLC 4+1 FAC 4+1*
Stockport Co *(Loaned on 23/11/2006) FL 2+2*
Sheffield U *(Loaned on 24/7/2009) FL 12+4/1 FLC 0+1*
Preston NE *(Signed on 1/2/2010) FL 8+9/2*

TREMARCO Carl Philip
Born: Liverpool, 11 October 1985
Height: 5'9" **Weight:** 12.2
Carl jumped at the chance to sign for Macclesfield from Blue Square Premier side Wrexham last summer, giving him the opportunity to re-establish himself at League level. He was one of the best signings made by the late Keith Alexander, playing left-back with vigour and determination. He is a combative player who can pick up cautions along the way but he quickly established himself as a fans' favourite. Ever-present until the end of January when he underwent a hernia operation, he tried to return in late March but problems following the operation left him sidelined again until he played in the last three matches. Carl's hard work was rewarded with an extension to his contract to June 2012.
Tranmere Rov *(From trainee on 2/4/2004) FL 34+18/1 FAC 2 Others 3+1*
Wrexham *(Free on 18/1/2008) FL 10*
Darlington *(Loaned on 30/1/2009) FL 2*
Macclesfield T *(Free on 3/7/2009) FL 27+2 FLC 1*

TRIPPIER Kieran John
Born: Bury, 19 September 1990
Height: 5'10" **Weight:** 11.0
International Honours: E: Yth
Signed on a month's loan from Manchester City in February, Kieran made his debut for Barnsley the same day at Middlesbrough. A footballing full-back, whose ability to read the game got him to the ball early, he showed that he was a good passer and was used to take the corners in his short time at Barnsley. An ankle injury cut short his time at Oakwell and he returned to City early.
Manchester C *(From trainee on 15/10/2007)*
Barnsley *(Loaned on 9/2/2010) FL 3*

TROTMAN Neal Anthony
Born: Manchester, 26 April 1987
Height: 6'2" **Weight:** 13.7
Club Honours: AMC '10
Neal made just one Preston appearance in 2009-10 before spending the season

on loan at Southampton and Huddersfield as he attempted to catch up on over a year out with injury and what an impact he made. He came on as a substitute in the Carling Cup win over Morecambe and 12 seconds later was celebrating his first goal for the club with a powerful header from a corner. Despite that he was allowed to go out on loan to Southampton a few days later as new manager Alan Pardew was assessing the squad he had inherited. Neal proved a godsend. A solid, dashing central defender, he worked well in several defensive permutations and it was something of a surprise when his loan was not extended after an excellent Boxing Day performance against Exeter at St Mary's, in which he scored his second goal for Saints, in their 3-1 win. His next loan spell saw him arriving at Huddersfield during the January transfer window to add strength to the back line. After a shaky start to his new surroundings the physical defender added sheer muscle to the back four and provided a powerful outlet at set pieces. After making his debut in the away victory at Yeovil, the team went unbeaten in eight games and Neal formed a formidable partnership with team captain Peter Clarke in defence. Always strong in the air and able to shackle opposing defenders Neal enjoyed a two-goal return during the course of the season as the Terriers pushed on towards the play-offs.
Oldham Ath *(From trainee at Burnley on 15/9/2006) FL 16+2/1 FLC 0+1 FAC 3+1/2 Others 1*
Preston NE *(£500,000 on 31/1/2008) FL 2+1 FLC 0+1/1*
Colchester U *(Loaned on 19/3/2009) FL 5+1*
Southampton *(Loaned on 20/8/2009) FL 17+1/2 Others 1+1*
Huddersfield T *(Loaned on 22/1/2010) FL 21/2 Others 2*

TROTTER Liam Antony
Born: Ipswich, 24 August 1988
Height: 6'2" **Weight:** 12.2
Club Honours: FAYC '05
Liam was offered contracts by Ipswich and Scunthorpe during the summer and having decided to stay with Ipswich featured in 12 games during the first three months of the season. However, despite the number of games played he was not able to put together a confidence building run together and faded from the first team scene before joining Millwall on loan in January. Returning to the Den, having previously played three games in 2006 on loan there, the tall and agile centre-back

showed himself to be comfortable on the ball, never being rushed into hasty distribution, and good in the air. His only League goal came in added time and rescued a point in the draw with Southampton.
Ipswich T *(From trainee on 30/8/2006)* FL 15+8/2 FLC 2 FAC 1+1
Millwall *(Loaned on 31/8/2006)* FL 1+1 Others 0+1
Grimsby T *(Loaned on 19/9/2008)* FL 15/2 Others 1
Scunthorpe U *(Loaned on 23/2/2009)* FL 4+8/1 Others 1+1
Millwall *(Loaned on 5/1/2010)* FL 20/1 Others 3

TRUNDLE Lee Christopher
Born: Liverpool, 10 October 1976
Height: 6'0" **Weight:** 13.3
Club Honours: AMC '06
A former favourite with Swansea, Lee returned to the Liberty Stadium on an initial three-month loan from Bristol City in late August and scored from the penalty spot in his first game back at the stadium, against Sheffield United. His loan was extended until the end of the season when the January transfer window opened but apart from two starts, all of his appearances came from the substitutes' bench. Was out of contract at the end of June.
Wrexham *(£60,000 from Rhyl, ex Burscough, Chorley, Stalybridge Celtic, Southport, on 16/2/2001)* FL 73+21/27 FLC 0+2 FAC 1 Others 4+1/3
Swansea C *(Free on 14/7/2003)* FL 135+8/77 FLC 3 FAC 13+1/7 Others 5+8/1
Bristol C *(£1,000,000 on 31/7/2007)* FL 25+29/7 FLC 1+3 FAC 0+1 Others 3/1
Leeds U *(Loaned on 9/1/2009)* FL 7+3/1
Swansea C *(Loaned on 28/8/2009)* FL 2+17/5 FAC 0+1

TUDGAY Marcus
Born: Shoreham, 3 February 1983
Height: 6'3" **Weight:** 13.2
Linked in the close season with a move to Burnley, Marcus eventually signed a new contract for Sheffield Wednesday, but it was a disappointing season for him. His versatility meant that he was used in some games as a right-sided midfielder instead of being up front. Wherever he played, he put in his usual hard-working shift in games but lacked the killer instinct he had shown previously. He was hoping to improve on his goal tally of the previous season but never looked like doing so. Marcus remains a popular player with the fans but needs to be played as an out-and-out striker to get the best from him. Hopefully, his future career will continue at Hillsborough, as he is now one of the

mainstays of the team.
Derby Co *(From trainee on 16/7/2002)* FL 53+39/17 FLC 2 FAC 4+1/1
Sheffield Wed *(Signed on 1/1/2006)* FL 163+15/47 FLC 5 FAC 6/1

Marcus Tudgay

TUDUR JONES Owain
Born: Bangor, 15 October 1984
Height: 6'2" **Weight:** 12.0
Club Honours: AMC '06
International Honours: W: 4; U21-3
Having signed the tall and athletic midfielder from Swansea in June, a series of niggling injuries hampered his progress at Norwich. Unfortunately for this Welsh international those injuries coincided with the arrival of new manager Paul Lambert at Carrow Road and when he regained his fitness the Canaries were well on their way to promotion with a settled team. A loan spell with Yeovil allowed him to get some matches under his belt, but the form of others continued to keep him on the sidelines when he returned to Norfolk. A powerful presence in the midfield area, he uses the ball intelligently and likes to get forward in support of his strikers. Will be hoping for an injury free 2010-11.
Swansea C *(£5,000 from Bangor C on 4/8/2005)* FL 26+16/3 FLC 4 FAC 2+1 Others 5+3/1
Swindon T *(Loaned on 9/3/2009)* FL 11/1
Norwich C *(£250,000 on 16/6/2009)* FL 2+1/1 FLC 1 FAC 0+1 Others 1
Yeovil T *(Loaned on 27/1/2010)* FL 6/1

TULLY Stephen (Steve) Richard
Born: Paignton, 10 February 1980
Height: 5'9" **Weight:** 11.0
Devon-born Steve put in another round of solid performances for Exeter as he made the right-back position his own.

Found himself out of favour for several games when manager Paul Tisdale changed his defensive set up but fought his way back into the team. An excellent passer with good awareness, he formed part of a City rearguard that conceded only 20 League goals at St James' Park. He ended a three-year spell without a goal by scoring in the 3-0 win over Brentford at the end of October.
Torquay U *(From trainee on 18/5/1998)* FL 90+16/3 FLC 5+1 FAC 4+1 Others 8 *(Freed during during 2002 close season)*
Exeter C *(Free from Weymouth, ex Weymouth, Exeter C, on 16/1/2007)* FL 71+3/1 FLC 1+1 FAC 2 Others 2

Steve Tully

TUNA Tamer Hakan
Born: Bexley, 19 October 1991
Height: 5'9" **Weight:** 11.5
Another product of Charlton's Academy, Tamer started the season on the bench for the first nine games, making a late appearance against Tranmere in August. He then made his first start against Barnet in the Johnstone's Paint Trophy and scored his first senior goal. At the end of the year he was loaned to Staines Town to gain experience and further loan spells followed at Woking and Welling United. Tamer possesses a powerful shot, has a good work ethic and should feature more regularly next season.
Charlton Ath *(Trainee)* FL 0+3 Others 1/1

[TUNCAY] SANLI Tuncay
Born: Sakarya, Turkey, 16 January 1982
Height: 5'11" **Weight:** 11.4
International Honours: Turkey: 74; U21-14; Yth
Following Middlesbrough's relegation

from the Premier League, it was accepted by the Boro faithful that Tuncay would be one of the first players to leave the club. Therefore it came as a welcome surprise to the supporters that he was still at the club when the season started. However, he only featured as a substitute as manager Gareth Southgate was reluctant to risk injury and jeopardise any possible big money transfer and following three matches, in which he scored twice, he was on his way to Stoke at the end of August. The signing of the enigmatic Turkish forward sent shockwaves of excitement buzzing through the ranks of the Stoke

supporters when it was announced, though since then it would be fair to say that it was a case of mixed fortunes for the player. It took a long time for Tony Pulis to commit him to a regular first team slot and even then he found himself in and out of the starting line-up, as Stoke struggled to find an effective strike partnership to address their lack of goals. On occasion Tuncay looked out of place amidst Stoke's bustling and often direct football, but at other times his undoubted skill and finishing qualities came shining through. Tuncay is a popular player with supporters and once he is effectively

accommodated into Stoke's rigid style of play he will show what he is made of.
Middlesbrough (Free from Fenerbahce, Turkey, ex Sakaryaspor, on 10/7/2007) P/FL 57+13/17 FLC 1 FAC 4+3/1
Stoke C (£5,000,000 on 28/8/2009) PL 13+17/4 FLC 2 FAC 2+3/1

TUNCHEV Aleksandar
Born: Pazardzhik, Bulgaria, 10 July 1981
Height: 6'2" **Weight:** 13.3
Club Honours: Div 1 '09
International Honours: Bulgaria: 20
Leicester's classy Bulgarian international centre-half would not be out of place in the Premier League. Unfortunately, when Aleksandar returned for City from a cruciate ligament injury in late August he soon suffered further knee problems that resulted in another bout of surgery, causing him to miss almost the entire season.
Leicester C (£375,000 from CSKA Sofia, Bulgaria, ex Hebar Pazardzhik, Belasitsa Petrich, Lokomotiv Plovdiv, on 6/8/2008) FL 20+2/1 FLC 2 FAC 4 Others 1

TUNNICLIFFE James
Born: Denton, 7 January 1989
Height: 6'4" **Weight:** 12.3
Having been signed from Stockport in the summer, a series of steady performances earned James the respect of the Brighton supporters despite him being unable to establish himself in the side as the management tinkered with the line-up. Equally at home in the air or with the ball at his feet, the big central defender contributed two goals during the campaign and was identified as one for the future by new manager Gus Poyet. However, to gain further experience he joined MK Dons on loan in February to help cover an injury-crisis, his debut coming in a 5-0 shellacking at Carlisle. Although he started in each of the following eight games the team struggled to find any sort of consistent form and after completing two months with the Dons he returned back to his parent club.
Stockport Co (From trainee on 7/7/2006) FL 32+9 FAC 5 Others 3+1
Brighton & Hove A (Signed on 15/7/2009) FL 17/2 FAC 2 Others 0+1
MK Dons (Loaned on 11/2/2010) FL 9/1

TURNBULL Paul Daniel
Born: Handforth, 23 January 1989
Height: 6'0" **Weight:** 12.7
Paul spent much of the season vying with fellow product of Stockport's youth system, Greg Tansey, for a spot in the centre of the park. Undoubtedly the

Tuncay

highlight of his season would be the 5-0 thrashing of Tooting & Mitcham in the FA Cup, when Paul scored the fourth and fifth goals in the space of five minutes. He also set up the opener, scored by Peter Thompson, and was named as the 'Man of the Match'.
Stockport Co *(From trainee on 15/5/2006) FL 51+33/1 FLC 2 FAC 4+1/2 Others 10*

TURNBULL Ross
Born: Bishop Auckland, 4 January 1985
Height: 6'4" **Weight:** 13.5
International Honours: E: Yth
A highly-rated young goalkeeper who joined Chelsea from Middlesbrough after his contract lapsed. As the club's number-three 'keeper, Ross made only fitful appearances, being forced to wait because of the excellent form shown by Petr Cech and Hilario. He made his debut as a first-half substitute for the injured Portuguese 'keeper in the Carling Cup fourth round against Bolton and contributed to yet another home clean sheet. His full debut followed six weeks later against Apoel Nicosia in the Champions League and after three months back in the reserves, he dramatically returned to the spotlight when injuries ruled out both Cech and Hilario for the Champions League knock-out tie against Jose Mourinho's Inter Milan. He was completely unfazed by the media frenzy surrounding the match and put in a confident display, beaten only by a clinical finish by Samuel Eto'o. With the new Premier League ruling on home developed players Ross has a great opportunity to move up in the goalkeeping pecking order.
Middlesbrough *(From trainee on 6/7/2002) PL 27 FLC 2*
Darlington *(Loaned on 14/11/2003) FL 1*
Barnsley *(Loaned on 22/4/2004) FL 3*
Bradford C *(Loaned on 6/8/2004) FL 2*
Barnsley *(Loaned on 6/10/2004) FL 23 FAC 1*
Crewe Alex *(Loaned on 4/8/2005) FL 29*
Cardiff C *(Loaned on 31/7/2007) FL 6 FLC 2*
Chelsea *(Free on 2/7/2009) PL 2 FLC 0+1 Others 2*

TURNER Benjamin (Ben)
Howard
Born: Birmingham, 21 January 1988
Height: 6'4" **Weight:** 14.4
International Honours: E: Yth
The strapping Coventry central defender had a disastrous season with injuries. He started as first choice central defender and played 13 of the first 15 games, doing well despite a few

inconsistencies. Then disaster struck with an ankle ligament injury that turned out to be more serious than first thought and required surgery. It ruled him out for the season.
Coventry C *(From trainee on 1/7/2006) FL 55+3 FLC 4+1 FAC 7*
Peterborough U *(Loaned on 15/9/2006) FL 7+1 FLC 1 Others 1*
Oldham Ath *(Loaned on 23/2/2007) FL 1*

TURNER Christopher (Chris) Jack Michael
Born: Burnley, 26 August 1990
Height: 5'10" **Weight:** 11.7
A valued young Accrington squad member who is a left-footer but can play on the left or right-wing, Chris is in his second season as a pro at Stanley after progressing through the youth system. With both pace and the ability to get great crosses over, he has plenty of potential. Scored two League goals during the campaign.
Accrington Stanley *(From trainee on 8/8/2008) FL 25+22/2 FLC 0+1 Others 1*

TURNER Michael Thomas
Born: Lewisham, 9 November 1983
Height: 6'4" **Weight:** 12.6
Having started the season in his familiar berth at the heart of Hull's defence, Michael's hugely successful three years at the KC Stadium came to a controversial end as the transfer window closed. Rumoured to be an eight-figure target for Aston Villa, Everton and Liverpool during the summer, he moved to Sunderland for a much lower fee even though it was a new club record. By coincidence, his Black Cats' debut was against City when he notably did not join in the celebrations despite being heavily involved in the first goal and received a very warm ovation for the return fixture in Hull. Settling down to become one of Sunderland's most important players, he even attracted speculation that he might become a contender for England and stood in as team captain whenever the club were without regular skipper Lorik Cana. Dominant in the air, Michael showed himself to be the centre-half on which Steve Bruce – no mean centre-back himself – could build his defensive platform. Very harshly sent off at Manchester City for what looked an innocuous aerial challenge, he had his ban extended to Sunderland's astonishment following an appeal. Having been one of only two outfield players to play every minute of the previous Premier League season, Michael was sent off again on the final day of the campaign and will thus miss

the start of 2010-11 through suspension.
Charlton Ath *(From trainee on 6/3/2001)*
Leyton Orient *(Loaned on 26/3/2003) FL 7/1*
Brentford *(Signed on 6/8/2004) FL 91/3 FLC 1 FAC 14 Others 4*
Hull C *(£350,000 on 12/7/2006) P/FL 128+1/12 FLC 6+1 FAC 7/1 Others 3*
Sunderland *(Signed on 31/8/2009) PL 29/2 FLC 2 FAC 1*

TWISS Michael John
Born: Salford, 26 December 1977
Height: 5'11" **Weight:** 13.3
Club Honours: AMC '01
One of Morecambe's recent legends was allowed to leave in the New Year after failing to hold on to a first team place. He was largely out of the side at the start of the campaign but had a good run around Christmas which tied in with a successful run of results. Found goals difficult to come by and scored only twice, although he hit the woodwork on a regular basis, including four times in two games. After becoming increasingly frustrated at his lack of starts, he was allowed to leave and joined former boss Jim Harvey at Stalybridge Celtic.
Manchester U *(From trainee on 5/7/1996) FLC 1 FAC 0+1*
Sheffield U *(Loaned on 7/8/1998) FL 2+10/1 FAC 2+2*
Port Vale *(Free on 27/7/2000) FL 15+3/3 FLC 2 FAC 0+2 Others 1+1 (Freed during 2001 close season)*
Morecambe *(Free from Chester C, ex Leigh RMI, on 8/5/2004) FL 71+19/10 FLC 4/1 FAC 1+1 Others 7+1*

TYSON Nathan
Born: Reading, 4 May 1982
Height: 5'10" **Weight:** 11.12
International Honours: E: Yth
Despite being a forward by trade, Nathan was used as a winger by Nottingham Forest, looking comfortable on either flank. A pacy player who has developed into a good team man, he does not mind coming back to help his defenders when needed. He will be disappointed with only two League goals for his season's work.
Reading *(From trainee on 18/3/2000) FL 9+24/1 FLC 0+2 FAC 2+1 Others 0+2*
Swansea C *(Loaned on 30/8/2001) FL 7+4/1*
Cheltenham T *(Loaned on 22/3/2002) FL 1+7/1*
Wycombe W *(Free on 2/1/2004) FL 76+2/42 FLC 3/2 FAC 3 Others 1+2*
Nottingham F *(£675,000 on 11/11/2005) FL 111+43/33 FLC 3+2/1 FAC 11+2/6 Others 4*

UV

UDDIN Anwar
Born: Stepney, 1 November 1981
Height: 6'2" **Weight:** 13.0
Club Honours: FC '07
Anwar found himself as fourth choice at centre-back for Dagenham following an ankle injury at the start of the season and spent a month on loan to Blue Square Grays Athletic to assist his recovery. His first appearance of the season came as a last-minute substitute against Macclesfield in March but he then found himself back in the starting line-up due to injuries. The powerful centre-back continues to work closely with local Asian children to encourage more to participate in the game.
West Ham U (From trainee on 9/7/2001)
Sheffield Wed (Free on 28/2/2002)
Bristol Rov (Free on 2/7/2002) FL 18+1/1 FLC 1 Others 1+1
Dagenham & Redbridge (Free on 4/8/2004) FL 53+11/1 FLC 2 FAC 2+1 Others 5+1

UPSON Edward (Ed) James
Born: Bury St Edmunds, 21 November 1989
Height: 5'10" **Weight:** 11.7
International Honours: E: Yth
Ed made his debut for Ipswich as a substitute in the Carling Cup tie at Shrewsbury and also came on in the subsequent tie at Peterborough. Apart from being on the bench at West Bromwich he saw no other first team action and joined Barnet on loan in March. Initially he was restricted to a few substitute appearances, but after extending his loan deal until the end of the season he started in a number of key games as the Bees battled their way to safety. Ed scored his only goal for Barnet in sensational fashion in the home defeat to Macclesfield. Was released by Ipswich at the end of the season.
Ipswich T (From trainee on 5/12/2006) FLC 0+2
Barnet (Loaned on 12/3/2010) FL 5+4/1

UPSON Matthew James
Born: Diss, 18 April 1979
Height: 6'1" **Weight:** 11.4
Club Honours: PL '02
International Honours: E: 19; U21-11; Yth
The central defender is the club captain at West Ham and leads by example. All season, Matthew put in assured displays with some great interceptions and superb tackles. He is always calm and collected and was a colossus at Aston Villa in January in the 0-0 draw. He also had a superb game at Chelsea in March, as he nullified the threat of Didier Drogba. At international level, he was always around the England squad and was included in the 23 to travel to the World Cup finals.
Luton T (From trainee on 24/4/1996) FL 0+1 Others 1
Arsenal (£1,000,000 on 14/5/1997) PL 20+14 FLC 8 FAC 3+1 Others 8+2
Nottingham F (Loaned on 8/12/2000) FL 1
Crystal Palace (Loaned on 2/3/2001) FL 7
Reading (Loaned on 6/9/2002) FL 13+1 FLC 1/1
Birmingham C (£2,000,000 + on 23/1/2003) P/FL 112+1/5 FLC 7 FAC 8
West Ham U (£6,000,000 + on 31/1/2007) PL 101/4 FLC 4+1 FAC 5

UTAKA John Chukwudi
Born: Legugnu, Nigeria, 8 January 1982
Height: 5'10" **Weight:** 12.12
Club Honours: FAC '08
International Honours: Nigeria: 43
The enigmatic Nigerian had another sporadic season. Injuries limited John's appearances for Portsmouth, with the highlight of his season coming against Sunderland in the FA Cup fourth round, where his two goals earned the Blues a 2-1 win. Bursting with talent, pace and skill, John remains a mystery to most Portsmouth fans as he drifts in and out

Matthew Upson

of games and often fails to live up to his own high standards. He was in the Nigerian squad for the World Cup finals and there could be further summer activity for him. Many clubs are sure to be clamouring for his signature as Portsmouth's financial problems suggest they will have to cash in on their most valuable assets.

Portsmouth (£7,000,000 from Stade Rennais, France, ex Enuga Rgrs, Arab Contractors, Ismaily, Al-Sadd, RC Lens, on 18/7/2007) PL 39+26/7 FLC 6+1/1 FAC 7+5/2 Others 1+1

UWEZU Michael
Born: Nigeria, 12 December 1990
Height: 5'6" **Weight:** 12.2
Having started his career at the Arsenal Academy before joining Fulham, Michael shows plenty of promise as a striker who picks up chances in and

around the box. Three times an unused sub for Fulham's Europa League group matches, he arrived at Lincoln on loan, along with Matthew Saunders, in January. Michael's three appearances for Lincoln all came from the substitutes' bench before injury robbed him of an extended spell at Sincil Bank. Was out of contract in the summer.

Fulham (From Arsenal juniors on 28/5/2009)
Lincoln C (Loaned on 1/1/2010) FL 0+2 FAC 0+1

VALENCIA Luis **Antonio**
Born: Lago Agrio, Ecuador, 4 August 1985
Height: 5'10" **Weight:** 12.4
Club Honours: FLC '10
International Honours: Ecuador: 41
An exciting young winger who became Manchester United's first summer

signing from Wigan for an estimated £16-million, Antonio made his competitive debut in the FA Community Shield against Chelsea at Wembley, when he replaced the injured Nani in the 62nd minute. Scoring his first Premier League goal for the Reds, the winner against Bolton in October, his first Champions League goal followed four days later in a 1–0 away victory against CSKA Moscow. As the season wore on, Antonio became more influential, as was demonstrated in the Carling Cup final against Aston Villa when his pinpoint cross produced the winner for Wayne Rooney. Sir Alex Ferguson's desire to have an orthodox winger in his side has been a feature of his reign and Antonio looks to be well on his way to filling the bill.

Wigan Ath (Signed from Villareal, Spain, ex CD El Nacional, Recreativo - loan, on 10/8/2006) PL 78+6/7 FLC 3 FAC 2
Manchester U (£16,000,000 on 30/6/2009) PL 29+5/5 FLC 2+2 FAC 0+1 Others 6+4/2

Ryan Valentine

VALENTINE Ryan David
Born: Wrexham, 19 August 1982
Height: 5'10" **Weight:** 11.11
International Honours: W: U21-8; Yth
Ryan was predominantly used as Hereford's left-back, although he also popped up occasionally on the right flank. A strong defender who was always willing to get forward, Ryan's competitive style made him a strong favourite at Edgar Street although two red and a dozen yellow cards indicate that he could take matters to extremes. Ryan also proved a reliable performer

Antonio Valencia

with penalties when his cool temperament was a big asset, his successful spot-kicks earning important wins against Chesterfield and Shrewsbury.
Everton *(From trainee on 1/9/1999)* FL 151+11/4 FLC 4 FAC 6 Others 4
Wrexham *(Free on 3/8/2006)* FL 46+2/2 FLC 3 FAC 2 Others 2
Darlington *(Free on 18/1/2008)* FL 43+5 FLC 1 FAC 2
Hereford U *(Free on 2/7/2009)* FL 40/4 FLC 1 FAC 2/1 Others 1

VALERO Borja
Born: Madrid, Spain, 12 January 1985
Height: 5'9" **Weight:** 11.7
International Honours: Spain: Yth
The Spanish-born attacking central midfielder featured in just two games for West Bromwich, as a substitute against Ipswich in the Championship and against Rotherham in the Carling Cup. Despite the club having high hopes for him, he was unable to command a regular place in the team and was subsequently loaned out to his former club, Real Mallorca, until May.
West Bromwich A *(£4,700,000 from Real Mallorca, Spain, Ex Real Madrid Castilla, on 26/8/2008)* P/FL 27+4 FLC 2 FAC 1+2

VAN AANHOLT Patrick
Born: Hertogenbosch, Holland, 29 August 1990
Height: 5'9" **Weight:** 10.8
International Honours: Holland: U21-4; Yth
As one of Chelsea's promising youngsters, the Dutch left-back arrived at Coventry on the eve of the campaign to fill the club's problem position and during his five-month stay at the Ricoh he was a virtual ever-present. A cool defender with a cultured left foot, Patrick showed his attacking ability with strong overlapping runs and generally good quality crosses. At the end of January he was recruited on loan by Newcastle as cover for the injured Enrique and he slotted seamlessly into the position, looking very much at home in the Championship's leading side. Comfortable and assured on the ball with a sound positional sense he minimized the loss of Enrique and was given a great reception by the Toon Army when he played his last game in the victory at Watford. Patrick made a timely return to Chelsea during an injury crisis at full-back in March and made consecutive Premier League substitute appearances against Portsmouth and Aston Villa. Nominally a left-back, he has also appeared in

central defence for the Chelsea reserve side and is a very accomplished player anywhere along the back line. Having been tipped for a glittering future, like so many of Chelsea's young stars he looks sure to feature more this coming season.
Chelsea *(From trainee, ex junior at PSV Eindhoven, Holland on 6/9/2007)* PL 0+2
Coventry C *(Loaned on 7/8/2009)* FL 19+1
Newcastle U *(Loaned on 29/1/2010)* FL 7

VANDEN BORRE Anthony
Born: Likasi, DR Congo, 24 October 1987
Height: 6'1" **Weight:** 12.8
International Honours: Belgium: 20
The Belgian full-back joined Portsmouth on loan from Italian side Genoa in the summer and arrived on the south coast with a high reputation. Anthony became a steady performer for the Blues, both at full-back and in midfield. Quick and direct, his defensive capabilities also improved markedly as the season drew to a close and as a result Pompey were hoping to retain his services.
Portsmouth *(Loaned from Genoa, Italy, ex Anderlecht, Fiorentina, on 13/8/2009)* PL 15+4 FLC 4/1 FAC 2

VAN DEN BROEK Benjamin
Born: Gellen, Holland, 21 September 1987
Height: 6'2" **Weight:** 13.3
An attacking right-sided midfield player who is also comfortable in the centre or playing behind the strikers, he signed for Shrewsbury in February from Dutch side HFC Haarlem, looking to break into English football. He made his debut from the bench in the 3-0 defeat at Grimsby. Strong and fast, he was involved in 11 League games, providing the cross for one of the goals in the 3-0 win at Crewe in April, and bagged his first goal with a good finish in the 3-2 defeat by Morecambe in May.
Shrewsbury T *(Free from Haarlem, Holland, ex NAC Breda, on 13/2/2010)* FL 5+6/1

VAN DER GUN Cedric
Born: Den Haag, Holland, 5 May 1979
Height: 5'10" **Weight:** 11.11
International Honours: Holland: U21
The former Ajax wide midfield player was signed by Swansea following a trial period shortly after the start of the season and soon displayed good skill in either wide position. He scored his first Swansea goal in the away win at Scunthorpe and remained a regular

inclusion in Paulo Sousa's starting line-up until he suffered a hamstring injury in January.
Swansea C *(Free from FC Utrecht, Holland, ex Den Bosch, Ajax, Willem II Tilburg - loan, ADO Den Haag, Borussia Dortmund, on 10/9/2009)* FL 20+5/2 FAC 1

VAN DER SAR Edwin
Born: Leiden, Holland, 29 October 1970
Height: 6'5" **Weight:** 13.6
Club Honours: FLC '06, '10; PL '07; '08, '09; CS '07; UEFACL '08
International Honours: Holland: 130
Veteran Manchester United and Dutch international goalkeeper, Edwin suffered an early season to forget. Having sustained a finger injury during the Audi Cup pre-season tournament, he missed the first 12 matches of the new campaign. Returning to action in October, when he played in United's 2-1 victory over Bolton, four Premiership games later, he was struck down with a knee injury in the Everton game. He returned to Holland to be reviewed by the Dutch team doctor and while there, his wife Annemarie was taken seriously ill. Edwin was given compassionate leave by United, Annemarie recovered and he returned to first team action in in January for a 3-0 win over Burnley at Old Trafford. Showing his undoubted class in the Champions League quarter-final against Bayern Munich at Old Trafford in April, he could not prevent the Germans from progressing to the semi-finals. He signed a one-year extension to his contract in February and, veteran or not, his air of total calm continues to be a vital element in United's success.
Fulham *(£7,000,000 from Juventus, Italy, ex Noordwijk, Ajax, on 10/8/2001)* PL 126+1 FLC 1 FAC 15 Others 11
Manchester U *(£2,000,000 on 10/6/2005)* PL 153 FLC 5 FAC 11 Others 51

VAN HEERDEN Elrio
Born: Port Elizabeth, South Africa, 11 July 1983
Height: 5'6" **Weight:** 10.3
International Honours: South Africa: 33
Elrio arrived at Blackburn with the warning that he needed strength work before he could play in the Premier League. He left in the January transfer window having seen action only as a substitute in two Carling Cup games. Anxious to play regularly so that he can cement his place in the home team for the World Cup, Elrio was only too happy to move to Turkey.

Blackburn Rov *(Free from Club Bruges, Belgium, ex University of Port Elizabeth, FC Copenhagen, on 29/6/2009) FLC 0+2*

VAN PERSIE Robin
Born: Rotterdam, Holland, 6 August 1983
Height: 6'1" **Weight:** 11.2
Club Honours: CS '04; FAC '05
International Honours: Holland: 43; U21
Robin started the season as the attacking lynchpin of Arsenal's new 4-3-3 formation and although he did not score in the early games, he was central to everything Arsenal did well in the final third. After opening his account at Manchester City, he went on a scoring spree that included the winner at Fulham and a brace at home to Tottenham. Yet, as with every season he has been at the club, injury was to disrupt his campaign again after he was hurt on international duty for Holland in early November and remained out of action until the middle of April. If he could stay fit for a season there is no question that Robin could be as influential for the Gunners as Wayne Rooney and Didier Drogba are for their respective clubs. He is a great finisher, leads the line well, brings others into play and can set up chances effortlessly. He featured 16 times in the Premier League, scoring nine goals, and four times in the Champions League adding one goal. His late return to club fitness was of great benefit to Holland as he could lead their attacking options in the World Cup.
Arsenal *(£2,750,000 from Feyenoord, Holland on 17/5/2004) PL 93+38/48 FLC 7+1/5 FAC 10+4/7 Others 30+14/13*

Robin Van Persie

VARNEY Luke Ivan
Born: Leicester, 28 September 1982
Height: 5'11" **Weight:** 11.7
Luke played in attack when Derby lost to Rotherham in the Carling Cup and made one Championship appearance as a substitute before spending the remainder of the season on loan to Sheffield Wednesday, where he had also been in 2008-09. Arriving at Hillsborough, he made himself an integral part of the side, always being full of endeavour and enthusiasm, and played either as part of a front-two pairing or as an attacking left-sided midfielder. Wherever he was asked to play he gave his all for the side and he gained much from the experience before departing for Derby.
Crewe Alex *(Signed from Quorn on 25/3/2003) FL 68+27/27 FLC 4+1/1 FAC 2+1 Others 5/7*
Charlton Ath *(£2,000,000 on 21/5/2007) FL 39+18/10 FLC 1+1 FAC 2*
Derby Co *(£1,000,000 + on 27/11/2008) FL 9+2/1 FLC 0+1 FAC 1+1*
Sheffield Wed *(Loaned on 20/3/2009) FL 3+1/2*
Sheffield Wed *(Loaned on 21/8/2009) FL 32+7/9*

VAUGHAN David Owen
Born: Abergele, 18 February 1983
Height: 5'7" **Weight:** 10.10
International Honours: W: 17; U21-8; Yth
The Blackpool midfielder was one of the most composed players in the Championship throughout the season. His intelligence on the ball is something which warrants his inclusion in the Welsh national squad and he started three games for them in the season. Although of small build, David is surprisingly tenacious in the tackle and is an astute reader of the game, full of tactical awareness, making him one of the most consistent performers in the League. Playing in a five-man midfield suits his style as he is able to drop off and collect the ball from deep – something he struggled to do in a quartet. He would like to score more than his three goals, one of them coming for Wales away in Liechtenstein.
Crewe Alex *(From trainee on 6/2/2001) FL 166+19/18 FLC 10 FAC 9/1 Others 5/1*
Blackpool *(£200,000 from Real Sociedad, Spain on 8/8/2008) FL 63+11/2 FLC 1+1/1 FAC 2 Others 3*

VAUGHAN James Oliver
Born: Birmingham, 14 July 1988
Height: 5'11" **Weight:** 12.8
International Honours: E: U21-3; Yth
Everton's Birmingham-born striker enjoyed an upturn in the 2009-10

campaign after a couple of injury-blighted seasons. Although a brief loan spell at Derby and knee problems kept him out of the first team early in the season, the Premier League's youngest ever scorer made seven successive appearances from the bench around the turn of the year, impressing again with his determination and enthusiasm. A rare start against Carlisle in the FA Cup was rewarded with a first Everton goal in two years before he joined up with Leicester on loan to assist the club's push for a play-off place. His pace can clearly cause problems for defences, as he demonstrated when netting his first Foxes' goal in a one-on-one confrontation with Watford. Unfortunately, niggling hamstring problems kept him out of the play-offs.
Everton (From trainee on 14/9/2005) PL 8+38/7 FLC 1+2 FAC 2+4/1 Others 0+4/1

Derby Co (Loaned on 18/9/2009) FL 2
Leicester C (Loaned on 11/3/2010) FL 2+6/1

[VEIGA] DA VEIGA Jose Manuel Monteiro
Born: Lisbon, Portugal, 18 December 1976
Height: 6'2" **Weight:** 13.3
International Honours: Cape Verde: 11
Having operated without a back-up goalkeeper in 2008-09, Macclesfield decided that one should be signed. Veiga moved from Hereford in August and was given his chance in four consecutive matches in August and September. With the side struggling to achieve a victory, he returned to the bench. He made two further appearances, in the first round FA Cup defeat at MK Dons and in the final match of the season at Lincoln, where he kept a clean sheet.

Hereford U (Free from Atherstone Town, ex Benfica, Alverca, Levante, Real Valladolid, Estrela de Amado, Olhanense, Tamworth, on 24/12/2008) FL 1
Macclesfield T (Free on 4/8/2009) FL 5 FAC 1

VELA Carlos Alberto
Born: Cancun, Mexico, 1 March 1989
Height: 5'9" **Weight:** 11.5
International Honours: Mexico: 28; Yth
Carlos was yet another in a long line of Arsenal players who endured an injury-plagued season. The Mexican forward rarely featured for long periods and while his ability has often come to the fore in Carling Cup games, where Arsenal field second-string teams, he has still to truly convince at the top level. Carlos does possess great skill and can finish exquisitely at times but he now needs to impose himself on games on a much more regular basis if he is going to become a permanent fixture in the first team. He appeared 11 times in the Premier League, although only two of those were starts, scoring once, five times in the Champions League, twice in the FA Cup and twice in the Carling Cup, adding a further goal. Is a member of the Mexico World Cup squad.
Arsenal (£125,000 + from Guadalajara, Mexico, via CA Osasuna, on 31/1/2007) PL 3+22/2 FLC 4+1/5 FAC 5+1/1 Others 4+9

VELICKA Andrius
Born: Kaunas, Lithuania, 5 April 1979
Height: 6'1" **Weight:** 12.8
International Honours: Lithuania: 21
On loan from Glasgow Rangers, the Lithuanian international striker's time at Bristol City was curtailed by cruciate ligament damage to his left knee just five minutes after coming on as a substitute for his Ashton Gate debut against Queens Park Rangers in August.
Heart of Midlothian (Signed from FBK Kaunas, Lithuania, via loans at Anzhi Makhachkal and Irtysh Pavlodar, on 8/9/2006) SL 39+819 SLC 1+4/2 SC 3/4 (£1,000,000 to Viking Stavanger, Norway on 26/2/2008)
Glasgow Rgrs (£1,000,000 from Viking Stavanger, Norway on 17/6/2008) SL 6+2/4 SC 1/1
Bristol C (Loaned on 15/8/2009) FL 0+1

VENNEGOOR OF HESSELINK Johannes (Jan)
Born: Oldenzaal, Holland, 7 November 1978
Height: 6'3" **Weight:** 13.5
International Honours: Holland: 19
Although Hull were unable to secure a big name signing during the summer

Jan Vennegoor of Hesselink

transfer window, they were able to recruit the services of one of the longest-named players two days after the window closed as big Jan was a free agent following his release by Glasgow Celtic. Having trained with FC Twente during much of the close season, he was made aware of the qualities of East Yorkshire's Premier League club by their new coach and ex-Tiger Steve McClaren. With his strength and awareness both in the air and on the ground, his experience was of obvious benefit to his younger colleagues in a struggling team. Jan's goals featured in wins against Wigan and Stoke plus a crucial draw against Wolverhampton. Often used as a lone striker, his bravery in the box was demonstrated when he was out cold for five minutes and suffered concussion in the game with Aston Villa in April. Although his season at Hull ended in relegation and he was unable to regain his place in the Holland squad for the World Cup, Jan certainly left a favourable impression amongst the City followers before being released in the summer.

Glasgow Celtic (Signed from PSV Eindhoven, Holland, ex Twente Enschede, on 25/8/2006) SL 63+15/4 SLC 4+1/1 SC 11/7 Others 11+3/2
Hull C (Free on 3/9/2009) PL 17+14/3 FLC 1 FAC 1

VERMA Aman Kumar
Born: Leicester, 3 January 1987
Height: 6'0" **Weight:** 10.0
On the staff of Leicester, Aman was an early season signing for Crewe on a loan basis. Following a substitute appearance in the Carling Cup game against Blackpool, the attack-minded midfielder made his first full appearance in the League at Grimsby. However, being unable to command a regular place in the side he returned to the Walkers Stadium early.
Leicester C (Free from Redditch U, ex Bedworth U, on 12/12/2008)
Crewe Alex (Loaned on 10/8/2009) FL 5+2 FLC 0+1 Others 1

VERMAELEN Thomas
Born: Antwerp, Belgium, 14 November 1985
Height: 6'0" Weight: 11.11
International Honours: Belgium: 28; U21-5
Thomas arrived at Arsenal in the summer as the only new signing and his impact was immediate. He scored on his debut at Everton, went on to register an impressive seven goals in the Premier League and had a penchant for scoring with superlative strikes. His goals in the home games against Wigan

and Blackburn were both tremendous efforts. Thomas was signed as a central defender and formed a strong partnership with William Gallas, playing every minute of Arsenal's Premier League campaign until injury forced him off during the game at Aston Villa in January. He made a quick return to the side but a calf injury suffered away in the North London derby ended his season early. The Belgian international played 33 times in the Premier League, had 11 games in the Champions League, adding a further goal, and played once in the FA Cup. He was named in the PFA Premier League 'Team of the Season'.
Arsenal (£10,000,000 from Ajax, Holland, via loan at RKC Waalwijk, on 19/6/2009) PL 33/7 FAC 1 Others 11/1

VERNON Scott Malcolm
Born: Manchester, 13 December 1983
Height: 6'1" **Weight:** 11.6
The hard-working striker enjoyed a superb start to the season when scoring three goals for Colchester in August. However, he soon found himself out of favour when Aidy Boothroyd succeeded Paul Lambert as manager in September and decided to have a spell on loan at Gillingham in mid-October. Unfortunately, his time there was cut short when he injured his ankle on his debut at MK Dons. Following two months on the sidelines, Scott then joined Colchester's Essex rivals Southend on loan, arriving at Roots Hall in the January transfer window along with fellow Colchester player Pat Baldwin. He immediately gained a regular place in the side and although adept at holding the ball up to bring colleagues into play he was unable to find the net more than four times during his five-month spell, two of those goals coming from the penalty spot. Back at the Weston Homes Community Stadium, Scott was released in the summer.
Oldham Ath (From trainee on 3/7/2002) FL 43+32/20 FLC 1 FAC 3+2/1 Others 5+2/6
Blackpool (Loaned on 10/9/2004) FL 4/3
Blackpool (Signed on 17/6/2005) FL 37+33/16 FLC 5/2 FAC 4+2/1 Others 0+2/1
Colchester U (Loaned on 17/3/2006) FL 4+3/1
Colchester U (Signed on 31/1/2008) FL 27+30/12 FLC 2+1 FAC 0+1 Others 4+1
Northampton T (Loaned on 20/3/2009) FL 4+2/1
Gillingham (Loaned on 15/10/2009) FL 1 FAC 1
Southend U (Loaned on 29/1/2010) FL 17/4

VIDAL Javan Noel
Born: Manchester, 10 May 1989
Height: 5'10" **Weight:** 10.10
International Honours: E: Yth
It was hoped that Javan would strengthen Derby's right flank, either at full-back or in midfield. He made only one substitute appearance before a combination of injury and a virus took him back to Manchester City.
Manchester C (From trainee on 3/7/2007)
Grimsby T (Loaned on 1/9/2008) FL 2+1 Others 0+1
Aberdeen (Loaned on 16/1/2009) SL 8+4 SC 1/1
Derby Co (Loaned on 1/2/2010) FL 0+1

VIDIC Nemanja
Born: Subotica, Serbia, 21 October 1981
Height: 6'2" **Weight:** 13.3
Club Honours: PL '07, '08, '09; CS '07; UEFACL '08; FLC '09, '10
International Honours: Serbia: 45
Manchester United and Serbian central defender who is recognised as one of the best in the Premiership, Nemanja was an absentee from the two opening Premiership games but started his season in fine form before being hit by a run of injury woes. In October, he was sent off against Liverpool in a 2–0 defeat at Anfield, confirming a trend for this fixture. This marked his third consecutive red card when playing against Liverpool. He notched his first Premier League goal of the campaign against Wolverhampton at Old Trafford in December. Blighted by injury lay-offs, he came back to full form and fitness for the all-important run-in as United chased major honours on two fronts. A real hero at Old Trafford, his partnership with Rio Fedinand is still one of the most formidable in the Premier League.
Manchester U (£7,200,000 from Spartak Moscow, Russia, ex Red Star Belgrade, on 4/1/2006) PL 123+3/9 FLC 4+4 FAC 14 Others 38/4

VIEIRA Patrick
Born: Dakar, Senegal, 23 June 1976
Height: 6'4" **Weight:** 13.0
Club Honours: PL '98, '02, '04; FAC '98, 02, '05; CS '98, '99, '02
International Honours: France: 107 (WC '98, UEFA '00); U21
In his prime the former Arsenal and French international midfielder was one of the most dynamic and influential players of his generation. At the age of 33, however, he was only an occasional performer for Jose Mourinho's Inter Milan. Soon after taking over at Manchester City, his former Inter manager Roberto Mancini rescued him

from obscurity by offering him a short-term contract at Eastlands in January. Unfortunately, as soon as Patrick signed for City he was sidelined with a calf injury and had to wait a month to make his debut at Hull and his first start against Bolton when he provided an assist for Emmanuel Adebayor in a 2-0 victory. Thereafter he alternated with Gareth Barry and Nigel de Jong in central midfield and scored his first City goal in the 6-1 victory at Burnley. It is hard to say that the signing was vindicated as City failed to clinch fourth place in the Premiership despite being well placed with a month to go.
Arsenal *(£3,500,000 from AC Milan, Italy, ex Cannes, on 14/8/1996) PL 272+7/28 FLC 7 FAC 45+2/2 Others 71+1/2 (£18,000,000 to Juventus, Italy on 14/7/2005)*
Manchester C *(Signed from Inter Milan, Italy on 8/1/2010) PL 8+5/1 FAC 0+1*

VIGNAL Gregory
Born: Montpellier, France, 19 July 1981
Height: 5'11" **Weight:** 12.3
Club Honours: FAC '01; UEFAC '01; ESC '01; FLC '03
International Honours: France: U21-4; Yth (UEFA U18 '00)
Signed by Birmingham from Lens, Gregory showed up impressively in the early matches. His quality on the ball and defensive capabilities - he loved a tackle and was on his way to becoming a bit of a cult hero - came over. He was injured and then Liam Ridgewell took his chance at left-back and played so well Gregory could not get back in. Returned right at the season's end and performed soundly before being released in the summer.
Liverpool *(£500,000 from Montpellier, France on 29/9/2000) PL 7+4 FLC 3 FAC 0+1 Others 4+1*
Glasgow Rgrs *(Loaned on 5/8/2004) SL 29+1/3 SLC 4 SC 1 Others 6+1*
Portsmouth *(Free on 12/7/2005) PL 13+1 FLC 1 FAC 2 (Freed during 2007 close season)*
Southampton *(Loaned from RC Lens, France on 1/8/2007) FL 20/3 FLC 0+1 FAC 2/1*
Birmingham C *(Signed from RC Lens, France on 13/8/2009) PL 6+2 FAC 1*

VILHETE Mauro Alexandre da Silva
Born: Rio de Mauro, Sintra, Portugal, 10 May 1993
Height: 5'9" **Weight:** 11.9
Local boy Mauro was handed a professional contract at Barnet on his 17th birthday, following a number of impressive displays at youth level and a

League debut. Despite interest from Aston Villa, Mauro chose to sign for his local side and was rewarded with his debut as a substitute in the penultimate game of the season, making him the youngest ever player to turn out for the Bees. He then started Barnet's final game of the season at home to Rochdale and showed much promise.
Barnet *(Trainee) FL 1+1*

VINCELOT Romain
Born: Poitiers, France, 29 October 1985
Height: 5'10" **Weight:** 11.3
Romain arrived at Dagenham in January after applying to the club for a trial. The French-born player made his debut for the Daggers as a substitute at right-back against Shrewsbury and had an assured game. Upon the return to Portsmouth of Marlon Pack in April, Romain made the central midfield role his own, partnering Peter Gain for the final month of the season and scoring a 25-yard goal against Burton in the process.
Dagenham & Redbridge *(Free from Gueugnon, France, ex Chamois Niortais, on 22/1/2010) FL 7+2/1 Others 3*

VINCENT Ashley Derek
Born: Oldbury, 26 May 1985
Height: 5'10" **Weight:** 11.8
Ashley's first full season at Colchester was severely limited by an ankle injury that kept him out for the best part of six months. The speedy right-winger played a key role in the U's flying start to the campaign but then badly injured his ankle in the process of scoring at Swindon in September – new manager Aidy Boothroyd's second game in

charge. Ashley was eased back into the side from the end of February onwards and soon began to rediscover his early season form. Coincidentally, his only goal following his return came in the reverse match against Swindon.
Cheltenham T *(From trainee at Wolverhampton W on 2/7/2004) FL 50+60/8 FLC 4+3/1 FAC 4+3/2 Others 4+3/2*
Colchester U *(Signed on 19/3/2009) FL 20+5/4 FLC 1 Others 1*

VINCENT James Michael
Born: Manchester, 27 September 1989
Height: 5'11" **Weight:** 11.5
In just his second season as a professional, James found himself starting the majority of Stockport's games. Usually in the middle of the park, he was at times called upon to play on either wing or occasionally at right-back, to cover for Johnny Mullins. Despite all his games, he managed to keep himself out of trouble, picking up only one yellow card all season. James' form was recognised by County's supporters' club who nominated him 'Young Player of the Year'.
Stockport Co *(From trainee on 1/7/2008) FL 38+13/2 FLC 0+1 FAC 2+1/1 Others 2+2*

VINCENT Jamie Roy
Born: Wimbledon, 18 June 1975
Height: 5'10" **Weight:** 11.8
Having played a number of games on loan in 2003-04, Walsall supporters knew exactly what they were getting with Jamie – a quality, experienced left-back able to help a young defence. He showed his versatility by switching to

Ashley Vincent

centre-half when the club had only one fit regular central defender available. His excellent reading of the game helped him in this position although he was vulnerable in the air and sometimes exposed to the trickery of experienced strikers, giving away two penalties. Jamie was Walsall's 'Players' Player of the Season'.

Crystal Palace (From trainee on 13/7/1993) FL 19+6 FLC 2+1/1 FAC 1
Bournemouth (Loaned on 18/11/1994) FL 8
Bournemouth (£25,000 + on 30/8/1996) FL 102+3/5 FLC 7+1 FAC 8 Others 9/1
Huddersfield T (£440,000 + on 25/3/1999) FL 54+5/2 FLC 3+2 FAC 2
Portsmouth (£800,000 on 23/2/2001) FL 43+5/1 FLC 1
Walsall (Loaned on 17/10/2003) FL 12 FAC 0+1
Derby Co (Free on 16/1/2004) FL 22/2 FLC 1
Millwall (Loaned on 5/8/2005) FL 15 FLC 2
Yeovil T (Free on 31/1/2006)
Millwall (Loaned on 15/3/2006) FL 3+1
Swindon T (Free on 28/7/2006) FL 84 FLC 1 FAC 3 Others 1
Walsall (Loaned on 31/7/2009) FL 37+1 FLC 1 Others 1

VINE Rowan Lewis
Born: Basingstoke, 21 September 1982
Height: 6'1" **Weight:** 12.2
Club Honours: Div 1 '05
Along with a clutch of Queens Park Rangers' team-mates, Rowan spent the season trying to recover his form after suffering a broken leg in 2007-08. Rowan had returned towards the end of 2008-09 and would have been hoping to be back to full fitness for 2009-10, but things never quite went for him. He was always in and around the squad and made a staggering 20 appearances off the bench, but his eight League starts yielded just one goal and he will be looking to turn things around in time for the new season.

Portsmouth (From trainee on 27/4/2001) FL 3+10
Brentford (Loaned on 7/8/2002) FL 37+5/10 FLC 1+1/1 FAC 3/2 Others 3
Colchester U (Loaned on 7/8/2003) FL 30+5/6 FLC 1 FAC 5+2/4 Others 4+2/2
Luton T (Signed on 6/8/2004) FL 90+12/31 FLC 2+2/1 FAC 5/1
Birmingham C (£2,500,000 on 12/1/2007) P/FL 10+7/11 FLC 2
Queens Park Rgrs (£1,000,000 on 2/10/2007) FL 42+27/8 FLC 3

VIRGO Adam John
Born: Brighton, 25 January 1983
Height: 6'2" **Weight:** 13.7

Club Honours: SPD '06
International Honours: S: B-1
A disappointing season started with Adam as Brighton team captain and ended with his release from a club that he had served admirably in two spells. Played mostly in his preferred position at centre-half, he struggled along with the rest of the Brighton defence for a considerable time as he looked in vain for some consistency, and conceded the captaincy to Andrew Crofts in November. In the New Year he began to turn in some sterling performances but just as he was enjoying his best form of the season, a second red card saw him lose his place to Adam El-Abd and he made only one more start. A robust defender willing to give everything, Adam leaves with the best wishes of all the fans at Brighton.

Brighton & Hove A (From juniors on 4/7/2000) FL 65+8/10 FLC 2 FAC 1 Others 4+2/1
Exeter C (Loaned on 29/11/2002) FL 8+1
Glasgow Celtic (£1,500,000 on 20/7/2005) SL 3+7 SLC 1 SC 0+1
Coventry C (Loaned on 7/8/2006) FL 10+5/1 FAC 1
Colchester U (Loaned on 18/8/2007) FL 30+6/1 FAC 1
Brighton & Hove A (Free on 2/7/2008) FL 56+5/4 FLC 3/2 FAC 5 Others 7/1

VOKES Samuel (Sam) Michael
Born: Lymington, 21 October 1989
Height: 5'10" **Weight:** 11.13
Club Honours: Ch '09
International Honours: W: 5; U21-14
Having scored for Wales against Montenegro three days before the domestic season began, the young Wolverhampton striker came on as a sub for the first four League games, heading wide a good chance against Hull. To further his football education he was loaned out to Leeds in October to cover for the injured Luciano Becchio and made his debut in the 2-1 win against the eventual League One champions, Norwich. Returning to Molineux after scoring just one goal in ten appearances, his starts in 2010 were restricted to three games in the FA Cup, while in the League he might have scored the equalizer against Manchester United had he come off the bench earlier than the 89th minute and been given time to get into the game.

Bournemouth (From trainee at Brockenhurst College on 29/11/2007) FL 38+16/16 FLC 1 FAC 1+1 Others 2
Wolverhampton W (£250,000 on 29/5/2008) P/FL 4+37/6 FLC 2 FAC 4+1/2

Leeds U (Loaned on 19/10/2009) FL 8/1 Others 1+1

VORONIN Andriy Viktorovych
Born: Odessa, Ukraine, 21 July 1979
Height: 5'10" **Weight:** 11.11
International Honours: Ukraine: 62
When the Ukrainian international striker left Liverpool in the summer of 2008 for a season's loan with Hertha Berlin, it was assumed that he would not come back. With the German club not making an acceptable offer in the summer and the Reds' manager Rafa Benitez short of forwards, Andriy returned but with even less success than in his first spell. After being used as a substitute for the first two months of the season, he was given a run of three starts in late October. The third was a vital Champions League fixture away to Olympique Lyon which Liverpool had to win to remain in the competition. Having missed a one-on-one chance in the first half to translate Liverpool's dominance of the game into a lead, he was later substituted and never played in the first team again, while the Reds, although scoring late on, could not hold on to their lead. In the January transfer window he moved to Dynamo Moscow for a fee of £1.8 million.

Liverpool (Free from Bayer Leverkusen, Germany, ex Chornomorets Odessa, Borussia Moenchengladbach, FSV Mainz 05, FC Cologne, on 12/7/2007) PL 14+13/5 FLC 2 FAC 0+1 Others 5+5/1

VUCKIC Haris
Born: Ljubljana, Slovenia, 21 August 1992
Height: 6'2" **Weight:** 12.8
International Honours: Slovenia: Yth
Haris is a stylish, attacking, midfield player at Newcastle who is rated highly, and who featured in the pre-season friendly at Blyth Spartans. He made his competitive debut as a late substitute on the left-wing in the Carling Cup tie against Huddersfield, and five days later was called up from the bench in the League game against Leicester. His first start came a month later in the Carling Cup tie against Peterborough but in October he suffered knee and ankle injuries requiring surgery. He marked his return for the reserves in April with a couple of goals and was an unused substitute in the final game of the season at Queens Park Rangers.

Newcastle U (Signed from NK Domzale, Slovenia on 16/1/2009) FL 0+2 FLC 1+1

W

WAGHORN Martyn Thomas
Born: South Shields, 23 January 1990
Height: 5'10" **Weight:** 13.0
International Honours: E: Yth
Having joined Leicester on loan from
Sunderland, the highly-rated young
striker, scored on his City debut on
the bench in the seasonal opener and
continued to find the net regularly to
finish the campaign as Leicester's
leading League marksman. He was the
club's choice as 'Young Player of the
Season' and scored the fans' choice of
'Goal of the Season', curling in an effort
against Queens Park Rangers. He was
denied a goal at Cardiff in the League
when an assistant referee failed to spot
his in-swinging corner crossing the goal
line before being cleared and he nearly
repeated the effort to produce what

would have been a last-minute winner
in the play-offs at the same venue, but
his corner was pushed against the
woodwork by a scrambling goalkeeper.
Always a willing runner, he regularly
induced terrace chants of "sign him
up" at the Walkers Stadium but, after
the success of his loan, Sunderland
manager Steve Bruce may well be
looking to promote Martyn into the
Black Cats' first team squad.
Sunderland (From trainee on 1/2/2008)
PL 2+2 FAC 1
Charlton Ath (Loaned on 17/11/2008)
FL 4+3/1
Leicester C (Loaned on 6/8/2009) FL
27+16/12 FLC 0+1 FAC 1 Others 1+1

WAGSTAFF Scott Andrew
Born: Maidstone, 31 March 1990
Height: 5'10" **Weight:** 10.3
Scott is hard working, very quick and
likes to run with the ball at defenders.
He can operate on either flank but is
essentially right sided. He made his full

debut for Charlton in the Carling Cup
at Hereford, and started both
Johnstone's Paint Trophy games, scoring
with a glorious volley against Barnet. It
was December before he started in the
League, scoring Charlton's second goal
at Brighton. He scored five goals in all
and his best was a 35-yard volley
against Hartlepool. Despite only starting
a dozen games, Scott was the only
player to feature in the named squad
for every game and was voted
Charlton's 'Young Player of the Year'.
Charlton Ath (Trainee) FL 9+25/4 FLC 2
FAC 1+1 Others 2+2/1
Bournemouth (Loaned on 21/8/2008)
FL 3+2 Others 1

WAINWRIGHT Neil
Born: Warrington, 4 November 1977
Height: 6'0" **Weight:** 11.5
The experienced winger was another
Morecambe player whose season was
hit by injury. An Achilles tendon
problem made him miss pre-season and
he went out on loan to Barrow to work
on his match fitness. After a successful
spell with the Blue Square Premier team
he returned to Morecambe but started
only five League games as he suffered a
recurrence of his injury problems.
Despite this, he was offered a new one-
year contract by manager Sammy
McIlroy and will be another player
hoping for much better luck.
Wrexham (From trainee on 3/7/1996)
FL 7+4/3 FAC 1 Others 1
Sunderland (£100,000 + on 9/7/1998)
P/FL 0+2 FLC 5+1
Darlington (Loaned on 4/2/2000) FL
16+1/4
Halifax T (Loaned on 13/10/2000) FL
13 FAC 1 Others 2
Darlington (£50,000 on 17/8/2001) FL
167+68/24 FLC 2+3 FAC 10+3/2 Others
7+3
Shrewsbury T (Loaned on 25/10/2007)
FL 2+1
Mansfield T (Loaned on 21/3/2008) FL
1+4
Morecambe (Free on 2/7/2008) FL
37+18/1 FLC 1+1 FAC 2 Others 2+2

WAITE Gareth
Born: Stockton, 16 February 1986
Height: 6'1" **Weight:** 13.1
Gareth made the step up from local
football at Spennymoor United with
apparent ease and soon settled in to
the hurly-burly of midfield in League
Two with Darlington. He is strong in the
air and a good ball winner, who loves to
get forward into the box, scoring his
first goal against Rotherham at home in
February. An injury sustained against
Barnet in late March necessitated an
operation and he was ruled out for the

Martyn Waghorn

remainder of the season.
Darlington *(Free from Spennymoor T on 18/1/2010) FL 14/1*

WALCOTT Theo James
Born: Stanmore, 16 March 1989
Height: 5'7" **Weight:** 10.10
International Honours: E: 11; B-1; U21-21; Yth
Theo endured another season of frustration as injury deprived him of a regular place in the Arsenal team. He also continues not to convince when given the chance at the highest level. His greatest asset is his lightning-quick pace and most defenders simply cannot cope with him in a foot race, yet at times he seems unsure and lacking in belief about how best to exploit this. He possesses a good shooting range but he still needs to work on his final ball. His greatest moments came against Barcelona in the Champions League quarter-final as he scored the first goal in the 2-2 home draw and set up Nicklas Bendtner for the opening goal in the away leg. Theo played 23 times in the Premier League, scoring three goals, six times in the Champions League, scoring twice, and once in the FA Cup. He was named in England's provisional 30-man World Cup squad and it was a surprise when Fabio Capello did not pick him to go to South Africa for the finals.
Southampton *(Trainee) FL 13+8/4 FLC 0+1 FAC 0+1/1*
Arsenal *(£9,100,000 on 20/3/2006) PL 44+42/9 FLC 10/2 FAC 6+3/1 Others 15+16/6*

WALKER Adam Richard
Born: Coventry, 22 January 1991
Height: 5'6" **Weight:** 9.0
A graduate of Coventry's Academy, Adam, like many of his young colleagues, played in the Carling Cup defeat at home to Hartlepool. Without a reserve team at Coventry, the midfielder struggled for match practice and was loaned to Nuneaton Town in October. He impressed for the non-League outfit and returned to Nuneaton in April after being released by the Sky Blues.
Coventry C *(From trainee on 29/6/2009) FL 0+2 FLC 1*

WALKER James Luke Newton
Born: Hackney, 25 November 1987
Height: 5'11" **Weight:** 11.13
International Honours: E: Yth
A strong, bustling forward, James has struggled to live up to the fee Southend paid Charlton for his services in June 2008, and has rarely commanded a starting place in the first team. Having

been consigned to impact appearances from the bench, as a result in September he was loaned to Hereford for two months and made a big impression on his Edgar Street debut with a spectacular 30-yard strike against Dagenham. He also found the net from distance in similar style as Hereford progressed against Aldershot in the Johnstone's Paint Trophy and many at Edgar Street were disappointed when he decided to go back to Southend at the end of his month. However, he opted to return to Roots Hall to fight for a place in the team, but failing to crack the starting line-up he was released from his contract during January to allow him to join Gillingham on a free transfer. Although he looked lively in his two starts for the Gills, at Brentford and Yeovil, he was short of match fitness and as a result saw little first team action.
Charlton Ath *(From trainee on 9/12/2004)*
Hartlepool U *(Loaned on 1/1/2006) FL 1+3*
Bristol Rov *(Loaned on 27/9/2006) FL 3+1/1 Others 1*
Leyton Orient *(Loaned on 23/11/2006) FL 9+5/2 FAC 1+1/1*
Notts Co *(Loaned on 15/3/2007) FL 2+6*
Yeovil T *(Loaned on 19/10/2007) FL 11+2/3 FAC 1 Others 1*
Southend U *(£200,000 on 15/2/2008) FL 25+20/6 FLC 1+1 FAC 2+2/2 Others 3*
Hereford U *(Loaned on 25/9/2009) FL 6/1 Others 1/1*
Gillingham *(Free on 1/2/2010) FL 2+3*

WALKER Joshua (Josh)
Born: Newcastle, 21 February 1989
Height: 5'11" **Weight:** 12.0
International Honours: E: Yth
Fresh from captaining England under-20s at the FIFA World Cup in Egypt in the summer, Josh was hoping to push for a regular place in Middlesbrough's first team squad. However, the classy central midfielder was overlooked and had to be content with reserve team football. In November, new Boro boss Gordon Strachan allowed him to move on a two-month loan deal to League Two side Northampton, but after only four games he suffered a serious shoulder injury and had to return back to the Riverside. Having recovered from his injury he made a surprise comeback to the Boro starting line-up in a home game against Peterborough in February, but that was to be his final action for the Teesside club before he was loaned to League Two side Rotherham at the end of February. Brought in to add passing ability and guile to United's midfield he did just that.

He also produced the bonus of three cracking goals, all from distance, including direct from a free kick against Port Vale and a superb strike at Accrington. Generally adjusted well to the bustle of League Two and will have learned from the experience.
Middlesbrough *(From trainee on 4/3/2006) P/FL 3+5 FLC 0+1 FAC 1+2*
Bournemouth *(Loaned on 9/3/2007) FL 5+1*
Aberdeen *(Loaned on 29/1/2008) SL 3+5 SLC 1 SC 1+1 Others 2/1*
Northampton T *(Loaned on 19/11/2009) FL 3 FAC 1*
Rotherham U *(Loaned on 27/2/2010) FL 15/3*

WALKER Kyle Andrew
Born: Sheffield, 28 May 1990
Height: 5'10" **Weight:** 11.6
International Honours: E: U21-1; Yth
Kyle was one of two Tottenham defenders signed from Sheffield United during the close season. He was immediately allowed to return to Bramall Lane where he was a regular at right-back with the odd appearance as a central defender. His tackling was well judged and using his speed and anticipation he often intercepted the danger. With an excellent first touch and always comfortable on the ball, he looked to use it well and was a threat going forward to produce well-judged crosses. Recalled by Spurs a few hours before the January deadline, he made just two starts at right-back and confirmed his earlier promise. Kyle has also progressed from the England under-19 team to the under-21 team, playing at this level against Greece in March.
Sheffield U *(From trainee on 3/7/2008) FL 2 FAC 2 Others 3*
Northampton T *(Loaned on 13/11/2008) FL 9*
Tottenham H *(Signed on 22/7/2009) PL 2*
Sheffield U *(Loaned on 5/8/2009) FL 26 FAC 1+1*

WALKER Mitchell (Mitch) Charles Alan
Born: St Albans, 24 September 1991
Height: 6'2" **Weight:** 13.0
A most promising young Brighton goalkeeper, Mitch was a scholar at the start of the season, but was included in the squad in August and signed a two-year professional contract a few days later. Showing considerable authority for his years, he continued to impress in the reserves and youth team, and in March, with Michel Kuipers injured, became the regular back-up for Peter Brezovan. Mitch played one Blue Square Premier game in an emergency for Eastbourne Borough and was rewarded

by Albion for his excellent progress with his League debut in the last match, when he gave a near faultless performance to keep a clean sheet.
Brighton & Hove A (From trainee on 10/9/2009) FL 1

WALKER Richard Martin
Born: Birmingham, 8 November 1977
Height: 6'0" **Weight:** 12.0
Club Honours: AMC '02
The experienced striker had a difficult first season with Burton after joining the League newcomers on a two-year deal. His craft and ability to lead the line were never doubted, but a scarcity of goals and a variety of fitness problems saw him slip into the background as younger, more mobile and prolific strikers such as Shaun Harrad and Greg Pearson caught the eye of manager Paul Peschisolido. Richard had virtually no part to play for the Brewers in the second half of the campaign.
Aston Villa (From trainee on 13/12/1995) PL 2+4/2 FLC 1+1 FAC 0+1 Others 1
Cambridge U (Loaned on 31/12/1998) FL 7+14/3 Others 1+2/1
Blackpool (Loaned on 9/2/2001) FL 6+12/3
Wycombe W (Loaned on 13/9/2001) FL 10+2/3 FAC 1/1
Blackpool (£50,000 + on 21/12/2001) FL 38+24/12 FLC 0+1 FAC 1+2 Others 3+1/3
Northampton T (Loaned on 21/10/2003) FL 11+1/4 FAC 4/2 Others 3/2
Oxford U (Free on 17/3/2004) FL 3+1
Bristol Rov (Free on 2/8/2004) FL 115+28/46 FLC 4+2/2 FAC 9+4/5 Others 12+2/9
Shrewsbury T (Loaned on 29/7/2008) FL 16+11/5 FLC 1 FAC 1 Others 2+1/1
Burton A (Free on 2/7/2009) FL 10+7/3 FLC 1 FAC 1 Others 1

WALLACE James Robert
Born: Kirkby, 19 December 1991
Height: 5'11" **Weight:** 12.8
The goalscoring midfielder made his Everton debut against Sigma Olomouc in the Europa League as a substitute in August but was unlucky that a double hernia operation kept him out of the first team picture until into the New Year.
Everton (From trainee on 24/12/2008) Others 0+1

WALLACE Ross
Born: Dundee, 23 May 1985
Height: 5'8" **Weight:** 10.0
Club Honours: SC '04; SPD '06; SLC '06; Ch '07
International Honours: S: 1; B-1; U21-4; Yth

Ross is an enigma who divides opinion at Preston. A left-winger who can beat his man with pace and guile on the ball, he often loses opportunities to cross by over elaborating, which frustrates colleagues and fans alike, as he can whip the ball in with accuracy when fully on his game. He is really dangerous from free kicks around the box but his seven goals were counterbalanced by no less than 13 bookings, many of them unnecessary, and he was suspended twice at important points of the season. The coming season is an important one for Ross if he is to fully develop his undoubted potential as a match-winning player.
Glasgow Celtic (From juniors on 12/5/2002) SL 18+19/1 SLC 3+1/3 SC 2+2 Others 1+6
Sunderland (Signed on 31/8/2006) P/FL 38+15/8 FLC 1 FAC 1
Preston NE (Signed on 5/8/2008) FL 74+6/12 FLC 4 FAC 3 Others 2

WALSH Philip (Phil) Andrew
Born: Hartlepool, 4 February 1984
Height: 6'3" **Weight:** 13.4
Phil arrived at Dagenham in January from Dorchester Town, where he had spent the season deputizing at centre-back. The centre-forward causes goalkeepers plenty of problems with his aerial ability at corners and set pieces. Although he did not open his Daggers' account before the end of the season, his presence caused opponents to make mistakes that allowed other players to score. Phil is still to make his first start for the club.
Dagenham & Redbridge (Signed from Dorchester T, ex Bath C, Newport Co, on 5/1/2010) FL 0+9 Others 0+2

WALTERS Jonathan (Jon) Ronald
Born: Birkenhead, 20 September 1983
Height: 6'1" **Weight:** 12.0
International Honours: RoI: U21-1; Yth
Despite being one of the first names on

Ross Wallace

Roy Keane's team-sheet, Jon's season reflected that of Ipswich in being very disappointing. His taking over of the captaincy coincided with their first win, against Derby, but his overall performances were still below the standards he set two seasons earlier and which brought him to the attention of other clubs. He played in all but three of the matches and finished as the club's leading scorer thanks to two goals in April against Reading and Newcastle. As in previous seasons he played mainly on the right side of midfield with occasional outings on the left or leading the attack. He had the distinction of scoring his side's first and last goals of the season, at Coventry and Newcastle respectively.

Blackburn Rov *(From trainee on 3/8/2001)*
Bolton W *(Signed on 30/4/2002) PL 0+4 FLC 1 FAC 0+1*
Hull C *(Loaned on 24/2/2003) FL 11/5*
Barnsley *(Loaned on 12/11/2003) FL 7+1 FAC 3 Others 0+1*
Hull C *(£50,000 on 5/2/2004) FL 9+28/2 FLC 1 FAC 0+2/1 Others 1*
Scunthorpe U *(Loaned on 4/2/2005) FL 3*
Wrexham *(Free on 3/8/2005) FL 33+5/5 FLC 1 FAC 1 Others 1*
Chester C *(Free on 1/8/2006) FL 24+2/9 FLC 1 FAC 5/1 Others 0+1*
Ipswich T *(Signed on 27/1/2007) FL 123+12/30 FLC 4+2/1 FAC 4/1*

WALTON Simon William
Born: Sherburn-in-Elmet, 13 September 1987
Height: 6'1" **Weight:** 13.5
Signed by Crewe on a season-long loan from Plymouth, Simon played consistently in midfield. He made his debut in the home game against Macclesfield in September and proved to be both a steady player and a hard worker.

Leeds U *(From trainee on 14/9/2004) FL 26+8/3 FLC 1+1 FAC 2*
Charlton Ath *(£500,000 + on 10/7/2006)*
Ipswich T *(Loaned on 18/8/2006) FL 13+6/3*
Cardiff C *(Loaned on 31/1/2007) FL 5+1*
Queens Park Rgrs *(£200,000 on 9/8/2007) FL 1+4*
Hull C *(Loaned on 29/1/2008) FL 5+5*
Plymouth Arg *(£750,000 on 7/8/2008) FL 12+1 FLC 1*
Blackpool *(Loaned on 26/3/2009) FL 0+1*
Crewe Alex *(Loaned on 31/8/2009) FL 26+5/1 FAC 1 Others 0+1*

WARD Daniel (Danny) Carl
Born: Bradford, 11 December 1990
Height: 5'11" **Weight:** 12.5

Signed from Leeds at the age of 16, Danny finally made his first team debut for Bolton as a substitute in the opening day defeat to Sunderland. A promising striker who can also play in midfield, his appearance in the following game at Hull was his last prior to joining Swindon on loan in November. The young striker was soon a main component of Town's successful campaign and it was no real surprise that manager Danny Wilson made moves to extend the deal until the end of the season. Usually utilised on the left flank as an attacking wide midfielder, cum winger, he demonstrated his ability with a string of fine attacking performances. Showing a great attitude and high work rate throughout, he delivered many dangerous crosses for his forwards and was also willing to get into the box to take chances of his own, scoring a number of useful goals.

Bolton W *(From trainee on 12/12/2008) PL 0+2*
Swindon T *(Loaned on 26/11/2009) FL 24+4/7 FAC 1 Others 3/2*

WARD Darren Philip
Born: Harrow, 13 September 1978
Height: 6'0" **Weight:** 12.6
Darren returned to Millwall, whom he had joined eight years earlier, in September on loan from Wolverhampton and signed a contract in January to strengthen the central defensive area. He quickly recovered his assured displays that the fans were used to, but with added experience he made it look simple. Very good in the air, his confidence in his ability spread to his colleagues, especially Paul Robinson.

Watford *(From trainee on 13/2/1997) P/FL 56+3/2 FLC 6/1 FAC 2 Others 0+1*
Queens Park Rgrs *(Loaned on 17/12/1999) FL 14 FAC 1*
Millwall *(£500,000 on 3/10/2001) FL 135+7/4 FLC 3 FAC 12 Others 4*
Crystal Palace *(£1,100,000 on 1/6/2005) FL 62+1/5 FLC 1 FAC 4/1 Others 1*
Wolverhampton W *(£500,000 on 4/7/2007) FL 30+1 FLC 1 FAC 2*
Watford *(Loaned on 30/9/2008) FL 9/1*
Charlton Ath *(Loaned on 30/1/2009) FL 16*
Millwall *(Free on 11/9/2009) FL 30+1/1 FAC 2 Others 3*

WARD Elliott Leslie
Born: Harrow, 19 January 1985
Height: 6'2" **Weight:** 12.0
Elliott was out of favour at Coventry, being behind Stephen Wright and Ben Turner when the season began, but injuries saw him start in four League games and giving everything despite looking a shade rusty. A big-hearted central defender who can win the ball in the air against most strikers in the division, Elliott was loaned to Doncaster on the morning of their midweek game against Sheffield Wednesday at Hillsborough in mid-February after Jason Shackell and Shelton Martis had both suffered injuries on the previous Saturday. He made an immediate impact by snuffing out the Wednesday attacks and scoring a terrific goal after 41 minutes with a scissor-kick following a corner to set the Rovers on the winning trail for a first ever League win at Hillsborough. With his month up, Elliott joined Preston on loan and made five appearances in all, helping the club to stave off any lingering worries about relegation, before going back to the Ricoh. Was out of contract in the summer.

West Ham U *(From trainee on 23/11/2002) P/FL 13+2 FLC 3 Others 3*
Bristol Rov *(Loaned on 29/12/2004) FL 0+3*
Plymouth Arg *(Loaned on 22/11/2005) FL 15+1/1*
Coventry C *(£1,000,000 on 7/7/2006) FL 111+6/14 FLC 4 FAC 5+1/2*
Doncaster Rov *(Loaned on 15/2/2010) FL 6/1*
Preston NE *(Loaned on 23/3/2010) FL 4*

WARD Jamie John
Born: Birmingham, 12 May 1986
Height: 5'5" **Weight:** 9.4
International Honours: NI: U21-7; Yth
Jamie began the season for Sheffield United in excellent form. Playing on either flank or down the middle, his speed as he ran at defenders caused constant problems. Playing with confidence and inventiveness he was a threat in the area, being quick to react and with a hard accurate shot. He damaged a hamstring in the Sheffield derby in September and when he returned had a lengthy run in the side but was not always quite as effective. His hamstring problem recurred at Peterborough and again at home to Barnsley when his season came to an early end.

Aston Villa *(From trainee on 16/5/2004)*
Stockport Co *(Loaned on 7/3/2006) FL 7+2/1*
Torquay U *(Free on 18/7/2006) FL 21+4/9 FLC 1 FAC 2/2 Others 1*
Chesterfield *(Signed on 31/1/2007) FL 58+9/29 FLC 2 FAC 4/2 Others 1*
Sheffield U *(£330,000 on 20/1/2009) FL 32+12/9 FAC 1+2/1 Others 1+1*

WARD Joel Edward Philip
Born: Emsworth, 29 October 1989
Height: 6'2" **Weight:** 11.13
Defender Joel broke into Portsmouth's
side for his debut in a Carling Cup tie
against Hereford in August but did not
make another start until April at Wigan.
However, still young and clearly
talented, local lad Joel looks set to stay
on at Pompey in the Championship for
the season ahead, where he will hope
first team opportunities are easier to
come by.
Portsmouth (From trainee on
4/7/2008) PL 1+2 FLC 1
Bournemouth (Loaned on 8/8/2008) FL
16+5/1 FLC 1 FAC 2 Others 1

WARD Stephen Robert
Born: Dublin, 20 August 1985
Height: 5'11" **Weight:** 12.1
Club Honours: Ch '09
International Honours: Rol: B; U21-3;
Yth
Stephen held on to the left-back spot at
Wolverhampton for the first three
games, but went off in the last. A tear
in his cartilage needed surgery and kept
him out until late November, and the
defence looked more balanced when he
returned to the team. Stephen made a
fine saving tackle against Bolton as
Wolves won three successive matches
that he played in. Defeat at Liverpool
followed, though Wolves were looking
comfortable at 0-0 until Stephen was
sent off. He always gave his best, but
lost his place in March. He had one
more game, against Blackburn, when
he had a shot blocked and made a goal
with a fine cross. A couple of days later
he had an exploratory knee operation.
Wolverhampton W (Signed from
Bohemians, ex Portmarnock, on
19/1/2007) P/FL 90+21/3 FLC 1+1 FAC
3+2 Others 0+2

WARNE Paul
Born: Norwich, 8 May 1973
Height: 5'9" **Weight:** 11.2
Back for his second spell at Rotherham,
his popularity being reflected in a
tumultuous welcome when he went on
as substitute on the opening day. He
responded by scoring the last-minute
winner against Accrington. In the
veteran stage but has looked after
himself and is a great example to others
with his enthusiasm and effort. It was a
pity that a foot injury chopped a huge
chunk out of his season, but he was
involved behind the scenes as fitness
coach and energetically took the pre-
match warm-ups. Is a great character to
have around the club.
Wigan Ath (£25,000 from Wroxham
on 30/7/1997) FL 11+25/3 FLC 0+1 FAC

1 Others 1+2/1
Rotherham U (Free on 15/1/1999) FL
173+57/28 FLC 6+6/1 FAC 10/1 Others 5
Mansfield T (Loaned on 26/11/2004)
FL 7/1
Oldham Ath (Free on 4/7/2005) FL
80+6/18 FLC 2 FAC 8/3 Others 4
Yeovil T (Free on 18/7/2007) FL
64+13/5 FLC 3/1 FAC 1+2 Others 3
Rotherham U (Free on 18/7/2009) FL
8+6/2 FLC 1/1 FAC 0+1 Others 0+1

WARNER Anthony (Tony)
Randolph
Born: Liverpool, 11 May 1974
Height: 6'4" **Weight:** 13.9
Club Honours: Div 2 '01
International Honours: Trinidad &
Tobago: 1
The much-travelled goalkeeper played
for Hull in the final of the Barclays Asia
Trophy against Tottenham in July,
having had previous experience of the
prestigious pre-season tournament
during his time with Fulham. Tony's only
other appearance for the Tigers came in
the Carling Cup win over Southend
before his contract was cancelled in
January. He joined League One Charlton
on a two-month contract in March but
did not add to his appearances tally.
Liverpool (From juniors on 1/1/1994)
Swindon T (Loaned on 5/11/1997) FL 2
Glasgow Celtic (Loaned on
13/11/1998) SL 3
Aberdeen (Loaned on 31/3/1999) SL 6
Millwall (Free on 16/7/1999) FL 200
FLC 10 FAC 10 Others 5
Cardiff C (Free on 3/7/2004) FL 26 FLC
2 FAC 2
Fulham (£100,000 on 12/8/2005) PL
19+2 FLC 2 FAC 3
Leeds U (Loaned on 4/8/2006) FL 13 FLC 1
Norwich C (Loaned on 2/3/2007) FL 13
Barnsley (Loaned on 31/1/2008) FL 3
Hull C (Free on 17/7/2008) FLC 1 FAC 1
Leicester C (Loaned on 13/3/2009) FL 4
Charlton Ath (Free on 25/3/2010)

WARNOCK Stephen
Born: Ormskirk, 12 December 1981
Height: 5'7" **Weight:** 12.1
Club Honours: ESC '05
International Honours: E: 1; Yth; Sch
Stephen contributed little to
Blackburn's season. Having started the
first game conscious of Aston Villa's
interest in him he was then left out of
the match at Sunderland before
signing for the Villans. Villa had been
crying out for a top left-back since
Wilfred Bouma suffered a serious injury
and Nicky Shorey fell out favour and
Stephen quickly showcased his ability
as a tough-tackling competitor. During
his first season at Villa he formed a
good understanding with Ashley

Young and Stewart Downing,
depending on which of the wingers
joined him down the left flank.
Stephen is comfortable in possession, a
competent passer of the ball and has a
willingness to push forward and
overlap as well as carry out his
defensive duties. Martin O'Neill
described him as a "warrior" after
witnessing numerous performances
when the slightly-built player put his
body on the line, only to return for
more of the same. In fact, his refusal
to shirk challenges even at the risk of
injury to himself, eventually caught up
with him when his form dipped slightly
during the second half of the season
due to an accumulation of knocks.
Even so, his performances for Villa
were enough to keep him in England
contention and he was called into
Fabio Capello's provisional squad for
the World Cup in South Africa.
Liverpool (From trainee on 27/4/1999)
PL 27+13/1 FLC 7+1 FAC 2+1 Others
10+6
Bradford C (Loaned on 13/9/2002) FL
12/1
Coventry C (Loaned on 31/7/2003) FL
42+2/3 FLC 2 FAC 2+1
Blackburn Rov (Loaned on
23/1/2007) PL 88/5 FLC 3+2 FAC 7+1
Others 8/1
Aston Villa (Signed on 27/8/2009) PL
30 FLC 5/1 FAC 6

WARRINGTON Andrew
(Andy) Clifford
Born: Sheffield, 10 June 1976
Height: 6'3" **Weight:** 12.13
Club Honours: Div 3 '04
Named 'Man of the Match' on the
opening day of the season at the very
moment that Rotherham's winning goal
was going in against Accrington, the
goalkeeper maintained those high
standards across the nine months.
Made so many vital saves in the
opening part of the season and
maintained his pretty good one-on-one
record, including one in stoppage time
of a 2-1 Carling Cup win over Derby. He
was ever-present, playing in all 55
games, and was again a reassuring
presence for his defenders. Topped his
season with two outstanding saves in
the League Two play-off final that were
highly acclaimed from all sides and
were worthy of any match at Wembley,
whatever the level.
York C (From trainee on 11/6/1994) FL
61 FLC 7 FAC 4 Others 4
Doncaster Rov (Free on 8/6/1999) FL
89 FLC 7 FAC 3
Bury (Free on 23/11/2006) FL 20 FAC 1
Rotherham U (Free on 11/7/2007) FL
130 FLC 7 FAC 6 Others 9

Andy Warrington

WATKINS Marley Joseph
Born: Lewisham, 17 October 1990
Height: 5'10" **Weight:** 10.3
Young winger Marley spent his first full season as a professional with Cheltenham. The Welshman, promoted from the scholarship scheme in the summer, made a handful of starts on the right of midfield in the first half of the season, after which most of his appearances were from the substitutes' bench. A quick, tricky winger, Marley scored his first goal as a substitute in a 2-1 defeat at Northampton. At the end of the season, he was the only player with a contract for the following campaign and aims to make further progress.
Cheltenham T (From trainee on 6/3/2009) FL 8+17/1 FAC 0+1 Others 1

WATSON Benjamin (Ben)
Born: Camberwell, 9 July 1985
Height: 5'10" **Weight:** 10.11
International Honours: E: U21-2
Ben burst back into the Wigan first team in April after spending the vast majority of the season on loan at both Queens Park Rangers and West Bromwich. Following the appointment of Roberto Martinez last July, the attacking midfielder found himself out of the first team picture and was loaned to the London club until the end of January, scoring two goals in the opening four games before finding himself red carded on two occasions. On his return to the DW stadium in January, Ben netted in the FA Cup tie at Notts County before being loaned out again. At the Hawthorns for a little over a month, Ben scored Albion's opening goal in their 3-2 home win over Preston

as the race for the Premiership started to hot up. He made seven appearances for the Baggies and when he left manager Roberto di Matteo said: "He gave us something different...he did well". Back at Wigan, an injury to Hendry Thomas saw him recalled, netting on his first start in the League when giving a 'Man of the Match' performance in the amazing fight-back against Arsenal. A dead-ball specialist, who is a constant danger from corners and free kicks, he added to his reputation as a tough-tackling player who can distribute the ball effectively. He leads by example, covering most of the field, and is always available to take charge of the middle of the park.
Crystal Palace (From trainee on 12/8/2004) P/FL 145+24/18 FLC 8+3 FAC 5 Others 3+1/2
Wigan Ath (£2,000,000 on 26/1/2009) PL 10+5/3 FLC 1 FAC 0+2/1
Queens Park Rgrs (Loaned on 1/9/2009) FL 16/2
West Bromwich A (Loaned on 22/2/2010) FL 6+1/1

WATSON Benjamin (Ben)
Charles
Born: Shoreham, 6 December 1985
Height: 5'10" **Weight:** 11.2
Ben's season at Exeter in 2009-10 was plagued by a calf injury and his attempts to make a full recovery were stalled by a constant recurrence of the problem. He made his one appearance this season when he came on as a substitute in the home against by Stockport.
Exeter C (Signed from Grays Ath on 12/3/2008) FL 4+9/2 FAC 0+1 Others 1

WATT Herschel Oulio **Sanchez**
Born: Hackney, 14 February 1991
Height: 5'11" **Weight:** 12.0
International Honours: E: Yth
The young Arsenal striker scored his first goal for the first team when he netted the opener in the Carling Cup third round win over West Bromwich. Quick and nimble on the ball, he played all the games in the Gunners' Carling Cup run, scoring once before going to Southend on a month's loan in February. Sanchez went straight into the starting line-up for the trip to Colchester and immediately showed up as being extremely pacy with abundant skill on the ball. He played four times on the wing for the Shrimpers and when Southend manager Steve Tilson decided against extending his loan spell for a second month he moved to Leeds on loan for the rest of the season, creating a couple of goals on his debut in a 4-1 win against MK Dons at Elland Road.

Arsenal (From trainee on 2/7/2008) FLC 1+2/1
Southend U (Loaned on 2/2/2010) FL 4
Leeds U (Loaned on 25/3/2010) FL 1+5

WATTS Adam James
Born: Hackney, 4 March 1988
Height: 6'1" **Weight:** 11.9
International Honours: E: Yth
Central defender Adam was Chris Sutton's first signing as Lincoln manager, initially joining the club on loan from Fulham before making the move permanent on a two-year contract. Some no-nonsense performances at the heart of the defence made him a regular feature in the Imps' starting line-up, but his season was cruelly ended in February when he suffered a broken leg in the local derby at Grimsby.
Fulham (From trainee on 7/2/2007) MK Dons (Loaned on 22/3/2007) FL 1+1
Northampton T (Loaned on 26/3/2009) FL 3+2
Lincoln C (Signed on 20/10/2009) FL 18 FAC 2

WEALE Christopher (Chris)
Born: Chard, 9 February 1982
Height: 6'2" **Weight:** 13.3
Club Honours: FAT '02; FC '03; Div 2 '05
International Honours: E: SP-4
After Leicester had been forced to use six different goalkeepers during 2008-09, Chris proved to be a model of consistency between the sticks, only missing an ever-present tag through being rested for the regular season's closing game against Middlesbrough. He produced a string of excellent saves and match-winning or saving performances throughout the campaign, and vied closely in the voting with Jack Hobbs for the club's 'Player of the Year' accolade.
Yeovil T (From juniors on 5/6/2000) FL 97+1 FLC 5 FAC 11 Others 2
Bristol C (Free on 4/7/2006) FL 5+4 FLC 4 FAC 1
Hereford U (Loaned on 9/8/2007) FL 1
Hereford U (Loaned on 27/11/2008) FL 1
Yeovil T (Loaned on 16/3/2009) FL 10/1
Leicester C (Free on 2/7/2009) FL 45 FLC 2 FAC 2 Others 2

WEBB George Andrew
Born: Poole, 1 May 1991
Height: 5'10" **Weight:** 11.6
The young defender made a number of substitute appearances for Bournemouth before moving to Gosport Borough at the end of October. He had become available due to the Cherries being unable to sign players under an embargo and was quickly

snapped up by the non-League side.
Bournemouth *(From trainee on 7/8/2009) FL 0+2 Others 0+2*

WEBBER Daniel (Danny) Vaughn

Born: Manchester, 28 December 1981
Height: 5'9" **Weight:** 10.8
International Honours: E: Yth
It was a difficult season for the speedy striker signed by Portsmouth as a free agent in the summer after the end of his Sheffield United contract. Danny was used predominantly as an 'impact' substitute, so usually started on the bench. He scored in Carling Cup ties against Carlisle and Stoke, as well as a late equaliser in the League match against West Ham in January. However, his frustrating season was cruelly cut short against Tottenham in March, when a cruciate knee ligament injury brought it to an abrupt end and ruled him out for at least six months. After a turbulent season, Pompey will be keen to retain Danny's services for the Championship, where his pace and finishing could be vital components.
Manchester U *(From trainee on 7/1/1999) FLC 1+1 Others 0+1*
Port Vale *(Loaned on 23/11/2001) FL 2+2 Others 0+1*
Watford *(Loaned on 28/3/2002) FL 4+1/2*
Watford *(Loaned on 13/8/2002) FL 11+1/2*
Watford *(Signed on 7/7/2003) FL 48+7/17 FLC 3+1 FAC 1+3*
Sheffield U *(£500,000 on 24/3/2005) P/FL 72+42/23 FLC 6+2/2 FAC 2+1/1*
Portsmouth *(Free on 10/9/2009) PL 4+13/1 FLC 3/2 FAC 1+3*

WEBSTER Aaron Denton

Born: Burton-on-Trent, 19 December 1980
Height: 6'2" **Weight:** 12.2
Club Honours: FC '09
Aaron was one the finest products of Burton's youth system and went with them from the Southern League to the Football League, winning UniBond League and Blue Square Premier championship medals on the way. A raiding, wide midfield player in his younger days, Aaron was moulded into a stylish left-back during Nigel Clough's reign as Burton manager, though his versatility meant he was also used in the centre of defence and, occasionally, up front. Blessed with a lovely left foot, Aaron also made a reputation as a dangerous opponent at set pieces, from where he scored many headed goals in his non-League days. Aaron had fitness problems that delayed his League debut but went on to make a useful

contribution, though it was not enough to win him a new contract
Burton A *(From juniors on 30/1/1998) FL 18+6/4 FAC 2*

WEBSTER Byron Clark

Born: Sherburn-in-Elmet, 31 March 1987
Height: 6'4" **Weight:** 13.12
Byron was signed at the beginning of the season by Doncaster after a successful trial period. A tall and cultured centre-back, he had spent two seasons in the Czech First Division and was given an early chance in the Rovers' team, where he did well but suffered an elbow injury after falling awkwardly. After recovering from this setback he then suffered a broken metatarsal in his foot which effectively ended his season. Hopefully the next season will see him make his mark.
Doncaster Rov *(Free from SIAD Most, Czech Republic, ex York C, Harrogate T, Whitby T, on 6/8/2009) FL 1+4 FLC 1+1*

WEDDERBURN Nathaniel Carl

Born: Wolverhampton, 30 June 1991
Height: 6'1" **Weight:** 13.5
International Honours: E: Yth
The tall, powerful midfielder made a good early impression as he inspired one of Hereford's best performances of the first half of the season with a win at Northampton on his debut. However, he struggled to maintain that level of performance as Hereford's form also dipped and he returned to Stoke at the end of his month's loan. Was out of contract at the end of June.
Stoke C *(From trainee on 27/11/2008)*
Notts Co *(Loaned on 27/11/2008) FL 3+6 FAC 2*
Hereford U *(Loaned on 26/11/2009) FL 3*

WEIR Tyler Carlton

Born: Gloucester, 21 October 1990
Height: 5'10" **Weight:** 11.8
Local boy Tyler was handed a debut at left-back for Hereford in a Johnstone's Paint Trophy area semi-final and proved that in terms of temperament and talent he was well up to the job. Further appearances followed as a left-back in League matches which all served to prove that he is a young player with a promising future.
Hereford U *(From juniors on 21/7/2009) FL 3 Others 1*

WEISS Vladimir

Born: Bratislava, Slovakia, 30 November 1989
Height: 5'9" **Weight:** 10.10
International Honours: Slovakia: 8; U21

A product of the Manchester City Academy, the Slovakian-born winger, and son of a former Czech and Slovak international, played a starring role in City's FA Youth Cup triumph of 2008. In 2009-10 his only City appearances came in Cup competitions – three times a substitute in the Carling Cup, including scoring the final goal in the 3-0 defeat of Arsenal in December. He was also included in the starting line-up for the FA Cup match at Middlesbrough in January but shortly afterwards was shipped out on loan to Bolton for the remainder of the season. An outstanding prospect, Vladimir arrived at the Reebok in a bid to add some pace and creativity to the side and made his debut as a late substitute in the 1-0 home win over Burnley. Showing enough in those few minutes to suggest that he could prove to be a real asset during the remainder of the season, he made sporadic appearances from the bench and, despite impressing, expressed some frustration at the lack of minutes he was spending on the pitch. He made his first League start in the home draw with Portsmouth in April and retained his place in the remaining two games of the season, generally impressing. An exceptionally quick player with a fondness for tricks and step-overs, Vladimir showed on numerous occasions that he is capable of delivering pinpoint balls into the box and is certainly a name to look out for in the near future. Made his international debut for Slovakia, a team managed by his father, during the season and was included in the World Cup squad.
Manchester C *(From trainee on 11/9/2007) PL 0+1 FLC 0+3/1 FAC 1*
Bolton W *(Loaned on 25/1/2010) PL 3+10*

WELBECK Daniel (Danny) Nii Tackie Mensah

Born: Manchester, 26 November 1990
Height: 6'1" **Weight:** 11.7
Club Honours: FLC '09, '10
International Honours: E: U21-4; Yth
The Manchester United winger, cum striker, started 2009-10 on a high when he rounded off a brilliant one-two with Michael Owen to score the club's only goal in the Carling Cup win over Wolverhampton in September. He followed that up by scoring in his second successive Carling Cup game, netting against Barnsley in the 2-0 win, and once again his partnership up front with Michael Owen took most of the plaudits. In November he made his Champions League debut in the 0-1 defeat to Besiktas, a defeat that put the

Reds' young stars under a lot of criticism as they surrendered a four-year home unbeaten record in Europe. Having committed his future to the club by signing a new contract, Danny went out on loan to Preston, where he made an instant impact with his pace and skill on the ball. However, his time there was cut short by injury. In less than a month he played eight times, scoring twice, with both goals being memorable for different reasons. His first was an exquisite chip over the Ipswich 'keeper from 20 yards, whilst his second, against Barnsley, saw him pounce on a poor back pass in a flash. Sadly, his knee injury required surgery and he returned to Old Trafford in February, having shown glimpses of why he is regarded so highly there.
Manchester U (From trainee on 11/7/2008) PL 2+6/1 FLC 7+1/2 FAC 4+2/2 Others 2
Preston NE (Loaned on 25/1/2010) FL 8/2

WELLENS Richard (Richie) Paul
Born: Manchester, 26 March 1980
Height: 5'9" **Weight:** 11.6
Club Honours: AMC '02, '04
International Honours: E: Yth
A talented midfield general who regularly directed Leicester's performances throughout, the only thing missing for Richie appeared to be an entry in the goals column, a fact he put right with a cheekily chipped penalty in the seasonal closer against Middlesbrough. Otherwise, he brought out the best in youngsters Andy King and Jay Spearing as the campaign progressed and could be a key barometer of the Foxes' fortunes in 2010-11.
Manchester U (From trainee on 19/5/1997) FLC 0+1
Blackpool (Signed on 23/3/2000) FL 173+15/16 FLC 8+1 FAC 10+2/2 Others 12+5/1
Oldham Ath (Signed on 4/7/2005) FL 87/8 FLC 2 FAC 8 Others 3+1
Doncaster Rov (Free on 23/7/2007) FL 84/9 FLC 3/1 FAC 6 Others 3+1
Leicester C (Signed on 7/7/2009) FL 41/1 FLC 1 FAC 2 Others 2

WELSH Andrew (Andy) Peter David
Born: Manchester, 24 January 1983
Height: 5'8" **Weight:** 9.8
International Honours: S: Yth
Having signed for Yeovil two years ago, the left-winger had an extremely creative season, with his assists total running into double figures. An innate ability to deliver quality set pieces and

strong running down the flank won him lots of admirers during the season, a campaign that saw him feature 45 times in total. Scored twice too, his first goals since 2005-06, and provided an outlet for the defence on numerous occasions, turning defence into attack in seconds.
Stockport Co (From trainee on 11/7/2001) FL 44+31/3 FLC 1+2 FAC 2 Others 3+2
Macclesfield T (Loaned on 30/8/2002) FL 4+2/2
Sunderland (£15,000 on 24/11/2004) P/FL 15+6/1 FLC 1+1 FAC 1+1/1 (Freed on 23/3/2007)
Leicester C (Loaned on 1/3/2006) FL 4+6/1
Leicester C (Loaned on 16/10/2006) FL 4+3 FLC 1
Blackpool (Free from Toronto FC, Canada on 31/8/2007) FL 3+18 FLC 1+1 FAC 1
Yeovil T (Free on 4/9/2008) FL 51+28/2 FLC 1 FAC 1+1 Others 1

WELSH John Joseph
Born: Liverpool, 10 January 1984
Height: 5'7" **Weight:** 11.6
International Honours: E: U21-8; Yth
John, a central midfielder and former England under-21 international, was signed by Tranmere manager John Barnes on a one-year deal following a successful pre-season trial. He enjoyed consistent and impressive form, earning several 'Man of the Match' awards and ending second, by only one game, in the appearance table. John was influential at all times and always worked hard, playing the holding role and netting four goals in the process. Many of his well-judged passes led to scoring opportunities but he also knows how to tackle and when to track back. Unsurprisingly, John was offered a new contract at Prenton Park.
Liverpool (From trainee on 29/1/2001) PL 2+2 FLC 0+3 FAC 1 Others 0+2
Hull C (Signed on 23/8/2005) FL 38+12/3 FLC 3+1
Chester C (Loaned on 1/1/2008) FL 6
Carlisle U (Loaned on 28/10/2008) FL 2+2 FAC 1+1
Bury (Loaned on 26/3/2009) FL 3+2 Others 0+1
Tranmere Rov (Free on 13/7/2009) FL 44+1/4 FLC 2 FAC 4 Others 1

WESTCARR Craig Naptali
Born: Nottingham, 29 January 1985
Height: 5'11" **Weight:** 11.8
Club Honours: Div 2 '10
International Honours: E: Yth
Notts County moved quickly to sign Craig when he became available from Blue Square Premier Kettering. He was

originally developed on the other side of the River Trent when manager Ian McParland worked for Nottingham Forest. Craig showed tremendous flexibility as a wide midfield player on both flanks and also as a striker. His goal tally of 11 included a hat-trick against Hereford and he created even more goals than he scored. He proved to himself and everyone else that he is more than capable of playing League football.
Nottingham F (From trainee on 31/1/2002) FL 2+21/1 FLC 1+1 FAC 0+1 (Freed during 2005 close season)
Lincoln C (Loaned on 31/12/2004) FL 5+1/1
MK Dons (Loaned on 24/3/2005) FL 0+4
Notts Co (Free from Kettering T, ex Cambridge U, Kettering T, Stevenage Borough, on 1/6/2009) FL 33+9/9 FLC 0+1 FAC 5+1/1 Others 1/1

WESTLAKE Darryl James
Born: Sutton Coldfield, 1 March 1991
Height: 5'9" **Weight:** 11.0
Darryl got his chance at right-back for Walsall when Rhys Weston picked up a red card early in the season. In a run of nine consecutive games, he showed remarkable maturity and calmness for one so young. There were times when he was overawed – the defeat at Southampton being a particular example - but he has learned enormously from his debut season. Likely to be the club's first choice right-back in the coming season, he has set himself a high standard and can be proud of his first season as a professional. He was voted the club's 'Young Player of the Season'.
Walsall (From trainee on 6/7/2009) FL 20+2 FAC 0+1 Others 1

WESTLAKE Ian John
Born: Clacton, 10 July 1983
Height: 5'9" **Weight:** 12.0
Ian was one of Peter Taylor's main signings for Wycombe in the summer, after his release by Cheltenham. The experienced midfielder missed the start of the season with a hamstring injury but, in the club's third game, made his debut against former club Leeds. He was then a regular but, after Taylor's departure in October, played only two games under new manager Gary Waddock, the last being in the 1-0 defeat at Southampton in December. A training injury in January, requiring surgery, put him out for two months and he ended the season in the reserves. Ian is an intelligent left-sided midfielder, a good passer, and has a year left on his contract.

Ipswich T (From trainee on 9/8/2002)
FL 90+24/15 FLC 3+2/1 FAC 3 Others 4
Leeds U (Signed on 4/8/2006) FL
29+18/1 FLC 2+1/1 FAC 1 Others 1
Brighton & Hove A (Loaned on
4/3/2008) FL 11/2
Cheltenham T (Free on 24/10/2008) FL
22/2 FAC 4
Oldham Ath (Loaned on 19/3/2008) FL 5
Wycombe W (Free on 15/7/2009) FL
7+2 Others 1

WESTON Curtis James
Born: Greenwich, 24 January 1987
Height: 5'11" **Weight:** 11.9
A very gifted Gillingham midfielder with
an eye for goal, Curtis started life in
League One in fine form and had
doubled his tally for 2008-09, netting
eight goals before the Christmas period,
including a goal of the season
contender against former club Millwall
and a rare header against Wycombe.
Sadly he seemed to suffer a significant
loss of form at the turn of the year and,
although still an important first team
player, his performances lacked the
impact shown earlier on.
Millwall (From trainee on 17/3/2004)
FL 2+2 FAC 0+2

Swindon T (Free on 12/7/2006) FL
21+6/1 FLC 0+1 FAC 2 Others 1
Leeds U (Free on 10/8/2007) FL 1+6/1
FLC 0+1 FAC 1+1 Others 1
Scunthorpe U (Loaned on 4/3/2008) FL
2+5
Gillingham (Free on 1/8/2008) FL
79+5/11 FLC 2 FAC 7/2 Others 5+1

WESTON Myles Arthur
Eugene Wesley
Born: Lewisham, 12 March 1988
Height: 5'11" **Weight:** 12.0
The speedy outside-left joined Brentford
from Notts County in the close season.
Due to injuries Myles started the
campaign playing up front, scoring twice
on his debut at Carlisle. He struggled in
this position, however, before disputing
the left-wing slot with Sam Wood.
Having pulled a hamstring in November,
causing him to miss five games, he
established himself at outside-left on his
return, giving some pulsating
performances with his darting runs and
precision left-footed crosses that excited
the crowd. As well as scoring twice on
the opening day he also scored braces
against Gateshead in the FA Cup, Carlisle
again and Gillingham.

Charlton Ath (From trainee on
16/6/2006)
Notts Co (Free on 15/3/2007) FL
59+14/3 FLC 0+3/1 FAC 3+1 Others
0+1
Brentford (Signed on 2/7/2009) FL
32+8/8 FLC 1 FAC 3/2 Others 1

Myles Weston

WESTON Rhys David
Born: Kingston, 27 October 1980
Height: 6'1" **Weight:** 12.3
International Honours: W: 7; U21-4.
E: Yth, Sch
In his third season at Walsall, Rhys
continued to produce solid and reliable
performances at right-back. An over-
exuberant challenge in the Carling Cup
at Accrington saw him pick up a red
card. He lost his place for the next nine
games due to the form of Darryl
Westlake, whom he was always willing
to help and pass on advice. He likes to
get forward whenever possible and is a
good crosser of the ball. Rhys left
Walsall at the end of the season,
intending to find a club close to his
family home in Scotland.
Arsenal (From trainee on 8/7/1999) PL
1 FLC 1+1
Cardiff C (£300,000 on 21/11/2000) FL
170+12/2 FLC 10 FAC 14+1 Others 7
(Free to Viking FK, Norway on
31/8/2006)
Port Vale (Free from Viking FK, Norway
on 9/2/2007) FL 15
Walsall (Free on 23/7/2007) FL 96+6/1
FLC 1 FAC 7 Others 1

WESTWOOD Ashley Roy
Born: Nantwich, 1 April 1990
Height: 5'9" **Weight:** 10.8
Since emerging from Crewe's youth
team ranks in the previous season with

Curtis Weston

two substitute appearances, Ashley has made massive progress in his second year as a professional. Confident and a hard worker in midfield, he won the club's 'Player of the Year' award from the supporters. He also made a useful contribution with his goals.
Crewe Alex (From trainee on 23/5/2008) FL 34+4/6 FLC 1 FAC 1

Ashley Westwood

WESTWOOD Christopher (Chris) John
Born: Dudley, 13 February 1977
Height: 6'0" **Weight:** 12.2
Club Honours: Div 2 '07
Wycombe signed this vastly experienced defender after his release by Peterborough in the summer. Although starting the first game at Charlton, Chris played one more League match before falling out of favour. He returned for the team's, and probably his, worst game of the season in the 6-0 mauling at Huddersfield in November. Ironically it proved to be turning point, as he was then virtually ever-present in central defence until the end of the season, forming a particularly good partnership with Adam Hinshelwood. Chris is dominant in the air and has especially good positional sense.
Wolverhampton W (From trainee on 3/7/1995) FL 3+1/1 FLC 1+1 (Freed during 1998 close season)
Hartlepool U (Signed from Telford U on 24/3/1999) FL 244+6/7 FLC 8 FAC 15/2 Others 20
Walsall (Free on 1/7/2005) FL 64+5/5 FLC 3 FAC 1+1 Others 2
Peterborough U (Free on 12/7/2007) FL 45+8 FLC 2+1 FAC 2+1 Others 2
Cheltenham T (Loaned on 5/1/2009) FL 9/2

Wycombe W (Free on 9/7/2009) FL 28/2 FLC 1 FAC 1 Others 1

WESTWOOD Keiren
Born: Manchester, 23 October 1984
Height: 6'1" **Weight:** 13.10
Club Honours: Div 2 '06
International Honours: RoI: 5
Keiren continued where he left off the previous season with Coventry, putting in consistently high levels of performance and living up to his rating as the best goalkeeper outside the Premiership. His performances deservedly earned him selection to the Republic of Ireland squad as deputy to Shay Given. Keiren gave some outstanding displays, especially away from home, often saving Coventry from bigger defeats. He had an excellent game in the victory at Watford when he single-handedly kept City in the game as his defence was at sea in the first half. Great displays followed at Queens Park Rangers and Leicester and he made a great penalty save from Scunthorpe's Gary Hooper in the home victory. Another strength is his kicking, usually long and accurate, and during the season his kicks created a few goals. Transfer speculation was again rife in the January window but no club came in for him and the summer could test Coventry's resolve to keep him as Premier League clubs circle over the Ricoh, knowing that Keiren has only one more year on his contract with the Sky Blues.
Manchester C (From juniors on 25/10/2001)
Carlisle U (Free on 13/9/2004) FL 127 FLC 3+1 FAC 4 Others 11
Coventry C (£500,000 on 30/6/2008) FL 90 FAC 5

WHALEY Simon
Born: Bolton, 7 June 1985
Height: 5'11" **Weight:** 11.7
A goalscoring right-winger with a direct style, Simon arrived at Norwich after being signed by Bryan Gunn from Preston and made a good pre-season impact. However, a change of manager and formation saw him loaned out to Rochdale in September, where he provided a classy presence on either wing during his two month stay, scoring in big wins against Hereford and Bournemouth as Dale moved up to second in the table. Back at Carrow Road, Simon immediately joined Bradford on a six-week loan and started five games, being employed on both wings, and scored a half-volley from 25 yards at Grimsby on his full debut. Having negotiated his release from Norwich, Simon joined Chesterfield in

January as a free agent and came off the bench to score on his debut. He injured a knee after just five more appearances, and an operation to clean the affected area finished the attack-minded wide midfielder's season. Was out of contract in the summer.
Bury (From trainee on 30/10/2002) FL 48+25/11 FLC 2 FAC 2+2 Others 1+5
Preston NE (£250,000 on 9/1/2006) FL 74+46/14 FLC 2+1/1 FAC 4+2/2 Others 0+2
Barnsley (Loaned on 7/11/2008) FL 4/1
Norwich C (Signed on 24/7/2009) FL 3 FLC 2 Others 1
Rochdale (Loaned on 18/9/2009) FL 8+1/2
Bradford C (Loaned on 20/11/2009) FL 5+1/1
Chesterfield (Free on 19/2/2010) FL 5+1/1

WHEATER David James
Born: Redcar, 14 February 1987
Height: 6'4" **Weight:** 12.12
International Honours: E: U21-11; Yth
David started like a house on fire at Middlesbrough, alongside Robert Huth. There were four clean sheets in the first four games and a big reason for this was the centre-half pairing. David's game suffered after the German international left for Stoke and he seemed unsettled by the constant changes in the back four; over the season he had seven different central defensive partners. His pairing with loan signing Sean St Ledger did not run as planned and a couple of uncharacteristic mistakes from David led to costly goals. He improved with the calming influence of Steve McManus alongside him and regained his knack of being a threat in the opposing box. After having a couple of goals dubiously chalked off, he finally found the net at Ipswich in February. With three games to go, he suffered an ankle ligament injury that ended his season. He was voted Boro's 'Community Player of the Year' for the third season running, this time jointly with Danny Coyne, as he constantly attended events and clubs in the area.
Middlesbrough (From trainee on 16/2/2005) P/FL 112+4/6 FLC 4 FAC 10/2 Others 0+1
Doncaster Rov (Loaned on 10/2/2006) FL 7/1
Wolverhampton W (Loaned on 29/9/2006) FL 1
Darlington (Loaned on 1/1/2007) FL 15/2 Others 1

WHELAN Glenn David
Born: Dublin, 13 January 1984
Height: 6'0" **Weight:** 12.5

International Honours: RoI: 20; B; U21-18; Yth
The Irishman had to fight for his place for much of the season but went on to appear in 25 of Stoke's 38 League games. His performances particularly impressed the Republic of Ireland manager Giovanni Trapattoni, who went so far as to liken the midfielder to a young Patrick Vieira for his efforts in helping to take his country to within a whisker of World Cup qualification. Stoke are not noted for their subtle midfield play, but most of the constructive football in the middle of the team comes from Glenn's efforts. He always tries to play football and if some of what he attempts does not come off, it is often because his team-mates were not quite on the same page. He had only two League goals but both were important, especially the 87th-minute drive at Tottenham that enabled Stoke to pull off their best win of the season.
Manchester C (From trainee on 25/1/2001) Others 0+1
Bury (Loaned on 29/9/2003) FL 13 FAC 1 Others 1
Sheffield Wed (Free on 7/7/2004) FL 136+6/12 FLC 8/2 FAC 6/1 Others 3/1
Stoke C (£500,000 on 31/1/2008) P/FL 59+14/4 FLC 5/2 FAC 5

WHELAN Noel David
Born: Leeds, 30 December 1974
Height: 6'2" **Weight:** 12.3
Club Honours: FAYC '93
International Honours: E: U21-2; Yth (UEFA-U18 '93)
Noel was one of Steve Staunton's first signings for Darlington, joining the club as a free agent and made his debut at Dagenham in October for his first Football League game in four years since leaving Boston United. However, he had to retire with a leg injury after half-an-hour and did not appear again until late January when he broke down with a recurrence of this injury just two minutes after coming on as a substitute against Northampton. He started one more game against Barnet and showed all his experience and strength in shielding the ball, which could have proved so vital to Darlington's survival had he stayed fit.
Leeds U (From trainee on 5/3/1993) PL 28+20/7 FLC 3+2/1 FAC 2 Others 3
Coventry C (£2,000,000 on 16/12/1995) PL 127+7/31 FLC 6/1 FAC 15+1/7
Middlesbrough (£2,200,000 on 4/8/2000) PL 33+28/6 FLC 4/2 FAC 5+3/3
Crystal Palace (Loaned on 7/3/2003) FL 7+1/3

Millwall (Free on 5/8/2003) FL 8+7/4 FLC 1
Derby Co (Free on 29/1/2004) FL 3+5 Aberdeen (Free on 5/8/2004) SL 18+2/5 SC 2+1
Boston U (Free on 11/7/2005) FL 8+7/4 FLC 0+1 Others 1
Livingston (Free on 10/3/2006) SL 5+3/1
Dunfermline Ath (Free on 10/7/2006) SL 1 (Freed on 4/1/2007)
Darlington (Free from Harrogate T, following a spell out of the game, on 8/10/2009) FL 2+1

WHELPDALE Christopher (Chris) Mark
Born: Harold Wood, 27 January 1987
Height: 6'0" **Weight:** 12.8
Wide man Chris missed the first seven games for Peterborough and the last six because of injury. In between these times, he was the Chris that the fans have come to expect. A quick wide midfield player with nimble feet, he loves to attack defences. To that, he adds a powerful shot and is good in the air. An injury-free season could see Chris back to his best.
Peterborough U (Free from Billericay T, ex Maldon T, on 17/5/2007) FL 85+18/11 FLC 3+1/1 FAC 7+1 Others 1+1

WHING Andrew (Andy) John
Born: Birmingham, 20 September 1984
Height: 6'0" **Weight:** 12.0
Brighton's Player of the Season from 2008-09 made just 11 appearances in 2009-10 and ended the campaign on loan to Chesterfield. Although he started as the first choice right-back, he got off to a miserable start with an own goal in the first match and then underwent a hernia operation in September that ruled him out for a couple of months. Andy returned for four games, but then the on-loan Gavin Hoyte took over and when Inigo Calderon was signed it was clear that his opportunities were limited and the wholehearted defender moved to Saltergate for the remainder of the season in March. In his new surroundings, Andy found himself operating in an unfamiliar role in central midfield as the club tried to maintain play-off form. Six bookings in eight games told a story of a player lacking match fitness and this counted against him in the end, with him seeing out the season on the substitutes' bench.
Coventry C (From trainee on 7/4/2003) FL 87+19/2 FLC 4+3 FAC 5+1
Brighton & Hove A (Loaned on 7/10/2006) FL 12 Others 3

Brighton & Hove A (Free on 3/7/2007) FL 91 FLC 5 FAC 6 Others 7+1
Chesterfield (Loaned on 5/3/2010) FL 9+2

WHITAKER Daniel (Danny) Philip
Born: Wilmslow, 14 November 1980
Height: 5'10" **Weight:** 11.2
If you were looking for a good, solid midfield man then Oldham's Danny would spring to mind every time. Packs a thunderbolt of a shot and is always looking to unleash it on unsuspecting defences. A tricky, crafty player who is not frightened of taking players on, he made 44 appearances but was not always the first choice and many of them came from the bench. Surprisingly, he was released by Oldham at the end of his contract, following three good years at Boundary Park.
Macclesfield T (Signed from Wilmslow Albion on 5/7/2000) FL 156+15/23 FLC 6/5 FAC 12/2 Others 12+1/2
Port Vale (Free on 8/7/2006) FL 80+6/14 FLC 5/1 FAC 5/1 Others 2
Oldham Ath (Free on 19/7/2008) FL 61+19/8 FLC 3 FAC 1+1/1 Others 2/2

WHITBREAD Zak Benjamin
Born: Houston, Texas, USA, 4 March 1984
Height: 6'2" **Weight:** 11.6
International Honours: USA: U23; Yth
A highly regarded central defender, Zak joined Norwich from Millwall in January and while injury restricted his impact at Carrow Road in the promotion campaign, he displayed much promise for the seasons ahead in his limited game time. Very strong in the air, he also has excellent positional sense and is always prepared to play his way out of defence, thus combining the ruggedness required of any defender with the ability to contribute more to his team.
Liverpool (From trainee on 8/5/2003) FLC 4 FAC 1 Others 1+1
Millwall (Free on 24/11/2005) FL 93+7/3 FLC 4 FAC 9/1 Others 6
Norwich C (Signed on 8/1/2010) FL 1+3

WHITE Aidan Peter
Born: Otley, 10 October 1991
Height: 5'7" **Weight:** 10.0
International Honours: E: Yth
Still only 18, the speedy Leeds' left-back struggled with a niggling knee injury early in the campaign. He made only a handful of League appearances but is highly regarded by Leeds, manager Simon Grayson revealing that Aidan often suffered from cramp because of nervous energy while playing for the

first team. Much will be expected on the young defender, who can also play as a left-winger, in the forthcoming season.
Leeds U (From trainee on 5/12/2008) FL 9+4 FLC 1+1 FAC 1+5 Others 3

WHITE Alan
Born: Darlington, 22 March 1976
Height: 6'1" **Weight:** 13.2
Alan made a surprise but welcome return on loan to his home-town club, Darlington, in January after leaving for Luton in the summer. He continued where he had left off, as a colossus in the heart of the defence, with his powerful aerial presence and no-nonsense clearances. He established a good understanding with skipper Ian Miller in the centre of the defence and added one goal to his Darlington total with a powerful header in the victory at Burton on Easter Saturday. He has now played more than 100 games for the Quakers.
Middlesbrough (From trainee on 8/7/1994) Others 1
Luton T (£40,000 on 22/9/1997) FL 60+20/3 FLC 3+3 FAC 2 Others 4
Colchester U (Loaned on 12/11/1999) FL 4 Others 1
Colchester U (Free on 19/7/2000) FL 128+11/4 FLC 7+1 FAC 6+2 Others 6
Leyton Orient (Free on 6/7/2004) FL 26 FLC 1 FAC 2 Others 2
Boston U (Free on 4/3/2005) FL 48/4 FLC 1 FAC 3 Others 1/1
Notts Co (Free on 3/7/2006) FL 32+3/5 FLC 3 FAC 1 Others 1
Peterborough U (Loaned on 20/3/2007) FL 7/3
Darlington (Free on 4/7/2007) FL 75/3 FLC 1 FAC 3 Others 6/2 (Free to Luton T on 27/7/2009)
Darlington (Loaned from Luton T on 15/1/2010) FL 23+1/1

WHITE John Alan
Born: Maldon, 26 July 1986
Height: 5'10" **Weight:** 12.1
Out of favour with Colchester manager Paul Lambert, John began the 2009-10 campaign on loan at Southend, where he fitted in well alongside fellow loanee Matt Heath and the experienced Adam Barrett. Having sorted out manager Steve Tilson's left-back problem, temporarily at least, he also proved to be adept at right-back and a real testament to his defensive qualities was the fact that Southend lost only once in his six appearances for the Roots Hall outfit. Upon his return to Colchester, he was installed at right-back under new boss Aidy Boothroyd and enjoyed one of his best seasons at the club. Starting virtually every game from thereon, the loyal clubman was consistently solid and even

filled in at left-back on the odd occasion.
Colchester U (From trainee on 23/2/2005) FL 134+23 FLC 3+1 FAC 12 Others 6+1
Southend U (Loaned on 30/7/2009) FL 5 FLC 1

Dean Whitehead

WHITEHEAD Dean
Born: Abingdon, 12 January 1982
Height: 5'11" **Weight:** 12.1
Club Honours: Ch '05, '07
Perhaps the surprise package of the Stoke season, Dean had a tough time in winning over the crowd after he first signed, but he quickly settled into his stride and became an integral member of the first team, with his box-to-box play and tough tackling. His strengths lie in his tireless engine, which sees him keep going at full pace from the first minute through to the last, and his refusal to consider any situation on the field to be a lost cause. Dean also showed that he can turn his hand to covering at right-back and while he is far more useful to the team as a midfielder, that versatility served Stoke well midway through the season when injuries and suspensions hit the team hard and left them struggling to fill certain positions.
Oxford U (From trainee on 20/4/2000) FL 92+30/9 FLC 5+1 FAC 3+2 Others 1+2
Sunderland (Signed on 2/8/2004) P/FL 176+9/13 FLC 5+3 FAC 7/1
Stoke C (£3,000,000 on 24/7/2009) PL 33+3 FAC 4/1

WHITTINGHAM Peter Michael
Born: Nuneaton, 8 September 1984
Height: 5'10" **Weight:** 10.5
Club Honours: FAYC '02

International Honours: E: U21-17; Yth
Cardiff's Peter enjoyed his best season ever - 25 goals in League and Cups. He was the Championship's joint top scorer on 20 goals and netted twice in the play-offs. By the end of the season Premier League and top Championship clubs were keen on the wide midfield player. Has top quality technique, is left-footed and has an outstanding delivery from set pieces. Peter played much of the season on the right for Cardiff, but was given the freedom to drift inside where he loved to go for goal. The former Aston Villa player is always a potential match-winner. His Cardiff contract runs until the summer of 2011.
Aston Villa (From trainee on 2/11/2002) PL 32+24/1 FLC 6+3/1 FAC 1
Burnley (Loaned on 14/2/2005) FL 7 FAC 2
Derby Co (Loaned on 16/9/2005) FL 11
Cardiff C (£350,000 on 11/1/2007) FL 107+27/32 FLC 7+3/4 FAC 11+1/4 Others 3/2

Peter Whittingham

WICKHAM Connor Neil Ralph
Born: Hereford, 31 March 1993
Height: 6'0" **Weight:** 14.1
International Honours: E: Yth
Roy Keane's faith in the striker's ability was demonstrated at the start of the season when, controversially, he sold Jordan Rhodes to Huddersfield. Connor rewarded him by improving throughout the season and finishing as an Ipswich regular. He started with a brace of goals at Shrewsbury in the Carling Cup and gained experience with substitute appearances throughout the season. His first League goal came in injury time against Scunthorpe when he controlled

Brian Murphy's long kick on the edge of the box, held off two defenders with his strength on the ball and calmly fired past the 'keeper. Easter proved to be a significant time for him as he signed his first professional contract with the club and scored at Derby which prompted Ipswich legend Ray Crawford to say that he would be happy for Connor to break his Ipswich scoring record. He scored again at Newcastle in a game that proved he was perfectly capable of playing up front on his own.

Ipswich T (From trainee on 11/5/2010) FL 9+19/4 FLC 1+1/2 FAC 0+1

WIDDOWSON Joseph (Joe)
Born: Forest Gate, 29 March 1989
Height: 6'0" **Weight:** 12.0
Signed on a three-year contract by Grimsby following on a loan spell in the previous season, Joe was to be a first team regular apart from a winter absence with an ankle injury. This neat and tidy left-back showed his attacking qualities during a relegation battle, his contribution to Town's only 'double' of the term at Hereford (1-0) in April earning a place in the League Two 'Team of the Week' on the FL website.

West Ham U (From trainee on 6/7/2007)
Rotherham U (Loaned on 12/2/2008) FL 3
Grimsby T (Free on 2/1/2009) FL 55+3/1 FLC 1 FAC 1 Others 1

WIGGINS Rhoys Barrie
Born: Uxbridge, 4 November 1987
Height: 5'8" **Weight:** 11.5
International Honours: W: U21-9; Yth
A talented Welsh under-21 international left-back who moved to Norwich from Crystal Palace in the summer, his senior opportunities were limited by the consistency of Adam Drury and he spent the last three months of the season on loan at Bournemouth. Having previously been at the club on loan in 2008-09, Rhoys was ever-present in his time at Dean Court and further enhanced his popularity with the Cherries' faithful. Brave and quick in the tackle he has a cultured left foot that enables him to distribute the ball accurately over long and short distances.

Crystal Palace (From trainee on 28/7/2006) FL 1
Bournemouth (Loaned on 15/1/2009) FL 12+1
Norwich C (Signed on 24/7/2009) FAC 0+1 Others 2
Bournemouth (Loaned on 29/1/2010) FL 19

WILBRAHAM Aaron Thomas
Born: Knutsford, 21 October 1979
Height: 6'3" **Weight:** 12.4
Club Honours: AMC '08; Div 2 '08
Aaron finished his fourth season with MK Dons with another double figure League scoring tally, being a pivotal figure throughout in manager Paul Ince's attacking game plan. Leading the line with good physical presence, he linked up well with his attacking partners and was always looking to play in colleagues. Captaining the team on a few occasions brought out the best in him, scoring the club's 'Goal of the Season' in one of those games at Charlton, and though occasionally dividing opinion with Dons' supporters, his all-round willingness to contribute to the team makes him one of the major players.

Stockport Co (From trainee on 29/8/1997) FL 118+54/35 FLC 5+2/1 FAC 3+1 Others 2
Hull C (£100,000 on 9/7/2004) FL 10+9/2 FAC 1
Oldham Ath (Loaned on 29/10/2004) FL 4/2 Others 1
MK Dons (Free on 8/7/2005) FL 135+31/47 FLC 5+1/2 FAC 5+3 Others 10+2/5
Bradford C (Loaned on 3/3/2006) FL 5/1

WILDIG Aaron Keith
Born: Hereford, 15 April 1992
Height: 5'9" **Weight:** 11.2
International Honours: W: Yth
A central midfield player who came through Cardiff's trainee ranks, Hereford-born teenager Aaron made his mark in the first team when injuries gave him chances. A neat and tidy player, whose movement and distribution are good, Aaron is highly rated by manager Dave Jones. His senior contract runs until the summer of 2012.

Cardiff C (From trainee on 15/4/2009) FL 4+7/1 FLC 0+3 FAC 3

WILKINSON Andrew (Andy) Gordon
Born: Stone, 6 August 1984
Height: 5'11" **Weight:** 11.0
If you are looking for an all-action hero who is willing to run through a brick wall for the team, then look no further than Andy. The local lad is a firm favourite with the Stoke fans because of his wholehearted approach and the way he does not shy away from putting his head where others may fear to dip in a toe. The full-back is totally committed and often has supporters out of their seats when he goes on one of his surges forward. That first goal in a Stoke shirt cannot be too far away.

He is not always a regular first choice for a manager who likes big players across the back but Andy bides his time when he is not in the side and always delivers a storming performance when he does get back into the team. It is no surprise that the papers have linked him with moves to other Premier League clubs.

Stoke C (From trainee on 8/7/2002) P/FL 64+20 FLC 5+1 FAC 3+2 Others 0+1
Partick Thistle (Loaned on 13/7/2004) SL 9+3/1 SLC 2 Others 1+2
Shrewsbury T (Loaned on 8/3/2005) FL 9
Blackpool (Loaned on 23/11/2006) FL 5+2

WILLIAMS Andrew (Andy)
Born: Hereford, 14 August 1986
Height: 5'11" **Weight:** 11.2
Andy started the season on the transfer list and looked to be on his way out of Bristol Rovers. However, his attitude and performances convinced manager Paul Trollope that he should be given a further opportunity. He scored a superb stoppage-time winner at Southampton, picking up the ball on the edge of the Saints' penalty area and curling in a superb left-foot shot over the 'keeper. He considered the goal as his best career strike and that lifted his confidence. He was always a threat with his pace down the right or when he linked up as a partner with striker Jo Osei-Kuffour.

Hereford U (From Pershore College on 14/3/2006) FL 30+11/8 FLC 1+1 FAC 2+2 Others 0+1/1
Bristol Rov (Signed on 19/7/2007) FL 37+51/8 FLC 1+3/1 FAC 8+1/1 Others 1
Hereford U (Loaned on 1/9/2008) FL 19+7/2 FAC 2 Others 0+1

WILLIAMS Ashley Errol
Born: Wolverhampton, 23 March 1984
Height: 6'0" **Weight:** 11.2
International Honours: W: 20
Swansea City's Ashley was voted 'Welsh Footballer of the Year' and 'Club Player of the Year' for 2009, captaining Wales in the international friendly against Scotland at Cardiff's new stadium in November. He continued to be a regular inclusion in John Toshack's Welsh side, as an extremely reliable, pacy centre-back, who was always a threat at set pieces. In April he was voted by his fellow professionals into the PFA 'Championship Team of the Season'.

Stockport Co (Free from Hednesford T on 31/12/2003) FL 159+3/3 FLC 5 FAC 6/1 Others 3
Swansea C (£350,000 on 27/3/2008) FL 94+1/7 FLC 1 FAC 4

West Ham U (£250,000 on 9/12/2004) PIFL 7+3/1 FLC 1
Ipswich T (£300,000 on 9/11/2005) FL 47+7/3 FAC 4+1
Bristol C (£300,000 on 19/7/2008) FL 26+23/3 FLC 2+1 FAC 0+2/1
Yeovil T (Loaned on 11/3/2010) FL 7+1/5

WILLIAMS Luke Anthony
Born: Middlesbrough, 11 June 1993
Height: 6'1" **Weight:** 11.5
International Honours: E: Yth. RoI: Yth
Luke became the youngest Middlesbrough player for over a century when he made his debut as a substitute in a 2-1 defeat at Barnsley in December. Aged 16 years and 200 days, he was Boro's second youngest player after Thomas Murray who was 38 days younger in 1905. Luke started the season as a Republic of Ireland youth international, but switched to his home country when picked for the England under-17 squad. A knee injury kept him out for two months later in the season but he recovered enough to start for the first time in the penultimate match, at home to Coventry. He also started at Leicester and his strong, direct running down the right wing brought admiring comments from his manager and pundits alike. He is a great prospect.
Middlesbrough (Trainee) FL 2+2 FAC 0+1

WILLIAMS Marcus Vincent
Born: Doncaster, 8 April 1986
Height: 5'8" **Weight:** 10.9
Club Honours: Div 1 '07
Scunthorpe's first choice left-back Marcus had a good season back in the Championship. He started 37 of the club's 46 League games and always won his place straight back after missing out through injury. Confident on the ball, he is a very energetic player who loves to get forward and linked up well with Martyn Woolford down the left. His form during the second half of the season was particularly impressive, but he missed four of the closing five games because of a niggling injury. Marcus signed a three-year contract with Reading in May.
Scunthorpe U (From trainee on 3/8/2005) FL 152+14 FLC 10 FAC 10+2 Others 7+1

WILLIAMS Marvin Travis
Born: Sydenham, 12 August 1987
Height: 5'11" **Weight:** 11.6
Club Honours: Div 2 '09
The fast and tricky outside-right was selected as a substitute for Brentford's first six fixtures but came on only once, against Bristol City in the Carling Cup,

Ashley Williams

WILLIAMS Benjamin (Ben) Philip
Born: Manchester, 27 August 1982
Height: 6'0" **Weight:** 13.4
International Honours: E: Sch
Goalkeeper Ben enjoyed an outstanding debut season at Colchester. Playing every League game, Ben consistently pulled off a string of breathtaking saves throughout the campaign and was deservedly named 'Player of the Season'. He hardly made a mistake all season and could not really be blamed when his side conceded 12 goals in two games in January. Ben kept 17 clean sheets in all competitions.
Manchester U (From juniors on 3/7/2001)
Chesterfield (Loaned on 30/12/2002) FL 14
Crewe Alex (Free on 19/3/2004) FL 134+1 FLC 7 FAC 2 Others 4
Carlisle U (Free on 6/8/2008) FL 31 FLC 2 FAC 2 Others 1
Colchester U (Signed on 10/7/2009) FL 46 FAC 3

WILLIAMS Gavin John
Born: Pontypridd, 20 June 1980
Height: 5'10" **Weight:** 11.5
Club Honours: FC '03; Div 2 '05
International Honours: W: 2
The skilful midfielder was frustrated due to being on the Bristol City substitutes' bench for much of the season, only making four starts. No doubt he felt a measure of relief in mid-March when he returned on loan to Yeovil, the club he left for West Ham in 2004. Despite playing only seven times in his brief time at Huish Park, the Welsh wizard reminded everyone there of what they had missed since he left the club. With five goals and five assists making it a memorable return to Somerset for one of the best midfielders ever to play for Yeovil, he showed the form that won him the move to the Championship in the first place and was a wonderful addition to the team just at the right time.
Yeovil T (£20,000 from Hereford U on 16/5/2002) FL 54+1/11 FLC 1+1 FAC 5/3 Others 2/1

before joining Torquay on a free transfer. Unfortunately, his opportunities were limited at Plainmoor and he was unable to secure a longer deal.
Millwall (From trainee on 11/1/2006) FL 27+24/7 FAC 3/1 Others 1
Torquay U (Loaned on 6/3/2007) FL 2/1
Yeovil T (Signed on 9/8/2007) FL 8+15 FLC 1
Brentford (Signed on 7/7/2008) FL 21+13 FLC 1+1 FAC 1/1 Others 1/1
Torquay U (Free on 1/9/2009) FL 1+3

WILLIAMS Rhys
Born: Perth, Australia, 7 July 1988
Height: 6'1" **Weight:** 11.3
International Honours: W: U21-10. Australia: 3
Rhys enjoyed a great season, which culminated in his being voted the Middlesbrough official supporters' club 'Young Player of the Year'. Along the way, he earned his first three full caps for Australia, although the last was blighted when he received a red card after 18 minutes. Usually a centre-half, he was surprisingly used by then Boro boss Gareth Southgate in central midfield in pre-season. After scoring four goals in five games, he started against Sheffield United in that position and played the majority of the season there, as a ball-winning midfielder who protects the back four. Rhys still managed to score twice, netting against Coventry and Scunthorpe. He suffered towards the end of the season with a pelvic injury and once Boro had failed to make the play-offs, manager Gordon Strachan rested him. Rhys signed a new contract in February which will take him to 2013.
Middlesbrough (From trainee on 5/4/2007) P/FL 31+1/2 FLC 1+1 FAC 1
Burnley (Loaned on 31/1/2009) FL 17

WILLIAMS Robert (Robbie)
Ian
Born: Pontefract, 2 October 1984
Height: 5'10" **Weight:** 11.13
The left-back started in Huddersfield's opening day draw at Southend but gave away a penalty and looked out of sorts. Normally efficient and committed, Robbie delivers some useful crosses and, after a spell on the substitutes' bench, returned to the side with some quality displays. His work rate was solid and he was named League One 'Player of the Month' in November. His three goals came from two successful free kicks and a rare right-foot volley to round off a sweet team move. Was out of contract at the end of June.
Barnsley (From trainee on 2/7/2004) FL 44+22/4 FLC 5/1 FAC 3+1 Others 1+2

Blackpool (Loaned on 21/3/2007) FL 9/4 Others 3/1
Huddersfield T (Signed on 24/8/2007) FL 68+9/4 FLC 2/1 FAC 6/2 Others 2+2

WILLIAMS Samuel (Sam)
Born: Solihull, 9 June 1987
Height: 5'11" **Weight:** 10.8
The 22-year-old striker joined Yeovil last summer and ended 2008-09 on a low note with a serious knee injury that kept him out for several weeks. He scored four goals this season but created many others for colleagues with his unselfish hold-up play and often came off battered and bruised for the cause. Another player who doubled his career games total this season, the tall forward will be looking to hit the ground running when the new campaign comes around.
Aston Villa (From trainee on 10/6/2005)
Wrexham (Loaned on 20/1/2006) FL 14+1/2
Brighton & Hove A (Loaned on 29/9/2006) FL 3/1 Others 1
Colchester U (Loaned on 3/11/2008) FL 1 FAC 1 Others 1/1
Walsall (Loaned on 31/1/2009) FL 0+5/1
Brentford (Loaned on 9/3/2009) FL 5+6/2
Yeovil T (Free on 21/7/2009) FL 28+6/4 FLC 1 FAC 1 Others 1

WILLIAMS Stephen (Steve)
Born: Preston, 24 April 1987
Height: 6'4" **Weight:** 13.5
Steve gladly downed his scissors and put a career as a barber on hold after signing for Bradford. The centre-half kept his hand in by cutting the hair of several Valley Parade team-mates but it was his performances on the field that really got him noticed. A quick and agile defender, Steve uses the ball intelligently as well as possessing an aerial threat at set pieces. He looks to have a good future in the game if he continues to progress.
Bradford C (Free from Bamber Bridge, ex Charnock Richard, Chorley, Bamber Bridge, Hyde U, Fleetwood T, on 17/7/2009) FL 36+3/4 FLC 1 FAC 1 Others 2

WILLIAMS Thomas (Tom)
Andrew
Born: Carshalton, 8 July 1980
Height: 6'0" **Weight:** 11.8
International Honours: Cyprus: 1
A full-back who likes to play a bit and loves getting to the by-line to send in telling crosses, a loss of form and an injury saw him lose his starting place in Peterborough in October. Loaned out to

Queens Park Rangers for the third time in his career, he only enjoyed five appearances before returning to London Road, but, remarkably, his short stay saw him play under three different managers in Jim Magilton, Steve Gallen and Paul Hart. Although Tom got back into the United team at Xmas he followed Darren Ferguson to Preston on loan in February as cover for Callum Davidson at left-back and fitted in well. Injured for three weeks, he returned for the run-in and generally impressed with his willingness to support the attack and deliver telling crosses into the box as an addition to his defensive efforts. Was out of contract in the summer.
West Ham U (£60,000 from Walton & Hersham on 3/4/2000)
Peterborough U (Free on 22/3/2001) FL 32+4/2 FLC 1+1 FAC 4+1 Others 1
Birmingham C (£1,000,000 on 12/3/2002) FL 4
Queens Park Rgrs (Loaned on 8/8/2002) FL 22+4/1 FLC 1 FAC 2 Others 2+2
Queens Park Rgrs (Loaned on 4/8/2003) FL 4+1
Peterborough U (Free on 1/2/2004) FL 20+1/1 FAC 1
Barnsley (Free on 4/6/2004) FL 38+1 FLC 2 FAC 1 Others 1
Gillingham (Free on 1/9/2005) FL 13 FLC 1+1 FAC 1 Others 2
Swansea C (£50,000 on 1/1/2006) FL 30+16 FLC 0+1 FAC 2 Others 0+3
Wycombe W (Free on 7/8/2007) FL 6+4 FLC 1 FAC 1 Others 1
Peterborough U (Free on 1/1/2008) FL 39+8 FLC 3/1 FAC 4 Others 1
Queens Park Rgrs (Loaned on 9/11/2009) FL 5
Preston NE (Loaned on 15/2/2010) FL 8+2

WILLIAMSON Lee Trevor
Born: Derby, 7 June 1982
Height: 5'10" **Weight:** 10.4
Lee joined Sheffield United in the summer but a back problem sidelined him until October and, having missed most of the pre-season training, he took time to get fully involved. Playing either in central midfield or on the right he worked hard and looked good going forward. He contributed three goals, one gaining a draw in the Sheffield derby. After that game his back problem re-emerged and required further surgery.
Mansfield T (From trainee on 3/7/2000) FL 114+30/3 FLC 3+3 FAC 8+1 Others 7
Northampton T (Signed on 9/9/2004) FL 31+6 FLC 1 FAC 2/1 Others 3/1
Rotherham U (Signed on 28/7/2005) FL 54+2/9 FLC 3/1 FAC 1+1 Others 1

Watford *(Signed on 5/1/2007) P/FL*
57+14/4 FLC 3/1 FAC 2 Others 2
Preston NE *(Loaned on 26/3/2009) FL*
5/1
Sheffield U *(£500,000 on 18/6/2009)*
FL 14+6/3 FAC 2+1/1

Mike Williamson

WILLIAMSON Michael (Mike) James
Born: Stoke-on-Trent, 8 November 1983
Height: 6'4" **Weight:** 13.3
Club Honours: Ch '10
Mike made an excellent start to the season, turning in two 'Man of the Match' performances in Watford's first six matches and scoring twice. However, once he became aware of transfer interest from Portsmouth, he made it clear that he wanted to go and duly left for Fratton Park at the end of August for a sizeable fee. Unable to get a game at Pompey, Mike was signed by Newcastle initially on an emergency loan deal so that he could make his debut the following day against Crystal Palace. Having delivered a 'Man of the Match' performance on his debut, he then signed a three-and-a-half-year contract and became a regular at the heart of the defence until a broken hand suffered when exercising at home sidelined him for three weeks in March. Tall and assured, but unruffled on the ball, he formed a solid partnership with Fabricio Coloccini to ensure that the run-in to the Championship title stayed on the rails. His performances offered promise that at last Newcastle may have found the commanding centre-back they have been seeking for so long.
Torquay U *(Trainee) FL 3 Others 1*
Southampton *(£100,000 on 21/11/2001)*
Torquay U *(Loaned on 15/9/2003) FL*

9+2 Others 1
Wycombe W *(Free on 20/7/2004) FL*
132+11/11 FLC 9/1 FAC 5 Others 8+1
Watford *(£150,000 on 27/1/2009) FL*
21/2 FLC 2/1
Portsmouth *(Signed on 1/9/2009)*
Newcastle U *(Signed on 27/1/2010) FL 16*

WILSHERE Jack Andrew
Born: Stevenage, 1 January 1992
Height: 5'7" **Weight:** 10.3
International Honours: E: U21-5; Yth
Having starred for Arsenal in the pre-season Emirates Cup tournament, with the club retaining high hopes that he will blossom into a great player he went on loan to Bolton in January in order to obtain regular first team football. In his new surroundings Jack was a huge success, proving to be Bolton's most impressive and consistent player during that period. He was excellent in the 2-0 defeat at Manchester City in February and retained his place in the team for much of the remainder of the season, scoring his only goal for the club with an excellent finish in the 2-1 victory at West Ham and showing some solid tackling ability in that game too. Jack really does appear to have the world at his feet - even at such a young age he plays with confidence, industry and tenacity. He has exceptional close ball control and his vision when picking out pinpoint passes is particularly impressive. Owen Coyle was hopeful of retaining Jack's services but with current form it cannot be long before the youngster breaks into the Arsenal first team and perhaps the England team too.
Arsenal *(From trainee on 2/7/2009) PL*
0+2 FLC 5/1 FAC 1+2 Others 1+4
Bolton W *(Loaned on 29/1/2010) PL*
13+1/1

WILSON Brian Jason
Born: Manchester, 9 May 1983
Height: 5'10" **Weight:** 11.0
Having played in four of the first eight matches of the season after deciding to accept the club's offer of a new contract, the Bristol City wing-back suffered a broken shin just a couple of minutes into a 7-0 reserve game win at Bournemouth in October and was out of action until the end of the campaign. Also unlucky with injuries during the previous campaign, at his best Brian is a skilful, pacy player who can perform well on either flank. Was out of contract in the summer.
Stoke C *(From trainee on 5/7/2001) FL*
1+5 FLC 0+1 Others 1
Cheltenham T *(Loaned on 12/12/2003)*
FL 7 FAC 1
Cheltenham T *(Signed on 25/3/2004)*

FL 105+13/15 FLC 5/1 FAC 9/1 Others
10+1/2
Bristol C *(£100,000 on 12/11/2007) FL*
53+7/1 FLC 2+2/1 FAC 1

WILSON Callum Eddie Graham
Born: Coventry, 27 February 1992
Height: 5'11" **Weight:** 10.5
A home-grown young Coventry striker who along with many of his age group, was given a debut against Hartlepool in the Carling Cup in August. While 14 minutes of football as a substitute was insufficient to judge him, his contract was extended for another year and he may have more chances to shine. In March, he became the first Coventry player to win the 'Apprentice of the Year' award.
Coventry C *(Trainee) FLC 0+1*

WILSON James Steven
Born: Chepstow, 26 February 1989
Height: 6'2" **Weight:** 12.13
Club Honours: Div 2 '09
International Honours: W: U21-3; Yth
The cultured defender joined Brentford for a second loan spell in August, but with the Bees now playing in League One James found this spell tougher than in League Two the previous year. He played at both centre-back and right-back before losing his place and returning to Bristol City.
Bristol C *(From trainee on 22/4/2006)*
FL 0+2
Brentford *(Loaned on 7/8/2008) FL 14*
FLC 1 Others 1
Brentford *(Loaned on 20/8/2009) FL 13*
FAC 1

WILSON Kelvin James
Born: Nottingham, 3 September 1985
Height: 6'2" **Weight:** 12.3
After missing the start of the season with an ankle injury, Kelvin returned to the Nottingham Forest side against Plymouth in September and soon re-established himself, forming a good central defensive partnership with Wes Morgan and missing only one further League game. He was made captain against Scunthorpe on the last day of the season.
Notts Co *(From trainee on 20/7/2004)*
FL 71+7/3 FLC 2+1/1 FAC 5 Others 2
Preston NE *(Signed on 10/3/2006) FL*
16+11/1 FLC 1 FAC 2/1
Nottingham F *(£300,000 on 20/7/2007) FL 110+3 FLC 3 FAC 5+1*
Others 2

WILSON Kyle Philip
Born: Bebington, 14 November 1985
Height: 5'10" **Weight:** 13.1
Kyle moved to Macclesfield last summer from Unibond Premier League side FC

United of Manchester where he was top scorer the previous season. He made his League debut in the home match against Notts County as a 79th-minute substitute. He was on again as substitute in the following match, after which a series of niggling injuries kept him out for six weeks. He went on loan to his former club FC United in January, returning to Town in March following the death of manager Keith Alexander. Was out of contract at the end of the season.

Crewe Alex *(From trainee on 17/7/2003. Freed during 2006 close season)*
Macclesfield T *(Free from FC United of Manchester, ex Altrincham - loan, Barrow, Droylsden, Fleetwood T, on 3/7/2009) FL 0+4*

WILSON Laurence (Laurie) Thomas
Born: Huyton, 10 October 1986
Height: 5'10" **Weight:** 11.0
International Honours: E: Yth
The exciting young left-back signed in the summer from relegated Chester and was an instant hit at Morecambe. A good solid defender, he also gained a reputation for his attacking runs down the left and scored one of the best goals of the season in a 5-0 victory over Bournemouth, one of his three League goals. Laurie was nominated for the 'Player of the Year' awards and was a firm fans' favourite but the only downside was his ten yellow cards.
Everton *(From trainee on 12/11/2004)*
Mansfield T *(Loaned on 10/2/2006) FL 14+1/1*

Chester C *(Free on 1/8/2006) FL 108+7/4 FLC 3 FAC 6+1/2 Others 5/2*
Morecambe *(Free on 14/7/2009) FL 41/3 FLC 1 FAC 2 Others 3*

WILSON Marc David
Born: Belfast, 17 August 1987
Height: 6'2" **Weight:** 12.7
International Honours: RoI: U21-1; Yth; NI: Yth
Marc established himself as an integral part of Portsmouth's side. Drafted in at centre-half, the tall Irishman put in steady and assured performances throughout the season. Strong and good in the air, Marc also possesses cultured ball skills. Innately two-footed, Marc's distribution and passing is second to none. As a result, he was pushed forward into his preferred position in central midfield as the season developed and he excelled there. Energetic and classy, Marc earned his first international call to the Republic of Ireland squad and played a vital role in Pompey's FA Cup run that took them all the way to the final. With all the indications being that Portsmouth will have to sell their assets after a disastrous season, Marc is likely to be in demand.
Portsmouth *(From trainee on 7/7/2005) PL 30+1 FLC 1+2 FAC 8 Others 1*
Yeovil T *(Loaned on 10/3/2006) FL 1+1*
Bournemouth *(Loaned on 5/1/2007) FL 19/3*
Bournemouth *(Loaned on 21/9/2007) FL 7 Others 1*
Luton T *(Loaned on 16/11/2007) FL 4*

WILSON Mark Antony
Born: Scunthorpe, 9 February 1979
Height: 5'11" **Weight:** 13.0
Club Honours: AMC '07
International Honours: E: U21-2; Yth; Sch
Mark had his best season in midfield for Doncaster. After starting 2009-10 on the bench, he cemented his place in the midfield with some fine displays. A cultured footballer, he goes about his job in a workmanlike but unspectacular fashion.
Manchester U *(From trainee on 16/2/1996) PL 1+2 FLC 2 Others 3+2*
Wrexham *(Loaned on 23/2/1998) FL 12+1/4*
Middlesbrough *(£1,500,000 on 9/8/2001) PL 6+10 FLC 5/2 FAC 2+1 (Freed during 2005 close season)*
Stoke C *(Loaned on 14/3/2003) FL 4*
Swansea C *(Loaned on 12/9/2003) FL 12/2 Others 1*
Sheffield Wed *(Loaned on 22/1/2004) FL 3*
Doncaster Rov *(Loaned on 2/9/2004) FL 1+2 Others 1*

Marc Wilson

Livingston (Loaned on 24/1/2005) SL 4+1 SC 1
Doncaster Rov (Free from Dallas Burn, USA, via trial at Bradford C, on 15/11/2006) FL 84+26/3 FLC 3+1 FAC 3+1 Others 3+3
Tranmere Rov (Loaned on 20/11/2008) FL 4+1

WINDASS Dean
Born: Hull, 1 April 1969
Height: 5'10" **Weight:** 12.6
Veteran striker Dean came to Darlington as assistant manager to Colin Todd in the summer and after initially saying he had hung up his boots, started the opening game at Aldershot. His vast experience and guile were evident in his passing ability and reading of the game. Alas, after just three starts and four substitute appearances he left the club after Colin Todd resigned in September and reappeared as a television pundit for both BBC and Sky later in the season.
Hull C (Free from North Ferriby U on 24/10/1991) FL 173+3/57 FLC 11/4 FAC 6 Others 12/3
Aberdeen (£700,000 on 1/12/1995) SL 60+13/21 SLC 5+2/6 SC 7/3 Others 6/1
Oxford U (£475,000 on 6/8/1998) FL 33/15 FLC 2 FAC 3/3
Bradford C (£950,000 + on 5/3/1999) P/FL 64+10/16 FLC 6/2 FAC 2 Others 6/3
Middlesbrough (£600,000 + on 15/3/2001) PL 16+21/3 FLC 2 FAC 4+3
Sheffield Wed (Loaned on 6/12/2001) FL 2
Sheffield U (Loaned on 11/11/2002) FL 4/3
Sheffield U (Signed on 16/1/2003) FL 16/3 Others 2
Bradford C (Free on 14/7/2003) FL 138+4/60 FLC 5/4 FAC 7/2 Others 1
Hull C (£150,000 on 18/1/2007) P/FL 45+15/20 FLC 1+1/1 FAC 0+1/2 Others 3/2
Oldham Ath (Loaned on 9/1/2009) FL 9+2/1
Darlington (Free on 2/7/2009) FL 3+3 FLC 0+1

WINFIELD David (Dave)
Thomas
Born: Aldershot, 24 March 1988
Height: 6'3" **Weight:** 13.7
Club Honours: FC '08
Dave is a towering centre-half who came up through Aldershot's youth ranks, developing from a fringe player into an established defender as the season went on and coping well with big physical forwards. He scored against Cheltenham and Bury before his season went slightly sour in late October with a red card for violent conduct at Shrewsbury. Made his 100th

appearance for the Shots, as a substitute against Bournemouth, before missing six games with a hamstring injury. However, he was back in time for the disappointing play-off defeat by Rotherham.
Aldershot T (From juniors on 15/7/2005) FL 28+7/2 Others 1+1

WINNARD Dean
Born: Wigan, 20 August 1989
Height: 5'9" **Weight:** 10.3
The young defender signed for Accrington in the summer following his release from Blackburn, where he had captained the reserve side. A committed professional with a fantastic attitude, Dean played at left-back in almost every game during the season, but is versatile enough to play in the centre of the defence or further forward in a wide position if needed. Good on the ball, Dean is always looking for attacking options.
Blackburn Rov (From trainee on 13/3/2007)
Accrington Stanley (Free on 4/8/2009) FL 44 FLC 2 FAC 5 Others 3/1

WISEMAN Scott Nigel
Kenneth
Born: Hull, 9 October 1985
Height: 6'0" **Weight:** 11.6
International Honours: E: Yth
Re-signed in the summer after initially being released by Rochdale for cost-

cutting reasons, Scott was injured after only one game of the season. However, when he was restored to the side Dale won the next four games. Scott became the regular first choice at right-back for the remainder of the promotion campaign, though he did miss some games through further injuries. Happy to join the attack on overlapping runs, he scored his first Dale goal in the home victory over Macclesfield.
Hull C (From trainee on 8/4/2004) FL 10+6 FLC 1 FAC 0+1 Others 0+1
Boston U (Loaned on 18/2/2005) FL 1+1
Rotherham U (Loaned on 4/8/2006) FL 9+9/1 FLC 1+1 Others 1
Darlington (Free on 8/3/2007) FL 12+5 FAC 1 Others 2
Rochdale (Free on 4/8/2008) FL 63+5/1 FAC 2 Others 1+2

WOOD Bradley Alan
Born: Leicester, 2 September 1991
Height: 5'9" **Weight:** 11.0
This young defender was to provide one of the high points of Grimsby's season. An excellent debut at home to Darlington in September brought selection for the League Two 'Team of the Week' on the FL website, Bradley notably winning most headers and tackles from right-back. Also seen as an emergency left-back and central defender, the teenager was awarded a four-year contract just before manager

Scott Wiseman

Mike Newell's exit. Although Bradley was overlooked after Christmas, he ended the term by hitting the only goal to defeat Shrewsbury in the Midlands Floodlit Youth Cup final.
Grimsby T *(From trainee on 19/10/2009) FL 7+1 FAC 1 Others 1+1*

WOOD Christopher (Chris) Grant

Born: Auckland, New Zealand, 7 December 1991
Height: 6'3" **Weight:** 12.12
International Honours: New Zealand: 9; Yth
Coming on as a second-half substitute in the 3-1 home League win over Doncaster, 17-year-old striker Chris scored West Bromwich's third goal with a truly stunning right-foot shot five minutes from time, becoming the 13th Albion player to find the net during the early stages of the season. His other goal clinched a 2-0 fourth round FA Cup win at Huddersfield. Unfortunately, with so many strikers at the club the Kiwi's first team chances were restricted to just six starts, although he was used effectively as a substitute no less than 17 times by manager Roberto di Matteo. Chris – Albion's 'Young Player of the Year' – was named in New Zealand's squad for the 2010 World Cup finals in South Africa.
West Bromwich A *(From trainee on 27/5/2009) P/FL 6+14/1 FLC 0+3 FAC 0+2/1*

WOOD Richard Mark

Born: Ossett, 5 July 1985
Height: 6'3" **Weight:** 11.11
Richard's Sheffield Wednesday career came to an end in October with a temporary loan move to Coventry, which was made permanent in January. He had been unsettled for a time, due in part to losing the Owls' captaincy to new signing Darren Purse. Chris Coleman had pursued the pacy and dependable centre-back for over a year and finally got his man despite intense competition from Ipswich. With Ben Turner injured, Richard went straight into the team and his impact was immediate as he helped shore up a dodgy defence as well as giving a new option from attacking corners. In his second game, he scored a late headed equaliser at Queens Park Rangers and two further goals followed. Strong in the air and in the tackle, the former Owl gave an authority that the defence had lacked since Scott Dann's departure. Following James McPake's return from injury around Christmas, Coleman paired Richard with the combative defender and after an initial

hiccup at Ipswich the two were outstanding at the heart of the defence. Their performances were a major factor in Coventry's rise up the table, with the two complementing each other well.
Sheffield Wed *(From trainee on 7/4/2003) FL 162+9/7 FLC 6+1/1 FAC 3+2 Others 5+1*
Coventry C *(Loaned on 18/11/2009) FL 22+2/3 FAC 2*

WOOD Samuel (Sam) James

Born: Bexley, 9 August 1986
Height: 6'0" **Weight:** 11.4
Club Honours: Div 2 '09
After his hugely successful first season at Brentford, when he was voted 'Player of the Year', Sam signed a new improved contract in the summer. In a season at a higher level, he struggled at times but, through determination and hard work, ultimately had another good campaign. Sam was the only Brentford player selected in either the starting line-up or on the bench for every one of the Bees' first team games. Appearing at left-back and left of midfield as well as on the right, he could always be relied upon.
Brentford *(Free from Bromley, ex Cray Wanderers, on 16/6/2008) FL 74+9/3 FLC 1 FAC 4+1 Others 0+2*

WOODARDS Daniel (Danny) Mark

Born: Forest Gate, 7 October 1983
Height: 5'11" **Weight:** 11.1
Danny's first season with MK Dons was in-and-out due mainly to a series of niggling injuries he suffered. When available for selection he was generally the first choice right-back, where he showed good positional awareness and tackling ability. When switched to a central defensive slot, his pace and aerial ability also came to the fore. Less happy when getting further forward down the flank, he will be hoping for a more sustained first team run under the club's new manager.
Chelsea *(From trainee on 11/7/2003. Freed during 2005 close season)*
Crewe Alex *(£30,000 + from Exeter C on 31/1/2007) FL 80+4 FLC 4 FAC 2+1 Others 3*
MK Dons *(Free on 2/7/2009) FL 23+6 FLC 1 FAC 2 Others 4*

WOODGATE Jonathan Simon

Born: Middlesbrough, 22 January 1980
Height: 6'2" **Weight:** 13.0
Club Honours: FAYC '97; FLC '08
International Honours: E: 8; U21-1; Yth
The England international defender had avoided injury for most of his Tottenham career until this season,

when he managed only three starts in October and November. These were against Stoke, when he was replaced after 14 minutes, and then in home wins against Sunderland and Wigan. Jonathan is a cultured central defender, but his season was in turmoil due to a persistent and mysterious groin injury for which he has sought assistance from as far afield as Australia. Jonathan captained the side in the historic 9-1 win over Wigan, which was his last game of 2009-10.
Leeds U *(From trainee on 13/5/1997) PL 100+4/4 FLC 7 FAC 11 Others 20*
Newcastle U *(£9,000,000 on 31/1/2003) PL 28 FAC 2 Others 7 (£13,400,000 to Real Madrid, Spain on 20/10/2005)*
Middlesbrough *(£7,000,000 from Real Madrid, Spain on 31/8/2006) PL 46 FAC 6*
Tottenham H *(£8,000,000 on 29/1/2008) PL 49/2 FLC 5/1 FAC 1 Others 9*

WOODMAN Craig Alan

Born: Tiverton, 22 December 1982
Height: 5'9" **Weight:** 9.11
Once again Craig made most appearances for Wycombe, missing only two League games in the left-back spot he has made his own. He is above all a solid and safe defender, also liking to push up to deliver into the box and normally takes the dead-ball kicks. He scored his customary single goal, shooting from the edge of the box into the top corner at Gillingham. He was voted 'Players' Player of the Season' for the second consecutive year. Was given the captain's armband when Michael Duberry departed, only to lose it later to Adam Hinshelwood.
Bristol C *(From trainee on 17/2/2000) FL 71+19/1 FLC 3 FAC 4+2 Others 13*
Mansfield T *(Loaned on 25/9/2004) FL 8/1 Others 1*
Torquay U *(Loaned on 6/12/2004) FL 20+2/1*
Torquay U *(Loaned on 3/11/2005) FL 2 FAC 2*
Wycombe W *(Free on 1/8/2007) 117+2/2 FLC 3 FAC 4 Others 5*

WOODS Martin Paul

Born: Airdrie, 1 January 1986
Height: 5'11" **Weight:** 11.11
International Honours: S: U21-2; Yth
Martin took over as captain and playmaker of the Doncaster midfield when Brian Stock was sidelined through injury. He had a good season until he was struck down by a tear to a groin muscle in January that ended his involvement
Leeds U *(From trainee on 3/1/2003) FL 0+1*

Hartlepool U *(Loaned on 10/9/2004)*
FL 3+3 FLC 1 Others 1
Sunderland *(Free on 7/7/2005)* PL 1+6
FLC 1
Rotherham U *(Free on 4/8/2006)* FL
31+5/4 FLC 2 Others 1
Doncaster Rov *(Free on 28/7/2007)* FL
64+16/6 FLC 4+1/1 FAC 6 Others 2+1/2
Yeovil T *(Loaned on 15/2/2008)* FL 3

WOOLFORD Martyn Paul

Born: Castleford, 13 October 1985
Height: 6'0" **Weight:** 11.9
International Honours: E: SP-2
Left-winger Martyn's second season as a
professional saw him continue to
progress with his tricky wing play, pace
and directness causing problems for a
number of Championship defences. He
appeared in 40 of Scunthorpe's 46
League games although 11 were as a
substitute, often due to the team
changing formation. Continued to show
his eye for the big occasion with all his
five goals being vital – the late winner in
the home opener against Derby, a 94th-
minute equaliser against Leicester, the
winner in the relegation six-pointer
against Plymouth and, famously, both
goals as Scunthorpe beat champions
Newcastle 2-1 in October.
Scunthorpe U *(Signed from York C, ex
Glasshoughton Welfare, Frickley Ath,
on 14/8/2008)* FL 61+18/9 FLC 3+1 FAC
5 Others 9+1/3

WORDSWORTH Anthony
Daniel

Born: Camden, 3 January 1989
Height: 6'1" **Weight:** 12.0
Versatile midfield player Anthony
enjoyed a superb season and was
deservedly named 'Young Player of the
Season'. Played mainly on the left of
midfield, the technically gifted Anthony
confirmed himself as one of the
brightest prospects in the division. He
scored 11 goals, including three in two
games against Essex rivals Southend
and a brace in the 3-0 home win over
Swindon. His goals were largely made
up of curling free kicks and long-range
strikes. Anthony possesses a deadly
corner and is also an aerial threat in
open play. A self-titled central
midfielder, he was tried as a supporting
striker in the last two games.
Colchester U *(From trainee on
4/7/2007)* FL 46+28/14 FLC 2+1 FAC
2+1 Others 3+1

WORLEY Harry

Born: Warrington, 25 November 1988
Height: 6'4" **Weight:** 13.3
Club Honours: AMC '09
Unable to hold down a regular place at
Leicester, the centre-back joined Crewe

on loan in mid-August and made his
debut in the 4-0 win at Grimsby the
same month. He remained at Crewe for
the whole season and did sterling work
in a defensive role. He scored just one
goal in the season.
Chelsea *(From trainee, having been
signed from Stockport Co juniors for
£150,000, on 5/12/2005)*
Doncaster Rov *(Loaned on 6/3/2007)*
FL 10
Carlisle U *(Loaned on 31/8/2007)* FL 1
Leicester C *(Free on 6/3/2008)* FL 1+1
Luton T *(Loaned on 19/9/2008)* FL 6+2
Others 1+1
Crewe Alex *(Loaned on 14/8/2009)* FL
21+2/1 Others 1

WORRALL David Richard

Born: Manchester, 12 June 1990
Height: 6'0" **Weight:** 11.3
The 19-year-old attacking Bury
midfielder, able to play both on the
wing and in the centre, was voted the
'Youth Player of the Season' at the
club's annual awards. David scored five
great goals in the campaign, four of
which were nominated for the 'Goal of
the Season'. Full of pace and flair and
excellent at creating scoring
opportunities, David is seen as one of
the most promising prospects for the
forthcoming season.
Bury *(Trainee)* FL 0+1
West Bromwich A *(From trainee on
8/8/2007)* FLC 0+1
Accrington Stanley *(Loaned on
22/8/2008)* FL 1+3 Others 1
Shrewsbury T *(Loaned on 25/2/2009)*
FL 7+2 Others 1+2
Bury *(Free on 6/8/2009)* FL 34+6/4
Others 2/1

WORTHINGTON Jonathan
(Jon) Alan Spencer

Born: Dewsbury, 16 April 1983
Height: 5'9" **Weight:** 11.0
The midfield hard man joined Oldham
from Huddersfield in the summer and
never shirked a tackle. Jon came a
cropper when landing awkwardly in the
game against Swindon and the injury
forced him to miss two-thirds of the
campaign. When fully fit, he is a
handful in midfield with his crunching
tackles and crafty passing. He will hope
for better times in the season ahead.
Huddersfield T *(From trainee on
10/9/2001)* FL 184+29/12 FLC 7/1 FAC 7
Others 9+1/1
Yeovil T *(Loaned on 30/1/2009)* FL 9
Oldham Ath *(Free on 2/7/2009)* FL
11+5 FLC 1

WOTTON Paul Anthony

Born: Plymouth, 17 August 1977
Height: 5'11" **Weight:** 12.0

Club Honours: Div 3 '02; Div 2 '04;
AMC '10
Although a back-up player rather than a
regular first choice these days, Paul
had a busy and successful season, playing
an essential role in Southampton's
billionaire- assisted revival. Never one to
elaborate, never mind over-elaborate,
Paul keeps it simple and mostly faultless.
To such an extent it is not always clear if
he has been selected on his own merit or
is deputizing for someone; an instance
being his sterling central-midfield
performance alongside Dean Hammond
in the Johnstone's Paint Trophy final at
Wembley.
Plymouth Arg *(From trainee on
10/7/1995)* FL 359+35/54 FLC 10+1/2
FAC 23/5 Others 9+1/2
Southampton *(Free on 10/7/2008)* FL
30+25 FLC 5 FAC 2+1 Others 3+2

WRIGHT Andrew David

Born: Liverpool, 15 January 1985
Height: 6'1" **Weight:** 13.7
Andrew's season was off to a
disappointing start when a broken
metatarsal in the first home game
sidelined him for six weeks. The
Scunthorpe utility man started only two
more games before Christmas, when a
festive return against West Bromwich
ended in a red card. An ankle injury in
training in January added further
disruption and it was not until March
that he enjoyed a decent run in the
team. Comfortable on the ball, he was
used primarily as a right-back but also
filled in at left-back and in the midfield
holding role as required. He signed a
two-year contract extension during a
season that also featured a spectacular
own goal in the home defeat by
Blackpool in April.
Scunthorpe U *(Free from University of
West Virginia, USA, ex trainee at
Liverpool, on 14/1/2008)* FL 30+19 FLC
1+1 FAC 1 Others 3+1

WRIGHT Benjamin (Ben)

Born: Munster, Germany, 1 July 1980
Height: 6'3" **Weight:** 14.0
Ben moved from Lincoln to Macclesfield
last summer and appeared in almost
every match, although about a third of
his appearances were from the bench.
As a target man, he has the ability to
hold the ball especially when acting as
the sole striker. After a frustrating time,
he eventually scored in his 20th League
appearance in the home win against
Hereford. A second goal followed at the
end of December, but he then had to
wait until the middle of March when he
hit a purple patch, scoring four goals in
six matches. A groin strain kept Ben out
of contention for the final matches and

he was released in the summer.
Bristol C (£30,000 + from Kettering T on 10/3/1999) FL 0+2 (Freed on 18/12/2000)
Lincoln C (Free from IK Start, Norway, ex Viking Stavanger, Moss FK - loan, on 1/8/2007) FL 41+26/17 FLC 2/1 FAC 3+1 Others 0+2
Macclesfield T (Free on 6/7/2009) FL 25+14/6 FLC 1 FAC 1

WRIGHT Benjamin (Ben)

Born: Basingstoke, 20 August 1988
Height: 6'2" **Weight:** 13.3
The young Peterborough front man was given limited chances to show what he could do in 2009-10 and was loaned out to non-League Luton, Grimsby and Barnet. Having spent a month at Luton, Ben was initially signed by Grimsby on a two-month loan deal at the end of November, his move to Blundell Park being described as a 'friendship agreement' following Ryan Bennett's transfer to Peterborough. The big striker impressed on his full debut at Macclesfield, but as more experienced players returned from injury his time was ended early. His next stop was at Barnet in March and the day after his arrival he made his debut as a substitute in the home defeat to Accrington. However, injury curtailed Ben's stay at the club, making two more appearances from the bench before returning to the Posh in early April and appearing in three of the last four matches.
Peterborough U (£50,000 from Hampton & Richmond Borough, ex Basingstoke T, on 29/1/2009) FL 0+5 FLC 0+1
Grimsby T (Loaned on 26/11/2009) FL 1+1
Barnet (Loaned on 11/3/2010) FL 0+3

WRIGHT David

Born: Warrington, 1 May 1980
Height: 5'11" **Weight:** 10.8
International Honours: E: Yth
Liam Rosenior's form at right-back meant that David was again required to switch to the left to stay in the Ipswich team, but he is equally at home on either flank, breaking up attacks and bursting forward, although when on the left he tends to cut in so that he can cross with his right foot. He scored the goal that gave the club their first win of the season when he was on hand to head Rosenior's cross high into the net. He faced competition from Jaime Peters and, latterly, Shane O'Connor for the left-back berth and did not make as many appearances as in previous seasons. David has played his last game for Ipswich because he has not been offered a new contract.

Crewe Alex (From trainee on 18/6/1997) FL 206+5/3 FLC 10+1 FAC 12 Others 3+1
Wigan Ath (£500,000 on 28/6/2004) P/FL 26+19 FLC 3 FAC 1
Norwich C (Loaned on 17/11/2005) FL 5
Ipswich T (Signed on 12/1/2007) FL 117+3/5 FLC 3 FAC 5

WRIGHT Jake Maxwell

Born: Keighley, 11 March 1986
Height: 5'11" **Weight:** 10.7
Signed from Crawley Town primarily as cover for the injured Jimmy McNulty, Jake had little opportunity to establish himself at Brighton as he was also sidelined by a couple of injuries. Struggling at times at left-back, he played only once in his preferred role of centre-back, giving a good account of himself at Leyton Orient in the Johnstone's Paint Trophy. With eight Albion appearances to his name, Jake was allowed to join Oxford United in the New Year, on loan until the end of the season, and played his part in their successful campaign to regain League status via the play-offs.
Bradford C (From trainee on 4/7/2005) FL 0+1 (Freed during 2006 close season)
Brighton & Hove A (Signed from Crawley T, ex Halifax T, on 31/7/2009) FL 4+2 FLC 1 Others 1

WRIGHT Joshua (Josh) William

Born: Bethnal Green, 6 November 1989
Height: 5'9" **Weight:** 11.10
International Honours: E: Yth
Central midfielder Josh stepped up to Championship level after being released by League One Charlton and looked a fantastic acquisition on a free transfer. Had to wait until September to make the starting line-up but did not look back in the following four months, sitting deep in midfield and keeping possession with some excellent, accurate passing. By mid-January he was arguably the club's player of the season and was attracting interest from bigger clubs until he was struck down by a virus and never regained his early form. A toe injury at Newcastle in March also hindered his progress but he will be expecting to figure again regularly in 2010-11.
Charlton Ath (From trainee on 4/7/2007) FL 2 FAC 1
Barnet (Loaned on 31/8/2007) FL 31+1/1 FAC 3
Brentford (Loaned on 19/9/2008) FL 5 Others 1
Gillingham (Loaned on 24/3/2009) FL 5 Others 3
Scunthorpe U (Free on 6/7/2009) FL 24+11 FLC 3+1 FAC 1+1

WRIGHT Mark Anthony

Born: Wolverhampton, 24 February 1982
Height: 5'11" **Weight:** 11.4
Club Honours: Div 2 '07, '08; AMC '08
A lanky winger with a reputation for scoring goals, Mark joined Brighton from MK Dons in the summer and started well, showing glimpses of his best form. However, finding it hard to settle in Sussex he was allowed to move to Bristol Rovers after just three weeks of the campaign. He had been a long-time target for Rovers, primarily due to his ability to play wide on the right or left of midfield and it was hoped he would be a valuable asset. Unfortunately, Mark failed to make much impression and was regularly substituted before failing to appear from the bench in the final months of the season.
Walsall (From trainee on 26/1/2001) FL 94+30/9 FLC 3+2 FAC 6 Others 6
MK Dons (Free on 19/7/2007) FL 58+8/18 FLC 2+1 FAC 2 Others 6+1/2
Brighton & Hove A (Free on 2/7/2009) FL 2+2 FLC 0+1
Bristol Rov (Signed on 1/9/2009) FL 19+5 FAC 1

WRIGHT Richard Ian

Born: Ipswich, 5 November 1977
Height: 6'2" **Weight:** 13.0
Club Honours: FAC '02; PL '02
International Honours: E: 2; U21-15; Yth; Sch
Richard started the season as Ipswich's number-one goalkeeper but uncharacteristic mistakes forced the manager to bring in Asmir Begovic from Portsmouth to steady the defence. Begovic's recall by Pompey meant that Richard was back in the side for the visit to Cardiff but he twisted his knee after 25 minutes and was replaced by Arran Lee-Barrett. The injury sidelined him for four months and although he did make it back to the substitutes' bench in April, Brian Murphy had established himself as the top 'keeper. It looks as if Richard has played his last game in Town colours as his contract will not be renewed.
Ipswich T (From trainee on 2/1/1995) P/FL 240 FLC 27 FAC 13 Others 11
Arsenal (£6,000,000 on 13/7/2001) PL 12 FLC 1 FAC 5 Others 4
Everton (£3,500,000 + on 26/7/2002) PL 58+2 FLC 7 FAC 4
West Ham U (Free on 6/7/2007) FLC 3
Southampton (Loaned on 20/3/2008) FL 7
Ipswich T (Signed on 22/7/2008) FL 58 FLC 3 FAC 2

WRIGHT Stephen John

Born: Liverpool, 8 February 1980
Height: 6'2" **Weight:** 12.0
Club Honours: UEFAC '01; Ch '05
International Honours: E: U21-6; Yth

The experienced full-back who has had more than his share of injuries over the years kept largely injury-free with Coventry. In the first quarter of the season he played a number of games in central defence owing to injuries and always competed well physically. He did, however, look more comfortable at right-back, where he played for the rest of the season. His worst moment came at Queens Park Rangers where, for the second season running, he was shown a red card for a second yellow, costing him a two-match ban. A captain who leads by example, Stephen's contract expired in the summer.

Liverpool (From trainee on 13/10/1997) PL 10+4 FLC 1+1 FAC 2 Others 2+1/1
Crewe Alex (Loaned on 6/8/1999) FL 17+6 FLC 1
Sunderland (£3,000,000 on 15/8/2002) P/FL 88+4/2 FLC 1+2 FAC 10
Stoke C (Loaned on 7/8/2007) FL 14+2 FLC 1
Coventry C (Free on 8/8/2008) FL 55 FLC 2 FAC 5

WRIGHT Thomas (Tommy) Andrew

Born: Kirby Muxloe, 28 September 1984
Height: 6'0" **Weight:** 11.12
International Honours: E: Yth

Signed by Grimsby from Aberdeen in the January transfer window to aid their relegation fight, Tommy's lack of match fitness and a later ankle injury meant he was unable to provide the goals that the Mariners desperately needed. The forward though was always a presence in attack, finally ending his drought with a run and shot in April against Chesterfield.

Leicester C (From trainee on 10/6/2003) P/FL 3+18/2 FLC 1 FAC 0+2
Brentford (Loaned on 12/9/2003) FL 18+7/3
Blackpool (Loaned on 31/8/2005) FL 10+3/6 Others 2
Barnsley (£50,000 on 1/1/2006) FL 11+23/2 FLC 2 FAC 1+1 Others 0+3
Walsall (Loaned on 23/11/2006) FL 5+1/2
Darlington (Signed on 16/1/2007) FL 46+7/17 FLC 1/1 FAC 2/1 Others 2
Aberdeen (£100,000 on 8/8/2008) SL 4+14/1 SLC 0+1 SC 2+1/1
Grimsby T (Signed on 28/1/2010) FL 13+1/1

WRIGHT-PHILLIPS Bradley Edward

Born: Lewisham, 12 March 1985
Height: 5'8" **Weight:** 11.0
International Honours: E: Yth

Following Southampton's relegation to League One, Bradley was released from his contract and in July signed a two-year deal with Plymouth. After recovering from a pre-season knee injury, he made his debut in September against Watford. Unfortunately the knee injury recurred and he was sidelined for another long spell. Bradley made his long awaited return for Argyle in the FA Cup against Newcastle in January and his first start against Coventry in March. His first goal for the Pilgrims came against Bristol City in March and he scored another three, including an injury-time header to beat Doncaster in April. A natural finisher he will be looking forward to an injury-free season.

Manchester C (From trainee on 2/7/2002) PL 1+31/2 FLC 0+2 FAC 2+4
Southampton (£1,000,000 on 20/7/2006) FL 58+53/22 FLC 5/3 FAC 3+2
Plymouth Arg (Free on 15/7/2009) FL 12+3/4 FAC 0+1

WRIGHT-PHILLIPS Shaun Cameron

Born: Greenwich, 25 October 1981
Height: 5'6" **Weight:** 10.1
Club Honours: Div 1 '02; PL '06; CS '05; FLC '07; FAC '07
International Honours: E: 31; U21-6

It was a tale of two halves for the mercurial Manchester City and England right-winger. The first half of the season under manager Mark Hughes was excellent, virtually ever-present and scoring five goals, mostly his trademark cross-shot from the right side of the penalty box. However, he suffered an ankle injury in the home match against Sunderland – which proved to be Hughes' last in charge – and when fit again he started only seven games under new manager Roberto Mancini, in five of which he was withdrawn, while coming off the bench in 11 games. His indifferent form in the second half of the season cast doubts on his England future but Fabio Capello retained his faith in Shaun and took him to the World Cup finals. Earlier, he enjoyed an excellent cameo performance against Egypt when, as a second-half substitute, he scored the second goal and provided the cross for Peter Crouch as England came from behind to win 3-1.

Manchester C (From trainee on 28/10/1998) P/FL 130+23/26 FLC 9+4/3

FAC 8+1/1 Others 4+2/1
Chelsea (£21,000,000 on 19/7/2005) PL 43+39/4 FLC 7+2/1 FAC 11+3/4 Others 4+16/1
Manchester C (£9,000,000 on 29/8/2008) PL 46+11/9 FLC 6/2 FAC 2+1/1 Others 9/3

WROE Nicholas (Nicky)

Born: Sheffield, 28 September 1985
Height: 5'11" **Weight:** 10.7

A skilful midfield playmaker who struggled to find his best form for Torquay early in the season before finally forming an excellent partnership with Lee Mansell whose work rate and tackling complemented Nicky's vision and passing skills. In addition to his creative ability, he likes to have a shot on goal, although nine of his 13 goals in the season were from the penalty spot, including two in an FA Cup hat-trick against Cheltenham. Captained the side in the second half of the season after Chris Hargreaves' departure

Barnsley (From trainee on 6/8/2004) FL 34+15/1 FLC 6 FAC 1+2 Others 1
Bury (Loaned on 9/2/2007) FL 4+1
Hamilton Academical (Free on 2/7/2007) Others 1 (Freed on 29/8/2007)
Torquay U (Free from York C on 2/7/2008) FL 45/9 FLC 1 FAC 2/3 Others 2/1

WYNTER Alex James

Born: Lambeth, 16 September 1993
Height: 6'0" **Weight:** 13.4

A young Crystal Palace Academy central defender who, despite making only a few reserve team appearances, was fast-tracked to the first team last season when he made one appearance in the FA Cup as a substitute at Sheffield Wednesday in January.

Crystal Palace (Associated Schoolboy) FAC 0+1

WYNTER Thomas (Tom) Lenworth

Born: Ashford, Kent, 20 June 1990
Height: 5'7" **Weight:** 11.11

A natural left-footer, Tom is equally comfortable playing at left-back or centre-half and is in his second year as a professional at Gillingham after progressing through the youth team. Although not the tallest of defenders, he is excellent in the air and enjoys the more physical aspect of the game. He was thrust into the side on Boxing Day following Josh Gowling's red card against Brentford and caught the eye with a series of lively, battling displays. Was out of contract at the end of June.

Gillingham (From trainee on 4/8/2008) FL 4+4 FAC 1

XYZ

[XISCO] TEJADA JIMENEZ Francisco
Born: Palma de Mallorca, Spain, 26 June 1986
Height: 6'1" **Weight:** 13.3
International Honours: Spain: U21-11
Newcastle striker Xisco began the season with two early substitute appearances, and then moved to Racing Santander on a season-long loan. His showing in those games was disappointing, perhaps explained by his reported comments that he was more interested in a move away from Newcastle.
Newcastle U (£5,700,000 from Deportivo La Coruna, via UD Vecindario - loan, on 3/9/2008) P/FL 3+4/1 FLC 0+1 FAC 1

YAKUBU Aiyegbeni
Born: Benin City, Nigeria, 22 November 1982
Height: 6'0" **Weight:** 13.1
Club Honours: Div 1 '03
International Honours: Nigeria: 52
Recovery from a serious ruptured Achilles injury dating back to November 2008 meant that Everton's Nigerian international was not at full throttle for most of the season. Aiyegbeni was used mostly as a substitute, but there were

still flashes of the style and natural ability that makes him one of the Premier League's most natural goal-poachers. Understandably the striker saved his best form for the last months of the season, netting some crucial League goals, and producing a match-winning cameo from the bench at Blackburn. A smoothly clinical operator in front of goal, the forward has greater skills outside of the box than he is generally given credit for.
Portsmouth (£1,800,000 from Maccabi Haifa, Israel, ex Julius Berger, Hapoel Kfar Saba - loan, Dynamo Kiev - loan, on 13/1/2003) P/FL 76+5/35 FLC 2+3/4 FAC 6/3
Middlesbrough (£7,500,000 on 13/7/2005) PL 67+6/25 FLC 1+1 FAC 15/8 Others 5+9/2
Everton (£11,250,000 on 30/8/2007) PL 49+19/24 FLC 5+1/4 FAC 0+1 Others 13+5/4

YAKUBU Ismail Salami
Born: Kano, Nigeria, 8 April 1985
Height: 6'1" **Weight:** 12.9
Club Honours: FC '05
International Honours: E: SP-6
Long-serving centre-back Ismail had something of a mixed season at Barnet. He began in terrific form and was recognised for this with the League Two 'Player of the Month' award for August. However, injury brought a premature end to his season. He did not feature for the Bees from late January, suffering

a number of setbacks to his recovery. A popular figure at the club, in the first half of the season he notched four goals from defence. Was out of contract in the summer.
Barnet (From juniors on 30/4/2005) FL 144+2/9 FLC 4 FAC 16/4 Others 6/1

YATES Adam
Born: Stoke-on-Trent, 28 May 1983
Height: 5'10" **Weight:** 10.9
International Honours: E: SP-3
The dependable Port Vale right-back had to wait for his chance, but following the retirement of Sam Stockley proved that he could do the job with equal aplomb. Good in the tackle, he got on with his job with no fuss and became more regular following the switch to 4-4-2, helping Vale to go close to play-offs. He scored once, a strike just before half-time in the FA Cup tie with Stevenage.
Crewe Alex (From trainee on 6/2/2001. Freed during 2004 close season)
Morecambe (Signed from Leek T on 11/8/2006) FL 74+2 FLC 3 FAC 3 Others 7
Port Vale (Free on 2/7/2009) FL 25+7 FLC 1+1 FAC 2/1 Others 1

YEATES Mark Stephen Anthony
Born: Dublin, 11 January 1985
Height: 5'9" **Weight:** 10.7
International Honours: Rol: U21-4; Yth
After an impressive 2008-09 season with Colchester, Mark became

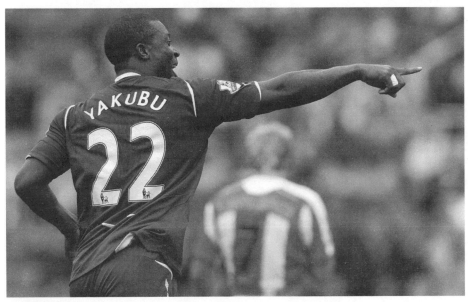

Aiyegbeni Yakubu

Middlesbrough's first signing of the season when joining in July for a sizeable fee. After playing well in pre-season, he started the first game against Sheffield United on the right-hand side of midfield. Even though the team began the season well, Mark found himself struggling for form and soon found himself in and out of the starting line-up. This continued with the change of manager in October, when Gordon Strachan took the helm. In November he was recalled to play against Peterborough and in the next game, at Queens Park Rangers, he had his best game in a Boro shirt as well as scoring the final goals in a thumping 5-1 win. However, he still could not cement his place in the team and in the January transfer window it was announced that Sheffield United had agreed a undisclosed fee for him. Playing wide on the right, but sometimes during play operating on the left, he used his skill and speed to attack the defenders and create chances with his crosses. Ever-present in the squad after his arrival, about half his appearances were from the bench, but he ended his season with a fine display and goal at Ipswich.

Tottenham H *(From trainee on 25/7/2002) PL 1+2 FAC 0+1*
Brighton & Hove A *(Loaned on 14/11/2003) FL 9 Others 1*
Swindon T *(Loaned on 27/8/2004) FL 3+1*
Colchester U *(Loaned on 5/8/2005) FL 42+2/5 FLC 1 FAC 5/1 Others 1+1*
Hull C *(Loaned on 10/8/2006) FL 2+3 FLC 1+1*
Leicester C *(Loaned on 31/1/2007) FL 5+4/1*
Colchester U *(£100,000 on 27/7/2007) FL 71+1/20 FLC 3 FAC 2 Others 1+3/1*
Middlesbrough *(£500,000 on 25/6/2009) FL 11+8/1 FLC 1 FAC 0+1*
Sheffield U *(Signed on 19/1/2010) FL 11+9/2*

YEBDA Hassan
Born: Saint-Maurice, France, 14 May 1984
Height: 6'2" **Weight:** 12.2
International Honours: France: Yth; Algeria: 9
The highly-rated Algerian midfield player joined Portsmouth from Benfica in the summer. He went on to become a regular fixture in the Blues' engine room, showing the energy and skill that led to him becoming one of the most sought after prospects in European football. His headed goal to make it 1-0 at Wolverhampton earned Pompey their first victory of the League campaign and he also scored the winning penalty in a

2-1 success at Burnley. As he returned to Benfica at the conclusion of his loan, the classy and confident Hassan looks sure to have a bright future. He was a member of Algeria's squad in the World Cup finals and they were pitched against England in the group stage in South Africa.
Portsmouth *(Loaned from Benfica, Portugal, ex KV Mechelen, Stade Lavallois - loan, Le Mans, on 1/9/2009) PL 15+3/2 FLC 3 FAC 2*

YOBO Joseph Phillip
Born: Kano, Nigeria, 6 September 1980
Height: 6'2" **Weight:** 11.6
International Honours: Nigeria: 66
It was a frustrating campaign for one of David Moyes' first signings at Everton, with ongoing hamstring problems causing him to miss large parts of the season and also forcing an early return from the African Cup of Nations. The Nigerian international was his usual

steady self in the opening months of the campaign, captaining the side in Phil Neville's absence, until picking up his first injury at the end of November. On his return in the New Year, the good form of Phil Jagielka and Sylvain Distin meant only sporadic appearances from the bench. The speedy centre-half has been a key part of the Moyes revolution at Goodison and is in the midst of a five-year deal.
Everton *(£4,500,000 from Olympique Marseille, France, ex Mechelen, Standard Liege, on 6/8/2002) PL 204+16/8 FLC 12 FAC 6+2 Others 18+1/2*

YOUGA Kelly Alexandre
Born: Bangui, Central African Republic, 22 September 1985
Height: 6'1" **Weight:** 12.0
Able to play in central defence or at full-back, Kelly was the first choice left-back at Charlton, starting every game in

Kelly Youga

all competitions until he injured a knee against Bristol Rovers in late November. It was the second of two consecutive games that Kelly had started at right-back to cover for the injured Frazer Richardson. The injury did not seem serious at the time but it would not clear up and it transpired Kelly had sprained his posterior cruciate ligament and sustained some bone bruising. He was to take no further part in the season.
Charlton Ath *(Free from Lyon, France on 30/6/2005) FL 61+1/1 FLC 2 FAC 4+1 Others 2*
Bristol C *(Loaned on 14/10/2005) FL 4 FAC 1*
Bradford C *(Loaned on 31/1/2007) FL 11*
Scunthorpe U *(Loaned on 11/7/2007) FL 18+1/1 FLC 1*

YOUNG Ashley Simon
Born: Stevenage, 9 July 1985
Height: 5'9" **Weight:** 9.13
International Honours: E: 7; U21-10
Ashley is firmly established as a

favourite of Aston Villa boss Martin O'Neill and is one of the club's biggest assets. He switched from his usual position on the left wing to the right for half of the season, although the manager encourages his wide players to swap flanks during games. Ashley is rated among the Premier League's trickiest wingers with his pace, quick feet and ability to turn markers inside out before delivering dangerous crosses. He is sometimes criticised for crossing from deep rather than getting to the by-line and he is also accused of going to ground too easily under challenges. Although Ashley did not hit the heights of the previous year, his strike rate of nine League and Cup goals and ten Premier League assists proved that he was among Villa's most dangerous attackers. O'Neill regularly purrs with praise for the winger who has to contend with teams double marking him to nullify his threat. Fabio Capello not completely convinced and after giving Ashley a couple of opportunities,

left him out of England's World Cup squad. Ashley has another two years left on his contract but his form has attracted interest from top clubs.
Watford *(From juniors on 12/7/2002) P/FL 73+25/19 FLC 7+1/2 FAC 0+1 Others 3/1*
Aston Villa *(£8,000,000 + on 23/1/2007) PL 121+2/22 FLC 6+1/2 FAC 10/2 Others 10/2*

YOUNG Jamie Iain
Born: Brisbane, Australia, 25 August 1985
Height: 5'11" **Weight:** 12.9
International Honours: E: Yth
Jamie once again dropped to second choice 'keeper at Wycombe, after Scott Shearer returned from injury. His appearances were restricted to two Cup games early on and a humbling 6-0 reverse at Huddersfield in November, when the whole team had an off day. In January he was told his contract would not be renewed and was cancelled by mutual consent. Jamie was a particular favourite of the fans and his departure was greeted with disappointment. A strong, confident Australian-born keeper of Scottish/Sri Lankan descent, he joined Aldershot as a non-contract player in mid-March, making his debut when coming on for Marvin Morgan following Mikhael Jaimez-Ruiz's dismissal in the final minutes of the win at Bury in late March. Although beaten by the resultant penalty kick, the following week he was a starter at Macclesfield and saved a penalty after just two minutes. From thereon, Jamie's presence strengthened the spine of the team as they successfully reached the League Two play-offs. Unfortunately, he sustained a bad knee injury in the first half of the home leg of the semi-final against Rotherham and missed the return leg four days later.
Reading *(From trainee on 20/10/2003) FL 0+1*
Rushden & Diamonds *(Loaned on 21/7/2005) FL 19+1 FLC 1 FAC 3*
Wycombe W *(Free on 3/8/2006) FL 36+3 FLC 5 FAC 2 Others 2*
Aldershot T *(Free on 11/3/2010) FL 8+1 Others 1*

YOUNG Lewis Jack
Born: Stevenage, 27 September 1989
Height: 5'10" **Weight:** 11.0
Lewis began his loan spell at Hereford with a promising display in a win over Bradford, where his pace and ability to cross the ball marked him out as a promising performer. After that, however, the brother of the Aston Villa and England star Ashley Young found the physical nature of League Two less easy to overcome and he returned to

Ashley Young

Watford at the end of his month. Was out of contract in the summer.
Watford *(From trainee on 2/7/2008) FL 0+1 FLC 1+2*
Hereford U *(Loaned on 19/3/2010) FL 5+1*

Luke Young

YOUNG Luke Paul
Born: Harlow, 19 July 1979
Height: 5'11" **Weight:** 12.4
Club Honours: FLC '99
International Honours: E: 7; U21-12; Yth
Having become a Villa Park favourite during his first campaign, Luke then suffered second season syndrome through no fault of his own. A pre-season curtailed by injury hardly helped and then the defender suffered personal tragedy when his half-brother was killed in a holiday accident. Luke's place at right-back was filled by either new signing Habib Beye or, more regularly, converted central defender Carlos Cuellar and he struggled to get back in. He made 14 Premier League starts and four Cup appearances, but was left on the bench for the Carling Cup final and FA Cup semi-final defeats at Wembley. On several occasions he deputized at left-back, as he had done in the previous campaign. Luke also announced his decision to retire from international football last November after England coach Fabio Capello sounded him out about a potential recall for the friendly against Brazil. He was one of a host of fringe players made available for transfer by Aston Villa.
Tottenham H *(From trainee on 3/7/1997) PL 44+14 FLC 1+3 FAC 9+2 Others 2+1*
Charlton Ath *(£3,000,000 + on 27/7/2001) PL 181+6/4 FLC 12 FAC 9*

Middlesbrough *(£2,500,000 on 10/8/2007) PL 35/1 FLC 2 FAC 5*
Aston Villa *(£5,000,000 on 8/8/2008) PL 47+3/1 FLC 1 FAC 5 Others 7*

YUSSUFF Rachid Olatokunbo Oladobe
Born: Poplar, 23 September 1989
Height: 6'1" **Weight:** 10.7
A free transfer summer signing from Charlton, Rachid is a left-footed midfielder who joined Gillingham after impressing on trial in pre-season. He had to wait for his opportunity but looked good in his rare outings with a good range of passing and a decent turn of pace. Was out of contract in the summer.
Charlton Ath *(From trainee on 8/3/2008) FAC 0+1*
Gillingham *(Free on 3/8/2009) FL 2+6 Others 0+1*

ZABALETA Pablo Javier
Born: Buenos Aires, Argentina, 16 January 1985
Height: 5'9" **Weight:** 11.9
International Honours: Argentina: 7; U23-9; Yth
With the influx of so many stellar players at Eastlands in the summer, the Manchester City and Argentine defender was not expected to play a large part. To his credit, due to his versatility coupled with the form of Micah Richards, he was one of City's success stories of the season, playing in 35 games and starting 30 of them. Pablo can play in either full-back positions while favouring the right, in the defensive holding role, or on the right side of midfield. He did not make his first start until October, replacing Richards for eight games, but following the arrival of new manager Robert Mancini he played in every game bar three when he was suspended.
Manchester C *(£6,750,000 from Espanyol, Spain, ex San Lorenzo, on 1/9/2008) PL 49+7/1 FLC 5 FAC 4+1 Others 11*

ZAHA Dazet Wilfried Armel
Born: Ivory Coast, 10 November 1992
Height: 5'11" **Weight:** 10.5
With their first team short on numbers towards the end of last season, Crystal Palace promoted some of their promising youngsters, several of whom had only made a scattering of appearances at reserve level. Striker Wilfried was part of Palace's FA Youth Cup side that reached the quarter-finals the previous season and made his only appearance at home as a substitute against Cardiff. He signed professional terms with Palace in the summer.
Crystal Palace *(Trainee) FL 0+1*

ZAKI Amr Hassan
Born: Mansoura, Egypt, 1 April 1983
Height: 6'1" **Weight:** 11.11
International Honours: Egypt: 57
Having enjoyed a sensational first season in the Premier League, Amr returned to England during the January transfer window at strugglers Hull. As the talented forward was largely lacking match fitness having suffered an injury during the first-half of the season at his parent club Zamalek, he was chiefly used for the bench. The first Egyptian to play for Hull, Amr also became the first Tiger to play in an international match at Wembley since 1977 when he was recalled to the Egypt team for the friendly with England. He followed in the City footsteps of Alan Jarvis (Wales), Terry Neill (Northern Ireland) and Dave Roberts (Wales). Unfortunately, he suffered a knee injury during new manager Iain Dowie's first training session which led to his loan deal being cut short in April.
Wigan Ath *(Loaned from Zamalek, Egypt, ex Al-Mansoura, ENPPI, Lokomotiv Moscow, on 31/7/2008) PL 22+7/10 FLC 2+1/1*
Hull C *(Loaned from Zamalek, Egypt on 18/1/2010) PL 2+4*

ZAKUANI Gabriel (Gabby)
Born: Kinshasa, DR Congo, 31 May 1986
Height: 6'0" **Weight:** 10.10
International Honours: DR Congo: 1
Centre-back Gabby was hit by injuries but, despite an in-out-season with Peterborough, still had time to show what a fine player he is. Good in the air, quick on the ground and strong in the tackle, he is a no-frills defender and if the ball needs putting over the stand that is exactly where it will go.
Leyton Orient *(From trainee on 1/6/2005) FL 84+3/3 FLC 2 FAC 7 Others 2*
Fulham *(£1,000,000 on 12/7/2006) FLC 1 FAC 2*
Stoke C *(Loaned on 30/1/2007) FL 9*
Stoke C *(Loaned on 31/8/2007) FL 11+8 FAC 1*
Peterborough U *(Signed on 13/9/2008) FL 60+1/1 FLC 3 FAC 5*

ZAMORA Robert (Bobby) Lester
Born: Barking, 16 January 1981
Height: 6'0" **Weight:** 11.0
Club Honours: Div 3 '01; Div 2 '02
International Honours: E: U21-6
An outstanding performer for Fulham throughout the whole season, his 18 goals included a number of sensational strikes, not least in the Europa League ties against Shakhtar Donetsk and at Wolfsburg, where his first-minute goal

proved crucial. His best European performance was reserved for the vital group tie in Basel when he netted his only double of the campaign. A target man, he holds the ball well, bringing others into play, and in addition to scoring goals was often instrumental in making them. Unfazed by the number of different forward partners, he linked particularly well with Erik Nevland, Diomansy Kamara and Zoltan Gera. Bobby was deployed on occasions as a lone striker when the team adopted a 4-5-1 formation. During the final month of the season he sustained an Achilles injury and although he battled bravely through key Europa League games, he needed an operation after the end of the season, putting paid to any chance of a widely speculated late inclusion in the England World Cup squad.
Bristol Rov (From trainee on 1/7/1999) FL 0+4 FLC 0+1 FAC 0+1
Brighton & Hove A (Loaned on

11/2/2000) FL 6/6
Brighton & Hove A (£100,000 on 10/8/2000) FL 117+2/70 FLC 4/2 FAC 6/4 Others 1/1
Tottenham H (£1,500,000 on 22/7/2003) PL 6+10 FLC 1/1 FAC 0+1
West Ham U (Signed on 3/2/2004) P/FL 85+45/30 FLC 5/4 FAC 3+6/2 Others 7+1/4
Fulham (Signed on 16/7/2008) PL 59+3/10 FLC 1 FAC 7+2/5 Others 16+1/8

ZAYATTE Kamil
Born: Conakry, Guinea, 7 March 1985
Height: 6'2" **Weight:** 14.2
International Honours: Guinea: 21
Although he prefers playing as a defensive midfield anchor, the Guinea international performed admirably at right-back in Hull's early season Premier League games against Bolton and Wolverhampton. The fearless performer then reverted to his more familiar

Tigers' role of centre-back at Sunderland where he scored for both sides. Although Kamil then enjoyed a two-game stint in his preferred midfield role, for much of the remainder of the campaign he formed a formidable central defensive partnership with Anthony Gardner. Unfortunately, he suffered a season-ending injury in a typically wholehearted challenge with Arsenal's Sol Campbell in what was to become manager Phil Brown's last game in charge.
Hull C (£2,500,000 from Young Boys of Berne, Switzerland, RC Lens, on 1/9/2008) PL 52+3/3 FLC 1 FAC 6/1

ZEBROSKI Christopher (Chris) Matthew
Born: Swindon, 29 October 1986
Height: 6'1" **Weight:** 11.8
The striker had the best possible start to the season, scoring twice in Wycombe's 3-2 defeat at Charlton on the opening day. Both goals were well taken, a looping header into the far corner and a one-on-one with the 'keeper. His all-action, committed style kept him in the team under Peter Taylor, but he fell down the pecking order under new manager Gary Waddock and, after joining Torquay on loan in November, he joined them permanently in January. At Plainmoor he operated extremely effectively as a powerful and pacy central striker before Christmas, hitting four goals in one three game spell. He was subsequently withdrawn into a wide midfield role, sometimes on the left and sometimes on the right, in order to give the team a more solid shape. Although this limited his goalscoring opportunities, he contributed fully to the team with his prodigious work rate enabling him to cover his full back, work the flank, and still carry an attacking threat.
Plymouth Arg (From trainee on 28/7/2006) FL 0+4 FLC 0+1
Millwall (Free on 8/9/2006) FL 10+15/3 FLC 1 FAC 4 Others 1+1
Wycombe W (Free on 10/7/2008) FL 43+5/9 FLC 1+1 FAC 2+2 Others 0+1
Torquay U (Signed on 20/11/2009) FL 30/6

ZENDEN Boudewijn (Bolo)
Born: Maastricht, Holland, 15 August 1976
Height: 5'9" **Weight:** 11.5
Club Honours: FLC '04; ESC '05; CS '06
International Honours: Holland: 54
Signed by Sunderland in mid-season as a free agent, the former Holland international started only one League and one Cup game but was reported to have played sufficient games as a

Bobby Zamora

substitute to trigger a new one-year contract offer dependent upon appearances. Invariably offering quality on the ball, Bolo's class indicated why he had several of Europe's elite clubs on his CV including Marseille, where he had played the previous season with his Sunderland captain Lorik Cana. Scoring his first Sunderland goal back at one of his former clubs, Chelsea, Bolo subsequently rendered a club 'Goal of the Season' competition redundant by sublimely volleying a stunning goal in a victory over Spurs that drew comparisons with his countryman Marco van Basten's iconic effort at Euro '88.
Chelsea *(£7,500,000 from Barcelona, Spain, ex PSV Eindhoven, on 10/8/2001) PL 24+19/4 FLC 2+3 FAC 1+6 Others 3+1*
Middlesbrough *(Signed on 30/8/2003) PL 67/9 FLC 6+1/2 FAC 3+1/1 Others 10/3*
Liverpool *(Free on 4/7/2005) PL 14+9/2 FLC 2 Others 14+8 (Freed during 2007 close season)*
Sunderland *(Free from Olympique Marseille, France on 16/10/2009) PL 1+19/2 FAC 1*

ZHIRKOV Yuri Valentinovich
Born: Tambov, Russia, 20 August 1983
Height: 5'11" **Weight:** 11.11
Club Honours: PL '10; FAC '10
International Honours: Russia: 34
Chelsea's left-sided full-back or winger, Yuri was known as the 'Russian Ronaldinho' having won every domestic honour and being an influential member of Guus Hiddink's national side that did so well at Euro 2008. Yuri's outstanding performances saw him elected into the 'Team of the Tournament'. The first half of Yuri's initial English season was hampered by a persistent knee injury and he only had a run in the side in the wake of Ashley Cole's serious ankle injury at Everton but two matches later he was forced off at Wolves with a nasty calf injury. Earlier in the match he had shown a flash of real quality when, following clever link-up play with Michael Ballack, he dribbled to the by-line to set up a goal for Didier Drogba. Upon his return he formed a devastating left-sided partnership with Florent Malouda. In one memorable match the pair bamboozled the Aston Villa right flank with their interplay and Yuri earned two penalties when surging runs were halted in the box. He dropped down to the bench for the last three matches of the League season when Cole reappeared but the acquisition of two medals in his first English season is particularly satisfying.
Chelsea *(£18,000,000 from CSKA*

Moscow, Russia, ex Spartak Tambov, on 6/7/2009) PL 10+7 FLC 2 FAC 4 Others 3+1

Yuri Zhirkov

ZOLA-MAKONGO Calvin
Born: Kinshasa, DR Congo, 31 December 1984
Height: 6'3" **Weight:** 12.0
Calvin was established as Crewe's main striker in his second season at Gresty Road. He did well after signing from Tranmere but it was not until this season that his scoring potential flourished. A real handful for central defenders, he finished as leading scorer and could well have had more goals but for an injury kept him out of the side for a time.
Newcastle U *(From trainee on 17/1/2002)*
Oldham Ath *(Loaned on 30/8/2003) FL 21+4/5 FAC 1/1 Others 2/1*
Tranmere Rov *(Free on 9/7/2004) FL 55+41/16 FLC 2+2/1 FAC 4+2 Others 1+1/1*
Crewe Alex *(Signed on 1/7/2008) FL 48+13/20 FLC 2/1 FAC 2+3/1 Others 3/1*

ZUBAR Ronald
Born: Les Abymes, Guadeloupe, 20 September 1985
Height: 6'1" **Weight:** 12.8
International Honours: France: U21-15. Guadeloupe: 1
Arriving at Wolverhampton from Marseille, Ronald had some distractions in the early weeks which meant it took longer for him to settle in and his first start did not come until October 17, at Everton. He had four games but in the last of them scored an own goal and also hurt his thigh. However, in January he lined up at right-back against Crystal

Palace, scoring a stunning goal to keep Wolves in the FA Cup. He kept his place from then on with some valiant defending, as well as venturing forward to score with a superb low drive at West Ham. He was still full of running and he set up Wolves' last goal of the season.
Wolverhampton W *(Signed from Olympique Marseille, France, ex SM Caen, on 4/7/2009) PL 23/1 FLC 1 FAC 2/1*

Ronald Zubar

ZUIVERLOON Gianni Michel Eugene
Born: Rotterdam, Holland, 30 December 1986
Height: 5'10" **Weight:** 11.0
International Honours: Holland: U21-17
Gianni missed a handful of games for West Bromwich during the first half of the season due to a niggling hamstring injury and then, late on, lost his place because of some poor performances coupled with further injuries, being replaced by Steven Reid. Earlier, the attacking right wing-back had been in excellent form and netted his first League goal for Albion with a fine individual strike in the 5-0 home win over Watford in October. He later added three more to his tally including a vital equaliser at Cardiff (1-1) before starting to lose his way, admitting: "I suddenly lacked confidence but the manager told me that I need not worry…it happens to us all!"
West Bromwich A *(£3,200,000 from SC Heerenveen, Holland, ex Feyenoord, RKC Waalwijk - loan, on 25/7/2008) P/FL 59+4/4 FLC 2 FAC 3+2/1*

FA Barclays Premiership and Coca-Cola Football League Clubs

Summary of Appearances and Goals for 2009-10

KEY TO TABLES: P/FL = Premier/Football League. FLC = Football League Cup. FAC = FA Cup. Others = Other first team appearances.
Left hand figures in each column list number of full appearances + appearances as substitute. Right hand figures list number of goals scored.

ACCRINGTON STANLEY (Div 2: 15th)

Player	P/FL App	Goals	FLC App	Goals	FAC App	Goals	Others App	Goals
BLACK Adam	0 + 1							
BOUZANIS Dean	12 + 2				3 + 1		1	
DUNBAVIN Ian	27				2		2	
EDWARDS Phil	46	8	2		5		4	1
FLYNN Johnny	6 + 2							
GRANT Robert	41 + 1	14	0 + 2	1	5	2	4	1
JOYCE Luke	36 + 5	1	2		2 + 1		3 + 1	
KEE Billy	15 + 22	9	1 + 1		1 + 2		2	
KEMPSON Darran	40	1	2		5		3	
KING Chris	1		1				1	
KING Gary	3 + 5	1			1		1	1
LEES Tom	39				4		3	
McCARTEN James	1							
McCONVILLE Sean	14 + 14	1	1 + 1		3 + 2		0 + 1	
MARTIN Alan	7		2				1	
MILES John	32 + 4	3	2		4	1	2 + 1	
MULLIN John	1 + 2							
MULLIN Paul	4		1	1				
MURPHY Peter	5 + 5		1		1 + 1		2 + 1	
PROCTER Andy	44	5	2		5		4	
RICHARDSON Leam	2						0 + 1	
RYAN Jimmy	36 + 3	3	2		5	1	3 + 1	
SYMES Michael	39 + 2	13	1	1	5	3	4	2
TURNER Chris	11 + 13	2	0 + 1				1	
WINNARD Dean	44		2		5		3	

ALDERSHOT TOWN (Div 2: 6th)

Player	P/FL App	Goals	FLC App	Goals	FAC App	Goals	Others App	Goals
BLACKBURN Chris	36 + 6		1		2		1	
BOZANIC Olly	19 + 6	2			0 + 2	1		
BROWN Aaron	12	1					2	
CHALMERS Lewis	19 + 4		1		3		1	
CHARLES Anthony	32 + 1	4			3		2	
CONNOLLY Reece	0 + 3						0 + 1	
DONNELLY Scott	42 + 1	13	1		3	1	3	
GERMAN Antonio	2 + 1						1	
GRANT John	5 + 12	3	0 + 1		0 + 2			
HALLS John	10 + 6		1		0 + 2		2	
HARDING Ben	28 + 5	1	1		0 + 2			
HENDERSON Stephen	8							
HERD Ben	33 + 1				3		3	
HINSHELWOOD Adam	13 + 2		1		1		1	
HOPKINSON Bobby	0 + 1						0 + 1	
HOWELL Dean	0 + 3	1						
HUDSON Kirk	24 + 10	4	1		1		1 + 1	1
HYLTON Danny	5 + 16	3	0 + 1		0 + 1		1	
JACKSON Marlon	18 + 4	1			2		2	
JAIMEZ-RUIZ Mikhael	30				3		2 + 1	
MASTERS Clark	0 + 1		1					
MORGAN Dean	8 + 1	4					2	
MORGAN Marvin	36 + 4	15	1	1	3		2	
PARRETT Dean	4							
RIZA Omer	0 + 1							
SANDELL Andy	29	5	1		3		1	
SOARES Louie	28 + 8	7	1		3	1	1	1
SPENCER Damian	3 + 9						0 + 2	
STRAKER Anthony	35 + 2	2			3		3	
WINFIELD Dave	19 + 6	2					1 + 1	
YOUNG Jamie	8 + 1						1	

ARSENAL (PREM: 3rd)

Player	P/FL App	Goals	FLC App	Goals	FAC App	Goals	Others App	Goals
ALMUNIA Manuel	29						7	
ARSHAVIN Andrei	25 + 5	10			0 + 1		7 + 1	2
BARAZITE Nacer	0 + 1							
BARTLEY Kyle					1			
BENDTNER Nicklas	13 + 10	6	1		1		7	5
CAMPBELL Sol	10 + 1				1		2	1
CLICHY Gael	23 + 1						9	
COQUELIN Francis			1 + 1		1			
CRUISE Thomas								
DENILSON	19 + 1	3			1	1	5 + 2	1
DIABY Abou	26 + 3	6			0 + 1		9 + 1	1
DJOUROU Johan	0 + 1							
EASTMOND Craig	2 + 2		2		1			
EBOUE Manu	17 + 8	1	1				6 + 4	2
EDUARDO	13 + 11	2	1		1 + 1	1	2 + 3	2
EMMANUEL-THOMAS Jay					1			
FABIANSKI Lukasz	4		2		2		2	
FABREGAS Cesc	26 + 1	15	1				8	4
GALLAS William	26	3	1				8	1
GIBBS Kieran	3		2				2	
GILBERT Kerrea			2				1	
LANS Henri	0 + 1							
MANNONE Vito	5						3	
MERIDA Fran	0 + 4	1	2		1		1	
NASRI Samir	22 + 4	2	1		0 + 1		6	3
RAMSEY Aaron	7 + 11	3	3		1 + 1	1	1 + 5	
RANDALL Mark			0 + 2					
ROSICKY Tomas	14 + 11	3	1				5 + 2	
SAGNA Bacary	31 + 4				1		7 + 1	
SENDEROS Philippe			2					
SILVESTRE Mikael	9 + 3	1	3		2		2 + 1	
SONG Alexandre	25 + 1	1	1				10	
SUNU Gilles			1				0 + 1	
SZCZESNY Wojciech			1					
TRAORE Armand	9		2		1			
VAN PERSIE Robin	14 + 2	9					4	1
VELA Carlos	1 + 10	1	1 + 1	1	2		2 + 3	
VERMAELEN Thomas	33	7	1				11	1
WALCOTT Theo	12 + 11	3	1				2 + 4	1
WATT Sanchez			1 + 2	1				
WILSHERE Jack	0 + 1		2		1		1 + 2	

ASTON VILLA (PREM: 6th)

Player	P/FL App	Goals	FLC App	Goals	FAC App	Goals	Others App	Goals
AGBONLAHOR Gabriel	35 + 1	13	6	2	2	1	0 + 2	
ALBRIGHTON Marc	0 + 3		0 + 1		1		0 + 1	
BEYE Habib	5 + 1		1		2		2	
CAREW John	22 + 11	10	1 + 2		3 + 2	6	1	1
CLARK Ciaran	1							
COLLINS James	26 + 1	1	5		5		1	
CUELLAR Carlos	36	2	6		4	1	2	
DAVIES Curtis	2	1			0 + 1		2	
DELFOUNESO Nathan	0 + 9	1	0 + 1		2 + 1	2		
DELPH Fabian	4 + 4		1 + 1		4	1	1	
DOWNING Stewart	23 + 2	2	4	1	6			
DUNNE Richard	35	3	5		4			
FRIEDEL Brad	38		1		3			
GARDNER Craig	0 + 1		1				1	
GUZAN Brad			5				2	
HESKEY Emile	16 + 15	3	5	2	3 + 1		2	
LOWRY Shane					0 + 1		0 + 2	
MILNER James	36	7	6		4 + 1		2	1
PETROV Stiliyan	37		6		3	1	1	
REO-COKER Nigel	6 + 4		1		1		1	
SHOREY Nicky	3		1				1	
SIDWELL Steve	12 + 13		0 + 3		1 + 3		1	
WARNOCK Stephen	30		5	1	6			
YOUNG Ashley	37	5	5	2	6	2	2	1
YOUNG Luke	14 + 2		1		3			

BARNET (DIV 2: 21st)

Player	P/FL App	Goals	FLC App	Goals	FAC App	Goals	Others App	Goals
ADOMAH Albert	37 + 8	5	1		1 + 1		1	
BOLASIE Yala	14 + 8	2	1		3		2	
BREEN Gary	25				1			
BUTCHER Calum	3				1			
CHARLES Elliott	0 + 3		0 + 1				0 + 2	
COLE Jake	46		1		3		2	
DEEN Ahmed	12 + 4	1			3		1	
DEVERA Joe	31 + 2		0 + 1				2	
DEVERDICS Nicky	4 + 12	1			1 + 2		1	
FURLONG Paul	31 + 7	5	1		3			
GILLET Kenny	31 + 6		1		3			
HART Danny	0 + 1						0 + 2	
HUGHES Mark	40 + 1	2	1		2		2	
HYDE Jake	17 + 17	6	0 + 1		0 + 2		2	1
HYDE Micah	41	1	1		3	1	1	
JAMES Chris	0 + 2							
JARRETT Albert	33 + 12	2	1		2 + 1		1 + 1	
KAMDJO Clovis	14 + 1				0 + 1		1	
LEACH Daniel	12 + 1		1		1		1	

	P/FL App	Goals	FLC App	Goals	FAC App	Goals	Others App	Goals
LIVERMORE David	11 + 3	1						
LOCKHART-ADAMS Kofi	0 + 1							
LOCKWOOD Matt	19	2						
McALLISTER Craig	4 + 1							
MEDLEY Luke	0 + 1							
O'FLYNN John	31 + 5	12			3	3	2	1
O'NEILL Ryan	11 + 4		1					
SAWYER Lee	4 + 3	1						
SINCLAIR Dean	2 + 1	1			0 + 1			
TABIRI Joe	2 + 3						0 + 1	
UPSON Ed	5 + 4	1						
VILHETE Mauro	1 + 1							
WRIGHT Ben	0 + 3							
YAKUBU Ismail	25	2	1		3	1	2	1

BARNSLEY (CHAMP: 18th)

	P/FL App	Goals	FLC App	Goals	FAC App	Goals	Others App	Goals
ADAM Jamil	0 + 2							
ANDERSON	25 + 6	3	3 + 1	1	1			
BIALKOWSKI Bart	2							
BOGDANOVIC Daniel	20 + 9	11	2 + 1	3	1			
BUTTERFIELD Jacob	10 + 10	1	2 + 2		1			
CAMPBELL-RYCE Jamal	8 + 5		2 + 1		0 + 1			
COLACE Hugo	41	7	3	1	1			
DEVANEY Martin	6 + 5							
DICKINSON Carl	27 + 1	1			1			
DOYLE Nathan	32 + 2							
EL HAIMOUR Mounir	2		1					
FOSTER Steve	42	2	4		1			
GRAY Andy	19 + 11	6			1			
GRAY Julian	1 + 4		2					
HALLFREDSSON Emil	22 + 5	3	2		1			
HAMMILL Adam	31 + 8	4	3		0 + 1			
HASSELL Bobby	22 + 2	1	1		1			
HUME Iain	17 + 18	5	1 + 1					
KOZLUK Rob	12 + 2		4					
MACKEN Jon	27 + 4	4	4	1	0 + 1			
MOORE Darren	33 + 2	1	2					
NOBLE-LAZARUS Reuben	0 + 2							
ODEJAYI Kayode	2 + 3		2					
POTTER Luke	12 + 2		2					
PREECE David	5 + 1		1					
RODRIGUEZ Jay	1 + 5	1	1					
SHOTTON Ryan	30				1			
SODJE Onome	0 + 1							
STEELE Luke	39		3		1			
TAYLOR Alastair	0 + 1							
TEIXEIRA Filipe	14							
THOMPSON O'Neil	1		0 + 1					
TRIPPIER Kieran	1							

BIRMINGHAM CITY (PREM: 9th)

	P/FL App	Goals	FLC App	Goals	FAC App	Goals	Others App	Goals
BENITEZ Christian	21 + 9	3	1		3 + 2	1		
BOWYER Lee	34 + 1	5	1 + 1	1	4 + 1			
CARR Stephen	35		1		4			
CARSLEY Lee	3 + 4		1	1	1			
DANN Scott	30		1		4	1		
ESPINOZA Gio			2					
FAHEY Keith	18 + 16		0 + 1		3 + 2			
FERGUSON Barry	37		1		5	2		
GARDNER Craig	10 + 3	1			0 + 2			
HART Joe	36				5			
JEROME Cameron	32	11			4			
JERVIS Jake					0 + 1			
JOHNSON Damien	0 + 1				1 + 1			
JOHNSON Roger	38				5			
LARSSON Sebastian	26 + 7	4			4			
McFADDEN James	32 + 4	5	0 + 1		4			
McSHEFFREY Gary	1 + 4		2		0 + 2			
MICHEL	3 + 6							
O'CONNOR Garry	5 + 5	1	1 + 1					
O'SHEA Jay	0 + 1		2					
PARNABY Stuart	6 + 2		2		1			
PHILLIPS Kevin	2 + 17	4	1		1 + 3			
PRESTON Dan			0 + 1					
QUEUDRUE Franck	6		1					
RIDGEWELL Liam	30 + 1	3	1		5	1		
SAMMONS Ashley			1					
TAINIO Teemu	5 + 1							
TAYLOR Maik	2		2					
VIGNAL Gregory	6 + 2				1			

BLACKBURN ROVERS (PREM: 10th)

	P/FL App	Goals	FLC App	Goals	FAC App	Goals	Others App	Goals
ANDREWS Keith	22 + 10	1	1 + 2					
BASTURK Yildiray	1							

	P/FL App	Goals	FLC App	Goals	FAC App	Goals	Others App	Goals
BROWN Jason	3 + 1		2		1			
CHIMBONDA Pascal	22 + 2	1	3 + 1		1			
DIOUF El Hadji	24 + 2	3			1			
DI SANTO Franco	15 + 7	1	0 + 1		1			
DUNN David	20 + 3	9	3 + 1	1	1			
EMERTON Brett	17 + 7		5	2				
GALLAGHER Paul	0 + 1							
GIVET Gael	33 + 1	2	3		1			
GRELLA Vince	10 + 5		0 + 2					
HANLEY Grant	1							
HOILETT David	8 + 15		3 + 1	1	1			
JACOBSEN Lars	11 + 2		1 + 1					
JONES Phil	7 + 2		2		1			
KALINIC Nikola	14 + 12	2	6	4	1	1		
KHIZANISHVILI Zurab			1		0 + 1			
LINGANZI Amine	1							
McCARTHY Benni	7 + 7	1	3 + 2	3				
NELSEN Ryan	25 + 3	4	4 + 1					
N'ZONZI Steven	33	2	5					
OLSSON Martin	19 + 2	1	4 + 1	1	1			
PEDERSEN Morten Gamst	27 + 6	3	5	2	0 + 1			
REID Steven	1 + 3		3 + 2	1	1			
RIGTERS Maceo					0 + 1			
ROBERTS Jason	15 + 14	5	1 + 1					
ROBINSON Paul	35		4					
SALGADO Michel	16 + 5		4		1			
SAMBA Chris	30	4	3					
VAN HEERDEN Elrio			0 + 2					
WARNOCK Stephen	1							

BLACKPOOL (CHAMP: 6th)

	P/FL App	Goals	FLC App	Goals	FAC App	Goals	Others App	Goals
ADAM Charlie	41 + 2	16	2		1		3	2
ALMOND Louis	0 + 1							
BANGURA Al	2 + 7		2					
BANNAN Barry	8 + 12	1					0 + 2	
BOUAZZA Hameur	11 + 8	1	0 + 1				0 + 3	
BURGESS Ben	20 + 15	6	2	2			0 + 3	
BUTLER Andy	4 + 3							
CAMPBELL DJ	14 + 1	8					3	3
CLARKE Billy	9 + 9	1	3		1			
COID Danny	1							
COLEMAN Seamus	9		1				3	
CRAINEY Stephen	41		1		1		3	
DE MONTAGNAC Ishmel	1 + 7		1 + 1		0 + 1			
DOBBIE Stephen	6 + 10	4	1				0 + 3	1
EARDLEY Neal	22 + 2		1 + 1		1			
EASTHAM Ashley	0 + 1		1					
EDWARDS Rob	19 + 2		3		0 + 1		0 + 1	
EMMANUEL-THOMAS Jay	6 + 5	1	1					
EUELL Jason	23 + 10	4	0 + 1		1			
EVATT Ian	35 + 1	4	1		1		3	
GILKS Matty	26		3				3	
HUDSON Mark			1					
HUSBAND Stephen	1 + 2							
JOHN-BAPTISTE Alex	42		3		1		3	
MARTIN Joe	4 + 2		2		0 + 1			
NARDIELLO Danny	1 + 4		1	1				
NOWLAND Adam			1	1				
ORMEROD Brett	27 + 9	11	2		1	1	3	3
RACHUBKA Paul	20		1					
SEIP Marcel	7	2						
SOUTHERN Keith	43 + 2	2	0 + 1		1		3	1
TAYLOR-FLETCHER Gary	26 + 6	6	1 + 1	1	1		3	1
VAUGHAN David	37 + 4	1	1	1	1		3	

BOLTON WANDERERS (PREM: 14th)

	P/FL App	Goals	FLC App	Goals	FAC App	Goals	Others App	Goals
AL-HABSI Ali			1		1			
BASHAM Chris	2 + 6		0 + 1		0 + 1			
CAHILL Gary	29	5	3	1	2	1		
COHEN Tamir	26 + 1	3	0 + 1		2 + 2			
DAVIES Kevin	37	7	2	1	3	1		
DAVIES Mark	5 + 12		2	1	0 + 2	1		
DAVIS Sean	3		1					
ELMANDER Johan	15 + 10	3	1 + 2	1	1 + 3	1		
GARDNER Ricardo	11 + 10	1	2		3			
HOLDEN Stuart	1 + 1				3			
JAASKELAINEN Jussi	38		2		3			
KLASNIC Ivan	12 + 15	8	2		3			
KNIGHT Zat	35		1	3	3			
LEE Chung-Yong	27 + 7	4	0 + 2		3 + 1	1		
McCANN Gavin	5 + 6		1 + 1					
MUAMBA Fabrice	35 + 1	1	3		4			
O'BRIEN Andy	6				2 + 1			
RICKETTS Sam	25 + 2		3		3			

	P/FL App	Goals	FLC App	Goals	FAC App	Goals	Others App	Goals
RIGA	0 + 1				0 + 2			
ROBINSON Paul	24 + 1		2					
SAMUEL JLloyd	12 + 1		3		2			
STEINSSON Gretar	25 + 2		1		3	1		
TAYLOR Matt	29 + 8	8	3		3			
WARD Danny	0 + 2							
WEISS Vladimir	3 + 10							
WILSHERE Jack	13 + 1	1						
BOURNEMOUTH (DIV 2: 2nd)								
BARTLEY Marvin	24 + 10		0 + 1		1 + 1		2	
BRAD Lee	43 + 1	1	1		2		2	
CONNELL Alan	19 + 19	5			2	2	2	1
COOPER Shaun	6							
CUMMINGS Warren	27 + 7		1		2		2	
EDGAR Anthony	2 + 1						1	
FEENEY Liam	44	5	1		2		1	
FLETCHER Steve	31 + 14	4	0 + 1		0 + 2			
GARRY Ryan	33 + 1	1	1		2		2	
GOULDING Jeff	3 + 14	1	1					
GUYETT Scott	6 + 3						1	
HOLLANDS Danny	37 + 2	6			1 + 1		1	1
IGOE Sammy	15 + 6	2	1		2	1	1	
INGS Danny							0 + 1	
JALAL Shwan	44		1		1		1	
McQUOID Josh	9 + 20	1	0 + 1		0 + 2		1	
MOLESLEY Mark	10	1	1				0 + 1	
PARTINGTON Joe	4 + 7							
PEARCE Jason	39	1	1		2			
PITMAN Brett	46	26	1		2	1	1	1
ROBINSON Anton	43 + 1	4	1		2		2	
STECH Marek	1							
STOCKLEY Jayden	0 + 2						0 + 1	
THOMAS Dan	1 + 1				1		1	
TINDALL Jason							1 + 1	
WEBB George	0 + 1						0 + 2	
WIGGINS Rhoys	19							
BRADFORD CITY (DIV 2: 14th)								
BATESON Jon	14 + 7		1		1		3 + 1	
BOLDER Adam	14	1						
BOULDING Michael	9 + 12	3	0 + 1		0 + 1	1	2	
BOULDING Rory	0 + 2							
BRANDON Chris	14 + 6	2					2 + 2	1
BULLOCK Lee	41		1		1		2	
CLARKE Matthew	20 + 1	1	1				3	
COLBECK Joe	3 + 2		1					
DALEY Omar	6 + 8	1					0 + 1	
DEAN Luke	0 + 1							
EASTWOOD Simon	22		1		1		4	
EVANS Gareth	38 + 5	11	1		1		2	
FLYNN Mike	41 + 1	6	1		1		4	2
GLENNON Matty	17							
GRANT Gavin	7 + 4							
HANSON James	33 + 1	12	1		1		2 + 1	1
HARRISON Ryan	0 + 1							
HORNE Louis	0 + 1							
KENDALL Ryan	2 + 4	2						
McCAMMON Mark	2 + 2							
McLAUGHLIN Jon	7							
NEILSON Scott	18 + 5	1	1		1		4	1
O'BRIEN Jamie	15 + 8	2	0 + 1		1		2 + 1	
O'BRIEN Luke	39 + 4	1	1		1		4	
O'LEARY Stephen	4 + 3							
OLIVER Luke	7	2						
OSBORNE Leon	5 + 7				0 + 1		1 + 1	
RAMSDEN Simon	30 + 1	1	1				3	
REHMAN Zesh	36 + 2	2	1		1		2	
SHARRY Luke	0 + 1						1 + 1	
THORNE Peter	4 + 3						1 + 1	
THRELFALL Robbie	17	2						
WHALEY Simon	5 + 1	1					1	
WILLIAMS Steve	36 + 3	4	1		1		2	
BRENTFORD (DIV 1: 9th)								
AINSWORTH Lionel	1 + 8							
AKINDE John	2							
BALKESTEIN Pim	14	1						
BEAN Marcus	25 + 6				4		1	
BENNETT Alan	11 + 2		1		3			
BLAKE Ryan	0 + 1							
BOSTOCK John	9	2			1			
BULL Nikki	5 + 1	1						

	P/FL App	Goals	FLC App	Goals	FAC App	Goals	Others App	Goals
CORT Carl	16 + 12	6			1 + 1	1		
DIAGOURAGA Toumani	20							
DICKSON Ryan	26 + 1	2	1		4			
FOSTER Danny	32 + 4		1		4		1	
GRABBAN Lewis	7	2						
HUNT David	18 + 6	3	1		0 + 4		1	
KABBA Steve	3 + 7		1				1	
LEGGE Leon	28 + 1	2			3	1	1	
MacDONALD Charlie	39 + 1	15			3	2		
MOORE Simon	0 + 1							
MURPHY Rhys	1 + 4				0 + 1			
O'CONNOR Kevin	43	4	1		4	1	1	
OSBORNE Karleigh	13 + 6		0 + 1		1		1	
PHILLIPS Mark	19 + 3		1					
PRICE Lewis	13				4		1	
SAUNDERS Sam	15 + 11	1	1		1 + 1		1	
SMITH Tommy	8							
STREVENS Ben	20 + 5	6			3 + 1	1		
SZCZESNY Wojciech	28							
TAYLOR Cleveland	8 + 4	1			1 + 1		1	
WESTON Myles	32 + 8	8	1		3	2	1	
WILLIAMS Marvin			0 + 1					
WILSON James	13				1			
WOOD Sam	37 + 6	2	1		3		0 + 1	
BRIGHTON & HOVE ALBION (DIV 1: 13th)								
ARISMENDI Diego	3 + 3							
BARNES Ashley	4 + 4	4						
BENNETT Elliott	43	7			4	2		
BREZOVAN Peter	20							
CALDERON Inigo	19	1			1			
CAROLE Seb	7 + 2				0 + 1			
CASKEY Jake	0 + 1							
COX Dean	9 + 12		1		3 + 1		1	
CROFTS Andrew	44	5	1		5	2		
DAVIES Arron	7						1	
DAVIES Craig	0 + 5				1 + 1			
DICKER Gary	33 + 9	2			4 + 1			
DICKINSON Liam	17 + 10	4	1		3 + 1	2		
DUNK Lewis	1							
EL-ABD Adam	33 + 2	1	0 + 1		3			
ELPHICK Tommy	43 + 1	3	1		4	1	1	
FORSTER Nicky	23 + 4	13	1		4 + 1	3		
HART Gary	1 + 16				0 + 1		1	
HAWKINS Colin	0 + 1							
HENDRIE Lee	6 + 2							
HOLROYD Chris	5 + 8							
HOYTE Gavin	16 + 2				3			
KUIPERS Michel	20		1		3			
LIVERMORE David							0 + 1	
LUA-LUA Kazenga	9 + 2				1 + 1		0 + 1	
McLEOD Kevin	2 + 3				1 + 1		0 + 1	
McNULTY Jimmy	5 + 3				2		1	
MURRAY Glenn	25 + 7	12	0 + 1		3	2	1	
NAVARRO Alan	31 + 5		1		2 + 1		1	
PAINTER Marcos	18 + 1							
SMITH Graeme	5 + 1				2 + 1		1	
SMITH Jamie	1 + 1							
THORNHILL Matt	3 + 4		1				1	
TUNNICLIFFE James	17	2			2		0 + 1	
VIRGO Adam	20 + 5	1	1		4		1	
WALKER Mitch	1							
WHING Andy	9		1		1			
WRIGHT Jake	4 + 2	1					1	
WRIGHT Mark	2 + 2		0 + 1					
BRISTOL CITY (CHAMP: 10th)								
AGYEMANG Patrick	5 + 2							
AKINDE John	0 + 7		1 + 1		0 + 2			
BASSO Adriano	4							
BLACKMAN Andre			1 + 1					
CAMPBELL-RYCE Jamal	13 + 1							
CAREY Louis	36 + 1	2	2		2			
CLARKSON David	10 + 16	4	2		1			
ELLIOTT Marvin	33 + 6	1	2		1 + 1			
FONTAINE Liam	31 + 5	2	2		2			
GERKEN Dean	39		2		2			
HARTLEY Paul	36 + 4	5	2		2			
HAYNES Danny	29 + 9	7	2		1			
HENDERSON Stephen	3							
IWELUMO Chris	7	2						
JOHNSON Lee	18 + 10	1	2					
McALLISTER Jamie	31 + 2		1		2			

Player	P/FL App	Goals	FLC App	Goals	FAC App	Goals	Others App	Goals
McCOMBE Jamie	13 + 3	1	0 + 1					
MAIERHOFER Stefan	1 + 2							
MAYNARD Nicky	40 + 2	20	1	1	2			
NYATANGA Lewin	33 + 4	1			1			
ORR Bradley	38 + 1	2	1		2			
RIBEIRO Christian	5		1					
SABORIO Alvaro	11 + 8	2			0 + 2			
SAWYER Gary	2							
SKUSE Cole	39 + 4	2	2		2			
SNO Evander	16 + 8	3			1			
SPROULE Ivan	8 + 22	1	0 + 2		1			
VELICKA Andrius	0 + 1							
WILLIAMS Gavin	2 + 12		2		0 + 1	1		
WILSON Brian	3		0 + 1					

BRISTOL ROVERS (DIV 1: 11th)

Player	P/FL App	Goals	FLC App	Goals	FAC App	Goals	Others App	Goals
ANDERSEN Mikkel	39							
ANTHONY Byron	37		2		1			
BALDWIN Pat	6							
BLIZZARD Dominic	22 + 12	1	1 + 1		1		1	
BROWN Wayne	3 + 1							
CAMPBELL Stuart	46		2		1		1	
COLES Danny	36	1						
DICKSON Chris	10 + 4	4						
DUFFY Darryl	15 + 15	4	2	2	0 + 1	1	1	
ELLIOTT Steve	21	1	1	1	1		1	
EVANS Rhys	3		2		1		1	
FORSTER Fraser	4							
HEFFERNAN Paul	11	4						
HUGHES Jeff	44	12	2		1			
HUNT Ben	0 + 2							
JONES Dan	17							
LAMBERT Rickie	1	1						
LESCOTT Aaron	23 + 1	2	1				1	
LINES Chris	41 + 1	10	2		1		1	
OSEI-KUFFOUR Jo	42	14	2		1		1	
PIPE David	5 + 2	2					1	
REECE Charlie	5 + 9		0 + 1				0 + 1	
REGAN Carl	32 + 3		2		1		1	
RICHARDS Eliot	0 + 5							
RIGG Sean			1					
SWALLOW Ben	6 + 17		0 + 2		0 + 1		1	
WILLIAMS Andy	18 + 25	3	0 + 1				1	
WRIGHT Mark	19 + 5				1			

BURNLEY (PREM: 18th)

Player	P/FL App	Goals	FLC App	Goals	FAC App	Goals	Others App	Goals
ALEXANDER Graham	33	7			2	1		
BIKEY Andre	26 + 2	1	2		1			
BLAKE Robbie	20 + 11	2	0 + 1		1 + 1			
CALDWELL Steve	12 + 1	1			1			
CARLISLE Clarke	27		1					
CORK Jack	8 + 3	1						
CORT Leon	15							
DUFF Michael	10 + 1		0 + 1		2			
EAGLES Chris	20 + 14	2	2	1	1			
EASTON Brian			1					
ECKERSLEY Richard			2		1			
EDGAR David	2 + 2		1		1			
ELLIOTT Wade	34 + 4	4			2			
FLETCHER Steven	35	8	1 + 1	3	1	1		
FOX Danny	13 + 1	1						
GUDJONSSON Joey	1 + 9		2		1 + 1			
GUERRERO Fernando	0 + 7		2					
JENSEN Brian	38		1		2			
JORDAN Stephen	23 + 2							
KALVENES Christian	3 + 3		1		1			
McCANN Chris	7							
McDONALD Kevin	15 + 11	1	2		2			
MEARS Tyrone	38							
NIMANI Frederic	0 + 2							
NUGENT David	20 + 10	6						
PATERSON Martin	17 + 6	4	1 + 1		0 + 1			
PENNY Diego	0 + 1		1 + 1					
RODRIGUEZ Jay			1 + 1					
THOMPSON Steve	1 + 19	4	1		1 + 1			

BURTON ALBION (DIV 2: 13th)

Player	P/FL App	Goals	FLC App	Goals	FAC App	Goals	Others App	Goals
AUSTIN Ryan	18	2	1		2	1	1	
BOCO Romauld	3 + 5							
BOERTIEN Paul	33 + 1	1	1				1	
BRANSTON Guy	18 + 1	1			2		1	
BROWN Aaron	1				0 + 2			
CADOGAN Kieron	2				1			

Player	P/FL App	Goals	FLC App	Goals	FAC App	Goals	Others App	Goals
CORBETT Andy	32 + 2	1	1				0 + 1	
EDWORTHY Marc	1							
GILROY Keith	4 + 4							
GOODFELLOW Marc	0 + 3						1	
HARRAD Shaun	35 + 7	21			2	1	1	
JACKSON Richard	4 + 1							
JAMES Tony	42	1	2				1	
KABBA Steve	18 + 5	6	1					
KELLY Shaun	2 + 2							
KRYSIAK Artur	38		1				1	
McGRATH John	44 + 1	1	1		1		1	1
MAGHOMA Jacques	24 + 11	3	1		1	1	1	
MAKOFO Serge	0 + 2				0 + 2			
PARKES Tom	21 + 1	1	1					
PEARSON Greg	24 + 18	14	1		0 + 2		0 + 1	
PENN Russell	34 + 6	4	1		2			
PHILLIPS Jimmy	19 + 5	1	0 + 1	1	1		0 + 1	
POOLE Kevin	5 + 1		1					
REDMOND Shane	3				1			
SHROOT Robin	4 + 3							
SIMPSON Michael	20 + 4	2	1		2			
STRIDE Darren	5 + 4							
TAYLOR Cleveland	23 + 1	4						
THOMPSON O'Neil	1 + 1							
WALKER Richard	10 + 7	3	1		1		1	
WEBSTER Aaron	18 + 6	4			2			

BURY (DIV 2: 9th)

Player	P/FL App	Goals	FLC App	Goals	FAC App	Goals	Others App	Goals
BAKER Richie	7 + 7	1	0 + 1		1		1 + 2	
BARRY-MURPHY Brian	46	1	1		1		2 + 1	
BELFORD Cameron	5 + 2						1	
BISHOP Andy	12 + 13	3					1	
BROWN Wayne	41		1		1		2	
BUCHANAN Dave	37 + 1		1		1		2	
CARLTON Danny	1 + 6						1	
CRESSWELL Ryan	24 + 4				1		2	
DAWSON Stephen	45	4	1		1		3	
ELLIOTT Tom	7 + 9	1			1		1	
FUTCHER Ben	29 + 3		1		0 + 1		3	
HEWSON Sam	1 + 6							
JOHNSON Simon	1 + 3		0 + 1				1	
JONES Mike	36 + 5	5	1		1		2	2
LOWE Ryan	34 + 5	18	1		1		1 + 1	
MORRELL Andy	25 + 7	9					0 + 1	
NARDIELLO Danny	6	4						
NEWEY Tom	29 + 3				1		3	
PARKER Keigan	2							
POOLE James	4 + 5							
RACCHI Danny	10 + 12	1	1				2	1
ROBERTSON Jordan	4	1					1	
ROUSE Domaine	1 + 3		0 + 1				0 + 1	
SCOTT Paul	26 + 4	1	1		0 + 1		2	
SODJE Efe	39	2	1		1		1	
WORRALL David	34 + 6	4					2	

CARDIFF CITY (CHAMP: 4th)

Player	P/FL App	Goals	FLC App	Goals	FAC App	Goals	Others App	Goals
BLAKE Darcy	15 + 3				1 + 2		3	
BOTHROYD Jay	40	11	2	1	3	1	3	
BURKE Chris	38 + 6	9	2		2 + 1	1	3	
CAPALDI Tony	10 + 5		3					
CHOPRA Michael	36 + 5	16	2 + 1	1	3 + 1	2	3	2
COMMINGES Miguel	0 + 1		1					
ENCKELMAN Peter	3 + 1		3					
ETUHU Kelvin	7 + 9	1					0 + 3	
FEENEY Warren	1 + 1				0 + 1			
GERRARD Anthony	39	2	3		4		0 + 1	
GYEPES Gabor	16	1	2		2			
HUDSON Mark	26 + 1	2	1		2		3	
KENNEDY Mark	25 + 5				2 + 1		3	
LEDLEY Joe	27 + 2	3	1		3		3	1
McCORMACK Ross	21 + 13	4			3 + 1	1	0 + 3	
McNAUGHTON Kevin	20 + 1				2		3	
McPHAIL Stephen	21				2		3	
MAGENNIS Josh	1 + 8		0 + 1	1				
MARSHALL David	43				4		3	
MATTHEWS Adam	24 + 8	1	1		2			
MORRIS Aaron	0 + 1							
QUINN Paul	16 + 6		2		2			
RAE Gavin	28 + 9	1	3	1	2			
SCIMECA Riccy	2 + 2		1 + 1					
TAIWO Sol	2 + 6				0 + 2			
WHITTINGHAM Peter	41	20	3	2	4	1	3	2
WILDIG Aaron	4 + 7	1	0 + 3		3			

CARLISLE UNITED (DIV 1: 14th)

	P/FL App	Goals	FLC App	Goals	FAC App	Goals	Others App	Goals
ALDRED Tom	4 + 1						0 + 1	
ANYINSAH Joe	20 + 8	9	3		2 + 2	1	1 + 4	1
BOWMAN Ryan	0 + 6							
BRIDGE-WILKINSON Marc	6 + 13		1 + 1				2 + 3	1
BURNS Michael							1	
CLAYTON Adam	28	1			2 + 1		5	2
COLLIN Adam	29				2		5	
DOBIE Scott	24 + 15	5	2 + 1	2	1 + 3		3 + 2	3
DUFFY Darryl	7 + 1	1						
GILLESPIE Mark	0 + 1							
HARTE Ian	45	16	3	1	4	1	6 + 1	
HORWOOD Evan	31 + 1				4		6 + 1	
HURST Kevan	30 + 3	2	2		3 + 1	2	5	1
KANE Tony	1 + 3						1	
KAVANAGH Graham	28 + 1	2	1 + 1		4		5	3
KEOGH Richard	41		3 + 1	1	4	1	6	1
LIVESEY Danny	38	2	3		4		4	
MADINE Gary	6 + 14	4	0 + 2	1			1 + 2	1
MARSHALL Ben	11 + 9	3						
MURPHY Peter	12 + 4		2		1		4 + 1	1
OFFIONG Richard	2 + 13	1	1				2 + 1	
PERICARD Vincent	10	4			4	2	2	
PIDGELEY Lenny	17		3		2		2	
PRICE Jason	8 + 1	4						
RAVEN David	14 + 2		3				2	
ROBSON Matty	39	4	3		4		7	3
ROTHERY Gavin	0 + 1		0 + 2				1 + 1	
TAIWO Tom	30 + 5	1	3		3		4 + 2	
TAYLOR Cleveland	1							
THIRLWELL Paul	24 + 4	1	2				2	

CHARLTON ATHLETIC (DIV 1: 4th)

	P/FL App	Goals	FLC App	Goals	FAC App	Goals	Others App	Goals
BAILEY Nicky	43 + 1	12	0 + 1		1		3	1
BASEY Grant	14 + 5		1				2	
BORROWDALE Gary	10						2	
BURTON Deon	35 + 4	13	0 + 1		0 + 1		2 + 1	1
DAILLY Christian	44	1			1		4	
DICKSON Chris	1 + 4							
ELLIOT Rob	33		1				1	
FLEETWOOD Stuart			0 + 1					
FORSTER Nicky	8	2					0 + 2	
GRAY Andy	0 + 2		1					
HOLDEN Luke							0 + 1	
IKEME Carl	4						1	
JACKSON Johnnie	4							
LLERA Miguel Angel	23 + 2	4					2	
McKENZIE Leon	0 + 12		1		0 + 1		0 + 1	1
McLEOD Izale	3 + 8	2	1		1		1	1
MAMBO Yado							0 + 1	
MOONEY Dave	20 + 8	5					3	1
OMOZUSI Elliott	7 + 2				1			
RACON Therry	36	1			1		2 + 1	
RANDOLPH Darren	9 + 2				1		2	
REID Kyel	11 + 6	4					1	
RICHARDSON Frazer	37 + 1	1					2	
SAM Lloyd	40 + 3	4	1		1		3	
SEMEDO Jose	35 + 3	1	1		1		3	
SHELVEY Jonjo	19 + 5	4			1		1 + 1	
SMALL Wade			1					
SODJE Akpo	10 + 15	5					0 + 1	
SODJE Sam	24 + 3	4	1		1		1	
SOLLY Chris	2 + 7						1	
SPRING Matthew	7 + 5		1				2	
STAVRINOU Alex	0 + 1						0 + 1	
TUNA Tamer	0 + 1						1	1
WAGSTAFF Scott	9 + 21	4	1		0 + 1		2 + 2	1
YOUGA Kelly	18		1		1		1	

CHELSEA (PREM: 1st)

	P/FL App	Goals	FLC App	Goals	FAC App	Goals	Others App	Goals
ALEX	13 + 3	1	1		6		2	
ANELKA Nicolas	31 + 2	11			3 + 1	1	7 + 1	3
BALLACK Michael	26 + 6	4	2		3 + 1	1	5 + 2	
BELLETTI Juliano	4 + 7		3		2 + 1		4 + 1	
BORINI Fabio	0 + 4		1		0 + 2		0 + 1	
BOSINGWA Jose	8						0 + 1	
BRUMA Jeffrey	0 + 2		0 + 1					
CARVALHO Ricardo	22				1		6	1
CECH Petr	34				2		7	
COLE Ashley	25 + 2	4	0 + 1		2		5	
COLE Joe	14 + 12	2	3		3 + 2		2 + 3	
DECO	14 + 5	2	2	1	2		2 + 3	
DROGBA Didier	31 + 1	29	0 + 2	2	4	3	6	3
ESSIEN Michael	13 + 1	3	0 + 1				6 + 1	1
FERREIRA Paulo	11 + 2		3	1	4			
HILARIO	2 + 1		3		4		0 + 1	
HUTCHINSON Sam	0 + 2		1					
IVANOVIC Branislav	25 + 3	1	3		3		7	
KAKUTA Gael	0 + 1		0 + 1		0 + 1		1	
KALOU Salomon	11 + 12	5	3	3	2 + 2	1	5 + 2	3
LAMPARD Frank	36	22	0 + 1		6	3	7 + 1	2
MALOUDA Florent	26 + 7	12	3	1	4 + 2	2	8 + 1	
MATIC Nemanja	0 + 2				0 + 1			
MIKEL John Obi	21 + 4		2		3		5	
SHEVCHENKO Andrei	0 + 1							
STURRIDGE Daniel	2 + 11	1	1		3 + 1	4	0 + 2	
TERRY John	37	2	0 + 1		5	1	9	
TURNBULL Ross	2		0 + 1				2	
VAN AANHOLT Patrick	0 + 2							
ZHIRKOV Yuri	10 + 7		2		4		3 + 1	

CHELTENHAM TOWN (DIV 2: 22nd)

	P/FL App	Goals	FLC App	Goals	FAC App	Goals	Others App	Goals
ALMOND Louis	2 + 2							
ALSOP Julian	21 + 20	4	0 + 1		1		0 + 1	
ANDREW Danny	9 + 1							
ARTUS Frankie	7						1	
BIRD David	35 + 2		1		1		1	
BOZANIC Olly	4							
BROWN Scott	0 + 1							
BROWN Scott	46		1		1		1	
COX Sam	1							
DENTON Tom	1 + 1		0 + 1				1	
DIALLO Drissa	17 + 1				1		1	
DUFF Shane	11						1	
EASTHAM Ashley	18 + 2							
ELITO Medy	12	3						
EYJOLFSSON Holmar	4							
GALLINAGH Andy	35 + 4	1	1		0 + 1		1	
HAMMOND Elvis	14 + 10	4	1	1	1			
HAYLES Barry	23 + 16	7	1		0 + 1		0 + 1	
HAYNES Kyle	6 + 7				0 + 1		0 + 1	
HUTTON David	14 + 11		1					
LABADIE Joss	11							
LEE Jake	0 + 1							
LESCOTT Aaron	7 + 1							
LEWIS Theo	9 + 6				1	1		
LOW Josh	35 + 4	4	0 + 1		1		1	1
MARSHALL Ben	6	2						
PIPE David	7 + 1							
POOK Michael	31 + 4	5	1		1			
RICHARDS Justin	39 + 5	15	1		1		1	
RIDLEY Lee	26 + 1	1	1		1			
ROSE Romone	1							
TABOR Jordan							1	
THORNHILL Matt	16 + 1	3						
TOWNSEND Michael	34	3	1				1	
WATKINS Marley	4 + 9	1					1	

CHESTERFIELD (DIV 2: 8th)

	P/FL App	Goals	FLC App	Goals	FAC App	Goals	Others App	Goals
ALLOTT Mark	45	2	1		1		3	
ARTUS Frankie	2 + 1							
AUSTIN Kevin	14 + 5		1				2	
BODEN Scott	5 + 30	6			1		1	
BOSHELL Danny	3 + 6							
BOWERY Jordan	2 + 8		1		0 + 1		0 + 2	1
BRECKIN Ian	41 + 1		1		1		3	
CONLON Barry	15 + 4	7						
CROSSLEY Mark	4							
CURRIE Darren	2 + 2		0 + 1	1			0 + 1	1
DE MONTAGNAC Ishmel	10	3						
DJILALI Kieron	8	1						
DOWNES Aaron	7	1						
GOODALL Alan	17							
GRAY Dan	16 + 3		1				1 + 2	
GREEN Dominic	10	2						
GRITTON Martin	2 + 7	1	1					
HALL Danny	5 + 2	1	1		1			
HARSLEY Paul	0 + 3		1				0 + 1	
LEE Tommy	42				1		3	
LESTER Jack	27 + 2	11			1	1	3	
LEWIS Terrell	0 + 1							
LITTLE John	12				1		1	
LOWRY Jamie	13	5					2	1
McDERMOTT Donal	13 + 2	5	1				2 + 1	
MADINE Gary	2 + 2							
MORRIS Ian	7							
NIVEN Derek	28 + 11	2	0 + 1		0 + 1		1	

Ashley Cole (Chelsea)

	P/FL App	P/FL Goals	FLC App	FLC Goals	FAC App	FAC Goals	Others App	Others Goals
PAGE Rob	38 + 1	1					2 + 1	
PERKINS David	11 + 2	1			1			
PICKEN Phil	20 + 1		0 + 1				1 + 1	
ROBERTSON Gregor	8 + 2				1		3	
RUNDLE Adam	12 + 4							
SMALL Wade	24 + 3	4			1		1	2
SOMMA Davide	1 + 2							
TALBOT Drew	26 + 4	6	1		1		3	4
WHALEY Simon	5 + 1	1						
WHING Andy	9 + 2							
COLCHESTER UNITED (DIV 1: 8th)								
BALDWIN Pat	6 + 1		1					
BATTH Danny	16 + 1	1	1		1			
BEEVERS Lee	4		1					
BENDER Thomas	0 + 1							
COUSINS Mark			1				1	
ELITO Medy	0 + 3				0 + 1			
FOX David	15 + 3	3			2		1	
GILLESPIE Steven	8 + 22	1			2 + 1	1		
GUY Jamie	0 + 1							
HACKNEY Simon	9 + 8	1	1	1	3	1	1	
HAMMOND Dean	2		0 + 1					
HEATH Matt	13 + 5						1	
HENDERSON Ian	6 + 7	2						
IFIL Phil	15 + 12	2			2 + 1			
IZZET Kemi	31 + 6		1		1 + 1		1	
LISBIE Kevin	35 + 6	13	1		1			
LOCKWOOD Matt	1						1	
MAY Alan	1 + 1		1					
ODEJAYI Kayode	19 + 9	9			3	1		
OKUONGHAE Magnus	44		1		3	1		
O'TOOLE John-Joe	30 + 1	2			2		1	
PAYNE Josh	2 + 1							
PERKINS David	0 + 5	1	1				0 + 1	
PLATT Clive	36 + 5	7	1		1 + 1	1	1	1
PRUTTON David	18 + 1	3						
QUEUDRUE Franck	3							
REID Paul	10 + 2				2			
RIBEIRO Christian	2							
THOMAS Joel	0 + 4				0 + 2		0 + 1	
TIERNEY Marc	41				3			
VERNON Scott	4 + 3	3	0 + 1				1	
VINCENT Ashley	15 + 4	3	1				1	
WHITE John	38 + 1				3		1	
WILLIAMS Ben	46				3			
WORDSWORTH Anthony	36 + 5	11			1 + 1		0 + 1	
COVENTRY CITY (CHAMP: 19th)								
BAKER Carl	14 + 8							
BARNETT Leon	19 + 1							
BELL David	20 + 8	2			2	1		
BEST Leon	25 + 2	9			1 + 1	1		
CAIN Ashley	0 + 2		1					
CAMERON Nathan			0 + 1					
CLARKE Jordan	6 + 6		1					
CLINGAN Sammy	32 + 2	5			2			
CORK Jack	20 + 1							
CRANIE Martin	38 + 2	1			2			
DEEGAN Gary	9 + 8	2						
EASTWOOD Freddy	21 + 15	8	1		1 + 1			
GRANDISON Jermaine	1 + 2		1		0 + 1			
GUNNARSSON Aron	34 + 6	1			2			
HALL Marcus	7 + 1							
HUSSEY Chris	1 + 7							
JEFFERS Shaun	0 + 4		1					
KONSTANTOPOULOS Dimi	2 + 1		1		0 + 1			
McINDOE Michael	38 + 2	1	1		2			
McKENZIE Leon	0 + 1							
McPAKE James	17				2			
MADINE Gary	0 + 9							
MORRISON Clinton	38 + 8	11	0 + 1		2			
OSBOURNE Isaac	12 + 3		1					
SEARS Freddie	3 + 7							
STEAD Jon	9 + 1	2						
TURNER Ben	13		1					
VAN AANHOLT Patrick	19 + 1							
WALKER Adam			1					
WARD Elliott	4 + 4							
WESTWOOD Keiren	44				2			
WILSON Callum			0 + 1					
WOOD Richard	22 + 2	3			2			
WRIGHT Stephen	38		1		2			

	P/FL App	P/FL Goals	FLC App	FLC Goals	FAC App	FAC Goals	Others App	Others Goals
CREWE ALEXANDRA (DIV 2: 18th)								
ADA Patrick	16 + 2		1		1		1	
BAILEY James	20 + 1		1		1			
BOGDAN Adam	1							
BRAYFORD John	45		1		1		1	
BUTTON David	10							
CLEMENTS Chris					0 + 1			
COLLIS Steve	1							
DAVIS Harry	0 + 1							
DONALDSON Clayton	28 + 9	13	0 + 1		0 + 1			
ELDING Anthony	4 + 6		0 + 1				0 + 1	
GARDNER Danny	0 + 2							
GRANT Joel	41 + 2	9	1		1	1	1	
JONES Billy	10 + 1	2	1				1	
LEGZDINS Adam	6		1				1	
LEITCH-SMITH Ajay	0 + 1							
MARTIN Carl	1 + 5	1						
MILLER Shaun	22 + 11	7					0 + 1	
MITCHEL-KING Mat	31 + 1		1		1		1	
MOORE Byron	13 + 19	3	1		1		1	
MURPHY Luke	24 + 8	3	1		0 + 1			
O'DONNELL Danny	27							
PHILLIPS Steve	28				1			
SCHUMACHER Steve	27 + 5	4					1	
SHELLEY Danny	7 + 12	1			1			
STOKES Chris	2							
TOOTLE Matt	26 + 2	1						
VERMA Aman	5 + 2		0 + 1				1	
WALTON Simon	26 + 5	1			1		0 + 1	
WESTWOOD Ashley	34 + 2	6	1		1		1	
WORLEY Harry	21 + 2	1					1	
ZOLA-MAKONGO Calvin	30 + 4	15	1		1	1	1	1
CRYSTAL PALACE (CHAMP: 21st)								
AMBROSE Darren	44 + 2	15	2	2	5	3		
ANDREW Calvin	13 + 14	1			0 + 5	1		
BUTTERFIELD Danny	36 + 1	1	1		4	3		
CARLE Nick	14 + 8	1	0 + 1		3			
CLYNE Nathaniel	19 + 3	1	1		5			
COMLEY James					0 + 2			
DANNS Neil	41 + 1	8	2		5	1		
DAVIS Claude	19 + 2				5			
DERRY Shaun	46		2		5			
DJILALI Kieron	2 + 6	1	0 + 1		0 + 2			
ERTL Johnny	29 + 4		0 + 1		4	1		
FLAHAVAN Darryl	1							
FONTE Jose	22	1	2		1			
HILL Clint	43	1	2		3			
HILLS Lee	10 + 9							
JOHN Stern	7 + 9	2						
LAWRENCE Matt	14 + 4				2 + 1			
LEE Alan	33 + 9	6	1		5	1		
McCARTHY Paddy	20		2					
MOSES Victor	14 + 4	6	2		1			
N'DIAYE Alassane	12 + 14	3	2		1			
SCANNELL Sean	11 + 15	2	0 + 2		1			
SEARS Freddie	11 + 7		1					
SMITH Ryan	0 + 5		0 + 1					
SPERONI Julian	45		2		5			
WYNTER Alex					0 + 1			
ZAHA Wilfried	0 + 1							
DAGENHAM & REDBRIDGE (DIV 2: 7th)								
ANTWI Will	19	1	1		1		1	
ARBER Mark	41	4	1		1		4	
BENSON Paul	45	17	1		1	1	4	4
BINGHAM Billy	0 + 2							
CARLOS Joao	0 + 1							
CURRIE Darren	5 + 11							
DAY Jamie	8							
DEAN Harlee	0 + 1							
DOE Scott	40 + 2		1		1		3	
FOLLY Yoann	5 + 2							
GAIN Peter	43	3	1		1		4	
GREEN Danny	45 + 1	13	1		1		3 + 1	1
GRIFFITHS Scott	13	1	1				1	
KILBEY Tom							1	
LOCKWOOD Matt	4							
McCRORY Damien	20						3	
MILLER Adam	8							
MONTGOMERY Graeme	4 + 13	2	0 + 1		0 + 1		1 + 2	
NURSE Jon	30 + 8	7			1		4	1

	P/FL App	Goals	FLC App	Goals	FAC App	Goals	Others App	Goals
OFORI-TWUMASI Nana	8	2						
OGOGO Abu	27 + 3	2	0 + 1				4	
PACK Marlon	17	1						
ROBERTS Tony	46		1		1		4	
SCOTT Josh	36 + 4	10	0 + 1	1	1		3 + 1	5
SPILLER Danny	7 + 3							
TAIWO Solomon	4		1					
TEJAN-SIE Tommy	1 + 2				1		0 + 1	
THOMAS Wes	3 + 20	3	1		0 + 1		1	
THURGOOD Stuart	17		1		1			
UDDIN Anwar	3 + 3						0 + 1	
VINCELOT Romain	7 + 2	1					3	
WALSH Phil	0 + 9						0 + 2	

DARLINGTON (DIV 2: 24th)

	P/FL App	Goals	FLC App	Goals	FAC App	Goals	Others App	Goals
ARNISON Paul	17 + 1	1	1				2	
BAINS Rikki	3 + 1						0 + 1	
BARNES Corey	4 + 2				1		1	
BARNETT Moses	4				1			
BENNETT James	3 + 1						0 + 1	
BOWER Mark	12 + 1	1	1				1	
BURN Dan	2 + 2							
BYRNE Richie	2 + 2							
CHANDLER Jamie	12 + 2	1	1				1	
CHISHOLM Ross	2 + 1							
COLLINS James	5 + 2	2			1			
CONVERY Mark	9 + 12				1		1 + 1	1
COOK Jordan	4 + 1							
DAVIS David	5				1			
DEANE Patrick	0 + 10							
DEMPSEY Gary	24	1						
DEVITT Jamie	5 + 1	1			1			
DIOP Serigne	18 + 5	2			0 + 1	1		
DOWSON David	6 + 4	1	1				0 + 1	
FOSTER Stephen	15 + 1	1	1		1		1	
GALL Kevin	9 + 1	2					2	
GIDDINGS Stuart	22							
GRAY Josh	10 + 17	1			0 + 1			
GROVES Danny	8 + 8						1	
HALL Danny	3							
HARSLEY Paul	3							
HOGG Jonathan	5	1						
HOULT Russell	6							
JONES Ashlee	1							
KANE Tony	4							
KNIGHT David	7		1				1	
LIVERSEDGE Nick	13				1		1	
LUMSDON Chris	2		1					
McREADY John	3 + 1							
MADDEN Simon	13 + 2							
MAIN Curtis	12 + 14	3	0 + 1		0 + 1		0 + 1	
MARSHALL Jordan	0 + 3							
MILLER Ian	40	1	1				2	
MILNE Andrew	12 + 1							
MOORE Chris	8 + 3							
MULLIGAN Nathan	10 + 6	1						
PLUMMER Matt	5 + 3		0 + 1		1		2	
PORRITT Nathan	4 + 1							
PURCELL Tadhg	22	9						
REDMOND Shane	19							
SMITH Gary	32 + 2	1	1		1		2	
SMITH Jeff	22 + 2		1		1		1 + 1	
SMITH Michael	3 + 4	1						
THOMAS Simon	7	1	1		1			
THORPE Lee	7 + 1	1	1				1	1
WAITE Gareth	14							
WHELAN Noel	2 + 1							
WHITE Alan	23 + 1	1	1					
WINDASS Dean	3 + 3		0 + 1					

DERBY COUNTY (CHAMP: 14th)

	P/FL App	Goals	FLC App	Goals	FAC App	Goals	Others App	Goals
ADDISON Miles	10 + 3	2	1		2			
ANDERSON Russell	9 + 6	1						
BALL Callum	0 + 1							
BARKER Shaun	33 + 2	5			2 + 1			
BUXTON Jake	19	1	1		4			
BYWATER Stephen	42		1		4			
CAMPBELL DJ	6 + 2	3						
COMMONS Kris	11 + 9	3			3 + 1	1		
CONNELLY Ryan	0 + 1							
CONNOLLY Paul	17 + 4		1		1			
CROFT Lee	14 + 5	1	1		1			
CYWKA Tomasz	4 + 1							
DAVIES Steve	7 + 11	1	1		1 + 2	1		

	P/FL App	Goals	FLC App	Goals	FAC App	Goals	Others App	Goals
DEENEY Saul	2 + 1							
DICKOV Paul	10 + 6	2						
GREEN Paul	30 + 3	2			4			
HENDRIE Lee	4 + 5				1			
HUGHES Bryan	3							
HULSE Rob	30 + 7	12			2 + 1			
HUNT Nicky	20 + 1				2			
JOHNSON Lee	4				2 + 1			
LEACOCK Dean	13 + 4							
LIVERMORE Jake	11 + 5	1						
McEVELEY Jay	28 + 5	2	0 + 1		1 + 1	2		
MARTIN David	2							
MARTIN Dave	2 + 9	1						
MENDY Arnaud	0 + 1							
MILLS Greg	0 + 2							
MOXEY Dean	27 + 3		1		3			
PEARSON Stephen	34 + 3	1			4			
PORTER Chris	11 + 10	4			3			
PRINGLE Ben	1 + 4		1					
SAVAGE Robbie	45 + 1	2	1		3			
STOOR Fredrik	10 + 1							
SUNU Gilles	6 + 3	1						
TEALE Gary	21 + 7	2	1	1	0 + 2			
TONGE Michael	18	2			1			
VARNEY Luke	0 + 1		0 + 1					
VAUGHAN James	2							
VIDAL Javan	0 + 1							

DONCASTER ROVERS (CHAMP: 12th)

	P/FL App	Goals	FLC App	Goals	FAC App	Goals	Others App	Goals
CHAMBERS James	43		1 + 1		2			
COPPINGER James	38 + 1	4	1	1	2			
DUMBUYA Mustapha	0 + 3							
EMMANUEL-THOMAS Jay	12 + 2	5						
FAIRHURST Waide	2 + 4	2	0 + 1					
FORTUNE Quinton	3 + 3	1	0 + 1					
GILLETT Simon	10 + 1							
GUY Lewis	1 + 12		2		0 + 1			
HAYTER James	29 + 9	9	1 + 1		0 + 1			
HEFFERNAN Paul	6 + 11				0 + 1			
HIRD Sam	21 + 15		1		0 + 2			
LOCKWOOD Adam	10 + 6	2	2					
McDAID Sean	0 + 1							
MARTIS Shelton	13 + 1	1						
MUTCH Jordon	5 + 12	2						
O'CONNOR James	33 + 5		1		2	1		
OSTER John	36 + 4	1	2		2			
ROBERTS Gareth	40 + 2	3	2		2			
SHACKELL Jason	20 + 1	1			2			
SHARP Billy	32 + 1	15			2			
SHIELS Dean	25 + 13	6	1		2			
SMITH Ben	1 + 1		2					
SPICER John	9 + 11		1 + 1		0 + 1			
STOCK Brian	15		1		2			
SULLIVAN Neil	45				2			
WARD Elliott	6	1						
WEBSTER Byron	1 + 4		1 + 1					
WILSON Mark	29 + 6		1		2			
WOODS Martin	21 + 3	4	2	1				

EVERTON (PREM: 8th)

	P/FL App	Goals	FLC App	Goals	FAC App	Goals	Others App	Goals
AGARD Keiran	0 + 1		0 + 1		0 + 1		1 + 2	
AKPAN Hope							0 + 1	
ANICHEBE Victor	6 + 5	1						
ARTETA Mikel	11 + 2	6			0 + 1		2	
BAINES Leighton	37	1	1		2	1	8	
BAXTER Jose	0 + 2						1 + 4	
BIDWELL Jake							1	
BILYALETDINOV Diniyar	16 + 7	6	1		2		6 + 1	1
CAHILL Tim	33	8	1		2 + 1	1	7	1
COLEMAN Seamus	0 + 3				0 + 1		3	
CRAIG Nathan							0 + 1	
DISTIN Sylvain	29		2		1		6	2
DONOVAN Landon	7 + 3	2			1		2	
DUFFY Shane							1 + 1	
FELLAINI Marouane	20 + 3	2	1 + 1		2		7	1
FORSHAW Adam							1	
GOSLING Dan	3 + 8	2	2	1			6 + 1	
HEITINGA Johnny	29 + 2		2		2			
HIBBERT Tony	17 + 3		2		1		7	
HOWARD Tim	38		2		2		9	
JAGIELKA Phil	11 + 1						0 + 1	
JO	6 + 9		1 + 1	1			5 + 2	1
LESCOTT Joleon	1							
MUSTAFI Shkodran							0 + 1	

	P/FL App	P/FL Goals	FLC App	FLC Goals	FAC App	FAC Goals	Others App	Others Goals
NASH Carlo							1	
NEILL Lucas	10 + 2		1 + 1		1			
NEVILLE Phil	22 + 1				2		4	
OSMAN Leon	25 + 1	2	1	1	0 + 1	1	6 + 1	
PIENAAR Steven	30	4			2		6	3
RODWELL Jack	17 + 9	2	2				6 + 2	2
SAHA Louis	26 + 7	13	1		1		3 + 2	2
SENDEROS Philippe	1 + 1						1	
VAUGHAN James	0 + 8	1			1 + 1	1	0 + 1	
WALLACE James							0 + 1	
YAKUBU Aiyegbeni	9 + 16	5	2	1			4 + 5	
YOBO Joseph	14 + 3	1					6	1
EXETER CITY (DIV 1: 18th)								
ARCHIBALD-HENVILLE Troy	13 + 2				0 + 1		1	
BURNELL Joe	4 + 4							
CORR Barry	17 + 17	3			2	3	1	
COZIC Bertie	21 + 8	2	1		2		1	
DUFFY Richard	41 + 1	1	1		1			
DUNNE James	18 + 5	3			1 + 1		1	
EDWARDS Rob	17 + 4							
FLEETWOOD Stuart	16 + 11	4			2		0 + 1	1
FRIEND George	13	1						
GOLBOURNE Scott	30 + 4		1		2		0 + 1	
HABER Marcus	3 + 2							
HARLEY Ryan	43 + 1	10	1		2			
JANSSON Oscar	7							
JONES Paul	26		1					
LOGAN Richard	4 + 30	4	0 + 1				1	
McALLISTER Craig	0 + 4		1					
MARRIOTT Andy	13				2		1	
NOONE Craig	7	2						
NORWOOD James	2 + 1		0 + 1					
RUSSELL Alex	27 + 2	1	1		2			
SAUNDERS Neil	2 + 4						0 + 1	
SEABORNE Danny	17 + 2		1		2		1	
SERCOMBE Liam	25 + 3	1	1		0 + 1		1	
STANSFIELD Adam	19 + 8	7			0 + 2	1	1	
STEWART Marcus	36 + 5	2	1		1			
TAYLOR Matt	46	5	1		2	2	1	
TAYLOR Ryan	3 + 4							
TULLY Steve	36 + 2	1	0 + 1		1		1	
WATSON Ben	0 + 1							
FULHAM (PREM: 12th)								
ANDERSON Joe			0 + 1					
BAIRD Chris	29 + 3		1		3		13 + 3	
DAVIES Simon	12 + 5		1		3 + 1	1	11	2
DEMPSEY Clint	27 + 2	7			1 + 1		6 + 7	2
DIKGACOI Kagisho	7 + 5		0 + 1		1 + 1			
DUFF Damien	30 + 2	6			4	2	10 + 4	1
ELM David	3 + 7	1	0 + 1		1 + 2		0 + 2	
ETUHU Dickson	14 + 6				3		14	2
GERA Zoltan	19 + 8	2	1	1	3 + 1	1	18	6
GREENING Jonathan	15 + 8	1	1		2 + 1		6 + 1	
HANGELAND Brede	32	1			4		16	2
HUGHES Aaron	34				5		16 + 1	
JOHNSON Andrew	7 + 1				1		4	3
JOHNSON Eddie	0 + 2		1				0 + 1	
KALLIO Toni	0 + 1				1			
KAMARA Diomansy	5 + 4	1					3 + 1	2
KELLY Stephen	7 + 1		1		3		9 + 1	
KONCHESKY Paul	27	1			2		13	
MURPHY Danny	25	5			3		13	2
NEVLAND Erik	12 + 11	3			1	1	2 + 7	
OKAKA CHUKA Stefano	3 + 8	2			0 + 2	1		
PANTSIL John	22						9 + 1	
RIISE Bjorn Helge	5 + 7		1		2 + 1		7 + 5	
SCHWARZER Mark	37				5		18	
SEOL Ki-Hyeon	0 + 2		1				0 + 2	1
SHOREY Nicky	9				2			
SMALLING Chris	9 + 3		1		1		4	
STOCKDALE David	1		1				1	
STOOR Fredrik	0 + 2		1					
ZAMORA Bobby	27	8			4	3	16 + 1	8
GILLINGHAM (DIV 1: 21st)								
BARCHAM Andy	38 + 4	7	2	1	2 + 1		2	
BENTLEY Mark	34 + 2	2	1		3	1	1	
BRANDY Febian	5 + 2	1			2	1		
DENNEHY Darren	19							
DICKSON Chris	4 + 5	1						
ERSKINE Jacob	0 + 4						1 + 1	
FRY Matt	11				2			
FULLER Barry	35 + 1		2		3		1	
GOWLING Josh	29 + 1	2	2		3		1	
HOWE Rene	18	2						
JACKMAN Danny	21 + 1		0 + 1				1	
JACKSON Simeon	34 + 8	14	2	2	3		0 + 1	1
JULIAN Alan	30				1		2	
LEWIS Stuart	16 + 4	1			3		0 + 1	
McCAMMON Mark	3 + 11		1 + 1		0 + 3		2	
MAHER Kevin	21 + 5		2		0 + 2		0 + 1	
MILLER Adam	22 + 4	4	1				2	
NUTTER John	32 + 3	1	2		1 + 2		1	
OLI Dennis	23 + 13	3	1		1 + 1			
PALMER Chris	16 + 4	1	1 + 1		3		2	
PAYNE Jack	14 + 5		0 + 1				1	
PLUMMER Tristan	2							
RICHARDS Garry	16		1				2	
ROONEY Luke	2 + 11	2	0 + 1				2	
ROYCE Simon	16 + 1		2		2			
VERNON Scott	1							
WALKER James	2 + 3							
WESTON Curtis	36 + 3	6	2		3	2	1 + 1	
WYNTER Tom	4 + 4				1			
YUSSUFF Rachid	2 + 6						0 + 1	
GRIMSBY TOWN (DIV 2: 23rd)								
AKPA AKPRO Jean-Louis	26 + 10	5	1		1		0 + 2	
ATKINSON Rob	37	2	1		1		2	
BENNETT Ryan	13		1				1	
BORE Peter	37 + 3				1		1	
BOSHELL Danny	5 + 1		1		1		1	
CHAMBERS Ashley	2 + 2	2						
CLARKE Jamie	9 + 4						1 + 1	
COLGAN Nick	35		1		1		2	
CONLON Barry	7 + 9	5	1		1		0 + 1	
COULSON Michael	28 + 1	5						
COWAN-HALL Paris	0 + 3							
DEVITT Jamie	15	5						
FEATHERSTONE Nicky	7 + 1							
FLETCHER Wes	1 + 5	1						
FORBES Adrian	8 + 5	1					2	
FORECAST Tommy	4							
FULLER Josh	2 + 3				0 + 1		1	
HEGARTY Nick	5 + 4		1					
HEYWOOD Matt	1							
HUDSON Mark	11 + 5	2						
JARMAN Nathan	2 + 5						1	
JONES Chris	6 + 1	1			0 + 1			
LANCASHIRE Ollie	24 + 1	1					1	
LEARY Michael	19 + 9		0 + 1		1		1 + 1	
LILLIS Josh	4							
LINWOOD Paul	23 + 5	1			1			
McCRORY Damien	10						1	
MAGENNIS Josh	1 + 1							
MENDY Arnaud	1							
NORTH Danny	9 + 8	1	0 + 1		0 + 1		1	
OXLEY Mark	3							
PEACOCK Lee	14 + 3	2						
PROUDLOCK Adam	14 + 13	1	1				1	1
SHAHIN Jammal	4 + 1				1		1	
SINCLAIR Dean	16	3						
STIRLING Jude	2 + 2							
STOCKDALE Robbie	8		1					
SWEENEY Peter	36 + 4	4	1				2	2
WIDDOWSON Joe	36 + 2		1		1		1	
WOOD Bradley	7 + 1				1		1 + 1	
WRIGHT Ben	1 + 1							
WRIGHT Tommy	13 + 1	1						
HARTLEPOOL UNITED (DIV 1: 20th)								
AUSTIN Neil	36 + 3	3			1		1	
BEHAN Denis	21 + 8	6	2		1		0 + 1	
BJORNSSON Armann	10 + 8	3					1	
BOYD Adam	25 + 15	7	1 + 1	2	1		0 + 1	
BROWN James	19 + 13	4	0 + 1					
CHEREL Julien	1							
CLARK Ben	6 + 5							
COLLINS Sam	44		2		1		1	
FLINDERS Scott	46		2		1		1	
FOLEY David	0 + 2							
FREDRIKSEN Jon Andre	4 + 8		1 + 1					
GAMBLE Joe	22	2						
GREULICH Billy	0 + 4				0 + 1			
HARTLEY Peter	38	2	2		1			
HASLAM Steve	15		2				1	

	P/FL App	Goals	FLC App	Goals	FAC App	Goals	Others App	Goals
HUMPHREYS Ritchie	33 + 5				1		1	
JONES Richie	22 + 11	4	2		0 + 1			
LARKIN Colin	10 + 12	1	0 + 2		1		1	
LIDDLE Gary	40	3	2		1		1	
MACKAY Michael	0 + 1							
McSWEENEY Leon	24 + 7	1	2				1	
MONKHOUSE Andy	43	11	2		1		1	
O'DONOVAN Roy	15	9						
POWER Alan	0 + 2							
ROWELL Jonny	0 + 6						1	
SWEENEY Antony	32 + 10	2	2		1			

HEREFORD UNITED (DIV 2: 16th)

	P/FL App	Goals	FLC App	Goals	FAC App	Goals	Others App	Goals
ADAMSON Chris	1							
AJDAREVIC Astrit	0 + 1							
BARTLETT Adam	45 + 1		2		2		4	
BLANCHETT Danny	13				2		1	
CONSTANTINE Leon	25 + 10	6	1		1		3	2
DENNEHY Darren	6 + 1		1 + 1				1	
DONE Matty	7 + 13		0 + 1		0 + 1		1 + 2	
DOWNING Paul	6							
ELFORD-ALLIYU Lateef	1							
GODSMARK Jonny	7 + 1	1	2	1	1		0 + 2	
GREEN Ryan	31	1	2		1		2	
GWYNNE Sam	21 + 5		0 + 2		0 + 1		2	
JACKSON Marlon	2 + 3		0 + 1				1	
JERVIS Jake	5 + 2	2						
JONES Craig	1		1					
JONES Darren	40 + 1	3	1		2		3	
KING Craig	22 + 4	3			2		2	
LOWE Keith	17 + 2	1	1		2		2 + 1	
LUNT Kenny	42	1	2		2		4	
McCALLUM Gavin	20 + 7	8			1 + 1		2	
McQUILKIN James	20 + 2	2	1					
MANSET Mathieu	16 + 13	3			1 + 1	1	0 + 2	1
MARSHALL Mark	8						2	
MORRIS Lee	5 + 7		1				1	
MUTCH Jordon	3				1		1	
PLUMMER Tristan	4 + 1	3	1		1			
PRESTON Dan	4							
PUGH Marc	39 + 1	13	1		1 + 1		3	
ROSE Richard	22 + 3		2				3	
SONKO Eddy	5 + 5				1		1 + 1	
SOUTHAM Glen	5 + 1		2				0 + 1	
TOLLEY Jamie	6 + 4		0 + 1				1 + 1	
VALENTINE Ryan	40	4	1		2	1	1	
WALKER James	6	1			1		1	1
WEDDERBURN Nathaniel	3							
WEIR Tyler	3				1			
YOUNG Lewis	5 + 1							

HUDDERSFIELD TOWN (DIV 1: 6th)

	P/FL App	Goals	FLC App	Goals	FAC App	Goals	Others App	Goals
AINSWORTH Lionel	2 + 9		0 + 2		1 + 1		1 + 1	
BERRETT James	2 + 7		0 + 1		0 + 1		1	
BUTLER Andy	10 + 1		1				1	
CLARKE Nathan	15 + 2	1	1		3	1	2 + 1	1
CLARKE Peter	46	5	2		3		3	1
CLARKE Tom	15 + 6		1		0 + 2		1	
COLLINS Michael	23 + 5	3	1		3		2 + 1	
DRINKWATER Danny	27 + 6	2	1		0 + 1		2	
ECCLESTON Nathan	4 + 7	1					0 + 1	
GOODWIN Jim	3 + 2						2	
HEFFERNAN Dean	15							
KAY Antony	38 + 2	6	2		3		3	
NOVAK Lee	24 + 13	12	1		3		3 + 1	
PEARCE Krystian	0 + 1							
PELTIER Lee	42		2		3		3	
PILKINGTON Anthony	42 + 1	7	2		2		4	2
RHODES Jordan	43 + 2	19	2	3	3	1	3	
ROBERTS Gary	40 + 3	7	1		3	2	3	
ROBINSON Theo	17 + 20	13	1 + 1	3	0 + 3		0 + 1	
SIMPSON Robbie	4 + 9		0 + 2				1	1
SKARZ Joe	14 + 1		2		1		2	
SMITHIES Alex	46		2		3		4	
TROTMAN Neal	21	2					2	
WILLIAMS Robbie	13 + 4	2			2	1	1 + 2	

HULL CITY (PREM: 19th)

	P/FL App	Goals	FLC App	Goals	FAC App	Goals	Others App	Goals
ALTIDORE Jozy	16 + 12	1	1	1	0 + 1			
ATKINSON Will	2		1					
BARMBY Nick	6 + 14		2					
BOATENG George	26 + 3	1	1		0 + 1			
BULLARD Jimmy	13 + 1	5						
CAIRNEY Tom	10 + 1	1	2	1	1			
COOPER Liam	1 + 1		2					
COUSIN Daniel	1 + 2							
CULLEN Mark	2 + 1	1			0 + 1			
DAWSON Andy	35	1						
DOYLE Nathan			1					
DUKE Matt	11		1					
FAGAN Craig	20 + 5	2	1					
FEATHERSTONE Nicky			2					
FOLAN Caleb	7 + 1	2						
GARCIA Richard	14 + 4				1			
GARDNER Anthony	24							
GEOVANNI	16 + 10	3	0 + 1	1	1		1	1
GHILAS Kamel	6 + 7	1	1 + 1		1			
HALMOSI Peter			2		1			
HUNT Stephen	27	6						
KILBANE Kevin	15 + 6	1	0 + 2		1			
McSHANE Paul	26 + 1		0 + 1					
MARNEY Dean	15 + 1	1	0 + 1					
MENDY Bernard	15 + 6		1		1			
MOUYOKOLO Steven	19 + 2	1	1		1			
MYHILL Bo	27							
OLOFINJANA Seyi	11 + 8	1						
SONKO Ibrahima	9							
TURNER Michael	4							
VENNEGOOR OF HESSELINK Jan	17 + 14	3	1		1			
WARNER Tony			1					
ZAKI Amr	2 + 4							
ZAYATTE Kamil	21 + 2	2	1		1			

IPSWICH TOWN (CHAMP: 15th)

	P/FL App	Goals	FLC App	Goals	FAC App	Goals	Others App	Goals
AINSLEY Jack			1					
BALKESTEIN Pim	8 + 1		1					
BEGOVIC Asmir	6							
BROWN Troy	0 + 1							
BRUCE Alex	12 + 1	1	2					
CLARK Billy	0 + 3							
COLBACK Jack	29 + 8	4	2		2	1		
COUNAGO Pablo	11 + 16	2	1		0 + 1	1		
DELANEY Damien	36		1		2			
EASTMAN Tom	1							
EDWARDS Carlos	21 + 7	2			1 + 1			
GARVAN Owen	14 + 11		1		1 + 1	1		
HEALY Colin	3		2					
HEALY David	5 + 7	1						
JOHN Stern	5 + 2	1			2			
LAMBE Reggie			1					
LEADBITTER Grant	36 + 2	3			2			
LEE-BARRETT Arran	12 + 1				2			
McAULEY Gareth	40 + 1	5			2			
MARTIN Lee	9 + 7	1	1		0 + 1			
MURPHY Brian	16							
MURPHY Daryl	18	6						
NORRIS David	24	1	1					
O'CONNOR Shane	11 + 1		0 + 1					
PETERS Jaime	22 + 10	1			2			
PRISKIN Tamas	9 + 8	1	1	1	0 + 1			
QUINN Alan	8 + 11		2	1				
ROSENIOR Liam	26 + 3	1			2			
SMITH Tommy	11 + 3		1					
STEAD Jon	13 + 9	6						
SUPPLE Shane			1					
TROTTER Liam	11 + 1							
UPSON Ed			0 + 2					
WALTERS Jon	43	8	0 + 2		2			
WICKHAM Connor	9 + 17	4	1 + 1	2	0 + 1			
WRIGHT David	25 + 1	1	2		1			
WRIGHT Richard	12		1					

LEEDS UNITED (DIV 1: 2nd)

	P/FL App	Goals	FLC App	Goals	FAC App	Goals	Others App	Goals
ANKERGREN Casper	27 + 2				6		4	
BECCHIO Luciano	32 + 5	15	1 + 2		3 + 2	2	1 + 1	
BECKFORD Jermaine	38 + 4	25	2		6	5	2	1
BROMBY Leigh	31 + 1	1			5		2	
CAPALDI Tony	3		1 + 1					
COLLINS Neill	9							
CROWE Jason	16 + 1	1	3		3 + 1		3	2
DICKOV Paul	1 + 3							
DOYLE Micky	42		3		6		1	
EPHRAIM Hogan	1 + 2						1	
GRADEL Max	11 + 21	6					2 + 1	
GRELLA Mike	3 + 14	1	2 + 1		1 + 3	3	3 + 1	1
HIGGS Shane	19				3			
HOWSON Jonny	39 + 6	4	3		6	1	2	

	P/FL App	Goals	FLC App	Goals	FAC App	Goals	Others App	Goals
HUGHES Andy	38 + 1		3		5		4	
HUNTINGTON Paul			1					
JOHNSON Brad	26 + 10	7	3		4		2 + 2	
KANDOL Tresor	0 + 10	2			0 + 1	1	2	
KILKENNY Neil	24 + 11	2	0 + 3		5		4 + 1	2
KISNORBO Paddy	29	1	2		3		0 + 1	
LOWRY Shane	11						1	
McSHEFFREY Gary	9 + 1	1					1	
MARTIN David							1	
MICHALIK Lubo	7 + 6	1	2		3 + 1		4	
NAYLOR Richard	29	2			3		5	
PARKER Ben	2 + 2							
PRUTTON David	1 + 5						2 + 1	
ROBINSON Andy	0 + 6						1 + 1	1
RUI MARQUES	5		1					
SHOWUNMI Enoch	0 + 7		1 + 2	1			0 + 2	
SNODGRASS Rob	40 + 4	7	3	2	5 + 1		4	1
SOMMA Davide							0 + 1	
VOKES Sam	8	1					1 + 1	
WATT Sanchez	1 + 5							
WHITE Aidan	4 + 4				1 + 4			

LEICESTER CITY (CHAMP: 5th)

	P/FL App	Goals	FLC App	Goals	FAC App	Goals	Others App	Goals
ADAMS Nicky	1 + 17		2	1				
BERNER Bruno	34 + 1	4					2	
BROWN Wayne	38 + 1				1			
BRUCE Alex	2 + 1						2	
CAMPBELL DJ	0 + 3							
DICKOV Paul	0 + 1		0 + 1					
DYER Lloyd	25 + 8	3	0 + 1		1		2	
FRYATT Matty	26 + 3	11	2	1	1 + 1		1 + 1	1
GALLAGHER Paul	31 + 10	7	1		1 + 1		2	
GRADEL Max			0 + 1					
HOBBS Jack	44		1		2		2	
HOWARD Steve	17 + 19	5	1		1		1	
KERMORGANT Yann	9 + 11	1	0 + 1		1 + 1		0 + 2	
KING Andy	37 + 6	9	1		1		2	1
LOGAN Conrad	1 + 1							
McGIVERN Ryan	9 + 3				2			
MORRISON Michael	30 + 1	2	2		2		1	
NEILSON Robbie	19		1		1			
N'GUESSAN Dany	16 + 11	3	2	1	1 + 1	2	0 + 1	
OAKLEY Matt	37 + 1		2		2			
O'NEILL Luke	0 + 1		1					
POWELL Chris	2		2					
SOLANO Nobby	6 + 5						2	
SPEARING Jay	6 + 1	1					1 + 1	
TUNCHEV Aleksandar	1 + 1		1					
VAUGHAN James	2 + 6	1						
WAGHORN Martyn	27 + 16	12	0 + 1		1		1 + 1	
WEALE Chris	45		2		2		2	
WELLENS Richie	41	1	1		2		2	

LEYTON ORIENT (DIV 1: 17th)

	P/FL App	Goals	FLC App	Goals	FAC App	Goals	Others App	Goals
ADAMS Nicky	6							
ASHWORTH Luke	7 + 3				1	1	2	
BAKER Harry	0 + 4						2	
BRIGGS Matt	1							
CAVE-BROWN Andrew	12 + 4						2	
CHAMBERS Adam	26 + 3	1	0 + 1		1		2	
CHORLEY Ben	42	1	2		2		1	
DANIELS Charlie	40 + 1		2		2		2	
DEMETRIOU Jason	29 + 10	1	2		2		2	1
DORAN Aaron	6							
JARVIS Ryan	34 + 8	8	1 + 1		0 + 2		2	
JONES Jamie	36		1				2	
LICHAJ Eric	9	1						
McGLEISH Scott	36 + 6	12	0 + 1		2			
MELLIGAN JJ	14 + 2	1	2	1	1			
MKANDAWIRE Tamika	43	7	2		1		1	
MORRIS Glenn	10 + 1		1 + 1		2			
O'LEARY Kris	1 + 2							
PATULEA Adrian	4 + 17	1	2	1	1 + 1		1 + 1	1
PIRES Loick	0 + 8		0 + 1		1		1 + 1	
PURCHES Stephen	30 + 1	1	2		2			
SCOWCROFT James	13 + 13		1		1		1 + 1	
SMITH Jimmy	34 + 6	2	1		2			
SPICER John	9	1						
SUMMERFIELD Luke	14						1	
TEHOUE Jonathan	5 + 11	2						
THORNTON Sean	28 + 2	7	0 + 1		2		0 + 1	
TOWNSEND Andros	17 + 5	2	2				1 + 1	

LINCOLN CITY (DIV 2: 20th)

	P/FL App	Goals	FLC App	Goals	FAC App	Goals	Others App	Goals
ADAMS Nathan	0 + 2							
ANDERSON Joe	23				1			
BAKER Nathan	17 + 1							
BENNETT Lee	0 + 1							
BROUGHTON Drewe	7							
BROWN Aaron	14 + 3		1		1	1	1	
BURCH Rob	46		1		3		1	
BUTCHER Richard	10 + 5		1					
CLARKE Jamie	14 + 6	1	1		2	3		
CLARKE Shane	21 + 8		1		2		1	
CLUCAS Sam							1	
COLEMAN-CARR Luca	0 + 1							
CONNOR Paul	8 + 7	1	1				1	
FACEY Delroy	9 + 1	1						
FAGAN Chris	10 + 3	3	0 + 1		2	1	0 + 1	
GILMOUR Brian	14 + 2	2			1 + 1			
GORDON Michael	4 + 1							
GREEN Paul	13 + 2				1			
HEATH Joe	3 + 1				1			
HERD Chris	20	4			2			
HONE Daniel	16 + 1	1					1	
HOWE Rene	14 + 3	5	1		1 + 1		1	
HUGHTON Cian	41	4	1		3		1	
HUTCHINSON Andrew	0 + 10						1	
JOHN-LEWIS Lenny	7 + 17	1			1 + 1		0 + 1	
KELTIE Clark	9 + 2							
KERR Scott	36 + 3				2		1	
KOVACS Janos	14	1			2			
LENNON Steven	15 + 4	3						
LICHAJ Eric	6							
OAKES Stefan	11 + 5		1					
PEARCE Ian	5 + 5				0 + 1			
PULIS Tony	7				1			
SAUNDERS Matthew	17 + 1	3			1			
SMITH Khano	4 + 1				1			
SOMMA Davide	14	9						
STEPHENS David	3							
SWAIBU Moses	29 + 5	1	1		2		1	
TORRES Sergio	7 + 1	1			1		1	1
UWEZU Michael	0 + 2				0 + 1			
WATTS Adam	18				2			

LIVERPOOL (PREM: 7th)

	P/FL App	Goals	FLC App	Goals	FAC App	Goals	Others App	Goals
AGGER Daniel	23				1		12	1
AQUILANI Alberto	9 + 9	1	0 + 1		1 + 1		3 + 2	1
AURELIO Fabio	8 + 6		1				3 + 4	
AYALA Daniel	2 + 3							
BABEL Ryan	9 + 16	4	2		0 + 1		5 + 5	2
BENAYOUN Yossi	19 + 11	6	0 + 1		1 + 1		9 + 3	3
CARRAGHER Jamie	37		1		2		13	
CAVALIERI Diego			2		1		1	
DARBY Stephen	0 + 1				1		1	
DEGEN Philipp	3 + 4		2		1		0 + 1	
DOSSENA Andrea	1 + 1		1				1 + 1	
ECCLESTON Nathan	0 + 1		0 + 1					
EL ZHAR Nabil	1 + 2						0 + 4	
GERRARD Steven	32 + 1	9	0 + 1		2	1	13	2
INSUA Emiliano	30 + 1		1	1	2		10	
JOHNSON Glen	24 + 1	3	0 + 1				9	
KELLY Martin	0 + 1						1 + 1	
KUYT Dirk	35 + 2	9	1		2		13	2
KYRGIAKOS Sotirios	13 + 1	1	2				3 + 2	
LUCAS	32 + 3						12 + 1	1
MASCHERANO Javier	31 + 3		1				12 + 1	1
N'GOG David	10 + 14	5	2		1 + 1		5 + 4	2
PACHECO Daniel	0 + 4						0 + 3	
PLESSIS Damien			1					
REINA Pepe	38				1		13	
RIERA Albert	9 + 3		1				2 + 1	
ROBINSON Jack	0 + 1							
RODRIGUEZ Maxi	14 + 3	1						
SKRTEL Martin	16 + 3	1	1 + 1		1 + 1		5 + 1	
SPEARING Jay	1 + 2		2					
TORRES Fernando	20 + 2	18			2		7 + 1	4
VORONIN Andriy	1 + 7						1 + 2	

MACCLESFIELD TOWN (DIV 2: 19th)

	P/FL App	Goals	FLC App	Goals	FAC App	Goals	Others App	Goals
BELL Lee	37 + 5	2	0 + 1		1			
BENCHERIF Hamza	19	5	1				1	
BOLLAND Paul	17 + 10	1	1				1	
BRAIN Jon	41		1				1	
BRISLEY Shaun	29 + 4	1	1		1		1	1

	P/FL App	Goals	FLC App	Goals	FAC App	Goals	Others App	Goals
BROWN Nat	37 + 1	4			0 + 1		1	
BUTCHER Richard	8	2						
DANIEL Colin	34 + 4	3	1		1		1	
DRAPER Ross	28 + 1	1	1		1			
HESSEY Sean	27							
KIRK Tyrone			1					
LINDFIELD Craig	12 + 6	2						
LOWE Matt	7 + 3							
MILLS Greg	0 + 1							
MORGAN Paul	35 + 1		1		1			
MUKENDI Vinny	8 + 1	1						
REED Steve							1	
REID Izak	34 + 3		0 + 1		1		1	
ROONEY John	14 + 11	1	1		1		0 + 1 1	
SAPPLETON Ricky	18 + 6	7			0 + 1		1	
SINCLAIR Emile	33 + 9	7			1		1	
THOMAS Michael	0 + 4							
TIPTON Matthew	11 + 20	5	0 + 1		0 + 1		1	
TREMARCO Carl	27 + 2		1		1			
VEIGA	5							
WILSON Kyle	0 + 4							
WRIGHT Ben	25 + 14	6	1		1			

MANCHESTER CITY (PREM: 5th)

	P/FL App	Goals	FLC App	Goals	FAC App	Goals	Others App	Goals
ADEBAYOR Emmanuel	25 + 1	14	2 + 1		2			
BARRY Gareth	34	2	6	1	2 + 1			
BELLAMY Craig	26 + 6	10	4 + 1		1 + 2	1		
BENJANI	1 + 1		0 + 2		2	1		
BOYATA Dedryck	1 + 2		2		2			
BRIDGE Wayne	23		3		2			
CUNNINGHAM Greg	0 + 2				0 + 1			
DE JONG Nigel	30 + 4		4 + 1		3			
DUNNE Richard	2							
FULOP Marton	3							
GARRIDO Javier	7 + 2	1	2		1			
GIVEN Shay	35		6		3			
IBRAHIM Abdi	0 + 1				1			
IRELAND Stephen	16 + 6	2	4 + 1	1	3			
JOHNSON Adam	14 + 2	1						
JOHNSON Michael	0 + 1		0 + 1	1				
KOMPANY Vincent	21 + 4	2	3 + 1		3			
LESCOTT Joleon	17 + 1	1	4	1	2			
NIELSEN Gunnar	0 + 1							
NIMELY Alex	0 + 1							
ONUOHA Nedum	5 + 5	1	0 + 1		2	1		
PETROV Martin	8 + 8	4	0 + 1		3	1		
RICHARDS Micah	19 + 4	3	4		2			
ROBINHO	6 + 4		1		1	1		
SANTA CRUZ Roque	6 + 13	3	1	1	0 + 2			
SYLVINHO	6 + 4		1 + 1		2 + 1	1		
TAYLOR Stuart					1			
TEVEZ Carlos	32 + 3	23	6	6	0 + 1			
TOURE Kolo	31	1	3	1	1			
VIEIRA Patrick	8 + 5	1			0 + 1			
WEISS Vladimir			0 + 3	1	1			
WRIGHT-PHILLIPS Shaun	19 + 11	4	6	2	1 + 1	1		
ZABALETA Pablo	23 + 4		4		3 + 1			

MANCHESTER UNITED (PREM: 2nd)

	P/FL App	Goals	FLC App	Goals	FAC App	Goals	Others App	Goals
ANDERSON	10 + 4	1	3		1		5	
BERBATOV Dimitar	24 + 9	12	2		1		2 + 5	
BROWN Wes	18 + 1		4 + 1		1		2 + 2	
CARRICK Michael	22 + 8	3	4 + 1	1			7 + 2	1
DE LAET Ritchie	2		1 + 2					
DIOUF Biram	0 + 5	1	0 + 1					
EVANS Jonny	18		5		1		4	
EVRA Patrice	37 + 1		3				8 + 2	
FABIO	1 + 4		2		1		2 + 1	
FERDINAND Rio	12 + 1		1				7	
FLETCHER Darren	29 + 1	4	3				7 + 1	1
FOSTER Ben	9		1				3	
GIBSON Darron	6 + 9	2	2 + 1	2	1		3 + 1	1
GIGGS Ryan	20 + 5	5	2	1	0 + 1		1 + 3	1
HARGREAVES Owen	0 + 1							
KING Josh			0 + 1					
KUSZCZAK Tomasz	8		3		1		2	
MACHEDA Federico	1 + 4	1	2 + 1				2	
NANI	19 + 4	4	2 + 1				9	3
NEVILLE Gary	15 + 2		2 + 1		1		6	
OBERTAN Gabriel	1 + 6		2		1		1 + 2	
O'SHEA John	12 + 3	1	1				3 + 1	
OWEN Michael	5 + 14	3	3 + 1	2	0 + 1		3 + 4	4
PARK Ji-Sung	10 + 7	3					6 + 1	1
RAFAEL	8		2				3 + 1	

	P/FL App	Goals	FLC App	Goals	FAC App	Goals	Others App	Goals
ROONEY Wayne	32	26	2 + 1	2	1		7 + 1	6
SCHOLES Paul	24 + 4	3	1 + 1	1			7 + 1	3
TOSIC Zoran			0 + 2					
VALENCIA Antonio	29 + 5	5	2 + 2		0 + 1		6 + 4	2
VAN DER SAR Edwin	21		2				6	
VIDIC Nemanja	24	1	2				7	
WELBECK Danny	1 + 4		3	2	1		2	

MIDDLESBROUGH (CHAMP: 11th)

	P/FL App	Goals	FLC App	Goals	FAC App	Goals	Others App	Goals
ALIADIERE Jeremie	16 + 4	4	1		1			
ARCA Julio	26 + 8		1		1			
BENNETT Joe	10 + 2		0 + 1					
BENT Marcus	3 + 4		1		1			
COYNE Danny	22 + 1		1		1			
DIGARD Didier	4 + 5							
EMNES Marvin	12 + 4	1	1		0 + 1			
FLOOD Willo	11	1						
FOLAN Caleb	0 + 1	1						
FRANKS Jonathan	9 + 14	3			1			
GROUNDS Jonathan	16 + 4							
HINES Seb	2							
HOYTE Justin	23 + 7	1	1		1			
HUTH Robert	4		1					
JOHNSON Adam	25 + 1	11	1	1	1			
JONES Brad	24							
KILLEN Chris	15 + 2	3	1					
KITSON Dave	6	3						
LITA Leroy	23 + 17	8	0 + 1					
McDONALD Scott	12 + 1	4						
McMAHON Tony	20 + 1		0 + 1		1			
McMANUS Stephen	16	1						
MILLER Lee	6 + 4							
NAUGHTON Kyle	12 + 3							
O'NEIL Gary	35 + 1	4	1		1			
OSBOURNE Isaiah	9							
O'SHEA Jay	1 + 1							
POGATETZ Manny	13							
RIGGOTT Chris	4 + 2				1			
ROBSON Barry	18	5						
ST LEDGER Sean	14 + 1	2						
TAYLOR Andrew	8 + 4		1					
TUNCAY	0 + 3	2						
WALKER Josh	1							
WHEATER David	42		1		1			
WILLIAMS Luke	2 + 2				0 + 1			
WILLIAMS Rhys	31 + 1	2	1		1			
YEATES Mark	11 + 8	1	1		0 + 1			

MILLWALL (DIV 1: 3rd)

	P/FL App	Goals	FLC App	Goals	FAC App	Goals	Others App	Goals
ABDOU Jimmy	43		1		5		4	
ALEXANDER Gary	8 + 7	1	2	1			1 + 2	
BARRON Scott	12 + 11		2		0 + 1		3	
BATT Shaun	10 + 6	3					1	
BOLDER Adam	5 + 6		0 + 1		0 + 1		0 + 1	
CRAIG Tony	29 + 1	2			2		3	
DUNNE Alan	29 + 3	2	2		3 + 1	1	1	
FORDE David	46		2		5		3	
FRAMPTON Andy	20 + 1	2	2		4		1 + 1	
FRIEND George	4 + 2						1	
FUSEINI Ali	10 + 5		2				1	
GRABBAN Lewis	5 + 6		0 + 1		3 + 1	1		
GRIMES Ashley	2 + 2		0 + 2		0 + 2		0 + 1	
HACKETT Chris	34 + 6	2	2		5		0 + 1	
HARRIS Neil	21 + 11	13	2	4	1	1	3	
HENRY James	6 + 3	5						
HUGHES-MASON Kiernan	0 + 1							
LAIRD Marc	17 + 3		1 + 1		5		1 + 1	
MARQUIS John	0 + 1							
MARTIN Dave	16 + 4	3	1		3 + 1		1	
MORISON Steve	42 + 1	20	1		5	2	3	1
OBIKA Jonathan	0 + 12	2						
PRICE Jason	5 + 10	1	0 + 1		1 + 2	2	1	
ROBINSON Paul	34	4			5	1	4	2
SCHOFIELD Danny	28 + 8	7			2 + 2	2	2	
SMITH Jack	30 + 1		2		4 + 1	1	1	
SULLIVAN John							1	
TROTTER Liam	20	1					3	
WARD Darren	30 + 1	1			2		3	

MILTON KEYNES DONS (DIV 1: 12th)

	P/FL App	Goals	FLC App	Goals	FAC App	Goals	Others App	Goals
BALDOCK Sam	11 + 9	5			2 + 1	2	2 + 2	3
BRIDGES Michael	0 + 1	1	1					
CARRINGTON Mark	15 + 5	4	1				3	1
CHADWICK Luke	39 + 1	2	0 + 1		2 + 1		4	
CHICKSEN Adam	4 + 2							

	P/FL App	P/FL Goals	FLC App	FLC Goals	FAC App	FAC Goals	Others App	Others Goals
COLLINS Charlie	2							
DAVIS Sol	5 + 5		1				2 + 1	
DEVANEY Martin	4 + 1				1 + 1	1		
DORAN Aaron	2 + 2						1	1
DOUMBE Mathias	29 + 4	1	1		2		3	
EASTER Jermaine	32 + 4	14	1	1	2 + 1	1	4 + 1	3
FLANAGAN Tom	0 + 1							
GLEESON Stephen	26 + 3				3		3 + 1	
GOBERN Lewis	7 + 13		1		0 + 1	1	1 + 3	
GOBERN Oscar	0 + 1							
GUERET Willy	43		1		3		6	
HOWELL Luke	17 + 12		1		1 + 1		3	
IBEHRE Jabo	3 + 7	1					1 + 1	
JOHNSON Jemal	12 + 5	1	1				2	
LEVEN Peter	26 + 5	4			3		3 + 3	
LEWINGTON Dean	42				3		5	1
McCRACKEN David	41		1		2		4	
MORGAN Dean	1 + 8	1			0 + 1	1	1 + 1	
O'HANLON Sean	3 + 3							
PARTRIDGE Richie	1 + 3						1	
POWELL Daniel	2	1						
POWELL Darren	19 + 5		0 + 1		2			
PUNCHEON Jason	23 + 1	7	0 + 1		2 + 1		4	1
QUASHIE Nigel	6 + 1	2					1	
RAE Alex	2 + 1						0 + 1	
RANDALL Mark	12 + 4						1 + 1	1
SEARLE Stuart	3							
STIRLING Jude	1 + 8				0 + 1		1 + 1	
SWAILES Danny	2						1 + 1	
TOWNSEND Andros	8 + 1	2						
TUNNICLIFFE James	9	1						
WILBRAHAM Aaron	31 + 4	10			3		4 + 1	2
WOODARDS Danny	23 + 6		1		2		4	
MORECAMBE (DIV 2: 4th)								
ADAMS Danny	15 + 2		1		1			
ARTELL Dave	33 + 4	7	1		1		3	1
BENTLEY Jim	27 + 1	3			1		2	
CRANEY Ian	16	2			1 + 1			
CURTIS Wayne	9 + 26	4			0 + 1		2 + 1	1
DAVIES Scott	1						0 + 1	
DRUMMOND Stewart	41 + 2	9	1		1		2	
DUFFY Mark	24 + 11	4	1		0 + 2	1	3	1
HACKNEY Simon	8	1						
HAINING Will	28 + 4	1	1		1		1	
HUNTER Garry	26 + 5	2			2		2	1
JEVONS Phil	40	18			2		1 + 1	
McLACHLAN Fraser	1							
McSTAY Henry	0 + 2		0 + 1				0 + 1	
MOSS Darren	13 + 3	1	1				3	
MULLIN Paul	36 + 2	12			2		2	
PANTHER Manny	14 + 5						0 + 1	
PARRISH Andy	34 + 1				2		2 + 1	
POOLE Matty			0 + 1					
ROCHE Barry	42		1		2		3	
SMITH Ben	3							
STANLEY Craig	31 + 9	4	1		2		2	
TAYLOR Aaron	0 + 3							
TWISS Michael	18 + 8	1	1	1	1 + 1		1	
WAINWRIGHT Neil	5 + 12		0 + 1		1		1	
WILSON Laurie	41	3	1		2		3	
NEWCASTLE UNITED (CHAMP: 1st)								
AMEOBI Shola	11 + 7	10	0 + 1	1	1 + 1			
BARTON Joey	8 + 7	1						
BEST Leon	6 + 7							
BUTT Nicky	10 + 7		1		2			
CARROLL Andy	33 + 6	17			2 + 1	2		
COLOCCINI Fabricio	37	2			3			
DONALDSON Ryan	0 + 2		1		0 + 2			
DUFF Damien	1	1						
GEREMI	3 + 4		1 + 1	1				
GUTHRIE Danny	36 + 2	4	2	1	2 + 1			
GUTIERREZ Jonas	34 + 3	4	0 + 1		2 + 1			
HALL Fitz	7							
HAREWOOD Marlon	9 + 6	5						
HARPER Steve	45							
ENRIQUE	33 + 1	1	1		2			
KADAR Tamas	6 + 7		1		2			
KHIZANISHVILI Zurab	6 + 1							
KRUL Tim	1 + 2		2		3			
LOVENKRANDS Peter	19 + 10	13	1		1 + 1	3		
LUA-LUA Kazenga	0 + 1		2					
NOLAN Kevin	44	17	1 + 1	1	2			

	P/FL App	P/FL Goals	FLC App	FLC Goals	FAC App	FAC Goals	Others App	Others Goals
PANCRATE Fabrice	5 + 11	1			3			
RANGER Nile	4 + 21	2	2		1 + 2			
ROUTLEDGE Wayne	15 + 2	3						
SIMPSON Danny	39		1		1			
SMITH Alan	31 + 1		0 + 1		2			
TAVERNIER James	1							
TAYLOR Ryan	19 + 12	4	2		3			
TAYLOR Steven	21	1	1		1			
TOZER Ben	0 + 1		1					
VAN AANHOLT Patrick	7							
VUCKIC Haris	0 + 2		1 + 1					
WILLIAMSON Mike	16							
XISCO	0 + 2							
NORTHAMPTON TOWN (DIV 2: 11th)								
AKINFENWA Bayo	36 + 4	17	0 + 1		2		0 + 1	
BECKWITH Dean	37 + 1		1		1		2	
BENJAMIN Joe	2 + 1						0 + 1	
BODEN Luke	4						1	
BROWN Simon	2							
CURTIS John	18 + 1		0 + 1		1			
DAVIS Liam	13 + 4	2			0 + 1		1	
DUNN Chris	29		1		2		3	
DYER Alex	4 + 16	2	0 + 1		0 + 1		1 + 1	
GILBERT Peter	30				1			
GILLIGAN Ryan	41 + 1	8	1		2	1	3	2
GUINAN Steve	19 + 9	4	1		2		2 + 1	3
GUTTRIDGE Luke	24 + 7	4			2	2	1	
HARRIS Seb	0 + 9	1			0 + 1			
HERBERT Courtney	8 + 15	2					0 + 1	
HINTON Craig	38 + 2		1		2		3	
HOLT Andy	31	3	1		2		2	
JACOBS Michael							1 + 1	
JOHNSON John	36	5			1		1	
KANYUKA Pat	3				1		1	
LUMLEY Billy	2							
McCREADY Chris	13 + 1		1				2 + 1	
McKAY Billy	29 + 11	8			0 + 1		0 + 1	
MARSHALL Ben	11 + 4	2	1				2	
MULLIGAN Gary	2 + 7						3	
O'FLYNN Steve	0 + 5							
OSMAN Abdul	26 + 4	2	1				1 + 1	
RODGERS Paul	24 + 7				2		2	
ROSE Romone	0 + 1		1					
STEELE Jason	13							
SWAILES Danny	3							
THORNTON Kevin	4 + 7	1						
THRELFALL Robbie	1 + 3						1	
WALKER Josh	3				1			
NORWICH CITY (DIV 1: 1st)								
ADEYEMI Tom	2 + 9		2				4	
ALNWICK Ben	3		2				1	
ASKOU Jens Berthel	21 + 1	2	1		1		3	
CURETON Jamie	3 + 3	2					2	
DALEY Luke	3 + 4		1				1 + 1	
DAWKIN Josh					0 + 1		1 + 1	
DOHERTY Gary	38	5	2		2		2	1
DRURY Adam	35		1		2		1	
DUMIC Dario							0 + 1	
ELLIOTT Stephen	4 + 6	2						
FORSTER Fraser	38				1		3	
FRANCOMB George	2						1	
GILL Matt	5 + 3		1				0 + 1	
HOLT Grant	39	24	2	3	2	3	1	
HOOLAHAN Wes	36 + 1	11	2	2	2	1	1	
HUGHES Stephen	12 + 17	3	0 + 1		0 + 1		2 + 1	
JOHNSON Oli	4 + 13	4						
LAPPIN Simon	42 + 2		1 + 1		2		2	
McDONALD Cody	4 + 13	3	1 + 1		0 + 2		1 + 3	1
McNAMEE Anthony	7 + 10	1						
McVEIGH Paul	4 + 5						2	
MARIC Goran			0 + 1				1	
MARTIN Chris	36 + 6	17	0 + 1		2	4	3	2
MARTIN Russell	26						1	
NELSON Michael	28 + 3	3			2		3	
OTSEMOBOR Jon	12 + 1	1	1		1		1 + 1	
ROSE Michael	11 + 1	1						
RUDD Declan	4 + 3				1			
RUSSELL Darel	34 + 1	3			2		2	
SMITH Korey	36 + 1	4	0 + 1		2			
SPILLANE Michael	10 + 3	1	2				1	
STEPHENS David							0 + 1	
THEOKLITOS Michael	1							

	P/FL App	P/FL Goals	FLC App	FLC Goals	FAC App	FAC Goals	Others App	Others Goals
TUDUR JONES Owain	2 + 1	1	1		0 + 1		1	
WHALEY Simon	3		2				1	
WHITBREAD Zak	1 + 3							
WIGGINS Rhoys					0 + 1		2	

NOTTINGHAM FOREST (CHAMP: 3rd)

	P/FL App	P/FL Goals	FLC App	FLC Goals	FAC App	FAC Goals	Others App	Others Goals
ADEBOLA Dele	13 + 20	3	0 + 2		1 + 1		0 + 1	1
ANDERSON Paul	33 + 4	4	2 + 1	1	1 + 1		1 + 1	
BLACKSTOCK Dexter	30 + 9	12	3	1	1		2	
BOYD George	5 + 1	1						
CAMP Lee	45				2		2	
CHAMBERS Luke	17 + 6	3	1	1	2			
COHEN Chris	44	3	3		2		2	1
DAVIES Arron			2					
EARNSHAW Rob	20 + 12	15	2		1		1 + 1	2
GARNER Joe	14 + 4	2	1 + 1		0 + 1			
GUNTER Chris	44	1	2		1 + 1		2	
LYNCH Joel	9 + 1		2					
McCLEARY Garath	1 + 23		1		1 + 1			
McGOLDRICK David	18 + 15	3	0 + 2		1		0 + 2	
McGUGAN Lewis	6 + 12	3	1 + 1	1	1		0 + 1	
McKENNA Paul	35		2 + 1		1		2	
MAJEWSKI Radoslaw	31 + 4	3	2	1	1		2	
MORGAN Wes	44	3	3		2		2	
MOUSSI Guy	21 + 6	3			1			
PERCH James	14 + 3	1			2		2	
SHOREY Nicky	9							
SMITH Paul	1		3					
TYSON Nathan	17 + 16	2	2 + 1		1 + 1		2	
WILSON Kelvin	35		1				2	

NOTTS COUNTY (DIV 2: 1st)

	P/FL App	P/FL Goals	FLC App	FLC Goals	FAC App	FAC Goals	Others App	Others Goals
AKINBIYI Ade	1 + 9				1			
BISHOP Neal	39 + 4	1	1		6		1	
CAMPBELL Sol	1							
CANHAM Sean	0 + 1							
CLAPHAM Jamie	17 + 13	1	1		5		1	
DAVIES Ben	45	15			6		1	
EDWARDS Mike	37 + 3	5	1		4		1	
FACEY Delroy	7 + 11	2			0 + 1		1	1
FOX Nathan	0 + 1							
HAMSHAW Matt	2 + 18				0 + 3			
HAWLEY Karl	14 + 17	3	1		2 + 3	1	1	
HOULT Russell	3 + 1		1		1			
HUGHES Lee	39	30	0 + 1		5	3		
HUNT Stephen	32	1	1		5	2		
JACKSON Johnnie	20 + 4	2			6	1		
JONES Dan	7						1	
LEE Graeme	31 + 1	4			3		1	
MOLONEY Brendon	18	1			1			
RAVENHILL Ricky	40	3	1		6		1	
RITCHIE Matt	12 + 4	3			1 + 1		0 + 1	
RODGERS Luke	27 + 15	13	1		0 + 5			
SCHMEICHEL Kasper	43				5		1	
THOMPSON John	38 + 2		1		5		1	
WESTCARR Craig	33 + 9	9	0 + 1		5 + 1	1	1	1

OLDHAM ATHLETIC (DIV 1: 16th)

	P/FL App	P/FL Goals	FLC App	FLC Goals	FAC App	FAC Goals	Others App	Others Goals
ABBOTT Pawel	38 + 1	13	0 + 1		1			
ALESSANDRA Lewis	0 + 1		0 + 1					
ALJOFREE Hasney	1							
BEMBO-LETA Djeny					0 + 1			
BLACK Paul	12 + 1	1						
BLACKMAN Nick	6 + 6	1			1			
BRILL Dean	28		1		1			
BROOKE Ryan	2 + 13	1			0 + 1		0 + 1	
BYFIELD Darren	0 + 3		1					
COLBECK Joe	18 + 9	1			1			
EAVES Tom	0 + 15							
FLAHAVAN Darryl	18							
FURMAN Dean	32 + 6		1		1		1	
GILBERT Peter	5		1					
GOODWIN Jim	8							
GREGAN Sean	46	1	1		1		1	
GUY Lewis	12	3						
HAZELL Reuben	41	3	1		1		1	
HEFFERNAN Paul	4	1						
HILLS Lee	3				1			
HOLDSWORTH Andy	11 + 1		1		1			
JACOBSON Joe	14 + 1							
LEE Kieran	16 + 8	1			0 + 1		1	
LOMAX Kelvin	11 + 4							
MARROW Alex	26 + 6	1			1			
MILLAR Kirk	2 + 4							

	P/FL App	P/FL Goals	FLC App	FLC Goals	FAC App	FAC Goals	Others App	Others Goals
NARDIELLO Danny	2							
O'GRADY Chris			1					
PARKER Keigan	17 + 10	2	0 + 1		1			
PRICE Jason	7	1	1					
ROWNEY Chris	0 + 1						0 + 1	
SHEEHAN Alan	8	1					1	
SMALLEY Deane	23 + 6	3			1			
STEPHENS Dale	24 + 2	2						
TAYLOR Chris	27 + 5	1	1		1			
TIMAR Krisztian	2							
WHITAKER Danny	31 + 10	2	1		0 + 1		1	1
WORTHINGTON Jon	11 + 5		1					

PETERBOROUGH UNITED (CHAMP: 24th)

	P/FL App	P/FL Goals	FLC App	FLC Goals	FAC App	FAC Goals	Others App	Others Goals
AMOS Ben	1							
ANDREW Danny	2							
BATT Shaun	5 + 15	2	2 + 2		0 + 1			
BENNETT Ryan	20 + 2	1	1		1			
BOYD George	32	9	4	3	1			
COUTTS Paul	13 + 3		1		1			
DAY Jamie	2 + 3		0 + 1					
DIAGOURAGA Toumani	18 + 1		4					
DICKINSON Liam	9	3						
FRECKLINGTON Lee	26 + 9	2	4	2	1			
GEOHAGHON Exodus	17 + 2	1						
GILBERT Kerrea	7 + 3							
GREEN Dominic	6 + 5	1			0 + 1			
GRIFFITHS Scott	20				1			
KEATES Dean	2 + 4	1	0 + 1					
KORANTENG Nathan	3 + 1							
LEE Charlie	28 + 5	2	2 + 1		1			
LEWIS Joe	43		4		1			
LITTLE Mark	9							
LIVERMORE Jake	9	1						
McCRAE Romone	0 + 2							
MACKAIL-SMITH Craig	39 + 4	10	3	1	1			
McKEOWN James	2 + 2		0 + 1					
McLEAN Aaron	30 + 5	7	4	1	1			
McLEOD Izale	2 + 2							
MARTIN Russell	8 + 2		2 + 2					
MILLS Danny	1 + 2							
MORGAN Craig	33 + 1	1	3		1			
PEARCE Krystian	0 + 2		2 + 1					
REID Reuben	5 + 8							
ROSE Danny	4 + 2							
ROWE Tommy	26 + 6	2	3		1			
SIMPSON Josh	8 + 13	2						
TORRES Sergio	7 + 2							
WHELPDALE Chris	27 + 2	1	1 + 1	1	1			
WILLIAMS Tom	14 + 1		2	1	1			
WRIGHT Ben	0 + 4		0 + 1					
ZAKUANI Gabby	28 + 1		3					

PLYMOUTH ARGYLE (CHAMP: 23rd)

	P/FL App	P/FL Goals	FLC App	FLC Goals	FAC App	FAC Goals	Others App	Others Goals
ARNASON Kari	32	2			2			
BARKER Chris	10 + 4				2			
BARNES Ashley	3 + 4	1	0 + 1		1			
BHASERA Onismor	7							
BLAKE Darcy	5 + 2				2			
BOLASIE Yala	8 + 8	1			1			
CHESTER James	2 + 1							
CLARK Chris	28 + 9	1	0 + 1		2			
COOPER Kenny	0 + 7							
DUGUID Karl	40 + 2	1	1		2			
ECKERSLEY Richard	7							
FALLON Rory	25 + 8	5	1		2			
FLETCHER Carl	41	4			2			
FOLLY Yoann	4 + 3							
GOW Alan	8 + 6	2						
GRAY David	12							
JOHNSON Damien	20	2						
JOHNSON Reda	23 + 2							
JUDGE Alan	28 + 9	5	1		2			
LARRIEU Romain	25		1		2			
LEONARD Ryan	0 + 1							
LOWRY Shane	13							
MACKIE Jamie	42	8	1		1			
MacLEAN Steve	3		1					
McNAMEE David	6 + 3		1		0 + 2			
MASON Joe	5 + 14	3						
NGALA Bondz	9							
NOONE Craig	3 + 14	1	0 + 1		0 + 1			
PATERSON Jim	11 + 1		1					
SAWYER Gary	28 + 1	1	1		2			

	P/FL App	Goals	FLC App	Goals	FAC App	Goals	Others App	Goals
SEIP Marcel	5		1					
SHERIDAN Cillian	5 + 8				0 + 1			
STOCKDALE David	21							
SUMMERFIELD Luke	9 + 3		1	1	2			
TIMAR Krisztian	6 + 1	1						
WRIGHT-PHILLIPS Bradley	12 + 3	4			0 + 1			
PORTSMOUTH (PREM: 20th)								
ASHDOWN Jamie	5 + 1		1					
BASINAS Angelos	7 + 5		2		1 + 2			
BEGOVIC Asmir	8 + 1		3		3			
BELHADJ Nadir	16 + 3	3	4		2 + 1	1		
BEN HAIM Tal	21 + 1		1		1			
BOATENG Kevin	20 + 2	3			5	2		
BROWN Michael	22 + 2	2	2 + 1		6			
DINDANE Aruna	18 + 1	8	2	1	3	1		
DIOP Papa	9 + 3				5 + 2			
DISTIN Sylvain	3							
FINNAN Steve	20 + 1				4			
HREIDARSSON Hermann	17	1	1		5			
HUGHES Richard	9 + 1		2 + 1	1	1 + 2			
JAMES David	25				4			
KABOUL Younes	19	3	4		2			
KANU	6 + 17	2	0 + 4	2	0 + 1			
KRANJCAR Niko	4		1	1				
MAHOTO Gauthier			0 + 1					
MOKOENA Aaron	21 + 2		2 + 1		4	1		
MULLINS Hayden	15 + 3		2		4 + 2			
NUGENT David	0 + 3		0 + 1					
O'HARA Jamie	25 + 1	2			3	1		
OWUSU-ABEYIE Quincy	3 + 7				0 + 1	1		
PIQUIONNE Frederic	26 + 8	5	2 + 2	3	6 + 1	3		
RITCHIE Matt	1 + 1							
ROCHA Ricardo	10				2			
SMITH Tommy	12 + 4	1			2			
SOWAH Lennard	3 + 2							
UTAKA John	10 + 8	1	3	1	3 + 4	2		
VANDEN BORRE Anthony	15 + 4		4	1	2			
WARD Joel	1 + 2		1					
WEBBER Danny	4 + 13	1	3	2	1 + 3			
WILSON Marc	28		1 + 1		6			
YEBDA Hassan	15 + 3	2	3		2			
PORT VALE (DIV 2: 10th)								
ANYON Joe	7							
COLLINS Lee	45	1	3		3		2	
DAVIES Craig	22 + 2	7						
DODDS Louis	33 + 11	6	1		1 + 1	1	2	1
FRASER Tommy	33 + 5	1	3		1		2	
GLOVER Danny	0 + 3				0 + 1			
GRIFFITH Anthony	38 + 2		2 + 1		3		1 + 1	
GUY Jamie	0 + 3				0 + 1		1 + 1	
HALDANE Lewis	29 + 8	3	1		3		1 + 1	1
HORSFIELD Geoff	1 + 8		0 + 2		0 + 1			
HOWLAND David	0 + 4				0 + 1		0 + 1	
JARRETT Jason	7 + 2				2 + 1		1	
JORGENSEN Claus	0 + 4		0 + 1					
LAWRIE James	0 + 3						0 + 1	
LOFT Doug	21 + 11	3	3		2		2	
McCOMBE John	37 + 3	3	3		3		2	1
McCRORY Damien	2 + 3							
MARTIN Chris	39		3		3		2	
MORSY Sam	0 + 1							
OWEN Gareth	40		3		1		2	
PROSSER Luke	2	1			1			
RICHARDS Marc	45 + 1	20	3	2	3		1 + 1	1
RICHMAN Simon	0 + 5		0 + 1					
RIGG Sean	9 + 17	3						
STOCKLEY Sam	8 + 1		2				1	
TAYLOR Kris	38 + 3	3	3	1	3		2	
TAYLOR Rob	25 + 14	8	2 + 1	1	2		1	1
YATES Adam	25 + 7		1 + 1		2		1	
PRESTON NORTH END (CHAMP: 17th)								
BARTON Adam	1							
BROWN Chris	24 + 19	6	2 + 1	4	2		1	
CARTER Darren	11 + 12		3		2	1		
CHAPLOW Richard	29 + 2	2	0 + 2		2			
CHILVERS Liam	20 + 3		3					
COLLINS Neill	19 + 2	1			1			
COUTTS Paul	13	1						
DAVIDSON Callum	25 + 2	5			2			
ELLIOTT Stephen	3 + 6	1	3	1	0 + 1			
HART Michael	10 + 1		3		1			

	P/FL App	Goals	FLC App	Goals	FAC App	Goals	Others App	Goals
HENDERSON Wayne	1 + 1							
JAMES Matthew	17 + 1	2						
JONES Billy	42 + 2	4	2		1			
LONERGAN Andy	45		3		2			
MAWENE Youl	18 + 1		2		1			
MAYOR David	4 + 3				0 + 1			
MELLOR Neil	29 + 10	10	0 + 3	1	0 + 2			
NICHOLSON Barry	3 + 1		1	1				
NOLAN Eddie	15 + 4		2		1			
PARKIN Jon	26 + 17	10	1		1 + 1	3		
PARRY Paul	12 + 5	2	1 + 1					
PROCTOR Jamie	0 + 1							
ST LEDGER Sean	30	2	1		2			
SEDGWICK Chris	25 + 9	1	2		2	1		
SUMULIKOSKI Velice	9 + 6		2		0 + 1			
TONGE Michael	7							
TREACY Keith	8 + 9	2						
TROTMAN Neal			0 + 1	1				
WALLACE Ross	40 + 1	7	2		2			
WARD Elliott	4							
WELBECK Danny	8	2						
WILLIAMS Tom	8 + 2							
QUEENS PARK RANGERS (CHAMP: 13th)								
AGYEMANG Patrick	5 + 12	3	2		2			
AINSWORTH Gareth	0 + 1		0 + 1					
BALANTA Angelo	1 + 3							
BENT Marcus	2 + 1							
BORROWDALE Gary	18 + 3		2 + 1		2			
BROWN Lee	0 + 1							
BUZSAKY Akos	29 + 10	10	3		2	1		
CERNY Radek	29		1		2			
CONNOLLY Matthew	17 + 2	2	2					
COOK Lee	8 + 8	1						
EPHRAIM Hogan	16 + 6		2 + 1	2	0 + 1			
FAURLIN Alejandro	36 + 5	1	1		2			
GERMAN Antonio	5 + 8	2			0 + 1			
GORKSS Kaspars	40 + 1	3	3		2			
HALL Fitz	12 + 2							
HEATON Tom			2					
HELGUSON Heidar	3 + 2	1			0 + 1			
HILL Matt	15 + 1							
IKEME Carl	17							
LEIGERTWOOD Mikele	39 + 1	5	3		2			
MAHON Gavin	5 + 2	1	1 + 1					
OASTLER Joe	0 + 1							
PARKER Josh	1 + 3							
PELLICORI Alessandro	1 + 7		0 + 2	1				
PRISKIN Tamas	13	1						
QUASHIE Nigel	4							
RAMAGE Peter	29 + 4	2	1					
REID Steven	1 + 1							
ROSE Romone	0 + 1							
ROUTLEDGE Wayne	25	2	2 + 1	4	2			
ROWLANDS Martin	5 + 1		1					
SIMPSON Jay	34 + 5	12	1		2	1		
STEWART Damion	30	1	3		2	1		
TAARABT Adel	32 + 9	7	0 + 2		0 + 1			
TOSIC Dusko	5							
VINE Rowan	8 + 23	1	3					
WATSON Ben	16	2						
WILLIAMS Tom	5							
READING (CHAMP: 9th)								
ANTONIO Michail	0 + 1		0 + 1					
ARMSTRONG Chris			1					
BERTRAND Ryan	44	1	1		6			
BIGNALL Nick	0 + 1		2	2				
CHURCH Simon	22 + 14	10			5 + 1	2		
CISSE Kalifa	14 + 3	1			2			
CUMMINGS Shaun	8							
DAVIES Scott	3 + 1		1					
FEDERICI Adam	46				6			
GRIFFIN Andy	21				4			
GUNNARSSON Brynjar	18 + 8		1		4 + 1			
HAMER Ben			2		0 + 1			
HARPER James	0 + 3		2					
HENRY James	1 + 2		2		0 + 1			
HOWARD Brian	30 + 4	2			3 + 2	1		
HUNT Noel	5 + 5	2	0 + 2					
INGIMARSSON Ivar	25				6			
KARACAN Jem	19 + 8				4			
KEBE Jimmy	30 + 12	10			3 + 2	2		
KELLY Julian			1					

	P/FL App	Goals	FLC App	Goals	FAC App	Goals	Others App	Goals
KHIZANISHVILI Zurab	12 + 3							
LONG Shane	22 + 9	6			2 + 3	3		
McANUFF Jobi	36	3			5			
MATEJOVSKY Marek	13 + 2		2					
MILLS Matthew	22 + 1	2	1		6			
MOONEY Dave			2	2				
O'DEA Darren	7 + 1							
PEARCE Alex	24 + 1	4	2		0 + 1			
RASIAK Grzegorz	14 + 15	9			3 + 2			
ROBSON-KANU Hal	4 + 13				0 + 1			
ROSENIOR Liam	5		1					
SIGURDSSON Gylfi	32 + 6	16	1	1	5	3		
TABB Jay	27 + 1		0 + 1		2 + 1			
THORVALDSSON Gunnar	2 + 2				0 + 1			

ROCHDALE (DIV 2: 3rd)

	P/FL App	Goals	FLC App	Goals	FAC App	Goals	Others App	Goals
ARTHUR Kenny	15		1		1		1	
ATKINSON Will	15	3						
BRIZELL Josh			0 + 1					
BROWN Chris							0 + 1	
BUCKLEY Will	12 + 3	3	1		0 + 1		1	
DAGNALL Chris	45	20	1		2		1	
DAWSON Craig	40 + 2	9	1		2	1	1	1
FIELDING Frank	18							
FLITCROFT Dave							1	
FLYNN Matt	7 + 3						1	
GLOVER Danny	0 + 2							
GRAY Reece	0 + 2							
HAWORTH Andy	3 + 4							
HEATON Tom	12							
HIGGINBOTHAM Kallum	6 + 23	3	0 + 1		0 + 2			
HOLNESS Marcus	7 + 4		1		2		1	
JONES Gary	32 + 2	4	1		2			
KENNEDY Jason	40 + 2		1		2		1	
KENNEDY Tom	44	3	1		2		1	
LE FONDRE Adam	0 + 1							
LILLIS Josh	1							
McARDLE Rory	17 + 3				2			
MANGA Marc	0 + 2				0 + 1			
OBADEYI Temitope	5 + 6	1						
O'GRADY Chris	43	22			2			
RUNDLE Adam	6 + 6	1	1		2		1	
SHAW Jon	0 + 1		0 + 1					
SPENCER Scott	0 + 4						0 + 1	
STANTON Nathan	37 + 1		1					
STEPHENS Dale	3 + 3	1						
TABERNER Danny					1			
TAYLOR Jason	23	1						
THOMPSON Joe	27 + 9	6	1		2	2	1	
TONER Ciaran	7 + 6							
WHALEY Simon	8 + 1	2						
WISEMAN Scott	33 + 3	1					0 + 1	

ROTHERHAM UNITED (DIV 2: 5th)

	P/FL App	Goals	FLC App	Goals	FAC App	Goals	Others App	Goals
BELL-BAGGIE Abdulai	2 + 9						0 + 1	
BROGAN Stephen	1 + 4	1			2 + 1	1		
BROUGHTON Drewe	6 + 10	3			1 + 1	1	0 + 2	
CUMMINS Micky	6 + 9	1	1		1			
ELLISON Kevin	36 + 3	8	1 + 1	1	2	1	4	1
FENTON Nick	34 + 1		2		2		3	
GREEN Jamie	14 + 5		2				1	
GUNNING Gavin	21						3	
HARRISON Danny	32 + 5	4	1		2 + 1		4	
JOSEPH Marc	11 + 4		1		1		1	
LAW Nicky	41 + 1	2	2		3		4	
LE FONDRE Adam	43 + 1	25			3	2	4	3
LIDDELL Andy	0 + 2		1 + 1				1	
LYNCH Mark	21 + 2				2		3	
McALLISTER Craig	7 + 1							
MARSHALL Marcus	13 + 9						0 + 1	
MILLS Pablo	34 + 3		2		1		3	
NICHOLAS Andy	7		0 + 1		2			
POPE Tom	26 + 9	3	2		2			
ROBERTS Gary	11 + 2	3			2			
RUNDLE Adam	4							
SHARPS Ian	44		1		3		4	
TAYLOR Jason	2		1				0 + 1	
TAYLOR Ryan	3 + 16		0 + 1		1 + 1		3 + 1	2
TONGE Dale	18 + 3		2		1		1	
WALKER Josh	15	3						
WARNE Paul	8 + 6	2	1	1	0 + 1		0 + 1	
WARRINGTON Andy	46		2		3		4	

SCUNTHORPE UNITED (CHAMP: 20th)

	P/FL App	Goals	FLC App	Goals	FAC App	Goals	Others App	Goals
BYRNE Cliff	34 + 2	2	2		2			
CANAVAN Niall	4 + 3	1	2 + 1	1				
FORTE Jonathan	6 + 22	2	3 + 1	1	1 + 1			
FRIEND George	2 + 2							
HAYES Paul	45	9	4	2	2	2		
HOOPER Gary	31 + 4	19	1 + 2	1	1			
JONES Rob	28	1	2		2			
LILLIS Josh	6 + 2		1		1			
McCANN Grant	36 + 6	8	2	1	1			
McDERMOTT Donal	4 + 5							
McNULTY Jimmy	2 + 1							
MAY Ben	0 + 1							
MILNE Kenny	4				0 + 2			
MIRFIN David	37	1	3		2			
MOLONEY Brendon	1 + 2							
MORRIS Ian	2 + 1							
MURPHY Joe	40		3		1			
NGALA Bondz	0 + 2							
O'CONNOR Michael	23 + 9	2	3 + 1					
RAYNES Michael	12							
SLOCOMBE Sam	0 + 1		0 + 1					
SPARROW Matt	22 + 8	1	3	1	0 + 1			
SPENCE Jordan	9		2					
THOMPSON Gary	22 + 14	9	1 + 1		2			
TOGWELL Sam	33 + 8	2	1 + 3		2			
WILLIAMS Marcus	37		4		2			
WOOLFORD Martyn	29 + 11	5	3 + 1		2			
WRIGHT Andrew	13 + 6		1					
WRIGHT Josh	24 + 11		3 + 1		1 + 1			

SHEFFIELD UNITED (CHAMP: 8th)

	P/FL App	Goals	FLC App	Goals	FAC App	Goals	Others App	Goals
BARTLEY Kyle	10 + 4							
BENNETT Ian	4 + 1		1					
BROMBY Leigh			1					
BUNN Mark	31 + 1				3			
CAMARA Henri	9 + 14	4			2			
CONNOLLY Paul	7							
COTTERILL David	3 + 11	2			2 + 1	2		
CRESSWELL Richard	28 + 3	12			2 + 1			
DAVIES Andrew	7 + 1							
EVANS Ched	21 + 12	4			2 + 1			
FORTUNE Jon	3 + 2	1			1			
FRANCE Ryan	3 + 6		1					
GEARY Derek	5 + 2				2			
HARPER James	31 + 3	4			2			
HENDERSON Darius	28 + 4	12			1 + 1			
HOWARD Brian	3 + 1		1					
IKEME Carl	2							
KALLIO Toni	8							
KENNY Paddy	2							
KILGALLON Matthew	21		1		1			
LITTLE Glen	7 + 9		1		0 + 1			
LOWTON Matthew	1 + 1							
MONTGOMERY Nick	39	1	0 + 1		3			
MORGAN Chris	37	2			3			
NAYSMITH Gary	2							
NOSWORTHY Nyron	19							
QUINN Stephen	38 + 6	4	1		3			
REID Kyel	0 + 7		1					
ROBERTSON Jordan			0 + 1					
SEIP Marcel	5 + 1				1 + 1			
SHARP Billy			1	1				
SIMONSEN Steve	7							
STEWART Jordan	15 + 8							
TAYLOR Andy	22 + 4		1		3			
TREACY Keith	12 + 4	1	0 + 1					
WALKER Kyle	26				1 + 1			
WARD Jamie	25 + 3	7			1 + 2	1		
WILLIAMSON Lee	14 + 6	3			2 + 1	1		
YEATES Mark	11 + 9	2						

SHEFFIELD WEDNESDAY (CHAMP: 22nd)

	P/FL App	Goals	FLC App	Goals	FAC App	Goals	Others App	Goals
BEEVERS Mark	32 + 3		2		1			
BUXTON Lewis	28				0 + 1			
CLARKE Leon	18 + 18	6			1			
ESAJAS Etienne	5 + 15	2	2		0 + 1			
FEENEY Warren	0 + 1							
GRANT Lee	46		2		1			
GRAY Michael	27 + 3	2	0 + 1		1			
HINDS Richard	7 + 4		1 + 1					
JEFFERS Francis	1 + 12		1 + 1		1			
JOHNSON Jermaine	29 + 5	5	1 + 1	2	0 + 1			

	P/FL App Goals	FLC App Goals	FAC App Goals	Others App Goals
McALLISTER Sean	5 + 7	2		
MILLER Tommy	10 + 10 1	2		
NOLAN Eddie	14 1			
O'CONNOR James	44 3	0 + 1	1	
POTTER Darren	46 3	2	1	
PURSE Darren	39 2	1	1	
SIMEK Frankie	9 + 3	2	1	
SOARES Tom	17 + 8 2		1	
SODJE Akpo	0 + 11	0 + 1		
SPURR Tommy	46 1	2	1	
TUDGAY Marcus	41 + 2 10	2	1	
VARNEY Luke	32 + 7 9			
WOOD Richard	10 + 1 2			
SHREWSBURY TOWN (DIV 2: 12th)				
ARESTIDOU Andreas	2			
BRADSHAW Tom	1 + 5 3			
BRIGHT Kris	4 + 22 2	0 + 1	0 + 1	1
BUTTON David	26			
CANSDELL-SHERRIFF Shane	41 1	1 1	1	1
COUGHLAN Graham	36 2	1	1	1
CURETON Jamie	10 + 2			
DEVITT Jamie	8 + 1 2			
DISLEY Craig	16 + 2 1	1		
DUNFIELD Terry	28 + 2 2	0 + 1		
ELDER Nathan	9 + 10 2		0 + 1	1
FAIRHURST Waide	10 4			
GREY Andre	0 + 4			0 + 1
HIBBERT David	37 + 1 14	1 1	1	
HOLDEN Dean	37	1		
HOOMAN Harry	1 + 1		1	1
LABADIE Joss	11 + 2 5		1	1
LANGMEAD Kelvin	44 3	1	1	1
LESLIE Steven	21 + 13 6			
McINTYRE Kevin	43 + 2 1	1	1	1
MURRAY Paul	25 + 2	1	1	1
NEAL Chris	7	1	1	1
NEAL Lewis	21 + 8 2		1	1
PHILLIPS Steve	11			
RICHARDS Will				0 + 1
RIZA Omer	1 + 7	0 + 1		
ROBINSON Jake	15 + 19 3	1 1	1	
SIMPSON Jake	14 + 4		0 + 1	0 + 1
SKARZ Joe	20			
TAYLOR Danny	2 + 1			
TAYLOR Jon	0 + 2			
VAN DEN BROEK Benjamin	5 + 6 1			
SOUTHAMPTON (DIV 1: 7th)				
ANTONIO Michail	14 + 14 3		3 + 2 2	5 + 1 2
BARNARD Lee	14 + 6 9		1 + 1	
BIALKOWSKI Bart	6 + 1		1	2
CONNOLLY David	9 + 11 5		1 2	1 + 1
DAVIS Kelvin	40	2	4	4
FONTE Jose	21			3
GILLETT Simon	0 + 2	0 + 1	0 + 1	1 + 1
GOBERN Oscar	0 + 4	0 + 1	0 + 2	
HAMMOND Dean	40 5		4 1	5
HARDING Dan	42 3	2	4	5 1
HOLMES Lee	2 + 3		1 + 1	0 + 1
JAIDI Radhi	26 + 1 1		4	3
JAMES Lloyd	28 + 2 2	2	3	4 + 1
LALLANA Adam	44 15	2 2	5 1	5 2
LAMBERT Rickie	44 + 1 30	2 1	5 2	6 3
LANCASHIRE Ollie	1 + 1	1	0 + 2	
McNISH Callum	0 + 1			
MARTIN Aaron	2			
MELLIS Jacob	7 + 5	1		1 + 1
MILLS Joseph	8 + 8		1 + 2	2 + 1
MURTY Graeme	5 + 1	2	1	
OTSEMOBOR Jon	19			
OXLADE-CHAMBERLAIN Alex	0 + 2			
PAPA WAIGO	11 + 24 5		3 1	4 + 2 4
PATERSON Matt	4 + 3 1	1 + 1	0 + 1	
PERRY Chris	11 + 1	1	4	3 + 1
PUNCHEON Jason	19 3			
RASIAK Grzegorz	1 + 2	0 + 1		
SAGANOWSKI Marek	3 + 3	1		0 + 1
SCHNEIDERLIN Morgan	35 + 2 1	1 + 1	4	4
SEABORNE Danny	11 + 5			
THOMAS Wayne	10 + 5	2	4 1	4 + 1 1
THOMSON Jake	0 + 4	0 + 1		
TROTMAN Neal	17 + 1 2			1 + 1
WOTTON Paul	12 + 14	2	2 + 1	3 + 2

	P/FL App Goals	FLC App Goals	FAC App Goals	Others App Goals
SOUTHEND UNITED (DIV 1: 23rd)				
ASANTE Kyle		0 + 1		
BALDWIN Pat	18 1			
BARNARD Lee	25 15	2 2		1
BARRETT Adam	41 2	1	1	1
BETSY Kevin	0 + 2	0 + 1		
CHRISTOPHE Jean-Francois	31 + 5 1	2	1	1
CRAWFORD Harry	2 + 5 1			
FRANCIS Simon	45 1	2	1	1
FREEDMAN Dougie	9 + 11 1	0 + 1	1	0 + 1
FRIEND George	5 + 1 1			
GRANT Anthony	38	2	1	
HEATH Matt	4	2		
HERD Johnny	17 + 3			
IBEHRE Jabo	4			
JOYCE Ian	2			
LAURENT Francis	28 + 7 6		1	1
McCORMACK Alan	40 + 1 3	2		
MALONE Scott	15 + 2			
MILDENHALL Steve	44	2	1	1
MILNER Marcus	0 + 1			
MORRISON Sean	8			
MOUSSA Franck	41 + 2 5	2 1	1	1
M'VOTO Jean-Yves	15 + 2 1	2		
O'DONOVAN Roy	3 + 1 1			1
OKAI Julian			0 + 1	
O'KEEFE Stuart	3 + 4	1		0 + 1
PATERSON Matt	9 + 7 2			
REVELL Alex	1 + 2	1 + 1		
SANKOFA Osei	10 + 2			1
SAWYER Lee	0 + 6	0 + 2		1
SCANNELL Damian	15 + 10 1		0 + 1	
SPENCER Scott	5 + 7 4			
VERNON Scott	17 4			
WALKER James	2 + 11	1 + 1	1	
WATT Sanchez	4			
WHITE John	5			
STOCKPORT COUNTY (DIV 1: 24th)				
BAKER Carl	19 + 1 9	1	1 1	2 3
BARNES Sam	2			
BIGNALL Nick	11		1	1 1
BRIDCUTT Liam	15	2		2 1
DONNELLY George	16 + 3 4			
EDWARDS Declan	0 + 1			
FISHER Tom	0 + 1		0 + 1	
FON WILLIAMS Owain	44	2		
GERRARD Paul	1			1
GRIFFIN Adam	9 + 9	0 + 1	1	1
HALLS Andy	8 + 3			1
HAVERN Gianluca	7			2
HUNTINGTON Paul	26			
IBEHRE Jabo	20 5			
JOHNSON Jemal	14 + 2 2			
JOHNSON Oli	4 + 12 1	1	1 + 1	
McNEIL Matty	4 + 1			
MULLINS Johnny	36 1	1	2	2
PARTRIDGE Richie	20 + 2 1			
PERKINS David	22			
PILKINGTON Danny	10 + 19 1	0 + 1	1	1 + 1
POOLE David	29 + 7	1 1	2 1	1 + 1
RAYNES Michael	24 + 1 1	1	1	1
RIBEIRO Christian	7			
RIGBY Lloyd	2			1
ROSE Michael	24 2	1	1	2
ROWE Danny	0 + 4			
SADLER Mat	20			
SWAILES Danny	20			
TANSEY Greg	25 + 7 2	1	1 + 1	0 + 2
THOMPSON Peter	14 + 8 2	1	2 1	1 + 1
TURNBULL Paul	24 + 6	1	2	2 2
VINCENT James	30 + 4	0 + 1	2	1 + 1
STOKE CITY (PREM: 11th)				
ARISMENDI Diego	2			
BEATTIE James	11 + 11 3	1	1	
BEGOVIC Asmir	3 + 1		1	
COLLINS Danny	22 + 3		4 + 1	
CORT Leon		3	1	
CRESSWELL Richard	1 + 1	1		
DAVIES Andrew	0 + 1	0 + 1		
DELAP Rory	34 + 2		4 + 1	
DIAO Salif	11 + 5 1		2 + 1	

	P/FL App	Goals	FLC App	Goals	FAC App	Goals	Others App	Goals
DICKINSON Carl			1					
ETHERINGTON Mattie	33 + 1	5	0 + 1	1	3	1		
DIAGNE-FAYE Abdoulaye	30 + 1	2			1			
FAYE Amdy	1							
FULLER Ricardo	22 + 13	3	0 + 1	1	5	4		
GRIFFIN Andy			2 + 1	1				
HIGGINBOTHAM Danny	23 + 1	1	2	1	3			
HUTH Robert	30 + 2	3			5			
KITSON Dave	10 + 8	3	2		0 + 2	1		
LAWRENCE Liam	14 + 11	1	2		2 + 2			
MOULT Louis	0 + 1		0 + 2					
PUGH Danny	1 + 6	1	3		0 + 3			
SHAWCROSS Ryan	27 + 1	2			3	1		
SHOTTON Ryan	1							
SIDIBE Mama	19 + 5	2	0 + 1		4 + 1			
SIMONSEN Steve	2 + 1		1		0 + 1			
SOARES Tom			2 + 1					
SONKO Ibrahima	1							
SORENSEN Thomas	33				5			
TONGE Michael			2 + 1					
TUNCAY	13 + 17	4	2		2 + 3	1		
WHELAN Glenn	25 + 8	2	1		4			
WHITEHEAD Dean	33 + 3				4	1		
WILKINSON Andy	21 + 4		1		2			

SUNDERLAND (PREM: 13th)

	P/FL App	Goals	FLC App	Goals	FAC App	Goals	Others App	Goals
BARDSLEY Phil	18 + 8				2			
BENJANI	1 + 7							
BENT Darren	38	24			2	1		
CAMPBELL Fraizer	19 + 12	4	3	1	1 + 1	2		
CANA Lorik	29 + 2		2		2			
CATTERMOLE Lee	19 + 3							
COLBACK Jack	0 + 1							
COLLINS Danny	3							
DA SILVA Paulo	12 + 4		3		2			
EDWARDS Carlos			1					
FERDINAND Anton	19 + 5		0 + 1					
FULOP Marton	12 + 1				1			
GORDON Craig	26				3		1	
HEALY David	0 + 3		0 + 2		0 + 2			
HENDERSON Jordan	23 + 10	1	3	1	2			
HUTTON Alan	11							
JONES Kenwyne	24 + 8	9	3		1			
KILGALLON Matthew	6 + 1							
LEADBITTER Grant	0 + 1		1					
LIDDLE Michael					0 + 1			
McCARTNEY George	20 + 5		2		1			
MALBRANQUE Steed	30 + 1		1 + 2		1	1		
MENSAH John	14 + 2	1	1					
MEYLER David	9 + 1				2			
MURPHY Daryl	2 + 1		1 + 2		1			
NOBLE Ryan					0 + 1			
NOSWORTHY Nyron	7 + 3		2 + 1					
REID Andy	18 + 3	2	2 + 1	2	0 + 1			
RICHARDSON Kieran	28 + 1	1	2		1			
TAINIO Teemu			1	1				
TURNER Michael	29	2	2		1			
ZENDEN Bolo	1 + 19	2	2		1			

SWANSEA CITY (CHAMP: 7th)

	P/FL App	Goals	FLC App	Goals	FAC App	Goals	Others App	Goals
ALLEN Joe	13 + 8				1			
BAUZA Guillem	3 + 3		0 + 1					
BEATTIE Craig	12 + 11	3	1					
BESSONE Fede	21		1					
BODDE Ferrie	2 + 2							
BOND Chad	1				1			
BRITTON Leon	35 + 1		2					
BUTLER Tommy	9 + 16	1	1					
COLLINS Matty	1				1			
CORNELL David			1					
COTTERILL David	14 + 7	3			1	1		
DE VRIES Dorus	46							
DOBBIE Stephen	4 + 2		1 + 1	3	0 + 1			
DYER Nathan	37 + 3	2	2					
EDGAR David	5		1					
GOWER Mark	25 + 6	1	1 + 1		0 + 1			
IDRIZAJ Besian	1 + 3		0 + 1					
JORDI LOPEZ	7 + 5		2					
KUQI Shefki	14 + 6	5	1					
MacDONALD Shaun	2 + 1							
MONK Garry	22 + 1		2	1	1	1		
MORGAN Kerry	1 + 2		1 + 1					
ORLANDI Andrea	22 + 8	1	1					
PAINTER Marcos	4		1		1			

	P/FL App	Goals	FLC App	Goals	FAC App	Goals	Others App	Goals
PINTADO Gorka	16 + 16	2	1		1			
PRATLEY Darren	33 + 3	7	1		1			
RANGEL Angel	37 + 1		1 + 1		1			
RICHARDS Ashley	10 + 5							
SERRAN Albert	3 + 3				1			
TATE Alan	39	1	2		1			
THOMAS Casey	0 + 1							
TRUNDLE Lee	2 + 17	5			0 + 1			
VAN DER GUN Cedric	20 + 5	2	1					
WILLIAMS Ashley	45 + 1	5						

SWINDON TOWN (DIV 1: 5th)

	P/FL App	Goals	FLC App	Goals	FAC App	Goals	Others App	Goals
AMANKWAAH Kevin	33 + 3	3	2		3		4 + 1	
AUSTIN Charlie	29 + 4	19	1		2		3 + 2	1
CUTHBERT Scott	39	3	1		3		5	
DARBY Stephen	12						1 + 2	
DOUGLAS Jonathan	43		2		2		5	
EASTON Craig	2 + 10		1		0 + 1		1	
FERRY Simon	40	2			3		3	
GREER Gordon	43 + 1	1	2		3	1	4	
HUTCHINSON Ben	6 + 4	1			2 + 1		2	
KENNEDY Callum	4 + 4		1 + 1		1			
LESCINEL Jean-Francois	27 + 6		1		1		4	
LUCAS David	41				2		3	
McGOVERN Jon-Paul	45	1	2	1	3		5	
MACKLIN Lloyd	1 + 8		1 + 1		0 + 1			
McNAMEE Anthony	14 + 3	1	2		1		1 + 1	1
MARSHALL Mark	1 + 6		0 + 2					
MORRISON Sean	8 + 1	1	1					
NOUBLE Frank	3 + 5							
OBADEYI Temitope	9 + 3	2	1		1			
O'BRIEN Alan	3 + 6		0 + 1		0 + 1		1 + 2	
PAYNTER Billy	37 + 5	26	2	2	3	1	3	
PEACOCK Lee	0 + 4				0 + 2		0 + 1	
PERICARD Vincent	2 + 12						0 + 2	
REVELL Alex	7 + 3	2					2	
RITCHIE Matt	0 + 4							
SHEEHAN Alan	22	1			2		2	
SMITH Phil	5 + 1				1		2 + 1	
TIMLIN Michael	6 + 15		1		1 + 2		1 + 1	
WARD Danny	24 + 4	7			1		3	2

TORQUAY UNITED (DIV 2: 17th)

	P/FL App	Goals	FLC App	Goals	FAC App	Goals	Others App	Goals
BARNES Ashley	6							
BENYON Elliot	31 + 14	11	0 + 1		3	3	2	1
BEVAN Scott	17 + 1		1		2		2	
BRANSTON Guy	16							
BROUGH Michael	0 + 1		0 + 1					
CAMARA Mo	2							
CARAYOL Mustapha	11 + 9	6	0 + 1					
CARLISLE Wayne	20 + 4	2	1		3		1 + 1	
CHARNOCK Kieran	22 + 2		1		3		2	
COLLIS Steve	1							
COX Sam	1 + 2							
ELLIS Mark	25 + 2	3			1		1	
HARGREAVES Chris	21 + 2	3			2			
HODGES Lee	2 + 3						0 + 1	
MACKLIN Lloyd	3 + 1							
MANSELL Lee	35 + 4	2			3		1	
MILLS Danny	0 + 2							
NICHOLSON Kevin	23 + 4		1		1 + 2		2	
O'KANE Eunan	5 + 11	1						
POKE Michael	28 + 1				1			
RENDELL Scott	28 + 7	12	1		2 + 1	1	1 + 1	
ROBERTSON Chris	45	2	1		2		2	
ROWE-TURNER Lathaniel	5 + 1							
SILLS Tim	12 + 6	2	1	1	1 + 2		2	1
SMITH Adam	16							
STEVENS Danny	16 + 11	1	1		0 + 3		1 + 1	2
THOMPSON Tyrone	17 + 7		1		2		2	
THOMSON Jake	13 + 2	1	1		3			
TODD Chris	9	1	1				1	
WILLIAMS Marvin	1 + 3							
WROE Nicky	45	9	1		2	3	2	1
ZEBROSKI Chris	30	6						

TOTTENHAM HOTSPUR (PREM: 4th)

	P/FL App	Goals	FLC App	Goals	FAC App	Goals	Others App	Goals
ALNWICK Ben	1							
ASSOU-EKOTTO Benoit	29 + 1	1	1		3			
BALE Gareth	18 + 5	3	3		8			
BASSONG Sebastien	25 + 3	1	3		7			
BENTLEY David	11 + 4	2	4	1	4 + 1	1		
BOATENG Kevin	0 + 1							
BUTTON David	0 + 1							

	P/FL App	P/FL Goals	FLC App	FLC Goals	FAC App	FAC Goals	Others App	Others Goals
CORLUKA Vedran	29	1	1 + 1		5			
CROUCH Peter	21 + 17	8	2 + 1	4	6	1		
CUDICINI Carlo	6 + 1		1					
DAWSON Michael	25 + 4	2	3		8			
DEFOE Jermain	31 + 3	18	2	1	6 + 1	5		
GIOVANI	0 + 1		2					
GOMES Heurelho	31		3		8			
GUDJOHNSEN Eidur	3 + 8	1			1 + 2	1		
HUDDLESTONE Tom	33	2	3 + 1	2	5 + 1			
HUTTON Alan	1 + 7		4		2			
JENAS Jermaine	9 + 10	1	2		2			
KABOUL Younes	8 + 2							
KEANE Robbie	15 + 5	6	2 + 1	2	1 + 1	1		
KING Ledley	19 + 1	2			1			
KRANJCAR Niko	19 + 5	6			5 + 3	2		
LENNON Aaron	20 + 2	3	1 + 1					
LIVERMORE Jake	0 + 1							
MODRIC Luka	21 + 4	3			7			
NAUGHTON Kyle	0 + 1		1		0 + 1			
O'HARA Jamie	0 + 2		1		1			
PALACIOS Wilson	29 + 4	1	3		6 + 1			
PAVLYUCHENKO Roman	8 + 8	5	2	1	2 + 4	4		
ROSE Danny	1	1	0 + 1		1 + 2			
WALKER Kyle	2							
WOODGATE Jonathan	3							

TRANMERE ROVERS (DIV 1: 19th)

	P/FL App	P/FL Goals	FLC App	FLC Goals	FAC App	FAC Goals	Others App	Others Goals
BAIN Kithson	0 + 10						1	
BAKAYOGO Zoumana	29				5			
BARNETT Charlie	1 + 6	1	0 + 1		1		1	
BROOMES Marlon	31	1	1		3			
CAROLE Seb	4						1	
COLLISTER Joe	1 + 2							
CRESSWELL Aaron	13 + 1		2		5		1	
CURRAN Craig	38 + 5	5	2	1	5	1	1	1
DANIELS Luke	37		2		5		1	
EDDS Gareth	24 + 11	3	1 + 1	1	4		1	
FRAUGHAN Ryan	1 + 5		0 + 1				0 + 1	
GOODISON Ian	44	3	2		5		1	
GORDON Ben	4							
GORNELL Terry	18 + 9	2	1 + 1		3	1		
GULACSI Peter	5							
GUNNING Gavin	6							
LABADIE Joss	5 + 4	3						
LOGAN Shaleum	32 + 1		1		5			
McCREADY Chris	8							
McLAREN Paul	36 + 2		2	1	2 + 1			
MAHON Alan	8 + 8	1	2		1		1	
MARTIN David	3							
O'NEILL Luke	4							
RICKETTS Michael	7 + 5	2	0 + 1		1 + 3			
ROBINSON Andy	3 + 2	1						
SAVAGE Bas	10 + 3							
SHUKER Chris	16 + 10	2	2		3 + 1	1		
SORDELL Marvin	6 + 2	1						
TAYLOR Ash	27 + 6	1	1 + 1		5	1	1	
THOMAS-MOORE Ian	41 + 2	13	1	1	3 + 1	1	0 + 1	
WELSH John	44 + 1	4	2		4		1	

WALSALL (DIV 1: 10th)

	P/FL App	P/FL Goals	FLC App	FLC Goals	FAC App	FAC Goals	Others App	Others Goals
ADKINS Sam	0 + 1							
BRADLEY Mark	19 + 9				2			
BYFIELD Darren	31 + 6	10			2		1	
DEENEY Troy	42	14	0 + 1		2		1	
GILMARTIN Rene	22		1				1	
GRAY Julian	17 + 1	4						
HUGHES Mark	24 + 2	1			2			
INCE Clayton	24 + 1				2			
JONES Steve	25 + 5	9	1		2	1	0 + 1	
McDONALD Clayton	24 + 2	1					1	
MATTIS Dwayne	34	2	1		2		1	
NICHOLLS Alex	20 + 17	4	1	1	0 + 1		0 + 1	
O'KEEFE Josh	8 + 5							
PARKIN Sam	7 + 17	3	1		0 + 1		0 + 1	
RICHARDS Matt	39 + 1	4	1		2		1	
ROBERTS Steve	1		1					
SANSARA Netan	17				2			
SMITH Manny	30 + 3	4	1		2		1	
TAUNDRY Richard	24 + 6	3	1				1	
TILL Peter	18 + 10				0 + 1		1	
VINCENT Jamie	37 + 1		1				1	
WESTLAKE Darryl	20 + 2				0 + 1		1	
WESTON Rhys	23 + 4		1		2			

WATFORD (CHAMP: 16th)

	P/FL App	P/FL Goals	FLC App	FLC Goals	FAC App	FAC Goals	Others App	Others Goals
BENNETT Dale	8 + 2							
BROOKS Kurtney			0 + 1					
BRYAN Michael	1 + 6							
BUCKLEY Will	4 + 2	1						
CATHCART Craig	12							
CLEVERLEY Tom	33	11	1		1			
COWIE Don	40 + 1	2	2		1			
DeMERIT Jay	25 + 2				1			
DOYLEY Lloyd	43 + 1	1	2		1			
ELLINGTON Nathan	2 + 15	1	0 + 1					
EUSTACE John	39 + 3	4	2		1			
GRAHAM Danny	37 + 9	14	2		1			
HARLEY Jon	20 + 18	1	0 + 1		0 + 1			
HELGUSON Heidar	26 + 3	11						
HENDERSON Liam	0 + 13		0 + 1		0 + 1			
HODSON Lee	29 + 2		2		1			
HOSKINS Will	5 + 13	3	1					
JENKINS Ross	21 + 3		1		0 + 1			
LANS Henri	34 + 3	5	0 + 1		1			
LEE Richard			2					
LOACH Scott	46				1			
McANUFF Jobi	3				1			
McGINN Stephen	2 + 7							
MARIAPPA Adrian	46	1	2		1			
MASSEY Gavin	0 + 1							
OSHODI Eddie	0 + 1							
SEVERIN Scott	4 + 5		1	1	1			
SMITH Tommy	4	2	1					
SORDELL Marvin	1 + 5	1	0 + 1	1				
TAYLOR Martin	17 + 2	2						
WILLIAMSON Mike	4	1	2		1			

WEST BROMWICH ALBION (CHAMP: 2nd)

	P/FL App	P/FL Goals	FLC App	FLC Goals	FAC App	FAC Goals	Others App	Others Goals
BARNES Giles	1 + 8							
BARNETT Leon	0 + 1		3					
BEATTIE Craig	0 + 3		2	2				
BEDNAR Roman	21 + 6	11	1		4			
BRUNT Chris	39 + 1	13			3			
CARSON Scott	43				4			
CECH Marek	29 + 4	2	1		2 + 1			
COX Simon	17 + 11	9	3	1	3			
CUMMINGS Shaun	3				1			
DORRANS Graham	42 + 3	13	3	2	4	3		
GREENING Jonathan	2							
JARA Gonzalo	20 + 2	1	1		3			
KIELY Dean	3 + 2		3					
KOREN Robert	26 + 8	5	1		3 + 1	3		
MARTIS Shelton	10 + 3	2	1		1			
MATTOCK Joe	26 + 3		1 + 1		2 + 1	1		
MEITE Abdou	16 + 4		1 + 1		2			
MILLER Ishmael	4 + 11	2			0 + 1			
MOORE Luke	23 + 3	4	1		1 + 1			
MORRISON James	5 + 6	1			0 + 1			
MULUMBU Youssuf	35 + 5	3	0 + 2		3 + 1			
NOUBLE Frank	3							
OLSSON Jonas	43		2		3	1		
REID Reuben	0 + 4		2		0 + 1			
REID Steven	10	1						
SLORY Andy	1 + 5							
TAMAS Gabriel	23	2			2 + 1			
TEIXEIRA Filipe	1 + 8		2	1	1			
THOMAS Jerome	22 + 5	7	1		1	1		
THORNE George	0 + 1							
VALERO Borja	0 + 1		1					
WATSON Ben	6 + 1	1						
WOOD Chris	6 + 12	1	0 + 3		0 + 2	1		
ZUIVERLOON Gianni	26 + 4	4	2		2 + 1			

WEST HAM UNITED (PREM: 17th)

	P/FL App	P/FL Goals	FLC App	FLC Goals	FAC App	FAC Goals	Others App	Others Goals
BEHRAMI Valon	24 + 3	1			1			
BOA MORTE Luis	1		1					
COLE Carlton	26 + 4	10	1 + 1					
COLLINS James	3							
COLLISON Jack	19 + 3	2	1					
DA COSTA Manuel	12 + 3	2	1					
DAPRELA Fabio	4 + 3							
DIAMANTI Alessandro	18 + 9	7	1		1	1		
DYER Kieron	4 + 6		1					
EDGAR Anthony					0 + 1			

	P/FL App	Goals	FLC App	Goals	FAC App	Goals	Others App	Goals
FAUBERT Julien	32 + 1	1	1 + 1		1			
FRANCO Guille	16 + 7	5						
GABBIDON Danny	8 + 2		1					
GREEN Robert	38		2		1			
HINES Zavon	5 + 8	1	1 + 1	1				
ILAN	6 + 5	4						
ILUNGA Herita	16		1	1				
JIMENEZ Luis	6 + 5	1			1			
KOVAC Radoslav	27 + 4	2	2		1			
KURUCZ Peter	0 + 1							
McCARTHY Benni	2 + 3							
MIDO	5 + 4							
NGALA Bondz			0 + 1					
NOBLE Mark	25 + 2	2	1					
NOUBLE Frank	3 + 5		0 + 1		1			
PARKER Scott	30 + 1	2	2					
PAYNE Josh			1					
SEARS Freddie	0 + 1				0 + 1			
SPECTOR Jonathan	22 + 5		2					
SPENCE Jordan	0 + 1							
STANISLAS Junior	11 + 15	3	1	2	1			
TOMKINS James	22 + 1		2		1			
UPSON Matthew	33	3	0 + 1		1			

WIGAN ATHLETIC (PREM: 16th)

	P/FL App	Goals	FLC App	Goals	FAC App	Goals	Others App	Goals
AMAYA Antonio			1	1	2			
BOYCE Emmerson	23 + 1	3	1		2			
BRAMBLE Titus	35	2			3			
BROWN Michael	2							
CALDWELL Gary	16	2			1			
CHO Won-Hee	1 + 3							
DIAME Mohamed	34	1	1		2			
EDMAN Erik	2 + 1		1					
FIGUEROA Maynor	35	1			3			
GOHOURI Steve	4 + 1	1			0 + 1			
JORDI GOMEZ	11 + 12	1			2			
KAPO Olivier	0 + 1							
KING Marlon	0 + 3		1					
KIRKLAND Chris	32							
KOUMAS Jason	6 + 2	1			2			
McCARTHY James	19 + 1	1	1		2 + 1	1		
MELCHIOT Mario	32				1			
MORENO Marcelo	9 + 3							
MOSES Victor	2 + 12	1						
N'ZOGBIA Charles	35 + 1	5			0 + 3	2		
POLLITT Mike	2 + 2		1					
RODALLEGA Hugo	38	10	0 + 1		2 + 1			
SCHARNER Paul	30 + 8	4	1		1			
SCOTLAND Jason	14 + 18	1	1		3	1		
SINCLAIR Scott	1 + 17	1	1		3	1		
STOJKOVIC Vladimir	4				2			
THOMAS Hendry	27 + 4		0 + 1		1			
WATSON Ben	4 + 1	1	1		0 + 2	1		

WOLVERHAMPTON WANDERERS (PREM: 15th)

	P/FL App	Goals	FLC App	Goals	FAC App	Goals	Others App	Goals
BERRA Christophe	32		2		2			
CASTILLO Segundo	7 + 1		1					
COLLINS Neill			1					
CRADDOCK Jody	33	5	1		2			
DOYLE Kevin	33 + 1	9	1 + 1		0 + 1			
EBANKS-BLAKE Sylvan	12 + 11	2	1		2 + 1			
EDWARDS David	16 + 4	1	0 + 1					
ELOKOBI George	17 + 5		2		1 + 1			
FOLEY Kevin	23 + 2		1		3			
FRIEND George	1							
GUEDIOURA Adlene	7 + 7	1						
HAHNEMANN Marcus	25		2					
HALFORD Greg	12 + 3				0 + 1			
HENNESSEY Wayne	13				3			
HENRY Karl	34		1		3	1		
HILL Matt	2		1					
IWELUMO Chris	2 + 13				1 + 1			
JARVIS Matt	30 + 4	3	0 + 1		1	1		
JONES David	16 + 4	1	2		1 + 1	1		
KEOGH Andy	8 + 5	1	0 + 2					
KIGHTLY Michael	3 + 6		1					
MAIERHOFER Stefan	1 + 7	1	1					
MANCIENNE Michael	22 + 8				3			
MENDEZ-LAING Nathaniel			1					
MILIJAS Nenad	12 + 7	2	0 + 1		2			
MUJANGI BIA Geoffrey	1 + 2				1 + 1			

	P/FL App	Goals	FLC App	Goals	FAC App	Goals	Others App	Goals
STEARMAN Richard	12 + 4	1			2			
SURMAN Andrew	3 + 4		1		1			
VOKES Sam	0 + 5		1		2 + 1			
WARD Stephen	18 + 4				1 + 1			
ZUBAR Ronald	23	1	1		2	1		

WYCOMBE WANDERERS (DIV 1: 22nd)

	P/FL App	Goals	FLC App	Goals	FAC App	Goals	Others App	Goals
AINSWORTH Gareth	12 + 2	2						
AKINDE John	4 + 2	1						
BEAVON Stuart	14 + 11	3	1		0 + 1		1	
BENNETT Alan	6		1					
BETSY Kevin	35 + 4	5			2			
BLOOMFIELD Matt	8 + 6	2	1		0 + 1			
CHAMBERS Ashley	0 + 3	1					0 + 1	
COBB Joe							0 + 1	
DAVIES Scott	14 + 1	3			2	1		
DOHERTY Tommy	11 + 1				2			
DUBERRY Michael	18				1			
GREEN Stuart	10 + 3		1		1			
HARRIS Kadeem	0 + 2							
HARROLD Matt	29 + 7	8			2	2		
HEATON Tom	16							
HINSHELWOOD Adam	13		1					
HUNT Lewis	26 + 1				1			
JOHNSON Leon	5		1		1		1	
KEATES Dean	13	1			1			
KELLY Julian	9		1					
McLEOD Kevin	8 + 3							
MONCUR TJ	4							
MONTROSE Lewis	11 + 3						1	
MOUSINHO John	37 + 2	1	1		1			
OLIVER Luke	19 + 4		1		1			
PACK Marlon	7 + 1						1	
PAYNE Josh	3	1						
PHILLIPS Matt	18 + 18	5	0 + 1		2		1	
PITTMAN Jon-Paul	21 + 21	7	1		1 + 1	1	1	2
REVELL Alex	11 + 4	6						
SHEARER Scott	29				2			
SMITH Adam	3						1	
SPENCE Lewwis							0 + 1	
SPILLER Danny			1					
WESTLAKE Ian	7 + 2						1	
WESTWOOD Chris	28	2	1		1		1	
WOODMAN Craig	44	1	1		2		1	
YOUNG Jamie	1		1				1	
ZEBROSKI Chris	12 + 3	2	0 + 1		0 + 2			

YEOVIL TOWN (DIV 1: 15th)

	P/FL App	Goals	FLC App	Goals	FAC App	Goals	Others App	Goals
ALCOCK Craig	39 + 3	1			1			
AYLING Luke	1 + 3							
BOWDITCH Dean	26 + 4	10						
CAULKER Steven	44		1		1			
DAVIES Arron	4 + 6							
DAVIES Craig	2 + 2							
DAVIES Scott	4							
DOWNES Aidan	2 + 3							
FORBES Terrell	35 + 3	1	1		1		1	
HUTCHINS Danny	4 + 3				0 + 1		1	
JONES Nathan	18		1		1			
KAMUDIMBA KALALA Jean-Paul	32 + 2	1						
LINDEGAARD Andy	2 + 3						0 + 1	
McCARTHY Alex	44		1					
McCOLLIN Andre	0 + 2						0 + 1	
MacDONALD Shaun	31	3			1			
MARTIN Richard	2 + 1		1		1			
MASON Ryan	26 + 2	6			1			
MURRAY Scott	10 + 10	2	1					
MURTAGH Kieran	13 + 14	3			1		1	
OBIKA Jonathan	13 + 9	6	0 + 1		1		0 + 1	1
O'CALLAGHAN George	7 + 5		1		0 + 1		1	
SCHOFIELD Danny	4	1	1					
SMITH Nathan	27 + 7		0 + 1				1	
STAM Stefan	18	1	1					
TOMLIN Gavin	29 + 6	7	1				1	
TUDUR JONES Owain	6	1						
WELSH Andy	28 + 14	2	1				1	
WILLIAMS Gavin	7 + 1	5						
WILLIAMS Sam	28 + 6	4	1		1		1	

These are reported transfers between 1 and 9 July, which relate to players appearing within these pages and not being mentioned within their text. It does not include those who have left the Premiership and Football League to play in other leagues.

ARTELL Dave (Morecambe - Crewe Alexandra) Free
ASHWORTH Luke (Leyton Orient - Rotherham United) Free
AYLING Luke (Arsenal - Yeovil Town) Free
BAILEY Nicky (Charlton Athletic - Middlesbrough) £1,400,000
BARRETT Adam (Southend United - Crystal Palace) Free
BARRY-MURPHY Brian (Bury - Rochdale) Free
BATT Shaun (Peterborough United - Millwall) Undisclosed
BECKFORD Jermaine (Leeds United - Everton) Free
BELL Lee (Macclesfield Town - Crewe Alexandra) Free
BENAYOUN Yossi (Liverpool - Chelsea) Undisclosed
BENNETT Ian (Sheffield United - Huddersfield Town) Free
BERRETT James (Huddersfield Town - Carlisle United) Undisclosed
BLAKE Robbie (Burnley - Bolton Wanderers) Free
BOGDANOVIC Daniel (Barnsley - Sheffield United) Free
BRAIN Jon (Macclesfield Town - Walsall) Free
BROWN Aaron (Aldershot Town - Leyton Orient) Free
BROWN Wayne (Leicester City - Preston North End) Free
BULL Nikki (Brentford - Wycombe Wanderers) Free
BURCH Rob (Lincoln City - Notts County) Free
BUTCHER Richard (Lincoln City - Macclesfield Town) Free
CANHAM Sean (Notts County - Hereford United) Free
CARAYOL Mustapha (Torquay United - Lincoln City) Undisclosed
CHALMERS Lewis (Aldershot Town - Macclesfield Town) Free
COLLINS Michael (Huddersfield Town - Scunthorpe United) Undisclosed
CONNOLLY Paul (Derby County - Leeds United) Free
COX Dean (Brighton & Hove Albion - Leyton Orient) Free
COX Sam (Tottenham Hotspur - Barnet) Free
CRESSWELL Ryan (Bury - Rotherham United) Undisclosed
CURRAN Craig (Tranmere Rovers - Carlisle United) Free
CYWKA Tomasz (Wigan Athletic - Derby County) Free
DAGNALL Chris (Rochdale - Scunthorpe United) Free
DAVIES Arron (Brighton & Hove Albion - Peterborough United) Free
DAVIES Craig (Brighton & Hove Albion - Chesterfield) Free
DAWSON Stephen (Bury - Leyton Orient) Free
DERRY Shaun (Crystal Palace - Queens Park Rangers) Free
DICKINSON Liam (Brighton & Hove Albion - Barnsley) Undisclosed
DICKSON Ryan (Brentford - Southampton) Undisclosed
DOHERTY Gary (Norwich City - Charlton Athletic) Free
DUFF Shane (Cheltenham Town - Bradford City) Undisclosed
ERTL Johannes (Crystal Palace - Sheffield United) Free
FLEETWOOD Stuart (Charlton Athletic - Hereford United) Undisclosed
FLETCHER Steven (Burnley - Wolverhampton Wanderers) Undisclosed
FORBES Terrell (Yeovil Town - Leyton Orient) Free
FORSTER Nicky (Brighton & Hove Albion - Brentford) Free
FOSTER Ben (Manchester United - Birmingham City) Undisclosed
FOSTER Danny (Brentford - Wycombe Wanderers) Free
FOX David (Colchester United - Norwich City) Undisclosed
FRIEND George (Wolverhampton Wanderers - Doncaster Rovers) Free
GILLETT Simon (Southampton - Doncaster Rovers) Free
GILMARTIN Rene (Walsall - Watford) Undisclosed
GOULDING Jeff (Bournemouth - Cheltenham Town) Free
GRIFFIN Andy (Stoke City - Reading) Undisclosed
GUDJONSSON Joey (Burnley- Huddersfield Town) Free
GUY Lewis (Doncaster Rovers - Milton Keynes Dons) Free
HAWORTH Andy (Blackburn Rovers - Bury) Free
HEATON Tom (Manchester United - Cardiff City) Free
HEFFERNAN Paul (Doncaster Rovers - Sheffield Wednesday) Free
HIBBERT David (Shrewsbury Town - Peterborough United) Free
HILL Clint (Crystal Palace - Queens Park Rangers) Free
HOSKINS Will (Watford - Bristol Rovers) Free
HUDSON Kirk (Aldershot - Brentford) Undisclosed
HUNT Stephen (Hull City - Wolverhampton Wanderers) Undisclosed
IWELUMO Chris [Wolverhampton Wanderers - Burnley) Undisclosed
JACKSON Johnnie (Notts County - Charlton Athletic) Free
JARRETT Albert (Barnet - Lincoln City) Free
JEVONS Phil (Huddersfield Town - Morecambe) Free
JONES Darren (Hereford United - Aldershot Town) Undisclosed
JONES Richie (Hartlepool United - Oldham Athletic) Free
KENNEDY Tom (Rochdale - Leicester City) Free
KENNY Paddy (Sheffield United - Queens Park Rangers) £750,000
KEOGH Richard (Carlisle United - Coventry City) Free
LANGMEAD Kelvin (Shrewsbury Town - Peterborough United) Undisclosed
LEE Richard (Watford - Brentford) Free
LEGZDINS Adam (Crewe Alexandra - Burton Albion) Undisclosed

LEWIS Stuart (Gillingham - Dagenham & Redbridge) Free

LITTLE Mark (Wolverhampton Wanderers - Peterborough United) Free

LOWE Keith (Hereford United - Cheltenham Town) Free

McCALLUM Gavin (Hereford United - Lincoln City) Undisclosed

McCANN Grant (Scunthorpe United - Peterborough United) Free

McCOMBE John (Bristol City - Huddersfield Town) Undisclosed

McCRACKEN David (Milton Keynes Dons - Brentford) Undisclosed

McDAID Sean (Leeds United - Carlisle United) Free

MACKLIN Lloyd (Swindon Town - Torquay United) Free

McSHEFFREY Gary (Birmingham City - Coventry City) Free

MARNEY Dean (Hull City - Burnley) Undisclosed

MARSHALL Marcus (Blackburn Rovers - Rotherham United) Free

MARTIN Dave (Millwall - Derby County) Undisclosed

MARTIN David (Liverpool - Milton Keynes Dons) Free

MORGAN Craig (Peterborough United - Preston North End) £400,000

MOUSINHO John (Wycombe Wanderers - Stevenage Borough) Free

MOUYOKOLO Steven (Hull City - Wolverhampton Wanderers) Undisclosed

MULLINS Johnny (Stockport County - Rotherham United) Free

MURTAGH Kieran (Yeovil Town - Wycombe Wanderers) Free

NAYSMITH Gary (Sheffield United - Huddersfield Town) Free

NEWEY Tom (Bury - Rotherham United) Free

N'GALA Bondz (West Ham United - Plymouth Argyle) Free

O'DONOVAN Roy (Sunderland - Coventry City) Free

O'KEEFE Josh (Walsall - Lincoln City) Free

OMOZUSI Elliot (Fulham - Leyton Orient) Free

PANTHER Manny (Exeter City - Aldershot Town) Free

PETROV Martin (Manchester City - Bolton Wanderers) Free

PHILLIPS Steve (Bristol Rovers - Crewe Alexandra) Free

PRICE Jason (Millwall - Carlisle United) Free

PRUTTON David (Colchester United - Swindon Town) Free

PUGH Marc (Hereford United - Bournemouth) Undisclosed

PURCELL Tadhg (Darlington - Northampton Town) Free

PURCHES Stephen (Leyton Orient - Bournemouth) Free

RAVEN David (Carlisle United - Shrewsbury Town) Free

REID Steven (Blackburn Rovers - West Bromwich Albion) Free

RENDELL Scott (Peterborough United - Wycombe Wanderers) Undisclosed

RICHARDSON Frazer (Charlton Athletic - Southampton) Undisclosed

ROSE Michael (Stockport County - Swindon Town) Free

ROYCE Simon (Gillingham - Brentford) Free

RUNDLE Adam (Chesterfield - Morecambe) Free

SAM Lloyd (Charlton Athletic – Leeds United) Free

SAWYER Gary (Plymouth Argyle - Bristol Rovers) Free

SCANNELL Damian (Southend United - Dagenham & Redbridge) Free

SCHUMACHER Steve (Crewe Alexandra - Bury) Free

SCOTT Paul (Bury - Morecambe) Free

SEDGWICK Chris (Preston North End - Sheffield Wednesday) Free

SENDEROS Philippe (Arsenal - Fulham) Free

SHACKELL Jason (Wolverhampton Wanderers - Barnsley) Undisclosed

SHARP Billy (Sheffield United - Doncaster Rovers) £1,150,000

SHARPS Ian (Rotherham United - Shrewsbury Town) Free

SIMEK Frank (Sheffield Wednesday - Carlisle United) Free

SIMONSEN Steve (Stoke City - Sheffield United) Free

SKARZ Joe (Huddersfield Town - Bury) Free

SPARROW Matt (Scunthorpe United – Brighton & Hove Albion) Free

SPENCER Damian (Kettering Town - Aldershot Town) Free

SPILLANE Michael (Norwich City - Brentford) Undisclosed

SPRING Matthew (Charlton Athletic - Leyton Orient) Free

STREVENS Ben (Brentford - Wycombe Wanderers) Free

SURMAN Drew (Wolverhampton Wanderers - Norwich City) Undisclosed

SWEENEY Peter (Grimsby Town - Bury) Free

TAMAS Gabriel (Auxerre - West Bromwich Albion) Undisclosed

THOMSON Jake (Southampton - Exeter City) Free

THRELFALL Robbie (Liverpool - Bradford City) Free

TOMLIN Gavin (Yeovil Town - Dagenham & Redbridge) Free

UDDIN Anwar (Dagenham & Redbridge - Barnet) Free

UPSON Ed (Ipswich Town - Yeovil Town) Free

VINCENT Jamie (Walsall - Aldershot Town) Free

WALLACE Ross (Preston North End - Burnley) Undisclosed

WEDDERBURN Nathaniel (Stoke City - Northampton Town) Free

WHITAKER Danny (Oldham Athletic - Chesterfield) Free

WIDDOWSON Joe (Grimsby Town - Rochdale) Free

WILLIAMS Andy (Bristol Rovers - Yeovil Town) Free

WOODMAN Craig (Wycombe Wanderers - Brentford) Undisclosed

WRIGHT David (Ipswich Town - Crystal Palace) Free

WRIGHT Jake (Brighton & Hove Albion - Oxford United) Free

WRIGHT Tommy (Grimsby Town - Darlington) Free

Where Did They Go?

Below is a list of all players who were recorded in the previous edition as making a first-team appearance in 2008-09, but failed to make the current book. They are listed alphabetically and show their last league club, their approximate leaving dates, as well as their next club for which a minimum stay of three months is the requisite. Of course, they may well have moved on by now, but space does not allow further reference.

* Shows that the player in question is still with his named club but failed to make an appearance in 2009-10, the most common reason being injury.

+ Players retained by Luton Town and Chester City, who were relegated to the Conference.

Player	Last Club	Date	Next Club
ABBEY George	Crewe Alex	05.09	Retired
ABBEY Nathan	MK Dons	06.09	Rushden & Diamonds
ACHTERBERG John	Tranmere Rov	06.09	Retired
ADEMENO Charles	Southend U	06.09	Crawley T
ADEMOLA Moses	Brentford	01.10	Woking
AGUSTIEN Kemy	Birmingham C	05.09	RKC Waalwijk (Holland)
AHMED Adnan	Tranmere Rov	06.09	Ferencvaros (Hungary)
AINGE Simon	Bradford C	06.09	Bradford Park Avenue
AKURANG Cliff	Barnet	08.09	Rushden & Diamonds
ALBERTI Matteo	Queens Park Rgrs	*	
ALBRECHTSEN Martin	Derby Co	08.09	Midtjylland (Denmark)
ALGAR Ben	Chesterfield	05.09	Matlock T
ALLEN Chris	Swindon T	06.09	Weymouth
ALONSO Xabi	Liverpool	08.09	Real Madrid (Spain)
ALUKO Sone	Birmingham C	09.08	Aberdeen
ALVES Afonso	Middlesbrough	09.09	Al-Saad (Qatar)
AMEOBI Toni	Doncaster Rov	06.09	
ANDERSON Lloyd	Brentford	06.09	Whitehawk
ANDERTON Darren	Bournemouth	12.08	Retired
ANDREASEN Leon	Fulham	07.09	Hannover 96 (Germany)
ANDREWS Wayne	Luton T	12.08	Retired
ANYA Ikechi	Northampton T	07.09	Sevilla Atletico (Spain)
ANTWI Godwin	Liverpool	06.09	Vejle BK (Denmark)
ARBELOA Alvaro	Liverpool	07.09	Real Madrid (Spain)
ARMSTRONG Craig	Cheltenham T	01.09	Kidderminster Hrs
ASAFU-ADIAYE Ed	Luton T	+	
ASHBEE Ian	Hull C	*	
ASHIKODI Moses	Shrewsbury T	05.09	Kettering T
ASHTON Dean	West Ham U	12.09	Retired
ASHTON Nathan	Wycombe W	05.09	AFC Wimbledon
ASHTON Neil	Shrewsbury T	06.09	Chester C
ASKHAM Lee	Chesterfield	05.09	Guiseley
ASSOUMANI Mansour	Leeds U	03.09	Wrexham
BALL Michael	Manchester C	06.09	
BARKER Richie	Rotherham U	05.09	Retired
BARNES Phil	Grimsby T	03.09	Gainsborough Trinity
BARRY Anthony	Chester C	01.10	Fleetwood T
BASHAM Steve	Exeter C	06.09	Luton T
BATES Matty	Middlesbrough	*	
BAUDET Julien	Crewe Alex	06.09	Colorado Rapids (USA)
BEARDSLEY Jason	Derby Co	09.09	Tampa Bay Rowdies (USA)
BEAVAN George	Luton T	+	
BECKETT Luke	Huddersfield T	11.08	Gainsborough Trinity
BECKWITH Rob	Barnet	01.09	Grays Ath
BELL James	Accrington Stanley	08.09	Marine
BELSON Flavien	MK Dons	05.09	AS Cannes (France)
BENNETT Julian	Nottingham F	*	
BERCHICHE Yuri	Tottenham H	*	
BERRY Tyrone	Gillingham	01.09	Grays Ath
BEUZELIN Guillaume	Coventry C	06.09	Hamilton Academical
BIGNOT Marcus	Millwall	01.10	Kidderminster Hrs
BIRCHALL Adam	Barnet	06.09	Dover Ath
BIRCHALL Chris	Brighton & Hove A	05.09	Los Angeles Galaxy (USA)
BIRCHAM Marc	Yeovil T	01.09	Retired
BISCHOFF Amaury	Arsenal	06.09	Academica Coimbra (Portugal)
BLACK Tommy	Barnet	03.09	Grays Ath
BLACKETT Shane	Peterborough U	07.09	Luton T
BLINKHORN Matty	Morecambe	06.09	Sligo Rov
BLUNDELL Gregg	Darlington	06.09	Chester C
BOARDMAN Jon	Dagenham & Redbridge	06.09	Woking
BOJINOV Valeri	Manchester C	*	
BOLAND Willie	Hartlepool U	10.09	Retired
BOOTH Andy	Huddersfield T	05.09	Retired
BOPP Eugene	Crewe Alex	05.09	Portsmouth
BOUAOUZAN Rachid	Wigan Ath	04.10	Helsingborgs (Sweden)
BOUMA Wilfred	Aston Villa	*	
BOWES Gary	Millwall	06.09	AFC Hornchurch
BRAMMER Dave	Port Vale	06.09	Retired
BRKOVIC Ahmet	Millwall	05.09	Dubrovnik (Croatia)
BROADBENT Danny	Huddersfield T	06.09	Harrogate T
BROOKER Steve	Doncaster Rov	*	
BROWN Seb	Brentford	06.09	AFC Wimbledon
BUDTZ Jan	Hartlepool U	06.09	Eastwood T
BURGE Ryan	Barnet	01.09	Machida Zelvia (Japan)
BURGMEIER Franz	Darlington	06.09	FC Vaduz (Liechtenstein)
BURNS Robbie	Leicester C	*	
BUTLER Martin	Grimsby T	10.08	Burton A
BUTLER Paul	Chester C	02.09	Retired
BYRNE Mark	Nottingham F	*	
CACAPA	Newcastle U	06.09	Cruzeiro (Brazil)
CADAMARTERI Danny	Huddersfield T	05.09	Dundee U
CAICEDO Felipe	Manchester C	*	
CAINES Gavin	Cheltenham T	06.09	Kidderminster Hrs
CAMPION Darren	Carlisle U	01.09	Solihull Moors
CAMPO Ivan	Ipswich T	06.09	AEK Larnaca (Cyprus)

Name	Club	Date	Destination
CANN Steve	Rotherham U	06.09	Aberystwyth T
CAREW Ashley	Barnet	03.09	Eastleigh
CARNEY Dave	Sheffield U	08.09	FC Twente (Holland)
CARR Michael	Morecambe	02.09	Kidderminster Hrs
CARROLL Roy	Derby Co	08.09	Odense BK (Denmark)
CARSON Trevor	Sunderland	*	
CASAL Yinka	Swindon T	01.10	CFR Cluj (Romania)
CASEMENT Chris	Ipswich T	06.09	Dundee
CAUNA Sasa	Watford	05.09	Skonto Riga (Latvia)
CAVANAGH Peter	Accrington Stanley	08.09	Fleetwood T
CHADWICK Nick	Shrewsbury T	05.09	Chester C
CHARGE Daniel	Dagenham & Redbridge	08.09	Grays Ath
CHARLES Ryan	Luton T	+	
CHRISTIE Malcolm	Leeds U	01.09	Retired
CISSE Djibril	Sunderland	05.09	Panathinaikos (Greece)
CIVELLI Luciano	Ispwich T	*	
COCHRANE Justin	Aldershot T	06.09	Hayes & Yeading U
COKE Giles	Northampton T	06.09	Motherwell
COLE Andrew	Nottingham F	10.08	Retired
CONVEY Bobby	Reading	02.09	San Jose Earthquakes (USA)
COOK Steve	Brighton & Hove A.	*	
CORCORAN Sam	Colchester U	*	
COSTLY Carlos	Birmingham C	05.09	GKS Belchatow (Poland)
COYNE Chris	Colchester U	07.09	Perth Glory (Australia)
CRADDOCK Josh	Walsall	08.09	University
CRADDOCK Tom	Luton T	+	
CROOKS Leon	Wycombe W.	05.09	Ebbsfleet U.
CROSBY Andy	Scunthorpe U	06.09	Retired
CUMBERS Luis	Gillingham	*	
DACOURT Olivier	Fulham	05.09	Standard Liege (Belgium)
DANBY John	Chester C	+	
DAVENPORT Calum	West Ham U	*	
DAVIDSON Ross	Port Vale	*	
DAVIES Richard	Walsall	*	
DAWKINS Simon	Tottenham H	06.09	
DAY Rhys	Aldershot T	06.09	Oxford U
DAYTON James	Crystal Palace	06.09	Glenn Hoddle Academy
DE LA CRUZ Ulises	Birmingham C	04.09	LDU Quito (Ecuador)
DE MAGALHAES Jeremy	Barnet	04.09	L' Entente SSG (France)
DENNIS Kristian	Macclesfield T	*	
DERBYSHIRE Matt	Blackburn Rov	01.09	Olympiakos (Greece)
DE RIDDER Daniel	Wigan Ath	*	
DERVITE Dorian	Tottenham H	*	
DIARRA Lassana	Portsmouth	01.09	Real Madrid (Spain)
DI CARMINE Samuel	Queens Park Rgrs	05.09	Fiorentina (Italy)
DI MICHELE David	West Ham U	05.09	Torino (Italy)
DINNING Tony	Chester C	05.09	Stafford Rgrs
DIXON Jonny	Brighton & Hove A	07.09	Retired
DOBSON Craig	Brentford	04.09	Mansfield T
DOIG Chris	Northampton T	05.09	Central Coast Mariners (Australia)
DOLMAN Liam	Northampton T	06.09	Kidderminster Hrs
DONK Ryan	West Bromwich A	05.09	Brugge (Belgium)
DOUALA Rudi	Plymouth Arg	05.09	Lierse SK (Belgium)
DOYLE Colin	Birmingham C	*	
DUDLEY Mark	Derby Co	*	
DUFFY Ayden	Lincoln C	05.09	Gainsborough Trinity
DUNCAN Derek	Wycombe W	01.09	Ebbsfleet U
DURRANT Jack	Cheltenham T	*	
EASTON Clint	Hereford U	04.09	Ebbsfleet U
EDWARDS Paul	Port Vale	06.09	Barrow
EHIOGU Ugo	Sheffield U	05.09	Retired
ELANO	Manchester C	07.09	Galatasaray (Turkey)
ELLAMS Lloyd	Chester C	+	
ELLIOTT Stuart	Doncaster Rov	01.10	Hamilton Academical
ELVINS Rob	Aldershot T	06.09	Worcester C
EMANUEL Lewis	Luton T	+	
EMERY Josh	Cheltenham T	*	
ENNIS Paul	Stockport Co	06.09	Stalybridge Celtic
FAIRCLOUGH Ben	Notts Co	*	
FERNANDES Gelson	Manchester C	07.09	St Etienne (France)
FERREIRA Fabio	Chelsea	06.09	Esmoriz (Portugal)
FINNIGAN John	Cheltenham T	06.09	Kidderminster Hrs
FLEMING Greg	Oldham Ath	*	
FLO Tore Andre	MK Dons	05.09	Retired
FOJUT Jaroslaw	Bolton W	02.09	Slask Wroclaw (Poland)
FONTE Rui	Arsenal	06.09	Sporting Lisbon (Portugal)
FORAN Richie	Darlington	01.09	Inverness CT
FORRESTER Jamie	Notts Co	06.09	Lincoln U
FORTUNE Clayton	Darlington	06.09	Weston-super-Mare
FORTUNÉ Marc-Antoine	West Bromwich A	05.09	Glasgow Celtic
FOTHERINGHAM Mark	Norwich C	04.09	Dundee U
FOWLER Robbie	Blackburn Rov	12.08	North Queensland (Australia)
FRANCIS Damien	Watford	10.08	Retired
FRASER-ALLEN Kyle	Tottenham H	06.09	Hayes & Yeading U
GALLEN Kevin	Luton T	+	
GARCIA Omar	Rotherham U	01.09	
GARNER Glyn	Shrewsbury T	01.10	Grays Ath
GASMI Romain	Southampton	05.09	Strasbourg (France)
GEKAS Theofanis	Portsmouth	05.09	Bayer Leverkusen (Germany)
GERBA Ali	MK Dons	06.09	Toronto FC (Canada)
GIANNAKOPOULOS Stelios	Hull C	01.09	Larissa (Greece)
GIBSON Billy	Watford	*	
GILBERTO	Tottenham H	07.09	Cruzeiro (Brazil)
GILL Ben	Cheltenham T	01.09	Crawley T
GILL Jerry	Cheltenham T	10.08	Forest Green Rov
GILLESPIE Keith	Bradford C	05.09	Glentoran
GLAUBER	Manchester C	06.09	Sao Caetano (Brazil)
GNAPKA Claude	Luton T	+	
GONZALEZ Nacho	Newcastle U	06.09	Valencia (Spain)
GRAHAM David	Lincoln C	03.09	Sheffield FC
GRAHAM Richie	Dagenham & Redbridge	06.09	Grays Ath
GRANVILLE Danny	Leyton Orient	06.09	Hemel Hempstead T
GRAY Bradley	Leyton Orient	06.09	Salisbury C
GRAY Wayne	Leyton Orient	06.09	AFC Hornchurch
GREEN Franny	Macclesfield T	06.09	Kettering T
GREENACRE Chris	Tranmere Rov	05.09	Wellington Phoenix (New Zealand)
GRIFFIT Leandre	Crystal Palace	01.09	URS du Centre (Belgium)
GRIFFITHS Rostyn	Blackburn Rov	02.09	Adelaide U (Australia)
GRIGG Will	Walsall	*	
HADFIELD Jordan	Macclesfield T	06.09	Ashton U
HALL Asa	Luton T	+	
HAMANN Didi	Manchester C	06.09	MK Dons
HANSON Mitchell	Derby Co	*	
HARRIS Jay	Chester C	06.09	Enköpings SK (Sweden)
HARRISON Lee	Barnet	*	
HARVEY Neil	Macclesfield T	06.09	Retford U
HATCH Liam	Peterborough U	06.09	Luton T
HAYES Jonny	Leicester C	07.09	Inverness CT
HAZELL Justin	Southend U	*	

Name	Club	Date	Destination
HECKINGBOTTOM Paul	Bradford C	06.09	Mansfield T
HEMMINGS Ashley	Wolverhampton W	*	
HENDERSON Paul	Leicester C	06.09	North Queensland (Australia)
HENRY Paul	Tranmere Rov	06.09	Witton A
HESLOP Simon	Barnsley	*	
HINDMARCH Steve	Shrewsbury T	06.09	Workington
HODGE Bryan	Blackburn Rov	06.09	Patrick Thistle
HODGKISS Jared	West Bromwich A	06.09	Forest Green Rov
HOEFKENS Carl	West Bromwich A	05.09	Brugge (Belgium)
HOGAN David	Dagenham & Redbridge	*	
HOLLAND Matt	Charlton Ath	06.09	Retired
HOLMES Danny	Tranmere Rov	06.09	The New Saints
HOLMES Peter	Rotherham U	06.09	Ebbsfleet U
HOLT Gary	Wycombe W	06.09	Lowestoft T
HOPE Richard	Grimsby T	02.09	Retired
HOWARD Mike	Morecambe	06.09	Llanelli
HOWARTH Chris	Carlisle U	06.09	Droylsden
HOWELLS Jake	Luton T	*	
HUDSON-ODOI Bradley	Hereford U	06.09	Histon
HUGHES Stephen	Walsall	06.09	Retired
HUKE Shane	Dagenham & Redbridge	01.09	Central Coast Mariners (Australia)
HULBERT Robin	Darlington	06.09	Barrow
HUMPHREY Chris	Shrewsbury T	06.09	Motherwell
HUNT James	Grimsby T	06.09	Gainsborough Trinity
HURST Glynn	Bury	06.09	Gainsborough Trinity
HYYPIA Sami	Liverpool	06.09	Bayer Leverkusen (Germany)
IFIL Jerel	Swindon T	08.09	Aberdeen
IFILL Paul	Crystal Palace	06.09	Wellington Phoenix (New Zealand)
IRELAND Danny	Coventry C	*	
IRIEKPEN Izzy	Bristol C	06.09	Hamilton Academical
JACKSON Mike	Shrewsbury T	01.10	Retired
JARVIS Rossi	Luton T	+	
JEFFERY Jack	West Ham U	06.09	Maldon T
JENNINGS James	Macclesfield T	06.09	Kettering T
JENNINGS Steve	Tranmere Rov	07.09	Motherwell
JOHNSON Brett	Brentford	06.09	AFC Wimbledon
JOHNSON Eddie	Chester C	02.09	Austin Aztex (USA)
JOHNSON Michael	Notts Co	05.09	Retired
JONES Ben	Chester C	03.10	Colwyn Bay
JONES Mark	Rochdale	06.09	Wrexham
JOYCE Ben	Swindon T	06.09	Torquay U
JUTKIEWICZ Lucas	Everton	08.09	Motherwell
KADOCH Ran	Barnet	05.09	Bnei Yehuda (Israel)
KAMARA Malvin	Huddersfield T	06.09	Barrow
KAY Adam	Burnley	*	
KAY Michael	Sunderland	*	
KAZIMIERCZAK Prez	Darlington	06.09	Oldham Ath
KAZIMIERCZAK Przemyslaw	Derby Co	05.09	Vitoria Setubal (Portugal)
KEANE Keith	Luton T	+	
KENNEDY John	Norwich C	12.08	Glasgow Celtic
KENTON Darren	Cheltenham T	01.09	Rochester Rhinos (USA)
KERRY Lloyd	Chesterfield	*	
KIERNAN Rob	Watford	*	
KIM Do-Heon	West Bromwich A	07.09	Suwon Bluewings (South Korea)
KING David	MK Dons	*	
KING Simon	Gillingham	*	
KINGSON Richard	Wigan Ath	*	
KISHISHEV Radostin	Leicester C	12.08	Litex Lovech (Bulgaria)
KISSOCK John-Paul	Everton	06.09	Hamilton Academical
KLEIN-DAVIES Josh	Bristol Rov	05.09	Weston-super-Mare
KOROMA Omar	Portsmouth	06.09	
KUPISZ Tomasz	Wigan Ath	*	
KYLE Kevin	Coventry C	01.09	Kilmarnock
LAMBERT Kyle	Rochdale	01.09	Leigh Genesis
LANGE Rune	Hartlepool U	05.09	Kvik Halden (Norway)
LASTUVKA Jan	West Ham U	05.09	PC Dnipro (Ukraine)
LAUREN	Portsmouth	06.09	Cordoba (Spain)
LAURSEN Martin	Aston Villa	05.09	Retired
LAWRENCE Dennis	Swansea C	06.09	San Juan Jabloteh (Trinidad)
LEA Michael	Scunthorpe U	06.09	Chester C
LEDESMA Emmanuel	Queens Park Rgrs	02.09	Salernitana (Italy)
LEDGISTER Aaron	Cheltenham T	06.09	Worcester C
LEIJER Adrian	Fulham	08.09	Melbourne Victory (Australia)
LEKEJ Rocky	Sheffield Wed	07.09	Sandefjord (Norway)
LEON-AYARZA Diego	Barnsley	06.09	UD Las Palmas (Spain)
LIBURD Patrece	Macclesfield T	05.09	Farsley Celtic
LIPTAK Zoltan	Southampton	04.09	Ujpest (Hungary)
LLEWELLYN Chris	Grimsby T	06.09	Neath Ath
LLOYD Paul	Morecambe	01.09	Forest Green Rov
LOKANDO Peggy	Southend U	06.09	Leyton
LOOVENS Glenn	Cardiff C	08.08	Glasgow Celtic
LOPEZ Walter	West Ham U	06.09	Brescia (Italy)
LUCKETTI Chris	Huddersfield T	*	
LUPOLI Arturo	Sheffield U	06.09	Ascoli (Italy)
LUSCOMBE Nathan	Sunderland	*	
MACAULEY Josh	Tranmere Rov	*	
McCANN Ryan	Morecambe	01.09	Queen of the South
McCUNNIE Jamie	Hartlepool U	06.09	East Fife
MacDONALD Alex	Burnley	*	
MacDONALD Sherjill	West Bromwich A	07.09	Germinal Beerschot (Belgium)
McEVILLY Lee	Rochdale	06.09	Grays Ath
MacKENZIE Neil	Notts Co	01.09	Mansfield T
McLAGGON Kayne	Southampton	*	
MacLEOD Jack	Hereford U	06.09	Guildford C
McMANAMAN Callum	Wigan Ath.	*	
McMANUS Paul	Chester C	02.09	Bangor C
McMANUS Scott	Crewe Alex	12.09	
McPHEE Stephen	Blackpool	05.10	Retired
MAGNAY Carl	Chelsea	*	
MAGUIRE Danny	Queens Park Rgrs	06.09	
MAHON Craig	Wigan Ath	06.09	
MAINWARING Matty	Stockport Co	*	
MAKUKULA Ariza	Bolton W	08.09	Kayserispor (Turkey)
MALBON Anthony	Port Vale	*	
MANNIX David	Chester C	07.09	
MANUCHO	Manchester U	07.09	Real Valladolid (Spain)
MARIN Nicolas	Plymouth Arg	01.09	Bastia (France)
MARSHALL Andy	Coventry C	06.09	Aston Villa
MARSHALL Paul	Manchester C	*	
MARTINS Oba	Newcastle U	07.09	Vfl Wolfsburg (Germany)
MATTEO Dominic	Stoke C	06.09	Retired
MAYO Kerry	Brighton & Hove A	05.09	Retired
MAYO Paul	Notts Co	01.09	Mansfield T
MENDES Junior	Aldershot T	06.09	Ayr U
MENDES Pedro	Portsmouth	08.08	Glasgow Rgrs
MENSEGUEZ Juan Carlos	West Bromwich A	06.09	San Lorenzo (Argentina)
MERELLA Dominic	Blackpool	01.09	Weymouth

MIFSUD Michael	Coventry C	06.09	Valletta (Malta)
MILLAR Christian	Macclesfield T	06.09	Buxton
MILLER Kern	Lincoln C	*	
MILLER Liam	Sunderland	05.09	Hibernian
MILLS Leigh	Tottenham H	02.09	Retired
MILSOM Robert	Fulham	*	
MINEIRO	Chelsea	06.09	Schalke 04 (Germany)
MITCHELL Paul	MK Dons	01.09	Retired
MITCHLEY Danny	Blackpool	*	
MODEST Nathan	Sheffield Wed	*	
MOLYNEUX Lee	Southampton	*	
MONTAGUE Ross	Brentford	06.09	AFC Wimbledon
MOORE Karl	Manchester C	*	
MOSTTO Miguel	Barnsley	01.09	Total Chabco (Peru)
MOUTAOUAKIL Yazz	Charlton Ath	*	
MOZIKA Damien	Chester C	05.09	
MPENZA Emile	Plymouth Arg	06.09	FC Sion (Switzerland)
MULLARKEY Sam	Lincoln C	06.09	Lincoln U
MULLER Heinz	Barnsley	06.09	FSV Mairrz (Germany)
MURDOCK Colin	Accrington Stanley	05.09	Retired
MURPHY David	Birmingham C	*	
MURPHY Tom	Gillingham	*	
MURRAY Fred	Exeter C	06.09	Luton T
MURRAY Matt	Wolverhampton W	*	
MVUEMBA Arnold	Portsmouth	08.09	Lorient (France)
MYRIE-WILLIAMS Jennison	Bristol C	06.09	Dundee U
NAFTI Mehdi	Birmingham C	06.09	Aris Salonika (Greece)
NALIS Lilian	Swindon T.	6.09	Bastia (France)
NEMETH Krisztian	Liverpool	*	
NEWBOLD Adam	Nottingham F	05.09	Hucknall T
NEWMAN Ricky	Aldershot T	06.09	Retired
NEWTON Adam	Brentford	06.09	Luton T
N'GOTTY Bruno	Leicester C	06.09	Retired
NICHOLLS Kevin	Luton T	+	
NICOLAU Nicky	Barnet	05.09	Woking
NIX Kyle	Bradford C	06.09	Mansfield T
NOBLE David	Bristol C	06.09	Exeter C
NOEL WILLIAMS Gifton	Millwall	01.09	Austin Aztex (USA)
NORMINGTON Grant	Grimsby T	*	
NWOKEJI Mark	Dagenham &Redbridge	*	
OAKES Andy	Darlington	06.09	Retired
OBERSTELLER Jack	Exeter C	06.09	Grays Ath
O'BRIEN Joey	Bolton W	*	
O'BRIEN Mark	Derby Co	*	
OCHOA Lewis	Brentford	06.09	Maidenhead U
O'CONNOR Garreth	Luton T	01.09	St Patricks Ath
ODHIAMBO Eric	Leicester C	01.09	Inverness CT
O'HALLORAN Stephen	Aston Villa	*	
OJI Sam	Hereford U	02.09	Ljungskile (Sweden)
ONIBUJE Fola	Accrington Stanley	09.08	Weymouth
OOIJER Andre	Blackburn Rov	06.09	PSV Eindhoven (Holland)
ORENUJA Femi	Southend U	03.09	Everton
OSBORNE Junior	Aldershot T	12.08	
OWEN James	Chester C	+	
OWENS Graeme	Middlesbrough	06.09	Kilmarnock
OWUSU Lloyd	Cheltenham T	06.09	Adelaide U (Australia)
PALMER Aiden	Leyton Orient	06.09	Cambridge U
PAMAROT Noe	Portsmouth	06.09	Hercules Alicante (Spain)
PAREJO Daniel	Queens Park Rgrs	01.09	Real Madrid (Spain)
PARKES Jordan	Watford	*	
PATRICK Jordan	Luton T	*	
PATTERSON Marlon	Dagenham & Redbridge	01.09	Histon
PATTISON Matty	Norwich C	08.09	Mamelodi Sundowners (South Africa)
PEAD Craig	Brentford	06.09	Retired
PEKHART Tomas	Tottenham H	01.09	Slavia Prague (Czech Republic)
PELE	West Bromwich A	06.09	Falkirk
PENNANT Jermaine	Liverpool	06.09	Real Zaragoza (Spain)
PENTNEY Carl	Leicester C	*	
PEREPLOTKINS Andrejs	Derby Co	01.09	Skonto Riga (Latvia)
PERRY Kyle	Port Vale	06.09	Mansfield T
PETTEFER Carl	Bournemouth	09.08	Bognor Regis T
PHILLIPS Demar	Stoke C	01.09	Aalesund (Norway)
PILKINGTON George	Luton T	+	
PILKINGTON Kevin	Notts Co	*	
PINNEY Nathaniel	Crystal Palace	*	
PLATT Kristian	Chester C	+	
POOLE Glenn	Brentford	06.09	Grays Ath
POOM Mart	Watford	04.09	Retired
PORTER Joel	Hartlepool U	06.09	Gold Coast U (Australia)
PORTER Levi	Leicester C	*	
POSSEBON Rodrigo	Manchester U	*	
PRESTON Carl	Bournemouth	06.09	Weymouth
PRIJOVIC Aleksandar	Derby Co	01.10	FC Sion (Switzerland)
PRIMUS Linvoy	Portsmouth	12.09	Retired
PRYCE Ryan	Bournemouth	09.09	Salisbury C
PUDDY Will	Cheltenham T	*	
PUGH Andy	Gillingham	*	
PURDIE Rob	Darlington	05.09	Oldham Ath
PUYGRENIER Sebastien	Bolton W	05.09	Zenit St Petersburg (Russia)
QUARESMA Ricardo	Chelsea	05.09	Inter Milan (Italy)
RANKINE Michael	Bournemouth	11.08	Rushden & Diamonds
RAZAK Hamdi	Swindon T	05.09	Red Star St Ouen (France)
REICH Marco	Walsall	01.09	Jag Bialystok (Poland)
REID James	Nottingham F	*	
RHODES Alex	Rotherham U	06.09	Oxford U
RICE Robbie	Wycombe W	06.09	Basingstoke T
RICHARDS Matt	Wycombe W	06.09	
RIX Ben	Crewe Alex	01.09	Nea Salarnis (Cyprus)
ROBERTS Kevin	Chester C	+	
RONALDO	Manchester U	06.09	Real Madrid (Spain)
ROPER Ian	Luton T	06.09	Kettering T
ROUTLEDGE Jon	Wigan Ath	*	
RUDDY John	Everton	*	
RULE Glenn	Chester C	+	
RUSSELL Sam	Rochdale	05.09	Wrexham
RUTHERFORD Paul	Chester C	06.09	Barrow
RYAN Tim	Darlington	06.09	Chester C.
SAAH Brian	Leyton Orient	06.09	Cambridge U
SAEIJS Jan-Paul	Southampton	05.09	Roda JC (Holland)
ST AIMIE Kieron	Barnet	02.09	Hitchin T
SALIFOU Moustapha	Aston Villa	*	
SAMSON Craig	Hereford U	04.09	Ayr U
SANCHEZ Cesar	Tottenham H	01.09	Valencia (Spain)
SAVIO	West Ham U	09.09	Fiorentina (Italy)
SHAWKY Mohamed	Middlesbrough	01.10	Kayserispor (Turkey)
SHEPHARD Chris	Exeter C	*	
SHITTU Danny	Bolton W	*	
SIBIERSKI Antoine	Wigan Ath	06.09	Retired
SINCLAIR Frank	Lincoln C	06.09	Wrexham